1 MONTH OF
FREE
READING

at
www.ForgottenBooks.com

By purchasing this book you are eligible for one month membership to ForgottenBooks.com, giving you unlimited access to our entire collection of over 1,000,000 titles via our web site and mobile apps.

To claim your free month visit:
www.forgottenbooks.com/free1210855

ISBN 978-0-428-71324-9
PIBN 11210855

REPORTS

FROM

COMMISSIONERS, INSPECTORS,

/ / ./   ,

AND OTHERS:

FORTY-FIVE VOLUMES.

— *(32.)* —

LUNACY (SCOTLAND);
PAUPER LUNATICS (SCOTLAND)
DIETING;
POLICE (COUNTIES AND BOROUGHS);

Session
16 *January* 1902 —— 18 *December* 1902.

VOL. XLI.

1902.

REPORTS

FROM

COMMISSIONERS, INSPECTORS,

AND OTHERS:

1902.

FORTY-FIVE VOLUMES:—CONTENTS OF THE

THIRTY-SECOND VOLUME.

N.B.—*THE* Figures *at the* beginning of the line, *correspond with the* N° *at the foot of each* Report; *and the* Figures *at the* end of the line *refer to the* MS. Paging *of the Volumes arranged for The House of Commons.*

155118

FORTY-FOURTH ANNUAL REPORT

OF THE

GENERAL BOARD OF COMMISSIONERS IN LUNACY FOR SCOTLAND.

Presented to both Houses of Parliament by Command of His Majesty.

GLASGOW:
PRINTED FOR HIS MAJESTY'S STATIONERY OFFICE
By JAMES HEDDERWICK & SONS,
At "The Citizen" Press, St. Vincent Place.

And to be purchased, either directly or through any Bookseller, from
OLIVER & BOYD, Edinburgh ; or
EYRE & SPOTTISWOODE, East Harding Street, Fleet Street, E.C., and
32 Abingdon Street, Westminster, S.W. ; or
E. PONSONBY, 116 Grafton Street, Dublin.

1902.

[Cd. 1046.]   *Price* 1s. 1d.

CONTENTS OF THE REPORT.

APPENDICES.

FORTY-FOURTH ANNUAL REPORT.

TO THE RIGHT HONOURABLE

LORD BALFOUR OF BURLEIGH,

His Majesty's Secretary for Scotland.

GENERAL BOARD OF COMMISSIONERS IN LUNACY
FOR SCOTLAND, EDINBURGH.

February 1902.

MY LORD,
We have the honour to lay before you our
Forty-fourth Annual Report on the Condition and Management of
Lunatics and Lunatic Asylums in Scotland.

I. THE NUMBER OF THE INSANE ON 1ST JANUARY 1902.

Number of Lunatics on 1st January 1902.

The number of the insane in Scotland on 1st January of the
present year, exclusive of insane persons maintained at home by
their natural guardians, is shown in the tabular statement on
page xiv.

It appears from this statement that at 1st January, 1902, there
were in Scotland 16,288 insane persons of whom we had official
cognisance, including the inmates of Training Schools for Imbecile
Children and of the Lunatic Department of the General Prison at
Perth. Of these, 2401 were maintained from private sources, 13,841
by parochial rates, and 46 at the expense of the State. As the
total number at 1st January, 1901, was 15,899, an increase has
taken place during the past year of 389.

II. THE STATISTICS OF LUNACY FROM 1858 TO 1902.

CHANGES IN NUMBER AND MODE OF DISTRIBUTION.

The Statistics of Lunacy from 1858 to 1902.

In Table I. of Appendix A we give the number of private and
pauper lunatics of whom we had official cognisance, exclusive of
the inmates of the Lunatic Department of H.M. General Prison,
and of Training Schools for Imbecile Children, at 1st January 1858,
the average number in each quinquenniad from 1861 to 1880, and
the number at 1st January of each subsequent year up to the
present time, distinguishing the numbers of each category accommodated in establishments and in private dwellings, and also distinguishing between the sexes.

The Statistics
of Lunacy from
1858 to 1902.

Increase of
Number since
1858.

Table II. of Appendix A shows that from 1st January 1858, when we entered on our functions, to 1st January 1902, the total number of lunatics officially known to the Board, including the inmates of the Lunatic Department of H.M. General Prison, and also the inmates of Training Schools for Imbecile Children, has increased from 5824 to 16,288, showing an increase of 10,464, which was distributed as follows :—

	Increase since 1858.
1. Private Patients :—	
a. Resident in Establishments, . .	1122
b. Resident in Private Dwellings, .	110
2. Pauper Patients :—	
a. Resident in Establishments, . .	7997
b. Resident in Private Dwellings, .	847
Total, . . .	10,076
Increase of number in Training Schools, and the Lunatic Department of the General Prison, ...	388
Total Increase, ...	10,464

Changes in
Mode of
Distribution.

Table II. further shows the mode in which lunatics of all classes were provided for on the 1st of January 1858, and the mode in which they have been provided for since that time. The following statement shows the numbers provided for in the various ways at the beginning and at the end of the whole period :—

	At 1st January 1858.	At 1st January 1902.	Increase since 1858.	Decrease since 1858.	Net Increase.
In Royal or Public Asylums, .	2380	4,287	1907	...	...
,, District Asylums, . . .	...	7,002	7002	...	...
,, Private Asylums, . . .	745	130	...	615	...
,, Parochial Asylums . . .	576	550	..	26	...
,, Lunatic Wards of Poorhouses, .	264	1115	851	...	...
,, Private Dwellings, . . .	1804	2761	957	...	...
,, H.M. General Prison, . .	26	46	20	...	...
,, Training Schools, . .	29	397	368	...	...
Total Increase or Decrease,	5824	16,288	11,105	641	10,464

These figures show an increase under every head except private asylums, which have long ceased to receive pauper patients and are now few in number, and parochial asylums, which have also decreased in number, owing to the erection of District Asylums.

Increase of
Lunacy in
proportion to
Population.

INCREASE OF LUNACY IN PROPORTION TO POPULATION.

Since 1858, the number of lunatics under the jurisdiction of the Board has increased 180 per cent. The increase of the population during the same period has been 49 per cent. Table III. of Appendix A shows from 1858 to the present year the pro-

portions per 100,000 of population of private lunatics, of
pauper lunatics, and of both classes combined; and also shows the
proportions of each class disposed of respectively in asylums and
in private dwellings. The two last columns show further the proportion of ordinary paupers to population and the proportion of
pauper lunatics to ordinary paupers. The proportions from 1891
onwards have been recalculated this year on the corrected populations founded upon the results of the Census of 1901, which showed
a population somewhat in excess of the estimate.

The figures in Table I. show that the number of private patients
in asylums has increased during the past year by 44 and in private
dwellings by 6, an increase of 50 in all. The number of pauper
patients in establishments has increased during the year by 358
and in private dwellings has decreased by 38, showing a net
increase of the total number of pauper lunatics during the year of
320, excluding the inmates of Training Schools. The average
annual increase of pauper patients in establishments during the past
ten years has been 274. The increase during the past year has therefore been 84 in excess of the average of the past ten years. The
number of pauper patients in establishments has risen during these
ten years from 8207 to 10,950, that is, by 2743, a number which it
would require five of our larger District Asylums to accommodate.
Had the proportion of pauper lunatics in establishments during the past
remained the same in 1902 as it was in 1892 the increase of
population would alone have accounted for 910 of the total increase.
The proportion to population has, however, been rising steadily
throughout the ten years and now stands at 244 per 100,000,
instead of 203 as it was in 1892. The increase during the last year
alone shows a rise of 5 pauper lunatics in establishments per 100,000
inhabitants of Scotland. The increase of 2743 shown in the ten
years, in so far as it is not the result of increase of population,
must be due to an increased number of admissions in proportion to
population, or to accumulation arising from an excess in the
number of admissions over the number of discharges and deaths, or
to both these causes combined.

The number of pauper lunatics in private dwellings has increased
during the past ten years from 2435 to 2631. This increase of 196
has not been quite sufficient to maintain the proportion to population of ten years ago, which was 60, and is now 59. In 1895 and
1896 the proportion rose as high as 64. The largest actual number
of pauper patients under private care was attained in 1900, when
it stood at 2703. Both subsequent years show a considerable fall,
which will be afterwards referred to (*see* page xlii). The fall in the
number of pauper patients provided for under private care
accounts to a small extent for the increased number accommodated
in asylums.

The proportion per 100,000 of population of private patients in
asylums, who, it should be kept in view, include a considerable
number of patients drawn from England and Ireland, has risen
during the past ten years from 42 to 47. It has remained at the
latter figure without change during the past five years. The
proportion to population of private patients under care in private
dwellings has remained unchanged for many years.

Admissions to Register and Removals therefrom.

.The Statistics of Lunacy from 1858 to 1902.
  Table IV. (Appendix A) shows the total number of private and pauper lunatics on the register at 1st January of each year from 1874 to 1902, the number placed on the register during each year

Number placed on and removed from Register.
from 1874 to 1901, and the number removed therefrom each year by discharge or death. It further shows, for each year, the excess of the number placed on the register over the number removed from the register, and the proportion of deaths per cent. on the average number on the register.

  It will be observed that the average annual excess of the number placed on the register over the number removed from the register is 348 for the quinquenniad 1895–99, and that the excess of admissions to the register over removals from it was 370 in 1901, being thus 22 above the average for the quinquenniad 1895–99.

Number Registered for first time.
  Table V. (Appendix A) shows for each year from 1874 to 1901 the total number of private and pauper lunatics registered during the year, who had never previously been registered as lunatics, and the proportion of such lunatics per 100,000 of population. In the case of private patients, the proportion to population remains practically the same throughout the 28 years included in the Table. In the case of pauper patients, there has been a fairly steady rise in the proportion throughout the period. A slight fall is shown in the figures for 1901, but, as will be inferred from an examination of those for earlier years, this fall has probably no significance.

Admissions, Discharges, and Deaths in Establishments.
  Tables VI., VII., VIII., and IX. (Appendix A) give statistics relating to the number of private and of pauper patients admitted to establishments, the number discharged from establishments recovered and unrecovered, and the number removed by transfer or death, for each year since 1858.

Statistics of Lunacy for the Year 1901.

III. STATISTICS OF LUNACY FOR THE YEAR 1901.

Changes in the Distribution of the Insane during the Year.

Changes in the Number and Distribution of the Insane.
  With regard to the distribution of the insane in the different classes of establishments and in private dwellings, as shown in the Table on page xiv, the following differences appear in the manner of distribution of *registered* * lunatics at 1st January 1902, when compared with what it was at 1st January 1901.

  In Royal Asylums there is an increase of 35 private patients and of 88 pauper patients.

  In District Asylums there is an increase of 2 private patients and 194 pauper patients.

  In Private Asylums there is an increase of 4 private patients.

  In Parochial Asylums there is an increase of 6 pauper patients.

  In Lunatic Wards of Poorhouses there is an increase of 70 pauper patients.

  In Private Dwellings there is an increase of 6 private patients and a decrease of 38 pauper patients.

  * The inmates of Training Schools for Imbeciles and of the Lunatic Department of the General Prison are recorded in separate books, and, not being on the Board's General Register of Lunatics, are not included in this statement.

The general results during 1901, as compared with 1900, are, in Statistics of Lunacy for the Year 1901. regard to *registered** lunatics, as follows :—(1) There was a total increase of 370, of whom 50 were private patients and 320 were pauper patients. (2) The total increase of 370 arises from an Changes in the Number and Distribution of the Insane. increase of the number in establishments by 402, and a decrease of the number in private dwellings by 32. (3) Of the increased number of 402 in establishments, 44 were private patients and 358 were pauper patients. As the average increase in the number of private patients in establishments in the five years from 1st January 1896 to 1st January 1901 was 31, and of pauper patients 327, the increase for both classes during the year 1901 has been above the average increase of that quinquenniad. (4) All pauper lunatics in establishments continue to be provided for in institutions of a public character.

In the number of non-registered lunatics the following changes occurred during 1901 :—

In the Lunatic Department of the General Prison the number is the same as last year.

In Training Schools for Imbecile Children there was an increase of 19.

---

* The inmates of Training Schools for Imbeciles and of the Lunatic Department of the General Prison are recorded in separate books, and, not being on the Board's General Register of Lunatics, are not included in this statement.

[TABLE

Statistics of Lunacy for the year 1901.

Number of Lunatics at 1st January 1902.

Number of Lunatics at 1st January 1902.

MODE OF DISTRIBUTION.	Male.	Female.	Total.	PRIVATE.			PAUPER.		
				M.	F.	T.	M.	F.	T.
In Royal Asylums,	2,032	2,255	4,287	856	941	1,797	1,176	1,314	2,490
„ District Asylums,	3,510	3,492	7,002	95	112	207	3,415	3,380	6,795
„ Private Asylums,	44	86	130	44	86	130	...	...	...
„ Parochial Asylums, i.e. Lunatic Wards of Poorhouses with unrestricted Licenses,	268	282	550	...	...	...	268	282	550
„ Lunatic Wards of Poorhouses with restricted Licenses,	583	532	1,115	...	...	...	583	532	1,115
„ Private Dwellings,	1,100	1,661	2,761	49	81	180	1,051	1,580	2,631
	7,587	8,308	15,845	1,044	1,220	2,264	6,493	7,088	13,581
„ Lunatic Department of General Prison,	39	7	46	88	49	137	...	...	...
„ Training Schools,	246	151	397	...	...	...	158	102	260
TOTALS,	7,892	8,466	16,288	1,132	1,269	2,401	6,651	7,190	13,841

CHANGES FROM THE PAUPER TO THE PRIVATE CLASS,
AND *vice versa.* .

Statistics of
Lunacy for the
year 1901.

Changes from
Pauper to
Private Class,
and *vice versa.*

It must be kept in view, in connection with the statistical Tables giving the number of lunatics classified into private and pauper patients, that each patient does not necessarily continue till his discharge in the class to which he belonged on being placed on the Board's register. The results shown depend partly on the number of persons who, while continuing on the Board's register, cease to be private patients and become paupers, and *vice versa.* The following tabular statement shows the average number of pauper patients who have become private patients, and of private patients who have become pauper patients, for the quinquenniads 1885-89 1890-94, and 1895-99, and the numbers for the subsequent years:—

'YEARS.		Number of Registered Patients transferred from Pauper to Private Class.	Number of Registered Patients transferred from Private to Pauper Class.
1885–89		23	42
1890–94	Average Numbers	22	41
1895–99		32	45
1900, ...		28	46
1901, ...		20	34

ESTABLISHMENTS FOR LUNATICS.

Under the term Establishments, as used in this Report, we include Royal, District, Private, and Parochial Asylums, Lunatic Wards of Poorhouses, Training Schools for Imbecile Children, and the Lunatic Department of the General Prison. But it is necessary to point out that the Tables in the Appendix take no account of figures referring either to the Training Schools or to the General Prison, except where this is specially stated.

ADMISSIONS TO ESTABLISHMENTS.

(1) *Admissions directly under a Sheriff's Order, the Sanction of the Board, or other Statutory Authority.*

In arriving at the number of persons admitted to establishments who thereby add to the gross number of asylum patients, the number of admissions which refer to a mere transfer from one establishment to another must be deducted. In Table VII. the number of admissions for each year is therefore given after deducting transfers; and it shows (1) that the number of private patients admitted during last year was 538, being 5 less

Statistics of
Lunacy for
1901.

(1) Direct
Admissions to
Establish-
ments.

than in the preceding year, and 4 less than the average for the quinquenniad 1895–99 ; and (2) that the number of pauper patients admitted was 2962, being 63 more than the number during the preceding year, and 223 more than the average for the quinquenniad 1895–99.

(2) Admissions
by Transfer.

(2) *Admissions by Transfer.*

It will be seen from Table VI. that the number of patients transferred from one establishment to another during 1901 was 477, which is 81 less than the number transferred during the preceding year, and 155 below the average for the five years 1895–99. The number of pauper patients transferred was, as it always is, larger in proportion to the total admissions than the number of private patients transferred. This is due to the fact that private patients are usually placed at once in the asylums in which it is intended they should stay during their whole term of asylum residence; while pauper patients are frequently placed, in the first instance, in the asylums of the districts in which they are resident, and are afterwards removed to the asylums of the districts to which they belong. The following tabular statement shows the transfers which occurred. They were authorised in 40 instances by Sheriffs, and in 437 by the Board.

Removed from	To Royal and District Asylums.				To Private Asylums.				To Parochial Asylums		To Lunatic Wards of Poor-houses.		Total Transfers.	
	Private.		Pauper.		Private.		Pauper.		Pauper.		Pauper.		Private.	Pauper.
	M.	F.	M.	F.	M.	F.	M.	F.	M.	F.	M.	F.		
Royal and District Asylums,	20	11	91	118	...	2	...	...	1	8	101	53	33	372
Private Asylums, . .	8	2	...	...	...	...	...	...	...	...	...	...	5	...
Parochial Asylums, .	...	...	5	9	...	...	...	...	1	13	...	...	...	26
Lunatic Wards of Poor-houses, . . .	...	...	24	15	...	...	...	...	...	...	...	...	...	39
TOTALS, . .	23	13	120	142	..	2	...	...	2	21	101	53	38	439

(3) Admission
of Voluntary
Patients to
Establish-
ments.

(3) *Admission of Voluntary Patients.*

Voluntary patients are persons who, with the sanction of the Board, granted on a simple application signed by the patient, voluntarily enter asylums for treatment of mental disorder, but whose mental condition is not such as to render it legal to grant certificates of insanity in their case. They cannot be detained for more than three days after giving notice of their intention or desire to leave. They are not registered as lunatics, but a record is made of their names and other particulars regarding them. The whole number of such persons admitted into asylums in 1901 was 90. The average number admitted for the ten years 1892–1901 was 82. The number resident at 1st January 1902 was 75.

We have for many years been able to state that nothing has Statistics of Lunacy for 1901. occurred to indicate any difficulty or disadvantage traceable to the presence of this class of patients in asylums; and we continue to be of opinion that it is a useful provision of the law which permits (3) Admission of Voluntary Patients to Establishments. persons who desire to place themselves under care in an asylum to do so in a way which is not attended with troublesome or disagreeable formalities. At the visits of the Medical Commissioners to asylums all voluntary inmates are seen, and they have then an opportunity of making statements in regard to their position, should they desire to make any. When there is reason to suppose that they in any way fail to understand the conditions of their residence, these conditions are explained to them.

DISCHARGES FROM ESTABLISHMENTS.

Discharges from Establishments.

The remark we made, when speaking of the admissions to establishments, in regard to the necessity for the exclusion of such admissions as were merely transfers from one establishment to another, is applicable also to the discharges from establishments. The general statistics of the discharges for each year, after deducting transfers, are given in Table VIII. (Appendix A).

(1) *Discharges of the Recovered.*

Discharges from Establishments of Recovered Patients.

It will be seen from Table VIII. of Appendix A that there were 227 private patients discharged recovered during 1901, which is 12 below the number for the preceding year, and 6 below the average for the five years 1895–99. The number of pauper patients discharged recovered was 1268, which is 8 below the number for the preceding year, and 59 above the average for the five years 1895–99. Table IX. (Appendix A) shows the proportion of recoveries per cent. of the numbers admitted into each class of establishment. The following tabular statement shows these percentages for the quinquenniads 1890–94 and 1895-99, and for the two subsequent years:—

CLASSES OF ESTABLISHMENTS.	Recoveries per cent. of Admissions.			
	1890-1894.	1895-1899.	1900.	1901.
In Royal and District Asylums,	39	37	38	39
,, Private Asylums, . .	38	38	44	43
,, Parochial Asylums, . .	43	42	60	51
,, Lunatic Wards of Poorhouses,	7	5	4	4

It will be observed that in this statement private and pauper patients are not distinguished from one another. Regard would require to be had to this fact, and also to the nature of the cases received into each class of establishment, and even into each in-

b

dividual establishment, before these percentages could be accurately appreciated. Very erroneous inferences might be drawn from the figures if due weight were not given to these and other circumstances which have been discussed in previous Reports.

(2) *Discharges of the Unrecovered.*

The number of private patients discharged unrecovered, excluding transfers, during 1901, was, as shown in Table VIII. (Appendix A), 114, which is 19 below the average of the five years 1895–99. The number of pauper patients discharged unrecovered was 403, which is 16 above the number so discharged in the preceding year, and 1 above the average for the five years 1895–99.

The following tabular statement shows the different modes in which the discharge of unrecovered patients took place during the year 1901 :—

		Number of Patients removed Unrecovered from Asylums during 1901.		
			Pauper.	
MODES OF DISCHARGE.	Private.	Re-mained Pauper Lunatics.	Removed from Poor Roll.	Total.
By Friends,	95	...	...	95
,, Minute of Parish Council,	...	144	180	324
,, Escape or Absence over 28 days,	4	...	24	28
,, Expiry of period of Liberation on Probation,	7	14	11	32
,, Expiry of Emergency Certificate,	...	...	1	1
,, Expiry of Interim Order under Sec. 15 of 25 & 26 Vict. c. 54,	...	...	...	...
,, Warrant of Sheriff, and sent to England, Ireland, and other countries,	...	...	26	26
,, Order of Court to undergo Trial,	...	...	...	...
,, Withdrawal of Sheriff's Order,	...	..	...	...
,, Being placed in Perth Prison as a King's Pleasure Lunatic,	...	...	..	...
,, Transference to Training Schools for Imbecile Children,	...	3	...	3
,, Authority of Medical Officer under Sec. 17 of 25 & 26 Vict. c. 54,	...	...	...	...
,, Expiry of Warrant granted under Sec. 6 of 34 & 35 Vict. c. 55,	8	...	...	8
,, Defective admission papers,	...	...	..	...
,, Determination of Order under Sec. 7 of 29 & 30 Vic. c. 51,	...	...	...	...
Totals,	114	161	242	517

DEATHS IN ESTABLISHMENTS.

The number of private patients who died in establishments during 1901 is shown by Table VIII. of Appendix A to have been 170, which is the same as in 1900, and 25 more than the average of the five years 1895–99. The number of pauper patients who died was 917, which is 41 less than in 1900, and 98 above the average of the five years 1895–99.

The following statement, derived from Table IX. of Appendix A, shows the death-rate for private and pauper patients in establishments per cent. of the average number resident for the quinquenniads 1890-94 and 1895-99, and for the two subsequent years:—

CLASSES OF PATIENTS.	Proportion of Deaths per cent. on Number Resident in all Establishments.			
	1890–94.	1895–1899.	1900.	1901.
Private Patients, .	7·6	7·2	8·2	8·0
Pauper Patients, .	8·7	8·5	9·2	8·5
Both Classes, .	8·5	8·2	9·0	8·4

The rate of mortality per cent. of the number resident in different classes of establishments for the quinquenniads 1890–94 and 1895–99 and for the years 1900 and 1901 is shown in the following statement:—

CLASSES OF ESTABLISHMENTS.	Proportion of Deaths per cent. on Number Resident.			
	1890–94.	1895–99.	1900.	1901.
Royal and District Asylums, . .	8·8	8·4	9·4	8·8
Private Asylums, ...	6·3	9·0	7·8	4·7
Parochial Asylums, ...	9·6	10·5	9·9	9·0
Lunatic Wards of Poorhouses, .	4·6	4·5	4·5	5·1

Table X. (Appendix A) gives for each sex the number of deaths, and the number of deaths from various specified causes, in all establishments, for each year from 1870 to 1901, together with the absolute annual average number of deaths from each cause, and the average percentage of deaths from each cause, during each period of five years.

Table XXII. of Appendix A shows the number of deaths, from the various causes specified, in each establishment during the past year.

REMOVALS FROM ESTABLISHMENTS ON STATUTORY PROBATION.

At 1st January 1901, 68 patients were absent from asylums on probation, with the sanction of the Board. Of these, 36 have been finally discharged as recovered, 12 were sent back, and 20 remained on the expiry of the period under the care of friends. In the course of 1901, 152 patients were discharged on probation. Of these, 23 have been finally discharged as recovered; 14 whose period of probation has expired remain under the care of friends; 27 have been returned to asylums, and 1 died. The number still on probation at the close of the year was 87.

The following statement shows the average number of patients liberated on probation in each period of ten years from their authorisation in 1862 to 1892, and the number so liberated for each of the subsequent nine years:—

Year.	Number of Patients Liberated on Probation.
1862-3-72, ⎫	130
1873-82, ⎬ Average Numbers, . . ⎰	118
1883-92, ⎭	122
1893, ...	141
1894, ...	172
1895, ...	138
1896, ...	148
1897, ...	109
1898, ...	123
1899, ...	136
1900, ...	134
1901, ...	152

Of the 4950 patients liberated on probation since 1862, 1070 or 22 per cent. were replaced, before the expiry of the period of probation, in the asylums from which they had been removed.

The numbers liberated on probation from the different establishments in 1901 are shown in the following statements :—

Aberdeen Royal Asylum, .	9	Westermains Private Asylum, .	0
Argyll District Asylum, . .	6	Greenock Parochial Asylum, .	0
Ayr District Asylum,	11	Paisley Parochial Asylum, Craw	
Banff District Asylum, . .	3	Road, ...	0
Crichton Royal Institution, .	14	Paisley Parochial Asylum, Riccarts-	
Dundee Royal Asylum, . .	3	bar, ...	1
Edinburgh Royal Asylum, .	13	Aberdeen East Poorhouse, .	0
Elgin District Asylum, . .	0	Aberdeen West Poorhouse, .	0
Fife District Asylum, . .	0	Buchan Poorhouse, . . .	0
Glasgow Royal Asylum, . .	5	Cunninghame Poorhouse, .	0
Glasgow District Asylum (Gartloch),	4	Dumbarton Poorhouse, . .	0
,, ,, ,, (Woodilee),	0	Dundee East Poorhouse, .	0
Govan District Asylum, . .	1	Dundee West Poorhouse, .	0
Haddington District Asylum, .	0	Edinburgh Poorhouse, . .	0
Inverness District Asylum, .	44	Govan Poorhouse, . . .	0
Kirklands Asylum, . . .	1	Hamilton Poorhouse, . .	0
Lanark District Asylum, . .	0	Inveresk Poorhouse, . .	0
Midlothian District Asylum, .	2	Kincardine Poorhouse, . .	0
Montrose Royal Asylum, . .	1	Linlithgow Poorhouse, . .	0
Murray's Royal Asylum, . .	0	Old Monkland Poorhouse, .	0
Perth District Asylum, . .	1	Perth Poorhouse, . . .	0
Roxburgh District Asylum, .	26	Wigtown Poorhouse, . .	1
Stirling District Asylum, . .	5		
Mavisbank Private Asylum, .	0		
Saughtonhall Private Asylum, .	1	Total,	152

In the numbers above given, patients liberated on trial for periods not exceeding twenty-eight days are not included. Such trials can be made without the sanction of the Board, and they are frequently made use of by some Superintendents. The statutory removal on probation is not granted by the Board for a period exceeding one year, and its special use is to permit of the conditional liberation of patients whose fitness for permanent discharge cannot be determined without trial for a longer period than twenty-eight days. It is frequently found that patients who appear while in the asylum to have improved so much that they are fit for private care become unsettled when the influences of the asylum are removed. It is not, however, justifiable to retain permanently in the asylum all patients in whose cases a possibility of such unsettlement is thought to exist. The large majority of patients liberated 'on probation undergo no deterioration, and many are benefited by the change. By liberating patients on probation there is an opportunity given for testing their fitness for permanent discharge, and they can be replaced in the asylum without the expense attending a Sheriff's order, if they prove unfit. A more frequent use of removal on probation in some establishments would probably lead to a larger number of permanent discharges than takes place at present.

It must not, however, be inferred from the figures given above that the number of liberations on probation from any particular asylum is an indication of the frequency with which trial is made in it of the fitness of unrecovered patients for residence in private dwellings. In some asylums from which few or no discharges on statutory probation take place, the removal of unrecovered patients is freely resorted to either by severing their connection with the asylum at once or after the trial of twenty-eight days, which, as already explained, may take place by permission of the Superintendent, and without the authority of the Board.

[margin note: Statistics of Lunacy for 1901.]

[margin note: Removals on Probation.]

LIST OF ESTABLISHMENTS AND NUMBER OF LUNATICS IN EACH.

[margin note: Distribution of Lunatics in Establishments.]

Table XV. (Appendix A) shows the number of private and pauper lunatics in each Royal, District, Private, and Parochial Asylum and Licensed Poorhouse on 1st January 1902, and also the number of pauper lunatics from each county in each Royal, District, and Parochial Asylum and Licensed Poorhouse. With very few exceptions, the pauper lunatics of Scotland are disposed of either in asylums erected for them by the Boards of the lunacy districts to which they belong, or in asylums with which such Boards have made contracts.

SHERIFFS' ORDERS.

[margin note: Orders granted by Sheriffs during the Year.]

Table XIX. (Appendix A) gives the statutory return exhibiting the number of orders granted by Sheriffs for the admission of lunatics into any Public, Private, District or Parochial Asylum, or House, stating the Asylum or House to which such order referred, during the year ending 31st December 1901. The number of orders granted during the year was 3457.

LICENCES GRANTED BY THE BOARD FOR ESTABLISHMENTS.

[margin note: Licences granted by the Board to Asylums and Lunatic Wards of Poorhouses.]

Table XX. (Appendix A) gives the statutory return exhibiting the number of licences granted by us for the continuance or establishment of charitable institutions, private asylums, and lunatic wards of poorhouses, and the transfer of any licence from one establishment to another, during the year ending 31st December 1901. The number of licences amounted to 23, and they were granted for the renewal of the licences of 2 charitable institutions, 3 private asylums, and 18 wards or portions of poorhouses set apart for lunatics.

RESULTS OF TREATMENT IN ESTABLISHMENTS.

In the several sections of Table XXI. (Appendix A) we give
the average number resident, the number admitted, and the
results of treatment for each establishment. We have already
alluded to the general results which these Tables exhibit when
commenting on Tables VII., VIII., and IX.

Table XXII. (Appendix A) gives a classification of the causes of
death of those patients who died in establishments during the year
1901, giving each class of establishment and each establishment
separately.

CHANGES AMONG ATTENDANTS AND SERVANTS IN ESTABLISHMENTS.

The whole number of attendants and servants who left, were dismissed, or died, during 1901, was 977, which is 67 less than the
number for the previous year. The number who resigned their
situations voluntarily is 706, which is 97 fewer than last year.

In addition to the 706 who resigned voluntarily, 50 left on
account of ill - health, 5 died during their term of service, 29
absconded, 52 were dismissed for incompetence or unsuitability, 6 on
account of services not being longer required, and 129 for misconduct.

We recommend that the administrators of institutions in which
changes among attendants occur frequently should enquire carefully into the causes, and should endeavour to remove them by
offering increased inducements to good attendants to remain, and to
a better class to take service. Our experience tends to show that
in the case of men a high class of attendant and security for permanent service are best obtained by increasing the number of
married attendants. We therefore recommend, in all cases in
which it has not already been done, that comfortable cottages for
married attendants should be provided, wherever such accommodation is not to be had in the immediate neighbourhood of the
asylum.

It is proper to observe, however, in reference to the figures given
above, that we have ascertained that the great bulk of the changes
occurs in the case of attendants and servants who have only been a
short time in asylum service. As the number of attendants and
servants who resigned voluntarily constitutes no less than 72 per
cent. of the whole number of changes during the last year, it may
be inferred that, although the inducements to enter asylum service
are not pecuniarily unattractive to those who seek employment, the
service is found on trial to be congenial to a comparatively small
number. This may be due in part to the trying nature of the
service, and possibly still more to the general want of freedom
inseparable from the discipline of a large institution, which causes
a preference to be given to employments, perhaps less well paid, in
which the workers' time, after certain hours, is wholly at their own
disposal. In the case of male attendants, the somewhat similar
prison service proves more attractive than asylum employment, on
account of the pensions to which prison warders become entitled
after long service.

Statistics of
Lunacy for
1901.

Changes among
Attendants
and Servants
in Establish-
ments.

It should further be borne in mind that these figures include
many persons who are not engaged in the special duty of attending
on the insane, such as artisans of all kinds, farm-workers, hall-
maids, laundrymaids, &c.

We register the name of every attendant and servant dismissed
from an asylum for misconduct, and when any name so registered
reappears among the notices of engagement transmitted to us, we
intimate the facts to the superintendent by whom the engagement
has been made, with a view to his ascertaining whether the
engaged person is identical with that dismissed. In this way it
frequently happens that the fact of dismissal from another asylum,
which has been concealed on re-engagement, is detected. When the
fault concealed has been serious, dismissal for a second time follows,
but when it has not been of a grave nature, and the person's
character has otherwise been good, another chance is usually given.
We have no doubt that attendants and servants dismissed from
asylums would much more frequently engage in the service of
other asylums, if it were not generally known among them that the
facts as to dismissal will be communicated by the Board to any
asylum in Scotland in which they re-engage.

Escapes from
Establish-
ments.

ESCAPES FROM ESTABLISHMENTS.

The whole number of escapes during 1901 was 190. Of these,
96 were brought back within twenty-four hours, 45 within a week,
and 19 after a week. There were 30 still absent on the expiry of
twenty-eight days from the date of escape. Of the 30 patients
not brought back, 2 were removed from the asylum registers as
recovered, 11 as relieved, 15 as not improved, 1 died, and the mental
state of 1 was unknown.

The following statement shows the number of escapes that
have taken place during each of the ten years from 1892 to 1901 :—

Years.	Number of Escapes.	Not brought Back.		Number of Escapes per 1000 of Patients in Establishments.
		Removed from Register as Unrecovered.	Removed from Register as Recovered.	
1892, . . .	176	15	1	18
1893, . . .	201	26	4	20
1894, . . .	236	17	4	18
1895, . . .	196	21	...	18
1896, . . .	180	17	2	16
1897, . . .	177	17	3	15
1898, . . .	217	33	2	18
1899, . . .	186	19	...	12
1900, . . .	190	27	3	15
1901, . . .	190	26	2	15
Totals, .	1,949	218	21	

It appears from this statement that the number of escapes during
1901 per 1000 patients was lower than the average shown during
the last ten years. Very few of the patients not brought back before

Statistics of
Lunacy for
1901.
——
Escapes from
Establish-
ments.
the expiry of the twenty-eight days during which the law permits of their being received into the asylum without new certificates and new Sheriff's order are permanently lost sight of, and many are ultimately replaced in asylums. Those discharged recovered were as a rule convalescent patients whose discharge was in contemplation at the time of escape.

Accidents in
Establish-
ments,

ACCIDENTS IN ESTABLISHMENTS.

The whole number of accidents reported to us as having taken place during the year 1901 was 264. Of these, 17 ended fatally, death in 8 of these cases being due to suicide.

Of the deaths by suicide, 2 were caused by strangulation produced by tying, in one case a neckerchief, and in another a sheet, round the neck and fastening the detached portion to the bedpost : 1 by hanging, through suspending a strip of the cover of a mattress from a ventilation aperture in a window shutter; 1 by cutting the throat with a razor which an attendant had omitted to lock up : 1 by swallowing artificial teeth; 1 by swallowing poisonous liniment; 1 by swallowing two pieces of stick; and 1 by escaping from an attendant and being run over by a railway train. One case occurred of attempted suicide through swallowing the greater portion of the contents of a bottle containing chloral, bromide, and Indian hemp. Of the 9 accidental deaths not due to suicide, 1 was that of a patient who absented himself from the asylum by breaking his parole, and died in England from an overdose of morphia. taken, it is believed, without suicidal intention; 2 were caused by suffocation in bed during epileptic fits; 3 by food obstructing the air passages in the case of patients in a feeble condition; 1 by scalding with hot water from a basin; 1 by fracture of the ribs, found after death, and caused in some manner unascertained, in the case of a patient labouring under acute mania and difficult to restrain; and 1 by escape and being run over by a railway train under circumstances which pointed to the occurrence being purely accidental. The circumstances of all the deaths by suicide and accident were investigated by the Crown authorities and ourselves.

In 69 further cases the accidents involved fracture of bones or dislocation of joints, and in 18 cases injuries to the head. These were occasioned in 53 cases by falls, and in 24 cases by struggling with fellow-patients or attendants, or by assaults of fellow-patients. In 6 cases the fractures were unintentionally self-inflicted, and in 4 cases the cause was unascertained. There were reported in addition 15 accidental wounds, contusions, doubtful fractures, &c., of a more or less serious character, and 144 minor injuries. Most. if not all, of these latter were in themselves of a trifling character, such as bruises, scratches, &c., and would probably not have been recorded in the Register of Accidents prior to the Board's circular letter of 14th January 1901, referred to and printed in our last Report, which enjoined their recognition and entry as a protective measure, in view of the significance which might attach to them as bearing upon the general treatment of the insane.

In every case of death by accident, of sudden or unexpected death, or death under circumstances of apparent or alleged suspicion, occurring in an asylum, the Superintendent is required to give immediate intimation not only to the Board, but also to the Procurator-Fiscal of the county in which the asylum is situated, who makes such inquiry as he may deem necessary.

Statistics of Lunacy for 1901.

Accidents in Establish-ments.

PROGRESSIVE HISTORY OF PATIENTS FIRST ADMITTED INTO ESTABLISHMENTS IN THE YEAR 1898.

Progressive History of Patients first admitted in 1898.

On page xxxi of our Fourteenth Annual Report will be found a Table showing the changes which occurred among 1297 patients admitted to asylums for the first time in 1858 during that year, and the eleven subsequent years ending 1869. The results of that enquiry are further discussed on page xxxv of our Sixteenth Report. A similar series of Tables was begun in our Eleventh Report, relating to 1326 (subsequently corrected to 1319) patients admitted for the first time in 1868. The thirtieth and last of these Tables was given in our Fortieth Report, with a discussion of the inferences which may be drawn from the results.

The following is the fourth of a third series of such Tables dealing with the progressive history of 2539 patients admitted to asylums for the first time in 1898:—

		Progressive History of Patients first admitted into Asylums in 1898.							
YEAR.	New Cases Admitted.	Re-admitted during Year.				Removed Recovered.	Removed Unrecovered.	Died.	Remaining at 31st December
		Once.	Twice.	Thrice.	Total Number of Re-admissions.				
1898	2,539	71	3	...	77	678	135	247	1,556
1899	...	128	2	...	132	390	123	160	1,015
1900	...	93	9	...	111	93	45	113	875
1901	...	79	1	...	81	51	30	56	819

It will be observed from this Table that at the close of the second year 209 re-admissions had occurred, and at the close of the fourth year the re-admissions numbered 401. Of these, 371 had been re-admitted once during the four years, and 15 twice (the latter number counting as 30 re-admissions). The total number of re-admissions during the four years is equal to 15·8 per cent. of the original number admitted. Calculated on the original number admitted, the recoveries during the first two years amounted to 42·1 per cent., discharges unrecovered 10·2, and deaths 16 per cent., the removals from all causes thus representing 68·3 per cent. during the first two years of the original number admitted. During the succeeding two years the removals from all causes only amounted to 15·3 per cent. of the original admissions.

Calculated on the mean number resident (the mean for the first year being taken at half the number resident at 31st December), the recoveries during the first year amounted to 87·1 per cent., and the deaths to 31·7 per cent. In the fourth year these percentages had fallen respectively to 6·0 and 6·6.

IV. PRESENT CONDITION OF ESTABLISHMENTS FOR THE INSANE.

Establishments for the insane in Scotland arrange themselves in the followings groups :—(a) Royal and District Asylums, (b) Private Asylums, (c) Parochial Asylums, (d) Lunatic Wards of Poorhouses, (e) Training Schools for Imbecile Children, and (f) the Department for Criminal or State Patients in the General Prison.

The Royal or Chartered Asylums are institutions which were in existence previous to the enactment of the Lunacy Act of 1857. They are 7 in number. Five of these—the Royal Asylums of Aberdeen, Dundee, Edinburgh, Glasgow, and Montrose—were at their origin erected out of funds derived from legacies, subscriptions, and donations, including in all cases contributions of greater or less amount from parochial sources. The other two institutions, the Crichton Royal Institution at Dumfries, and Murray's Royal Asylum at Perth, were erected out of funds provided by the benefactors whose names they bear. All the 7 Royal Asylums received both pauper and private patients at the time of the passing of the Act of 1857; but the Directors of Murray's Royal Asylum resolved, soon after the passing of that Act, to devote the institution to the care and treatment of private patients only, and a like resolution was subsequently come to by the Directors of the Glasgow Royal Asylum.

District Asylums are institutions created under the provisions of the Lunacy Act of 1857. Asylums of this class are provided out of funds furnished by county and burgh assessments, and are intended for the accommodation of the pauper lunatics of localities where such accommodation is not otherwise provided. At present there are 16 such asylums in occupation.

Private Asylums are establishments conducted by their proprietors for profit ; and only private patients are received into them. There are 3 such establishments at present.

Parochial Asylums are establishments erected out of funds furnished by the poor-rate of the parishes to which they belong. These establishments are called Parochial Asylums for convenience, but they are technically lunatic wards of poorhouses which have been licensed by the Board to receive pauper patients suffering from all forms of insanity, that is, those who are curable and dangerous as well as those who are regarded as incurable and harmless. There are three establishments of this class at present.

The name of Lunatic Wards of Poorhouses is given specially to portions of poorhouses which have been set apart for the accommodation of pauper lunatics who are regarded as incurable and not dangerous. Such sections exist at present in 15 poorhouses.

The National Institution for the Training of Imbecile Children at Larbert, and the Baldovan Asylum for Imbecile Children, are both charitable institutions erected by voluntary subscription. In addition to children received gratuitously, both receive private and pauper children whose board is paid respectively by their friends and their parishes.

The lunatic department of the General Prison at Perth provides accommodation for insane prisoners and convicts, and also for persons detained during His Majesty's pleasure, who have either been acquitted on account of insanity of the offences with which they had been charged, or have been found to be insane in bar of trial. *Present Condition of Establishments.*

Different Classes of Establishments.

The Reports by the Commissioners of their inspection of the different establishments are given in Appendix B. These Reports are entered in the books of the respective establishments on the occasion of the statutory visits of the Medical Commissioners to the several institutions, and they form the basis of the following remarks :—

(a) ROYAL AND DISTRICT ASYLUMS.

Royal and District Asylums.

Aberdeen Royal Asylum, Aberdeen.

The new hospital divisions of the Aberdeen Royal Asylum afford accommodation for newly admitted cases, for sick and infirm cases, and for convalescent patients. The provision of separate accommodation for the latter class is highly commended because it will tend to prevent, to a large extent, the necessity for placing such cases in the chronic wards of the asylum. The fittings and general equipment of these hospitals are said to be in every respect excellent. When the asylum is relieved of the Aberdeen City patients, it is hoped that the Directors will proceed with their scheme for the reconstruction and renovation of the main asylum. The accommodation for private patients at Elmhill is again favourably commented upon, and it is reported that Elmhill Villa, in its immediate vicinity, has been prepared for the reception of patients and is now occupied by 16 ladies. The general condition of the patients, their freedom from excitement and the small number of complaints made by them are alluded to.

It is understood that owing to the recent drought and the scarcity of water in the Argyll and Bute District Asylum during the past summer, the District Board have ordered arrangements to be made for adding extensively to the present water reservoirs. The filter recently erected is said to work efficiently in freeing the water of peaty matter which formerly gave it a deep brown colour and which interfered with the proper working of the stop-cocks throughout the institution. The recently-constructed additions to the female side are reported to be in occupation. They consist of two large dayrooms, one of which in conjunction with the adjoining dormitory is used as infirmary accommodation. The whole of the work in connection with this extension, with the exception of the slating, was done by the asylum artisan staff and by the patients. The various parts of the institution have been connected by telephone. It is pointed out that the facilities for escape in case of fire from the Argyll and new Cowal male and the Bute female dormitories are incomplete, and it is recommended that fixed outside iron staircases should be erected in connection with these dormitories. *Argyll and Bute District Asylum, Lochgilphead.*

Present Condition of Establishments.

Royal and District Asylums.

Ayr District Asylum, Ayr.

It is pointed out that the margin of spare accommodation on the male side of the Ayr District Asylum is now very smalll, and the District Board are urged to take timely action in providing for the future. The numerous changes among the attendant staff are commented upon, and it is recommended that suitable cottages for married male attendants should be erected. The fatal assault committed by two attendants upon a male patient was made the subject of a special enquiry by the Medical Commissioners and later by the whole Board, who held a conference with the District Board at the asylum in order to discuss various matters connected with its management. This unfortunate case was immediately enquired into by the Procurator-Fiscal, and as a result of his enquiry the two attendants were apprehended, tried at the Ayr Sheriff Court, and sentenced each to three months' imprisonment. The treatment to which this patient was subjected is said to have been of a cruel character. The dayrooms in this asylum are reported to be comfortably furnished and well supplied with objects of interest and decoration.

Banff District Asylum, Ladysbridge.

It is reported that a night attendant has been appointed to each side of the Banff District Asylum. By this means the needs of the sick are better attended to at night, the safety of the suicidal and epileptic is better secured, and the defective habits of the demented are improved. In view of the unfortunate recurrence of enteric fever in the asylum it is recorded with satisfaction that the District Board have resolved to carry out the recommendations contained in the report of Professor Matthew Hay, the only modification being that in lieu of a system of sewage filtration it is proposed, if leave can be obtained, to have the sewage carried to the sea. Plans for the erection of filters and a reservoir capable of storing 27,000 gallons of water are in course of preparation. This storage will secure an ample supply of pure water to the asylum and as the water will also be supplied to the hydrants around the buildings the means for extinguishing fire will be greatly increased. The male side of the asylum is reported to be much too full, but progress is being made with the erection of a new separate villa for male patients.

Crichton Royal Institution, Dumfries.

A new separate block for female patients working in the laundry has been opened in connection with the Crichton Royal Institution, Dumfries. The internal arrangements and fittings of the block are reported to be elaborate and elegant in appearance. All the patients who work in the laundry and the paid laundresses reside in this building. This additional accommodation has greatly relieved the wards on the female side of the Second House. In this house it is recorded with satisfaction that an extended system of night nursing and supervision has been introduced, and that there are at present 70 female patients under constant supervision each night. These include new and suicidal cases and those whose habits are faulty. It is hoped that in time as many as possible of the noisy and restless inmates may be placed under the same treatment, and it is recommended that the system should be extended to the male side of the Second House. The provision by which over 20 per cent. of the patients of this asylum are accommodated in detached Present Con- houses is again favourably commented upon, and it is suggested dition of Estab-lishments. that, should further extensions of the institution be at any time required, houses similar to Brownhall, Rosebank, and Rosehall, in Royal and District Asylums. which conditions approaching domestic life exist to the fullest possible extent, should be multiplied. Crichton Royal Institution, Dumfries.

The Directors continue to carry out the charitable function of the institution in a liberal manner. The annual rate of board for patients of limited means belonging to the Southern Counties is £25, the lowest rate for private patients in Scotland. Contributions are also made to the funds of the institution towards reducing this rate when the circumstances of the patients or their relatives are shown to require them. In the case of patients paying the nominal rate of £40 annually, corresponding reductions are made from the funds of the institution. The benefits of this charity are considered to be important and far reaching.

The new block for private patients in connection with the Dundee Royal Asylum, Dundee. Dundee Royal Asylum is reported to be comfortably and handsomely furnished, and its several departments have been equipped with arrangements of a modern description. Extensive views of the surrounding scenery are obtained from all parts of the building, and the surrounding grounds are being laid out with plants and sheltering belts of trees. All parts of the main asylum were found clean and in good order; several sections of the male side have been repainted and repapered, and the floors of the general bath-room and dressing-rooms have been laid with tiles, and the baths refitted with larger pipes and taps. The reconstruction of the lavatories has been completed, and their arrangements are said to be in every way satisfactory. The drying closets in the laundry are reported to be so inefficient as to interfere with the proper supply of clean linen to the asylum. Changes among the nursing staff are stated to be less numerous than formerly. A recommendation is made that the cottages for married attendants should be increased in number, and that the detached hospital presently used for the accommodation of nurses should be trebled in size and converted into a comfortable nurses' Home.

It is pointed out that about 27 per cent. of the deaths in the Royal Edinburgh Asylum, Edinburgh. Royal Edinburgh Asylum are due to general paralysis of the insane, and that in June upwards of 14 per cent. of the male inmates of the West House were general paralytics. The large number of deaths from senile decay, uncomplicated by any active physical disease, is commented upon, and it is pointed out that in the majority of such cases the residence in the asylum has been short (under two years), from which it is inferred that a large number of feeble and decrepit cases are annually admitted to the institution. It is reported that the number of pauper patients on the male side is now as large as can be accommodated, and that overcrowding exists in the female wards. During the past five years the annual admission of parish patients has increased from 308 to 400. This rise, if it continues, will, it is said, lead to serious

Present Condition of Establishments. overcrowding in the near future, unless the Edinburgh District Board provide speedily their proposed new accommodation at Bangour.

Royal and District Asylums. The condition of the case books and the pathological journals is favourably referred to, and attention is directed to the efficient nursing and medical care of acute and physically ailing patients. The individual care bestowed upon the patients in Craig House attracted notice, and it is stated that every advantage is taken of the environment and of the prevailing skilful treatment, efficient nursing and good feeding, to secure recovery and to promote the happiness and well-being of the patients. In each of the gentlemen's dining-rooms a butler has charge of the service of the tables, and a lady-superintendent is in charge of the kitchen and the cooking of the food.

Royal Edinburgh Asylum, Edinburgh.

Elgin District Asylum, Elgin. The Elgin District Asylum is said to be very nearly full, there being 10 empty beds on the male side and 4 on the female side. It is, however, pointed out that there are in the institution 1 man and 20 women chargeable to Orkney parishes. The changes among the attendants in this asylum have been few, and the length of service of the present staff shows an average duration of 5 years. This is attributed to tactful management, and to the fact that much attention is bestowed upon the comfort of the attendants. It is recorded with satisfaction that the single rooms and corridors are now heated by a system of low-pressure hot-water pipes. The institution is said to be kept in admirable order and scrupulously clean.

Fife and Kinross District Asylum, Cupar. It is observed that the numbers resident in the Fife and Kinross District Asylum are slowly increasing, and that there are now only about 7 vacant beds in the institution, 5 on the male side and 2 on the female side. It is therefore understood with satisfaction that plans are being prepared with the object of providing hospital accommodation for acute and recent cases. It is observed that it was possible to pass from end to end of the female division of the asylum without the use of a key, and that, with one exception, the doors of all the female wards were unlocked, so that the great majority of the female patients can pass at will into the open air. Practically the same freedom prevails on the male side. The "open door" system is therefore more in force in this asylum (which was one of the first to introduce it) than in any similar institution in Scotland. It is stated that all the butcher meat, milk, and vegetables consumed by the inmates are supplied from the asylum farm.

Glasgow Royal Asylum, Gartnavel, Glasgow. The resignation by Dr. Yellowlees of the post of Physician Superintendent of the Glasgow Royal Asylum is thus referred to:— "It is learned with much regret that Dr. Yellowlees' retirement "was due to an affection of the eyesight. During a long and "successful professional career, wholly devoted to the study and "treatment of insanity, Dr. Yellowlees occupied a very distinguished "position in the esteem of his fellows, both on account of his wide

"knowledge and his sound judgment; and by his kindly and
"genial nature he has won the affectionate regard of all with whom
"he has been associated. His retirement from the more active duties
"of the management of this asylum creates a notable blank, not
"only in connection with the institution, but in the specialty of
"which he was an eminent member."

Present Condition of Establishments.

Royal and District Asylums.

Glasgow Royal Asylum, Gartnavel, Glasgow.

Dr. Yellowlees has been succeeded by Dr. L. R. Oswald, Medical
Superintendent of the Glasgow District Asylum at Gartloch. The
asylum is reported to be in good order, and the care the patients
receive is favourably commented upon.

It is reported that the spare accommodation for patients in the
Glasgow District Asylum at Gartloch has become exhausted.
Consequently the District Board have resolved to provide five
additional blocks capable of containing in all upwards of 200
patients. The plans for these additions show a house for 45
working patients in the vicinity of the farm steading, a house for
45 chronic male patients, and two houses each to contain 45 chronic
female patients; finally, an isolation hospital for the treatment of
phthisical patients of both sexes. On the second occasion on
which the asylum was visited, during the year the Register of
Restraint and Seclusion contained 182 entries, 156 of which referred
to the seclusion of one female patient on account of violent excitement. The wards of the asylum are, it is stated, in excellent order,
bright and cheerful in appearance, and comfortably furnished. It
is reported that Dr. Oswald has resigned the post of Medical
Superintendent on his promotion to the similar position of Physician
Superintendent of the Glasgow Royal Asylum. He has been
succeeded in office by Dr. W. A. Parker, the Senior Assistant
Physician.

Glasgow District Asylum, Gartloch, near Glasgow.

The need for extension of the accommodation in the Glasgow
District Asylum at Woodilee is said to be urgent. It is therefore
recorded with satisfaction that the District Board have resolved to
erect hospital accommodation for 240 patients, and a home for 110
nurses and servants. The hospital is to be of the segregate type,
and is to consist of separate blocks for newly admitted cases, for
the convalescent, for noisy and restless patients, for epileptics, for
phthisical cases, for the physically sick, and for the isolation of
cases of infectious diseases. It is also proposed to add an
administrative block, a kitchen, a store, a hall and a pathological
laboratory. The whole institution is now lighted by electricity. It
is reported that Dr. Blair, after 17 years' faithful and conscientious
service, has resigned the post of Medical Superintendent. Dr.
Hamilton Marr, the Deputy Superintendent, was unanimously
appointed his successor. The condition of the asylum is favourably commented upon, and the absence of excitement among the
inmates is noted.

Glasgow District Asylum, Woodilee, Lenzie.

It is pointed out that the accommodation at the disposal of the
Govan District Board is gradually becoming diminished, and it is
suggested that timely consideration should be given to this fact in

Govan District Asylum, Hawkhead Paisley.

Present Condition of Establishments.

Royal and District Asylums.

Govan District Asylum, Hawkhead, Paisley.

order that the District Asylum may not become too full. At the same time it is observed that a comparatively large number of acute alcoholic cases exist among the admissions, and it is suggested that the parochial authorities should consider whether, in some of these cases, appropriate medical treatment could not be given elsewhere than in the asylum for the short time that is often all that is required to complete recovery. It is also suggested that besides testing the control which can in this or other ways be exercised upon the admissions to the asylum, it would also be advisable to deal with the accumulation within the asylum by means of boarding out suitable cases. It is proposed to house from 12 to 14 men in the farm steading, and to accommodate about 20 male patients in the workshop block. It is reported that the District Board has acquired a lease of the adjoining farm, extending to about 145 acres. The asylum is said to be as usual in excellent order, and scrupulously clean.

Haddington District Asylum, Haddington.

Considerable alterations and structural changes are reported to be going on in the Haddington District Asylum. The drainage has been completely renewed, and a new system of heating the asylum by hot water is being introduced. Electric lighting has also been adopted. To provide a sufficiency of steam for heating, cooking, and electric lighting, it was found necessary to provide a new boiler and to enlarge the boiler-house. The laundry has also been enlarged and fitted with modern improvements. The wards and dormitories have been brightened and made comfortable by the addition of arm-chairs and ornaments of various kinds. Much of the flooring in the older apartments is being replaced by new pitch-pine flooring. Night attendants have recently been appointed, and, it is reported, with good effect and benefit to the patients.

Inverness District Asylum, Inverness.

The new female hospital of the Inverness District Asylum is now open, so that ample hospital provision is now made for the population of the asylum. The construction of the hospital, which is similar to that on the male side, is said to be in accordance with the best modern principles, combining the benefits of good classification with efficiency of working and supervision. The finish of the internal construction and the style of the furnishings are said to be in every respect admirable, and the District Board are congratulated on the provision of hospital accommodation, which will compare favourably with that in any asylum in the kingdom. It is pointed out that the asylum is becoming too full, and it is recommended that a serious effort should be made to transfer all those patients to care in private dwellings who have ceased to require care and treatment in a fully-equipped asylum like this. The overcrowding of the dining-hall and the consequent excitement which arises from this cause are referred to, and the suggestion to erect two new dining-halls, one in connection with each hospital, is commended. The asylum, it is said, continues to be managed in an enlightened and progressive manner, and it is evident that no effort is spared to render the care of the patients as efficient as possible.

· There is reported to be great need for properly designed and equipped hospital accommodation in the Kirklands Asylum, Bothwell. It is understood that the question of providing better accommodation for nurses and unmarried attendants and of erecting cottages for married attendants is at present being considered by the Committee. The building of the new laundry is making satisfactory progress. Full use is, it is stated, being made of the land recently acquired by the asylum, and it is hoped that the question of permanently acquiring more land for agricultural purposes may not be forgotten. All sections of the establishment are said to be maintained in good order; the day-rooms are well supplied with books, newspapers, and indoor games; the condition of the dormitories and bedding was found satisfactory, and the asylum is stated to be well managed.

[margin: Present Condition of Establishments. Royal and District Asylums. Kirklands Asylum, Bothwell.]

The death of Dr. Campbell Clark, Medical Superintendent of the Lanark District Asylum, is thus referred to by the Visiting Commissioners:—" While writing this report the news of Dr. " Clark's death has reached us. On the sad event it is not here " fitting to comment beyond expressing the opinions that his life's " work in all that concerned the interests of the insane has always " been greatly esteemed by his professional brethren, and that by " his death the County of Lanark has lost an able and high- " minded official."

Dr. Kerr, the Senior Assistant Physician, has been in charge of the asylum during Dr. Clark's long illness. The patients are reported to have been found, as a rule, quiet and contented, with the exception of the women in one of the divisions of the upper ward, who were noisy, which is explained by the fact that this ward is too large for the class of patient presently accommodated in it. The institution was found clean throughout and in excellent order.

[margin: Lanark District Asylum, Hartwood, Shotts.]

The extensive additions and other improvements in the Midlothian and Peebles District Asylum, such as the heating of the whole asylum by a system of hot-water pipes and radiators, electric lighting, increased water supply, and sewage filtration, all of which have been in progress for a considerable time, are now completed. The new hospitals are said to be admirably suited for their purpose. The day-rooms and dormitories in the extensions are suitably furnished, and the lavatories and bath-rooms attached to them have been equipped with arrangements of the most modern design. The enlargement of the dining and recreation halls is completed, and the ample space provided in these halls is favourably alluded to. The kitchen has been supplied with boilers of the newest and best description, and the dispensary, which adjoins the kitchen, has been converted into a scullery. The laundry has also been renovated and supplied with new machinery. The carrying out of these changes has had the effect of adapting the asylum to the requirements of the district, and has greatly increased the efficiency of the institution in all its departments. The patients, who are now free from overcrowding, bore, it is reported,

[margin: Midlothian and Peebles District Asylum, Rosewell, Roslin.]

Present Condition of Establishments.

Royal and District Asylums.

Montrose Royal Asylum, Montrose.

every evidence of being well cared for. They were found, with few exceptions, tranquil and contented, and the dress of both sexes was good and neat in appearance.

The new villa for 60 male patients in connection with the Montrose Royal Asylum is said to be of a pleasing design, and its internal arrangements are all that could be desired for quiet and convalescent patients. The whole house has been suitably and comfortably furnished, and the day-rooms are enlivened by pictures, plants, and other objects of interest. One of the rooms contains a billiard table. The Managers are congratulated on the excellence of this extension of the asylum, and upon the very moderate cost per bed at which it has been provided. The villa contains only 3 patients less than the number for which it was built, and its opening is calculated to have provided only 6 empty beds on the male side of the main portion of the institution. The female accommodation for pauper patients is said to be still much overcrowded, and it is recorded with satisfaction that the Managers have under consideration a proposal to erect a female villa corresponding to the male villa described above. The wards throughout the main building and hospital are reported to be clean, well ventilated, and in good order, and it is further reported that the condition of the patients as regards clothing and personal neatness was highly satisfactory.

Murray's Royal Asylum, Perth.

The Perth Royal Asylum is said to be full, and even overcrowded, in the male division, and it is suggested that the time has now come when the great success of the institution warrants its further extension. Plans of a new detached villa have been prepared by Dr. Urquhart, which it is understood may be approved of by the Directors. The reconstruction of the gallery on the ground floor of the ladies' division has been completed, and the result is stated to be an improvement beyond what was deemed possible. It is now a well lighted, well ventilated, artistically decorated, and comfortably furnished section of the asylum. The bath-room, lavatories, and other arrangements are of the most modern kind, and every detail in the reconstruction has been considered with the view of securing the welfare of the patients. All sections of·the institution are stated to be maintained in good order, and the accommodation throughout presented a cheerful and handsomely furnished appearance.

Perth District Asylum, Murthly.

It is reported that the wards of the Perth District Asylum at Murthly contain 38 men and 34 women in excess of the proper accommodation, and it is understood that the direction which any future extension of the asylum may take is at present occupying the attention of the District Board. It is pointed out that there are manifestly only two methods of extending—namely, the erection of hospital accommodation for acute cases, or the erection of additional villas for the more chronic patients. It is further pointed out that the existing hospital accommodation in the main building might possibly be adapted to the requirements of the asylum and that villas for chronic patients could then be erected _{Present Con-} at not much more than half the cost per bed of a new hospital. _{lishments.} Reference is made to the valuable scientific researches which 'are being so systematically and successfully carried on by Dr. Bruce _{trict Asylums.} into the causes and treatment of mental diseases.

The male division of the Roxburgh District Asylum is reported _{Roxburgh} to contain 15 patients in excess of the number for which it is _{Asylum,} constructed, and this, coupled with the fact that there has been an _{Melrose.} increase in the resident numbers of 40 male patients during the past ten years, shows the need of an extension of the buildings. It is therefore learned with approval that plans for the erection of a male hospital have been prepared. The present sick-room, which can only properly accommodate 10 patients, contains as many as 26 patients, which seriously hampers the care and the treatment of the cases. The building of the new laundry is completed, and contracts for its internal equipment have been accepted. A new boiler-house with workshop and coal store is in course of erection. The condition of the asylum as regards cleanliness and good order, and also as regards the care and condition of the patients, is highly commended. It is, however, pointed out that, while the state of the female wards, the new female hospital, and various apartments such as the dining and recreation halls are modern and in excellent repair, many parts of the male side stand urgently in need of renovation.

Neither restraint nor seclusion has been used in the case of any _{Stirling Dis-} patient in the Stirling District Asylum during the past year. The _{Larbert.} nursing arrangements in this asylum are said to present many novel and interesting features. There is a trained nurse of considerable experience in charge of the whole male side, and a night superinten- dent, also a trained nurse, who supervises the whole night staff— male and female. There are, in addition, 3 assistant matrons, who are trained hospital nurses, who are in charge, respectively, of the male hospital and infirmary, of the female hospital and infirmary, and of the division for female chronic patients. The sick and infirm male patients are wholly under the charge of female nurses during the day; and the male infirm dormitory, containing 23 beds, is under the charge of 2 female nurses at night. All the dormi- tories except three are under continuous supervision at night, and there are, in all, 17 night attendants—9 on the male side and 8 on the female side. The single rooms are all occupied by quiet patients, by whom they are regarded as bedrooms and are looked upon as a privilege. The methods employed in the nursing of the patients receive favourable recognition. The sick and infirm are said to be suitably tended, the accommodation provided for them is sufficiently warm and comfortable, and those of them who required rest or attention in bed were so disposed of. The position of the recent and acute cases is said to have been equally satisfactory. It was judged that every acute case in the asylum requiring bed treatment was being so treated; the number of such cases in bed is said to be much above the average usually met with in asylums.

Present Condition of Establishments.

(*b*) PRIVATE ASYLUMS.

Private Asylums.

Mavisbank Private Asylum, Polton, Midlothian.

The general condition of the patients in the Mavisbank Asylum is very favourably alluded to, and it is stated that their individual requirements are carefully studied and liberally met. A most gratifying form of the medical care was witnessed in the bed treatment of so many of the acute and excited cases. It is understood that all really acute cases of mania and melancholia are systematically treated in bed; and it was also observed that the more excited among the chronic cases were reposing in bed after their forenoon walk and before going out again in the afternoon. It is remarked that a good deal of painting and furnishing is required throughout the institution, more especially on the male side.

Saughton Hall Private Asylum, near Edinburgh.

The care of the patients in Saughton Hall Asylum is, as usual, considered to be very satisfactory. It was observed with particular commendation that so many of the acute, recent, and recurrent cases were being treated by rest in bed—a system which in this asylum has for many years been used as one of the ordinary methods of treatment. The nursing of the patients, their medical care, and the elaborate method of case-taking are referred to. The institution, it is reported, was in excellent order throughout.

Westermains Private Asylum, Kirkintilloch, Dumbartonshire.

Westermains Asylum is, it is stated, maintained in very good order; it is comfortably and even handsomely furnished, and the grounds surrounding it presented a pleasant appearance. The patients are considered to be carefully attended to and kindly treated.

Parochial Asylums.

(*c*) PAROCHIAL ASYLUMS.

Greenock Parochial Asylum, Greenock.

In the Greenock Parochial Asylum two accidents alleged to be caused by the rough usage of attendants are referred to. The first case was one of fracture of the ulna. The matter was reported to the criminal authorities, and the attendant, who had to deposit £10 in bail, absconded. The second case was one of fracture of two ribs, and although the evidence was found insufficient for legal conviction, the attendant was dismissed. With a few exceptions the patients were found well-behaved and free from excitement, and the state of good order and cleanliness of the asylum is noticed.

Paisley Parochial Asylum, Craw Road, Paisley.

It is observed with satisfaction that the numbers resident in the Paisley Parochial Asylum, Craw Road, show a tendency to diminish. The number of acute cases was also fewer, so that the patients presented a quieter and more orderly appearance. The wards and dormitories are said to be nicely painted and decorated, and the day-rooms, dormitories, and bedding were found to be in good order.

Paisley Parochial Asylum, Riccartsbar, Paisley.

The whole of the female division of the Paisley Parochial Asylum, Riccartsbar, has, it is reported, been tastefully repainted, and consequently the appearance of the wards has been greatly improved. Fire-escape staircases from the first floor at each end of the main building are in course of construction. The excellence of the arrangements for the care of the patients in the new male hospital block again attracted favourable attention. The land in connection with the institution is fully taken advantage of and affords ample outdoor work for the male patients, while the supply of farm produce to the asylum is abundant. It is believed that the pecuniary interests of the asylum have in no way suffered, but on the contrary probably benefited, by the possession and cultivation of this land.

Present Condition of Establishments.
——
Parochial Asylums.
——
Paisley Parochial Asylum, Riccartsbar, Paisley.

(d) LUNATIC WARDS OF POORHOUSES.

Lunatic Wards of Poorhouses.

The dietary of the patients in the lunatic wards of the Aberdeen East Poorhouse is commented upon in very favourable terms. The state of the wards, which are old, is said to be as good as could be expected. The patients were found well-conducted, free from excitement, and generally contented.

Aberdeen East Poorhouse, Aberdeen.

The lunatic wards of the Aberdeen West Poorhouse were found in good order, but the floors of the dormitories are said to stand greatly in need of re-staining and re-varnishing. All the inmates who are able to work are daily employed in useful occupations.

Aberdeen West Poorhouse, Aberdeen.

It is reported that vacant accommodation exists in the lunatic wards of the Buchan Poorhouse for 4 men and 4 women, and it is recommended that these beds should be filled as soon as possible. The impression produced by the appearance of the patients was a very favourable one, and their dress is described as being neat, clean, and in good repair. The opinion is expressed that a female attendant who was allowed to resign should have been dismissed on account of her unkindness to some of the patients.

Buchan Poorhouse, New Maud, Aberdeenshire.

The condition of the Cunninghame Poorhouse lunatic wards is, as usual, favourably commented upon, but it is pointed out that the dress of the male patients does not compare favourably with that of the females. The attention of the Committee is directed to the state of the lavatories adjoining the dormitories on the first floor, and it is suggested that the relaying of the floors and the introduction of slop sinks would be an improvement. It is reported that operations are in progress for heating these wards in conjunction with the rest of the poorhouse by means of water heaters supplied by steam from a central boiler.

Cunninghame Poorhouse, Irvine, Ayrshire.

Many improvements are said to have recently been effected in the lunatic wards of the Dumbarton poorhouse. The day-rooms and dormitories have been tastefully repainted; woven spring mattresses have been fitted into the majority of the beds, and the lavatory and bathing arrangements are said to be now satisfactory. A square of linoleum has been laid in the female day-room and easy-chairs have been provided for both day-rooms.

Dumbarton Poorhouse, Dumbarton

Present Condition of Establishments.

Lunatic Wards of Poorhouses.

Dundee East Poorhouse, Dundee.

The accommodation provided for patients in the lunatic wards of the Dundee East Poorhouse is said to be in every respect satisfactory; the day-rooms and dormitories are clean and in admirable order; the beds are comfortable, and their coverings sufficiently warm and commendably clean. The employment of night attendants in each division has, it is stated, exercised a beneficial effect upon the mental condition and habits of several of the inmates.

Dundee West Poorhouse, Dundee.

It is pointed out that the large day-rooms of the lunatic wards of the Dundee West Poorhouse are dingy, low in the ceilings, and not well furnished. The patients are reported upon as being free from excitement and as being apparently contented. It is understood that an addition, consisting of a sick-room with four beds, and two bedrooms for attendants, is to be constructed in connection with the male side.

Edinburgh Poorhouse, Craiglockhart.

The lunatic wards of the Edinburgh Poorhouse at Craiglockhart have been extended by the acquirement on lease of the mansion-house of Middleton Hall, situated in the parish of Uphall, Linlithgowshire. This house has undergone various internal alterations in order to adapt it to its purpose. It is said now to provide excellent accommodation and plenty of outdoor garden work for the male inmates. There are 50 men and 10 women resident in the house, and their general care has produced a favourable impression on the Visiting Commissioners. The removal of so many patients from Craiglockhart has necessitated the transference of 16 male epileptic patients from the Royal Edinburgh Asylum to the wards of the poorhouse, and for the supervision of these at night a special attendant has been engaged.

Govan Poorhouse, Govan, Glasgow.

The lunatic wards of the Govan Poorhouse are said to present a very commendable state of good order and cleanliness. The furnishings are of a modern description and suitably chosen. With the exception of the corridor of communication and the renovation of the general bath-room, the extensive alterations which have been proceeding for the past two or three years are finished, and upon the result the Committee and Mr. Thomson may, it is said, be justly congratulated.

Inveresk Poorhouse, Inveresk.

The lunatic wards of the Inveresk Poorhouse were found generally in satisfactory order, and the condition of the inmates, judged by the state of their personal clothing, their general appearance, and the absence of excitement, is taken as an indication of adequate and conscientious care.

Kincardine Poorhouse, Stonehaven.

The patients in the lunatic wards of the Kincardine Poorhouse are said to be suitably dressed, to be free from excitement, and to exhibit indications of efficient care and an adequate dietary. Six men and five women enjoy the privilege of a day's pass from time to time, which they occupy in visiting their friends. The practice is commended.

The care of the patients in the lunatic wards of the Linlithgow Poorhouse is favourably referred to. The removal of the partition in the male dormitory, and the erection at one end of the dormitory of a room for the male attendant, is said to afford greater comfort to the attendant, and more light and air to the dormitory.

The lunatic wards of the Old Monkland Poorhouse are stated to be maintained in excellent order. The day-rooms, dining-halls, and corridors have been repainted, and the beds in the dormitories have been furnished with wire mattresses. The patients are said to have presented a satisfactory appearance, and the dietary is stated to be abundant and nutritious.

The personal clothing of the inmates of the lunatic wards of the Perth Poorhouse is reported to be satisfactory, and their wants appear to be properly attended to in every respect. The day-rooms and dormitories were found bright and clean. It is suggested that the erection of wooden porches at the outer doors of the male and female wards, respectively, would preserve the floors of the corridors and increase the comfort of the patients.

The general health of the patients in the lunatic wards of the Wigtown Poorhouse is stated to be satisfactory. It is reported that a much-needed addition to the supply of butter to the patients has been given effect to. The day-rooms and dormitories were found in good order.

(e) TRAINING SCHOOLS FOR IMBECILE CHILDREN.

Relief to the overcrowding of the Baldovan Institution is, the reports state, much required, but notwithstanding the overcrowding, every part of the house was found in good order, and the training of the children who are capable of useful work is carried on assiduously. As no restrictions are imposed as to the class of children received, the proportion of feeble and helpless ones is said to be large. Since these reports were written the overcrowding has been relieved by the occupation of the new buildings.

The Larbert Institution is reported to be doing excellent work in the education and training of feeble-minded children. There is reported to be an increase of over 20 in the numbers resident during the year, and it is pointed out that the Directors must sooner or later face the question of further extension. It is learned with satisfaction that there is a prospect of acquiring a small piece of land immediately to the west of the institution. This will, it is pointed out, enable the Directors to increase the accommodation without having to add to the present buildings, which are sufficiently large for the area of ground they cover. The personal clothing of the pupils, their general health, and the management of the institution by Mr. Skene are favourably commented upon.

Establishment for State and Criminal Lunatics.

Lunatic Department of H.M. General Prison at Perth.

(*f*) ESTABLISHMENT FOR STATE AND CRIMINAL LUNATICS.

The Lunatic Department of H.M. General Prison at Perth is maintained by the State for the confinement of those persons called criminal lunatics who are or who have been insane and who are still regarded as requiring detention in a prison.

During 1901, 6 patients were admitted to this establishment. The offences of which they were accused or were guilty, the places from which they were brought, and other facts regarding them, are shown in the following statement:—

H.M. General Prison, Perth—Admissions to Lunatic Department during 1901.

C/No.	Whence brought.	Date of Trial.	Initials of Names.	Date of Admission.	Offence of which Accused is Convicted.
197/1901	Glasgow, ...	21 Feb. 1889	A. R.	26 Jan. 1901	Con. Act 10 Geo. IV., cap. 32, sec. 2.
395/1901	Aberdeen, ...	29 March 1889	J. H.	30 March 1901	Murder.
407/1901	Dundee, ...	30 do.	G. G.	2 April 1901	Do.
(F) 171/1901	Main Prison, Perth, .	27 do.	C. K. or M'P.	4 May 1901	False registration and theft.
1105/1900	Do. do. . .	26 Oct. 1897	J. M'S.	5 June 1901	Theft and p.c.
951/1901	Aberdeen, ...	24 June 1897	W. S.	25 do.	Murder.

The subjoined figures show the changes among the inmates of the Department in 1901:—

Average Number of Inmates.		Admissions.		Discharges Recovered.		Discharges not Recovered.		Deaths.	
M.	F.	M.	F.	M.	F.	M.	F.	M.	F.
38·5	7·5	5	1	3	1	1	1	–	–

The inmates at 31st December 1901 were classified as follows:—

1. Found to be insane in bar of trial, and detained during His Majesty's pleasure, ...   31
2. Found to have been insane at time of committing offence, and detained during His Majesty's pleasure, ...   11
3. Sentenced to death, but respited, or sentence commuted on account of insanity, ...   1
4. Convicts whose sentences had expired, ...   —
5. Imprisonment prisoners whose sentences had expired, . . .   —
6. Convicts whose sentences had not expired, ...   3
7. Imprisonment prisoners whose sentences had not expired, . .   —

46

The reports on the Department state that the inmates were found in good health, that with a few exceptions they were quiet and free from excitement, and that the wards were found in good order. The house now occupied by the female inmates approaches, it is said, closely to the ideal of a private residence; the rooms are nicely decorated, comfortably furnished, and well lighted, and while everything has been done to ensure detention, the methods employed to this end are as inconspicuous as possible and in no

way interfere with the home-like character of the building. Any *Establishment for State and Criminal Lunatics.*
similar modification in the direction of improving the accommoda-
tion for the male inmates would, it is suggested, greatly add to
their comfort and react favourably on their mental health.

V. LUNATICS IN PRIVATE DWELLINGS.

Lunatics in Private Dwellings.

It will be useful to repeat here the brief statement which has
been given in previous Reports, describing the position occupied by *All Pauper Lunatics but not all Private Lunatics in Private Dwellings are under jurisdiction of Board.*
patients in private dwellings in Scotland, and the amount of official
supervision which they receive.

All private patients, if they are detained in establishments for
the insane, come under the supervision of the Board, and all pauper
patients, whether provided for in establishments or in private
dwellings, are intimated to the Board, placed on the register, and
brought under supervision.

But in the case of private patients in private dwellings—that is,
insane persons who are not paupers, and who are not placed in
establishments for the insane—it is not required by the statutes
that all of them should be under the supervision of the Board.
The circumstances which bring under the Board's supervision an
insane person who is not a pauper and who is not placed in an
establishment are the following:—

1. If he is kept in a private dwelling for profit, unless he is a
patient in regard to whom it is certified by a registered medical
practitioner that he is afflicted with a malady which is not con-
firmed, and that it is expedient to place him for a temporary
residence, not exceeding six months, in the house in which he is
so kept.

2. If, whether kept for profit or not, he has been insane for more
than a year, and is subjected to compulsory confinement to the
house, to restraint or coercion, or to harsh and cruel treatment.

3. If he possesses property which has been placed under curatory
by a Court of Law.

The Board have therefore no official knowledge of a large number
of insane persons living at home under the care of their natural
guardians, provided they are neither paupers, nor kept for profit,
nor restrained, nor cruelly used.

NUMBERS FOR 1901.

The number of private lunatics who were provided for in private *Number of Private Lunatics in Private Dwellings.*
dwellings, with the sanction of the Board, on the 1st of January
1902, was 130. Of these, 54 were persons whose means have been
placed under curatory by the Court of Session or by a Sheriff Court.
Of the whole number of private patients in private dwellings, 44
were in houses which possessed special licences for the reception of
not more than four patients, and 86 were placed singly in houses
which having only one patient, require no licence.

All pauper lunatics, wherever placed, come upon the register of *Number of Pauper Lunatics in Private Dwellings.*
the Board, and we are fully informed as to the mode in which they
are provided for, and of every important fact in their history.

Lunatics in
Private
Dwellings.

Number of
Pauper
Lunatics in
Private
Dwellings.

The relations of the central authority to every individual member of the pauper class of the insane is peculiar to Scotland. In no other country is every lunatic whose maintenance is contributed to from public sources under the direct supervision of the central authority. The number of pauper patients provided for with the sanction of the Board in private dwellings on 1st January 1902 was 2631, showing a decrease of 38 compared with the preceding year. Of these, 954 are boarded with guardians who are relatives, and 1677 with unrelated guardians. Of the pauper patients with unrelated guardians, about two-thirds are in private dwellings specially licensed to receive 2, 3, or 4 patients. The remainder, as well as almost all patients with related guardians, are accommodated singly in houses which, having only one patient, require no special licence. The number admitted during the year to the roll of pauper patients in private dwellings was 254, which is 6 more than last year. Of these, 94, or 6 less than last year, were resident in private dwellings when first reported to the Board and remained with our sanction under private care, and 160, or 12 more than last year, were removed from asylums. Of the total number of patients in private dwellings, 23 were certified sane during the year, 26 were removed from the poor-roll by their friends, 115 were removed to asylums, and 128 died—the death-rate being equal to 49 per 1000.

DECREASE IN NUMBER OF PAUPER PATIENTS IN PAST TWO YEARS.

Decrease in
Number of
Pauper
Lunatics in
Private
Dwellings.

As this is the second successive year in which a fall appears in the number of pauper lunatics provided for in private dwellings, it may be advisable to call attention to the progress of the number of this class of the insane during past years, and to consider whether any special significance is to be attached to the decrease.

The following Table shows the number of pauper patients so provided for at 1st January 1881, and at 1st January of each subsequent fifth year to 1896, and for each of the following six years to 1902, distinguishing between those resident with related guardians and those resident with unrelated guardians.

[TABLE.

Years.	Resident with Relatives.	Boarded with Strangers.	Total.
1881	906	610	1,516
1886	967	1,091	2,058
1891	1,043	1,446	2,489
1896	1,009	1.691	2,700
1897	1,009	1,658	2,667
1898	1,009	1,645	2,654
1899	1,039	1,663	2,702
1900	1,020	1,683	2,703
1901	987	1,682	2,669
1902	954	1,677	2,631

Lunatics in Private Dwellings.

Decrease in Number of Pauper Lunatics in Private Dwellings.

It will be observed that the total number rose throughout the period embraced in the Table, and sometimes with great rapidity, from 1516 in 1881 to 2700 in 1896, an increase during these fifteen years of 1184, or 78 per cent. Since 1896 the total number has fluctuated somewhat, but attained the highest point it has ever reached in 1900, when it was 2703. At 1st January 1901, however, a fall is recorded of 34, and at 1st January of the present year a further fall of 38.

On examining the column of the Table giving the number resident with relatives, it will be seen that a rise occurred in the ten years from 1881 to 1891, from 906 to 1043, which was mostly contributed by the Highland counties, and that during the succeeding eleven years a fall has taken place to an almost equal extent. During the year 1899, a fall occurred of 19, during 1900 of 33, and during 1901 of 33. It is important to note, therefore, that the fall during the past two years in the total number of patients in private dwellings occurred almost wholly among those residing with relatives.

The pauper insane boarded with unrelated guardians are those to whom alone the term "boarded out" is properly applicable. With few exceptions, they are patients who have been formerly inmates of asylums, from which they have been removed and placed as boarders under the private care of strangers while still in a condition of insanity.

An examination of the column dealing with those boarded with strangers shows that in the five years from 1881 a rise occurred of 481 ; in the five years to 1891 a rise of 355 ; and in the five years to 1896 a rise of 245—an increase during the fifteen years of 1081, or 177 per cent. The highest point yet reached of patients boarded with strangers is shown at 1st January 1896, and on the whole this point has been substantially maintained. In the following two years a fall occurred, succeeded by a rise in the three subsequent years. The figures for the last three years, as compared with those of 1896, show falls of 8, 9, and 14 respectively, which are in themselves unimportant considering the large total number of patients, and are quite insufficient to justify the conclusion that this mode of care is in any way losing favour with the parishes which have systematically followed it.

It must be borne in mind that the rate of increase which occurred between 1881 and 1896 could not possibly have been maintained. The number of patients in asylums suitable for being boarded out in private dwellings is not unlimited, and if the number had been maintained after 1896 at the same rate as before, a class of patient of doubtful fitness for that mode of care would soon have been reached, especially in the case of patients from the large parishes such as Edinburgh, Glasgow, Govan, and Dundee, which have shown the greatest activity in taking advantage of that manner of providing for their patients. There is indeed reason to believe that the arrested increase since 1896 is due to the fact that in the case of certain parishes the number of patients who are obviously suitable for that mode of care is to some extent temporarily exhausted. It is not doubted, however, that there are still patients in establishments connected with some of these large parishes who might with safety and propriety be removed to private care, and it is certain that among the patients in establishments chargeable to the smaller parishes there are a great many patients who might be removed to private care with advantage to themselves and to the ratepayers. The failure to remove such patients to private dwellings must be attributed to some or all of the following causes :—(1) The absence of energetic pressure for removal on the part of the asylum authorities ; (2) the unwillingness of parochial officials to take a step which involves the effort to find guardians and future personal trouble in supervising the patients ; (3) the fact that the difference between the cost of maintaining patients in private dwellings and in asylums is not quite so emphatic as it formerly was, though it is still in the case of most asylums considerable.

In considering the changes in the number of pauper patients in private dwellings, it cannot be overlooked that the fall or arrested increase shown has taken place notwithstanding an ever increasing number of patients in establishments, and that the proportion of patients in private dwellings both to the total number of the insane and to population is becoming smaller at a rate which the actual fall in their number does not disclose. This is a consideration to which due weight should be given ; but at the same time it should be borne in mind that the increased number of patients sent to, or kept in, asylums does not necessarily imply a corresponding growth of the number fitted for private care. So far as such increased number may consist of persons suffering from transitory attacks of acute insanity, or of persons broken down through old age or disease, they would not add to the number from which patients suitable for private care could be drawn.

In 1858, of the total number of registered pauper patients in Lunatics in Private Dwellings. private dwellings, 1335, or 79 per cent., were resident with relatives, and 358, or 21 per cent., with strangers. The proportion resident Decrease in Number of Pauper Lunatics in Private Dwellings. with relatives has ever since decreased, and the position of the two classes is now reversed, the number residing with relatives being 954, or 36 per cent. of the whole, while 1677, or 64 per cent., are resident with strangers. This change has in part occurred through the death, or removal following on the death of relatives, of patients who were not really suitable for private care, but whose residence at home was permitted either because the relatives would not part with them, or because the greater comforts of an asylum would probably not have compensated for the devoted care bestowed upon them at home. The gradual falling off in the number of pauper patients cared for in their own families is probably due to much the same causes as those which have led to an increase in the number of patients sent to asylums, such as the growing unwillingness among the poorer classes to submit to all that is involved in keeping at home insane and useless relatives who require constant attention for their proper care, and who may have peculiarities more or less unfitting them for home life. The tendency of the population throughout Scotland to migrate from country districts to towns must also have had an influence in reducing the number of patients cared for by their relatives, as insane persons who could easily be cared for by their families in the country would not be found suitable for such a mode of care in towns.

PRIVATE DWELLINGS SPECIALLY LICENSED.

The tabular statement below shows the number of private dwell- Private Dwellings specially Licensed. ings specially licensed for pauper patients, classified in accordance with the number of patients they contained, and the number and sex of the patients resident in each class, at 31st December 1901 :—

Classes of Houses Specially Licensed for Pauper Patients, containing at 31st December 1901.	Number of Specially Licensed Houses in each Class.	Sex of Patients in each Class.		Total Number of Patients in each Class.
		M.	F.	
Two Patients, . .	338	234	373	607
Three Patients, . .	97	70	209	279
Four Patients, . .	42	46	122	168
Totals, . .	477	350	704	1054

It will be seen from this statement that of all the pauper lunatics provided for in specially licensed houses, nearly two-thirds are in houses which contain only two patients, and that of the patients accommodated in houses containing three or four patients, more than two-thirds are females.

Lunatics in
Private
Dwellings.

GENERAL REPORTS ON THE VISITATION OF PATIENTS.

General
Reports on
Visitation of
Patients.

We present as usual in Appendix C the general reports on the visitation of patients in private dwellings.

Dr. John Macpherson, Commissioner, who visited the patients in private dwellings in Fifeshire, writes as follows of the impression left upon him by his inspection :—

" Considering that the boarded-out patients in Fife number " nearly 500, and that they are widely spread over the county, it was " both surprising and gratifying to find an almost uniformly satis- " factory standard of care prevailing throughout the houses in which " the patients live."

He adds further :—" The uniformity in the care of the insane in " this county is probably due to the long period of time during " which the system of boarding out has been organised there, to the " liberal and uniform allowance for maintenance paid by the two " parishes of Edinburgh and Glasgow, to which the majority of the " patients are chargeable, and to the regular supervision of the " houses by the officials of these parishes, as well as by the Dundee " Parish Council, which also boards out extensively in this county."

Dr. Sutherland in his report gives useful statistics for the districts visited by him with regard to the proportion of the resident insane to the populations of certain villages, rural localities, and parishes in five counties in which the boarded-out insane are un- usually numerous. Speaking of the percentages of the insane in these localities he says :—" The percentages in certain villages may be " regarded as already sufficiently high ; but it cannot be said that the " capacity to receive patients in all the rural districts and most of " the villages in these counties has been exhausted. In the villages " and rural districts of these five counties, in order to bring the per- " centage of either sex or both up to 5, a percentage by no means " excessive or likely to give a colour to the population, 2340 " additional patients would require to be boarded out. This " calculation gives a fair conception of what might be done to extend " boarding out in rural districts, in villages already to a slight " extent utilised, and in parishes in Scotland not yet made use of in " that way, provided sufficiently encouraging pecuniary inducements " were held out to suitable guardians, inducements much below the " cost of patients in asylums."

He further, speaking of the relative fitness of male and female patients for being placed under private care, and of the surroundings in which the patients of each sex may be expected to do best, makes the following remarks :—

" In alluding to certain villages with somewhat high percentages to " population, and in suggesting that the maximum had been reached, " it is proper to qualify this expression of opinion by observing that " in two of them, including the largest village colony—that of Gart- " more, with 58—the patients are all females with the exception of " two, and in seven more villages with 122 patients the females far " outnumber the males. There need be little doubt that the per- " centage in villages of females may safely, and with regard to all " interests, be double that of males, having regard to the facts that " unmanageable habits are less common among females than males,

"and also that female patients adapt themselves more readily to the Lunatics in Private Dwellings.
"kinds of employment, multifarious and light, which are to be met
"with in village dwellings. On the other hand, the percentage of General Reports on Visitation of Patients.
"patients, whether male or female, in rural districts may, in the
"interests of patients, their guardians and families, and without
"injury to the public, be double that of the villages, the dwellings
"or farmhouses being, as a rule, so far apart as to bar the suggestion
"of patients mingling with each other, or with sane neighbours who
"may or may not take in insane boarders. The difficulty of finding
"suitablework for many men in village homes too often leads to en-
"forced idleness and inactivity, and induces a condition of discontent
"which not unfrequently ends in return to the asylum. Thus it is
"that men do better in farming districts, to which they are sent in
"numbers almost identical with females, the ratio being 100 to 100.
"Females do equally well in village or country, some adapting them-
"selves to the small field and farm work, others to domestic duties.
"Of course farmers have a preference for males with a certain
"capacity for work."

Dr. Charles Macpherson, Deputy Commissioner, makes in his report the following observations on the condition of pauper lunatics in the Western Isles which he inspected for the first time this year :—

"I was very agreeably surprised with the condition of matters
"found generally in the Western Isles. One hears so often of the
"poverty of the people there that I feared, judging by the usually
"very small alimentary allowances given for the patients, that I
"would find many indications of defective care and diet. I, however,
"found that these patients generally would compare favourably as
"regards robust appearance with any in Scotland. The great
"majority of them are living with relatives in what has always been
"their home, and they share everything equally with the family.
"There may be a want of variety, but there is always plenty of food,
"such as porridge and milk, potatoes, fish, eggs, etc. The
"impression left on my mind was that while the money allowance
"could not as a rule repay the guardians anything like the cost of
"the food supplied, still the patients were as well fed as they would
"be if the allowance were doubled or trebled. As a contrast to the
"small money allowance, the supply of clothing—especially in the
"Lewis parishes—is very generous. Both bed and body clothing are
"of excellent quality and are liberally supplied. The small money
"allowance has, however, this disadvantage. It often makes it
"difficult for an Inspector of Poor to induce the relatives of an
"asylum patient to take him home; and when patients prove in any
"degree troublesome the guardians are very apt to demand their
"immediate removal; whereas, if the money paid as aliment was
"such as to form an important item of the household income they
"would put up with a certain amount of inconvenience rather than
"lose it."

He speaks as follows of the favourable conditions of a small colony of male patients from Paisley boarded in Benderloch, a district of Argyllshire lying to the north of Loch Etive, and of the excellence of the provision made for them by Paisley Parish Council:—

Lunatics in
Private
Asylums.
——
General
Reports on
Visitation of
Patients.

" The guardians are small farmers or large crofters. The houses
" are in a good state of repair. The patients were all in good physical
" condition, usefully employed, and none of them had any complaint
" to make as to the diet or their treatment by the guardians. They
" were all well clad in good tweed suits, and had ample supplies of
" underclothing. Each man was provided with a warm overcoat, a
" sailor's oilskin coat, and leggings, so that they are thoroughly pro-
" tected during wet weather. In addition to the statutory visits of
" the Inspector of Poor, the colony is visited once a year by a
" deputation from the Parish Council, and the Medical Officer
" immediately after each of his quarterly visits sends a report to the
" Inspector of Poor on each patient."

Dr. Macpherson was furnished with a list of patients in the
Inverness District Asylum who, it was believed, would be found
suitable for private care, and he gave what assistance was possible
to induce parochial authorities to find homes for them. Speaking
of the general success and usefulness of this work, and of the difficulty in finding guardians alleged to exist in some cases, he says :—
" A home may not be obtainable among the patient's friends, or even
" possibly in his native parish, but any Inspector who chooses to take
" some trouble, and to pay a suitable rate of maintenance, need have
" no difficulty in finding homes for quiet, inoffensive patients. The
" result of the work, while not as great as one could wish, has been
" on the whole a success. Thirty of these patients have been dis-
" charged on twelve months' probation since the month of September,
" and I know that arrangements are in progress for providing homes
" for a considerable number more. As far as I at present know, none
" of these probationary patients has as yet had to be returned to the
" asylum. I am strongly of opinion that if time could be found for
" such work much good could be done by the visitation of parishes
" in many districts for the special purpose of calling attention to
" cases suitable for being boarded out, and my experience has
" clearly shown me that more can be done by a few minutes'
" talk than by any amount of letter-writing."

Position of
Districts.
——
List of Dis-
tricts and
Counties
which form
them.

VI. POSITION OF DISTRICTS.

For lunacy purposes Scotland is at present divided into the
following Districts :—

Counties from which the different Districts are formed.	Lunacy Districts arranged geographically.
Shetland, ...	1. Shetland District.
Orkney, ...	2. Orkney do.
Caithness, ...	3. Caithness do.
Inverness, Nairn, Ross, and Sutherland,	4. Inverness do.
Elgin, ...	5. Elgin do.
Banff, ...	6. Banff do.
Aberdeen, ...	7. Aberdeen County, consisting of all the parishes of Aberdeenshire, except Aberdeen City Parish. 8. Aberdeen City, consisting of the parish of that name.
Kincardine, ...	9. Kincardine District.

Counties from which the different Districts are formed.	Lunacy Districts arranged geographically.	Position of Districts.
	⎰10. Forfar District, consisting of all the parishes of Forfarshire, except Dundee Combination.	List of Districts and
Forfar, ...	11. Dundee District, consisting of the parish of Dundee Combination.	Counties which form them.
Perth, ...	12. Perth District.	
Stirling, Dumbarton, Linlithgow, and Clackmannan, ...	13. Stirling do.	
Fife and Kinross, ...	14. Fife and Kinross District.	
	⎧15. Edinburgh District, consisting of the parish of Edinburgh.	
Edinburgh and Peebles, ...	16. Leith District, consisting of the parishes of Leith and Duddingston.	
	17. Midlothian and Peebles District, consisting of the remaining parishes of Midlothian and of the county of Peebles.	
Haddington, ...	18. Haddington District.	
Roxburgh, Berwick, and Selkirk .	19. Roxburgh do.	
	20. Glasgow. do.	⎱ Consisting respectively of the parishes of the same names.
	21. Govan do.	
Lanark, ...	22. Lanark do.	Consisting of remaining parishes of Lanarkshire.
Renfrew, ...	23. Renfrew do.	Consisting of parishes of Renfrewshire, including entire parishes of Cathcart and Eastwood which are partly within Lanarkshire.
Argyll, ...	24. Argyll do.	
Bute, ...	25. Bute do.	
Ayr, ...	26. Ayr do.	
Dumfries, Kirkcudbright, and Wigtown,	27. Dumfries do.	

The District of Shetland continues to be dependent on the Royal Asylum at Montrose for the accommodation of its pauper lunatics. No formal agreement with that asylum exists at present, but such an agreement is under consideration. *Shetland District.*

Pauper lunatics belonging to the Orkney District who require removal from home are received into the Edinburgh Royal Asylum. A considerable number of lunatics from parishes in Orkney who cannot at present be received into the Royal Edinburgh Asylum are temporarily accommodated in other asylums, but not under formal agreement. *Orkney District.*

Under an agreement with the Managers of the Montrose Royal Asylum, pauper lunatics belonging to the Caithness District who need asylum treatment continue to be sent to that establishment. A fresh agreement with the Montrose Asylum is under consideration. *Caithness District.*

The pauper lunatics of the Inverness District, which includes the counties of Inverness, Nairn, Ross, and Sutherland, continue to be accommodated in the District Ayslum at Inverness. *Inverness District.*

d

Position of Districts.

Elgin District.   The Elgin District Asylum provides adequately for the wants of the District.

Banff District.   The pauper lunatics of the Banff District are accommodated in the asylum at Ladysbridge. A plan of a new separate building to accommodate 50 male patients has been approved of.

Aberdeen County Lunacy District.   The pauper lunatics of the Aberdeen County Lunacy District, which consists of all the parishes of the county except Aberdeen City Parish, are accommodated in the Aberdeen Royal Asylum, under an agreement with the directors of the asylum, and in the lunatic wards of Buchan Poorhouse.

Aberdeen City District.   The pauper lunatics of the Aberdeen City Lunacy District are accommodated in the Aberdeen Royal Asylum and in the lunatic wards of the East and West Aberdeen Poorhouses. The District Board have entered into an agreement with the Directors of the Royal Asylum for the temporary accommodation of their lunatics until the completion of a District Asylum, to which eventually all their patients, both in the Royal Asylum and in the lunatic wards of the Poorhouses, will be removed. We have approved of plans for a District Asylum of the village type at Kingseat, 11¼ miles by rail from Aberdeen, and its erection is now considerably advanced.

Kincardine District.   The agreement between the Kincardine District Lunacy Board and the Managers of the Montrose Royal Asylum remains in force. The pauper lunatics of the District are accommodated in that Asylum and in the lunatic wards of the Kincardine Poorhouse at Stonehaven. A new agreement with the Montrose Asylum is under consideration.

Forfar District.   The pauper lunatics of the Forfar District, which consists of all the parishes in the county except Dundee, are accommodated in the Royal Asylums of Montrose and Dundee. On 21st March 1900, notice was given by us of the termination of the existing agreements within twelve months. New agreements with the Montrose and Dundee Royal Asylums are under consideration.

Dundee District.   The pauper lunatics of the Dundee Lunacy District are accommodated in the Royal Asylums of Dundee and Montrose and in the lunatic wards of the East and West Dundee Poorhouses. On 21st March 1900, notice was given by us of the termination of the existing agreements within twelve months. New agreements with the Dundee and Montrose Royal Asylums are under consideration.

Perth District.   The District Asylum at Murthly and the lunatic wards of the Perth Poorhouse provide accommodation for the pauper lunatics of the Perth District.

Stirling District.   The pauper lunatics of the Stirling District are adequately accommodated in the District Asylum at Larbert and in the lunatic wards of the Linlithgow and Dumbarton Poorhouses.

The pauper lunatics of the counties of Fife and Kinross con- Position of tinue to be provided for adequately in the District Asylum at Districts. Springfield, near Cupar.

Fife and Kinross District.

The Edinburgh District is at present supplied with asylum Edinburgh accommodation by the Royal Edinburgh Asylum and the lunatic District. wards of the Poorhouse at Craiglockhart, which have been extended by our licensing in connection with them the house known as Middleton Hall, near Uphall, for 50 men and 15 women. In consequence of the overcrowded condition of the Royal Asylum pauper lunatics of the District are also boarded in the Lanark and Stirling District Asylums. The District Board purchased in 1897 the lands of West Bangour, in the parish of Ecclesmachen and county of Linlithgow, about fourteen miles to the west of Edinburgh, with a view to the erection on them of a District Asylum of the village type. A private Act was obtained for the construction of a railway line to the asylum grounds and for other purposes, and this line it is understood has been almost completed. Plans of many of the proposed buildings of this asylum were submitted to us in the early part of the past year for our general approval. These plans afforded ample evidence that they had been prepared with much care and thought and they seemed to us, subject to a few suggested changes of a minor character, to be well adapted in their internal arrangements to the special purposes for which they were designed. Their cost, however, so far as could be judged from a probable estimate by the Architect, appeared to us to be unusually high, judging from our experience of the cost of similar buildings erected elsewhere in Scotland. We were therefore only able to give a general approval to some of the buildings, and even as regards these such approval was given subject to our being ultimately satisfied with regard to their cost. Whether or to what extent the high estimated expense of these buildings may be due to local circumstances which are beyond control we are unable at present to say, but we thought it our duty to point out that the buildings generally presented certain external features which, however good they might be from an architectural point of view, did not seem to us to be called for in the case of a district asylum, and we suggested that if these features were found to add materially to the cost of the buildings they should be omitted. No plans or estimates have been subsequently submitted to us, and in consequence we regret to have to report that beyond the making of roads, and the digging out of some foundations in the process of doing so, no progress has been made with the erection of buildings.

We understand that serious and unexpected difficulties have been found to exist in the construction of reservoirs owing to the porous nature of the only ground suitable from its elevation as a site for them.

The complete occupation of all the accommodation available in the neighbourhood of Edinburgh and the rapidly approaching exhaustion of the spare accommodation in all other asylums in Scotland throws a very grave responsibility upon the District Board. It is now nearly five years since that Board purchased

Position of
Districts.
———
Edinburgh
District.

Bangour estate with a view to the erection of an asylum, and they have already allowed a time to elapse which is usually considered as sufficient for the purchase of a site and the erection and occupation of a completed asylum, without so much as a single building having been begun. Looking to the great increase in the number of pauper lunatics and the present want of accommodation throughout the country, it is plain that unless the District Board take prompt measures a state of matters fraught with the most serious consequences must arise. Indeed, the District Board may be said to be already face to face with a difficulty which it is doubtful whether the utmost promptitude in proceeding with the erection of an asylum will enable them to meet, and which may have to be met by the adoption of some measure of a temporary nature to supply the most pressing of the requirements of the next four or five years.

Leith District.

Leith District is supplied with asylum accommodation by the Royal Edinburgh Asylum.

Midlothian
and Peebles
District.

The pauper lunatics of the Midlothian and Peebles District are accommodated in the District Asylum at Rosewell, and to a small extent in the lunatic wards of the Inveresk Combination Poorhouse. The large addition to the District Asylum recently begun has now been completed.

Haddington
District.

The pauper lunatics of the Haddington District are accommodated in the Haddington District Asylum, and to a small extent in the lunatic wards of Inveresk Combination Poorhouse.

Roxburgh
District.

The Roxburgh District Asylum at Melrose provides accommodation for the pauper lunatics of the counties of Roxburgh, Berwick, and Selkirk. The male side is overcrowded, and an extension similar to what has been carried out on the female side is under consideration.

Glasgow
District.

The pauper lunatics of the Glasgow District, which consists of the parish of Glasgow, are accommodated in the District Asylum at Lenzie (formerly the Barony Parochial Asylum) and in the District Asylum at Gartloch.

Govan District,

The pauper lunatics of the Govan District are accommodated in the District Asylum at Hawkhead, Paisley, in the Kirklands Asylum at Bothwell, and in the lunatic wards of Govan Poorhouse.

Lanark
District.

The pauper lunatics of the Lanark District are accommodated in the District Asylum at Hartwood, Shotts, in the Kirklands Asylum at Bothwell, and in the lunatic wards of the poorhouse at Old Monkland.

Renfrew
District.

The pauper lunatics of the Renfrew District are accommodated chiefly in the two Parochial Asylums of Paisley, at Riccartsbar and Craw Road, and in Greenock Parochial Asylum. The Parish

Council of Paisley has, however, terminated all agreements for the boarding in its asylums of patients from other parishes. These asylums and also the Greenock Asylum are full and the newly elected Renfrew District Lunacy Board are taking steps towards the purchase of a site for a District Asylum. The Order and Regulations fixing the boundaries of the Renfrew Lunacy District, providing for the election of a District Lunacy Board, and exempting the parishes of Paisley and Greenock from liability to assessment for lunacy purposes, so long as they continue as heretofore to provide asylum accommodation for their pauper lunatics to our satisfaction, will be found at page 167 of the Appendix to this Report.

The pauper lunatics of the Districts of Argyll and Bute are accommodated in the District Asylum at Lochgilphead. Including the ground occupied by buildings and roads, the extent of land attached to the asylum is only 50 acres, which is inadequate for an asylum of its size.

The pauper lunatics of the Ayr District are accommodated in the Ayr District Asylum and in the lunatic wards of the Cunninghame Combination Poorhouse.

The pauper lunatics of the Dumfries District, which consists of the Counties of Dumfries, Kirkcudbright, and Wigtown, are accommodated in the Crichton Royal Institution and in the lunatic wards of the Wigtown Poorhouse. New accommodation of a hospital character for the pauper patients who are provided for in the Second House is considerably advanced towards completion, and a handsome separate building for the accommodation of patients working in the laundry and their attendants is now completed.

VII.—WANT OF ACCOMMODATION FOR THE POORER CLASS OF PRIVATE PATIENTS.

We entered into a full discussion of this subject in our Thirty-ninth Annual Report. We repeat the opinion that permissive power should be given by statute to District Lunacy Boards to provide accommodation for private patients under the conditions we indicated as desirable, and we have reason to believe that legislation in the direction suggested would tend to relieve the rates and would be approved of by District Lunacy Boards.

VIII. INCREASE OF PAUPER LUNACY IN LEWIS, ROSS-SHIRE.

We have more than once had occasion to remark in former Reports that what has taken place and is still taking place in regard to the increase of registered pauper lunacy in Scotland can best be shown by the examination of the figures relating to limited areas. This can be done with special ease in the case of

Increase of
Pauper Lunacy
in Lewis,
Ross-shire
———

localities which do not form parts of great commercial and industrial centres, and are therefore not subject to the complicated considerations arising not only from migration or emigration, but from the constant influx in large numbers of adult persons drawn from other districts of Scotland or from other countries. A district as free from such complicated considerations as possible is that of Lewis in Ross-shire, consisting of the parishes of Stornoway, Lochs, Uig, and Barvas, having a present population of 28,949. The statistics of this area during the last twenty years show an increase of pauper lunacy so great that, if the figures were taken by themselves, without examination of the special circumstances connected with their production, and without comparison with what has happened in other parts of Scotland, they might well be held to indicate a widespread breakdown of the mental health of the community and to afford scope for almost any theory which might be formed to account for them. A consideration of the facts will, however, show that such conclusions and theories would be baseless, so far as they might rest only upon these figures.

The following two Tables are submitted :—

TABLE I. Showing in quinquennial periods from 1881 to 1901 the number and disposal of the pauper lunatics of each parish in Lewis and the population of each parish.

TABLE II. Showing for the quinquennial periods in Table I. the proportion to population of pauper lunatics, in asylums and private dwellings respectively, of each parish of Lewis, and the like proportions in all Scotland.

[TABLES.

TABLE I.

Showing in Quinquennial Periods from 1881 to 1901 the Number and Disposal of the Pauper Lunatics of each Parish in Lewis, and the Population of each Parish.

	1					2			3			4			5			6		
YEAR.	POPULATION.					STORNOWAY.			LOCHS.			UIG.			BARVAS.			THE FOUR PARISHES.		
						Number of Pauper Lunatics at 1st January of each Year.			Number of Pauper Lunatics at 1st January of each Year.			Number of Pauper Lunatics at 1st January of each Year.			Number of Pauper Lunatics at 1st January of each Year.			Number of Pauper Lunatics at 1st January of each Year.		
	Stornoway.	Lochs.	Uig.	Barvas.	Total.	In Asylums.	In Private Dwellings.	Tl.	In Asylums.	In Private Dwellings.	Tl.	In Asylums.	In Private Dwellings.	Tl.	In Asylums.	In Private Dwellings.	Tl.	In Asylums.	In Private Dwellings.	Tl.
1881	10,389	6,294	3,489	5,325	25,487	11	4	15	3	9	12	2	3	5	1	2	3	17	18	35
1886	11,094	6,358	3,574	5,512	26,538	16	8	19	6	10	16	2	1	3	3	3	6	27	17	44
1891	11,799	6,432	3,660	5,699	27,590	14	12	26	10	15	25	2	8	5	4	7	11	30	37	67
1896	12,391	5,558	4,078	6,218	28,270	16	18	34	8	13	21	6	12	18	5	11	16	35	54	89
1901	12,988	4,788	4,49	6,736	28,949	11	15	26	11	13	24	12	11	23	8	16	24	42	55	97

TABLE II.

Showing for the Quinquennial Periods in Table I. the Proportion to Population of Pauper Lunatics, in Asylums and Private Dwellings respectively, of each Parish in Lewis, and the like Proportions in all Scotland.

	1			2			3			4			5			6		
	STORNOWAY.			LOCHS.			UIG.			BARVAS.			THE FOUR PARISHES.			ALL SCOTLAND.		
	Proportion of Pauper Lunatics per 10,000 of Population.			Proportion of Pauper Lunatics per 10,000 of Population.			Proportion of Pauper Lunatics per 10,000 of Population.			Proportion of Pauper Lunatics per 10,000 of Population.			Proportion of Pauper Lunatics per 10,000 of Population.			Proportion of Pauper Lunatics per 10,000 of Population.		
YEAR.	In Asylums.	In Private Dwellings.	Total.	In Asylums.	In Private Dwellings.	Total.	In Asylums.	In Private Dwellings.	Total.	In Asylums.	In Private Dwellings.	Total.	In Asylums.	In Private Dwellings.	Total.	In Asylums.	In Private Dwellings.	Total.
1881	10·6	3·8	14·4	4·8	14·3	19·1	5·7	8·6	14·3	1·9	3·7	5·6	6·7	7·0	13·7	18·1	4·1	22·2
1886	14·4	2·7	17·1	9·4	15·7	25·1	5·6	2·8	8·4	5·4	5·4	10·8	10·2	6·4	16·6	18·8	5·3	24·1
1891	11·8	10·2	22·0	15·5	23·3	38·8	5·5	8·2	13·7	7·0	12·3	19·3	10·9	13·4	24·3	20·0	6·2	26·2
1896	12·9	14·5	27·4	14·3	23·3	37·6	14·7	29·4	44·1	8·0	17·7	25·7	12·4	19·1	31·5	21·6	6·5	28·1
1901	8·5	11·5	20·0	23·2	27·5	50·7	26·7	24·4	51·1	11·9	23·7	35·6	14·5	19·0	33·5	24·6	6·2	30·8

It will be seen from these Tables that the actual number of registered pauper lunatics chargeable to the four parishes has increased during the past twenty years from 35 to 97. Calculated per 10,000 of the sane population, this represents an increase from 13·7 to 33·5, or 145 per cent. The number of pauper lunatics from the four parishes provided for in asylums has risen from 17 to 42, and in private dwellings from 18 to 55. In proportion to 10,000 of population this represents a rise of from 6·7 to 14·5 of asylum patients and from 7·0 to 19·0 of patients in private dwellings, an increase during the past twenty years of 116 and 171 per cent. respectively. A further examination of the figures will show that those relating to Stornoway differ greatly from those referring to the other three parishes. The increase in Stornoway during twenty years has been 38 per cent. only, and the increase is due altogether to the larger number receiving relief under private care, the proportion of those in asylums to population having fallen from 10·6 in 1881 to 8·5 in 1901. The increases shown by Lochs, Uig, and Barvas have, on the other hand, been very great. The actual increase in Barvas, for instance, has been from 3 to 24—1 to 8 of asylum patients and 2 to 16 of patients in private dwellings. In proportion to population the number of registered insane poor was thus in Barvas seven times greater in 1901 than in 1881, the number being about equally contributed by patients in asylums and in private dwellings. Increases little less remarkable are shown by the figures relating to Lochs and Uig. If, however, the figures of Lochs, Uig, and Barvas are compared with those for all Scotland it will be seen that they merely trace the course in the case of these parishes of a rapid approximation within the last few years to standards which have for long been common in Scotland. Barvas, in which the increase has been specially great, has at the present time only a proportion, per 10,000 of population, of lunatics provided for in asylums of 11·9 as compared with 24·6 so provided for in all Scotland. Only in the parish of Uig has the proportion (26·7) risen within the last few years beyond that of pauper patients in asylums in Scotland as a whole. This, as well as the high proportion shown also in Lochs (23·2), is in all likelihood due to an accumulation of patients in the Inverness District Asylum which possibly might have been prevented by energetic parochial management, seeing that the results shown by the parish of Stornoway (8·5 per 10,000 of population) are so very different. The proportion to population of pauper lunatics in the parishes of Lochs, Uig, and Barvas provided for in private dwellings is four times as high as the like proportion for all Scotland. This is in accordance with the truth that when the number of lunatics receiving relief in their own homes is large in any area the standard of wealth in that area will be found to be low. In other words, the presence of a large number of such patients resident within a locality is not a proof that insanity is unusually prevalent in it, but merely that it is poor. Were the income of the inhabitants of these Lewis parishes doubled or trebled the pauper lunatics in private dwellings would disappear, so far as the official register is concerned. The same things cannot, however, be said of patients in asylums. In all parts of Scotland,

no less than in Lewis, removal to an asylum means pauperism even
to the most highly paid workmen. In very few parts of Scotland
will there be found more than 10 per cent. of the population able to
obtain asylum treatment otherwise than through application to the
Parish Council, and in Lewis that class of the population must be
exceedingly small. Leaving this class of the population out of
account, the only effect upon the number of pauper lunatics
in asylums coming from poor as compared with rich localities
is that the numbers sent from poor localities, with a rental
perhaps so low as to be sensitive to the charge of even a
single lunatic in an asylum, are apt to be restricted, owing to
reasons of economy which in richer districts are not so pressing.
The proportion of all patients on the pauper lunatic roll per
10,000 of population is for Stornoway 20·0, for Lochs 50·7, for Uig
51·1, and for Barvas 35·6; with which may be compared the similar
figures for all Scotland 30·8, for Ross (as a whole) 51·6, for Sutherland 48·7, for Caithness 56·1, for Orkney 39·7, and for Shetland
39·4. Of patients in Asylums, the proportions are Stornoway 8·5,
Lochs 23·2, Uig 26·7, Barvas 11·9; with which may be compared
the similar figures for all Scotland 24·6, Ross 29·0, Sutherland
31·1, Caithness 32·2, Orkney 25·8, and Shetland 22·0.

It is often, however, assumed that figures such as those in Table
I. prove a growing prevalence of mental defect among the com-
munities of isolated localities such as Lewis, and this assumption. is
naturally followed by speculation as to the causes of such growth,
among which may be mentioned the following:—

1. The evil effects of intermarriage.

2. The fact that the healthiest and most active members of the
community migrate, leaving behind them the imbecile, who thus
appear as the product of the population which remains, but are
really the product of a potentially larger population.

3. The leaving of the production of a future population to those
who have not migrated, who are assumed to be of inferior mental
and bodily physique.

4. Poor food and clothing, unhealthy houses, deficient education,
and the assumed mental stagnation due to a retired life and
remoteness from centres of mental activity.

It is not believed that there is any reason to attribute weight in
the case of Lewis to the class of suggested causes last named. The
condition of the population of Lewis in respect to most, if not all,
of these matters, has in all probability improved and not deteriorated
during the past twenty years. At all events that is the case judging
from the reports on the condition of the insane in the island.

With regard to the effects of intermarriage, it must be kept in
view that intermarriage must have been at least as common
hundreds of years ago in Lewis as it is to-day. It cannot, therefore, be reasonably supposed, whatever evil effects may be held to
be due to it, that such effects should have first manifested themselves between the year 1881 and the year 1901, as must be
assumed, if it is sought in that way to account for the difference
between the figures of these years.

With respect to the leaving behind of the mentally incapable
during a process of migration, there is undoubtedly a truth in this

which applies to all the country districts of Scotland.   But in this Increase of
respect Lewis presents a peculiarity not common to other rural Pauper Lunacy in Lewis,
districts of Scotland, which as a rule show a falling off in population Ross-shire.
notwithstanding a sustained birth-rate.   In other parts of rural and
insular Scotland in which no such remarkable increase of registered
pauper lunacy is recorded, the migration during the past twenty
years has been so great as to reduce the population materially.   In
Lewis also, which adds to its population almost altogether through its
birth-rate, it would appear that during that period between 4,000
and 5,000 persons have left the Island; but the Census Returns
show that in Lewis, notwithstanding the considerable migration
which has taken place, the population has increased during the
twenty years by 3,462.   The fact that the population of Lewis has
been increasing throughout the last twenty years shows that arguments founded upon migration apply with less force to it than to
most rural and insular parts of Scotland, where, notwithstanding a
high birth-rate and a falling population due to migration, no
increase approaching what has taken place in Lewis has occurred
during the past twenty years in the proportion to population of the
registered insane.

The same consideration comes into force with regard to the
suggestion that the propagation of the population is left to those
least likely to produce a healthy stock.   It is no doubt true that
the young men and women who leave Lewis are likely to be, as a
rule, among the most healthy and intelligent of the community,
but it would be quite unsafe to conclude that the bulk of those left
behind are not healthy and intelligent.   There is no reason to think
that the crofter's son who remains at home to carry on the croft is,
as a rule, less intelligent and capable of producing healthy and
intelligent children than his brothers who enter the Army or join
the Glasgow police.   But in any case as the rising population
shows that the amount of migration taking place from Lewis is
much below what is occurring in other insular and rural districts
of Scotland, arguments founded upon migration cannot account
for the exceptional rise during the last twenty years in the number
of registered pauper lunatics belonging to that island.

It is not possible to say whether the mass of imbecility and other
forms of mental unsoundness has increased or decreased in Lewis
during the past twenty years, but it has been shown above that
there is an inherent improbability that such possible causes of
mental deterioration as are above alluded to should have withheld their effects in Lewis from time immemorial until 1881,
and have from that time onwards manifested themselves in
a great and growing wave of insanity.   There is, in fact, no
reason to doubt that the insane (as distinguished from the
registered insane) in Lewis were as numerous in proportion
to population in 1881 as in 1901.   The increase shown in the
Tables submitted is believed to be sufficiently accounted for
by the reasonable supposition that a great many persons were
recognised as lunatics and sent to the asylum for treatment in 1900
who would not have been so recognised and treated in 1881.   This
change, though much less recent in most places than in Lewis, is

Increase of
Pauper Lunacy
in Lewis,
Ross-shire.

———

common to all Scotland, and is believed by the Board to account for
the general growth of pauper lunacy in Scotland. It has its chief
source primarily in (a) the more widely-spread and strong desire—
often eagerness—to look to the parish as bound to provide for the
mentally defective members of a family; and (b) the increased
willingness of Parish Councils to recognise claims for assistance
founded upon mental defect. These causes would probably have
operated had there been no Pauper Lunatic Grant; but there can
be no doubt that the Grant, especially in the poorer areas of the
country, has greatly stimulated both causes. An examination of
the Board's registers shows that in the parishes of Lewis persons
were often formally certified and intimated as pauper lunatics in
batches at one date. Many of these were already in receipt of relief
as ordinary paupers; many, both of paupers and non-paupers, were
at the time of formal certification as lunatics old or middle-aged
persons who had been imbecile from birth. Such things as a
change of Inspector of Poor in Highland parishes has often resulted
in the sudden appearance of a large number of pauper lunatics in a
parish which up to that time had presented a comparatively clean
register. The gradual change in views and circumstances which
has led to an increase in the number of registered lunatics throughout
Scotland has been, as might be expected, longer in taking effect
in Lewis and similar outlying districts, and the effect in such
districts has been more marked than in the wealthier parts of the
country because the great bulk of the people are poor, and claims
to relief on account of mental defect are therefore general and
difficult to resist. It will be seen from the figures relating to the
growth of registered lunacy in the Parish of Stornoway, as compared
with the growth in the three other parishes of Lewis, that even in
Lewis itself the increase of registered pauper lunacy is much less
marked where the standard of wealth and other social conditions
approaches more nearly the standard prevailing in other parts of
Scotland.

It further cannot be asserted on the authority of the figures
given that imbecility and other forms of mental unsoundness are at
the present time either more or less prevalent in Lewis than elsewhere in Scotland; because neither in Lewis nor elsewhere in Scotland have the Board any trustworthy guide as to the extent of
mental defect in the community. The mere fact of a low standard
of wealth in any area is certain of itself to bring eventually on the
register a larger number of pauper lunatics than would be so
brought in a richer area. Had the statistics relating to pauper
lunacy in Lewis been examined twenty years ago, it will be seen
by comparing the figures in Sections 5 and 6 of Table II. that the
figures referring to 1881 might have been used to prove that
insanity was much less prevalent in Lewis than in Scotland generally, though the figures relating to subsequent years show that any
such conclusion would have been quite unjustified.

Cost per
Patient in
District
Asylums of
Land, Build-
ing, &c.

IX. COST PER PATIENT IN DISTRICT ASYLUMS OF LAND, BUILDING, &c.

The annual assessments for lunacy purposes have been used as
the basis for the figures in the following Tables, which relate to the

cost of land and building. These assessments are levied on lands Cost per
and heritages within lunacy districts which possess district asylums. District
They include interest on all sums borrowed to purchase land, and to Asylums of
build or add to asylums, together with instalments in repayment of Land, Build-
principal sums borrowed (which must be repaid within thirty years ing, &c.
from the time of borrowing), and also such smaller outlays in
connection with the building as it is thought desirable to pay off
year by year. In the following Table the amount of these assessments in all Scotland, for each year included in the Table, has
been divided by the average number of patients resident during
that year in district asylums, and the result shows in column 2
the average amount assessed for per occupied bed. In making
the calculations in this Table no assessment of the kind made at
any time has been omitted. For instance, assessments for debt
incurred by the original Glasgow District Board have been
included, though the money raised by them did not result in the
erection of a district asylum.

TABLE I.

Showing for all District Asylums in Scotland (1) the average
number of patients resident in each year named, (2) the
amount of assessment for providing accommodation per head
of patients resident, (3) the expenditure for the maintenance
of each patient, and (4) the total cost per patient:—

Years.	Average Number of Patients Resident in District Asylums. 1.	Annual Assessment per Patient to provide Land and Buildings. 2.	Net Annual Cost per Patient of Food, Clothing, Management, &c. 3.	Total cost per Patient. 4.
		£ s. d.	£ s. d.	£ s. d.
1868–1869	1132	27 8 2	...	...
1878–1879	2553	12 3 2	...	...
1888–1889	2996	10 16 2	23 10 0	34 6 2
1889–1890	3057	12 5 4	24 2 8	36 8 0
1890–1891	3148	13 4 3	23 8 8	36 12 11
1891–1892	3223	12 15 11	23 11 4	36 7 3
1892–1893	3290	13 1 9	23 14 10	36 16 7
1893–1894	3346	15 2 7	22 10 4	37 12 11
1894–1895	3462	14 5 1	23 1 10	37 6 11
1895–1896	3951	14 18 8	23 11 4	38 10 0
1896–1897	4319	14 15 8	23 7 10	38 3 6
1897–1898	4898	15 6 4	24 12 6	39 18 10
1898–1899	5304	14 15 8	25 1 10	39 17 6
1899–1900	6353	15 18 9	25 5 7	41 4 4
1900–1901	6561	16 6 8	26 18 1	43 4 9

The first of the District Asylums which may be regarded as
having been erected as an immediate consequence of the passing of

Cost per
Patient in
District
Asylums of
Land, Build-
ing, &c.

the Lunacy Act of 1857 was opened in 1863, and the last of that original group in 1874. Expenses in connection with the erection of these asylums were necessarily incurred for many years before they were ready for the reception of patients, and even after they were opened, several years would elapse during which the accommodation provided would only be partially occupied. It is therefore not surprising to find that in 1868-69, the earliest year embraced in the Table, there were only 1132 patients resident in district asylums, and that the outlay on asylum lands and buildings, when calculated on the number of patients resident, shows the high average of £27 8s. 2d. Ten years after this period the expenses connected with providing asylums had fallen to £12 3s. 2d. per head of the patients resident, and ten years subsequent to that, in 1888-89, to £10 16s. 2d., though during these periods many additions to the accommodation must have been made. Soon, however, after the last-mentioned year the figures begin to be affected by the first steps towards providing a new group of large and expensive asylums. Up to 1888, and for many years later, the patients of the populous county of Lanark, including the city of Glasgow, were provided for chiefly in the Glasgow Royal Asylum, and in parochial asylums belonging to the large parishes connected with Glasgow. In 1888 the county, which until then had been one lunacy district, was divided into several districts, and expenses immediately began to be incurred through steps being taken towards the erection of district asylums. The last of the three large and costly asylums subsequently founded was only fully completed after May 1898. Many of the parts and adjuncts of these asylums will be able to provide eventually for a larger population than the buildings as at first completed could contain. The expense, for instance, of land, farm buildings, roads, superintendents' houses, kitchens, amusement halls, &c., will not require to be provided afresh to meet all future extensions. It may therefore be hoped that as the population grows the expense per bed will fall, as has happened in the case of the older asylums, even apart from the fall which may be expected eventually to occur to some extent through extinction of debt. The Table shows, however, that at May 1901 the pauper lunatics of Scotland maintained in district asylums were costing the country a yearly rent per bed of £16 6s. 8d., which, added to the average cost for the food, clothing, and management of the patients at that date, gives the total cost of pauper lunatics in all district asylums as £43 4s. 9d. per patient.

The Edinburgh and the Aberdeen City District Boards have taken steps towards the erection of new asylums, and assessments for preliminary expenses incurred by them are included in Table I.

The providing expenses (land, building, &c.) of most of the older district asylums for the past twenty years, as shown in the following Table, may in some respects, perhaps, convey a truer view of the facts with regard to the cost of asylums, when stated apart from the cost of the newer asylums which have not yet reached the limit of their capacity. We omit from this Table the Elgin District Asylum and the Kirklands Asylum, because they were not erected by the District Boards to which they belong, and the Stirling District Asylum, because, unlike the other district asylums, the earlier debts incurred on account of it were not spread over a series of years but were paid off at once by large assessments.

Cost per Patient in District Asylums of Land, Building, &c.

[TABLE.

TABLE II.

ASSESSMENTS on Counties and Burghs to defray Cost of Land and Buildings in the case of the Asylums named (including instalments in repayment of principal sums borrowed) per head of Patients accommodated in each Year named.

	All the Asylums named		Argyll (Opened 1863)		Ayr (Opened 1869)		Banff (Opened 1865)		Fife (Opened 1866)		Haddington (Opened 1866)		Inverness (Opened 1864)		Midlothian (Opened 1874)		Perth (Opened 1864)		Roxburgh (Opened 1872)	
Years	No. of Patients	Assessment per Patient	No. of Patients	Assessment per Patient	No. of Patients	Assessment per Patient	No. of Patients	Assessment per Patient	No. of Patients	Assessment per Patient	No. of Patients	Assessment per Patient	No. of Patients	Assessment per Patient	No. of Patients	Assessment per Patient	No. of Patients	Assessment per Patient	No. of Patients	Assessment per Patient
		£ s. d.		£ s. d.		£ s. d.		£ s. d.		£ s. d.		£ s. d.		£ s. d.		£ s. d.		£ s. d.		£ s. d.
1881-82	2253	10 18 5	365	8 9 5	259	9 15 1	129	12 11 0	344	8 14 5	102	7 12 11	419	7 12 9	221	20 7 3	267	11 4 9	246	16 5 2
1882-83	2301	10 17 8	351	6 11 1	280	8 18 7	122	13 16 1	327	10 7 11	99	7 13 6	421	9 10 0	207	19 6 6	253	12 13 0	241	14 10 5
1883-84	2256	11 13 1	357	13 8 0	300	8 6 8	126	13 8 8	327	10 11 0	101	7 6 6	437	9 3 1	215	18 12 1	251	10 15 2	201	15 18 5
1884-85	2258	11 8 5	356	12 0 6	280	8 6 1	129	14 15 10	349	10 11 0	109	6 12 1	433	9 4 9	223	17 7 10	290	10 7 8	206	19 8 4
1885-86	2288	11 14 9	381	11 7 6	300	8 6 1	137	10 8 4	358	8 18 9	100	7 4 0	427	8 8 7	223	17 13 9	296	12 8 1	201	19 18 0
1886-87	2277	11 6 11	384	12 4 1	396	8 14 6	136	11 7 2	362	6 18 1	102	7 1 2	431	8 14 0	205	17 18 9	272	12 2 8	202	19 16 0
1887-88	2285	10 12 8	365	10 18 3	399	8 13 0	141	8 19 2	367	6 16 3	102	6 7 5	431	8 4 9	205	19 14 1	290	11 10 6	199	18 10 4
1888-89	2426	10 12 8	354	12 6 7	397	8 8 4	143	7 18 2	378	7 16 8	106	6 2 8	440	7 4 5	204	23 0 9	285	10 10 6	210	18 15 0
1889-90	2506	10 8 9	360	12 8 7	312	6 8 2	141	7 15 11	383	7 16 8	114	6 2 10	457	7 4 5	231	19 9 7	303	10 11 3	210	17 17 2
1890-91	2540	9 14 0	360	12 10 0	342	5 17 0	133	8 0 7	400	7 10 0	118	6 18 8	477	7 10 12	229	12 11 1	312	11 4 4	229	17 18 10
1891-92	2649	9 7 11	371	14 0 4	351	2 17 0	139	12 9 2	426	7 0 10	126	5 11 1	496	6 19 11	235	13 0 1	315	9 16 10	210	17 17 2
1892-93	2685	9 0 10	373	10 19 10	359	2 15 9	130	8 17 6	442	6 15 9	125	6 8 0	484	5 13 8	233	23 12 1	310	7 1 11	227	16 10 5
1893-94	2659	9 9 4	396	11 4 7	398	11 4 7	140	8 5 0	446	6 15 6	128	6 5 0	410	6 14 2	231	21 12 11	316	6 19 3	237	15 16 5
1894-95	2750	9 1 4	411	11 6 2	422	5 18 6	141	8 16 5	443	9 0 7	130	5 0 0	433	6 7 0	231	19 1 2	318	6 5 9	242	15 9 11
1895-96	2822	8 15 1	411	11 4 7	429	5 16 7	145	7 12 5	448	6 7 6	139	3 19 2	457	7 6 7	239	19 11 1	313	6 5 6	242	15 9 11
1896-97	2929	8 0 3	414	11 16 9	442	5 13 1	149	2 7 1	471	6 7 6	146	4 3 7	460	5 10 5	256	14 16 7	333	6 0 1	259	15 8 11
1897-98	3008	8 8 7	421	10 16 2	450	6 13 4	153	2 5 4	488	6 14 0	144	5 4 2	518	5 15 10	229	15 5 8	342	6 8 8	254	17 19 10
1898-99	3166	8 14 10	440	10 9 1	483	7 4 11	154	4 16 10	515	6 15 11	141	4 12 2	544	6 17 10	234	17 1 11	292	6 1 7	295	17 9 8
1899-1900	3244	9 13 5	446	11 12 9	496	7 0 7	156	5 1 10	552	7 1 9	143	4 17 7	570	9 6 0	243	20 11 6	364	6 0 11	303	16 10 0
1900-1901	3240	9 7 9	434	8 7 6	488	7 3 5	169	3 5 8	533	6 11 4	135	5 18 10	588	9 1 10	248	24 3 10	358	6 14 1	296	15 18 10
Average Assessment per Patient during 50 Years—1851-1901	…	9 19 8	…	11 8 1	…	7 2 5	…	8 8 10	…	7 14 0	…	6 0 1	…	7 13 0	…	18 13 2	…	9 1 2	…	17 3 5

It appears from this Table that the average yearly cost per bed of all the asylums included in the Table has been, during the last twenty years, throughout which period they may all be regarded as having been in full occupation, £9 19s. 8d., and that in the case of individual asylums the average cost during that period ranges from £6 0s. 1d. in the Haddington Asylum to £18 13s. 2d. in the Midlothian Asylum.

(margin note: Cost per Patient in District Asylums of Land, Building, &c.)

The following Table shows for the District Asylums included in Table II. the average number of patients resident during the year 1900-1901, the expenditure per head for providing accommodation, the expenditure per head for the maintenance of patients, and the total cost per patient.

TABLE III.

ASYLUMS.	Average Number of Patients Resident.	Providing Expenses per Patient.	Net Maintenance Expenses per Patient.	Total Cost per Patient.
	1.	2.	3.	4.
		£ s. d.	£ s. d.	£ s. d.
1. Argyll, ...	434	8 7 6	27 5 1	35 12 7
2. Ayr, ...	488	7 3 5	27 4 6	34 7 11
3. Banff, ...	163	3 5 8	17 17 9	21 3 5
4. Fife, ...	533	6 11 4	25 13 2	32 4 6
5. Haddington, . . .	185	5 18 10	24 0 4	29 19 2
6. Inverness, . . .	583	9 1 10	25 18 1	34 19 11
7. Midlothian, . . .	248	24 3 10	34 17 3	59 1 1
8. Perth, . . .	358	6 14 1	28 0 9	34 14 10
9. Roxburgh, . .	296	15 18 10	29 8 7	45 7 5
Averages, . .	..	9 13 11	26 13 11	36 7 10

It will be seen from this Table that in the group of District Asylums included in it, which have all been opened for periods ranging from 39 to 28 years, and which have all been during that period more or less extensively added to and altered, the present payment towards providing accommodation is on the average £9 13s. 11d., varying from £3 5s. 8d. in the Banff Asylum to £24 3s. 10d. in the Midlothian Asylum; that the average present cost of maintaining the patients is £26 13s. 11d., varying from £17 17s. 9d. in the Banff Asylum to £34 17s. 3d. in the Midlothian Asylum; and that the present total average cost per patient in the whole group is £36 7s. 10d., at the two extremes being Banff with a total cost of £21 3s. 5d. and Midlothian with a total cost of £59 1s. 1d. It will be observed that the cost of maintenance does not vary so greatly as the cost of providing accommodation, and it is the latter figure which therefore chiefly determines variations in the total cost.

Some of the asylums embraced in the foregoing Tables accommodate private patients. These are few in number, and the rates of board paid are sometimes little, if at all, in excess of the rates paid for pauper patients. In cases where a profit is made it

e

Cost per
Patient in
District
Asylums of
Land, Build-
ing, &c.

is applied equally in the reduction of building and maintenance rates. The figures upon which the calculations are made therefore include private patients.

Expenditure
for Pauper
Lunatics.

X. EXPENDITURE FOR PAUPER LUNATICS.

Expenditure
by Parish
Councils—
Increase

The expenditure by the Parish Councils of each county, on account of pauper lunatics, is given in Table XXIII. (Appendix A), for the year ending 15th May 1901. From this Table it appears that, for the maintenance of 15,987 pauper lunatics, who were under care for longer or shorter periods during the year, in asylums, lunatic wards of poorhouses, and private dwellings, and for other expenses connected with them, a total sum of £345,660 was paid; of which £265,602 was for maintenance in asylums (including Institutions for Imbecile Children), £24,142 was for maintenance in lunatic wards of poorhouses, £46,672 was for maintenance in private dwellings, and £9244 was for certification, transport, and other expenses. Of this expenditure £19,127 was repaid by relatives and others, and £115,849 was contributed from the Local Taxation Account, in terms of Section 22 of the Local Government (Scotland) Act, 1889, and of Section 2 of the Education and Local Taxation Account (Scotland) Act, 1892.

The following statement shows the average annual expenditure for the maintenance of pauper lunatics for each period of five years, beginning with 1859–1863 and ending with 1895–1899, and for the years 1899-1900 and 1900–1901, extracted from Table XXIV., and also the average annual number* of patients relieved in each period :—

Years.	Asylums, including Institutions for Imbecile Children.		Lunatic Wards of Poorhouses with Restricted Licenses.		Private Dwellings.		Cost of Certifi-cation, rates, Trans-port, &c.	Total.	
	Average No. of Patients relieved.	Expendi-ture.	Average No. of Patients relieved.	Expendi-ture.	Average No. of Patients relieved.	Expendi-ture.		Average No. of Patients relieved.	Expendi-ture.
1859–1863	2,587	£61,735	836	£14,695	1,706	£14,763	£4,031	5,129	£95,224
1864–1868	3,007	73,416	979	19,241	1,547	15,157	4,400	5,533	112,214
1869–1873	4,200	105,018	613	10,952	1,474	16,345	4,806	6,287	137,121
1874–1879	5,127	138,278	616	12,790	1,401	17,787	4,809	7,144	173,664
1880–1884	6,220	164,001	699	13,792	1,599	22,554	6,188	8,518	206,536
1885–1889	6,572	169,720	829	15,835	2,125	32,574	6,654	9,527	224,783
1890–1894	7,355	184,564	869	16,558	2,497	40,007	8,193	10,721	249,322
1895–1899	8,584	217,507	872	16,011	2,682	44,515	9,529	12,138	287,562
1899–1900	9,527	253,541	900	17,446	2,706	45,883	9,246	13,134	326,116
1900–1901	9,781	265,602	1,057	24,142	2,650	46,672	9,244	13,437	345,660

* The average number of patients relieved is the number of patients who received relief *for a whole year*, that is, it is arrived at by taking the total number of days for which relief was given for each year and dividing that number by 365.

The Act of 1857 had for one of its main objects the provision of sufficient accommodation for pauper lunatics, which was then either wholly wanting or deficient in almost every county in Scotland, and it was not until the close of the quinquenniad 1874–79 that the Act can be considered to have attained its object in this direction. The results shown in the later years included in the Table cannot therefore be instructively compared with those shown in the earlier years. But comparing the average results shown by the quinquenniad 1880–84, when the legislation of 1857 may be regarded as having taken full effect, with the results shown by the latest year included in the Table, it will be found that the expenditure on patients in asylums has increased from £164,001 to £265,602, or 62 per cent.; in the Lunatic Wards of Poorhouses from £13,793 to £24,142, or 75 per cent.; in Private Dwellings from £22,554 to £46,672, or 107 per cent.; and that the whole expenditure increased from £206,536 to £345,660, or 67 per cent.

Expenditure for Pauper Lunatics.

Expenditure by Parish Councils.— Increase.

It will be seen, however, from the following statement of the annual expenditure per patient that the increased total expenditure from the quinquenniad 1874–1879 up to the quinquenniad 1890–94 was due solely to an increase of numbers, and not to a larger expenditure on each patient. The following quinquenniad, however, and each subsequent year shows a progressive rise in the cost per head :—

Expenditure per head.

	Expenditure per Patient.			
	In Asylums, including Institutions for Imbecile Children.	In Lunatic Wards of Poorhouses with Restricted Licenses.	In Private Dwellings.	Total.
	£ s. d.	£ s. d.	£ s. d.	£ s. d.
1859–1863	23 17 3	17 11 7	8 13 1	18 11 6
1864–1868	24 8 4	19 13 1	9 15 11	20 6 1
1869–1873	25 0 1	17 17 4	11 1 9	21 16 6
1874–1879	26 19 5	20 13 3	12 13 11	24 6 5
1880–1884	26 7 4	19 14 8	14 2 1	24 5 5
1885–1889	25 16 6	19 1 0	15 6 7	23 19 5
1890–1894	25 1 10	19 1 1	16 0 5	23 5 3
1895–1899	25 6 5	18 7 1	16 12 0	23 18 7
1899–1900	26 12 3	19 7 8	16 19 1	24 16 7
1900–1901	27 5 11	22 16 10	17 12 3	25 14 6

(*Average Annual Expenditure.*)

We repeat here the following summary of facts to which attention has been drawn at greater length in former Reports :—

Summary of Remarks on Expenditure by Parish Councils.

(1) The increase of the gross expenditure for the first fifteen or twenty years for which we possess statistics, in so far as it is the result of increased numbers of the insane poor maintained in asylums, was an inevitable outcome of what the Lunacy Act of 1857 was intended to accomplish, that is, the provision of sufficient asylum accommodation.

(2) The rise in the cost per patient in institutions during that period was due to such causes as increased price of food, and also to

Expenditure for Pauper Lunatics.

the fact that Royal Asylums, which in the earlier years maintained pauper lunatics at rates involving loss, raised the rates from time to time.

Summary of Remarks on Expenditure by Parish Councils.

(3) The expenditure per head on pauper lunatics rose until 1874-79, whence it fell until the year 1895-96, when a rise, which still continues, is again shown. The expenditure per head on patients in private dwellings has risen gradually throughout the whole period.

Cost of Land and Buildings only slightly represented in Expenditure Table.

It is necessary to bear in mind that the expenditure, as given in Table XXIV., refers only to the cost of maintenance, which is borne in the first instance by the poor-rate, and contributed to by the State and the relatives of paupers. It does not take into account the expenditure on the purchase of land, and the erection of asylums. These expenses are defrayed out of special assessments on all Lunacy Districts in which District Asylums have been provided, as already explained on pages lx-lxvi. In the case of patients boarded in Royal Asylums, or in District or Parochial Asylums not connected with the parishes to which the patients are chargeable, an addition to the charge for maintenance is made in most cases, in consideration of the accommodation having been provided by the institution, but this addition does not bear any definite relation to the actual cost of the accommodation.

Repayments by relatives.

The contributions towards the maintenance of pauper lunatics made by relatives and obtained from other private sources are shown in the second last column of Table XXIII. These contributions show a steady increase. In 1859 they amounted to £1877, in 1880-1 to £9290, in 1890-1 to £11,687, and in 1900-1901 to £19,127.

Contributions from State Funds.

The annual Parliamentary Grant in aid of the cost of maintenance of pauper lunatics, first given for the year 1874-75, ceased in 1889, and its place was taken by a fixed contribution towards the cost of maintenance of pauper lunatics of £90,500, in terms of Section 22 of the Local Government (Scotland) Act, 1889. This contribution towards the cost to parishes of maintaining pauper lunatics was supplemented by a further fixed contribution of £25,000 under Section 2 of the Education and Local Taxation Account (Scotland) Act, 1892.

These contributions are distributed among Parish Councils by the Secretary for Scotland, as nearly as may be in the manner in which the annual Parliamentary Grant was distributed. In allocating the Grant, all expenditure over 8s. a week is excluded. Expenditure under and up to 8s. a week is treated as "admissible expenditure," and the Grant is apportioned upon such expenditure at so much per £ as far as it will go. The State contribution for the year 1900-1901 was equal to about 3s. 8d. per week for each patient, however provided for, for whose maintenance a sum was paid equal to or exceeding 8s. a week.

The contributions from State funds towards the maintenance of pauper lunatics, for each of the twenty-six years in which such con-tributions have been made, are shown in the following Statement :—

Contributions from State Funds towards Maintenance of Pauper Lunatics.

For the year ending			For the year ending		
14th May 1875,	.	£59,483	14th May 1889,	.	91,335
,, 1876,	.	62,637	,, 1890,	.	90,474
,, 1877,	.	65,470	,, 1891,	.	90,450
,, 1878,	.	68,583	,, 1892,	.	115,574
,, 1879,	.	71,272	,, 1893,	.	115,717
,, 1880,	.	73,883	,, 1894,	.	115,789
,, 1881,	.	76,856	,, 1895,	.	115,407
,, 1882,	.	79,711	15th May 1896,	.	115,761
*,, 1883,	.	81,495	,, 1897,	.	115,778
,, 1884,	.	83,089	,, 1898,	.	115,736
,, 1885,	.	85,111	,, 1899,	.	115,885
,. 1886,	.	87,164	,, 1900,	.	115,920
,, 1887,	.	88,258	,, 1901,	.	115,849
,, 1888,	.	£89,072			

The average daily cost of maintenance of pauper patients in the different classes of establishments for the ten years 1891-92 to 1900-1901 is shown in Table XXV. (Appendix A). The general average rate is shown by the Table to be 1s. 5d. a day, which is ¼d. above that for the previous year.

Table XXVI. (Appendix A) shows, from returns furnished by Inspectors of Poor, the average daily rate of maintenance paid by Parish Councils for each mode of providing for pauper lunatics in each county during the year ending 15th May 1901, and the proportion in which each mode is adopted in each county. It appears from this Table that the daily cost of maintaining pauper lunatics in asylums, in licensed wards of poorhouses, and in private dwellings varies considerably in the different counties.

As regards asylums, the lowest average daily cost per head for a county is 1s. 0¼d. and the highest is 1s. 9d¼., which, calculated for the year, would be £18 12s. 7¼d. and £32 6s. 4¼d.

As regards the licensed wards of poorhouses, the lowest daily cost for a county is 10d. and the highest is 1s. 3¾d., or £15 4s. 2d. and £23 19s. 0¾d. per annum.

As regards private dwellings, the lowest average daily cost for a county is 6¼d. and the highest is 1s. 2¼d., or £9 17s. 8¼d. and £22 1s. 0¼d. per annum.

Table XXVII. (Appendix A) shows the present rates of board for pauper lunatics in each of the various classes of establishments, and the minimum rates for private patients in Royal and District Asylums.

From this Table it appears that the minimum rates of board at which pauper patients are received in the Royal or Chartered Asylums range from £24 per annum, which is the rate in the Crichton Royal Institution, to £33, which is the rate in the Royal Edinburgh Asylum. In District Asylums the rates for patients belonging to the respective districts range from £18 5s. in the Banff Asylum to £34 in the Midlothian District Asylum. In Parochial Asylums the estimated cost for the pauper lunatics of the parishes to which these establishments severally belong varies from £26 18s. 5d., which is the estimated cost in the Paisley Parochial Asylum at Craw Road, a small establishment, to £28 3s. 4d., which is the estimated cost in the Paisley Parochial Asylum at Riccartsbar.

Expenditure for Pauper Lunatics.

Rates of Board in Establishments.

The rates in District Asylums may be regarded as showing in these establishments the actual cost of the maintenance of patients as distinguished from the cost of their lodging. It is proper, therefore, when comparing these rates with those in Royal and Parochial Asylums, to keep in view that the expense of erecting and fitting up is in District Asylums defrayed out of county assessments; whereas in the case of Royal Asylums it is defrayed either out of endowments, or out of the profits derived from keeping private patients, or out of the board charged for paupers; and in the case of Parochial Asylums, *i.e.*, lunatic wards of poorhouses with unrestricted licences, it is defrayed out of the poor-rate, and is now taken more or less into account in the estimated cost given in the Table. In the rates given as representing the cost in the lunatic wards of poorhouses, which range from £15 17s. 5d. in the Buchan Poorhouse to £27 1s. 8d. in the Govan Poorhouse, the cost of the buildings is also to some extent taken into account.

The great differences in the estimated cost of patients shown in some instances between one establishment of the same class and another, both in the case of Parochial Asylums and Lunatic Wards of Poorhouses, are not accounted for by differences in these establishments in regard to dietary or accommodation.

Cost of Providing District Asylum Accommodation.

Table XXVIII. shows the expenditure by District Boards of Lunacy during the financial year 1900–1901, on lands, buildings, and furnishings of District Asylums, and other expenses connected therewith.* It refers entirely to expenditure on pauper lunatics paid out of county assessments, as distinguished from the expenditure which is met by poor-rates levied on parishes.

Column 11 of the Table shows that the net outlay on District Asylums during the year 1900–1901 for land, building, and furnishings, &c., was £150,963.

Column 12 of the Table shows that the amount of money borrowed by District Lunacy Boards on the security of assessments, to provide land and buildings, and remaining unpaid at 15th May 1901, was £1,190,682; and Column 13 shows that the total assessments on lunacy districts to provide the interest on sums borrowed, to repay instalments of principal, and to repair and maintain buildings, &c., amounted for the year ending 15th May 1901 to £107,162.

Cost of Maintenance of Patients in District Asylums.

Table XXIX. shows in detail the expenditure on the maintenance and management of pauper lunatics in each District Asylum during the financial year 1900–1901, and the net cost at which the patients of each asylum are maintained. The average cost of maintenance and management per patient for the year 1900–1901 is £27 12s. 11d., and after a deduction of farm profits the average net cost is £26 17s. 7d.,† which shows an increase in the net cost over the previous year of £1 12s. 8d. per patient, food, clothing, salaries and wages, and miscellaneous expenses all contributing to this rise. The expenditure under such heads of these Tables as embrace articles produced by asylum farms and gardens is liable to be more or less affected by varying estimates of value, but as an over or under estimate of the

* See pages lx–lxvi of this Report.
† These calculations, and those in the following Table, are made upon the average numbers of patients actually resident.

value of farm produce would only have the ultimate effect of increas- *Expenditure for Pauper Lunatics.* ing or diminishing the apparent profit on the farm account, they cannot affect the 'net maintenance expenses,' which are stated under deduction of farm profits. The following statement shows the total *Cost of Maintenance of Patients in District Asylums.* expenses per patient, as shown by the Table, in all District Asylums for the year 1900-1901, and the expenses under the six heads specified.

No.	YEAR 1900-1901. DISTRICT ASYLUM.	Food.	Tobacco (per male patient).	Wines, Spirits, and Malt Liquors.	Clothing, Boots and Shoes.	Salaries and Wages.	All other Expenses.	Total Maintenance Expenses, without deduction of profit on Farm &c.*
		£ s. d.	£ s. d.	£ s. d.	£ s. d.	£ s. d.	£ s. d.	£ s. d.
1	Argyll,	11 14 6	0 11 11	0 0 9	1 11 5	7 10 7	6 5 11	27 9 4
2	Ayr,	10 18 3	0 12 7	0 6 3	1 14 9	6 14 7	8 0 8	28 0 2
3	Banff,	9 3 5	0 8 8	0 3 1	1 0 7	4 15 0	5 13 1	20 19 9
4	Elgin,	9 10 2	0 13 5	0 5 7	1 15 10	5 0 9	6 4 6	23 2 5
5	Fife,	12 5 1	0 8 6	0 3 8	1 18 0	6 0 1	6 5 8	26 16 4
6	Glasgow (Gartloch),	10 6 6	0 7 7	0 0 10	2 4 0	7 13 6	8 14 7	29 3 6
7	Glasgow (Woodilee),	9 15 7	0 10 6	0 1 0	2 4 6	7 4 0	6 3 11	25 14 3
8	Govan,	11 14 4	0 13 9	0 1 6	1 11 8	8 14 0	11 0 4	33 8 5
9	Haddington,	9 13 3	0 13 7	0 7 8	1 5 6	8 1 4	5 7 7	25 1 4
10	Inverness,	10 12 8	0 13 1	0 3 7	2 1 10	6 17 2	6 11 8	26 13 7
11	Kirklands,	9 16 7	0 9 1	0 5 2	1 10 10	8 2 8	6 1 0	26 0 11
12	Lanark,	9 7 0	0 10 2	0 2 6	1 10 11	7 6 0	6 9 4	25 1 4
13	Midlothian,	11 7 6	0 9 5	0 5 3	1 13 3	9 10 7	10 0 11	33 2 1
14	Perth,	10 6 2	0 8 1	0 2 9	1 16 10	6 19 5	3 19 6	23 8 11
15	Roxburgh,	11 16 0	0 10 0	0 3 6	1 9 8	7 15 3	3 19 10	30 9 2
16	Stirling,	11 1 4	0 12 8	0 5 2	2 6 1	6 18 4	8 3 2	29 0 6
	Average,	10 13 4	0 10 10	0 3 2	1 17 1	7 4 1	7 9 11	27 12 10

This statement shows that in the year 1900-1901 the highest *Expenditure on Maintenance of Patients in District Asylums during past years.* expenditure under the head of Food was £12 5s. 1d. per patient, in the Fife Asylum; and the lowest £9 3s. 5d., in Banff Asylum, which is £1 9s. 11d. below the average of all District Asylums.

The following statement shows the expenditure per patient in eighteen District Asylums during each of the eighteen years for which the information is obtainable under the same heads as those given in the previous statement:—

Years.	Food.	Tobacco (per Male patient).	Wines, Spirits, and Malt Liquors.	Clothing, Boots and Shoes.	Salaries and Wages.	All other Expenses.	Total Maintenance Expenses, without deduction of Profit on Farm, &c.*
	£ s. d.	£ s. d.	£ s. d.	£ s. d.	£ s. d.	£ s. d.	£ s. d.
1883-84	11 15 0	0 9 3	0 5 7	1 14 5	6 4 0	5 1 4	25 4 8
1884-85	11 12 0	0 9 8	0 5 2	2 0 4	6 8 0	5 5 8	25 15 9
1885-86	11 6 0	0 9 8	0 5 4	1 17 2	6 9 0	5 14 10	25 17 1
1886-87	10 14 4	0 10 0	0 5 6	1 17 0	6 12 0	5 10 6	25 4 3
1887-88	10 4 6	0 9 3	0 5 9	1 17 2	6 9 2	5 9 2	24 10 3
1888-89	10 4 3	0 9 3	0 6 9	1 19 3	6 9 4	5 11 9	24 16 0
1889-90	10 9 7	0 9 3	0 6 5	1 19 11	6 9 8	6 1 2	25 11 4
1890-91	10 8 7	0 9 3	0 6 2	1 16 9	6 5 0	5 14 2	24 15 2
1891-92	10 11 1	0 9 5	0 6 3	1 17 2	6 4 4	5 15 4	24 18 11
1892-93	10 7 1	0 9 7	0 5 4	1 15 8	6 4 0	5 19 5	24 16 3
1893-94	9 16 10	0 9 1	0 4 2	1 13 5	6 3 8	5 10 10	23 11 9
1894-95	9 14 6	0 9 6	0 4 0	1 15 1	6 6 5	5 15 8	24 0 11
1895-96	9 16 1	0 10 3	0 4 8	1 16 2	6 12 3	5 8 9	24 2 10
1896-97	9 11 2	0 10 1	0 4 1	1 16 3	6 11 8	5 17 1	24 5 2
1897-98	10 4 4	0 10 2	0 4 2	2 0 5	6 19 6	5 16 1	25 14 11
1898-99	10 6 2	0 10 2	0 4 1	1 15 2	7 1 9	6 4 2	25 16 6
1899-1900	10 4 10	0 10 2	0 3 10	1 16 10	7 1 11	6 7 6	25 19 0
1900-1901	10 13 4	0 10 10	0 3 2	1 17 1	7 4 1	7 9 11	27 12 10

* The difference between the sum shown in the last column, and that shown by the addition of the figures in the columns preceding it, arises from the fact that the 'Total Maintenance Expenses' are calculated upon the total number of patients resident, while in the case of the column headed 'Tobacco,' the cost is calculated on the number of male patients only.

Expenditure for Pauper Lunatics.

Expenditure on Maintenance of Patients in District Asylums during past eighteen years.

The expenditure naturally fluctuates somewhat from year to year, but on the whole it will be seen that the gross expenditure fell gradually until the year 1893–94, since which there has been a rise, the total expenses in the first year dealt with being £25 4s. 8d. per patient, and in the last £27 12s. 10d. The main decrease has occurred under the head 'Food.' 'Salaries and Wages' and unclassified expenses have risen since 1883–84.

Quantities and Values of Articles consumed in District Asylums.

Table XXX. shows the quantity per inmate (including patients and officers and servants partially or wholly boarded) of each article of consumption in regard to which we have separate figures, supplied to each asylum during the year 1900–1901; and also the price at which each article has been supplied, whether by purchase or from the asylum lands, the price in the latter case being an estimate. The quantities given are derived from the weight or measure assigned to each article by the voucher which accompanied its delivery at the store.

Quantities and Values of Articles supplied by Farms and Gardens of District Asylums.

Farm and Garden Accounts of District Asylums.

Table XXXI. shows the quantity of each article supplied to District Asylum stores from each asylum farm and garden, and the prices at which the various articles have been estimated.

Table XXXII. shows under various heads the receipts during the year 1900–1901 of District Asylum farms and gardens from produce sold or supplied to the asylum, the expenses in detail during these years, and the profit on each year's transactions.

In comparing the various amounts of profits shown, it is necessary to take into consideration the different estimates of the value of the produce supplied to the asylums.

Dangerous Lunatics.

XI. DANGEROUS LUNATICS.

The following Statement shows the number of persons sent to asylums as dangerous lunatics, in each of the ten years 1892–1901, at the instance of the Procurator-Fiscal, under the provisions of the 15th Section of 25 & 26 Vict. cap. 54 :—

1892,	.	.	14	1897,	.	.	13
1893,	.	.	5	1898,	.	.	5
1894,	.	.	4	1899,	.	.	8
1895,	.	.	13	1900,	.	.	1
1896,	.	.	10	1901,	.	.	5

The figures in this statement, however, do not disclose the extent to which the provisions of the Section dealing with dangerous lunatics are taken advantage of. In the great majority of cases in which proceedings are begun under that Section, an undertaking is given at an early stage of the procedure, by an Inspector of Poor or some person interested, that arrangements will be made for the safe custody of the lunatic which will be satisfactory to the Sheriff. In these cases an engagement that the patient will be placed in an asylum on a Sheriff's order, obtained in the ordinary way, is usually regarded by the Sheriff as 'an arrangement to Dangerous Lunatics. his satisfaction,' and no further procedure under the Section takes place. The patient remains in the asylum as an ordinary patient to whom the statutory provisions relating to persons confined as 'dangerous lunatics' do not apply. This procedure saves unnecessary expenditure and prevents the creation of obstacles to the discharge of patients in many cases which from their nature require no greater precautions than are called for in regard to the discharge of all unrecovered patients. The insanity of persons against whom proceedings are instituted as 'dangerous lunatics' does not usually differ from the insanity of persons committed to asylums in the ordinary way. They fall into the hands of the police frequently under circumstances such as might occur in the case of almost any lunatic who is friendless, or has become suddenly insane, or whose case does not happen to have been brought under the notice of parochial authorities. In many cases with which the police are called on to deal, and where no serious act has been committed, the patient is simply handed over to the care of the parochial authorities or of his friends, and no procedure whatever is taken under the Section in question. In other cases the circumstances are such as to make it desirable that the preliminary steps prescribed by the Section dealing with dangerous lunatics should be instituted, so as to give the Sheriff an opportunity of judging as to whether the lunatic should be confined as a dangerous lunatic or not, and in a few of these cases it is found to be of advantage for the public safety that the Sheriff should commit the lunatic in such a way that, unless he recovers his sanity, he cannot be discharged without consent of the Procurator-Fiscal. We have had no reason to think that the statutory provisions in regard to dangerous lunatics do not secure the safety of the public as far as is practicable.

XII. ALIEN LUNATICS. Alien Lunatics.

During 1901, 26 pauper lunatics were removed from Scotland, from having no settlement in that country. Of these patients, all of whom were removed from asylums, 10 were sent to England and 16 to Ireland.

XIII. LUNATICS UNDER JUDICIAL FACTORS. Lunatics under Judicial Factors

At the end of December 1901 there were 1025 persons reported to us by the Accountant of the Court of Session as under Judicial Factory in consequence of mental unfitness for the management of their affairs. This number is exclusive of some of the cases in which the means of the wards have been exhausted, though the Factory has not been formally discharged by the Court.

These persons were disposed of in the following way :—

635 were in asylums in Scotland;
321 were in private dwellings in Scotland; and
  69 were resident either in asylums or private dwellings beyond the direct jurisdiction of the Board.

Lunatics under Judicial Factors. Of the 69 who were beyond the direct jurisdiction of the Board, 28 were in asylums in England, 26 were in private dwellings in England, 1 in asylum in Ireland, and 2 were in private dwellings in Ireland. Of the remainder, 4 were resident in Australia, 1 in Canada, 1 in the United States of America, 1 in Germany, 1 in Belgium, 1 in Ceylon, 2 in New Zealand, and 1 in West Indies.

All patients resident in Scotland whose estates are under the management of Judicial Factors were visited by our officers during the year, except some whose position and circumstances were otherwise satisfactorily known, and in whose cases visitation was thought undesirable.

XIV.—ORDER AND REGULATIONS ISSUED UNDER THE LUNACY DISTRICTS (SCOTLAND) ACT.

We have issued with the approval of the Secretary for Scotland an Order and Regulations altering the Renfrew and Lanark Lunacy Districts, and providing for the election of a Renfrew District Lunacy Board, and for the conditional exemption from assessment for lunacy purposes of the Parishes of Paisley and Greenock. The Order and Regulations will be found on page 167 of the Appendix to this Report.

We have the honour to be,

MY LORD,

Your most obedient humble Servants,

WALTER G. SCOTT, *Chairman.*
JOHN COWAN.
JOHN CHEYNE.
JOHN FRASER.
JOHN MACPHERSON.

T. W. L. SPENCE,
   Secretary.

Edinburgh, 20th March 1902.

CONTENTS OF APPENDICES.

APPENDIX A.

APPENDIX B.

APPENDIX C.

APPENDIX D.

APPENDIX A.—TABLE I.*

The Number of Lunatics in Establishments and in Private Dwellings, classifying as Private and Pauper Patients, and distinguishing between the Sexes, on 1st January of each Year from 1858 to 1902.

At 1st January.	Number of Private Lunatics.						Number of Pauper Lunatics.						Totals.		
	In Asylums.			As Patients in Private Dwellings under Sheriff's Order or Sanction of Board.			In Asylums and Lunatic Wards of Poorhouses.			In Private Dwellings.			Private.	Pauper.	Total.
	M.	F.	T.	M.	F.	T.	M.	F.	T.	M.	F.	T.			
1858	506	506	1012	10	10	20	1402	1551	2953	810	974	1784	1022	4737	5769
1859	503	508	1011	11	13	24	1447	1656	3103	838	1039	1877	1035	4980	6015
1860	486	485	971	8	13	21	1567	1812	3379	828	1019	1847	992	5226	6218
Average of the 5 Years, 1861-65.	502	522	1024	8	13	21	1678	1939	3617	746	945	1691	1045	5308	6353
Average of the 5 Years, 1866-70.	558	581	1139	14	18	32	2014	2269	4283	666	855	1521	1171	5804	6975
Average of the 5 Years, 1871-75.	603	649	1252	33	38	71	2356	2654	5010	625	829	1454	1323	6464	7787
Average of the 5 Years, 1876-80.	667	681	1348	45	63	108	2822	3200	6022	565	834	1399	1456	7421	8878
1881	719	692	1411	41	72	113	3167	3555	6722	604	912	1516	1524	8238	9762
1882	701	703	1404	45	71	116	3343	3664	7007	611	957	1568	1520	8575	10095
1883	706	708	1414	45	75	120	3325	3692	7017	664	1099	1693	1584	8710	10244
1884	710	731	1441	48	80	128	3352	3726	7078	790	1091	1811	1569	8889	10458
1885	715	747	1462	53	75	130	3401	3773	7174	743	1119	1861	1592	9035	10627
Average of the 5 Years.	719	716	1426	46	75	121	3318	3682	7000	668	1022	1690	1548	8639	10237
1886	707	762	1469	44	76	120	3484	3764	7248	803	1255	2058	1589	9308	10895
1887	708	781	1489	45	83	130	3541	3725	7266	887	1303	2140	1619	9406	11025
1888	728	813	1541	44	88	132	3612	3774	7386	876	1394	2270	1673	9656	11329
1889	759	877	1636	42	89	131	3721	3879	7600	894	1403	2297	1767	9897	11664
1890	773	864	1637	44	82	128	3789	3999	7788	975	1470	2445	1765	10233	11996
Average of the 5 Years.	735	819	1554	44	84	128	3629	3828	7457	877	1365	2222	1682	9780	11382
1891	771	908	1679	40	84	124	3884	4104	7988	903	1496	2489	1803	10477	12280
1892	788	914	1702	42	83	125	3963	4344	8307	973	1462	2435	1827	10642	12469
1893	825	948	1773	37	78	115	3979	4339	8318	996	1523	2519	1888	10837	12735
1894	861	940	1801	40	68	108	4062	4414	8476	1013	1552	2565	1909	11041	12950
1895	915	968	1883	37	76	113	4241	4575	8816	1073	1604	2677	1996	11493	13489
Average of the 5 Years.	832	936	1768	39	78	117	4026	4335	8361	1010	1527	2537	1885	10898	12783
1896	910	1025	1935	37	74	111	4282	4675	8957	1100	1600	2700	2046	11657	13703
1897	897	1048	1945	33	75	118	4496	4865	9361	1066	1601	2667	2063	12028	14086
1898	919	1099	2018	37	76	113	4700	5007	9707	1078	1376	2454	2131	12361	14442
1899	953	1104	2057	40	83	123	4877	5220	10,097	1089	1613	2702	2180	12799	14979
1900	960	1110	2070	47	78	125	5049	5282	10,331	1084	1619	2708	2195	13034	15229
Average of the 5 Years.	928	1077	2006	40	77	117	4681	5010	9691	1083	1602	2685	2122	12376	14498
1901	969	1121	2090	47	77	124	5197	5395	10,592	1064	1605	2669	2214	13261	15475
1902	995	1139	2134	49	81	130	5442	5508	10,950	1051	1580	2631	2264	13581	15845

* Inmates of Schools for Imbeciles and in the Lunatic Department of the General Prison are not included in this Table. Their numbers at 1st January of each year from 1858 to 1902 will be found in the Table following.

A

APPENDIX A.—Table II.

The different Modes in which Lunatics, both Private and Pauper
have been provided for on 1st January of each Year from
1858 to 1902.

YEARS	In Royal and District Asylums.	In Private Asylums.	In Parochial Asylums, Lunatic Wards of Poorhouses with Unrestricted License.	In Lunatic Wards of Poorhouses with Restricted License.	In Private Dwellings.	Total Number of Registered Lunatics.	In Lunatic Department of General Prison.	In Training Schools.	General Total.
1858	2380	745	840		1804	5769	26	29	5824
1859	2496	821	797		1901	6015	29	28	6072
1860	2632	852	866		1868	6218	33	22	6273
Average of 5 Years, 1861-1865.	2880	883	879		1712	6354	31	34	6419
Average of 5 Years, 1866-1870.	3824	69	459	569	1553	6975	47	91	7113
Average of 5 Years, 1871-1875.	4697	320	657	588	1525	7787	51	132	7971
Average of 5 Years, 1876-1880.	5459	192	1072	647	1506	8878	57	161	9096
1881	5920	157	1842	714	1629	9762	55	195	10012
1882	6187	156	1850	718	1684	10095	62	198	10355
1883	6189	149	1377	716	1813	10244	63	203	10510
1884	6239	163	1398	719	1939	10458	53	223	10739
1885	6305	148	1435	748	1991	10627	53	238	10918
Average of 5 Years.	6168	155	1380	723	1811	10237	57	212	10506
1886	6297	139	1445	836	2178	10895	62	230	11187
1887	6326	128	1444	857	2270	11025	56	228	11309
1888	6440	148	1460	879	2402	11329	52	228	11609
1889	6707	158	1493	878	2428	11664	57	233	11954
1890	6882	156	1511	876	2573	11998	58	246	12302
Average of 5 Years.	6530	146	1471	865	2370	11382	57	233	11672
1891	7116	152	1517	882	2613	12280	57	258	12595
1892	7347	163	1524	875	2560	12469	57	273	12799
1893	7488	157	1570	876	2634	12725	55	278	13058
1894	7648	158	1614	857	2673	12950	54	296	13300
1895	7957	152	1726	864	2790	13489	54	309	13852
Average of 5 Years.	7512	156	1590	871	2654	12783	55	283	13121
1896	8293	144	1614	841	2811	13703	57	333	14093
1897	8812	137	1505	852	2780	14086	62	352	14500
1898	9243	142	1419	921	2767	14492	56	358	14906
1899	10440	136	668	910	2825	14979	48	372	15399
1900	10696	121	679	905	2828	15229	52	382	15663
Average of 5 Years.	9497	136	1177	886	2802	14498	55	359	14912
1901	10967	126	544	1045	2798	15475	46	378	15899
1902	11289	130	550	1115	2761	15845	46	397	16288

APPENDIX A.—TABLE III.

Proportions, founded on the figures of Table I., of Private Lunatics and of Pauper Lunatics in Asylums and Private Dwellings per 100,000 of the Population; the Proportion of Registered Paupers per 100,000 of Population ; and the Proportion of Pauper Lunatics per 100,000 of Registered Paupers, for each Year from 1858 to 1902.

YEARS.	Population.*	Proportions per 100,000 of Population.						Total Number of Lunatics.	Number of Registered Paupers.	Proportion of Pauper Lunatics in every 100,000 of Registered Paupers.
		Private Lunatics.			Pauper Lunatics.					
		In Asylums	In Private Dwellings	Total	In Asylums and other Establishments	In Private Dwellings	Total			
1858	3,027,665	34	1	35	98	59	157	192	2630	5980
1859	3,041,812	33	1	34	102	62	164	198	2616	6287
1860	3,054,738	32	1	33	111	61	172	205	2581	6657
Average of 5 Years, 1861–1865.		33	1	34	117	54	171	205	2528	6770
Average of 5 Years, 1866–1870.		35	1	36	132	47	179	215	2411	7415
Average of 5 Years, 1871–1875.		37	2	39	147	43	190	229	2183	8727
Average of 5 Years, 1876–1880.		38	3	41	168	39	207	248	1759	11773
1881	3,742,564	38	3	41	181	41	222	263	1700	13,074
1882	3,770,657	38	3	41	187	42	229	270	1662	13,790
1883	3,798,961	38	3	41	186	45	231	272	1622	14,244
1884	3,827,478	38	3	41	186	48	234	275	1566	14,946
1885	3,856,307	38	3	41	187	49	236	277	1524	15,485
Av. of 5 Yrs.		38	3	41	186	45	231	272	1614	14308
1886	3,885,155	38	3	41	188	53	241	282	1515	15,931
1887	3,914,318	38	3	41	187	55	242	283	1516	15,970
1888	3,943,701	39	3	42	189	58	247	289	1499	16,455
1889	3,973,305	41	3	44	193	58	251	295	1483	16,924
1890	4,003,132	41	3	44	196	62	258	302	1466	17,573
Av. of 5 Yrs.		40	3	43	190	57	247	290	1495	16,571
1891	4,086,245	42	3	45	200	62	262	307	1435	18,244
1892	4,078,910†	42	3	45	203	60	263	308	1399	18,347
1893	4,122,029	43	3	46	204	62	266	312	1443	18,413
1894	4,165,606	44	2	46	206	62	268	314	1451	18,455
1895	4,209,645	45	3	48	212	64	276	324	1465	18,836
Av. of 5 Yrs.		43	3	46	205	62	267	313	1439	18559
1896	4,254,153	46	3	49	213	64	277	326	1474	18,786
1897	4,299,132	46	2	48	220	63	283	331	1497	18,884
1898	4,344,589	47	3	50	225	62	287	337	1504	19,121
1899	4,390,530	47	3	50	233	62	295	345	1496	19,691
1900	4,436,958	47	3	50	235	62	297	347	1469	20,204
Av. of 5 Yrs.		46	3	49	225	63	288	337	1488	19,337
1901	4,483,880	47	3	50	239	60	299	349	1457	20,520
1902	4,531,299	47	3	50	244	59	303	353	1443	20,997

* The number of Lunatics is taken at the 1st January of each year, and the number of ordinary Paupers at 15th May preceding. The calculations are made on the Population of the previous year—e.g., the calculations for 1902 are made on the Population for 1901—the Population being that of the middle of the year, as estimated by the Registrar-General.

† The proportions from 1892 onwards have been recalculated this year on the corrected populations founded upon the census of 1901.

APPENDIX A.—TABLE IV.

Showing the Total Number of Private and Pauper Lunatics on the Register at 1st January of each year, from 1874 to 1902, the Number placed on the Register, the Number removed therefrom each year by discharge or death, and the Proportion of Deaths per cent. of the Average Number on the Register.

YEARS.	Number of Lunatics at 1st January of each Year.	Average Number of Lunatics on the Register in each Year.	Number placed on the Register in each Year.	Removed from the Register in each Year.			Excess of Number placed on the Register in each Year over Number removed from Register, including deaths.	Proportion of deaths per cent. on Average Number on the Register in each Year.
				By Recovery or otherwise ceasing to be under the cognizance of the Board.	Died.	Total.		
1874	7885	7959·0	2033	1274	611	1885	148	7·7
1875	8033	8171·0	2259	1335	648	1983	276	7·9
1876	8309	8480·0	2464	1451	671	2122	342	7·9
1877	8651	8768·5	2441	1559	647	2206	235	7·4
1878	8886	9022·0	2414	1485	657	2142	272	7·3
1879	9158	9271·0	2347	1422	699	2121	226	7·5
Average of 5 Years.		8742·5	2385	1450	664	2114	270	7·6
1880	9384	9573·0	2548	1491	679	2170	378	7·1
1881	9762	9928·5	2616	1548	735	2283	333	7·4
1882	10095	10169·5	2435	1512	774	2286	149	7·6
1883	10244	10351·0	2682	1665	803	2468	214	7·8
1884	10458	10542·5	2595	1646	780	2426	169	7·4
Average of 5 Years.		10112·9	2575	1572	754	2326	249	7·5
1885	10627	10761·0	2543	1481	794	2275	268	7·4
1886	10895	10960·0	2451	1518	803	2321	130	7·3
1887	11025	11177·0	2524	1437	783	2220	304	7·0
1888	11329	11496·5	2643	1486	822	2308	335	7·1
1889	11664	11831·0	2703	1559	810	2369	334	6·8
Average of 5 Years.		11245·1	2573	1496	802	2298	274	7·1
1890	11998	12139·0	2749	1567	900	2467	282	7·4
1891	12280	12374·5	2917	1629	1099	2728	189	8·9
1892	12469	12597·0	2933	1691	986	2677	256	7·8
1893	12725	12887·5	3060	1840	995	2835	225	7·8
1894	12950	13219·5	3203	1746	918	2664	539	6·9
Average of 5 Years.		12633·5	2972	1694	980	2674	298	7·8
1895	13489	13593·0	3079	1765	1100	2865	214	8·1
1896	13703	13894·5	3125	1777	965	2742	383	6·9
1897	14086	14289·0	3301	1806	1089	2895	406	7·6
1898	14492	14735·5	3542	1973	1082	3055	487	7·3
1899	14979	15104·0	3440	1929	1261	3190	250	8·3
Average of 5 Years.		14323·8	3297	1850	1099	2949	348	7·5
1900	15229	15352·0	3454	1920	1288	3208	246	8·4
1901	15475	15660·0	3481	1892	1219	3111	370	7·8
1902	15845							

APPENDIX A.—TABLE V.

Showing for each year, from 1874 to 1901, the Total Number of Private and Pauper Lunatics in Scotland, Registered during the year who had never previously been Registered as Lunatics, and the Proportion of such Lunatics per 100,000 of Population.

YEAR.	Population of Scotland estimated to the middle of the Year.	Number of Private Lunatics Registered each year who had never previously been Registered.			Number of Pauper Lunatics Registered each year who had never previously been Registered.			Total Number of Lunatics Registered each year who had never previously been Registered.			Proportion of Lunatics Registered each year who had never previously been Registered, per 100,000 of the Population.		
		Establishments.	Private Dwellings.	Total.	Establishments.	Private Dwellings.	Total.	Private.	Pauper.	Total.	Private.	Pauper.	Total.
1874	3,477,704	394	18	387	1141	60	1201	387	1201	1588	9·7	34·5	44·2
1876	3,514,744	376	11	387	1238	134	1357	387	1357	1744	11·0	38·6	49·6
1876	3,552,183	417	6	423	1392	126	1478	423	1478	1901	11·9	41·6	53·5
1877	3,590,092	347	11	358	1424	80	1504	358	1504	1862	11·0	41·9	51·9
1878	3,628,968	332	8	340	1352	104	1456	340	1456	1796	9·4	40·1	49·5
1879	3,665,448	319	13	332	1315	87	1402	332	1402	1734	9·1	38·2	47·3
1880	3,705,995	340	15	355	1445	138	1578	355	1578	1933	9·6	42·6	52·2
1881	3,742,564	382	4	386	1531	122	1653	386	1653	1989	9·0	44·2	53·2
1882	3,770,657	303	4	307	1375	116	1491	307	1491	1798	8·1	39·5	47·6
1883	3,798,961	378	17	395	1492	129	1621	395	1621	2016	10·4	42·7	53·1
1884	3,897,478	368	9	377	1460	88	1548	377	1548	1925	9·9	40·4	50·3
1885	3,856,307	320	8	328	1414	117	1531	328	1531	1859	8·5	39·7	48·2
1886	3,885,165	347	9	356	1358	98	1456	356	1456	1812	9·1	37·5	46·6
1887	3,914,318	363	5	368	1404	112	1516	368	1516	1884	9·4	38·7	48·1
1888	3,943,701	387	6	393	1485	104	1589	393	1589	1982	10·0	40·3	50·3
1889	3,973,305	379	8	387	1480	151	1631	387	1631	2018	9·7	41·1	50·8
1890	4,003,182	413	7	420	1568	108	1671	420	1671	2091	10·5	41·7	52·2
1891	4,086,345	426	4	430	1642	97	1789	430	1789	2169	*10·7	43·1	53·8
1892	4,078,910	419	3	422	1718	115	1833	422	1833	2255	10·3	44·9	55·2
1893	4,122,020	417	7	424	1764	115	1879	424	1879	2308	10·3	45·6	55·9
1894	4,165,608	387	9	396	1924	127	2051	396	2051	2447	9·5	49·2	58·7
1895	4,209,645	417	5	422	1781	123	1904	422	1904	2326	10·0	45·2	55·2
1896	4,254,158	384	6	400	1882	112	1994	400	1994	2394	9·4	46·9	56·3
1897	4,299,182	439	11	445	1963	101	2064	445	2064	2509	10·4	48·0	58·4
1898	4,344,689	459	6	470	2080	124	2204	470	2204	2674	10·8	50·7	61·5
1899	4,390,530	456	6	462	2090	107	2197	462	2197	2659	10·5	50·0	60·5
1900	4,436,968	442	15	457	2141	99	2240	457	2240	2697	10·3	50·5	60·8
1901	4,483,880	444	10	454	2144	90	2284	454	2284	2688	10·1	49·8	59·9

* The proportions from 1891 onwards have been recalculated this year on the corrected populations founded upon the census of 1901.

APPENDIX A.—TABLE VI.

The Numbers of Private and Pauper Lunatics resident in Royal, District, Private, and Parochial Asylums, and in Lunatic Wards of Poorhouses, on 1st January of each year from 1858 to 1901; the Numbers thereinto Admitted; the Numbers therefrom Discharged Recovered and Not Recovered; the Numbers Transferred from one establishment to another; and the Numbers that Died therein in each of the said years.

YEARS	Number Resident at 1st January.		Number Admitted during Year (including Transfers).		Number Discharged during Year.						Number Transferred during Year.		Number of Deaths during Year.	
					Recovered.		Not Recovered.							
	Private.	Pauper.	Private.	Pauper.	Private.	Pauper.	Private.	Pauper.			Private.	Pauper.	Private.	Pauper.

* Including Patients transferred from one Establishment to another.

APPENDIX A.—TABLE VII.*

Number of Admissions to Asylums and other Establishments, excluding Transfers from one Establishment to another, in each Year from 1858 to 1901.

YEARS.	Number placed in Establishments, excluding Transfers from one Establishment to another.								
	Private.			Pauper.			General Total.		
	M.	F.	T.	M.	F.	T.	M.	F.	T.
1858..............	193	213	406	436	606	1042	629	819	1448
1859..............	201	190	391	476	555	1031	677	745	1422
Average of 5 Years, 1860–1864.	168	199	3·5	481	558	1039	667	757	1424
Average of 5 Years, 1865–1869.	210	221	431	582	660	1242	792	881	1673
Average of 5 Years. 1870–1874.	204	232	436	691	794	1485	895	1026	1921
Average of 5 Years, 1875–1879.	247	239	486	868	963	1831	1115	1202	2137
1880..............	201	248	449	915	1070	1985	1116	1318	2434
1881..............	213	226	439	976	1125	2101	1189	1351	2540
1882..............	194	221	415	896	1079	1975	1090	1300	2390
1883..............	221	241	462	1021	1124	2145	1242	1365	2607
1884..............	229	256	485	1021	1072	2093	1250	1328	2578
Average of 5 Years.	212	238	450	966	1094	2060	1178	1332	2510
1885..............	200	247	447	984	1076	2060	1184	1323	2507
1886..............	200	243	443	991	1006	1997	1191	1249	2440
1887..............	238	263	501	920	1077	1997	1158	1340	2498
1888..............	219	300	519	968	1127	2095	1187	1427	2614
1889..............	220	259	479	1032	1129	2161	1252	1388	2640
Average of 5 Years.	215	262	477	979	1083	2062	1194	1345	2539
1890..............	246	276	522	1075	1138	2213	1321	1414	2735
1891..............	268	305	578	1102	1251	2353	1370	1556	2926
1892..............	249	281	530	1167	1237	2404	1416	1518	2934
1893..............	271	260	531	1220	1293	2513	1491	1553	3044
1894..............	254	261	515	1313	1348	2661	1567	1609	3176
Average of 5 Years.	257	277	534	1175	1253	2428	1433	1530	2963
1895..............	229	286	515	1229	1305	2534	1458	1591	3049
1896..............	234	248	482	1286	1359	2645	1520	1607	3127
1897..............	269	301	570	1365	1348	2713	1634	1649	3283
1898..............	263	318	581	1452	1484	2936	1715	1802	3517
1899..............	275	288	563	1517	1351	2868	1792	1639	3431
Average of 5 Years.	254	287	542	1370	1369	2739	1624	1657	3281
1900..............	262	281	543	1442	1457	2899	1704	1738	3442
1901	255	283	538	1516	1446	2692	1771	1729	3500

* Patients sent to Training Schools for Imbecile Children and to the Lunatic Department of the General Prison are not included in this or the following Table.

APPENDIX A.—TABLE VIII.

The Numbers of Discharges from Asylums and other Establishments, excluding Transfers, and the Numbers of Deaths therein during each Year from 1858 to 1901.

YEARS.	Removals Recovered.		Removals not Recovered, excluding Transfers.		Removals by Death.		Total Removals.		
	Private.	Pauper.	Private	Pauper.	Private.	Pauper.	Private.	Pauper.	Total.
1858...............	171	452	146	90	80	290	397	832	1229
1859...............	162	442	125	66	84	276	371	784	1155
Average of 5 Years, 1860–1864.	156	463	127	159	74	330	357	952	1309
Average of 5 Years, 1865–1869.	183	527	124	149	83	372	390	1048	1438
Average of 5 Years. 1870–1874.	179	713	132	230	90	444	401	1387	1788
Average of 5 Years, 1875–1879.	194	861	161	265	99	482	454	1608	2062
1880...............	167	941	145	303	92	518	404	1762	2166
1881...............	206	982	123	312	100	539	429	1833	2262
1882.......... ...	150	962	123	459	107	566	380	1987	2367
1883...............	185	1035	146	458	92	605	423	2098	2521
1884...............	213	990	140	440	102	578	455	2008	2463
Average of 5 Years.	184	982	135	394	99	561	418	1937	2355
1885...............	161	920	141	506	117	581	419	2007	2426
1886...............	177	961	131	458	99	576	407	1995	2402
1887...............	209	876	125	422	88	596	422	1894	2316
1888..............	183	944	130	350	101	608	414	1902	2316
1889...............	201	944	162	452	99	593	462	1989	2451
Average of 5 Years.	186	929	138	437	101	591	425	1957	2382
1890.............	199	975	124	418	140	638	463	2031	2494
1891...............	226	959	156	415	152	776	534	2150	2684
1892...............	204	1112	124	447	121	745	449	2304	2753
1893...............	224	1185	122	463	144	723	490	2371	2861
1894...............	197	1130	139	470	106	712	442	2312	2754
Average of 5 Years.	210	1072	133	443	133	719	476	2284	2709
1895.,............	203	1164	131	419	125	814	459	2397	2856
1896...............	209	1131	126	394	131	721	466	2246	2712
1897...............	231	1168	125	385	147	808	503	2361	2864
1898...............	269	1293	142	409	159	816	570	2518	3088
1899...............	250	1289	143	403	165	934	558	2626	3184
Average of 5 Years.	233	1209	133	402	145	819	511	2430	2941
1900.....	239	1276	131	387	170	958	540	2621	3161
1901...............	227	1268	114	403	170	917	511	2588	3099

APPENDIX A.—TABLE IX.

The Results of Treatment in different classes of Establishments for each Year from 1858 to 1901.

(a) *Royal and District Asylums.*

ROYAL AND DISTRICT ASYLUMS.	Average Number Resident.			Admissions (including Transfers).			Recoveries.			Discharges not Recovered (including Transfers).			Deaths.			Proportion of Admissions per cent. on Number Resident.			Proportion of Recoveries per cent. on Admissions.			Proportion of Deaths per cent. on Number Resident.		
	M.	F.	T.	M.	F.	T.	M.	F.	T.	M.	F.	T.	M.	F.	T.	M.	F.	T.	M.	F.	T.	M.	F.	T.
Year 1858	1268·5	1167·5	2431·0	449	456	392	171	208	392	160	160	359	103	103	225	34·7	37·1	35·9	38·1	40·1	37·0	9·2	7·1	8·2
„ 1859	1207·0	1242·5	2449·5	458	450	382	146	186	382	126	160	326	98	90	200	36·5	36·3	36·1	38·1	40·8	38·5	8·1	7·4	7·8
Average of 5 Years 1860-1864	1434·8	446·4	2876·2	498	534	392	174	208	392	160	161	11	132	103	225	34·7	37·1	35·9	38·1	39·0	37·0	9·2	7·1	8·2
Average of 5 Years 1865-1869	1653·1	1885·0	3742·1	709	740	505	230	275	505	182	196	378	163	102	315	38·2	39·5	38·9	32·5	36·9	34·7	8·8	8·0	8·4
Average of 5 Years 1870-1874	2292·8	2845·3	4637·9	794	883	687	230	373	687	256	256	492	188	188	390	34·6	37·7	36·2	39·6	42·3	41·0	8·8	8·0	8·4
Average of 5 Years 1875-1879	2904·7	2774·3	5379·0	915	973	763	331	432	763	292	274	556	199	199	412	35·1	35·1	35·1	38·2	44·4	40·4	8·4	7·0	7·7
Average of 5 Years 1880-1884	3013·0	2961·5	5874·0	1002	1095	1878	340	460	879	282	299	581	133	183	440	33·9	34·5	34·2	41·1	41·9	40·4	7·4	7·4	7·4
„ 1885	3013·0	3118·5	6106·0	1031	1099	2013	377	470	870	291	310	611	181	181	461	30·6	34·4	32·8	41·2	41·9	38·4	7·5	7·8	7·0
„ 1886	3035·5	3186·5	6136·0	1031	1147	3029	351	470	870	305	376	681	250	282	390	33·6	34·6	35·0	38·4	43·8	40·5	7·8	8·0	8·9
„ 1887	3083·5	3186·5	6168·0	1066	1164	3168	419	600	919	346	385	681	252	250	497	34·6	35·0	34·7	41·8	43·5	43·5	8·2	8·0	8·8
„ 1888	3035·0	3237·0	6272·0	1066	1164	2222	446	674	920	330	406	756	262	251	497	35·4	35·0	34·7	41·4	43·7	43·1	8·6	8·0	8·9
Average of 5 Years	3009·5	3130·9	6131·4	974	1125	2099	388	472	860	303	340	651	240	248	488	32·5	35·9	35·9	39·8	43·9	41·0	8·5	7·7	8·0
Year 1885	3094·0	3245·0	6301·0	1087	1110	2147	400	440	604	389	441	630	267	267	420	34·2	34·1	34·1	40·1	41·4	41·6	8·6	9·0	8·9
„ 1886	3097·5	3287·5	6305·0	1018	1040	3075	418	440	885	327	348	684	266	244	460	35·7	34·7	35·1	40·1	43·6	41·4	8·6	8·4	8·8
„ 1887	3119·0	2287·5	6380·0	1007	1101	2064	385	418	886	300	349	684	257	244	468	31·6	35·7	35·7	34·6	43·1	43·9	10·1	7·2	8·8
„ 1888	3290·0	3368·5	6578·5	1039	1161	2260	389	469	488	300	307	607	253	253	608	32·8	34·7	34·7	38·1	40·3	37·9	9·5	8·0	8·8
„ 1889	3334·0	3470·0	6794·0	1043	1169	2215	388	468	646	339	380	692	254	240	609	31·7	33·6	33·6	38·4	39·6	38·1	9·0	7·8	7·4
Average of 5 Years	3136·5	3316·0	6474·5	1026	1119	2147	382	456	838	325	365	690	256	247	503	32·5	33·2	33·7	40·1	38·3	39·0	8·1	7·4	7·8
Year 1890	3413·0	3585·5	6999·5	1107	1178	2285	393	445	846	311	300	601	288	282	587	32·6	32·8	32·8	34·6	39·8	37·5	9·2	8·0	8·0
„ 1891	3507·0	3734·5	7241·5	1137	1347	2434	391	490	879	315	366	678	280	280	688	33·1	34·8	34·8	34·7	43·8	39·5	9·6	7·8	8·8
„ 1892	3520·0	3957·5	7490·0	1236	1298	2506	473	603	1093	318	341	671	289	319	653	34·2	34·2	34·2	34·7	46·8	42·2	8·5	8·1	8·9
„ 1893	3440·0	3957·5	7480·0	1231	1368	3157	479	600	1094	328	385	681	340	316	683	34·6	34·8	34·6	38·1	45·8	42·9	8·3	8·1	8·8
„ 1894	3776·5	4026·0	7802·5	1221	1366	2607	500	461	961	300	365	704	340	298	638	34·4	33·4	33·4	35·4	44·8	40·8	9·0	7·0	8·9
Average of 5 Years	3541·4	3822·4	7463·8	1263	1297	2460	448	521	941	394	341	665	342	308	650	33·6	33·7	33·6	36·5	40·5	38·6	9·5	9·2	9·1
Year 1895	3992·0	4254·0	8246·0	1434	1475	2909	474	544	1018	467	386	683	311	313	688	35·9	34·7	35·8	33·0	38·0	36·0	9·5	9·3	9·5
„ 1896	4104·5	4450·0	8556·5	1406	1499	2905	482	546	1048	345	369	683	330	313	654	34·3	34·4	34·0	33·9	37·8	36·1	8·3	9·0	8·8
„ 1897	4235·0	4702·0	9027·5	1403	1686	3003	480	608	1148	469	399	685	367	379	746	37·0	34·3	34·3	34·7	37·8	38·6	8·3	8·5	8·6
„ 1898	4464·5	4820·5	9285·0	1462	1690	3157	643	664	1307	345	385	730	347	334	772	35·6	34·6	33·8	33·9	38·4	37·8	9·4	9·0	9·2
„ 1899	5100·5	4485·0	10595·0	1607	1710	3317	655	723	1277	433	449	900	334	448	981	35·4	31·8	33·3	35·4	43·7	38·9	10·5	8·0	9·3
Average of 5 Years	4446·0	4786·3	9264·3	1570	1590	3161	558	620	1178	416	483	899	300	360	760	33·3	33·3	33·3	35·6	39·0	37·5	9·	7·7	8·4
Year 1900	5251·0	5340·5	10591·0	1603	1801	3404	662	693	1352	405	485	933	410	373	1018	34·3	33·8	33·3	39·0	40·0	38·0	9·3	9·9	9·4
„ 1901	5429·5	5695·0	11127·5	1772	1738	3517	660	708	1380	430	495	950	468	486	977	32·6	30·5	31·6	38·6	40·8	38·6	9·3	8·7	8·6

APPENDIX A.—TABLE IX.—*continued.*

The Results of Treatment in different classes of Establishments for each Year from 1858 to 1901.

(d) *Lunatic Wards of Poorhouses with Restricted Licences.*

LUNATIC WARDS OF POORHOUSES.	Average Number Resident.			Admissions (including Transfers).			Recovered.			Discharges not Recovered (including Transfers).			Deaths.			Proportion of Admissions per cent. on Number Resident.			Proportion of Recoveries per cent. on Admissions.			Proportion of Deaths per cent. on Number Resident.		
	M.	F.	T.	M.	F.	T.	M.	F.	T.	M.	F.	T.	M.	F.	T.	M.	F.	T.	M.	F.	T.	M.	F.	T.
Year 1858, 1859																								
Average of 5 Years, 1860–1864																								
Average of 5 Years, 1865–1869																								
Average of 5 Years, 1870–1874																								
Average of 5 Years, 1875–1879																								
Year 1880																								
„ 1881																								
„ 1882																								
„ 1883																								
„ 1884																								
Average of 5 Years																								
Year 1885																								
„ 1886																								
„ 1887																								
„ 1888																								
„ 1889																								
Average of 5 Years																								
Year 1890																								
„ 1891																								
„ 1892																								
„ 1893																								
„ 1894																								
Average of 5 Years																								
Year 1895																								
„ 1896																								
„ 1897																								
„ 1898																								
„ 1899																								
Average of 5 Years																								
Year 1900																								
„ 1901																								

		S FROM SPECIFIC CAUSES.													
		ABDOMINAL AFFECTIONS.						Fever, Erysipelas, Cancer, &c.		General Debility and Old Age.		Suicides and Accidents.		Cause Unknown.	
	Inflammation of stomach, Intestines, or peritoneum.		Disease of Liver, Kidneys, &c.		Dysentery and Diarrhoea.										
	M.	F.	M.	F.	M.	F.	M.	F.	M.	F.	M.	F.	M.	F.	
1870 . . .	8	7	4	6	8	6	8	11	26	46	8	4	8	.
Absolute Annual A 1874, . .	·0	7·2	5·5	8·6	5·2	9·3	7·4	10·4	28·0	42·2	7·6	5·6	0·6	0·6
Average Percentage ·4	·4	2·7	2·1	3·2	2·2	3·6	2·9	3·8	10·6	15·6	2·9	2·1	0·2	0·2
1875 . . .	2	7	8	13	7	12	9	15	30	51	15	6	.	.
1876 . .	5	14	7	3	5	7	8	14	27	53	10	4	.	:
1877 . .	8	1·	8	15	2	5	16	14	34	49	5	4	.	.
1878 . .	9	6	0	15	4	9	12	9	34	44	6	4	.	.
1879 . .	11	9	7	4	4	9	9	13	29	57	4	1	.	.
Absolute Annual A ·0	9·4	7·2	10·0	4·4	8·4	10·2	12·2	26·6	50·2	8·0	4·0	.	.
Average Percentage 3	3·4	2·4	3·6	1·5	3·0	3·6	4·6	9·5	18·2	2·6	1·4	.	.
1880 . . .	13	17	7	13	5	14	12	27	22	38	4	6	.	.
1881 . . .	6	10	9	8	6	7	16	15	26	66	8	3	.	.
1882 . .	7	11	12	8	5	6	12	21	34	55	8	.	.	.
1883 . .	9	14	7	7	2	3	10	19	31	57	10	7	.	.
1884 . . .	7	12	9	11	5	5	11	27	31	46	6	4	.	.
Absolute Annual Av ·4	12·8	8·2	9·4	4·6	7·0	12·2	21·8	28·8	52·4	7·2	4·0	.	.
Average Percentage ·5	3·9	2·7	2·9	1·4	2·1	3·7	6·6	8·7	15·9	2·2	1·2	.	.
1885 . . .	13	16	11	7	1	10	14	22	28	52	8	1	.	.
1886 . .	8	9	9	18	2	2	13	22	26	49	8	7	.	.
1887 . .	11	10	8	11	2	2	10	23	18	46	7	4	.	.
1888 . .	17	9	14	14	.	1	15	21	21	52	4	6	.	:
1889 . .	11	10	14	12	1	2	10	26	28	37	8	5	.	.
Absolute Annual Av 0	10·8	11·2	12·4	1·2	3·4	12·4	23·4	24·6	47·2	7·0	4·6	.	.
Average Percentage ·4	3·2	3·2	3·6	0·3	1·0	3·5	6·2	7·0	13·3	2·0	1·3	.	.
1890 . . .	9	12	14	10	5	2	19	26	29	42	8	1	.	.
1891 . . .	8	15	10	12	1	5	23	48	29	48	9	4	.	.
1892 . . .	9	13	14	7	1	3	19	27	24	40	13	5	.	.
1893 . .	8	18	13	6	1	1	26	27	30	54	5	4	.	.
1894 . . .	3	18	12	14	1	2	9	28	16	39	13	2	.	.
Absolute Annual Av 4	15·2	12·6	9·8	1·2	2·6	21·2	31·2	25·6	44·6	9·4	3·2	.	.
Average Percentage 6	3·7	2·3	2·4	0·4	0·6	4·3	7·7	5·7	11·0	2·1	0·8	.	.
1895 . . .	9	16	7	13	1	6	30	38	35	50	8	4	.	.
1896 . .	2	26	8	17	1	4	11	30	32	46	15	5	.	.
1897 . .	2	18	13	18	1	2	27	44	17	61	12	5	.	.
1898 . .	0	16	13	19	1	.	30	46	34	40	7	6	.	.
1899 . .	3	15	20	17	1	3	32	51	35	64	7	6	.	.
Absolute Annual Av 2	18·2	12·2	16·8	1·0	3·0	26·0	41·8	30·6	52·2	9·8	5·2	.	.
Average Percentage 7	3·9	2·3	3·6	0·2	0·6	5·2	9·9	6·2	11·2	2·0	1·1	.	.
1900 . . .	7	21	16	12	.	2	42	71	36	60	12	5	.	.
1901 . . .	0	19	11	12	1	3	30	32	36	59	13	7	.	.

APPENDIX A.—TABLE IX.—*continued.*

The Results of Treatment in different classes of Establishments for each Year from 1858 to 1901.

(d) *Lunatic Wards of Poorhouses with Restricted Licences.*

LUNATIC WARDS OF POORHOUSES	Average Number Resident.			Admissions (including Transfers).			Recoveries.			Discharged not Recovered (including Transfers).			Deaths.			Proportion of Admissions per cent. on Number Resident.			Proportion of Recoveries per cent. on Admissions.			Proportion of Deaths per cent. on Number Resident.		
	M.	F.	T.	M.	F.	T.	M.	F.	T.	M.	F.	T.	M.	F.	T.	M.	F.	T.	M.	F.	T.	M.	F.	T.

	flammation of mach, Intines, or isoneum.		Disease of Liver, Kidneys, &c.		Dysentery and Diarrhœa		Fever, Erysipelas, Cancer, &c.		General Debility and Old Age		Suicides and Accidents		Cause Unknown.	
		F.	M.	F.	M.	F.	M.	F.	M.	F.	M.	F.	M.	F.
1870 . . .	8	7	4	6	8	6	8	11	26	48	8	4	3	.
Absolute Annual A 1874, . .	·0	7·2	5·6	8·6	5·2	8·2	7·4	16·4	28·0	42·2	7·6	5·6	0·6	0·6
Average Percentag	·4	2·7	2·1	3·2	2·2	3·6	2·8	3·2	10·6	15·6	2·9	2·1	0·2	0·2
1875 . . .	2	7	8	13	7	12	9	15	30	51	13	6	.	.
1876 . . .	5	14	7	8	5	7	8	14	27	53	10	4	.	;
1877 . . .	8	11	8	15	2	5	16	14	24	49	5	5	.	.
1878 . . .	9	6	6	15	4	9	12	9	24	44	6	4	.	.
1879 . . .	1	9	7	4	4	9	9	12	29	57	4	1	.	.
Absolute Annual A	·0	9·4	7·2	10·0	4·4	8·4	10·8	12·8	28·6	50·8	8·0	4·0	.	.
Average Percentage	·3	3·4	2·4	3·6	1·5	3·0	3·6	4·6	9·5	18·3	2·6	1·4	.	.
1880 . . .	·13	17	7	13	5	14	12	27	22	38	4	6	.	.
1881 . . .	6	10	9	8	6	7	16	15	26	66	8	3	.	.
1882 . . .	7	11	12	8	5	6	12	21	24	55	8	.	.	.
1883 . . .	9	14	7	7	2	8	10	19	31	57	10	7	.	.
1884 . . .	7	12	9	11	5	5	11	27	31	46	6	4	.	.
Absolute Annual Av	·4	12·8	8·8	9·4	4·6	7·0	12·2	21·8	28·8	52·4	7·2	4·0	.	.
Average Percentage	·5	3·8	2·7	2·9	1·4	2·1	3·7	6·6	8·7	15·9	2·2	1·2	.	.
1885 . . .	·13	16	11	7	1	10	14	22	28	52	8	1	.	.
1886 . . .	8	9	9	18	2	2	13	22	26	49	8	7	.	.
1887 . . .	·1	10	8	11	2	2	10	23	18	46	7	4	.	.
1888 . . .	·7	9	14	14	.	1	15	21	21	52	4	6	.	:
1889 . . .	·1	10	14	12	1	2	10	28	28	37	8	5	.	.
Absolute Annual Av	·0	10·8	11·2	12·4	1·2	3·4	12·4	23·4	24·6	47·2	7·0	4·6	.	.
Average Percentage	·4	3·2	3·2	3·6	0·3	1·0	3·5	6·9	7·0	13·9	2·0	1·3	.	.
1890 . . .	9	12	14	10	5	2	19	26	29	42	8	1	.	.
1891 . . .	8	15	10	12	1	5	32	48	29	48	9	4	.	.
1892 . . .	9	13	14	7	1	2	19	27	24	40	13	5	.	.
1893 . . .	8	18	13	6	1	1	26	27	30	54	5	4	.	.
1894 . . .	3	18	12	14	1	2	9	28	16	39	12	2	.	.
Absolute Annual Av	·4	15·2	12·6	9·8	1·8	2·6	21·2	31·2	25·6	44·6	9·4	3·2	.	.
Average Percentage	·6	3·7	2·8	2·4	0·4	0·6	5·7	7·7	5·7	11·0	2·1	0·8	.	.
1895 . . .	9	15	7	13	1	6	30	38	35	50	8	4	.	.
1896 . . .	2	26	8	17	1	4	11	30	32	46	15	5	.	.
1897 . . .	2	18	13	18	1	2	27	44	17	61	12	5	.	.
1898 . . .	0	16	13	19	1	.	30	46	34	40	7	6	.	.
1899 . . .	3	16	20	17	1	8	32	51	35	64	7	6	.	.
Absolute Annual Av	·2	18·2	12·2	16·8	1·0	3·0	26·0	41·8	30·6	52·2	9·8	5·2	.	.
Average Percentage	·7	3·9	2·5	3·6	0·2	0·6	5·2	9·0	6·2	11·2	2·0	1·1	.	.
1900 . . .	·7	21	16	12	.	2	42	71	36	60	12	5	.	.
1901 . . .	0	19	11	12	1	3	30	32	36	59	13	7	.	.

APPENDIX A.—TABLE XI.

The Statistics of Pauper Lunatics in Private Dwellings for Forty-four Years, 1858–1901.

YEARS.	ADMITTED TO ROLL OF PATIENTS IN PRIVATE DWELLINGS.						CHANGES TO OR BY PATIENTS IN PRIVATE DWELLINGS.								Died.		On Roll at 31st December of each year.			Percentage of Recoveries on Admissions.			Percentage of Deaths on the Numbers at 31st December of each year.		
	Intimated by Inspectors of Poor.		Transferred from Asylums.		Total.		Recovered.		Removed from Roll by Friends.		Transferred to Asylums.														
	M.	F.	M.	F.	M.	F.	M.	F.	M.	F.	M.	F.	M.	F.	M.	F.	M.	F.	T.	M.	F.	T.	M.	F.	T.
During 1858	135	168	6	9	161	68	18	8	16	18	21	24	87	40	838	1089	1939	1677	14	18	54	43	47	54	47
" 1859	63	113	8	9	68	68	8	8	16	18	21	24	55	40	825	1013	1013	1647	19	13	43	49	53	59	47
Average of 5 Years, 1860–1864	54		14		58		8	14	18	13	20	39	48	48	746	945	1691	14	15	14	57	53	55	55
Average of 5 Years, 1865–1869	63		15		61		15	10	19	25	27	48	37	53	686	855	1521	9	11	10	55	82	59	58
Average of 5 Years, 1870–1874	39		33		59		11	12	17	20	27	43	36	49	626	829	1455	12	12	12	57	59	58	16
Average of 5 Years, 1875–1879	65		19		67		8	9	17	33	57	35	43	566	834	1399	6	6	7	62	52	51	52
Average of 5 Years, 1880–1884	74		63		116		17	12	20	39	70	34	88	648	1022	1680	7	6	51	53	51	52

-erness 10,782	Kincardine 31,532		Kinross 6,980		Kirk-cudbright 39,407		Lanark 1,314,772		Linlithgow 66,434		Nairn 8,721		Oling ;338		Sutherland 21,550		Wigtown 22,683	
Left in Prir. Dwel.	Sent to Asylum.	Left in Prir. Dwel.	Sent to Asylum.	Left in Prir. Dwel.	Sent to Asylum.	Left in Prir. Dwel.	Sent to Asylum.	Left in Prir. Dwel.	Sent to Asylum.	Left in Prir. Dwel.	Sent to Asylum.	Left in Prir. Dwel.	Sent to Asylum.	Left in Prir. Dwel.	Sent to Asylum.	Left in Prir. Dwel.	Sent to Asylum.	Left in Prir. Dwel.
6	17	...	3	...	19	1	230	7	13	...	1	..			2	5	2	3
6·4	12·4	0·6	1·0	...	14·2	1·8	244·0	11·4	10·8	1·0	1·8	...	4·	3·4	4·6	1·6	9·0	3·2
7	36	2	14	...	33	4	38	2	28	3	22	...	1	4	19	7	21	8
6·8	11·0	1·8	3·6	0·2	11·8	2·0	321·0	6·6	11·6	0·6	2·4	0·8	2·	0·4	4·6	2·2	9·4	3·8
8	32	5	50	3	28	5	46	1	29	1	26	9		...	19	9	23	9
3·2	11·8	1·2	1·2	0·8	11·4	2·2	405·8	3·4	13·4	0·2	1·6	0·2	3·	2·2	4·2	1·0	10·8	1·8
4	34	3	19	12	27	5	52	...	32	...	19	2	1	2	18	4	28	4
12	15	1	3	...	17	...	450	5	16	1	2	...		3	11	4	15	4
13	7	2	2	...	13	1	548	2	24	2	5	...		3	7	4	16	1
9	14	1	...	...	13	...	579	8	16	...	5	...	1	1	7	4	10	1
10	11	...	1	...	8	1	571	13	15	...	4	1	1	4	6	4	13	1
12	8	1	5	...	12	1	488	12	20	...	3	...		1	7	...	12	2
11·0	11·0	1·0	2·2	...	12·6	0·6	531·2	8·0	18·2	0·6	3·8	0·2	7·	2·4	7·6	3·2	13·2	1·8
12	31	3	35	...	30	1	61	1	43	1	44	2	2	2	33	14	34	5
16	19	1	2	...	14	1	531	20	24	1	8	...	1	1	10	3	13	1
18	17	...	5	...	22	2	545	13	27	...	10	...	1	1	6	5	17	2
20	12	2	1	1	15	...	539	18	24	1	5	...		2	12	2	11	4
18	18	...	3	...	16	1	571	18	24	1	5	...	1	4	10	...	11	2
17	14	...	6	...	12	...	608	9	18	2	3	...	1	2	11	7	13	4
17·8	16·8	0·6	3·4	0·2	16·2	0·8	562·8	15·6	23·4	1·0	6·2	...	11	2·0	9·8	3·4	13·0	2·6
20	45	2	56	3	38	2	60	2	53	2	70	...	2	44	15	34	7
22	14	...	1	1	23	2	552	13	19	...	7	...	1	9	2	9	4
11	13	...	4	...	19	1	538	9	24	...	10	...	1	9	3	13	5
21	17	...	2	...	13	2	578	13	25	1	8	2	1	10	2	17	2
17	11	...	4	...	16	...	614	14	28	1	6	...	3	9	5	20	3
19	13	1	2	3	17	2	594	12	28	2	5	...		...	15	6	19	4
18·0	13·8	0·2	2·6	0·8	17·4	1·4	574·2	12·2	24·8	0·8	7·2	0·4		1·2	10·4	3·6	15·8	3·8
20	38	1	42	13	42	3	57	1	51	2	78	4	1	47	18	42	10
18	14	1	3	...	16	2	607	18	22	2	11	...	3	13	...	16	...
14	17	...	6	...	15	...	718	18	23	...	8	...	...	14	1	15	...
13	13	...	4	...	19	...	656	15	25	1	5	1	4	15	...	15	1
10	20	...	5	...	20	...	641	19	29	1	5	...	2	11	...	12	1
19	14	...	4	...	18	1	696	18	35	1	4	1	3	15	2	22	2
14·8	15·6	0·2	4·4	...	17·6	0·6	653·6	16·6	26·8	1·0	6·6	0·4	10	2·4	13·6	0·6	16·2	0·8
16	44	1	66	...	4	2	61	2	50	2	78	5	2	62	3	45	2
19	16	...	8	...	19	1	666	29	17	...	14	2	2	10	1	13	...
15	15	...	5	...	19	1	675	13	27	...	3	...	3	18	1	15	1
19	17	...	6	1	12	...	760	30	30	...	9	...	1	14	...	11	3
13	19	...	4	...	11	5	795	24	25	...	12	...	1	30	4	13	...
10	14	...	·4	...	20	1	847	32	33	2	8	1	1	25	5	17	2
15·2	16·2	...	5·4	0·2	16·2	1·6	750·6	25·6	26·4	0·4	9·2	0·6	11	1·6	19·4	2·2	13·8	1·2
17	51	...	79	3	41	4	62	2	44	1	107	7	1	89	10	40	3
8	15	...	4	1	17	...	907	28	29	...	6	...	2	17	1	16	1
11	15	...	2	...	20	2	922	15	27	...	7	...	2	10	2	20	...

Table.

	Kincardine.		Kinross.		Kirk-cudbright.		Lanark.		Linlithgow.		Nairn.		Orkney.		Sutherland.		Wigtown.	
	Priv. Dwel. to Asylums.	Asylums to Priv. Dwel.	Priv. Dwel. to Asylums.	Asylums to Priv. Dwel.	Priv. Dwel. to Asylums.	Asylums to Priv. Dwel.	Priv. Dwel. to Asylums.	Asylums to Priv. Dwel.	Priv. Dwel. to Asylums.	Asylums to Priv. Dwel.	Priv. Dwel. to Asylums.	Asylums to Priv. Dwel.	Priv. Dwel. to Asylums.	Asylums to Priv. Dwel.	Priv. Dwel. to Asylums.	Asylums to Priv. Dwel.	Priv. Dwel. to Asylums.	Asylums to Priv. Dwel.
	.	1	.	.	2	.	2	.	.	.	2	.	.	1 2	1	.	3	.
	0·4	0·8	0·2	0·2	1·4	1·2	2·8	2·8	0·2	.	0·4	0·2	0·4	0·2 4	0·8	.	1·4	0·2
	1·1	2·3	2·8	2·8	3·3	2·8	0·4	0·4	0·5	.	4·3	2·4	1·2	0·6 5	3·3	.	3·3	0·5
	1·6	0·4	0·4	0·8	0·8	0·6	6·6	7·6	0·8	0·2	.	.	.	. 6	0·4	.	1·9	1·0
	4·6	1·1	5·9	11·8	1·9	1·4	8·9	1·1	2·9	0·5	.	.	.	. 7	1·7	.	2·5	2·5
	0·4	1·4	.	0·4	1·8	1·0	3·9	5·	0·2	0·8	.	.	0·4	0·6 4	0·6	.	0·8	0·6
	1·1	4·0	.	6·2	4·3	2·4	0·4	0·7	0·5	1·4	.	.	1·3	1·9 9	2·6	.	2·1	1·5
	5	.	.	.	.	2	11	6	.	1	.	1	1	.	.	1	.	.
	.	.	.	.	1	3	4	.	1	1	.	.	.	.	2	.	1	3
	.	.	.	.	.	.	2	6	.	.	1	.	1	1	1	.	.	.
	.	.	.	.	1	.	4	7	.	.	1	.	.	1	.	.	.	1
	.	.	.	.	.	1	5	27	.	.	.	.	.	.	.	.	1	1
	1·0	.	.	.	0·8	0·8	5·4	9·2	0·2	0·4	0·4	0·2	0·4	0·2 1	0·6	0·2	0·4	0·6
	2·8	.	.	.	1·9	1·9	0·6	1·1	0·5	0·9	4·6	2·3	1·3	0·6 1	2·6	0·9	1·0	1·5
	1	1	1	2	.	2	8	32	.	.	1	1	1	1	.	.	.	.
	1	.	.	1	.	.	11	13	.	1	1	3	1	.	.	.	.	.
	1	.	.	.	.	5	21	59	.	.	.	.	1	2	3	1	1	3
	1	.	.	2	3	3	14	51	.	.	.	1	1	2	.	.	1	8
	.	.	.	.	.	.	20	42	.	.	.	.	.	.	.	.	.	.
	0·8	0·2	0·2	0·6	0·4	2·0	14·8	39·2	.	0·8	0·2	0·4	0·6	1·0	0·6	0·2	0·4	2·2
	2·3	0·6	3·3	9·9	0·9	4·7	1·6	4·2	.	1·8	2·3	4·5	1·9	3·1	2·7	0·9	1·6	5·7
	1	1	.	1	2	2	18	51	1	.	1	.	1	3	1	.	.	.
	1	2	.	.	.	.	24	79	.	1	.	.	.	.	.	1	1	1
	2	.	.	.	1	3	26	60	3	1	1	.	.	1	.	2	1	2
	2	.	.	.	2	1	20	48	1	1	.	1	.	.	1	2	2	2
	.	.	.	.	.	.	25	62	.	3	1	.	.	.	.	.	.	.
	1·0	0·6	.	0·2	1·0	1·6	21·8	60·0	1·0	1·2	0·4	0·2	0·2	0·3	0·4	1·0	1·4	1·4
	2·8	1·7	.	.	2·4	3·9	2·2	6·0	2·1	2·5	4·2	2·1	0·6	2·6	1·8	4·5	3·7	3·7
	.	.	.	.	1	.	16	34	.	1	1	2	1	.	2	3	1	1
	.	.	.	.	2	.	23	38	4	4	.	1	.	.	1	.	.	.
	.	.	.	1	2	1	23	42	.	.	.	.	1	1	.	.	1	1
	.	.	.	.	1	1	28	41	.	.	.	.	.	1	.	1	1	1
	.	1	.	.	.	1	14	61	.	.	.	.	.	.	.	2	.	.
2	.	0·2	.	0·2	1·2	0·4	21·2	43·2	0·8	1·0	0·2	0·6	0·2	0·6	0·6	1·4	0·4	0·8
4	.	0·6	.	3·0	3·0	1·0	1·9	4·0	1·5	1·9	2·3	7·9	0·7	2·0	2·7	6·4	1·1	1·7
	.	.	.	1	1	.	21	38	.	1	.	1	2	.	1	.	.	.
	.	.	.	.	1	2	14	32	.	.	.	.	1	.	2	1	.	2
	.	.	.	.	1	2	26	35	1	1	.	.	3	1	2	2	.	.
	.	.	.	1	1	.	35	66	.	3	.	1	.	3	1	2	3	.
	.	.	.	.	.	.	35	56	1	3	.	.	.	.	1	2	.	1
	.	.	.	0·2	0·8	1·0	26·2	45·6	0·4	1·0	.	0·4	1·2	1·2	1·2	1·0	0·4	0·6
	.	.	.	2·9	2·0	2·5	2·2	3·8	0·7	1·7	.	4·6	4·1	4·1	5·5	4·6	1·2	1·7
	...	...	...	...	...	...	81	69	1	...	1	...	8	1	...	1	...	...
	...	...	...	1	...	..	87	63	1	2	...	...	...	2	1	...	2	...

Kincardine. 31,532		Kinross. 6,980		Kirk-cudbright. 39,407		Lanark. 1,314,772		Linlithgow. 66,434		Nairn. 8,721		Orkney. 28,698		Peel 15,	Sutherland. 21,550		Wigtown. 33,688	
Estab.	Priv. Dwel.	Estab.	Priv. Dwel.	Estab.	Priv. Dwel.	Estab.	Priv. Dwel.	Estab.	Priv. Dwel.	Estab.	Priv. Dwel.	Estab.	Priv Dwel.	Estab.	Estab.	Priv. Dwel.	Estab.	Priv. Dwel.
53	29	12	6	57	27	580	102	37	11	14	9	16	33	13	18	35	41	47
55·	24·6	9·3	5·4	62·0	29·0	631·6	106·8	37·4	11·2	13·6	8·4	21·2	34·4	13·2	18·6	32·4	43·2	44·8
160	71	137	76	146	68	99	17	96	29	163	161	65	106	117	77	134	103	105
58·4	23·2	14·2	7·2	60·6	35·8	796·6	104·4	45·8	10·2	15·2	5·0	22·2	29·8	21·8	29·0	26·8	50·8	47·2
168	7	198	100	144	85	114	15	114	25	164	54	70	94	185	94	112	126	117
64·6	18·0	16·6	9·0	66·4	32·8	965·0	103·8	48·6	8·8	13·8	5·2	21·8	27·8	24·6	22·4	21·4	60·0	42·8
184	51	257	139	159	78	123	13	117	21	165	62	70	89	201	96	92	155	110
64	12	20	9	72	23	1104	92	49	11	12	6	27	30	24	34	21	72	38
60	·13	21	9	69	24	1189	87	52	10	15	5	29	39	22	31	24	76	36
62	·13	20	7	71	22	1243	91	50	10	12	3	32	33	26	39	23	73	33
60	11	21	7	70	21	1274	99	56	10	16	3	35	34	26	44	24	77	30
59	12	25	4	66	22	1304	121	60	10	16	2	38	31	34	41	23	80	32
61·0	12·2	21·4	7·2	69·6	22·4	1222·8	98·0	53·4	10·2	14·2	3·8	32·2	33·4	24·4	37·8	23·0	75·6	33·6
173	35	342	115	166	53	141	11	125	24	165	44	102	105	188	166	101	195	97
67	12	19	4	62	24	1357	157	62	11	16	2	41	33	23	45	26	78	33
62	12	21	4	68	23	1431	156	76	11	23	2	41	35	23	44	30	84	33
60	11	16	6	66	23	1446	200	75	14	19	2	43	39	22	51	29	82	33
67	10	17	6	62	27	1462	230	70	14	22	2	42	35	21	55	27	71	35
72	9	17	6	61	24	1515	248	70	16	19	3	47	33	24	60	31	56	38
65·6	10·8	18·0	5·2	63·8	24·2	1442·2	198·2	70·6	13·2	20·2	2·2	42·8	35·0	22·6	51·0	28·6	74·2	34·2
185	30	297	86	151	57	153	21	160.	30	228	25	134	109	165	228	128	192	39
67	9	16	7	70	25	1587	283	72	15	21	2	50	34	23	61	28	61	41
73	8	16	8	73	25	1606	330	72	16	27	2	51	34	28	51	31	66	42
74	10	16	8	73	25	1653	362	75	16	29	4	51	36	25	47	31	71	41
73	7	16	8	67	23	1733	379	82	16	24	4	53	34	23	51	36	72	44
74	6	15	10	72	22	1780	403	84	21	24	3	53	34	26	53	41	70	44
72·2	8·0	15·8	8·2	71·0	24·0	1663·2	351·4	77·0	16·8	25·0	3·0	51·6	34·4	25·6	52·6	33·4	68·0	42·2
203	22	256	133	173	58	168	35	159	35	265	32	165	110	176	238	151	182	113
76	7	17	8	76	23	1828	415	85	21	26	4	58	35	26	56	43	75	43
81	6	19	7	77	19	1928	413	85	16	29	5	64	33	27	61	43	77	40
81	6	20	6	90	17	1980	427	92	16	28	6	65	36	27	62	38	75	39
87	6	19	5	90	16	2013	430	96	15	19	6	69	37	27	49	36	74	37
83	6	19	5	87	16	2073	474	110	14	19	7	76	43	27	50	40	82	37
81·6	6·2	18·3	6·2	84·0	18·6	1966·4	431·8	93·6	16·4	24·2	5·6	66·4	36·8	28·1	55·6	40·2	76·6	39·2
230	17	282	93	210	47	180	40	175	31	284	66	218	121	19	254	194	212	109
77	6	21	5	90	16	2156	491	108	15	27	8	76	41	3	46	38	79	33
75	6	26	4	89	15	2249	487	110	15	20	6	77	45	5	55	38	80	31
78	6	23	5	90	16	2437	498	118	12	23	5	74	44	5	54	35	75	29
83	6	28	5	90	19	2532	531	112	12	27	5	72	45		63	37	74	27
84	6	27	4	94	19	2647	537	116	15	31	7	70	47		72	38	67	27
79·4	6·0	26·0	4·6	90·6	17·0	2404·2	506·8	112·8	13·8	25·6	6·2	73·8	44·4	33	58·0	37·2	75·0	29·4
248	19	381	67	228	43	200	42	188	23	297	72	250	150	22	267	171	218	96
77	6	24	4	92	19	2775	569	119	10	33	6	74	40		67	38	66	28
81	6	23	4	91	20	2893	582	128	11	32	6	78	47	5	66	36	71	21

January 1902; and the Number of Pauper Lunatics from each Co...orhouse.

IN WHICH THE PARISH OF SETTLEMENT IS SITUATED.

	Forfar		Haddington		Inverness		Kincardine		Kinross		Kirkcud-bright		Lanark		Linlithgow		Stirling		Sutherland		Wigtown	
	M.	F.	M.	F.	M.	F.	M.	F.	M.	F.	M.	F.	M.	F.	M.	F.	M.	F.	M.	F.	M.	F.
	...	...	...	...	...	...	1	1	...	...	40	51	...	...	...	...	...	...	...	...	...	...
	142	195	...	...	...	...	...	1	...	...	...	...	...	1	...	...	...	...	...	...	29	22
	...	...	...	...	...	...	...	...	...	...	...	...	...	1	...	...	...	...	...	1	...	...
	167	176	...	...	...	...	24	39	...	...	...	...	...	...	...	...	...	...	...	...	...	...
	...	...	...	...	4	3	...	...	...	...	...	...	...	...	...	...	...	...	...	...	...	...
	...	...	...	...	...	...	...	...	...	...	...	...	...	1	...	...	...	...	...	...	...	...
	...	...	...	...	...	...	...	...	4	19	...	...	...	...	...	...	...	...	...	...	...	...
	...	...	...	...	...	...	...	...	...	...	...	...	293	278	...	...	...	...	...	...	...	...
	...	...	...	...	...	...	...	...	...	...	...	...	445	405	...	...	...	...	...	...	...	...
	1	...	...	...	...	...	...	...	...	...	...	...	233	216	...	...	...	...	...	...	...	...
	...	...	57	65	...	...	...	...	...	...	...	...	...	...	...	...	...	...	...	...	...	...
	1	1	...	...	147	135	...	...	...	...	...	...	...	...	...	...	...	...	31	35	...	...
	...	...	...	...	...	...	...	...	...	...	...	...	82	95	...	...	...	...	...	...	...	...
	2	...	...	1	...	...	...	...	...	...	...	...	340	272	2	...	...	...	...	...	...	...
	...	1	...	...	...	1	...	...	...	...	...	...	...	...	...	...	...	...	...	...	...	...
	1	...	...	...	...	...	...	1	...	...	...	...	1	...	61	42	4	125	...	...	...	...
	314	373	57	66	151	139	25	42	4	19	40	51	1394	1269	63	42		125	31	35	29	22
	...	...	...	...	...	...	...	...	...	...	...	...	...	...	...	...	...	...	...	...	...	...
	...	...	...	...	...	...	...	...	...	...	...	...	...	...	...	...	...	...	...	...	...	...
	...	...	...	...	...	...	...	...	...	...	...	...	...	...	...	...	...	...	...	...	...	...
	...	...	...	...	...	...	...	...	...	...	...	...	...	...	...	...	...	...	...	...	...	...
	...	...	...	...	...	...	...	...	...	...	...	...	...	...	...	...	...	...	...	...	...	...
	...	...	...	...	...	...	...	...	...	...	...	...	1	...	...	...	...	...	...	...	...	...
	43	56	...	...	...	...	...	...	...	...	...	...	...	...	...	...	3	...	...	...	...	...
	37	37	...	...	...	...	...	...	...	...	...	...	...	...	...	...	...	...	...	...	...	...
	...	...	...	...	...	...	...	...	...	...	...	...	92	84	...	...	...	...	...	...	...	...
	...	...	5	8	...	...	...	...	...	...	...	...	...	...	...	...	...	...	...	...	...	...
	4	3	...	...	...	...	5	9	...	...	...	...	...	...	...	...	...	...	...	...	...	...
	...	...	...	...	...	...	...	...	...	...	...	...	2	1	14	9	2	...	...	...	...	...
	...	...	...	...	...	...	...	...	...	...	...	...	24	20	...	...	1	...	...	...	...	...
	...	...	...	...	...	...	...	...	...	...	...	...	2	4	...	...	...	...	...	...	...	...
	...	...	...	...	...	...	...	...	...	...	...	...	...	...	...	...	...	...	...	...	10	10
	84	96	5	8	...	...	5	9	...	...	...	...	121	109	14	9	6	...	...	...	10	10
	398	469	62	74	151	139	30	51	4	19	40	51	1515	1378	77	51		131	31	35	39	32

APPENDIX A—TABLE XVI.

Return showing the Number of Pauper Lunatics of each Sex chargeable to each County in Scotland on 1st January 1902, and the manner of their disposal.

		Number of Pauper Lunatics at 1st January 1902.			DISPOSAL OF PAUPER LUNATICS.											
COUNTIES.	Population in 1901.				In Establishments.						In Private Dwellings and under sanction of the Board.					
					In Asylums and in Wards of Poorhouses with Unrestricted Licenses.			In Ward of Poorhouses with Restricted Licenses.			With Relatives.			With Strangers and Alone.		
		M.	F.	T.	M.	F.	T.	M.	F.	T.	M.	F.	T.	M.	F.	T.
1. Aberdeen,	313,806	461	526	987	316	358	674	100	98	198	19	28	47	27	47	78
2. Argyll,	73,685	214	215	429	114	171	285	56	50	106	16	24	40	37	24	61
3. Ayr,	254,436	311	360	671	228	272	500	...	...	...	35	18	58	12	20	32
4. Banff,	61,457	110	120	230	86	80	165	...	...	...	28	18	28	8	25	37
5. Berwick,	30,811	63	56	108	40	40	80	...	...	...	15	9	15	7	6	13
6. Bute,	18,786	32	41	78	29	28	67	2	5	7	3	3	3	5	10	13
7. Caithness,	33,860	81	108	189	49	56	105	2	2	4	57	2	57	5	10	20
8. Clackmannan,	32,019	38	39	77	29	29	58	27	27	52	4	3	4	7	19	11
9. Dumbarton,	113,870	110	130	240	77	82	159	25	25	...	8	2	8	6	6	28
10. Dumfries,	72,569	101	92	198	80	81	170	...	...	...	11	5	11	6		12
11. Edinburgh—Urban Dist.,	487,912	562	621	1,188	290	848	647	131	87	218	15	20	35	117	166	293
Mid-Lothian Dist.,	44,806	107	114	241	113	205	206	7	4	11	6	8	13	7	10	12
12. Elgin (or Moray),	218,843	270	322	508	289	80	140	...	9	...	10	12	22	4	10	16
13. Fife,	284,078	457	605	1,062	289	984	508	84	96	180	13	13	29	46	43	61
14. Forfar,	38,662	67	81	148	314	373	687	5	8	18	18	7	40	8	109	155
15. Haddington,	90,752	242	257	499	57	66	123	...	...	...	18	6	...	1	1	3
16. Inverness,	31,582	33	54	87	151	139	290	6	9	14	65	70	126	38	48	84
17. Kincardine,	6,960	6	21	27	25	42	67	...	...	...	...	2	3	2	1	3
18. Kinross,	39,407	45	66	111	4	19	28	5	...	...	1	1	1	1	1	7
19. Kirkcudbright,	1,314,773	1,741	1,784	3,476	40	61	91	...	...	...	9	9	8	2	1	8
20. Lanark,	66,484	52	82	130	1,394	1,989	2,683	121	109	230	44	62	106	182	294	476
21. Linlithgow,	8,721	22	16	38	63	42	106	14		28	4	5	6	4	...	5
22. Nairn,	28,696	56	69	125	18	14	32	...	...	...	2	1	8	...	1	15
23. Orkney,	15,066	19	18	37	33	45	78	...	...	...	13	2	27	10	2	20
24. Peebles,	123,262	261	247	508	16	16	34	17	15	32	16	14	7	1	1	1
25. Perth,	298,461	196	348	652	187	182	369	...	...	...	1	5	2	41	39	80
26. Renfrew,	76,421	196	208	898	272	292	564	17	16	82	64	69	87	36	46	82
27. Ross and Cromarty,	45,798	69	98	167	114	113	227	...	...	...	8	8	2	17	21	38
28. Roxburgh,	23,339	58	66	122	94	85	149	3	...	...	8	8	89	8	5	8
29. Selkirk,	28,195	58	64	132	64	36	60	...	...	...	2	2	4	...	1	1
30. Shetland,	142,888	187	184	381	35	38	71	1	2	3	16	9	89	4	9	9
31. Stirling,	21,550	43	59	102	154	125	279	3	6	9	9	18	14	5	24	29
32. Sutherland,	32,683	46	46	92	29	35	61	10	10	20	7	11	18	3	6	12
Totals,	**4,472,000**	**6,493**	**7,088**	**13,681**	**4,859**	**4,976**	**9,835**	**688**	**582**	**1,116**	**404**	**550**	**964**	**647**	**1,080**	**1,677**

APPENDIX A.—TABLE XVII.

The Manner in which the Pauper Lunatics chargeable to each County, placed on the Register of the Board during 1901, were disposed of, and the Changes that have taken place during the year in the Disposal of those on the Register on 1st January of that year.

COUNTIES	No. of Pauper Lunatics at 1st January 1901 — In Establishments		In Private Dwellings as Single Patients		Number Intimated during the Year 1901		A. Disposal of Establishment Patients.* — Placed in Establishments — Of Patients Intimated during 1901		Of Single Patients transferred		Discharged from Establishments — Recovered		Removal from Poor-Roll		Died		B. Disposal of Single Patients. — Exempted from Removal of Single Patients intimated		Transferred from Establishments		Removed from Jurisdiction of Board. — By Recovery		By Friends		Died	
	M	F	M	F	M	F	M	F	M	F	M	F	M	F	M	F	M	F	M	F	M	F	M	F	M	F
1. Aberdeen																										
2. Argyll																										
3. Ayr																										
4. Banff																										
5. Berwick																										
6. Bute																										
7. Caithness																										
8. Clackmannan																										
9. Dumbarton																										
10. Dumfries																										
11. Edinburgh— Urban District Midlothian																										
12. Elgin																										
13. Fife																										
14. Forfar																										
15. Haddington																										
16. Inverness																										
17. Kincardine																										
18. Kinross																										
19. Kirkcudbright																										
20. Lanark																										
21. Linlithgow																										
22. Nairn																										
23. Orkney																										
24. Peebles																										
25. Perth																										
26. Renfrew																										
27. Ross & Cromarty																										
28. Roxburgh																										
29. Selkirk																										
30. Shetland																										
31. Stirling																										
32. Sutherland																										
33. Wigtown																										
TOTALS	8197	8260	1064	1600	1414	1627	1465	1692	53	82	622	646	148	114	445	472	49	48	64	98	10	13?	16	10	47	81

* Inmates of Schools for Imbeciles are not included in this Table.

APPENDIX A.—TABLE XVIII.

Proportion for each County, per 100,000 of Population, of Pauper
Lunatics annually placed on the Register in the Years
1892-1901, also of those at 1st January 1902 in Asylums,
Lunatic Wards of Poorhouses, and in Private Dwellings·
and the Proportion of Registered Paupers of all classes.

COUNTIES	Average number Intimated as Pauper Lunatics during the years 1892-1901.			Total number of Pauper Lunatics at 1st Jan. 1902.	Pauper Lunatics in Establishments at 1st Jan. 1902.			Pauper Lunatics in Private Dwellings at 1st Jan. 1902.	Paupers of all Classes at 16th May 1901.
	Sent to Asylums.	Left in Private Dwellings.	Total.		In Asylums and in Wards of Poorhouses with Unrestricted Licences.	In Wards of Poorhouses with Restricted Licences.	Total in Establishments.		
1. Aberdeen,	50	2	52	315	215	61	276	38	1421
2. Argyll,	73	6	79	582	445	...	445	124	2282
3. Ayr,	55	2	57	264	196	42	238	26	1333
4. Banff,	54	6	60	374	269	...	269	106	1843
5. Berwick,	38	5	43	350	260	...	260	91	1473
6. Bute,	55	1	56	389	303	...	303	85	1315
7. Caithness,	49	17	66	558	310	21	331	227	2921
8. Clackmannan,	49	3	52	240	181	13	194	47	1012
9. Dumbarton,	49	1	50	211	139	46	185	25	1169
10. Dumfries,	49	1	50	266	234	...	234	32	1386
11. Edinburgh,	67	2	69	292	175	47	222	70	1270
12. Elgin,	83	5	88	406	324	...	324	83	2285
13. Fife,	46	1	47	271	230	...	230	41	1025
14. Forfar,	68	2	70	374	242	63	305	69	1470
15. Haddington,	76	2	78	383	318	34	352	31	1596
16. Inverness,	76	15	91	550	320	...	320	230	2785
17. Kincardine,	50	...	50	276	213	44	257	19	1119
18. Kinross,	66	3	69	387	330	...	330	57	1017
19. Kirkcudbright,	44	3	47	281	231	...	231	51	1850
20. Lanark,	57	2	59	264	203	17	220	44	1326
21. Linlithgow,	43	1	44	209	158	35	193	17	1085
22. Nairn,	84	5	89	436	367	...	367	69	2007
23. Orkney,	47	15	62	436	272	...	272	164	2178
24. Peebles,	40	1	41	246	226	...	226	20	962
25. Perth,	67	2	69	412	299	26	325	87	1330
26. Renfrew,	63	...	63	222	192	...	192	30	1208
27. Ross and Cromarty,	61	18	79	521	297	...	297	224	3154
28. Roxburgh,	58	3	61	342	305	...	305	37	1357
29. Selkirk,	65	5	70	279	257	...	257	21	1230
30. Shetland,	50	12	62	433	252	11	263	170	2810
31. Stirling,	56	2	58	283	196	6	202	30	1255
32. Sutherland,	77	7	84	473	306	...	306	167	3452
33. Wigtown,	48	3	51	281	156	61	217	64·	2350
SCOTLAND,	58	3	61	304	220	25	245	59·	1446

* Calculated on Populations of '901·

APPENDIX A.—TABLE XIX.

Return exhibiting the Number of Orders granted by the Sheriffs for Admission of Lunatics into any Public, Private, District, or Parochial Asylum or House, stating the Asylum or House to which such Order was sent, during the Year ended 31st December 1901.

Orders granted by the Sheriffs of the County of	For the Admission of Patients into the Asylum or House of	No. of Orders Granted.	Total.
1. Aberdeen	Royal Asylum, Aberdeen .	245	
	Do. Montrose .	1	
			246
2. Argyll	District Asylum, Argyll .	48	
			48
3. Ayr	Crichton Royal Institution, Dumfries	4	
	Royal Asylum, Glasgow .	1	
	District Asylum, Ayr	126	
			131
4. Banff	District Asylum, Banff .	39	
			39
5. Berwick	District Asylum, Midlothian .	1	
	Do. Roxburgh .	6	
			7
6. Bute	Crichton Royal Institution, Dumfries,	1	
	Royal Asylum, Glasgow .	1	
	Private Asylum, Saughton Hall	1	
	District Asylum, Argyll .	10	
			13
7. Caithness	Royal Asylum, Montrose	17	
			17
8. Clackmannan	District Asylum, Fife .	1	
	Do. Stirling	10	
			11
9. Dumbarton	Royal Asylum, Glasgow .	1	
	Private Asylum, Westermains .	2	
	District Asylum, Glasgow (Woodilee)	9	
	Do. Stirling .	25	
			37
10. Dumfries	Crichton Royal Institution, Dumfries,	138	
			138
11. Edinburgh	Royal Asylum, Edinburgh	396	
	Private Asylum, Mavisbank .	16	
	Do. Saughton Hall	8	
	District Asylum, Haddington .	2	
	Do. Midlothian .	56	
			478
12. Elgin	Royal Asylum, Montrose .	1	
	District Asylum, Elgin .	33	
			34
13. Fife	Royal Asylum, Perth .	2	
	Private Asylum, Saughton Hall	1	
	District Asylum, Fife .	101	
			104
14. Forfar	Royal Asylum, Dundee .	139	
	Do. Montrose .	132	
	Do. Murray's, Perth	2	
			273
15. Haddington	District Asylum, Haddington .	24	
			24
16. Inverness	Royal Asylum, Aberdeen .	1	
	District Asylum, Argyll .	2	
	Do. Inverness	101	
			104
17. Kincardine	Royal Asylum, Montrose .	6	
			6
	Carry Forward .		1,710

APPENDIX A.—TABLE XIX.—*continued.*

Orders granted by the Sheriffs of the County of	For the Admission of Patients into the Asylum or House of	No. of Orders Granted.	Total.
	Brought Forward .	.	1,710
18. Kinross , . . .	Murray's Royal Asylum, Perth . . .	1	
	District Asylum, Fife	2	
			3
19. Kirkcudbright . .	Crichton Royal Institution, Dumfries . .	8	
			8
20. Lanark . . .	Crichton Royal Institution, Dumfries . .	2	
	Royal Asylum, Glasgow	99	
	Do. Montrose	2	
	District Asylum, Argyll	1	
	Do. Glasgow (Gartloch) .	253	
	Do. Glasgow (Woodilee) .	235	
	Do. Govan . . .	230	
	Kirklands Asylum, Bothwell . . .	77	
	District Asylum, Lanark	185	
	Do. Stirling. . . .	2	
	Parochial Asylum, Paisley (Riccartsbar) . .	1	
			1,087
21. Linlithgow . . .	District Asylum, Lanark	1	
	Do. Stirling	15	
			16
22. Nairn	Royal Asylum, Aberdeen	1	
	District Asylum, Inverness . . .	7	
			8
23. Orkney	Royal Asylum, Edinburgh	8	
	District Asylum, Elgin	1	
			9
24. Peebles	Royal Asylum, Edinburgh	1	
	District Asylum, Midlothian . . .	5	
	Do. Stirling	1	
			7
25. Perth	Crichton Royal Institution, Dumfries . .	1	
	Royal Asylum, Montrose	1	
	Do. Murray's, Perth . .	28	
	District Asylum, Glasgow (Gartloch) .	91	
	Do. Perth	1	
			122
26. Renfrew . . .	Crichton Royal Institution, Dumfries . .	3	
	Royal Asylum, Glasgow . . .	5	
	District Asylum, Glasgow (Woodilee) .	1	
	Do. Govan . . .	3	
	Do. Stirling . . .	1	
	Parochial Asylum, Greenock . . .	63	
	Do. Paisley (Craw Road) .	27	
	Do. Do. (Riccartsbar) .	98	
			201
27. Ross . . .	Royal Asylum, Montrose	1	
	District Asylum, Inverness . . .	27	
			28
28. Roxburgh . . .	District Asylum, Roxburgh . . .	37	
			37
29. Selkirk . . .	District Asylum, Roxburgh . . .	1	
			1
30. Shetland . . .	Royal Asylum, Montrose . . .	21	
			21
31. Stirling . . .	Royal Asylum, Glasgow . . .	1	
	District Asylum, Stirling . . .	174	
			175
32. Sutherland . . .	District Asylum, Inverness . . .	4	
			4
33. Wigtown . . .	Crichton Royal Institution, Dumfries . .	19	
	District Asylum, Ayr	1	
			20
	TOTAL, .		3,457

APPENDIX A.—TABLE XX.

Return exhibiting the Number of Licences granted by the General Board of
Commissioners in Lunacy for Scotland, for the Continuance, Establishment,
or Renewal of Charitable Institutions, Private Asylums, and Lunatic Wards
of Poorhouses, and the Transfer of any such Licence from any one Asylum
to another, during the year ended 31st December 1901.

Name.	Number of Licences granted for Continuance or Renewal.	Number of Licences granted for Establishment.	Number of Licences Transferred.	Total.
1. Charitable Institutions . . .	2	...	...	2
2. Private Asylums	3	...	...	3
3. Lunatic Wards of Poorhouses . .	18	...	...	18
TOTAL	23	...	...	23

APPENDIX A.—TABLE XXI.

Average Number of Patients Resident, and the Results of Treatment in each Asylum or other Establishment, for the Year 1901.

(a) *Royal and District Asylums.*

ROYAL AND DISTRICT ASYLUMS.		Average Number Resident.		Admissions (including Transfers).		Recoveries.		Discharged not Recovered (including Transfers).		Deaths.		Proportion of Recoveries per cent. on Admissions.		Proportion of Deaths per cent. on Average Number Resident.	
		M.	F.	M.	F.	M.	F.	M.	F.	M.	F.	M.	F.	M.	F.
1. Aberdeen Royal Asylum,	Private patients,														
	Pauper do.,														
	Total,														
2. Argyll District Asylum,															
3. Ayr District Asylum,															
4. Banff District Asylum,															
5. Crichton Royal Institution, Dumfries,	Private patients,														
	Pauper do.,														
	Total,														
6. Dundee Royal Asylum,	Private patients,														
	Pauper do.,														
	Total,														
7. Edinburgh Royal Asylum,	Private patients,														
	Pauper do.,														
	Total,														
8. Elgin District Asylum,															
9. Fife District Asylum,															
10. Glasgow Royal Asylum,															
11. Glasgow District Asylum, Gartloch,															
12. Glasgow District Asylum, Woodilee,															
13. Govan District Asylum,															
14. Haddington District Asylum,															
15. Inverness District Asylum,															
16. Kirklands Asylum at Bothwell,															
17. Lanark District Asylum,															
18. Midlothian District Asylum,															
19. Montrose Royal Asylum,	Private patients,														
	Pauper do.,														
	Total,														
20. Murray's Royal Asylum, Perth,															
21. Perth District Asylum,															
22. Roxburgh District Asylum,															
23. Stirling District Asylum,															
GENERAL RESULTS,															

APPENDIX A.—TABLE XXI.—*continued.*

Average Number of Patients Resident, and the Results of Treatment in each Asylum or other Establishment, for the Year 1901

(b) *Private Asylums.*

PRIVATE ASYLUMS.	Average Number Resident.		Admissions (including Transfers).		Recoveries.		Discharges not Recovered (including Transfers).		Deaths		Proportion of Recoveries per cent. on Admissions.		Proportion of Deaths per cent. on Average Number Resident.	
	M.	F.	M.	F.	M.	F.	M.	F.	M.	F.	M.	F.	M.	F.
1. Mavisbank,............	20·5	24·5	5	12	5	7	2	4	3	2	100·0	58·3	14·6	8·2
2. Saughton Hall,.......	23·0	46·0	3	8	...	1	1	...	...	1	...	12·5	...	2·2
3. Westermains,.........	2·0	12·0	...	2	...	..	...	...	...	...	...	...	...	...
GENERAL RESULTS,...	45·5	82·5	8	22	5	8	3	4	3	3	62·5	36·4	6·6	3·6

(c) *Parochial Asylums.*

(Lunatic Wards of Poorhouses with Unrestricted Licences.)

PAROCHIAL ASYLUMS.	Average Number Resident.		Admissions (including Transfers).		Recoveries.		Discharges not Recovered (including Transfers).		Deaths.		Proportion of Recoveries per cent. on Admissions.		Proportion of Deaths per cent. on Average Number Resident.	
	M.	F.	M.	F.	M.	F.	M.	F.	M.	F.	M.	F	M.	F.
1. Greenock,.............	113·0	116·5	42	44	27	21	3	3	12	13	64·3	47·7	10·6	11·2
2. Paisley, Craw h d.	47·5	61·0	9	20	4	7	6	7	2	4	44·4	35·0	4·2	6·6
3. „ Riccartsbar,	106·5	102·5	52	57	29	27	11	24	7	11	55·7	47·4	6·6	10·7
GENERAL RESULTS,	267·0	280·0	103	121	60	55	20	34	21	28	58·3	45·5	7·9	10·0

APPENDIX A.—TABLE XXI.—*continued.*

Average Number of Patients Resident, and the Results of Treatment in each Asylum or other Establishment, for the Year 1901.

(d) *Lunatic Wards of Poorhouses with Restricted Licences.*

LUNATIC WARDS OF POORHOUSES.	Average Number Resident.		Admissions (including Transfers).		Recoveries.		Discharges and Recovered (including Transfers).		Deaths.		Proportion of Recoveries per cent. on Admissions.		Proportion of Deaths per cent. on Average Number Resident.	
	M.	F.	M.	F.	M.	F.	M.	F.	M.	F.	M.	F.	M.	F.
1. Aberdeen (East),	41·5	39·5	5	5	...	...	3	4	1	2	...	...	2·4	5·1
2. Aberdeen (West),	26·5	26·0	1	4	1	2	5	1	...	...	100·0	50·0	...	...
3. Buchan (New Maud), ...	26·0	26·0	2	1	...	...	1	1	1	...	...	...	3·8	...
4. Cunninghame (Irvine),	48·0	45·0	3	5	...	...	...	2	2	4	...	...	4·2	8·
5. Dumbarton,	25·0	27·5	11	6	...	...	3	...	...	1	...	...	...	3·6
6. Dundee East,	44·0	55·5	7	9	...	...	7	7	2	1	...	...	4·5	1·8
7. Dundee West,	37·0	37·0	8	6	...	1	3	4	5	1	...	16·7	13·5	2·7
8. Edinburgh (City),	103·0	76·0	65	15	2	...	7	2	6	3	3·1	...	5·8	3·9
9. Govan (Glasgow),	93·0	78·5	8	16	...	...	6	...	4	5	...	...	4·3	6·4
10. Inveresk (Musselburgh),	15·5	15·5	1	...	...	...	2	1	...	...	...	...	...	...
11. Kincardine (Stonehaven),	20·0	20·5	2	3	...	...	1	1	1	3	...	...	5·0	14·6
12. Linlithgow,	17·0	17·0	1	1	...	...	1	1	...	...	...	...	...	...
13. Old Monkland,	24·0	22·5	1	3	...	1	...	2	1	3	...	33·3	4·2	13·3
14. Perth,	19·5	19·5	7	4	...	1	5	2	3	2	...	25·0	15·4	10·3
15. Wigtown (Stranraer),	19·0	15·0	5	1	...	...	1	1	4	...	...	...	21·1	...
GENERAL RESULTS,	559·0	521·0	127	79	3	5	45	29	30	25	2·4	6·3	5·4	4·8

APPENDIX A.—TABLE XXI.—*continued.*

Average Number of Patients Resident, and the Results of Treatment in each Asylum or other Establishment, for the Year 1901.

(e) *Training Schools for Imbecile Children.*

INSTITUTIONS.	Average Number Resident.		Admissions.		Recoveries.		Discharges not Recovered.		Deaths.	
	M.	F.	M.	F.	M.	F.	M.	F.	M.	F.
Baldovan, ...	68·5	44·0	16	10	...	...	5	...	14	10
Larbert,...............	170·5	105·0	36	24	...	...	12	8	7	12
TOTAL, ,..	239·0	149·0	52	34	...	...	17	8	21	22

APPENDIX A—TABLE XXII.

Classification of the Causes of Death of Patients who died in Asylums and other Establishments in the Year 1901.

(a) Royal and District Asylums.

NUMBER OF DEATHS OF MALES AND FEMALES FROM SPECIFIC CAUSES.

ROYAL AND DISTRICT ASYLUMS.	Average Number Resident (M)	Average Number Resident (F)	Total Number of Deaths (M)	Total Number of Deaths (F)	Number of foregoing Deaths which took place within a Year after Admission (M)	Number of foregoing Deaths which took place within a Year after Admission (F)
Aberdeen	422·0	484·5	29	30	14	17
Argyll	220·5	214·0	11	9	16	4
Ayr	229·5	269·5	17	29	12	17
Banff	85·5	80·0	3	3	1	1
Crichton Royal	350·5	380·0	31	31	8	12
Dundee	176·5	240·5	24	21	14	13
Edinburgh	478·5	476·0	63	60	40	32
Elgin	74·5	104·0	11	7	6	5
Fife	242·0	288·0	21	23	9	4
Glasgow Royal	176·5	283·5	24	10	12	
Glasgow District (Gartloch)	288·0	266·0	31	32	13	19
Glasgow District (Woodilee)	425·0	410·5	40	34	26	9
Govan	281·0	281·5	33	29	29	21
Haddington	62·5	75·5	3	7	8	
Inverness	312·0	294·0	21	10	6	2
Kirklands	99·5	93·0	17	11	8	14
Lanark	376·5	329·5	18	27	7	8
Midlothian	134·0	127·0	6	14	1	20
Montrose	310·5	364·5	28	48	11	
Murray's Royal	68·0	61·0	3	3	5	3
Perth	184·0	176·0	13	5	5	
Roxburgh	141·5	169·0	7	5	2	
Stirling	344·5	330·0	31	44	18	27
TOTAL,	**5429·5**	**5698·0**	**496**	**481**	**287**	**238**

(Table continues with columns for: Apoplexy and Paralysis; Epilepsy and Convulsions; General Paralysis; Mania and Melancholic Exhaustion; Organic Disease of Brain, Tumours, etc.; Consumption; Inflammation of Lungs and Membranes, and other forms of Pulmonary Disease; Disease of the Heart, Aneurism, etc.; Inflammation of Stomach, Intestines, or Peritoneum; Disease of Liver, Kidneys, etc.; Diarrhœa, Dysentery and; Fever, Erysipelas, Cancer, etc.; Old Age, General Debility and; Suicides and Accidents; Cause unknown — each subdivided into Male and Female.)

APPENDIX A.—TABLE XXII.—*continued.*

Classification of the Causes of Death of Patients who died in Asylums and other Establishments in the Year 1901.

(b) *Private Asylums.*

NUMBER OF DEATHS OF MALES AND FEMALES FROM SPECIFIC CAUSES.

PRIVATE ASYLUMS.	Average Number Resident. M.	F.	Total Number of Deaths. M.	F.	Number of foregoing Deaths which took place within a Year after Admission. M.	F.	Apoplexy and Paralysis. M. F.	Epilepsy and Convulsions. M. F.	General Paralysis. M. F.	Mania, Melancholia, Exhaustion. M.	F.	Organic Disease of Brain, Tumours, etc. M.	F.	Consumption. M. F.	Inflammation of Lungs and Membranes, and other forms of Pulmonary Disease. M.	F.	Disease of the Heart, Aneurism, etc. M.	F.	Inflammation of Stomach, Intestine, or Peritoneum. M.	F.	Disease of Liver, Kidney, etc. M.	F.	Dysentery and Diarrhœa. M. F.	Fever, Erysipelas, Cancer, etc. M. F.	General Debility and Old Age. M. F.	Suddenly and Accidents. M. F.	Cause unknown. M. F.
Mavisbank	90·5	24·5	3	2	1	1	1		1			1		1		1						1	
Saughton Hall	28·0	46·0		2																			
Wellermains	2·0	12·0		1								1											
TOTALS,	**46·5**	**82·5**	**3**	**3**	**1**	**1**	**1**		**1**			**1**		**1**		**1**				**1**		**1**	

(c) *Parochial Asylums.*

(Lunatic Wards of Poorhouses with Unrestricted Licences.)

PAROCHIAL ASYLUMS.	Average Number Resident. M.	F.	Total Number of Deaths. M.	F.	Number of foregoing Deaths which took place within a Year after Admission. M.	F.	Apoplexy and Paralysis. M. F.	Epilepsy and Convulsions. M. F.	General Paralysis. M. F.	Mania, Melancholia, Exhaustion. M.	F.	Organic Disease of Brain, Tumours, etc. M.	F.	Consumption. M. F.	Inflammation of Lungs and Membranes, and other forms of Pulmonary Disease. M.	F.	Disease of the Heart, Aneurism, etc. M.	F.	Inflammation of Stomach, Intestine, or Peritoneum. M.	F.	Disease of Liver, Kidney, etc. M.	F.	Dysentery and Diarrhœa. M. F.	Fever, Erysipelas, Cancer, etc. M. F.	General Debility and Old Age. M. F.	Suddenly and Accidents. M. F.	Cause unknown. M. F.
Greenock	118·0	116·5	12	13	7	4	1	2	1	1	1		1 1	1					1			3	1
Paisley (Craw Road)	47·5	61·0	2	4	1	1		2				2	1	1		1						3	1
„ (Riccartsbar)	106·5	102·5	7	11	4	9	1	2	1	1	1		1		1							3	1
TOTALS,	**247·0**	**280·0**	**21**	**28**	**12**	**14**	**2**	**5**	**3**	**2**	**2**	**2**	**2 4**	**2**	**1**	**1**			**1**			**8**	**2**

APPENDIX A.—TABLE XXII.—continued.

Classification of the Causes of Death of Patients who died in Asylums and other Establishments in the Year 1901.

(d) Lunatic Wards of Poorhouses with Restricted Licences.

NUMBER OF DEATHS OF MALES AND FEMALES FROM SPECIFIC CAUSES.

LUNATIC WARDS OF POORHOUSES.	Average Number Resident. M.	F.	Total Number of Deaths. M.	F.	Number of foregoing Deaths which took place within a Year after Admission. M.	F.
Aberdeen East	41·5	39·5	1	2	2	1
Aberdeen West	26·5	26·0	1	1		
Buchan	26·0	26·0	2			
Cunninghame	48·0	45·0	2	4		1
Dumbarton	25·0	27·5	2	2	3	
Dundee East	44·0	55·5	5	6		
Dundee West	37·0	37·0	4	3		1
Edinburgh	103·0	76·0		5		
Govan	93·0	78·5				
Inverisk	15·5	15·5	1	1		2
Kincardine	20·0	29·5	3	3	2	
Linlithgow	17·0	17·0				
Old Monkland	24·0	22·5	3	3	1	
Perth	19·5	19·5	3	2		1
Wigtown	19·0	15·0	4			
TOTALS,	569·0	521·0	30	25	4	6

(Table continues with columns for Cerebral and Spinal Affections [Apoplexy and Paralysis; Epilepsy and Convulsions; General Paralysis; Maniacal and Melancholic Exhaustion; Organic Disease of Brain, Tumour, etc.], Thoracic Affections [Consumption; Inflammation of Lungs and Membranes, and other forms of Phthisis Pulmonary Disease; Disease of the Heart, Aneurism, etc.], Abdominal Affections [Inflammation of Stomach, Intestines, or Peritoneum; Disease of Liver, Kidneys, etc.; Dysentery and Diarrhœa], Fever, Erysipelas, Cancer, etc.; General Debility and Old Age; Suicides and Accidents; Cause unknown — for Males and Females.)

APPENDIX A.—TABLE XXII.—*continued.*

Classification of the Causes of Death of Patients who died in Asylums and other Establishments in the Year 1901.

(b) *Private Asylums.*

| | Average Number Resident. | | Total Number of Deaths. | | | Number of foregoing Deaths which took place within a Year after Admission. | | Apoplexy and Paralysis. | | Epilepsy and Convulsions. | | General Paralysis. | | Mania, Melancholia and Exhaustion. | | Organic Disease of Brain, Tumours, etc. | | Consumption. | | Inflammation of Lungs and Membranes, and other forms of Pulmonary Disease. | | Disease of the Heart, Aneurism, etc. | | Inflammation of Stomach, Intestines, or Peritoneum. | | Disease of Liver, Kidneys, etc. | | Dysentery and Diarrhoea. | | Fever, Erysipelas, Cancer, etc. | | General Debility and Old Age. | | Suicides and Accidents. | | Cause unknown. | |
PRIVATE ASYLUMS.	M.	F.	M.	F.		M.	F.	M.	F.	M.	F.	M.	F.	M.	F.	M.	F.	M.	F.	M.	F.	M.	F.	M.	F.	M.	F.	M.	F.	M.	F.	M.	F.	M.	F.	M.	F.
Maviabank	20·5	24·5	3			1		1					1							1							1	1					1					
Saughton Hall	28·0	46·0		2																			1	1													
Westermains	2·0	12·0		1																																	
TOTALS,	**45·5**	**82·5**	**3**	**3**		**1**	**1**	**1**					**1**							**1**			**1**	**1**			**1**	**1**			**1**		**1**					

(c) *Parochial Asylums.*
(Lunatic Wards of Poorhouses with Unrestricted Licences.)

| | Average Number Resident. | | Total Number of Deaths. | | | Number of foregoing Deaths which took place within a Year after Admission. | | Apoplexy and Paralysis. | | Epilepsy and Convulsions. | | General Paralysis. | | Mania, Melancholia and Exhaustion. | | Organic Disease of Brain, Tumours, etc. | | Consumption. | | Inflammation of Lungs, etc. | | Disease of the Heart, etc. | | Inflammation of Stomach, etc. | | Disease of Liver, Kidneys, etc. | | Dysentery and Diarrhoea. | | Fever, Erysipelas, Cancer, etc. | | General Debility and Old Age. | | Suicides and Accidents. | | Cause unknown. | |
PAROCHIAL ASYLUMS.	M.	F.	M.	F.		M.	F.	M.	F.	M.	F.	M.	F.	M.	F.	M.	F.	M.	F.	M.	F.	M.	F.	M.	F.	M.	F.	M.	F.	M.	F.	M.	F.	M.	F.	M.	F.
Greenock	118·0	116·5	12	13		7	4	1	1	2	2	1	1	1	1	1	1	1	4	2		1		1								1		1			
Paisley (Craw Road)	47·5	61·0	2	4		1	1	1		2	2	1		1				1														1		1			
" (Riccartsbar)	106·5	102·5	7	11		4	9		1	2	2	1	2			1		1	1		2		1	1							1	1				1	
TOTALS,	**267·0**	**280·0**	**21**	**28**		**12**	**14**	**1**	**2**	**2**	**5**	**3**	**3**	**3**	**1**	**1**	**2**	**2**	**4**	**2**	**2**	**1**		**2**	**1**			**2**			**1**	**2**	**1**	**1**			**1**	

APPENDIX A.—TABLE XXII.—*continued.*

Classification of the Causes of Death of Patients who died in Asylums and other Establishments in the Year 1901.

(d) *Lunatic Wards of Poorhouses with Restricted Licences.*

NUMBER OF DEATHS OF MALES AND FEMALES FROM SPECIFIC CAUSES.

LUNATIC WARDS OF POORHOUSES	Average Number Resident M	Average Number Resident F	Total Number of Deaths M	Total Number of Deaths F
Aberdeen East	41·5	39·5	1	2
Aberdeen West	26·5	26·0	1	1
Buchan	26·0	26·0	2	4
Cunninghame	48·0	45·0	1	2
Dumbarton	25·0	27·5	2	1
Dundee East	44·0	55·5	2	5
Dundee West	37·0	37·0	6	3
Edinburgh	103·0	76·0	4	5
Govan	93·0	78·5		
Inveresk	15·5	15·5	1	3
Kincardine	20·0	29·5		
Linlithgow	17·0	17·0	1	3
Old Monkland	24·0	22·5	3	2
Perth	19·5	19·5	2	4
Wigtown	19·0	15·0		
TOTALS	**559·0**	**521·0**	**30**	**25**

Specific cause columns (headers): Number of foregoing Deaths which took place within a year after Admission (M, F); Cerebral and Spinal Affections — Apoplexy and Paralysis, Epilepsy and Convulsions, General Paralysis, Mania and Melancholic Exhaustion, Organic Disease of Brain, Tumours, etc.; Thoracic Affections — Consumption, Inflammation of Lungs and Membranes and other forms of Pulmonary Disease, Disease of the Heart, Aneurism, etc.; Abdominal Affections — Inflammation of Stomach, Intestion, or Peritoneum, Disease of Liver, Kidneys, etc., Dysentery and Diarrhœa; Fever, Erysipelas, Cancer, etc.; General Debility and Old Age; Suicides and Accidents; Cause unknown.

	COUNTIES.	Number of Pauper Lunatics Relieved during the Year.		Proportion per cent. of Days of Relief.		
				In Royal, District, and Parochial Asylums, and Training Schools for Imbecile Children.	In Lunatic Wards of Poorhouses with Restricted Licences.	In Private Dwellings.
		M.	F.			
1	Aberdeen, ...	523	60 62	67·3	20·0	12·7
2	Argyll, ...	248	23 64	79·1	...	20·9
3	Ayr, ...	390	41 06	73·5	15·3	11·2
4	Banff, ...	125	13 67	70·2	...	29·8
5	Berwick, ...	56	5 17	72·4	...	27·6
6	Bute, ...	36	3 94	76·4	...	23·6
7	Caithness, ...	92	12 89	65·3	2·9	31·8
8	Clackmannan, ...	46	02	72·5	5·7	21·8
9	Dumbarton, ...	142	15 29	69·0	18·8	12·2
10	Dumfries, ...	115	1 57	87·7	...	12·3
11	Edinburgh, ...	322	8 57	61·4	12·9	25·7
12	Elgin, ...	105	12 43	79·7	...	20·3
13	Fife, ...	322	3 63	84·1	0·1	15·8
14	Forfar, ...	530	7 80	64·9	17·0	18·1
15	Haddington, ...	79	19	80·8	10·7	8·5
16	Inverness, ...	275	2 55	56·3	...	43·7
17	Kincardine, ...	42	38	73·7	18·6	7·7
18	Kinross, ...	8	02	85·8	...	14·2
19	Kirkcudbright, ...	55	12	82·8	...	17·7
20	Lanark, ...	2,101	2,1 91	76·8	6·8	16·4
21	Linlithgow, ...	82	24	74·4	16·2	9·4
22	Nairn, ...	27	24	83·6	...	16·4
23	Orkney, ...	54	96	65·0	...	35·0
24	Peebles, ...	19	67	88·5	...	11·5
25	Perth, ...	302	2 74	72·1	6·2	21·7
26	Renfrew, ...	391	4 19	87·6	...	12·4
27	Ross, ...	213	2 91	54·9	...	45·1
28	Roxburgh, ...	75	1 53	88·6	...	11·4
29	Selkirk, ...	36	08	89·0	...	11·0
30	Shetland, ...	56	54	53·9	2·3	43·8
31	Stirling, ...	193	2 95	84·1	2·4	13·5
32	Sutherland, ...	51	43	62·5	1·0	36·5
33	Wigtown, ...	52	51	50·7	23·4	25·9
	Totals and Averages, ...	7,663	8,3 46	72·4	7·9	19·7

TABLE XXIII
Pauper Lunatics during the
89

In Royal Asylums.	In District Asylums.	In A...ar.	...tal ...diture ...g the ...ar.	Amount of foregoing Expenditure Contributed by Relatives or Others.	Amount of foregoing Expenditure Contributed by Government.	COUNTIES.
£ s. d.	£ s. d.	£	s. d.	£ s. d.	£ s. d.	
19,968 13 4	152 1 7		16 9	1,006 17 9	8,397 6 11	1. Aberdeen.
...	8,688 1 6		16 4	212 8 11	3,859 9 2	2. Argyll.
5 19 4	12,338 11 6		15 8	1,636 7 5	5,601 17 8	3. Ayr.
37 6 6	2,963 16 9		17 11	196 2 3	1,741 1 4	4. Banff.
...	1,919 18 11		6 10	136 0 3	895 3 9	5. Berwick.
2 10 6	1,469 5 11		3 6	160 19 0	641 0 9	6. Bute.
3,083 16 10	86 12 2		4 2	25 0 8	1,518 17 5	7. Caithness.
...	1,499 10 2		3 9	172 13 0	667 19 2	8. Clackmannan.
15 6 6	4,216 14 9		10 2	529 9 9	1,902 11 6	9. Dumbarton.
3,993 9 3	7 9 7		2 6	99 8 6	1,743 7 5	10. Dumfries.
17,389 15 6	9,208 13 7		17 10	2,311 7 3	12,451 10 11	11. Edinburgh.
9 6 3	3,082 5 5		5 5	168 8 2	1,594 3 0	12. Elgin.
38 15 6	13,620 14 6		16 1	1,566 16 1	5,173 18 11	13. Fife.
20,660 2 2	182 6 0		17 4	564 0 6	9,590 17 7	14. Forfar.
35 10 8	2,583 9 0		14 6	192 10 5	1,304 17 11	15. Haddington.
...	7,174 19 9		8 1	140 4 8	3,784 12 8	16. Inverness.
1,968 2 11	34 11 6		10 2	114 17 8	735 0 9	17. Kincardine.
...	652 13 11		6 2	125 4 9	219 0 1	18. Kinross.
2,140 12 0	8 0 5		15 9	58 15 7	992 7 6	19. Kirkcudbright.
83 18 6	65,347 0 7		9 6	4,956 6 6	30,328 6 8	20. Lanark.
2 19 8	2,583 9 11		0 10	200 18 3	1,144 14 10	21. Linlithgow.
...	832 3 10		14 6	87 14 0	321 13 3	22. Nairn.
1,288 10 8	1,105 19 1		17 3	135 14 2	924 7 8	23. Orkney.
...	1,060 14 1		9 7	72 10 6	357 14 2	24. Peebles.
33 2 8	9,395 5 4		10 2	1,194 14 5	4,284 14 3	25. Perth.
41 10 4	347 0 10	13,9...	8 7	1,383 16 7	5,653 8 4	26. Renfrew.
...	5,643 1 7		1 11	121 16 9	2,924 2 9	27. Ross.
7 2 5	3,515 19 8		17 9	403 4 7	1,370 11 11	28. Roxburgh.
23 12 9	1,406 18 7		1 1	171 4 3	533 16 4	29. Selkirk.
1,892 7 0	...		15 11	83 11 3	781 11 4	30. Shetland.
...	7,469 0 6		14 5	672 3 7	2,882 12 3	31. Stirling.
14 6 3	1,703 17 8		17 0	181 12 9	759 4 4	32. Sutherland.
1,070 15 6	26 15 7		17 11	44 0 1	766 10 4	33. Wigtown.
74,207 13 0	170,342 4 2	14,...	5 4	19,126 15 3	115,848 12 10	Totals and Averages.

APPENDIX A.—TABLE XXIV.

Expenditure by Parish Councils on account of Pauper Lunatics for each Year from 1859 to 1900–1901.

YEARS.	In Asylums, and Schools for Imbeciles.	In Lunatic Wards of Poorhouses.	In Private Dwellings.	For Certificates, Cost of Transport, &c.	Total Expenditure.
Average of 5 Years 1859–1868	61,735	14,695	14,763	4031	95,225
Average of 5 Years	73,416	19,241	15,157	4400	112,214
1869	99,754	11,415	15,509	5032	131,710
1870	102,248	10,978	15,826	4547	133,598
1871	102,769	10,799	16,167	4447	134,182
1872	104,545	10,869	17,018	4738	137,165
1873	115,778	10,702	17,211	5267	148,959
Average of 5 Years	105,018	10,952	16,345	4806	137,122
1874–75	124,663	11,758	17,098	4288	157,807
1875–76	130,776	12,530	17,340	4616	165,261
1876–77	137,879	13,302	17,890	4517	173,588
1877–78	147,015	13,029	18,088	5252	183,383
1878–79	151,056	13,332	18,518	5373	188,280
Average of 5 Years	138,278	12,790	17,787	4899	173,664
1879–80	155,333	13,101	19,366	5787	193,586
1880–81	161,145	13,788	20,533	5603	201,068
1881–82	168,448	12,958	21,830	6314	210,551
1882–83	168,140	13,970	24,593	6506	213,209
1883–84	166,938	14,148	26,449	6730	214,265
Average of 5 Years	164,061	13,793	22,554	6188	206,536
1884–85	169,681	14,641	28,184	6241	218,747
1885–86	170,170	15,855	31,203	6823	224,052
1886–87	169,725	16,604	33,107	6546	225,982
1887–88	168,336	16,186	34,717	6551	225,789
1888–89	170,688	15,887	35,662	7110	229,347
Average of 5 Years	169,720	15,835	32,575	6654	224,783
1889–90	174,671	15,962	38,256	7376	236,265
1890–91	180,627	16,665	39,175	7646	244,113
1891–92	186,831	17,115	39,435	8247	251,628
1892–93	189,102	16,476	40,781	8663	255,021
1893–94	191,590	16,570	42,389	9035	259,585
Average of 5 Years	184,564	16,558	40,007	8193	249,322
1894–95	197,994	15,842	44,172	9331	267,339
1895–96	207,691	15,023	44,959	9193	276,866
1896–97	215,849	15,646	44,618	9259	285,372
1897–98	228,486	16,280	43,994	10,118	298,878
1898–99	237,514	17,265	44,832	9,745	309,356
Average of 5 Years	217,507	16,011	44,515	9529	287,562
1899–1900	253,541	17,446	45,883	9,246	326,116
1900–1901	265,602	24,142	46,672	9,244	345,660

APPENDIX A.—TABLE XXV.

The Average Daily Cost of Maintenance of Pauper Lunatics in the different Classes of Establishments and in Private Dwellings in each of the Ten Years 1891–92 to 1900–1901.

ASYLUMS.	1891–2	1892–3	1893–4	1894–5	1895–6	1896–7	1897–8	1898–9	1899–1900	900–190
	s. d.	s. d.	s. d.	s. d.	s. d.	s. d.	s. d.	s. d.	s. d.	s. d.
In Royal and District Asylums, Private Asylums, Parochial Asylums, and Schools for Imbeciles,	1 4½	1 4½	1 4¼	1 4¼	1 4⅓	1 4⅔	1 5	1 5	1 5½	1 6
In Lunatic Wards of Poorhouses,	1 0¾	1 0½	1 0¾	1 0¼	0 11¾	1 0⅓	1 0	1 ½	1 0¾	1 3
In Private Dwellings,	0 10½	0 10¾	0 10¾	0 10¾	0 11	0 11	0 11	0 11	0 11¼	0 11½
GENERAL AVERAGES,	1 3¼	1 3¼	1 3¼	1 3¼	1 3½	1 3½	1 3¾	1 4¼	1 4¾	1 5

APPENDIX A.—Table XXVI.

The Daily Rate of Maintenance for each mode of providing for Pauper Lunatics in each County during the Year ending 15th May 1901.

COUNTIES.	In Royal, District, and Parochial Asylums, and Training Schools for Imbecile Children.	In Licensed Wards of Poorhouses with Restricted Licences.	In Private Dwellings.	General Averages. (This also includes the Extra Expenditure for Certificates of Lunacy, Cost of Transport, &c.)	Percentage of Patients.		
					In Royal, District, and Parochial Asylums, and Training Schools for Imbecile Children.	In Licens'd Wards of Poorhouses with Restricted Licences.	In Private Dwellings.
	s. d.	s. d.	s. d.	s. d.			
1. Aberdeen, .	1 3¾	1 0½	0 10½	1 6¼	67·3	20·0	12·7
2. Argyll, .	1 4¾	...	0 10½	1 4	79·1	...	20·9
3. Ayr, .	1 4½	0 11	0 9¾	1 3¼	73·5	15·3	11·2
4. Banff, .	1 0¼	...	0 9¾	1 0	70·2	...	29·8
5. Berwick, .	1 4½	...	0 10½	1 3¼	72·4	...	27·6
6. Bute, .	1 4¾	...	0 11¼	1 3¾	76·4	...	23·6
7. Caithness, .	1 6¼	...	0 9¼	1 3¾	65·3	2·9	31·8
8. Clackmannan, .	1 6	...	1 0½	1 5¼	72·5	5·7	21·8
9. Dumbarton, .	1 6½	0 10	1 1¼	1 5	69·0	18·8	12·2
10. Dumfries, .	1 3¾	...	0 11¼	1 3¾	87·7	...	12·3
11. Edinburgh, .	1 9¼	2 0¼	1 2½	1 8½	61·4	12·9	25·7
12. Elgin, .	1 1¼	...	0 10¼	1 1¼	79·7	...	20·3
13. Fife, .	1 5¾	...	1 0	1 5¼	84·1	0·1	15·8
14. Forfar, .	1 8¾	1 0½	1 0½	1 6¼	64·9	17·0	18·1
15. Haddington, .	1 2½	0 10	0 11¼	1 2¼	80·8	10·7	8·5
16. Inverness, .	1 5½	...	0 8½	1 2	56·3	...	43·7
17. Kincardine, .	1 8¼	0 10¾	0 11	1 6¼	73·7	18·6	7·7
18. Kinross, .	1 6	...	1 0¼	1 5½	85·8	...	14·2
19. Kirkcudbright, .	1 4	...	0 10¾	1 3½	82·3	...	17·7
20. Lanark, .	1 5¼	1 3½	1 1	1 4¾	76·8	6·8	16·4
21. Linlithgow, .	1 6	1 3¾	0 11½	1 5½	74·4	16·2	9·4
22. Nairn, .	1 5¼	...	0 11	1 4¾	83·6	...	16·4
23. Orkney, .	1 9	...	0 8½	1 6	65·0	...	35·0
24. Peebles, .	1 8½	...	1 0	1 8	88·5	...	11·5
25. Perth, .	1 5¼	1 2	1 1	1 4¾	72·1	6·2	21·7
26. Renfrew, .	1 5	...	1 2	1 5	87·6	...	12·4
27. Ross, .	1 5¼	...	0 8	1 1¾	54·9	...	45·1
28. Roxburgh, .	1 4½	...	1 1	1 4½	88·6	...	11·4
29. Selkirk, .	1 4¾	...	0 10	1 4½	89·0	...	11·0
30. Shetland, .	1 8¾	...	0 6½	1 3¼	53·9	2·3	43·8
31. Stirling, .	1 6¼	1 1	1 0¾	1 6	84·1	2·4	13·5
32. Sutherland, .	1 5½	...	0 8	1 2¾	62·5	1·0	36·5
33. Wigtown, .	1 4¼	1 0¼	0 11¼	1 2¾	50·7	23·4	25·9
General Averages,	1 6	1 3	0 11½	1 5	72·4	7·9	19·7

APPENDIX A.—TABLE XXVII.

Present Rates of Board per annum in Royal and District Asylums and in Training Schools, and the estimated Annual Cost of Patients in Parochial Asylums and Poorhouses.

ROYAL OR CHARTERED ASYLUMS.	Rates for Pauper Patients.		Minimum Rates for Private Patients.*	
	From the District.	From beyond the District.	Special or District Rate.	General Rate.
	£ s. d.	£ s. d.	£ s. d.	£ s. d.
Aberdeen Royal Asylum, . .	23 0 0	...	...	30 0 0
Crichton „ „	24 0 0	...	25 0 0	40 0 0
Dundee „ „ . .	22 10 0	...	22 10 0	22 10 0
Edinburgh „ „ . .	23 0 0	23 0 0	...	31 0 0
Glasgow „ „ . .	...	...	...	40 0 0
Montrose „ „ . .	22 0 0	24 0 0	25 0 0	42 0 0
Murray's „ „ . .	...	...	30 0 0	54 0 0
DISTRICT ASYLUMS.				
Argyll & Bute District Asylum,	27 14 3	...	27 14 3	29 0 0
Ayr „ „	27 6 0	...	...	...
Banff „ „	18 5 0	...	...	...
Elgin „ „	22 0 0	30 0 0	25 0 0	30 0 0
Fife „ „	27 0 0	...	35 0 0	...
Glasgow District Asylum (Gartloch)	26 0 0	...	...	...
Glasgow „ „ (Woodilee)	26 0 0	...	...	...
Govan „ „	31 4 8	...	...	33 0 0
Haddington „ „	23 0 0	...	30 0 0	40 0 0
Inverness „ „	24 0 0	...	35 0 0	...
Kirklands Asylum, Bothwell,	24 14 0	...	...	...
Lanark District Asylum,	29 15 0	32 0 0	...	32 0 0
Midlothian „ „	24 0 0	...	34 0 0	40 0 0
Perth „ „	26 0 0	...	...	...
Roxburgh „ „	23 0 0	...	26 0 0	40 0 0
Stirling „ „	26 0 0	31 10 0	35 0 0	40 0 0

PAROCHIAL ASYLUMS.	‡Estimated Annual Cost of Patients belonging to Parish or Combination.	Rates charged for Board-ers from other Parishes.	PAROCHIAL ASYLUMS. (Continued.)	‡Estimated Annual Cost of Patients belonging to Parish or Combination.	Rates charged for Board-ers from other Parishes.
	£ s. d.	£ s. d.		£ s. d.	£ s. d.
Greenock Parochial Asylum, . . .	27 1 8	32 10 0	Paisley (Riccartsbar),	26 3 4	32 10 0
Paisley (Craw Road),	26 15 5	32 10 0			

LUNATIC WARDS OF POORHOUSES.			LUNATIC WARDS OF POORHOUSES. (Continued.)		
Aberdeen (East), .	22 8 6	23 8 0	Govan, . . .	27 1 8	...
Aberdeen (West), .	21 6 10	23 8 0	Inveresk, . . .	19 13 3	...
Buchan, . .	15 17 5	...	Kincardine, . .	17 17 2	30 0 0
Cunninghame, . .	21 12 4	...	Linlithgow, . .	23 12 10	22 15 0
Dumbarton, . .	20 10 7	...	Old Monkland, .	21 11 2	22 2 0
Dundee, East, .	23 10 2	...	Perth, . . .	20 13 10	...
Dundee, West, .	20 6 3	...	Wigtown, . .	18 5 0	20 17 0
Edinburgh, . .	23 0 7	...			

TRAINING SCHOOLS FOR IMBECILE CHILDREN.	Rates charged for Pauper Patients.	Minimum Rate for Private Patients.
		£ s. d.
Baldovan	£25	25 0 0
Larbert	£27 10 0 and £30	42 0 0

* Most, if not all, of the Royal Asylums receive special cases at lower rates.
‡ The rent is taken as the proportion allocated to the lunatic wards of the gross rental in the valuation roll for the year, divided by the number of inmates for which the wards are licensed.

APPENDIX A.—TABLE XXVIII

The Expenditure of District Lunacy Boards during the Financial Year 1900–1901, in Providing, Building, Repairing, and Fitting up and Furnishing District Asylums; and the amount of Monies Borrowed and Assessed for by District Lunacy Boards under the provisions of the Act 20 & 21 Vict., c. 71.

DISTRICT ASYLUMS.	Providing Expenditure from 18th May 1900 to 16th May 1901.												Amount of Monies Borrowed remaining due as at 16th May 1901.	Assessments for Lunacy Purposes on the Landward parts of Counties and Burghs of each District in the year to 15th May 1901.	Amount of Assessment raised for or applied to Reduction of Debt.
	Land.		Buildings, Improvements, Alterations, and Additions. 4.	Expenditure on Farm (Erection of Buildings and Improvements). 5.	† Furniture and Furnishings. 6.	Miscellaneous Expenses. 7.	Interests on Monies Borrowed. 8.	Total Expenditure under Heads 1 to 8. 9.	‡ Deduct Proportion payable to the Providing Account of Profit on keeping Private Patients, Rent of Lands, &c. 10.	Net Providing Expenditure excluding Instalments of Loans repaid. (See Col. 14.) 11.				
	Purchase of Land other than Feued Lands. 1.	* Rent or Feu-duty of Asylum Grounds. 2.	Total. 3.									12.	13.	14.
1. Aberdeen,		21	21	4,313	165	949	467	5,907	380	5,537	13,553	2,140	467
2. {Argyll, § {Bute, §		31	31	3,010		457	484	4,460	172 143	4,369	} 15,233	3,000	1,161 210
3. Ayr,		140	140	4,718		67	50	117	108		1,879	635	210
4. Banff,	625	24	24	1,864		157	688	5,750		5,537	23,010	8,600	1,460
5. Edinburgh,		435	435	497	459	4,975	43	1,147	728	1,147	990	483	90
6. Elgin,		29	29	1,004		64	1,444	9,086	191	8,940	87,648	5,399	1,922
7. Fife,						625	389	866	487	694	8,019	1,000	414
8. Glasgow {Gartloch}, {Woodilee}							1,372	3,494		3,007	83,134	8,600	1,706
9. Govan,		21	21	18,668		1,488	1,388	4,301	374	22,267	200,063	15,313	17,973
10. Haddington,		19	19	3,080	2,171	1,015	1,393	4,117	1,834	16,402	140,655	16,184	7,889
11. Inverness,		4	4	4,953		879	784	6,480	394	11,306	185,137	12,701	811
12. Lanark,		384	384	9,293	74	777	101	1,393	107	1,286	6,104	302	1,729
13. Midlothian,		110	110	6,454	148	1,290	698	13,659	102	13,557	42,440	5,300	9,146
14. Perth,		168	168	22,774	31	87	1,177	14,002	1,994	12,418	213,021	17,700	4,122
15. Renfrew,		16	16	2,915		1,809	691	26,386	50	26,336	61,602	6,000	1,245
16. Roxburgh,				2,477			208	767	89	2,626	32,728	2,400	1,810
17. Stirling,		107	107	9,407	400	425 180	668	1,101 2,291	169 379	2,632 6,561	35,224 68,744	4,150 6,400	2,010 2,544
Totals,	626	1,320	1,835	96,943	8,407	7,804	14,887	167,492	6,529	160,963	1,190,692	107,169	54,816

* Rents or feu-duties of farm lands proper form a part of the Maintenance Expenditure, and appear in Table XXXII, showing the receipts and expenses of Asylum farms.
† Under this heading appears such expenditure as is needed for the complete equipment of the Asylum and additions to it, and articles rendered necessary by increase of population. The Current Expenditure under this heading is given in the Table following.
‡ The profit from private patients is divided equally between the Providing and Maintenance Accounts.
§ The Counties of Argyll and Bute, although served by one District Asylum, have separate District Lunacy Boards. The expenditure stated for Argyll Asylum under heads 1 to 6 inclusive is the combined expenditure of the two Boards; the transactions of each Board under other heads are, however, shown separately.

ASYLUMS.	Average Number of Patients Resident during the Financial Year.	MAINTENANCE EXPENDITURE FROM									
		1. Butcher Meat, Fresh, Cured, and Tinned; Condensed Preparations of Meat, Poultry, and Game.		2. Fish, Fresh and Cured.		11. Fresh and Dry Fruits and Minor Articles of Food.		12. Tobacco.		13. Household Requisites.	
		Total.	Per Patient.	Total.	Per Patient.	Total.	Per Patient.	Total.	Per Male Patient.	Total.	Per Patient.
		£	£ s. d.	£	£ s. d.	£	£ s. d.	£	£ s. d.	£	£ s. d
1. Argyll, . . .	434	1414	3 5 2	265	0 12 3	101	0 4 8	132	0 11 11	111	0 5 1
2. Ayr, . . .	488	1189	2 8 9	163	0 7 6	102	0 4 2	141	0 12 7	79	0 3 3
3. Banff, . . .	168	346	2 2 5	30	0 3 8	25	0 3 1	37	0 8 8	23	0 2 10
4. Elgin, . . .	182	492	2 14 1	51	0 5 7	78	0 8 7	51	0 13 5	32	0 9 0
5. Fife, . . .	533	2287	4 3 11	121	0 4 6	268	0 10 1	103	0 8 6	316	0 11 10
6. Glasgow (Gartloch),	522	1626	3 2 4	211	0 8 1	242	0 9 3	103	0 7 7	261	0 10 0
7. Glasgow (Woodilee),	818	2359	2 17 8	407	0 9 11	178	0 4 4	216	0 10 6	106	0 2 7
8. Govan, . . .	442	1659	3 13 5	131	0 5 11	194	0 8 7	148	0 13 9	84	0 3 9
9. Haddington, . .	185	348	2 11 7	39	0 5 9	65	0 9 3	40	0 13 7	64	0 9 6
10. Inverness, . .	583	1960	3 7 3	179	0 6 2	205	0 7 0	196	0 13 1	353	0 12 1
11. Kirklands, . .	179	478	2 13 5	38	0 4 3	92	0 10 3	41	0 9 1	68	0 7 7
12. Lanark, . . .	690	1582	2 4 5	483	0 14 0	181	0 5 3	186	0 10 2	309	0 8 11
13. Midlothian, . .	248	682	2 15 0	75	0 6 1	131	0 10 7	57	0 9 5	138	0 11 2
14. Perth, . . .	358	1148	3 4 2	92	0 5 2	113	0 6 4	75	0 8 1	196	0 10 11
15. Roxburgh, . .	298	853	2 17 3	148	0 9 11	102	0 6 10	69	0 10 0	107	0 7 2
16. Stirling, . . .	657	2231	3 7 11	259	0 7 11	281	0 8 7	212	0 12 8	544	0 15 7
Totals and Averages,	6740	20554	3 1 0	2715	0 8 1	2356	0 7 0	1807	0 10 10	2841	0 8 5

those payable out of the Poor Rate. The expenses in
tted, and all fractions above ½d. have been reckoned
the replacement or repair of what has been worn

15th MAY 1900 TO 15th MAY 1901.

	14.		15.		16.		21.		22.	23.		
	Laundry Requisites.		Clothing, Boots, and Shoes.		Medicines and Surgical Appliances	TOTAL MAINTENANCE EXPENSES.			DEDUCT OR ADD, AS THE CASE MAY BE:—Profit or Loss on Farm and Garden, Profit from keeping Private Patients, Receipts for Work done by Patients or Attendants other than for Asylums, &c.	NET MAINTENANCE EXPENSES.		ASYLUMS.
Total.	Per Patient.	Total.	Per Patient.	Total.	Per Patient	Per Patient.				Total.	Per Patient.	
£	£ s. d.	£	£ s. d.	£	£ s.	£ s. d.			£	£	£ s. d.	
73	0 3 4	682	1 11 5	105	0 4	27 9 4			— 91	11829	27 5 1	1. Argyll.
158	0 6 6	847	1 14 9	160	0 6	28 0 2			— 383	13366	27 4 6	2. Ayr.
73	0 3 11	168	1 0 7	44	0 5	20 19 9			— 505	2916	17 17 9	3. Banff.
46	0 5 1	336	1 15 10	42	0 4	23 2 5			— 252	3956	21 14 9	4. Elgin.
212	0 7 11	1013	1 18 0	129	0 4	26 16 4			— 618	13675	25 13 2	5. Fife.
156	0 6 0	1149	2 4 0	119	0 4	29 3 6			— 276	14954	28 12 11	6. Glasgow (Gartloch).
227	0 5 7	1821	2 4 6	262	0 6	25 14 3			— 563	20471	25 0 6	7. Glasgow (Woodilee).
161	0 7 1	715	1 11 8	139	0 6	33 8 5			— 662	14444	31 19 1	8. Govan.
23	0 3 5	172	1 5 6	44	0 6	25 1 4			— 142	3242	24 0 4	9. Haddington.
205	0 7 0	1219	2 1 10	107	0 3	26 13 7			— 454	15101	25 15 1	10. Inverness.
53	0 5 11	276	1 10 10	64	0 7	26 0 11			— 16	4646	25 19 1	11. Kirklands.
142	0 4 1	1067	1 10 11	211	0 6	25 1 4			— 711	14584	24 10 8	12. Lanark.
51	0 4 1	412	1 13 3	84	0 6	33 2 1			+ 436	8646	34 17 3	13. Midlothian.
136	0 7 7	660	1 16 10	113	0 6	28 8 11			— 147	10037	28 0 9	14. Perth.
116	0 7 9	442	1 9 3	59	0 4	30 9 2			— 306	8770	29 8 7	15. Roxburgh.
248	0 7 7	1515	2 6 1	280	0 8	29 0 6			— 467	18603	28 6 4	16. Stirling.
2980	0 6 2	12484	1 17 1	1962	0 5	27 12 10			—5157	181160	26 17 7	Totals and Averages.

connection with land, buildings, furnishings, &c.

as 1d.

out or destroyed. The cost of furniture and fur

and of Tobacco and Fuel, supp

ASYLUMS.	Average Number of Inmates.			1. Fresh Butcher Meat.		2. Cured Butcher Meat.		3. Tinned Butcher Meat.		4. Poultry and Game.		12. Cheese.		13. Bread.		14. Flour.	
	Patients.	Officers and Servants Boarded.	Total.	Quantity per Inmate.	Price per cwt.	Quantity per Inmate.	Price per cwt.	Quantity per Inmate.	Price per cwt.	Quantity per Inmate.	Price per cwt.	Quantity per Inmate.	Price per cwt.	Quantity per Inmate.	Price per cwt.	Quantity per Inmate.	Price per cwt.
				lbs.	£ s. d.	lbs.	£ s. d.	lbs.	£ s. d.	lbs.	£ s. d.	lbs.	£ s. d.	lbs.	£ s. d	lbs.	£ s.
1. Argyll, .	434	62	496	109	2 8 5	3	3 4 5	16	2 14 9 (²) .	.	10	2 6 7	.	.	300	0 16
2. Ayr, . .	488	76	564	77	2 8 0 (²) .	.	.	17	2 13 4 (²) .	.	13	3 4 0	93	0 13 3	207	0 9
3. Banff, .	163	19	182	71	2 16 10 (²) .	.	.	1	2 14 10	5	2 2 0 9	1 18 3	428	0 7 7	9	0 11
4. Elgin, . .	182	25	207	85	3 0 0	2	5 4 9	.	.	1	2 16 8 14	2 6 11	337	0 8 9	18	1 0
5. Fife, . .	533	73	606	125	2 19 4 (²) .	.	.	12	3 5 0 (²) .	.	17	2 11 0	396	0 9 11	25	0 9
6. Glasgow (Gartloch),	522	85	607	95	2 13 5	3	3 5 4	13	2 11 3	2	3 2 9 5	2 14 6	301	0 9 1	12	0 8
7. Glasgow (Woodilee),	818	122	940	86	2 15 6	3	3 5 2	13	2 8 1 (²) .	.	4	2 11 11	13	0 13 5	268	0 8
8. Govan, .	452	86	538	120	2 13 2	8	3 2 5	.	.	(²) .	5	2 16 2	41	0 10 9	231	0 9
9. Haddington,	135	16	151	92	2 14 3 (²) .	.	.	2	2 18 6 (²) .	.	4	2 14 1	324	0 10 3	20	0 11
10. Inverness, .	583	90	673	115	2 18 9	1	5 2 11	2	2 15 6	1	3 9 2 7	2 11 5	333	0 9 11	29	0 10
11. Kirklands, .	179	34	213	86	2 6 4	3	5 3 10	13	2 13 8 (²) .	.	7	2 17 4	300	0 9 4	29	0 11
12. Lanark, .	690	105	795	91	2 5 1 (²) .	.	.	3	2 10 5 (²) .	.	3	3 4 2	.	.	245	0 8
13. Midlothian, .	248	39	287	96	2 6 2	2	4 2 2	11	3 6 3 (²) .	.	11	2 14 7	361	0 9 8	14	0 11
14. Perth, .	356	55	413	93	2 9 3	1	4 13 5	29	2 13 6 (²) .	.	5	2 3 1	330	0 10 2	21	0 9
15. Roxburgh, .	298	37	335	97	2 10 9	1	4 3 1	10	2 19 2 (²) .	.	0	2 18 6	366	0 9 10	15	0 9
16. Stirling, .	657	107	764	85	2 17 5	2	5 9 2	24	2 17 3	2	2 19 6 7	2 11 1	.	.	284	0
Totals & Averages,	6740	1031	7771	95	2 12 4	3	4 5 2	12	2 15 10	2	2 18 0 9	2 12 9	(¹)345 49	0 10 4	(¹)256 19	0 9

Table **XXX.**

to each District Asylum, during th

| | 15. | | 16. | | 17. | | 25. | | 26. | | 27. | | 28. | | 29. | |
	Meal.		Barley.		Peas, &c.		Tea.		Wines and Spirits.		Malt Liquors.		Tobacco.		Fuel.		ASYLUMS.
Quantity per inmate.	Price per cwt.	Quantity per inmate.	Price per cwt.	Quantity per inmate.	Price per cwt	Quantity per inmate.	Price per cwt.	Quantity per inmate.	Price per gal.	Quantity per inmate.	Price per gal.	Quantity per Male Patient.	Price per cwt.	Quantity per inmate.	Price per ton.	
lbs.	£ s. d.	lbs.	£ s. d.	lbs.	£ s.	lbs.	£ s. d.	gills.	£ s. d.	pints.	£ s. d.	ozs.	£ s. d.	cwts.	£ s. d.	
7	0 10 2	18	0 9 0	7	0 9	6	8 1 3	1	0 16 0	1	0 0 11	51	21 0 6	61	0 16 10	1. Argyll.
82	0 10 6	7	0 9 5	39	0 11	6	8 3 4	10	0 17 3	.	.	56	19 13 2	75	0 12 2	2. Ayr.
16	0 10 5	12	0 9 9	22	0 9	5	7 19 2	3	0 18 10	10	0 0 9	36	21 13 7	83	1 3 11	3. Banff.
34	0 10 11	15	0 6 0	11	0 6	8	7 0 2	4	0 12 1	28	0 0 9	61	19 13 9	35	1 4 3	4 Elgin.
6	0 11 4	11	0 8 7	29	0 10	4	7 5 6	5	0 16 5	3	0 1 5	38	19 17 7	60	0 11 1	5. Fife.
46	0 11 3	6	0 10 3	7	0 12	6	7 18 8	1	0 16 2	1	0 2 0	35	19 6 8	116	0 12 3	6. Glasgow (Gartloch).
44	0 12 8	13	0 10 7	20	0 13	7	7 18 8	1	0 15 9	1	0 2 0	48	19 14 11	53	0 13 4	7. Glasgow (Woodilee).
44	0 10 11	3	0 8 10	14	0 8	7	8 4 8	2	0 19 5	.	.	60	20 12 4	143	0 12 6	8. Govan.
34	0 14 7	22	0 8 7	4	0 9	4	8 4 3	5	0 16 5	38	0 0 11	55	22 4 6	34	0 16 2	9. Haddington.
39	0 10 10	22	0 8 1	21	0 9	5	8 5 2	4	0 17 4	5	0 1 4	55	21 6 1	51	0 19 11	10. Inverness.
23	0 10 1	12	0 9 2	20	0 11	6	8 8 5	6	0 18 2	4	0 2 0	39	21 0 0	55	0 13 1	11. Kirklands.
4	0 11 8	8	0 9 4	19	0 12	6	7 12 0	3	0 19 3	2	0 2 0	43	21 6 11	103	0 11 8	12. Lanark.
36	0 11 10	9	0 8 10	25	0 11	5	8 8 0	8	0 18 0	2	0 1 3	48	19 10 1	127	0 11 6	13. Midlothian.
53	0 10 7	11	0 9 5	22	0 9	4	8 3 4	3	0 10 7	16	0 0 9	35	20 17 2	46	0 17 11	14. Perth.
54	0 11 11	12	0 9 9	21	0 10	5	8 17 4	1	1 5 4	11	0 1 7	41	22 3 1	84	0 16 7	15. Roxburgh.
54	0 11 6	19	0 8 2	22	0 9	5	8 13 11	5	0 17 5	7	0 1 11	56	20 9 2	76	0 9 8	16. Stirling.
75	0 11 4	13	0 9 0	19	0 10	6	8 1 6	4	0 17 2	9	0 1 5	47	20 13 1	72	0 15 2	Totals & Averages.

were respectively in asylums which do, and wh
dietary, but the quantity used was below 1 l

APPENDIX A.—TABLE XXXI.

Quantities and Estimated Values of Articles supplied to District Asylums from Asylum Farms and Gardens during the Financial Year 1900–1901; and the Prices at which the Produce supplied has been Estimated.

Quantities and Estimated Value of Supplies to Asylums from Asylum Farms and Gardens.

Farms and Gardens* of District Asylums.	Butcher Meat.		Poultry and Game.		Milk.		Butter.		Eggs.		Potatoes.		Green Vegetables.		Fresh Fruits.		Sundries.	Total Estimated Value.
	cwt.	£	lbs.	£	gals.	£	lbs.	£	lbs.	£	cwt.	£	cwt.	£	lbs.	£	£	£
1. Argyll,	190	444	50	2	23442	777	.	.	310	8	327	70	542	161	396	5	88	1555
2. Ayr,	.	.	.	.	.	.	.	.	.	.	.	.	441	151	438	6	47	204
3. Banff,	67	201	900	17	7360	307	.	.	887	22	324	49	162	55	1305	10	97	758
4. Elgin,	.	.	228	6	6864	228	.	.	832	21	369	55	214	57	1540	7	.	374
5. Fife,	383	1012	.	.	27668	850	.	.	.	.	1100	194	916	201	1646	18	25	2300
6. Glasgow (Gartloch),	475	1291	896	25	20999	826	780	46	1192	44	1324	286	577	125	1150	13	476	3132
7. Glasgow (Woodilee),	723	2006	364	10	35838	1493	.	.	1809	70	1177	254	954	197	2129	22	388	4440
8. Govan	.	.	30	1	25768	966	308	21	871	29	500	98	449	170	.	.	286	1521
9. Haddington,	27	70	.	.	4401	184	.	.	920	20	227	57	140	38	2604	29	17	415
10. Inverness,	365	1060	.	.	.	.	.	.	.	.	666	183	381	135	88	1	35	1364
11. *Kirklands,	3	9	52	2	.	.	.	.	299	11	340	77	249	41	1294	9	1	150
12. Lanark,	5	9	246	7	29625	1043	656	38	1442	56	1150	226	721	186	3572	22	48	1635
13. Midlothian,	12	42	64	2	12532	522	.	.	456	19	302	61	412	73	6790	34	83	836
14. Perth,	.	.	90	2	10610	383	.	.	361	9	447	55	677	174	2936	28	30	681
15. *Roxburgh,	40	100	.	.	.	.	.	.	.	.	59	10	300	88	1689	25	5	228
16. Stirling,	28	67	.	.	.	.	.	.	32	1	1001	186	1298	238	1260	18	80	590
Totals and Averages,	2318	6311	2920	74	200307	7579	1741	105	9411	310	8313	1811	8433	2090	38837	247	1656	20183

Prices at which Produce supplied to Asylums has been Estimated.

Farms and Gardens* of District Asylums.	Butcher Meat.	Poultry and Game.	Milk.	Butter.	Eggs.	Potatoes.	Green Vegetables.	Fresh Fruits.
	per cwt. £ s. d.	per cwt. £ s. d.	per gal. £ s. d.	per cwt. £ s. d.	per cwt. £ s. d.	per cwt. £ s. d.	per cwt. £ s. d.	per cwt. £ s. d.
1. Argyll.	2 6 9	4 9 6	0 0 8	.	2 17 10	0 4 8	0 5 11	1 8 3
2. Ayr.	.	.	.	.	.	.	0 6 10	1 10 8
3. Banff.	3 0 0	2 2 4	0 0 10	.	2 15 7	0 3 0	0 6 9	17 2
4. Elgin.	.	18 11	0 0 8	.	2 16 6	0 3 0	0 5 4	0 10 2
5. Fife.	2 12 10	.	0 0 9	.	.	0 3 6	0 4 5	1 4 6
6. Glasgow (Gartloch).	2 14 4	3 2 6	0 0 9	6 12 1	4 2 8	0 4 4	0 4 4	1 5 4
7. Glasgow Woodilee),	2 15 6	3 1 6	0 0 10	.	4 6 8	0 4 4	0 4 2	1 3 2
8. Govan.	.	3 14 8	0 0 9	7 15 3	3 14 7	0 3 11	0 7 7	.
9. Haddington.	2 11 10	.	0 0 10	.	2 8 8	0 5 0	0 5 5	1 5 0
10 nverness	2 18 1	.	.	.	.	0 4 0	0 7 1	1 5 5
11. *Kirklands.	3 0 0	4 6 2	.	.	4 2 5	0 4 6	0 3 4	0 15 7
12. Lanark.	1 16 0	3 3 9	0 0 8	6 9	4 7 0	0 3 11	5 2	0 13 10
13. Midlothian.	3 10 0	3 10 0	0 0 10	.	4 13 4	0 4 0	0 3 7	0 11 3
14. Perth.	.	2 9 9	0 0 9	.	2 15 10	0 2 6	0 5 2	1 1 4
15. *Roxburgh.	2 10 0	.	.	.	.	0 3 5	0 5 10	1 18 2
16. Stirling.	2 7 10	.	.	.	3 10 0	0 3 9	0 3 8	1 12 0
Totals and Averages.	2 14 5	2 16 9	0 0 9	6 15 1	3 13 9	0 4 4	0 4 11	0 19 2

* Those marked with an asterisk are gardens only.

C

APPENDIX A.—TABLE XXXII.

Acreage of Farms attached to District Asylums; Receipts and Expenses of such Farms and Gardens during the Financial Year 1900–1901; and Profit shown on the Year's Transactions.

FARMS AND GARDENS* or DISTRICT ASYLUMS.	Acreage of Farm and Garden.			Receipts.															Expenditure.											Profit + or Loss —.
	Arable or in Pasture, manured Pasture*	Non-Arable	Total	Valuation of Stock at 16th May 1901	2. Butcher Meat	3. Poultry and Game	4. Milk	5. Butter and Cheese	6. Eggs	7. Potatoes	8. Green Vegetables	9. Fresh Fruits	10. Grain	11. Live Stock	12. Wool, Hides, Skins	13. Grazing, Cartage, and Sundries	14. Total	1. Valuation of Stock at 16th May 1900	2. Rents	3. Interest on Unpaid Outlay from Providing Account of Stock and Implements	4. Live Stock	5. Implements and Harness	6. Seeds and Plants	7. Fodder, Roots, and Feeding Stuffs	8. Manures	9. Paid Labour	10. Miscellaneous	11. Total	
1. Argyll,	20	19	39	1086	444		529		5	70	161			206	24	205	2439	1043	40	54	406	24	24	1092	5	208	143	2154	+ 18
2. Ayr,	60	9	69	290							131	6		583		97	1067	1043	30		576	16	49			306	1	664	— 383
3. Banff,	206	10	216	1407	201	17	307	22		69	55	10	194	375	15	28	2696	177	100		99	29	29	121	48	77	39	2139	+ 548
4. Edinburgh,	660	118	778	3657		6			31	43	90	7	108	1747		265	5708	1662	166	100	949	134	109	166	36	125	129	4655	+ 50
5. Elgin,	108	5	118	1009	1018	6	598	31		43	201	18	108	243	57	8	1788	680	363		113	43	43	43	37	43	97	1387	+ 179
6. Fife,	229	5	234	1450		25	557		73	194	106	16	22	244		120	4370	950	302	36	100	109	50	100	28	108	132	2731	+ 520
7. Glasgow (Gartloch),	183	140	323	3070	3004	35	841	46	73	286	135	13	22	175	108	221	6380	2048	166		1990	79	71	318	184	444	569	5310	+ 570
8. Glasgow (Woodilee),	409	5	414	8901		11	1670	73	29	254	197	22	260	440	128	168	9155	1840	632	21	1840	123	117	1044	143	466	296	6092	+ 442
9. Govan,	99	47	146	7113	70	5	1310	21		96	170			747		225	4729	1069	1160		786	23	117	610	8	301	242	4216	+ 519
10. Haddington,	125	6	141	998			184		30	188	38	29	184	318	2	1840	3196	1082	478		383	28	12		24	31	30	2123	+ 63
11. Inverness,	116	60	176	1044	1090				11	138	135	1		71	97	189	5810	877	94		778	22		116	44	110	48	2169	+ 448
12. *Kirkland,	15		15							77	41	9		86		1	288		52		8		30	48	7	113	9	392	+ 6
13. Lanark,	246	325	571	1994	9	8	1043	68	23	296	168	33		1894	15	73	4623	1789	200		919	29	104	676	201	206	190	4637	+ 498
14. Midlothian,	735	3	328	1890	42		948	19	9	61	83	85	96	810		90	2770	1395	378		350	63	164	325	201	434	78	2848	+ 678
15. Perth,	60	34	108	461	100	3	335			25	174	39	94	319		30	1455		90		170	80	30	241	31	111	49	1288	— 168
16. *Roxburgh,	23	45	68	163					11	10	58	18	5	72	8	21	485	443	10		104	30	25		37	60	6	866	+ 130
17. Stirling,	67		67	957	66			1		186	288			814	11	118	2498	911	154		465	74	135	85	45	168	109	2164	+ 260

* Those marked with an asterisk are gardens only.　　† Includes proceeds of sale of stones from Quarry, and House Rent.

APPENDIX B.

ENTRIES MADE BY THE COMMISSIONERS IN THE PATIENTS'
BOOKS OF ASYLUMS AND POORHOUSES.

ROYAL AND DISTRICT ASYLUMS.

Appendix B.

Commissioners'
Entries.

Royal and
District
Asylums.

Aberdeen
Royal Asylum.

ABERDEEN ROYAL ASYLUM,
3rd, 4th, and *5th April* 1901.

The changes which have taken place in the population of the asylum since
last visit are as follows :—

	PRIVATE PATIENTS.		PAUPER PATIENTS.		TOTALS.
	M.	F.	M.	F.	
On Register 22nd October 1900,	115	137	278	349	879
Admitted, ...	18	20	47	41	126
Discharged recovered, . .	4	11	22	19	56
,, unrecovered, . .	1	2	7	11	21
Died, ...	4	5	11	14	34
On Register 3rd April 1901, .	124	139	285	346	894

In the above figures effect has been given to the transference since last visit
of 1 male and 1 female from the private to the pauper list, and of 3 females
from the pauper to the private list. With the exception of 1 man and 2
women absent on statutory probation all the patients were resident and were
seen during the visit.

The following are the assigned causes of the 34 deaths—gross brain disease,
7 cases ; heart disease, 6 cases ; phthisis and tuberculosis, 4 cases ; pneumonia
and congestion of lungs, 4 cases ; senile decay, 4 cases ; general paralysis, 3 cases ;
enteritis and colitis, 3 cases ; and cancer, bronchitis, and epilepsy, 1 case each.
Post mortem examinations were made in 22 instances.

There are no entries in the Register of Accidents or in the Register of
Escapes. There are 21 entries in the Register of Restraint and Seclusion.
These refer to the restraint of two female patients on account of violence, the
one on four occasions for two hours on each occasion, the other on seventeen
occasions for one day on each occasion. Both patients are impulsive and
dangerous, and both have previously been the cause of augmenting considerably
the record of restraints in this asylum. The total number of patients engaged
in work was 411 ; of these 174 were men and 237 women.

Eight attendants and nurses have resigned and 19 have been engaged since
last visit. The causes of the disparity between these figures are that an
increased number of nurses and attendants had to be engaged on account of
the new additions to the hospital buildings, and that the night staff has been
increased. There are now 13 attendants on night duty in the whole asylum,
being a proportion of 1 attendant to about 68 patients. Of these 3 men and
3 women are on duty in the main asylum ; 3 men and 3 women in the

D

hospital, and 1 woman at Elmhill. The newly admitted cases, the epileptics, the sick, and a certain proportion of those whose habits are faulty are under constant night supervision. It would be advantageous if this system were extended to all those patients who are noisy, restless, or careless in their habits at night, but the smallness of the dormitories and the large number of single rooms in the old buildings make it a difficult matter to include that class of patient, although they of all others have, in other asylums, been observed to benefit most by night nursing. But until the old buildings are reconstructed internally there is no prospect of such an extended scheme being put into effect.

The population of the asylum has increased by 15 since last visit. Fortunately the opening of the admission wards in connection with the hospital and the restoration of the buildings at Daviot have postponed the overcrowding with which the asylum was threatened. In one or two of the male wards in the old asylum there was apparent overcrowding, for these wards are so small and so unadaptable that excess in the number of patients occupying them produce an uncomfortable degree of congestion. It is hoped that no unreasonable delay may occur in carrying out the proposed alteration of the older asylum buildings, for their present condition is not compatible with modern requirements for the medical treatment of the insane.

The admission blocks for new cases in connection with the hospitals are a marked improvement and provide for an accurate and satisfactory classification of the patients. The hospital divisions now afford separate accommodation for newly-admitted cases, for sick and infirm cases, and for convalescent cases. The provision for the latter is highly commendable for it largely prevents recoverable cases from passing into the chronic wards of the asylum. The fittings and equipment of the new divisions are in every respect excellent and quite in keeping with those of the earlier constructed parts of the hospital. It would have increased the efficiency of these divisions if in addition provision had been made for the bed treatment of some of the recent cases of insanity, but when the reconstruction of the main building is completed, means no doubt will be found for putting into effect this highly advantageous adjunct to the treatment of the insane, which is certain in the near future to become an important feature in modern asylum administration.

The condition of the patients was highly satisfactory. They were, as a general rule, suitably and warmly clothed ; they bore evidence in their appearance of an adequate dietary ; and there was throughout the wards an absence of noise, excitement, or discontent. The complaints made by individual patients had no reference to their treatment or to the administration of the institution. The various wards and dormitories were in good order, and the beds, and their coverings, were everywhere found comfortable and clean.

The accommodation for private patents at Elmhill continues to deserve the commendation with which it has been referred to in previous reports. Elmhill Villa, immediately adjoining Elmhill, has been prepared for the reception of patients and is now occupied by 16 ladies. The rooms in this house have been tastefully furnished and decorated, and electric light has been introduced. This villa forms a valuable addition to the accommodation for patients paying the higher rates of board.

The Daviot Branch of the asylum has been restored and is now occupied by 49 men and 41 women. The rearrangement of the buildings is an improvement on the older form, and the furnishing and decoration of the interior are pleasing and comfortable. This mansion house affords commodious and in all respects satisfactory accommodation for the pauper patients occupying it, while the arable land in connection with it, the gardens, the laundry, kitchen, and general house work, provide ample and suitable employment for the inmates, all of whom were engaged in some kind of useful work at the time of the visit.

The case books and the registers of the asylum were examined and found carefully and correctly kept.

ABERDEEN ROYAL ASYLUM,
30th September and 1st and 2nd October 1901.

There were on the 30th ultimo 913 patients on the registers of the asylum. Of these, 2 were voluntary inmates, 120 men and 133 women were private patients, and 305 men and 353 women were paupers. Since last visit 3 males and 2 females have been transferred from the private to the pauper list, and 3 males from the pauper to the private list. Effect has been given to these changes in the above figures. Five private males, 4 private females, and 1 pauper female were absent on statutory probation, and 1 pauper male was absent on pass. The number resident was 902, all of whom were seen during the three days over which the visit extended.

Since 3rd April 1901, the date of the preceding entry, the following changes in the population of the asylum have taken place :—

	PRIVATE PATIENTS.		PAUPER PATIENTS.		TOTALS.
	M.	F.	M.	F.	
Admitted, . ' . .	12	11	50	48	121 .
Discharged recovered, .	7	4	18	28	57
Discharged unrecovered, .	1	7	6	3	17
Died, ...	8	4	6	12	30

One gentleman and 1 lady have been admitted as voluntary inmates.

By these changes the number of patients on the registers has increased by 19, and the number resident by 11. There is a decrease of 8 in the number of private patients and an increase of 27 paupers.

The deaths are registered as due to brain lesions in 5 cases, to general paralysis in 6 cases, to heart disease in 5 cases, to pneumonia in 4 cases, to phthisis pulmonalis in 3 cases, to senile decay in 3 cases, to cancer in 2 cases, and to mastoid abscess and to puerperal mania complicated with influenza in 1 case each. *Post mortem* examinations were made in 17 cases, or 56·6 per cent. of the deaths.

The Register of Restraint and Seclusion contains 6 entries. They refer to the use of the camisole in the case of a female patient in order to prevent her doing violence to herself and others. No accident involving injury to any patient has occurred. Three escapes have taken place in which the patients were absent from the asylum at least one night before being brought back.

The changes in the staff are as follows :—8 attendants and 15 nurses have resigned, 1 attendant has been dismissed, and 9 attendants and 17 nurses have been engaged. The attendant who was dismissed concealed the fact that he had been in the service of, and had been discharged from, another asylum. This information was communicated to Dr. Reid by the General Board. The changes among the nurses have been numerous, many of which were due to their having been trained and taught so as to enable them to obtain the nursing certificate of the Medico-Psychological Association. Soon after passing this examination they secured more lucrative appointments in nursing establishments in England.

It is learned with regret that the Directors have decided in the meanwhile to postpone the reconstruction of the main asylum. The defects in many of its arrangements, the want of adequate dining and amusement halls, and the overcrowded condition of the majority of its day-rooms have been repeatedly pointed out. It is hoped, however, that when the asylum is relieved of the paupers chargeable to Aberdeen, which will admit of sections of the old buildings being temporarily vacated, the Directors will make use of this opportunity and proceed with the reconstruction scheme which is so much required in the interests of the patients.

The two new wings of the hospital are valuable additions to this section of the asylum. In each is a spacious, lofty, and well-lighted day-room which can be divided into two apartments if this is thought desirable. On the ground floor, in addition to this day-room, are six single rooms, also bath, dressing, and boot rooms. The dressing-room is divided into cubicles which afford privacy to the patients while undressing and dressing. On the upper floor is a large observation dormitory in which the melancholic and suicidal sleep under continuous observation. This is a good and safe provision for this class of patients. The furniture and furnishings are throughout these extensions of the same tasteful and substantial character as that in other sections of the hospital. The excellence of this accommodation merits the warmest approval. The hospital, which by these additions has been made complete in all its arrangements, can now receive all patients requiring special supervision and treatment, and at the same time it admits of a classification which places patients in circumstances most likely to conduce to their mental and bodily improvement.

Elmhill continues to provide in the most liberal manner for patients paying the higher rates of board. It is a well-appointed residence suitable in every respect for persons belonging to the refined and wealthy classes.

Elmhill Cottage has all the characteristics of a private home, and the daily life of the patients resident there is made as far as possible like that of a private household. It is comfortably and handsomely furnished and was found in admirable order. Sixteen ladies are in residence.

The branch establishment at Daviot is now more efficiently staffed. An attendant who was for many years at Elmhill is now in charge of the male side and of the stores. There are in addition three male attendants. A grieve has been appointed to the farm. The more satisfactory condition of the patients as to clothing and personal neatness showed that they were better cared for than when one person, as was formerly the case, had charge of both the patients and the farm. The staff on the female side consists of a matron, three nurses, a cook, and a kitchen maid. The whole house was in excellent order, and its appearance was one of brightness, cheerfulness, and comfort. The room to the right of the entrance door has been furnished as a board-room. A system of electric bells has been introduced between the dormitories and the bedrooms of the charge attendants, and between these bedrooms and the apartments of the officials. This is a useful improvement from an administrative point of view. The number resident is 90—49 males and 41 females. All the men are daily engaged in useful work : 35 are engaged as field labourers, 6 as farm servants, 2 as gardeners, 1 as storekeeper, 1 as stoker, 1 as painter, and 1 as messenger. The day-rooms for the men are overcrowded, and it is understood with approval that the old Glack House is to be put into order. When this is completed, not only will these day-rooms be relieved, but additional accommodation will be obtained for 15 men. This establishment will, when the old house is renovated and equipped, be able to accommodate 110 patients.

Much that was seen during the visit bore evidence of Dr. Reid's assiduous attention to his duties and of his kindly management of the asylum. The patients generally were contented, and their condition was highly satisfactory. No complaints as to care and treatment were made except those which were manifestly the outcome of delusions. Except in one section on the female side of the main asylum the behaviour of the patients was quiet and orderly. All parts of the asylum were in good order.

As new piggeries have been erected on the Ashgrove Estate, it is hoped that no time will now be lost in removing the old ones, and in converting their site into garden or pleasure ground.

The books and registers were examined and found regularly and accurately kept.

ARGYLL AND BUTE DISTRICT ASYLUM,
19th and 21st January 1901.

There are 435 patients on the register of the asylum at this date. Of these, 12 males and 20 females are private patients, and 212 men and 191 women are paupers. All are resident and were seen, except 1 male and 3 female pauper patients who are absent on statutory probation. Effect has been given in the above figures to the transference since last visit of 1 female from the private to the pauper list and of 2 males from the pauper to the private list.

The changes among the patients since 6th July 1900, the date of last visit, have been as follows :—

	PRIVATE PATIENTS.		PAUPER PATIENTS.		TOTALS.
	M.	F.	M.	F.	
Admitted, . . .	3	3	18	10	34
Discharged recovered, .	1	0	9	10	20
Discharged unrecovered,	0	2	4	4	10
Died, ...	1	1	6	4	12

These figures show that the removals from all causes have exceeded the admissions by 8. This is mainly due to a high recovery rate, which since last visit is 58·8 per cent. on the admissions. The discharge of patients who have improved and who do not require a fully equipped asylum for their proper care frequently meets with strenuous opposition on the part of Parish Councils. The distance of the asylum from the homes of the patients and the expense of the journey stand in the way of a trial being given of home care to many patients. As a result of a falling off in the number discharged, and of consequent accumulation, the proportion per 100,000 of the population of pauper lunatics in this asylum is 415, the highest of any lunacy district in Scotland. In other districts, such as Stirling and Roxburgh, the proportion per 100,000 of population of pauper lunatics in asylums is 193 and 227 respectively.

The rate of mortality has been low, and the deaths were due to natural causes. *Post mortem* examinations were made in 4 cases, or in 33·3 per cent. of the deaths. The consent of relatives was refused in the other 8 cases. The results of these examinations are carefully recorded. The recommendation as to the erection of a separate mortuary contained in a previous entry is repeated. Its site should be a secluded one.

The Register of Restraint and Seclusion contains 12 entries. They refer to the restraint of one patient in order to prevent persistent destructive tendencies. One accident is recorded, a fracture of the tibia and fibula in the case of an old woman of 80, whose foot was twisted when being lifted from her chair by two attendants. She made a good recovery. Dr. Cameron fully investigated the occurrence, and did not consider the attendants blameworthy. There has been no escape.

The staff, which has been increased by 3, consists of 23 men and 24 nurses for day duty, and 3 men and 5 nurses for night duty. This gives a ratio of 1 attendant to 9½ patients and of 1 nurse to 9 patients for day duty, a proportion which indicates an adequate staff. An increase in the night staff is recorded with approval, as it allows of a larger number of patients being under constant night supervision. The comfort, safety, and good conduct of the patients are promoted by constant and efficient attention during the night. There was only one wet bed on the morning of the 17th instant. The changes among the staff have been very numerous. On the male side 14 men have resigned, 5 have been dismissed, and 21 have been engaged since 6th July 1900. The causes of dismissal do not include any misconduct affecting the patients. Five nurses have resigned and 6 have been engaged. Twelve, or 46 per cent., of the male attendants have only been six months, and 10, or 34 per cent., of the nurses have only been a year in the service of the asylum. Attention has been drawn in a former report to the inadequacy and unsuitability of the present accommodation for the staff. A small dormitory in which the beds are so crowded as almost to touch each other is the accommodation given to 10 nurses. One male attendant left immediately on being shown the unsatisfactory bedroom he was to occupy. The married attendants are provided with suitable cottages, and the duration of their services is excellent, but unless better and more comfortable provision is made for the nurses and junior male staff, constant changes will continue to occur, to the detriment of the patients. The erection of a nurses' home would contribute greatly to the securing and retaining of an intelligent class of nurses. The accommodation of the whole staff, official and ordinary, should be early considered by the District Board.

The filter recently erected frees the water of the vegetable *débris* which formerly made it of a deep brown colour. The water at this date was clear and almost colourless. It would, however, be advisable to have it again analysed so as to make sure of its fitness for domestic use. It was seen that the filter interferes only to a slight degree with the pressure necessary to throw the water on to the roof in case of fire. The whole pressure from the reservoir can, however, in a minute or two be secured by turning on a tap in the main pipe. The enlargement of the reservoir is a matter which should not be further delayed. Fortunately there have been three wet summers, but if a drought occur the serious evils which were experienced in former dry seasons from a deficient water supply would recur.

The new additions to the female side are now in occupation. They consist of two large dayrooms, one of which, in conjunction with the adjoining dormitory, is used as infirmary accommodation. The whole of the work in connection with these extensions, except the slating, has been done by the asylum artisan staff and by the patients. These additions are valued at

Appendix B.

Commissioners'
Entries.

Royal and
District
Asylums.

Argyll and
Bute District
Asylum.

£8983, their cost was only £3427, and they provide accommodation for 102 persons. In no asylum in Scotland have additions to the accommodation been made at so small a cost to the ratepayers. The employment of the patients in useful work is organised by Dr. Cameron in a most systematic manner. Artisan attendants receive a pecuniary reward for teaching patients their respective occupations, and this is attended with successful results. The number of patients thus employed is as follows:—Eight as tailors, 6 as joiners, 7 as masons, 5 as upholsterers, 5 as painters, 2 as bakers, 2 as plumbers, 2 as shoemakers, 2 as blacksmiths, and 2 as plasterers. The sum of work annually done in the various departments is most commendable. The small amount of land in connection with the asylum continues a defect in the arrangement for the employment of the patients in healthy outdoor work. There are only about 11 acres under cultivation. The District Board are strongly urged in the interests of the patients and of the asylum to secure more land at as early a date as possible.

The dayroom and dormitory accommodation of the asylum is, in consequence of recent additions and a rearrangement of rooms, as follows :—dayroom space for 258 men and 240 women, and dormitory accommodation for 211 men and 242 women. There is at present spare dayroom space for 34 men and 29 women. There is vacant bed space for 31 women, but there are 13 patients in excess of the male sleeping accommodation. Progress is, however, being made with the extension of the Cowal wing, which, when completed, will contain an observation dormitory for 30 men.

Almost without exception the patients were quiet, orderly, and contented. All complaints were in regard to undue detention by those who, on investigation, were found unfit for discharge. The patients were seen at supper. The bread and-butter was abundant, and the tea was satisfactory. The clothing was neat in appearance, sufficient, and of good quality. There were 6 men and 9 women in bed, and it was evident that they receive skilful treatment and efficient nursing.

The dayrooms and dormitories are maintained in excellent order, and presented a bright and comfortable appearance. Repainting and redecoration are constantly in progress, and the work is tastefully done. The heating arrangements are efficient—every section was of a comfortable warmth, and improvements in these arrangements and in the supply of hot water at the East House have recently been effected. The stairs throughout the asylum have been provided with hand rails.

The case books were found written up to date, and the registers were examined and found regularly and correctly kept.

ARGYLL AND BUTE DISTRICT ASYLUM,
8th and 9th October 1901.

Since the date of last entry the following changes in population have taken place :—

	PRIVATE PATIENTS.		PAUPER PATIENTS.		TOTALS.
	M.	F.	M.	F.	
On the Register,					
21st January 1901, .	12	20	212	191	435
Admitted, . . .	3	1	26	26	56
Discharged recovered, .	2	2	14	7	25
Discharged unrecovered,	0	0	5	3	8
Died, ...	1	1	9	6	17
On the Register,					
9th October 1901, .	12	18	210	201	441

With the exception of two men who were absent on statutory probation and one woman who was absent on pass, all the patients were resident and were seen during the visit.

There are no entries in the Register of Restraint and Seclusion, and no escape is recorded in which the patients were absent overnight from the asylum. Eight men and seven women were confined to bed. This is not a large proportion, but so far as could be seen, it included the majority of those

whose physical health required such treatment. It is understood with
approval that all recent acute cases of mental affection admitted to the asylum
are placed in bed for some days after admission. The number of wet beds
on the night of the 7th instant was two. This is as small a proportion as
could possibly be expected and is undoubtedly due to the large night staff.
There are 3 night attendants on the male and 5 on the female side of the
asylum. It is understood that when the new addition to the Cowal Division
on the male side is completed a larger number of male patients will be placed
under supervision.

There are 34 entries in the Register of Accidents, all of which, with the
exception of two, refer to bruises or marks of a trifling kind. The two more
serious accidents are a fracture of the neck of the femur caused by an accidental fall, and the fracture of two ribs. In the latter case the patient, a
male, stated that the injury was caused by a blow given by an attendant.
The matter was reported to the Procurator-Fiscal and to the General Board.
The evidence, though not of such a nature as to justify the prosecution of the
attendant for assault, was sufficient to render it undesirable to retain his
services in the asylum, and he was accordingly dismissed.

The following are the assigned causes of death:—Tuberculosis, 6 cases;
pneumonia, 4 cases; heart disease, 4 cases; apoplexy, 2 cases; bronchitis, 1
case. *Post mortem* examinations were made in 9 of the 15 cases of death, and
the results of these examinations are very carefully and graphically recorded
in a book kept for the purpose. The condition of the case books attracted
favourable attention.

Twenty-seven attendants—17 men and 10 women—have left the service of
the asylum since last visit. Of that number, 6 men were dismissed. Thirty
attendants—18 men and 12 women—have been engaged. These changes are
more numerous than is desirable, looking only to the interests of the patients.

The average general condition of the inmates of the asylum was satisfactory.
With the exception of one of the female wards in which there was noisy
excitement, the patients were quiet and seemingly contented, and few of them
made any statement beyond the usual demand for release. They had every
appearance of being suitably fed and no exception could be taken to the state
of their clothing.

Every part of the institution was found clean and in good order. Since
last visit the new female hospital day-room has been completed. It adjoins
and opens off the hospital dormitory, and the patients (exceeding 50 in
number) in both rooms are under one charge nurse. All the recent acute
cases, and those who for any reason require special treatment, are resident in
this section. The new ward is of good proportion, well heated, and comfortably furnished. It was observed with approval that the furnishings include
comfortable chairs, couches, and a piano. There is now telephonic communication between the various divisions of the asylum, in the matron' and head
male attendants' rooms, the general store and the Medical Superintendent's
office. The administration of the asylum must be greatly facilitated by
means of these instruments. The small Bute dormitory on the female side
has been converted into a series of 6 cubicles for female attendants, which
arrangement has the advantage of giving a separate sleeping compartment to
each of these nurses.

The facilities for escape from the various dormitories in case of fire were
inquired into, and it is judged advisable to recommend that fixed outside iron
staircases should be erected in connection with the Argyll male dormitory,
the Bute female dormitory, and the new Cowal male dormitory.

The unsatisfactory condition of the present mortuary has been referred to
in previous entries. It is strongly recommended that it should be removed
from its present position. The existing joiners' shop could easily be converted into suitable mortuary and *post mortem* rooms, while a new workshop
for joiners could more easily and cheaply be provided than a new mortuary.

It is understood that owing to the recent drought and the scarcity of water
in the asylum during the past summer months the District Board have
ordered arrangements to be made for adding extensively to the present water
reservoirs.

The resident population of the asylum has not greatly increased since last
visit. This is partly due to the fact that the admission rate has not recently
been so high and that more patients have been discharged unrecovered.

Should some of the larger parishes in the county continue to indicate a desire to board out suitable cases, it is hoped that every encouragement will be afforded them by the asylum authorities; for in this way only can the necessity for increased accommodation for patients in the asylum be checked and the rate-payers relieved from additional expenditure upon buildings and maintenance.

The books and registers were examined and found correctly kept.

AYR DISTRICT ASYLUM,
22nd and 23rd March 1901.

On the 22nd instant there were 224 men and 262 women on the register of the asylum. Of these, 1 man and 1 woman were absent on statutory probation. The number resident is 484, all of whom were seen in the course of the visit.

The following statement shows the changes on the population since the date of the preceding entry :—

PAUPER PATIENTS.

	M.	F.	TOTALS.
Admitted, ...	31	23	54
Discharged recovered, ...	20	11	31
Discharged unrecovered, . . .	9	5	14
Dead, ...	13	13	26

The number resident has decreased by 14—9 males and 5 females. The admission rate has for the past year been lower than that of recent years, but in view of the increasing population of the county this rate, it is feared, will not continue. The margin of spare accommodation on the male side is a small one, consisting of only 5 empty beds. Attention has been drawn in previous entries to this condition of the male division. The accommodation should at all times be ahead of the demand, and not drag laggingly behind. By the time another male villa can be erected and equipped, most of its accommodation will in all likelihood be required. It is therefore hoped that the District Board will take timely action in providing for the future.

The condition of the accommodation for female patients is, from this point of view, satisfactory, there being 29 empty beds.

The deaths are registered as due to diseases of the brain in 7 cases, to phthisis pulmonalis in 6 cases, to heart disease in 3 cases, to inflammatory chest affections in 2 cases, to chronic diarrhœa in 3 cases, and to violence, senile decay, post partum hæmorrhage, peritonitis, and Bright's disease, each in 1 case.

The causes of death were ascertained or verified only in 13 instances, or 50 per cent. of the whole by *post mortem* examinations. In 6 cases or 14 per cent. of 43 deaths in 1898, in 11 cases or 19·6 per cent. of 56 deaths in 1899, and in 24 cases or 45·3 per cent. of 53 deaths in 1900 were *post mortem* examinations made. It is a matter of regret that so few autopsies should have been made here in comparison with other asylums, as great importance is attached to the practice. In some asylums from 80 to 100 per cent. of the deaths are followed by *post-mortem* examinations. It is a matter of still greater regret that in this asylum no record is kept of the results of these examinations, and that the abundant material for pathological research, which gives a scientific interest to the cases and fosters the medical spirit, is not utilised in this direction. It is recommended that a second medical assistant or a clinical clerk be appointed for this important work. It is the duty of all asylums to aid in carrying on investigations which will elucidate the nature of insanity and influence its treatment. A Pathological Journal should be at once obtained and carefully kept.

The supervision of the institution is as follows :—A daily visit is paid by the Medical Superintendent to every section, during which all patients are seen ; an evening visit by the Assistant Medical Officer to patients in the main asylum, and frequent visits by the Matron and head male attendant. It is usual in other institutions for a morning visit to be paid by the Assistant Medical Officer previous to that of the Medical Superintendent, and it is recommended that the medical supervision be increased to that extent.

The Register of Restraint and Seclusion contains 36 entries. Of these 28

Appendix B.

Commissioners'
Entries.

Royal and
District
Asylums.

Ayr District
Asylum.

refer to the use of restraint by means of the strait jacket in the cases of 10 patients. The number of hours restraint was resorted to was 524. The reason stated for its use is in 9 cases to prevent suicide, and in 1 case to prevent stripping. In some asylums restraint is never used to prevent suicide, as it is thought to fix the morbid determination more deeply in the mind : vigilance of day and night supervision, removal of obvious means of self-destruction, and remedial bodily treatment being the plan successfully adopted. Eight entries refer to the use of seclusion in 4 cases ; the total period of seclusion amounted to 56 hours.

One escape has taken place, in which the patient was absent overnight before being brought back.

Eleven accidents are recorded, eight of which were not of a serious character ; two involved fracture of a bone—one of these was at the left wrist and due to a fall, and the other was due to an accidentally self-inflicted blow by a hammer on a finger. The most serious accident consists of a fatal assault on a male patient by two attendants. The circumstances of this assault were made the subject of a special enquiry by the Medical Commissioners, and the results were reported to the Board. The case was immediately reported to the Procurator-Fiscal, and as a result of his inquiry two male attendants were apprehended, tried at the Ayr Sheriff Court, and each sentenced to 3 months' imprisonment. The ill-usage in this case was of a cruel character.

The changes among the attendants are far more frequent than is desirable. Thirteen male and 5 female attendants have resigned, 5 males and 1 female have been dismissed, 1 female absconded, and 16 men and 9 females have been engaged. The duration of service of the present male staff cannot be said to be satisfactory. Of the 5 change attendants, only 1 has been in the service of the asylum for over 5 years, 1 for over 3 years, 2 for over 2 years, and 1 for only 4 months. Of the under-staff, only 1 has two years' service, 2 over 1 year, the average service of 8 is only 4 months, and of 3 only 13 days.

Fifty per cent. of the male attendants may be said to be inexperienced, their average service being barely 3 months. The recovery and comfort of the patients depend to a considerable extent on the tact and capabilities of experienced attendants, whereas recently appointed men are generally a source of anxiety and doubt to all concerned in the work of an asylum. If suitable cottages were erected for a large proportion of the day and night attendants, which would enable them to marry and settle down permanently in the service of the asylum, a well-conducted, trustworthy, and efficient male staff would be secured. At present there are only 3 cottages available—1 for the head attendant, 1 for the gardener, and 1 for the joiner. The head attendant, who is suitably accommodated, has been over 11 years in the service of the institution.

The number of male patients employed in healthy outdoor work is comparatively small, being only 26·4 per cent. In asylums possessed of farms there are over 42 per cent. of the male inmates daily engaged in farm work. The fields belonging to this asylum, about 50 acres in extent, are let for grazing, and consequently afford no employment for the patients. If the District Board were to add to the land they already possess, or lease an adjoining farm, and produce all the milk, potatoes, and even the butcher-meat which the asylum requires, abundant outdoor occupation would be available for the patients ; and there is every reason for believing that a farm can be worked in connection with the asylum with financial success. In one asylum the rate of board is reduced by about £3 per patient on account of the profit from its farm.

All the patients had the opportunity of making statements as to their care and treatment. None complained of ill-usage. The patient who has at each visit made complaints against the management of the asylum was specially interviewed. On this occasion he had nothing adverse to say about the treatment of his fellow patients, or as to the food, clothing, bedding, or bathing arrangements. His only request was to have his eyes, which are diseased, examined by a specialist, and this Dr. Skae undertook to do. Appeals for discharge were made, but investigation proved that further detention was necessary. The dress of both sexes was suitable and in proper order, and personal neatness was satisfactory. The dinner on the 22nd inst.

consisted of broth, fish, and potatoes, was abundant and well cooked, but the fish and potatoes were almost cold before being served. There is no hotplate in the dining-hall; one should be provided, upon which the carving of meat can be done, and with compartments underneath in which the whole of the patients' dinner can be kept warm. Enquiry elicited no complaint either as to the quantity or quality of the dietary. Apart from those in bed, the general health and physical condition of the inmates was good. Of the 52 epileptics, 46 sleep under continuous observation, the remaining 6, who have to live in single rooms, being frequently visited. Seventy-one men and 67 women sleep in dormitories in which night attendants are in constant charge. The hall for Sunday services and entertainments is no longer used as a dormitory, and consequently the monotony of asylum life is now relieved by regular dances, concerts, and other associated amusements.

The asylum throughout was found in excellent order. The dayrooms are comfortably furnished and well supplied with objects of interest and decoration. The large number of easy chairs and sofas for the senile, infirm, and restless is a praiseworthy feature in the furnishing of the wards. It cannot be doubted but that this is one of the causes which lead to the quiet and orderly behaviour which prevailed among the patients. The grounds around the new villa for women have been put into admirable order by the work of the patients and staff; all that is now required to add to their appearance is the planting of shrubs, such as rhododendrons. The same work in reference to the men's villa, which was contracted for, has only now been commenced.

It is hoped that the District Board will favourably consider the recommendation contained in the previous entry in reference to the installation of the electric light. Its great and many advantages are now so well known that it is needless to state them.

The registers were examined and found to be regularly and correctly kept.

AYR DISTRICT ASYLUM,
10th and 11th October 1901.

The asylum was last visited on 22nd March of the present year. Since then the following changes in population have taken place:—

				PAUPER PATIENTS.		
				M.	F.	TOTALS.
On Register at last visit,	.	.	.	224	262	486
Admitted,	.	.	.	44	40	84
Discharged recovered,	.	.	.	18	6	24
Discharged unrecovered,	.	.	.	15	7	22
Died,	.	.	.	10	12	22
On Register, 11th October 1901	.	.	225	277	502

Five men and two women are absent on statutory probation, but with these exceptions all the patients were resident and were seen during the visit.

There are 44 entries in the Register of Restraint and Seclusion referring to the restraint of 2 persons and the seclusion of 12 persons. Two patients escaped and were absent from the asylum for at least one night before being brought back. There are 12 entries in the Register of Accidents, of which 8 are of a minor nature. The more important refer to a fracture of the bones of the forearm, and to two dislocations of the shoulder joint, all three of which occurred in female patients and were of an accidental and unpreventible nature. The fourth entry refers to a cut on the back sustained by a male patient who jumped through a window.

Twenty-five attendants—14 men and 11 women—have been engaged; 7 men and 15 women have resigned; and 3 men have been dismissed. With the object of improving the stability of the service of male attendants, it is understood that the District Board propose to erect in the meantime four cottages for married men.

The deaths are registered as due to the following diseases:—gross brain disease, 3 cases; senile decay, 3 cases; cerebral effusion, 2 cases; peritonitis, 2 cases; melancholia, 2 cases; heart disease, 2 cases; inanition, general paralysis, bronchitis, chronic abscess, paralysis, phthisis, epilepsy, and acute rheumatism, 1 case each. *Post mortem* examinations were made in 10 instances, the permission to perform such examinations being refused in the remaining cases.

The record of the employment of patients remains much the same as formerly, except that the number of men working outside in the garden and grounds has been slightly increased. It will be observed by reference to the tabular statement at the commencement of this entry that while the number of female patients has not practically increased, the male patients on the register have increased by 13 since last visit. The margin of spare beds on the male side is now only about six. Unless the asylum authorities and some of the larger Parish Councils in the district can co-operate in removing from the asylum a number of cases for whom treatment in an institution is no longer necessary, there seems to be no course left but to add to the accommodation for male patients. It is understood that the District Board have under consideration the question of erecting a second male villa. The present villa is not fully occupied because, it is stated, of the difficulty of selecting suitable patients to place in it. In that case it would of course be inadvisable to erect, meantime, a villa for chronic, able-bodied male patients. In the male wards in the main asylum there were observed many senile, infirm, and harmless patients. If a villa were erected for the accommodation of such cases it would set free in the main buildings space which is at present urgently required for the hospital and bed treatment of acute and recent and physically sick patients.

The condition of the patients at the time of the visit was quite satisfactory. They were generally free from excitement, and complaints of every description were less numerous than usual. The dinner on the first day of the visit was substantial and apparently popular. The inmates presented the appearance o receiving an adequate dietary and no reference to the question of food was made by any of them. The clothing of both sexes was suitable and sufficient. The beds and bed-coverings wherever examined were found in good order, warm, and comfortable.

The admission dormitory has been enlarged by the removal of a partition and the inclusion of another adjoining apartment, with the result that 26 patients are now under the direct observation of the night attendant. This is a marked improvement.

It is suggested that the District Board should satisfy themselves as to whether the staircases leading to the dormitories in the male and female villas respectively form a sufficient egress in case of fire.

Considerable progress has been made during the past few months with the formation of the terrace in front of the main asylum and with the improvement of the walks in the neighbourhood of the garden.

The books and registers were examined and found correct.

BANFF DISTRICT ASYLUM,
9th February 1901.

There are 168 patients—88 men and 80 women—resident at this date. The main part of the asylum is overcrowded. There are upwards of 80 men occupying the dayroom space, which can only properly accommodate about 50, and in the female dormitories shakedowns require to be used for the surplus number, for whom it is impossible to place bedsteads. Under the kindly management of Mr. and Mrs. Fowler the patients suffer the least inconvenience from the state of matters described, but it was apparent that the administration of the institution is being carried on in circumstances of exceptional difficulty. There is, therefore, urgent need that the construction of the new villa for male patients should be expedited.

Since the asylum was last visited, 18 patients—11 men and 7 women—have been admitted ; 9 patients—4 men and 5 women—have been discharged recovered ; 4 patients—1 man and 3 women—have been discharged unrecovered ; and 1 man has died. The cause of this death, which was general paralysis, was verified by *post mortem* examination.

There are 19 entries in the Register of Restraint and Seclusion referring to the restraint of 1 person for surgical reasons. An injury to the nose of

(margin notes) Appendix B. Commissioners Entries.

Royal and District Asylums.

Ayr District Asylum.

Banff District Asylum.

Appendix B.

Commissioners'
Entries.

Royal and
District
Asylums.

Banff District
Asylum.

a male patient, caused by a blow received from a fellow-patient, is the only accident of a serious kind recorded. One hundred and thirty-five patients were industrially employed at the time of the visit. Of these, 34 men were engaged in farm work, and 45 women were employed either sewing and knitting or working in the kitchen and laundry.

The bodily health of the patients was good, only 3 women being confined to bed on account of illness. It is recorded, with regret, that another case of enteric fever has occurred within the past few days. The subject was a female attendant, and the origin of the infection is apparently as obscure as that of the previous cases. The only course open to the District Board in the unfortunate circumstances is to carry out in their entirety the recommendations contained in the report recently made by Professor Hay upon the sanitary condition of the asylum.

It is understood that a night nurse is to be immediately engaged for the female side of the institution, and it is hoped that in time the same course will be adopted on the male side. Should a regular system of night supervision be established, the question of how far such a system may modify the structural proposals with regard to the erection of new single rooms in connection with the main asylum will require to be considered.

The patients at Woodpark were quiet and free from excitement, but there was a good deal of noise in one of the female wards in the old building. The male patients presented as good an appearance as could possibly be expected in the crowded state of the wards. All the inmates—both male and female—were suitably clothed, and they presented every indication of an adequate dietary and proper care. The various parts of the asylum were found in good order.

It is hoped that when the new boiler-house is erected the question of heating the main building with hot water will receive the attention it deserves. It is understood that the price at present paid for gas is high. It might be found on enquiry that electric lighting would not cost more, in which case the advantage of the latter over gas lighting is so superior for public institutions that there ought to be no hesitation in adopting it. Attention is directed to the state of the scullery in the main building. It is too small for its purpose, and at the time of the visit the steam from the cooking boilers situated therein filled the apartment and passed freely into the adjoining kitchen. If it is found impossible to enlarge the scullery, its relative position to the kitchen might perhaps be changed by removing the partition between them or otherwise. In any case the arrangement for extracting steam requires immediate attention.

The books and registers were examined and found correctly kept.

BANFF DISTRICT ASYLUM,
24th and 25th July 1901.

On the 25th instant there were 164 patients on the register of the asylum. Of these, 84 were men and 80 were women. All were seen in the course of the visit except one man who is absent on statutory probation.

Since the date of the preceding entry, 9th February 1901, the following changes have taken place :—

	PAUPER PATIENTS.		
	M.	F.	TOTALS.
Admitted, ...	7	11	18
Discharged recovered, ...	5	7	12
Discharged unrecovered, . . .	5	4	9
Died, ...	1	1	2

The recovery rate has been high during the period to which the above figures refer, being 61 per cent. on the number admitted. The number discharged unrecovered or improved is large, and it is recommended that, in view of the overcrowded condition of the asylum, continued efforts be made to remove to domestic care all patients who have become harmless and easily managed, and for whom treatment in a fully equipped asylum is unnecessary. Though there has been a small decrease in the number of men resident, yet the male division

continues seriously overcrowded, and a condition of matters exists which is
fraught with many evils and difficulties. One of the three dayrooms on the
male side has now to be used as a dormitory, and the boot-room is the only
place in which temporary dayroom accommodation can be found. It is therefore hoped that the District Board will urge upon the contractors to hasten the
completion of the new male block, so as to have it ready for occupation at the
earliest possible moment.
The deaths are registered as due in one case to fatty degeneration of the
heart and congestion of the lungs, and in one case to typhoid fever and phthisis
pulmonalis. It is much to be regretted that the causes of death in these cases
were not verified by *post mortem* examinations. In some asylums an autopsy
is performed after every death, and the Board recently issued a circular pointing
out the importance of these examinations, both from a scientific point of view
and on account of the protective influence over the living which results from
the knowledge that in all cases of death such examinations will be made.
The Register of Restraint and Seclusion contains 3 entries referring to the
use of seclusion in the treatment of one patient on account of violent excitement. Two accidents are recorded : one involved the fracture of two ribs, due
to slipping and falling against a chair, and one was an injury to a finger which
a patient sustained when working in the quarry. One escape has taken place
in which the patient was absent for a night before being brought back.
The changes in the staff are few, and consist of the resignation of 1 attendant
and of 1 nurse, and of the engagement of 2 attendants and 3 nurses. There is
now a night attendant in each side of the asylum, and the results are said to
be admirable. A wet bed is now a very rare occurrence, and the restless
patients, in lieu of being shut up in single rooms, now sleep in associated dormitories under supervision. By these improved nursing arrangements the
needs of the sick are carefully attended to during the night, the safety of the
suicidal and epileptic is better secured, and the defective habits of the demented
are improved. Straw-bags which wet patients used to sleep on have now been
found unnecessary.
It will be seen that the cause of one of the deaths was typhoid fever. In
view of the unfortunate recurrence of this disease at the asylum, it is recorded
with satisfaction that the District Board have resolved to carry out the
recommendations contained in the report by Professor Mathew Hay, the only
modification being that in lieu of a system of sewage filtration the District
Board intend, if leave can be obtained, to have the sewage carried by a drain
to the sea. It is hoped that no difficulties will be experienced in effecting so
desirable a scheme for the disposal of the sewage. All open drains around the
grounds of the main asylum and of Woodpark are, it is understood, to be laid
with suitable pipes, and the sanction of the County Council has been applied
for in reference to substituting pipes for the open ditch at the roadside. Plans
for the erection of filter beds and a storage tank capable of containing 27,000
gallons of water are in course of preparation. The tank is to be connected by
a 4-inch pipe to the asylum. This storage will secure an ample supply of
filtered water, and as it will also be connected to the hydrants around the
asylum, the means for extinguishing fire will be greatly increased. The old
well in the garden has been filled up. These provisions will, it is earnestly
hoped, so improve the sanitary condition of the institution as to render it in
the future free from all diseases due to septic causes.
A suitable and convenient site has been selected for the new boiler-house,
and plans for its erection are being prepared. It is proposed to heat the new
male block by means of a low-pressure hot-water system, and it is recommended
that these heating arrangements be extended to the dayrooms, dormitories, and
single rooms of the main building.
The management of the asylum under the difficulties which exist at present,
especially in the male division, is highly creditable. The condition of the
patients in regard to clothing and personal neatness was very satisfactory.
With one exception they were quiet and orderly in conduct, and a general air
of contentment was evident.
The food of the inmates is abundant, and ample allowance is made for the
requirements of working patients. Fresh fish is now given once a week for
dinner in summer, and the dietary has been otherwise more varied.
The industrial employment of the patients continues to receive great and
praiseworthy attention. The asylum farm gives healthy outdoor work to a

large percentage of the male patients, and it is worked in a way which proves financially advantageous to the institution.

The condition of the grounds, the garden, the farm, and the interior of the farm buildings is excellent and deserves special commendation.

The net profit on the farm for the last financial year was £502. In addition to this profit, carting for the new block has been done to the value of £75.

The whole of the interior of Woodpark has been repainted and tastefully redecorated.

The registers were examined and found written up to date.

CRICHTON ROYAL INSTITUTION,
18th, 19th, 20th, and 21st March 1901.

There were on the 18th instant 734 patients on the registers of the institution. Of these, 12 were voluntary patients, 418 were private patients, and 304 were paupers. Three male and 6 female private patients, and 3 female pauper patients were absent on statutory probation. Effect has been given in the foregoing figures to the transference, since last visit, of 2 female patients from the private to the pauper list, and of 1 female from the pauper to the private list. The number resident is 722.

Since the institution was last visited the following changes have taken place :—

	PRIVATE PATIENTS.		PAUPER PATIENTS.		TOTALS.
	M.	F.	M.	F.	
I. Certificated Patients :—					
Admitted, ...	15	15	17	13	'60
Discharged recovered, .	5	6	7	6	24
Discharged unrecovered,	6	6	2	0	14
Died, ...	7	9	5	8	29
II. Voluntary Inmates :—					
Admitted, ...	4	2	.	.	6
Left, ...	6	3	.	.	9

The deaths are registered as due to cerebral and spinal diseases in 7 cases, to phthisis pulmonalis in 9 cases, to inflammatory lung affections in 5 cases, to heart disease in 2 cases, to peritonitis in 2 cases, and to lumbar abscess, pyæmia, pulmonary abscess, and suicide by cut throat each in 1 case. No death is registered as due to general paralysis of the insane. Thirty-one per cent. of the deaths were due to consumption, but investigation showed that of the 9 patients who died of this cause, 4 were consumptive on admission, and in 3 there was an hereditary predisposition to tubercular disease. The causes of death were ascertained or verified by *post mortem* examination in 51 per cent. of the cases. This percentage is not a high one, and the great importance of making these examinations whenever the consent of relatives can be obtained should be kept steadily in view. The mortuary is not at present provided with a room suitable for relatives or friends who come to pay the last token of respect to a deceased patient, but this defect is to receive immediate attention.

The work in the Pathological Laboratory has recently been developed in the direction of chemical investigation into the toxic bases of brain and nervous affections, and there is every reason to believe that important results bearing on the treatment of insanity will be obtained. The equipment of the laboratory in apparatus and material is complete, and the medical staff are to be congratulated on having the means of carrying on scientific investigations of value and importance. The clinical records in the case books indicate that the history and symptoms of the patients are carefully and ably studied.

The Register of Restraint and Seclusion contains no entry. Two accidents are recorded—a contused wound on scalp sustained by an attendant from being struck by a piece of coal thrown by a patient, and a suicide by cut throat. An attendant had neglected to lock up a razor he had been using, and a patient who had been placed under special observation on account of suicidal tendencies, but who was culpably allowed to walk alone in the

Appendix B.

Commissioners
Entries.

Royal and
District
Asylums.

Crichton Royal
Institution,
Dumfries.

gallery, got hold of the razor, went into a lavatory and cut his throat. One of the attendants was summarily dismissed, and the other is under a month's notice to leave. Dr. Rutherford purposes calling in all ordinary razors and providing each gallery with a safety one. Four patients have escaped, and were absent for at least one night before being brought back.

The present staff comprises 46 male and 52 female attendants. The proportion for day duty is 1 attendant to 7 patients, a ratio which is indicative of a staff of adequate strength. In the First House there is 1 night attendant in the gentlemen's division, and 1 in the ladies'; but this number is increased as occasion demands. In the Second House there are 2 on the male and 4 on the female side, which gives a proportion of 1 to 75 in the male, and 1 to 65 on the female division. The number of wet beds on the morning of the 18th instant was 5. All epileptics whom it is possible to place in associated dormitories sleep under continuous observation. The changes among the attendants continue to be far more numerous than are desirable in the interests of the patients. Fourteen men and 15 women have resigned, 1 man has been dismissed, and 15 men and 16 women have been engaged. The provision of additional cottages for married attendants would be an effective way of increasing the stability of the male staff. This is clearly proved by the following statement, which shows the average duration of service of the present married and single attendants :—

	FIRST HOUSE.		SECOND HOUSE.	
	DURATION OF SERVICE.			
	YRS.	MOS.	YRS.	MOS.
Married attendants, . . .	11	7	11	11
Single attendants, ...	0	11	2	3

The institution generally is maintained in excellent order. The central portion and staircase on the male side of the First House has been greatly improved and rendered brighter by tasteful repainting and redecoration. In the Second House a new visiting room has been provided, day-rooms and corridors have been repapered, and the kitchen tiled from roof to floor. The back wings of this house on the female side are greatly in need of thorough renovation. The inadequacy and unsuitability of the male sickroom accommodation were very apparent at this visit. The new male infirmary cannot therefore be ready for occupation at too early a date. Unfortunately no progress has been made with the building of the new infirmaries. The making of a permanent road to their site and difficulties with the contractors have been the cause of delay. Matters have, it is understood, been now adjusted, and building operations are at once to be proceeded with. Trees should at once be planted to the north-east of the site, so as to shelter the infirmaries from the bitterly cold winds that often prevail from that direction. The laundry house is approaching completion. Externally it is a handsome building, and internally it is well designed and excellently equipped. Being adjacent to the laundry buildings it will be a most convenient home for the laundry staff and workers. The addition to one of the wings of the First House, which contains an escape staircase and lavatory and sanitary arrangements, is being finished internally, and is a valuable and useful extension. The safety of the patients in the First House will, in case of fire, be secured, if a similar addition is made to each wing. It is understood that this is to be done. A large, level turfed area for cricket and other outdoor games has been formed by the work of the patients and staff, and constitutes a great improvement to the grounds. A neat wooden pavilion has been erected at the south boundary.

During the visit the patients were given the opportunity of making any statement they desired. No complaint of a reasonable character was made. Generally speaking, the patients showed much contentment with their treatment, which is evidently kind and considerate. A freedom from irksome discipline has always been a noteworthy and commendable feature in Dr. Rutherford's able management, and it is one which is productive of the best results. Unlocked doors are the rule, not the exception. Eighteen patients enjoy the privilege of parole beyond the grounds, and 73 are granted parole within the grounds. The personal condition and clothing of

Appendix B.

Commissioners'
Entries.

Royal and
District
Asylums.

Crichton Royal
Institution
Dumfries.

both sexes were, with a few exceptions among the men in the Second House, satisfactory. The dinners which were seen in the course of the visit were well cooked, abundant, and greatly relished. Enquiry made relative to the dietary elicited favourable comments. The behaviour of the patients was almost without exception quiet and orderly. Industrial occupation is systematically attended to. Healthy outdoor work is found for 49 male private patients, and 73 male paupers. Fifty-four per cent. of the patients are registered as daily engaged in either indoor or outdoor occupations. The number attending Divine Service last Sunday in the Crichton Memorial Church was 293.

The distribution of the patients throughout the various sections of the institution continues generally as stated in previous entries. There are 574, or 79·5 of the patients in the First and Second Houses, and 148 or 20·5 per cent. in the detached houses. A larger percentage of the patients could be placed in separate dwellings, and it is suggested that, should further extensions of the institution be at any time required, houses similar to Brownhall, Rosebank, and Rosehall, in which the conditions of domestic life exist in an admirable manner, should be multiplied. The state of real comfort, contentment, and happiness which prevails in these home-like dwellings could not be surpassed in any other mode of provision. In segregated asylums the cooking is done in a central kitchen, and the food conveyed in a waggon to each block or house. Dr. Rutherford has found that the cooking can efficiently, and without additional expense, be done in each house. It is an interest and occupation to the inmates and staff, and adds completeness to the domesticity of the arrangements.

The Directors continue to carry out the charitable function of the institution in a liberal and enlightened manner. The annual rate of board for private patients of limited means belonging to the counties of Dumfries, Kirkcudbright, and Wigtown is £25, the lowest rate for private patients in Scotland. It would be a great boon in other lunacy districts if asylum care could be obtained for this class of patients at such a low rate. But, beyond this, the Directors make contributions from the funds of the institution towards reducing this rate when the circumstances of the patients or of their relatives are shown to require them. There are at present 61 patients at the £25 rate, and of these 47 receive contributions from the funds amounting to £728 annually. Of the 47 patients, 1 pays £22 annually, 1 £15, 4 £12, 31 £10, and 10 only £5. It will be evident that if it were not for these reductions on the rate of board the stigma of pauperism would have to be incurred by these patients in order to obtain or retain asylum care. The same can be said relative to many patients whose rate of board is nominally £40 per annum. Twenty-six patients at this rate receive contributions amounting to £619 annually. The contributions vary from £8 to £40 annually, according to the necessities of the case. The total contributions for the year amount to £1347. It may thus be truly said that of the £7425 paid to the institution by parishes for the maintenance of their pauper inmates, the ratepayers receive back indirectly about a fifth part of their outlay. In this way the parochial rates of the three counties are relieved of a very considerable burden, a fact which should be widely recognised. All applications for reduction of these rates, in order to retain the patients on the private list, are carefully and liberally considered and are annually subjected to review. It is well to state that no one in the institution except the Physician Superintendent knows which of the private patients have or have not their rates of board reduced by contributions from the funds. The benefits of this charitable function of the institution are great and far-reaching.

The registers were examined and found to be kept in an especially neat and accurate manner.

CRICHTON ROYAL INSTITUTION, DUMFRIES,
14th, 15th, and 16th October 1901.

The institution was last visited on the 18th March of the present year. Since then the following changes have taken place in the population :—

	PRIVATE.		PAUPER.		TOTALS.	
I. Certificated Patients.	M.	F.	M.	F.		Appendix B.
On Register 18th March 1901, .	199	220	142	161	722	Commissioners' Entries.
Admitted since, ...	30	37	26	24	117	
Discharged recovered, . .	11	17	6	18	52	Royal and District Asylums.
Discharged unrecovered, . .	5	9	2	5	21	
Died, ...	8	7	5	8	28	
On Register 14th October 1901, .	205	225	155	153	738	Crichton Royal Institution Dumfries
II. Voluntary Inmates.						
Resident at last visit, . .	7	5	—	—	12	
Admitted since, ...	7	5	—	—	12	
Left, ...	5	5	—	—	10	
Died, ...	—	—	—	—	—	
Resident at this date, . .	9	5	—	—	14	

In the above figures effect has been given to the transference of one male and two females from the private to the pauper list, and of two males and two females from the pauper to the private list.

There are no entries in the Register of Restraint and Seclusion.

The number of patients who escaped and were absent for at least one night before being brought back is five.

There are four entries in the Register of Accidents. These refer to the fracture of the right humerus in the case of a private female patient, to the fracture of the fibula in the case of a male private patient, to an incised wound of the face in the case of a male pauper patient, and to an assault upon an attendant by a patient.

The number of patients attending Divine service last Sunday was 327, of whom 156 were men and 171 were women.

The record of the employment of patients shows that at the time of the visit 423 individuals were usefully employed, of which number no less than 71 males and 117 females were private patients.

The following are the assigned causes of the 28 cases of death :—phthisis pulmonalis 7 cases, heart disease 4 cases, peritonitis 3 cases, gross disease of the brain 3 cases, general paralysis of the insane 2 cases ; and the following 9 diseases in one case each—septicæmia, senile decay, ovarian tumour, enteritis, bronchitis, morphia poisoning, mania, rheumatic fever, and pneumonia. *Post mortem* examinations were made in 14 instances.

Twenty-two nurses and attendants have been engaged, and twenty-six have left the service of the institution since last visit.

The First House was found in excellent order, and the patients residing in it were as usual surrounded with comfort and bore every evidence of sufficient care. The only structural change calling for special notice is the completion of the newly-constructed staircase, with conjoined lavatories, bath-rooms, and boot-rooms in one of the ladies' wings. This addition supplies another exit from the building in case of fire as well as for daily use, and increases the sanitary conveniences of the section. The accommodation for the nursing of the sick in the first house, and in the portion of the Second House set apart for private patients is not so good as could be wished. In the case of the more affluent patients who can afford separate rooms and special attendance, such accommodation is not required, but for the majority, whose means are limited, there can be no question as to the advantages of well-equipped hospital wards. Probably the only solution of the difficulty would be the erection of a small separate hospital for all classes of private patients. The new segregated asylum for pauper patients from the southern counties, now in course of erection, will provide accommodation of a modern kind for sick cases. It is clear that for private patients a similar provision is equally needed.

It was learned that there is a proposal now before the Directors to erect a special hospital for the isolation and treatment of phthisis. The proposal is an excellent one both in the interest of sufferers from that disease and also as a means of protecting healthy inmates from infection.

Another proposal which, it is understood, is presently engaging the attention of the Directors, is that of providing cottages for more of the married attendants. Such a scheme, if carried out, would probably be found to have

E

Appendix B.
Commissioners'
Entries.

Royal and
District
Asylums.

Crichton Royal
Institution,
Dumfries.

an equally good effect here as in other institutions, where it has conduced towards securing the permanent services of a reliable class of male attendants.

The new block for laundry patients is now occupied. The impression produced by the inspection of it was very favourable. The internal arrangements, the finishing of the woodwork, the tiling of the lavatories and of the kitchen, the details of the plumber work, of the heating, and of the lighting, are all elaborate, highly finished, elegant in appearance, and, it is believed, efficient. All the patients who work in the laundry, and the paid laundresses, reside in this building. There is, in addition, a staff of nurses and a cook, for, in accordance with Dr. Rutherford's established method, the cooking in this, as in all the villas and cottages in connection with the institution, is done in the separate houses.

The opening of this block has greatly relieved the wards on the female side of the Second House. It was observed with satisfaction that an extended system of night nursing and supervision has been introduced into the latter house, and that there are at present 70 female patients under constant supervision each night. These include new and suicidal cases, and those whose habits are faulty. It is hoped that in time as many as possible of the noisy and restless inmates may be subjected to the same treatment. It is recommended that the system should as soon as possible be extended to the male side of the Second House.

As has been frequently pointed out in previous entries, the accommodation for physically sick patients in the Second House is, as regards dormitory space, much too limited; but in view of the erection of the new buildings for pauper patients no further comment is needed. It was observed that in the female hospital dayroom the noisier inmates of the ward were separated from the quieter patients and placed in an adjoining room opening off the larger apartment. Although so simple an arrangement may seem scarcely deserving of notice, its regular adoption is a matter of considerable importance to a large class of the insane whose physical weakness renders them peculiarly susceptible to the disturbing excitement of even a minority of their fellows. The simple expedient referred to is therefore highly commended as a measure not alone suitable for hospital wards but for all asylum wards where noisy and quiet patients are intermingled.

The private and pauper patients who reside in the various villas and cottages over the asylum estate, and who number about 20 per cent. of all the inmates, were again considered to exhibit the physical and mental advantages which life under such conditions undoubtedly bestows even when it is conceded that the patients are selected on account of their suitability for residence in separate houses with the minimum of supervision.

The medical work of the institution is carried on by Dr. Rutherford and three assistants, one of whom (the second) also acts as pathologist. The Pathological Laboratory has since last visit undergone considerable alteration, more especially as regards fittings and appliances. The supply of instruments is apparently very generous, and ought to stimulate and encourage the prosecution of original research among the junior members of the medical staff. It is understood that the present pathologist has for some time been engaged in interesting investigations upon the infection of milk by tubercular bacillus.

The books and registers were examined, and found regularly and correctly kept.

DUNDEE ROYAL ASYLUM,
11th and 12th June, 1901.

The changes in the population since last visit are given in the following statement :—

	PRIVATE PATIENTS.		PAUPER PATIENTS.		TOTALS.
	M.	F.	M.	F.	
On Register, 18th October, 1900,	45	44	124	193	406
Admitted, ...	8	12	32	34	86
Discharged Recovered, . .	3	3	6	15	27
Discharged Unrecovered, .	4	3	6	6	19
Died, ...	4	3	14	11	32
On Register, 12th June, 1901,	42	47	130	195	414

With the exception of 1 man who was absent on pass and 1 woman who was absent on statutory probation, all the patients were resident and were seen during the visit.

The deaths are registered as due to organic brain disease and paralysis in 10 cases, to general paralysis of the insane in 6 cases, to phthisis in 5 cases, to heart disease in 4 cases, to senile decay in 3 cases, to epilepsy in 2 cases, and to puerperal septicæmia and pneumonia in 1 case each. *Post mortem* examinations were made in 18 cases ; permission to perform such examination was refused in the remaining instances. There are no entries in the Register of Restraint and Seclusion. There are 3 entries in the Register of Accidents, one of which refers to an intracapsular fracture of the head of the femur due to an accidental fall, the other two are unimportant.

There are 15 male and 26 female attendants on day duty and 3 male and 6 female attendants on night duty. The following changes have taken place in the nursing staff since last visit :—6 men and 20 women have been engaged, 1 man and 13 women have resigned, and 3 men and 2 women have been dismissed. From this statement it will be seen that out of 32 female attendants 20 have been less than 9 months in the service of the institution. These numerous changes are not conducive to the good of the patients, and steps ought to be taken to reduce them. While the existence of social causes as one of the sources of this unrest must be admitted, experience has shown that much may be done to improve the stability of asylum service by increasing the comfort of the staff in the matter of extended leave, better food, and more suitable quarters. In one asylum the opening of a new Nurses' Home has been followed by unexpected and satisfactory results in this respect.

The number of patients attending Divine service last Sunday was 189. The absence of a proper hall or chapel for these services is a defect which ought to be remedied as soon as possible. The number of patients industrially employed at the time of the visit was 233, of whom 111 were men and 122 were women.

The asylum was found clean in every part and in very good order. The new block for private patients is rapidly approaching completion. Its construction has been planned with care, and its internal fittings and decorations are pleasing and elaborate in detail. One feature referred to in the preceding entry—the carrying of the heating pipes close to the ceiling in some of the rooms—must again be alluded to, as it is not only suggestive to suicidal patients, but forms a convenient arrangement for suspension. Unless some precautionary measures of a structural kind are taken by the Directors to obviate this risk they must be prepared to face the occurrence of a fatality of a disagreeable nature at any time. It is understood that the lease of Gray House expires within the next few months and that it is not to be renewed. The loss is a regrettable one, for the rural amenities and quietness of this charming country house cannot be replaced by the new asylum.

It is understood that the drying horses in the laundry are defective and that several hours are required to dry clothes which ought under more perfect conditions to be prepared for ironing in a few minutes, and that serious inconvenience is experienced in consequence. It was judged that this defect could be remedied by rapidly propelling hot air through the chambers, and by minor alterations of a structural kind, upon which it would be advisable to obtain the advice of a skilled engineer

The patients had every appearance of being suitably fed, and their clothing was, almost without exception, in a very satisfactory condition. The men were, with two exceptions, quiet and orderly, but there was a considerable amount of noise and excitement among the female patients. It is not improbable to suppose that the frequent changes among the nurses may have some effect in the causation of this excitement.

The medical element in the care of the patients and in the management of the asylum continues to be a prominent feature in the administration of the institution. The case books are admirably kept, and any information regarding the patients is easily obtained by referring to them. The sickrooms are conducted exactly like the wards of an ordinary hospital, and the instruction of the attendants in nursing and in the treatment of the insane is perseveringly carried on by Dr. Rorie.

The books and registers were examined and found to be carefully and correctly kept.

Appendix B.

Commissioners' Entries.

Royal and District Asylums.

Dundee Royal Asylum.

Appendix B.

'Commissioners'
Entries.

Royal and
District
Asylums.

Dundee
Royal Asylum.

DUNDEE ROYAL ASYLUM,
7th and 8th November 1901.

There were on the 7th instant 419 patients on the registers of the asylum. Of these, 1 is a voluntary inmate, 38 men and 46 women are private patients, and 137 males and 197 females are paupers. Since last visit 1 male and 1 female have been transferred from the private to the pauper list, and 1 female from the pauper to the private list. Effect has been given to these changes in the above figures. One female pauper was absent on pass. The number resident is 418, all of whom were given in the course of the visit an opportunity of making any statement they desired.

The following changes in the population have taken place since 12th June 1901, the date of preceding report :—

| | PRIVATE PATIENTS. | | PAUPER PATIENTS. | | TOTALS. |
	M.	F.	M.	F.	
Admitted, . . .	4	4	21	21	50
Discharged recovered, . .	1	2	5	6	14
Discharged unrecovered, . .	3	2	4	9	18
Died, ...	3	1	6	4	14

During the period under review there has been a decrease of 5 in the number of private patients and an increase of 9 in the number of paupers. The amount of vacant accommodation in this asylum is large. It is understood that the Directors, in consideration of this fact, are not to renew the lease of Gray House. The main building and the new block for private patients, which is practically ready for occupation, can properly accommodate 486 patients, and as the number resident is 418 it will be evident that there are vacant beds for 68 patients. In view of the overcrowding in other asylums, it is a matter of regret in the interests of the patients that advantage is not taken of the large margin of spare accommodation in this asylum.

The deaths are registered as due to organic lesions of the brain and nervous diseases in 4 cases ; to heart affections in 2 cases ; to senile decay in 2 cases ; to tubercular diseases in 2 cases ; and to cancer, pneumonia, chronic bronchitis, and suffocation during an epileptic fit, each in 1 case. *Post mortem* examinations were made in 7 cases, or in 50 per cent. of the deaths. In the remaining 7 cases the consent of the relatives to an autopsy was withheld. The Pathological Journal containing the record of these examinations is well kept, and much valuable pathological work is done by Dr. Rorie and his staff. The manner in which the case books are kept and illustrated by excellent photographs is worthy of praise. The medical work in this institution is of a high standard.

Neither restraint nor seclusion has been resorted to in the treatment of any patient since 24th October 1889. The Register of Accidents contains 4 entries. They refer in 2 cases to a fracture of the thigh bone, due in each instance to an accidental fall ; in 1 case to a fracture of a rib and bruises on the face, due to ill-usage by an attendant ; and in 1 case to suffocation during an epileptic fit. The patient, who slept in an observation dormitory, appears to have turned silently on his face during a fit unobserved. This death was the subject of enquiry by the Procurator-Fiscal, and no blame was attributed to the attendant in charge. The facts in reference to the case of ill-usage by an attendant should have been reported to the Procurator-Fiscal, especially as it is understood that the attendant acknowledged himself guilty of the assault. He was summarily dismissed. The number of patients who have escaped and were absent for at least one night before being brought back is 4.

It is satisfactory to report that the changes among the attendants and nurses have not been so numerous as formerly—2 attendants and 6 nurses have resigned, 3 attendants have been dismissed, and 4 attendants and 6 nurses have been engaged. It will be seen from the following statement that the duration of service of the male staff is far more satisfactory than that on the female side :—

Length of Service.		Attendants.	Nurses.
From 11 to 20 years, ...		5	0
,, 6 ,, 7 ,, ...		2	2
,, 2 ,, 4 ,, ...		3	10
Over 1 year, ...		4	7
Under 1 year, ...		6	10

The six members of the male staff who have been longest in the service of the asylum are married men. If suitable cottages were provided for married attendants the average duration of service among the male staff would, without doubt, be largely increased. The detached hospital is used as accommodation for nurses and servants. If it were trebled in size and converted into a comfortable Nurses' Home, the changes among the female staff would certainly be fewer, and an intelligent and capable class of nurses would be retained. From the fact that there are 15 of the present staff who have obtained the certificate of proficiency in nursing granted by the Medico-Psychological Association, it will be evident that the training and teaching of the attendants is attended with a large measure of success.

The condition of the patients was in all respects satisfactory, and the manifestations of excitement were fewer than at any previous visit. The clothing of both sexes was suitable for the season, and generally neat and tidy in appearance. The dinners served during the visit were liberal in amount, and favourable comments were voluntarily made as to the dietary by several patients. Eleven men and 17 women were in bed. The number of epileptics is 26, of general paralytics 7, and of those under special observation on account of active suicidal tendencies 7. Twenty-two male and 6 female private patients are induced to engage daily in useful work, and the number of paupers industrially employed is 91 men and 116 women.

All parts of the asylum were found clean, bright, and in excellent order. Several sections of the male side have been repainted and repapered, and their appearance made cheerful and pleasing. The floors of the general bath and dressing rooms have been laid with tiles, and the baths refitted with larger pipes and taps. As the filling or emptying of the baths now only takes a minute, each patient can have clean water, and yet the bathing operations are expeditiously accomplished. The reconstruction of the lavatories is completed, and their arrangements are in every way admirable. The condition of the sheets and pillow-cases, especially on the male side, calls for unfavourable comment: they were not so clean as is desirable. It is understood that this state of matters is due to the inefficient condition of the drying-closets. It was demonstrated during the visit that sheets which had been for hours in these closets were only partially dry in the centre and quite wet at the edges. In these circumstances a weekly change in the underclothing of both men and women and of the bed-linen is not possible. It will be evident that no time should be lost in putting these drying-closets into proper order. Porcelain tubs are gradually being substituted for the old wooden ones. A new and larger boiler has recently been erected in the boiler-house, and additions to the electric plant are about to be made in order to meet the requirements of the new private block. A pipe is in process of being laid to convey the sewage of the asylum to the drainage system at Bullionfield Works. The fields which have been used for the disposal of the sewage by irrigation are too near the new building to render the continuance of this system satisfactory from a sanitary point of view.

The new private block is being comfortably and handsomely furnished, and its several departments have been equipped with arrangements of the best and most modern description. The accommodation throughout the building will provide for patients belonging to the upper and middle classes in a way which cannot fail to be conducive to their mental and bodily well-being. Extensive views of the surrounding scenery are obtained from all parts of the building. The laying out of the grounds and the planting of sheltering belts of trees are in progress.

The registers were examined and found regularly and accurately kept.

Appendix B, ..

Commissioners Entries.

Royal and District Asylums.

Dundee Royal Asylum.

ROYAL EDINBURGH ASYLUM.
17th, 18th, 19th, and 21st June 1901.

Royal Edinburgh Asylum.

The following statement shows the changes in population since the asylum was last visited :—

I. Certificated Patients—

		PRIVATE.		PAUPER.		TOTALS.
		M.	F.	M.	F.	
On Register, 20th November, 1900,		188	176	308	302	974
Admitted, ...		24	17	105	109	255
Discharged Recovered, . .		5	13	21	43	82
Discharged Unrecovered, .		11	4	90	41	146
Died, ...		5	6	26	30	67
On Register, 17th June, 1901,		197	169	270	298	934

II. Voluntary Inmates—

Resident at last visit, , .		9	3	0	0	12
Admitted, ...		0	3	0	0	3
Left, ...		2	2	0	0	4
Resident at this date, . .		7	4	0	0	11

In the above figures effect has been given to the transference of 3 females from the private to the pauper list, and of 6 males and 2 females from the pauper to the private list.

The total number resident at this date is 945 as against 986 at the date of last visit. The decrease of 41 patients has occurred entirely among the pauper patients, and is due to the removal of 78 men and 33 women to other asylums in Scotland, and to lunatic wards of poorhouses, with the object of relieving the pressure upon the accommodation of the West House. That the removal of 111 patients in this way has only had the effect of reducing the population by about 40 is a fact which, considering the unfortunate delay in the construction of the new asylum at Bangour, renders the prospect for the immediate future a very serious one. During the year ending 31st December, 1900, no less than 400 cases, chargeable to the parishes of Edinburgh, Leith, and Duddingston, were admitted to the asylum, an increase of 20·5 per cent. over the average of the past five years. The Managers of the Royal Asylum have hitherto done everything in their power to avert serious over-crowding, but unless the Edinburgh District Lunacy Board can provide more accommodation for some of their patients at an early date, either at Bangour or elsewhere, it is impossible to see how such a calamity can long be postponed.

The chief assigned causes of the 67 deaths are as follows :—general paralysis, 17 cases ; senile decay, 14 cases ; phthisis or tuberculosis, 8 cases ; gross disease of the brain or spinal cord, 7 cases ; exhaustion from mania, complicated or not by gross brain disease, 6 cases ; heart disease, 4 cases ; pneumonia, or congestion of the lungs, 3 cases ; cancer, 2 cases ; bronchitis, 2 cases ; alcoholism, 2 cases ; syncope, 1 case ; and cirrhosis of the liver and kidneys, 1 case. *Post mortem* examinations were made in 59 instances, or in 88 per cent. of the cases, a fact which shows that the medical work of the asylum continues to be sedulously performed. The only points which attract notice in the list of the causes of death are the numbers under the heads of general paralysis and senile decay. Seventeen deaths from general paralysis (25 per cent. of the whole) is for a Scottish asylum a new and startling proportion. It was also ascertained in the course of the visit that about 14 per cent. of the present male patients in the West House are general paralytics—a fact which reflects seriously upon the social health of a large section of the city population. The number of deaths from senile decay, uncomplicated by any active organic disease, is also remarkable. The average age of 10 of these cases was 69 years, and their average stay in the asylum 1½ years. It is satisfactory to note that no deaths have occurred from dysentery, diarrhœa, or enteric fever—diseases which are peculiarly liable to break out in institutions with a congested population. It is understood that since the new drainage has been introduced the asylum has been remarkably free from these and similar diseases.

There are 71 entries in the Register of Restraint and Seclusion, which refer to the Restraint of 4, and the seclusion of 19 persons. Seclusion was resorted to on account of maniacal, violent, or homicidal excitement, in each instance for short periods of time. Three patients were restrained for surgical reasons only, and 1 female patient was restrained by means of a camisole on three occasions to prevent determined attempts at suicide, after all other preventive means had been tried without success. The number of patients who escaped since last visit, and who have been absent for at least one night before being brought back, is 11. There are 4 entries in the Register of Accidents, 3 of which relate to fractures of the skull, of the humerus, and of the fore-arm respectively. All these were due to accidental falls, and none of them were followed by serious consequences. The fourth describes a cut accidentally received by the breaking of an earthenware vessel.

Four hundred and seventy-eight patients, including 25 gentlemen and 65 ladies in Craig House, were industrially employed at the time of the visit. The number of patients attending Divine service last Sunday was 466.

Excluding heads of departments, there are 71 male attendants and 73 nurses employed on day duty in the institution, and 6 men and 7 women on night duty. The following changes have occurred in the nursing staff since last visit :—18 men and 18 women have been engaged, 13 men and 13 women have resigned, and 3 men and 1 woman have been dismissed.

Notwithstanding the demand upon the accommodation of the West House, the patients occupying it were, as a whole, found in a highly satisfactory state as regards their physical health, their clothing, and the circumstances of their care and treatment. The weather during the greater part of the visit was warm and fine, and the inmates of the hospitals, both in the male and female sides of the building, were all in the open air during several hours each day. Even the bed-ridden were carried out and placed on couches and mattresses in the gardens attached to these buildings, which are sheltered from the wind and abundantly shaded by trees and shrubs. The wards on the ground floor of the main building were as usual found with their doors unlocked, so that the patients occupying them are able to pass unrestrainedly into the grounds at all hours during the daytime. With the exception of the new cases in the admission wards, both on the male and female sides, and the chronic patients in one of the female wards, there was no noisy excitement observed during the visit. The dinners at the West House were seen on two days. The food at these meals was abundant and apparently relished, and no complaint was made by those partaking of it. A new cooking range has been introduced into the kitchen, and is said to be working satisfactorily. A great deal of painting and papering of the wards and corridors in this division has recently been done, and much more is in progress. The effect of this decoration has been to add markedly to the cheerfulness and brightness of the apartments.

The condition of the patients at Craig House was eminently satisfactory in every respect. The space is fully occupied, but it is judiciously limited to the number which it can conveniently accommodate without pressure. It was satisfactory to observe that the accommodation for patients paying the highest rates of board was equally taken advantage of, which is a sign both of financial prosperity and of the public appreciation of the management of the asylum under Dr. Clouston. The individual attention to the wants of each patient, the great diversity which characterises the classification, the location, and the surroundings of the various patients, and the multiplicity of the means adopted for their employment and amusement are all interesting and instructive features in the administration. At this season of the year cricket, tennis, golf, and gardening are largely engaged in by the patients. A lady possessing the South Kensington certificate has been engaged to come twice a week to teach the lady patients fancy needlework. She goes to each ward and villa in turn. It is understood that this work has greatly interested some of the patients, and that many ladies who seemed formerly to take no interest in anything are now accomplished and enthusiastic workers. Considering the engrossing effect of needlework upon the healthy female mind, its introduction into an asylum as a curative and ameliorative measure is certainly commendable on account of its usefulness and originality. Since last visit a trained and certificated cook has been engaged as lady superintendent of the kitchen department. This change is said to have produced a marked improvement not only in cooking but in the administration of this department. A head butler has also been engaged.

The grounds immediately surrounding Craig House have now fully assumed under careful culture the aspect of relief to the buildings and to the extremely advantageous surroundings of the situation which was originally intended when they were first laid out. Their appearance was effective and pleasing. Another piece of land, on the opposite side of the road to the lower field at Craig House, has been purchased with the object primarily of protecting the grounds from being overlooked by new buildings. This finally

Appendix B.

Commissioners' Entries.

Royal and District Asylums.

Royal Edinburgh Asylum.

secures the whole boundary of the estate from encroachment of this kind. The grounds at the West House have undergone many important changes. The waste portion to the north of the building has been reclaimed, partially levelled, and converted into a fruit and vegetable garden; while the arable field to the west of the Chapel has been entirely set apart for the cultivation of garden vegetables. It is understood that the supply of vegetables to the asylum from these gardens is now abundant.

' The review of the preceding list of changes has prevented any lengthy allusion to the more purely medical work of the institution, which Dr. Clouston and his assistants continue to prosecute with zeal and with great success.

The case books were examined, and were seen to contain voluminous accounts of the treatment and progress of the various patients under care.

The registers of the asylum are carefully and correctly kept.

ROYAL EDINBURGH ASYLUM,
25th, 26th, 27th, and 28th November 1901.

There were on the 27th instant 956 patients on the registers of the asylum. Their position is shown in the following statement :—

		M.	F.	TOTALS.
1. Certified Patients—				
(1) Private,	· · · · ·	195	172	367
(2) Pauper,	· · · · ·	278	299	577
2. Voluntary inmates,	· · · ·	8	4	12
		481	475	956

Effect has been given in the foregoing figures to the transference since last visit of 1 male and 2 females from the pauper to the private list. There are 1 male and 3 females absent on statutory probation, and 1 female absent on pass. Four gentlemen and 2 ladies are at present residing in the seaside house at Cockenzie.

Since the 17th June 1901, the date to which the figures in the preceding entry refer, the following changes in the asylum population have taken place:—

	PRIVATE.		PAUPER.		TOTALS.
	M.	F.	M.	F.	
1. Certified Patients—					
Admitted, · · ·	15	20	72	73	180
Discharged recovered, ·	5	5	15	32	57
Discharged unrecovered, ·	7	11	25	19	62
Died, · · · ·	6	3	23	19	51
2. Voluntary inmates—					
Admitted, · · , ·	3	1	0	0	4
Left, · · · ·	2	1	0	0	3

The increase in the number on the register during the period under review is fortunately small, consisting of 1 private patient and of 9 paupers, or 10 in all. The number of pauper patients on the male side is as large as can be accommodated, and overcrowding exists in the female wards. The Managers and Dr. Clouston have during recent years taken advantage of the vacant accommodation available in other asylums in order to relieve the institution from overcrowding, and no less than 140 patients chargeable to Edinburgh have in this way been provided for. It is, however, doubtful whether spare accommodation will continue to be found which will receive the annual increase of paupers which takes place. It is understood that already intimation has been received from the Stirling District Board to remove the Edinburgh paupers boarded in the Larbert Asylum. During the past five years the annual pauper admissions to this institution have risen from 308 to 400, an increase of 92. Should this rise in the admission rate continue, as in all likeli-hood it will, and perhaps even be greater, as the increase is progressive, the number of paupers admitted will in all probability be about 500 in 1906. The annual admissions from the parish of Edinburgh have risen from 243 in 1895 to 311 in 1900, an increase of 68 in five years. Notwithstanding the large number removed to other establishments, the Edinburgh pauper patients

Appendix B.

Commissioners'

Entries.

Royal and District Asylums.

Royal Edinburgh Asylum.

resident in the institution have increased from 348 in 1895 to 416 in 1901. These figures point in no uncertain manner to a most serious condition of matters as to overcrowding in the near future unless the Edinburgh District Board provide without further delay, as it is clearly their duty to do, accommodation at Bangour to meet the great and increasing requirements of their district.

It is unsatisfactory to have to report that owing to the congested condition of the West House only one private patient at the lowest rate of board has been admitted since last visit. As has been repeatedly pointed out, the reception of private patients in straitened circumstances is a duty incumbent on the institution from its foundation.

The deaths were all due to natural causes, and in 37 instances, or 72·5 per ent. of the deaths, a *post mortem* examination was made. The consent of relatives to an autopsy was withheld in the remaining cases. The most fatal cause was general paralysis, which accounted for 29·4 per cent. of the deaths. The percentage from gross brain lesions is 19·6, from phthisis pulmonalis 13·7, and from senile decay 11·7. It is satisfactory to note that no death was due to zymotic disease, and that the patients in the West House have been remarkably free from epidemic or zymotic ailments since its drainage has been put into proper order. The pathological journals were examined, and found to contain full and intelligent records of the *post mortem* examinations. Much valuable pathological work is done by the medical staff, in conjunction with the Scottish Asylums' Laboratory.

The Register of Restraint and Seclusion contains 36 entries. They refer in 4 instances to the use of restraint in one case for surgical reasons, and 5 occasions in another case in order to prevent determined attempts at suicide by self-strangulation. Twenty-seven of the entries refer to the use of seclusion in the case of six patients on account of acute and violent maniacal excitement. Seven escapes have occurred ; in 2 instances the patients were absent for twenty-eight days, and consequently their names fell to be removed from the register, and in 5 instances the patients were absent for at least one night before being brought back. Two casualties are recorded—a dislocation of the right shoulder due to a fall, and a fracture of the right humerus sustained during a struggle with an attendant, the patient falling against a corner of a window No blame was, on investigation, attributed to the attendant, a verdict in which the patient is understood to have acquiesced.

The changes among the attendants and nurses are as follows—11 attendants and 17 nurses have resigned, 2 attendants and 1 nurse have been dismissed, and 15 attendants and 16 nurses have been engaged. It is understood, with approval, that the night staff in the West House is to be increased by 2, 1 in each division. This addition will increase the efficiency of the night supervision of the suicidal, the epileptic, and of those of defective habits. It is now fully recognised that a complete system of night nursing is productive of the best results in every direction. The teaching and training of the attendants and nurses continues to be carried on in a careful and successful manner Twenty-nine members of the Craig House staff and 20 of that in the West House have passed the prescribed examination, and obtained the certificate and medal granted by the Medico-Psychological Association for proficiency in mental nursing. As an incentive to take an interest in this teaching and training. and to make themselves proficient in their duties, the Managers have agreed to give an increase of 30s. in the wages of the attendants and nurses who pass this examination. It is also given as a reward to all who have already obtained the certificate.

The patients in the West House are, except for overcrowding, especially in the hospital sections, well provided for. Their requirements are liberally met, and their condition as to clothing and personal neatness was highly satisfactory. When the large number of admissions to this section, and the acute character of the bulk of the new cases are considered, the manifestations of excitement were few. The dinners seen during three days of the visit in the two dining halls were well-cooked, palatable, and abundant meals, and no reasonable complaint was made, though many patients were questioned as to the quality and quantity of their food. The dinner to the nurses was also seen, and the extremely neat manner in which the meal was served in their mess-room merits commendation. The consideration thus given to their comfort at meal times cannot fail to promote contentment

Appendix B.

Commissioners'
Entries.

Royal and
District
Asylums.

Royal Edin-
burgh Asylum.

among the female staff in this department. Every ward was found scrupulously clean, and many improvements were observed which indicated that this house is being maintained in excellent order. The dormitory for acute cases in the female hospital is in respect of equipment and appearance of comfort and brightness all that can be desired. No. 1 Female Day-room has been most effectively renovated and refurnished, and several wards, both in the male and female divisions, have been repainted. It is recommended that the male acute sick-ward be furnished with beds similar to those in the female hospital. The benches in the amusement hall have been replaced by chairs, which are found much more convenient. The effective isolation of consumptive patients is practically impossible on the male side, owing to the overcrowding of the hospital; but in the female division Dr. Clouston is able to reserve a small wing of the hospital, containing a series of single rooms, for the segregation and treatment of acute female consumptives. This is a matter which is at present receiving much attention, and it is hoped that separate accommodation will ere long be provided in all asylums for the care and treatment of those who are the subjects of tubercular lung disease. From a return furnished by the medical staff, there are among the patients in the West House 29 in the first stage of consumption, 11 in the second stage, and 1 in the third.

The impression produced by the visit to Craig House and its adjoining villas was one of its great efficiency, both in regard to the classification of the patients and as to their treatment. Each patient is provided for according to his or her mental condition and social requirements. Individual care is a marked feature in the management, and evidently everything is done by environment, skilful treatment, good feeding, and efficient nursing to secure recovery and to promote the happiness and well-being of the patients. All sections are replete with comfort, and the profusion of flowers and decorative plants attracted favourable notice. The dinners in the series of dining-rooms were seen and found excellent, both as to the quality of the food and the service of the meals. In each of the gentlemen's dining-rooms a butler has charge of the arrangements. A lady-superintendent has been appointed to supervise the work of the kitchen, and the cooking and prompt service of meals have consequently been greatly improved. Contracts have been entered into for the erection of cooking apparatus of the newest and best design.

The grounds, both at Craig House and the West House, are even at this season of the year in admirable order. The garden ground has been considerably extended, and the supply of vegetables has practically been doubled. The greenhouses are evidently under efficient management, and all sections of the asylum are abundantly supplied with flowers and plants.

It was clear during the visit, which extended over four days, that Dr. Clouston's management is characterised by earnestness, energy, and ability. The institution holds a very high position among establishments for the insane, commands public confidence, and is deservedly prospering in all directions.

The case books are kept in a manner highly creditable to the Assistant Medical Staff, and the registers were found accurate and written up to date.

ELGIN DISTRICT ASYLUM,
8th February 1901.

The changes in population which have occurred since last visit are shown in the following statement :—

PRIVATE AND PAUPER PATIENTS.

	M.	F.	TOTALS.
On register 18th August 1900, . . .	72	107	179
Admitted since, ...	15	5	20
Discharged recovered, . . .	4	0	4
Discharged unrecovered, . . .	2	1	3
Died, ...	2	7	9
Resident 8th February 1901, . . .	79	104	183

Of those resident at this date, 6 men and 2 women are private patients.

The causes of the 9 deaths are as follows :—in 3 cases phthisis pulmonalis Appendix B.
(2 of these cases were transfers from another institution, and were suffering
from the disease at the time of their admission to this asylum), in 2 cases Commissioners' Entries.
gross cerebral disease, in 2 cases heart affection, in 1 case cancer, and in 1
case senile decay. A *post mortem* examination was made in 1 case. Royal and
There are 2 entries in the Register of Restraint and Seclusion referring to District
the restraint of one person for surgical reasons. The Register of Accidents Asylums.
contains 1 entry descriptive of a fracture of the forearm sustained by an
elderly female patient through slipping and falling on the floor of one of the Elgin District Asylum.
lavatories. One hundred and thirty-five patients were industrially employed
at the time of the visit in the following manner ·

	M.	F.
Assisting in housework, .	16	23
Garden and farm work, ...	37	0
Artisans, ...	6	0
Kitchen and laundry, ...	0	26
Knitting and needlework, . . .	0	27

There are 8 attendants, including 1 farm servant, in charge of the male
patients, and 8 female attendants, including 2 laundresses, have charge of
the female patients.

There are 3 night attendants—1 man and 2 women.

Since last visit 1 male and 2 female attendants have resigned, and others
have been engaged in their places.

The length of service of the asylum staff is highly satisfactory, and shows
an average duration of 5 years.

2 have served upwards of 20 years.
2 ,,   ,,   ,,   ,, 10   ,,
2 ,,   ,,   ,,   ,,   8   ,,
2 ,,   ,,   ,,   ,,   5   ,,
4 ,,   ,,   ,,   ,,   3   ,,
6 ,,   ,,   ,,   ,,   1 year.
6 ,,   ,,   under   1   ,,

The present staff is said to be efficient and satisfactory, and every effort
is made to render the conditions of their service and their circumstances as
light and agreeable as possible.

All the patients in the asylum were seen during the visit. Their general
physical health was satisfactory, and the nursing and medical care of 9 of
their number, who were confined to bed on account of illness, appeared to
be in every respect careful, kindly, and efficient. The inmates were free
from excitement, and those of them who were conversed with frankly
expressed themselves as contented with the treatment they receive. Their
personal clothing was in every instance suitable, and in good repair ; many
of the women were neatly and tastefully dressed. The beds were comfortable, and the bedcoverings were sufficient for the season of the year and
beautifully clean.

The asylum was found in excellent order and in an unexceptionable state
of cleanness. The work of heating the single rooms with hot-water pipes
has been completed, and the result has not only secured the comfort of the
patients who occupy these rooms, but it has also materially improved the
temperature in the corridors, staircases, and other parts of the building.
The old stone pavement in the corridors leading to the sick wards has been
removed and replaced by pitch pine wood flooring, covered by linoleum.
This also is a marked improvement.

The patients occupying the farm-house of Bilbohall were found in good
health and bearing evidence of sufficient care.

It is gratifying to be able to report that the well-being of the patients
appears to be successfully promoted under the present administration of the
institution.

The books and registers were examined and found correctly kept.

Appendix B.

Commissioners'
Entries.

Royal and
District
Asylums.

Elgin District
Asylum.

ELGIN DISTRICT ASYLUM,
24th July 1901.

There are 187 patients resident in the asylum at this date. Of these, 7 men and 4 women are private patients, and 69 men and 107 women are paupers. In the above figures effect has been given to the transference of 1 male from the pauper to the private list. Of the 176 paupers resident, 1 male and 20 females are chargeable to parishes in Orkney.

The following changes have taken place since 8th February 1901, the date of previous report :—

	PRIVATE AND PAUPER PATIENTS.		
	M.	F.	TOTALS.
Admitted, ...	5	16	21
Discharged recovered, . . : : .	4	3	7
Discharged unrecovered, . . .	0	3	3
Died, ...	4	3	7

The margin of spare accommodation in this asylum is getting small. The number of empty beds for males is 3 in the main asylum and 7 at Bilbohall, and for females there are only 4. It will be evident that no more female patients from Orkney should be received.

The deaths are registered as due to cerebral disease in 3 cases, to epilepsy in 1 case, to heart disease in 1 case, to phthisis pulmonalis in 1 case, and to chronic bronchitis in 1 case. In 3 instances, or in 42·8 per cent. of the deaths, a *post mortem* examination was made.

The Register of Restraint and Seclusion contains 2 entries. They refer to the use of restraint in 1 case to prevent self-injury, and in 1 case to secure the safety of a patient who was acutely excited. One escape has occurred in which the patient was absent for a night before being brought back. No patient has been the subject of an accident.

The changes in the staff have been few—2 men and 1 woman have resigned and the vacancies have been filled. The causes of leaving are as follows :—1 on account of ill-health, 1 to nurse a sick mother, and 1 for a more lucrative situation. The fewness of these changes, coupled with the highly satisfactory average duration of service of the present staff, as is shown in the previous entry, indicates tactful and successful management. The introduction of satisfactory arrangements for the night supervision of the patients has rendered it safe and proper to give each day attendant a separate and well furnished bedroom. The staff is therefore more comfortably accommodated than was formerly the case.

The patients were with one exception quiet and orderly in behaviour, their appearance bore every evidence of efficient care, good feeding, and abundant open-air exercise. A well cooked and palatable dinner was served during the visit. The dining-hall is now too small for the present number of inmates, a larger percentage than is desirable having to take their meals in the wards. Fifty-eight men and 77 women are actively employed in useful work, which promotes good health and contentment. The number confined to bed was only 8, the majority of whom were suffering from the infirmities of old age. It was evident that they were kindly and efficiently nursed.

It is recorded with satisfaction that the single rooms and corridors are now heated during the winter months by a system of low-pressure hot-water pipes. This and the flooring of the corridors with pitch pine are two decided improvements which contribute materially to the comfort of the patients.

The asylum was throughout in admirable order and scrupulously clean. The walls of the new dayroom, dormitories, and single rooms on the female side are now sufficiently dry to be painted and decorated, and it is hoped this work will be done without further delay. The woodwork around the sinks and basins has been renewed in several of the lavatories, and it is understood that more is to be done in this direction.

The books and registers were examined and found regularly and accurately kept.

Appendix B.

Commissioners' Entries.

Royal and District Asylums.

Fife and Kinross District Asylum.

FIFE AND KINROSS DISTRICT ASYLUM,
28th and 31st May, 1901.

Since last visit the following changes have taken place in the population of the asylum :—

PRIVATE AND PAUPER PATIENTS.

	M.	F.	TOTALS.
On the Register 4th October, 1900,	242	290	532
Admitted,	38	45	83
Discharged recovered,	15	14	29
Discharged unrecovered,	7	16	23
Died,	10	15	25
On the Register 31st May, 1901,	248	290	538

Of those on the register at this date 6 women are private patients.

It is observed that the numbers resident are slowly increasing, and that there are now only about 7 vacant beds in the asylum—5 on the male and 2 on the female side. Fortunately the admission rate for the past year has been somewhat lower than the average of previous years, and the numbers discharged have been maintained at the usual high rate, otherwise the population would by this time have exceeded the accommodation. It is understood that plans are to be shortly prepared with the object of providing hospital accommodation for acute and recent cases. The two alternative proposals regarding the situation and character of the additions were described informally by Dr. Turnbull, and it was judged that either might be satisfactory ; but it is suggested that, before finally deciding to adopt the one or the other, sketch plans of both should be prepared by the architect and submitted to the General Board in order that an interchange of views may take place between that Board and the District Board on this important subject.

The assigned causes of the 25 deaths are as follows :—Phthisis or tuberculosis, 7 cases ; gross brain disease, 5 cases ; pneumonia, 3 cases ; general paralysis, cancer, heart disease, and exhaustion from mania, 2 cases each ; anæmia, 1 case ; and 1 death was due to the intentional swallowing of a poisonous liniment. In the last-mentioned case the patient, a woman, was considered to be convalescent, and was removed to a ward where for such cases the rigour of close supervision is properly relaxed. While there she unfortunately obtained access to a cupboard in which a bottle of liniment was kept, and swallowed the contents. The death of this patient was immediately reported to the General Board and to the Procurator-Fiscal, and an investigation was conducted by the latter into all the circumstances attending it. *Post mortem* examinations were made in 22 instances. In the 3 remaining cases the consent of the relatives to such examination was refused.

Four patients escaped and were absent for at least one night since the date of last visit. There are no entries in the Register of Restraint and Seclusion. The more important entries in the Register of Accidents refer to the suicide already mentioned, to a fracture of the humerus in a female patient caused by the sudden twisting of her arm by another patient, and to the accidental fracture of two ribs in a male patient.

The changes among nurses and attendants since last visit have been as follows :—Eight men and 13 women have been engaged, 2 men and 6 women have resigned, and 5 men and 1 woman have been dismissed. The day nursing staff consists of 22 persons on the male side, 3 of whom are women, and 27 nurses on the female side. There are 4 male and 5 female night attendants, the allocation of whom secures that 34 female and 26 male patients are under continuous night supervision, and that 70 female and 42 male patients are, though less rigorously watched, yet always under supervision.

The night nursing of the chronic insane has been in force in this asylum for the past ten years, and Dr. Turnbull states it has exercised a salutary effect upon the health and the conduct of the patients subjected to it.

It was observed during the visit that, with one exception, all the doors of the wards on the female side of the asylum were unlocked, and that it was possible to pass from one end of the division to the other without the use of a key. It was also observed that, with the exception of those in the ward

Appendix B.

Commissioners'
Entries.

Royal and
District
Asylums.

Fife and Kinross District
Asylum.

mentioned, any of the female patients who have liberty to do so may pass freely from the wards into the open air. On the male side the same freedom prevails, with the exception of some parts of the main building. As this asylum was one of the first to adopt the open-door system, it is gratifying to see that it still in large part maintains it, and any possible extension of the system will be welcomed.

It is recorded with satisfaction that all the butcher meat now used in the asylum is killed on the farm, and that all the milk and vegetables consumed are also produced at home. In time it is hoped that most of the food supply of the institution will come from the land attached to it. It is worth considering whether it might not be an advantage to bake the bread required for the asylum instead of contracting for it as at present.

The asylum was found clean and in good order, and the condition of the patients was satisfactory. The dresses of the women deserve attention on account of their neatness and the variety and colour of the material of which they are made.

The increase in the number of patients during the past few years is such that the work thrown upon the Assistant Medical Officer (although in the present instance most capably performed) is greater than is generally considered consistent with efficiency. The opening of an addition to the asylum would, of course, necessitate the appointment of a second Assistant Medical Officer, but the subject is now referred to as it seems probable that before then the number of patients may require it.

The books and registers were examined and found to be regularly and correctly kept.

FIFE AND KINROSS DISTRICT ASYLUM,
4th and 5th November 1901.

There are at this date, 5th November 1901, 532 patients on the register of the asylum. Of these, 6 females are private patients, and 239 males and 287 females are paupers. One male is absent on pass, and 1 female absent by escape.

Since last visit, on 31st May 1901, the following changes in the population have taken place :—

| | | PRIVATE AND PAUPER PATIENTS. | |
	M.	F.	TOTALS.
Admitted, ...	21	28	49
Discharged recovered, . . .	10	11	21
Discharged unrecovered, . . .	9	8	17
Died, ...	11	6	17

The number of male patients has, during the year under review, decreased by 9, and that of the females has increased by 3. The admission rate for the past year has been lower than that of previous years, but it is inadvisable to entertain any hope of a continuance of the decrease in the number of admissions. Unfortunately, the experience of other lunacy districts is that a low admission rate has sooner or later been followed by a large influx of patients, and a return to the usual annual increase in the admissions. The margin of spare accommodation in the asylum is, as has been previously pointed out, very small, and it may at any time be fully occupied. It is therefore learned with approval that plans for the erection of two wings to the present hospital block have been prepared and are at present under the consideration of the District Board. It is hoped that it will be found possible to admit the patients directly into these new buildings. The present plan of receiving patients at the administrative section, and of taking them through many doors and corridors before they reach the ward in which they are to be treated, creates an unpleasant impression which is not beneficial. In our newest asylums the arrangements in the hospital blocks for the admission of patients are such as not to cause anxiety or distrust, and this is important from a curative point of view.

Of the 17 patients discharged unrecovered, 4 were transferred to other asylums, 3 were removed from the register after an absence of 28 days by escape, and 10 were sent to the care of relatives and were at the same time removed from the poor roll. Constant efforts have been and are being made by Dr. Turnbull to keep down the growth of the asylum population by the discharge of patients who have so far improved as to warrant their trial under domestic care. A large proportion of these patients do well and remain permanently at home, but unfortunately in the cases of other patients mental changes occur, often after years of residence outside, which necessitate their return to the asylum. Of the 532 patients at present resident in the asylum, 168 or 31·5 per cent. have been tried either at their own homes or in private dwellings under suitable guardians and had to be readmitted. In 28 of these cases a trial had been given twice or oftener. From these facts it can be concluded that there has been no undue detention. If it were not for this liberal policy of discharge on the part of Dr. Turnbull the population of the asylum would have been much larger than it is at this date.

The deaths are registered as due to brain or spinal lesions in 4 cases, to exhaustion from acute mental diseases in 2 cases, to general paralysis in 3 cases, to phthisis pulmonalis and other tubercular affections in 6 cases, and to heart disease in 2 cases. In 12 cases, or in 70 per cent. of the deaths, a *post mortem* examination was made. In the remaining 5 cases, the consent of the relations was withheld.

The medical staff remains at the same strength as when the population of the asylum was less than half its present number. A second assistant medical officer is needed, and his appointment is strongly recommended. It is impossible for the present staff, with their large amount of medical and administrative work, to engage in any of the finer pathological investigations usually done in other asylums. It is, however, only just to state that the case books and other medical records were found carefully kept and written up to date.

The Register of Restraint and Seclusion contains 5 entries. In 3 instances they refer to the use of restraint for the purpose of preventing self-injury, and in 2 instances to the use of seclusion in the treatment of one patient. Five accidents are recorded ; four were slight injuries such as bruises, and one was a fracture of the ulna due to slipping on the polished floor. Six escapes have taken place ; three of the patients remained absent for 28 days and were removed from the register, but one of these has since been readmitted, and the other two are known to be doing well ; one patient is still absent, and two were away for at least one night before being brought back.

The changes among the attendants and nurses have not been numerous—5 nurses have resigned, 1 attendant has died, and 1 attendant has been dismissed for misconduct, not, however, affecting the patients, and 2 attendants and 4 nurses have been engaged. The attendant who died, Alexander Duncan, had been in the service of the asylum for over 28 years and was a most trustworthy, industrious, and capable servant. The ratio of the day staff to patients is 1 to 11, a proportion which indicates a staff of adequate strength. In regard to duration of service it is satisfactory to find that a good percentage of the attendants and nurses have had considerable asylum experience. On the male side 25 per cent. of the staff have an average duration of service of 12 years, and 42 per cent. an average of over 2 years. Thirty-three per cent. have not yet completed a year's service. In the female division 15 per cent. of the nurses have an average duration of service of over 10 years, and 53 per cent. an average of over 2 years. Thirty-two per cent. have been under a year in the service of the asylum. The arrangements for the night supervision, and especially for the continuous night supervision of the suicidal, of the epileptic, and of those of defective habits, were inquired into and found satisfactory. The ratio of the night staff to patients is 1 to 59.

The condition in which the patients were found throughout the asylum was in every respect highly satisfactory, and there was abundant evidence of kindly and sympathetic consideration in their general treatment. Their dress was neat, tidy, and suitable for the season. The dinners seen during the visit were liberal and palatable meals, of which appreciation was expressed by those of whom enquiries were made. The arrangements in the hospital section provide every requirement necessary for the efficient care and treatment of the sick and infirm. Nine men and 14 women were confined to bed. The number of patients regarded as actively suicidal is 10 males and 11 females ; the general paralytics are 3 men and 1 woman ; and those subject

Appendix B.

Commissioners' Entries.

Royal and District

Fife and Kinross District Asylum.

to epilepsy are 19 men and 8 women. The number returned as daily engaged in useful occupations is 167 males and 196 females, being 69 per cent. and 67 per cent. respectively. Divine service was last Sunday attended by 145 men and 119 women, a total of 264, which is 50 per cent. of the population.

The day-rooms and dormitories were in excellent order, and the bedding was clean and sufficient. The day-rooms, which were bright with an abundance of flowers, presented a cheerful and comfortable appearance. Several wards have been repainted in a tasteful manner, and work of this kind is always in progress. In this way the interior of the asylum is maintained in proper order.

The extended farm is proving a financial success as well as being of great advantage in many other directions. The rate of board has recently been reduced £1, and it is understood that it was the profits on the farm which enabled the District Board to make this reduction. The meat consumed in the asylum is from cattle fattened on the farm, and its quality at the time of the visit was excellent. It has been possible to introduce greater variety in the dinners to the patients and attendants since the cattle were killed on the farm. The home supply of potatoes and milk is sufficient for the requirements of the institution.

Telephonic communication has been established between the asylum and the office of the Clerk of the District Board. It would be of great administrative convenience if this was extended between the Board-room and the principal sections of the asylum, and also the house of the Medical Superintendent.

The registers were examined and found regularly and correctly kept.

GLASGOW ROYAL ASYLUM,
18th and 19th June 1901.

On the 18th instant there were 431 patients on the registers of the asylum. Of these, 3 gentlemen and 12 ladies were voluntary inmates—173 gentlemen and 239 ladies were private patients, and 3 males and 1 female were paupers. One gentleman was absent on statutory probation, and 6 ladies were resident at a seaside villa at Ardrossan. The remaining 424 patients were individually seen in the course of the visit.

Since 4th December, 1900, the date of the preceding report, the following changes have taken place :—

Certificated Patients—

	PRIVATE.		PAUPER.		TOTALS.
	M.	F.	M.	F.	
Admitted, ...	28	33	0	0	61
Discharged Recovered, . .	6	6	0	0	12
Discharged Unrecovered, .	9	3	1	2	15
Died, ...	19	7	0	0	26
Voluntary Inmates—					
Admitted, ...	3	4	0	0	7
Left, ...	3	6	0	0	9

It will be seen from the above figures that there is an increase of 17 in the number of ladies resident and a decrease of 6 gentlemen, of 2 paupers and of 2 voluntary inmates.

The institution is practically full in the ladies' divisions, but there are about 30 empty beds on the male side.

The deaths are registered as due to diseases of the brain or spinal cord in 11 cases, to cardiac disease in 4 cases, to senile decay in 5 cases, and in 1 case to each of the following causes:—nephritis, phthisis pulmonalis, bronchiectasis, peritonitis, œsophagotomy, and tumour in neck. In 18 instances or in 69 per cent. of the deaths a *post mortem* examination was made.

The Register of Restraint and Seclusion contains 45 entries. They refer to the restraint of 3 persons—1 on account of destructive habits, 1 to prevent determined attempts at suicide, and 1 to prevent interference with the dressings after a surgical operation. Seven patients were on, in all, 36 occasions secluded for periods varying from 1 to 8 hours on account of maniacal and dangerous excitement. The only accidents calling for notice are (1) a fracture of the humerus due to an accidental fall, and (2) swallowing lower plate of artificial teeth with suicidal intent. The upper plate had been removed, and the fact that there was a lower plate was unknown. The patient swallowed the plate, and as all efforts to extract it proved unsuccessful, œsophagotomy was performed. Death unfortunately ensued in four days after the operation.

No escape has occurred. The changes in the staff have been numerous—28 attendants have resigned, 23 have been engaged, and 1 has been dismissed. Six male attendants left for military service in South Africa. The staff at present consists of 36 male and 40 female attendants for day duty, and 4 of each sex for night duty. The proportion of attendants to patients is 1 to 5 on the male side, and 1 to 6 in the female division.

The patients continue to be well cared for, and generally speaking they showed great contentment with their treatment. All had an opportunity of making any statement they desired, and private interviews were given to several patients. Except on the ground of detention there were no complaints, and those who appealed in regard to undue detention were manifestly unfit for discharge.

The mental and bodily condition of every patient is carefully studied with a view to improvement or recovery.

The medical treatment and the hospital care of those suffering from bodily disease or acute mental illness are highly satisfactory. The dinner to those paying the lower rates of board was a substantial and well-cooked meal, and enquiry into the dietary elicited favourable replies from the more intelligent patients in the dining hall. Sixty gentlemen and 98 ladies are registered as daily engaged in useful work. Two hundred and one patients or 46·7 per cent. attended Divine service last Sunday. Sixty patients are on parole within the grounds, and outdoor games, such as cricket, croquet, and golf are well provided for. Associated entertainments are held weekly, and indoor games, books and newspapers are well supplied.

The institution is evidently managed with great ability and conscientiousness. Of the 61 patients admitted the rate of board of 17 was £40, and in 1 case the rate accepted was only £20.

As has been repeatedly pointed out in previous entries, a large number of patients are most liberally treated in the matter of accommodation. They are detained in galleries at lower charges than those which the other patients in competent circumstances pay. In maintaining these patients at unremunerative rates and in preserving their social status in the institution the Directors and Dr. Yellowlees are in an admirable manner fulfilling its charitable function.

It is understood with satisfaction that the Directors and Dr. Yellowlees contemplate taking on lease for a number of years a country house to which patients can be sent for change of air and scene. This house would be an acceptable extension of the accommodation of the institution, and would prove to be a boon much appreciated by the patients. The change of residence and of scene would in not a few cases hasten recovery.

The asylum throughout was scrupulously clean and in excellent order. The different galleries presented a cheerful and comfortably furnished appearance. Each section is furnished in a manner consonant with the class of patients resident. One gallery in the West House was in course of renovation, for which new furnishings are to be provided. New carpeting has been laid at the foot of and between the beds in the hospital wards.

Improvements in the heating arrangements and in the supply of hot water to the West House are in progess.

The dynamos are now being driven by electricity conveyed by cable from the Corporation Electrical Works.

The books and registers were examined and found regularly and accurately kept.

Appendix B.

Commissioners' Entries.

Royal and District Asylums.

Glasgow Royal Asylum.

GLASGOW ROYAL ASYLUM,
12th and 13th December 1901.

The following changes have taken place in the population since last visit :—

F

		CERTIFICATED PATIENTS.		VOLUNTARY INMATES.		TOTALS.
		M.	F.	M.	F.	
On Register 18th June 1901,	.	176	240	3	12	431
Admitted, ...	.	26	25	5	6	62
Left, ...	.	—	—	5	6	11
Discharged recovered, .	.	5	11	—	—	16
Discharged unrecovered,	.	10	5	—	—	15
Died, ...	.	5	4	—	—	9
On Register 12th December 1901,.		182	245	3	12	442

Of the certificated patients, 3 men and 1 woman are paupers.

With the exception of 2 male and 3 female patients who were absent on statutory probation and 1 male patient who was absent on pass, all the patients were seen during the visit.

The causes of death in the nine cases who died are registered as follows:—four were due to general paralysis, 2 to gross brain disease, 2 to abdominal disease, and 1 to heart disease. *Post mortem* examinations were made in 7 cases.

There are 8 entries in the Register of Accidents. Of these, only two—a fracture of the radius and a fracture of the clavicle—are sufficiently serious to demand notice here. In neither case was blame directly attributable to those in immediate charge of the patients.

There are 5 entries in the Register of Restraint and Seclusion. Of these, two refer to the seclusion of individuals on account of violence and excitement, two to the use of locked gloves and locked boots respectively to prevent the removal of surgical dressings, and one to the use of locked gloves to aid in the prevention of persistent attempts at suicide.

The number of patients attending Divine service last Sunday was 211.

No less than 166 patients—65 gentlemen and 101 ladies—were industrially employed at the time of the visit. Of that number, 24 gentlemen were working in the garden, and 43 ladies were engaged at needlework.

The asylum was found in all its departments in excellent order.

With the exception of one or two of the ladies in the East House, who became excited and were noisy, the state of the patients was wholly satisfactory.

The various living and sleeping rooms presented a comfortable and cheerful appearance. They were sufficiently warm and properly ventilated.

Since the date of the last visit Dr. Yellowlees has resigned the position of Physician Superintendent, and he has been succeeded in the office by Dr. L. R. Oswald, Medical Superintendent of the Glasgow District Asylum at Gartloch.

It is learned with much regret that Dr. Yellowlees' retirement was due to an affection of the eyesight. During a long and successful professional career wholly devoted to the study and treatment of insanity, Dr. Yellowlees occupied a very distinguished position in the esteem of his fellows, both on account of his wide knowledge and his sound judgment ; and by his kindly and genial nature he has won the affectionate regard of all with whom he has been associated. His retirement from the more active duties of the management of this asylum creates a notable blank not only in connection with the institution, but in the speciality of which he was an eminent member.

The books and registers were examined and found to be accurately and correctly kept.

GLASGOW DISTRICT ASYLUM, GARTLOCH.
14th and 15th May 1901.

There were on the 14th instant 278 men and 260 women, in all 538 patients, on the register of the asylum. One woman is absent on statutory probation, and 1 man absent on pass. The number resident was 536, all of whom were individually seen in the course of the visit.

Since 21st November, 1900, the date of the preceding entry, the following changes in the population have taken place :—

Appendix B.

Commissioners Entries.

Royal and District Asylums.

Glasgow District Asylum, Gartloch.

	PAUPER PATIENTS.		
	M.	F.	TOTALS.
Admitted, ...	59	70	129
Discharged recovered, ...	24	22	46
Discharged unrecovered, ...	14	17	31
Died, ...	18	22	40

The number resident has increased by 12, the admissions have been 129, and the discharges from all causes 117. These figures show a very active movement of the population, and the number resident at this date would have been larger had not the death rate been high, and had not Dr. Oswald and the parochial officials been successful in discharging 23 unrecovered but improved patients either to the care of their relatives or to homes in country districts. Notwithstanding these energetic efforts to board out suitable patients, the spare accommodation of the asylum is being rapidly occupied. There are only 2 empty beds in the male and 23 in the female division of the main asylum. The male division is practically full, and the margin of spare accommodation on the female side is, in view of the high female admission rate, not large. In these circumstances it is understood with satisfaction that the District Board have resolved to provide additional accommodation, and that plans are being prepared for the erection of five blocks capable of accommodating 230 chronic patients. It is intended to erect what may be called an industrial home near the farm steading for 40 men and 5 women who are engaged at farm work, and a block for 45 chronic male cases near the site of the old gasworks. Two blocks, each for 45 chronic female cases, are to be provided, and the field to the west, that between the farm buildings and the hospital, appears to be an admirable and convenient site for these buildings. In connection with these extensions it is the desire of Dr. Oswald to have a small hospital for the isolation and treatment of consumptive patients. This provision would be an important advance in the medical classification of the patients. The communicability of consumption has been long recognised, and the isolation of patients subject to this disease is therefore a duty in the interests of the other inmates. The deaths from phthisis pulmonalis during the last six months were 5, or 12½ per cent. of the mortality during this period. Of these patients, 1 was consumptive on admission, and 4 were free of the physical signs of the disease when admitted. The District Board are strongly recommended to provide an hospital which will not only secure the isolation of such patients, but also the treatment, and probably the cure, of their malady.

The deaths are registered as due to organic brain disease in 20 cases, to phthisis pulmonalis in 5 cases, to inflammatory lung affections in 4 cases, to senile decay in 4 cases, to heart disease in 2 cases, and in 1 case to each of the following causes:—carbuncle, puerperal septicæmia, exophthalmic goitre, cancer, and septic pneumonia after tracheotomy. It is creditable to the medical staff to be able to report that in 95 per cent. of the deaths the causes were ascertained or verified by *post mortem* examination. It is noted with approval that a pathologist has recently been appointed, and will shortly enter on duty.

The Register of Restraint and Seclusion contains 75 entries. Seventy-one of these entries refer to the case of a female patient whose impulsive attacks were dangerous to others. Though in a locked room, the window was widely open, and she was able to sew or knit. The other entries refer to the use of seclusion in the cases of 4 patients for periods varying from 15 minutes to 7 hours. Five accidents are recorded—a fracture of right collar bone due to jumping from a window, a cut inflicted on a nurse by a patient, a fracture of a rib caused by a kick from a fellow-patient, a contused wound over hip joint from a fall, and a case of choking in a general paralytic. This patient was provided with a diet of mince meat, but he took a piece of meat from the plate of a fellow-patient, and in his hurry to swallow it was choked. Prompt measures were taken to relieve him, but he died the following day from septic pneumonia. Three escapes have taken place, but none was from among the 93 patients who enjoy the privilege of parole in the grounds. This large amount of liberty granted to patients is a most commendable feature in the management.

The changes among the attendants and nursing staff have been few. Six attendants and 5 nurses have been engaged, and 1 attendant and 4 nurses have resigned. There have been no dismissals. The increase in the staff, as indicated by the above figures, is due to 2 extra attendants being engaged to take the place of those on holiday, and to the fact that a larger staff is required since extensions of leave have been granted. Both the day and night staff is therefore maintained at an adequate strength. The causes which led to the 5 resignations are as follows,—1 attendant left because he was severely censured, 1 nurse to take up hospital work, 1 because of ill health, and 2 because their services were not considered satisfactory. The efforts of the District Board and of Dr. Oswald to prevent unnecessary changes, and to secure a suitable staff, may be said to have been very successful during the past year. The changes have been at a minimum, and it is hoped that they will continue so. The comforts of the Nurses' Home and of the accommodation for the male attendants in the administrative block are all that could be desired, the amount of leave of absence is most liberal, and their diet is varied and plentiful. The duration of service among the charge attendants and charge nurses is most satisfactory. Of the 7 charge attendants, 2 entered the service at the opening of the asylum, and the other 5 in the following year, and of the 9 charge nurses, 1 entered the service of the asylum in 1896, 5 in 1897, and 2 in 1898. These attendants and nurses could not have been longer in the service, as they were engaged as the various wards were opened.

The majority of the female patients were seen in the field adjoining the loch, sitting on the grass enjoying the fine weather, and some were knitting or sewing. On Sunday afternoon a concert of sacred music by the asylum band is held in this field, hymns are sung, and the whole service is said to be much appreciated by the patients. The behaviour of both sexes throughout the asylum was with few exceptions quiet and orderly, and no complaints calling for attention were made. Their personal neatness and clothing were quite satisfactory—only 3 females were found wearing special dresses on account of destructive habits. The industrial employment of the inmates is well organised, and a large amount of useful outdoor and indoor work is daily done. A party consisting of about 12 female patients from the hospital wards under the charge of two nurses is daily engaged in garden work, and they are found to be greatly improved both mentally and bodily by this healthy and interesting employment. Religious services for the Protestant and Catholic patients are held every Sunday morning at 10 a.m., and in winter a service or sacred concert is held at 7 p.m. Associated entertainments are regularly provided, and are varied in character. The male patients and staff engage daily in outdoor games such as cricket and bowls. These amusements and recreations are as necessary for the wellbeing of the staff as for that of the patients.

The visit to the hospital left a most pleasant impression as to the high standard of the medical treatment of the patients, the efficiency of the nursing arrangements, and the comforts surrounding its inmates. The curable insane have every chance of recovery, those suffering from bodily diseases are skilfully treated, and those who are the subjects of the infirmities of old age are carefully nursed. A great improvement has been effected both in the male and female sections by the removal of a partition wall between a dayroom and a dormitory, and by converting the two rooms into a dayroom dormitory. By this change supervision will be facilitated, and a better classification of the acute cases will be rendered possible.

The wards were in excellent order, bright and cheerful in appearance, and comfortably furnished. The condition of the dormitories and of the beds and bedding was very satisfactory. A bath, a water-closet, and a sink have been provided on the two dormitory floors of each block of the main building, and have proved of great service in the practical working of these sections. The grounds around the asylum and the hospital are rapidly getting into good order. A great deal has been done since they were last seen, and the work now in progress appears to be well considered.

The books and registers were examined, and found to be regularly and accurately kept.

GLASGOW DISTRICT ASYLUM, GARTLOCH,
17th and 18th December 1901.

On the 14th May of this year, the date of last visit, there were 538 patients on the register, of whom 278 were men and 260 were women. Since then the following changes have occurred :—

	PAUPER PATIENTS.			Appendix B.
	M.	F.	TOTALS.	Commissioners'
Admitted,	81	72	153	Entries.
Discharged recovered,	33	24	57	
Discharged unrecovered,	20	15	35	Royal and District
Died,	14	14	28	Asylums.

There were 571 patients on the register on the 15th instant, of whom 292 were males and 279 were females. These figures show an increase, within the period referred to, of 33 patients. All the patients were resident and were seen during the visit. Of the 35 patients discharged unrecovered, 9 were boarded out, 9 were sent to the care of friends, 12 were transferred to other asylums, 3 escaped, and 2 were discharged on expiry of their warrants.

The deaths were registered as due to general paralysis in 13 cases, to cerebral haemorrhage in 5 cases, to tuberculosis in 3 cases, to pneumonia in 2 cases, and to each of the following diseases in 1 case—viz., cardiac disease, epilepsy, melancholia, senile decay, and cancer of the uterus. *Post mortem* examinations were made in every instance with one exception, in which permission was refused.

There are no less than 182 entries in the Register of Restraint and Seclusion. These refer to the seclusion of 1 woman on account of violent excitement on 156 occasions, of 1 woman on 10 occasions, of 1 woman on 7 occasions, of 1 woman on 4 occasions, and of 4 women and 1 man each on one occasion. It is satisfactory to be able to record that the patient who among these has been most frequently secluded has now been found to be capable of tolerable behaviour while residing in one of the sick-room dormitories.

Three patients escaped and were absent for 28 days, after which the order for their detention expired.

There are 5 entries in the Register of Accidents. They refer to the fracture of the femur caused by jumping from a dormitory window, to a fracture of the leg caused by slipping on a floor, to the crushing of a finger in the ironing machine in the laundry, to a fracture of the olecranon process, and to a suspected fracture of a rib caused by being jammed between a cart and a gate-post.

The number of patients attending Divine service last Sunday forenoon was 318, and 290 patients attended a concert of sacred music on the evening of the same day.

Three hundred and sixty-seven patients—205 men and 162 women—were usefully employed at the time of the visit. The above figures, both as regards church attendance and regular work, are eminently satisfactory. It has again to be recorded that the changes in the nursing staff of this asylum continue to be exceptionally low. During the period covered by this report only 6 nurses out of a total staff of 69 individuals have left the service.

Since the asylum was last visited Dr. Oswald has resigned on his appointment to the important post of Physician Superintendent to the Glasgow Royal Asylum. He has been succeeded in the office of Medical Superintendent by Dr. W. A. Parker, the senior Assistant Physician.

The asylum was found, as usual, in excellent order, and the condition of the patients as a whole produced a favourable impression.

The books and registers were examined and found to be carefully and correctly kept.

GLASGOW DISTRICT ASYLUM, WOODILEE,
27th, 28th, and 29th May 1901.

There were on the register of the asylum on the 27th instant 438 male and 411 female patients, total 849. All were resident and individually seen in the course of the three days over which the visit extended.

Since 8th November, 1900, the date of the preceding entry, the following changes in the population have taken place :—

Appendix B.

·Commissioners'
Entries.

Royal and
District
Asylums.

·Glasgow District Asylum,
Woodilee.

PAUPER PATIENTS.

	M.	F.	TOTALS.
Admitted,	88	68	156
Discharged Recovered,	23	25	48
Discharged Unrecovered,	9	19	28
Died,	19	22	41

During the period to which the foregoing statistics refer, a little over six months, there has been an increase of 39 patients—37 men and 2 women. The total accommodation of the asylum is as follows :—males, 445, females, 405, Idiot Home, 35, in all 885. The number resident is 849, and consequently the margin of spare accommodation throughout all sections of the institution consists at this date of only 36 empty beds. In view of the increase in the admission rate, from 233 for the year ending 15th May, 1900, to 323 for the year to 15th May, 1901 (an increase of 90 patients), and of the increase of 115 patients in the number resident since May, 1900, the amount of spare accommodation is, it will be clear, utterly inadequate to meet the large and inevitable growth in the population. The need of providing additional buildings is urgent. It is therefore recorded with satisfaction that the District Board have resolved to erect hospital accommodation for 240 patients, and a Home capable of accommodating 110 nurses and servants. It is hoped no time will be lost in having the plans prepared for the erection of these buildings. Dr. Blair and Dr. Marr have reported on the special requirements which should be provided for in the new hospital so as to ensure proper classification and efficient care and treatment. It is recommended in the report that the hospital be of the segregate type, and that blocks be erected suitable for the recently admitted, the convalescent, the acute and noisy, the epileptic, the consumptive, for those suffering from bodily diseases, and for those who are the subjects of infectious diseases. It is also proposed to have an administrative block, a kitchen, a store, a hall, and a scientific laboratory. Plans embodying these views will have the careful consideration of the General Board.

The deaths are registered as due to organic brain diseases in 10 cases, to general paralysis in 9 cases, to cardiac disease in 7 cases, to acute chest affections in 5 cases, to senile decay in 5 cases, to phthisis pulmonalis or tubercular diseases in 3 cases, and to gangrene of the leg and cancer of the intestines in 1 case each. *Post mortem* examination was made in 70 per cent. of the deaths.

The Register of Restraint and Seclusion contains 17 entries referring to the seclusion of 9 patients for periods varying from 2 to 8 hours on account of epileptic or acute and dangerous excitement. The Register of Accidents contains 18 entries. Of these, 9 refer to minor casualties, such as bruises, small cuts, etc., 8 to fractures of bones, and 1 to sudden death, the cause of which was found on investigation by the Procurator-Fiscal to be due to heart disease. A special enquiry was held in the case of a fractured rib, but the evidence was not considered sufficient to justify a charge being brought against the attendant implicated. There have been 7 escapes, and in one instance, as the patient was not brought back before 28 days, he was discharged.

The changes among the attendants and nurses are numerous—14 attendants and 18 nurses have resigned, 7 attendants have been dismissed, and 16 attendants and 18 nurses have been engaged. The dismissals were due to intemperance and breaches of the rules. The District Board have erected 7 cottages and other 7 are in course of building for married attendants. It is hoped that these cottages and the improved accommodation in the Home to be erected will have the effect of materially lessening the changes among the staff. The total number of attendants and nurses, when present vacancies are filled up, is 81—40 in the male and 41 in the female division. The ratio of attendants is 1 to 11, and of nurses 1 to 10½, for day duty, which indicates a staff of adequate strength. It is recommended that a deputy head attendant be appointed, so as to increase the lay supervision of the male division. A novel feature of the training of the nurses has recently been introduced. A course of lessons in cookery is at present being given to the charge and under-charge nurses. A trained teacher from Glasgow attends once weekly, and the object of the course is to demonstrate practically the

methods of preparing food and invalid beverages for the sick. It is intended
that every nurse before qualifying for the Medico-Psychological certificate
shall have attended a course of 12 lectures in this branch of cookery. This
useful innovation in the training of nurses is one which is worthy of being
adopted in other asylums.

The patients in all sections of the asylum were, generally speaking, quiet and
well behaved, only a few of those recently admitted being noisy and excited.
No complaints were made which on investigation appeared to be well founded.
The clothing of both sexes was very satisfactory, and no one was seen wearing
a strong dress. Fifteen men and 30 women were confined to bed, the majority
of whom appeared to be suffering from the infirmities of old age. The number
of epileptics is 85—50 males and 35 females. All except 12, whose fits are
infrequent and not severe, sleep under continuous supervision. Twenty-two
patients are the subjects of consumption, 6 of whom are acutely phthisical, and
in 16 the malady is as yet in the incipient stage. A separate block for the
isolation and treatment of phthisical patients is one of the provisions in the new
hospital scheme. In regard to the infectious nature of consumption no
authority at the present day has any doubt, and the isolation of those who
are phthisical is therefore necessary for the well-being of the other
patients.

The number of inmates industrially employed is 336 men and 362 women,
being 76 per cent. of the former and 63 per cent. of the latter. Three hundred
and seventy-six patients attended the Protestant service last Sunday, and 75
the Catholic service.

The condition of the asylum, except for the dirty state of the walls and
ceilings, the effects of the oil-gas, was highly satisfactory. The whole house
practically requires repainting, and it is understood this is to be effected
directly the introduction of the electric light. which is now in progress, is completed. The boiler-house has been considerably enlarged, new boilers erected,
and accommodation for the electric plant provided. Two additional rooms, a
bathroom and new lavatory and water-closets, are in process of being built at
the gate lodge. The lavatory arrangements in the administrative block have
been found deficient : this defect has been remedied on the male side by the
conversion of a room which formed part of the store into a well-equipped
lavatory, and on the female side one of the kitchen store-rooms is to be
similarly dealt with. A separate milk-house with store-rooms for the cook
is to be erected on the ground between the kitchen and general bath-
room.

The new Home for idiot children contains 11 boys and 10 girls. The
commendation on the excellence of its arrangements bestowed in the previous
entry is fully endorsed, and this praise of their suitability is justified by the
experience of their working since the Home was occupied. Care should be
taken that only ineducable children are admitted. Two girls appeared not to
belong to this class ; they spoke well, and their expression did not indicate any
great defect in intelligence. It is a matter for consideration whether these
girls should not be sent to a training school for imbeciles.

The case books are kept with care, and contain full records of the family and
antecedent history and of the bodily and mental condition of each patient.
Dr. MacDonald, the pathologist, has just been appointed to the Senior
Assistantship of another asylum.

The registers were examined and found regularly and correctly kept.

GLASGOW DISTRICT ASYLUM, WOODILEE,
11th, 12th, and 13th November 1901.

The asylum was last visited on the 27th May 1901. Since then the following
changes have taken place :—

PAUPER PATIENTS.

				M.	F.	TOTALS.
On Register at last visit,	.	.	.	438	411	849
Admitted,	.	.	.	75	51	126
Discharged recovered,	.	.	.	34	23	57
Discharged unrecovered,	.	.	.	14	18	32
Died,	.	.	.	22	14	36
On Register 11th November 1901,	.			443	407	850

All the patients were resident and were seen during the visit.

The deaths are registered as due to organic brain disease in 10 cases, to phthisis in 8 cases, to general paralysis of the insane in 7 cases, to epilepsy in 5 cases, to heart disease in 3 cases, and to senile decay, pneumonia, and intestinal hæmorrhage in 1 case each. *Post mortem* examinations were performed in 26 instances.

The Register of Accidents contains 8 entries, of which 7 refer to minor casualties and 1 to the death of a female patient, the subject of excited melancholia, caused by swallowing small pieces of wood, chiefly obtained from the corset she was wearing.. Every effort was made to save the patient's life, but she succumbed to intestinal hæmorrhage.

There are 14 entries in the Register of Restraint and Seclusion referring to the seclusion of 5 persons. Three patients escaped and were absent for at least one night before being brought back.

The present staff of attendants consists of 43 day and 9 night female nurses, and of 34 day and 5 night male attendants — a total of 91 individuals. Since last visit 20 have left the service, of whom 12 resigned and 8 were dismissed, and 23—12 men and 11 women—have been engaged. These changes are more numerous than is desirable, but it is hoped that the action of the District Board in erecting, at considerable cost, 12 admirably constructed cottages for married attendants, and in including in the plans for the proposed extension of the asylum a provision for the erection of a Nurses' Home for the accommodation of the female staff, may have a salutary effect in checking this tendency to movement on the part of the nursing staff.

The industrial employment of the patients continues to be very thoroughly attended to. At the time of the visit no less than 611 patients—345 men and 266 women—were engaged at work. Of the men, 251 were working on the farm or in the garden.

It was learned that at a meeting of the District Board held on the 13th instant the resignation of Dr. Blair was accepted, and that Dr. Hamilton Marr, the Senior Assistant Medical Officer, was appointed Medical Superintendent of the asylum.

The population of the asylum has not materially increased since last visit, although there are 40 more patients than at this time last year. The increase, which is wholly confined to male patients, reduces the number of vacant beds in the asylum to a very small number.

The patients were on the whole quiet and free from excitement except in one of the female divisions, where they became excited. The complaints and statements made by them had reference wholly to the subject of detention. The general physical appearance of the inmates, both male and female, was satisfactory. A marked improvement was observable in this respect in the case of many of the patients, especially those occupying the farm homestead. On two of the days of the visit the dinner in the large hall was seen being partaken of. It was observed with satisfaction that an allowance of bread is now given to each patient at this meal. The dinners appeared to be sufficient in quantity and properly cooked, and the service of the food was careful and expeditious.

The various wards and dormitories were found, as usual, clean and in good order.

The personal clothing of the patients was satisfactory ; that of the male inmates was universally in good order, and that of the women was neat and varied in colour.

The asylum is now lighted throughout by electricity, and although the installation is still in the hands of the contractors it is regarded as promising to fulfil its purpose satisfactorily.

In a previous entry attention was directed to the darkness of the main corridors leading from the administrative block to the wards. In the dull weather which prevailed at the time of the visit one of these corridors was so dark that it was impossible to pass along it without groping. Dr. Marr showed how, by utilising the verandah opposite the chapel entrance, a very bright and handsome corridor could be obtained, and it is hoped that the District Board may see their way to adopt his suggestion.

A new milk-house—a detached building in the female courtyard--is approaching completion. The interior of this building, which is tiled, is so constructed as to ensure as far as possible the purity of the milk. The present milk-house, which is within the kitchen premises, is to be converted into a

bread-cutting room. It is also proposed to convert the meat store, which
opens off the kitchen, into a messroom for the patients who work in the
kitchen.

The case books and the *post mortem* register continue to be kept in a
manner which is highly creditable to the medical staff.

The books and registers were examined and found correct.

GOVAN DISTRICT ASYLUM, HAWKHEAD,
4th and 5th March 1901.

There were on the 4th instant 463 patients on the register of the asylum. Of these, 4 men and 3 women are private patients, and 215 men and 241 women are paupers. In the foregoing figures effect has been given to the transference since last visit of 1 male from the pauper to the private list. All were resident and seen except two women who were absent on statutory probation, and 1 man who was absent by escape.

Since 17th July 1900, the date of the preceding entry, the following changes in the asylum population have taken place :—

	PRIVATE PATIENTS.		PAUPER PATIENTS.		TOTALS.
	M.	F.	M.	F.	
Admitted, . . .	2	3	66	77	148
Discharged recovered, .	0	0	21	29	50
Discharged unrecovered,	0	0	18	22	40
Died, ...	0	3	23	17	43

Of the 40 discharged unrecovered or mentally improved, 6 were sent to the care of relatives, 7 were boarded out with guardians in rural districts, 12 were transferred to the lunatic wards of Govan Poorhouse, and 15 were transferred to other asylums. It is understood that a minute of the Parish Council has been obtained in the cases of 4 patients for removal either to the care of relatives or to suitable homes in the country. It is also understood that 18 patients are about to be transferred to the lunatic wards of Govan Poorhouse.

The following table shows the number in establishments of patients chargeable to the Govan Parish on 1st January of each of the last five years :—

1st January.	1897.	1898.	1899.	1900.	1901.
In District Asylum, Hawkhead, . .	232	285	440	468	451
In Lunatic Wards of Govan Poorhouse,	168	157	121	127	167
In Kirklands Asylum, . . .	59	58	61	75	92
In other Establishments, . . .	107	108	24	21	15
Totals, . . .	566	608	646	691	725

It will be seen that the number in establishments has increased from 566 in 1897 to 725 in 1901, an increase of 159 in five years. The increase during the coming five years will in all likelihood be larger, as the rate of increase is unfortunately becoming greater each quinquennaid. The District Board will therefore have to provide asylum accommodation for at least 884 patients by 1st January 1906 to meet the requirements of the district. The accommodation at present possessed by the District Board is as follows :—for 510 at the Hawkhead Asylum, for 200 in the lunatic wards of Govan Poorhouse, and for 95 at the Kirklands Asylum, total 805. There will in all probability be a deficiency in the accommodation by 1906 to the extent of either 90 or 100 patients. Timely consideration should be given to these figures in order that the asylum accommodation may be provided ahead of the demand, and not dragged laggingly behind.

The rate of mortality has been high. The deaths are registered as due to diseases of the brain and spinal cord in 21 cases, to heart affections in 7 cases, to tubercular disease in 5 cases, to pneumonia in 3 cases, to senile decay in 2 cases, and to jaundice, acute peritonitis, bronchitis, puerperal fever, and septicæmia each in 1 case. In 39·5 per cent. of the deaths was the cause verified by *post mortem* examination. This is a low percentage, but Dr. Watson states that difficulty is experienced in obtaining the consent of the relatives to an autopsy.

The Register of Restraint and Seclusion contains 78 entries. Sixty-four of these entries, 60 in the case of one man, and 4 in the cases of 2 men, refer to the use of restraint in order to prevent interference with surgical dressings which were essential to proper treatment. Fourteen entries refer to the use of seclusion in the cases of 10 patients on account of their maniacal and violent condition. Six accidents are recorded—5 consisted of small cuts or bruises due to accidental falls, and 1 of a fracture at elbow-joint sustained by an excited patient during a struggle with an attendant. Dr. Watson, after full inquiry, did not consider the attendant blameworthy. One escape has occurred; the patient is still absent, and no anxiety is entertained as to his welfare.

The changes among the nurses have been comparatively few, only 5 nurses having resigned and 1 having been dismissed; but those among the male attendants have been more numerous, due mainly to 8 men having left for service in South Africa. Only 2 of the male attendant staff are provided with house accommodation on the asylum estate. If suitable houses were erected for the married members of the male staff a great inducement would be held out to trustworthy and efficient attendants to remain permanently in the service of the asylum. The day staff consists of 20 men and 24 women, which gives a proportion of 1 to 11 on the male, and 1 to 10 on the female, side. The night supervision of the patients, is as follows:—on the main asylum 1 attendant on each side is in constant charge of the epileptic dormitory, and 1 attendant in each division visits the single rooms and the other dormitories at regular intervals; on the hospital section 1 attendant is in constant charge of each sickroom, 1 of each observation dormitory, and 1 regularly visits the single rooms and the other dormitories. When necessary, a second observation dormitory is instituted, and an attendant placed in constant charge of it.

A case of smallpox is at present under treatment in the asylum. The patient was admitted in November last, and the disease developed on 27th January. The infection appears to have been brought by a woman who was admitted on 15th January, her husband having been under hospital treatment for smallpox. This woman slept in the bed next to the patient who became affected. It is a matter of regret that from want of room all recently admitted patients cannot be isolated for 12 or 14 days before mingling with the other inmates. The affected patient is at present thoroughly isolated in the infectious section of the hospital. All the patients, officials, and attendant staff have been vaccinated, and great watchfulness is being generally exercised.

The patients of both sexes were sufficiently and neatly clothed, and their personal condition was very satisfactory. Their behaviour during the visit was, with only two exceptions, most orderly. Several appeals in reference to undue detention were made, but investigation disclosed the unfitness of the patients for discharge. The dinners were abundant, well cooked, and most palatable, and the food generally was warmly commended by those who were spoken to on the subject. At breakfast both porridge and milk and tea and bread and butter are given to those who desire them. The special dietetic requirements of the sick and delicate are carefully and liberally attended to. The hospital deserves commendation for the excellence of its arrangements for the care of recently admitted patients, and for those labouring under bodily disease. Six men and 11 women were confined to bed. Thirty-one per cent. of the inmates attended Divine service last Sunday. This percentage is a small one and might with advantage be increased. The chapel in connection with the mortuary has been provided with seats, and services are to be regularly held there for the Roman Catholic inmates. Eighty per cent. of the patients are registered as daily engaged in useful employment.

The asylum was throughout in excellent order and comfortably heated. Appendix B.
It is learned with approval that the District Board have acquired the lease
of the adjoining farm. This additional land, extending to 146 acres, will Commissioners'.
afford further facilities for employing the patients in healthy outdoor work, Entries.
and there is every reason for believing that it can be worked in connection Royal and
with the asylum with financial profit.   District
A closed tank with a grit chamber has recently been added to the arrange- Asylums.
ments for the purification of the sewage. Brick clinkers have been
substituted for ashes in the filter beds. It is fully anticipated that these Govan District
improvements will render the effluent as innocuous as it is possible to make it. Asylum,
The case-books were found written up to date, and the registers are Hawkhead.
kept with accuracy and regularity.

GOVAN DISTRICT ASYLUM, HAWKHEAD,
14th and 15th November 1901.

Since the asylum was last visited the following changes in population have
taken place :—

PRIVATE AND PAUPER PATIENTS.

	M.	F.	TOTALS.
On Register 4th March 1901, . . .	219	244	463
Admitted, ...	112	80	192
Discharged recovered, ...	46	45	91
Discharged unrecovered, ...	20	33	53
Died, ...	22	21	43
On Register 14th November 1901, . .	243	225	468

With the exception of 1 man, who was absent on pass, all the patients
were seen during the visit.
Of the numbers resident, 6 men and 4 women are private patients. The
number of male patients has increased by 24 and the number of females has
decreased by 19, so that the net increase is 5 since last visit. Last year the
female population preponderated in this asylum, and the present greater
number of males is due to the fact that during the past nine months the
excess of the male admission over the female has been 32, and that a somewhat larger number of women were discharged unrecovered. From the
comparatively large number of acute alcoholic cases seen among the men, it
is not improbable that the larger male admission rate this year may be due to
alcoholism. If that is so, it might be proper that the parochial authorities
should consider whether, in some cases, appropriate medical treatment could
not be given elsewhere than in the asylum for the short time that is often all
that is required to complete recovery.
The rapid admission rate necessarily gives rise to uneasiness as to the
accommodation for lunatics at the disposal of the parish of Govan. But
before proceeding to consider the question of increasing that accommodation,
it would be well to test the control which can be exercised first upon the
numbers sent to the asylum, and second upon the accumulations within the
asylum. The desire to have in the asylum that number of patients which
will render it workable at a reasonable maintenance cost is entirely sym-
pathised with, but with the rapidly growing population of Govan there is
unfortunately every reason for believing that in the course of a very few
years, despite every endeavour to postpone it, the question of extending the
asylum must be faced. In the meantime, therefore, there is all the more
reason why the exclusion of cases unsuitable for treatment in the asylum,
and the removal of all cases suitable for boarding out, should be vigorously
dealt with.
The deaths are registered as due to gross disease of the brain and nervous
system in 15 cases ; to phthisis in 6 cases ; to general paralysis in 4 cases ; to
heart disease in 4 cases ; to mania in 3 cases ; to epilepsy in 2 cases ; to
pneumonia in 2 cases ; and to senile decay, alcoholic neuritis, acute enteritis,
Bright's disease, empyema, anæmia, and septicæmia in 1 case each. *Post
mortem* examinations were made in 24 instances.
The need for a laboratory for pathological investigation by the Medical
Officers was evident. The site for such a laboratory ought undoubtedly to

Appendix B.

Commissioners' Entries.

Royal and District Asylums.

Govan District Asylum, Hawkhead.

be at the mortuary, and a small addition to the present mortuary buildings would fully meet this requirement.

Of the entries in the Register of Accidents, one refers to the death of a female attendant and one to the death of a bricklayer employed at work on the farm buildings. The nurse, returning from Glasgow, had entered by mistake the wrong train—an express—and on finding that it did not stop at the station for the asylum, she, it is supposed, jumped out, and was instantly killed. The workman fell off a scaffold upwards of 20 feet high and fractured his skull, from the effects of which he expired within a few hours. Of the remaining entries, the only serious one records the accidental fracture of the radius in a female patient.

There are 21 entries in the Register of Restraint and Seclusion, referring to the restraint of 3 persons for surgical reasons and the seclusion of 12 persons on account of violence or excitement or both.

Seven patients have escaped since last visit, and were each absent for at least one night before being brought back.

The record of the industrial employment of the patients at the time of the visit is very good. One hundred and eighty-six men and 177 women were usefully employed. Of these, 105 men were engaged at farm or garden work, 42 women were working in the laundry and kitchens, and 74 women were knitting or sewing.

The proposal to house 12 or 14 men in the farm homestead was explained by Dr. Watson, and the accommodation was examined. It appears to be perfectly satisfactory, provided that more wash-hand basins are added to the lavatory and that the existing arched partition in the kitchen be removed so as to make that apartment large enough to permit of the patients receiving their meals in it. It would be an advantage if an additional water-closet seat were provided for the patients. The proposal to place about 20 male patients in the workshop block was also inquired into. With respect to this it may be said that no objection can be taken to the character of the buildings in themselves, but that the consent of the General Board must depend upon the nature of the structural adaptations to the requirements of living and sleeping rooms for the insane.

The patients were found in a satisfactory state of physical health. They were all suitably and neatly clothed, and gave every indication of receiving a liberal dietary. There was a marked absence of noisy excitement among the acute cases. It was observed that a large proportion of the recent and acute cases were being treated by rest in bed with very successful results. This method of treatment is rational and humane, and it greatly relieves the anxiety and responsibility of those in charge of such cases.

Every section of the institution was, as usual, found scrupulously clean and in the best of order. It was observed that the gas light in the hospital section is very inferior, and there is reason to believe that it is no better in other parts of the asylum. If, as it is learned, a high price is paid for this gas, the District Board should either insist on a better supply or adopt electricity, which is now in use in almost every similar institution in the country.

The case books are carefully written up and contain full information regarding the patients. The usual examination of the statutory books and registers was made, and they were found accurately and neatly kept.

Haddington District Asylum.

HADDINGTON DISTRICT ASYLUM,
8th May, 1901.

As will be seen from the following tabular statement, the number of patients resident in the asylum is less than at the date of last visit :—

	PRIVATE AND PAUPER PATIENTS.		
	M.	F.	TOTALS.
Resident on 10th October, 1900, . . .	62	76	138
Admitted, ...	8	8	16
Discharged recovered, ...	3	4	7
Discharged unrecovered, . . . -	2	1	3
Died, ...	2	5	7
Resident at this date, ...	63	74	137

Of those resident, 8 men and 10 women are private patients, and 1 man is
a voluntary inmate.

The assigned causes of the 7 deaths are as follows :—Senile decay, general
paralysis, pneumonia, phthisis, heart disease, anæmia, and kidney disease.
Post mortem examinations were made in every instance except one, in which
the consent of the relatives was refused. This fact is significant of the active
and scientific interest which the Medical Officer takes in the performance of
his duties.

There are no entries in the Register of Restraint and Seclusion, in the
Register of Escapes, or in the Register of Accidents. Upon such an uneventful
record the administration is to be congratulated.

Since last visit 2 male and 7 female attendants have been engaged, 2 female
attendants have resigned, and 3 have been dismissed. The reasons assigned
for dismissal are incompetency, intemperance, and roughness in dealing with
patients. There are 5 male and 6 female attendants on day duty, and 1 male
and 1 female attendant on night duty. The appointment of night attendants
is said to have been very beneficial ; that statement is borne out by the fact
that at the time of the visit there were no wet beds in the institution, and it is
understood that practically since the establishment of the system of night
supervision all patients of faulty habits have been carefully attended to in
this respect.

Forty-six men and 69 women were industrially employed at the time of the
visit. Of these, 28 men were engaged in farm or garden work, 36 women at
knitting or needlework, and 13 in the kitchen and laundry.

The patients' clothing attracted favourable attention. The men's suits were
neat and in good repair and well fitting, and their underclothing was in
excellent order. Forty complete suits of clothing and underclothing for male
patients have been made at the asylum by the matron, Mrs. M'Rae, with the
assistance of a tailor who was specially hired for this work. The clothing of
the female patients was neat and tasteful in every instance, and much of this
has also been made by the matron. The patients presented a healthy and
well-nourished appearance. They were, with few exceptions, quiet and
orderly in their demeanour, and no complaints of ill-usage or statements indicative of discontent were received.

The appearance of the wards on the female side was highly pleasing. Comfortable basket chairs, a good supply of ordinary chairs, and the breaking up
of the floor space by means of small tables are noticeable improvements which
conduce towards comfort and lessen what may be termed the institutional
character of the rooms. A considerable amount of papering and painting has
added to the brightness of these apartments. The dormitories throughout
have been furnished with new bedsteads, in which the old straw palliasses have
been replaced by metal springs. The question of reflooring the sleeping
apartments with pitch pine wood is, it is understood, presently under consideration. The present flooring has served since the opening of the institution
upwards of 30 years ago, and although, mechanically, it might be
regarded as efficient for some years to come, it is pointed out that in
many places it is much worn, and that from a sanitary point of view
its replacement is desirable. The proposals for improving the ventilation
of the steam from the kitchen range were explained. It is suggested that a more effective scheme, and one that would facilitate the kitchen
work, would be the removal of the dividing wall between the kitchen and
scullery, placing he boilers in the centre of the enlarged apartment, and
ventilating the whole from a central point in the kitchen roof.

In connection with the drainage and steam heating operations now in
progress, the present position of the bathrooms deserves notice. If the
relative positions of the bathrooms and bootrooms on both sides of the house
were reversed, the advantages gained would be (1) that the baths would stand
in a single-storied building which would be easily ventilated ; (2) that the size
of the new bathrooms would permit of an additional bath being inserted, and
(3) that the piping and drainage would be nearer the outside of the building.
An exit from the kitchen premises to the courtyard is much required for
bringing in coals and removing refuse. This can easily be obtained by converting the window of one of the several small rooms opening off the
kitchen corridor into a doorway.

Considering the extensive operations in which the District Board are at

Appendix B.

Commissioners
Entries.

Royal and
District
Asylums.

Haddington
District
Asylum.

present engaged with a view to improving the condition of the asylum, it is not without some hesitation and consideration that the above recommendations are made, but it must be kept in mind that every institution requires from time to time not only repair but also adaptation to modern requirements.

With regard to the question of electric lighting, all that need be said is that if its cost is found on investigation not to materially exceed the price now paid for gas the District Board will be acting wisely in adopting a method of illuminating which is now used in most of the asylums in this country and which has been found to be more efficient and more sanitary than gas.

Operations for the erection of a new boiler-house, for ventilating the present water-closets, and for the enlargement of the existing laundry are in progress. In connection with the latter, it may be pointed out that the replacement of the present wooden washing-tubs by others of a more modern description would be an improvement. The general condition of the asylum as to cleanliness and order and the medical and lay care of the patients produced a favourable impression.

The books and registers were examined and were found regularly and correctly kept.

HADDINGTON DISTRICT ASYLUM,
12th September 1901.

There are 141 patients on the register of the asylum at this date. Of these, 9 men and 10 women are private patients, and 56 men and 66 women are paupers. Since last visit 1 man has been transferred from the pauper to the private list. No patient was absent either on probation or on pass. The voluntary inmate who was resident at last visit has left.

Since 8th May 1901, the date of the previous entry, the following changes have taken place :—

| | PRIVATE AND PAUPER PATIENTS. | | |
	M.	F.	TOTALS.
Admitted, ...	7	8	15
Discharged recovered, . . .	3	4	7
Died, ...	1	2	3

During the period to which the foregoing statistics refer, there is an increase of 5—3 males and 2 females—in the number resident. It is observed that there has been no discharge of improved patients since last visit. As the margin of spare accommodation is not large, it is hoped that the boarding out of patients who are suitable for domestic care will be kept steadily in view.

The deaths are registered as due to acute nephritis, empyema, and phthisis pulmonalis. *Post mortem* examinations were made in every case and the cause of death verified. These examinations are of great importance in asylums, and the attention they receive in this institution merits commendation. The knowledge that in all cases of death such examinations will be made has a protective influence over the living.

Neither restraint nor seclusion has been resorted to in the treatment of the patients since last visit. No accident has occurred, a fact creditable to the management in view of the building and other operations now in progress. Two patients escaped and were absent for several days before being brought back.

The following changes in the staff have taken place :—3 attendants and 3 nurses have resigned, 1 attendant has been dismissed as unsuitable, and 3 attendants, 3 nurses, and 1 servant have been engaged. A nurse now attends to the needs and comforts of the sick during the night, and regularly supervises those of defective habits. The results are very satisfactory—the reduction in the amount of dirty linen is considerable, and the destruction of bedding and other material is prevented. The appointment of a trained nurse to assist the matron and take charge during her absence is recommended.

Every day-room, dormitory, and single room has been repapered, repainted, and revarnished, and the work has been done with much taste and thoroughness. The appearance of the wards has been greatly improved ; it is now one of brightness and cheerfulness. Considerable additions have been made to the furniture and furnishings ; basket chairs, small tables, new tiled fireplaces, and objects of interest and decoration now contribute largely to give the day-rooms

Appendix B.

Commissioners'
Entries.

Royal and
District
Asylums.

Haddington
District
Asylum.

a comfortable and pleasing aspect. The dormitories have been practically refurnished : new iron bedsteads with wire mattresses have been provided— the hair in the mattresses and bolsters has been reteased, the pillows filled with cleaned feathers, and the ticking generally renewed. One important improvement remains to be effected, viz., the relaying of the floors of the dormitories with pitch pine, and as this would be a renovation of sanitary importance, it is understood with satisfaction that the District Board have resolved to carry it out. The dormitories will then compare favourably with those in the most modern institutions for the insane. The reconstruction of the kitchen is in progress—the partition between the kitchen and scullery has been removed, and new boilers are about to be placed in the centre of the floor. A tea infuser of the most efficient kind has been procured. The floor of the kitchen is of stone flags, which are much worn in certain places. It would be an improvement if tiles of moderate cost were substituted ; they are easily kept clean and would greatly add to the appearance of the kitchen. A central hatch of good size between kitchen and dining hall, with a hot plate at base upon which the meat could be served and kept warm is much required. This would admit of the carving table in the dining hall being used for the service of patients. The dining hall appeared at this date scarcely adequate for the present number.

The erection of a boiler-house is almost completed, and the new boiler is already *in situ.*

The storage for hot and cold water is being largely increased ; four cold-water tanks are at present being erected above the kitchen, and two hot water cisterns are being added to each division of the asylum. It is believed that when these new arrangements are in operation an ample supply of hot and cold water will be available for the weekly bathing of the patients. The laundry is being enlarged, and it is recommended that fireclay tubs be substituted for the wooden ones. Additional tubs are required. The woodwork around the present tubs is rotten ; it should be removed and all pipes should be exposed so as to be easy of access. Radiators have been placed in the dining hall, but the question of heating the dormitories and single rooms by hot-water pipes is one which requires attention. The single rooms are generally tenanted by patients who are of low vitality, restless, and who do not keep themselves covered by bedclothes, and consequently the safety and comfort of patients of this class require that these rooms should be comfortably heated during winter.

Effect is being given to the recommendations in previous entry relative to bath and shoe rooms. Two excellent bathrooms are in course of construction, and on the dormitory floor a lavatory with basins, water-closets, and sinks of modern design are being provided on each side of the asylum. If a door were made between the dayroom and bathroom, the former would then serve as a convenient dressing-room.

The District Board have decided to introduce electric lighting throughout the institution, and wiring of the house is now in progress. It is needless at this time to comment on the many advantages of this light for asylums—its safety, coolness, cleanliness, and efficiency have been universally acknowledged.

Telephonic communication has been established between the institution and Dr. Ronaldson's house.

All these additions, alterations, and renovations will greatly improve the character of the accommodation and facilitate the efficient administration of the asylum.

All the patients had an opportunity of making any statement they may have desired. None made any reasonable complaint, and the appeals for discharge were comparatively few. The condition of the inmates was most satisfactory. A marked improvement in their clothing was noted ; every patient was well dressed, and the neatness of their personal appearance attracted attention. The dinner at this date consisted of pea soup, bread, fresh herrings and potatoes—it was a well cooked and ample meal. Milk is given as a beverage for dinner twice a week. The general health of the patients is good ; only 1 man and 2 women being confined to bed. The asylum is under painstaking and energetic direction, and the patients are evidently treated in a kindly and judicious manner.

The books and registers were examined and found regularly and accurately kept.

Appendix B.

Commissioners'
Entries.

Royal and
District
Asylums.

Inverness
District
Asylum.

INVERNESS DISTRICT ASYLUM,
5th and 6th February 1901.

The following statement shows the changes in population which have
taken place since the asylum was last visited :—

PRIVATE AND PAUPER PATIENTS.

	M.	F.	TOTALS.
On register 16th August 1900, . .	304	291	595
Admitted since, ...	35	27	62
Discharged recovered, ...	21	17	38
Discharged unrecovered, . . .	3	3	6
Died, ...	6	10	16
On register 5th February 1901, . .	309	288	597

Of those at present on the register, 1 man and 1 woman are private
patients. Twelve patients—7 men and 5 women—are absent on statutory
probation, so that the actual number resident is 585. The above figures
show that the increase in the number of patients since last visit has been
immaterial, but that is clearly due to the comparatively small number
admitted in the interval. In view of the fact, referred to in the preceding
entry, that the asylum is now full, it would be unsafe to base any hope for
the future upon the present drop in the number of admissions. On the
contrary, such pauses in otherwise progressive admission rates are from time
to time incidental to most lunacy districts, and are not infrequently of short
duration. There seems, unfortunately, no possibility of averting an approaching state of overcrowding in the institution except by an early consideration
of the whole subject on the part of the District Board. In this connection
the condition of the general dining hall may be referred to. At the time of
the visit the hall was much too full for comfort, and the expeditious service
of the food was interfered with to a considerable extent. The close
arrangement of the tables prevented free access to all parts of the hall, and
the proximity of the patients to one another gave rise to more noise and
excitement than is usually met with. It is understood that the District
Board have this question under consideration. Taken by itself, and without
reference to the general question of overcrowding above referred to, the
best solution of this difficulty would undoubtedly be the erection of a small
dining hall in connection with each of the present hospitals. By this means
the hospital patients, many of whom are weakly, would be saved the long
walk three times a day to the central dining hall, and their withdrawal from
it would provide the required accommodation for the remaining patients who
use the hall. This suggestion is, however, provisional and dependent on
the decision of the District Board with regard to the major and more
important question of the increase of the asylum accommodation, because the
initiation of a suitable scheme to that effect would have the effect of relieving the pressure in the dining hall for some time to come.

Attention must again be directed to the absence of heating in the corridors
and single rooms in the main portion of the asylum. The weather at the
time of the visit was inclement, and thermometers hung in the upstairs
corridors and single rooms registered a temperature at mid-day of from
32 degs. to 35 degs. Fahr.

It is understood that the change in the method of night nursing, whereby
patients who, on account of noise or troublesome habits, formerly occupied
single rooms now sleep in associated dormitories under constant supervision, has already had a good effect upon the mental condition of these
patients. This is shown by the fact that on the night of the 4th inst. there
was only one wet bed in the whole asylum. This change has also had the
effect of setting free a large number of single rooms for other purposes, and
it was observed with approval that advantage has been taken of the
opportunity to provide each of the male attendants who sleep in the asylum
with a separate bedroom. If the furnishing of these rooms were somewhat
improved, and a chest of drawers or a wardrobe provided for each man,
the character of this accommodation would certainly help to retain in the
service a good class of male attendants.

Appendix B.

Commissioners'
Entries.

Royal and
District
Asylums.

Inverness
District
Asylum.

The new female hospital is now occupied. The wards presented a bright and cheerful aspect, and they are lighted, heated, and ventilated in a manner that leaves little to be desired. The construction of the hospital, which is similar to that on the male side, is in accordance with the best modern principles, combining the benefits of good classification with efficiency of working and supervision. The finish of the internal construction and the style of the furnishing are in every respect admirable. The hospitals—the most important sections of the institution—are now in full working order, and the District Board are to be congratulated on having provided accommodation for their sick, recent and acute, cases, which will compare favourably with that in any asylum in the kingdom.

The alterations on the laundry block are making satisfactory progress. It is understood that the District Board has still under consideration proposals to divert the road which passes immediately behind and to the north of the asylum to the south and lower border of the grounds, and to erect cottages for married attendants and officials in the vicinity of the asylum.

The 16 deaths are registered as due to phthisis or tuberculosis in 4 cases, to heart disease in 4 cases, to pneumonia in 2 cases, to cancer in 2 cases, to cerebral hæmorrhage and softening in 2 cases, to general paralysis in 1 case, and to meningitis in 1 case. A *post mortem* examination was made in every case except 1.

The Register of Restraint and Seclusion contains 11 entries referring to the restraint of 2 persons in order to prevent the removal of surgical dressings. Three patients escaped and were absent for at least one night before being brought back. No accident of a serious nature has occurred since the asylum was last visited. Three hundred and sixty patients—200 men and 160 women—attended Divine service last Sunday. Four hundred and fifty-nine patients—219 men and 240 women—were industrially employed at the time of the visit. The general health of the inmates was good, only 8 men and 16 women being confined to bed on account of physical illness. The medical treatment and the nursing of these cases were to all appearance eminently satisfactory, and the infirmary wards had that air of quiet and restfulness which is so necessary for the comfort of the sick and the convalescent.

All the patients in residence were seen during the visit. Their general appearance indicated that they are suitably fed, and their evident contentment and the absence of all complaints pointed to the conclusion that their wants are thoughtfully and systematically attended to. The personal clothing of all the patients, but especially that of the women, was neat, warm, and in an excellent state of preservation.

The asylum was found throughout in very good order, and even those parts of it which stand very much in need of redecoration and repair bore evidence of that careful attention to cleanliness which is always characteristic of minute and equable administration.

The case-books contain full records of the histories and progress of the various cases under treatment, and the various registers are regularly and correctly kept.

INVERNESS DISTRICT ASYLUM,
22nd and 23rd July 1901.

On the 22nd instant there were 611 patients on the register of the asylum. Of these, 1 male and 3 females were private patients, and 310 men and 297 women were paupers. Nine males and 7 females were absent on statutory probation, and 1 man and 1 woman were absent by escape. The number resident was 593, all of whom were seen and given an opportunity of making any statement they desired. No complaint was made calling for special mention. The appeals for discharge were not numerous.

Since the date of last visit the following changes among the patients have taken place :—

	PRIVATE AND PAUPER PATIENTS.		
	M.	F.	TOTALS.
Admitted, ...	44	41	85
Discharged recovered, . . .	23	21	44
Discharged unrecovered, . . .	5	4	9
Died, ...	14	4	18

Among the admissions were two private females.

G

The deaths are registered as due to diseases of the brain and spinal cord in 4 cases, to acute pulmonary affections in 6 cases, to phthisis pulmonalis (in 1 case complicated with diabetes mellitus) in 3 cases, to heart disease in 3 cases, and to cancer in 2 cases. It is highly creditable to Dr. Keay that in the case of every death a *post mortem* examination was made. It is most important that the cause of death should be verified by an examination and found to be a natural one. These examinations are not only important in the interests of science, but also on account of the protective influence over the living which results from the knowledge that in all cases of death such examinations will be made.

Neither restraint nor seclusion has been employed in the treatment of any patient since last visit. Three accidents are recorded, (1) a fall from which a patient sustained bruises on cheek and nose; (2) bruises on chest which on investigation could not be satisfactorily accounted for by those in charge of the patient, and consequently Dr. Keay rightly discharged those implicated; and (3) two bruises in face which similarly could not be satisfactorily explained, the result being the dismissal of the attendant in charge. It will be seen from these facts that misconduct on the part of the attendants affecting the patients is promptly followed by dismissal. There have been 7 escapes in which the patients were absent from the asylum for at least one night before being brought back.

The number on the register has increased by 14 since last visit. The day-room space is more than fully occupied, and the sleeping accommodation is overcrowded to the extent of 45 patients In view of this it is recommended that a serious effort be made to transfer all those patients to care in private dwellings who have ceased to need care and treatment in a fully equipped asylum. Dr. Keay has drawn up a list of patients who he considers are suitable for domestic care—the number being 52 males and 30 females, 82 in all. Considerable difficulties have been experienced by Dr. Keay in getting many of the Parish Councils and Inspectors of Poor to co-operate in the removal of patients to private dwellings, but it is believed that if earnest efforts are made the asylum will be relieved of those patients for whom its accommodation and equipment are not necessary for their proper care. The population of the asylum is still growing, and unless a considerable reduction in number is effected in this manner further extensions will be inevitable.

The congested condition of the dining hall, which has been referred to in previous entries, is a matter which urgently calls for action. The excitement and confusion which prevail during the meals, and which are due to over-crowding, are far from satisfactory, and it is therefore hoped that the District Board will early decide on some scheme by which additional dining hall accommodation will be provided. The suggestion contained in the previous entry as to the erection of dining halls in connection with the hospital sections is an excellent one. In other asylums this provision has been a decided success. The close proximity of dining accommodation to the hospital wards is of great advantage to the sick, infirm, and aged.

Except in those sections of the male side which are at present in process of renovation and the lavatories in F and G male wards, the asylum was found in excellent order. One ward in the male division has been refloored with pitch pine, and the walls painted and decorated in a tasteful manner. New furniture has been provided, and the aspect of this renovated section is one of brightness and comfort. It will be a great improvement from a sanitary point of view when the whole of the male side is similarly dealt with. There should be no delay in remodelling the lavatories in F and G wards. Their arrangements are antiquated and their present condition is most unsatisfactory. They are quite out of harmony with the rest of the asylum. The new female hospital wards are in every way admirably adapted for the purpose for which they were built, and the nurses' home in the basement is an important and valuable addition to the equipment of the institution. It is learned with approval that the District Board have resolved to erect cottages for married attendants—the need of which has long been felt. Good progress is being made with the reconstruction of the wash-house. The enlargement of the laundry is completed; it is now a spacious, well lighted department with ample space for the sorting and despatch of clean clothing. The new drying-closets are proving efficient. Telephonic communication has been installed between the various sections of the asylum and between the Medical Superintendent's house and the institution

Appendix B.

Commissioners'
Entries.

Royal and
District
Asylums.

Inverness
District
Asylum.

Kirklands
Asylum.

—fifteen stations in all. It is proving a great convenience from an administrative point of view. The extension of the hospital heating arrangements to the whole of the asylum is necessary for the health and comfort of the patients. Pneumonia was the cause of 33 per cent. of the deaths since last visit, and it is feared that this may have been due to the coldness of the dormitories and single rooms during the winter months.

The asylum continues to be managed in an enlightened and progressive manner. It was evident that no effort is spared to render the care of the patients as efficient as possible, and to promote the recovery of the curable. The sick, the suicidal, the epileptic, and those of noisy and defective habits now sleep under constant night supervision, and good results, such as freedom from accidents, greater comfort, and improved conduct, have been obtained. The clothing of both sexes was in good repair, and that of the women was varied, well made, and tasteful in appearance. Every patient capable of employment is encouraged to engage in useful work. The number registered as industrially employed is 235 men and 247 women. One hundred and seventy-one men and 160 women attended ivine service last Sunday.

The important question of the isolation of consumptive patients has been ably and fully brought before the District Board by Dr Keay in his last annual report. The grounds set forth in this report for the separate accommodation of phthisical patients are fully endorsed. It has been proved beyond doubt that consumption is a communicable disease, and it has therefore become a duty to separate the phthisical from the healthy. This is especially necessary as regards the phthisical insane, who expectorate their bacilli-laden sputum on the bedclothes and floors. This morbid excretion when it dries becomes dust and is inhaled. In this way consumption is generated in those predisposed to the disease and in those who are weakened by nervous and bodily aliments. It appears from a statement prepared by Dr. Keay that the number of patients who are at present the subjects of this disease is very large, 30 of whom are in the third stage. It is therefore hoped that the District Board will carefully consider the question of providing for the isolation and treatment of an infectious class of patients in a manner which scientific medicine of the present day directs

The staff of attendants is an adequate one. There are 27 attendants and 3 nurses in the male, and 35 nurses in the female division. The ratio on the male side is 1 attendant to 10 patients, and in the female division 1 to 8. The night staff consists of 4 attendants and 4 nurses. The appointment of a night matron to supervise this staff is a matter worthy of consideration. The changes among the attendants and nurses are not so numerous as in other asylums—3 have resigned and 7 have been dismissed. Of the dismissals, 4 were due to misconduct towards the patients, 1 to inefficiency, and 2 to breaches of discipline.

It is understood with satisfaction that the Committee appointed by the District Board to effect the divergence of the public road which passes through the asylum grounds have secured the consent of the county and local authorities to the proposed change of route. It is earnestly hoped that no insurmountable difficulties will now be encountered in the furtherance of such a desirable alteration in the interests of the patients.

The case books were found to contain full records of the condition and progress of the patients, and the registers were written up to date and accurately kept.

KIRKLANDS ASYLUM, BOTHWELL,
16th February 1901.

There are 190 patients—99 men and 91 women—on the register of the asylum at this date. All are resident and were seen during the visit except 1 woman who is absent on statutory probation.

Since 5th November 1900, the date of the preceding report, the following changes have taken place :—

PAUPER PATIENTS.

	M.	F.	TOTALS.
Admitted,	25	3	28
Discharged recovered,	3	3	6
Discharged unrecovered,	4	3	7
Died,	3	2	5

Among the admissions were 20 patients transferred from the Royal Edinburgh Asylum and chargeable to the parish of Edinburgh. Of the remaining 170 patients, 94 are chargeable to Govan and 76 to landward parishes of Lanarkshire.

Of the 5 deaths, 3 are registered as due to cerebral disease, 1 to chronic phthisis pulmonalis, and 1 to heart disease and chronic bronchitis. In 3 cases the causes of death were verified by *post mortem* examinations, and in 2 cases the consent of the relations for an autopsy was refused.

The Register of Restraint and Seclusion contains no entry. One accident has occurred—injuries to the right hand through its being caught in the mangle. There has been one escape in which the patient was absent for a night before being brought back.

The changes among the staff are as follows :—2 have resigned, 1 has been dismissed, and 2 have been engaged. The accommodation for the attendants is far from what is considered desirable at the present day. Nine nurses sleep in a small dormitory in which it will be evident they can have no privacy, and the night nurse occupies this dormitory during the day. Each nurse should have a room to herself. Cottages for married male attendants or artizans are much required, and it is recommended that early consideration be given to this matter.

Plans for the erection of a separate laundry have been prepared, and a special report on them has been laid before the General Board. The site selected is a suitable and convenient one.

The patients were found efficiently cared for. The dress and personal neatness of both sexes were most satisfactory ; all the men have tweed suits, and the pleasing variety and good taste of the women's clothing attracted favourable attention. Nothing has greater influence on the behaviour of the female patients than the proper care of their personal appearance. There was a remarkable absence of excitement during the whole of the visit, and a general air of contentment prevailed among the patients. The dinner was a well-cooked and evidently popular meal, and it was served in perfect order. Three men and six women were confined to bed. These patients were chiefly in single rooms. As has been previously pointed out, a great defect in this asylum is the want of well-designed and properly-equipped hospital accommodation.

Fifty-one per cent. of the men and 74 per cent. of the women are registered as daily engaged in useful work. It is hoped that, now that the asylum is to continue permanently as accommodation for pauper patients, the Committee will lose no opportunity of securing by purchase additional land. It will be required as sites for necessary and useful extensions of the institution, and for the full employment of the male inmates in healthy outdoor work.

Fifty-six men and 48 women attended Divine service last Sunday, and regular services are now held for those patients and members of the staff who belong to the Roman Catholic Church.

All sections of the establishment are maintained in good order. The dayrooms are well supplied with books, newspapers, and indoor games. The condition of the dormitories and bedding was very satisfactory. The asylum continues to be well managed.

The books and registers were examined and found regularly and accurately kept.

KIRKLANDS ASYLUM, BOTHWELL,
7th November 1901.

The changes which have occurred in the population of the asylum since last visit are set forth in the following tabular statement :—

				PAUPER PATIENTS.		
				M.	F.	TOTALS.
Resident 16th February 1901,	.	.	.	99	91	190
Admitted since,	.	.	.	28	34	62
Discharged recovered,	.	,	.	9	13	22
Discharged unrecovered,	.	.	.	8	11	19
Died,	.	.	.	12	10	22
Resident at this date,	.	.	.	98	91	189

From the above statement it will be seen that the number of patients remains practically the same as at last visit.

‽ The causes of death are registered as follows :—gross brain disease, 6 cases; heart disease, 5 cases ; epilepsy, 3 cases ; general paralysis, 3 cases ; phthisis, 2 cases ; pneumonia, 1 case ; and two fatal accidents. The first of these accidents was the death by scalding of an old and bedridden female patient. It seems that a nurse was filling a hot water bottle in the hospital ward, and that during the process she placed the bottle in a basin in order to preserve the furniture and floor. In the process of filling, some of the hot water overflowed into the basin. While the nurse's back was turned the patient got up, overturned the basin, and scalded herself on the arms and chest. Dr. Skeen is of opinion that in a younger subject death would not have resulted from this injury, and he is further of opinion that there is not sufficient ground for attributing blame to the nurse. The second accident was the death by choking of a male patient, labouring under general paralysis, during a meal. Every effort was made by the doctor to save this patient's life, but without avail. Besides these two fatal accidents a third serious accident, the fracture of the bones of the left forearm in a female patient, took place. This patient made a satisfactory recovery,

There are 61 entries in the Register of Restraint and Seclusion referring to the restraint of 4 persons, entirely for surgical reasons and to prevent the removal of surgical dressings, and to the seclusion of 1 person on one occasion. Four patients escaped and were absent from the asylum for at least one night before being brought back.

Since last visit, 6 attendants—1 man and 5 women—have resigned ; 2 men have been dismissed ; and 9—3 men and 6 women—have been engaged.

More than one-half of the patients attended Divine Service last Sunday. The proportion of the inmates who were usefully employed at the time of the visit was between 60 and 70 per cent. ; of these, 21 men were seen working in the garden and on the piece of arable land which has recently been rented with so much advantage. It was learned with satisfaction that the question of acquiring some permanent land for agricultural purposes has come under the attention of the Committee.

The state of the patients, both in respect to their mental and physical health, was as satisfactory as could be expected. There was a universal absence of noisy excitement, and the statements made by two or three of the inmates had reference solely to the question of undue detention. The personal clothing of the patients of both sexes was in good order, neatly fitting and clean. The dinner this day was expeditiously served, and there was no hurry or disorder of any kind in the dining-room. The food was well-cooked, and appeared to be enjoyed by the patients.

The day-rooms and dormitories were clean and in excellent order. It is understood that the question of providing better accommodation for the unmarried attendants and of erecting cottages for the married attendants is at present under consideration by the Committee. These proposals are certain to meet the approval of the General Board, for experience has shown that similar efforts in other institutions have tended towards securing the permanent services of reliable attendants. Should it be the intention of the Joint Committee to engage in any scheme for the alteration and enlargement of the asylum, it is hoped that the urgent need for better and more commodious hospital accommodation will not be lost sight of.

The books and registers were examined and found to be regularly and correctly kept.

LANARK DISTRICT ASYLUM, HARTWOOD, *7th and 8th March* 1901.

There were on the 8th instant 708 patients on the register of the asylum. Of these, 19 men and 28 women are private patients, and 356 men and 305 women are paupers. In the above figures effect has been given to the transference of one man from the pauper to the private list. All are resident and were seen in the course of the visit.

Of the 661 paupers resident, 593 are chargeable to parishes in Lanark Lunacy District, 50 to the parish of Edinburgh, 7 to the parish of Cathcart, 6 to Orkney parishes, and 5 to other parishes outwith the district.

The following statement shows the changes in the population of the asylum since 27th November, 1900, the date of last visit :—

	PRIVATE PATIENTS.		PAUPER PATIENTS.		TOTALS.
	M.	F.	M.	F.	
Admitted, . . .	4	2	23	21	50
Discharged recovered, .	2	1	7	10	20
Discharged unrecovered,	0	0	2	1	3
Died, ...	1	0	2	5	8

The deaths are registered as due to tubercular disease in 3 cases, to heart affections in 2 cases, and to dysenteric diarrhœa, cerebral softening, and kidney disease in one case each. A *post mortem* examination was made in every case, and the results of these examinations are recorded with completeness. The appointment of a resident pathologist is recorded with approval. Researches into minute cerebral changes require much time and labour, and can only be undertaken by one specially appointed for the work. Our knowledge of the essential nature of brain disorders is advanced by investigations into the structural changes affecting the nervous system in insanity, and it is therefore clearly one of the duties of asylums to encourage and aid the prosecution of scientific work of this nature.

The Register of Restraint and Seclusion contains 14 entries. They refer to the use of seclusion for periods varying from 4 to 8 hours in the treatment of 4 patients. A male patient was in seclusion at the time of the visit on account of excited and violent conduct. There has been no escape. Two accidents are recorded ; one consisted of a fracture of the 5th and 6th ribs and a bruise on ear, and the second of a double fracture of the lower jaw, a fracture of the olecranon process of left ulna, and flesh wounds. The first was caused during a struggle with an attendant, and was the subject of investigation by the Procurator-Fiscal. Though no further steps were taken by the Fiscal, yet the attendant was dismissed, as his treatment of the patients had on other occasions been rough. The injuries in the second accident were caused by the patient jumping over the bridge which crossed the railway ; he ran his barrow to the parapet and sprang over. It is understood that the Board have called attention to a recommendation made in an entry in 1897 as to the necessity for heightening the parapet in order to prevent such accidents, and the District Board have, it is learned, decided to erect a paling on the parapet of sufficient height to prevent the recurrence of such an accident. This patient is progressing satisfactorily, and his mental condition has much improved since the accident. It was noted with satisfaction that the deep cutting of the asylum railway is now protected by a suitable fence.

The changes in the staff have been as follows :—5 have resigned, 3 have been dismissed, and 8 have been engaged. The staff of attendants, when vacancies have been filled up, will include for day duty 34 men and 5 nurses on the male, and 33 nurses on the female side. This number gives a proportion of 1 to 11 in the male, and 1 to 10 in the female division. The night staff comprises 6 male attendants and 6 nurses, giving a ratio of 1 to 62 on the male, and 1 to 55 on the female side. There are 97 male and 94 female patients under continuous supervision during the night. A most commendable feature in the accommodation for the staff in this asylum is the large number of houses provided for married male attendants. The artisan attendants are in all large asylums generally well supplied with house accommodation, but the attendants whose sole duty is the care of the insane are not so amply provided with suitable houses as at this institution. Of the 36 houses on the asylum estate, 21 are occupied by the following members of the male attendant staff :—1 by head-attendant, 1 by deputy head-attendant, 3 by charge attendants, 4 by night attendants, and 12 by members of the under staff. The results of this provision as seen in the duration of service are most satisfactory. This asylum was opened 5 years and 10 months ago. The average duration of the head, deputy, and charge attendants is 5 years and 8 months, of the 4 night attendants 2 years and 11 months, and of the 12 under attendants 2 years and 4 months. These facts clearly show that a stable

male staff can be secured by providing house accommodation for married
male attendants.

Satisfactory precautions are being taken in view of the epidemic of smallpox now prevailing in Glasgow and elsewhere. Every patient admitted to the asylum is placed for fourteen days in a section of the hospital wards on each side, which have been partitioned off. At the end of this period they are transferred to the wards. So far, no patient has shown signs of the disease. All inmates, as well as officials, attendants, and persons resident on the asylum estate, have been vaccinated.

The dayrooms presented a most comfortably furnished appearance, and were brightened with plants and other objects of interest. They are well provided with books, newspapers, and means of amusement. The temperature throughout every section of the building was even and comfortable. The dormitories were in excellent order, and the bed-coverings ample for this season of the year. The ventilation of some of the boot-rooms was not so effective as is desirable, and the introduction of Blackman fans worked by electric motors is recommended.

The condition of the patients as to personal neatness was very satisfactory. The dress of the female inmates is varied in material, well fitting, and tasteful in appearance, and reflects great credit on those in charge of them. The men have tweed suits, well made and of good quality. The dinners on each day of the visit were abundant and palatable meals, and served in a manner which always attracts favourable attention on account of its complete orderliness. General contentment prevailed relative to the quality and quantity of the food. The behaviour of the patients was with few exceptions quite satisfactory. Appeals for discharge were made, but it was found on investigation that those making them were properly detained. The inmates of the hospital wards evidently receive skilful treatment and efficient nursing. The number daily employed in useful work is 484, or 68 per cent. of the patients. The sum of work yearly done by the patients who are employed on the farm, garden, and grounds is a large and profitable one. All who are employed in the asylum, and all unfit for work and able to walk, are daily taken for exercise within the asylum grounds. Everything seen during the visit indicated competent and energetic management.

Owing to the serious illness of Dr. Clark, the asylum has for some time been deprived of his valuable services, but his place is ably filled by Dr. Kerr, the senior assistant. Dr. Kerr showed during the visit an intimate knowledge of the condition of the patients and of all administrative details. He is assisted by the junior Medical Officer and the Pathologist, who is also a Medical Officer. It is understood with satisfaction that Dr. Clark is recovering, and it is hoped that the District Board will grant him prolonged leave of absence, so that his health and strength may be completely restored.

The case-books and registers were examined and found to be carefully and regularly kept.

LANARK DISTRICT ASYLUM,

26th and 27th November 1901.

The following changes have taken place in the population of the asylum since last visit :—

	PRIVATE PATIENTS.		PAUPER PATIENTS.		TOTALS.
	M.	F.	M.	F.	
On Register 8th March, 1901,	21	28	354	305	708
Admitted, . . .	7	9	78	57	151
Discharged recovered, .	5	4	32	30	71
Discharged unrecovered,	4	3	13	5	25
Died, ...	·1	4	15	13	33
On Register 26th November, 1901,	18	26	372	314	730

In these figures effect has been given to the transference of 1 male from the private to the pauper list, and of 3 males from the pauper to the private list.

The deaths are registered as due to cardiac affections in 12 cases ; to

Appendix B.

Commissioners' Entries.
—
Royal and District Asylums.

Lanark District Asylum, Hartwood.

pneumonia and bronchitis in 7 cases ; to tuberculosis in 5 cases ; to general paralysis in 4 cases ; to cerebral hæmorrhage in 2 cases ; and to strangulated hernia, cancer of the stomach, and extensive burns on the body received prior to admission in 1 case each. *Post mortem* examinations were performed in 31 instances. This is a remarkably high proportion and exceedingly creditable to the Medical Officers.

There are three entries in the Register of Accidents which record simple fractures of the clavicle and ulna in two male patients respectively, and of the neck of the femur in a female patient. The descriptions given of these fractures raise no doubt as to the fortuitous nature of the occurrences which caused them.

There are 50 entries in the Register of Restraint and Seclusion referring to the seclusion of 14 persons on account of noise or violence or excitement. One patient escaped and was absent for at least one night before being brought back.

The record of the employment of patients shows that at the time of the visit 268 men and 248 women were usefully employed. Of the men no less than 200 were working on the farm and garden, while of the women about 60 were working in the laundry and kitchen, and about 100 at sewing or knitting.

Twenty-seven persons, 17 men and 10 women, have been engaged as attendants and nurses, and 14 men and 10 women employed in that capacity have left the service of the institution ; of the latter 4 men and 3 women were dismissed. The present staff consists of 31 male and 38 female attendants for day duty, and of 6 males and 6 females for night duty. This allows a proportion over all of 1 attendant to 10·5 patients during the day, and of 1 to about 60 during the night.

The patients were found, as a rule, quiet and contented, with the exception of the women in one of the divisions in the upper ward who were noisy. This ward is too large for the accommodation of this class of patient, for it was evident that a few more turbulent cases had the effect of exciting the others. Several of the male patients were clamorous for release and submitted various complaints. With one exception those so demanding release were judged to be insane and properly detained. The appeal of the case referred to is receiving attention. The dress of the patients was universally neat, warm, and in good repair. The dinner on the first day of the visit consisted of salt herrings, potatoes, and suet pudding, and on the second day of broth, potatoes, and boiled beef. The service of the food was orderly and expeditious.

Every part of the institution was found, as usual, in excellent order. It was learned with much regret that Dr. Campbell Clark's illness has lately assumed a more serious aspect. Dr. Kerr, the senior assistant physician, was in charge of the asylum at the time of the visit. While writing this report the news of Dr. Clark's death has reached us. On the sad event it is not here fitting to comment, beyond expressing the opinions that his life's work in all that concerned the interests of the insane has always been greatly esteemed by his professional brethren, and that by his death the county of Lanark has lost an able and high minded official.

The case books and *post mortem* records continue to be kept with great care ; the statutory registers were examined and found correct.

Midlothian and Peebles District Asylum.

MIDLOTHIAN AND PEEBLES DISTRICT ASYLUM,
19th February 1901.

Since the asylum was last visited the following changes in population have taken place :—

			PRIVATE AND PAUPER PATIENTS.		
			M.	F.	TOTALS.
On register, 29th September 1900,	.	.	124	126	250
Admitted since,	.	.	13	14	27
Discharged recovered,	.	.	2	3	5
Discharged unrecovered,	.	.	2	3	5
Died,	.	.	3	9	12
On register, 19th February 1901,	.	.	130	125	255

There are 3 men and 4 women absent on probation, so that the numbers resident to-day are 248, of whom 127 are men and 121 are women. Of those resident, 4 men and 12 women are private patients, and 1 of these men is a voluntary inmate.

The deaths are registered as due to gross brain disease in 6 cases, to cancer in 2 cases, to general paralysis in 2 cases, to senile decay in 1 case, and to exhaustion from acute mania in 1 case. *Post mortem* examinations were made in 9 instances.

The asylum was seen under very unfavourable conditions. Scarcely any part of it was free from workmen, and the patients were found partly in the new buildings and partly in the old. It is therefore impossible, on this occasion, to comment either favourably or unfavourably upon the general order or arrangement of the institution. A regrettable fact, which has been referred to in previous entries, is that it has been found necessary, during the somewhat lengthy progress of the building operations, to place so many patients in single rooms during the day. The completion of these buildings appears now definitely in view, and it is earnestly hoped that their arrangements will permit of all patients being treated in association during the day.

All the patients in residence were seen during the visit. They were found free from any appearance of excitement, and none of them made any complaint of a rational kind beyond the usual demands for release. Both the men and the women were suitably, and, with one or two exceptions, neatly clothed, and their physical condition indicated a careful and systematic supervision and an adequate dietary. Twenty-two men and 19 women were confined to bed chiefly on account of physical ailments, but it was observed with approval that among that number were several patients labouring under acute forms of mental affection who were being treated by means of prolonged rest in bed. The extension of this system of treatment to all suitable cases cannot be too highly recommended. It was ascertained that among the sick confined to bed there were no cases of phthisis, and that there are no patients in the asylum at present who, so far as is known to the medical officers, manifest any sign or symptom of that disease. Out of 273 deaths which have occurred in the institution since the year 1888, only 34, or 12·4 per cent., have been caused by tuberculosis in any of its forms. As *post-mortem* examinations were made in upwards of 80 per cent. of the patients who died during the period referred to, the accuracy of the above statement may be generally conceded. No doubt many factors—climate, the situation of the asylum, its heating and ventilation—have contributed to the diminution of this disease to which the insane are believed to be peculiarly liable, but without careful treatment and suitable food such general conditions would have been largely inoperative.

The dinner to-day, which was served to 168 patients in the new dining hall, consisted of vegetable broth, bread, and suet dumpling. It was well cooked and sufficiently popular. The dining hall is a spacious room capable of accommodating with ease a larger number of patients than occupied it to-day ; its lighting and ventilation are in every respect satisfactory. The new hospital wards are now in use. They appear to be admirably adapted for their purpose, being in the form of dayroom dormitories and having single rooms, stores, kitchens, and lavatories attached. The buildings are one-storeyed, well lighted, comfortably heated, and ventilated by extracting fans driven by electricity. The furnishing of the wards has been tastefully carried out. The new acute blocks are partially occupied by some of the chronic patients from those parts of the old building where the wards are at present undergoing alterations.

Since last visit 13 attendants—3 men and 5 women—have been engaged, and 10 men and 4 women have resigned. There are 11 attendants on day duty on each side of the house, being a proportion of 1 attendant to about 11 patients. This is a smaller proportion than the average in modern asylums in this country, where the proportion is 1 to 10, in many instances 1 to 9. It is understood that it is proposed to increase the staff as soon as the new buildings are completed. The night staff has recently been increased by one additional attendant on each side, and it is learned with approval that it also is to be further augmented.

The Register of Restraint and Seclusion contains 31 entries referring to

Appendix B.

Commissioners'
Entries.

Royal and
District
Asylums.

Midlothian
and Peebles
District
Asylum.

the seclusion of 8 persons on account of violence and excitement. Two minor accidents descriptive of bruises are recorded.

The case-books contain full and creditable accounts of the patients, and the various registers were found to be regularly and correctly kept.

MIDLOTHIAN AND PEEBLES DISTRICT ASYLUM,
23rd October 1901.

There are 259 patients on the registers of the asylum at this date. Of these, 1 male is a voluntary inmate, 5 males and 13 females are private patients, and 132 males and 108 females are paupers. One female has since last visit been transferred from the private to the pauper list. Two males are absent on statutory probation.

Since 19th February 1901, the date of the preceding report, the following changes in the population have taken place :—

	PRIVATE PATIENTS.		PAUPER PATIENTS.		TOTALS.
	M.	F.	M.	F.	
Admitted, ...	3	7	25	21	56
Discharged recovered, . .	0	4	8	17	29
Discharged unrecovered, . .	1	1	5	2	9
Discharged not insane, . .	0	0	1	0	1
Died, ...	0	1	6	7	14

The rate of recovery has during the period embraced in the above figures been high, being 51·7 per cent. on the number admitted.

The mortality has been low. The deaths are registered as due to gross brain lesions in 3 cases, to melancholic exhaustion in 2 cases, to heart disease in 2 cases, to pneumonia in 2 cases, to diarrhœa in 2 cases, and to cancer, general tuberculosis, and choking, each in 1 case. In 12 cases, or in 85·7 per cent. of the deaths, the cause was ascertained or verified by a *post mortem* examination. This is highly creditable to the medical staff, and affords protection to the insane against injuries which might not otherwise be discovered. The Pathological Journal was examined, and found to contain full details of these examinations. The medical records in the case books show that the mental and bodily condition of each patient is carefully studied.

The Register of Restraint and Seclusion contains 26 entries. They refer to the use of seclusion for periods varying from half-an-hour to 8 hours in the treatment of 9 patients. Three casualties have occurred—(1) a scald, not of a serious character, sustained by a patient during bathing operations ; (2) a blow inflicted on an attendant by a patient by means of the poker which had been obtained from the hospital kitchen, the door of which had carelessly been left open ; and (3) a case of suffocation by means of a small piece of meat which became impacted in the larynx. This patient was an old man who was confined to bed on account of weak heart and senile infirmity. All efforts to extract the piece of meat were unsuccessful—it was found at the *post mortem* examination beneath the vocal cords. Three escapes have taken place in which the patients were absent for one night before being brought back.

The changes in the staff since last visit have been as follows :— 3 attendants, 3 nurses, and 8 servants have resigned, 2 attendants and 1 servant have been dismissed, 1 attendant has died, and 6 attendants, 5 nurses, and 10 servants have been engaged. The causes of dismissal were neglect of duty and intemperance. To meet increased requirements due to the opening of the new wards 1 attendant and 2 nurses have been added to the staff. The proportion of day attendants to the patients is now 1 to 10, which indicates a day staff of adequate strength. The ratio of the night staff is 1 to 68 on the male and 1 to 60 on the female side. In some asylums it is as high as 1 to 43, which is a proportion which more thoroughly secures the safety and comforts of the patients during the night. It is therefore understood with satisfaction that the number of night attendants is to be increased. The duration of service cannot be considered as wholly satisfactory. Of the 13 male attendants, only 2 have been in the service of the asylum over 2 years, 4 over 1 year, and 7 under 9 months. Of the 12 nurses, 3 have 3 years' service, 1 over 2 years, 3 over 1 year, and 5 from 1 to 6 months. The senior night attendant has over

3 years' service, and the senior night nurse over 4 years. It is hoped that as more comfortable accommodation for the staff has been provided in the recent extensions, and the difficulties and disturbances occasioned by building operations are at an end, there will be a longer duration of service in the future.

Appendix B.

Commissioners'
Entries.

Royal and
District
Asylums.

Midlothian
and Peebles
District
Asylum.

The impression produced by the visit on this occasion was highly satisfactory. The patients, who are now free from overcrowding, bore every evidence of being well cared for. They were, with few exceptions, tranquil and contented, and the dress of both sexes was good and neat in appearance. The dinner at this date consisted of Irish stew and bread—4 oz. of the latter for men and 2 oz. for the women. The meal was an abundant and palatable one, and every patient of whom enquiry was made expressed decided approval. The dietary of the working inmates has recently been increased by the issue of a lunch consisting of 4 oz. of bread and 2 oz. of cheese. This addition causes the dietary to be of the energy standard necessary for such patients. Twenty men and 15 women were confined to bed, of whom 8 were in single rooms. One man, a recently admitted patient, was in seclusion on account of homicidal tendencies. Fourteen men and 4 women are epileptic, and 5 men and 12 women are suicidal. These patients have the protection of continuous night supervision, and this is also being more and more extended to those of wet and dirty habits. The number daily engaged in useful work is 97 men and 78 women, the percentage being 64 of each sex. A party of women are during the summer months employed on the farm and garden. The number who attended Divine service last Sunday was 40 men and 52 women.

The extensive additions and other improvements, such as the heating of the whole asylum by a system of hot-water pipes and radiators, electric lighting, increased water supply, and sewage filtration, all of which have been in progress for a considerable time, are now completed. The new hospital sections are lofty, spacious, well lighted, and efficiently ventilated wards, and are furnished with every appliance necessary for the care and comfort of the sick and infirm. They are admirably suited for their purpose, and will enable the patients to be much more efficiently treated and cared for than has previously been possible. The day-rooms and dormitories in the extensions to the main building are in occupation on the female side, but only partially on the male side. They have been suitably furnished, and the lavatories and bathrooms have been equipped with arrangements of the most modern design. The enlargement of the dining and amusement halls is completed. The ample space in the new dining hall permits of the meals being served in a most orderly and expeditious manner. The kitchen has been supplied with boilers and other cooking apparatus of the newest and best description, and the dispensary which adjoins the kitchen has been converted into a scullery. Useful improvements have been made in the laundry and wash-house—the latter has been refloored with cement, a washing machine has been provided, and a fan in the roof effectively removes the steam. The laundry has been furnished with an ironing calender, the drying-closets have been made efficient, and an enlarged distributing room has been added. A double boiler, which will, it is hoped, be able to supply sufficient steam for the kitchen, the laundry, the electric machinery, and the heating arrangements, is in process of being fitted into the boiler-house. Two boilers are at present required to do this work, and the consumpt of coal has in consequence been very large. An economiser is to be erected, and this, coupled with the use of one boiler, will, it is expected, effect a considerable saving in the expenditure for coal. The majority of the stairs in the asylum are unprovided with handrails. This is a defect which should be remedied, as these rails are most helpful to feeble and senile patients going both up and down stairs, and they also save accidents when patients stumble or are pushed when going down stairs.

The general result of the recent extensions and improvements is that the District Board now possesses an asylum which affords excellent and sufficient accommodation to meet the requirements of the district for many years, and one in which the efficiency of every department has been greatly increased.

The present rate of board is high, being £34 a year. The expenditure of the asylum has recently been the subject of careful investigation both by the General Board and by the District Board. It is fully anticipated that this will, as a result of these inquiries, be reduced in many directions without the interests and good care of the patients being affected.

The registers were examined and found regularly and accurately kept.

·Appendix B.

Commissioners'
Entries.

Royal and
District
Asylums.

Montrose
Royal Asylum.

MONTROSE ROYAL ASYLUM,
6th and 7th June 1901.

Since the institution was last visited the following changes have taken place in the population :—

I. Certificated Patients—

		PRIVATE PATIENTS.		PAUPER PATIENTS.		TOTALS.
		M.	F.	M.	F.	
On the Register, 23rd October, 1900,		47	60	249	294	650
Admitted,	. . . . .	8	24	41	48	121
Discharged Recovered,	.	4	9	8	16	37
Discharged Unrecovered,	. .	1	0	7	8	16
Died,	. . . . . .	2	4	10	20	36
On the Register, 6th June, 1901,	.	48	71	265	298	682

II. Voluntary Inmates—

		M.	F.	M.	F.	
Resident at last visit,	. . .	1	3	0	0	4
Admitted,	. . . . .	5	1	0	0	6
Left,	. . . . .	3	2	0	0	5
Resident at this date,	. . .	3	2	0	0	5

In the above figures effect has been given to the transference since last visit of 1 female from the private to the pauper list and of 2 females from the pauper to the private list. With the exception of 1 man who was absent on pass all the patients were resident and were seen during the visit.

The number of private patients has increased by 13 and the number of pauper patients by 20. The increase in the private patients, which appears to be steadily progressive, is satisfactory, and shows that the excellent accommodation which the Managers have provided for such cases is becoming more widely known and appreciated. The increase in the number of pauper patients is a more doubtful benefit, and the hope may be expressed that it is exceptional and not likely to continue.

The following statement shows the distribution of the inmates of the institution, excluding Carnegie House, in which there are 43 patients :—

						M.	F.	TOTALS.
Main Asylum,	.	.	.	.	.	186	249	435
Hospital,	.	.	.	.	.	72	82	154
New Villa,	.	.	.	.	.	43	0	43
Gate Lodge,	.	.	.	.	.	0	12	12
						301	343	644

The accommodation in these divisions amounts to 588 beds, and the number of patients at present resident in them is 644, an excess of 84. At present there are about 40 more female than male patients, and it is therefore proposed to take advantage of the removal of the male patients to the villa by placing 25 female patients in one of the male dormitories. The basement dormitory on the male side of the hospital has also been furnished with 18 beds, and an internal staircase leading to the sick-room of the hospital is being constructed, so that the patients using the dormitory may reside in the hospital, in which there is said to be sufficient day-room space for this additional number. When all has been done the fact remains that the institution is overcrowded to the extent of about 80 patients, which is, significantly, the number now in the asylum belonging to the parish of Dundee.

The deaths are registered as due to heart disease in 8 cases, to general paralysis in 6 cases, to organic brain diseases in 6 cases, to phthisis in 6 cases, to senile decay in 5 cases, to acute mania in 2 cases, and to pneumonia, peritonitis, and Bright's disease in 1 case each. *Post mortem* examinations were made in 21 cases, in the remaining 15 cases the consent of the relatives to such an examination was refused.

There are 81 entries in the Register of Restraint and Seclusion. These refer to the restraint of 1 man and 1 woman on account of homicidal and impulsive conduct, and of 2 women for surgical reasons ; also to the seclusion of 1 man and 1 woman on account of violent conduct, and of 1 man for excitement after epileptic fits.

Five patients escaped and were absent for at least 1 night before being brought back. There is only 1 entry in the Register of Accidents, descriptive of a fracture of the thigh bone sustained by a male patient through being pushed over by a fellow patient.

The number of patients attending Divine service last Sunday was 332. Three hundred and eighty patients, 171 men and 209 women, were usefully employed at the time of the visit. This proportion (55 per cent.) is somewhat small and might advantageously be increased, especially in the direction of employing a greater number of the male patients at field labour, for which there is, fortunately, unlimited scope in connection with the asylum.

The staff of attendants and nurses consists of 31 men and 30 women for day duty, and of 5 men and 5 women for night duty. While the male staff is amply sufficient, that on the female side, especially in the main building and hospital, appears to be slightly below the average, both for day and night work. The changes which have taken place in the nursing staff since last visit are as follows :—17 men and 11 women have been engaged, 10 men and 10 women have resigned, and 4 men have been dismissed.

The general condition of the patients was highly satisfactory. They were suitably and neatly clothed, and the appearance of the female patients in the main asylum and in the hospital was in this respect more than usually creditable. The state of health of the patients indicated that they are adequately and judiciously fed, and in the course of numerous conversations with individual inmates no reference was made to any defect in dietary or to the want of any personal comfort. There was no undue excitement in the wards at the time of the visit, but it was evident that in almost every part of the house there were excitable patients who were capable of creating disturbances. This is not due to the fact that patients in this asylum are particularly prone to excitement, but because there exists no rigid system of classification. In this connection it may be pointed out that it is now unusual in asylums to have no wards set apart for the reception and treatment of the newly-admitted cases.

The asylum was found in excellent order—bright, clean, and well-ventilated. On the female side of the main building and hospital the floral and other decorations were especially attractive. It is unnecessary to refer to Carnegie House, for it maintains fully the ideals of those who constructed it, and continues to deserve the favourable opinions which have so often been expressed regarding it.

Several improvements and alterations were observed in the course of the visit. Among them may be mentioned the erection of a gate lodge and the formation of an avenue leading to Carnegie House. The construction of the new garden is making satisfactory progress. A new oven has been added to the bakehouse, and the kitchen in the main building has been completely renovated and fitted with cooking apparatus of a modern type. The latter improvement has added greatly to the facility of operation and to the comfort of those who work in this department. Telephones for connecting the various parts of the institution are in course of being erected by the electrical engineer of the asylum. These will be found to facilitate administration and to increase the central control over the outlying portions of the institution. Many portions of the asylum estate which are incapable of arable cultivation have been very wisely planted with trees. It is understood that the Directors have agreed to take on lease from the town of Montrose a part of the lands known as Haugh of Kinnaber, lying beside the North Esk and adjacent to lands cultivated by the asylum. The arable land farmed by the institution will then amount to fully 300 acres.

It was learned with approbation that the Directors have joined the scheme of the Pathological Laboratory of the Scottish Asylums. The commendable feature of this scheme is the voluntary combination of almost all the asylum Boards in this country with the object of scientifically furthering our knowledge of the causes of a widespread and terrible affliction. If science is ever to succeed in unravelling the mysteries connected with the causes and prevention of this disease it may safely be assumed that it will be through investigations conducted in such laboratories.

The books and registers were examined and found to be carefully and correctly kept.

Appendix B.

Commissioners' Entries.

Royal and District Asylums.

Montrose Royal Asylum.

Appendix B.

Commissioners'
Entries.

Royal and
District
Asylums.

Montrose
Royal Asylum.

MONTROSE ROYAL ASYLUM,
27th and 28th September 1901.

There were on the 27th instant 684 patients on the registers of the asylum. Of these, 5 are voluntary inmates, 43 males and 71 females are private patients, and 265 males and 300 females are paupers. Effect has been given in these figures to the transference since last visit of 2 males from the private to the pauper list, and of 1 female from the pauper to the private list. All were resident, and every patient was given an opportunity of making any statement desired.

The following changes have taken place since 6th June 1901 :—

	PRIVATE PATIENTS.		PAUPER PATIENTS.		TOTALS.
	M.	F.	M.	F.	
Admitted, . . .	10	7	15	25	57
Discharged recovered, .	5	5	12	7	29
Discharged unrecovered, .	2	0	0	0	2
Died, ...	6	3	5	15	29

There have been no changes among the voluntary inmates.

Since last visit the number resident has decreased by 3, but the number of paupers has increased by 2. The decrease is evidently due to the high death rate during the period to which the foregoing statement refers. The admission rate continues undiminished, and there does not appear to be any ground for anticipating that the progressive increase of the number of patients, which has characterised the statistics of the asylum in past years, will be arrested. In these circumstances, the adequacy of the accommodation to meet the present and future requirements of those lunacy districts with which the Managers desire to enter into contracts, calls for consideration. The accommodation of an asylum should be in advance of the demand. Calculated on the minimum floor space allowed for each patient, the main building can only properly accommodate 176 patients of each sex. The occupation of the new villa has reduced the number of male patients in the main building to 170, or 6 less than it should contain. In the female division there are 76 patients in excess of the proper number. A dormitory containing 25 beds on the second storey on the male side has been shut off and used for female patients. This, however, does not relieve the congestion in the female day-rooms. It will be evident that the provision of additional female accommodation is urgently required, and it is therefore understood with satisfaction that the Managers have resolved to erect a villa for females. It is hoped that there will be no further delay in providing this extension. The day-room accommodation for females in the hospital is overcrowded, but adequate dormitory space is obtained by utilising rooms originally intended for the hospital staff. The male villa contains 3 less than the number for which it was built. The margin of spare accommodation for male pauper patients throughout the asylum is small, and it will be obvious that the erection of a villa for 60 female patients will not wholly relieve the overcrowding in the female sections which at present exists.

The deaths are registered as due to brain lesions in 8 cases, to general paralysis in 7 cases, to senile decay in 4 cases, to pneumonia in 3 cases, to phthisis pulmonalis in 2 cases, and to cancer, ovarian tumor, chorea, ulceration of bowels, and suicide by hanging in 1 case each. *Post mortem* examinations were made in 15 cases, or in 51·7 per cent. of the deaths.

The Medical Records in the Case Books and the Pathological Journal were examined and found to be well and intelligently kept. The appointment of a Pathologist, as third Medical Officer or as Clinical Clerk, whose whole time could be devoted to scientific research and who would work in connection with the Pathological Laboratory of the Scottish Asylums is worthy of consideration.

The Register of Restraint and Seclusion contains 9 entries. They refer to the use of the camisole in 2 cases on account of maniacal excitement with homicidal violence, and in 1 case for surgical reasons. One accident is recorded—a suicide by hanging. This patient had been in the asylum for six weeks, and had during that time manifested no suicidal tendencies. He was placed in a single room on account of noisy excitement, and during an interval

between the visits of the night attendant he contrived to secure a strip of his Appendix B.
mattress in a small ventilating aperture at the top of the shutter, and to hang Commissioners' Entries.
himself by it. Two escapes have occurred in which the patients were absent
for at least one night before being brought back.

The changes among the attendants, nurses, and servants have not been Royal and District Asylums.
numerous. Three attendants, 2 nurses, and 5 servants have resigned, 2 nurses
have been dismissed as unsuitable, and 4 attendants, 6 nurses, and 5 servants
have been engaged. The duration of service among the senior staff is most Montrose Royal Asylum.
satisfactory ; 14 attendants have served from 30 to 5 years, and 10 nurses from
20 to 5 years. Of the whole staff, 24, or 32 per cent., have been in the service
of the asylum over 5 years, and 40, or 53 per cent., have over 2 years' service.
It is noted with approval that the arrangements for the continuous night supervision of female patients in associated dormitories in the main building have
been made similar to those which have for some time obtained on the male
side. An additional nurse has been engaged to give effect to this extension of
the night supervision. The night staff at present consists of 5 attendants and 6
nurses.

The asylum is evidently under able and energetic administration. The condition of the patients as regards clothing and personal neatness was highly
satisfactory. No patient made any complaint as to care and treatment, and
the appeals for discharge were comparatively few. The dinners seen during
the visit were abundant and palatable meals, with which the more intelligent
patients expressed hearty approval. The number of pauper patients daily
engaged in useful work is 164 men and 199 women, which gives a percentage
of 61 and 66 respectively. The number on parole is large—81 within and 53
beyond the grounds. It is evident that parole is granted to every patient
whose mental condition warrants the privilege, and the result is increased
happiness and contentment. This is a feature in the management which merits
commendation. Twelve men and 23 women were confined to bed, and everything seen regarding these patients bore testimony to skilful treatment and
efficient nursing. The number of epileptics is 30—19 men and 11 women ;
24 patients—18 men and 6 women—are the subjects of general paralysis ; and 39
men and 31 women are returned as actively suicidal. The Sunday Services are
usually attended by 50 per cent. of the inmates.

The new male villa is a pleasing building externally, and its accommodation is
all that could be desired for the quiet and convalescent patients. On the
ground floor are three day-rooms, a dining-room, kitchen, lavatories, and boot-
room. On the first floor are three dormitories, attendants' rooms, bathroom,
dressing-room and lavatories, and on the second floor three dormitories and
accommodation for the attendants. The whole house has been suitably and
comfortably furnished and the day-rooms are enlivened by pictures, plants,
and other objects of interest. One of the rooms is provided with a billiard
table. The brightness, cheerfulness, and comfort of the patients' environments
in this house cannot fail to have a most beneficial effect. The Managers are
to be congratulated on the excellence of this extension of the asylum, and it
is satisfactory to learn that it has been provided at a moderate cost per bed.

The wards throughout the main building and hospital were clean, in good
order, and well ventilated. The relief from overcrowding on the male side of
the main building is attended with satisfactory results, the patients being, with
one or two exceptions, free from manifestations of irritability and excitement.
The change from the experience at former visits was most marked. The new
internal staircase to the basement male dormitory permits of the latter being
used by patients resident in the hospital. Formerly, the dormitory was
occupied by patients belonging to the main building who had to go outside
to get to it, an arrangement which was not satisfactory during winter months.
Telephonic communication has been established between the principal sections
of the institution, and is proving a great convenience in their administration.
The equipment of the kitchen is completed and the arrangements of this
important department have been made thoroughly efficient. The electric light
has been extended to the large dining-hall, high dormitories, workshops, and
farm-steading, and a small combined set has been provided for running during
the night when few lights are required. The foundations for duplicating the
large combined set are ready. The asylum is now included in the Hillside
Drainage District, and the disposal of the sewage will in future be unattended
with any difficulties or outlay.

Appendix B.
———
Commissioners'
Entries.
———
Royal and
District
Asylums.
———
Montrose
Royal Asylum.

The great comfort and elegance of the internal arrangements of Carnegie House never fail to attract favourable attention. It is in every way a desirable residence for patients belonging to the cultured and wealthy classes. Sixteen gentlemen and 27 ladies are in residence, and they are made as happy as it is possible for them to be during their mental illness. A large extent of ground to the south has been laid out as a flower and fruit garden, and the field to the east has been planted with trees. Walks have been formed in the garden and around and through this field for the use of patients. The erection of a summer house, which would afford shelter from the sun and rain, is recommended.

The registers were examined and found regularly and accurately kept.

Murray's
Royal Asylum,
Perth.

MURRAY'S ROYAL ASYLUM, PERTH,
1st May 1901.

There are 135 patients at this date on the registers of the asylum. Of these, 67 gentlemen and 59 ladies are certificated patients, and 6 gentlemen and 3 ladies are voluntary inmates. Five gentlemen were at the date of the visit resident at the seaside villa at Elie, 1 gentleman was absent on pass, and 1 gentleman, a voluntary inmate, was temporarily absent from the institution. The number of patients resident in the asylum is 128, all of whom were individually seen and interviewed.

Since 17th December 1900, the date of the previous entry, the following changes have taken place:—

	PRIVATE PATIENTS.		
	M.	F.	TOTALS.
Certificated Patients—			
Admitted,	8	8	16
Discharged recovered,	4	5	9
Discharged unrecovered,	3	3	6
Died,	1	3	4
Voluntary Inmates—			
Admitted,	2	0	2
Left,	0	0	0

The deaths are registered as due to apoplexy in 1 case, to cardiac disease in 2 cases, and to senile debility in 1 case. It is creditable to the medical administration of the asylum that in every instance the cause of death was verified by *post mortem* examination.

The Register of Restraint and Seclusion contains 14 entries, referring to the use of restraint in the cases of 3 patients in order to prevent interference with surgical dressings. One accident is recorded, a contused scalp wound which an epileptic patient sustained during a struggle. There has been no escape.

With few exceptions in the ladies' division, the behaviour of the patients was quiet and orderly. There was among them generally an air of contentment which was indicative of kind and considerate treatment. Individual requirements are carefully attended to, as large an amount of liberty is granted as is compatible with safety, and industrial employment, both in the wards and in the grounds, is successfully encouraged. Carriage drives, outdoor games, and indoor amusements and entertainments are liberally provided. In fact, everything seen during the visit showed that Dr. Urquhart endeavours by every means to promote the recovery of all in whom this result is possible, and the contentment, happiness, and comfort of everyone committed to his care.

The institution is full, and even overcrowded in the male division, and the time has now come when its great success warrants its further extension. It is understood that the directors and Dr. Urquhart have under consideration how further provision should be made consonant with modern ideas of asylum accommodation.

The reconstruction of the gallery on the ground floor of the ladies' division has been completed, and when its former dismal condition is considered, the result is beyond what was deemed possible. It is now a well-lighted, well-ventilated, artistically decorated, and comfortably furnished section of the asylum. The bathroom, lavatory, and other sanitary arrangements, are of

the most modern kind, and every detail in its reconstruction has been con- Appendix B
sidered with the view of securing the welfare of the patients. The other
sections of the institution are maintained in excellent order, and the accom- Commissioners'
modation throughout presented a cheerful and handsomely-furnished appear- Entries.
ance. The grounds and garden, which afford healthy outdoor work for about Royal and
20 gentlemen, are kept in admirable order. District
The case-books, pathological register, and official registers, were found Asylums.
written up to date. The medical records indicate the high standard of clinical
work bestowed on the study of the condition and history of the patients. Murray's
Royal Asylum,
Perth.

MURRAY'S ROYAL ASYLUM, PERTH,
4th December 1901.

The asylum was last visited on the 1st May, at which date there were 135
patients resident. Of these, 67 gentlemen and 59 ladies were certificated, and
6 gentlemen and 3 ladies were voluntary inmates.
Since then the following changes have occurred :—

	VOLUNTARY PATIENTS.		CERTIFICATED PATIENTS.		TOTALS.
	M.	F.	M.	F.	
Admitted, . . .	1	2	10	12	25
Discharged recovered, .	—	—	5	3	8
Discharged unrecovered, .	—	—	3	7	10
Left, ...	2	2	—	—	4
Died, . . .	—	—	—	—	—

At the present time there are 139 patients in the asylum, of whom 69
gentlemen and 61 ladies are certificated and 6 gentlemen and 3 ladies are
resident of their own accord. With the exception of 2 gentlemen who were
absent on pass, all the patients were seen during the visit.
There has been no death during the period covered by this report.
There are 36 entries in the Register of Restraint and Seclusion referring to
the restraint of 4 persons. In three instances the restraint was technical and
employed solely as a medicament in the form of the wet pack ; in the fourth
it was employed to prevent the removal of medical applications in a case of
erysipelas.
There have been two escapes in which the patients were each absent for at
least one night before being brought back.
Among the entries in the Register of Accidents three are of a sufficiently
serious character to demand notice. These refer to a cut on the scalp in the
case of a lady, and a fracture of the rib and a fracture of the thigh in the case
of two gentlemen respectively. The descriptions given of these accidents are so
explicit as to raise no doubt as to the fortuitous nature of the causes which
account for them.
Fifty-three gentlemen and 44 ladies were employed at useful work at the
time of the visit. Of these, 20 gentlemen were employed in the garden and 23
ladies at needlework of various kinds.
The number of patients on parole continues to be comparatively large.
Eleven gentlemen and 7 ladies are permitted to go beyond the asylum
boundaries, and 17 gentlemen and 11 ladies are confined to the grounds.
The bulk of the patients are distributed between the main building and
Kincarrathie House. A few were still at the seaside house at Elie, and two
ladies occupied a cottage near the asylum. The recent increase of patients
makes it necessary to consider means of enlarging the accommodation, and an
excellent plan of a detached villa was exhibited by Dr. Urquhart which it is
understood may be approved of by the Directors.
The condition of the patients, the care of their mental and physical health,
and the recorded progress of their cases as seen in the case books, was highly
satisfactory.
The whole institution was found, as usual, in excellent order.
The books and registers were examined and found correct.

H

Appendix B.

Commissioners'
Entries.

Royal and
District
Asylums.

Perth District
Asylum.

PERTH DISTRICT ASYLUM,
11th *May* 1901.

There are 358 patients—181 men and 177 women—on the register of the asylum at this date. All are resident and were individually seen in the course of the visit.

Since 18th December, 1900—the date of the previous entry—the following changes have taken place :—

PAUPER PATIENTS.

	M.	F.	TOTALS.
Admitted, ...	13	22	35
Discharged Recovered, ...	7	5	12
Discharged Unrecovered, ...	5	5	10
Died, ...	4	2	6

It is interesting to note that senile cases are very few among the 35 patients admitted. Only 1 was over 70 years of age, and 5 between 60 and 70. Twenty-two of the patients were between 30 and 60, and 7 were between 17 and 30. The subjects of acute senile insanity require skilful care, and are generally a heavy task upon the nursing resources of an asylum. It is shown in the Forty-Second Report of the Board of Lunacy to be a mistake to think that the increased number of pauper lunatics resident in asylums is in an important degree due to the greater frequency with which persons suffering from the mental decay of old age are sent to asylums.

At the end of the six months to which the foregoing statistics refer, there is an increase of 7 patients. The women have increased by 10, and the men have decreased by 3. Though it is understood that the admission rate has during the last twelve months been lower than that of the immediately preceding years, yet there is, on account of the large percentage of incurable cases admitted, only a decrease of 8 in the number resident since 5th June, 1900. The decrease in the population of the county will, it is feared, have no effect in diminishing the admission rate. It is the able-bodied and mentally sound who emigrate, and the old and defective in mind and body who are left behind. This is a well known fact in regard to Ireland, from which millions have emigrated, and yet the number of lunatics is yearly increasing at a rapid rate. The shortage in the accommodation of the main asylum was dealt with in a previous entry, and it practically remains the same at this date. There are in the dayrooms of the main asylum 38 men and 34 women in excess of what they can properly accommodate. This indicates an overcrowding which is inimical to the welfare of the patients. The accommodation of an institution for the insane should be kept in advance of the demand, not in arrear as is the case in this asylum. It is therefore hoped that the District Board will no longer delay in deciding on the nature and amount of accommodation, and in taking steps to provide it.

The rate of mortality has been low. Of the 6 deaths, 3 are registered as due to diseases of the brain, 2 to phthisis pulmonalis, and 1 to pneumonia and heart affection. In 4 cases, or in 66·6 per cent. the cause of death was verified by *post mortem* examination.

The Register of Restraint and Seclusion contains 13 entries. They refer to the use of seclusion for periods varying from 1¾ to 8 hours in the treatment of 3 males and 3 females on account of threatening homicidal violence or acute epileptic excitement. No accident to any patient has occurred, and there has been no escape.

A fairly adequate day staff continues to be maintained, giving 1 attendant for every 12 males and 1 nurse for every 11 females. The night staff is numerically strong, consisting of 4 men and 4 nurses, the ratio to patients being 1 to 45 in the male, and 1 to 44 in the female division. The continuous supervision of the patients in three dormitories of each side continues as described in previous reports, and is productive of the best results as to their comfort, safety, and improvement in habits and behaviour.

The extension of the villa in which the nurses dine and in which 14 of them sleep is strongly recommended. It should be enlarged so as to accommodate the whole of the nursing staff. This provision would be a boon to the nurses, and would without doubt tend to secure and retain the services of an intelligent and trustworthy staff of nurses. It is now getting to be recognised that it is only right and proper that the nurses should have a separate home to go to after the harassing duties of the day are over.

The patients continue to be well cared for. Their dress and personal neatness were quite satisfactory. The clothing of the women attracted favourable attention on account of its variety and tastefulness. One or two patients were inclined to be noisy, but the others were quiet and orderly. The only complaint of ill-usage was by a male patient who at every visit makes incredible charges against the management of the asylum This man was stripped and carefully examined, but no bruises or marks could be found. Generally speaking, the patients were contented, and many expressed appreciation of the care and treatment they receive. The dinner consisted of pea soup and Irish stew made with tinned meat. The soup was well cooked and savoury. It is recommended that a 2-oz. slice of bread be added to this meal. Industrial employment of the inmates is well attended to—112 men and 120 women are registered as daily engaged in useful occupations. Two men are granted parole beyond the grounds, and 49 men and 4 women have the privilege of parole within the grounds. The fact that there has been no escape shows that the patients are well selected for liberty in the grounds.

All the wards were found scrupulously clean and in good order. They are suitably and comfortably furnished, well supplied with plants and other objects of decoration, and liberally provided with books and means of amusement. The kitchen has been re-modelled, its walls tiled, and its lighting and ventilation greatly improved. New boilers of the most modern pattern have been provided, so that the kitchen has now been made an efficient department. A meat store is in course of being fitted out, and its site on the kitchen court appears to secure the necessary coolness and ventilation. A great amount of repainting and repapering has been done, and more is in progress. This work, though tastefully, is yet economically done by the patients and the asylum staff. It is recommended that as the straw palliasses become worn out, wire mattresses should be substituted. The levelling and turning of the cricket field has been completed, and a cricket match between the asylum team and a Blairgowrie club was in progress during the visit.

The medical work in the institution is characterised by marked ability, and scientific investigations have been made which are of value both clinically and therapeutically. Other important work in this direction is in progress. The staff is taught clinically in a manner which deepens their interest in the patients under their charge.

The official registers were examined, and found regularly and correctly kept.

PERTH DISTRICT ASYLUM, MURTHLY,
5th December 1901.

The following statement shows the changes which have taken place in the numbers resident since last visit :—

	PAUPER PATIENTS.		
	M.	F.	TOTALS.
On Register 11th May 1901, . . .	181	177	358
Admitted, ...	28	36	64
Discharged recovered, ...	7	17	24
Discharged unrecovered, . . .	9	9	18
Died, ...	8	3	11
On Register to-day, ...	185	184	369

With the exception of one man who was absent on pass, all the patients were resident and were seen during the visit.

In three cases the deaths are registered as due to senile decay, and in two to general paralysis of the insane. The remaining cases are attributed to each of the following causes—phthisis, exhaustion from mania, exhaustion from epilepsy, cancer of the liver, disease of the kidneys, and apoplexy. *Post mortem* examinations were made in 7 instances.

The number of entries in the Register of Restraint and Seclusion is 56. These refer to the seclusion of 11 persons.

Appendix B.

Commissioners'
Entries.

Royal and
District
Asylums.

Perth District
Asylum.

The Register of Accidents contains three entries. One of these refers to an injury of the scrotum and two to fractures of ribs. In one of the latter cases the patient died, but whether as a direct result of the injury cannot be determined. The patient—a man—was labouring under mania with great excitement, and the cause of the injury was not ascertained. The matter was referred to the Procurator-Fiscal, who held an investigation and ordered a *post mortem* examination.

Nine attendants—3 men and 6 women—have been engaged ; 1 man and 4 women have voluntarily left the service ; 2 men have been dismissed ; and 2 women have absconded.

Two hundred and thirty-one patients—116 men and 115 women—were industrially employed at the time of the visit. Of that number about 60 men were employed at work on the farm or garden ; 30 women were working in the kitchen and laundry, and 49 at needlework.

The various sections of the asylum were found in very good order, and comfortably heated and ventilated. There was evidence of overcrowding in the rooms which collectively form what are known as the "Homes" in the main building, and a tendency towards excitement among the patients due to this reason was apparent.

The patients in the hospitals were found under the most favourable conditions as regards care and treatment. Every case of acute insanity that ought to be in bed was so disposed of, and the number of beds for the accommodation of the sick and infirm was ample. The very advanced methods used in the treatment of mental diseases in this asylum, and the valuable scientific researches which are being so successfully and systematically instituted into the causes of these diseases, are worthy of the fullest recognition.

The patients occupying the detached villas were found in excellent health and suitably provided for.

Progress is being made with the building for the enlargement of the Nurses' Home.

It is understood that the question of the direction which any future extension of the asylum should take is occupying the attention of the District Board. There are manifestly only two methods of extending—namely, the erection of hospital accommodation for acute cases, or the erection of additional villas for the more chronic patients. In deciding between these two forms of extension it is worthy of consideration that the existing hospitals might possibly be adapted to the requirements of the district, and also that a new hospital, to be efficient and modern, must cost very much more per bed than ordinary accommodation for physically robust patients.

The dress of the inmates was satisfactory ; in almost every instance it was neat, in good repair, and suitable. The dinner on the day of the visit was seen being partaken of. The food was properly cooked and wholesome, and the meal appeared to be appreciated.

The books and registers were examined and found correct.

ROXBURGH DISTRICT ASYLUM,
14th May 1901.

Since last visit the following changes in the population of the asylum have occurred :—

	PRIVATE AND PAUPER PATIENTS.		
	M.	F.	TOTALS.
On Register, 10th December 1900,	143	164	307
Admitted,	12	11	23
Discharged recovered,	5	1	6
Discharged unrecovered,	2	3	5
Died,	6	2	8
On Register at this date,	142	169	311

Thirteen men and 12 women are private patients. With the exception of 1 man and 9 women, who were absent on statutory probation, all the patients were seen during the visit.

The deaths are registered as due to general paralysis in 4 cases, heart disease in 3 cases, and myelitis in 1 case. *Post mortem* examinations were made in each instance.

There are no entries in the Register of Restraint and Seclusion or in the Register of Escapes. There are 4 entries in the Register of Accidents, 2 of which describe simple fractures of bones due to accidental falls in both instances. The other two are unimportant. Appendix B.

Commissioners' Entries.

The changes among attendants and nurses have been comparatively few. Three men and 4 women have been engaged, 4 men and 4 women have resigned, and 1 woman has been dismissed. There are in all 24 ordinary attendants on day duty, being a proportion of 1 to 12½ of the resident patients, and there are 5 attendants on night duty, a proportion of 1 to 60 patients. Royal and District Asylums.

Roxburgh District Asylum.

The number of patients attending divine service last Sunday was 174. Two hundred and twenty-four patients were industrially employed at the time of the visit.

The patients, as a whole, were free from noisy excitement. They were remarkably communicative and unreserved in their conversation and criticisms, which, taken in conjunction with the fact that there was a total absence of irritable discontent, indubitably indicates that care is considerate and kindly. The general health of the inmates was, with the exception of those suffering from acute mental or physical ailments, highly satisfactory, and they presented all the usual appearances of a liberal dietary. They were suitably clothed.

The condition of the asylum as regards cleanliness and good order was very satisfactory. Otherwise, it presented an unequal appearance. Some parts, including the female hospital, the kitchen, dining-room, and recreation hall, are new, and fulfil all the requirements which the standard of modern institutions for the insane throughout the United Kingdom has established. Other parts of the asylum, especially on the male side, are urgently in need of renovation and repair. The male hospital is overcrowded by, it is understood, over 25 per cent. of its normal capacity. Consequently the sick, senile, and infirm patients cannot receive that amount of care and attention to which they are entitled, and for the newly-admitted male patients there is no such provision for hospital treatment as on the female side. It is learned, however, that plans are being prepared for the erection of a hospital wing for male cases.

Progress is being made with the erection of the new laundry, and at the time of the visit the roof was being put on. This building is simple in construction, but will apparently be sufficiently large and efficient for its purpose. The partitions are formed of glazed bricks, and the interior of the building is lined with the same materials. This is now a common procedure in the construction of modern asylums and public laundries, and when the cost of ordinary bricks and plaster is taken into account the excess in cost is well expended on the durability and cleanliness which is thus ensured.

Plans for the construction of three cottages for married attendants and officials have been submitted for the approval of the General Board. The erection of such houses is commendable, in so far as it tends to ensure a permanent staff in the service of the asylum, whereby the comfort of the patients and the confidence of the public in the administration of the institution cannot fail to be increased.

The books and registers were examined and were found to be neatly, regularly, and correctly kept.

ROXBURGH DISTRICT ASYLUM,
17th October 1901.

There are 312 patients on the register of the asylum at this date. Of these, 12 males and 11 females are private patients, and 134 males and 155 females are paupers. There are 3 pauper males and 4 pauper females absent on statutory probation. The number resident is 305, all of whom were seen during the visit.

Since 14th May 1901, the date of the preceding entry, the following changes in the population have taken place :—

Appendix B.		PRIVATE PATIENTS.		PAUPER PATIENTS.		TOTALS.
		M.	F.	M.	F.	
Commissioners' Entries.	Admitted, . . .	1	0	10	7	18
	Discharged recovered, .	1	1	1	6	9
Royal and District Asylums.	Discharged unrecovered, .	0	0	3	1	4
	Died, ...	1	0	1	2	4

Roxburgh District Asylum.

The recovery rate has been high, being 50 per cent. on the number admitted The death rate has been low. The number of private patients has decreased by 2, and that of the paupers has increased by 3.

The deaths are registered as due to varicose ulcers and cellulitis of leg, to old age and heart disease, to phthisis pulmonalis, and to apoplexy and softening of the brain. In the cases of 3 of the 4 patients who died, a *post mortem* examination was made.

Neither restraint nor seclusion has been resorted to in the treatment of any patient since 19th August 1900. Six accidents are recorded—3 were wounds sustained from falls due to epileptic seizures or to stumbling, 1 was a fracture of the clavicle from falling against a bedstead, 1 consisted of cuts got by pushing a hand through a window, and 1 of injuries inflicted by a patient on an attendant by means of an old knife found in the grounds. One escape has occurred in which the patient was absent for one night before being brought back.

The changes in the staff have not been numerous—1 attendant, 1 nurse, and 2 servants have resigned, and 2 attendants, 2 nurses, and 3 servants have been engaged. Great credit is due to Dr. Johnstone for the attention he bestows on the teaching and training of the attendants and nurses by lectures and practical demonstrations. Six attendants and seven nurses have obtained the certificate of proficiency in nursing granted by the Medico-Psychological Association, and it is understood that other five of the staff are to present themselves at the next examination. The building of three cottages for married members of the male staff is in progress. This accommodation will prevent the asylum losing the services of trustworthy and capable attendants who desire to marry. It has been found that married attendants have a good and steadying influence on the younger members of the male staff, and secure a more considerate supervision of the patients.

The patients were, except in a few cases, quiet and orderly in behaviour, and many of the more intelligent spoke voluntarily of the kindly manner in which they are treated. Much ability and conscientiousness continue to be shown in the management of the asylum and in the medical treatment of the acutely insane and of those suffering from bodily ailments. Six patients were confined to bed ; 3 men and 1 woman are the subjects of general paralysis ; 16 men and 8 women are epileptic ; and 21 men and 21 women are returned as suicidal. Seventeen epileptics who have frequent fits, and 8 patients who are acutely suicidal, sleep under continuous observation. One hundred and five men and 126 women are daily engaged in useful work, the percentage employed being 73 and 77 respectively. The number who attended Divine service last Sunday was 80 men and 84 women. Associated amusements are usually attended by 76 men and 90 women. The patients generally were in a satisfactory condition as to bodily health. The dinner at this date consisted of broth, bread, boiled beef, potatoes, and mashed turnips; it was an abundant meal, of which the patients, in reply to enquiries, expressed cordial approval. The enlarged dining-hall permits of the meals being served in an orderly and expeditious manner. The reconstructed kitchen gives every facility for the increased work of this department.

The wards in the female division were in excellent order. Several of its corridors have been repainted and furnished with a dado of wood. The female hospital again attracted favourable attention on account of the great excellence of its accommodation and arrangements. The condition of the male wards is not satisfactory, all of them stand greatly in need of repainting and thorough renovation. It is recommended that a painter-attendant be engaged. There is sufficient work to keep him, and one or two patients who could be trained to assist him, fully and constantly employed.

It is learned with approval that plans for the erection of a male hospital have been prepared and are about to be submitted to the General Board. There cannot be the least doubt as to the necessity for this addition to the accommodation and equipment of the asylum. The present sick-room, which *Appendix B.* can only properly accommodate 10 patients, contained at this date 26 inmates requiring hospital treatment. During the night 16 patients occupy this room, five of whom have to sleep on shakedowns. It will be at once evident that in these circumstances the care and treatment of the patients must be seriously hampered by overcrowding. The male side contains 15 in excess of its proper number, and this, coupled with the fact that there has been an increase of 40 on the male side during the last ten years, a growth which in all likelihood will continue, clearly proves the need of an extension to provide for present and future requirements.

Commissioners' Entries.

Royal and District Asylums.

Roxburgh District Asylum.

The building of the new laundry is completed, and contracts for its internal equipment have been made. The present boilers underneath the kitchen have been pronounced insufficient to meet the increased requirements as to power and steam, and their position is neither a safe nor a convenient one. A new boiler-house with workshop and storage for coals is in course of erection on a suitable site. Boilers are to be provided which will supply sufficient steam for the laundry, the kitchen, and the heating arrangements. An iron escape-staircase has been erected in connection with the amusement hall. By it the safety of the patients is secured should a fire prevent egress by the internal staircases. It is strongly recommended that the piggeries be removed from their present position. They are far too near the female hospital, and their condition both from age and design is not satisfactory from a sanitary point of view.

The additional land acquired by the District Board about four years ago is of great service. It affords healthy outdoor work for the male patients. It is being drained, and a road has been made around it; paths of good width have also been formed through its upper wooded portion, from which extensive views of the surrounding scenery are obtained. The exercise parties have now varied and interesting walks within this piece of ground.

The case books and registers were examined and found regularly and intelligently kept.

STIRLING DISTRICT ASYLUM, *Stirling Dis-* *27th and 28th June* 1901. *trict Asylum.*

On the 27th instant there were 688 patients on the register of the asylum. Of these, 45 are private patients and 643 are paupers. Effect has been given in the foregoing figures to the transference of 1 male and 1 female from the pauper to the private list. Except 1 private male and 1 male pauper, who are absent on statutory probation, all the patients were individually seen and afforded an opportunity of making any statement they desired.

Of the 642 paupers resident, 594 are chargeable to parishes in the Stirling Lunacy District, 34 to the parish of Edinburgh, 11 to Orkney parishes, and 3 to other parishes.

Since 29th November 1900, the date to which the figures given in the previous entry refer, the following changes have taken place :—

	PRIVATE PATIENTS.		PAUPER PATIENTS.		TOTALS.
	M.	F.	M.	F.	
Admitted, . . .	7	8	71	88	174
Discharged Recovered, .	1	6	28	32	67
Discharged Unrecovered,	0	1	15	10	26
Died, ...	3	3	20	30	56

Among the admissions were 15 paupers transferred from the Royal Edinburgh Asylum. The increase in the number on the register since last visit is 25, of whom 1 is a private patient and 24 are paupers. According to present requirements as to floor space, the asylum can, from calculations made by Dr. Robertson, accommodate 710 patients, 365 on the male and 345 on the female side. The margin of spare accommodation is becoming small, being only sufficient for 13 men and 9 women. This fact should be borne in mind in view of the large increase in the general population of the district during the last decade, and of the consequent increase in the admission rate. In these circumstances the propriety of receiving additional pauper boarders is doubtful. Until the new asylum for the Edinburgh Lunacy District is erected and ready for occupation, which will not be for some years, it will practically be impossible to get free of Edinburgh and Orkney patients.

The deaths are registered as due to diseases of the brain in 10 cases, to general paralysis in 7 cases, to phthisis pulmonalis in 10 cases, to cardiac affections in 9 cases, to senile decay in 6 cases, to pneumonia in 4 cases, to typhoid fever in 2 cases, to influenza complicated with acute pulmonary affections in 2 cases, to acute pleurisy, acute pulmonary tuberculosis, and fractured ribs in 1 case, and to the following causes, cancer, general tuberculosis, chronic nephritis, pernicious anæmia, and cut throat with septicæmia each in 1 case. The two patients who died from typhoid fever were suffering from this disease on admission, and there are 3 recently admitted patients who are suspected of being the subjects of this fever. In the case of cut throat, the injury was self-inflicted before admission. The causes of death were ascertained or verified in 32 cases, or in 57 per cent. of the deaths.

Neither restraint nor seclusion has since last visit been resorted to in the treatment of any patient. Two accidents are recorded, a fracture of the right clavicle due to being pushed over by a fellow-patient, and fracture of two ribs sustained during a struggle with attendants. This patient was impulsive and extremely violent, requiring five attendants to control him. He was at the time the subject of acute pleurisy and acute pulmonary tuberculosis. The case was reported to, and fully investigated by, the Procurator-Fiscal, and Crown Counsel saw no cause to proceed further. There have been 4 escapes in which the patients were absent for at least one night before being brought back.

The nursing arrangements in this asylum possess many novel and interesting features which are worthy of record. There are 3 Assistant Matrons who are trained hospital nurses of good social position—1 is in charge of the male hospital and infirm wards, which are staffed by nurses, 1 of the infirm and ordinary wards on the female side of the old asylum, and 1 of the female side of the Succursal Block. There are also a trained nurse of considerable experience in charge of the whole of the male side during the day, and a night superintendent, a trained nurse, who supervises the whole of the night staff. The influence and control of these trained nurses have been found to be most beneficial, both as to the patients and staff. Gentler methods of dealing with the patients, better order, and more efficient care and supervision are among the results obtained. There are 10 nurses on duty on the male side—4 in the sick-room and 6 in the infirm wards. The sick and infirm male patients are therefore wholly under the care of nurses during the day, and the male infirm dormitory, containing 23 patients, is under the charge of 2 night nurses. These arrangements are said to be working most successfully, and to be productive of kindlier care and more efficient nursing. The constant presence of women in these male wards acts as a deterrent to refractory conduct, and the patients are found to be more obedient to the nurses, and are thus more easily managed. Their behaviour during the visit was most orderly, and the condition of these wards was all that could be desired. The supervision of the male division of the asylum by a trained nurse has been found to be advantageous in various ways. The men's clothing has been much improved, and the clothes-store is a model as to neatness of what such a store should be. The night staff consists of 10 nurses and 7 male attendants, 9 on the male and 8 on the female side, being in the proportion of 1 to 41 in the male and 1 to 42 in the female division. All the dormitories except 3 are under continuous night supervision. There are 54 epileptics, 33 men and 21 women, all of whom are under constant night supervision. The single rooms have now all to be occupied on account of the increase in the population, but they are given to quiet patients as a privilege. These rooms are gradually being furnished with chairs, tables, and pictures. The night staff assist in the morning in dressing the patients and in putting the dormitories into order ; consequently each morning's work is well advanced before breakfast. The night superintendent visits at intervals all sections of the asylum, and sees that the duties of the night staff are properly performed.

The District Board are recommended to take into consideration the erection of a separate hospital for the care and treatment of consumptive patients. Of the 56 deaths since last visit, 10, or 17·8 per cent., were due to consumption, and among the patients resident there are 12 suffering from the acute stages of this disease, and 28 from either its first or second stages. Medical science has

for many ears shown that consumption is a communicable disease. The
isolation of the subjects of this malady is therefore a duty in the interests and
well-being of the other inmates of the asylum. A separate hospital would not
only secure isolation, but also enable modern methods of treatment to be
adopted for the cure or arrestment of this malady.
The management of the asylum is characterised by marked ability. The
patients bore every evidence of efficient care, and were remarkably quiet and
orderly in behaviour. The improvement in the conduct of many of the
patients, largely the result of good night nursing, was most satisfactory.
Except for a few appeals for discharge there were no complaints. The dinner
on the first day of the visit was seen served in an orderly manner to 209
patients in the hall of the main asylum, and on the second day to 310 patients
in the hall of the Succursal Block. Both meals were liberal in amount, well
cooked, and evidently much appreciated. A patient played on the piano in
the orchestra in the latter hall during the dinner. The sick, the infirm, and
the acutely insane are skilfully treated and carefully nursed. The number
industrially employed is 214 men and 225 women. Eighty-four men are
engaged at outdoor work ; this number gives a much smaller percentage than
that in asylums possessed of large farms. If more outdoor work were
available, there is no doubt that this number could be considerably increased.
It is therefore hoped that the District Board will endeavour to secure additional
land without any unavoidable delay.

The asylum is maintained in excellent order and was throughout scrupulously clean. The dayrooms are well supplied with plants and other
decorative objects. The supply of newspapers, periodicals, books, and indoor
games is liberal. Three dayrooms, a bathroom, a bootroom, corridors, and
single rooms in the female section of the main asylum have been repainted
and tastefully redecorated. A separate milk store is required near the
kitchen in which the cooking for the whole asylum is done.

The books and registers were examined and found to be regularly and
accurately kept.

STIRLING DISTRICT ASYLUM,
2nd and 3rd December 1901.

The asylum was last visited on the 27th June 1901. The following changes
have taken place since then :—

	PRIVATE PATIENTS.		PAUPER PATIENTS.		TOTALS.
	M.	F.	M.	F.	
On Register 27th June, .	26	19	326	317	688
Admitted, . . .	5	1	50	43	99
Discharged recovered, .	3	2	21	19	45
Discharged unrecovered, .	—	—	16	15	31
Died, . . .	1	1	12	11	25
On Register 3rd December, .	28	16	326	316	686

In the above figures effect has been given to the transference of 1 male from
the pauper to the private list and of 1 female from the private to the pauper
list.

With the exception of 2 men and 1 woman who were absent on pass, all the
patients were seen in the course of the visit.

The number of male patients has increased by 2 and that of the female
patients has decreased by 4, since last visit, so that there is practically little
change in the state of the population. According to calculations made by Dr.
Robertson, which are quoted in last entry, there are at present only 11 beds
vacant on the male side and 13 on the female side. As there are a number of
female boarders from the Edinburgh district in the asylum, the accommodation of the female side need not be further referred to, but the small
margin of vacant space on the male side is deserving of the serious attention of
the District Board. It is believed that the present time is particularly suitable for again urging upon the larger parishes the many advantages of
boarding out their patients in private dwellings ; but should that for any
reason fail to diminish materially the resident population, the question of
further extension alone remains to be considered.

Appendix B.

Commissioners'
Entries.

Royal and
District
Asylums.

Stirling Dis-
trict Asylum.

The deaths are registered as due to general paralysis of the insane in 5 cases, to apoplexy in 4 cases, to heart disease in 3 cases, to phthisis in 3 cases, to pneumonia in 2 cases, to acute delirious insanity in 2 cases, to septicæmia in 2 cases, and to gastritis, senile decay, pleurisy, and nephritis in 1 case each. *Post mortem* examinations were made in 17 instances.

There are no entries in the Register of Restraint and Seclusion, and no patient was absent over night by escape since last visit.

There are two entries in the Register of Accidents, one of which refers to the fracture of the forearm in the case of a female attendant, and the other to a fracture of the jaw, unfortunately followed by fatal result, in the case of a male patient. In the description of the latter accident it is stated that this patient, an epileptic of violent habits, on the 20th September last attempted to assault one of the male attendants without any warning. The latter closed with him, and both fell on the floor, the patient, owing to the fall, sustaining a fracture of both rami of the lower jaw. Septicæmia intervened, and ten days afterwards the patient died. The case was reported at the time the accident took place to the Procurator-Fiscal, who held an inquiry, and afterwards ordered a *post mortem* examination.

Two hundred and nine men and 225 women were industrially employed at the time of the visit. The proportion of men employed is slightly under 80 per cent., which is a lower proportion than the average in similar asylums. Only 76 men were employed at outdoor work on the farm and garden. If this small proportion (21 per cent.) is due to the want of land it is earnestly recommended that the District Board should secure such an amount of ground as will provide healthy labour for at least twice as many male lunatics as are at present employed in this manner.

Twenty-seven nurses and attendants—11 men and 16 women—have left the service of the asylum in the period covered by this report. Of these, 4 men and 4 women have been dismissed. Twenty-four—7 men and 17 women—have been engaged.

The institution was found in very good order. The methods employed in the nursing of the patients are such as are deserving of recognition by those interested in the advance of the treatment of insanity. The sick and infirm are suitably tended, the accommodation provided for them is sufficiently warm and comfortably furnished, and those of them who require rest or attention in bed are so disposed of. The position of the recent and acute cases was equally satisfactory. It was judged that every acute case in the asylum requiring bed treatment was being so treated; the number of such cases in bed was much above the average usually met with in asylums.

The patients with some exceptions, were quiet and orderly. The personal clothing both of the men and the women was suitable, and they had every appearance of receiving a generous dietary.

The books and registers were examined and found correct.

PRIVATE ASYLUMS.

Private
Asylums or
Licensed
Houses.

Mavisbank
Asylum.

MAVISBANK ASYLUM,
16th May 1901.

There are 23 gentlemen and 26 ladies resident at this date, of whom 5 gentlemen and 3 ladies are voluntary inmates. Since the 13th December 1900, the date of last visit, the following changes have taken place among the certificated patients—5 gentlemen and 1 lady have been admitted; 5 gentlemen and 5 ladies have been discharged, and 1 gentleman has died. The cause of death was brain-softening. During the same period the changes among the voluntary patients consisted in the admission of 6 gentlemen and 2 ladies, and in the departure of 4 gentlemen and 4 ladies.

Appendix B.

Commissioners'
Entries.

Private
Asylums or
Licensed
Houses.

Mavisbank
Asylum.

There are no entries in the Register of Accidents or in the Register of Escapes. The Register of Restraint and Seclusion contains 162 entries referring to the seclusion of one for short periods on 38 occasions, and to the restraint of 5 ladies for the following reasons:—One lady was restrained on 103 occasions on account of homicidal violence. The irresponsible behaviour of this unfortunate patient has been the means of augmenting the entries in this register on previous occasions, and from the accounts received of her from Dr. Wilson there is reason to believe that her symptoms are of an exceptional character. Another lady was restrained on 12 occasions, a third on 5 occasions, a fourth on 1 occasion, and a fifth on 3 occasions. The last four patients were restrained in order to prevent the removal of surgical dressings.

The medical care of the patients again attracted favourable attention. The opportunities which an institution of this size affords for the treatment of individual cases appears to be amply taken advantage of. The idiosyncrasies of each case are separately studied and every effort is made to assist recovery, or to mitigate symptoms by companionable association with members of the staff. But the most obvious and gratifying form of the medical care was witnessed in the bed treatment of so many of the acute and excited cases. It is understood that all really acute cases of mania and melancholia are systematically confined to bed, and several such were seen during the visit. It was also observed that the more excited among the chronic patients were reposing in bed after their forenoon walk and before going out again in the afternoon. Such instances as those mentioned are indicative of a desire to benefit the inmates by the adoption of medical measures which are not only theoretically sound but which have recently been sanctioned by authoritative experience in more than one country in Europe.

The house was found in good order, but it was evident that a good deal of furnishing and decoration is still required, more especially on the male side. The opening of a door from the male sickroom in order to give easier access to the lawn would add greatly to the comfort and convenience of the patients who occupy that part of the building. It is recommended that this structural alteration should be carried out.

The various books and registers were examined and found correct.

MAVISBANK ASYLUM,
18th September, 1901.

There are at this date 47 patients on the register of the asylum. Of these, 7 gentlemen and 3 ladies are voluntary inmates, and 16 gentlemen and 21 ladies are certificated patients. One voluntary inmate, a gentleman, is absent on pass, but he came to the asylum and was seen during the visit.

Since 16th May 1901, the date of the preceding entry, the changes among the certificated patients are as follows:—2 gentlemen and 3 ladies have been admitted, 2 gentlemen and 1 lady have been discharged recovered, 2 ladies have been discharged unrecovered, and 2 gentlemen and 2 ladies have died. Six gentlemen have been received as voluntary inmates, 3 gentlemen have left, and 1 gentleman has died.

The deaths are registered as due to general paralysis in 2 cases, to Bright's disease and peritonitis in 1 case, to carcinoma in 1 case, and to diabetes and heart disease in one case. In the cases of 2 of the 5 patients who died a *post mortem* examination was made.

The Register of Restraint and Seclusion contains 59 entries. In 56 instances they refer to the use of the camisole in the case of a lady who persistently made homicidal attacks upon her fellow-patients and on the nurses. This lady has been transferred to another asylum. Another lady has been restrained on one occasion, and the two remaining entries refer to the use of padded straps in order to prevent interference with surgical dressings. No casualty has occurred and there has been no escape.

The general condition of the patients was highly satisfactory. Their individual requirements are carefully studied and liberally met. It was abundantly evident that the medical treatment of the patients is in the hands of a skilful physician deeply interested in his work. The most approved and advanced methods of treatment are adopted, and the results are gratifying. Since the visit on 13th December 1900, 11 patients have been admitted, and during this period 11 patients have been discharged recovered—the rate of recovery being 100 per cent. on the admissions.

Appendix B.
Commissioners'
Entries.

Private
Asylums or
Licensed
Houses.

The establishment was in good order, but several sections require redecoration and renewal of floorcloth and furnishings. The necessity for the erection of a wider and better lighted staircase to the sick-room in the ladies' division has been pointed out in a previous entry, and it is hoped that effect will soon be given to this recommendation.

The case-records are kept in an exceptionally careful and able manner.

Saughton Hall
Asylum.

SAUGHTON HALL ASYLUM,
9th *May* 1901.

There are at this date 74 patients—24 gentlemen and 50 ladies—resident. Five of the ladies are voluntary inmates. Since last visit on the 1st October 1900, 8 gentlemen and 8 ladies have been admitted ; 7 gentlemen and 4 ladies have been discharged or left, and 1 gentleman has died. The cause of death was general paralysis.

There are 11 entries in the Register of Restraint and Seclusion referring to the restraint of 3 persons on account of violence and excitement. There are no entries in the Register of Escapes or Register of Accidents.

The care of the patients was as usual very satisfactory. Owing to the judicious division of the accommodation into small sitting-rooms the patients enjoy the greatest amount of privacy, and a classification suitable for individuals of varied tastes, proclivities, and mental peculiarities is consequently adopted with advantage. The individual treatment of the patients was evident in the careful and elaborate system of case-taking and in what may be termed the hospital treatment of acute cases. It was particularly gratifying to observe so many of the acute, recent, and recurrent cases being treated by repose in bed. This system, which is now becoming very general in continental institutions, is based upon sound medical and physiological reasons, and has been shown to be, when properly carried out, an essential adjunct to the medical treatment of acute insanity. Although it has not, as yet, been adopted to any considerable extent in Great Britain, it is right to acknowledge that in this asylum it has for many years been used as one of the ordinary forms of treatment, and that by this means, among others, the nursing of the acutely insane has been brought into line with the physically sick in ordinary hospitals. It is believed that the results of this painstaking treatment have fully justified its adoption and its continuation.

The patients were generally quiet, free from excitement, and no complaints were submitted. The institution was in excellent order throughout. The various registers were examined and found correct.

SAUGHTON HALL ASYLUM,
6th *September* 1901.

There are at this date 76 patients on the registers of the asylum. One gentleman and 6 ladies are voluntary inmates, and 24 gentlemen and 45 ladies are under certificates. Twenty-four gentlemen and 26 ladies are in residence at Saughton Hall, 1 gentleman and 15 ladies at Balgreen, and 10 ladies at Gullane House.

Since last visit the changes among the certificated patients are as follows :— 1 gentleman and 2 ladies have been admitted, 1 gentleman and 1 lady have been discharged unrecovered, and 1 lady has died. The cause of death has been registered as bronchitis : the patient's age was 75, and she had been an inmate of the asylum for 39 years. One gentleman and 1 lady have been admitted as voluntary inmates.

The Register of Restraint and Seclusion contains 2 entries referring to the use of the camisole to prevent self-mutilation. One casualty is recorded — a patient slipped into the head attendant's room, seized a bottle of medicine containing chloral, bromide of potassium, and canabis indica, and swallowed the greater portion of its contents. No injurious results followed, as effective measures were taken in due course. The lock on this room was found to be defective, and a new one has been provided.

The care and treatment of the patients continue to be characterised by ability, liberality, and kindly consideration. No complaints calling for attention were made, and the appeals for discharge were from patients who were manifestly insane. Only one lady, the subject of acute melancholia, was noisy and excited; the other patients were quiet, orderly, and generally contented.

The gentlemen were seen in the gardens, in which there are several shelters from sun and rain. Only 3 ladies were confined to bed, and the nursing of these patients was of a most efficient character—water beds and other similar arrangements being in use. The fulness of the records in the case books as to the history, condition, and treatment of each patient deserves commendation.

All sections of the asylum were found in admirable order. Renovations and redecorations are attended to, and the accommodation throughout is of a most comfortable and home-like character. Gullane House, the seaside adjunct to the asylum, is surrounded by a garden over 2 acres in extent. The patients resident there enjoy great privacy, and the change of air and of scene cannot fail to be beneficial both bodily and mentally. Parties of from 8 to 10 reside there from May to September.

The registers were examined and found regularly and accurately kept.

Appendix B.
—
Commissioners'
Entries.
—
Private
Asylums or
Licensed
Houses.
—
Saughton Hall
Asylum.

WESTERMAINS ASYLUM.
29th May 1901.

Westermains
Asylum.

There are 17 patients on the registers of the asylum at this date. Of these, 3 ladies are voluntary inmates, and 2 gentlemen and 12 ladies are certificated patients. One lady, a voluntary inmate, was absent at the time of the visit.

Since 10th November 1900, the date of previous report, 1 lady has been admitted under a Sheriff's order, and 2 ladies as voluntary boarders. The latter appear to be proper cases to be received in that capacity. There has been no discharge and no death.

The patients bore evidence of being carefully attended to and kindly treated.

Two ladies have been 24 years, 1 gentleman and 2 ladies 18 years, and 3 ladies over 10 years inmates of this asylum.

The establishment is maintained in very good order, handsomely furnished, and throughout there was great cleanliness. The grounds are well kept and present a most pleasing appearance.

The registers were written up to date.

WESTERMAINS ASYLUM,
13th November 1901.

There are 16 patients resident in the asylum at this date. Of these, 1 lady is a voluntary inmate, and 2 gentlemen and 13 ladies are certificated.

Since last visit one lady has been admitted on sheriff's order. There has been no death. Two ladies who were here as voluntary patients have left.

There has been no escape or accident since the asylum was last visited.

The patients were found in a satisfactory state of bodily health; they were suitably clothed, and bore evidence of kindly care and good supervision. They manifested no excitement, and none of them made any complaint.

The house was found as usual in excellent order, well ventilated, properly heated and clean. The furniture and furnishings of the rooms again attracted favourable notice.

The books and registers were found correctly kept.

PAROCHIAL ASYLUMS.

Parochial
Asylums.
—
Greenock
Parochial
Asylum.

GREENOCK PAROCHIAL ASYLUM,
17th January 1901.

There are 229 patients, 115 men and 114 women, on the register of the asylum at this date. All were resident and seen during the visit except one woman who is absent by escape.

Appendix B.

Commissioners'
Entries.

Parochial
Asylums.

Greenock
Parochial
Asylum.

Since 19th July 1900, the date of last visit, the following changes have taken place :—

	PAUPER PATIENTS.		
	M.	F.	TOTALS.
Admitted, ...	22	22	44
Discharged recovered, . . .	12	19	31
Discharged unrecovered, . . .	2	1	3
Died, ...	4	4	8

These figures show that the number in the asylum has increased by 2. This establishment was during a period of great deficiency of asylum accommodation in Lanarkshire licensed for 290 patients, but according to present requirements as to floor space it can only properly accommodate 246 patients. If the pauper insane are to be adequately provided for, this number should not be exceeded. The asylum proper can only contain 184 patients, and those portions of the poorhouse which were not designed as accommodation for the insane, and can only be regarded as used temporarily for that purpose, can contain 62 patients. Calculations based on the rate of increase during the last ten years of patients in the asylum chargeable to Greenock show that their number will probably be 255 in 1910, or 9 more than can be efficiently provided for in all the sections now used as asylum accommodation. It would, however, be safer to take the rate of increase during the last five years, and if this is done, the number of Greenock patients would probably be 279 in 1910. The increase during the five years 1890-1895 was 22, but during the last five years 1895-1900 it was 46. It will therefore be evident that Greenock will in the course of a few years require all its present asylum accommodation for its own patients.

The percentage of recoveries continues very high, being 70 per cent. on the admissions since last visit. The deaths are registered as due to diseases of the brain in 3 cases, to inflammatory chest affections in 3 cases, to heart disease in 1 case, and to phthisis pulmonalis in 1 case. The causes of death were ascertained or verified by *post-mortem* examinations in 4 instances, or in 50 per cent. of the cases. The consent of the relatives was withheld in the remaining 4 cases.

The Register of Restraint and Seclusion contained 30 entries. They refer to the use of restraint in 3 cases for surgical reasons and in 1 case to prevent impulsive and dangerous attacks, and to the use of seclusion in the treatment of 2 patients. Three accidents are recorded—fracture of two ribs, caused by a fall during an epileptic seizure ; fracture of the right ulna, believed to be due to the rough usage of an attendant ; and fracture of two ribs, also believed to be due to ill-treatment by an attendant. These two cases were reported to the Procurator-Fiscal. In the former case the attendant, who had to deposit £10 as bail, absconded before his trial, and in the latter case, though the evidence was considered legally insufficient to convict, the attendant was dismissed. Two escapes have taken place in which the patients were absent for at least one night before being brought back.

The changes among the staff are far more numerous than is desirable in the interests of the patients. Nine have resigned, 2 have been dismissed, 1 absconded, and 13 have been engaged.

The asylum was found clean, in excellent order, and of a suitable temperature. The sanitary arrangements on the male side are being remodelled in a manner similar to what has been done in the female division. The fireplaces are being reconstructed in order to make them more efficient. The washtubs in the laundry, which are of wood, are in an unsatisfactory condition, and they should be replaced by those made of porcelain. The floor of the wash-house also needs renewal.

The patients generally were well behaved, and their clothing and personal neatness were satisfactory. An abundant dinner of broth, boiled beef, and bread was served during the visit, and enquiries regarding their food elicited favourable answers. The overcrowding of the dining hall has ceased since the reopening of the male ward in the poorhouse. Useful employment is found for 79 per cent. of the men and 76 per cent. of the women. The

general health of the patients is very satisfactory, only 1 man and 1 woman Appendix B.
being confined to bed.

The registers were examined and found regularly and correctly kept.

Commissioners
Entries.

GREENOCK PAROCHIAL ASYLUM, Parochial
Asylums.
11th July 1901.

There are 240 patients, 121 men and 119 women, on the register at this date. Greenock
Parochial
Asylum.
With the exception of 1 man who was absent on probation, all the patients
were seen during the visit. Since the 17th January of the present year, the
date of last visit, the following changes have occurred in population :—

	PAUPER PATIENTS.		
	M.	F.	TOTALS.
Admitted, ...	18	31	49
Discharged recovered, . . .	9	15	24
Discharged unrecovered, . . .	0	3	3
Died, ...	3	8	11

The numbers resident have thus increased by 11 since last visit.

The deaths are registered as due to phthisis in 3 cases, to senile decay in 2
cases, to gross disease of the brain and spinal cord in 2 cases, and to each of
the following diseases in 1 case :—heart disease, epilepsy, bronchitis, and
exhaustion following acute mania. *Post mortem* examinations were made in 7
cases.

There are 3 accidents recorded ; one refers to a scalding of the right leg
sustained by an attendant, the others to a cut on the head and a lacerated
wound of the hand in the case of 2 male patients respectively. The wound of
the hand was caused by the patient jumping through a window while in a
state of acute mania. Dr. Wallace is strongly of opinion that some protecting
mechanism should be applied to the windows of the apartments inhabited by
such patients. This is a point which may safely be left to the Committee
under the guidance of their medical adviser, but it may be pointed out that
such protection of the windows, if decided upon, should be wholly ornamental
and unsuggestive of its purpose.

The Register of Restraint and Seclusion contains 22 entries. No less than
21 of these refers to 1 woman whom it is found necessary to restrain partially
from time to time during long periods of excitement. Two patients have
escaped and have been absent for at least one night before being brought back.
The changes among the attendants have been as follows :—7 men and 4
women have been engaged, and 6 men and 5 women have resigned. One
hundred and eighty-five patients, 99 men and 86 women, were usefully
employed at the time of the visit. Of the 99 men employed, 54 were engaged
in outdoor work on the farm and garden. These figures are highly satisfactory.

The patients with a few exceptions were quiet, free from excitement, and
orderly in their demeanour. They were seen partaking of a very ample and
well-cooked dinner, and they bore every appearance of regularly receiving an
adequate dietary. Their clothing was neat and in good repair.

Every section of the asylum was found clean and well aired.

The books and registers were examined and found to be carefully and
correctly kept.

PAISLEY PAROCHIAL ASYLUM, CRAW ROAD, Paisley
Parochial
Asylum,
Craw Road.
11th January 1901.

There are 111 patients, 50 men and 61 women, on the register of the
asylum at this date. All are resident.

Since 16th July 1900, the date of last visit, the following changes have
taken place :—

	PAUPER PATIENTS.		
	M.	F.	TOTALS.
Admitted, ...	4	8	12
Discharged recovered, . . .	2	2	4
Discharged unrecovered, . .	1	1	2
Died, ...	0	7	7

Appendix B.
——
Commissioners'
Entries.
——
Parochial
Asylums.
——
Paisley
Parochial
Asylum,
Craw Road.

The patients admitted were chargeable to the following parishes—3 to Paisley, 5 to Eastwood, 3 to Mearns, and 1 to Eaglesham. Of the 111 patients resident at this date, 64 are chargeable to Paisley, 27 to Eastwood, 10 to Mearns, 5 to Eaglesham, and 5 to Lochwinnoch. The asylum contains 12 inmates in excess of its license. Seven patients have to sleep on shake-downs. In these circumstances it is difficult to see how the asylum is to provide for the future and increasing requirements of those parishes whose lunatics it has contracted to accommodate. Should the increase of patients from Paisley, Eastwood, Mearns, Eaglesham, and Lochwinnoch continue as it has done during the last ten years, the numbers in excess of the accommodation would probably be 27 in 1910 and 37 in 1920. If, however, the calculation is made on the increase of the last five years, then the numbers beyond what the asylum can properly receive would probably be 39 in 1910 and 61 in 1920. Early consideration should be given to this matter, so that contracting parishes can make timely arrangements for the accommodation of their lunatics.

The deaths are registered as due to diseases of the brain and nervous system in 4 cases, to pneumonia in 1 case, to bronchitis in 1 case, and to senile decay in 1 case. *Post mortem* examinations were made in 2 cases, or in the proportion of 28·5 per cent. of the deaths. This is a very low percentage, but it is understood from Dr. Graham that the consent of the relatives was refused in the other cases.

The Register of Restraint and Seclusion contains one entry referring to the use of the strait-jacket and seclusion in the case of a female patient who, during the visit, became very excited and violent and assaulted the nurses with a chair. It is recommended that she be transferred to Riccartsbar Asylum. One accident consisting of slight injuries to face and trunk is recorded. These were due to a struggle with an attendant, and after investigation the Superintendent did not consider the attendant blame-worthy. There has been no escape.

Five attendants have been engaged, 3 have resigned, 1 absconded, and 1 has been dismissed for intemperance. The staff consists of 4 male attendants and 5 nurses for day duty, and 1 male attendant and 1 nurse for night duty. This gives a proportion of about 1 to every 12 patients for day duty, which is not a strong staff.

The patients were, with the exception of two females, quiet and contented. The general health of the inmates is good, only 1 man and 3 women being confined to bed. The dress and personal neatness of the patients was quite satisfactory. The stock of clothing is ample. All the patients have Sunday suits or dresses, and much good taste is shown in the choice of material and in the making of the women's clothing. A dinner of broth, boiled beef, and bread was served in an orderly manner during the visit. The broth was pleasant to the taste, and the meal was a good and abundant one. All expressed approval of their dietary. Useful employment is found for 78 per cent. of the men and 70 per cent. of the women. Thirty-two men work on the land attached to the asylum.

The dayrooms, dormitories, and bedding were clean and in good order. It is understood with approval that the straw palliasses, many of which are becoming old and unsatisfactory, are being replaced by wire mattresses. The linoleum in some of the passages on the female side needs renewal. The floors of the dormitories, especially those of the sick wards, should be varnished and waxed so as to avoid wet scrubbing, which is not conducive to good health. The new shoe-room serves its purpose in an efficient manner and is altogether a useful addition.

The registers were examined and found to be regularly and correctly kept.

PAISLEY PAROCHIAL ASYLUM, CRAW ROAD,
10th *July* 1901.

There are 104 patients on the register of the asylum at this date. Of these, 44 are men and 60 women. With the exception of 1 woman who was absent on pass, all these patients were seen in the course of the visit. Since the 14th January of the present year, the date of last visit, 1 man and 11 women have been admitted, 2 men and 2 women have been discharged recovered, 4 men and 8 women have been discharged unrecovered, and 1 man and 2 women have died. The assigned causes of death are epilepsy, pernicious anæmia, and Appendix B. pneumonia. A *post mortem* examination was made in 1 case ; in another the Commissioners Entries. permission of the relatives was not obtained ; and the third case died while absent from the asylum on pass.

There is one entry in the Register of Restraint and Seclusion, referring to the Parochial Asylums. seclusion of one woman for a short period on account of maniacal excitement. There have been no escapes and no accidents since last visit. Thirty-nine Paisley Parochial Asylum, Craw Road. men and 45 women, over 80 per cent. of the resident population, were industrially employed at the time of the visit. This is a large and creditable proportion.

The changes among the staff have been numerous. Two men and 7 women have been engaged, 1 man and 6 women have resigned, and 1 man and 1 woman have been dismissed.

The patients were seen partaking of dinner. The meal, which consisted of soup, boiled beef, and bread, appeared to be appreciated, and those who were questioned professed themselves satisfied with it. In the wards the patients were exceptionally quiet and orderly. None of them made any complaint of a rational kind, and they seemed on the whole to be contented.

The wards and dormitories were nicely painted and decorated. One of the female dormitories, to the decoration of which it is understood some members of the Committee personally contributed, was especially attractive. In some of the rooms the carpeting is worn and ought to be replaced.

It is satisfactory to observe that the numbers resident have diminished since last visit.

The books and registers were examined and found correct.

PAISLEY PAROCHIAL ASYLUM, RICCARTSBAR, Paisley Parochial Asylum, Riccartsbar.
15th January 1901.

There are 211 patients, 107 men and 104 women, on the register of the asylum at this date. All are resident and were seen except one man who is absent by escape.

Since 20th July 1900, the date of last visit, the following changes have taken place :—

	PAUPER PATIENTS.		
	M.	F.	TOTALS.
Admitted, ...	19	15	34
Discharged recovered, . . .	12	7	19
Discharged unrecovered, . . .	0	4	4
Died, ...	6	3	9

The number resident in the asylum is 6 in excess of its accommodation. There is room for 5 additional male patients, but in the female side there are at present 11 patients beyond what the establishment can properly accommodate. The number of lunatics in this asylum from Paisley and other Renfrewshire parishes has increased from 137 in 1890 to 211 at this date, an increase of 74 in ten years. It will be at once apparent that this establishment, which is more than full, cannot, without serious and dangerous overcrowding, continue to meet the requirements as to lunacy accommodation of those parishes with which it has contracts. The Asylum Committee is therefore recommended to give intimation to these parishes, in order that they may make timely arrangements for the accommodation of their lunatics. Calculations based on the increase during the last five years of lunatics, chargeable to Paisley show that in the course of about ten years Paisley will probably require all its asylum accommodation at Riccartsbar and Craw Road for its own pauper insane.

The deaths are registered as due to brain disease in 4 cases, to acute pneumonia in 2 cases, to heart disease in 2 cases, and to acute peritonitis in 1 case.

Post mortem examinations were made in 6 cases, or in 66·6 per cent. of the deaths. The consent of the relatives was refused in the remaining 3 cases.

The Register of Restraint and Seclusion contains no entry. One slight accident is recorded—a flesh wound over the right eyebrow, due to slipping while being bathed. Two patients have escaped—one was absent for a night before being brought back, and one is still absent.

I

Appendix B.

Commissioners'
Entries.

Parochial
Asylums.

Paisley
Parochial
Asylum,
Riccartsbar.

The changes among the staff are very numerous—5 male attendants and 4 nurses have resigned, 1 nurse absconded, and 6 male attendants and 4 nurses have been engaged. These changes involve 50 per cent. of the staff. The ratio of day attendants to patients is 1 to 10½ on the male side, and 1 to 11 in the female division, proportions which are adequate. The night staff consists of 2 men and 2 women, or 1 to about 52 patients. One attendant on each side of the house is in continuous night charge of the suicidal, the epileptic, and the sick, and the second attendant periodically visits the remaining sections of his or her division. There were only 2 wet beds last night.

Reconstruction of the female sickroom is urgently required. This section is low in the roof and quite unsuitable in many ways as hospital accommodation. Its lavatory and sanitary arrangements are antiquated and inadequate. Plans should be prepared for its reconstruction and submitted to the General Board.

The patients were found in a satisfactory condition, and their conduct generally was quiet and orderly. The sick and acutely insane receive skilful treatment, and their special requirements are met in a praiseworthy manner. The clothing of the patients is suitable and sufficient. The dinner was a palatable and abundant meal. Bread at dinner and bread and butter at supper are now put on a plate in the centre of each table, and the patients help themselves *ad libitum.*

The whole of the female division has been tastefully repainted, and consequently the appearance of these wards has been greatly improved as to brightness and cheerfulness. Fire escape stairs from the first floor at each end of the main building are in course of construction. The excellence of the arrangements for the care of the patients in the new male hospital block attracted favourable attention. The dayroom in Riccartsbar House is not satisfactory—the building is an old one, damp permeates its walls, its roof is low, it is badly lighted, and altogether the room is a cheerless apartment. Its continuance as satisfactory dayroom accommodation is doubtful.

The registers were examined and found regularly and accurately kept.

PAISLEY PAROCHIAL ASYLUM, RICCARTSBAR,
11*th July* 1901.

The following statement shows the changes in population which have taken place since last visit.

	PAUPER PATIENTS.		
	M.	F.	TOTALS.
On the Register, 15th January, 1901, .	107	104	211
Admitted since, ...	34	33	67
Discharged recovered, ...	16	14	30
Discharged unrecovered, . . .	6	18	24
Died, ...	4	7	11
On the Register at this date, . .	115	98	213

With the exception of 1 woman who was absent on pass and 3 who were out on statutory probation all the patients on the register were seen during the visit.

The above figures indicate a very active change in the population, which is highly satisfactory in so far as it points to an endeavour to avoid overcrowding by promoting the discharge of recoverable cases and by removing suitable cases to other institutions or to private care.

The deaths are registered as due to exhaustion from brain disease, tubercular disease of the bowels, puerperal septicæmia, pleurisy, senile decay, general paralysis, apoplexy, exophthalmic goitre, alcoholism, phthisis, and acute delirious mania. *Post mortem* examinations were made in six cases, in the remaining five cases the permission of the relatives was not granted.

Two accidents, a fracture of the humerus and a fracture of the femur, are recorded. So far as the responsibility of the staff is concerned these accidents appear to have been unavoidable. One hundred and sixty-six patients (79 per cent. of the population) were employed usefully at the time of the visit. This is a large and very creditable proportion. There are no entries in the Register

of Restraint and Seclusion. Three patients escaped in the interval since last
visit and they were each absent for at least one night before being brought
back. The changes which have occurred in the nursing staff are as follows :—
Eight attendants, 3 men and 5 women, have resigned, and one man has been
dismissed ; 4 men and 5 women have been engaged.

The condition of the patients was wholly satisfactory. They were free from
excitement and apparently contented ; their clothing was neatly fitting and
suitable ; they made no complaints as to their treatment ; and their food,
judging from the dinner on the day of the visit, is nutritious, properly cooked,
and palatable.

Every part of the institution was found clean, well aired, and in excellent
order. The plans for the renovation and enlargement of the female sickroom
have obtained the sanction of the General Board, and it is expected that
building operations will begin at an early date.

The land in connection with the institution is fully taken advantage of : it
affords ample work for the male patients, and the supply of farm produce to the
institution is abundant. It is satisfactory to learn that the pecuniary interests
of the asylum have in no way suffered, but on the contrary have benefited, by
the possession and cultivation of this land.

The impression produced by the visit was very favourable. The present
management of the asylum appears to be energetic and thorough, the methods
of administration are modern and efficient, and are characterised by a conscientious desire to promote the comfort and welfare of the inmates.

The books and registers were examined and were found to be regularly and
correctly kept.

Appendix B.

Commissioners'
Entries.

Parochial
Asylums.

Paisley
Parochial
Asylum,
Riccartsbar.

--- --- --- --- --- ---

LUNATIC WARDS OF POORHOUSES.

Lunatic Wards
of Poorhouses.

Aberdeen East
Poorhouse.

LUNATIC WARDS, ABERDEEN EAST POORHOUSE,
12th February 1901.

These wards were last visited on the 18th October 1900, at which date
there were 83 patients—43 men and 40 women—resident.

Since then, 5 men and 2 women have been admitted, 3 men have been discharged, and 1 woman has died. The numbers resident at this date are 45
men and 41 women, all of whom were seen during the visit.

The death was due to pneumonia in a tubercular subject ; a *post mortem*
examination was held. Forty-nine patients—29 men and 20 women—were
industrially employed at this date. There has been no casualty or escape,
and no change in the staff since last visit.

With the exception of 2 women confined to bed, the patients were found in
a good state of physical health. One of these women, M. D. or M'L., is
broken down permanently through old age and infirmity ; she has been
constantly confined to bed for the past eight weeks, and is helpless, demented,
and of faulty habits. The care which her nursing demands is too great a
strain upon the limited staff of an institution such as this, and her removal to
the asylum is therefore recommended.

The dinner provided on the day of the visit was a palatable, temptingly-
cooked meal, consisting of pea soup, stewed meat, and potatoes. The patients
get four regular meals per diem, and their quiet and contented demeanour
and the good average state of their health is no doubt largely due to this
liberality in diet. The clothing both of the men and the women is made of
substantial material suitable for the season of the year.

The dormitories were very comfortable, and fires were burning in them
early in the afternoon. The beds had an amply sufficient supply of good,
clean coverings.

Apart from the state of the wards, which are now old and somewhat cheer-

134 *Appendix to the Forty-fourth Report of the General Board of*

Appendix B.
Commissioners'
Entries.

Lunatic Wards
of Poorhouses.

Aberdeen East
Poorhouse.

less in appearance, it was evident that the patients are in other respects comfortably treated and well cared for.

The books and registers are regularly and correctly kept.

LUNATIC WARDS, ABERDEEN EAST POORHOUSE,
26th July 1901.

There are 43 men and 40 women, 83 patients in all, as inmates of the wards at this date. There are vacant beds for 1 male and 10 females, and efforts should be made to have them occupied by patients transferred from the Royal Asylum.

Since last visit 1 man and 2 women have been admitted, 2 men and 3 women have been discharged, and 1 man has died. The death in this case was sudden, and it is unsatisfactory to have to report that there was no *post mortem* examination. It should have been made in order to ascertain, for the information of all concerned in the administration of the wards, whether or not the cause of death was a natural one. The value of these examinations from this point of view is great.

No accident is recorded, and there has been no escape. Two male attendants have resigned, and 2 have been engaged.

The establishment was found in good order. The dining hall and. dayrooms on the female side have been repainted, and the work has been well and tastefully done.

No patient was confined to bed, and the physical condition of the inmates indicated a liberal dietary and sufficient exercise in the open air. The dinner served during the visit consisted of pea-soup, bread, fresh fish, sauce, and mashed potatoes. It was an abundant and well-cooked meal, and was generally approved of by the patients. The dress and personal neatness of both sexes were satisfactory. The regular employment of the inmates in useful work continues to receive due attention. The wards are evidently managed in a careful and conscientious manner.

The registers were examined and found accurately kept.

Aberdeen
West
Poorhouse :

LUNATIC WARDS, ABERDEEN WEST POORHOUSE,
11th February 1901.

There are 56 patients—29 men and 27 women—resident in the wards at this date.

Since the 19th October 1900, the date of last visit, 3 women have been admitted and 1 man and 2 women have been discharged. No accident, escape, or death has occurred among the patients, and none of them has been subjected to any form of restraint or seclusion. A male attendant resigned, and another has been engaged in his place.

Thirty-six patients were industrially employed to-day, the majority of the men being engaged in wood-cutting, and the larger proportion of the women at laundry work and at sewing and knitting.

The patients were quiet, free from excitement, and none of them made any statement or complaint bearing on the manner of their treatment. They were warmly and suitably clad, and their general appearance and state of contentment indicated a suitable dietary. The wards were comfortable and pleasantly heated.

The books and registers were examined and found correctly kept.

LUNATIC WARDS, ABERDEEN WEST POORHOUSE,
26th July 1901.

At this date there are 26 men and 26 women, or 52 patients in all, as inmates of the wards. Vacant accommodation exists for 4 men and 4 women, and suitable patients should be removed from the Royal Asylum to fill the empty beds.

Since last visit, on the 11th February 1901, 1 woman has been admitted, and 3 men and 2 women have been discharged. No death has occurred. The patient admitted is a boarder from a parish in Caithness.

No patient has been the subject of any casualty. One escape has taken place, but the patient was brought back in the course of a few hours. A female attendant resigned on being charged with neglect of duty, 1 male attendant has been appointed to another appointment in the poorhouse, and 2 male attendants have resigned. One female and 3 male attendants have been engaged.

The patients were quiet and orderly and entirely free from complaints. Their physical health and appearance bore evidence of a suitable and liberal dietary and abundant outdoor exercise. Their clothing is kept in proper repair, and the suits and dresses for Sundays and special occasions are of good quality and neatly made. All the inmates who are able to work are daily employed in useful occupations.

The annual picnic took place on the 19th June, and at this date a strawberry treat is to be given to all the inmates in the male exercise ground. Such breaks in the monotony of institutional life are most beneficial and give great pleasure.

The wards were in good order; but the floors of the dormitories stand greatly in need of re-staining and re-varnishing. This, it is understood, is to be done.

The registers were examined, and found written up to date and accurately kept.

(margin) Appendix B. Commissioners Entries. Lunatic Wards of Poorhouses. Aberdeen West Poorhouse.

LUNATIC WARDS, BUCHAN POORHOUSE,
11th February 1901.

(margin) Buchan Poorhouse.

These wards were last visited on the 20th October 1900. Since then no change of any kind has occurred in the population. There has been no casualty or escape to record, and no change has taken place in the staff. Upon these negative facts, those concerned in the management of the institution are to be congratulated.

There are 52 patients—26 men and 26 women—resident in the wards at this date. They were all seen during the visit and found, with one exception—an old man confined to bed on account of physical debility—in the enjoyment of good health. They were also quiet and orderly in their demeanour, and no sign of discontent was manifested by any of them. The physical condition of the patients of both sexes was highly satisfactory. It is not often that such a large average of the inmates of any single institution present so healthy and so robust an appearance. They gave the impression of being not only liberally but judiciously fed, and that they are thoughtfully cared for was apparent from the excellent state of their personal clothing. Most of the men were out working, and each of these had on warm underclothing, a well-fitting shirt with a knitted jersey worn over it, a well-cut suit of clothes, and a pair of neatly-buttoned leggings. Many of them also wore woollen mittens. They all looked smart and clean, and there was a total absence of slovenliness in their appearance. The dress of the women was equally neat and good and varied by nicely coloured shawls.

The state of cleanliness, brightness, and good order of the dayrooms was in every respect commendable; they are comfortably furnished and provided with arm chairs and couches. The dormitories were also in excellent order, and the arrangement and comfort of the beds and the quality and quantity of their coverings left little to be desired. It is unnecessary to add that the impression produced by the inspection of these wards was entirely favourable.

The books and registers were examined and found correct.

LUNATIC WARDS, BUCHAN POORHOUSE,
27th July 1901.

There are 52 patients, 26 men and 26 women, as inmates of the wards at this date.

Since last visit 2 men have been admitted, 1 man has been discharged, and man has died. The death is registered as due to valvular disease of the

Appendix B.

Commissioners' Entries.

Lunatic Wards of Poorhouses.

Buchan Poorhouse.

heart. No *post mortem* examination was made. Such examinations are important, and should be made unless the consent of relatives is withheld.

No accident has occurred and there has been no escape. Three changes have taken place in the female staff. The conduct of the female attendant who last resigned was so unsatisfactory as to have justified Mr. and Mrs. Fraser in dismissing her. It is to be regretted that this was not done, as her dismissal would in all likelihood have prevented her being re-engaged as an attendant on the insane. Complaints were made by a patient as to this attendant's treatment of the inmates. On being severely reprimanded for her behaviour, she resigned.

Except in regard to this matter the patients were free from complaint. They bore every evidence of being liberally provided for and well fed. The dinner seen during the visit was an abundant meal. The neatness and good quality of their clothing are highly creditable to the management, and the stores of spare and sundry clothing are kept in a most orderly manner. Nineteen of both sexes are engaged in useful work. The land in connection with the poorhouse affords healthy and interesting outdoor labour to 14 men. Four cows are kept, and the supply of milk is abundant for the requirements of the inmates.

The wards were found scrupulously clean and in admirable order. One of the dormitories on the male side has been provided with new iron bedsteads with wire mattresses, and similar bedsteads are to be placed in a female dormitory after it has been repapered and repainted. This improvement in the furnishing of the wards is recorded with satisfaction. The condition of the patients and of the wards was clearly indicative of careful and intelligent management.

The registers were examined and found accurately kept.

Cunninghame Poorhouse.

LUNATIC WARDS, CUNNINGHAME POORHOUSE,
9th May, 1901.

There are as inmates of these wards 47 men and 44 women. There are vacancies for 8 patients.

Since 6th October 1900, the date of last visit, 2 men and 2 women have been admitted, 3 women have been discharged, and 3 men and 3 women have died. The rate of mortality has been high during the last seven months. The proportion of deaths to the numbers resident has for many years in this establishment been a low one. Of the 6 patients who died, 1 was 84 years of age, 4 were over 60, and 1 was 52 years. The deaths are registered as due to brain disease in 3 cases, and to senile debility, peritonitis, and struma, each in 1 case. A *post mortem* examination was made in 1 case. Whenever the consent of the relatives can be obtained the cause of death should, in the interests of all concerned in the administration of the wards, be verified by an autopsy.

One accident, very slight in character, is recorded. There has been no escape. One change in the staff has taken place. The average duration of service of the present staff is very satisfactory. The head nurse has completed 6 years, and the garden attendant 20 years of service.

The condition of the inmates as regards physical health was satisfactory; only one patient was confined to bed. The clothing, except that of some of the men, was neat in appearance and of good quality. The patients generally were very contented, and bore evidence of judicious and kindly care. The dinner consisted of broth, beefsteak pie, and bread, and was a liberal and palatable meal. The inmates are well employed—85 per cent. of the men and 75 per cent. of the women are daily engaged in useful work. Three men have parole beyond the grounds, and 8 men and 3 women are granted parole within the grounds.

Many improvements were observed in the state of the wards. Several day-rooms, dormitories, and single rooms have been effectively painted, which has added greatly to their brightness, and it is understood that the remaining rooms are to be similarly renovated. Linoleum has been laid in the dormitories, and furnishings have been renewed. The escape staircases are of a satisfactory width, and have been well placed to secure the egress of the patients in the case of fire.

The attention of the House Committee is drawn to the insanitary condition of the straw palliasses, the majority of which are old and stained. It is strongly recommended that these should be condemned and wire mattresses substituted. The compartments in the bathrooms containing the water-closets are open in front, which is not a satisfactory arrangement, and it is recommended that these be provided with dwarf doors, as explained to Mr. Lockhart.

The registers were examined and found regularly and correctly kept.

Appendix B.

Commissioners, Entries.

Lunatic Wards of Poorhouses.

Cunninghame Poorhouse.

LUNATIC WARDS, CUNNINGHAME POORHOUSE,
11th October 1901.

There are 94 patients resident at this date. Of these, 48 are men and 46 are women.

Since the wards were last visited on 9th May of the present year, 1 man and 4 women have been admitted ; 1 woman has been discharged; and 1 woman has died. The cause of death, which was verified by *post mortem* examination, was phthisis.

There has been no accident or escape since last visit, and there are no entries in the Register of Restraint and Seclusion. Seventy-five patients, 40 men and 35 women, were industrially employed at the time of the visit.

The patients were found in good health, free from excitement, and generally contented. The dress of the female patients was bright, neat, and clean. That of the men was not, comparatively, in the same good order.

The wards were found, as usual, clean and well kept. The attention of Committee is directed to the condition of the lavatories adjoining the upstairs dormitories. It would be an undoubted advantage if the floors were relaid with new wood and proper slop sinks introduced into these apartments. Operations are in progress for heating the lunatic wards in conjunction with the rest of the poorhouse by means of steam conveyed from a central boiler to water heaters placed throughout the buildings. It is hoped that by this means a more uniform and at the same time a more economical system of heating the institution may be obtained.

The books and registers were examined and found neatly and correctly kept.

LUNATIC WARDS, DUMBARTON POORHOUSE,
5th February 1901.

Dumbarton Poorhouse.

There are 47 patients, 22 men and 25 women, in the wards at this date.

There is vacant accommodation for 8 men and 5 women, and it is recommended that the Parish Councils of the Combination be informed to this effect.

Since last visit 1 man has been admitted, 2 men and 1 woman have been discharged, and 2 men and 2 women have died.

The deaths are registered as due to the following causes:—general debility, congestion of liver and jaundice, chronic diarrhœa, and senile decay. Attention is drawn to the fact that no *post mortem* examination was made. An autopsy should be made in order to verify the cause of death in every case in which the consent of the relatives can be obtained.

There has been no accident. One escape has occurred, and the patient was absent for 28 days. His name consequently fell to be removed from the register. He is reported to be maintaining himself.

Many improvements have recently been effected in the wards. The two dayrooms and four dormitories have been tastefully repainted and their appearance rendered brighter and more cheerful. A large square of linoleum has been laid in the female dayrooms, easy chairs have been provided, and the beds in one dormitory on each side have been furnished with spring mattresses. The lavatory and bathing arrangements are very satisfactory.

The wants of the inmates are liberally met. The dinner served during the visit consisted of broth, bread, and pudding—the meal was an abundant one, and the broth and pudding were well made and pleasant to the taste.

The clothing and personal cleanliness of the patients were satisfactory.

Their employment in useful work is well attended to. The condition of the inmates and of the wards is creditable to the present management.

The registers were examined and found regularly and correctly kept.

Appendix B

Commissioners'
Entries.

Lunatic Wards
of Poorhouses.

Dumbarton
Poorhouse.

LUNATIC WARDS, DUMBARTON POORHOUSE,
9th July 1901.

There are 52 patients, 25 men and 27 women, in the wards at this date. Since last visit, on 5th February of the present year, 4 men and 3 women have been admitted, 1 man has been discharged, and 1 woman has died. The cause of death was acute Bright's disease. There have been no accidents, no escapes, no changes in the staff, and no patient has been restrained or secluded since last visit.

Thirty-nine patients, 20 men and 19 women, were industrially employed at the time of the visit.

The patients were quiet and orderly in their demeanour, and beyond a few appeals for release there was no appearance of discontent. Their clothing was neat and clean, and they had every appearance of being suitably fed and properly cared for.

The wards and dormitories were clean and in good order.

Woven wire mattresses have been fitted into the majority of the beds in the dormitories, and are a great improvement upon the old straw mattresses. Two easy chairs have been added to the furnishings of each day-room, and these increase the comfort and improve the appearance of these rooms.

There is still room for 5 men and 3 women in the wards, and it is hoped that these vacancies may be occupied before next visit.

The books and registers were examined and found correct.

Dundee East
Poorhouse.

LUNATIC WARDS, DUNDEE EAST POORHOUSE,
21st February 1901.

When these wards were last visited, on 5th September 1900, there were 44 men and 56 women resident. Since then 3 men and 3 women have been admitted, 4 men and 4 women have been discharged, and 1 man has died. The death was due to intestinal obstruction, and the cause was verified by *post mortem* examination. There are 42 men and 55 women resident at this date. There has been no accident to any of the inmates since last visit One escape in which the patient was absent for a night has occurred. There has been no change in the staff.

All the patients were seen during the visit. Their general physical condition was highly satisfactory ; they presented a healthy, well-nourished appearance, and their personal clothing was neatly fitting, clean, and in good repair. Demands for release were frequent, but otherwise there was no indication of excitement or discontent. Twenty-nine men and 43 women were usefully employed at the time of the visit.

The accommodation provided for patients in these wards is in every respect satisfactory. The dayrooms and dormitories were clean and in admirable order. The beds in the dormitories were comfortable, and their coverings were sufficiently warm and commendably clean.

The employment of a night attendant on the male and female sides of the wards respectively has, as might have been expected, had a most beneficial effect upon the mental health and habits of several of the inmates.

The books and registers were examined and found correct.

LUNATIC WARDS, DUNDEE EAST POORHOUSE,
9th July 1901.

There are 98 patients, 44 men and 54 women, as inmates in the wards at this date.

Since last visit 3 men and 3 women have been admitted, 1 man and 3 women have been discharged, and 1 woman has died. Of the 4 patients discharged, 2 were boarded out and 2 were returned to the asylum as unsuitable for care in these wards. The death is registered as due to cardiac failure and senile dementia. There was no *post mortem* examination.

The Register of Accidents contains only one entry ; it refers to a cut on the forehead, due to an accidental fall. There has been one escape in which the patient was absent for two nights before being brought back. One change has

taken place in the staff, the female night attendant resigned, and one was
engaged in her stead.

The management of the patients continues judicious and kindly; their occupation in useful work, which is so essential in securing good order, tranquillity, and physical well-being, receives careful attention. Eleven men are engaged in garden work, which benefits them both bodily and mentally, and 17 are usefully occupied either at trades or in assisting in keeping the wards in order.

Twenty-five women work in the laundry, 10 at sewing or knitting, and 8 assist the attendants in the wards. The condition of the patients as regards clothing and personal neatness was satisfactory, and their general health was indicative of a suitable and liberal dietary.

The wards throughout were in excellent order, and the aspect of both day-rooms and dormitories was bright, cheerful, and comfortable. It is recorded with satisfaction that practically all the beds have been provided with wire mattresses, which is found to be a great improvement. Much that was seen during the visit showed that the establishment is managed in a conscientious and progressive manner.

The registers were examined and found accurately and regularly kept.

LUNATIC WARDS, DUNDEE WEST POORHOUSE,
21st February 1901.

There are 78 patients—40 men and 38 women—resident in the wards at this date. Since the 5th of September 1900, the date of last visit, 6 men and 4 women have been admitted, 4 men and 1 woman have died, and there is an increase of 2 men and 3 women in the number resident.

The assigned causes of the 5 deaths are cancer of internal organs in 2 cases, and senile decay, cardiac failure, and cerebral haemorrhage in 1 case each. A *post mortem* examination was held in 1 case. There has been no accident or escape since last visit, and no form of restraint has been applied to any of the patients. One male attendant has resigned and 1 has been engaged.

With the exception of 1 man and 3 women who were confined to bed, the patients were in good bodily health, and the majority of them were usefully employed. The laundry and kitchen of the institution supply work for the more active among the females, but at this season of the year, when garden work is suspended, the men have no proper form of exercise and no interesting employment. Sixteen of them were engaged in rope-teasing, which is neither congenial nor healthy occupation for the insane, and the reporter hopes that the recommendation contained in the preceding entry regarding the advisability of introducing such an occupation for the men as wood-cutting and splitting will soon be given effect to.

The patients were free from excitement, none of them made any complaint regarding their treatment, and their general condition was satisfactory,

The dormitories were comfortable, and the beds were suitably supplied with coverings.

The large dayrooms where the patients dine and sit are dingy, low in ceiling, and their furnishings are not good when compared with the standard of more modern institutions for the insane.

The books and registers were examined and found regularly and correctly kept.

LUNATIC WARDS, DUNDEE WEST POORHOUSE,
9th and 18th July 1901.

There are 78 patients, 39 men and 39 women, as inmates of the wards at this date.

Since 21st February, the date of last visit, 3 men and 4 women have been admitted, 1 man and 2 women have been discharged, and 3 men and 1 woman have died.

The deaths are registered as due to pneumonia in 2 cases and to cardiac disease in 2 cases. In only 1 case was a *post mortem* examination made. The importance of these examinations should be kept in view, and whenever the consent of relations can be obtained an autopsy should be made.

Appendix B. The Register of Accidents contains no entry. There has been no escape. It
is recorded with satisfaction that there has been no change in the staff since
Commissioners' last visit. The nurse and laundress attendant have each completed over three
Entries. years service in the wards.

Lunatic Wards A plan for the alterations of the present workshops has been approved of by
of Poorhouses. the Board. By these alterations suitable workshops will be obtained in which
the patients can be employed in wood cutting and bundling and in which they
Dundee West will do this work under healthy conditions.
Poorhouse. It is proposed by the Parish Council to extend the accommodation of the
wards on the male side by an addition to contain rooms for the two attendants
and a sickroom for four patients. This extension will add to the efficiency of
the wards ; the sick will be provided for in a more satisfactory manner, and
the staff will be more comfortably accommodated. A door and an outside
staircase are also provided, leading from the sickroom to the exercise court.
On the ground floor of the extension will be a visiting room and an enlarged
mortuary. It is recommended that a water-closet be provided next the
sick-room. Space for this can be obtained between the sick ward and one
of the attendants' rooms, which is of large size. Should effect be given
to this alteration, the Board are recommended to approve of the plans for the
extension.

The dining halls have been repainted and have been rendered as bright and
as cheerful as their low ceilings and indifferent lighting will allow. The floor
of the hall on the female side has been laid with linoleum and floorcloth,
and additions have been made to the furniture. Further additions to the
furniture would be advantageous and give these rooms a more comfortable
appearance.

The dormitories were clean and in good order, and the worn-out straw
palliasses are gradually being replaced by wire mattresses.

The patients are well cared for and their health and physical condition are
satisfactory. Only one man was confined to bed. The dinner was a well-cooked
and abundant meal.

Rope teasing as an employment for the men has been abandoned, and
garden work substituted. The laundry and kitchen afford employment for 15
women, 7 assist in the work of the wards, and 7 are engaged at either sewing
or knitting.

The registers were examined and found regularly and accurately kept.

Edinburgh
Poorhouse,
Craiglockhart.

LUNATIC WARDS, EDINBURGH POORHOUSE, CRAIGLOCKHART,
29th January 1901.

There were 150 patients—79 men and 71 women—resident on the 24th
August 1900, the date of last visit.

Since then the following changes have taken place in the population :—

						M.	F.	TOTALS.
Admitted,	.	.	.	.	.	8	2	10
Discharged,	.	.	.	.	.	6	0	6
Died,	.	.	.	.	.	2	1	3

At this date there are 151 patients—79 men and 72 women—in the wards.
The three deaths are registered as due to heart disease, anæmia, and
emphysema respectively. *Post mortem* examinations were made in two
instances. Since last visit one patient escaped and was absent for at least
one night before being brought back. There has been no accident, and
none of the inmates have been subjected to any kind of restraint or seclusion.

The number of patients attending Divine service last Sunday was 111 or
74 per cent. of the population—a very creditable proportion. One hundred
and five patients—66 men and 39 women—were industrially employed at this
date. The proportion of women usefully employed is somewhat small, and
although the provision of work of a suitable kind for female patients is always
attended with considerable difficulty, it is hoped that in a large institution
like this means may perhaps be devised for remedying, to some extent at
any rate, a defect which is not consistent with the general welfare of the
patients.

The physical health of the inmates was very satisfactory, only 2 females, both suffering from chronic bodily ailments, being confined to bed A substantial dinner, consisting of bread, broth, and boiled beef, was seen being partaken of. The food was of good quality, and it was satisfactory to observe that, while it was judiciously distributed, the quantity supplied to each patient was liberal and in every instance sufficient. The personal clothing of the inmates, both male and female, was of good material and generally well-fitting. All parts of the wards were found in good order, and the female section was especially clean, bright, and attractive in its arrangements. Appendix B.
——
Commissioners'
Entries.
——
Lunatic Wards
of Poorhouses.
——
Edinburgh
Poorhouse,
Craiglockhart.

The inmates at the time of the visit were quiet, free from excitement and restlessness, and none of them made any complaint of a rational kind.

It is understood that a number of patients are this week to be sent to Middleton Hall, and that their places will be filled by fresh cases from the Royal Edinburgh Asylum. There are, excluding heads of departments, 10 ordinary attendants on day duty at present, and a male night attendant is to be engaged. While this staff is sufficient for the class of inmate presently occupying the wards, it is right to point out, should patients of a more acute type be transferred to the institution, it will be necessary to increase the number of attendants.

The books and registers are correctly kept.

LUNATIC WARDS, EDINBURGH POORHOUSE, CRAIGLOCKHART,
2nd and 3rd July 1901.

There are at present on the register of the wards 124 men and 77 women, or 201 patients in all.

Since 29th January 1901, the date of last visit, the following changes have taken place:—

PAUPER PATIENTS.

	M.	F.	TOTALS.
Admitted, ...	47	9	56
Discharged unrecovered, ...	2	1	3
Died, ...	0	3	3

The deaths are registered as due to chronic hemiplegia, valvular heart disease, and phthisis pulmonalis respectively.

In 2 of the 3 deaths a *post mortem* examination was made.

This establishment now consists of two sections—the wards in Craiglockhart Poorhouse, and the mansion-house Middleton Hall at Uphall. The latter was opened for the reception of patients on 1st February 1901, and at present contains 59 patients—49 men and 10 women. In the wards at Craiglockhart are 142 patients—75 men and 67 women.

All parts of the wards at Craiglockhart were found in excellent order, and presented an aspect of cleanliness, cheerfulness, and comfort. The condition of the beds and bedding was satisfactory. The patients during the visit were quiet and well conducted, and except the usual appeals for discharge there were no complaints. The clothing of both sexes was of good quality and tidy in appearance, that of the women especially so. The neatness of the personal appearance of the women is highly creditable to the head and other nurses in charge. The dinner consisted of broth, bread, and Irish stew, and was abundant and well liked. It was observed with approval that the special dietetic requirements of certain patients receive attention, rice broth, or rice and milk, and pudding being provided for those unable to take the ordinary fare. Among the men transferred from the Royal Asylum since last visit are 16 epileptics, and an attendant has been engaged for their supervision at night. It is regretted that on account of the size of the dormitories these epileptics cannot be accommodated in one room so as to secure continuous night supervision. They, however, sleep in three adjacent dormitories, and it is understood that the night attendant is constantly on patrol between these rooms.

The number of women industrially employed has increased from 39 to 48, or from 54 to 62 per cent. The rate of mortality has been low, and the

Appendix B.

Commissioners'
Entries.

Lunatic Wards
of Poorhouses.

Edinburgh
Poorhouse,
Craiglockhart.

general health of the inmates is good. One accident, not of a serious character, is recorded. There has been no escape.

The impression produced by the visit to Middleton Hall was highly satisfactory. This mansion house is proving excellently adapted for the purpose it is for a period intended to serve. The internal alterations to render it suitable for the accommodation of the insane and to facilitate administration have evidently been carefully considered and efficiently carried out. Adequate and excellent bathing and water-closet arrangements have been provided, and the supply of cold and hot water is sufficient. The furniture has been well selected, the beds are of good design and substantially made, the bedding and bed coverings are of good quality, the floors of the dormitories are covered with waxcloth, strips of carpet are laid between the beds, and the day-rooms and dining hall have been suitably furnished. In one of the day-rooms is a grand piano, which is proving most useful at the evening entertainments. It is understood to be the gift of a lady member of the Parish Council. The lighting of the house is by lamps, and it was evident that everything is done to render them as safe as possible. They are placed out of reach of the patients in the day-rooms and are encased in wire netting receptacles in the dormitories. The drying arrangements in the laundry are at present defective, but are soon to be made efficient. The patients are evidently well cared for and judiciously treated. The absence of the ordinary asylum arrangements in the building is a decided advantage, and some of the more intelligent patients expressed satisfaction with their new surroundings. Suitable employment is found for every inmate, and a most creditable amount of outdoor work has been done since the house was occupied. The grounds have been put into good order, and a large piece of land has been converted into a garden. The supply of vegetables promises to be abundant. Dr. Stewart of Uphall visits daily, and due provision has been made for religious services on Sundays. The staff consists of Mr. and Mrs. Henry, who are in charge, a cook, a laundress, and 3 male attendants ; and the management of this section appears to be quite satisfactory in every detail.

Of the 10 female patients, 4 work in the laundry, 3 in the kitchen, 1 as a housemaid, and 2 at sewing.

The registers were examined and found written up to date.

Govan
Poorhouse.

LUNATIC WARDS, GOVAN POORHOUSE,
1st *February* 1901.

There are 166 patients, 93 men and 73 women, resident in the wards at this date. There is vacant accommodation for 7 men and 27 women.

Since 13th July 1900, the date of last visit, 12 men and 8 women have been admitted, 1 woman has been discharged, and 3 men and 2 women have died. Of the 20 patients admitted, 12 were transferred from the Govan District Asylum, 4 from the Larbert Imbecile Institution, 3 from their own homes, and 1 from being boarded out.

The deaths are registered as due to cerebral affections in 2 cases, to cancer in 1 case, to heart disease in 1 case, and to chronic Bright's disease in 1 case. *Post mortem* examinations were made in 3 cases, and the sanction of the relatives was refused in 2 cases.

There is no entry in the Register of Restraint and Seclusion. Two accidents are recorded, a flesh wound on left forearm from thrusting arm through window, and a scalp wound from being pushed down by a fellow-patient. One patient escaped and was absent for a night before being brought back. Four attendants have resigned and four have been engaged.

The condition of the inmates bore evidence of their being well cared for. They were quiet and orderly in behaviour and their clothing and personal neatness were satisfactory. The dinner was an abundant and well-cooked meal, and was evidently much liked. Complaints were made as to the porridge being cold at breakfast. The cause of this should be seen to and remedied.

The wards, which have been most successfully reconstructed, presented a bright and comfortable appearance. The heating arrangements are very efficient—steam can be turned on to each radiator as required, and consequently the temperature of each room can be regulated by using one or more radiators. The floor of the sewing room has been relaid with pitch pine, and its walls are about to be repainted. The substitution of spring mattresses for the straw palliasses is again recommended. Opaque green blinds have been provided for all the windows.

A great improvement has been effected in the appearance of the grounds adjoining the wards by the removal of the wall and the high, prison-like railing which surrounded the male and female exercise courts. A series of greens, divided and fenced by low iron railings, now flank the buildings. To the south a large bowling green has been completed by the patients and attendants.

The registers were examined and found regularly and accurately kept.

Appendix B.

Commissioners' Entries.

Lunatic Wards of Poorhouses.

Govan Poorhouse.

LUNATIC WARDS, GOVAN POORHOUSE,
12th July 1901.

There are 176 patients on the register at this date, of whom 94 are men and 82 are women. With the exception of 1 man who was absent on pass, all the patients were seen at the time of the visit.

Since the 1st February 1901, the date of last visit, the numbers resident have increased by 10 and the following changes have occurred in the population :—

	PAUPER PATIENTS.		
	M.	F.	TOTALS.
Admitted, ...	7	12	19
Discharged, ...	4	0	4
Died, ...	2	3	5

The deaths are registered as due to cancer of the bowel, heart disease with pneumonia, epilepsy, cerebral softening, and cerebral hæmorrhage. *Post mortem* examinations were made in three instances. There are no entries in the Register of Restraint and Seclusion. One patient escaped and was absent for at least one night before being brought back. One accident is recorded which is of an unimportant nature.

One hundred and forty-six patients, or the remarkably high proportion of 83 per cent. of the population, were industrially employed at the time of the visit ; of this number it is satisfactory to record that 50 men were employed at garden or field labour. It is understood that 12 acres of arable land have recently been acquired by the institution, which will amply meet the requirements of the male patients in respect to outdoor work. The grounds surrounding the department for the insane were in admirable order, and the removal of the massive iron railings has had the effect of greatly improving their appearance and of removing from the sight of the patients an object which was so suggestive of restraint. The new railing is open and ornamental.

The wards and dormitories were found in a very commendable state of good order and cleanliness. The furnishings are of a modern description and suitably chosen. Wire mattresses have been fitted into all the beds in the dormitories, which is a change of considerable importance from a sanitary point of view. With the exception of the corridor of communication and the renovation of the general bathroom, the extensive alterations which have been proceeding for the past two or three years are finished, and upon the results the Committee and Mr. Thomson may justly be congratulated.

The general health of the patients was satisfactory, and only three persons, one man and two women, were confined to bed. No exception could be taken to their personal clothing or to the quality or cooking of the food which was being prepared for their dinner. Their demeanour was quiet and orderly, and no complaint of a rational nature was submitted by any of them.

It is satisfactory to record that out of a staff of 17 nurses and attendants, only one change has taken place since last visit.

The books and registers were examined and found to be regularly and correctly kept.

Appendix B.
—
Commissioners'
Entries.
—
Lunatic Wards
of Poorhouses.
—
Inveresk
Poorhouse.

LUNATIC WARDS, INVERESK POORHOUSE.
31st January 1901.

There are at this date 16 men and 16 women in the wards. There has been no change in the population since 29th August 1900, the date of last visit. It is satisfactory to record that no death, accident, or escape has occurred among the inmates since the wards were last visited.

The health of the inmates was satisfactory with the exception of one man, 75 years of age, who was admitted to the wards last July, and who is now confined to bed, suffering from bronchitis, heart affection, and senile decay. Such cases are as a rule more suited for treatment in asylums which possess special facilities for the care of sick and infirm patients.

The wards were found throughout in good order, and the condition of the inmates, judged by the state of their personal clothing, their general appearance, and the absence of excitement and signs of discontent, indicated that they are conscientiously and adequately cared for.

The medical journal and the books and registers were examined and found regularly and correctly kept.

LUNATIC WARDS, INVERESK POORHOUSE,
4th September 1901.

There are 30 patients—15 men and 15 women—resident in the wards at this date.

Since last visit 1 man has been admitted, and 2 men and 1 woman have been discharged. There has been no death. The three patients discharged were transferred to the asylum on account of their being unsuitable for care and treatment in an establishment of this kind. The Register of Accidents and Escapes contains no entry.

Practically there has been no change in the staff. The female attendant, who has been in the service of the wards for 3 years, had to leave for some months on account of domestic reasons, but has now returned.

The condition of the patients as regards cleanliness and personal neatness was exceedingly satisfactory, and suitable for the season. The dinner at this date consisted of pea soup, boiled beef, and bread, and it was a well cooked and abundant meal. It is recommended that potatoes be given more frequently—at present they are given only twice a week, once as Irish stew and once at the fish dinner. The diets would be made quite satisfactory by this change and by giving extras to working patients, otherwise they are good and varied.

The cleanliness and good order which prevailed throughout the wards merit commendation. The water supply and the bathing arrangements continue defective, and until the former is ample the bathing of the patients cannot be as satisfactory as in other establishments for the insane. The straw palliasses are old, and, as their condition must be an insanitary one, they should be discarded and wire mattresses substituted.

The registers were examined and found regularly and correctly kept.

Kincardine
Poorhouse.

LUNATIC WARDS, KINCARDINE POORHOUSE,
12th February 1901.

There were 43 patients in the wards on the 20th October 1900, the date of last visit. Since then 1 man and 1 woman have been discharged, and 1 man has died. There are at this date 40 patients on the register, of whom 19 are men and 21 are women. All are resident, with the exception of one man who is out on a week's pass and who is at present working for a neighbouring farmer. All the patients were seen during the visit. It is understood that the Governor has satisfied himself that this patient who is on pass is properly fed and treated during his absence from the institution.

The single death is registered as due to softening of the brain. There has been no change in the staff, no escape, and no accident since last visit. About 25 of the inmates—13 men and 12 women—are usefully employed from day to day.

The health of the majority of the patients was satisfactory, only 1 woman, suffering from bronchitis and weakened by successive attacks of

influenza, being confined to bed. Attention must, however, be directed to
the following 2 patients, both of whom were admitted to the wards about
6 months ago:—(1) C. S. is in feeble health, his heart's action is weak, and
his feet are consequently swollen; he is so demented that he cannot dress
himself. (2) H. B. or C. also suffers from heart disease, and her feet are
swollen; there is an ulcer on one of her legs; she is unfit to do any kind
of work; her age is given as 67, but she herself says she is 80 years of
age, and her appearance is more in accordance with her own statement.

Appendix B.

Commissioners'
Entries.

Lunatic Wards
of Poorhouses.

Kincardine
Poorhouse.

Both patients are unsuitable subjects for the lunatic wards of a poorhouse, where there exist no means or appliances for the care or nursing
of senile or infirm patients, and their removal back to the asylum is therefore recommended.

The wards and dormitories were clean and in excellent order. The
patients, who were all suitably dressed, were free from excitement and
exhibited every indication of efficient care and of an adequate dietary.

The books and registers were found regularly and correctly kept.

LUNATIC WARDS, KINCARDINE POORHOUSE,
27th July 1901.

There are 20 men and 21 women in the wards at this date.

Since 12th February 1901, the date of last visit, 2 men and 2 women have
been admitted, 1 man and 1 woman have been discharged, and 1 woman has
died. The cause of death is registered as heart disease. No *post mortem*
examination was made. The value of these examinations in institutions for
the insane is great—a fact which should be kept in view.

No accident occurred. A male patient recently escaped, and has not yet
been brought back. It is believed he is on his way to his home near Kirrie-
muir, and there appears to be no ground for anxiety as to his welfare. A
change in the staff on the male side has taken place.

Both in regard to the care and treatment of the patients and the management
of the establishment, the visit left a most favourable impression. The
appearance of the patients indicates good feeding and plenty of exercise in the
open air.

All were quiet and orderly, and none had any complaint to make. The
present inmates appear to be suitable for an establishment of this character.

Two women were confined to bed, one from general debility and one on account
of an ulcer on the leg. One man was absent visiting his relatives; and it is
understood that 6 men and 5 women are given a day's leave from time to time
to visit their friends. This privilege is greatly appreciated, and promotes
happiness and contentment, and is never abused.

Ten of the men do useful and profitable work, either on the land belonging
to the poorhouse, or in wood cutting and bundling.

Thirteen women are engaged at either household work or at sewing and
knitting.

The wards were in admirable order, and presented throughout an aspect of
brightness and comfort.

The registers were examined and found accurately kept.

LUNATIC WARDS, LINLITHGOW POORHOUSE,
28th February 1901.

There are 34 patients—17 men and 17 women—inmates of the wards at
this date. The only changes since last visit are the admission of 1 man and
the discharge of 1 man.

There has been no accident and no escape. One change in the staff
has occurred, a nurse having resigned and one having been engaged in her
stead.

The male attendant has been in the service of the wards for nearly twelve
years. There is great kindliness in the relations between the patients
under his charge and himself.

The establishment continues to be efficiently managed. The dayrooms
and dormitories were clean, in excellent order, and comfortably furnished.

Appendix B.

Commissioners'
Entries.

Lunatic Wards
of Poorhouses.

Linlithgow
Poorhouse.

Repainting is well attended to, and consequently both the rooms and passages are bright and cheerful in appearance. It is understood that the conversion of the two male dormitories into one, which would be a great improvement, is to be carried out at an early date. The patients are, with one exception, suitable for care in this institution. The removal of J. P. to the asylum, on account of her defective habits, has been called for. The condition of the inmates as to physical health, personal neatness, and tidiness of clothing was very satisfactory. The dinner was a well-cooked and liberal meal; it consisted of pea-soup, bread, and boiled beef. All the patients, with one exception, in each division are daily engaged in useful work. Contentment, the result of kindly and judicious treatment, prevailed among the inmates.

The registers were examined and found correctly kept.

LUNATIC WARDS, LINLITHGOW POORHOUSE,
23rd *November* 1901.

The number of patients resident at this date is the same as at the date of the last visit—17 men and 17 women. In the interval 1 man and 1 woman have been admitted, and 1 man and 1 woman have been discharged. There have been no deaths. There is an entry in the Register of Accidents, referring to an injury to the knee of a male patient, which was fortunately not of a serious nature. With the exception of one man and one woman, all the patients are employed usefully. They all looked healthy and well fed, and their clothing was, in every instance, well fitting, clean, and in good repair. A suitable dinner, consisting of broth, bread, and stewed meat, was served during the visit. The day-rooms, dormitories, and the various accessory apartments were found, as usual, in excellent order. The removal of the partition in the male dormitory and the erection at one end of it of a room for the male attendant has proved already the wisdom of the proposal, for the alteration gives greater comfort to the attendant and more air and light to the dormitory.

The books and registers were examined and found to be correctly kept.

Old Monkland
Poorhouse.

LUNATIC WARDS, OLD MONKLAND POORHOUSE,
6th *May* 1901.

There are 24 men and 22 women at this date as inmates of the wards.

Since last visit on 30th November 1900, 1 woman has been admitted and 2 women have died. The cause of death in each case was apoplexy. A *post mortem* examination was made in one case, but the consent of the relatives for an autopsy was refused in the other. It is desirable and important in the interests of all concerned in the administration of the wards that the causes of death should be verified by an examination whenever the consent of relatives can be obtained for it.

There has been no accident to any patient, no escape, and no case of seclusion or restraint.

The wards are maintained in excellent order, and were throughout scrupulously clean. The day-rooms, dining-halls, and corridors have been tastefully repainted and made bright and cheerful in appearance. Linoleum has been laid in the day-rooms and dining-halls, and is a great improvement. The beds in the male dormitories have been furnished with wire mattresses, and those in the other dormitories are to be similarly equipped.

The recommendation in the previous entry as to placing a piece of felt between the wire and hair mattresses, and a blanket between the under sheet and hair mattress has been carried out. The baths have now been fitted with arrangements which give an ample supply of hot water. The outlet from the baths is too small, and entails delay in emptying. If it can be enlarged it should be done, as it would enable the attendants to give clean water to each patient without loss of time. The large wardrobe in the room which was formerly a surgery is a useful addition, and admits of the female clothing being kept in an orderly manner. A smaller press in the same room would be serviceable in holding the spare crockery of the wards.

The patients were neatly and comfortably clothed, and their personal cleanliness satisfactory. Their aspect was indicative of a liberal dietary and abundant outdoor exercise or work. The dinner was a well-cooked and abundant meal, with which the more intelligent patients expressed cordial approval. The industrial occupation of all capable of employment is well attended to. The patients were entirely free from complaints and excitement, and everything seen during the visit reflects creditably on the present management of the wards.

J.W. or S. has become very defective in her habits, both during the day and night. As there is no prospect of improvement her removal to the asylum is recommended.

The registers were examined and found correctly and neatly kept.

Appendix B.

Commissioners' Entries.

Lunatic Wards of Poorhouses.

Old Monkland Poorhouse.

LUNATIC WARDS, OLD MONKLAND POORHOUSE,
16th December 1901.

There were 46 patients—24 men and 22 women—resident on the 6th May of the present year, at which date the wards were last visited. Since then 1 man and 3 women have been admitted, 1 woman has been discharged recovered, 2 women have been discharged unrecovered, and 1 woman has died.

There are 46 patients—25 men and 21 women—resident at this date.

The death is registered as due to phthisis.

One male attendant has resigned and one has been engaged. There have been no accidents or escapes, nor has any patient been secluded or restrained during the period embraced in this report.

The patients were free from excitement, their physical health was apparently good, and their personal clothing was in every respect suitable. One of the female patients named M. L. is suffering from Addison's disease. It is recommended that she should be removed to an asylum for the prolonged nursing which her symptoms require.

The day-rooms and dormitories were found clean, properly heated, and in excellent order. A proper supply of hot water has now been provided for the baths and lavatories on the male and female sides respectively.

In respect of adaptation to their purpose of the care and management of the patients, and of good order and cleanliness, these wards will compare favourably with any similar institution in the country.

The books and registers were examined and found accurately and correctly kept.

LUNATIC WARDS, PERTH POORHOUSE,
28th March 1901.

Perth Poorhouse.

There are 37 patients—19 men and 18 women—in the wards at this date. Since last visit, one female has been discharged recovered, and one man and one woman have died. The cause of death in both cases is registered as heart disease. No *post mortem* examination was made ; in one case the sanction of relatives for an examination was refused, and in the other case it was not applied for. It is important that an examination should be made whenever the consent of relatives can be obtained, in order to verify the cause of death.

No accident has occurred, and there has been no escape. A male attendant has been dismissed for intemperance and one has been appointed in his stead.

The patients were quiet and well behaved, and in a satisfactory condition as regards dress and personal neatness. Two females were in bed—one from a temporary ailment, and one on account of the infirmities of old age. M. S. has again become wet in her habits and requires night supervision for her proper care. Her transfer to the District Asylum is recommended.

The inmates were seen at dinner, which was a well cooked and abundant meal. It consisted of broth, boiled beef, bread, and pudding. Regular employment is provided for 14 men and 10 women. The workshop, in which 11 men are engaged in bundling firewood, is a very satisfactory feature of this institution. It is spacious, well lighted, efficiently ventilated, and comfortably heated.

K

Appendix B.

Commissioners'
Entries.

Lunatic Wards
of Poorhouses.

Perth
Poorhouse.

Wigtown
Poorhouse.

The wards are maintained in excellent order. The day-rooms have been repapered, and the dormitories presented a clean, bright and well furnished appearance. The bed clothes were ample for the season.

The satisfactory condition of the establishment deserves commendation.

The registers were examined and found correctly kept.

LUNATIC WARDS, PERTH POORHOUSE,
5th December 1901.

Since the last visit to these wards 6 men and 4 women have been admitted, 4 men and 2 women have been discharged, and 1 man and 1 woman have died. The number resident at this date is 39, of whom 20 are men and 19 are women. This shows an increase of one patient of each sex as compared with the numbers at last visit. The two deaths are registered as due to senile decay and fatty degeneration of the heart respectively. There has been no accident or escape during the period covered by this report.

The patients were found in good physical health, all except one woman, M. S., who has been bedridden since September last owing to bodily weakness and infirmity. As, in addition, she frequently suffers from attacks of diarrhœa, her case is evidently one which could be better nursed in an asylum hospital, and her removal to the district asylum is therefore recommended.

The personal clothing of the inmates was satisfactory, and their wants appear to be properly attended to in every respect. The dayrooms and dormitories were, as usual, bright, clean, and in excellent order. It is worthy of consideration whether the comfort of the inmates would not be increased and the floors of the corridors better preserved if wooden porches were erected at the outer doors of the male and female wards respectively.

It is also suggested that it would add materially to the convenience of the cleansing and other arrangements if hot water were introduced into the male division of the wards.

The books and registers were examined and found correct.

LUNATIC WARDS, WIGTOWN POORHOUSE,
21st March 1901.

There are 16 men and 14 women at present inmates of the wards.

Since last visit, 1 man has been admitted and 4 men have died. One death was due to valvular disease of the heart and old age (84), and 3 were due to influenza complicated with acute chest affections. Influenza is and has been prevalent in the district, and the rate of mortality among the general population has, it is understood, been high. One patient who has been seriously ill from influenza and pneumonia is evidently going to make a good recovery. Investigation into the care of these patients showed that everything was done to secure their constant day and night supervision. The medical records by Dr. Anderson relative to these cases are very complete and indicate skilful and liberal treatment.

There has been no accident and no escape in which the patient was absent overnight. Two male attendants have resigned and two have been engaged. These frequent changes are undesirable in the interests of the patients. Every reasonable inducement should be offered to efficient and trustworthy attendants to remain in the service of the institution.

The patients continue to be kindly and judiciously treated. The men were seen at supper—the tea was satisfactory, the bread sufficient, but the butter was scanty. The allowance of butter should be increased. The women have tea at 3 p.m. and at 6 p.m., and none had any complaints. The clothing of the inmates has been much improved in recent years. Nine men are daily engaged in garden work and one in house work. Nine women are usefully employed.

The wards were in good order, the bedding clean, and the bedclothes ample for the season. The management continues to be painstaking and satisfactory.

The registers were examined and found regularly and correctly kept.

LUNATIC WARDS, WIGTOWN POORHOUSE,
12th October 1901.

Appendix B.

Commissioners'
Entries.

Lunatic Wards
of Poorhouses.

Wigtown
Poorhouse.

There are 34 patients in the wards at this date—viz., 19 men and 15 women.

Three men and 1 woman have been admitted since last visit, and 1 woman who was at that time on probation has been removed from the roll. There has been no death or accident and there is no entry in the Register of Restraint or Seclusion. There have been 2 escapes where 2 male patients were absent over night. One was away for four days, and had travelled to a relation's house at Hurlford, from which he was sent back; the other escaped while the attendant was engaged looking for this man, and was returned from Glenluce on the following day. One of the male patients recently admitted—W. C. C.—is slovenly as regards his clothing, and is said to be defective in his habits, and it is recommended that he should be returned to the asylum.

Two male attendants have resigned and 2 have been engaged since last visit.

The day being very wet, all the patients were found in the house, but in suitable weather 14 men are regularly employed at garden work, and one is employed assisting the attendant in the wards. Of the females, 10 are engaged regularly in house and laundry work, knitting, &c. The general health of the patients was very satisfactory, and all who were questioned expressed themselves as quite satisfied with their treatment. They were seen at dinner, and the meal consisted of an unlimited supply of good broth, a fair quantity of boiled beef, and bread. Effect has been given to Dr. Fraser's recommendation regarding the supply of butter; each patient is said now to receive nearly double the former allowance.

The day-rooms and dormitories were clean, well aired, and in good order, and the supply of clothing was ample, of good quality, and well made. Improvement has been begun as regards the bedding by the introduction of a few spring mattresses. The supply of bed clothing was sufficient and of good quality.

The books and registers were examined and were found regularly and correctly kept.

INSTITUTIONS FOR IMBECILE CHILDREN.

BALDOVAN INSTITUTION,
22nd February 1901.

Institutions
for Imbeciles.

Baldovan
Institution.

The numbers resident have increased from 105 on the 12th September 1900, the date of last visit, to 114 at this date. Of the latter number, 2 boys and 3 girls are private pupils, 1 boy is supported by the funds of the institution, and 67 boys and 41 girls are chargeable to various parishes throughout the country.

Since last visit 13 boys and 9 girls have been admitted, 5 boys and 2 girls have been discharged, and 4 boys and 2 girls have died. The assigned causes of death are epilepsy (3 cases), phthisis, heart failure, and bronchitis.

Seven children were confined to bed, the majority of them on account of trivial ailments. During the past five months no epidemics or debilitating affections of a marked kind have operated unfavourably upon the general health of the inmates. The children were found in as satisfactory a state of physical condition as could be expected, considering the somewhat large proportion of weakly and helpless cases which the institution accommodates. Allowing for that fact, however, the general appearance of the children was distinctly favourable; they were well nourished, cheerful, tidily dressed, and the relations existing between them and Miss Butter were

150 *Appendix to the Forty-fourth Report of the General Board of*

Appendix B.
Commissioners'
Entries.

Institutions
for Imbeciles.

Baldovan
Institution.

evidently cordial and characterised by confidence on their part and affection on hers. There are four regular meals a day—breakfast, dinner, tea, and supper. The dinner to-day was witnessed. The food was suitable and of adequate quantity, and the order prevailing in the dining-rooms, though not of a disciplinary character, was perfectly pleasant, considering that many of the children are unable to feed themselves.

The employment of the children is carefully attended to, everyone who is able to do any work being encouraged to do a little. Apart from light household work, in which as many as 40 are induced to participate to a greater or less extent, the following modes of employment may, among others, be mentioned :—4 boys work in the garden, 8 boys and 5 girls are employed in the laundry and kitchen, and 10 boys and 8 girls either knit or sew. The usual amount of attention continues to be devoted to school training.

It is expected that the new buildings will be ready for occupation about the beginning of August, and that the present house will then be relieved to the extent of about 50 inmates. Such a relief is much required, for the number resident is greatly in excess of that for which the establishment is licensed and which it can properly accommodate.

Every part of the house was found in good order, the rooms were bright and well ventilated, and the beds in the dormitories were comfortable and suitably supplied with coverings.

The books and registers were examined and found correct.

BALDOVAN INSTITUTION,
18th July 1901.

There are 70 boys and 46 girls as pupils in the institution at this date. Of these, 3 boys and 3 girls are private pupils, 1 boy is maintained out of the funds of the institution, and 66 boys and 43 girls are paid for by Parish Councils. Two pauper boys were absent on holiday.

Since 22nd February 1901, the date of last visit, 8 boys and 5 girls have been admitted, 3 boys have been discharged, and 5 boys and 3 girls have died. Except in 1 instance, the admission of a private boy boarder, these changes refer to pauper pupils.

The rate of mortality has been high. The deaths are registered as due to tubercle of the lungs in 3 cases, to tuberculous enteritis in 3 cases, to epilepsy in 1 case, and to atrophy and debility in 1 case. A *post mortem* examination was made in 5 cases.

The changes in the staff have been very few, a fact which is highly creditable to Miss Butter, and indicative of her tactful management. One of the governesses has resigned, and there has been only 1 change among the nursing staff. Two additional servants have been engaged.

The number in the register has increased by 2. Serious overcrowding is an unsatisfactory feature in the condition of the present institution, and as overcrowded dwellings are the real breeding places of tuberculosis it is hoped that relief will be speedily obtained by the opening of the new buildings. The new institution was inspected, and it was found that it will yet be two months or more before it will be ready for occupation. Relief of the present house to the extent of 50 pupils will then be obtained. It is recommended that until the new buildings are opened no fresh cases be received.

It was observed that no direct access to the grounds has been provided in the hospital section of the new institution. The pupils in this section, who will be of the most helpless class, will have to be taken—in many instances they will have to be carried—along the corridor to the front door in order to get to the grounds. It is recommended that one of the windows of the sick ward be converted into a door and a suitable porch erected outside. This improvement should be effected without delay. Immediate access to the grounds will better secure the open-air treatment which is now found so beneficial to those who are the subject of tuberculous disease, as a large percentage of imbecile and idiot children are.

It was abundantly evident during the visit that the children are efficiently cared for. Their condition in regard to cleanliness and clothing was highly satisfactory. Every child was neatly and tastefully dressed ; and in this way their sense of self-respect is promoted. A pride in appearance judiciously cultivated never fails to have a beneficial effect on habits and conduct, and this Appendix B. is especially true of weak-minded children. The stores of Sunday and special clothing were inspected, and their quality, variety, and tastefulness were all Commissioners' Entries. that could be desired. Great credit is due to Miss Butter for the attention she bestows on this section of her duties.

The training of those children who are capable of useful work is carried on Institutions for Imbeciles. assiduously, and the teaching staff for the school now consists of an additional governess. As no restrictions are imposed as to the class of children received, Baldovan Institution. the proportion of the feeble and helpless is a very large one, and this entails a great amount of labour. The staff of nurses will require to be increased when the new buildings are in occupation.

The management of the institution continues to merit the commendations expressed in previous entries.

The registers were examined and found accurately kept.

LARBERT INSTITUTION, Larbert Institution.
13th May 1901.

There are 260 pupils on the books of the institution at this date. Of these, 27 boys and 17 girls are private pupils, 52 boys and 34 girls are elected pupils, and 83 boys and 47 girls are paid for by Parish Councils. One boy was absent on holiday.

Since last visit, 14th November 1900, the following changes have taken place :—

	PRIVATE.		ELECTED.		PAUPER.		TOTALS.
	M.	F.	M.	F.	M.	F.	
Admitted	1	0	0	0	11	4	16
Discharged	0	0	1	1	3	1	6
Died	0	2	3	2	3	5	15

During the period to which the foregoing figures refer, there has been a decrease of 5 in the number resident. The private and elected pupils have decreased by 1 and 7 respectively, and the pauper inmates have increased by 3. It has been pointed out in previous reports that the accommodation for private pupils is fully occupied, and that as a result of the well merited and widely spread reputation of the institution, applications for admission for this class of pupils continue to be received. If these are to be met, an extension of the private section will have to be provided in order to accommodate these pupils in a manner consonant with the higher rates of board.

The rate of mortality has, during the last six months, been high. Of the 15 deaths, 6 are registered as due to epilepsy, 3 to general tuberculosis, 2 to phthisis pulmonalis, and one to each of the following causes—hydrocephalus, pneumonia, tubercle of brain, and tubercular peritonitis. In 1 case a *post-mortem* examination was made. Such a large number of deaths means a great amount of sickness requiring hospital care. Many of the children who died were under treatment for long periods. The present sick wards are not satisfactory, their site especially so. The children going to the covered playground have to pass through the passage between the two sickrooms, and to-day, they were, as usual, very noisy, as is to be expected, and in one of the sick wards was a boy seriously ill with pneumonia. Such an arrangement cannot possibly be regarded as satisfactory, and it is therefore hoped that the Directors will favourably consider the erection of a separate hospital of modern construction on a suitable site. This is without doubt the next improvement in the equipment of the institution which should be provided. To obtain a suitable site the field adjoining the covered playground would require to be purchased. The acquisition of this piece of ground would be of great benefit in this and many other ways, and a most desirable investment in the interests of the institution.

The general care of the children was found most satisfactory. Their personal neatness and the tastefulness of their clothing cannot be too highly commended. These are features in their condition which cannot fail to attract favourable notice and to give assurance of the great efficiency of Mr. Skene's management of the institution. The careful attention given to the children's dress tends to check destructive, slovenly, and uncleanly habits, and the expenditure and care in this direction are fully compensated by the improvement in behaviour effected. The dinner was served in an orderly manner, and a considerable number of the elder girls are trained in the duties of the table. The children had every appearance of being happy and contented, and of being on the best of terms with those in charge of them.

The covered playground can unhesitatingly be pronounced a great success. The children were seen at play there, and the usefulness and advantages of this unique addition to the institution were at once evident. The children thoroughly enjoyed themselves, running freely about, some skipping, some with hoops, and some with hand-balls or footballs. The great amount of exercise which they obtain in this way cannot fail to be highly beneficial to them, both mentally and bodily. Play of this description brightens their intellect, develops their muscles, and makes them sleep better. It has been observed that the children now play in the park during summer more readily and freely than when they were confined to dayrooms, as was formerly the case, during the winter. They forgot, in fact, how to play on account of idling about the dayrooms all winter. A good musical instrument is required in this building to aid in the drills and manual and other exercises conducted there. It is hoped that it will be at once provided.

The institution is doing excellent work in the education and training of the children. A class of boys and girls read with considerable fluency, their writing was decidedly good, and their sums in compound division showed how efficiently they were taught. In regard to the other children at school, it was evident that no efforts are spared by the teachers to develop and expand the intelligence of the pupils according to the measure of its strength and capability. In the workroom section, where the children are taught to sew, knit, and do fancy work, the motor and co-ordinating powers are trained and developed, and the results are of a gratifying character. Useful occupations receive careful attention—112 boys and 102 girls are registered as being industrially employed. In this way the pupils are trained to be useful members of a household on leaving the institution.

All sections of the establishment are maintained in excellent order. The dayrooms are comfortably furnished, and abundantly supplied with objects of interest and decoration. The condition of the dormitories, beds, and bedding was satisfactory. Repainting is being gradually overtaken, and the work is well and tastefully done. New and improved grates have been provided in the private section of the establishment. A verandah is much required at the west door where the goods for the store are received, and where the ash-buckets are kept. The erection of a mortuary supplies a long felt want. The new office for the Superintendent, the new Board and visiting room, and the sitting room for the nurses are all most useful additions, from an administrative point of view.

The staff of the institution is numerically strong, consisting in all of 62 persons. Among the officials are the Superintendent, the Matron, Assistant Matron, and 3 Governesses. The female staff consists of a head nurse, 20 nurses, 2 cooks, 4 laundresses, 2 hall maids, and 20 ward cleaners. There are 5 men employed—an engineer, a gardener, a tailor, a coachman, and a labourer. Of the latter, one resides within the grounds so as to be available in any case of emergency, such as a fire during the night. It is worthy of note that among the staff there are 7 servants who were formerly pupils. These are fed and clothed and receive wages according to the value of their work. These facts strikingly illustrate the usefulness and philanthropy of the institution. It is also worthy of record that many imbeciles who have been trained in this establishment are now known to be maintaining themselves by their industry.

The registers were examined and found to be regularly and accurately kept.

LARBERT INSTITUTION,
3rd December 1901.

* Since the 13th May—the date of last visit—the following changes have occurred in the number resident :—

	PRIVATE.		ELECTED.		PAUPER.		TOTALS.	
	M.	F.	M.	F.	M.	F.		
On Register 13th May, .	27	17	52	34	83	47	260	
Admitted, . . .	5	4	11	6	8	10	44	
Discharged, . . .	2	1	4	7	2	0	16	
Died, ...	1	1	1	1	1	1	6	
On Register 3rd December, .	28	19	59	32	88	56	282	

In the above figures effect has been given to the transference of 1 boy from the private to the elected list.

The deaths are registered as due to brain disease in 1 case, to tuberculosis in 2 cases, and to German measles in 2 cases. *Post mortem* examinations were made in 2 instances.

An epidemic of German measles has recently visited the institution, and no less than 50 children were infected.

Two hundred and fifty-four children, 160 boys and 90 girls, were attending school to-day. Of that number, 17 boys and 40 girls are being instructed in needlework and knitting, and, judging from the samples of work seen, with excellent results. Many of the pupils were also engaged in useful work in the garden, laundry, and kitchen. A highly interesting exhibition was given in the covered playground by a number of the pupils. It consisted of songs, musical drill, and various exercises. The performance was undoubtedly creditable to those who have charge of the instruction of the children.

The principal governess has resigned, and another has been engaged, who is to enter on her duties to-morrow.

The dinner and tea meals were seen to-day. The food was good and wholesome, and the conduct of the children and the service of the meals were entirely satisfactory.

The personal clothing of the pupils attracted very favourable attention. It was not only warm, suitable, and in good repair, but in almost every instance neat and varied, and, what is more important to note, indistinguishable in its appearance from the clothing worn by children of the same age in ordinary circumstances. The various living and sleeping apartments were found, as usual, in excellent order.

There is an increase of 22 in the number resident as compared with last visit, which number exceeds by 32 the licensed capacity of the institution. The Directors will have, sooner or later, to face the question of further extension, and it is well known by experience that the consideration of this question cannot be undertaken too soon. It may be suggested that the class for whom new accommodation is more urgently required is the private class, and it is worthy of consideration whether such extension should be in the form of separate houses or villas. The advantages of segregate buildings for all institutions are now becoming widely recognised, but in the case of children who are particularly subject to epidemic infection their value is greatly enhanced. For this and other reasons it is learned with much satisfaction that there is a prospect of acquiring the small piece of land to the west of the institution. The existing buildings are already sufficiently large for the area of ground they cover, and it would not be advisable to add to them except in case of necessity. The erection of a villa for pupils paying the higher rates of board would set free accommodation in the main buildings which is required for other inmates. It is hoped that when the new piece of ground referred to is acquired, the Directors will not lose sight of the proposal to erect a small hospital.

The books and registers were examined and found correct.

LUNATIC DEPARTMENT OF H.M. GENERAL PRISON.

PERTH, 28th *March* 1901.

To the Secretary of the General Board of Lunacy.

SIR,—I have to report that at this date I visited the Lunatic Department of Perth General Prison.

Appendix B.

Commissioners
Entries.
———
H.M. General
Prison, Perth.

On 19th December 1900, the date of last visit, there were 37 men and 8 women resident. Since then, 2 men have been admitted, 1 man and 1 woman have been discharged as pauper lunatics to District Asylums, and 1 man has been discharged to the Penal Department. The above changes leave 37 men and 7 women resident at this date.

During the inspection all inmates were given an opportunity of making any statement they desired. Only one man made complaints as to his treatment, but investigation disclosed that they were the outcome of delusions of suspicion. Several complained of their detention.

The clothing and personal neatness of the inmates were satisfactory, and their physical health and condition indicated a suitable and liberal dietary. With very few exceptions their behaviour was quiet and orderly. One man and one woman were in seclusion, the former on account of physical illness and the latter on account of mania. It is recommended that a Register of Seclusion be kept, similar to that in use in asylums. At present its use is entered in the case records of each inmate secluded.

The male wards have been repainted and redecorated, and made brighter and more cheerful in appearance. The brackets and pipes in connection with the cisterns of the water-closets have been encased in wood, and the facilities for suicide have consequently been lessened.

The female department was in excellent order, scrupulously clean, and comfortably furnished.

PERTH, 6th *December* 1901.

To the Secretary of the General Board of Lunacy.

Sir,—I have to report that I this day visited the Lunatic Department of the Perth General Prison. There are 39 men and 7 women resident at present. Since the 28th March of the present year, the date of the last official visit by one of the Commissioners in Lunacy, 4 men and 1 woman have been admitted, 1 man has been sent to an ordinary asylum, and 1 man and 1 woman have, with the sanction of the Secretary of State, been placed in private dwellings. There has been no death during the period covered by this report.

The wards were found in good order. The house now occupied by the female inmates approaches closely to the ideal of a private residence. The rooms are nicely decorated, comfortably furnished and well lighted. While everything has been done to ensure detention, the methods employed to this end are as inconspicuous as possible and in no way interfere with the home-like character of the building. Any similar modification in the direction of improving the accommodation for the male inmates would add greatly to the comfort of the latter and would undoubtedly react favourably on their mental health. The inmates of the wards as a whole were, with one or two exceptions, quiet and free from excitement, and their physical wants seem to be liberally and judiciously attended to.

The living rooms were properly heated and the sleeping apartments were clean and comfortably supplied with bed coverings. The good supply of books and newspapers throughout the wards attracted favourable attention.

APPENDIX C.

Appendix C.

Reports on
Patients in
Private
Dwellings.

Report by
Dr. John
Macpherson.

GENERAL REPORTS ON THE CONDITION OF PATIENTS IN PRIVATE DWELLINGS.

REPORT BY DR. JOHN MACPHERSON.

I have to report that during the past year I visited the patients resident in private dwellings in the county of Fife. The following statement shows the number of patients and their classification :—

	M.	F.	T.
Single Patients—			
(a) Private and Curatory,	5	15	20
(b) Pauper,	30	54	84
Pauper Patients in Specially Licensed Houses,	126	260	386
	161	329	490

A separate report upon the condition of each patient was, as usual, transmitted to the Board immediately after the patient was visited. With one or two exceptions, I have not felt called upon to report in an unfavourable sense on the management or care of any of the patients, and any recommendations which may have been made in the direction of improving the circumstances or increasing the comfort of individual cases have, as a rule, been promptly attended to.

Considering that the boarded-out patients in Fife number nearly 500 and that they are widely spread over the county, it was both surprising and gratifying to find an almost uniformly satisfactory standard of care prevailing throughout the houses in which the patients live. As might be expected, some of the houses liberally exceeded the ordinary requirements, and perhaps many more fell below the average standard, but it is worthy of record that in few instances was it suspected that the food, personal clothing, or the sleeping arrangements for the patients were defective. The reasons for adverse criticism or for recommending the removal of patients were entirely based upon either personal defects in the guardians or upon the unsuitability o the patients for private care.

The uniformity in the care of the insane in this county is probably due to the long period of time during which the system of boarding-out has been organised there, to the liberal and uniform allowance for maintenance paid by the two parishes of Edinburgh and Glasgow, to which the majority of the patients are chargeable, and to the regular supervision of the houses by the officials of these parishes as well as by the Dundee Parish Council, which also boards out extensively in this county.

Appendix C.

Reports on
Patients in
Private
Dwellings.

Report by Dr.
J. F. Suther-
land.

REPORT BY DR. J. F. SUTHERLAND.

SIR,—I beg to submit the following general report, and accompanying statistical returns, bearing upon the work accomplished by me during 1901, in the visitation of the private and pauper insane in private dwellings, resident in the counties specified in the subjoined Tables.

TABLE I.

1901. Counties Visited.	Parishes Visited.	A.—Private and Curatory Patients.			B.—Pauper Patients.						Total of B.	Total of A and B.	Number of Visits Made.
					Single Patients.			In Specially Licensed Houses.					
		M.	F.	T.	M.	F.	T.	M.	F.	T.			
Aberdeen .	47	7	7	14	34	62	96	8	6	14	110	124	124
Ayr . . .	25	2	8	10	33	26	58	21	72	93	151	161	219
Bute & Arran .	6	7	4	11	17	14	31	4	6	10	41	52	92
Caithness .	10	–	–	–	32	46	78	1	1	2	80	80	80
Elgin . .	12	5	5	10	16	17	33	–	4	4	48	48	48
Fife—Markinch & Kennoway	2	–	1	1	7	15	22	42	85	127	149	150	} 780
Fife — Other Parishes	42	5	14	19	23	39	62	84	175	259	321	340	
Kincardine .	10	3	3	6	2	5	7	3	9	12	19	25·	25
Kinross . .	4	1	–	1	3	1	4	19	32	51	55	56	98
Kirkcudbright .	11	3	4	7	4	16	20	–	–	–	20	27	27
Nairn . .	3	1	–	1	4	4	8	–	–	–	8	9	9
Orkney . .	16	1	1	2	21	22	43	–	–	–	43	45	45
Perth . .	50	16	17	33	52	44	96	80	101	181	277	310	509
Ross . .	27	2	4	6	60	61	121	–	–	–	121	127	128
Shetland .	13	2	–	2	19	28	47	–	–	–	47	49	49
Sutherland .	12	1	–	1	9	21	30	–	–	–	30	31	31
Wigtown .	10	–	–	–	8	15	23	–	–	–	23	23	23
Total, .	300	56	68	124	345	437	782	261	490	751	1533	1657	2186

From the foregoing Table referable to the 300 parishes in the 16 specified counties, with a population of 1,281,670, it would appear that 1657 patients were visited, and that 2186 visits were made. Of the patients visited, however, those in Fifeshire, numbering 490, were visited by Mr. Commissioner Macpherson, of whom 290 were a second time visited by me. The number of patients visited by me was thus 1457, and the total number of visits paid by me, including the revisitation of districts in which aggregations occurred, was 1986. Of the total insane poor visited, 606 were males and 927 females, the sex ratio thus being 100 to 153.

GENERAL OBSERVATIONS.

Reviewing my work for the year, I desire to make special reference to two or three aspects of boarding out—*first*, the sex ratio of the insane found in private dwellings ; *second*, the distribution of the small colonies, and the percentage of insane to population in the villages and rural districts in which there are aggregations ; and *third*, the relative adaptability of the sexes for domestic care. With regard to the disposal of the insane, it would appear that in the half of Scotland which I have officially visited, the number placed singly is nearly the same as that in the licensed houses in which 2, 3, or 4 are lodged. In the former there were 782 provided for, in the latter 751. The proportion of males to females among the single patients is 100 to 126 ; among the groups of two, three, and four 100 to 186, a ratio which favours the generally accepted view that the female insane in association do better than

Appendix C.

Reports on
Patients in
Private
Dwellings.

———

Report by Dr.
J. F. Suther-
land.

males. The average ratio for both in all the 16 counties is 100 to 153, the three counties of Aberdeen, Caithness, and Kinross approximating it, while the six counties of Kirkcudbright (100:400), Kincardine (100:280), Sutherland (100:230), Fife (100:200), Wigtown (100:181), and Ayr (100:180) exceed it as much on the one hand as the four counties of Shetland (100:100), Ross (100:101), Orkney (100:104), and Perth (100:110) fall below it. The sex ratio of the aggregations in the 18 rural districts of the five counties of Fife, Perth, Kinross, Ayr, and Arran, with 211 patients, is 100 to 100, but in the 24 villages of these counties (Table II.), with 431 patients, it is 100 to 280, or nearly three to one. In 8 of the villages—Gartmore, Scone, Ballantrae, Craigrothie, Kilconquhar, Bilmullo, Largo, and Milton of Balgonie—with 180 insane, 173 are females, and only 7 males.

In the 27 parishes in the five counties referred to there is a population of 66,200 and 662 insane, or 43 per cent. of all visited, giving a percentage to population of 1. The percentages in certain villages may be regarded as already sufficiently high, but it cannot be said that the capacity to receive patients of all the rural districts and most of the villages in these counties has been exhausted. In the villages and rural districts of these five counties, in order to bring the percentage of either sex or both up to 5, a percentage by no means excessive or likely to give a colour to the population, 2340 additional patients would require to be boarded out. This calculation gives a fair conception of what might be done to extend boarding-out in rural districts, in villages already to a slight extent utilised, and in parishes in Scotland not yet made use of in that way, provided sufficiently encouraging pecuniary inducements were held out to suitable guardians, inducements much below the cost of patients in asylums. I am satisfied, having now traversed almost every parish in Scotland, and visited patients in 600 parishes, that the possibilities are great if only inspectors of poor as a whole, following the excellent example of a few, bestowed the time, labour, trouble, and care necessary to make boarding-out a success.

In alluding to certain villages with somewhat high percentages to population, and in suggesting that the maximum had been reached, it is proper to qualify this expression of opinion by observing that in two of them, including the largest village colony—that of Gartmore, with 58—the patients are all females with the exception of two, and in seven more villages with 122 patients the females far outnumber the males. There need be little doubt that the percentage in villages of females may safely, and with regard to all interests, be double that of males, having regard to the facts that unmanageable habits are less common among females than males, and also that female patients adapt themselves more readily to the kinds of employment, multifarious and light, which are to be met with in village dwellings. On the other hand, the percentage of patients, whether male or female, in rural districts may, in the interests of patients, their guardians and families, and without injury to the public, be double that of the villages, the dwellings or farmhouses being, as a rule, so far apart as to bar the suggestion of patients mingling with each other, or with sane neighbours who may or may not take in insane boarders.

The difficulty of finding suitable work for many men in village homes too often leads to enforced idleness and inactivity, and induces a condition of discontent which not unfrequently ends in return to the asylum. Thus it is that men do better in farming districts, to which they are sent in numbers almost identical with females, the ratio being 100 to 100. Females do equally well in village or country, some adapting themselves to field and farm work, others to domestic duties. Of course the small farmers have a preference for males with a certain capacity for work.

Appendix C.

TABLE II.

Reports on Patients in Private Dwellings.

Report by Dr J. F. Sutherland.

Showing the Number and Sex of the Aggregations of Lunatic Poor Boarded-out in the Village and Rural Districts of Fife, Perth, Kinross, Ayr, and Arran.

County and Parish.	Districts.	1901 Popula- tion.	Patients.			Percentage of Patients to Population.
			M.	F.	T.	
I. FIFE—						
1. Markinch	Thornton Village	1,385	6	14	20	*1·4*
	Milton of Balgonie, Village	471	–	23	23	*4·9*
	Windygates ,,	913	10	3	13	*1·4*
	Markinch Rural	4,034	2	17	19	*·4*
2. Kennoway	Kennoway Village	800	9	14	23	*2·8*
	Star ,,	220	8	16	24	*10·9*
	Kennoway Rural	485	4	2	6	*1·2*
3. Falkland	Freuchie Village	880	10	20	30	*3·4*
	Falkland ,,	809	4	3	7	*·8*
	,, Rural	540	1	4	5	*·9*
4. Strathmiglo	Strathmiglo Village	966	6	8	14	*1·4*
	,, Rural	650	2	2	4	*·6*
5. Auchtermuchty	Dunshalt Village	300	–	9	9	*3·*
	Auchtermuchty Village	1,429	11	22	33	*2·3*
6. Collessie	Ladybank ,,	1,340	7	2	9	*·6*
	Collessie Rural	821	2	5	7	*·8*
7. Kettle	Kettle Parish	1,757	6	25	31	*1·7*
8. Leuchars	Balmullo Village	320	1	12	13	*4·*
9. Largo	Largo ,,	1,341	1	8	9	*·6*
10. Kilconquhar	Kilconquhar ,,	334	3	11	14	*4·1*
11. Ceres	Craigrothie ,,	129	–	12	12	*9·3*
	Totals for 15 Villages	11,637	76	177	253	*2·1*
	Totals for 7 Rural	8,287	17	55	72	*·8*
	Both	19,924	93	232	325	*1·6*
II. PERTH—						
1. Port of Menteith	Gartmore Village	350	2	56	58	*16·5*
	Port of Menteith Rural	738	11	4	15	*2·1*
2. Kincardine	Thornhill Village	388	2	7	9	*2·3*
3. Ardoch	Ardoch Parish	916	17	–	17	*1·8*
4. Blackford	Blackford ,,	1,539	7	–	7	*·4*
5. Scone	Scone Village	1,585	2	20	22	*1·3*
6. Auchtergave	Bankfoot and Waterloo } Villages	755	10	6	16	*2·*
7. Cargill	Wolfhill Village	132	4	5	9	*6·7*
8. Kinclaven	Kinclaven Parish	637	6	2	8	*1·2*
	Total for 5 Villages	3,210	20	94	114	*3·5*
	Total for 4 Rural	3,830	41	6	47	*1·2*
	Both	7,040	61	100	161	*2·2*
III. KINROSS—						
1. Portmoak	Kinneswood Village	225	8	9	17	*7·5*
	Wester Balgedie ,,	78	6	3	9	*11·5*
	Portmoak Rural	524	5	1	6	*1·1*
2. Orwell	Milnathort Village	1,052	3	6	9	*·9*
IV. AYR—						
1. Ballantrae	Ballantrae Village	600	–	29	29	*4·8*
	,, Rural	524	4	9	13	*2·4*
2. Colmonell	Colmonell Parish	1,950	2	8	10	*·5*
3. Kirkoswald	Kirkoswald ,,	1,577	10	1	11	*·7*
4. Dunlop	Dunlop ,,	1,542	–	10	10	*·6*
V. ARRAN—						
1. Kilmore	Kilmore Parish	2,311	17	12	29	*1·2*
2. Kilbride	Kilbride ,,	2,532	9	4	13	*·5*
	Grand Total for Villages	16,202	113	318	431	*2·6*
	Grand Total for Rural	23,077	105	106	211	*·9*
	Grand Total for Both	39,279	218	424	642	*1·6*

This return refers to 642 patients (m. 218, f. 424), for the most part chargeable to the urban parishes of Edinburgh, Glasgow, Govan, Dundee, and Leith, and residing in 27 parishes in the five counties of Fife, Perth, Kinross, Ayr, and Arran. Males are to females in the proportion of 100 to 194. The village colonies in these parishes number 24, and in the aggregate amount to 431 patients, males being to females in the ratio of 100 to 280. The rural colonies, numbering 18, have 211 patients, males being to females as 100 to 100.

Appendix C.

Reports on Patients in Private Dwellings.

Report by Dr. J. F. Sutherland.

The principal village colonies are those in Fifeshire of Thornton 20, Milton of Balgonie 23 (all females), Kennoway 23, Star 24, Freuchie 30, Strathmiglo 14, Auchtermuchty 33, Kilconquhar 14, Balmullo 13 (all females save one), ·Craigrothie 12 (all females), and Dunshalt 9 (all females) ; in Perthshire, Gartmore 58 (all females save two), Scone 22 (all females save two), Bankfoot and Waterloo 16, Wolfhill 9 ; in Kinross, Kinneswood 17, Wester Bargeddie 9 ; and in Ayrshire, Ballantrae 29 (all females).

The chief rural aggregations are to be found in Fifeshire in the parishes of Markinch 19, Kettle (village and rural) 31 ; in Perthshire, Port of Monteith 15, Ardoch 17 (all males) ; in Ayrshire, Ballantrae 13, Colmonell 10, Kirkoswald 11, Dunlop 10 ; and in Arran, Kilbride 13, Kilmore 29.

In the 24 village aggregations the percentages to population which exceed 5 are to be found in Star 10·9, Craigrothie (females) 9·3, Gartmore (females) 16·5, Wolfhill 6·7, Kinneswood 7·5, Wester Balgedie 11·5. The highest rural percentage, viz. 2·4, is to be found in Ballantrae parish. Having visited Fifeshire for the first time six years ago I am in a position to compare the results of my visit of 1896 with that of 1901. Considerable changes have taken place, not least that in the 11 parishes specified in the foregoing table there has been in the interval a diminution of 102 patients, or 23 per cent., and the 15 villages in these parishes contribute no less than 94 of this reduction, the principal contributors being Thornton, Windygates, Kettle and Kettlebridge, Ladybank, Kennoway, Star, and Strathmiglo.

On the other hand there have been slight increases at Freuchie and Craigrothie.

It is safe to say that the capacity of many of these villages and rural districts for receiving suitable cases has not by any means been exhausted.

TABLE III.

Changes during 1901 among the Lunatic Poor in private dwellings chargeable to the 16 counties enumerated *infra*.

COUNTIES.	(a)					(b) Admissions.			Balances + or –
	Died.	Recovered.	Removed to Asylums.	Removed from Roll.	Total.	Discharged from Asylum Unrecovered.	Intimated by Inspectors of Poor.	Total.	
Aberdeen	5	1	4	–	10	4	4	8	– 2
Ayr	4	–	4	4	12	1	4	5	– 7
Bute and Arran	1	1	1	–	3	–	–	–	– 3
Caithness	7	–	1	1	9	–	5	5	– 4
Elgin	·2	–	1	–	3	–	–	–	– 3
Fife	9	1	3	1	14	2	5	7	– 7
Kincardine	–	–	–	–	–	–	–	–	–
Kinross	–	–	–	1	1	1	–	1	–
Kirkcudbright	1	–	–	–	1	–	2	2	+ 1
Nairn	–	–	–	–	–	–	–	–	–
Orkney	1	–	–	–	1	2	6	8	+ 7
Perth	5	1	6	–	12	7	–	7	– 5
Ross	10	–	3	1	14	5	8	13	– 1
Shetland	2	–	2	–	4	–	3	3	– 1
Sutherland	2	1	1	–	4	–	2	2	– 2
Wigtown	–	–	2	–	2	–	–	–	– 2
	49	5	28	8	90	22	39	61	– 29

Apendix C.

Reports on
Patients in
Private
Dwellings.

Report by Dr.
J. F. Suther-
land.

The outstanding fact revealed by this return is that there are 29 fewer patients this year in private dwellings chargeable to parishes in these 16 counties than last year, and this in spite of the fact that the death-rate has been low. With the exception of Orkney it may be said that the balance of admissions over deaths, &c., is on the wrong side.

ADMISSIONS.

The mental defects and derangements met with among the 98 (males 35, females 63) residing in, although not all chargeable to, the 16 counties specified, who were seen and examined for the first time during the current year were as follows :—

Imbecility (congenital or acquired in early life),	28
Dementia,	36
Senile Dementia,	9
Paranoia and Delusional Insanity,	16
Melancholia,	6
Mania,	2
General Paralysis of the Insane,	1
	—
	98

Dementia thus accounts for 33 per cent., senile dementia 9 per cent., and both combined 42 per cent. ; imbecility for 28 per cent., and delusional insanity 16 per cent. The only observation which these figures call for is that relative to dementia and other disorders the proportion of imbeciles is much smaller than in former years.

Of the 98, 23 were left with or placed under the care of related guardians, 75 with strangers. The relative position of related and unrelated guardians is also being reversed.

The following figures give the number of patients in each of the divisions into which the ages naturally and conveniently divide :—

Under 15.	15–20	21–30	31–40	41–50	51–60	61–70	71–80	Above 80.	Total.
2	11	14	18	9	21	15	8	–	98

From this analysis it would appear that the ages of 23, or 23 per cent., of the entrants exceeded 60 years, and 8, or 8 per cent., 70 years. The majority of the twenty-three patients of an age exceeding 60 were suffering from senile dementia more or less in evidence, and many of them struck one as belonging to that dependent class in the community who in years not very remote would have been classed as ordinary paupers.

REMOVAL TO ASYLUMS.

Removals took place in 63 instances, 29 being males and 34 females. Considering that in private dwellings males are to females in the proportion of 100 to 153, it is plain that the male sex contributes considerably more than its share of these returns. The excess may be put at 7, or 24 per cent. The percentage of such returns may be expressed by 4, by no means a large figure, rather a remarkably small one, and one calculated to encourage asylum superintendents and inspectors of poor to make the fullest trial of the private dwelling.

It may be of interest to note that, of sixty-one of those removed to asylums whose cases I have investigated, 16, or 26 per cent., were under 1 year in private dwellings ; 27, or 42 per cent., under 2 years ; 17, or 28 per cent., between 3 and 10 years ; and 15, or 25 per cent., from 11 up to 30 years. The return of those whose stay might be considered brief was necessitated by the manifestation either of wandering tendencies or unmanageable dispositions, both of which are difficult of control in family. In the case of those who had spent a large part of their lives in private dwellings their return was due to faulty habits, physical diseases, and the infirmities inseparable from old age.

The principal cause, and the numbers referable to each cause as stated in intimations made by inspectors of poor, may be summarised as follows :—*First*, requiring institutional treatment and appliances because of physical disease and exacerbation of mental malady, 15 ; *second*, unmanageable, impulsive, quarrelsome, nocturnally noisy, discontented, &c., 20 ; *third*, wandering and unsettled habits, 7 ; *fourth*, sexual risks arising from eroticism or inefficient guardianship, 3 ; *fifth*, bad or indifferent care, and inability of inspectors of poor at the time to find suitable guardians, 6 ; and *sixth*, on educational grounds there were sent to imbecile training institutions, 3. While these six caus s combined account for 54, or 85 per cent., of all who were removed, the second and third account for no less than 27 transfers (14 males, 13 females), or 50 per cent. It is evident that males in proportion to their numbers are much more prone to the wandering habit and noxious propensities than females. Were the liability in this direction uniform, then, instead of 14 males, the number should be 8, or 42 per cent. less.

Appendix C.

Reports on Patients in Private Dwellings.

Report by Dr. J. F. Sutherland.

RECOVERIES AND REMOVALS FROM ROLL.

Residing in the counties referred to, of recoveries there were 13, and of removals 11, six being males and five females—one of the latter, after a very brief residence, becoming impulsive and not easily managed.

The causes of the 64 deaths as certified by the Parochial Medical Officers were as undermentioned :—

1. Cerebral and Spinal Affections :—
   (1) Apoplexy, Hemiplegia, &c., 14
   (2) Chronic Hydrocephalus . 1
   (3) Convulsions . . . 2
   (4) General Paralysis . . 1
   (5) Diffuse Myelitis . . 1
   ———
   19

2. Thoracic Affections :—
   (1) Heart Disease . . . 15
   (2) Pneumonia . . . 5
   (3) Bronchitis . . . 5
   (4) Phthisis 1
   (5) Congestion of Lungs . 1
   ———
   27

3. Abdominal Affections :—
   (1) Acute Peritonitis . . 1
   (2) Malignant Tumour . . 1
   ———
   2

4. Specific Diseases :—
   (1) Influenza 1
   (2) Septicæmia . . . 1
   (3) Acute Tuberculosis . . 1
   ———
   3

5. Other Diseases :—
   (1) Senile Debility, Senile Decay, Senile Marasmus 7
   (2) Senile Gangrene . . 1
   (3) General Debility . . 3
   (4) Retained Menses . . 1
   (5) Unascertained . . . 13
   ———
   64

The percentage death-rate of patients residing in the 16 counties, calculated on those seen and on the small number not seen owing to their coming upon the register after official visitation of the district had been made, is, as near as possible, four. This may be considered a low death-rate, and much lower than last year, and indeed most years. To brain and spinal lesions 30 per cent. of the deaths are set down, to pulmonary and cardiac diseases 42 per cent., and to various senile causes 17 per cent.

Of the 64 deaths, 29 were those of males, 35 those of females. Males in proportion to their numbers yield 7, or 24 per cent., more deaths than females.

The number of deaths at certain age periods is as follows :—

[TABLE.

Appendix C.

	Under 20.	20–30.	31–40.	41–50.	51–60.	61–70.	71–80.	Above 80.	Total.
Reports on Patients in Private Dwellings. Report by Dr. J. P. Sutherland.	3	7	6	7	10	15	11	5	64

It will be observed that the ages of 25 per cent. exceed 70 years, and 48 per cent. 60 years, and, further, that of the 64, 8, or 12 per cent., have been on the register of the insane in private dwellings for less than 1 year; 28, or 43 per cent., less than 5 years; 19, or 30 per cent., between 5 and 10; and above 20 years, 12, or 18 per cent. The longevity which so many attain, and the long periods of life spent amid natural and normal conditions, may be referred to in support of the private dwelling as the most suitable destiny for a large proportion of the insane poor, in addition to many other strong reasons which need not be urged now. ·

Twenty-one resided with related guardians, 43 with unrelated.

PRIVATE AND CURATORY PATIENTS.

Of these there were visited 124, 56 being males and 68 females. Save in two cases the position of each was satisfactory, one of the two being a male imbecile whose treatment in several respects did not indicate much consideration, the other being an elderly female suffering from carcinoma of the breast, and who required hospital treatment. In three more instances minor recommendations were made to curators, relatives, and guardians to improve somewhat upon what was being already done to promote the happiness and well-being of those, many of them advanced in years, whose person and property were committed to the care of others.

The deaths of twelve was made known, 8 being curatory and 4 private; 10 were females and 2 males. Seventeen were seen for the first time, 13 (5 m. and 8 f.) being curatory and 4 (2 m. and 2 f.) private cases.

REPORT BY DR. CHARLES MACPHERSON.

Appendix C.

Reports on Patients in Private Dwellings.

Report by Dr Charles Macpherson.

I have the honour to submit the following report of the work done by me in connection with the visitation of the insane in private dwellings during the year 1901.

The district visited includes seventeen counties, and the number of the patients visited is shown in the following Table :—

TABLE I.

Counties Visited.	Parishes Visited.	Private and Curatory Patients.			Pauper Patients.						Number of Patients Visited.	Number of Visits Paid.
					Single Patients.			In Specially Licensed Houses.				
		M.	F.	T.	M.	F.	T.	M.	F.	T.		
Argyll, . .	21	3	6	9	42	34	76	8	11	19	104	104
Banff, . -	16	1	2	3	28	34	62	–	5	5	70	70
Berwick, -	10	–	2	2	7	13	20	2	2	4	26	26
Clackmannan, -	3	–	1	1	2	2	4	–	2	2	7	7
Dumbarton, -	9	3	4	7	4	8	12	2	–	2	21	21
Dumfries, -	16	2	3	5	12	11	23	–	2	2	30	30
Edinburgh, -	18	24	40	64	26	40	66	2	13	15	145	145
Forfar, -	26	2	6	8	28	37	65	3	18	21	94	94
Haddington, -	8	2	2	4	5	8	13	–	–	–	17	17
Inverness, -	19	5	5	10	52	85	137	11	20	31	178	257
Lanark, -	21	15	9	24	46	93	139	24	73	97	260	336
Linlithgow, -	5	1	–	1	3	5	8	–	–	–	9	9
Peebles, -	3	2	1	3	1	3	4	–	–	–	7	7
Renfrew, -	12	6	7	13	7	9	16	–	2	2	31	32
Roxburgh, -	8	3	4	7	9	14	23	–	–	–	30	30
Selkirk, -	4	1	–	1	2	6	8	–	–	–	9	9
Stirling, - -	18	7	12	19	20	20	40	60	99	159	218	338
Western Isles,-	13	1	–	1	59	66	125	–	–	–	126	126
Totals, -	230	78	104	182	353	488	841	112	247	359	1382	1558

As usual, a report on each individual case was forwarded to the Board immediately after the visit.

With the exception of the counties of Dumfries, Edinburgh, and Inverness, the whole of the district visited was, to me, new ground. The impression left by the visit was, on the whole, a favourable one. As must always occur when dealing with such large numbers, it was found necessary in a few cases to recommend removal of patients to other guardianship or to an asylum. In other cases there were minor defects which required only to be pointed out to be rectified. I saw no patient who bore the slightest appearance of being insufficiently fed. The most frequent defects to which I had to call attention were insufficient bed-clothing and defective attention to cleanliness, and in the great majority of these cases the guardians at once promised to have the defects remedied.

I was very agreeably surprised with the condition of matters found generally in the Western Isles. One hears so often of the poverty of the people there that I feared, judging by the usually very small alimentary allowances given for the patients, that I would find many indications of defective care and diet. I, however, found that these patients generally would compare favourably as regards robust appearance with any in Scotland. The great majority of them are living with relatives in what has always been their home, and they share every-

Appendix C.

Reports on
Patients in
Private
Dwellings.

Report by Dr.
Charles.
Macpherson.

thing equally with the family. There may be a want of variety, but there is always plenty of food, such as porridge and milk, potatoes, fish, eggs, etc. The impression left on my mind was that while the money allowance could not as a rule repay the guardians anything like the cost of the food supplied, still the patients were as well fed as they would be if the allowance were doubled or trebled. As a contrast to the small money allowance, the supply of clothing—especially in the Lewis parishes—is very generous. Both bed and body clothing are of excellent quality and are liberally supplied. The small money allowance has, however, this disadvantage. It often makes it difficult for an Inspector of Poor to induce the relatives of an asylum patient to take him home; and when patients prove in any degree troublesome the guardians are very apt to demand their immediate removal: whereas, if the money paid as aliment was such as to form an important item of the household income they would put up with a certain amount of inconvenience rather than lose it.

At Benderloch in Argyllshire there is a small colony of male patients chargeable to Paisley which is in my opinion an ideal one. There are no licensed houses; all are single patients. The guardians are small farmers or large crofters. The houses are in a good state of repair. The patients were all in good physical condition, usefully employed, and none of them had any complaint to make as to the diet or their treatment by the guardians. They were all well clad in good tweed suits and had ample supplies of under-clothing. Each man was provided with a warm overcoat, a sailor's oilskin coat, and leggings, so that they are thoroughly protected during wet weather. In addition to the statutory visits of the Inspector of Poor, the colony is visited once a year by a deputation from the Parish Council, and the Medical Officer immediately after each of his quarterly visits sends a report to the Inspector of Poor on each individual case. The district is a most suitable one for patients, and their number might with advantage be increased. It is satisfactory to know, on the authority of the Inspector of Poor, that, notwithstanding the very liberal treatment of the patients, the cost to the parish is less than that incurred in the asylum, and that his Council are willing and anxious to board out, on similar lines, all the patients they can get from the asylum.

The Glasgow Parochial Authorities continue to develop their boarding-out system in a praiseworthy manner, and I have been informed recently by Mr. Motion, that he is at present selecting homes for 30 patients from Woodilee Asylum. A regular system is now pursued regarding every asylum patient chargeable to this parish. The assistant Inspector of the part of the parish from which the patient has been removed visits the asylum at stated intervals, sees these patients, and hears as to their present condition from the attendants in charge, and, when necessary, from the Medical Officer. He then reports to the Inspector what he has learned—the work each patient is engaged in; whether noisy, impulsive, or epileptic; his habits as to cleanliness, speech, and behaviour generally, and the conclusions he has come to as to his suitability for private care. These reports are carefully revised by the Inspector, and a list of the patients is drawn up for discussion with the Medical Superintendent as to their fitness for removal from the asylum. There is no doubt that the result of this course of action will be the removal of an increased number of patients, as the attention of the Medical Superintendent will thus be frequently drawn to individual cases whose fitness for private care might not otherwise be specially noticed among such large numbers.

Changes.

During the year there have been 66 deaths among the patients resident. Forty-six patients have been returned to the asylum, this number, however, including several who were out on probation and had only been out for a very short time. Six have been discharged recovered, and 11 have been removed from the roll.

Deaths.

The death-rate has been considerably lower than that of last year, and amounts to about 4·7 per cent. of the cases visited. There is an absence of all epidemic causes. Influenza was certified as the cause of a large number of

Appendix C.

Reports on
Patients in
Private
Dwellings.

Report by Dr.
Charles
Macpherson.

deaths in 1900, but during last year no death has been certified as due to influenza. The average age at death was 60·8 years.

1 was 92.	7 were between 40 and 50.	
11 were between 80 and 90.	2 „ „ 30 „ 40.	
19 „ „ 70 „ 80.	4 „ „ 20 „ 30.	
8 „ „ 60 „ 70.	1 was „ 16 „ 20.	
13 „ „ 50 „ 60.		

The causes of death, as certified by the medical attendants, may be grouped as follows, viz. :—

1. Cerebral Affections :—
   (a) Apoplexy and Paralysis - - - - - 11
   (b) Epilepsy and Convulsions - - - - - 2
   — 13
2. Thoracic Affections :—
   (a) Phthisis Pulmonalis - - - - - - 2
   (b) Pneumonia or Bronchitis - - - - - 11
   (c) Disease of the Heart - - - - - - 10
   — 23
3. Abdominal Affections :—
   (a) Inflammatory - - - - - - - 5
   (b) Disease of Liver, Kidneys, &c. - - - - 2
   (c) Cancer - - - - - - - - 3
   — 10
4. General Debility and Senile Decay - - - - 17
5. Drowning (Suicidal) - - - - - - - 1

   Total - - - 64

The last-mentioned case was that of an old woman of 74 who was found drowned in a well. She had been in a private dwelling for many years and had never shown any suicidal tendencies. An inquiry was held by the Procurator-Fiscal and the evidence showed that no blame could be attached to the guardian.

REMOVALS TO ESTABLISHMENTS.

These have been rather numerous. In some cases the removal was undoubtedly due to defective guardianship. Three were epileptics, whose seizures had become more severe ; 7 were inclined to wander ; 20 were returned as noisy, excitable, or unmanageable ; 3 were sent in for medical or surgical treatment ; 2 on account of the death of their guardians, and the difficulty at the time of procuring suitable guardians for them ; and 1 was sent to Baldovan Institution.

There are no special circumstances to report regarding the recoveries or removals from the poor-roll.

In addition to my usual work in connection with the boarded-out insane, I assisted, during the year, at the visitation of 17 institutions. While visiting the Inverness District Asylum, along with Mr. Commissioner Fraser, attention was directed to the number of patients in that institution who did not appear to require asylum treatment, and at Dr. Fraser's request Dr. Keay sent me a list of all those who he considered might be tried in private dwellings. The list contained the names of 82 patients chargeable to 51 different parishes in the Counties of Nairn, Inverness, Ross and Sutherland. At the request of the Board I undertook to give what assistance I could to induce the Parochial Authorities to find suitable homes for these patients, and, in pursuance of this object, I paid special visits to the Inspectors and, in some cases, to the Chairmen and Medical Officers of 32 of these parishes. My ordinary work prevented me from overtaking the visitation of the other 19 parishes, but in these cases I communicated with the Inspector by letter, calling his attention to the names of the patients considered suitable for private care. In most cases the matter was taken up very heartily, though,

Appendix C.

Reports on f
Patients in
Private
Dwellings.

Report by Dr.
Charles
Macpherson.

as was to be expected, there were, in several instances, circumstances known to the Inspectors of Poor regarding the former conduct of some of these patients which seemed to make it undesirable to have them at home from the risk of their being either kept too closely confined, or becoming public nuisances. It was advised that these patients should not be removed from the asylum until further investigation had been made. In other cases —mostly in those regarding whom I had written and had not visited—I was assured that it was impossible to find homes for them. This, as we know by the experience of the Inspectors of the larger parishes, is not correct. A home may not be obtainable among the patient's friends, or even possibly in his native parish, but any Inspector who chooses to take some trouble, and to pay a suitable rate of maintenance, need have no difficulty in finding homes for quiet inoffensive patients. The result of the work, while not as great as one could wish, has been on the whole a success. Thirty of these patients have been discharged on twelve months' probation since the month of September, and I know that arrangements are in progress for providing homes for a considerable number more. As far as I at present know, none of these probationary patients has as yet had to be returned to the asylum. I am strongly of opinion that if time could be found for such work much good could be done by the visitation of parishes in many districts for the special purpose of calling attention to cases suitable for being boarded out, and my experience has clearly shown me that more can be done by a few minutes talk than by any amount of letter writing. I intend during the coming year to visit the 19 parishes which other work prevented me from visiting, and to see whether anything further can be done towards removing such of their patients still in the asylum as may be suited for domestic care. This experience in connection with Inverness District Asylum brings clearly home to one's mind the very large number of patients who, while not requiring asylum treatment, must be filling up the wards in almost all the Scottish asylums, thus causing overcrowding and the necessity for additional accommodation.

APPENDIX D.

Lunacy Districts (Scotland) Act, 1887 [50 & 51 *Vict.,* Ch. 39].
Prisons (Scotland) Act, 1877 [40 & 41 *Vict.,* Ch. 53, *Section* 61].

ORDER AND REGULATIONS ISSUED BY THE GENERAL BOARD
OF COMMISSIONERS IN LUNACY FOR SCOTLAND, IN
REGARD TO ALTERING AND VARYING THE RENFREW
LUNACY DISTRICT AND THE LANARK LUNACY DISTRICT.

THE ORDER.

Applications having been made to the General Board of Commissioners
in Lunacy for Scotland by the Parish Councils of Cathcart and of Eastwood
to alter and vary the Renfrew Lunacy District, at present consisting of the
County of Renfrew, and also to alter and vary the Lanark Lunacy District, at
present consisting of all parts of the County of Lanark which are not within
the Glasgow Lunacy District or the Govan Lunacy District, the General
Board of Commissioners in Lunacy for Scotland do hereby, in virtue of the
powers conferred upon them by the Lunacy Districts (Scotland) Act, 1887,
alter and vary the Renfrew Lunacy District and also the Lanark Lunacy
District in the following manner :—
1. The Renfrew Lunacy District shall consist of the County of Renfrew,
together with those portions of the Parishes of Cathcart and Eastwood which
are in the County of Lanark.
2. The Lanark Lunacy District shall consist of all parts of the County of
Lanark which are not within the Glasgow Lunacy District, the Govan Lunacy
District, or the Renfrew Lunacy District as defined in the immediately preceding paragraph.

THE REGULATIONS.

The General Board of Commissioners in Lunacy for Scotland do further, in
virtue of the powers conferred upon them by the Lunacy Districts (Scotland)
Act, 1887, make and issue the following Regulations which they consider
necessary in consequence of the alteration of the Renfrew and the Lanark
Lunacy Districts made by the foregoing Order :—
1. In consideration of the fact that the Parishes of Paisley and Greenock
have been wholly exempted by the Board from assessments for lunacy purposes
so long as they continue to provide asylum accommodation for their pauper
Lunatics to the satisfaction of the Board, the Burghs of Paisley and Greenock,
which are wholly situated within these Parishes, shall have no representation
on a District Lunacy Board for the Renfrew Lunacy District during such time
as these Parishes are wholly exempted from assessments for lunacy purposes.
2. There shall be elected to be the District Lunacy Board for the Renfrew
Lunacy District a Board consisting of Fourteen persons, of whom Nine shall
be elected by the County Council of Renfrew, Three by the Magistrates of the
Burgh of Glasgow, One by the Magistrates of the Burgh of Port-Glasgow, and
One by the Magistrates of the Burgh of Renfrew.
3. The County Council of Renfrew and the Magistrates of the Burghs of
Glasgow, Port-Glasgow, and Renfrew shall elect their respective representatives
on the Renfrew District Lunacy Board within twenty-eight days from the date
at which this Order and Regulations come into force, and the members of the
Board so elected shall meet and elect a Chairman, and Committees as soon

thereafter as may be convenient, at a time and place to be fixed by the General Board. The District Board so elected shall hold office only until the election of a new Board in the manner provided for in Regulation No. 4.

4. The County Council aforesaid shall elect representatives to serve on the Renfrew District Lunacy Board at their Statutory Meeting in December of the current year, and thereafter at their Annual Statutory Meeting in December of each year following ; and the Magistrates of the Burghs aforesaid shall elect representatives to serve on the Renfrew District Lunacy Board not earlier than the third lawful day after the first Tuesday in November and not later than the third Tuesday in December of the current year, and thereafter at a date within the above-mentioned days in each year following ; and the Board so elected shall meet and elect a Chairman and Committees as soon thereafter as may be convenient, at a time and place to be fixed by the General Board.

5. The constitution of the Lanark District Lunacy Board as determined by Regulation No. 4 of the Order and Regulations issued by the Board and approved of by the Secretary for Scotland on 25th July, 1888, shall remain unaltered.

6. The General Board reserve the power from time to time to alter and amend these Regulations as the public interest may require and experience suggest, and also, if requested, to hear and determine all questions or disputes which may arise out of the alteration of the Renfrew and Lanark Lunacy Districts by the foregoing Order, or as to the interpretation, meaning, or effect of, or any other question arising out of, the foregoing Order and these Regulations, or any of them, or otherwise in any manner of way.

7. The foregoing Order and Regulations shall come into force on the date when they receive the sanction of the Secretary for Scotland.

WALTER G. SCOTT, *Chairman.*
JOHN COWAN.
JOHN CHEYNE.
JOHN FRASER.
JOHN MACPHERSON.

GENERAL BOARD OF LUNACY,
     EDINBURGH, *26th June*, 1901.

BALFOUR OF BURLEIGH,
     His Majesty's Secretary for Scotland.

SCOTTISH OFFICE, WHITEHALL,
     8th July, 1901.

GLASGOW : PRINTED BY JAMES HEDDERWICK & SONS,
FOR HIS MAJESTY'S STATIONERY OFFICE.

REPORT ON DIETING OF PAUPER LUNATICS IN ASYLUMS AND LUNATIC WARDS OF POOR-HOUSES IN SCOTLAND, by DR. J. C. DUNLOP.

SUPPLEMENT

TO THE

FORTY-THIRD ANNUAL REPORT

OF THE

GENERAL BOARD OF COMMISSIONERS IN LUNACY FOR SCOTLAND.

Presented to both Houses of Parliament by Command of His Majesty.

GLASGOW:
PRINTED FOR HIS MAJESTY'S STATIONERY OFFICE
By JAMES HEDDERWICK & SONS,
At "The Citizen" Press, St. Vincent Place.

And to be purchased, either directly or through any Bookseller, from
OLIVER & BOYD, Edinburgh; or
EYRE & SPOTTISWOODE, East Harding Street, Fleet Street, E.C., and
32 Abingdon Street, Westminster, S.W.; or
E. PONSONBY, 116 Grafton Street, Dublin.

1902.

[Od. 955.]   Price 5½d.

SUPPLEMENT

TO THE

FORTY-THIRD ANNUAL REPORT.

TO THE RIGHT HONOURABLE

LORD BALFOUR OF BURLEIGH,

His Majesty's Secretary for Scotland.

GENERAL BOARD OF LUNACY,
EDINBURGH, 24th *January*, 1902.

MY LORD,

We have the honour to lay before you as a Supplement to our Forty-third Annual Report, and in accordance with the intention therein expressed, a Report furnished to us by Dr. James Craufurd Dunlop, Edinburgh, on the Dieting of Pauper Lunatics in Asylums and Lunatic Wards of Poorhouses in Scotland.

The Board are glad to observe that in the great majority of institutions the diets may be regarded as satisfactory, and that there are only a few cases in which they can be said to fall considerably short of the scientific standard adopted by Dr. Dunlop.

While the Board have no desire to suggest absolute uniformity in dietaries, they do not doubt that a careful study of this Report will suggest still further improvements in the dieting of the insane in our institutions.

We have the honour to be,

MY LORD,

Your most obedient humble Servants,

WALTER G. SCOTT, *Chairman.*
JOHN COWAN.
JOHN CHEYNE.
JOHN FRASER.
JOHN MACPHERSON.

T. W. L. SPENCE,
Secretary.

REPORT

TO THE

GENERAL BOARD OF LUNACY FOR SCOTLAND

ON THE

DIETING OF PAUPER LUNATICS IN ASYLUMS AND LUNATIC WARDS OF POORHOUSES IN SCOTLAND.

BY

JAMES CRAUFURD DUNLOP,
M.D., F.R.C.P., Edin.

CONTENTS.

REPORT TO THE GENERAL BOARD OF LUNACY FOR SCOTLAND ON THE DIETING OF PAUPER LUNATICS IN ASYLUMS AND LUNATIC WARDS OF POORHOUSES IN SCOTLAND.

I have the honour to submit to the Board my report on the dieting of pauper lunatics in Asylums and Lunatic Wards of Poorhouses in Scotland.

In the month of March, 1900, in compliance with instructions issued by the Board, a record was made of the actual issues of food in all asylums and poorhouses where pauper lunatics are treated, and the result of these records, together with details of the dietary regulations of the institutions, were returned to the Board on prescribed schedules. It is on the statements incorporated in these schedules that my report is founded. I have examined the schedules critically; and by correspondence in some cases, and by visits to the institutions in others, have satisfied myself that the facts recorded in them are reasonably correct. A copy of one of these schedules as filled up is given later. To save space copies of the others are omitted, and only the main facts stated.

In the report I shall give :—

1. Composition of those foodstuffs found to be used in asylum dietaries.

2. Tests for deciding the sufficiency and suitability of the diets.

3. A copy of a schedule as issued and filled up.

4. Details of, and remarks on, the dietaries of all asylums and poorhouses in Scotland where pauper lunatics are received.

5. General remarks on results got by the application of the tests referred to.

6. Suggestions for ensuring that all pauper lunatics are sufficiently and properly fed.

4

I. COMPOSITION OF FOODSTUFFS.

The large number of diets and the large number of foodstuffs in use made individual analysis of the foods and dishes a practical impossibility, and consequently I have utilised reliable average analyses. In the following Table the figures used in preparing this report are shown. The majority are taken from Bulletin 28, U.S. Board of Agriculture, Office of Experimental Station (Revised Edition), and some are from private analyses.

ANIMAL FOOD.

	Composition.		
	Proteid.	Fat.	Carbo-hydrate.
Beef, forequarter	18.3	18.9	—
,, hindquarter	19.3	18.3	—
,, sides	18.8	18.8	—
,, ribs	14.4	20.0	—
,, heads, hough, &c.	9.7	3.9	—
,, liver	20.7	4.5	1.5
,, heart	16.0	20.4	—
,, tripe	14.1	3.1	—
,, tinned	26.3	18.7	—
Mutton, sides	13.0	24.0	—
,, tinned	28.8	22.8	—.—
,, pluck (as liver)	23.1	9.0	5.0
Pork	12.0	29.8	—
Ham	14.5	33.2	—
Cod, fresh	16.7	.3	—
Haddock, fresh	17.2	.3	—.-
,, Findon	23.3	.2	—
Herring, fresh	11.2	3.9	—
,, red	20.5	8.8	—
Stock fish	27.3	.3	—
Suet	4.7	81.8	—
Lard	—	100.0	—
Dripping	—	97.7	—
Margarine	1.2	83.0	—
Butter	1.0	85.0	—
Eggs	11.9	9.3	—
Milk, whole	3.3	4.0	5.0
,, skimmed	3.4	.3	5.1
,, butter	3.0	.5	4.8
,, condensed	8.8	8.3	54.1
Cheese	27.7	36.8	4.1

VEGETABLE FOOD

	Composition.		
	Proteid.	Fat.	Carbo-hydrate.
Bread, white - - - - -	9.2	1.3	53.1
„ brown - - - -	5.4	1.8	47.1
Buns - - - - - - -	6.3	6.5	57.3
Oatmeal - - - - -	16.1	7.2	67.5
Flour - - - - - -	11.4	1.0	75.6
Peas - - - - - -	24.6	1.0	62.0
Beans - - - - - -	22.5	1.8	59.6
Lentils - - - - -	25.7	1.0	59.2
Barley - - - - -	8.5	1.1	77.8
Rice - - - - - -	8.0	.3	79.0
Sago - - - - - -	9.0	.4	78.1
Tapioca - - - - -	.4	.1	88.0
Cornflour - - - - -	7.1	1.3	78.4
Sugar - - - - - -	—	—	100.0
Syrup and treacle - - -	—	—	69.3
Jam and marmalade - - -	.6	.1	84.5
Potatoes - - - - -	1.8	.1	14.7
Fresh vegetables (as cabbage) -	1.4	.2	4.8
Currants - - - - -	2.4	1.7	74.2
Raisins - - - - -	2.3	3.0	68.5
Apples - - - - - -	.3	.3	10·8

CONDIMENTS.

	Composition.		
	Proteid.	Fat.	Carbo-hydrate.
Tea - - - - - -	—	—	—
Coffee - - - - -	—	—	—
Coffee Essence - - - -	—	—	—
Cocoa - - - - -	21.6	28.9	37.7
Ginger - - - - -	—	—	—
Pepper - - - - -	15.5	8.5	63.0
Beer* - - - - - -	.5	—	11.5

For convenience, and to facilitate comparison of the results with standards, the quantities of foodstuffs used have all been converted into grammes or cubic centimetres, and the quantities of food principles are similarly expressed as grammes. The energy values of the diets are expressed as Calories, the large Calorie, which is the amount of heat necessary to raise the temperature of one litre of

* The isodynamical value of alcohol is included in carbo-hydrate value. (Bul. 75, U.S. Department of Agriculture Office of Experimental Stations, page 17.)

water one degree centigrade, being taken as the convenient standard.
Rübner's formulæ have been used in estimating these energy
values.

II. TESTS FOR DECIDING THE SUITABILITY
OF THE DIETS.

1. *The Energy Value.*

The two most important functions of food are to supply material
for the repair and growth of tissue, and to supply the energy
necessary to sustain life and do work. The former is a special
function of the proteids of the food, the latter is a function common
to all three organic food principles. Of these two great functions
the latter is the one which up to the present time has been more
thoroughly examined, and consequently is the first which will here
be used as a test of sufficiency.

Our present knowledge of the requirement of energy by the human
subject points to that requirement being a definite quantity, influ-
enced very slightly if at all by individual variation, but varying
through wide limits according to physiological law. As proof of
this assertion I can advance three arguments:— (1) That it is the
general opinion of all authorities on the scientific aspects of dietetics,
such as Atwater, Von Voit, König, and Von Noorden; (2) that
it has been found by dietary studies that there is a great
similarity in the food value of the diets of labouring men
living on very different dietaries in widely distant towns and
countries; and (3) that if a number of men of different individual
character, but leading similar lives, be fed by a rigidly fixed diet,
and that diet be even slightly altered, the effect on the well-being
of the men is practically universal. A comparison between the
dietaries of the labouring men of different countries will be found in
Atwater's "Investigations on the Chemistry and Economy of Food,"
Bul. 21, U.S. Department of Agriculture, Office of Experimental
Stations, and in Paton, Dunlop, and Inglis' "Study of the Diet of
the Labouring Classes in Edinburgh," Schulze & Co., Edinburgh,
1901. A record of the effects of the alteration of a regulation
diet on a number of men is to be found in a paper on "Food Requirements of Varying Labour" communicated by me to the
International Medical Congress, Paris, 1900, and published in the
Scottish Medical Journal of May, 1901.
The more important physiological factors influencing food
requirement are sex, work, size, and age. These should all be considered when stating a standard energy requirement for asylum
dietaries. I shall first give my opinion as to that standard for
adult male working patients of average size, and afterwards state
how the various factors influence that standard.
For dietary purposes the male working lunatic may be considered
as an able-bodied man doing a moderate day's work. It appears
from the schedules that in most asylums the working male patient is
employed about six or seven hours a day at agricultural or

other manual labour, and although such a day's work does not amount to the severity of some forms of the free man's labour, yet it certainly amounts to what may fairly be considered moderate labour. The standard of energy value necessary for these working male pauper lunatics is consequently the same as that found to be necessary for moderate labourers, which according to Atwater* is 3500 calories. Smaller standards have been advanced as sufficient for moderate labour, but because Atwater's observations are not only the most recent but also the most extensive yet published, and because I have been able to satisfy myself of the accuracy of his standards† I feel justified in adopting his figure as the necessary standard of energy value of the food of the working male pauper lunatic.

But with the influencing factors already enumerated it would not be right to use that standard for all male patients. Excess of work, idleness, exceptional size, and extremes of age all must be considered.

Hard work certainly requires more food than this standard. It has been shown that a dietary worth 4000 or 4500 calories is necessary for such work. From the detail of the schedules it is impossible to estimate what addition should be made to the standard for unusually severe work; but from the fact that work heavier than the average is occasionally undergone by pauper lunatics, it is necessary to bear in mind that a standard of 3500 calories, which is an energy value sufficient for moderate labour, is not necessarily sufficient for each working man at all times. The returns show that this is no new principle in asylum dietaries; in several asylums extra food is reported as being given during the harvest and other times when the labour is more severe than usual.

Inability or unwillingness to work is a factor which influences the average diet of lunatic asylums more than the excess of work. Atwater's standard for the idle, i.e. a man doing no work and taking no exercise, is 2700 calories, but of such the number in asylums dieted by the ordinary scale is presumably so small that they may be left out of account. Atwater's light labour standard, the standard for sedentary labour, for gentle exercise, &c., is 3100 calories, and this may be taken as the standard for those pauper patients who are not engaged in the more active employments, but who have exercise and may do some light work. For convenience, in this report they are spoken of as idlers.

The amount to which this influencing factor may be taken into account depends on the relative numbers of working and idle patients in asylums. The following Table is prepared from figures stated in the schedules; in it patients are grouped as working when they are employed at outdoor work on farm garden, &c., or in workshops, laundries, kitchens, or sewing rooms. Only patients dieted by the ordinary scales are included. It will be seen in the Table that 56 per cent. of the patients dieted by the ordinary scales are workers, and that 44 per cent. are idlers.

*U.S. Department of Agriculture Office of Experimental Stations, Bulletin 21.
† "Food Requirements of Varying Labour." Scottish Medical and Surgical Journal, May, 1901.

8

TABLE SHOWING RELATIVE NUMBERS OF WORKING AND IDLE
MALE PAUPER PATIENTS.

	Total Number.	Number Returned as Workers.	Per cent. Working.
Royal Asylums . . .	997	610	61
District Asylums . . .	3,156	1,637	52
Parochial Asylums . . .	320	217	67
Lunatic Wards . . .	418	291	69
Total . . .	4,891	2,755	56

Taking the number of idle patients at half of the total number of patients, the energy value of the average must not be reduced to less than 3300 calories. Such an average diet, if properly divided, would allow of a diet worth 3500 calories for the half of the patients who are working, and a diet worth 3100 calories to the other half who are idle.

With a reduction from a standard sufficient for all patients, one proviso is essential, and that is, that the food must be so divided that workers get more than idlers, for without that the workers would be insufficiently and the idlers excessively fed. There are at least two means of doing this, the one to allow some food at meal times *ad libitum*, the other to make the ordinary rations of all sufficient for idlers only, and give extra rations to workers. Both appear to be used in asylums, and provided they are properly carried out they are equally good. A combination of the two is probably the best means of ensuring a correct division of the food.

The size of the individual as a complicating factor would have to be considered were individual rations the point at issue, but when it is an average diet which is being discussed, it need not necessarily be allowed for. Direct observation has shown that the average size of the lunatic pauper in the various asylums is fairly constant. Patients of exceptional size are met with, but they are nowhere so numerous as to materially influence the average. Allowance for large patients should be made in the distribution of food, but is unnecessary in fixing the average diet.

Age as a complicating factor in fixing a standard is of importance when the extremes are dealt with. Juveniles and aged persons require less food than ordinary adults. For juveniles there is no occasion to make allowance, for their number in the asylums is so small that they cannot materially affect the average diet. Aged patients are a factor which should be considered, but for want of sufficient scientific information it is impossible to properly estimate for them. The fact that these aged persons require less food than younger adult patients, and that they have not been specially allowed for, prevents the standard of average requirement being rigidly applied. The presence of many aged inmates would warrant the reduction of the average diet. Direct observation shows that the average age of the pauper inmates in asylums varies but slightly, for in 36 out of the 39 institutions included in this report the average age is between 40 and 50.

Females, for at least two reasons, require less food than males. The one reason is that their average size is smaller, the other is that proportionally to their weight they have less active tissue, muscle, than males. Atwater's estimate of their requirement is at four-fifths of that of a man, and his estimate is generally accepted as correct. Using that figure, the standard for women may be taken as 2800 calories for workers, 2500 calories for idlers, and an average diet of 2650 calories in asylums where half are workers and half are idlers and where the individual rations are not fixed. As to the influence of women of exceptional size and of old age, little need be said further than that with them, as with men, the presumption is that exceptional sizes should balance themselves, and that it is impossible to make a fair deduction for the presence of old women.

From these remarks as to the necessary energy value of asylum dietaries it may be concluded:—

1. That the requirements of male and female patients are different, and that an equal diet for the two sexes would be faulty. Such a diet must entail either under-feeding or waste.

· 2. That the average male asylum dietary should have an energy value of 3300 calories.

3. That the diet for working male patients should have an energy value of 3500 calories.

4. That the diet of comparatively idle male patients should have an energy value of 3100 calories.

5. That the average female asylum dietary should have an energy value of 2650 calories.

6. That the diet for the working female patients should have an energy value of 2800 calories.

7. That the diet of comparatively idle female patients should have an energy value of 2500 calories.

2. *The Proteid Value.*

The question of what is the requisite amount of proteid to maintain health has been largely studied, but so far no very definite conclusion has been arrived at. Voit fixed the standard proteid requirement at 118 grms. per diem for a man at moderate labour, and his standard has been upheld by many subsequent observers, including Atwater. Other observers, notably Hirschfeld, Kumagawa, and Pechsel, have advanced evidence that health can be maintained on a smaller amount of proteid. With such contradictory opinions it would not be right at present to apply any proteid standard very rigidly, but with the more general consensus of opinion being that at least 118 grms. are necessary, that quantity will be here adopted as the standard for the male dietaries, the female standard being assessed at four-fifths of that, namely 94 grms.

A factor influencing this standard is the nature of the proteid taken, for there is great difference in the absorbability of the different varieties. Animal proteids as a class are well absorbed, vegetable proteids as a class are less perfectly absorbed, and some vegetable proteids, as for example those of peas, beans, and the husk of wheat, are very imperfectly absorbed. These differences may be allowed for in a general way by insisting on the standard being fully met when vegetable proteid is in excess, and allowing some relaxation of the standard when animal proteid is in excess.

To what extent the proteid standard should be increased to meet the requirements of the more severe forms of labour is also an uncertain point. It is well known that men in athletic training require a large amount of proteid, but such men are hardly comparable to lunatic patients. The athlete requires exceptional quantities of tissue-forming food, to encourage the growth and provide for the repair of muscle, and no very large amount of stored nutriment, as their exertion is not long sustained. The fully worked asylum patient wants not so much a large growth of muscular tissue as a large store of nutriment, and consequently the cases are not comparable. On general principles it may be stated that for severe work the patients require an all-round increase of food, and that with that all-round increase the proteid value of the diet should be proportionately increased.

In examining the diets, the use of a proteid standard will not be found of the same utility as the use of an energy-value standard, for as a matter of fact it is rarely found that a diet of sufficient energy value is deficient in proteid.

3. The Amount of Fat and Carbohydrate in the Diets.

The amount of fat and carbohydrate in a diet was at one time considered an important test for the sufficiency of the diet, but now that it has been clearly shown that the functions of these two food principles are identical, that they are both energy providers, and that their combined quantity can be best estimated in terms of energy, it is not now considered necessary to insist on any standard of each of these foods being in a diet. From the time when Playfair published his dietary studies, until recently, a fat standard and a carbohydrate standard have habitually been stated, but the more modern method, introduced by Atwater, of suppressing these and in terms of Rübner's formulæ expressing the energy value of the diet, is found more convenient and more reasonable.

One point in connection with the amount of carbohydrate must be considered, and that is that the total quantity of that food principle should not much exceed 550 grms. in a day's diet. The reason of this limitation is twofold, in the first place carbohydrate-containing food is more bulky food than fatty food, and there is a limit to the total bulk of a diet, and in the second place, it is generally allowed that excess of carbohydrate, be it sugar or be it starch, is apt to cause disorders of digestion. With this limitation, it follows that when a diet has to be raised to a high energy value the increase should not be one of carbohydrate only, but of proteid and fat proportionally.

4. *The Average Weight of Patients.*

In addition to the dietary schedules already referred to, returns stating average age, height, length of residence, and weight of patient have been received from the institutions. To ensure uniformity of these returns, all patients not in regular employment, all patients over 70 years of age, and all patients who have not been in residence for at least one year were excluded, and all weighings were taken before breakfast, the patients wearing their ordinary clothing, except boots and coats.

To use weight as a test of proper nourishment it is necessary to have some standard for comparison. In the following Table the standards of Hutchison[*] and Wells,[†] and the averages found in Scottish asylums are shown.

Height.	Hutchison's Standard.	Wells' Standard.	Asylum Average.	Number of Institutions in Average.
Inches.	*Lbs.*	*Lbs.*	*Lbs.*	
63	133	141	131	1
64	139	144	138	4
65	142	148	140	19
66	145	152	145	12
67	147	157	151	3

In the Table it may be seen that the average weight of the patients is found to fairly closely agree with Hutchison's standard, and consequently it may be inferred that the averages found may themselves be fairly used as standards. Wells' standards are based on an enormous number of weighings; their inclusion in the Table is instructive, as they show that Hutchison's standards and the asylum averages are not excessive. The asylum averages as stated in the above Table are adopted as the standard of weight for use in this report.

5. *Other Tests.*

In addition to these four tests which I have selected as the most important, there are other points which may be considered essential for a good diet, and which consequently may also be used as tests. Among these are a proper division of the diet into meals,

* " Encyclopædia Medica "—article " Life Insurance," Edinburgh, 1901.
† Green's " Life Insurance." New York, 1901.

a proper variety of food, a proper use of condiments, and a proper use of antiscorbutic food.

The importance of a proper division of the food into meals is obvious. Were a pittance only given for two meals and excess for a third, there would inevitably be a waste at the full meal, and though the daily average appeared good, the diet would in reality be short. For institution feeding it is essential to have not only a daily sufficiency, but a sufficiency at each meal.

A proper variety of food is essential, a monotonous diet leads to a want of relish, and that is followed by a poorer digestion and absorption. The feeding of a man or animal has been compared to the stoking of an engine. The simile is a good one, both require energy, and both get that energy from the food or fuel supplied; but the use of the simile has a limit. The man is not the simple machine a steam engine is. There is the governing nervous mechanism to consider, there are the various functions connected with digestion and absorption which are not found in the simple machine. Allowance must be made for these complicating factors, and it has been found that variety of food is necessary.

The proper use of condiments is also essential for institution dietaries. The inmates of asylums are necessarily deprived of many of the more stimulating pleasures of life, and must tend to get into a more or less atonic condition. Such a condition would inevitably reduce the powers of assimilation and digestion, and to counteract that loss the use of condiments is essential. The same argument applies to the necessity of a proper and pleasing variety of food. The term "condiment" here is used in its wider significance as including not only mustard, pepper, ginger, and the like, but also tea, coffee, beer, and other tasty and stimulating beverages. It is, in fact, used as synonymous with the German term "Genussmittel."

The use of antiscorbutic food is at the present day hardly necessary to refer to, as its importance is invariably acknowledged and acted on. A good diet must have a sufficiency of fresh potato or other vegetable food to ensure a sufficiency of antiscorbutic properties.

From what has been said, the essential points of a good institution dietary may be summed up as follows :—

1. It must contain sufficient energy-producing food. Energy-value standards have been stated.

2. It must contain sufficient proteid.

3. It must not contain excess of carbohydrate.

4. There must either be a classification of patients both as to sex and work, or food allowed at discretion.

5. It must be divided into meals of reasonable amount.

6. It must be sufficiently varied and pleasing.

7. It must contain a sufficient allowance of condiments.

8. It must contain a fair allowance of potato or fresh vegetable.

III. A SCHEDULE AS SUBMITTED AND RETURNED.

The following shows the queries regarding dietary as issued to all asylums and the answers returned by one of them. The return from Roxburgh District Asylum has been taken as an illustration. This return was selected on account of the very careful and complete manner in which it was filled up:—

ROXBURGH DISTRICT ASYLUM.

RETURN to the General Board of Lunacy regarding the Dietary of Pauper Patients in Scottish Lunatic Asylums, with special reference to the amount of Food supplied to Pauper Patients and to Private Patients receiving the same dietary as pauper patients, exclusive of patients on special diet, during the Four Weeks beginning Sunday, 4th March, 1900.

Numbers during Four Weeks beginning 4th March 1900.

	M.	F.
1. Daily average number of staff receiving food in Asylum,	13·	23·
2. Daily average number of patients of all classes,	136·4	158·0
3. Daily average number of pauper patients, and of private patients receiving the same food as pauper patients, *exclusive of patients of these classes on special diet,**	136·4	158·0
4. Daily average number of patients of the same class as those in Query 3, but excluded from the number returned in answer to that query because of receiving special diet on account of physical sickness, acute insanity, convalescence, &c.,	0	0

Patients on Special Diet.

5. Is there a specially fixed diet for patients on special diet, or is it ordered in special cases by the Medical Officers ?—No. "Extras" are ordered, as required, by the Medical Officers.
6. If the former, state shortly the differences that exist between the fixed special dietary referred to and that of the ordinary chronic patients.—The "extras" consist of milk, bread, eggs, beef-tea, puddings, &c. During the four weeks the daily average number of patients receiving such extras (in addition to the ordinary dietary) was— Males, 74; females, 33.

Working Patients.

	M.	F.
7. How many patients are employed at outdoor work on the farm, garden, &c. ?—Including Sundays,	47·	0
Excluding Sundays,	54·7	0
8. How many hours a day do such patients work ?	6·	0
On Saturdays,	3·	0
9. How many patients are employed in workshops, laundries, kitchens, and sewing-rooms ?—Including Sundays,	9·5	65·6
Excluding Sundays,	10·6	74·3

* The answers and returns for all the queries which follow are to be given in reference only to the patients included in the numbers given in answer to QUERY 3, unless when anything to the contrary is expressly stated or implied.

B

		M.	F.
10.	How many hours a day do such patients work? Males, 3 hours on Saturdays. (Laundry patients work nearly 7 hours daily, but 3½ on Wednesdays).	6·	6·

Breakfast.

11. What is the breakfast hour?—8 a.m.

		M.	F.
12.	How many patients work outside the wards in the early morning before breakfast? . .	5	10

13. Is any food given to these patients before sending them out to work?—No.
14. If so, state generally the kind and quantity of the articles of food given to the patients.
15. Daily Breakfast—

Name of Article.	Quantity per Patient. M.	Quantity per Patient. F.	*Price of Article.
Oatmeal, ...	7 oz.	5 oz.	£12 4s. ton
New milk, ...	½ pint	½ pint	9½d. gall.
Skimmed milk, ...	—	—	—
Buttermilk, ...	—	—	—
†Bread (wheaten), . .	8 oz.	6 oz.	1·103d. lb.
Bread (other kinds), . .	—	—	—
Butter, ...	½ oz.	½ oz.	11·464d. lb.
Margarine, ...	—	—	—
Tea, ...	⅛ oz.	⅛ oz.	1s. 5d. lb.
Coffee, ...	—	—	—
Sugar, ...	½ oz.	½ oz.	1·901d. lb.
‡Milk, ...	·26 pint (cream).	·26 pint (cream).	9½d. gall.
§Flour, ...	—	—	

		M.	F.
16.	How many patients get porridge and milk only for breakfast?	83·9	70
17.	How many get tea or coffee with bread and butter only?	35·5	30
18.	How many get both porridge and milk with tea or coffee and bread and butter?‖ . . .	17·	58

The quantities for patients who get both are—

	Oatmeal.	Milk.	Bread.	Butter.	Tea.	Sugar.
	ozs.	pt.	ozs.	oz.	oz.	oz.
M. .	3½	½	8	½	⅛	¾
F. .	2½	½	3	¼	1/16	¼

Dinner.

19. What is the dinner hour?—1.15 p.m.
20. In the case of working patients employed outside the wards or at *constant* work within the wards, is any food given between breakfast and dinner?—Many male patients get lunch; all female patients get lunch.

* Where article is produced on Asylum Farm write "Farm" instead of price.
† Where bread is baked at Asylum give quantity used but not price.
‡ Milk used in tea or coffee only.
§ Where bread is not purchased give price of flour only, and state kind or kinds of flour used.
‖ If in any case tea or coffee and bread is given without butter, the fact to be stated.

21. If so, state generally the kind and the approximate quantities per patient.—Males (generally), bread, 4 ozs.; milk, ½-pint. Females (generally), bread, 1½ ozs.; milk, ½-pint. Laundry workers get— bread, 3 ozs.; cheese, 1 oz.; tea, ⅛ oz.; sugar, ½ oz.; milk, ¾ oz. (= ·26 pint).

22. Daily Dinner—

Days of Week.	* Menu.	†Quantity of each Article per Patient.	
		M.	F.
		oz.	oz.
Sunday, . .	Rice soup (not limited), . . .	40	40
	Bread, ...	4	3
	Meat (fresh beef or mutton fore-quarter or salted pork), . .	8	8
	Potatoes (or turnips), . .	12	12
Monday, . .	Barley broth (not limited), . .	40	40
	Bread, ...	4	3
	Meat (tinned Sydney mutton princi-pally), ...	4	4
	Potatoes, ...	12	12
Tuesday, . . .	Barley broth (not limited), . .	40	40
	Bread, ...	4	3
	Meat (fresh beef or mutton fore-quarter), ...	8	8
	Potatoes, ...	6	6
	Haricot beans, ...	1½	1½
Wednesday, .	Rice soup (not limited), . . .	40	40
	Bread, ...	4	3
	Dumpling (not limited), . .	12	12
Thursday, .	Barley broth (not limited), . .	40	40
	Bread, ...	4	3
	Meat (fresh beef or mutton fore-quarter), ...	8	8
	Potatoes, ...	6	6
	Cabbage (not limited), . .	6	6
Friday, . .	Fresh fish (haddocks), . . .	16	12
	Potatoes, ...	12	12
	Bread, ...	4	3
	Cheese, ...	1	1
Saturday, .	Pea soup (not limited), . . .	40	40
	Potatoes, ...	12	12
	Bread, ...	4	3

* Where a larger routine of dinner is given than can be comprehended within one week, they are to be detailed on separate sheets exactly following this form and in the order in which they are usually given.

† In all cases where the quantity of the cooked article is not limited, state "not limited," and give average quantity. Otherwise give exact quantities.

Butcher meat must be defined as "fresh," "salt," or "tinned," as "beef," "mutton," or "pork." The weight of all butcher meat is to be estimated uncooked and with bone, except in tinned meats. Further, the parts of the carcase used must be specified, thus—"Fresh beef hindquarter," "Fresh mutton forequarter," "Fresh beef, shank bones," &c., &c.

Fish to be sufficiently described thus, "fresh cod," "dried ling," &c. Weight to be estimated after cleaning and trimming, but before cooking.

Vegetables to be separately specified and defined as "green" or "dried," as "turnips," "cabbage," &c. Weight to be estimated after being cleaned and prepared for cooking.

23. Is the fresh butcher meat purchased or supplied by the Asylum Farm ?—In both ways.
24. If in both ways, state precisely the method by which the supply to the Asylum from both sources is arranged and regulated.—The bulk of the supply is got by contract. This is supplemented by pork from the Asylum Piggery, and mutton from sheep which are bought, fattened, and killed in the autumn and winter season.
25. What is the average price per pound paid for (a) fresh beef 5d., (b) fresh mutton 6¼d., (c) fresh pork 4½d., (d) tinned mutton 5·333d., (e) tinned beef 4·714d., (f) fresh fish 2¼d., (g) salt fish 2·303d.
26. What kinds of fish are supplied ?—Fresh haddocks as a rule; fresh herrings occasionally. Salt cod, ling, or tusk only when no fresh fish is procurable.
27. State as nearly as possible the quantities of the various ingredients in the following articles :—

		Quantity per Patient.
(1) Stewed Meat— * Butcher meat, † Vegetables, ‡ Stock and fat,		
(2) Meat Pies— * Butcher meat,	Fresh beef (hindquarter mainly), un-cooked and free from bone,	8 ozs.
‡ Stock and fat, † Vegetables, Pastry,	Flour, 4 ozs. ; lard, 1½ ozs.	
(3) Irish Stew— * Butcher meat,	Cooked and free from bone, sometimes altogether or in part tinned beef, &c.,	4 „
Potatoes, ‡ Stock and fat, † Vegetables,	Peeled,	16 „
	Turnips, carrots, onions, or leeks, vary-ing with the seasons, to about	3 „
(4) § Scotch Broth— (a) ‡ Stock,	Fresh beef (forequarter principally),	4 „
(b) Barley,		1½ „
(c) Vegetables,	Cabbages, turnips, carrots, parsnips, parsley, onions, or leeks, varying with the seasons, from about	ozs. 2 to 7
	Whole peas,	½ oz.
(5) § Rice Soup— (a) ‡ Stock, (b) Rice, (c) Parsley, (d) † Vegetables,	Same as No. 4, rice taking place of barley.	
(6) Potato Soup— (a) ‡ Stock, (b) Potatoes, (c) † Vegetables,		
(7) Fish Soup— (a) ‡ Stock, (b) Fish, (c) † Vegetables,		

* Mention kind used.
† Specify each green or dried vegetable separately. Meal, flour, and other thickening substances to be entered separately.
‡ The kind of stock used to be definitely stated, thus—"Bones," "beef," "mutton," "pork," "ham," &c.
§ NOTE.—The beef boiled in the broth and soup is served as the ration of meat.

		Quantity per Patient.

(8) § Pea or Lentil
    Soup—
  (a) ‡ Stock,   Meat (beef, mutton, or pork), . . 4 ozs.
  (b) Peas or lentils, Split peas, ... 4½ „
  (c) † Vegetables,   Turnips, carrots, parsnips, parsley, onions,
       green,   or leeks, varying with the seasons, to
           about 3 ounces per ration.

(9) Rice and Milk—
  (a) Rice, ... 3 „
  (b) Milk, ... 10 „
                            (½ pt.)
  (c) Sugar, ... ¾ oz.
  (d) Fat,

(10) Stewed or
   baked Fruit—Rice and rhubarb—
  (a) Fruit,   Rice, ... 3 ozs.
  (b) Sugar,   Rhubarb, ... 16 „
           Sugar, ... 3 „
           Milk, ... 5 „
                        (¼ pt.)

(11) Pastry—   Rhubarb tart—
  (a) Flour, ... 4 ozs.
  (b) Lard, ... 1½ „
  (c) Sugar, ... 3 „
  (d) Rhubarb, ... 16 „

(12) Suet Pudding—Dumpling—
  (a) Flour, ... 4 ozs.
  (b) Bread crumbs,
  (c) Rice,
  (d) Raisins,
  (e) Currants, ... ½ „
  (f) Suet, ... 1 „
  (g) Treacle, ... ½ „

(13) Sauce with Fish—
  (a) Flour,
  (b) Butter,
  (c) Milk,
   Rice and syrup—Rice, 3 ounces } per ration.
                 Syrup, 2 „

Tea.

28. What is the tea hour?—6.15 p.m.

29. Is any food given to working patients between dinner and tea?—
No.

30. If so, state generally the kind and approximate quantities of each
article given to each patient.

† Specify each green or dried vegetable separately. Meal, flour, and other thickening
substances to be entered separately.

‡ The kind of stock used to be definitely stated, thus—"Bones," "beef," "mutton,"
"pork," "ham," &c.

§ NOTE.—The beef boiled in the broth and soup is served as the ration of meat.

31. Daily Tea—

Name of Article.	Quantity per Patient.		* Price of Article.
	M.	F.	
Oatmeal, ...	7 oz.	5 oz.	£12 4s. ton.
New milk, ...	½ pint	½ pint	9¼d. gall.
Skimmed milk, . .	—	—	—
Bread (wheaten), . .	8 oz.	6 oz.	1·103d. lb.
Bread (other kinds), .	—	—	—
Butter, ...	½ oz.	½ oz.	11·464d. lb.
Margarine, . . .	—	—	—
Tea, . ·. . ·. ·.	⅛ oz.	⅛ oz.	1s. 5d. lb.
Coffee, ...	—	—	—
Sugar, ...	½ oz.	½ oz.	1·901d. lb.
†Milk, ...	·26 pint (cream).	·26 pint (cream).	9¼d. gall.
Jam (jam, marmalade, etc., is given in place of butter occasionally), . . Marmalade, . . .	1·163 oz.	1·163 oz.	Home-made.

* Where any article is exclusively produced on Asylum Farm put "Farm" in place of price.
† Used with tea or coffee only.

	M.	F.
32. How many patients get porridge and milk only?	27·5	23·5
33. How many get tea or coffee with bread and butter only?	108·9	134·5
34. How many get both porridge and tea or coffee with bread and butter?	0	0

Supper.

35. If supper is given after and in addition to tea, state the hour at which it is served, the number and kind of patients that partake of it, and the quantity in which each article composing the meal is distributed to each patient.—No regular supper is given, but at 7.30 some of the patients on "extras" get food as described in Answer 6.

General.

36. State what precautions (if any) are taken to secure (a) a uniform nutritive standard of the milk supplied to the Asylum, and (b) to ensure its freedom from infection or impurity.—(a) The milk is examined and tested in the usual practical ways. (b) No special precautions are taken. The milk is all got from one contractor, who supplies no other persons. His dairy is visited from time to time by the Medical Superintendent and the County Officers of Health.

37. Are all patients regularly weighed?—Yes.
38. If so, how often?—All recent and special cases once a fortnight; all others every three months.
39. How are their weights recorded for reference?—In "Weight Books" kept for the purpose, and in the Case Books.

Average Weekly Allowances.

40. State on the accompanying forms the average weekly allowance of food, during the four weeks beginning on Sunday, 4th March, 1900,

to those patients who are embraced in the answer to Query 3—that is, to pauper patients and private patients receiving the same diet as pauper patients, but excluding such patients of these classes as are on special diet.

STATEMENT showing Average Weekly Allowance of Food, during the Four Weeks beginning on Sunday, 4th March 1900, to those patients who are embraced in the answer to Query 3—that is, to Pauper Patients, and Private Patients receiving the same diet as pauper patients, but excluding such patients of these classes as are on special diet.

FOOD.	Is Quantity Limited ? "Yes" or "No."	Averge* quantity per week per Patient.	
		Males.	Females.
1. Oatmeal, . . .	Yes.	43·235 oz.	27·136 oz.
2. Milk—			
(a) New milk, . .	,,	3·615p'ts.	6·612p'ts.
(b) Skimmed milk (not used).			
(c) Buttermilk (not used).			
3. Bread—			
(a) Wheaten, . .	,,	94·602 oz.	84·731 oz.
(b) (State kind)—	—	—	—
4. Butter, ...	Yes.	4·155 ,,	4·286 ,,
5. Margarine (not used).			
6. Tea, ...	,,	1·036 ,,	1·069 ,,
7. Coffee (not used).			
8. Sugar, . . .	,,	4·593 ,,	4·286 ,,
9. Flour (not in bread), .	,,	3·879 ,,	3·879 ,,
10. Beef—			
(a) Fresh forequarter, .	,,	19·346 ,,	19·346 ,,
†(b) Fresh hindquarter, .	—	—	—
11. Mutton, . . .	Yes.	4·079 ,,	4·079 ,,
12. Pork, ...	,,	3·782 ,,	3·782 ,,
13. Ox heads, bones, shanks, &c. (none received as such).			
14. Tinned meat, . .	,,	2·122 ,,	2·122 ,,
15. Fresh Fish—			
(a) Cod, . . .	—	—	—
(b) Haddock, . .	Yes.	16· ,,	12· ,,
(c) Herring, fresh, .	—	—	—
16. Cured Fish—			
(a) Ling, dried, . .	—	—	—
(b) (State kind)—	—	—	—
17. Suet (see also No. 36, Lard), ...	Yes.	·324 ,,	·324 ,,
18. Potato, . . .	,,	60·072 ,,	60·072 ,,
19. Cabbage, . . .	,,	10·860 ,,	10·860 ,,
20. Carrot, . . .	,,	·800 ,,	·800 ,,
21. Turnip, . . .	,,	11·030 ,,	11·030 ,,

* These averages to be calculated on the numbers stated in answer to Query 3 of Return.
† None of the articles thus marked used during the four weeks to which this statement refers.

Food.	Is Quantity Limited? "Yes" or "No."	Average* quantity per week per Patient.	
		Males.	Females.
22. Peas—			
(a) Green, . . .	—	—	—
(b) Split, . . .	Yes.	4·098 oz.	4·098 oz.
(c) Whole dried, . .	„	2·169 „	2·169 „
23. Beans—			
†(a) Green, . . .	—	—	—
(b) Dried, . . .	Yes.	1·454 „	1·454 „
24. Lentils (not used).			
25. †Onions, . . .	—	—	—
26. †Parsley, . . .	—	—	—
27. Vegetables (state kind)—			
Leeks, . . .	Yes.	·775 „	·775 „
Parsnips, . . .	„	·254 „	·254 „
28. Barley, ...	„	3·975 „	3·975 „
29. Rice, ...	„	2·618 „	2·618 „
30. Fruit (state kind)—			
Currants, dried, . .	„	·430 „	·430 „
31. Jam (or jelly), . .	„	·872 „	·872 „
32. Treacle, . . .	—	—	—
33. †Syrup, . . .	—	—	—
34. †Marmalade, . .	—	--	--
35. Cheese, ...	Yes.	1·770 „	1·770 „
36. Other Foods (state kind)— Lard (see also No. 17,			
Suet), ...	„	·536 „	·536 „

* These averages to be calculated on the numbers stated in answer to Query 3 of Return.
† None of the articles thus marked used during the four weeks to which this statement refers.

RETURN showing weight of male working inmates. (Only those who have been resident for at least one year in the asylum, and who are under 70 years of age, are included in this Return.)

ROXBURGH DISTRICT ASYLUM.

NUMBER OF PATIENTS EMPLOYED AT 4TH APRIL 1901.

Nature of Employment.	Male Patients.
Assisting attendants in the wards, ...	24
As garden or field labourers, ...	40
„ farm servants, ...	1
„ clerks, ⎫	1
„ storekeepers, ⎭	
„ messengers, ...	—
„ stokers, ...	2
„ bakers, ...	—
„ tailors, ...	3
„ shoemakers, ...	3
„ upholsterers, ...	2
„ painters, ...	1
„ joiners, ...	1
„ plumbers, ...	—
„ masons, ...	—
„ slaters, ...	—
In kitchen, ...	1
Total, ...	79

No.	Names of Working Male Patients.	Age.	Nature of Mental Malady.	Length of Residence. Yrs. Ms.	Height in Inches.	Weigh in Pounds*
(1) 1308	J. A. - -	69	Secondary dementia.	8 8	63½	141½
(2) 1569	R. B. - -	34	Chronic mania.	4 4	65½	135
(3) 953	J. B. - -	40	Secondary dementia.	15 8	69¾	164¼
(4) 1092	T. B. - -	44	do.	12 9	66¾	151½
(5) 1795	J. B. - -	39	Chronic mania.	1 2	70	152¼
(6) 1538	J. H. B. -	28	Chronic melancholia.	4 10	68	132
(7) 1674	J. B. - -	46	Chronic mania.	2 11	71¾	212
(8) 1392	A. B. - -	58	Secondary dementia.	7 6	65½	117
(9) 557	G. B. - -	47	Congenital.	21 9	64	137
(10) 906	T. C. - -	50	Chronic melancholia.	16 4	70	170¼
(11) 1647	H. C. - -	36	Congenital.	3 3	65¼	130
(12) 1687	W. D. - -	31	Secondary dementia.	2 10	70	168
(13) 1707	R. D. D. -	22	Chronic melancholia.	2 7	73	178
(14) 1715	R. D. - -	24	Secondary dementia.	2 5	64½	158½
(15) 1578	A. D. - -	44	Chronic mania.	4 3	64¾	191
(16) 1611	A. D. - -	48	Chronic melancholia.	3 11	66¼	139¼
(17) 1706	R. D. - -	43	Secondary dementia.	2 7	65	149¾
(18) 1624	J. D. - -	35	do.	3 9	63½	138
(19) 1469	R. D. - -	52	Congenital.	5 7	69¼	137
(20) 58	A. D. - -	59	Secondary dementia.	33 0	70¾	161½
(21) 255	J. D. - -	52	Acquired epilepsy.	26 8	65¾	150¼
(22) 699	J. D. - -	49	Chronic mania.	19 7	68	122
(23) 1056	P. D. - -	35	Secondary dementia.	13 6	65¼	155
(24) 1797	G. D. - -	64	Chronic mania.	1 2	69	149
(25) 1457	W. E. - -	23	Secondary dementia.	6 2	67	144¼
(26) 625	A. E. - -	48	do.	20 7	64	129
(27) 1735	J. F. - -	39	Chronic mania.	2 1	69¾	181½
(28) 1179	A. F. - -	58	Chronic melancholia.	10 10	69¼	171
(29) 827	J. F. - -	50	Secondary dementia.	17 7	66	121¼
(30) 1435	J. G. - -	45	Congenital.	6 8	68¼	164
(31) 1052	J. S. or G. -	44	Secondary dementia.	13 7	70	150
(32) 1434	W. G. - -	47	Congenital.	6 8	69	166½

* Patients to be weighed before breakfast with their ordinary clothing except coats and boots.

No.	Names of Working Male Patients.	Age.	Name of Mental Malady.	Length of Residence.	Height in Inches.	Weight in Pounds*
				Yrs. Ms.		
(33) 350	R. G. - -	63	Chronic mania.	25 2	64¾	131½
(34) 1242	J. G. - -	26	Congenital.	9 9	69¾	164
(35) 1353	T. G. - -	50	Secondary dementia.	8 -	63½	143½
(36) 1747	R. G. - -	50	Chronic mania.	1 11	66	137¾
(37) 1433	T. G. - -	50	Congenital.	6 8	67½	135
(38) 853	R. G. - -	69	Chronic mania.	17 1	66¾	143½
(39) 605	J. H. - -	43	Secondary dementia.	20 10	71½	152½
(40) 1384	J. H. - -	36	do.	7 7	61½	121¾
(41) 1673	J. H. - -	21	Congenital.	2 11	72¾	163
(42) 1280	T. H. - -	45	Secondary dementia.	9 1	66½	149¾
(43) 989	T. H. - -	43	do.	14 10	66½	126
(44) 781	A. H. - -	19	Acute mania.	1 5	70¾	143
(45) 1545	W. H. -	19	Acquired epilepsy.	4 9	68½	148½
(46) 1477	W. H, - -	47	do.	5 11	65¾	140
(47) 735	J. I. - -	51	Chronic mania.	19 -	69¾	214½
(48) 142	A. K. - -	49	Secondary dementia.	28 9	67¼	130
(49) 736	N. K. - -	43	do.	19 -	67¼	152½
(50) 941	T. L. - -	49	do.	15 10	68	191½
(51) 49	G. L. - -	59	Congenital.	34 -	60½	124
(52) 1445	J. L. - -	38	Chronic mania.	6 6	70	164½
(53) 1638	W. M. -	19	Congenital.	3 6	64½	104
(54) 1650	T. M. - -	27	Chronic mania.	3 3	68¼	142
(55) 1364	R. M'M.	34	do.	7 10	68½	135
(56) 1591	D. D. M. -	34	do.	4 1	65	151¾
(57) 1257	J. M'M.	35	do.	9 5	68½	161¼
(58) 1160	J. O. - -	37	Congenital.	11 5	66½	150¾
(59) 997	R. R. - -	35	Chronic mania.	14 8	71¾	148
(60) 1594	J. R. - -	49	do.	4 1	69½	151½
(61) 1684	R. R. - -	69	do.	2 10	65¼	156½
(62) 1710	J. R. - -	51	Secondary dementia.	2 6	69	210
(63) 218	W. A. or R. -	63	Chronic mania.	27 4	69½	170½
(64) 780	G. R. - -	40	Congenital.	18 3	61¾	134½

* Patients to be weighed before breakfast with their ordinary clothing except coats and boots.

No.	Names of Working Male Patients.	Age.	Nature of Mental Malady.	Length of Residence.	Height in Inches.	Weight in Pounds*
				Yrs. Ms.		
(65) 91	J. S. - -	50	Secondary dementia.	30 6	72	150½
(66) 146	W. S. - -	53	do.	28 8	68½	132½
(67) 1417	J. S. - -	59	Chronic mania.	6 11	66½	148
(68) 1229	G. S. - -	40	Secondary dementia.	10 -	66½	114½
(69) 1801	W. T. S. -	34	Acquired epilepsy.	1 1	69¾	166½
(70) 1157	J. T. - -	37	Chronic mania.	11 5	67	140½
(71) 1671	A. T. - -	37	do.	3 -	66½	132
(72) 1482	J. T. - -	28	Secondary dementia.	5 11	67½	150
(73) 61	J. T. - -	68	do.	32 9	70¼	198½
(74) 502	R. V. - -	61	Chronic mania.	22 5	67½	132
(75) 1808	J. W. - -	23	Acute melancholia.	1 -	65¼	125
(76) 1311	J. W. - -	68	Secondary dementia.	8 8	67½	158
(77) 868	R. W. - -	38	do.	16 10	60	122
(78) 1314	G. W. - -	39	do.	8 8	69	164
(79) 1771	R. W. - -	39	Acquired epilepsy.	1 7	69¼	158

* Patients to be weighed before breakfast with their ordinary clothing except coats and boots.

IV. DESCRIPTION AND CRITICISM OF DIETARIES.

(1.) Royal Asylums.

ABERDEEN ROYAL ASYLUM.

Breakfast.—The majority get porridge and milk along with either tea bread and butter, or oatcake, or milk and bread. Some receive porridge and milk only, and a considerable number, mostly females, receive tea bread and butter only.

Dinner.—There are three different dinners served, two in the asylum, one being for working, the other for non-working patients, the third at the Daviot branch. The weekly routine of dinners for non-working patients includes potato soup on two days, once along with suet pudding, and once with fresh beef; broth on four days, once with potato, twice with green vegetable and potato, and once with beef, potato, and rice; and pea soup with fish and potato on one day. Oatcake is given in addition with all seven dinners. Working patients get dinners similar to the non-working patients, but with an allowance of beef on four additional days, making six days in all. The routine of dinners at Daviot branch includes rice and milk with suet pudding on one day, broth with meat and potato on four days, pea soup with pork or corned beef and potato on one day, and potato soup with fish and potato on one day; bread is given daily. The cooking of the beef is varied.

Evening Meal.—The majority get porridge and milk, either alone or with oatcake and butter. The remainder get tea and bread, with either butter, syrup, or jam.

Extras for Working Patients.—In addition to the difference made at dinner, working patients receive a lunch of oatcake cheese and beer, and tea and bread in the afternoon.

Dietary for Females differs from that for males in that the rations are rather smaller.

Table showing the Average Weekly Composition of Dietaries.

	MALE.					FEMALE.				
	Quantity.		Proteid.	Fat.	Carbo-hydrate	Quantity.		Proteid.	Fat.	Carbo-hydrate
	Oz.	Grms.				Oz.	Grms.			
Beef, ...	14·0	397·6	74·45	74·12	..	12	340·8	63·78	63·55	..
Heads, bones, &c., . .	·5	14·2	1·37	·55	..	·5	14·2	1·37	·55	..
Fish (Fresh), . .	5·5	156·2	26·86	·46	..	5·5	156·2	26·86	·46	..
Fish (Salt, &c.), .	2·63	74·69	15·72	5·27	..	2·01	57·08	12·02	4·01	..
Suet, . . .	·4	11·35	·53	9·29	..	·4	11·36	·53	9·29	..
Butter, ...	1·7	48·28	·48	41·08	..	3·0	85·2	·85	72·42	..
Eggs, ...	·64	18·17	2·16	1·68	..	·49	13·91	1·65	1·92	..
Milk, ...	138·0	3919·2	129·33	156·76	195·96	100	2840·	93·72	113·6	142·0
Cheese, . . .	1·7	48·28	13·27	17·76	1·97	1·4	39·76	11·01	14·63	1·63
Bread, ...	54·4	1544·96	142·13	20·08	820·37	52·4	1488·16	136·91	19·34	790·21
Oatmeal, ...	107·3	3047·32	490·61	219·4	2056·94	76·4	2169·76	349·33	156·22	1464·58
Flour, ...	3·0	85·2	9·71	·85	64·41	3·0	85·2	9·71	·85	64·41
Peas, ...	2·4	68·16	16·76	·68	42·25	2·0	56·8	13·97	·56	35·71
Barley, ...	4·5	127·8	10·96	1·4	99·42	4·25	120·7	10·25	1·32	93·9
Rice, ...	2·5	71·0	5·68	·21	56·09	2·0	56·8	4·54	1·7	44·87
Sugar, ...	4·5	127·8	..	..	127·8	7·4	210·16	..	..	210·16
Syrup and Treacle, . .	1·0	28·4	..	..	19·68	2·0	56·8	..	..	39·36
Potatoes, ...	80·0	2272·0	40·89	2·27	333·98	70·0	1988·0	35·78	1·98	292·23
Fresh Vegetables, .	29·0	823·6	11·53	1·64	39·43	28·0	795·2	11·13	1·59	33·16
Currants, Raisins, . .	·4	11·36	·26	·22	8·26	·4	11·36	·26	·22	8·26
Tea, ...	·7	19·88	..	..	..	1·3	36·92	..	..	..
Beer, ...	17·	482·8	2·41	..	48·62	6·	170·4	·85	..	19·6
Total, . .	..	..	995·11	553·67	3915·28	..	..	784·52	463·58	3345·08

Food Values.—The average daily food values of the male and female dietaries, all routines included, are as follows :—

	Proteid.	Fat.	Carbo-hydrate.	Energy Value.
Male	142·2	79·1	559·3	3612
Female . . .	112·1	66·2	463·6	2976

Average height of male working patients is 66½ inches; their average weight at the asylum is 153·3 lbs., at Daviot branch 148 lbs.*

Critical Remarks.—From the detail of the diet shown above it may be gathered that the dietaries of this asylum are all of ample quantity. They all meet the requirements of the standards as stated earlier in the report. The energy value of both the average male dietary and the average female dietary is in excess of the standards, the proteid values are ample, and the amount of carbohydrate is not excessive. The special wants of the working patients appear to be amply provided for. They receive extra food at dinner time, and they get small extra meals in the forenoon and in the afternoon. The application of the weight test (see page 11) shows that the working patients both at the asylum and at Daviot branch are properly fed.

A scrutiny of the use of individual food-stuffs shows three faults in the dietaries—a too small use of meat, an excessive use of oatmeal, and a too small use of condiment. The average use of meat is only 14 oz. for males and 12 oz. for females weekly. When with these figures it is remembered that working patients get three times as much meat as idle patients, it is seen how small the allowance of meat for idle patients is; as a fact it is only 7½ oz. per week for males, and the same for females. This sparse use of meat is to some extent compensated by a free use of milk, but is principally compensated by a very large use of the proteid-rich cereal, oatmeal. The use of oatmeal is larger in this asylum than in any other in Scotland. It is on the table in some form at every meal. Its average quantity consumed provides fully half the nutriment of the entire diet. Many of the patients get porridge and milk night and morning, and oatcake and soup daily for dinner, along with vegetables, suet pudding, or meat, and never get white bread. I am aware that in Aberdeenshire and neighbouring counties the labouring household uses oatmeal to an extent which is not now found in other parts of the country, but even allowing for that, the monotony of an almost exclusively oatmeal diet in an asylum seems hardly right. The use of condiment is too small. The weekly average allowance of tea is less than three-quarters of an ounce per male patient.

The dietary would be greatly improved by giving a tea with bread and butter meal once daily, instead of a porridge meal. This change would vary the diet without unduly reducing its nutritive value. Meat should be used oftener and more freely.

CRICHTON ROYAL INSTITUTION.

Breakfast.—All males and the majority of females receive porridge and milk only. Some females get tea, bread and margarine, and some both porridge and tea with bread and margarine.

* These averages include only patients who have been resident in the asylum for at least a year. The weights were taken before breakfast with ordinary clothing, boots and coats excepted. This applies to similar averages which are stated along with remarks on the diets of other asylums.

Dinner.—The dinner routine contains bread daily, rice soup twice weekly, once with tart and milk, the other time with meat pie and potato, broth four times a week, twice being followed by beef and potato, once by suet pudding and milk, and once by fish and potato, and pea soup once a week along with mutton, potato, and milk. Meat is given four times a week; the cooking of it is varied.

Evening Meal.—Tea, bread, and margarine for all.

Extras for Working Patients.—A fuller allowance of oatmeal (about 1 oz. extra) is served at the farm where most of the outside workers live. Female patients working in the laundry, kitchen, and dining halls get tea, bread and margarine both forenoon and afternoon.

Dietary for Females differs from that for males by the allowances being smaller, and in the service of the extras already noted.

Table showing the Average Weekly Composition of Dietaries.

	MALE.					FEMALE.				
	Quantity.		Proteid.	Fat.	Carbo-hydrate	Quantity.		Proteid.	Fat.	Carbo-hydrate
	Oz.	Grms.				Oz.	Grms.			
Beef, ...	16·2	462·92	86·97	86·12	..	12·36	352·16	66·25	66·46	..
Heads, Bones, &c., .	4·25	120·7	11·7	4·7	..	3·87	110·76	10·74	4·31	..
Mutton, ...	6·89	195·96	25·47	47·08	..	4·48	127·8	16·61	30·67	..
Fish (Fresh), . . .	11·	312·4	52·94	·92	..	8·14	232·98	39·48	·69	..
Suet, ...	4·5	127·8	6·0	99·33	..	4·0	118·6	5·33	92·92	..
Margarine, . . .	5·4	153·36	1·84	127·28	..	4·5	127·8	1·53	106·07	..
Milk (Whole), . . .	103·2	2930·89	96·71	117·23	146·54	103·2	2930·98	96·71	117·23	146·54
Milk (Skimmed), . .	61·8	1755·12	59·67	5·28	89·51	61·8	1755·12	59·67	5·26	89·51
Bread, ...	90·86	2581·56	227·5	33·56	1370·8	70·67	2007·88	184·72	26·1	1066·18
Oatmeal, ...	38·5	1093·2	176·0	78·71	737·91	28·45	807·98	130·08	58·17	545·38
Flour, ...	14·3	406·12	46·29	4·06	307·02	12·66	359·26	40·95	3·59	271·6
Peas, ...	4·89	139·16	34·23	1·39	86·27	3·82	107·92	26·54	1·07	66·91
Barley, . . , .	4·25	120·7	10·25	1·32	93·9	3·67	105·08	8·98	1·15	81·75
Rice, ...	3·62	102·24	8·17	·3	80·76	2·44	68·16	5·45	·2	53·84
Sugar, ...	8·61	244·64	..	..	244·64	10·27	292·52	..	..	292·52
Syrup, Jam, &c., . .	3·47	97·98	·5	·08	80·63	2·59	73·34	·25	·05	60·23
Potatoes, ...	81·85	2325·96	41·86	2·32	341·91	60·67	1722·88	31·02	1·72	253·41
Fresh Vegetables, .	58·17	1652·88	23·14	3·3	79·33	48·5	1377·4	19·28	2·75	66·11
Currants, Raisins, .	1·42	39·76	·92	·92	28·36	1·42	39·76	·92	·92	28·36
Tea, ...	1·0	28·4	..	..	..	1·32	36·92	..	..	..
Total, . .	..	..	930·16	612·63	3687·58	..	..	744·56	518·33	3022·94

Food Values.—The average daily food values of the male and female dietaries are as follows:—

	Proteid.	Fat.	Carbo-hydrate.	Energy Value.
Male	131·4	87·7	526·8	3514
Female . . .	106·4	74·0	431·7	2894

Average height of male working patients is 66·8 inches, average weight 141·6 lbs.

Critical Remarks.—The dietaries of this asylum appear to be good in most respects, they fully meet the energy-value standard, the proteid allowances are ample, carbohydrates are not given to excess, some allowances for the special wants of the working patients appear to be made, the routine is varied, and condiments and fresh vegetables are used in reasonable amount. The average weight of male working patients is below the standard, 141 lbs. as against 145 lbs.; this may be attributed to their not receiving sufficient extra food.

DUNDEE ROYAL ASYLUM.

Breakfast.—Two-thirds of the male and one-third of the female patients receive porridge. The remainder get tea bread and margarine.

Dinner.—The weekly routine includes pea soup with beef and potato once, rice and milk with bread and cheese once, and broth five times, twice being given with beef and potato, once with potato and bread, once with fish and bread, and once with suet pudding and bread. Meat is given four times a week, on three of these occasions it is fresh meat, on one tinned meat. Bread is only given on three days a week.

Evening Meal.—All the females and most of the males receive tea bread and margarine, a few men get porridge and milk.

Extras for Working Patients.—Some working females receive a lunch consisting of bread cheese and beer. At harvest time some male patients get a similar lunch.

Dietary for Females differs from that for males by having smaller rations and by including relatively more bread and less oatmeal.

[TABLE.

Table showing the Average Weekly Composition of Dietaries.

	MALE.					FEMALE.				
	Quantity.		Proteid.	Fat.	Carbo-hydrate	Quantity.		Proteid.	Fat.	Carbo-hydrate
	Oz.	Grms.				Oz.	Grms.			
Beef,.	18	511·2	93·54	96·61	..	12	340·8	62·36	64·41	..
Mutton, .	4	113·6	32·71	25·9	..	3	85·2	24·53	19·42	..
Fish (Fresh), .	12	340·8	57·75	1·02	..	12	340·8	57·75	1·02	..
Suet, .	·66	18·74	·38	15·32	..	·66	18·74	·88	15·32	..
Margarine, .	6·1	173·24	2·07	143·78	..	8·6	244·24	2·98	202·71	..
Milk (Whole), .	103	2925·2	96·53	117·00	146·26	55	1562	51·54	62·48	78·1
Cheese, .	2	56·8	15·73	20·9	2·33	2	56·8	15·73	20·9	2·33
Bread, .	85·1	2416·84	222·34	31·41	1283·34	83·7	2377·08	218·69	30·9	1262·22
Oatmeal, .	35·17	998·82	180·71	71·91	674·2	12·7	360·68	58·06	25·96	243·45
Flour, .	3·2	90·88	10·36	·9	68·7	3·2	90·88	10·36	·9	68·7
Peas, .	5·25	149·1	36·67	1·49	92·44	5·25	149·1	36·67	1·49	92·44
Barley, .	7·5	213	18·1	2·34	165·71	7·5	213	18·1	2·34	165·71
Rice, .	3	85·2	6·81	·25	67·3	3	85·2	6·81	·25	67·3
Sugar, .	7	198·8	..	..	198·8	9·4	266·96	..	..	266·96
Syrup, .	·25	7·1	..	..	4·92	·25	7·1	..	..	4·92
Potatoes, .	72	2044·8	36·8	2·04	300·58	72	2044·8	36·8	2·04	300·58
Fresh Vegetables, .	24	681·6	9·54	1·36	32·71	24	681·6	9·54	1·36	32·71
Currants, Raisins, .	·50	14·2	·33	·33	10·12	·50	14·2	·33	·33	10·12
Tea,.	1	28·4	..	..	..	1·5	42·6	..	..	..
Total, .	..	..	800·87	532·56	3047·41	..	..	611·08	451·88	2595·54

Food Values.—The average daily food values of the male and female dietaries are as follows:—

	Proteid.	Fat.	Carbo-hydrate.	Energy Value.
Male .	114·4	76·1	435·7	2969
Female .	87·3	64·5	370·8	2478

Average height of working male patients is 65 inches, their average weight 144·1 lbs.

Critical Remarks.—The results got from the returns from this asylum are contradictory. On the one hand the dietaries, both male and female, appear to be insufficient, as they appear to contain too little proteid and to have insufficient energy values, and there appears to be no special allowance made for the wants of working male patients, but on the other hand the average weight of those patients is such as to show that they are being properly fed. I am unable to explain this contradiction, especially so as I am assured by the Medical Superintendent of the asylum that the regulation dietary is closely adhered to, and that both the dietary schedule and the weight returns were correctly made out.

The details in the schedule show these dietaries, though appearing to be short in quantity, to be of excellent quality, they are varied, they contain a reasonable amount of fresh vegetable and condiments. The allowance of bread and meat are both below the average, a freer use of these two foodstuffs would greatly improve the diets. Some extra food for male working patients appears necessary.

EDINBURGH ROYAL ASYLUM.

Breakfast.—The majority of both sexes get tea, bread and butter; the remainder of the males get porridge and milk; of the remainder of the females a few receive porridge and milk only, the rest both porridge with milk and tea with bread and butter.

Dinner.—The weekly routine includes broth on six days, on three broth days beef and potato are given, on one potato and dumpling, on one fish and potato, and on one bread and cheese. On the day on which broth is not given the dinner consists of Irish stew and bread. Meat is thus given on four days a week, on one of these tinned meat is used. Bread is only given with two dinners weekly.

Evening Meal.—All the patients get tea bread and butter only. A few men and a considerable number of females receive porridge and milk as a supper.

Extras for Working Patients.—All the more actively worked inmates receive a luncheon of bread and cheese, the male inmates getting half a pint of beer in addition.

It is to be noted in the schedule that special extra food is largely used in this asylum, no less than 20 per cent. of the males and 25 per cent. of the females are excluded from the returns as receiving such extras. It is also to be noted that the routine diet is varied in summer, rice and stewed rhubarb being frequently given in place of broth.

Dietary for Females.—The differences between the dieting of the males and that of the females are that some of the latter get both porridge and bread for breakfast, that more of them have the late supper, that their bread allowance per meal is less, 5 oz. as against 7½ oz., and that they do not get beer.

[TABLE.

Table showing the Average Weekly Composition of Dietaries.

	MALE.					FEMALE.				
	Quantity.		Proteid.	Fat.	Carbo-hydrate	Quantity.		Proteid.	Fat.	Carbo-hydrate.
	Oz.	Grms.				Oz.	Grms.			
Beef, ...	25·5	724·2	142·75	136·60	..	25·5	724·2	142·75	136·60	..
Heads, Bones, &c., .	8·0	227·2	22·03	8·86	..	8·0	227·2	22·03	8·86	..
Fish (Fresh), . .	6·0	170·4	29·3	·51	..	6·0	170·4	29·3	·51	..
Suet, ...	·5	14·2	·66	11·61	..	·5	14·2	·66	11·61	..
Butter, ...	4·0	113·6	1·12	96·56	..	6·0	170·4	1·7	144·84	..
Milk (Whole), . .	40	1136·0	37·48	45·44	56·8	40	1136·0	37·48	45·44	56·8
Milk (Skimmed), . .	35	994·0	33·79	2·98	50·69	60	1704·0	57·93	5·11	86·9
Cheese, ...	6·75	191·7	53·09	70·53	7·86	5·0	142·0	39·33	52·25	5·92
Bread, ...	118	3351	308·3	43·56	1779·48	109·0	3096·6	284·79	40·24	1643·76
Oatmeal, ...	21·66	615·14	99·03	44·29	415·21	24·67	700·62	112·79	50·44	472·91
Flour, ...	3·0	85·2	9·71	·85	64·41	3·0	85·2	9·71	·85	64·41
Peas, ...	4·5	127·8	31·43	1·27	79·23	4·4	124·96	30·74	1·24	77·47
Barley, ...	7·5	213·0	18·1	2·34	165·71	7·3	207·32	17·62	2·28	161·29
Rice, ...	3·0	85·2	6·81	·25	67·3	3·0	85·2	6·81	·25	67·3
Sugar, ...	5·5	156·2	..	..	156·2	8·0	227·2	..	..	227·2
Potatoes, . . .	108·0	3067·2	55·2	3·06	450·96	104·0	2953·6	53·16	2·94	434·16
Fresh Vegetables, .	12·7	360·68	5·04	·72	17·31	12·7	360·68	5·04	·72	17·31
Currants, . . .	·5	14·2	·34	·24	10·53	·5	14·2	·34	·24	10·53
Tea, Coffee, . . .	1·9	53·96	..	..	..	2·5	71·0	..	..	..
Beer, ...	47	1334	6·67	..	150·08	..	..	..	..	..
Total, . .	..	..	860·85	469·67	3471·67	..	..	852·18	504·42	3325·96

Food Values.—The average daily compositions of the male and female dietaries are as follows:—

	Proteid.	Fat.	Carbo-hydrate.	Energy Value.
Male	123	67·1	496	3162
Female . . .	121·7	72·1	475·1	3117

Average height of male working patients is 65·6 inches, average weight 143 lbs.

Critical Remarks.—A comparison of the food values of the diets of this asylum with the male and female standards shows that the male diet is somewhat below the standard and the female in considerable excess of the standard. When in any institution, as is here to be seen, the male and female diets are of nearly equal value it may be assumed that both are not correct; in this instance the chief fault is excessive feeding of females, their diet being nearly 18 per cent. too much, the male diet being only about 4 per cent. too small. Notwithstanding the shortage of the male diet the male workers are found to average more than standard weight, a contradiction which is due to their receiving an ample luncheon. In other respects these diets are very good, they are varied and condiment is sufficiently used. One necessary improvement that becomes evident by a critical examination of them is an increase of the food allowance of the male patients; this could readily be brought about by giving bread with all dinners instead of only twice weekly as at present. The allowance of fresh fish for the weekly fish dinner is too small, and might with advantage be doubled.

MONTROSE ROYAL ASYLUM.

Breakfast.—The majority get porridge and milk only. The remainder, about 25 per cent. of the males and 40 per cent. of the females, get tea bread and butter in addition.

Dinner.—The weekly routine includes broth on four days, once with Irish stew, once with fish and potato, and twice with beef and potato, lentil soup with tinned beef on one day, potato soup with fruit dumpling on one day, and pea soup with mealy pudding on one day. Fresh meat is given on three days a week, tinned beef on one. Bread is given daily with dinner.

Evening Meal.—For all inmates this consists of tea bread and butter. Syrup and jam are given once weekly.

Extras for Working Patients.—Tea with bread and butter is given to a few who do early work in the morning. Female patients working in the laundry on Monday and at "spring cleaning" get bread and beer in the forenoon and tea with bread and butter or jam in the afternoon.

Dietary for Females differs from that for males by having smaller portions, notably of bread and soup.

[TABLE.

Table showing the Average Weekly Composition of Dietaries.

	MALE.					FEMALE.				
	Quantity.		Proteid.	Fat.	Carbo-hydrate.	Quantity.		Proteid.	Fat.	Carbo-hydrate.
	Oz.	Grms.				Oz.	Grms.			
Beef, ...	20	568	115·28	105·75	..	19	539·6	107 81	100·44	..
Pork, ...	4	113·6	13·63	33·85	..	4	113·6	13·63	33·85	..
Fish (Fresh), . .	7	198·8	33·62	·59	..	7	198·8	33·62	·59	..
Suet, ...	·25	7·1	·33	5·8	..	·25	7·1	·33	5·8	..
Butter, ...	7	198·8	1·96	168·96	..	7	198·8	1·96	168·96	..
Milk (Whole), . .	90	2556	84·34	102·24	127·8	90	2556	84·34	102·24	127·8
Cheese, . . .	2	56·8	15·73	20·	2·33	2	56·8	15·73	20·9	2·33
Bread, ...	106	3010·4	276·95	39·13	1598·52	83	2357·2	216·96	30·64	1251·67
Oatmeal, . . .	23·6	670·24	107·9	48·25	452·41	23·6	670·24	107·9	48·25	452·41
Flour, . . .	3	85·2	9·71	·85	64·41	3	85·2	9·71	·85	64·41
Peas, Lentils, . .	9	255·6	64·27	2·54	154·68	8	227·2	57·13	2·26	138·68
Barley, ...	4·57	134·9	11·46	1·48	104·96	4·25	120·7	10·25	1·32	93·9
Rice, ...	1·1	31·24	2·49	·09	24·67	1·1	31·24	2·49	·09	24·67
Sugar, ...	10·5	298·2	..	..	298·2	10·5	298·2	..	..	298·2
Treacle, Marmalade, &c.,	3·5	99·4	·34	·05	77·51	3·5	99·4	·34	·05	77·51
Potatoes, . . .	80	2272	40·89	2·27	333·96	80	2272	40·89	2·27	333·96
Fresh Vegetables, .	24·1	684·44	9·58	1·96	32·85	24·1	684·44	9·58	1·96	32·85
Currants, Raisins, .	1·25	35·5	·84	·78	25·52	1·25	35·5	·84	·78	25·52
Tea, ...	1·75	49·7	..	..	..	1·75	49·7	..	..	..
Total, . .	..	..	789·32	534·89	3298·03	..	..	713·41	520·65	2922·93

Food Values.—The average daily food values of the male and female dietaries are as follows :—

	Proteid.	Fat.	Carbo-hydrate.	Energy Value.
Male	112·8	76·4	471·1	3105
Female . . .	101·9	74·4	417·7	2822

Average height of male working patients is 66·4 inches, average weight 147·5 lbs.

Critical Remarks.—The dietaries of this asylum are in most respects excellent. The food is varied, fresh vegetable and condiments are sufficiently used, but the male diet falls short of the standard, both as regards energy value and the proteid value. This shortage may be ascribed to male breakfasts being insufficient. The schedule states that the majority of male patients receive porridge and milk only, and that their allowance of oatmeal is only three ounces per head. The doubling of that allowance would make the porridge breakfast a reasonable quantity, and would correct this imperfection of the diet. The female dietary appears to be ample. A luncheon for male workers is desirable.

(2.) District Asylums.

ARGYLL DISTRICT ASYLUM.

Breakfast.—The majority have porridge and milk only, while a few of both sexes get tea bread and butter only.

Dinner.—The weekly routine contains one dinner of rice and milk and bread and cheese, one of broth beef and potato, one of pea soup beef and potato, two dinners of broth fish and potato, one of broth suet pudding and bread, and one of Irish stew. Fresh meat is given on two days, tinned meat on one day, fish on two. Bread is given on two days only.

Evening Meal.—This for all consists of tea bread and butter, and marmalade one night weekly.

Extras for Working Patients.—Patients doing a fair day's work get milk and bread for lunch. Some women workers get tea and bread in the early morning and again in the course of the afternoon. Some male patients and a few female patients get an allowance of porridge as a supper.

Dietary for Females differs from that for males by having smaller rations of many foods, especially bread, oatmeal, soup, and fish. The freer use of extras to some females has been noted.

TABLE.

34

Table showing the Average Weekly Composition of Dietaries.

	MALE					FEMALE				
	Quantity		Proteid.	Fat.	Carbo-hydrate	Quantity		Proteid.	Fat.	Carbo-hydrate
	Oz.	Grms.				Oz.	Grms.			
Beef, ...	18·13	514·88	102·53	98·26	..	14·51	412·07	83·15	74·16	..
Heads, Hough, &c.,	6·14	174·37	16·91	6·8	..	6·14	174·37	16·91	6·8	..
Fish (Fresh), . .	11	312·4	52·87	·93	..	8	227·2	38·50	·68	..
Fish (Salt), . . .	7·8	225·52	46·23	19·34	..	7·8	225·52	46·23	19·34	..
Suet, ...	1·5	42·6	2·0	34·84	..	1·5	42·6	2·0	34·84	..
Butter, ...	4·49	127·51	1·27	108·38	..	4·49	127·51	1·27	108·38	..
Eggs, ...	2·96	84·06	10·0	7·81	..	2·96	84·06	10·0	7·81	..
Milk (Whole), . .	125·40	3561·36	117·52	142·45	178·06	125·40	3561·36	117·52	142·45	178·06
Milk (Condensed), .	·53	15·05	1·32	1·24	8·14	·53	15·05	1·32	1·24	8·14
Bread, ...	102·91	2922·64	268·88	37·99	1561·92	81·88	2325·39	213·93	30·23	1234·73
Oatmeal, ...	33·18	942·31	151·71	67·84	636·05	26·54	753·73	121·35	54·26	508·76
Flour, ...	4·46	126·66	14·43	1·26	95·75	4·46	126·66	14·43	1·26	95·75
Peas, ...	3·04	86·33	21·23	·86	53·52	3·04	86·33	21·23	·86	53·52
Barley, ...	5·08	144·27	12·26	1·58	112·24	5·08	144·27	12·26	1·58	112·24
Rice, ...	2·49	70·71	5·65	·21	55·96	2·49	70·71	5·65	·21	55·96
Sugar, ...	9·5	156·2	..	..	156·2	9·5	156·2	..	..	156·2
Jam, Treacle, &c., .	4·28	121·54	·4	·06	94·41	4·28	121·54	·4	·06	94·41
Potatoes, . . .	96	2726·4	49·04	2·72	400·76	96	2726·4	49·04	2·72	400·76
Fresh Vegetables, .	31	880·4	12·32	1·76	42·25	31	880·4	12·32	1·76	42·25
Currants, . . .	·71	19·38	·47	·33	14·75	·71	19·38	·47	·33	14·75
Tea, ...	1·57	44·58	..	..	..	1·57	44·58	..	..	..
Total, . .	..	..	887·04	530·16	3400·01	..	..	767·98	489·47	2955·58

Food Values.—The average daily composition of the male and female dietaries is as follows:—

	Proteid.	Fat.	Carbo-hydrate.	Energy Value.
Male	126·7	75·7	485·7	3215
Female . . .	109·7	69·9	422·2	2831

Average height of male working patients is 65·6 inches, average weight 147·3.

Critical Remarks.—The energy value of the average male dietary nearly coincides with the standard. That of the female dietary is some excess of the standard. The proteid values of both are in excess of the standards. The quality of the diet appears to be excellent, the use of fresh vegetable and of condiments is ample, and variety is sufficient. The special wants of the working patients are allowed for. The average weight of the male working patients is satisfactory.

AYR DISTRICT ASYLUM.

Breakfast.—About half of the male and nearly all the female patients get both porridge and milk, and tea with bread and butter. Of the other half of the male patients the most get porridge and milk only. A few male and female patients get tea with bread and butter only.

Dinner.—The weekly routine includes one dinner of rice and milk and bread and cheese, one of pea soup, meat stewed with vegetable and potato, one of broth, bread, and pudding, one of broth, fish, and potato, one of lentil soup, meat stewed with vegetable, and potato or Irish stew, and two of rice soup with beef and potato. Fresh meat is given on three days, and tinned meat on one day. Bread is given on two days only.

Evening Meal.—This consists of tea with bread and butter for all.

Extras for Working Patients.—A few male patients get milk, bread, and butter in the afternoon. Females in the laundry get milk or beef tea or custard and bread in the forenoon, and those in the kitchen and laundry get tea, bread and marmalade in the afternoon.

Dietary for females differs from that for males by having smaller rations of oatmeal and bread.

Table showing the Average Weekly Composition of Dietaries.

	MALE.					FEMALE.				
	Quantity.		Proteid.	Fat.	Carbo-hydrate	Quantity.		Proteid.	Fat.	Carbo-hydrate
	Oz.	Grms.				Oz.	Grms.			
Beef, ...	18·0	511·2	110·56	94·22	..	18·0	511·2	110·56	94·22	..
Heads, Bones, &c.,.	8·0	227·2	22·08	8·86	..	8·0	227·2	22·08	8·86	..
Fish (Fresh), . .	8·0	227·2	37·94	·68	..	8·0	227·2	37·94	·68	..
Suet, ...	·75	21·3	1·0	17·42	..	·75	21·3	1·0	17·42	..
Butter, ...	5·5	156·2	1·56	132·77	..	5·5	156·2	1·56	132·77	..
Milk (Whole), . .	100	2840·0	98·72	113·6	142·0	100	2840·0	98·72	113·6	142·0
Cheese, . . .	2·0	56·8	15·73	20·9	2·33	2·0	56·8	15·73	20·9	2·33
Bread, ...	106·0	3010·4	276·95	39·13	1598·52	80·0	2272·0	209·02	29·53	1206·53
Oatmeal, , . . .	35·0	994·0	160·08	71·56	670·95	17·5	497·0	80·02	35·78	335·47
Flour, ...	4·0	113·6	12·95	1·13	85·88	4·0	113·6	12·95	1·13	85·88
Peas, Lentils, . .	11·0	312·4	78·25	3·11	190·10	11·0	312·4	78·25	3·11	190·10
Barley, ...	3·0	85·2	7·24	·93	66·23	3·0	85·2	7·24	·93	66·23
Rice, ...	7·0	198·8	15·9	·59	157·05	7·0	198·8	15·9	·59	157·05
Sugar, ...	4·5	127·8	..	..	127·8	4·75	134·9	..	..	134·9
Syrup, Marmalade,.	3·25	92·3	·5	·08	76·90	3·25	92·3	·5	·08	76·90
Potatoes,. . . .	80·0	2272·0	40·89	2·27	333·98	80·0	2272·0	40·89	2·27	333·98
Fresh Vegetables, .	23·25	660·3	9·24	1·32	31·69	23·25	660·3	9·24	1·32	31·69
Tea, ...	1·0	28·4	..	..	..	1·5	42·6	..	..	..
Total, . .	..	..	884·49	506·57	3483·48	..	..	736·55	463·19	2763·11

Food Values.—The average daily food values of the male and female dietaries are as follows:—

	Proteid.	Fat.	Carbo-hydrate.	Energy Value.
Male	126·4	72·6	467·6	3234
Female . . .	105·2	66·2	394·7	2665

Average height of male working patients is 66·5 inches, average weight 152·3 lbs.

Critical Remarks.—These are in all ways excellent diets. The food values of both closely agree with the standard, variety is sufficient, the use of fresh vegetable and condiment is ample, and the special wants of working patients are provided for. The average weight of working patients is satisfactory.

BANFF DISTRICT ASYLUM.

Breakfast.—Nearly all the male inmates have porridge and milk and bread, about one-third of them get tea in addition. Most of the females get porridge and milk and tea with bread and butter, while some get porridge and milk and bread only. A few of both sexes receive tea bread and butter only.

Dinner.—The weekly routine contains one dinner of rice milk and cheese, three of broth, meat and potato, one of pea soup and pudding, one of Irish stew, and one of beef, green vegetable and oatmeal brose. Bread is given with every dinner. Meat is given on four days a week. The composition of the broth is varied.

Evening Meal.—The majority of male patients receive porridge and milk and tea with bread and butter, a few get tea with bread and butter only. Of the female patients the majority get tea bread and butter only, a few get porridge in addition.

Extras for Working Patients.—A few of both sexes receive brose and bread with either milk or tea as an early breakfast. All more actively worked patients get bread with either syrup or jam and either coffee or milk in the forenoon, and tea with bread and either butter or jam in the afternoon. Laundry and kitchen workers have as an addition twice weekly either fresh fish or an egg in the forenoon. Some kitchen workers have some milk and bread as a supper.

Dietary for females differs from that of the males in having smaller rations of bread, oatmeal, potato, and beef.

Table showing the Average Weekly Composition of Dietaries.

	MALE.					FEMALE.				
	Quantity.		Proteid.	Fat.	Carbo-hydrate	Quantity.		Proteid.	Fat.	Carbo-hydrate
	Oz.	Grms.				Oz.	Grms.			
Beef, ...	20·0	568·0	106·20	105·98	..	16·0	454·4	84·85	84·85	..
Heads, Bones, &c., .	4·0	113·6	11·02	4·43	..	4·0	113·6	11·02	4·43	..
Fish (Fresh), . .	..	..	..	..	..	2·0	56·8	9·77	·17	..
Suet, ...	1·0	28·4	1·32	23·22	..	1·0	28·4	1·32	23·22	..
Butter, ...	4·0	113·6	1·12	96·56	..	4·0	113·6	1·12	96·56	..
Eggs, ...	..	..	..	..	..	·66	18·74	2·23	1·73	..
Milk (Whole), . .	120	3402·0	112·96	136·08	170·1	80	2272·0	74·97	90·98	113·6
Cheese, ...	3·0	85·2	23·6	31·85	3·49	2·0	56·8	15·73	20·9	2·33
Bread, ...	140·0	3976·0	365·79	51·98	2111·25	100·0	2840·0	261·28	36·92	1508·04
Oatmeal, . . .	66·0	1874·4	301·77	134·95	1265·22	40·0	1136·0	182·28	81·78	766·8
Flour, ...	2·5	71·0	8·09	·71	53·68	2·0	56·8	6·47	·56	42·94
Peas, ...	7·0	198·8	43·9	1·98	123·25	7·0	198·8	43·9	1·98	123·25
Barley, ...	3·0	85·2	7·24	·93	66·28	3·0	85·2	7·24	·93	66·28
Rice, ...	3·0	85·2	6·81	·25	67·3	3·0	85·2	6·81	·25	7·3
Sugar, ...	4·5	127·8	..	..	127·8	6·0	170·4	..	..	170·4
Syrup, Jam, . .	1·5	42·6	·17	·08	33·93	3·0	85·2	·34	·05	67·87
Potatoes, . . .	62·0	1760·8	31·69	1·76	258·83	52·0	1476·8	26·58	1·47	217·08
Fresh Vegetables, .	26·25	745·5	10·43	1·49	35·78	22·25	631·9	8·84	1·26	30·23
Currants, Raisins, .	1·0	28·4	·67	·66	20·25	1·0	28·4	·67	·66	20·25
Tea, Coffee, . .	·9	25·56	..	..	..	2·1	59·64	..	..	..
Total, . .	..	..	1087·08	592·06	4337·06	..	..	751·02	448·6	3196·27

Food Values.—The average daily food values of the male and female dietaries are as follows :—

	Proteid.	Fat.	Carbo-hydrate.	Energy Value.
Male	148·5	84·6	619·6	3934
Female . . .	107·3	64·1	456·6	2907

Average height of male working patients is 67·2 inches, average weight 151·9 lbs.

Critical Remarks.—The energy and proteid values of both male and female dietaries not only satisfy the standard, but are in excess. Carbohydrate is somewhat excessive in the male diet. Ample allowance is made for the special wants of working patients. Fresh vegetables are sufficiently used. By the free use of oatmeal the diets are adapted to the custom of the part of Scotland in which the asylum is situated, but the use of oatmeal is not carried to excess. The average weight of the male working patients is satisfactory. The allowance of tea, specially at breakfast, might with advantage be increased.

ELGIN DISTRICT ASYLUM.

Breakfast.—One-third of the male patients receive porridge and milk only, the remainder of the male patients and all the female patients get tea with bread and butter either alone or along with porridge. The rations of oatmeal, milk, and bread vary according to whether the patients get porridge and bread, or porridge only.

Dinner.—The weekly routine contains one dinner of broth and cheese, three of broth and pudding, one of broth, beef and potato, one of rice soup and Irish stew, and one of pea soup, fish and potato. Bread is given with all dinners. A small quantity of meat is given daily in the soup, separate meat rations are given on two days only. The puddings are varied.

Evening Meal.—This consists of tea with bread and butter for all, and porridge and milk in addition for many.

Extras for Working Patients.—Some working females get tea with bread and marmalade in the early morning. All working women receive milk with bread and marmalade in the forenoon, and tea with bread and marmalade or jam in the afternoon. Male working patients get in the forenoon an extra consisting of bread and marmalade.

Dietary for females differs from that for males by having smaller rations of bread, meat, and potatoes, by all receiving tea for breakfast, and by the freer use of extras.

Table showing the Average Weekly Composition of Dietaries.

	MALE.					FEMALE.				
	Quantity.		Proteid.	Fat.	Carbo-hydrate	Quantity.		Proteid.	Fat.	Carbo-hydrate
	Oz.	Grms.				Oz.	Grms.			
Beef, ...	26·5	752·6	127·72	142·24	..	24·5	695·8	127·33	131·5	..
Fish (Fresh), . .	12·0	340·8	58·6	1·02	..	8	227·2	39·06	·68	..
Suet, ...	3·0	85·2	4·0	69·69	..	3	85·2	4·0	69·69	..
Butter, ...	6·75	191·7	1·91	162·94	..	7·5	213	2·13	181·05	..
Milk (Whole), .	145	4116·0	185·89	164·72	205·9	122	3464·8	114·33	138·59	173·21
Cheese, ...	3	85·2	23·6	31·35	3·49	3	85·2	23·6	31·35	3·49
Bread, ...	106	3010·4	276·95	39·13	1506·52	111	3152·4	290·02	40·98	1708·92
Oatmeal, . . .	31·5	894·6	144·03	64·41	603·25	18·5	525·4	84·58	37·82	354·64
Flour, ...	10·5	298·2	33·99	2·98	225·43	8·5	241·4	27·51	2·41	182·49
Peas, ...	4	113·6	27·94	1·13	71·43	4	113·6	27·94	1·13	71·43
Barley, ...	6	170·4	14·48	1·87	132·57	6	170·4	14·48	1·87	132·57
Rice, ...	4	113·6	9·08	3·4	89·74	4	113·6	9·08	3·4	89·74
Sugar, ...	9·5	269·8	..	..	269·8	11·5	326·6	..	..	326·6
Syrup, Marmalade, .	8·5	241·4	1·1	·18	195·34	7·5	213	·98	·15	171·34
Potatoes, . . .	42	1192·8	21·47	1·99	175·34	36	1022·4	18·4	1·02	150·29
Fresh Vegetables, .	31·75	901·7	12·62	1·8	43·28	31·75	901·7	12·62	1·8	43·28
Tea, ...	1·5	42·6	..	..	..	2·2	62·48	..	..	..
Total, . .	..	..	908·28	688·25	3614·69	..	..	796·01	643·44	3403·03

Food Values.—The average daily food values of the male and female dietaries are as follows:—

	Proteid.	Fat.	Carbo-hydrate.	Energy Value.
Male	120·0	98·5	516·4	3561
Female . .	113·7	91·9	486·1	3314

Average height of male working patients is 66·8 inches, average weight 143·8 lbs.

Critical Remarks.—The diets of this asylum appear to be good. Their only fault, and that is not a bad one, is that they are rather excessive; the female diet is especially so. They are varied, the wants of working patients are allowed for, and the use of condiments is sufficient. The average weight of the male working patients is satisfactory.

FIFE AND KINROSS DISTRICT ASYLUM.

Breakfast.—The majority of patients both male and female get both porridge and milk and tea with bread and butter, some of both sexes get porridge and milk only, and some tea with bread and butter only.

Dinner.—The weekly routine includes a dinner of rice and milk tinned beef and bread and cheese, two of broth, beef and potato, two of broth, bread and suet pudding, one of broth, fish and potato, and one of stewed meat with vegetable and potato. Meat is given four times a week, twice being fresh meat and twice tinned meat. Bread is given with three dinners.

Evening Meal.—The female patients get tea with bread and butter or marmalade every evening. On four evenings in the week the male patients have tea and bread and butter or marmalade. On three evenings they have porridge and milk, or tea and bread and butter.

Extras for Working Patients.—A few get an early breakfast. A luncheon of bread and cheese is given to all working patients. Female patients working in laundry get tea. A supper consisting of coffee and bread is given to some male patients who do extra work.

Dietary for females differs from that for males in that the rations of bread, meal, and potatoes are smaller.

[TABLE.

Table showing the Average Weekly Composition of Dietaries.

	MALE					FEMALE				
	Quantity.		Proteid.	Fat.	Carbo-hydrate	Quantity.		Proteid.	Fat.	Carbo-hydrate
	Oz.	Grms.				Oz.	Grms.			
Beef, ...	24·8	704·32	144·33	132·72	..	20·6	585·04	119·77	110·25	..
Heads, Bones, &c., . .	5·7	161·88	15·7	6·31	..	5·7	161·88	15·7	6·31	..
Pork, ...	2·7	76·68	9·0	22·85	..	2·5	71	8·52	21·15	..
Fish (Fresh), . . .	4·3	122·12	20·39	·36	..	4·3	122·12	20·39	·36	..
Stock Fish, . . .	4·2	119·28	32·56	3·57	..	4·2	119·28	32·56	3·57	..
Suet, ...	1·5	42·6	2·0	34·34	..	1·5	42·6	2·0	34·84	..
Butter, ...	2·8	79·52	·79	67·59	..	3·7	105·08	1·05	89·31	..
Milk (Whole), . . .	120	3402	112·26	136·08	170·1	84	2385·6	78·72	95·42	119·28
Cheese, ...	4·9	139·16	38·54	51·21	5·7	4·9	139·16	38·54	51·21	5·7
Bread (White, Brown), .	123	3498·2	300·96	48·10	1822·51	113	3209·2	277·97	43·96	1676·81
Oatmeal, ...	38	1079·2	173·75	77·7	728·46	25	710	114·31	51·12	479·25
Flour, ...	9·2	261·28	29·78	2·61	197·52	6·9	195·96	22·33	1·95	148·14
Lentils, ...	3·3	93·72	24·07	·93	55·48	3·3	93·72	24·07	·93	55·48
Barley, ...	4	113·6	9·65	1·24	88·38	4	113·6	9·65	1·24	88·38
Rice, ...	3·1	88·04	7·04	·26	69·55	3·1	88·04	7·04	·26	69·55
Sugar, ...	6	170·4	..	..	170·4	7·7	218·68	..	..	218·68
Syrup, Jam, &c., . .	4·3	122·12	·69	·11	102·32	4·3	122·12	·69	·11	102·32
Potatoes, ...	101	2866·4	51·63	2·86	421·65	67	1902·8	34·24	1·9	279·71
Fresh Vegetables, . .	31·1	883·24	12·56	1·76	42·39	31·1	883·24	12·36	1·76	42·39
Currants, Raisins, . .	2·4	68·16	1·59	1·59	48·62	2·4	68·16	1·59	1·59	48·62
Tea, ...	1	28·4	.	..	..	1·3	36·92	..	..	..
Total, . .	..	..	986·99	592·69	3923·08	..	..	821·5	517·26	3334·31

Food Values.—The average daily food values of the male and female dietaries are as follows :—

	Proteid.	Fat.	Carbo-hydrate.	Energy Value.
Male . . .	141·0	84·7	560·4	3663
Female . . .	117·3	73·9	476·3	3121

Average height of male working patients is 65·6 inches, average weight 143·7 lbs.

Critical Remarks.—Both the male and female dietaries appear to be of ample quantity, they both more than meet the standards. The female dietary is in considerable excess of the standard. The special wants of working patients are amply provided for. Fresh vegetables and potatoes are freely used, and the food is varied.

41

The allowances of meat are ample, but the dietary would be improved by giving fresh meat oftener and tinned meat more seldom. The average weight of the male working patients is satisfactory.

GLASGOW (GARTLOCH) ASYLUM.

Breakfast.—On week days all get porridge and milk and tea with bread and margarine. On Sundays an extra allowance of bread and some marmalade is given in lieu of porridge.

Dinner.—The weekly routine of dinners in this asylum is subject to frequent change. From the routines submitted it is seen that soup is given five or six times a week, rice and milk once a week, fish once or twice a week, pudding or stewed fruit once or twice a week, potato about six times a week, bread only once or twice a week, and cheese occasionally. On several occasions during the month the dinner served in the hospital dining hall was different from that served in the general dining hall.

Evening Meal.—All get tea bread and margarine daily, with jam as an addition once weekly.

Extras for Working Patients.—Females working in the kitchen and laundry get tea with bread or jelly in the forenoon and in the afternoon. Extra food is not as a rule given to male workers.

Dietary for females differs from that for males by having smaller rations of bread, meat, and fish.

[TABLE.

42

Table showing the Average Weekly Composition of Dietaries.

	MALE.				FEMALE.				
	Quantity.		Proteid.	Fat.	Carbo-hydrate	Quantity.		Proteid.	Fat.	Carbo-hydrate
	Oz.	Grms.				Oz.	Grms.			
Beef, . . .	28·4	805·56	155·27	130·98	..	23·6	670·24	131·24	109·82	..
Heads, Hough, &c., .	8	227·2	22·03	8·96	..	8	227·2	22·03	8·96	..
Mutton Sides, . . .	4	113·6	14·76	27·26	..	3	85·2	11·07	20·44	..
Pork, ...	4	113·6	13·63	33·65	..	3	85·2	10·22	25·38	..
Fish (Fresh), . .	11	312·4	52·55	·93	..	9	255·6	43·0	·76	..
Stock Fish, . . .	1·5	42·6	11·62	·12	..	1·25	35·5	9·69	·1	..
Suet, ...	·5	14·2	·06	11·61	..	·5	14·2	·06	11·61	..
Margarine, . . .	5·9	167·56	2·01	130·07	..	5·9	167·56	2·01	130·07	..
Milk (Whole), . . .	95	2698	89·08	107·92	134·9	95	2698	89·08	107·92	134·9
Cheese, ...	1	28·4	7·96	10·45	1·16	1	28·4	7·96	10·45	1·16
Bread, ...	112	3180·8	292·63	41·35	1689·0	82	2328·8	214·24	30·27	1236·59
Oatmeal, ...	19	539·6	86·87	33·85	364·23	19	539·6	86·87	33·85	364·23
Flour, ...	4	113·6	12·96	1·12	85·38	3·25	92·3	10·52	·92	69·77
Peas, Lentils, . . .	5	142	25·54	1·41	86·44	5	142	25·54	1·41	86·44
Barley, ...	3	85·2	7·24	·93	66·23	3	85·2	7·24	·93	66·23
Rice, ...	4·9	139·16	11·13	·41	109·93	4·9	139·16	11·13	·41	109·93
Sago, ...	·5	14·2	1·27	·05	11·09	·5	14·2	1·27	·05	11·09
Sugar, ...	7·6	215·84	..	..	215·84	7·6	215·84	..	..	215·84
Syrup, Jam, &c., . .	3	85·2	·34	·05	67·67	3	85·2	·34	·05	67·67
Potatoes, . . .	90	2556	46·0	2·55	375·73	90	2556	46·0	2·55	375·73
Fresh Vegetables, . .	34	965·6	13·51	1·93	46·34	34	965·6	13·51	1·93	46·34
Currants, Raisins, . .	2·2	62·48	1·45	1·68	43·60	2·2	62·48	1·45	1·68	43·60
Tea, Coffee, . . .	1·5	42·6	..	..	..	1·56	44·37	..	..	..
Ginger, ...	·06	1·77	..	..	..	..	..	..	..	..
Total, . .	..	..	878·35	561·74	3296·09	..	..	754·92	513·46	2829·57

Food Values.—The average daily food values of the male and female dietaries are as follows:—

	Proteid.	Fat.	Carbo-hydrate.	Energy Value.
Male	125·5	80·2	471·1	3192
Female . . .	107·8	73·3	404·2	2781

Average height of male working patients is 65·5 inches, their average weight is 134·8 lbs. Male patients working outside have an average height of 65·7 inches and an average weight of 135·1 lbs.

Critical Remarks.—A very commendable feature of the dietary of this asylum is variety. This is specially noticeable in the dinner routine. The male diet is in some ways faulty. The average food value is too small, and it does not allow for the special wants of the working patients. These assertions are based on a comparison of the food value to the standard, and by the result of the weight test, which shows the average weight of working patients to be decidedly too small, 134·8 lbs. as against 140 lbs. These assertions are further supported by notes I made when visiting the asylum and inspecting the service of a dinner; I reproduce them:—" Dinner consisted of potato soup, ginger pudding, and bread. Quantities limited, a portion to each table, which was equally divided. Absolutely no food left over." The female dietary appears to be sufficient and good in all respects. The male dietary of this asylum would be much improved if some food such as bread or oatcake were given *ad libitum* with all dinners, and were the working patients given some luncheon during the forenoon. The dietary is amply sufficient for idle inmates, but not for those doing a moderate day's work.

GLASGOW (WOODILEE) ASYLUM.

Breakfast.—Nearly two-thirds of the male patients get porridge and milk and bread, the remainder get porridge and milk and tea with bread and margarine. Of the female patients about two-thirds get tea bread and margarine only, the remainder getting porridge and milk in addition.

Dinner.—The routine of dinners is varied and is not the same on any two weeks of a month. Soup is given five or six times a week, rice and milk is usually given once, meat is given three or four times a week, fish once or twice a week, pudding about twice a week, potato four times a week, bread to male patients only when potato is not given, to female patients it is given daily, coffee is given once weekly, and cheese occasionally. A great variety of dishes appear in these routines; especially is this so with regard to puddings, for no fewer than nine different puddings are mentioned in the schedule.

Evening Meal.—This consists of tea bread and butter for all, jam and marmalade being occasionally given.

Extras for Working Patients.—A few men and a considerable number of women get an early breakfast, consisting of tea, bread and margarine. No lunch is given to either sex. Afternoon tea is given to females working in the laundry and kitchen.

Dietary for females differs from that for males by having the different breakfast already noted, by having a small daily ration of bread at dinner, by having smaller rations of meat, fish, and dinner bread on days when no potato is given, and by a more liberal use of margarine.

[TABLE.

Table showing the Average Weekly Composition of Dietaries.

	MALE					FEMALE				
	Quantity		Proteid.	Fat.	Carbo-hydrate	Quantity		Proteid.	Fat.	Carbo-hydrate
	Oz.	Grms.				Oz.	Grms.			
Beef, ...	25·5	724·2	144·44	185·58	..	18·25	518·3	106·19	96·69	..
Heads, Hough, &c., .	1	28·4	2·74	1·1	..	1	28·4	2·74	1·1	..
Mutton Sides, . .	1	28·4	3·69	6·81	..	1	28·4	3·69	6·81	..
Pork, ...	1	28·4	3·4	8·46	..	·5	14·2	1·7	4·23	..
Fish (Fresh), .	8	227·2	38·50	·68	..	6	170·4	28·37	·50	..
Stock Fish, . .	3	85·2	23·25	·25	..	3	85·2	23·25	·25	..
Suet, . . .	2·5	71	3·33	58·07	..	2·5	71·0	3·33	58·07	..
Margarine, . .	4·4	124·96	2·49	103·71	..	5	142	1·7	117·86	..
Milk (Whole), . .	96	2726·4	89·97	109·05	136·22	60	1704	56·23	68·16	85·2
Cheese, . . .	1	28·4	7·96	10·45	1·16	·75	21·3	5·9	7·84	·87
Bread, . . .	98	2784·8	253·44	35·81	1462·79	91	2584·4	237·76	33·59	1372·31
Oatmeal, . . .	24	681·6	109·78	49·07	460·08	5·2	147·68	23·77	10·63	99·68
Flour, . . .	3	5·2	9·71	·85	64·41	3	85·2	9·71	·85	64·41
Peas, Lentils, &c., .	2·75	78·1	19·13	·38	47·47	2·75	78·1	19·13	·38	47·47
Barley, . . .	3·75	106·5	9·05	1·17	82·85	3·75	106·5	9·05	1·17	82·85
Rice, . . .	3·25	92·6	7·38	2·76	72·91	3·25	92·6	7·38	2·76	72·91
Tapioca, .	·5	14·2	·06	·01	12·49	·5	14·2	·06	·01	12·49
Sugar, . . .	6·5	184·6	..	..	184·6	9·5	269·8	..	.	269·8
Treacle, Marmalade, &c.,	2·25	63·9	·25	·04	50·75	2·25	63·9	·25	·04	50·75
Potatoes, . . .	85	2414	43·45	2·41	354·85	85	2414	43·45	2·41	354·85
Fresh Vegetables, .	29	823·6	11·53	1·64	39·53	29	823·6	11·53	1·64	39·53
Currants, . .	·5	14·2	·34	·24	10·53	·5	14·2	·34	·24	10·53
Tea, Coffee, . .	1·25	35·5	..	..	..	2	56·7	..	..	..
Total, . .	..	..	783·73	529·04	2980·74	..	.	595·92	415·73	2563·65

Food Values.—The average daily food values of the male and female dietaries are as follows:—

	Proteid.	Fat.	Carbo-hydrate.	Energy Value.
Male	112·0	75·6	425·8	2908
Female . . .	85·1	59·4	366·2	2403

The average height of male working patients is 65 inches, their average weight 138·1 lbs. The average height and weight of those male working patients who reside at the farm is 65¼ inches and 131 lbs.

Critical Remarks.—The dietaries of this asylum, like those of Gartloch Asylum, are commendable on account of their quality, but are wanting in quantity. Variation of diet is very amply provided, no other asylum gives its pauper inmates so large a number of different dishes. As to quantity these dietaries are both wanting, for neither the male nor female satisfies the standards for idle inmates, far less the standards for working inmates. The energy values of both are too small, and so are the proteid values. Combined with this shortage it is to be noted that practically no allowance is made for the extra food requirement of the working patients, and it consequently is not surprising to find that their average weight is below the standard. The inmates of the farm have an average height of 65·5 inches, their average weight is 131 lbs., which is 9 lbs. less than the standard. A service of bread *ad libitum* with all dinners, and a small luncheon to working patients, would correct the faults of these in many ways excellent diets.

GOVAN DISTRICT ASYLUM.

Breakfast.—All patients get porridge with milk and tea with bread and margarine.

Dinner.—The weekly routine contains two dinners of rice and milk and pudding, one of broth mutton and potato, one of pea soup, meat stewed with vegetable and potato, one of pea soup, beef and potato, one of rice soup and meat pie, and either a dinner of broth, beef and potato, or one of fish, potato and pudding. Bread is given daily. Meat is given four or five times a week. The puddings are varied.

Evening Meal.—All patients receive tea and bread with either margarine, jam, or marmalade.

Extras for Working Patients.—Females working in the laundry, kitchen and official blocks get tea, bread and margarine in the forenoon and again in the afternoon, jelly is sometimes given instead of margarine, and soup instead of tea.

Dietary for females differs from that for males by having smaller rations of oatmeal, bread, rice and milk pudding, meat, and potatoes.

[TABLE.

D

46

Table showing the Average Weekly Composition of Dietaries.

	MALE					FEMALE				
	Quantity		Proteid	Fat	Carbo-hydrate	Quantity		Proteid	Fat	Carbo-hydrate
	Oz.	Grms.				Oz.	Grms.			
Beef, ...	25	710	132·41	132·69	..	18·25	518·3	96·75	96·90	..
Heads, Hough, &c., .	8	227·2	23·03	8·96	..	8	227·2	23·03	8·96	..
Mutton Sides, . .	6·25	177·5	23·07	42·6	..	5·75	163·3	21·22	39·19	..
Stock Fish, . .	4·25	120·7	32·95	·36	..	4·25	120·7	32·95	·36	..
Suet, ...	7	198·8	9·34	162·61	..	7	198·8	9·34	162·61	..
Lard, ...	·9	25·56	..	25·56	..	·9	25·56	..	25·56	..
Margarine, . .	4·6	130·64	1·56	108·43	..	4·6	130·64	1·56	108·43	..
Eggs, ...	·75	21·3	2·53	1·98	..	·75	21·3	2·53	1·98	..
Milk (Whole), . .	150	4260	140·58	170·4	233·0	150	4260	140·58	170·4	233·0
Bread, Buns, . .	89	2527·6	227·17	42·44	1349·90	86·75	2463·7	221·19	41·61	1305·97
Oatmeal, . . .	20	568	91·44	40·89	383·4	20·25	575·1	92·59	41·4	388·19
Flour, . . .	7·25	205·9	23·47	2·05	155·66	6·75	191·7	21·85	1·91	144·92
Peas, ...	6	170·4	41·91	1·7	105·64	6	170·4	41·91	1·7	105·64
Barley, . . .	1·6	45·44	3·96	·49	35·35	1·6	45·44	3·96	·49	35·35
Rice, ...	7·5	213	17·04	·83	168·27	5·5	156·2	12·49	·46	123·39
Tapioca, . . .	·6	17·04	·06	·02	14·99	·6	17·04	·06	·02	14·99
Sugar, . . .	15	426	..	..	426·0	16·25	461·5	..	..	461·5
Treacle, Jam, &c., .	4·25	120·70	·61	·09	99·38	4·25	120·70	·61	·09	99·38
Potatoes, . . .	82	2328·8	41·91	2·32	342·33	43·5	1235·4	22·23	1·23	181·6
Fresh Vegetables, .	40·6	1153·04	16·14	23·06	55·34	40·6	1153·04	16·14	23·06	55·34
Currants, Raisins, .	·8	22·72	·53	·53	16·20	·8	22·72	·53	·53	16·20
Tea, Coffee, . . .	1·5	42·6	..	..	..	1·96	55·28	..	..	..
Total, . .	..	..	822·61	767·71	3385·46	..	..	760·42	726·69	3165·47

Food Values.—The average daily food values of the male and female dietaries are as follows:—

	Proteid.	Fat.	Carbo-hydrate.	Energy Value.
Male	118·4	109·7	483·6	3488
Female . . .	108·6	103·8	452·2	3265

Average height of male working patients is 66·5 inches, their average weight 141 lbs.

Critical Remarks.—Were some extra food given to male working patients these diets would be excellent. The average energy and proteid values are sufficient, the food is varied, condiments are used in proper quantity, and a reasonable supply of fresh vegetable is given. The weight of male working patients is below the standard, it is almost certainly due to their receiving no extras.

HADDINGTON DISTRICT ASYLUM.

Breakfast.—Nearly all the male and the majority of the female patients get porridge and milk only for breakfast, a considerable number of females and a few males get tea bread and butter in addition. A few of both sexes get tea bread and butter only. A special breakfast consisting of coffee, bread and butter, and ham is served to all patients on Sunday.

Dinner.—The weekly routine includes one dinner of pea soup three of broth, beef and potato, one of broth and suet pudding, one of broth, fish and potato, and one of broth, oatmeal pudding and potato. Bread is given daily. Meat is given three times a week, and the cooking of it is varied. When the supply of fish fails an extra meat dinner is given.

Evening Meal.—Tea with bread and butter or jam is given to all patients. A late supper consisting of beer and bread, or milk and bread, or gruel is given to patients desiring it.

Extras for Working Patients.—No special extras are given to working patients.

Dietary for females differs from that for males by having smaller rations of oatmeal, bread, soup, meat, potatoes, and pudding.

Table showing the Average Weekly Composition of Dietaries.

	MALE.					FEMALE.				
	Quantity.		Proteid.	Fat.	Carbo-hydrate	Quantity.		Proteid.	Fat.	Carbo-hydrate
	Oz.	Grms.				Oz.	Grms.			
Beef, ...	16·69	474·28	86·79	89·63	..	11·25	319·5	58·46	60·38	..
Heads, Hough, &c., .	3	85·2	8·26	3·82	..	1·66	47·14	4·57	1·63	..
Ham, ...	3	85·2	12·35	28·28	..	2	56·8	8·23	18·85	..
Fish (Fresh), . . .	6	170·4	28·45	·51	..	4	113·6	18·97	·34	..
Suet, ...	2·08	59·64	2·8	48·73	..	1·68	47·71	2·24	39·02	..
Butter, ...	5·74	161·88	1·61	137·59	..	4·64	130·64	1·3	111·04	..
Milk (Whole), . .	112·40	3192·16	105·34	127·68	159·6	77·90	2209·52	72·91	88·28	110·47
Bread, ...	138·62	3936·24	362·13	51·17	2090·14	82·69	2348·68	216·07	30·53	1247·14
Oatmeal, . . .	52·92	1502·36	241·87	108·16	1014·09	35·82	1016·72	163·69	73·2	686·28
Flour, ...	3·92	110·76	12·62	1·1	83·73	3·23	90·88	10·36	·9	68·7
Peas, ...	8·84	249·92	61·48	2·49	154·95	4·91	139·16	34·23	1·39	86·27
Barley, ...	11·88	337·96	28·72	3·71	262·98	5·94	168·98	14·36	1·85	131·46
Sugar, ...	5·53	156·2	..	..	156·2	6·87	195·96	..	..	195·96
Syrup, Jam, &c., . .	1·14	32·66	·12	·02	25·36	·82	23·28	·08	·01	18·28
Potatoes, . . .	60·89	1729·56	31·13	1·72	254·24	40·62	1153·04	20·75	1·15	169·49
Fresh Vegetables, .	26·28	746·92	10·45	1·49	35·85	13·35	380·56	5·82	·76	18·26
Currants, . . .	·92	25·56	·61	·43	18·96	·75	21·3	·51	·36	15·8
Apples, ...	·92	25·56	·07	·07	2·76	·75	21·3	·06	·06	3·3
Tea, Coffee, . . .	·94	26·69	..	..	..	1·16	32·94	..	..	.
Total, . .	..	..	994·8	606·15	4259·31	..	..	632·11	480·05	2751·41

Food Values.—The average daily food values of the male and female dietaries are as follows:—

	Proteid.	Fat.	Carbo-hydrate.	Energy Value.
Male	142·1	86·6	608·5	3872
Female . . .	90·3	61·4	393·1	2553

Average height of male working patients is 66·2 inches, their average weight 140·6 lbs.

Critical Remarks.—From the detail of the schedule the average male diet appears to be fully sufficient, while the average female diet appears to be barely sufficient, as it is wanting both in proteid and energy. Variety of food is provided for. Fresh vegetables are used in reasonable quantity. The allowance of tea for male patients is too small. The average weight of male working patients is below the standard, 140·6 lbs. as against 145 lbs. This may be ascribed to no special allowance being made for them. The dietaries would be improved by increasing the tea allowance of males, by giving another meat dinner weekly, and by giving a luncheon to workers of both sexes.

INVERNESS DISTRICT ASYLUM.

Breakfast.—The great majority of both male and female patients get porridge and milk, a few get tea bread and butter in addition.

Dinner.—The weekly routine includes one of broth and beef, one of rice soup and suet pudding, one of rice soup fish and potato, one of meat pie and potato, and one of pea soup and pork. Bread is given daily, meat four times a week.

Evening Meal.—This for all consists of tea with bread and either butter, jam, or marmalade.

Extras for Working Patients.—Females working in the laundry, kitchen, and dining hall get tea bread and cheese in the forenoon, and tea bread and butter in the afternoon. Male working patients get no extra food.

Dietary for females differs from that for males in having smaller rations of oatmeal and bread.

Table showing the Average Weekly Composition of Dietaries.

	MALE					FEMALE				
	Quantity.		Proteid.	Fat.	Carbo-hydrate	Quantity.		Proteid.	Fat.	Carbo-hydrate
	Oz.	Grms.				Oz.	Grms.			
Beef, ...	16·4	465·76	87·49	86·75	.	16·7	474·28	89·05	83·26	..
Heads, Hough, &c., .	1·03	29·25	2·83	1·14	..	1·04	29·53	2·86	1·15	..
Pork, ...	8·2	232·88	27·94	69·39	.	8·3	235·72	28·28	70·24	..
Fish (Fresh), . . .	10·3	292·52	45·81	3·22	..	10·5	298·2	46·45	3·44	..
Suet, ...	1·5	42·6	2·0	34·84	..	1·5	42·6	2·0	34·84	..
Butter, . . .	3·9	110·76	1·1	94·14	..	4·5	127·8	1·27	108·63	..
Milk (Whole), . .	86·60	2459·44	81·16	98·37	122·97	90	2556	84·34	102·24	127·8
Cheese, ...	..	..	..	..	..	1·06	30·1	8·33	11·07	1·23
Bread, ...	105·5	2996·2	275·65	38·96	1590·98	85·5	2428·2	223·39	31·56	1289·37
Oatmeal, ...	36	1022·4	164·6	73·61	690·12	30	852	137·17	61·34	575·1
Flour, ...	10·3	292·52	33·34	2·92	221·14	10·5	298·2	33·99	2·98	225·43
Peas, ...	5·6	159·04	39·12	1·59	96·6	5·7	161·88	39·82	1·61	100·36
Barley, ...	6·1	173·24	14·72	1·9	134·78	6·4	181·76	15·44	1·99	141·4
Rice, ...	9·2	261·28	20·9	·78	206·41	9·5	169·8	13·58	·5	134·14
Sugar, ...	5·1	144·84	..	..	144·84	6·2	176·08	..	..	176·08
Treacle, Jam, . .	1·55	44·02	·22	·08	36·11	1·56	44·30	·22	·03	36·30
Potatoes, . . .	32·9	934·36	16·81	·96	137·35	32·9	934·36	16·81	·98	137·35
Fresh Vegetables, . .	14·8	420·32	5·88	·84	20·17	16·15	458·66	6·42	·01	32·01
Currants, . . .	·5	14·2	·34	·24	10·53	·2	5·68	·13	·09	4·21
Tea, ...	1·1	31·24	..	..	..	1·3	36·92	..	..	..
Total, . .	..	..	819·91	519·54	3414·0	..	..	749·55	521·81	2970·78

Food Values.—The average daily food values of the male and female dietaries are as follows :—

	Proteid.	Fat.	Carbo-hydrate.	Energy Value.
Male	117·1	74·2	487·7	3169
Female . . .	107·1	74·5	424·4	2872

Average height of male working patients is 67 inches, their average weight 150·6 lbs.

Critical Remarks.—The male dietary appears to be rather small, as it meets neither the energy nor the proteid standards. It is sufficient for non-working patients, but not for working ones, and no special addition is made to satisfy their requirements ; their average weight, however, appears to be good. The female diet is ample to meet the requirements of female patients, being in slight excess of the energy and proteid standards. The allowances of potato, of fresh vegetable, and of milk are all below the average. The dietaries would be improved by giving milk more liberally, by giving potato oftener, and by giving male working patients some luncheon.

KIRKLANDS ASYLUM.

Breakfast.—All male and female patients get porridge and milk and tea bread and margarine.

Dinner.—The weekly routine includes one dinner of lentil soup, pudding and bread, one of rice soup, beef and potato, one of broth, beef and potato, one of broth, sheep plucks and potato, one of tinned beef, potato, turnip and pudding, one of potato soup, bread and pudding, and one of fish, potato and pudding. Fresh beef is given on two days, tinned beef on one day, sheep pluck on one day. A small quantity of fresh beef is also used in preparing potato and lentil soup. The puddings are varied. Bread is given with two dinners only. A second potato soup dinner is sometimes given in place of the sheep pluck dinner.

Evening Meal.—This for all consists of tea bread and margarine.

Extras for Working Patients.—Those who work in the early morning receive some tea and bread. Women working in the laundry get in the forenoon some tea bread margarine and cheese, and those working in the kitchen and laundry some tea and bread in the afternoon.

Dietary for females differs from that for males by having smaller rations of oatmeal and bread.

Table showing the Average Weekly Composition of Dietaries.

	MALE.					FEMALE.				
	Quantity.		Proteid.	Fat.	Carbo-hydrate.	Quantity.		Proteid.	Fat.	Carbo-hydrate
	Oz.	Grms.				Oz.	Grms.			
Beef, ...	23·6	670·24	131·27	126·45	..	23·6	670·24	131·27	126·45	..
Heads, Hough, &c., .	·1	2·84	·27	·11	..	·1	2·84	·27	·11	..
Mutton, ...	4·3	122·12	28·2	10·99	6·1	4·3	122·12	28·2	10·99	6·1
Fish, ...	11·5	326·6	55·38	·97	..	11·5	326·6	55·38	·97	..
Suet, ...	1·4	39·76	1·96	32·52	..	1·4	39·76	1·96	32·52	..
Margarine, . . .	4·2	119·28	1·43	99·0	..	3	85·2	1·02	70·71	..
Milk (Whole), . . .	136	3862·4	127·45	154·49	193·12	136	3862·4	127·45	154·49	193·12
Cheese, ...	..	..	..	.	..	·1	2·84	·78	1·04	·11
Bread, &c., . . .	101·9	2898·96	265·24	39·38	1533·11	83·5	2371·40	217·17	32·59	1260·63
Oatmeal, . . .	16·8	477·12	76·81	34·25	322·05	14·7	417·48	67·21	30·05	281·79
Flour, ...	5·4	153·36	17·48	1·53	115·94	5·4	153·36	17·48	1·53	115·94
Peas, Lentils, . .	4·3	122·12	30·94	1·19	73·40	4·3	122·12	30·94	1·19	73·40
Barley, ...	2·6	73·84	6·27	8·12	57·44	2·6	73·84	6·27	8·12	57·44
Rice, ...	2·8	79·52	6·36	·23	62·82	2·8	79·52	6·36	·23	62·82
Cornflour, . . .	·8	22·72	1·61	·29	17·87	·8	22·72	1·61	·29	17·87
Sugar, ...	6·4	181·76	..	..	181·76	6·4	181·76	..	..	181·76
Jam, Marmalade, . .	2·4	68·16	·4	·06	57·59	2·4	68·16	·4	·06	57·59
Potatoes, . . .	73·5	2087·4	37·57	2·08	306·84	73·5	2087·4	37·57	2·08	306·84
Fresh Vegetables, . .	29·7	843·48	11·8	1·68	123·99	29·7	843·48	11·8	1·68	123·99
Currants, Raisins, .	1·2	34·08	·81	·65	59·96	1·2	34·08	·81	·65	59·96
Tea, Coffee, . . .	1·8	51·12	..	..	..	1·8	51·12	..	..	..
Total, . . .	..	..	901·15	514·09	3116·99	..	..	742·85	475·75	2799·46

Food Values.—The average daily food values of the male and female dietaries are as follows :—

	Proteid.	Fat.	Carbo-hydrate.	Energy Value.
Male	114·5	73·4	445·3	2977
Female . . .	106·3	68·0	399·9	2717

The average height of male working patients is 65 inches, their average weight 128·1 lbs.

Critical Remarks.—The male dietary of this asylum appears to be of too small nutritive value. It satisfies neither the energy standard nor the proteid standard. Combined with that shortage, absence of extras for male working patients is to be noted, and consequently it is not surprising to find that their average weight is decidedly below par, being 128 lbs., or 12 lbs. below the standard. The quality of the dietary is excellent, there is plenty of variety, and condiment is sufficiently used. The female dietary appears to be excellent in all respects, it fully meets their wants, and allowance is made for the special requirements of workers. The male dietary should be increased. This might be done by increasing the allowance of oatmeal, by giving bread *ad libitum* with all dinners, and by giving working patients some luncheon.

LANARK DISTRICT ASYLUM.

Breakfast.—All male and female patients get porridge and milk and tea bread and margarine.

Dinner.—The weekly routine includes one dinner of potato soup, bread and fruit tart, one of péa and rice soup, beef and potato, one of fresh fish, potato and pudding, one of lentil soup and potato, and two of broth, beef and potato. Beef is given three times a week. Bone or a small quantity of meat is also used in preparing two soup dinners. Bread is only given once weekly.

Evening Meal.—This for all consists of tea bread and margarine.

Extras for Working Patients.—Females in laundry get an early breakfast of tea, bread, and margarine, and those in kitchen and laundry get in the forenoon tea and bread with margarine or jam. Male working patients get no extra food.

Dietary for female patients differs from that of the males by having smaller rations of all foods and by the use of the extras already referred to.

Table showing the Average Weekly Composition of Dietaries.

	MALE.					FEMALE.				
	Quantity.		Proteid.	Fat.	Carbo-hydrate	Quantity.		Proteid.	Fat.	Carbo-hydrate
	Oz.	Grms.				Oz.	Grms.			
Beef, ...	32	908·8	166·31	171·76	..	24	681·6	124·73	123·82	..
Fish (Fresh), . . .	10	284	45·13	·84	..	8	227·2	36·50	·68	..
Fish (Salt), . . .	9	255·6	69·77	·76·	..	7	198·8	54·27	·59	..
Suet, ...	·75	21·3	1·0	17·42	..	·5	14·2	·96	11·61	..
Margarine, ...	4	113·6	1·36	94·28	..	3·5	99·4	1·19	82·5	..
Milk (Whole), . . .	120	3402	112·26	136·08	170·1	120	3402	112·26	136·08	170·1
Bread, ...	96	2726·4	250·82	35·44	1447·71	71	2016·4	185·5	26·21	1070·7
Oatmeal, . . .	22	624·8	103·59	44·96	421·74	18	511·2	82·2	36·8	345·06
Flour, ...	13·5	383·4	43·7	3·83	289·35	11·25	319·5	36·42	3·19	241·54
Peas, Lentils, . . .	6·5	184·6	46·65	1·84	111·27	5·5	156·2	39·25	1·56	94·45
Barley, ...	3	85·2	7·24	·93	66·28	3	85·2	7·24	·93	66·28
Rice, ...	3	85·2	6·21	·25	67·3	3	85·2	6·21	·25	67·3
Sugar, ...	10	284	..	..	284·0	9	255·6	..	..	255·6
Jam, Marmalade, . .	2·25	63·9	·38	·06	53·99	2·25	63·9	·38	·06	53·99
Potatoes, ...	126	3578·4	64·43	3·57	526·02	98	2783·2	50·09	2·78	409·13
Fresh Vegetables, . .	15	426	5·96	·85	20·44	11	312·4	4·27	·62	14·99
Tea, Coffee, . . .	1·87	53·25	..	..	..	1·87	53·25	..	..	..
Total, . . .	..	..	923·41	512·39	3455·7	..	..	744·07	432·68	2789·14

Food Values.—The average daily food values of the male and female dietaries are as follows :—

	Proteid.	Fat.	Carbo-hydrate.	Energy Value.
Male . . .	132·6	73·3	494·1	3251
Female . . .	106·3	61·8	398·5	2644

Average height of male working patients 65·9 inches, their average weight 135·9 lbs.

Critical Remarks.—The energy values of both the male and female dietaries appear to closely correspond with the standard, and the proteid values of both to be sufficient. The weight test, however, shows the male workers to average 4 lbs. less than the standard. This contradiction may be ascribed to male workers receiving no extra food. The diets would be improved by allowing a discretionary use of bread with all dinners and giving a luncheon to all working patients. A fourth meat dinner and a freer use of fresh vegetables are also desirable.

MIDLOTHIAN DISTRICT ASYLUM.

Breakfast.—The great majority of male and female patients have porridge and milk only. A few get tea bread and butter in addition.

Dinner.—The weekly routine includes one dinner of rice and milk and cheese, one of broth, beef and potato, one of pea soup and pudding, one of lentil soup, fish and potato, and two of Irish stew. Bread is given daily. Meat is given three times a week.

Evening Meal.—This for all consists of tea with bread and butter, and sometimes jam.

Extras for Working Patients.—Females working in the laundry get during the forenoon some tea bread and butter. Field workers during extra busy times some bread cheese and beer. Otherwise no extras to working patients are given.

Dietary for female patients differs from that for males by having smaller rations of bread and meat.

[TABLE.

Table showing the Average Weekly Composition of Dietaries.

	MALE.					FEMALE.				
	Quantity.		Proteid.	Fat.	Carbo-hydrate	Quantity.		Proteid.	Fat.	Carbo-hydrate
	Oz.	Grms.				Oz.	Grms.			
Beef,	28	795·2	145·52	150·29	..	24	681·6	124·72	128·82	..
Fish (Fresh),	9	255·6	42·68	·76	..	9	255·6	42·68	·76	..
Suet,	·75	21·3	1·0	17·42	..	·75	21·3	1·0	17·42	..
Butter,	3	85·2	·85	72·42	..	3	85·2	·85	72·42	..
Milk (Whole),	90	2556	84·34	102·24	127·8	90	2556	84·34	102·24	127·8
Cheese,	2	56·8	15·73	20·9	2·33	2	56·8	15·73	20·9	2·33
Bread,	80	2272	191·74	31·79	1179·16	64	1817·6	149·94	25·89	937·87
Oatmeal,	30	852	137·17	61·34	575·1	30	852	137·17	61·34	575·1
Flour,	2	56·8	6·47	·56	42·94	2	56·8	6·47	·56	42·94
Peas, Lentils,	7·75	220·1	55·15	2·19	133·87	7·75	220·1	55·15	2·19	133·87
Barley,	2	56·8	4·32	·62	44·19	2	56·8	4·32	·62	44·19
Rice,	3	85·2	6·81	·25	67·2	3	85·2	6·81	·25	67·2
Sugar,	5·33	151·2	..	..	151·2	5·33	151·2	..	..	151·2
Jam,	3	85·2	·5	·08	71·96	3	85·2	·5	·08	71·96
Potatoes,	112	3180·8	57·25	3·18	467·57	112	3180·8	57·25	3·18	467·57
Fresh Vegetables,	21·25	603·5	8·44	1·2	28·96	21·25	603·5	8·44	1·2	28·96
Currants, &c.,	·50	14·2	·33	·33	10·12	·50	14·2	·33	·33	10·12
Tea,	1	28·4	..	..	..	1	28·4	..	..	..
Total,	..	..	758·3	465·57	2902·62	..	..	696·2	438·2	2661·23

Food Values.—The average daily food values of the male and female dietaries are as follows:—

	Proteid.	Fat.	Carbo-hydrate.	Energy Value.
Male	108·4	66·5	414·7	2761
Female . . .	99·5	62·6	380·2	2548

The average height of working male patients is 65·7 inches, their average weight 137·4 lbs.

Critical Remarks.—Both the male and the female dietaries appear to be of insufficient food value, as neither meets the energy standard. The male diet also contains too little proteid. No allowance at ordinary times is made for the special wants of the male workers. That the diets are short is supported by the result of the weight test, for it is found that the average weight of the male workers is only 137 lbs., or 3 lbs. below the standard. The female diet is relatively more generous than the male diet, it more

nearly approaches the energy standard, and with it allowance is made
for workers. The average issues to both males and females of
bread, of butter, and of tea are below the average. The male diet
would be much improved by giving more food at breakfast, either
more porridge or some tea bread and butter in addition to the
porridge, by increasing the allowance of bread at dinner time—at
present only 2 oz.—and by giving working patients some luncheon.
The female diet would be improved by giving more bread at dinner
time. Butter might be used more liberally with advantage.

PERTH DISTRICT ASYLUM.

Breakfast.—For practically all patients this consists of porridge
and milk only.

Dinner.—The weekly routine includes one dinner of rice and
milk, bread and cheese, one of broth, tinned mutton, vegetable and
bread, one of broth, beef, bread and rice or turnip, one of broth,
meat pie and potato, one of broth, fish and potato, one of pea soup,
pudding and bread, and one of broth and Irish stew. Fresh
meat is given only once a week, tinned mutton three times, once
cold, once in Irish stew, and once in meat pie. Additional small
quantities of fresh meat are used in making the soups. Bread is
given four times a week.

Evening Meal.—This for all consists of either tea or chocolate
with bread and butter or marmalade.

Extras for Working Patients.—Females working before breakfast
get tea and bread. Females in laundry get tea bread and cheese
during the forenoon, those in kitchen and sewing room tea and
bread in the forenoon. Other than these no extras are given to
working patients.

Dietary for females differs from that for males by having smaller
rations of oatmeal, bread, and pudding, and by the use of the extras
referred to.

[TABLE.

Table showing the Average Weekly Composition of Dietaries.

	MALE.					FEMALE.				
	Quantity.		Proteid.	Fat.	Carbo-hydrate	Quantity.		Proteid.	Fat.	Carbo-hydrate
	Oz.	Grms.				Oz.	Grms.			
Beef and Mutton, . .	27·9	792·36	173·16	149·04	..	27·9	792·36	173·16	149·04	..
Heads, Hough, &c., .	4·5	127·8	12·39	4·98	..	4·5	127·8	12·39	4·98	..
Fish (Fresh), . . .	10	284	43·13	·84	..	10	284	43·13	·84	..
Suet, ...	1·5	42·6	2·0	34·84	..	1·5	42·6	2·0	34·84	..
Lard, ...	·4	11·36	..	11·36	..	·4	11·36	..	11·36	..
Butter, ...	2·3	65·32	·65	55·52	..	2·3	65·32	·65	55·52	..
Milk (Whole), . . .	74	2101·6	69·25	84·06	105·06	74	2101·6	69·25	84·06	105·06
Cheese, ...	2·33	65·22	18·09	24·03	2·67	3·3	93·72	25·96	34·49	3·84
Bread, ...	90·4	2567·36	237·19	33·37	1363·27	94·2	2675·28	256·12	34·77	1420·57
Oatmeal, ...	31·25	887·5	142·88	63·9	599·06	28·2	800·88	128·94	57·66	540·59
Flour, ...	6·5	184·6	21·04	1·84	139·55	6·5	184·6	21·04	1·84	139·55
Peas, ...	8·6	244·24	60·08	2·44	151·42	8·6	244·24	60·08	2·44	151·42
Barley, ...	3·75	106·5	9·05	1·17	82·85	3·75	106·5	9·05	1·17	82·85
Rice, ...	3·4	96·56	7·72	·28	76·28	3·4	96·56	7·72	·28	76·28
Sugar, ...	5·75	163·2	..	..	163·2	5·75	163·2	..	..	163·2
Jam, Marmalade, . .	2·4	68·16	·4	·06	57·59	2·4	68·16	·4	·06	57·59
Potatoes, . . .	49	1391·6	25·04	1·39	204·56	49	1391·6	25·04	1·39	204·56
Fresh Vegetables, . .	23·1	656·04	9·18	1·31	31·48	23·1	656·04	9·18	1·31	31·48
Currants, . . .	·8	22·72	·54	·28	16·85	·8	22·72	·54	·28	16·85
Tea, Cocoa, . . .	1	28·4	·61	·82	1·07	1·16	32·94	·61	·82	1·07
Total, . .	..	..	837·5	471·63	2996·03	..	..	850·36	477·25	2996·03

Food Values. The average food values of the male and female dietaries are as follows:—

	Proteid.	Fat.	Carbo-hydrate.	Energy Value.
Male	119·6	67·4	427·9	2871
Female . . .	121·5	68·2	427·9	2886

The average height of the male working patient is 66·5 inches, their average weight 139·8 lbs.

Critical Remarks.—The male and female dietaries appear to be of the same food value, and consequently both cannot be correct. By comparison with the standard the male dietary is found to be too small by 13 per cent., and the female diet too large by 9 per cent. No special allowance is made for male working patients. The deficiency of the male diet is shown by the fact that the average weight of male workers is decidedly too small, it being 6 lbs. below the standard. The breakfasts for male patients are too small, it is exclusively a porridge and milk meal, and the allowances of both are no greater than those given in other asylums where bread and butter is given in addition. Fresh meat is given too seldom, and tinned meat too often. The weekly use of butter is too small, and so is that of potato. The dietaries of this asylum might with great advantage be completely revised and considerably increased.

ROXBURGH DISTRICT ASYLUM.

Breakfast.—More than one-half male and nearly one-half female patients have porridge and milk only. The remainder have tea bread and butter, either alone or with porridge and milk.

Dinner.—The weekly routine includes one dinner of rice soup, meat and potato, one of rice soup and pudding, one of broth, meat and potato, two of broth, meat, potato and vegetable, one of fish, potato and cheese, and one of pea soup and potato. Bread is given with all dinners. Meat is given four times a week.

Evening Meal.—The majority get tea bread and butter or jam, a few get porridge and milk only.

Extras for Working Patients.—Females working in laundry get tea bread and cheese. Many working male patients get bread and milk in the forenoon.

Dietary for females differs from that of the males by having less oatmeal and bread, and by them all having a luncheon consisting of bread and milk.

Additions to the ordinary dietary of this asylum are freely ordered by the medical officers. About 50 per cent. of the male and about 33 per cent. of the female patients daily receive such extras.

[TABLE.

Table showing the Average Weekly Composition of Dietaries.

	MALE.					FEMALE.				
	Quantity.		Proteid.	Fat.	Carbo-hydrate	Quantity.		Proteid.	Fat.	Carbo-hydrate
	Oz.	Grms.				Oz.	Grms.			
Beef, ...	21·42	608·32	116·13	114·84	..	21·42	608·32	116·13	114·84	..
Mutton, . . .	4·1	116·44	15·13	27·94	..	4·1	116·44	15·13	27·94	..
Pork, ...	3·78	107·35	12·38	31·99	..	3·78	107·35	12·38	31·99	..
Fish (Fresh), . .	16	454·4	78·12	1·26	..	12	340·8	58·6	1·02	..
Suet, ...	·32	9·06	·42	7·42	..	·32	9·06	·42	7·42	..
Lard, ...	·53	15·05	..	15·05	..	·53	15·05	..	15·05	..
Butter, ...	4·15	117·36	1·17	100·18	..	4·29	121·55	1·21	103·31	..
Milk (Whole), . .	72	2044·8	67·47	81·79	102·24	132	3748·8	122·71	149·95	187·44
Cheese, . . .	1·7	48·28	13·27	17·76	1·97	1·7	48·28	13·27	17·76	1·97
Bread, ...	94·6	2686·64	247·17	34·92	1426·6	84·7	2405·48	221·3	31·27	1277·3
Oatmeal, . . · . .	43·23	1227·73	197·66	88·39	823·71	27·13	770·49	124·04	55·47	590·08
Flour, ...	3·87	109·9	12·52	1·09	83·08	3·87	109·9	12·52	1·09	83·08
Peas, Beans, . .	7·71	218·96	52·99	2·51	134·76	7·71	218·96	52·99	2·51	134·76
Barley, ...	3·97	112·74	9·58	1·24	87·71	3·97	112·74	9·58	1·24	87·71
Rice, ...	2·6	73·84	5·9	·22	58·23	2·6	73·84	5·9	·22	58·23
Sugar, ...	4·6	130·64	..	..	130·64	4·3	122·12	..	..	122·12
Jam, ...	·87	24·7	·14	·02	20·87	·87	24·7	·14	·02	20·87
Potatoes, . . .	60·1	1706·84	30·72	1·7	250·9	60·1	1706·84	30·72	1·7	250·9
Fresh Vegetables, . .	23·71	673·08	9·42	1·34	32·2	23·71	673·08	9·42	1·34	32·3
Currants, . . .	·43	12·21	·29	·2	9·05	·43	12·21	·29	·2	9·05
Tea, ...	1·03	29·25	..	..	..	1·07	30·38	..	..	..
Total, . .	..	..	871·06	529·96	3167·16	..	..	806·35	564·34	2785·91

Food Values.—The average daily food values of the male and female dietaries are as follows:—

	Proteid.	Fat.	Carbo-hydrate.	Energy Value.
Male	124·5	75·7	452·4	3069
Female . . .	115·5	80·6	398.0	2855

The average height of the male working patient is 67·4 inches, their average weight is 150 lbs.

Critical Remarks.—The ordinary male dietary appears to be deficient in quantity, but this shortage appears not to affect the weight of working patients. This apparent contradiction may be ascribed to an ample luncheon which is given to them as an extra. Apart from that apparent deficiency these diets appear to be good. They are varied, and vegetables and condiments are sufficiently used.

STIRLING DISTRICT ASYLUM.

Breakfast.—On week days the majority of the male and one-third of the female patients get porridge and milk only. Of those remaining most get tea bread and margarine only, while some get porridge and milk and tea bread and margarine. On Sunday all get coffee bread and margarine.

Dinner.—The weekly routine includes one dinner of broth and pudding, three of broth, meat and potato, one of broth and mutton pie, one of broth and fish, and one of pea soup and pudding. Meat is given four times a week, on two of those days tinned meat is used. Bread is given with all dinners. The puddings and the cooking of the meat are varied.

Evening Meal.—This consists of tea bread and margarine for all. About one-third of all patients get a late supper of porridge and milk.

Extras for Working Patients.—Females in the kitchen get an early breakfast of tea bread and margarine. Females in kitchen and laundry get tea bread and margarine during the forenoon, those in the laundry get cheese in addition on three days a week. Male working patients receive no extra food.

Dietary for females differs from that for males by having smaller allowance of bread, and by the use of extras already referred to.

Table showing the Average Weekly Composition of Dietaries.

	MALE.					FEMALE.				
	Quantity.		Proteid.	Fat.	Carbo-hydrate	Quantity.		Proteid	Fat.	Carbo-hydrate
	Oz.	Grms.				Oz.	Grms.			
Beef, ...	19·69	559·16	111·82	104·12	..	19·69	559·16	111·82	104·12	..
Heads, Hough, &c.,	4·6	130·64	12·67	5·09	..	4·6	130·64	12·67	5·09	..
Mutton, ...	5·23	148·53	42·77	33·36	..	5·23	148·53	42·77	33·96	..
Pork, ...	2·85	80·94	9·71	24·12	..	2·85	80·94	9·71	24·12	..
Fish (Fresh), . . .	12	340·8	56·9	1·02	..	12	340·8	56·9	1·02	..
Suet, ...	1	28·4	1·32	23·22	..	1	28·4	1·32	23·22	..
Margarine, . . .	5·14	145·97	1·75	121·15	..	5·14	145·97	1·75	121·15	..
Milk (Whole), . . .	105	2982	96·4	119·28	149·1	105	2982	96·4	119·28	149·1
Cheese, ...	2·2	62·48	17·8	22·99	2·56	2·2	62·48	17·8	22·99	2·56
Bread, ...	156·49	4444·31	408·87	57·77	2859·92	108·66	2943·94	270·84	38·27	1563·23
Oatmeal, . . .	26·6	755·44	121·62	54·39	509·92	17·15	487·06	78·41	35·06	328·76
Flour, ...	3·4	96·56	11·0	·96	72·99	3·4	96·56	11·0	·96	72·99
Peas, ...	7·7	218·68	53·79	2·18	135·58	7·7	218·68	53·79	2·18	135·58
Barley, ...	6	170·4	14·48	1·87	132·57	6	170·4	14·48	1·87	132·57
Rice, ...	3·5	99·4	7·95	·29	78·53	3·5	99·4	7·95	·29	78·53
Sugar, ...	9·7	275·48	..	..	275·48	9·7	275·48	..	..	275·48
Syrup, ...	1·2	34·08	..	..	23·61	1·2	34·08	..	..	23·61
Potatoes, . . .	58·95	1674·18	30·13	1·67	248·1	58·95	1674·18	30·13	1·67	248·1
Fresh Vegetables, .	56	1590·4	22·26	3·18	76·32	56	1590·4	22·26	3·18	76·32
Tea, Coffee, . .	1·88	53·39	..	..	..	1·88	53·39	..	..	..
Total. . .	..	..	1022·74	577·16	4002·68	..	..	841·5	538·33	3084·33

Food Values.—The average daily food values of the male and female dietaries are as follows:—

	Proteid.	Fat.	Carbo-hydrate.	Energy Value.
Male	146·1	82·5	580·4	3745
Female . . .	120·2	76·9	440·7	2872

The average height of the male working patient is 66·1 inches, their average weight 141·2 lbs.

Critical Remarks.—Both the male and the female dietaries appear to be ample and to more than meet the requirements of the standards. Variation of food is good, the use of fresh vegetable and condiment is ample. The diet would be somewhat improved by restricting the use of tinned meat and giving more of the more savoury fresh meat; tinned meat twice weekly is too much. The weight test shows that male workers are not of standard weight, that may be attributed to their receiving no extra food.

(3.) Parochial Asylums.

Govan Parochial Asylum.

Breakfast.—The majority of male patients and about one-half of the female patients get porridge and milk only. The remainder get tea bread and margarine.

Dinner.—The weekly routine includes two dinners of potato soup, meat and bread, one of broth, meat and potato, one of broth, meat pie and bread, one of pea soup, meat and potato, one of rice soup, meat and potato, and one of rice soup, pudding and bread. Meat is given six times a week, is always fresh beef, and on five days a week is served as boiled beef, on one as a meat pie. Bread is given on four days a week.

Evening Meal.—This consists of tea, bread and margarine. Coffee is given once weekly in place of tea, and either jam or marmalade in place of margarine.

Extras for Working Patients.—No extra food is given to working patients.

Dietary for females differs from that for males by having smaller rations of bread.

Table showing the Average Weekly Composition of Dietaries.

| | MALE | | | | FEMALE | | | | |
| | Quantity. | | Proteid. | Fat. | Carbo-hydrate | Quantity. | | Proteid. | Fat. | Carbo-hydrate |
	Oz.	Grms.				Oz.	Grms.			
Beef,	34	965·6	176·7	182·49	..	34	965·6	176·7	182·49	..
Heads, Hough, &c.,	6	170·4	16·52	6·64	..	6	170·4	16·52	6·64	..
Suet,	1·5	42·6	2·0	34·84	..	1·5	42·6	2·0	34·84	..
Lard,	1·5	42·6	..	42·6	..	1·5	42·6	.	42·6	..
Margarine,	5	142	1·7	117·86	..	5	142	1·7	117·86	..
Milk (Whole), .	100	2840	93·72	113·6	142·0	100	2840	93·72	113·6	142·0
Bread,	108	3067·2	233·18	39·37	1628·68	88	2499·2	229·92	32·48	1327·07
Oatmeal, .	24	681·6	109·78	49·07	460·08	24	681·6	109·73	49·07	460·08
Flour,	8	227·2	25·9	2·26	171·76	8	227·2	25·9	2·26	171·76
Peas,	4	113·6	27·94	1·13	71·48	4	113·6	27·94	1·13	71·48
Barley,	4	113·6	9·65	1·24	88·38	4	113·6	9·65	1·24	88·38
Rice,	4	113·6	9·08	3·4	89·74	4	113·6	9·08	3·4	89·74
Sugar,	6	170·4	..	..	170·4	6	170·4	..	.	170·4
Treacle, Jam, .	2	56·8	·17	·03	43·67	2	56·8	·17	·03	43·67
Potatoes,	88	2499·2	44·98	2·49	367·38	80	2272	40·89	2·27	333·96
Vegetables,	16	454·4	6·36	·9	21·81	16	454·4	6·36	·9	21·81
Currants,	1	28·4	·68	·48	21·06	1	28·4	·68	·48	21·06
Tea, Coffee, .	1·50	42·6	..	..	..	1·50	42·6	..	..	..
Total, .	..	..	808·31	598·9	3276·29	..	..	750·96	591·29	2941·38

Food Values.—The average daily food values of the male and female dietaries are as follows :—

	Proteid.	Fat.	Carbo-hydrate.	Energy Value.
Male .	115·5	85·5	468·1	3188
Female .	107·3	84·5	420·2	2948

The average height of the male working patient is 64.6 inches, their average weight 132·7 lbs.

Critical Remarks.—Both the energy value and the proteid value of the male diet are rather below the standard. That diet is ample for idle patients but hardly sufficient for working patients, and as workers get no extra diet it is probable that they are not being fully fed. The weight test shows that that is so, the average weight of male ·workers being 5 lbs. below the standard. The female diet is ample for both idle and working female patients. The use of fresh vegetable and condiment is sufficient. The diets are sufficiently varied. The

E

use of bread with all dinners, and the giving of luncheon to workers, would make the dietaries of this asylum in all ways satisfactory.

GREENOCK PAROCHIAL ASYLUM.

Breakfast.—All the male and most of the female patients get porridge and milk, some get tea bread and margarine in addition. A few females get tea bread and margarine only.

Dinner.—The weekly routine includes one dinner of pea soup, bread and cheesé, one of broth, beef and potato, one of broth, beef cabbage and bread, one of broth, fish and 'potato, one of rice soup, suet pudding and potato, one of rice soup, beef, cabbage and bread, and one of lentil soup, beef, greens and bread. Meat is given four times a week, on one day weekly it is stewed with onion, on the other three days it is boiled. Bread is given four times a week.

Evening Meal.—This consists of tea bread and margarine for all.

Extras for Working Patients.—In the forenoon male patients get bread and cheese, and working females bread and coffee. No early breakfast or afternoon tea is given.

Dietary for females differs from that for males by having smaller rations of bread, oatmeal, meat, potato, and fish.

Table showing the Average Weekly Composition of Dietaries.

	MALE.					FEMALE.				
	Quantity.		Proteid	Fat.	Carbo-hydrate	Quantity.		Proteid.	Fat.	Carbo-hydrate
	Oz.	Grms.				Oz.	Grms.			
Beef, ...	41·5	1178·6	219·18	222·66	..	33	937·2	173·77	177·07	..
Heads, Hough, &c., .	12	340·8	33·05	13·29	..	10	284	27·54	11·07	..
Fish (Fresh), . . .	6	170·4	29·3	·51	..	4·5	127·8	21·98	·38	..
Fish (Salt), . . .	5	142	38·76	·42	..	4	113·6	31·01	·34	..
Margarine, . . .	5	142	1·7	117·86	..	5	142	1·7	117·86	..
Milk (Whole), . . .	80	2272	74·97	90·88	113·6	80	2272	74·97	90·88	113·6
Cheese, ...	4·5	127·8	35·4	47·03	5·23	4·5	127·8	35·4	47·03	5·23
Bread, · . . .	108	3067·2	283·18	39·37	1628·68	81	2300·4	211·63	29·9	1221·51
Oatmeal, ...	36	1022·4	164·6	73·61	690·12	30	852	137·17	61·34	575·1
Flour, ...	3	85·2	9·71	·35	64·41	3	85·2	9·71	·35	64·41
Peas, Lentils, . . .	6	170·4	42·53	1·69	105·06	6	170·4	42·53	1·69	105·06
Barley, ...	6	170·4	14·48	1·37	132·57	6	170·4	14·48	1·37	132·57
Rice, ...	4	113·6	9·08	3·4	89·74	4	113·6	9·08	3·4	89·74
Sugar, ...	7	198·8	..	..	198·8	9	255·6	..	..	255·6
Syrup, ...	1	28·4	..	..	19·08	1	28·4	..	..	19·08
Potatoes, ...	·57	1618·8	29·18	1·61	237·96	54	1533·6	27·6	1·53	225·43
Fresh Vegetables, .	35	994	13·91	1·99	47·71	35	994	13·91	1·99	47·71
Currants, . . .	1·5	42·6	1·02	·72	31·6	1·5	42·6	1·02	·72	31·6
Tea, Coffee, . . .	1·6	45·44	..	..	..	1·75	49·7	..	..	..
Total, . .	..	..	1000·0	618·26	3865·15	..	..	833·5	547·92	2887·22

Food Values.—The average daily food values of the male and female dietaries are as follows:—

	Proteid.	Fat.	Carbo-hydrate.	Energy Value.
Male	142·8	88·3	480·7	3378
Female . . .	119·1	78·3	413·4	2907

The average height of the male working patient is 65·8 inches, their average weight 138·8 lbs.

Critical Remarks.—The male dietary of this asylum appears to be good. Its energy value nearly coincides with the standard, its proteid value is ample, sufficient allowance is made for the special wants of workers, and the use of condiment and fresh vegetable is sufficient. The female diet is also good, it is in some excess of the standard and may be rather wasteful. The average weight of male workers approaches closely the standard. A service of bread with all dinners appears to be the only necessary improvement.

PAISLEY, CRAW ROAD, PAROCHIAL ASYLUM.

In this asylum patients are, for dietary purposes, divided into four classes.

Class C, corresponding to Class C of ordinary paupers, includes the able-bodied patients of both sexes.

Class D, corresponding to Class D of ordinary paupers, includes patients of over 60 years of age.

Class T, includes patients who cannot, or state that they cannot, take porridge, and who get tea bread and margarine in place of porridge.

*Class M, includes infirm patients selected by the Medical Officer.

At the time when the returns were made there were 109 patients in the asylum; of these 60 were in Class C, 20 in Class D, 12 in Class T, and 17, mostly women, in Class M.

Breakfast.—The breakfast for Classes C and D consists of porridge and milk, that for Classes T and M of tea bread and margarine. With Class C breakfast butter-milk is used, with Class D skimmed milk.† In porridge 5oz. of oatmeal per patient is allowed. The bread allowance is 6oz.

Dinner.—On Sundays rice and milk and bread is given to all patients. On all week days the dinner for patients in Class M consists of half a pint of sweet milk and half a pound of bread only. Patients in Classes C, D, and T on week days receive soup, meat

---

* Class M diet is included in this description because it is one of the regular dietaries of the institution, because details of it were returned on the schedule, and because a considerable number of the inmates, 15 per cent., were receiving it. It is not a "hospital diet" as it is given to inmates who feed in the general dining hall. (*Vide* query 40, page 18.)

† Since the return was made, sweet milk has been given with Class D breakfast.

and bread on five days a week, on three days the soup is broth, on one day rice soup and on one day pea soup. On the remaing week day the dinner for Classes C, D, and T consists of fish bread and potato. The meat allowance per patient is 6oz. cooked, equivalent to about 8oz. uncooked. On four days a week the meat is served boiled, on one day as a pie.

Evening Meal.—This for all classes consists of tea and bread, with either margarine or jelly.

Extras for Working Patients.—Patients working before breakfast get tea and bread, and females in the sewing room get tea bread and margarine in the forenoon. A considerable amount of extra food, consisting of eggs, steak, sweet milk, wine, and whisky, is given to patients in Class M.

Dietary for females is the same as that for males excepting that a larger number of females than of males are put into Class M.

Table showing Average Weekly Composition of Class C Dietary.

	MALE AND FEMALE.				
	Quantity.		Proteid.	Fat.	Carbohydrate.
	Oz.	Grms.			
Beef, ...	40	1136	207·88	214·69	...
Heads, Hough, &c., . .	6·66	187·83	18·36	7·37	...
Fish (Salt), ...	8	227·2	62·02	·68	...
Margarine, ...	2·5	71	·85	58·93	...
Milk (Whole), . . .	14·5	411·8	13·58	16·47	20·59
Milk (Butter), . . .	105	2962	88·86	14·81	142·17
Cheese, ...	3	85·2	23·6	31·35	3·49
Bread, ...	94	2669·6	245·6	34·7	1417·55
Oatmeal, ...	35	994	160·03	71·56	670·95
Peas, ...	9·5	269·8	66·37	2·69	167·27
Barley, ...	6	170·4	14·48	1·87	132·57
Rice, ...	8	227·2	18·16	6·8	179·48
Sugar, ...	5·75	163·3	...	...	163·3
Marmalade, . . .	2	56·8	·34	·05	47·99
Potatoes, ...	16	454·4	8·17	·45	66·79
Fresh Vegetables, . .	10	284	3·97	·56	13·63
Tea, ...	·9	25·56	...	...	...
Total, . . .	...	...	982·27	462·98	3025·78

Table showing Average Weekly Composition of Class D Dietary.

	MALE AND FEMALE.				
	Quantity.		Proteid.	Fat.	Carbo-hydrate.
	Oz.	Grms.			
Beef, ...	40	1136	207·88	214·69	...
Heads, Hough, &c., . .	6·66	187·38	18·36	7·37	...
Fish (Salt), ...	8	227·2	62·02	·68	...
Margarine, ...	2·5	71	·85	58·93	...
Milk (Whole), . . .	14·5	411·8	13·58	16·47	20·59
Milk (Skimmed), . .	105	2982	101·88	8·94	143·13
Cheese, . . .	3	85·2	23·6	31·35	3·49
Bread, ...	94	2669·6	245·6	34·7	1417·55
Oatmeal, ...	35	994	160·03	71·56	670·95
Peas, ...	9·5	269·8	66·87	2·69	167·27
Barley, ...	6	170·4	14·48	1·87	132·57
Rice, ...	8	227·2	18·16	6·8	179·48
Sugar, ...	5·75	163·3	...	...	163·3
Marmalade, . . .	2	56·8	·84	·05	47·99
Potatoes, ...	16	454·4	8·17	·45	66·79
Fresh Vegetables, . .	10	284	3·97	·56	13·63
Tea, ...	·9	25·56	...	...	...
Total, . . .	...	...	944·79	457·11	3026·71

[TABLE.

Table showing Average Weekly Composition of Class T Dietary.

	Quantity.		Proteid.	Fat.	Carbo-hydrate.
	Oz.	Grms.			
Beef, ...	40	1136	207·88	214·69	...
Heads, Hough, &c., . .	6·66	187·33	18·36	7·37	...
Fish (Salt), ...	6	170·4	46·51	·51	...
Margarine, ...	6	170·4	2·04	141·42	...
Milk (Whole), . . .	18·75	532·5	17·57	21·3	26·62
Bread, ...	128	2493·2	321·37	45·41	1854·88
Peas, ...	9·5	269·8	66·37	2·69	167·27
Barley, ...	6	170·4	14·48	1·87	132·57
Rice, ...	8	227·2	18·16	6·8	179·48
Sugar, ...	11	312·4	...	...	312·4
Marmalade, . . .	2	56·8	·34	·05	47·99
Potatoes, ...	16	454·4	8·17	·45	66·79
Fresh Vegetables, . .	10	284	3·97	·56	13·63
Tea, ...	1·75	49·7	...	...	...
Total, . .	...	...	725·22	443·12	2801·63

Table showing Average Weekly Composition of Class M Dietary.

	Quantity.		Proteid.	Fat.	Carbo-hydrate.
	Oz.	Grms.			
Margarine, ...	6	170·4	2·04	141·42	...
Milk (Whole), . . .	78·75	2236·5	73·8	89·46	111·82
Bread	140	3976	365·79	51·68	2111·25
Rice, ...	4	113·6	9·08	3·4	89·74
Sugar, ...	11	312·4	...	...	312·4
Marmalade, . . .	2	56·8	·34	·05	47·99
Tea, ...	1·75	49·7	...	...	...
Total, . .	...	...	451·05	286·01	2673·2

Table showing Total Composition of Extra Food given Weekly.

	MALE AND FEMALE.				
	Quantity.		Proteid.	Fat.	Carbo-hydrate.
	Oz.	Grms.			
Beef, ...	112	3180·8	747·48	648·88	...
Eggs (98), ...	...	5586	664·73	519·49	...
Milk (Whole), . . .	700	19880	656·04	795·2	994·0
Bread, ...	28	795·2	73·15	10·83	422·25
Total, . . .	...	...	2141·4	1973·9	1416·25

Table showing Composition of Average Dietary, all Patients' Extras included.

	MALE AND FEMALE.				
	Quantity.		Proteid.	Fat.	Carbo-hydrate.
	Oz.	Grms.			
Beef, ...	34·72	986·98	182·1	186·87	...
Heads, Hough, &c., . .	5·6	159·03	15·43	6·06	...
Fish (Salt), ...	5·8	164·92	44·96	·49	...
Margarine, ...	3·4	96·56	1·15	80·14	...
Eggs, ...	...	51·3	6·1	4·77	...
Milk (Whole), . . .	28·6	815·64	26·9	32·62	40·77
Milk (Skimmed), . .	15·5	440·2	14·96	1·32	22·45
Milk (Butter), . . .	57·5	1633	48·99	8·16	7·83
Cheese, ...	2·2	62·48	17·3	22·99	2·56
Bread, ...	104·65	2969·22	273·16	38·59	1576·65
Oatmeal, ...	26·5	752·6	121·16	54·18	506·0
Peas, ...	8	227·2	55·89	2·27	140·86
Barley, ...	5	142	12·07	1·56	110·47
Rice, ...	7·3	207·32	16·58	·62	163·78
Sugar, ...	7·1	201·64	...	...	201·64
Marmalade, . . .	2	56·8	·34	·05	47·99
Potatoes, ...	13·5	383·4	6·9	·38	56·35
Fresh Vegetables, . .	8·4	238·56	3·33	·47	11·45
Tea, ...	1·13	31·8	...	...	...
Total, . . .	...	...	847·31	441·54	2890·8

Food Values.—The average weekly food values of Classes C, D, T, and M diets and of the average diets of the whole asylum are as follows:—

	Proteid.	Fat.	Carbo-hydrate.	Energy Value.
Class C, male and female	133·2	66·1	432·2	2933
„ D, „ „ „	135·0	65·3	432·4	2933
„ T, „ „ „	103·6	63·3	400·2	2654
„ M, „ „ „	64·4	40·8	381·4	2210
* Average Diet male and female	121·0	63·1	413·0	2835

* Extras included.

The average height of the male working patient is 64·8 inches, their average weight 137·1 lbs.

Critical Remarks.—The system of dietary in this asylum is essentially different from that in use in all other asylums, as it is the only asylum where lunatic patients are classified like ordinary paupers. A similar method of classification is to a limited extent found in the lunatic wards of some poorhouses, it is undesirable there, but in an asylum where all forms of insanity are received and treated it is indefensible. The division of patients into Classes C and D in particular is faulty, the difference between the two diets points to the authorities of the asylum considering that lunatics upwards of 60 years of age require some luxury (skimmed milk instead of butter-milk), while lunatics under that age require no luxury, an opinion hardly in keeping with the modern principles of the treatment of insanity. Classes T and M may be more justifiable, they may be required for the carrying out of the special dietary treatment prescribed by the Medical Officer.

The food value of the diets of all four classes is for male patients deficient in quantity, and for female patients, Class M excepted, excessive, a condition of affairs which may always be expected when males and females are fed according to the same scale. No special allowances are made for the requirements of male workers. The use of potato and of fresh vegetable is much smaller than it should be. The diets of all classes are too monotonous, in Class M particularly so, for on that diet patients, if not getting special medical extras, receive on six days a week tea bread and margarine night and morning, and milk and bread for dinner, the only relaxation for them is on Sunday, when their dinner is rice and milk and bread, instead of milk and bread. It is only right to state that medical extras appear to be freely used with Class M diet. The dietary of this asylum is so far from what it should be that a complete revision is urgently needed; in reconstructing it the dietaries of any of the neighbouring parochial asylums, Greenock, Govan, or Riccartsbar, might be taken as a model.

It is to be observed that the average weight of male working patients nearly coincides with the standard.

PAISLEY, RICCARTSBAR, PAROCHIAL ASYLUM.

Breakfast.—All patients get porridge and milk, some tea bread and butter in addition.

Dinner.—The weekly routine includes one dinner of rice and milk and cheese, three of broth, meat and potato, one of pea soup and pudding, one of pea soup, fish and potato, and one of rice and pudding. Bread is given with all dinners. Meat is given three times a week, and a small quantity used on three other days in making soup. The meat is always fresh beef.

Evening Meal.—This consists of tea bread and butter for all. Jelly is used instead of butter on Sundays.

Extras for Working Patients.—A few of both sexes get an early breakfast. All working patients get a luncheon of tea, bread and butter. Females in the kitchen and laundry get in the afternoon tea bread and butter. Working patients also get an egg with evening meal.

Dietary for females differs from that for males by having smaller rations of oatmeal and bread.

Table showing the Average Weekly Composition of Dietaries.

	MALE.					FEMALE.				
	Quantity.		Proteid.	Fat.	Carbo-hydrate	Quantity.		Proteid.	Fat.	Carbo-hydrate
	Oz.	Grms.				Oz.	Grms.			
Beef, ...	24	681·6	124·72	123·62	..	24	681·6	124·72	123·62	..
Fish (Fresh), . .	3	85·2	14·22	·25	..	6	170·4	28·27	·50	..
Fish (Salt), . .	9	255·6	61·16	·76	..	6	170·4	46·51	·51	..
Suet, ...	4·5	127·2	6·0	99·33	..	4·5	127·8	6·0	99·33	..
Butter, . . .	4	113·6	1·12	96·56	..	4	113·6	1·12	96·56	..
Eggs, ...	4·2	119·28	14·19	11·09	..	8·2	232·88	27·71	21·65	..
Milk, ...	150	4260	140·58	170·4	233·0	150	4260·0	140·58	170·4	233·0
Cheese, . . .	2	56·8	15·73	20·9	2·32	2	56·8	15·73	20·9	2·32
Bread, . . .	88	2499·2	229·92	32·48	1327·07	72	2044·8	188·12	26·58	1085·78
Oatmeal, . . .	31	880·4	141·74	63·88	594·27	21	596·4	96·02	42·94	402·57
Flour, . . .	8	227·2	25·9	2·26	171·76	8	227·2	25·9	2·26	171·76
Peas, ...	10	284	69·84	2·84	176·08	10	284	69·84	2·84	176·08
Barley, . . .	6	170·4	14·48	1·87	132·57	6	170·4	14·48	1·87	132·57
Rice, . . .	4·5	127·8	10·22	·38	10·09	4·5	127·8	10·22	·38	10·09
Sugar, . .	4·75	134·9	..	..	134·9	4·75	134·9	..	..	134·9
Syrup, Jam, &c., .	3·5	99·4	·25	·04	75·35	3·5	99·4	·25	·04	75·35
Potatoes, . . .	64	1817·6	32·7	1·8	267·18	64	1817·6	32·7	1·8	267·18
Fresh Vegetables, .	12	340·8	4·77	·68	16·35	12	340·8	4·77	·68	16·35
Currants, . . .	1	28·4	·68	·48	21·06	1	28·4	·68	·48	21·06
Tea, ...	1·5	42·6	..	..	..	1·5	42·6	..	..	..
Total, . .	..	..	908·22	634·32	3162·0	..	..	834·22	618·54	2729·01

Food Values.—The average weekly food values of the male and female dietaries are as follows:—

	Proteid.	Fat.	Carbo-hydrate.	Energy Value.
Male	129·7	90·6	451·7	3227
Female . . .	119·2	88·4	329·6	2909

The average height of the male working patient is 65·6 inches, their average weight 135·5 lbs.

Critical Remarks.—The dietaries of this asylum, excepting that the male diet is rather short of standard value, appear to be excellent. The variety of food, the use of fresh vegetable and condiment, and the special allowance for working patients are all that can be desired. The average weight of male workers is 4½ lbs. below the average. The adddition of some bread to the present exclusively porridge breakfast would raise the energy value of the diet to the necessary amount.

(4.) Lunatic Wards of Poorhouses.

ABERDEEN EAST POORHOUSE.

Breakfast.—The majority of male patients get porridge and skimmed milk only. The majority of the females get porridge with milk and tea bread and butter. The remainder of both sexes get tea bread and butter only.

Dinner.—The weekly routine includes one dinner of rice soup bread and cheese, one of broth, mutton and potato, two of broth, beef and bread, one of pea soup, pudding and bread, one of pea soup, fish and potato, and one of rice soup, beef and pudding. Meat is given four times a week, on three days beef is given, on one mutton. The cooking of the beef is varied. The puddings are varied. An additional beef dinner is frequently given in place of the pea soup pudding and bread dinner. With all dinners, the rice soup, beef and pudding dinner excepted, either bread or potato is given *ad libitum*.

Evening Meal.—This consists of tea bread and butter for all, jam occasionally instead of butter. Nearly all the males, and about one-third of the females, get late supper consisting of porridge and milk.

Extras for Working Patients.—Male and female patients working before breakfast receive an allowance of tea bread and butter. All working patients get milk and bread for luncheon.

Dietary for females differs from that for males by having smaller rations of oatmeal and by fewer getting late supper.

Table showing the Average Weekly Composition of Dietaries.

	MALE					FEMALE				
	Quantity.		Proteid.	Fat.	Carbo-hydrate	Quantity.		Proteid.	Fat.	Carbo-hydrate
	Oz.	Grms.				Oz.	Grms.			
Beef, . . .	13	369·2	67·56	69·77	..	12	340·8	62·36	64·41	..
Mutton, . . .	4	113·6	14·76	27·26	..	4	113·6	14·76	27·26	..
Fish (Fresh), . .	2	56·8	9·62	·18	..	1·5	42·6	7·18	·13	..
Fish (Salt), . .	4·5	127·8	34·98	·38	..	3	85·2	23·25	·25	..
Suet, . . .	4	113·6	5·33	92·92	..	4	113·6	5·33	92·92	..
Butter, . . .	3·5	99·4	·98	84·48	..	7	198·8	1·96	168·96	..
Milk (Whole), . .	10	284	9·37	11·36	14·2	20	568	18·74	22·72	28·0
Milk (Skimmed), . .	280	7952	270·36	23·64	405·54	210	5964	202·77	17·89	304·16
Cheese, . . .	4	113·6	31·46	41·3	4·65	4	113·6	31·46	41·3	4·65
Bread, . . .	76	2158·4	198·57	28·06	1146·11	116	3294·4	303·08	42·82	1749·82
Oatmeal, . . .	82·5	2343	377·22	168·69	1581·52	37·7	1070·68	172·37	77·08	722·7
Flour, . . .	9	255·6	29·12	2·54	196·22	8	227·2	25·9	2·26	171·76
Peas, . . .	4	113·6	27·94	1·13	71·43	4	113·6	27·94	1·13	71·43
Barley, . . .	6	170·4	14·48	1·87	132·57	6	170·4	14·48	1·87	132·57
Rice, . . .	4	113·6	9·08	3·4	89·74	4	113·6	9·08	3·4	89·74
Sugar, . . .	3·5	99·4	..	..	99·4	7	198·8	..	..	198·8
Syrup, Jam, . .	1·5	42·6	·08	·01	31·67	1·5	42·6	·08	·01	31·67
Potatoes, . .	60	1704	30·67	1·7	250·48	50	1420	25·56	1·42	208·74
Fresh Vegetables, . .	10	284	3·97	·56	13·63	10	284	3·97	·56	13·63
Currants, Raisins, .	1·0	28·4	·67	·66	20·25	1·0	28·4	·67	·66	20·25
Tea, Coffee, . .	1·4	39·76	..	..	..	2·25	63·9	..	..	..
Total, . .	..	..	1136·12	560·6	4054·41	..	..	960·94	567·55	3747·42

Food Values.—The average daily food values of the male and female dietaries are as follows:—

	Proteid.	Fat.	Carbo-hydrate.	Energy Value.
Male	162·3	80·1	579·2	3785
Female . . .	135·8	81·1	535·3	3506

The average height of the male working patient is 65·5 inches, their average weight 144·2 lbs.

Critical Remarks.—The diets, both male and female, are in considerable excess of the standard; they may be wasteful, but they certainly are sufficient to secure that all inmates are fully fed. Ample provision is made for the wants of working patients. The variation of the diet and the use of condiment are both good. Oatmeal here is sufficiently used to meet local habit, but is not used to the exclusion of bread and meat. The excellence of the male dietary is corroborated by the weight test.

ABERDEEN WEST POORHOUSE.

Breakfast.—The majority of men, and one-third of the women, get porridge and milk only. The remainder get tea, bread and butter.

Dinner.—The weekly routine includes one dinner of rice and milk and cheese, two of broth, beef and potato, one of broth and suet pudding, one of potato soup, one of rice soup and beef, and one of pea soup and fish. Bread is given daily. Meat is given three times a week, it it invariably boiled beef. Small quantities of meat are also used in preparing the soup of other dinners.

Evening Meal.—The majority of the male patients, and about one-third of the female patients (the same number of both sexes as at breakfast), get porridge and milk only. The remainder get tea, bread, and butter.

Extras for Working Patients.—Male patients working in the forenoon receive some milk and bread; female patients working in the forenoon get some tea and bread, with some cheese as an addition on washing days.

Dietary for females differs from that for males by having smaller rations of porridge, smaller rations of bread at breakfast and tea, and by a larger number having tea bread and butter at breakfast and tea.

Table showing the Average Weekly Composition of Dietaries.

	MALE.					FEMALE.				
	Quantity.		Proteid.	Fat.	Carbo-hydrate	Quantity.		Proteid.	Fat.	Carbo-hydrate
	Oz.	Grms.				Oz.	Grms.			
Beef, ...	12	340·8	62·36	64·41	..	12	340·8	62·36	64·41	..
Heads, Hough, &c., .	1·5	42·6	4·13	1·66	..	1·5	42·6	4·13	1·66	..
Fish (Fresh), . . .	8	227·2	37·94	·68	..	8	227·2	37·94	·68	..
Suet, ...	2·5	71	3·23	58·07	..	2·5	71	3·23	58·07	..
Butter, ...	1·4	39·76	·39	33·79	..	4·9	139·16	1·39	118·28	..
Milk (Whole), . . .	180	5112	168·69	204·48	255·6	60	1704	56·23	68·16	85·2
Milk (Skimmed), . .	74	2101·6	71·45	6·2	107·18	56	1590·4	54·07	4·77	81·11
Cheese, ...	3	85·2	23·6	31·35	3·49	5	142	39·33	52·25	5·82
Bread, ...	74·1	2104·44	198·6	27·35	1117·45	90·5	2570·2	236·45	33·41	1364·77
Oatmeal, ...	69	1959·6	315·49	141·09	1322·73	22·5	639	102·87	46·0	431·32
Flour, ...	6·5	184·6	21·04	1·84	139·55	6·5	184·6	21·04	1·84	139·55
Peas, ...	5	142	34·92	1·42	88·04	5	142	34·92	1·42	88·04
Barley, ...	6	170·4	14·48	1·96	132·56	6	170·4	14·48	1·96	132·56
Rice, ...	4	113·6	9·08	3·4	89·74	4	113·6	9·08	3·4	89·74
Sugar, ...	1·5	42·6	..	..	42·6	8	227·2	..	..	227·2
Jam, ...	..	..	..	..	..	2·3	65·32	·39	·06	55·19
Potatoes, ...	56	1590·4	28·62	1·59	233·78	56	1590·4	28·62	1·59	233·78
Fresh Vegetables, . .	8	227·2	3·18	·45	10·9	8	227·2	3·18	·45	10·9
Tea, ...	·3	8·52	..	..	..	2·7	76·68	..	..	..
Total, . .	..	..	992·3	579·74	3543·62	..	..	709·21	458·21	2945·18

Food Values.—The average daily food values of the male and female dietaries are as follows:—

	Proteid.	Fat.	Carbo-hydrate.	Energy Value.
Male	141·8	82·8	506·2	3426
Female . .	101·4	65·5	420·7	2750

The average height of the male working patient is 65·9 inches, their average weight 137 lbs.

Critical Remarks.—The food values of both dietaries appear to be sufficient, but the weight test shows that the working male patients are not receiving a sufficiency, for their average weight is 3 lbs. below the standard. This anomaly may be ascribed to the extreme monotony of the diet. The twice daily porridge, the small use of meat, the invariable boiling of the meat, the meagre allowance of tea, the small use of fresh vegetable, all contribute to making the diet untempting and monotonous. I am of opinion that a diet of the same food value but of a more varied and pleasing description would be found to nourish the inmates better.

BUCHAN POORHOUSE.

Breakfast.—Nearly all the patients receive porridge and milk; the majority of females, and about half the males, get tea bread and butter in addition. The few who do not get porridge have tea bread and butter only.

Dinner.—The weekly routine includes one dinner of broth, bread and cheese, two of broth, beef and potato, one of broth, beef and bread, one of potato soup, bread and cheese, one of pea soup, bread and pudding, and one of pea soup, fish and bread. Meat is given on three days a week, and is invariably boiled beef. Bread is given three times a week. Rice and milk is given to some patients twice a week in lieu of pea soup.

Evening Meal.—All female and most male patients get tea bread and butter only. A few males get porridge and skim milk.

Extras for Working Patients.—Bread and syrup is given to all workers as luncheon daily, except on Monday when men get bread and cheese, and women bread and coffee.

Dietary for females differs from that for males by having smaller rations of porridge and bread.

[TABLE-

Table showing the Average Weekly Composition of Dietaries.

	MALE.					FEMALE.				
	Quantity.		Proteid.	Fat.	Carbo-hydrate	Quantity.		Proteid.	Fat.	Carbo-hydrate
	Oz.	Grms.				Oz.	Grms.			
Beef, ...	13	369·2	67·56	60·77	..	12	340·2	62·36	64·41	..
Fish (Salt), . . .	4	113·6	31·01	·34	..	4	113·6	31·01	·34	..
Suet, ...	1	28·4	1·32	23·22	..	1	28·4	1·32	23·22	..
Butter, ...	3	85·2	·85	72·42	..	2	56·8	·56	48·28	..
Milk (Skimmed), . .	140	3976	135·18	11·92	202·77	100	2840	96·56	8·52	144·84
Cheese, ...	4·5	127·8	35·4	47·02	5·23	4·5	127·8	35·4	47·02	5·23
Bread, ...	117·5	3337	307	43·38	1771·94	89	2527·6	232·53	32·95	1342·15
Oatmeal, ...	50	1420	228·62	102·24	968·5	30	852	137·17	61·34	575·1
Flour, ...	4	113·6	12·95	1·13	85·38	4	113·6	12·95	1·13	85·38
Peas, ...	6	170·4	41·91	1·7	106·64	5	142	34·92	1·42	88·04
Barley, ...	8	227·2	19·3	2·48	176·76	7	198·8	16·89	2·18	154·66
Rice, ...	5	142	11·36	·42	112·18	5	142	11·36	·42	112·18
Sugar, ...	4	113·6	..	..	113·6	4	113·6	..	..	113·6
Syrup, &c., . . .	2	56·8	..	..	39·36	2	56·8	..	..	39·36
Potatoes, ...	64	1817·6	32·7	1·8	267·18	48	1363·2	24·52	1·26	200·28
Fresh Vegetables, . .	16	454·4	6·36	·9	21·81	16	454·4	6·36	·9	21·81
Currants, Raisins, . .	·10	28·4	·67	·66	20·25	·50	14·2	·33	·33	10·12
Tea, Coffee, . . .	1·12	31·95	..	..	..	1·12	31·95	..	..	..
Total, . . .	..	:	932·19	379·4	3881·1	..	..	714·24	298·72	2893·25

Food Values.—The average daily food values of the male and female dietaries are as follows:—

	Proteid.	Fat.	Carbo-hydrate.	Energy Value.
Male	133·2	52·2	544·4	3323
Female . . .	102·0	41·9	413·3	2503

The average height of the male working patient is 65·9 inches, their average weight 139·1 lbs.

Critical Remarks.—The food value of the male diet is sufficient, that of the female barely so. Some extra food is given to workers. The weight test shows male working patients to average very nearly the standard weight. The diets, however, are faulty in two respects, the division into meals is unequal and the dinners are unduly monotonous. The inequality of meals is specially notice-able in the male dietary. In the schedule it is reported that about half of the male patients have a breakfast consisting of oatmeal 6 oz., skimmed milk 15 oz., bread 8 oz., butter 1 oz., sugar ½ oz., and tea; such a meal has an energy value of more than 1800 calories, which is more than one-half of the entire day's food, and from such a meal a very considerable waste may be expected. The monotony of the dinners is due to the routine including two soup bread and cheese dinners, and three boiled beef dinners. Desirable changes of these dietaries are a revision of the dinner routine, including more meat dinners, varying the cooking of the meat and using fresh vegetables more freely, and rearranging the issues of bread, giving less of it along with the ample porridge ration at breakfast time and more of it with the dinners.

CUNNINGHAM POORHOUSE.

Breakfast.—The majority of both sexes get porridge and skim milk only. The remainder get tea bread and margarine only.

Dinner.—The weekly routine includes three dinners of broth and boiled beef, one of broth and meat pie, one of pea soup and boiled beef, and one of broth, fish and potato. Bread is given daily, meat five times a week.

Evening Meal.—This consists of tea bread and margarine for all. On Sundays coffee is given in place of tea and jam in place of margarine.

Extras for Working Patients.—Working men get bread and cheese and some milk at breakfast time in addition to their ordinary breakfast. Working women get tea, bread and margarine in addition to their ordinary breakfast.

Dietary for females differs from that for males by having smaller rations of oatmeal and bread.

Table showing the Average Weekly Composition of Dietaries.

	MALE.					FEMALE.				
	Quantity.		Proteid.	Fat.	Carbo-hydrate	Quantity.		Proteid.	Fat.	Carbo-hydrate
	Oz.	Grms.				Oz.	Grms.			
Beef, ...	20	568	103·94	107·35	..	20	568	103·94	107·35	..
Fish (Fresh), . .	8	227·2	39·06	·68	..	8	227·2	39·06	·68	..
Margarine, . . .	3·5	99·4	1·19	82·5	..	6·5	184·6	2·21	153·21	..
Milk (Whole), . .	7	198·8	6·56	7·95	9·94	7	198·8	6·56	7·95	9·94
Milk (Skimmed), . .	285	8094	275·19	24·28	412·79	225	6390	217·26	19·17	325·89
Cheese, ...	14	397·6	110·13	146·31	16·3	2	56·8	15·73	20·9	2·33
Bread, ...	120	3408	313·53	44·3	1809·64	114	3237·6	297·85	42·08	1719·16
Oatmeal, ...	42	1192·8	192·04	85·88	805·14	35	994	160·03	71·56	670·95
Peas, ...	4·5	127·8	31·43	1·27	79·23	4·5	127·8	31·43	1·27	79·23
Barley, ...	10	284	24·14	3·12	230·95	10	284	24·14	3·12	230·95
Rice, ...	2	56·8	4·54	1·7	44·87	2	56·8	4·54	1·7	44·87
Sugar, ...	4	113·6	..	..	113·6	7	198·8	..	..	198·8
Jam, Marmalade, . .	1	28·4	·17	·03	23·99	1	28·4	·17	·03	23·99
Potatoes, . . .	16	454·4	8·17	·45	66·79	16	454·4	8·17	·45	66·79
Fresh Vegetables, .	37·5	1065	14·91	2·13	51·12	37·5	1065	14·91	2·13	51·12
Tea, Coffee, . . .	1·05	29·82	..	..	..	1·75	49·7	..	..	..
Total, . .	..	..	1125·0	507·95	3654·36	..	..	926·0	431·6	3414·02

Food Values.—The average daily food values of the male and female dietaries are as follows:—

	Proteid.	Fat.	Carbo-hydrate.	Energy Value.
Male	160·7	72·6	522·0	3474
Female . . .	132·3	61·6	483·7	3115

The average height of the male working patient is 65·3 inches, their average weight 146·2 lbs.

Critical Remarks.—Both dietaries are of ample energy value, and that they are so is supported by the result of the weight test. The working male patients average 6 lbs. more than the standard. The female dietary is in excess of the standard food value. The use of milk in these lunatic wards is exceptionally generous and is to be commended. In these dietaries potato is not sufficiently used, it is only given once a week in soup and never with meat. Desirable improvements of these dietaries could be effected by the freer use of potato, and by giving the working patients their extra food during the forenoon instead of at breakfast time.

DUMBARTON COMBINATION POORHOUSE.

Breakfast.—About one-half of the male patients get porridge and milk only, all others get porridge and milk and tea bread and margarine.

Dinner.—The weekly routine includes two dinners of broth, beef and bread, two of pea soup, dried ling and potato, one of broth beef and pudding, and one of rice soup, bread and cheese. Meat is given three times a week, invariably as boiled beef. Bread is given four times a week.

Evening Meal.—About one-half of the male patients get porridge and milk only (the same patients as do so at breakfast), the rest of the males get porridge and milk with tea bread and margarine. The females get tea bread and margarine only.

Extras for Working Patients.—A few get tea bread and margarine in the early morning. Women in the laundry get for lunch some bread and cheese and coffee. Working male patients receive the larger breakfast referred to above.

Dietary for females differs from that for males by having smaller rations of oatmeal, bread, cheese, and potato.

Table showing the Average Weekly Composition of Dietaries.

	MALE.					FEMALE.				
	Quantity.		Proteid.	Fat.	Carbo-hydrate	Quantity.		Proteid.	Fat.	Carbo-hydrate
	Oz.	Grms.				Oz.	Grms.			
Beef, ...	18	511·2	98·54	96·61	..	18	511·2	93·54	96·61	..
Heads, Hough, &c.,	8	227·2	22·03	8·96	..	8	227·2	22·03	8·96	..
Fish (Salt), . .	12	340·8	98·02	1·02	..	12	340·8	98·02	1·02	..
Suet, ...	1·5	42·6	2	34·84	..	1·5	42·6	2·0	34·84	..
Margarine, . .	3·3	98·72	1·12	77·78	..	7·5	213	2·55	176·79	..
Milk (Whole), . .	145	4113	136·89	164·72	205·9	86·8	2459·44	81·16	98·37	122·97
Cheese, ...	4	113·6	31·46	61·3	4·65	6·75	191·7	53·1	70·54	7·85
Bread, ...	58	1647·2	151·54	21·41	874·66	104	2953·6	271·73	38·39	1568·36
Oatmeal, . . .	84	2385·6	384·08	171·76	1610·28	28	795·2	128·02	57·25	536·76
Flour, ...	4	113·6	12·95	1·13	85·88	4	113·6	12·95	1·13	85·88
Peas, ...	6	170·4	41·91	1·7	105·64	6	170·4	41·91	1·7	105·64
Barley, ...	8	227·2	19·3	2·48	176·76	8	227·2	19·3	2·48	176·76
Rice, ...	1·5	42·6	3·4	·12	33·65	1·5	42·6	3·4	·12	33·65
Sugar, ...	4	113·6	..	..	113·6	9	255·6	..	..	255·6
Potatoes, . . .	96	2726·4	49·04	2·72	400·76	72	2044·8	36·3	2·04	300·58
Fresh Vegetables, .	11·75	333·7	4·67	·66	16·01	11·75	333·7	4·67	·66	16·01
Tea, Coffee, . ·. .	·9	25·56	..	..	..	2·4	68·16	..	..	..
Total, . .	..	..	1045·95	627·61	3627·79	..	..	866·18	590·8	3210·06

Food Values.—The average daily food values of the male and female dietaries are as follows:—

	Proteid.	Fat.	Carbo-hydrate.	Energy Value.
Male	149·4	89·6	518·3	3571
Female . . .	123·7	84·4	458·6	3172

The average height of the male working patient is 66·3 inches, their average weight 146·9 lbs.

Critical Remarks.—The energy and proteid values of these diets are both ample, they both exceed the standard. The requirements of working patients are fully met. The diet, however, is faulty on account of its monotony. Half of the male patients are restricted to porridge and milk twice daily, and never get tea. The twice weekly use of dried ling must also be found monotonous. The issues of milk and potato are both commendably generous. The diet would be greatly improved by giving a tea bread and butter supper to all patients, by varying the cooking of the meat, and by restricting the use of dried ling, giving more meat in its stead. The weight test shows that the average weight of male

F

workers is quite satisfactory. The monotony of the feeding of male workers is relieved by their having tea at breakfast time.

DUNDEE EAST POORHOUSE.

Breakfast.—The majority of male patients and a minority of female patients get porridge and skimmed milk only. The remainder get tea bread and butter only.

Dinner.—The weekly routine includes one dinner of lentil soup and meat, two of broth and meat, one of pea soup, meat and suet pudding, one of Irish stew, one of rice and milk, and one of broth and fish. Meat is given five times a week, and is always beef. On four days it is boiled, on one day stewed. Bread is given daily, except with the pea soup, beef and suet pudding dinner. Potato is given twice a week.

Evening Meal.—This consists of tea, bread and butter for all male and nearly all female patients. The remaining few females get porridge and milk. Jelly and marmalade are each given once weekly instead of butter.

Extras for Working Patients.—Working male patients are given a luncheon of bread with cheese or tinned mutton. Female patients receive smaller rations of the same with some tea in addition.

Dietary for females differs from that for males by their having a different breakfast, and smaller rations of oatmeal, bread, and pudding.

Table showing the Average Weekly Composition of Dietaries.

	MALE.					FEMALE.				
	Quantity.		Proteid.	Fat.	Carbo-hydrate	Quantity.		Proteid.	Fat.	Carbo-hydrate
	Oz.	Grms.				Oz.	Grms.			
Beef, . . .	23·6	670·24	122·65	126·67	..	23·2	661·72	121·09	125·06	..
Fish (Fresh), . .	9·3	264·12	44·1	·79	..	9	255·6	42·68	·76	..
Suet, ...	2	56·8	2·66	46·46	..	2	56·8	2·66	46·46	..
Butter, . . .	2·75	78·1	·78	66·38	..	6·1	173·24	1·73	147·25	..
Milk (Whole), .	38	1079·2	35·61	43·16	53·96	52	1476·8	48·73	59·07	73·84
Milk (Skimmed), .	96	2726·4	92·69	3·17	139·04	..	..	..	..	..
Cheese, . . .	5·7	161·88	44·84	59·57	6·63	2·7	76·68	21·24	28·21	3·14
Bread, . .	118·9	3376·76	310·66	43·89	1798·05	143·7	4081·08	375·45	53·05	2167·05
Oatmeal, . . .	38·5	1093·4	176·08	78·72	788·04	3·9	110·76	17·83	7·97	74·76
Flour, . . .	5·4	153·36	17·48	1·53	115·94	4·5	127·8	14·56	1·27	96·61
Peas, Lentils, . .	8·3	235·72	59·04	2·35	143·43	8·3	235·72	59·04	2·35	143·43
Barley, . . .	5·9	167·56	14·24	1·84	130·26	6·1	173·24	14·72	1·9	134·73
Rice, . . .	3	85·2	6·81	·25	67·3	2·6	73·84	5·9	·22	58·33
Sugar, . . .	4·6	130·64	..	..	130·64	8·6	244·24	..	..	244·24
Syrup, Jam, &c., .	3·25	92·3	·42	·07	74·75	4·55	129·22	·64	1	105·95
Potatoes, . . .	22·9	650·36	11·7	·65	96·6	24	681·6	12·26	·68	100·19
Fresh Vegetables, .	18·5	525·4	7·35	1·05	25·21	18·5	525·4	7·35	1·05	25·21
Currants, Raisins, .	1·0	28·4	·67	·66	20·25	·10	28·4	·67	·66	20·25
Tea, . . .	·9	25·56	..	..	..	1·9	53·96	..	..	..
Total, . .	..	..	947·73	482·21	3534·2	..	..	746·55	476·06	3247·73

Food Values. The average daily food values of the male and female dietaries are as follows :—

	Proteid.	Fat.	Carbo-hydrate.	Energy Value.
Male	135·4	68·9	504·9	3266
Female . . .	106·6	68·0	464·0	2973

The average height of the male working patient is 65·3 inches their average weight 133·8 lbs.

Critical Remarks.—The male dietary is of rather less than standard food value, the female is of ample food value. Special allowance is made for the wants of working patients. The use of potato for both sexes and of tea for males is too small. The weight test shows that average weight of male working patients is fully 6 lbs. below the standard; why this is so is not apparent. A freer use of potato would greatly improve the diet, and so would the addition of some bread to all breakfasts. A more generous allowance of tea for male patients is also desirable.

DUNDEE WEST POORHOUSE.

Breakfast.—About one-half of both male and female patients get porridge and skim milk only. The remainder get tea bread and butter only,

Dinner.—The weekly routine includes two dinners of broth, meat and bread, two of broth, meat and potato, one of broth and fish, one of lentil soup and meat, and one of lentil soup and pudding. Meat is given five times a week, it is invariably boiled beef. Bread is given daily.

Evening Meal.—About two-thirds of the patients get tea bread and butter only. The remainder get porridge and skim milk. No patients are restricted to porridge and milk twice daily to the exclusion of tea and bread.

Extras for Working Patients.—Working patients get a luncheon consisting of tea, bread and butter.

Dietary for females differs from that for males by having smaller rations of oatmeal, bread, and pudding.

[TABLE

Table showing the Average Weekly Composition of Dietaries.

| | MALE | | | | FEMALE | | | | |
| | Quantity. | | Proteid. | Fat. | Carbo-hydrate | Quantity. | | Prote d. | Fat. | Carbo-hydrate |
	Oz.	Grms.				Oz.	Grms.			
Beef, . .	34	965·6	176·7	132·49	..	34	965·6	176·7	132·49	..
Fish (Fresh), .	8·75	248·5	41·49	·74	..	8·75	248·5	41·49	·74	..
Suet, . .	·5	14·2	·66	11·61	..	·5	14·2	·66	11·61	..
Butter, . .	4	113·6	1·13	96·56	..	5	142	1·42	120·7	..
Milk (Whole), .	10	284	9·27	11·36	14·2	10	284	9·27	11·36	14·2
Milk (Skimmed), .	90	2556	86·9	7·66	130·35	60	1704	57·93	5·11	86·9
Bread, . .	107	3038·8	279·56	39·5	1613·6	104	2953·6	271·73	38·39	1568·36
Oatmeal, . .	37	1050·8	169·17	75·65	709·29	21	596·4	96·02	42·94	402·57
Flour, . .	6	170·4	19·42	1·7	123·62	5	142	16·18	1·42	107·25
Peas, Lentils, .	9·5	269·3	68·55	2·69	161·70	9·5	269·3	68·55	2·69	161·70
Barley, . .	10	284	24·14	3·12	220·95	10	284	24·14	3·12	220·95
Sugar, . .	4	113·6	..	..	113·6	5	142	..	..	142·0
Potatoes, . .	32	908·3	16·35	·9	133·59	32	908·3	16·35	·9	133·59
Fresh Vegetables, .	10·4	295·36	4·13	·59	14·17	10·4	295·36	4·13	·59	14·17
Raisins, . .	1	28·4	·65	·35	19·45	1	28·4	·65	·35	19·45
Tea, . .	1	28·4	..	..	..	1·25	35·5	..	..	..
Total, . .	..	..	896·22	435·42	3259·72	..	..	785·22	422·91	2871·24

Food Values.—The average daily food values of the male and female dietaries are as follows:—

	Proteid.	Fat.	Carbo-hydrate.	Energy Value.
Male	128·3	62.2	465·7	3014
Female . . .	112·2	60·4	410·2	2703

The average height of the male working patient is 65·2 inches, their average weight 125·9 lbs.

Critical Remarks.—The dietary for male patients is of insufficient food value, and although working patients receive some extra food they are decidedly below their normal weight; their average is no less than 14 lbs. below the standard. The female diet appears to be of ample quantity. Necessary improvements of these dietaries are a more liberal use of bread with all dinners, a fuller allowance of vegetables, and some variation in the cooking of the meat.

EDINBURGH (CRAIGLOCKHART) POORHOUSE.

Breakfast.—The male patients get porridge and butter-milk only. The female patients get tea bread and butter.

Dinner.—The weekly routine includes three dinners of broth, meat and potato, one of broth, meat and bread, one of pea soup with either meat pie or Irish stew, one of rice soup and fish, and one of rice soup and cheese. Bread is given with all dinners. Meat is given five times a week, it is invariably beef, and is served four times a week as boiled beef, and once a week as meat pie or Irish stew.

Evening Meal.—All males get tea, bread and butter only. All females get porridge and skim milk, a few of them get tea, bread and butter in addition.

Extras for Working Patients.—A few patients get an early breakfast, other than that no extras are given to workers.

Dietary for females differs from that for males by having smaller rations of oatmeal and cheese, by having skimmed milk with porridge, and by having pudding once weekly instead of beef.

Table showing the Average Weekly Composition of Dietaries.

	MALE.					FEMALE.				
	Quantity.		Proteid.	Fat.	Carbo-hydrate	Quantity.		Proteid.	Fat.	Carbo-hydrate
	Oz.	Grms.				Oz.	Grms.			
Beef, ...	44	1249·6	228·67	236·17	..	38	1079·2	197·49	203·96	..
Fish (Fresh), . .	12	340·8	57·75	1·02	..	12	340·8	57·75	1·02	..
Suet, ...	..	..	..	..	..	1·14	32·37	1·52	26·47	..
Butter, ...	3·5	99·4	·99	84·49	..	4	113·6	1·12	96·56	..
Milk,*	105	2982	89·46	14·91	143·13	60	1704	57·93	5·11	86·9
Cheese, . . .	4	113·6	31·46	41·8	4·65	2	56·8	15·73	20·9	2·33
Bread, ...	123	3493·2	321·37	45·41	1854·86	87·5	2485	228·62	32·3	1319·53
Oatmeal, . . .	42	1192·3	192·04	85·88	805·14	30	852	137·17	61·34	575·1
Flour, ...	1·5	42·6	4·85	·43	32·21	3·1	88·04	10·08	·88	66·65
Peas, . . .	5·5	156·2	38·42	1·55	96·94	6	170·4	41·91	1·7	105·64
Barley, ...	8	227·2	19·3	2·48	176·76	10	284	24·14	3·12	220·95
Rice, ...	4	113·6	9·08	3·4	89·74	2	56·8	4·54	1·7	44·37
Sugar, . . .	2·62	74·4	..	..	74·4	3	85·2	..	..	85·2
Potatoes, . . .	40	113·6	20·44	1·13	166·99	40	1136	20·44	1·13	166·99
Fresh Vegetables, .	28	795·2	11·13	1·59	38·16	28	795·2	11·13	1·59	38·16
Tea, ...	·9	25·56	..	..	..	1	28·4	..	..	..
Total, . .	..	..	1024·96	520·27	3482·9	..	..	809·52	457·78	2712·22

* Butter-milk for males, skimmed milk for females.

Food Values.—The average daily food values of the male and female dietaries are as follows:—

	Proteid.	Fat.	Carbo-hydrate.	Energy Value.
Male	146·4	74·3	497·5	3331
Female . . .	115·6	65·4	387·5	2671

The average height of the male working patient is 66·5 inches, their average weight 143·8 lbs.

Critical Remarks.—The quantity of both dietaries is ample, and the food values of both practically coincide with the standards. No special provision is made for the wants of working patients. The issue of tea appears to be too small. Were this increased, and were workers allowed some luncheon, the dietaries of these lunatic wards would be excellent. The weight test shows the average weight of working patients to be slightly below the standard.

INVERESK POORHOUSE.

Breakfast.—This consists of porridge and skimmed milk for all patients.

Dinner.—The weekly routine includes two dinners of broth, meat and vegetable, one of broth and Irish stew, one of rice soup, meat and suet pudding, one of rice soup, fish and potato, one of pea soup, meat and pease pudding, and one of coffee and cheese. Bread is given at all dinners, the fish dinner excepted. Meat is given five times a week, on three occasions as boiled beef, on one as boiled mutton, and on one as beef cooked in Irish stew.

Evening Meal.—This consists of tea bread and butter for all.

Extras for Working Patients.—An early breakfast is given to four working patients, other than that no extras are given to any working patients.

Dietary for females differs from that for males by having smaller rations of oatmeal, bread, cheese, meat, and fish.

Table showing the Average Weekly Composition of Dietaries.

| | MALE. | | | | | FEMALE. | | | | |
| | Quantity. | | Proteid. | Fat. | Carbo-hydrate | Quantity. | | Proteid. | Fat. | Carbo-hydrate |
	Oz.	Grms.				Oz.	Grms.			
Beef, ...	30	852	155·91	161·02	..	20	568	103·94	107·35	..
Heads, Hough, &c., .	·5	14·2	1·37	·55	..	·5	14·2	1·37	·55	..
Mutton, ...	6	170·4	23·15	40·39	..	4	113·6	14·76	27·26	..
Fish (Salt), . . .	8	227·2	62·02	·68	..	6	170·4	46·51	·51	..
Suet, ...	·5	14·2	·66	11·61	..	·5	14·2	·66	11·61	..
Butter, ...	1·75	49·7	·49	42·24	..	1·75	49·7	·49	42·24	..
Milk (Skimmed), . .	116	3294·4	112·0	9·88	168·01	116	3294·4	112·0	9·88	168·01
Cheese, ...	4	113·6	31·46	41·8	4·65	3	85·2	23·6	31·35	3·49
Bread, ...	104	2953·6	271·73	33·39	1568·26	80	2272	209·02	29·53	1206·58
Oatmeal, ...	42	1192·3	192·04	85·88	805·14	28	795·2	128·02	57·25	536·76
Flour, ...	4	113·6	12·95	1·13	85·88	4	113·6	12·95	1·13	85·88
Peas, ...	6·5	184·6	45·41	1·84	114·45	6·5	184·6	45·41	1·84	114·45
Barley, ...	6	170·4	14·48	1·37	132·57	6	170·4	14·48	1·37	132·57
Rice, ...	4	113·6	9·08	3·4	89·74	4	113·6	9·08	3·4	89·74
Sugar, ...	4	113·6	..	..	113·6	4	113·6	..	..	113·6
Syrup, Jam, &c., . .	2·5	71·0	·34	·05	57·83	2·5	71	·34	·05	57·83
Potatoes, . . .	34	965·6	17·38	·96	141·94	34	965·6	17·38	·96	141·94
Fresh Vegetables, . .	24	681·6	9·54	1·36	32·71	24	681·6	9·54	1·36	32·71
Tea, Coffee, . . .	1·1	31·24	..	..	..	1·1	31·24	..	..	..
Total, . . .	..	..	969·01	443·55	3314·88	..	..	749·55	322·14	2683·51

Food Values.—The average daily food values of the male and female dietaries are as follows:—

	Proteid.	Fat.	Carbo-hydrate.	Energy Value.
Male	137·0	63·4	473·5	3062
Female . . .	107·1	46·9	383·4	2447

The average height of the male working patient is 63·1 inches, their average weight 131·2 lbs.

Critical Remarks.—The diets, both male and female, appear to be of less than standard food value. They have sufficient proteid but insufficient energy. Both diets may be taken as sufficient for idle patients, but as insufficient for workers. No special allowance is made to meet the wants of workers. Of individual food-stuffs bread and potato may be selected as being issued in less than usual quantities. The diets in other ways are good, and are sufficiently varied. The diets would be made quite satisfactory by giving some luncheon to working patients, and by using potato more freely.

KINCARDINE POORHOUSE.

Breakfast.—The majority of both sexes get porridge and milk only, the remainder get tea, bread and margarine.

Dinner.—The weekly routine includes one dinner of broth and cheese, one of broth, salt beef and rice pudding, one of broth, salt beef with oatmeal pudding or mashed cabbage occasionally added, one of broth, fish and potato, one of broth and suet pudding, one of pea soup and Irish stew, and one of potato soup and stewed beef. Bread is given with all dinners. Meat is given four times a week, salt beef being used twice weekly and fresh beef twice weekly. The cooking of the meat is varied.

Evening Meal.—This consists of tea, bread and margarine for all.

Extras for Working Patients.—Tea, bread and either margarine or marmalade is given to some women as an early breakfast. A luncheon of tea, bread and either margarine or marmalade is given to all workers.

Dietary for females differs from that for males by having smaller rations of oatmeal, bread, and pudding.

Table showing the Average Weekly Composition of Dietaries.

	MALE.					FEMALE.				
	Quantity.		Proteid.	Fat.	Carbo-hydrate	Quantity.		Proteid.	Fat.	Carbo-hydrate
	Oz.	Grms.				Oz.	Grms.			
Beef, ...	26	738·4	157·83	138·98	..	26	738·4	157·83	138·98	..
Fish (Salt), . . .	8	227·2	62·02	·68	..	8	227·2	62·02	·68	..
Suet, ...	2·5	71	3·33	58·07	..	2·5	71	3·33	58·07	..
Butter, ...	4·8	136·22	1·96	115·87	..	4·8	136·22	1·96	115·87	..
Milk (Whole), . . .	44	1249·6	41·23	49·98	62·48	38	1079·2	35·61	43·16	53·96
Cheese, ...	2	56·8	15·73	20·9	2·33	2	56·8	15·73	20·9	2·33
Bread, ...	149·1	4234·44	389·56	55·04	2248·48	128·7	3655·08	336·36	47·51	1940·84
Oatmeal, ...	26·5	752·6	121·16	54·18	508·0	15·6	443·04	71·32	31·89	299·05
Flour, ...	8	227·2	25·9	2·26	171·76	8	227·2	25·9	2·26	171·76
Peas, ...	4·5	127·8	31·43	1·27	79·23	4·5	127·8	31·43	1·27	79·23
Barley, ...	10	284	24·14	3·12	220·25	10	284	24·14	3·12	220·95
Rice, ...	1	28·4	2·27	·85	22·43	1	28·4	2·27	·85	22·43
Sugar, ...	4·8	136·22	..	..	136·22	4·8	136·22	..	..	136·22
Jam, Treacle, &c., . .	4	113·6	·84	·05	47·99	4	113·6	·84	·05	47·99
Potatoes, ...	52	1476·8	26·58	1·47	217·08	52	1476·8	26·58	1·47	217·08
Fresh Vegetables, . .	69	1959·6	27·43	3·91	94·06	69	1959·6	27·43	3·91	94·06
Tea, ...	1·25	35·5	..	..	..	1·25	35·5	..	..	..
Total, . . .	..	..	930·31	506·63	3849·77	..	..	821·65	469·99	3325·96

Food Values.—The average daily food values of the male and female dietaries are as follows:—

	Proteid.	Fat.	Carbo-hydrate.	Energy Value.
Male	133·9	72·4	550·0	3412
Female . . .	117·4	67·1	475·1	3053

The average height of the male working patient is 64 inches, their average weight 137·3 lbs.

Critical Remarks.—The dietaries of these lunatic wards are good in all respects. Their energy and proteid values are both more than the standard, the food is varied, fresh vegetables and potato are freely used, condiment is used in reasonable quantity, and an ample allowance is made for the special wants of working patients. The result of the weight test is satisfactory.

LINLITHGOW POORHOUSE.

Breakfast.—This consists of tea, bread and butter for all. Jelly, syrup, and marmalade are sometimes given instead of butter.

Dinner.—The weekly routine includes one dinner of rice soup, one of rice soup and pudding, one of rice soup and fish, one of broth and meat, one of broth, meat and potato, one of broth and cheese, and one of pea soup and Irish stew. Bread is given with all dinners. Meat is given three times a week, and is always fresh beef, twice weekly served boiled, and once weekly as Irish stew. A completely different routine of dinners is used in warm weather, it includes ample allowances of milk and fish, but no meat other than a little used in soup-making.

Evening Meal.—All male patients get porridge and milk, and a few of them get tea, bread and butter in addition. All female patients get both porridge and milk, and tea bread and butter.

Extras for Working Patients.—Working patients get some bread and skimmed milk during the forenoon. This luncheon is occasionally varied by tea and bread with syrup, marmalade, or jelly.

Dietary for females differs from that for males by having smaller rations of oatmeal, bread, potato, meat, pudding, cheese, and fish.

[TABLE.

Table showing the Average Weekly Composition of Dietaries.

	MALE.					FEMALE.				
	Quantity.		Proteid.	Fat.	Carbo-hydrate	Quantity.		Proteid.	Fat.	Carbo-hydrate
	Oz.	Grms.				Oz.	Grms.			
Beef, ...	25	710	133·22	132·13	..	23	653·2	122·65	121·97	..
Mutton, ...	2	56·8	7·38	13·65	..	2	56·8	7·38	13·63	..
Fish (Fresh), . . .	3	85·2	14·22	·25	..	2	56·8	9·48	·17	..
Suet, . . .· .	·1	2·84	·01	2·32	..	·1	2·84	·01	2·32	..
Butter, ...	4·25	120·7	1·2	102·59	..	4·25	120·7	1·2	102·59	..
Milk (Whole), . . .	80	2272	74·97	90·88	113·6	90	2556	84·34	102·24	127·8
Milk (Skimmed), . .	60	1704	57·93	5·11	86·9	60	1704	57·93	5·11	86·9
Milk (Butter), . . .	20	568	17·04	2·84	27·26	20	568	17·04	2·84	27·26
Cheese, ...	4	113·6	31·46	41·8	4·65	4	113·6	31·46	41·8	4·65
Bread, ...	118	3351·12	306·3	43·56	1779·44	105	2982	274·34	38·76	1585·44
Oatmeal, ...	42	1192·8	192·04	85·38	806·14	21	596·4	96·02	42·94	402·57
Flour, ...	4·5	127·8	14·56	1·27	96·61	4·5	127·8	14·56	1·27	96·61
Peas, Lentils, . . .	5	142	35·23	1·41	88·24	5 _	142	35·23	1·41	88·24
Barley, ...	6	170·4	14·48	1·97	132·57	6	170·4	14·48	1·97	132·57
Rice, ...	5	142	11·26	·42	112·18	5	142	11·26	·42	112·18
Sugar, ...	3·75	106·5	..	..	106·5	7	198·3	..	..	198·3
Treacle, Jam, &c., . .	4·50	127·8	·68	·1	104·75	4·50	127·8	·68	·1	104·75
Potatoes, . . .	46	1306·4	23·51	1·3	192·04	40	1136	20·44	1·13	166·99
Fresh Vegetables, . .	12·25	347·9	4·87	·69	16·69	12·25	347·9	4·87	·69	16·69
Tea, Coffee, . . .	1·85	52·54	..	..	..	1·8	51·12	..	..	.
Total, . .	..	..	942·51	523·05	3666·57	..	..	803·42	480·26	3149·45

Food Values.—The average daily food values of the male and female dietaries are as follows:—

	Proteid.	Fat.	Carbo-hydrate.	Energy Value.
Male . . . · .	134·6	75·4	523·8	3401
Female . . .	114·8	68·7	449·9	2954

The average height of the male working patient is 65·6 inches, their average weight 145·8 lbs.

Critical Remarks.—Both the male and the female dietaries appear to be excellent. They are of sufficient energy and proteid value, they are varied, and sufficient allowance is made for the wants of working patients. The sufficiency of the diet is corroborated by the result of the weight test, for it is found that the average weight of the male working patients is above the standard. The diets of these lunatic wards may be taken as being satisfactory in every detail.

OLD MONKLAND POORHOUSE.

Breakfast.—This for all consists of tea, bread and margarine, and porridge with skim milk.

Dinner.—The weekly routine includes four dinners of broth and meat, one of pea soup and potato, one of rice and milk and suet pudding, and one of rice and milk and meat. Bread is given daily. Meat is given five times a week, it is always fresh beef, once weekly it is served as mince, all other times boiled. Potato is used only once a week.

Evening Meal.—This consists of tea, bread and margarine for all.

Extras for Working Patients.—Working patients get tea bread and cheese in the forenoon.

Dietary for females differs from that for males by having smaller rations of oatmeal and bread.

Table showing the Average Weekly Composition of Dietaries.

	MALE.					FEMALE.				
	Quantity.		Proteid.	Fat.	Carbo-hydrate	Quantity.		Proteid.	Fat.	Carbo-hydrate
	Oz.	Grms.				Oz.	Grms.			
Beef, ...	52	1476·8	270·25	279·11	..	52	1476·8	270·25	279·11	..
Fish (Salt), . . .	4	113·6	31·01	·34	..	4	113·6	31·01	·34	..
Suet, ...	1·25	35·5	1·66	29·03	..	1·25	35·5	1·66	29·03	..
Margarine, . . .	7	198·8	2·38	165·0	..	7	198·8	2·38	165·0	..
Milk (Whole), . .	28	795·2	26·24	31·8	39·76	108	3067·2	101·21	122·68	153·36
Milk (Skimmed), . .	154	4373·6	148·7	13·12	223·05	140	3976	135·18	11·92	202·77
Cheese, ...	21	596·4	165·25	219·47	24·45	20·3	576·52	159·69	212·15	23·63
Bread, ...	174·25	4943·7	455·28	64·33	2027·75	134·3	3828·22	352·2	49·76	2032·83
Oatmeal, ...	28	795·2	123·02	57·25	536·76	24·5	695·8	112·02	50·09	469·66
Flour, ...	2·25	63·9	7·28	·63	48·3	2·25	63	7·28	·63	48·3
Peas, ...	6	170·4	41·91	1·7	105·64	6	170·4	41·91	1·7	105·66
Barley, ...	8	227·2	19·2	2·48	176·76	8	227·2	19·2	2·48	176·76
Rice, ...	4	113·6	9·08	3·4	89·74	4	113·6	9·08	3·4	89·74
Sugar, ...	9·25	262·7	..	..	262·7	9·25	262·7	..	..	262·7
Potatoes, ...	8	227·2	4·08	·22	33·39	8	227·2	4·08	·22	33·39
Fresh Vegetables, . .	6·5	156·2	2·18	·31	7·49	6·5	156·2	2·18	·31	7·49
Currants, . . .	1·25	35·5	·85	·6	26·34	1·25	35·5	·85	·6	26·34
Tea, ...	1·75	49·7	..	..	..	1·75	49·7	..	..	..
Total, . .	..	..	1313·57	863·79	4202·13	..	..	1250·28	929·42	3632·61

Food Values.—The average daily food values of the male and female dietaries are as follows:—

	Proteid.	Fat.	Carbo-hydrate.	Energy Value.
Male	187·6	124·1	600·3	4385
Female . . .	178·6	132·8	518·9	4105

The average height of the male working patient is 65·6 inches, their average weight 153·4 lbs.

Critical Remarks.—The dietaries of these lunatic wards, both for the male and for the female patients, appear to be excessive in quantity. They both far exceed the standard, and are both very considerably larger than the corresponding dietaries of other lunatic wards and asylums. The female dietary appears to be of greater food value than any of the male dietaries of other institutions included in this report. There certainly is no underfeeding. The weight test shows the average weight of working patients to be no less than 13 lbs. more than the standard. Both dietaries contain an excess of carbohydrate. Looking at the issues of individual foods it may be noted that those of bread and beef are exceptionally large, that of the former especially so, it amounts to a daily average of nearly 25 oz. for males and 19 oz. for females. It may also be noted that the issues of some foods, viz. potato and fresh vegetable, are too small. The dinners appear to be too monotonous. A revision of these diets is desirable. Smaller but better selected diets would be found more satisfactory.

PERTH POORHOUSE.

Breakfast.—The majority of male patients have tea bread and butter, and porridge with skimmed milk, the remainder have porridge and skimmed milk only. The majority of female patients have tea bread and butter only, the remainder have porridge and skim milk only.

Dinner.—The weekly routine includes one dinner of rice and milk and Irish stew, three of broth and meat, and three of lentil soup and meat, with one of the latter suet pudding is also given. Bread is given daily. Meat is given seven times a week, six times being boiled beef, and once tinned mutton cooked as Irish stew.

Evening Meal.—The majority of males get tea bread and butter, and porridge and skim milk. The remainder get porridge and skim milk only. The female patients all get porridge and skim milk only.

Extras for Working Patients.—Working female patients are given a luncheon of tea bread and cheese. No extras are given to male working patients.

Dietary for females differs from that for males by having smaller rations of oatmeal and bread.

Table showing the Average Weekly Composition of Dietaries.

| | MALE. | | | | | FEMALE. | | | |
| | Quantity. | | Proteid. | Fat. | Carbo-hydrate | Quantity. | | Proteid. | Fat. | Carbo-hydrate |
	Oz.	Grms.				Oz.	Grms.			
Beef, ...	30·15	856·26	168·15	161·53	..	30·15	856·26	168·15	161·53	..
Suet, ...	1·5	42·6	2·0	34·84	..	1·5	42·6	2·0	34·84	..
Butter, ...	4	113·6	1·12	96·56	.	4	113·6	1·12	96·56	..
Milk (Whole), . . .	20	568	18·74	22·72	28·0	60	1704	56·22	68·16	85·2
Milk (Skimmed), . .	210	5964	202·77	17·89	304·16	90	2556	86·9	7·66	130·35
Cheese, ...	5·33	150·52	41·69	55·39	6·17	5·33	150·52	41·69	55·39	6·17
Bread, ...	119	3379·6	310·92	43·93	1794·56	94	2669·6	245·6	34·7	1417·55
Oatmeal, . . .	67	1902·8	306·35	187·0	1284·39	31·5	894·6	144·03	64·41	608·85
Flour, ...	4·05	115·02	13·11	1·15	86·96	4·05	115·02	13·11	1·15	86·96
Lentils, ...	13	369·2	94·88	3·69	213·56	13	369·2	94·88	3·69	213·56
Barley, ...	6·5	184·6	15·69	2·03	143·61	6·5	184·6	15·69	2·03	143·61
Rice, ...	6·5	184·6	14·76	5·53	145·83	6·5	184·6	14·76	5·53	145·83
Sugar, ...	4·75	134·9	..	..	134·9	4·75	134·9	..	..	134·9
Jam, &c., . . .	4·5	127·8	·76	·12	107·99	4·5	127·8	·76	·12	107·99
Potatoes, ...	19·1	542·44	9·76	·54	79·77	19·1	542·44	9·76	·54	79·77
Fresh Vegetables, . .	13·25	118·3	1·65	·23	5·67	13·25	118·3	1·65	·23	5·67
Currants, Raisins, . .	1·8	51·12	1·19	1·19	36·46	1·8	51·12	1·19	1·19	36·46
Tea, ...	1·75	49·7	..	..	..	1·75	49·7	..	..	..
Total, . . .	..	..	1203·54	584·34	4377·02	..	..	897·52	537·73	3202·86

Food Values.—The average daily food values of the male and female dietaries are as follows:—

	Proteid.	Fat.	Carbo-hydrate.	Energy Value.
Male	171·9	83·5	625·3	4045
Female . . .	128·2	76·8	457·5	3116

The average height of the male working patient is 64·9 inches, their average weight 145 lbs.

Critical Remarks.—Both dietaries appear to be in considerable excess of the requirements of the inmates. The diets are too monotonous, porridge and milk night and morning, with tea bread and butter added if wanted, boiled beef and soup six times a week for dinner. Potato is not sufficiently freely used, being only served once a week. The male diet has an excessive quantity of carbohydrate. These diets, require revision, as almost certainly smaller but better balanced diets would be found more satisfactory. The average weight of male working patients is found to be well over the standard.

WIGTOWN POORHOUSE.

Breakfast.—This consists of porridge and skim milk for all.

Dinner.—The weekly routine includes one dinner of rice soup and cheese, one of broth and Irish stew, three of broth and beef, one of broth, fish and potato, and one of pea soup and suet pudding. Bread is given with all except the fish dinner. Meat is given three times a week, being served twice as boiled beef and once as Irish stew. Some additional meat is used in the preparation of soup.

Evening Meal.—This consists of tea, bread and butter for male patients, for female patients bread and butter with either tea, coffee, or cocoa.

Extras for Working Patients.—Females working before the usual breakfast hour get an early breakfast of tea, bread and butter. No other extras are given.

Dietary for females differs from that for males by having smaller rations of oatmeal and bread, and by having two small tea meals in the afternoon in place of one larger tea meal.

Table showing the Average Weekly Composition of Dietaries.

	MALE.					FEMALE.				
	Quantity.		Proteid.	Fat.	Carbo-hydrate	Quantity.		Proteid.	Fat.	Carbo-hydrate
	Oz.	Grms.				Oz.	Grms.			
Beef, ...	15·5	440·2	82·67	81·91	..	15·5	440·2	82·67	81·91	..
Fish (Salt), . . .	8	227·2	62·02	·	..	8	227·2	62·02	·68	..
Suet, ...	1	28·4	1·32	23·22	..	1	28·4	1·32	23·22	..
Butter, ...	1·75	49·7	·49	42·24	..	3·5	99·4	·98	84·48	..
Milk (Skimmed), . .	105	2982	101·28	8·94	152·08	105	2982	101·28	8·94	152·08
Cheese, ...	2	56·8	15·73	20·9	2·32	2	56·8	15·73	20·9	2·32
Bread, ...	92	2612·8	240·27	33·96	1387·29	86	2442·4	224·7	31·75	1296·91
Oatmeal, ...	42	1192·8	192·04	85·88	805·14	35	994	160·03	71·56	670·95
Flour, ...	4	113·6	12·96	1·13	85·88	4	113·6	12·96	1·13	85·88
Peas, ...	6	170·4	41·91	1·7	105·64	6	170·4	41·91	1·7	105·64
Barley, ...	10	284	24·14	3·12	220·95	10	284	24·14	3·12	220·95
Rice, ...	2	56·8	4·54	1·7	44·27	2	56·8	4·54	1·7	44·27
Sugar, ...	4	113·6	..	..	113·6	7·5	213	..	..	213·0
Syrup, ...	·5	14·2	..	..	9·84	·5	14·2	..	..	9·84
Potatoes, ...	32	908·8	16·35	·9	133·59	32	908·8	16·35	·9	133·59
Fresh Vegetables, . .	20	568	7·95	1·13	27·26	20	568	7·95	1·13	27·26
Tea, Coffee, Cocoa, .	·9	25·56	..	..	..	2	56·8	3·68	4·92	6·42
Total, . .	..	..	803·86	307·41	3088·56	..	..	760·35	338·04	2969·71

Food Values.—The average daily food values of the male and female dietaries are as follows:—

	Proteid.	Fat.	Carbo-hydrate.	Energy Value.
Male	114·8	43·9	441·2	2688
Female . . .	108·6	42·3	424·2	2633

The average height of the male working patients is 66 inches, their average weight 138·5 lbs.

Critical Remarks.—The diet for the male inmates of these lunatic wards appears to be deficient in quantity, as it meets neither the energy nor the proteid standards. Its energy value is nearly 20 per cent. too small, and as no special provision is made for working patients, it is not surprising to find that the average weight of male workers is decidedly below what it should be. The female dietary is only slightly below standard value, but it appears to be insufficient for workers. The issues in the male dietary of meat, butter, bread, and tea are all too small. Both dietaries require revision. The diet for the male patients of these lunatic wards is the most meagre diet recorded in this report.

V. GENERAL REMARKS ON THE DIETARIES.

I.—*Energy Value.*—Standard for males 3300 calories, for females 2650 calories.

In the following Tables there are shown the energy values of the dietaries of all the institutions where pauper lunatics are cared for. The male dietaries are there divided into three groups, the first contains those dietaries which are at least 200 calories (6 per cent.) in excess of the standard, the second contains those dietaries which are approximately of standard value, 3200-3500 calories, the third contains those dietaries which are of less than standard value. The female dietaries are similarly grouped. In the Table showing the food value of the male dietaries the results of the weight test are included for comparison. The weight test was not applied to female inmates.

[TABLE.

Table showing Food Value of Male Dietaries and Result of Weight Test.

Institutions.	Food Value.		Weight Test.			
	Daily Average Calories.	Compared to Standard Calories.	Height. Average Inches.	Weight. Average Lbs.	Compared to Standard Lbs. +	−
GROUP I—Excessive. Eleven Dietaries.						
Old Monkland P.H.(1)	4385	+1085	65·6	153·4	13	—
Perth P.H.	4045	+745	64·9	145·1	7	—
Banff D.A.	3934	+634	67·2	151·9	—	1
Haddington D.A.	3872	+572	66·2	140·6	—	5 (2)
Aberdeen East P.H.	3785	+485	65·5	144·2	4	—
Stirling D.A.	3745	+445	66·1	141·2	—	4 (2)
Fife and Kinross D.A.	3663	+363	65·6	143·7	3	—
Aberdeen R.A.	3612	+312	66·5	153·3	8	—
Dumbarton P.H.	3571	+271	66·3	146·9	2	—
Elgin D.A.	3561	+261	66·8	143·8	—	2
Crichton R.A.	3514	+214	66·8	141·6	—	4 (2)
GROUP II.—Approximating the Standard. Thirteen Dietaries.						
Govan D.A.	3488	+188	66·5	141·0	—	4 (2)
Cunningham P.H.	3474	+174	65·3	146·2	6	—
Kincardine P.H.	3412	+112	64·0	137·3	0	1
Aberdeen West P.H.	3426	+126	65·9	137·0	—	3
Linlithgow P.H.	3401	+100	65·6	145·8	5	—
Greenock P.A.	3378	+78	65·8	138·8	—	2
Edinburgh P.H.	3331	+31	66·5	143·8	—	2
Buchan P.H.	3323	+23	65·9	139·1	—	1
Dundee East P.H.	3266	−34	65·3	133·8	—	7
Lanark D.A.	3251	−49	65·9	135·9	—	4 (2)
Ayr D.A.	3234	−66	66·5	152·3	7	—
Riccartsbar P.A.	3227	−73	65·6	135·5	—	5
Argyll D.A.	3215	−85	65·6	147·3	7	—
GROUP III.—Deficient. Fifteen Dietaries.						
Gartloch D.A.	3192	−108	65·5	134·8	—	6
Govan P.A.	3188	−112	64·6	132·7	—	6
Inverness D.A.	3169	−131	67·0	150·6	—	1
Edinburgh R.A.	3162	−138	65·6	143·0	3	—
Montrose R.A.	3105	−195	66·4	147·5	2	—
Roxburgh D.A.	3069	−231	67·4	150·0	—	1
Inveresk P.H.	3062	−238	63·1	131·2	—	?
Dundee West P.H.	3014	−286	65·2	125·9	—	14
Kirklands D.A.	2977	−323	65·0	128·1	—	12
Dundee R.A.	2969	−331	65·0	144·1	4	—
Woodilee D.A.	2908	−392	65·0	138·1	—	2
Perth D.A.	2871	−429	66·5	139·8	—	6
Craw Road P.A.	2835	−465	64·8	137·1	—	1
Midlothian D.A.	2761	−539	65·7	137·4	—	3
Wigtown P.H.	2688	−612	66·0	138·5	—	7

(1) R.A.—Royal Asylum. D.A.—District Asylum. P.A.—Parochial Asylum. P.H.—Lunatic Wards of Poorhouses.

(2) In these instances want of special allowance for working patients explains low-weight average.

Table showing Food Value of Female Dietaries.

Institutions.	Daily Average Calories.	Compared to] Standard Calories.
GROUP I.—Excessive. Twenty-five Dietaries.		
Old Monkland P.H. (1)	4105	+1455
Aberdeen East P.H.	3506	+856
Elgin D.A.	3314	+664
Govan D.A.	3265	+615
Dumbarton P.H.	3172	+522
Fife and Kinross D.A.	3121	+471
Edinburgh R.A.	3117	+467
Perth P.H.	3116	+466
Cunningham P.H.	3115	+465
Kincardine P.H.	3053	+403
Aberdeen R.A.	2976	+326
Dundee East P.H.	2973	+323
Linlithgow P.H.	2959	+309
Govan P.A.	2948	+298
Riccartsbar P.A.	2909	+259
Banff D.A.	2907	+257
Greenock P.A.	2907	+257
Perth D.A.	2886	+236
Crichton R.A.	2894	+229
Inverness D.A.	2872	+222
Stirling D.A.	2872	+222
Roxburgh D.A.	2855	+205
Craw Road P.A.	2835	+185
Argyll D.A.	2831	+181
Montrose R.A.	2822	+172
GROUP II.—Approximating the Standard. Eight Dietaries.		
Gartloch D.A.	2781	+131
Aberdeen West P.H.	2750	+100
Kirklands D.A.	2717	+67
Dundee West P.H.	2703	+53
Edinburgh P.H.	2671	+21
Ayr D.A.	2665	+15
Lanark D.A.	2644	−6
Wigtown P.H.	2633	−17
GROUP III.—Deficient. Six Dietaries.		
Haddington D.A.	2553	−97
Midlothian D.A.	2548	−102
Buchan P.H.	2503	−147
Dundee R.A.	2478	−172
Inveresk P.H.	2447	−203
Woodilee D.A.	2403	−247

(1) R.A.—Royal Asylum. D.A.—District Asylum. P.A.—Parochial Asylum. P.H.—Lunatic Wards of Poorhouses.

G

A scrutiny of these Tables brings out the following points:—

1. The majority of dietaries both male and female are in Groups I. and II., that is, are sufficient to satisfy the standard.

2. The number of dietaries which are classed in Group III. as deficient are greater among male than among female dietaries. 15 male dietaries, but only 6 female dietaries, are so classed.

3. Excessive feeding is more prevalent in female than in male departments. 25 female dietaries are classed as excessive. while only 11 male dietaries are so classed.

4. The variations of male dietaries are from 4385 Calories (Old Monkland Poorhouse) to 2688 Calories (Wigtown Poorhouse), or 30 per cent. over the standard to 20 per cent. below the standard. Female dietaries vary from 4105 Calories (Old Monkland Poorhouse) to 2403 Calories (Glasgow Woodilee District Asylum), or from 35 per cent. over to 10 per cent. under the standard.

5. The average of all the male dietaries is 3335 Calories, which is approximately the same as the standard, while the average of all female dietaries is 2890 Calories, or 9 per cent. more than the standard.

6. The weight test has with a few exceptions given results which corroborate the result of a comparison of the actual food value to a standard food value.

Of Group I. male dietaries, four instances only show a deficient average weight; in three of these four it is to be explained by want of any special food for workers, and in the remaining case —Elgin District Asylum—it is so small that it may be considered insignificant.

Of Group II. dietaries, nine are associated with deficient average weight, in four of them the deficiency is insignificant, 2 lbs. or less, in two the deficiency is due to want of special allowance for workers, while in three the deficiency is without apparent cause.

Of Group III. dietaries the majority are, as is to be expected, associated with deficient average weight, but there is a minority where the apparently deficient food is associated with satisfactory weighings. This minority includes three institutions, all of which are Royal Asylums. In one of these Royal Asylums—Edinburgh —the satisfactory average weight may be ascribed to the ample allowance of extra food which is there given to workers. The explanation of how in the other two Royal Asylums—Dundee and Montrose—the apparently deficient feeding comes to be associated with a satisfactory average weight is not evident.

7. A general conclusion to be got from this study of the energy value of the dietaries is that considerable improvement is possible. Some dietaries might safely be reduced, and others with much advantage increased. If the correctness of the standard adopted in this report is allowed, and the facts recorded in the schedules are correct, it appears that the food supply of male patients in 11 institutions and of female patients in 25 institutions may safely be reduced, a few materially, the remainder more or less slightly. On the other hand it appears that the male dietaries of 15 institutions, and the female dietaries of 6 institutions, require to be increased. Independent of any fixed standard the great variation found is by

itself reason for concluding that in many instances modification of the dietary scales is desirable.

II.—*Proteid Standard,* male 118 grammes, female 94 grammes. —It was pointed out earlier in this report why this test of the sufficiency of a diet is not of the same practical value as that of energy value. As a matter of fact in these studies there is not a single example of a dietary having sufficient energy and being deficient in proteid. Several have been pointed out as deficient in proteid, all of those have also been deficient in energy. Granted a reasonably mixed diet and a sufficient energy value, a sufficient proteid value may be taken for granted.

III.—*Carbohydrate Standard,* not over 550 grammes.—Excess of carbohydrate has been noted in the dietaries of three institutions only, Banff District Asylum and Perth and Old Monkland Poorhouses. In each of these three instances the dietaries are of excessive food value.

IV.—*Classification of Patients.*—It was earlier in the report explained that when there is any restriction of diet a proper classification of patients according to sex and severity of labour is essential. When the male and female dietaries of an institution are found to be approximately the same, it of necessity follows that both cannot be rightly estimated, and when it is found that working and idle inmates are given the same amount of food that also may be taken as demonstrating faulty estimation of their food requirements.

Male versus Female Dietaries.—In four institutions the dietaries appear to be faulty in that the male diet is restricted to the amount found necessary for females. These four institutions are Edinburgh Royal Asylum, Perth District Asylum, Paisley Craw Road Parochial Asylum, and Wigtown Poorhouse. In them the dietaries for the male and for the female patients are reported to be of equal or of nearly equal value, which is a condition of affairs that may be taken as a clear indication that both the male and female dietaries are not correct and that revision is called for.

Working versus Idle Patients.—In discussing the dietaries of the individual institutions it was in five instances necessary to adversely criticise on account of insufficient special allowance for active workers, where all other matters were satisfactory. In each of these five instances the weight test showed workers to average less than standard weight. These five instances were Crichton Royal Asylum, and Govan, Haddington, Lanark, and Stirling District Asylums. In each of these institutions the feeding would be materially improved by giving extra food to workers. The weight returns from Glasgow Woodilee District Asylum are instructive as showing how active work increases food requirement. The diet there does not comply with the standard and the average weight of all male workers is below the standards by 2 lbs. The most actively worked inmates of that asylum reside at a farm, they receive no extra food, and what appears to be the result of the insufficient diet combined with active work is that they average no less than 9 lbs. below the standard, or half a stone less than the less actively worked men in the same asylum.

V.—*Division into Meals.*—Under this head little adverse criticism of the institution dietaries has been given. An excessive breakfast in Buchan Poorhouse has been remarked on, and an increased allowance of food for breakfast has been suggested in some other institutions.

VI.—*Variation of Food.*—The want of proper variation of food has been remarked on when discussing the dietary of several institutions; more especially was this noted about Aberdeen Royal Asylum, Paisley Craw Road Parochial Asylum, Aberdeen West Poorhouse, Dumbarton Combination Poorhouse, and Perth Poorhouse. The more frequent causes of monotony of feeding appear to be excessive use of porridge and unvarying boiling of beef. Porridge and milk is doubtless splendid food and its use should be encouraged in all institutions, but two exclusively porridge meals daily are on account of their monotony to be condemned. The unvarying boiling of beef is a fault that should be easily rectified. Another matter which I have had occasion to adversely criticise is the too frequent use of tinned meat, for that must inevitably lead to monotony. The dietaries of the District Asylums of Perth, Fife and Kinross, and Stirling are faulty on this account. At Perth District Asylum tinned meat is reported to be used three times as often as fresh meat.

After drawing attention to faults of some of the dietaries in point of quantity it is only right to add that in many no adverse criticism of the variation and quality has been made. The dietaries of the two Glasgow asylums, Gartloch and Woodilee, and of the Govan District Asylum may be selected as specially good in respect of variation and quality. In these institutions great care has evidently been taken to ensure that the inmates are pleasingly fed.

The matter of variation of food will be referred to when making suggestions for securing the sufficient and proper feeding of all pauper lunatics.

VII.—*The Use of Condiments.*—In the dietaries under consideration, other than mustard, pepper, etc., tea is found to be the only condiment used habitually. This is as it should be, as it is now an essential part of all dietaries, and a very necessary part of the dietaries of persons under the depressing influence of asylum treatment. Loss of liberty must be depressing. In several institutions the dieting has been found fault with on account of the insufficient use of tea. That was done in the cases of Aberdeen Royal Asylum, Banff and Haddington District Asylums, and in several poorhouses.

VIII.—*The Use of Potato and Fresh Vegetable.*—The use of these in the great majority of institutions has been found sufficient, but in a minority insufficient. The institutions which can be selected as using potato and fresh vegetable in the most insufficient quantities are Paisley Craw Road Parochial Asylum, and Old Monkland Poorhouse, in the former the average use of the two combined is under 1½ lbs. weekly, in the latter less than 1 lb. weekly.

VI. SUGGESTIONS FOR ENSURING THE PROPER FEEDING OF PAUPER LUNATICS.

In making critical remarks of the individual dietaries various suggestions for improvement have been made. I propose now to supplement these by drawing up a scheme of what I consider should be the essentials of asylum feeding. It is not my intention to draw up a weekly bill of fare, as such detail may well be left to the management of the individual institutions.

1. *Bread should be given ad libitum with all Meals.*—Bread is the basis of ordinary diets, and should be freely used. An unlimited distribution of it with every meal will go far to ensure that every patient will receive a sufficiency of food. This I consider is an improvement called for in nearly all the asylum dietaries. There is little fear of the majority of the inmates abusing such discretionary power and wasting unduly.

2. *24 oz. of Meat, uncooked without bone, should be the minimum weekly allowance.*—This minimum allowance is intended to be sufficient for four meat dinners weekly. A proper supply of meat is wholesome, is necessary to counteract the proteid deficiency of bread, and is desirable to give proper variation of food.

3. *A fish dinner or a fifth meat dinner should be given weekly.*— The advisability of a fish dinner is open to question; in some institutions it appears to be appreciated as being a variety, but in others that is not so. For a fish dinner the minimum allowance of fresh fish should be 12 oz. (dressed), and that of dried fish 6 oz. When a fifth meat dinner is given the minimum weekly allowance of meat should be increased to from 24 oz. to 30 oz.

4. *Porridge and Milk must be given at least once daily.*—This national dish without a doubt should be freely used, it is cheap food, and is of special value in counteracting the proteid deficiency of bread. It also makes variety. Suggestion No. 1 if adopted will prohibit the exclusive porridge meals at present used in many asylums, and will permit of other food being secured for patients who, on account of dyspepsia or for other reason, are unable to eat porridge.

5. *The minimum weekly allowance of Potato should be 3 lbs., of other Fresh Vegetables 1¼ lbs.*—These minimum allowances will secure that patients receive a sufficiency of antiscorbutic food, and will assist in securing proper variety of food. The potato allowance should be sufficient for three services weekly. The vegetable allowance should be sufficient to provide for four services of well-seasoned broth and one service of a meat and vegetable stew.

6. *Tea or Coffee or Cocoa should be served ad libitum to Patients twice daily.*—I am strongly of opinion that a proper use of these condiments is essential. The stimulating properties of these beverages will help to counteract the flagging appetites caused by the depressing influence of confinement. The minimum weekly allowance of tea per inmate to secure two services daily should be 3 oz. That minimum need not be insisted on when coffee or cocoa is substituted.

7. *The minimum weekly allowance of Butter should be* 5 *oz.*—Butter or margarine, like tea, is universally used and doubtless should be included in asylum dietaries in reasonable quantity. It is of value in increasing the food value of the bread, and as a condiment to the bread. The use of butter in the dietaries is reported to vary enormously, the extremes are found at Montrose Royal Asylum, Old Monkland Poorhouse, and Aberdeen West Poorhouse; at the first two it is 7 oz. a week, at the last it is only 1·4 oz. a week. I am of opinion that 5 oz. would be a reasonable and not excessive minimum, and is one that will not entail a material increase in the majority of the asylums where the diet is reasonably good.

Margarine of a good quality may safely be used in place of butter, experience has shown it to be a good food and not disliked by the patients. One stipulation, however, is desirable when margarine is used, and that is that the weekly minimum allowance should be increased, and the reason for that is that it is found that margarine "does not go so far as butter," it is softer and soaks into the bread, and consequently if sparingly used does not give the same appetising appearance as butter, A minimum weekly allowance of margarine should not be less than 6 oz.

8. *The proper variation of diet should be insisted on.*—For variation of institution dietaries, variation of the dinner must to a great extent be depended on, and to secure that I would suggest the following:—

   a. No individual soup, broth excepted, should be given oftener than twice weekly.

   b. The meat and the cooking of it should be varied. Boiled beef should not be served oftener than thrice weekly.

   c. Puddings should sometimes be given, these must be sweetened or flavoured.

   d. The same dinner must not be given oftener than twice weekly.

   e. The weekly routine should be periodically revised and made to include seasonable dishes. Rhubarb, apples, etc., should be used when readily procurable.

9. *Extra Food for Working Patients.*—Suggestion No. 1 should to a great extent meet the special requirements of the more severely worked inmates, but as it has been found by experience in asylums that a luncheon is wholesome and appreciated, I am of opinion that it should be given to all inmates who do a moderate day's work.

JAMES CRAUFURD DUNLOP.

24 STAFFORD STREET,
EDINBURGH, *December* 1901.

GLASGOW: PRINTED FOR HIS MAJESTY'S STATIONERY OFFICE
BY JAMES HEDDERWICK & SONS.

ENGLAND AND WALES.

REPORTS of the Inspectors of Constabulary, for the Year ended 29th September 1901, made to His Majesty's Principal Secretary of State, under the Provisions of the Statute 19 & 20 Vict. c. 69.

TABLES.

(PRESENTED PURSUANT TO ACT OF PARLIAMENT.)

Ordered, by The House of Commons, *to be Printed,*
27 May 1902.

LONDON:
PRINTED FOR HIS MAJESTY'S STATIONERY OFFICE,
BY EYRE AND SPOTTISWOODE,
PRINTERS TO THE KING'S MOST EXCELLENT MAJESTY.

And to be purchased, either directly or through any Bookseller, from
EYRE AND SPOTTISWOODE, East Harding Street, Fleet Street, E.C., and
32, Abingdon Street, Westminster, S.W.; or
OLIVER AND BOYD, Edinburgh; or
E. PONSONBY, 116, Grafton Street, Dublin.

191.

INDEX

TO THE REPORTS UPON THE SEPARATE POLICE FORCÈS.

No. 1.—EASTERN COUNTIES, MIDLAND, AND NORTH WALES DISTRICT.

ANNUAL REPORT of the Hon. C. G. Legge, Inspector of Constabulary for the Eastern Counties, Midland, and North Wales District, for the Year 29 September 1901.

Northgate House, Warwick,
Sir, 30 November 1901.

In presenting my reports on the Police Forces of the Eastern and Midland Counties and North Wales, I have the honour to inform you that, following the precedents of the years 1881 and 1891, I have adhered to the enumeration of the census of 10 years ago, and have made no use of figures of this year's census, which, if obtainable, would have been unverified and misleading.

With the exception of the borough of Boston, all the forces in the district have been maintained efficiently in respect of management, numbers, and discipline. The Police Authority at Boston has, however, failed to provide proper cells for prisoners, or suitable accommodation for the police to carry out the duties required of them in the shape of offices.

There are 56 forces under inspection; 26 maintained by counties and 30 by boroughs. The force for the liberty of Peterborough is distinct from that for the county of Northampton, but is placed under the Chief Constable of that county, and is under the same conditions of service as the Northamptonshire police.

There are 17 boroughs with population (according to census of 1891) of from 11,008 to 59,474 persons watched by the police of the counties wherein they are situated.

COUNTY FORCES.

Number in Tables.	Name of Force.	Number in Tables	Name of Force.	Number in Tables.	Name of Force.
	ENGLAND.		**ENGLAND—cont.**		**N. WALES.**
1	Bedford.	28	Oxford.		
4	Buckingham.	31	Peterborough (Liberty of).(a)	1	Anglesey.
6	Cambridge.			2	Carnarvon.
8	Ely, Isle of.	33	Rutland.	3	Denbigh.
9	Essex.	34	Shropshire.	4	Flint.
11	Hertford.	36	Stafford.	5	Merioneth.
13	Huntingdon.	41	Suffolk (East).	6	Montgomery.
14	Leicester.	43	Suffolk (West).		
16	Lincoln.	44	Warwickshire.		
22	Norfolk.	48	Worcestershire.		
26	Northampton.(a)				

(a) Under one chief constable.

BOROUGH FORCES.

Number in Tables.	Name of Force.	Number in Tables.	Name of Force.	Number in Tables.	Name of Force.
29	Banbury.	37	Hanley.	27	Northampton.
2	Bedford.	42	Ipswich.	25	Norwich.
45	Birmingham.	49	Kidderminster.	30	Oxford.
17	Boston.	24	King's Lynn.	32	Peterborough.
7	Cambridge.	47	Leamington.	12	St. Albans.
5	Chepping Wycombe.	15	Leicester.	35	Shrewsbury.
10	Colchester.	20	Lincoln.	39	Walsall.
46	Coventry.	21	Louth.	40	Wolverhampton.
18	Grantham.	50	Luton.	50	Worcester.
19	Great Grimsby.	3	Newcastle - under - Lyme.		
23	Great Yarmouth.	38			

A

NAME OF BOROUGH.	Area in Acres.	Population in 1891.	Watched by Police of
Chelmsford - - - -	2,309	11,008	} Essex.
Southend-on-Sea - - -	3,441	12,333	
Loughborough - - - -	3,078	18,196	Leicestershire.
Wenlock - - - -	22,657	15,703	Shropshire.
Burslem - - - . -	2,585	31,999	
Burton-upon-Trent - - -	4,207	46,047	
Longton - - - -	1,948	34,327	
Smethwick - - -	1,872	36,106	Staffordshire.
Stafford - - - -	1,084	20,270	
Stoke-upon-Trent - -	1,881	24,027	
Wednesbury - - -	2,287	25,347	
West Bromwich - -	5,851	59,474	
Lowestoft - - - -	2,176	23,347	Suffolk (East).
Bury St. Edmunds - -	2,947	16,630	Suffolk (West).
Warwick - - -	5,613	11,903	Warwickshire.
Dudley - - - -	3,615	45,740	Worcestershire.
Wrexham - - -	1,306	12,552	Denbighshire.

The aggregate strength of the police force in the district is 6,598, an increase of 156 on the number in 1900. This increase is chiefly accounted for by an augmentation of 100 men for the city of Birmingham. There are also 118 " additional " constables appointed at private cost.

Two hundred and thirty constables belonging to the Army Reserve have been called up to join the colours during the past two years, and were accounted for as follows on 29th September:—rejoined the police 85, died 10, killed in action 3, still serving with their regiments 115. The remaining 17 had either re-engaged in the Army or had left the police service for other employment.

Four thousand five hundred and eighty-seven members of the several forces hold certificates from the St. John Ambulance Association, every force in the district having a good percentage of men able to render "first aid" except the county of Norfolk, where no steps have been taken to enable the police to render themselves efficient in this most useful qualification.

I append returns showing the number of vacancies in the various forces on 29th September, and of augmentations and reductions effected during the year.

NUMBER of VACANCIES in the STRENGTH of the various FORCES (exclusive of "Additional" Constables) on 29th September 1901.

No. 1.
Eastern Counties,
Midland,
and North Wales
District.

COUNTIES.			BOROUGHS.		
NAME OF FORCE.	Established Strength.	Number of Vacancies.	NAME OF FORCE.	Established Strength.	Number of Vacancies.
Bedford - - -	100	2	Bedford - - -	42	2
Buckingham - - -	154	3 .	Luton - - -	35	1
Cambridge - -	71	—	Chepping Wycombe	15	—
Ely (Isle of) - -	65	—	Cambridge - -	63 .	—
Essex - - -	393	—	Colchester - -	46	—
Hertford - - -	248	—	St. Albans - -	19	1
Huntingdon - -	54	—	Leicester - - -	215	—
Leicester - - -	167	—	Boston - - -	15	— .
Lincoln - - -	315	4	Grantham - -	16	—
Norfolk - - -	242	5	Great Grimsby -	65	—
Northampton - .	166	2	Lincoln - - -	49	—
Oxford - - -	111	—	Louth - - -	10	—
Peterborough (Liberty of) -	10	—	Great Yarmouth -	57	—
Rutland - - -	15	—	King's Lynn -	23	—
Shropshire - -	165	6	Norwich - -	120	—
Stafford - - -	690	17	Northampton -	113	—
Suffolk (East) - -	165	—	Banbury - -	13	—
Suffolk (West) -	113	—	Oxford - -	62	—
Warwick - - -	304	4	Peterborough - -	30	1
Worcester - -	357	—	Shrewsbury -	37	. —
			Hanley - - -	60	3
			Newcastle-under-Lyme -	18	—
NORTH WALES.			Walsall - -	78	3
			Wolverhampton -	93	—
Anglesea (Isle of) - -	30	—	Ipswich - - -	67	—
Carnarvon - -	32	—	Birmingham - -	800	56
Denbigh - - -	33	—	Coventry - -	88	1
Flint - - -	58	—	Leamington - -	40	—
Merioneth - -	35	—	Kidderminster -	29	1
Montgomery - -	36	—	Worcester - -	51	—
TOTAL - -	4,229	43	TOTAL - -	2,369	70

AUGMENTATIONS and REDUCTIONS in the STRENGTH of POLICE FORCES made during the Year ended 29th September 1901.

COUNTIES.		BOROUGHS.		BOROUGH.	
NAME OF FORCE Augmented.	No.	NAME OF FORCE Augmented.	No.	NAME OF FORCE Reduced.	No.
Essex - - -	3	Leicester - -	9	Ipswich - -	1
Worcester - -	6	Grimsby - -	2		
Carnarvon - -	2	Norwich - -	3		
Denbigh - -	1	Northampton - -	27		
		Banbury - -	1		
		Hanley - -	2		
		Birmingham - -	100		
TOTAL - -	12	TOTAL - -	144	TOTAL - -	1

The usual Tables will be found at the end of reports, viz.: (I.) The Authorised Strength of the Forces ; (II.) The Ranks, Numbers, and Rates of Pay ; (III.) Licensed Houses and Returns of Drunkenness ; (IV.) Prices paid for Constables' Clothing ; (V.) Return of Cost of the Police.

No. 1.
Eastern Counties,
Midland,
and North Wales
District.
———

In a very large proportion of forces the scale of pay has been revised and increased. The Standing Joint Committees of Norfolk, East and West Suffolk, and Cambridgeshire appointed representative members to confer on the question as it affected East Anglia with the result of coming to an almost uniform arrangement upon it.; and it would seem very desirable that so good an example should be generally followed, and that in areas where similar conditions as regards questions affecting the police service obtain joint action should be taken.

With regard to licensed houses and drunkenness it appears that during the last 10 years the number of public-houses has been reduced by 290 and that of beerhouses by 267. The number of persons proceeded against for drunkenness was 1,652 more in 1901 than in 1891, and of persons convicted 1,746 more, the proportion of convictions being 92·50 per cent. in 1801 and 93·25 per cent. in 1901. These figures, however, cannot afford any real indication of the growth or diminution of intemperance until the correct census figures of this year are available for comparison.

I have, &c.
(Signed) *C. G. Legge*,
H.M. Inspector of Constabulary.

To the Right Honourable
    C. T. Ritchie, M.P.,
        His Majesty's Principal Secretary of State
        for the Home Department.

REPORTS OF COUNTIES AND BOROUGHS RESPECTIVELY.

No 1.
Eastern Counties,
Midland,
and North Wales
District.

COUNTY OF BEDFORD.

Force - - - - - - - - - 100.*

Area in acres† - - - 297,605 | Acres to each constable - - - 2,976
Population in 1891† - - 102,906 | Population to ditto, as per census, 1891 1,029

Yearly Pay in £ and Shillings.

RANKS.	Chief Constable.	6 Superintendents.						5 Inspectors.			
		Deputy Chief Constable.	Chief Clerk.	1st Class.	2nd Class.	3rd Class.	4th Class.	Special Class.	1st Class.	2nd Class.	3rd Class.
Number of each Rank and Class -	1	1	1	2	1	1	-	1	-	1	1	2
Rates of Pay of each ditto - -	£ 550	£ 180	£ 135	£ 160	£ 145	£ 140	£ 135	£ 190	£ 110	£ 105	£ 100	£ 95

Weekly Pay in Shillings and Pence.

RANKS.	11 Sergeants.			Merit Class.	77 Constables.							2nd Class.	3rd Class.	Wanting to Complete.
	1st Class.	2nd Class.	3rd Class.		1st Class.									
Number of each Rank and Class -	-	3	3	2	3	-	16	8	2	11	14	15	6	3	2
Rates of Pay of each ditto - -	s. d. 33	s. d. 31 6	s. d. 30 4	s. d. 29 2	s. d. 28 7	s. d. 28 7	s. d. 27 5	s. d. 26 10	s. d. 26 3	s. d. 25 8	s. d. 25 1	s. d. 24 6	s. d. 22 9	s. 21	-

* Exclusive of one constable appointed under 3 & 4 Vict. c. 88, s. 19.
† The parish of Swineshead (acreage 1,354, population 178) is transferred from Huntingdonshire for police purposes, by order of Quarter Sessions, dated 18th October 1860. The parish of Tilbrook (acreage 1,683, population 314), is transferred to Huntingdonshire for police purposes, by order of Quarter Sessions, dated 17th October 1860.

Inspected in May, when there were vacancies for three constables.

The authorised establishment of the force is one chief constable, six superintendents, one of whom is deputy chief constable, and another is chief clerk, five inspectors, 11 sergeants, and 77 constables. There is also one constable appointed under 3 & 4 Vict. c. 88. s. 19.

Extra duties performed by the police :—

NATURE OF DUTY.	Chief Constable.	Superintendents.	Inspectors.	Sergeants.	Constables.	TOTAL.
Inspectors under Contagious Diseases (Animals) Act.	1	6	4	11	8	30
Inspectors under Explosives Act - -	—	5	1	—	—	6
Inspector under Food and Drugs Act -	—	—	1	—	—	1
Assistant Relieving Officer - -	—	1	—	—	—	1

Nine army reservists have been called up for service with the colours, of whom three were still serving in South Africa on 29th September, the other six having returned to the force, and were fit for the service.

There has been a reduction of three in the number of public-houses and of two beerhouses. Proceedings taken against persons for drunkenness show a decrease of 16, and convictions of 10.

Seventy-five members of the force hold certificates from the St. John Ambulance Association.

The Inspector visited all the stations, except the one at Sharnbrook, and found them clean and in good order.

The books and returns were well kept, and the management, numbers, and discipline of the force have been efficiently maintained.

A 3

A new scale of pay as under has been adopted :—

Superintendents—

		£	
On appointment	- - - -	135	per annum.
After 3 years' service -	- - -	140	,,
,, 6 ,, ,,	- - -	145	,,
,, 8 ,, ,,	- - -	150	,,
,, 10 ,, ,,	- - -	155	,,
,, 12 ,, ,,	- - -	160	,,

Inspectors --

On appointment	- - - -	95	,,
After 3 years' service -	- - -	100	,,
,, 6 ,, ,,	- - -	105	,,
,, 9 ,, ,,	- - -	110	,,

Sergeants—

		£	s.	d.	
On appointment -	- - -	1	8	7	per week.
After 3 years' service	- - -	1	9	2	,,
,, 6 ,, ,,	- - -	1	10	4	,,
,, 9 ,, ,,	- - -	1	11	6	,,
,, 12 ,, ,,	- - -	1	12	8	,,

Constables—

		£	s.	d.	
On appointment	- - -	1	1	0	,,
,, ,, as 2nd class constable -		1	2	9	,,
,, ,, ,, 1st ,, ,, -		1	4	6	,,
After 3 years' service as 1st class constable		1	5	1	,,
,, 6 ,, ,, ,, ,,		1	5	8	,,
,, 8 ,, ,, ,, ,,		1	6	3	,,
,, 10 ,, ,, ,, ,,		1	6	10	,,
,, 12 ,, ,, ,, ,,		1	7	5	,,

BOROUGH OF BEDFORD.

Force - - - - - - - - - 42.*

Area in acres - - - 2,223	Acres to each constable - - 53
Population in 1891 - - 28,023	Population to ditto, as per census 1891 667

Yearly Pay in £ and Shillings.

RANKS.	Chief Officer.	Superintendents.						2 Inspectors.				
		Deputy Chief Officer.	Chief Clerk.	1st Class.	2nd Class.	3rd Class.	4th Class.	1st Class.	2nd Class.	3rd Class.	4th Class.	5th Class.
Number of each Rank and Class -	1	-	-	-	-	-	-	1	1	-	-	-
Rates of Pay of each ditto - -	£ 300	-	-	-	-	-	-	£ 110	£ 105	£ 95	-	-

Weekly Pay in Shillings and Pence.

RANKS.	6 Sergeants.						33 Constables.								
	Clerk.	1st Class.	2nd Class.	3rd Class.	4th Class.	5th Class.	Detective.	Merit. Class.	1st Class.					2nd Class.	3rd Class.	Wanting to Complete.
Number of each Rank and Class -	1	1	3	1	-	-	1	1	4	3	1	6	5	8	2	-	2
Rates of Pay of each ditto - -	s. d. 39 3	s. d. 37 6	s. d. 33 10	s. d. 33 0	s. d. 33 1	s. d. 30 11	s. d. 34 6	s. d. 33 6	s. d. 31 6	s. d. 30 4	s. d. 29 2	s. 28	s. d. 26 10	s. d. 25 8	s. d. 24 6	s. d. 23 4	-

Inspected on 1st May, when there was a vacancy for one constable.

The authorised establishment of the force is one chief officer, two inspectors, six sergeants, one of whom is clerk, and 33 constables. The pay of the chief officer has been increased by 50*l.* a year.

Three army reservists belonging to this force rejoined the colours during the year, two were still serving with their regiments on 29th September, and one was on sick furlough.

Constables—
On appointment -   -   -   1 4 6 per week.
After 1 year's service -   - 1 5 8 ,,
,, 2 years' service -   - 1 6 10 ..
,, 4 ,, ,, -   - 1 8 0 ..
,, 6 ,, .. -   1 9 2 ..
,, 9 ,, .. -   - 1 10 4 ..
,, 11 .. .. -   - 1 11 6 ..

Sergeants—
On appointment -   -   - 1 12 8 ,,
After 2 years' service -   - 1 13 10 ..
,, 4 ,, ,, -   - 1 15 0 .
,, 6 .. -   - 1 16 2 ,,
,, 9 ,, ,, -   - 1 17 4 ,,

Inspectors on appointment 100*l.* per annum, with increments of 5*l.* at the discretion of the Watch Committee.

Chief Constable 300*l.* per annum.

BOROUGH OF LUTON.

Force - - - - - - - - - - 35.

Area in acres - - - - 3,134 | Acres to each constable - - 90.
Population in 1891 - - 30,056 | Population to ditto, as per census 1891 859

RANKS.	Chief Officer.	Superintendents.						2 Inspectors.				
		Deputy Chief Officer.	Chief Clerk.	1st Class.	2nd Class.	3rd Class.	4th Class.	Chief Inspector.	1st Class.	2nd Class.	3rd Class.	4th Class.
Number of each Rank and Class -	1	-	-	-	-	-	-	1	1	-	-	-
Rates of Pay of each ditto -	£ 340	-	-	-	-	-	-	£ 125	£ s. 102 14	-	-	-

Yearly Pay in £ and Shillings.

Weekly Pay in Shillings and Pence.

RANKS.	5 Sergeants.					27 Constables.									
	1st Class.	2nd Class.	3rd Class.	4th Class.	5th Class.	Detective.	1st Class.							2nd Class.	3rd Class.
Number of each Rank and Class -	3	1	1	1	-	1	11	1	1*	1	-	4	7	-	-
Rate of Pay of each ditto -	s. d. 36 2	s. 35	s. d. 34 5	s. d. 33 3	s. d. 33 1	s. d. 30 11	s. d. 33 0	s. d. 31 6	s. d. 30 4	s. d. 29 9	s. d. 29 2	s. 28	s. d. 26 10	s. d. 25 6	s. d. 24 6	s. d. 23 6

* With merit.

Inspected on 2nd May, when the force was complete.

The authorised establishment of the force is one chief officer, one chief and one other inspector, five sergeants, one of whom is clerk, and 27 constables. An inspector has been substituted for a sergeant.

No. 1.
Eastern Counties,
Midland,
and North Wales
District.

There has been no change in the number of public and beerhouses for several years. The number of persons proceeded against for drunkenness was 98, and of those convicted 92, an increase of eight and seven respectively on the number in 1900.

Thirty-four members of the force hold certificates from the St. John Ambulance Association.

The cells and police offices were clean and in good order.

The books and returns were well kept, and the management, numbers, and discipline of the force have been efficiently maintained.

A new scale of pay has been adopted as under :—

			£	s.	d.	
Constables—						
On appointment	-	-	1	4	6	per week.
After 1 year	-	-	1	5	8	,,
,, 2 years	-	-	1	6	10	..
,, 4 ,,	-	-	1	8	0	..
.. 6 ..	-	-	1	9	2	..
,, 9 ,,	-	-	1	10	4	..
,, 11 ..	-	-	1	11	6	..
Sergeants—						
On appointment	-	-	1	12	8	..
After 2 years	-	-	1	13	10	..
,, 4 ,,	-	-	1	15	0	..
:: 6 ,,	-	-	1	16	2	,,
,, 9 ,,	-	-	1	17	4	,,

Inspectors on appointment 98*l.* 16*s.* per annum, rising at the discretion of the Watch Committee, to 125*l.* per annum.

The detectives and chief clerk receive 1*s.* 6*d.* per week extra irrespective of rank.

There is also a " Merit Badge " (open to all ranks) awarded for conspicuous and meritorious conduct. The extra amount of pay is decided on, by the Watch Committee, according to the merits of each case, as recommended by the Chief Constable.

COUNTY OF BUCKINGHAM.

Force - - - - - - - - - 154.*

Area in acres † -	-	-	478,691	Acres to each constable	-	-	-	3,108
Population in 1891 † -	-	-	173,227	Population to ditto, as per census 1891				1,125

Yearly Pay in £ and Shillings.

RANKS.	Chief Con- stable.	6 Superintendents.					6 Inspectors.				
		Deputy Chief Constable.	Chief Clerk.	1st Class.	2nd Class.	3rd Class.	4th Class.	1st Class.	2nd Class.	3rd Class.	4th Class.	5th Class.
Number of each Rank and Class -	1	1	1	2	1	1	-	-	2	-	-
Rates of Pay of each ditto - -	£ 380	£ 180	£ s. 160 0	£ s. 152 10	£ s. 147 10	£ s. 142 10	£ s. 137 10	£ 110	£ 104	£ 99	£	£

Weekly Pay in Shillings and Pence.

RANKS.	22 Sergeants.				118 Constables.								
	Merit Class.	1st Class.	2nd Class.	3rd Class.	Merit Class.				1st Class.	2nd Class.	3rd Class.	4th Class.	5th Class.	Wanting to Com- plete.
Number of each Rank and Class -	-	5	8	10	26	5	15	27	14	26	11	-	-	2
Rates of Pay of each ditto - -	-	s. 31	s. 29	s. d. 28 6	s. 28	s. d. 26 10	s. d. 25 9	s. d. 24 6	s. d. 24 2	s. d. 22 1	s. d. 20 10	-	-	-

* Exclusive of eight constables appointed under 3 & 4 Vict. c. 88, s. 19.
† The parish of Stokenchurch (acreage 5,930, population 1,780), and part of the parish of Ibstone (acreage 272, population 137), have been transferred to Buckinghamshire from Oxfordshire.

Extra duties performed by the police :—

NATURE OF DUTY.	Chief Constable.	Super-intendents.	Inspectors.	Sergeants.	Constables.	TOTAL.
Inspectors under Contagious Diseases (Animals) Act.	1	5	5	20	—	31
Inspectors under Food and Drugs Act	—	5	—	—	—	5
Inspectors under Explosives Act	—	5	5	14	—	21

Ten members of this force, who belong to the Army Reserve, were called up to join their respective regiments, of whom five have returned ; four were still serving with the colours on 29th September, and one who was invalided did not rejoin the force on account of ill-health.

There has been a reduction of five in the number of beerhouses during the year, and of two refreshment houses with wine licenses ; and 50 fewer persons were proceeded against for drunkenness, and 50 fewer were convicted.

Eighty-four members of the force hold certificates from the St. John Ambulance Association.

The Inspector visited nine stations, and found them clean and in good order.

The books and returns were well kept, and the management, numbers, and discipline of the force have been efficiently maintained.

BOROUGH OF CHEPPING WYCOMBE.

Force - - - - - 15.

Area in acres - - - 687 | Acres to each constable - - 46
Population in 1891 - - - 13,435 | Population to ditto, as per census 1891 896

Yearly Pay in £ and Shillings.

RANKS.	Chief Officer.	Superintendents.						Inspectors.				
		Deputy Chief Officer.	Chief Clerk.	1st Class.	2nd Class.	3rd Class.	4th Class.	1st Class.	2nd Class.	3rd Class.	4th Class.	5th Class.
Number of each Rank and Class -	1	-	-	-	-	-	-	-	-	-	-	-
Rates of Pay of each ditto -	£ 208	-	-	-	-	-	-	-	-	-	-	-

Weekly Pay in Shillings and Pence.

RANKS.	3 Sergeants.					11 Constables.							
	1st Class and Long Service.	1st Class.	2nd Class.	3rd Class.	4th Class.	1st Class.				2nd Class.	3rd Class.	4th Class.	5th Class.
Number of each Rank and Class -	1	1	1	-	-	1	3	1	4	1	1	-	-
Rates of Pay of each ditto -	s. d. 34 8	s. d. 33 6	s. d. 31 2	s. d. 30 4	s. d. 29 2	s. 53	s. 30	s. d. 27 8	s. d. 26 6	s. d. 25 4	s. d. 34 2	s. 23	-	-

Inspected on 26th March, when the force was complete.

The authorised establishment of the force is one chief officer, three sergeants, and 11 constables. The pay of the chief officer has been raised from 180l. to 208l. a year.

The chief officer is inspector of common lodging-houses, and under the Dairies and Cowsheds Order ; he is also inspector under the Food and Drugs, Weights and Measures, Contagious Diseases (Animals), and Explosives Acts.

discipline of the force have been efficiently maintained.

COUNTY OF CAMBRIDGE.

Force - - - - 71.*

Area in acres † - 312,003	Acres to each constable - - 4,394
Population in 1891 † - 83,303	Population to ditto, as per census 1891 1,173

Yearly Pay in £ and Shillings.

RANKS.	Chief Constable	5 Superintendents.						2 Inspectors.				
		Deputy Chief Constable	Chief Clerk.	1st Class.	2nd Class.	3rd Class.	4th Class.	1st Class.	2nd Class.	3rd Class.	4th Class.	5th Class.
Number of each Rank and Class -	1	1	1	-	1	2	-	-	2	-	-	-
Rates of Pay of each ditto -	£ 350	£ 150	£ 190	£ 150	£ 135	£ 120	-	£ 105	£ s. 97 10	£ 90	-	-

Weekly Pay in Shillings and Pence.

RANKS.	6 Sergeants.						57 Constables.							
	Merit Class.	1st Class.	2nd Class.	3rd Class.	4th Class.	5th Class.	1st Class.						2nd Class.	3rd Class.	4th Class.	5th Class.
Number of each Rank and Class -	-	4	1	1	-	-	12	4	11	8	16	6	-	-
Rates of Pay of each ditto -	-	s. d. 30 11	s. d. 29 9	s. d. 28 7	s. d. 27 5	-	s. d. 27 5	s. d. 26 3	s. d. 25 1	s. d. 23 11	s. d. 23 9	s. d. 21 7	-	-

* Exclusive of one constable appointed under 3 & 4 Vict. c. 88. s. 19.

† The parishes of Great Chishall and Little Chishall and Haydon (acreage 4,964, population 746), were transferred from Essex by Order dated 27th May 1895, and of Papworth St. Agnes (acreage 475, population 54), from Huntingdon. The parish of Royston (acreage 19, population 439), part of Bassingbourne (acreage 174, population 673), and part of Melbourne (acreage 243, population 213) were transferred to Hertfordshire on 30th September 1895.

Inspected in May, when the force was complete.

The authorised establishment of the force is one chief constable, five superintendents, one of whom is deputy chief constable and another chief clerk, two inspectors, six sergeants, and 57 constables. There is also one constable appointed under 3 & 4 Vict. c. 88. s. 19.

Extra duties performed by the police :—

NATURE OF DUTY.	Chief Constable.	Super-intendents.	Inspectors.	Sergeants.	Constables.	TOTAL.
Inspector of Weights and Measures	1	—	—	—	—	1
Assistant Relieving Officers for Vagrants	—	2	1	—	—	3
Inspectors under Adulteration Act	1	4	2	—	—	7
Inspectors under Explosives Act	1	4	2	—	—	7
Inspectors under Sale of Coal Act	1	4	2	6	—	13
Inspectors under Contagious Diseases (Animals) Act.	1	4	2	—	—	7

A fully licensed house has been substituted for a beerhouse, and there is a decrease of 12 and 10 respectively in the number of persons proceeded against for drunkenness and convicted, as compared with 1900.

Four army reserve men were called up to join their regiments from the force, and were still abroad on 29th September.

BOROUGH OF CAMBRIDGE.

Force - - - - - 63.

Area in acres	-	-	- 3,233	Acres to each constable	-	- 51
Population in 1891	-	-	- 36,983	Population to ditto, as per census 1891		587

RANKS.	Yearly Pay in £ and Shillings.											
	Chief Officer.	Superintendents.						2 Inspectors.				
		Deputy Chief Officer.	Chief Clerk.	1st Class.	2nd Class.	3rd Class.	4th Class.	1st Class.	2nd Class.	3rd Class.	4th Class.	5th Class.
Number of each Rank and Class -	1	-	-	-	-	-	-	1	-	1	-	-
Rates of Pay of each ditto -	£ 400	-	-	-	-	-	-	£ 180	£ s. 134 16	£ s. 114 8	-	-

RANKS.	Weekly Pay in Shillings and Pence.													
	7 Sergeants.						53 Constables.							
	1st Class.				2nd Class.	3rd Class.	4th Class.	1st Class.					2nd Class.	3rd Class.	4th Class.
Number of each Rank and Class -	1	3	1	1	1	-		2	8	1	7	3	9	8	1	9
Rates of Pay of each ditto -	s. d. 41 5	s. d. 38 11	s. d. 37 4	s. d. 34 10	s. d. 33 10	-		s. d. 31 10	s. d. 30 9	s. d. 29 9	s. d. 28 8	s. d. 27 8	s. d. 26 7	s. d. 25 7	s. d. 24 7	s. d. 23 7

Inspected on 9th May, when there was one vacancy.

The authorised establishment of the force is now one chief officer, two inspectors, seven sergeants, and 53 constables.

Nine men were called up belonging to the Army Reserve, all of whom have resumed police duty except one, who re-engaged with the colours.

The chief officer acts as assistant relieving officer, inspector of hackney carriages and provisions, and under the Contagious Diseases (Animals) Act. An inspector is inspector of common lodging-houses.

A fully licensed house has been substituted for a beerhouse, and refreshment houses with wine licenses have increased by one.

The number of persons proceeded against for drunkenness was 10 less than in the previous year, and the number convicted nine less.

Forty-four members of the force hold certificates from the St. John Ambulance Association.

The temporary cells and police offices were in good order. The new station was nearly completed at the time of inspection and was expected to be ready for occupation in the following October.

The books and returns were well kept, and the management, numbers, and discipline of the force have been efficiently maintained.

No. 1.
Eastern Counties,
Midland,
and North Wales
District.

ISLE OF ELY.

Force - - - - - 65.

Area in acres * - - 238,107 | Acres to each constable - 3,663
Population in 1891 * - - 63,340 | Population to ditto, as per census 1891 944

RANKS.	Chief Constable.	3 Superintendents.					3 Inspectors (including Chief Clerk).				
		Deputy Chief Constable.	1st Class.	2nd Class.	3rd Class.	4th Class.	1st Class.	2nd Class.	3rd Class.	4th Class.	5th Class.
Number of each Rank and Class -	1	1	-	2	-	-	-	1	2	-	-
Rates of Pay of each ditto - -	£ 350	£ 150	£ 140	£ 120			£ 105	£ s. 97 10	£ 90	£ 80	-

RANKS.	8 Sergeants.						50 Constables.				
	Merit Class.	1st Class.	2nd Class.	3rd Class.	4th Class.	5th Class.	1st Class.			2nd Class.	3rd Class.	4th Class.	5th Class.
Number of each Rank and Class -	-	1	2	-	5	-	11	-	10	5	12	12	-	-
Rates of Pay of each ditto - -	-	s. d. 30 4	s. d. 29 2	28	s. d. 26 10	-	s. d. 26 10	s. d. 26 8	s. d. 24 6	s. d. 23 4	s. d. 22 2	s. 21	-	-

* The parish of Redmere (acreage 695, population 44) was transferred from the county of Norfolk on 1st October 1895, by Local Government Board's Provisional Order Confirmation (No. 9) Act, 1896.

Inspected in May, when the force was complete.

The authorised establishment of the force is one chief constable, three superintendents, one of whom is deputy chief constable, three inspectors, including the chief clerk, eight sergeants, and 50 constables.

One member of the force belonging to the Army Reserve was called up to join the colours, but has rejoined the force.

Extra duties performed by the police :—

NATURE OF DUTY.	Chief Constable.	Super-intendents.	Inspectors.	Sergeants.	Constables.	TOTAL.
Inspectors under Contagious Diseases (Animals) Act.	—	3	2	1	—	6
Inspectors under Explosives Act - -	1	3	2	—	—	6
Inspectors under Food and Drugs Act -	—	3	2	—	—	5
Inspectors of Common Lodging-houses -	—	3	1	—	1	5
Inspector of Public Gas Lamps -	—	1	—	—	—	1
Assistant Relieving Officers - - -	—	3	1	1	12	17
Keepers of Sessions House - -	—	2	—	—	—	2
Billet Masters - - - -	—	3	2	—	—	5

Public-houses have been reduced by one, and beerhouses by three, but refreshments houses with wine licenses have increased by three. Three fewer persons were proceeded against for drunkenness, and four fewer were convicted, than in 1900.

Forty-two members of the force hold certificates from the St. John Ambulance Association.

The Inspector visited all the stations except one, and found them clean and in good order.

The books and returns were well kept, and the management, numbers, and discipline of the force have been efficiently maintained.

COUNTY OF ESSEX.

Force - - - - 393.*

Area in acres † - - - 908,072 | Acres to each constable - - 2,312
Population in 1891 † - - 335,136 | Population to ditto, as per census 1891   853

RANKS.	Chief Constable	14 Superintendents.						12 Inspectors.			
		Deputy Chief Constable.	Chief Clerk.	1st Class.	2nd Class.	3rd Class.	4th Class.	1st Class.	2nd Class.	3rd Class.	4th Class.
Number of each Rank and Class -	1	1	1	1‡	4	3	4	4	4	2	2
Rates of Pay of each ditto -	£ 600	£ 250	£ 135	£ 200	£ 175	£ 150	£ 135	£ 115	£ 110	£ 105	£ 100

Yearly Pay in £ and Shillings.

Weekly Pay in Shillings and Pence.

RANKS.	51 Sergeants.				315 Constables.					
	1st Class.	2nd Class.	3rd Class.	4th Class.	1st Class.				2nd Class.	3rd Class.
Number of each Rank and Class -	22	6	7	16	47	47	31	189	38	13
Rates of Pay of each ditto -	s. d. 33 10	s. d. 32 8	s. d. 31 6	s. d. 30 4	s. 28	s. d. 26 10	s. d. 25 8	s. d. 29 2	s. d. 23 11	s. d. 22 2

* Exclusive of one inspector and three constables appointed under 3 & 4 Vict. c. 88. s. 19.
† The parishes of Great Chishall and Little Chishall and Heydon, with acreage of 4,954, and population 748, were transferred to Cambridgeshire by order, dated 27th May 1895; and by the same order, the parish of Kedington (acreage 722, population 136) was transferred to the county of Suffolk.
‡ Temporarily increased by 25l. for one year.

Inspected in May, when the force was complete.

The authorised establishment of the force, which has been augmented by three constables, is one chief constable, 14 superintendents, an officer of this rank having been substituted for an inspector, one of whom is deputy chief constable and another is chief clerk, 12 inspectors, 51 sergeants, and 315 constables. There are also an inspector and three constables appointed under 3 & 4 Vict. c. 88. s. 19.

Seven army reservists were called up from this force, four of whom were on active service in South Africa on 29th September, and three had returned to their police employment.

Scale of pay, as below, came into effect from 1st April 1901 :—

Constables—   £ s. d.
  3rd class (on appointment) - - 1 2 2 per week.
  2nd ,, - - - - 1 3 11 ,,
  1st ,, - - - - 1 5 8 ..
  After 2 years on 1st class - - 1 6 10 ..
  ,, 5 ,, ,, - - 1 8 0 ..
  ,, 8 ,, ,, - - 1 9 2 ..
Sergeants—
  On appointment - - - - 1 10 4 ..
  After 2 years - - - - 1 11 6 ..
  ,, 4 ,, - - - - 1 12 8 ..
  ,, 6 .. - - - 1 13 10 ..
Inspectors—
  On appointment - - - 100 0 0 per annum.
  After 2 years - - - 105 0 0 ,,
  ,, 4 ,, - - - 110 0 0 ,,
  .. 6 - - - 115 0 0 ..

No. 1.
Eastern Counties,
Midland,
and North Wales
District.

Superintendents—

		£	s.	d.	
On appointment	- - -	135	0	0	per annum.
After 5 years	- -	150	0	0	,,
,, 10 ,,	- -	175	0	0	,,
,, 15 ,,	- -	200	0	0	,,

Deputy Chief Constable—

| On appointment | - - - | 220 | 0 | 0 | ,, |

Extra duties performed by the police :—

NATURE OF DUTY.	Super-intendents.	Inspectors.	Sergeants.	Constables.	TOTAL.
Inspector of Common Lodging-houses - -	—	1	—	—	1
Inspectors under the Fertilisers and Feeding Stuffs Act.	13	11	—	—	24
Inspectors under Weights and Measures Act -	8	1	3	—	12
Inspectors under Food and Drugs Act -	8	1	3	—	12
Inspectors under Explosives Act - - -	13	7	—	—	20
Inspectors under Petroleum Act - -	6	2	—	—	8
Inspectors under Contagious Diseases (Animals) Act.	13	10	1	—	24
Inspectors of Horse-slaughtering Yards -	2	1	1	—	4
Inspectors of Hackney Carriages - -	1	2	5	18	26
Town Hall Keeper at Harwich - -	—	1	—	—	1
Assistant Relieving Officers - - - -	6	4	1	—	11

A new division has been formed by the separation of the Thorpe and
Clacton sub-divisions from the Colchester Division and placed under a
superintendent, with its headquarters at Thorpe.

There has been a decrease of four in the number of "on," and of nine in
the number of "off," licenses during the year, but refreshment houses with
wine licenses have increased by three. Twenty-nine fewer persons were
proceeded against, and 21 fewer convicted, for drunkenness than in 1900.

Two hundred and twenty-three members of the force hold certificates
from the St. John Ambulance Association.

The municipal boroughs of Chelmsford and Southend-on-Sea are watched
by the county police.

The Inspector visited 16 stations, and found them clean and in good order.

The books and returns were well kept, and the management, numbers, and
discipline of the force have been efficiently maintained.

BOROUGH OF COLCHESTER.

Force - - - - - - 46.*

Area in acres - - - 11,331	Acres to each constable - - 246
Population in 1891 - - 34,559	Population to ditto, as per census 1891 7,512

Yearly Pay in £ and Shillings.

RANKS.	Chief Officer.	Superintendents.					4 Inspectors.				
		Deputy Chief Officer.	Chief Clerk.	1st Class.	2nd Class.	3rd Class.	4th Class.	1st Class.	2nd Class.	3rd Class.	4th Class.	5th Class.
Number of each Rank and Class -	1	-	-	-	-	-	-	1	1	1	1	-
Rates of Pay of each ditto -	£ s. 355 4	-	-	-	-	-	-	£ 188	£ 115	£ s. 107 10	£ 100	-

Weekly Pay in Shillings and Pence.

RANKS.	6 Sergeants.						35 Constables.				
	Merit Class.	1st Class.	2nd Class.	3rd Class.	4th Class.	5th Class.	Merit Class.	1st Class.			2nd Class.	3rd Class.
Number of each Rank and Class -	1	3	-	1	-	-	3	5	7	5.	7	9	-
Rates of Pay of each ditto -	s. d. 43 3	s. d. 35 7	s. d. 34 5	s. d. 33 3	s. d. 32 1	-	s. d. 37 1	s. d. 30 11	s. d. 29 9	s. d. 36 7	s. d. 27 5	s. d. 26 3	s. d. 25 1

Inspected on 25th May, when the force was complete.

The authorised establishment of the force is one chief officer, four inspectors, six sergeants, a sergeant having been substituted for a constable during the year, and 35 constables. There are also eight constables appointed at private cost.

The chief officer is inspector of weights and measures, food and drugs, explosive substances, petroleum, and hackney carriages; he and one of the inspectors are assistant relieving officers, and an inspector is assistant inspector of weights and measures and food and drugs. Two of the inspectors are appointed inspectors under the Contagious Diseases (Animals) Act, and one of the inspectors acts as port sanitary inspector and water bailiff.

There is an increase of one in the number of public-houses, and of 10 in that of persons proceeded against for drunkenness, with an increase of 15 convictions.

Three army reservists belonging to the force were called up to join their regiments, one of whom has rejoined the force, one is still serving as such, and one has re-engaged in the Artillery.

Thirty-eight members of the force hold certificates from the St. John Ambulance Association.

The cells and police offices were in good order; but those in use were of a temporary character, pending the completion of the new town hall.

The books and returns were well kept, and the management, numbers, and discipline of the force have been efficiently maintained.

COUNTY OF HERTFORD.

Force - - - - - - - - - - 248.*

Area in acres † - - - 367,406 | Acres to each constable - - 1,481
Population in 1891 † - - 177,478 | Population to ditto, as per census 1891 716

Yearly Pay in £ and Shillings.

RANKS.	Chief Constable.	7 Superintendents.									8 Inspectors.					
		Deputy Chief Constable.	Chief Clerk.	1st Class.	2nd Class.	3rd Class.	4th Class.	5th Class.	6th Class.	7th Class.	8th Class.	1st Class.	2nd Class.	3rd Class.	4th Class.	5th Class.	6th Class.
Number of each Rank and Class	1	1	1	2	1	-	2	-	-	-	-	1	1	2	1	3	-
Rates of Pay of each ditto	£ 600	£ 220	£ 190	£ 160	£ 150	£ 145	£ 135	-	-	-	-	£ 115	£ s. 112 10	£ s. 107 10	£ 105	£ 100	-

Weekly Pay in Shillings and Pence.

RANKS.	29 Sergeants.				203 Constables.				
	1st Class.	2nd Class.	3rd Class.	4th Class.	Merit Class.	1st Class.	2nd Class.	3rd Class.	Probationary Class.
Number of each Rank and Class	6	8	6	9	10	46	19	38	68	31	1
Rates of Pay to each ditto	s. d. 33 10	s. d. 32 8	s. d. 31 6	s. d. 30 4	s. d. 30 3	s. d. 29 2	s. d. 28 0	s. d. 26 10	s. d. 25 8	s. d. 22 11	s. d. 21 7

* Exclusive of two sergeants and seven constables appointed under 3 & 4 Vict. c. 88. s. 19.
† The parish of Nettleden (acreage 504, population 415) and part of Ivinghoe (acreage 503, population 300) were transferred from Buckinghamshire by order, 30th September 1896, and the parish of Royston (acreage 19, population 439), part of Bassingbourne (acreage 174, population 573), part of Kneesworth (acreage 118, population 627), and part of Melbourn (acreage 243, population 31½) were transferred from Cambridgeshire to Hertfordshire on the same date.

Inspected in June, when there were vacancies for six constables.

The authorised establishment of the force is one chief constable, seven superintendents, one of whom is deputy chief constable, and another is chief clerk, eight inspectors, 29 sergeants, and 203 constables. There are also two sergeants and seven constables appointed under 3 & 4 Vict. c. 88. s. 19.

Eighteen members of the force were called out with the Army Reserve, of whom nine were still serving with the colours on 29th September, one was killed in action at Belmont, and four have left the police for good. Three of the nine still fulfilling their engagement with the Army are, however, performing police duty on " working furlough."

Extra duties performed by the police :—

NATURE OF DUTY.	Chief Constable.	Super-intendent.	Inspectors.	Sergeants.	TOTAL.
Chief Inspectors under Weights and Measures Act.	1	1*	—	—	2
Chief Inspector under Food and Drugs Act -	1	—	—	—	1
Chief Inspector under Explosives Act - -	1	—	—	—	1
			Inspectors.		
Chief Inspectors under Contagious Diseases (Animals) Act.	1	6	8	29	44
Inspectors of Common Lodging-houses - -	—	2	—	1	3
Assistant Relieving Officers - - -	—	4	1	1	6

* Chief clerk, who does the clerical work under the Act.

The number of public-houses has been reduced by one. Thirty-two fewer persons were proceeded against for drunkenness, and 46 fewer were convicted, than in 1900.

One hundred and sixty-one members of the force hold certificates from the St. John Ambulance Association.

The Inspector visited 12 stations, and found them clean and in good order.

The books and returns were well kept, and the management, numbers, and discipline of the force have been efficiently maintained.

A new scale of pay as under has been adopted :—

Constables—

	£	s.	d.	
On probation -	1	1	7	per week.
2nd Class -	1	3	11	,,
1st ,,	1	5	8	,,
,, ,,	1	6	10	,,
,, ,,	1	8	0	,,
,, ,,	1	9	2	,,
Merit -	1	10	2	,,

Sergeants—

4th Class	1	10	4	,,
,, ,, Merit	1	11	4	,,
3rd ,,	1	11	6	,,
,, ,, Merit -	1	12	6	,,
2nd ,,	1	12	8	,,
,, ,, Merit -	1	13	8	,,
1st ,,	1	13	10	,,
,, ,, Merit -	1	14	10	,,

Inspectors—

7th Class	100	0	0	per annum.
6th ,,	102	10	0	,,
5th ,,	105	0	0	,,
4th ,,	107	10	0	,,
3rd ,,	110	0	0	,,
2nd ,,	112	10	0	,,
1st ,,	115	0	0	,,

Superintendents—

14th Class	135	0	0	,,
13th ,,	140	0	0	,,
12th ,,	145	0	0	,,
11th ,,	150	0	0	,,
10th ,,	155	0	0	,,

Chief Constable   -   -   -   - 600 0 0   „

The superintendent appointed deputy chief constable receives 20*l.* per annum additional.

CITY OF ST. ALBANS.

Force   -   -   -   -   -   -   -   -   - 19.

| Area in acres   -   -   -   - | 997 | Acres to each constable   -   -   - | 52 |
| Population in 1891   -   - | 12,898 | Population to ditto, as per census 1891 | 679 |

RANKS.	Chief Officer.	Superintendents.						Inspectors.				
		Deputy Chief Officer.	Chief Clerk.	1st Class.	2nd Class.	3rd Class.	4th Class.	1st Class.	2nd Class.	3rd Class.	4th Class.	5th Class.
Number of each Rank and Class -	1	-	-	-	-	-	-	-	-	-	-	-
Rates of Pay of each ditto -	£ 150	-	-	-	-	-	-	-	-	-	-	-

RANKS.	3 Sergeants.			15 Constables.			
	1st Class.	2nd Class.	3rd Class.	1st Class.		2nd Class.	3rd Class.
Number of each Rank and Class -	1 - 2	-	-	- 2 3 -	2	7	-
Rates of Pay of each ditto -	*s.* 26 *s. d.* 33 10 *s. d.* 32 8	*s. d.* 31 6	*s. d.* 30 4	*s. d.* 29 9 *s. d.* 29 2 *s.* 28 *s. d.* 26 10	*s. d.* 25 8	*s. d.* 24 6	*s. d.* 23 4

Inspected on 3rd June, when there was a vacancy for one constable.

The authorised establishment of the force is one chief officer, three sergeants, and 15 constables.

Mr. W. H. Smith was, on the retirement of Mr. Blatch, from inspector in the borough of Cambridge force, appointed chief officer, at a salary of 150*l.* a year.

One member of the force who belonged to the Army Reserve was called up in 1899 to join the colours, and was still serving with his regiment in South Africa on 29th September.

There was no change during the year in the number of the licensed houses; but a decrease in proceedings taken against persons for drunkenness of 20, and of 21 persons convicted, as compared with 1900.

Eighteen members of the force hold certificates from the St. John Ambulance Association.

The cells and police offices were clean and in good order.

The books and returns were well kept, and the management, numbers, and discipline of the force have been efficiently maintained.

COUNTY OF HUNTINGDON.

Force - - - - - - 54.

| Area in acres* - - - - 234,162 | Acres to each constable - - - 4,336 |
| Population in 1891* - - - 55,015 | Population to ditto, as per census 1891 1,019 |

RANKS.	Chief Constable.	4 Superintendents.						2 Inspectors (including Chief Clerk).				
		Deputy Chief Constable.	1st Class.	2nd Class.	3rd Class.	4th Class.	5th Class.	1st Class.	2nd Class.	3rd Class.	4th Class.	5th Class.
Number of each Rank and Class -	1	1	1	1	1	-	-	-	-	2	-	-
Rates of Pay of each ditto -	£ 250	£ 180	£ 150	£ 135	£ 120	-	-	£ 105	£ s. 97 10	£ 90	£ -	-

Yearly Pay in £ and Shillings.

RANKS.	4 Sergeants.						43 Constables.				
	Clerk.	1st Class.	2nd Class.	3rd Class.	4th Class.	5th Class.	1st Class.	2nd Class.	3rd Class.	4th Class.	4th Class.
Number of each Rank and Class -	-	1	3	-	-	-	22 4 5 5 6 3	-	-		
Rates of Pay of each ditto -	s. d. -	s. d. 30 11	s. d. 29 3	s. d. 28 7	-	-	s. d. 27 3 26 3 25 1 23 11 22 9 21 7	-	-		

Weekly Pay in Shillings and Pence.

* The parish of Tilbrook (acreage 1,683, population 314) is transferred from Bedfordshire for police purposes by order of Quarter Sessions dated 17th October 1860, and part of the parish of Winwick is transferred from Northamptonshire by order, from 30th September 1895 (acreage 1,352, population 129). The parish of Swineshead (acreage 1,354, population 173) is transferred to Bedfordshire for police purposes by order of Quarter Sessions dated 18th October 1860; parts of Loddington, Sutton, and Thurning are transferred to Northamptonshire, and the parish of Papworth St. Agnes is transferred to Cambridgeshire, by order, from 30th September 1895.

Inspected on 4th May, when the force was complete.

The authorised establishment of the force is one chief constable, four superintendents, one of whom is deputy chief constable, two inspectors, four sergeants, and 43 constables. On the retirement of Major Rooper in the month of June Lieut.-Col. A. G. Chichester, of the Royal Irish Regiment, was appointed chief constable with a salary of 250*l.* a year.

Two members of the force belonging to the Army Reserve were called upon to join the colours, one of whom was still serving with them on 29th September. The other rejoined the force, but subsequently resigned.

There is an increase of one in the number of beerhouses, but a decrease of 43 in the number of persons proceeded against for drunkenness, and convicted.

Forty-two members or the force hold certificates from the St. John Ambulance Association.

The Inspector visited all the stations, and found them clean and in good order ; but the one at Ramsey should be reconstructed or a new one provided. A new station has been completed at Standground comprising two cells, charge office, and accommodation for a married officer.

The books and returns were well kept, and the management, numbers, and discipline of the force have been efficiently maintained.

COUNTY OF LEICESTER.

Force - - - - - - - - - 167.

| Area in acres | - | - | - | 524,200 | Acres to each constable | - | - | - | 3,139 |
| Population in 1891 | - | - | 201,464 | Population to ditto, as per census 1891 | 1,206 |

		Yearly Pay in £ and Shillings.							
RANKS.	Chief Constable.	8 Superintendents.						7 Inspectors.	
		Deputy Chief Constable.	1st Class.	2nd Class.	3rd Class.			1st Class.	2nd Class.
Number of each Rank and Class -	1	1	1	2	1	1	2	1	6
Rates of Pay of each ditto - -	£ 650	£ 205	£ 185	£ 170	£ 155	£ 145	£ 140	£ s. 112 10	£ 105

		Weekly Pay in Shillings and Pence.							
RANKS.	23 Sergeants.				128 Constables.				
	Only one Class.				Merit Class.		1st Class.	2nd Class.	3rd Class.
Number of each Rank and Class -	12	1	3	6	22	4	3	27	14	12	12	26	7
Rates of Pay of each ditto - -	s. d. 34 5	s. d. 34 1	s. d. 33 6	s. d. 33 2	s. d. 30 2	s. d. 29 0	s. d. 27 10	s. d. 29 2	s. d. 28 0	s. d. 26 10	s. d. 25 2	s. d. 24 6	s. d. 23 4

Inspected in March, when there was a vacancy for one constable.

The authorised establishment of the force is one chief constable, eight superintendents, one of whom is deputy chief constable and another is chief clerk, seven inspectors, 23 sergeants, and 128 constables.

Five army reserve men were called up to rejoin their regiments, of whom two were serving abroad on 29th September, the remainder having rejoined the force.

Extra duties performed by the police :—

NATURE OF DUTY.	Chief Constable.	Super-intendents.	Inspectors.	Sergeants.	Constables.	TOTAL.
Inspectors of Railway Cattle Trucks -	—	7	2	—	—	9
Inspectors of Weights and Measures -	1	3	1	1	—	6
Inspectors of Common Lodging-houses -	—	2	1	—	—	3
Inspectors under Food and Drugs Act -	1	7	2	—	—	10
Inspectors under Explosives Act -	1	7	2	—	—	10
Inspectors under Petroleum Act - -	1	7	2	—	—	10
Inspectors under Swine Fever Order (1893)	1	8	7	23	—	39
Inspectors under Fertilisers and Feeding Stuffs Act.	1	7	2	—	—	10

There is an increase of one in the number of beerhouses ; 72 more persons were proceeded against for drunkenness than in 1900, and 80 more were convicted.

One hundred and forty-eight members of the force hold certificates from the St. John Ambulance Association.

The municipal borough of Loughborough is watched by the county police.

The Inspector visited 10 stations, and found them clean and in good order.

The books and returns were well kept, and the management, numbers, and discipline of the force have been efficiently maintained.

No. 1.
Eastern Counties,
Midland,
and North Wales
District.

COUNTY BOROUGH OF LEICESTER.

Force - - - - - - - 215.

Area in acres - - - - 8,586	Acres to each constable - - - 40
Population in 1891 - - - 174,624	Population to ditto, as per census 1891 812

RANKS.	Chief Officer.	Yearly Pay in £ and Shillings.										
		4 Superintendents.						6 Inspectors.				
		Deputy Chief Officer.	Chief Clerk.	1st Class.	2nd Class.	3rd Class.	4th Class.	1st Class.	2nd Class.	3rd Class.	4th Class.	5th Class.
Number of each Rank and Class	1	-	1	1	1	1	-	2	1	1	1	-
Rates of Pay of each ditto - .	£ 600	-	£ s. 175 10	£ s. 182 0	£ s. 175 10	£ s. 186 0	-	£ 130	£ s. 134 16	£ s. 123 4	£ s. 119 12	-

RANKS.	Weekly Pay in Shillings and Pence.													
	33 Sergeants.				172 Constables.									
	1st Class.	2nd Class.	3rd Class.	4th Class.	1st Class.								2nd Class.	3rd Class.	4th Class.
Number of each Rank and Class -	5	4	11	12	1	13	16	15	23	22	20	9	-	29	24
Rates of Pay of each ditto - .	s. 40	s. 38	s. 36	s. 34	s. 34	s. 33	s. 32	s. 31	s. 30	s. 29	s. 28	s. 27	s. 26	s. 25	s. 24

Inspected on 11th March, when there were vacancies for two constables.

The authorised establishment of the force, which has been augmented by two sergeants and seven constables during the year, is one chief officer, four superintendents, one of whom is chief clerk, six inspectors, 32 sergeants, and 172 constables.

The chief officer acts as billet master.

Nine members of the force belonging to the Army Reserve were recalled to the colours, four of whom were still with their regiments on 29th September, two re-engaged in the Army, and three have rejoined the force.

The number of beerhouses has been reduced by two, and of persons proceeded against for drunkenness by 64, and 61 fewer were convicted than in 1900.

One hundred and sixty-nine members of the force hold certificates from the St. John Ambulance Association.

The Inspector visited all the sub-stations, of which there are six, and found the cells and offices there, as well as at the town hall, clean and in good order.

The books and returns were well kept, and the management, numbers, and discipline of the force have been efficiently maintained.

COUNTY OF LINCOLN.

Force - - - - - - - - - 315.*

Area in acres - - - 1,680,981 | Acres to each constable - - - 5,370
Population in 1891 - - 338,808 | Population to ditto, as per census 1891 1,082

RANKS.	Chief Constabl	22 Superintendents.								11 Inspectors.		
		Deputy Chief Constable.	Chief Clerk.	1st Class.	2nd Class.	3rd Class.	4th Class.	5th Class.	6th Class.	1st Class.	2nd Class.	3rd Class.
Number of each Rank and Class -	1	1	1	1	7	2	5	4	1	2	5	4
Rates of Pay of each ditto -	£ 700	£ 185	£ 125	£ 180	£ 160	£ 145	£ 135	£ 120	£ 110	£ 110	£ 100	£ 90

Yearly Pay in £ and Shillings.

Weekly Pay in Shillings and Pence.

RANKS.	38 Sergeants.					243 Constables.						
	1st Class.	2nd Class.	3rd Class.	4th Class.	Wanting to complete.	Merit Class.	1st Class.	2nd Class.	3rd Class.	4th Class.	5th Class.	Wanting to complete.
Number of each Rank and Class -	18	13	6	–	2	75	23	48	67	28	–	–	4
Rates of Pay of each ditto -	s. 33	s. 31	s. 30	–	–	s. d. 29	s. d. 28 3	s. d. 27 6	s. 26	s. 24	–	–	–

* Exclusive of three sergeants and three constables appointed under 3 & 4 Vict. c. 88. s. 19.

Inspected in July, when there were vacancies for one sergeant and one constable.

The authorised establishment of the force is one chief constable, 22 superintendents, one of whom is deputy chief constable and another chief clerk, 11 inspectors, 38 sergeants, and 241 constables. There are also three sergeants and three constables appointed under 3 & 4 Vict. c 88. s. 19.

The force is distributed as follows :—

	Super-intendents.	Inspectors.	Sergeants.	Constables.	TOTAL.
For Lindsey District -	14	4	20	139	177
For Kesteven District -	5	3	11	58	77
For Holland District -	2	4	4	40	50

The chief constable is chief inspector of weights and measures for the Lindsey district ; 21 superintendents are inspectors under the Sale of Food and Drugs Acts, and 16 under Explosives and Petroleum Acts. The two superintendents, three inspectors, and one sergeant in the Holland district are inspectors under the Contagious Diseases (Animals) Act.

Two full licenses have been substituted for two " off " licenses, and 139 fewer persons were proceeded against for drunkenness, and 128 fewer convicted than in 1900.

Ninety-five members of the force hold certificates from the St. John Ambulance Association.

The Inspector visited 21 stations, and found them clean and in good order.

The books and returns were well kept, and the management, numbers, and discipline of the force have been efficiently maintained.

No. 1.
Eastern Counties,
Midland,
and North Wales
District.

BOROUGH OF BOSTON.

Force - - - - - - - - - - 15.

Area in acres - - - - 2,765	Acres to each constable - - 184
Population in 1891 - - - 14,593	Population to ditto, as per census 1891 973

RANKS.	Chief Officer.	Superintendents.						Inspectors.				
		Deputy Chief Officer.	Chief Clerk.	1st Class.	2nd Class.	3rd Class.	4th Class.	1st Class.	2nd Class.	3rd Class.	4th Class.	5th Class.
Number of each Rank and Class -	1	-	-	-	-	-	-	-	-	-	-	-
Rates of Pay of each ditto -	£ 180	-	-	-	-	-	-	-	-	-	-	-

Yearly Pay in £ and Shillings.

Weekly Pay in Shillings and Pence.

RANKS.	3 Sergeants.						11 Constables.							
	Merit Class.	1st Class.	2nd Class.	3rd Class.	4th Class.	5th Class.	1st Class.				2nd Class.	3rd Class.	4th Class.	5th Class.
Number of each Rank and Class -	2	-	-	-	1	-	-	2	5	3	-	1	-	-
Rates of Pay of each ditto -	s. 33	s. 32	s. d. 31 7	s. 31	s. 30	s. 29	s. d. 29 6	s. 28	s. 27	s. 26	s. 25	s. 24	s. 23	-

Inspected on 15th July, when the force was complete.

The authorised establishment of the force is one chief officer, three sergeants, and 11 constables.

The chief officer is inspector of common lodging-houses and assistant relieving officer. He is also inspector under the Shop Hours, Petroleum, Explosives, and Contagious Diseases (Animals) Acts. A sergeant is coroner's officer.

The number of fully licensed houses is the same as in 1900, but there is a decrease of one " off " license and an increase of two refreshment houses with wine licenses. There is an increase of five in the number of persons proceeded against for drunkenness, but a decrease of nine in the number convicted, viz., 73 dismissals as against 95 convictions. The proportion of the former is unusually large in the borough.

Thirteen members of the force hold certificates from the St. John Ambulance Association.

The cells and police offices are wholly inadequate for the requirements of the force, and are insanitary, and as no apparent progress is being made to remedy these defects, the Inspector does not consider this force efficiently managed.

The books and returns were well kept.

BOROUGH OF GRANTHAM.

Force - - - - - - - - - 16.

| Area in acres | - | - | - | 1,833 | Acres to each constable | - | - | 115 |
| Population in 1891 | - | - | - | 16,746 | Population to ditto, as per census 1891 | | | 1,047 |

Yearly Pay in £ and Shillings.

RANKS.	Chief Officer.	Superintendents.						Inspectors.				
		Deputy Chief Officer.	Chief Clerk.	1st Class.	2nd Class.	3rd Class.	4th Class.	1st Class.	2nd Class.	3rd Class.	4th Class.	5th Class.
Number of each Rank and Class	1	-	-	-	-	-	-	-	-	-	-	-
Rates of Pay of each ditto -	£ 170	-	-	-	-	-	-	-	-	-	-	-

Weekly Pay in Shillings and Pence.

RANKS.	3 Sergeants.					12 Constables.				2nd Class.	3rd Class.
	1st Class.	2nd Class.	3rd Class.	4th Class.	5th Class.	1st Class.					
Number of each Rank and Class	1	-	1	1	-	5	1	1	1	2	2
Rates of Pay of each ditto -	s. d. 34 7	s. d. 33 6	s. d. 33 4	s. d. 31 2	s. d. 30 0	s. d. 29 0	s. 28	s. d. 27 0	s. d. 25 10	s. d. 24 8	s. d. 23 6

Inspected on 5th July, when the force was complete.

The authorised establishment of the force is one chief officer, three sergeants, and 12 constables.

The salary of the chief officer has been raised from 150l. to 170l. a year.

One member of this force was called up with the Army Reserve, and died while serving with his regiment in South Africa.

The chief officer is inspector under the Weights and Measures, Explosives, Petroleum, and Contagious Diseases (Animals) Acts, and of common lodging-houses; he is also high constable and billet master.

There has been no alteration in the number of licensed houses during the year, but a decrease of one in the number of persons proceeded against for drunkenness, and of one in the number convicted.

Eleven members of this force hold certificates from the St. John Ambulance Association.

The cells and police offices were clean and in good order.

The books and returns were well kept, and the management, numbers, and discipline of the force have been efficiently maintained.

The following new scale of pay has been adopted :—

Chief Constable - 170l. per annum, with 10l. in lieu of uniform.

		£	s.	d.	
Acting Inspector	- - - -	1	14	7	per week.
Sergeants—					
After 8 years	- - - -	1	13	6	,,
,, 5 ,,	- - - -	1	12	4	,,
,, 2 ,,	- - - -	1	11	2	,,
On joining	- - -	1	10	0	..
Constables—					
After 11 years	- - -	1	9	0	,,
,, 8 ,,	- - -	1	8	0	..
,, 5 ,,	- - - -	1	7	0	..
,, 3 ,,	- - -	1	5	10	..
,, 1 ,,	- - -	1	4	8	--
On joining	- - -	1	3	6	..

COUNTY BOROUGH OF GREAT GRIMSBY.

No. 1
Eastern Counties,
Midland,
and North Wales
District.

Force - - - - - - 65.

| Area in acres | - | - 2,832 | Acres to each constable | - | - 44 |
| Population in 1891 | - | - 51,934 | Population to ditto, as per census 1891 | | 799 |

RANKS.	Chief Officer.	1 Superintendent.						2 Inspectors.				
		Deputy Chief Officer.	Chief Clerk.	1st Class.	2nd Class.	3rd Class.	4th Class.	1st Class.	2nd Class.	3rd Class.	4th Class.	5th Class.
Number of each Rank and Class	1	-	1	1	-	-	-	-	-	-	2	-
Rates of Pay of each ditto - -	£ 300	-	£ s. 93 12	£ 156	-	-	-	£ 130	£ s. 124 16	£ s. 119 12	£ s. 114 8	£ s. 109 4

Yearly Pay in £ and Shillings.

RANKS.	12 Sergeants (including Chief Clerk).				49 Constables.									
	1st Class.						2nd Class.	3rd Class.	4th Class.	Merit Class.			1st Class.				2nd Class.	3rd Class.	4th Class.

| Number of each Rank and Class | 2 | 2 | - | 1 | 1 | 5 | - | - | - | 1 | 1 | 2 | - | 2 | 9 | 6 | 5 | 5 | 2 | 10 | 3 | 3 |
| Rates of Pay of each ditto - - | s. 40 | s. 39 | s. 38 | s. 37 | s. 36 | s. 35 | s. 34 | s. 33 | s. 32 | s. 37 | s. 36 | s. 35 | s. 34 | s. 33 | s. 32 | s. 31 | s. 30 | s. 29 | s. 28 | s. 27 | s. 26 | s. 25 | s. 24 |

Weekly Pay in Shillings and Pence.

Inspected on 8th July, when the force was complete.

The authorised establishment of the force is one chief officer, one super-intendent, two inspectors, 12 sergeants, one of whom is clerk, and 49 constables, showing an increase of two constables. On the death of Mr. Fisher, Mr. Stirling, Chief Officer of Police at Newcastle-under-Lyme, was appointed at a salary of 300*l.* a year.

The chief officer acts also as inspector of explosives, and the superintendent is inspector of hackney carriages.

Two members of the force belonging to the Army Reserve rejoined the colours; one was still on active service on 29th September, the other who had been wounded had rejoined the force.

There has been no change in the number of licensed houses, but an increase of 66 in the number of persons proceeded against for drunkenness, and of 65 in the number convicted.

Fifty-three members of this force hold certificates from the St. John Ambulance Association.

The cells and police offices were clean and in good order. The books and returns were well kept, and the management, numbers, and discipline of the force have been efficiently maintained.

The following scale of pay has been adopted :—

Superintendent—

				£	s.	d.	
On appointment	-	-	-	137	16	0	per annum.
After 2 years' service	-	-	-	143	0	0	,,
,, 4 ,, ,,	-	-	-	148	4	0	,,
,, 6 ,, ,,	-	-	-	156	0	0	,,
,, 8 ,, ,,	-	-	-	163	16	0	,,

Inspectors—

				£	s.	d.	
On appointment	-	-	-	109	4	0	,,
After 2 years' service	-	-	-	114	8	0	,,
,, 4 ,, ,,	-	-	-	119	12	0	,,
,, 6 ,, ,,	-	-	-	124	16	0	,,
,, 8 ,, ,,	-	-	-	130	0	0	,,

	£	s.	d.	
Sergeants—				
On appointment - - -	1	14	0	per week.
After 1 year's service - - -	1	15	0	,,
,, 2 years' ,, - - -	1	16	0	..
.. 4 ,, - - -	1	17	0	..
.. 6 .. .. - - -	1	18	0	..
, 8 .. .. - - -	1	19	0	..
,, 10 .. .. - - -	2	0	0	..
Constables—				
On appointment - - - -	1	4	0	..
After 6 months' service - .. -	1	5	0	..
,, 1 year's service - - -	1	6	0	,,
,, 2 years' ,, - - -	1	7	0	..
. 4 ,, .. - - -	1	8	0	..
.. 6 .. .. - - -	1	9	0	,,
,, 8 .. .. - - -	1	10	0	..
,, 10 .. .. - - -	1	11	0	..
,, 12 .. .. - - -	1	12	0	..
,, 14 .. .. - - -	1	13	0	,,

CITY AND COUNTY BOROUGH OF LINCOLN.

Force - - - - - - - 49.

Area in acres - - 3,747	Acres to each constable - - 76
Population in 1891 - - 41,491	Population to ditto, as per census 1891 847

Yearly Pay in £ and Shillings.

RANKS.	Chief Officer.	Superintendents.				2 Inspectors.					
		Deputy Chief Officer.	Chief Officer.	1st Class.	2nd Class.	3rd Class.	1st Class.	2nd Class.	3rd Class.	4th Class.	5th Class.	6th Class.
Number of each Rank and Class	1	-	-	-	-	-	1	1	-	-	-	-
Rates of Pay of each ditto - -	£ 360	-	-	-	-	-	£ s. 123 10	£ s. 110 10	£ 104	-	-	-

Weekly Pay in Shillings and Pence.

RANKS.	8 Sergeants.						38 Constables.								
	1st Class.	2nd Class.				3rd Class.	Merit Class.	1st Class.						2nd Class.	3rd Class.
Number of each Rank and Class	1	3	1	1	1	1	1	11	5	4	4	4	9	-	-
Rates of Pay of each ditto - -	s. 39	s. 38	s. 37	s. d. 35 7	s. d. 35 0	s. 34	s. d. 32 7	s. d. 30 10	s. d. 29 8	s. d. 28 6	s. d. 27 4	s. d. 26 2	s. d. 25 0	s. d. 24 6	s. 24

Inspected on 10th July, when the force was complete.

The authorised establishment of the force is one chief officer, two inspectors, eight sergeants, and 38 constables.

Four members of the force belonging to the Army Reserve were called upon to rejoin their regiments; two of them returned to the police, but resigned shortly after doing so, and the other two were still serving in South Africa on 29th September.

The chief officer is inspector under the Explosives and Canal Boats Acts; also of hackney carriages, assisted by one of the inspectors. A sergeant is inspector of weights and measures, and food and drugs; he is also engineer of the fire brigade, and two constables are assistant engineers.

There is no change in the number of licensed houses, with the exception of three additional refreshment houses. Proceedings against persons for drunkenness increased by nine, and convictions by 18, during the year.

Forty members of the force hold certificates from the St. John Ambulance Association.

The following new scale of pay has been adopted :—

	£	s.	d	
Inspectors—				
1st class - - - -	123	10	0	per annum.
2nd class - - -	110	10	0	,,
Sergeants—				
On appointment - - -	1	14	0	per week.
After 2 years' approved service - -	1	15	0	,,
,, 4 ,, ,, ,, - -	1	16	0	..
,, 6 ,, ,, ,, -	1	17	0	..
,, 9 ,, ,, ,, - -	1	18	0	..
,, 12 ,, ,, ,, - -	1	19	0	..
Constables—				
On appointment - - -	1	4	6	..
After 6 months' approved service -	1	5	0	..
,, 2 years' ,, ,, -	1	6	2	..
,, 4 ,, ,, ,, -	1	7	4	..
,, 6 ,, ,, ,, -	1	8	6	..
,, 9 ,, ,, ,, -	1	9	8	..
,, 12 ,, ,, ,, -	1	10	10	..
,, 15 ,, ,, ,, (with badge at the discretion of the Watch Committee) - -	1	12	0	..

First Merit, open to all ranks, 1d. per day, and badge.

Second Merit, open to all ranks, 1d. per day additional, with badge.

The cells and police offices were clean and in good order.

The books and returns were well kept, and the management, numbers, and discipline of the force have been efficiently maintained.

BOROUGH OF LOUTH.

Force - - - - - 10.

Area in acres	-	- 2,749	Acres to each constable	-	- - 275
Population in 1891	-	- 10,040	Population to ditto, as per census 1891		1,004

		Yearly Pay in £ and Shillings.										
RANKS.	Chief Officer.	Superintendents.						Inspectors.				
		Deputy Chief Officer.	Chief Clerk.	1st Class.	2nd Class.	3rd Class.	4th Class.	1st Class.	2nd Class.	3rd Class.	4th Class.	5th Class.
Number of each } Rank and Class	1	-	-	-	-	-	-	-	-	-	-	-
Rates of Pay of } each ditto - - }	£ 140	-	-	-	-	-	-	-	-	-	-	-

		Weekly Pay in Shillings and Pence.												
RANKS.		2 Sergeants.						7 Constables.						
	Merit Class.	1st Class.	2nd Class.	3rd Class.	4th Class.	5th Class.	Acting Sergeants.	Merit Class.	1st Class.	2nd Class.	3rd Class.	4th Class.	5th Class.	6th Class.
Number of each } Rank and Class	-	-	1	-	1	-	-	4	-	-	2	1	-	-
Rates of Pay of } each ditto - - }	-	s. d. 32 6	s. d. 31 2	s. d. 30 4	s. 29	-	-	s. d. 26 9	s. d. 26 2	s. d. 23 7	s. 24	s. 23	s. 23	-

Inspected on 8th July, when the force was complete.

The authorised establishment of the force is one chief officer, two sergeants, and seven constables. On 1st April, Mr. A. E. Danby, from Barnsley, where he was detective inspector, was appointed chief officer in succession to Mr. Barham, resigned.

The chief officer is inspector of common lodging-houses, and under the Petroleum and Weights and Measures Acts.

There is an increase of one in the number of refreshment houses, but a decrease of 15 persons proceeded against and convicted for drunkenness, compared with 1900.

Eight members of the force hold certificates from the St. John Ambulance Association.

The cells and police offices were clean and in good order.

The books and returns were fairly well kept, and the management, numbers, and discipline of the force have been efficiently maintained.

COUNTY OF NORFOLK.

Force - - - - - 242.*

Area in acres† - - 1,302,882	Acres to each constable - - - 5,384
Population in 1891† - - 318,202	Population to ditto, as per census 1891 1,315

Yearly Pay in £ and Shillings.

RANKS.	Chief Constable.	14 Superintendents.						9 Inspectors.				
		Deputy Chief Constable.	Chief Clerk.	1st Class.	2nd Class.	3rd Class.	4th Class.	1st Class.	2nd Class.	3rd Class.	4th Class.	5th Class.
Number of each Rank and Class }	1	1	1	8	4	-	-	7	2	-	-	-
Rates of Pay of each ditto - -}	£ 600	£ 190	£ 145	£ 145	£ 134	£ 118	-	£ s. 88 8	£ s. 83 4	-	-	-

Weekly Pay in Shillings and Pence.

RANKS.	21 Sergeants.					197 Constables.						
	Merit Class.	1st Class.	2nd Class.	3rd Class.	Acting Sergeants.	Merit Class.	1st Class.			2nd Class.	3rd Class.	4th Class.	Wanting to complete.
Number of each Rank and Class }	-	16	5	-	-	-	48	36	45	23	24	16	5
Rates of Pay of each ditto - -}	-	29	s. d. 27 6	-	-	-	s. 26	s. 25	s. 24	s. 23	s. d. 21 6	s. 20	-

* Exclusive of three constables appointed for the months of July, August, and September.
† The parish of Welney (acreage 1,817, population 668) has been transferred from the Isle of Ely by order, from 30th September 1896, and the parish of Redmere (acreage 1,112, population 44) are similarly transferred to the Isle of Ely at the same time.

Inspected in May, when there were vacancies for three constables.

The authorised establishment of the force is one chief constable, 14 superintendents, one of whom is deputy chief constable and another is chief clerk, nine inspectors, 21 sergeants, and 197 constables. There are also three constables appointed for the months of July, August, and September.

. Extra duties performed by the police :—

NATURE OF DUTY.	Superintendents.	Inspectors.	Sergeants.	Constables.	TOTAL.
Inspector under Food and Drugs Act - -	—	—	—	1	1
Inspectors under Explosives Act -	14	2	—	—	16
Inspectors under Petroleum Act -	14	2	—	—	16
Billet Masters - - - -	6	2	1	—	9
Inspectors under Contagious Diseases (Animals) Act.	The whole force.				

There is an increase of three in the number ʳof public-houses, and of 10 beerhouses. Eight fewer persons were proceeded against for drunkenness than in 1900, and 17 fewer convicted.

No. 1.
Eastern Counties,
Midland,
and North Wales
District.

The cells and police offices were clean and in good order.

The books and returns were well kept, and the management, numbers, and discipline of the force have been efficiently maintained.

A new scale of pay, as under, has been adopted :—

		£	s.	d.	
Inspectors—	On appointment	95	0	0	per annum.
	After 3 years	100	0	0	,,
	,, 6 ,,	105	0	0	..
Sergeants—	On appointment	1	10	11	per week.
	After 3 years	1	13	3	,,
	,, 6 ,,	1	15	0	..
Constables—	On appointment	1	3	4	..
	After 1 year	1	4	6	.
	,, 2 years	1	5	8	..
	3 ,,	1	6	10	..
	,, 5 ,,	1	8	0	..
	,, 10 ..	1	9	2	..
	,, 15 ,,	1	10	4	..

CITY AND COUNTY BOROUGH OF NORWICH.

Force - - - - - - 120.

Area in acres - - - 7,558	Acres to each constable - - 63
Population in 1891 - - 100,970	Population to ditto, as per census 1891 841

RANKS.	Chief Officer.	Superintendent.		4 Inspectors (including Chief Clerk).						
		Deputy Chief Officer.	Chief Clerk.	Chief Inspector.	1st Class.	2nd Class.	3rd Class.	4th Class.	5th Class.	
Number of each Rank and Class -	1	-	1	1	-	1	1	1	1	-
Rates of Pay of each ditto -	£ 350	-	£ s. 110 0	£ s. 141 6	£ 130	£ 126	£ 120	£ 115	£ 110	-

Yearly Pay in £ and Shillings.

RANKS.	18 Sergeants.						97 Constables.							
	Merit Class.	1st Class.	2nd Class.	3rd Class.	4th Class.	5th Class.	1st Class.							
Number of each Rank and Class -	6	-	3	4	5	4	26	17	1	7	12	10	14	10
Rates of Pay of each ditto -	s. 38	s. 37	s. 36	s. 35	s. .34	-	s. 31	s. 30	s. 29	s. 28	s. 27	s. 26	s. 25	s. 24

Weekly Pay in Shillings and Pence.

Inspected on 13th May, when the force was complete.

The authorised establishment of the force is one chief officer, one chief and three other inspectors, one of whom is chief clerk, 18 sergeants, and 97 constables.

Three constables belonging to the Army Reserve were called up to join their regiments, one was still serving with them on 29th September, but the other two had rejoined the force.

The chief officer is inspector of hackney carriages, and petroleum and other explosives, assisted by a sergeant; of street obstructions, and under the Weights and Measures Act; he is also billet master, and the whole force form the fire brigade.

There is a decrease of one in the number of full-licensed houses, but an increase of one in the number of refreshment houses with wine licenses. The number of persons proceeded against for drunkenness, and the number convicted was 50 and 41 respectively in excess of the number in 1900.

Ninety-three members of the force hold certificates from the St. John Ambulance Association.

The cells and police offices were clean and in good order. The importance of providing some sub-stations is, in the Inspector's opinion, a growing one.

The books and returns were well kept, and the management, numbers, and discipline have been efficiently maintained.

The following new scale of pay has been adopted :—

	£	s.	d.	
Chief Inspector - - - -	140	0	0	per annum.
Inspector—				
On appointment - - -	110	0	0	,,
After 2 years - - - -	115	0	0	,,
,, 4 ,, - - -	120	0	0	,,
,, 6 .. - - - -	125	0	0	,,
,, 8 .. - - -	130	0	0	..
Sergeant—				
On appointment - - -	1	14	0	per week.
After 2 years - - -	1	15	0	,,
,, 4 ,, - - -	1	16	0	..
,, 6 .. - - -	1	17	0	..
,, 8 .. - - -	1	18	0	..
Constable—				
On appointment - - -	1	4	0	,,
After 1 year - - -	1	5	0	,,
,, 2 years - - -	1	6	0	..
.. 4 ,, - - -	1	7	0	..
.. 6 .. - - -	1	8	0	..
.. 8 .. - - -	1	9	0	..
.. 10 .. - - -	1	10	0	..
,, 15 .. - - -	1	11	0	..

COUNTY OF NORTHAMPTON.

Force - - - 166.*

Area in acres † - - - 581,697 | Acres to each constable - - 3,504
Population in 1891† - - 203,281 | Population to ditto, as per census 1891 1,225

RANKS.	Chief Constable.	7 Superintendents.								9 Inspectors.			
		Deputy Chief Constable.	Chief Clerk.	1st Class.	2nd Class.	3rd Class.	4th Class.	5th Class.	6th Class.	1st Class.	2nd Class.	3rd Class.	4th Class.
Number of each Rank and Class -	1	1	1	1	–	4	–	–	–	1	7	–	1
Rates of Pay of each ditto -	£ 450	£ 205	£ 135	£ 165	£ 160	£ 155	£ 150	£ 145	£ 135	£ s. 112 16	£ s. 108 18	£ 105	95

RANKS.	19 Sergeants.				130 Constables.								
	1st Class.	2nd Class.	3rd Class.	4th Class.	Merit Class.			1st Class.			2nd Class.	3rd Class.	Wanting to complete.
Number of each Rank and Class -	1	7	6	5	2	4	1	7	–	4	20	30	21	29	10	2
Rates of Pay of each ditto -	s. 35	s. 33	s. 32	s. 30	s. 31	s. d. 30 6	s. 30	s. d. 29 6	s. 29	s. d. 28 6	s. d. 27 6	s. d. 26 6	s. 26	s. 24	s. 22	–

* Exclusive of two constables appointed under 3 & 4 Vict. c. 88, s. 19.

† The parishes of Luddington (acreage 497, population 81), Luton (acreage 345, population 49), and Thurning (acreage 811, population 101) have been transferred from Huntingdonshire by order, from 30th September 1896,¹ and by the same order the parish of Stoneton (acreage 737, population 32) has been transferred to Warwick, and the parish of Winwick (acreage 1,359, population 151) to Huntingdon.

No. 1.
astern Counties,
Midland,
nd North Wales
District.

Inspected in March, when there were vacancies for three constables.

The authorised establishment of the force is one chief constable, seven superintendents, one of whom is deputy chief constable and another is chief clerk, nine inspectors, 19 sergeants, and 130 constables. There are·also two constables appointed under 3 & 4 Vict. c. 88. s. 19.

The whole of the force are appointed inspectors under the Contagious Diseases (Animals) Act, and six superintendents and two inspectors are similarly appointed under the Explosives and Petroleum Acts.

Twelve members of the force belonging to the Army Reserve were called upon to join their regiments, eight of whom were still serving with them on the 29th September, and four had returned and rejoined the police service.

The number of public-houses has been reduced by 15 during the year, of beerhouses by 46, and of refreshment houses with wine licenses by four ; but the number of persons proceeded against for drunkenness and convicted increased by 10.

One hundred and thirty-eight members of the force hold certificates from the St. John Ambulance Association.

The Inspector visited eight stations, and found them clean and in good order. A new station has been provided at Rushden, comprising accommodation for a married inspector, a married sergeant, and three single constables, with three cells and necessary offices. The accommodation at Wellingborough has also been improved.

The books and returns were well kept, and the management, numbers, and discipline of the force have been efficiently maintained.

COUNTY BOROUGH OF NORTHAMPTON.

Force - - - - - - - - 113.

| Area in acres - - - - 3,392 | Acres to each constable - - - 30 |
| Population in 1891 - - 87,021 | Population to ditto, as per census 1891 770 |

Yearly Pay in £ and Shillings.

RANKS.	Chief Officer.	7 Inspectors (including Chief Clerk).									
		Deputy Chief Officer.	Chief Clerk.	Chief Inspector.	1st Class.	2nd Class.	3rd Class.	4th Class.	5th Class.	6th Class.	7th Class.
Number of each Rank and Class -	1	-	1	-	1	1	-	1	-		1
Rates of Pay of each ditto - -	£ 350	-	£ 135	-	£ s. 145 12	£ s. 130 -	£ s. 124 16	£ s. 119 12	£ s. 114 8	£ s. 109 4	£ 104

Weekly Pay in Shillings and Pence.

RANKS.	18 Sergeants.				87 Constables.							
	1st Class.	2nd Class.	3rd Class.	Acting Sergeants.	1st Class.	2nd Class.	3rd Class.	4th Class.	5th Class.	6th Class.	7th Class.	Pro-bationary.
Number of each Rank and Class -	1	3	4	4	1	3	1	1	6	8	6	2	6	7	12	4	10	-	-	34	2
Rates of Pay of each ditto - -	s. 40	s. 38	s. 36	s. 34	s. 33	s. 32	s. 31	s. 30	s. 33	s. 32	s. 31	s. 30	s. 29	s. 28	s. 27	s. 26	s. 25	-	-	s. 23	s. 22

Inspected on 18th March, when there were vacancies for eight constables.

The authorised establishment of the force is one chief officer, seven inspectors, including the chief clerk, 18 sergeants, and 87 constables. The force has been augmented by two inspectors, eight sergeants, and 17 constables, in consequence of the extension of the boundaries of the borough.

The chief officer and an inspector act as inspectors of hackney carriages, the latter also acting as inspector under the Weights and Measures and Explosives Acts. An inspector is coroner's officer and inspector of common lodging-houses; and the chief officer, five inspectors, 17 sergeants, and one constable are inspectors under the Contagious Diseases (Animals) Act.

There is an increase of 15 full and 47 " off " licenses. Eighty-one persons were proceeded against for drunkenness, and 80 convicted in excess of the numbers in 1900, but these increases are accounted for by the enlargement of the area of the borough.

One hundred and one members of the force hold certificates. from the St. John Ambulance Association.

The cells and police offices were clean and in good order.

The books and returns were well kept, and the management, numbers, and discipline of the force have been efficiently maintained.

No. 1.
Eastern Counties,
Midland,
and North Wales
District.

COUNTY OF OXFORD.

Force - - - - 111.*

Area in acres † - - 471,340	Acres to each constable - - - 4 246
Population in 1891† - - 130,985	Population to ditto, as per census 1891 1,180 .

Yearly Pay in £ and Shillings.

RANKS:	Chief Constable	Deputy Chief Constable and Chief Clerk	7 Superintendents					5 Inspectors						
			1st Class.	2nd Class.	3rd Class.	4th Class.	5th Class.	1st Class.	2nd Class.	3rd Class.	4th Class.	5th Class.	6th Class.	7th Class.
Number of each Rank and Class	1	1	1	--	2	3		--	--	3	2	--	--	--
Rates of Pay of each ditto -	£ s. 406 15	£ 290	£ s. 173 5	£ s. 166 15	£ s. 153 15	£ s. 147 5	£ s. 135 5	£ s. 121 16	£ s. 116 16	£ s. 111 16	£ s. 106 16	--	--	--

Weekly Pay in Shillings and Pence.

RANKS.	10 Sergeants.				90 Constables.‡					2nd Class.	3rd Class.	4th Class.
	1st Class.		2nd Class.	3rd Class.	1st Class.							
Number of each Rank and Class	--	--	3	7	--	3	18	37		17	10	5
Rates of Pay of each ditto -	s. d. 33 3	s. d. 31 7	s. d. 30 1	s. d. 28 7	s. d. 28 3	s. d. 27 3	s. d. 26 3	s. d. 25 3		s. d. 24 2	s. 22	s. d. 19 10

* Exclusive of two constables appointed under 3 & 4 Vict. c. 88. s. 19.
† The parish of Stokenchurch (acreage 2,873, population 1,780) was transferred to Buckinghamshire, and the parishes of Kingsey from Buckinghamshire (acreage 2,43, population 190), and part of Mollington from Warwickshire (acreage 683, population 97), were transferred to Oxfordshire by Order of Local Government Board, No. 14 A A, 1895.
‡ Two constables in excess to fill pending retirements.

Inspected in March, when the force was complete.

The authorised strength of the force is one chief constable, seven superintendents, one of whom is deputy chief constable and chief clerk, five inspectors, 10 sergeants, and 88 constables. There are also two constables appointed under 3 & 4 Vict. c. 88. s. 19.

Five constables belonging to the Army Reserve were called up to join their regiments, four of whom were still serving with them on 29th September, and one had rejoined the force.

Extra duties performed by the police :—

NATURE OF DUTY.	Chief Constable.	Super-intendents.	Inspectors.	Sergeants.	TOTAL.
Inspectors under Contagious Diseases (Animals) Act.	1	7	5	9	22
Inspectors under Explosives Act - -	—	7	5	—	12
Inspectors under Food and Drugs Act -	—	7	5	—	12
Inspectors of Common Lodging-houses -	—	5	2	5	12

The number of public-houses and beerhouses has in each case been reduced by one, and there are two refreshment houses with wine licenses fewer than in 1900, but 45 more persons were proceeded against, and 42 more convicted, for drunkenness than in that year.

Thirty members of the force hold certificates from the St. John Ambulance Association.

The Inspector visited 11 stations, and found them clean and in good order.

The books and returns were well kept, and the management, numbers, and discipline of the force have been efficiently maintained.

BOROUGH OF BANBURY.

Force - - - - - - 13.

Area in acres - - - 4,634	Acres to each constable - · - - 356
Population in 1891 - - - 12,768	Population to ditto, as per census 1891 905

Yearly Pay in £ and Shillings.

RANKS.	Chief Officer.	Superintendents.						Inspectors.				
		Deputy Chief Officer.	Chief Clerk.	1st Class.	2nd Class.	3rd Class.	4th Class.	1st Class.	2nd Class.	3rd Class.	4th Class.	5th Class.
Number of each Rank and Class	1	-	-	-	-	-	-	-	-	-	-	-
Rates of Pay of each ditto -	£ 180	-	-	-	-	-	-	-	-	-	-	-

Weekly Pay in Shillings and Pence.

RANKS.	3 Sergeants.					9 Constables.						
	Merit Class.	1st Class.	2nd Class.	3rd Class.	4th Class.	1st Class.					2nd Class.	3rd Class.
Number of each Rank and Class	1	1	1	- ·	-	-	6	-	1	-	2	-	-
Rates of Pay of each ditto -	s. d. 33 8	s. d. 30 4	s. d. 29 3	s. d. 28 7	s. d. 27 5	s. d. 25 1	s. 28	s. d. 26 10	s. d. 25 8	s. d. 24 6	s. d. 23 4	s. d. 22 3	s. 21

Inspected on 30th March, when the force was complete.

The authorised establishment of the force is one chief officer, three sergeants (an augmentation of one), and nine constables.

One member of this force belonging to the Army Reserve was called up to join his regiment, and died of enteric fever at Bloemfontein.

The chief officer is appointed inspector under the Weights and Measures, Explosives, Petroleum, Contagious Diseases (Animals), and Food and Drugs Acts ; also of public lamps.

A full licensed house has been substituted for an " off" license, and proceedings for drunkenness show an increase of 25, with 25 more convictions, as against 1900.

Twelve members of the force hold certificates from the St. John Ambulance Association.

The cells and police offices were clean and in good order.

The books and returns were well kept, and the management, numbers, and discipline of the force have been efficiently maintained.

CITY AND COUNTY BOROUGH OF OXFORD.

Force - - - - - - - - 62.*

| Areas in acres - - - 4,676 | Acres to each constable - - - 75 |
| Population in 1891 - - - 45,742 | Population to ditto, as per census 1891 738 |

RANKS.	Chief Officer.	Superintendents.						4 Inspectors (including Chief Clerk).				
		Deputy Chief Officer.	Chief Clerk.	1st Class.	2nd Class.	3rd Class.	4th Class.	1st Class.	2nd Class.	3rd Class.	4th Class.	5th Class.
Number of each Rank and Class	1	-	1	-	-	-	-	1	1	1	-	-
Rates of Pay of each ditto -	£ 300	-	£ s. 109 4	-	-	-	-	£ s. 119 12	£ s. 114 8	£ s. 111 16	£ s. 109 4	£. 88

Yearly Pay in £ and Shillings.

Weekly Pay in Shillings and Pence.

RANKS.	9 Sergeants.					48 Constables.						
	1st Class.				2nd Class.	Merit Class.		1st Class.			2nd Class.	3rd Class.
Number of each Rank and Class	1	2	3	1	1	14	3	9	7	5	2	7	1
Rates of Pay of each ditto -	s. 37	s. 36	s. 34	s. 33	s. 32	s. 30	s. 29	s. 28	s. 27	s. 26	s. 25	s. 24	s. d. 22 6

* Exclusive of two constables appointed at private post.

Inspected on 29th March, when the force was complete.

The authorised establishment of the force is one chief officer, four inspectors, including chief clerk, nine sergeants (one of this rank having been substituted for a constable during the year), and 48 constables. There are also two constables appointed at private cost.

One member of this force belonging to the Army Reserve was called up to rejoin the colours, and was still serving with his regiment on 29th September.

The chief officer and a sergeant are appointed inspectors under the Explosives and Petroleum Acts, and an inspector and a sergeant are inspectors of weights and measures.

There is a decrease of one public-house, but 16 more persons were proceeded against for, and convicted of, drunkenness than 1900.

Fifty-seven members of the force hold certificates from the St. John Ambulance Association.

The cells and police offices were clean and in good order.

The books and returns were well kept, and the management, numbers, and discipline of the force have been efficiently maintained.

LIBERTY OF PETERBOROUGH.

Force - - - - - - - 10.*

Area in acres - - - 51,587	Acres to each constable - - - 5,158
Population in 1891 - - 10,078	Population to ditto, as per census, 1891 1,007

RANKS.	Chief Constable.†	1 Superintendent.						Inspectors.				
		Deputy Chief Constable.	Chief Clerk.†	1st Class.	2nd Class.	3rd Class.	4th Class.	1st Class.	2nd Class.	3rd Class.	4th Class.	5th Class.
Number of each Rank and Class	1	-	1	1	-	-	-	-	-	-	-	-
Rates of Pay of each ditto -	£ 50	-	£ 10	£ 150		-	-	-	-	-	-	-

Yearly Pay in £ and Shillings.

RANKS.	1 Sergeant.						8 Constables.						
	Merit Class.	1st Class.	2nd Class.	3rd Class.	4th Class.	5th Class.	Merit Class.	1st Class.	2nd Class.	3rd Class.	4th Class.	5th Class.	6th Class.
Number of each Rank and Class	-	1	-	-	-	-	1	1	3	4	-	-	-
Rates of Pay of each ditto -	-	s. 33	-	-	-	-	s. d. 29 6	s. d. 27 6	s. d. 26 6	s. 26	-	-	-

Weekly Pay in Shillings and Pence.

* Exclusive of chief constable and chief clerk.   † Same officers as for the county of Northampton.

Inspected in March, when the force was complete.

The authorised establishment of the force, which is under the chief constable of Northamptonshire, and under the same conditions of service, pay, and pension as that force, is one superintendent, one sergeant, and eight constables.

There has been a reduction of three in the number of beerhouses during the year, a decrease of 15 in the number of persons proceeded against, and of 14 in the number convicted, for drunkenness as compared with 1900.

All the members of the force hold certificates from the St. John Ambulance Association.

The cells and police offices were clean and in good order.

The books and returns were well kept, and the management, numbers, and discipline of the force have been efficiently maintained.

CITY OF PETERBOROUGH.

Force - - - - - - 30.

Area in acres - - - 1,884	Acres to each constable - - - 62
Population in 1891 - - 25,171	Population to ditto, as per census, 1891 839

RANKS.	Chief Officer.	Superintendents.						1 Inspector.				
		Deputy Chief Officer.	Chief Clerk.	1st Class.	2nd Class.	3rd Class.	4th Class.	1st Class.	2nd Class.	3rd Class.	4th Class.	5th Class.
Number of each Rank and Class }	1	-	-	-	-	-	-	1	-	-	-	-
Rates of Pay of each ditto - }	£ 300	-	-	-	-	-	-	£ s. 119 12	£ s. 109 4	-	-	-

Yearly Pay in £ and Shillings.

RANKS.	5 Sergeants.						23 Constables.							
	Merit Class.	1st Class.	2nd Class.	3rd Class.	4th Class.	5th Class.	Merit Class.	1st Class.	2nd Class.	3rd Class.	4th Class.	5th Class.	6th Class.	Wanting to complete.
Number of each Rank and Class }	-	4	1	-	-	-	-	5	2	4	5	4	2	1
Rates of Pay of each ditto - }	-	s. 28	s. d. 25 6	-	-	-	s. d. 33 6	s. d. 31 6	s. d. 30 6	s. d. 29 6	s. d. 28 6	s. 27	s. 25	-

Weekly Pay in Shillings and Pence.

Inspected on 16th March, when the force was complete.

The authorised establishment of the force is one chief officer, one inspector, five sergeants, and 23 constables.

The chief officer acts as inspector of weights and measures, of food and drugs, of explosives, and of petroleum. The five sergeants are inspectors of common lodging-houses.

The number of licensed houses is the same as in 1900; with a decrease of 22 in the number of persons proceeded against for drunkenness, and of 23 in the number convicted.

Twenty-five members of the force hold certificates from the St. John Ambulance Association.

The cells and police offices were clean and in good order.

The books and returns were well kept, and the management, numbers, and discipline of the force have been efficiently maintained.

No. 1.
Eastern Counties,
Midland,
and North Wales
District.

COUNTY OF RUTLAND.

Force - - - - - 15.

Area in acres - - - 97,273 | Acres to each constable - - - 6,485
Population in 1891 - - 20,659 | Population to ditto, as per census 1891 1,377

RANKS.	Chief Constable	1 Superintendent.						1 Inspector.				
		Deputy Chief Constable.	Chief Clerk.	1st Class.	2nd Class.	3rd Class.	4th Class.	1st Class.	2nd Class.	3rd Class.	4th Class.	5th Class.
Number of each Rank and Class	1	1	-	-	-	-	-	1	-	-	-	-
Rates of Pay of each ditto -	£ 250	£ 105	-	-	-	-	-	£ 106	-	-	-	-

Yearly Pay in £ and Shillings.

RANKS.	1 Sergeant.						11 Constables.		
	Merit Class.	1st Class.	2nd Class.	3rd Class.	4th Class.	5th Class.	1st Class.	2nd Class.	3rd Class.
Number of each Rank and Class	-	-	1	-	-	-	6　1　1	2	1
Rates of Pay of each ditto -	-	s. d. 33 10	s. d. 32 8	s. d. 30 4	s. d. 29 2	s. 28	s. d. 29 2　28 0　26 10	s. d. 24 6	s. d. 22 4

Weekly Pay in Shillings and Pence.

Inspected on 15th March, when the force was complete.

The authorised establishment of the force is one chief constable, one superintendent and deputy chief constable, one inspector, one sergeant, and 11 constables.

The chief constable, superintendent, inspector, and sergeant are inspectors under the Contagious Diseases (Animals) and (excepting the sergeant) Adulteration Acts; and the chief constable is inspector under the Explosives Acts.

One constable was called up to join the colours of his regiment in 1899, and was still serving with it on 29th September last.

There is no alteration in the number of licensed houses, but a decrease of three and four persons respectively proceeded against and convicted for drunkenness, as compared with 1900.

Nine members of the force hold certificates from the St. John Ambulance Association.

The cells and police offices at Oakham and Uppingham were clean and in good order.

The books and returns were well kept, and the management, numbers, and discipline of the force have been efficiently maintained.

A new scale of pay, as below, has been adopted :—

```
                                          £   s.  d.
Constables—
   On appointment -     -      -      -   1   3   4   per week.
   Second class   -     -      -      -   1   4   6      „
   First class    -     -      -      -   1   5   8      „
   After 2 years in first class -   -  -  1   6  10      „
      „  5   „        „        -      -   1   8   0      „
      „  8   „        „        -      -   1   9   2      ..
Sergeants—
   On appointment-      -      -      -   1  11   6      ..
   After 3 years  -     -   -   -     -   1  12   8      ..
      „  6   „     -    -      -      -   1  13  10      „
Inspectors—
   On appointment -     -      -      - 100   0   0   per annum.
   After 5 years  -     -      -      - 105   0   0      „
      „ 10   „     -    -      -      - 110   0   0      „
```

The constable acting as clerk receives 4d. per diem in addition to the ordinary scale of pay.

COUNTY OF SHROPSHIRE.

Force - - - - - 165.*

Area in acres† - - - 858,276 | Acres to each constable - - - 5,201
Population in 1891† - - 209,860 | Population to ditto, as per census 1891 1,272

RANKS.	Chief Constable.	8 Superintendents.				4 Inspectors (including Chief Clerk).				
		Deputy Chief Constable.	1st Class.	2nd Class.	3rd Class.	1st Class.	2nd Class.	3rd Class.	4th Class.	5th Class.
Number of each Rank and Class	1	1	1	1	5	—	4	—	—	—
Rates of Pay of each ditto	£ 400	£ s. 177 5	£ s. 180 11	£ s. 141 8	£ s. 130 15	£ s. 100 6	£ s. 95 16	—	—	—

Weekly Pay in Shillings and Pence.

RANKS.	20 Sergeants.§			132 Constables.					
	1st Class.		2nd Class.	1st Class.			2nd Class.	3rd Class.	Wanting to complete.
Number of each Rank and Class	5	6	1	8	26‡	22‡	21‡	5	12	31	9	6
Rates of Pay of each ditto	s. 35	s. d. 33 3	s. d. 31 6	s. d. 29 9	s. d. 28 0	s. d. 26 10	s. d. 25 8	s. d. 25 1	s. d. 24 6	s. d. 23 4	s. d. 23 2	—

* Exclusive of eight constables appointed under 3 & 4 Vict. c. 88. s. 19.
† The parishes of Ludford (population 94, acreage 611) from Herefordshire, of Sheriffhales (population 525, acreage 2,907) from Staffordshire, and of Tittenley (population 34, acreage 580) from Cheshire, were transferred to Shropshire by Order of Local Government Board, which came into operation on 30th September 1895, and on the same date were transferred from Shropshire the parishes of Bobbington (population 22, acreage 491) to Staffordshire, of Dowles (population 91, acreage 711) to Worcestershire, and of Leintwardine (population 48, acreage 611) to Herefordshire.
‡ Seven constables at these rates receive 2d. a day "merit" pay in addition.
§ One sergeant in excess, there being a vacancy in the rank of superintendent.

Inspected in September, when there were vacancies for eight constables.

The authorised strength of the force is one chief constable, eight superintendents, one of whom is deputy chief constable and another is chief clerk, though an inspector is acting as such at present, four inspectors, 20 sergeants, and 132 constables. There are also eight constables appointed under 3 & 4 Vict. c. 88. s. 19.

Six constables belonging to the Army Reserve were called up to join the colours, of whom one had rejoined the force on 29th September.

Extra duties performed by the police:—

NATURE OF DUTY.	Chief Constable.	Super-intendents.	Inspectors.	Sergeants.	Constables.	TOTAL.
Inspectors under Contagious Diseases (Animals) Act.	1	8	4	20	91	124
Inspectors under Explosives Act -	—	7	3	17	4	31
Inspector under Lighting Act -	—	—	—	1	—	1
Inspector under Chimney Sweepers Act -	1	—	—	—	—	1
Inspectors of Common Lodging-houses -	—	—	—	4	—	4
Assistant Relieving Officers -	—	—	2	2	—	4

There is a decrease of three in the number of public-houses, and of three refreshment houses, as compared with 1900. One hundred and seventy-nine more persons were proceeded against for drunkenness, 176 more convicted, than in 1900.

One hundred and fifty-two members of the force hold certificates from the St. John Ambulance Association.

The Inspector visited 14 stations, and found the cells and police offices were clean and in good. A charge office has been provided at the station at Newport, and an additional bedroom for the resident officer.

No. 1.
Eastern Counties,
Midland,
and North Wales
District.

The books and returns are well kept, and the management, numbers, and discipline of the force have been efficiently maintained.

The following new scale of pay has been adopted :—

RANK.	PERIOD.	PAY.		REMARKS.
		Per Day.	Per Annum.	
		s. *d.*	£ *s.* *d.*	
Police constable, 3rd Class -	On appointment	3 2	—	3rd class constables
„ „ 2nd „ -	„	3 4	—	are promoted to 2nd
„ „ 1st „ -	„	3 6	—	class on passing as
„ „ „ „ -	After 3 years -	3 8	—	efficient.
„ „ „ „ -	„ 6 „ -	3 10	—	
„ „ „ „ -	„ 9 „ -	4 0	—	
Sergeants, 2nd Class -	On appointment	4 3	—	
„ „ „ -	After 3 years -	4 6	—	Merit badge, sergeants
„ 1st „ -	On appointment	4 9	—	and constables, 2d.
„ „ -	After 3 years -	5 0	—	per day additional.
Inspectors - - -	On appointment	—	95 16 3	Boot money for all
„ - -	After 5 years -	—	100 7 6	ranks 6d. per week.
Superintendents - -	On appointment	—	130 15 10	
„ - - -	After 5 years -	—	135 7 1	
„ - -	„ 9 „ -	—	141 8 9	Allowances are given
„ - - -	„ 12 „ -	—	146 0 0	towards house rent.
„ - -	„ 15 „ -	—	150 11 3	
Chief Superintendent - -	On appointment	—	167 5 10	
„ „ as D.C.C.	„	—	10 0 0	
Chief Clerk - - -	Special rate per annum in addition to pay of rank.			

BOROUGH OF SHREWSBURY.

Force - - - - - - 37.

Area in acres - - - - 3,525 | Acres to each constable - - - 95
Population in 1891 - - - 26,967 | Population to ditto, as per census 1891 729

RANKS.	Chief Officer.	Superintendents.						2 Inspectors (including Chief Clerk).				
		Deputy Chief Officer.	Chief Clerk.	1st Class.	2nd Class.	3rd Class.	4th Class.	1st Class.	2nd Class.	3rd Class.	4th Class.	5th Class.
Number of each Rank and Class	1	-	1	-	-	-	-	1	-	-	-	-
Rates of Pay of each ditto - -	£ 270	-	£ 120	-	-	-	-	£ 100	-	-	-	-

Yearly Pay in £ and Shillings.

RANKS.	4 Sergeants.						30 Constables.					
	1st Class.	2nd Class.	3rd Class.	4th Class.	5th Class.	6th Class.	Merit Class.	1st Class.	2nd Class.	3rd Class.	4th Class.	5th Class.
Number of each Rank and Class	2	2	-	-	-	-	-	21	1	8	-	-
Rates of Pay of each ditto - -	*s. d.* 33 11	*s. d.* 33 9	*s. d.* 31 7	-	-	-	-	*s.* 29	*s. d.* 28 1	*s. d.* 25 9	*s. d.* 23 8	-

Weekly Pay in Shillings and Pence.

Inspected on 13th April, when the force was complete.

The authorised establishment of the force is one chief officer, two inspectors, one of whom is chief clerk, four sergeants, and 30 constables.

The chief officer, the two inspectors, four sergeants, and two constables are appointed inspectors under the Contagious Diseases (Animals) Act. The chief officer and an inspector are inspectors of common lodging-houses, explosives, and petroleum, and the inspector is coroner's officer and inspector of hackney carriages.

There is one refreshment house with wine license less than in 1900. Thirty-one fewer persons were proceeded against for drunkenness, and 21 fewer convicted than in that year.

All the members of the force hold certificates from the St. John Ambulance Association.

The cells and police offices were clean and in good order.

The books and returns were well kept, and the management, numbers, and discipline of the force have been efficiently maintained.

The pay of the chief officer has been raised from 250*l.* to 270*l.* a year, and the following new scale has been adopted :—

	£.	s.	d.	
Chief Inspector - - - -	120	0	0	per annum.
Inspector - - - -	100	0	0	,,
Sergeants—				
On appointment - - -	1	11	7	per week.
After 1 year's service - - -	1	12	9	,,
,, 2 years' ,, - - -	1	13	11	..
Constables—				
On appointment- - - -	1	3	5	..
After 1 year's service - - -	1	5	9	..
,, 2 years' ,, - - -	1	8	1	..
,, 4 ,, ,, - - -	1	9	0	,,

Good conduct badges, at the rate of 6*d.* per week per badge, are granted for each five years' service clear of report, in addition to the above.

COUNTY OF STAFFORD.

Force - - - 690.*

| Area in acres† | - | - 731,542 | Acres to each constable | - | - 1,060 |
| Population in 1891† | | - 858,391 | Population to ditto, as per census 1891 | | 1,244 |

Yearly Pay in £ and Shillings.

RANKS.	Chief Constable.	18 Superintendents.										22 Inspectors.			
		Deputy Chief Constable.	Chief Clerk.	Chief Superintendent.		1st Class.			2nd Class.	3rd Class.	Wanting to complete.	1st Class.‡		2nd Class.	3rd Class.
Number of each Rank and Class	1	1	1	2	-	-	3	1	3	2	2	1	-	2	-	2	4	6	3	5
Rates of pay of each ditto -	£ 800	£ 315	£ 315	£ 265	£ 275	£ 265	£245	£ 225	£ 205	£ 190	£ 175	£ 160	£ 145	-	£ 135	£ 127 10	£ 120	£ 115	£ 110	£ 105

Weekly Pay in Shillings and Pence.

RANKS.	82 Sergeants.				567 Constables.								
	1st Class.	2nd Class.	3rd Class.	Merit Class.	1st Class.						2nd Class.	3rd Class.	Wanting to complete.
Number of each Rank and Class	13½ 2	34	11	11½	11	17	13	70	86	2	35	51	51	55 66	61	74	16
Rates of Pay of each ditto -	s. d. 39 8	s. d. 38 6	s. d. 37 6	s. d. 36 9	s. d. 36 2	s. d. 35 7	s. 35	s. d. 34 5	s. d. 33 8	s. d. 31 6	s. d. 30 11	s. d. 30 4	s. d. 29 9	s. d 29 2 s. d 28 7	s. 28	s. d. 26 3	s. d. 25 1	-

* Exclusive of one sergeant and 15 constables appointed under 3 & 4 Vict. c. 88. s. 19.
† Parts of the parishes of Bobbington from Salop (acreage 491, population 22), of Croxall from Derbyshire (acreage 1,586, population 210), and of Drayton Basset from Warwickshire (acreage four, population nil), were transferred to Staffordshire by Order of Local Government Board from 30th September 1895; and part of Sherifhales (acreage 2,907, population 822) was similarly transferred from Staffordshire to Shropshire on the same date.
‡ One in excess.
§ All the sergeants at 39s. 7d. and at 37s. 6d. and one at 36s. 2d. are in receipt of merit pay at 1s. 7d. a week; and two of the first receive 4s. a week, and one 2s. a week in addition as long service pay.

F

No. 1.
Eastern Counties,
Midland,
and North Wales
District

Inspected in April, when there were 30 vacancies.
The authorised establishment of the force is one chief constable, 18 superintendents, one of whom is deputy chief constable and another is chief clerk, 22 inspectors, 82 sergeants, and 567 constables. There are also a sergeant and 15 constables appointed under 3 & 4 Vict. c. 88. s. 19.
Extra duties performed by the police :—

NATURE OF DUTY.	Chief Constable.	Super-intendents.	Inspectors.	Sergeants.	Constables.	TOTAL.
Inspectors under Explosives Act - -	—	1	15	43	—	59
Inspectors of Common Lodging-houses -	—	5	2	3	—	10
Inspectors of Hackney Carriages - -	—	2	2	1	—	5
Inspectors under Petroleum Act - -	—	—	1	1	—	2
Assistant Relieving Officers - -	—	6	4	3	1	14
Relieving Officer for a Mendicity Society	—	—	—	—	1	1
Superintendent of a Recreation Ground -	—	1	—	—	—	1
Assistant Inspector of Canal Boats -	—	—	1	—	—	1

Twenty-eight constables belonging to the Army Reserve were called up to join, 17 of whom were still serving with their regiments on 29th September, seven had rejoined the police in good health, one died in South Africa, two joined the police there, and one resigned from the force.
The whole of the force carry out the provisions of the Diseases of Animals Acts in the administrative county, and in the borough of Stoke-upon-Trent ; two sergeants performing the duty in each of the boroughs of West Bromwich and Wednesbury.
The number of public-houses is the same as in 1900, but that of beerhouses has been increased by eight during the year ; refreshment houses have increased by 10, but the number of persons proceeded against for drunkenness is 116, and the number of convictions 166, less than in that year.
Four hundred and seventy-two members of the force hold certificates from the St. John Ambulance Association.
The county boroughs of Burton-upon-Trent, West Bromwich, and the municipal boroughs of Burslem, Longton, Smethwick, Stafford, Stoke-upon-Trent, and Wednesbury, are watched by the county police.
The Inspector visited 43 stations, and found them clean and in good order. A new station has been built at Darlaston, comprising charge room and offices, and accommodation for eight single constables. A dwelling-house for a married inspector is also attached to the station.
The books and returns were well kept, and the management, numbers, and discipline of the force have been efficiently maintained.
The following new scale of pay has been adopted :—

Constables—
	£	s.	d.
3rd class, on appointment - -	1	5	1 per week.
2nd class, after at least 12 months in 3rd class - -	1	6	3 ..
1st class, after at least 12 months in 2nd class - - -	1	8	0 ..
1st class, after 2 years in 1st class -	1	8	7 ..
„ „ 4 „ „ „ -	1	9	2 ..
„ „ 6 „ „ „ -	1	9	9 ..
„ „ 8 „ „ „ -	1	10	4 ..
„ „ 10 „ „ „ -	1	11	6 ..
Merit class, extra, to not more than 15 per cent. of the number of constables - - -	0	1	2 ..

Sergeants—
On appointment - - -	1	14	5 ..
After 2 years in rank - -	1	15	0 ..
„ 4 „ „ „ - -	1	15	7 ..
„ 6 „ „ „ - -	1	16	2 ..
„ 8 „ „ „ - -	1	16	9 ..
„ 10 „ „ „ - -	1	18	6 ..
Merit class, extra, to not more than 20 per cent. of rank - -	0	1	2 ..

Inspectors—		£	s.	d.	
On appointment	- - -	105	0	0	per annum.
After 2 years in rank	- -	110	0	0	,,
,, 4 ,, ,, ,,	- -	115	0	0	,,
,, 6 ,, ,, ,,		120	0	0	,,
,, 8 ,, ,, ,,	- -	127	10	0	,,
,, 10 ,, ,, ,,		135	0	0	,,
Acting Superintendent	- -	145	0	0	,,
Superintendents—					
On Appointment	- -	160	0	0	,,
After 2 years in rank	-	175	0	0	,,
,, 4 ,, ,, ,,	-	190	0	0	,,
,, 6 ,, ,, ,,	- -	205	0	0	,,
,, 8 ,, ,, ,,	-	225	0	0	,,
,, 10 ,, ,, ,,	- -	245	0	0	,,
Chief Superintendents—					
On appointment	- -	265	0	0	,,
After 3 years in rank	-	275	0	0	,,
,, 6 ,, ,, ,,	-	285	0	0	,,
Deputy Chief Constable, in addition to his pay as Chief Superintendent	- -	30	0	0	,,
Chief Clerk, in addition to the pay of his rank	- - -	30	0	0	,,

No. 1.
Eastern Counties,
Midland,
and North Wales
District.

LONG SERVICE PAY.

(Subject in each case to special grant by the Standing Joint Committee.)

	Inspectors.	Sergeants.	Constables.
After 30 years' service	2 6	2 0	1 6 per week.
,, 32 ,, ,,	5 0	4 0	3 0 ,,

COUNTY BOROUGH OF HANLEY.

Force - - - - - - 60.*

Areas in acres - - - 1,780	Acres to each constable - - - 30
Population in 1891 - - - 54,946	Population to ditto, as per census 1891 916

Yearly Pay in £ and Shillings.

RANKS.	Chief Officer.	Superintendents.						3 Inspectors.				
		Deputy Chief Officer.	Chief Clerk.	1st Class.	2nd Class.	3rd Class.	4th Class.	1st Class.	De-tective.	2nd Class.	4th Class.	5th Class.
Number of each Rank and Class -	1	-	1	-	-	-	-	1	1	1	-	-
Rates of Pay of each ditto - -	£ 300	-	£ s. 91 5	-	-	-	-	£ s. 192 19	£ s. 119 5	£ s. 190 15	-	-

Weekly Pay in Shillings and Pence.

RANKS.	6 Sergeants (including Chief Clerk).				50 Constables.						
	Merit Class.	1st Class.	2nd Class.	Wanting to complete.	Merit Class.	1st Class.				2nd Class.	3rd Class.	Wanting to complete.
Number of each Rank and Class -	1	1	1	1	-	3	4	6	10	6	11	3	5	3
Rates of Pay of each ditto -	s. d. 39 4	s. d. 38 9	s. d. 36 9	s. d. 35 7	-	s. d. 33 11	s. d. 33 4	s. d. 32 9	s. d. 32 2	s. d. 31 7	s. d. 31	s. 30	s. 28	s. 25

* Exclusive of three constables appointed at private cost.

No. 1.
Eastern Counties,
Midland,
and North Wales
District.

Inspected on 23rd April, when the force was complete.

The authorised establishment of the force is one chief officer, three inspectors, six sergeants, and 50 constables. There are also three constables appointed at private cost. The force has been increased by two constables.

Three members of the force were called up with the Army Reserve, one of whom was still serving with his regiment on 29th September, but the other two had rejoined the force.

On the retirement on pension of Mr. Windle, Mr. R. J. Carter, who had been chief officer of police at Windsor since 1st September 1898, was appointed to succeed him from 1st September last.

The chief officer and a constable act as inspectors of weights and measures ; the former and an inspector are also inspectors of common lodging-houses and hackney carriages and explosives, and the whole force act as fire brigade.

There is a decrease of one public-house, but an increase of 52 and 58 respectively in the number of persons proceeded against and convicted for drunkenness, as compared with 1900.

Thirty-four members of the force hold certificates from the St. John Ambulance Association.

The cells and police offices were clean and in good order.

The books and returns were well kept, and the management, numbers, and discipline of the force have been efficiently maintained.

BOROUGH OF NEWCASTLE-UNDER-LYME.

Force - - - - - - 18.

| Area in acres | - | - | 672 | Acres to each constable - | - | - | 32 |
| Population in 1891 | - | - | 18,452 | Population to ditto, as per census 1891 | | | 1,025 |

RANKS.	Chief Officer.	Deputy Chief Officer.	Chief Clerk.	1st Class.	2nd Class.	3rd Class.	4th Class.
Yearly Pay in £ and Shillings.							
Number of each Rank and Class -	1	-	1	-	-	-	-
Rates of Pay of each ditto - -	£ s. 180 0	-	£ s. 87 19	-	-	-	-

RANKS.	4 Sergeants.						13 Constables (including Chief Clerk).								
	Merit Class.	1st Class.	2nd Class.	3rd Class.	4th Class.	5th Class.	Merit Class.	1st Class.					2nd Class.	3rd Class.	4th Class.
Weekly Pay in Shillings and Pence.															
Number of each Rank and Class -	-	-	-	-	4	-	-	-	1	1	-	1	-	2	6	1	-
Rates of Pay of each ditto -	s. d. 37 11	s. d. 36 9	s. d. 36 9	s. 35	s. d. 33 10	s. d. 33 0	-	-	s. d. 31 6	s. d. 30 11	s. d. 30 4	s. d. 29 9	s. d. 28 7	s. d. 27 5	s. d. 26 3	s. d. 25 1	s. d. 23 11

Inspected on 23rd April, when the force was complete.

The authorised establishment is one chief officer, four sergeants, and 13 constables. The chief officer, Mr. Stirling, having removed to Great Grimsby, Mr. A. F. Richardson, an inspector in the Birmingham City Force, was appointed in his place at a salary of 180l. a year.

The chief officer acts as assistant relieving officer, and is inspector under the Food and Drugs and Explosives Acts, of markets, and of lodging-houses.

One of the sergeants also acts as inspector of markets, and two constables as assistant inspectors of common lodging-houses and of food and drugs.

The number of beer and refreshment houses have each increased by one during the year, and the number of persons proceeded against for drunkenness and convicted is eight and 14 more respectively than in 1900.

All the members of the force hold certificates from the St. John Ambulance Association.

The cells and police offices were clean and in good order.

The books and returns were well kept, and the management, numbers, and discipline of the force have been efficiently maintained.

No. 1.
Eastern Counties, Midland, and North Wales District.

COUNTY BOROUGH OF WALSALL.

Force - - - - - 78.

| Area in acres - - - 7,358 | Acres to each constable - - - 94 |
| Population in 1891 - - - 71,789 | Population to ditto, as per census 1891 - 920 |

Yearly Pay in £ and Shillings.

RANKS.	Chief Officer.	Superintendent.						6 Inspectors.				
		Deputy Chief Officer.	Chief Clerk.	1st Class.	2nd Class.	3rd Class.	4th Class.	1st Class.	2nd Class.	3rd Class.	4th Class.	5th Class.
Number of each Rank and Class -	1	-	-	-	-	-	-	2	1	3	-	-
Rates of Pay of each ditto -	£ 300	-	-	-	-	-	-	£ 117	£ s. 110 10	£ 104	-	-

Weekly Pay in Shillings and Pence.

RANKS.	11 Sergeants.						60 Constables.										
	1st Class.	2nd Class.	3rd Class.	Wanting to complete.	5th Class.	6th Class.	Special.	1st Class.						2nd Class.	3rd Class.	4th Class.	Wanting to complete.
Number of each Rank and Class -	1	8	1	1	-	-	1	4	2	4	5	9	11	13	-	9	2
Rates of Pay of each ditto -	s. 36	s. 33	s. d. 31 6	-	-	-	s. d. 31 6	s. d. 31 2	s. d. 30 7	s. 30	s. 29	s. 28	s. 27	s. 26	s. 25	s. 24	-

Inspected on 2nd April, when there were vacancies for two constables.

The authorised strength of the force is one chief officer, six inspectors, 11 sergeants, and 61 constables. The growing requirements of the town necessitate an augmentation of the force, as the night beats are too long.

Extra duties performed by the police :—

NATURE OF DUTY.	Chief Officer.	Inspectors.	Sergeants.	Constables.	TOTAL.
Inspectors of Hackney Carriages - -	1	1	—	—	2
Inspectors of Common Lodging-houses - -	1	1	—	—	2
Inspector of Public Markets - -	1	—	—	—	1
Inspectors under Explosives Act - -	1	1	—	—	2
Inspectors under Petroleum Act - -	1	1	—	--	2
Inspectors under Contagious Diseases (Animals) Act.	1	6	—	—	7
Assistant Relieving Officer - - -	1	—	—	—	1
Fire Brigade - - - -	1	3	3	7	14

The number of public-houses has been reduced by two. Thirty-nine more persons were proceeded against for drunkenness during the year than in 1900, and 20 more were convicted.

Six members of the force belonging to the Army Reserve were recalled to their regiments, four of whom had returned before the 29th September, and the other two were still serving with the colours on that date.

Forty-four members of the force hold certificates from the St. John Ambulance Association.

The cells and police offices were clean and good order.

The books and returns were well kept, and the number and discipline of the force have been efficiently maintained, but there appears to the Inspector that there is room for improvement in the management of this force.

COUNTY BOROUGH OF WOLVERHAMPTON.

Force - - - - - - - - 93.

Area in acres - - - - 3,525 | Acres to each constable - - - 38
Population in 1891 - - - 82,662 | Population to ditto, as per census 1891 889

RANKS.	Chief Officer.	1 Superintendent.					5 Inspectors (including Chief Clerk).					
		Deputy Chief Clerk.	Chief Clerk.	1st Class.	2nd Class.	3rd Class.	1st Class.	2nd Class.	3rd Class.	4th Class.	5th Class.	6th Class.
Number of each Rank and Class -	1	-	1	1	-	-	2	1	1	-	-	-
Rates of Pay of each ditto -	£450	-	£105	£160	-	-	£120	£115	£110	£104	-	-

Weekly Pay in Shillings and Pence.

RANKS.	11 Sergeants.				75 Constables.														
	Merit Class.	1st Class.	2nd Class.	3rd Class.	Merit Class.	1st Class.									2nd Class.	3rd Class.	4th Class.	Wanting to complete.
Number of each Rank and Class -	2	-	2	3	1	3	-	1	2	6	15	2	7	8	9	6	3	15	1	-
Rates of Pay of each ditto -	s. d. 39 8	s. d. 37 6	s. d. 38 6	s. d. 36 9	s. d. 35 7	36	s. d. 32 6	s. d. 31 6	s. d. 30 11	s. d. 32 8	s. d. 31 6	s. d. 30 6	s. d. 29 9	s. d. 29 2	s. d. 28 7	s. 28	s. d. 26 3	s. 25	s. 24	-

Inspected on 3rd April, when there were vacancies for six constables.

The authorised establishment of the force is one chief officer, one superintendent, five inspectors, one of whom is chief clerk, 11 sergeants, and 75 constables. The pay of the chief officer has been increased by 50l. a year.

Extra duties performed by the police :—

NATURE OF DUTY.	Chief Officer.	Super-intendents.	Inspectors.	Sergeants.	Constables.	TOTAL.
Inspectors of Common Lodging-houses -	—	—	1	—	3	4
Inspectors of Hackney Carriages - -	1	—	—	—	1	2
Inspectors under Explosives Act - -	1	—	—	—	1	2
Inspectors under Petroleum Act - -	1	—	—	—	1	2
Fire Brigade - - - -	1	1	—	3	19	24

There is one beerhouse more than in 1900, but 29 fewer persons were proceeded against for drunkenness than in that year, and 11 fewer convicted.

Fifty-eight members of the force hold certificates from the St. John Ambulance Association.

Ten constables were called up with the Army Reserve, one of whom was killed in action, one died, and four were still serving with their regiments on 29th September. The remaining four have rejoined the force.

The cells and police offices were clean and in good order.

The books and returns were well kept and the management, numbers, and discipline of the force have been efficiently maintained.

A new scale of pay as under has been adopted :—

Constables—

	£	s.	d.
3rd class, on appointment - - -	1	5	1 per week.
2nd class, after at least 12 months in 3rd class - - - - -	1	6	3
1st class, after at least 12 months in 2nd class - - - -	1	8	0
1st Class, after 2 years in 1st class -	1	8	7
„ „ 4 „ „ -	1	9	2
„ „ 6 „ „ -	1	9	9
„ „ 8 „ „ -	1	10	4
„ „ 10 „ „ -	1	11	6
Merit class, extra, to not more than 15 per cent. of number of constables -	0	1	2

Sergeants—

On appointment - - - -	1	14	5
After 2 years in ranks - -	1	15	0
„ 4 „ „ - - -	1	15	7
„ 6 „ „ - -	1	16	2
„ 8 „ „ - - -	1	16	9
„ 10 „ „ - - -	1	18	6
Merit class, extra, to not more than 20 per cent. of rank - - -	0	1	2

Inspectors—

On appointment - - -	105	0	0 per annum.
After 2 years in rank - - -	110	0	0 „
„ 4 „ „ - -	115	0	0
„ 6 „ „ - -	120	0	0
„ 8 „ „ - -	127	10	0
„ 10 „ „ - -	135	0	0

Superintendent—

On appointment - -	160	0	0
After 2 years in rank - - -	175	0	0
„ 4 „ „ - -	190	0	0
„ 6 „ „ - -	205	0	0
„ 8 „ „ - -	225	0	0
„ 10 „ „ - -	245	0	0

No. 1. Eastern Counties, Midland, and North Wales District.

COUNTY OF SUFFOLK (EAST).

Force - - - - - - 165.*

| Area in acres - - - - 549,744 | Acres to each constable - - - 3,332 |
| Population in 1891 - - - 183,478 | Population to ditto, as per census 1891 1,112 |

RANKS.	Chief Constable.	Yearly Pay in £ and Shillings.										
		6 Superintendents.						11 Inspectors (including Chief Clerk).			
		Deputy Chief Constable.	Chief Clerk.	1st Class.	2nd Class.	3rd Class.	4th Class.	1st Class.	2nd Class.	3rd Class.	4th Class.
Number of each Rank and Class -	1	1	1	1	2	2	-	1	3	6	-
Rates of Pay of each ditto - -	£ 400	£ s. 175 11	£ s. 88 4	£ s. 180 11	£ s. 139 18	£ s. 135 7	£ s. 130 15	£ s. 88 4	£ s. 86 13	£ s. 80 12	-

RANKS.	Weekly Pay in Shillings and Pence.											
	10 Sergeants.							137 Constables.				
	Merit Class.	1st Class.	2nd Class.	3rd Class.	4th Class.	5th Class.	Acting Sergeants.	Merit Class.	1st Class.	2nd Class.	3rd Class.	Wanting to complete.
Number of each Rank and Class -	-	3	7	-	-	-	-	21	55	34	27	-
Rates of Pay of each ditto - .	-	s. d. 29 9	s. d. 27 5	-	-	-	-	s. d. 26 3	s. d. 24 6	s. d. 22 2	s. d. 20 5	-

* Exclusive of nine constables appointed under 3 & 4 Vict. c. 88, s. 19.

Inspected in May, when there were vacancies for three constables.

The authorised establishment of the force is one chief constable, six superintendents, one of whom is deputy chief constable, 11 inspectors, including chief clerk, 10 sergeants, and 137 constables. There are also nine constables appointed under 3 & 4 Vict. c. 88. s. 19.

Extra duties performed by the police :—

NATURE OF DUTY.	Chief Constable.	Super-intendents.	Inspectors.	Sergeants.	Constables.	TOTAL.
Inspectors under Contagious Diseases (Animals) Act.	1	6	11	10	—	28
Inspectors under Food and Drugs Act -	1	6	—	—	—	7
Inspectors under Explosive Act -	—	6	—	—	—	6
Inspectors of Common Lodging-houses -	—	6	—	—	—	6
Assistant Relieving Officers - . -	—	1	6	2	5	14

Four constables belonging to the Army Reserve were called up to join their regiments, two were still serving with them on the 29th September, and two had rejoined the force.

There are four more public-houses but three fewer beerhouses than in 1900. The number of persons proceeded against for drunkenness was two less, and the number convicted eight less, than in that year.

One hundred and thirty-nine members of the force hold certificates from the St. John Ambulance Association.

The municipal borough of Lowestoft is watched by the county police. The want of a sub-station is increasingly felt in this growing town.

The Inspector visited eight stations, and found them clean and in good order.

The books and returns were well kept, and the management, numbers. and discipline of the force have been efficiently maintained.

The following conditions of pay were to take effect from 30th September :—

Superintendents—

	£	s.	d.	
After 10 years in the rank - -	- 170	0	0	per annum.
„ 5 „ „ „ -	- 150	0	0	„
On appointment - -	- 135	0	0	„

Inspectors —

After 10 years in the rank -	- 110	0	0	„
„ 5 „ „ „ -	- 100	0	0	„
On appointment - -	- 95	0	0	„

Sergeants—

After 10 years in the rank - -	- 1	13	3	per week.
„ 5. „ „ „ -	- 1	11	6	„
On appointment - -	- 1	10	4	„

Constables—

Merit class - - -	- 1	8	0	„
1st class, after 10 years in the class -	- 1	6	10	„
„ „ 5. „ „ „ -	- 1	5	8	„
„ on appointment - -	- 1	4	6	„
2nd class - - - -	- 1	3	4	„
3rd „ - - -	- 1	2	2	„

NOTES.—1. The chief clerk to hold a rank not below that of sergeant, and whether in that or any other superior rank to be in addition to the number of that rank ; his promotion to be at the discretion of the chief constable.

2. Men joining the force will be appointed 3rd class constables, and may at the discretion of the chief constable be promoted to a higher class at any time. An increase of pay because of length of service cannot be claimed as of right, and will only be granted according to merit, and as men are found to qualify themselves for their duties.

COUNTY BOROUGH OF IPSWICH.

Force - - - - - - 67.

Area in acres - - - - 8,110 | Acres to each constable - - - 121
Population in 1891 - - - 57,360 | Population to ditto, as per census 1891 - 856

RANKS.	Chief Officer.	Yearly Pay in £ and Shillings.										
		1 Superintendent.						3 Inspectors.				
		Deputy Chief Officer.	Chief Clerk.	1st Class.	2nd Class.	3rd Class.	4th Class.	1st Class.	2nd Class.	3rd Class.	4th Class.	5th Class.
Number of each Rank and Class -	1	-	1	-	-	-	-	2	-	-	-	-
Rates of Pay of each ditto - -	£ 324	-	£ 140	-	-	-	-	£ 115	£ s. 107 10	£ 100	-	-

RANKS.	Weekly Pay in Shillings and Pence.										
	7 Sergeants.					56 Constables.					
	1st Class.	2nd Class.	3rd Class.	4th Class.	5th Class.	1st Class.			2nd Class.		3rd Class.	4th Class.
Number of each Rank and Class -	4	2	1	-	-	24	5	6	6	10	5	-
Rates of Pay of each ditto -	s. d. 35 7	s. d. 34 5	s. d. 33 3	s. d. 32 1	-	s. d. 30 11	s. d. 29 9	s. d. 28 7	s. d. 27 5	s. d. 26 3	s. d. 25 1	s. d. 23 11

NOTE.—In addition to rates of pay shown above, 1s. a week is paid to all ranks after 26 years' service, of which two inspectors, one sergeant, and two constables were in receipt on 29th September.

Inspected on 23rd May, when the force was complete.

The authorised establishment of the force is one chief officer, one superintendent and clerk, two inspectors, seven sergeants, and 56 constables. The force having been reduced by one constable.

The superintendent acts as inspector of common lodging-houses, of hackney carriages, and under the Contagious Diseases (Animals) Act ; he is also assistant relieving officer for vagrants, and billet master.

One constable of this force belonging to the Army Reserve was called up, but has rejoined the police.

There is a decrease of two in the number of public-houses, but an increase of seven and eight respectively in the number of persons proceeded against for drunkenness and convicted, as compared with 1900. There is also one more beerhouse than in the previous year.

Twenty-eight members of the force hold certificates from the St. John Ambulance Association.

The cells and police offices were clean and in good order. A new station has been built with one cell and accommodation for a married constable.

The books and returns were well kept, and the management, numbers, and discipline of the force have been efficiently maintained.

A new scale of pay came into operation on the 1st of April 1901 as follows :—

Inspectors—

	£	s.	d.	
On appointment	100	0	0	per annum.
After 3 years	107	10	0	,,
,, 6 ,,	115	0	0	,,

Sergeants—

	£	s.	d.	
On appointment	1	12	1	per week.
After 2 years	1	13	3	,,
,, 4 ,,	1	14	5	..
,, 6 ..	1	15	7	..

Constables—

	£	s.	d.	
On appointment	1	3	11	..
After 1 year	1	5	1	..
,, 3 years	1	6	3	..
,, 5 ,,	1	7	5	..
,, 7 ..	1	8	7	..
,, 9 ..	1	9	9	..
,, 11 ..	1	10	11	..

N.B.—In addition to the above, 1s. extra per week is paid to all ranks after 26 years' approved service. No alteration was made in the pay of the superintendent.

COUNTY OF SUFFOLK (WEST).

Force - - - - - - 113.*

| Area in acres † | - | - | - 390,855 | Acres to each constable | - | - 3,459 |
| Population in 1891 † | - | - | - 121,708 | Population to ditto, as per census 1891 | | 1,077 |

RANKS.	Chief Constable	5 Superintendents						9 Inspectors.			
		Deputy Chief Constable.	Chief Clerk.	1st Class.	2nd Class.	3rd Class.	4th Class.	1st Class.	2nd Class.	3rd Class.	4th Class.
Number of each Rank and Class	1	1	1	1	1	2	-	2	1	3	3
	£	£ s.	£ s.	£ s.	£ s.	£ s.	£ s.	£ s.	£ s.	£ s.	£ s.
Rates of Pay of each ditto - -	300	159 18	71 9	150 11	139 18	135 7	130 15	100 7	88 4	86 13	80 13

Weekly Pay in Shillings and Pence.

RANKS.	9 Sergeants (including Chief Clerk).						89 Constables.							
	Merit Class.	1st Class.	2nd Class.	3rd Class.	4th Class.	5th Class.	Acting Sergeants.	Merit Class.	1st Class.	2nd Class.	3rd Class.	4th Class.	5th Class.	6th Class.
Number of each Rank and Class	-	3	6	-	-	-	-	10	38	24	17	-	-	-
		s. d.	s. d.					s. d.	s. d.	s. d.	s. d.			
Rates of Pay of each ditto - -	-	29 9	27 5	-	-	-	-	26 3	24 6	22 3	20 5	-	-	-

* Exclusive of four constables appointed under 3 & 4 Vict. c. 88. s. 19.
† Parts of the parishes of Woodditton and Newmarket (acreage 340, population 550) were transferred from Cambridgeshire to Suffolk, and part of the parish of Kiddington (acreage 722, population 36) was transferred from Essex to Suffolk, by Order of Local Government Board, as from 30th September 1895.

Inspected in May, when the force was complete.

The authorised establishment of the force is one chief constable, five superintendents, nine inspectors, nine sergeants, one of whom is chief clerk, and 89 constables. There are also four "additional" constables appointed under 3 & 4 Vict. c. 88. s. 19.

Two constables were called out with the Army Reserve, one of whom was still away on 29th September, but the other had rejoined the force.

There is an increase of 10 in the number of beerhouses and of one refreshment house. Four more persons were proceeded against for drunkenness and one more convicted than in 1900.

One hundred and six members of the force hold certificates from the St. John Ambulance Association.

The municipal borough of Bury St. Edmund's is watched by the county police.

The Inspector visited 11 stations, and found them clean and in good order.

The books and returns were well kept, and the management, numbers, and discipline of the force have been efficiently maintained.

A new scale of pay as follows was to take effect from 30th September :—

Constables—	£	s.	d.	
3rd class, on appointment -	1	2	2	per week.
2nd „ at discretion of chief constable	1	3	4	„
1st „ „ „ -	1	4	6	„
1st „ after 5 years in that class -	1	5	8	„
1st „ „ 10 „ „ -	1	6	10	„
Merit class, at discretion of chief constable - - - - -	1	8	0	„

<table>
<tr><td rowspan="3">No. 1.
Eastern Counties,
Midland,
and North Wales
District.</td></tr>
</table>

No. 1.
Eastern Counties,
Midland,
and North Wales
District.

Sergeants—

	£	s.	d.	
On appointment - - - -	1	10	4	per week.
After 5 years - - - -	1	11	6	,,
,, 10 ,, - - - -	1	13	3	..

Inspectors—

	£	s.	d.	
3rd class, on appointment -	90	0	0	per annum.
2nd ,, ,, -	95	0	0	,,
1st ,, ,, -	100	0	0	,,
,, ,, after 5 years in 1st class	110	0	0	..

Superintendents—

	£	s.	d.	
On appointment - -	135	0	0	,,
After 5 years - - -	150	0	0	,,
,, 10 ,, - - -	170	0	0	,,

COUNTY OF WARWICK.

Force - - - - - - - - 304.

Area in acres * - - 570,788	Acres to each constable - - - 1,877
Population in 1891 * - - 277,566	Population to ditto, as per census 1891 913

	Chief Constable.	Yearly Pay in £ and Shillings.										
RANKS.		9 Superintendents.							10 Inspectors.			
		Deputy Chief Constable.	Chief Clerk.	1st Class.	2nd Class.	3rd Class.	4th Class.	5th Class.	1st Class.	2nd Class.	3rd Class.	4th Class.
Number of each Rank and Class -	1	1	1	2	1	2	-	2	3	3	4	-
Rates of Pay of each ditto -	£ 400	£ 220	£ 200	£ 200	£ 175	£ 160	£ 150	£ 140	£ 115	£ s. 107 10	£ 100	-

	Weekly Pay in Shillings and Pence.											
RANKS.	33 Sergeants.						251 Constables.					
	Merit Class.	1st Class.	2nd Class.	3rd Class.	4th Class.	Wanting to complete.	1st Class.				2nd Class.	3rd Class.	4th Class.	Wanting to complete.
Number of each Rank and Class -	-	14	5	9	4	1	91	24	30	32	39	25	-	2
Rates of Pay of each ditto -	-	s. d. 33 3	s. d. 32 1	s. d. 30 11	s. d. 29 9	-	s. d. 29 2	s. 28	s. d. 26 10	s. d. 25 8	s. d. 24 6	s. d. 23 4	-	-

* The parish of Oldberrow (acreage 1,235, population 73) was transferred from Worcestershire by Order of Quarter Sessions dated 29th June 1837; and the parishes of Alderminster (acreage 3,239, population 433), Shipston (acreage 1,230, population 1,644), Tidmington (acreage 774, population 62), and Tredington (acreage 5,347, population 919) are also transferred from Worcestershire by Order of Quarter Session dated 28th June 1859. The parishes of Mollington (acreage 655, population 97) and of Drayton Bassett (acreage four) were transferred from Warwickshire to Oxfordshire and Staffordshire, respectively, and the parish of Stoneton (acreage 717, population 22) from Northamptonshire to Warwickshire, by Order of Local Government Board, on 30th September 1895.

Inspected in September, when there were vacancies for one sergeant and three constables.

The authorised establishment of the force is one chief constable, nine superintendents, one of whom is deputy chief constable and another is chief clerk, 10 inspectors, 33 sergeants, and 251 constables.

Extra duties performed by the police :—

NATURE OF DUTY.	Superintendents.	Inspectors.	Sergeants.	Constables.	TOTAL.
Inspectors under Contagious Diseases (Animals) Act.	8	8	25	—	41
Inspector under Food and Drugs Act -	1	—	—	—	1
Inspectors under Explosives Act -	8	—	—	—	8
Inspector under Petroleum Act -	—	1	—	—	1
Inspectors under Shop Hours Act -	8	9	—	1	18

(53)

Fifteen members of the force who belonged to the Army Reserve were called up to rejoin the colours, eight were still serving with their regiments on 29th September, one died in South Africa, and six had rejoined the force.

There is an increase of four in the number of beerhouses, and of seven refreshment houses. The number of persons proceeded against for drunkenness shows a decrease of 226, and of convictions a decrease of 180, as compared with the preceding year. This may be attributed to the reduction of the area of the county for police purposes.

Two hundred and twenty-four members of the force hold certificates from the St. John Ambulance Association.

The municipal borough of Warwick is watched by the county police.

The Inspector visited 19 stations, and found them clean and in good order.

The books and returns were well kept, and the management, numbers, and discipline of the force have been efficiently maintained.

No. 1.
Eastern Counties, Midland, and North Wales District.

CITY AND COUNTY BOROUGH OF BIRMINGHAM.

Force - - - - - - - - - 800.*

Area in acres - - - 12,705 | Acres to each constable - - - 16
Population in 1891 - - 478,113 | Population to ditto, as per census 1891 ' 60

Yearly Pay in £ and Shillings.

RANKS.	Chief Officer.	8 Superintendents.							25 Inspectors.					
		Deputy Chief Officer.	Chief Clerk.	1st Class.	2nd Class.	3rd Class.	4th Class.	5th Class.	Chief Inspector.	1st Class.		2nd Class.	3rd Class.	Wanting to complete.
Number of each Rank and Class -	1	1	1	2	1	2	–	1	–	1	1	3	2	10	5	2
Rates of Pay of each ditto -	£ 800	£ 300	£ 240	£ 250	£ 220	£ 210	£ 180	£ 170	£ 160	£ 160	£ 132	£ s. 125 4	£ 120	£ s. 119 12	£ s. 109 4	–

Weekly Pay in Shillings and Pence.

RANKS.	72 Sergeants.				694 Constables.							
	1st Class.		2nd Class.	Wanting to complete.	Merit Long Service Class.		1st Class.	2nd Class.	3rd Class.	4th Class.	5th Class.	Wanting to complete.
Number of each Rank and Class -	– 30 – 13 – 14 –	10	5	– 110 – – 99	122	– – 98 –	– 133 – 27	55	49
Rates of Pay of each ditto -	s. 42 41 40 39 38 37 36 35	s. 34	–	s. d. 34 32 32 6 32 31 6 31 30 6	s. 30	s. d. 29 28 6 28 27	s. d. 26 6 26 25 6 25	s. 24	–

* Exclusive of two inspectors, three sergeants, and 11 constables appointed at private cost.

Fourteen sergeants and 68 constables are in receipt of "merit" pay varying from 6d. to 2s. a week in addition to the rates shown.

Inspected on 19th and 20th April, when there were 90 vacancies.

The authorised establishment of the force is one chief officer, eight superintendents, one of whom is deputy chief officer and another is chief clerk, 25 inspectors, 72 sergeants, and 694 constables. There are also two inspectors, three sergeants, and 11 constables appointed at private cost. The force has been increased by one sergeant and 99 constables, and a further annual augmentation of 20 men is to take place automatically for six years in succession.

Fourteen members of the force belonging to the Army Reserve were recalled to the colours, seven of whom were all still serving away on 29th September, four have returned, and the remainder have left the force for good.

G 3

Extra duties performed by the police :—

NATURE OF DUTY.	Inspectors.	Sergeants.	Constables.	TOTAL.
Inspectors of Public Carriages - -	1	1	5	7
Inspector of Explosives - - -	1	—	—	1
Coroner's Summoning Officers - - -	1	1	1	3
Art Gallery, Free Library, and Law Courts -	—	—	6	6
Rate Department - - - -	1	—	—	1

The number of public-houses has been increased by three, but of beer-houses it has been reduced by 16, during the year, and the number of persons proceeded against for drunkenness shows a decrease of 184 on that for 1900, and of convictions a decrease of 154. There are nine more refreshment houses with wine licenses.

Six hundred and seventy-four members of the force hold certificates from the St. John Ambulance Association.

The Inspector visited all the police stations, and found the cells, offices, &c. clean and in good order.

The books and returns were well kept, and the management, numbers, and discipline of the force have been efficiently maintained.

CITY AND COUNTY BOROUGH OF COVENTRY.

Force - - - - - - - - 88

Area in acres - - - 4,147 | Acres to each constable - - - 47
Population in 1891 - - - 58,479 | Population to ditto, as per census 1891 665

	Yearly Pay in £ and Shillings.										
RANKS.	Chief Officer.	Superintendents.						5 Inspectors.			
		Deputy Chief Officer.	Chief Clerk.	1st Class.	2nd Class.	3rd Class.	4th Class.	Chief Inspector.	1st Class.	2nd Class.	3rd Class.
Number of each Rank and Class -	1	-	-	-	-	-	-	1	2	2	-
Rates of Pay of each ditto -	£ 250	-	-	-	-	-	-	£ 140	£ 130	£ s. 124 16	£ 117

	Weekly Pay in Shillings and Pence.												
RANKS.	8 Sergeants.						74 Constables.						
	1st Class.	2nd Class.	3rd Class.	4th Class.	5th Class.	Wanting to complete.	Merit and Long Service Class.	1st Class.	2nd Class.	3rd Class.	4th Class.	5th Class.	Probationary.
Number of each Rank and Class	2	2	1	-	2	1	1	9	6	5	21	10	18	4	
Rates of Pay of each ditto -	s. 38	s. d. 36 11	s. d. 34 10	s. d. 33 10	s. d. 32 10	-	s. d. 32 4	s. d. 31 10	s. d. 30 10	s. d. 29 9	s. d. 28 9	s. d. 26 8	s. d. 25 7	s. d. 24 7	s. d. 22 7

Inspected on 22nd March, when the force was complete.

The authorised establishment of the force is one chief officer, five inspectors, eight sergeants, and 74 constables.

The chief officer is inspector of hackney carriages, and under the Explosives Act ; he is also assistant relieving officer and billet master. The whole of the force act as inspectors under the Cattle Diseases Acts.

The number of licensed houses is the same as in 1900 ; but 134 more persons were proceeded against for drunkenness, and 111 more convicted, than in that year.

Eighty-four members of the force hold certificates from the St. John Ambulance Association.

Two constables belonging to the Army Reserve were called up to join their regiments, one was still serving in South Africa on 29th September, but the other had rejoined the force.

The cells and police offices were clean and in good order, but sub-stations are much required.

The books and returns were well kept, and the management, numbers, and discipline of the force have been efficiently maintained.

The following scale of pay came into effect on 1st April :—

Sergeants—

		£	s.	d.	
On appointment -	-	1	12	10	per week.
After 2 years -	-	1	13	10	,,
,, 4 ,,	-	1	14	10	,,
,, 6	-	1	16	11	,,
,, 9 ..	-	1	18	0	,,

Constables—

		£	s.	d.	
On joining -	-	1	4	7	..
After 1 year -	-	1	5	7	..
,, 2 years -	-	1	6	8	..
,, 4 ,,	-	1	8	9	..
,, 8 ,,	-	1	9	9	..
,, 11 ..	-	1	10	10	..
,, 15 ..	-	1	11	10	..

BOROUGH OF ROYAL LEAMINGTON SPA.

Force - - - - - - - 40.

Area in acres - - - 2,816 | Acres to each constable - - - 70
Population in 1891 - - - 26,930 | Population to ditto, as per census 1891 673

Yearly Pay in £ and Shillings.

RANKS.	Chief Officer.	Superintendents.					3 Inspectors.			
		Deputy Chief Officer.	Chief Clerk.	1st Class.	2nd Class.	3rd Class.	1st Class.	2nd Class.	3rd Class.	4th Class.
Number of each Rank and Class -	1	-	-	-	-	-	1	1	-	1
Rates of Pay of each ditto -	£ 300	-	-	-	-	-	£ s. 135 4	£ s. 121 15	£ s. 116 11	£ s. 110 1

Weekly Pay in Shillings and Pence.

RANKS.	6 Sergeants.						30 Constables.					
	Merit Class.	1st Class.	2nd Class.	3rd Class.	4th Class.	5th Class.	Merit Class.	1st Class.			2nd Class.	3rd Class.	Probationary Class.
Number of each Rank and Class -	-	2	1	3	-	-	3	4	8	5	2	-	4	4	2
Rates of Pay of each ditto -	s. d. 38 6	s. d. 37 6	s. d. 35 6	s. d. 34 4	-	-	s. 32	s. 31	s. d. 29 10	s. d. 29 3	s. d. 28 8	s. d. 27 6	s. 26	s. 24	s. 21

Inspected on 22nd March, when the force was complete.

The authorised establishment of the force is one chief officer, three inspectors, six sergeants, and 30 constables.

The chief officer is coroner's officer, billet master, and inspector of explosives ; he, two inspectors, and a sergeant are also appointed inspectors under the Contagious Diseases (Animals) Acts.

No. 1.
Eastern Counties,
Midland,
and North Wales
District.

One constable belonging to the force, in the Army Reserve, was alled up to rejoin his regiment, and died on active service in South Africa.

The number of licensed houses, with the exception of a reduction of one public-house, is the same as in the previous year ; but four more persons were proceeded against for drunkenness, and six more convicted, than in 1900.

Thirty-one members of the force hold certificates from the St. John Ambulance Association.

The cells and police offices were clean and in good order.

The books and returns were well kept, and the management, numbers, and discipline of the force have been efficiently maintained.

COUNTY OF WORCESTER.

Force - - - - - 357.*

Area in acres † - - - 463,613 | Acres to each constable - - 1,299
Population in 1891 † - - 314,772 | Population to ditto, as per census 1891 882

RANKS.	Chief Constable.	Yearly Pay in £ and Shillings.												
		11 Superintendents.								11 Inspectors.				
		Deputy Chief Constable.	Chief Clerk.	1st Class.	2nd Class.	3rd Class.	4th Class.	5th Class.	6th Class.	1st Class.	2nd Class.	3rd Class.	4th Class.	5th Class.
Number of each Rank and Class -	1	1	1	1	3	1	3	–	3	3	3	6	–
Rates of Pay of each ditto -	£ 600	£ s. 200 15	£ s. 100 7	£ s. 182 10	£ s. 178 7	£ s. 164 5	£ s. 155 2	146	£ s. 136 17	£ s. 118 12	£ s. 112 10	£ s. 106 9	£ s. 100 7	–

RANKS.	46 Sergeants.				Weekly Pay in Shillings and Pence.						
	1st Class.	2nd Class.	3rd Class.	4th Class.	288 Constables.					2nd Class.	3rd Class.
					1st Class.						
Number of each Rank and Class -	11	9	8	18	1	76	48	34	69	38	22
Rates of Pay of each ditto -	s. 36	s. d. 33 3	s. d. 31 6	s. d. 29 9	s. d. 29 3	s. 28	s. d. 26 10	s. d. 25 8	s. d. 24 6	s. d. 23 4	s. d. 22 2

* Exclusive of two inspectors and one constable appointed under 3 & 4 Vict. c. 88. s. 19.
† The parish of Upper Arley (acreage 3,969, population 847) is transferred from Staffordshire by order of Quarter Sessions dated 30th September 1890. The parish of Edvin Loach (acreage 533, population 48) is transferred (19th September 1892) to Herefordshire by Local Government Board Order Confirmation Act, 56 & 57 Vict. c. 133. The parishes of Cutsdean (acreage 1,560, population 196), Daylesford (acreage 670, population 89), and Evenlode (acreage 1,819, population 348), are transferred to Gloucestershire by order of Quarter Sessions dated 1st May 1880 ; and the parish of Teddington (acreage 747, population 99) is also transferred to Gloucestershire by order of Quarter Sessions dated 1st November 18-0. The parish of Oldberrow (acreage 1,236, population 73) was transferred to Warwickshire by order of Quarter Sessions dated 29th June 1857 ; and the parishes of Aldermaster (acreage 3,379, population 433), Shipston (acreage 1,220, population 1,516), Tidmington (acreage 774, population 62), and Tredington (acreage 3,347, population 919) are also transferred to Warwickshire by order of Quarter Sessions dated 29th June 1859. Dudley Castle Hill parish (acreage 69, population 16), although stated in Census Returns to form part of Worcestershire, is excluded here and included in Staffordshire. (H. O. V. 30,865.) The parish of Dowles (acreage 711, population 91) was transferred from Shropshire by Provisional Order of the Local Government Board, No. P. 1118, of 6th May 1895. Under the Malvern Link (Extension and Water) Act, 1896, an area (acreage 228, population 551) was transferred from Herefordshire to Worcestershire. The parishes of Aston Somerville (acreage 1,004, population 107), of Childswick Green (acreage 1,8-5, population 400) and of Hinton-on-the-Green (acreage 3,291, population 175) were transferred from Gloucestershire under agreement dated 23rd March 1898 ; and the parishes of Overbury (acreage 1,371, population 417) and of Oonderton (acreage 800, population 175) were similarly transferred to Gloucestershire. A portion of the parish of Oradley (acreage 60, population nil), and the parish of Stoke Bliss (acreage 1 163, population 149), were transferred from Herefordshire under Provisional Order of the Local Government Board P. 130, of 8th May 1897, and P. 1143, respectively, and the parishes of Acton, Beauchamp (acreage 1,544, population 216), and of Rural Mathon (acreage 3,036, population 379) were transferred from Herefordshire under the latter Order.

Inspected in August, when there was a vacancy for a constable.

The authorised establishment of the force, which has been augmented by one superintendent and five constables during the year, is one chief constable, 11 superintendents, one of whom is deputy chief constable and another is chief clerk, 11 inspectors, 46 sergeants, and 288 constables. Two "additional" inspectors and one constable are appointed under 3 & 4 Vict. c. 88. s. 19.

Ten members of the force belonging to the Army Reserve rejoined the colours, one of whom was killed in action, two have died, three have rejoined the force, and four were still serving with their regiments on 29th September.

Extra duties performed by the police :—

NATURE OF DUTY.	Chief Constable.	Super-intendents.	Inspectors.	Sergeants.	Constables.	TOTAL.
Inspectors under Weights and Measures Act.	1	3	—	—	—	4
Inspectors under Contagious Diseases (Animals) Act.'	1	9	4	5	1	20
Inspectors under Explosives Act - -	1	9	1	—	—	11
Assistant Relieving Officer - -	—	1	—	—	—	1

There is a decrease of six in the number of public-houses and of 13 in that of beerhouses, but an increase of eight in refreshment houses with wine licenses. Proceedings against persons for drunkenness were 228, and convictions 212, less than in 1900.

Two hundred and sixty-six members of the force hold certificates from the St. John Ambulance Association.

The county borough of Dudley is watched by the county police.

The Inspector visited 16 stations, and found them clean and in good order.

The books and returns were well kept, and the management, numbers, and discipline of the force have been efficiently maintained.

BOROUGH OF KIDDERMINSTER.

Force - - - - - - 28.*

| Area in acres - | - | - | - | 1,213 | Acres to each constable - | - | - | 43 |
| Population in 1891 - | - | - | 24,803 | Population to ditto, as per census 1891 | 886 |

RANKS.	Chief Officer.	Superintendents.						1 Inspector.				
		Deputy Chief Officer.	Chief Clerk.	1st Class.	2nd Class.	3rd Class.	4th Class.	1st Class.	2nd Class.	3rd Class.	4th Class.	5th Class.
Number of each Rank and Class -	1	-	-	-	-	-	-	1	-	-	-	-
Rates of Pay of each ditto -	£ 312	-	-	-	-	-	-	£ 117	-	-	-	-

Yearly Pay in £ and Shillings.

RANKS.	5 Sergeants.				22 Constables.							
	1st Class.			2nd Class.	3rd Class.	Merit Class and Long Service.			1st Class.	2nd Class.	3rd Class.	4th Class.	5th Class.	Wanting to complete.
Number of each Rank and Class -	-	1	-	2	-	-	2	-	-	-	1	2	7	-	3	2	5	1	-
Rates of Pay of each ditto -	s. d. 37	s. d. 35 8	s. d. 33 8	s. d. 32 6	s. d. 32 4	s. d. 31 4	s. d. 30 4	s. d. 29 2	£ 32	s. 31	s. 30	s. 29	s. 28	s. d. 26 10	s. d. 26 8	s. d. 25 8	s. d. 24 6	s d. 23 4	s. d. 22 2	-

Weekly Pay in Shillings and Pence.

* Exclusive of two constables appointed at private cost.

Inspected on 3rd April, when there was a vacancy for one constable.

The authorised establishment of the force is one chief officer, one inspector five sergeants, and 22 constables. There are also two constables appointed at private cost.

The chief officer is inspector of common lodging-houses and hackney carriages, and under the Weights and Measures, Petroleum, Explosives, and Contagious Diseases (Animals) Acts, and the inspector is assistant inspector of common lodging-houses, and under the Contagious Diseases (Animals) Act.

H

No. 1.
Eastern Counties,
Midland,
and North Wales
District.

One constable belonging to the Army Reserve was called up to join the colours, and was still serving with the regiment on 29th September.

There is no alteration in the number of licensed houses, but 41 more persons were proceeded against for drunkenness, and 42 more convicted, than in 1900.

Twenty-five members of the force hold certificates from the St. John Ambulance Association.

The cells and police offices were clean and in good order.

The books and returns were well kept, and the management, numbers, and discipline of the force have been efficiently maintained.

CITY AND COUNTY BOROUGH OF WORCESTER.

Force - - - - - - - - 51.

Area in acres - - - - 3,185 | Acres to each constable - - - 62
Population in 1891 - - - 42,908 | Population to ditto, as per census 1891 841

RANKS	Yearly Pay in £ and Shillings.					
	Chief Officer.	2 Inspectors.				
		1st Class.	2nd Class.	3rd Class.	4th Class.	5th Class.
Number of each Rank and Class	1	—	—		1	1
Rates of Pay of each ditto -	£ 335	£ s. 134 16	£ s. 119 12	£ s. 114 8	£ s. 109 4	£ 104

RANKS.	Weekly Pay in Shillings and Pence.										
	7 Sergeants.					41 Constables.					
	1st Class.	2nd Class.	3rd Class.	4th Class.	5th Class.	Merit Class.	1st Class.	2nd Class.	3rd Class.	4th Class.	5th Class.	Wanting to complete.
Number of each Rank and Class	2	1	2	1	1	1	2	7	11	6	4	2	3	3	1	1
Rates of Pay of each ditto -	s. 37	s. 36	s. 35	s. 34	s. 31	s. 33	s. 32	s. 31	s. 30	s. 29	s. 28	s. 27	s. 26	s. 25	s. 24	—

Inspected on 26th August, when the force was complete.

The authorised establishment of the force is one chief officer, two inspectors, seven sergeants, one of whom is clerk, and 41 constables.

The chief officer is inspector of hackney carriages, and under the Contagious Diseases (Animals) Act. He is also chief of the fire brigade, to which an inspector, four sergeants, and eight constables also belong.

Two members of the force belonging to the Army Reserve were called upon to rejoin their regiments, one was still serving in South Africa on 29th September, the other died there.

There is no change in the number of licensed houses, but a decrease of 21 in proceedings taken for, and 20 in convictions for, drunkenness.

Forty-three members of the force hold certificates from the St. John Ambulance Association.

The cells and police offices were clean and in good order.

The books and returns were well kept, and the management, numbers, and discipline of the force have been efficiently maintained.

NORTH WALES.

COUNTY OF ANGLESEY.

Force - - - - - 30.

Area in acres - - - - 175,826	Acres to each constable - - 5,861
Population in 1891 - - - 50,098	Population to ditto, as per census 1891 1,670

RANKS.	Chief Con-stable.	Yearly Pay in £. and Shillings.										
		1 Superintendent.					1 Inspector.					
		Deputy Chief Constable.	1st Class.	2nd Class.	3rd Class.		1st Class.	2nd Class.	3rd Class.	4th Class.	5th Class.	
Number of each Rank and Class -	1	-	1	-	-	-		-	-	1	-	-
Rates of Pay of each ditto -	£ 275	£ 131	£ 121	£ 115	-	-		£ 90	£ 85	£ s. 82 2	-	-

RANKS.	Weekly Pay in Shillings and Pence.												
	4 Sergeants.						23 Constables.						
	Merit Class.	1st Class.	2nd Class.	3rd Class.	4th Class.	5th Class.	Merit Class.	1st Class.	2nd Class.	3rd Class.	4th Class.	5th Class.	6th Class.
Number of each Rank and Class -	-	2	2	-	-	-	9	2	5	4	3	-	-	-
Rates of Pay of each ditto -	-	s. 29	s. 27	-	-	-	s. 26	s. 25	s. 24	s. 23	s. 22	-	-

Inspected in June, when the force was complete.

The authorised establishment of the force is one chief constable, one superintendent and deputy chief constable, one inspector, four sergeants, and 23 constables. The pay of the chief constable has been increased by £25 a year.

Two constables act as assistant relieving officers, and the whole force act as inspectors under the Contagious Diseases (Animals) Act, and under the Explosives Act.

There is no alteration in the number of licensed houses, but a decrease of 20 in the number of persons proceeded against for drunkenness, and of 24 in the number convicted, as compared with 1900.

Twenty-one members of this force hold certificates from the St. John Ambulance Association.

The Inspector visited seven stations, and found them clean and in good order.

The books and returns were well kept, and the management, numbers, and discipline of the force have been efficiently maintained.

COUNTY OF CARNARVON.

Force - - - - - 82.*

Area in acres † - - - 360,451	Acres to each constable - - - 4,396
Population in 1891 † - - 115,886	Population to ditto, as per census 1891 1,413

RANKS.	Chief Constable	Yearly Pay in £ and Shillings.										
		4 Superintendents.						3 Inspectors.				
		Deputy Chief Constable.	Chief Clerk.	1st Class.	2nd Class.	3rd Class.	4th Class.	1st Class.	2nd Class.	3rd Class.	4th Class.	5th Class.
Number of each Rank and Class	1	1	-	-	2	-	1	-	-	-	1	2
Rates of Pay of each ditto - -	£ 370	£ 175*		£ 165	£ 155	£ 145	£ 135	£ 120	£ 115	£ 110	£ 105	£ 100

RANKS.	Weekly Pay in Shillings and Pence.									
	13 Sergeants.				61 Constables.					
	Merit Class.	1st Class.	2nd Class.	3rd Class.	1st Class.				2nd Class.	3rd Class.	4th Class.
Number of each Rank and Class	2	5	2	4	19	6	7	17	8	7	-
Rates of Pay of each ditto - -	s. 35	s. d. 33 10	s. d. 32 8	s. d. 31 6	s. 30	s. 28	s. d. 27 6	s. 26	s. 25	s. 24	-

* Exclusive of two constables, whose appointment is sanctioned for the months of July, August, and September annually, at the expense of the urban district council of Llandudno, but included in "ranks," &c. above, and one similarly appointed for Pwllheli district.
† The parish of Llysfaen (acreage 1,878, population 1,700) is transferred to Denbighshire by order of Carnarvonshire Quarter Sessions dated 17th April 1890.

Inspected in June, when the force was complete.

The authorised strength of the force is one chief constable, four superintendents, one of whom is deputy chief constable, three inspectors, including one specially appointed to supervise licensed houses, 13 sergeants, and 61 constables. The force has been augmented by one sergeant and one constable.

Some further augmentation seems to the Inspector necessary at Bangor.

Two constables belonging to the Army Reserve were called upon to rejoin the colours, one was still with his regiment on 29th September, the other had rejoined the force.

There has been a reduction of four in the number of public-houses, but an increase of eight refreshment houses. Proceedings against persons for drunkenness, and convictions, show a decrease of 30 and 50 on the figures for 1900.

Sixty-two members of the force hold certificates from the St. John Ambulance Association.

The Inspector visited 15 stations, and found them clean and in good order.

The books and returns were well kept, and the management, numbers, and discipline of the force have been efficiently maintained.

A new scale of pay, as under, has been adopted :—

Constables—	£	s.	d.	
On appointment - - -	1	4	0	per week.
After 1 year (if promoted to 2nd class)	1	5	0	,,
,, 2 years (promoted to 1st class) -	1	6	0	,,
,, 4 ,, - - - -	1	7	6	..
,, 6 .. - - -	1	8	0	..
,, 8 .. - - - -	1	10	0	..

On appointment -	-	-	- 100	0 per annum.
After 2 years -	-	-	- 105 0 0	,,
,, 4 ,,	-	-	- 110 0 0	..
,, 6 ..	-	-	- 115 0 0	..
,, 8 ..	-	-	- 120 0 0	..

Superintendents—

On appointment -	-	-	- 135 0 0	..
After 2 years	-	-	- 145 0 0	..
,, 4 ,,	-	-	- 155 0 0	..
,, 6	-	-	- 165 9 0	..
Deputy chief constable (extra) -	-	- 10 0 0	..

COUNTY OF DENBIGH.

Force - - - - 83.*

Area in acres † - - - 429,493   Acres to each constable - - - 5,175
Population in 1891 † - - 120,807   Population to ditto, as per census, 1891 1,455

Yearly Pay, in £ and Shillings.

RANKS.	Chief Constable.	3 Superintendents.							3 Inspectors (including Chief Clerk).			
		Deputy Chief Constable.	Chief Clerk.	1st Class.	2nd Class.	3rd Class.	4th Class.	5th Class.	1st Class.	2nd Class.	3rd Class.	4th Class.
Number of each Rank and Class -	1	1	1	1	1	–	–	–	–	–	2	–
	£	£ s.	£	£ s.	£ s.	£. s.	£ s.	£ s.	£ s.	£ s.	£	£ s.
Rates of Pay of each ditto - -	330	178 9	105	156 12	114 1	109 10	104 10	100 7	110 16	104 6	105	91 5

Weekly Pay in Shillings and Pence.

RANKS.	3 Sergeants.			68 Constables.							
	1st Class.	2nd Class.	3rd Class.	1st Class.				2nd Class.	3rd Class.	4th Class.	5th Class.
Number of each Rank and Class -	2	3	3	19	10	3	11	8	10	7	–
	s.	s. d.	s. d.	s.	s.	s.	s. d.	s.	.	s.	
Rates of Pay of each ditto - -	35	33 10	32 8	30	29	28	27 6	26	25	24	–

* Exclusive of two constables appointed under 3 & 4 Vict. c. 88, s. 19.
† The parish of Llysfaen (acreage 1,879, population 1,700) is transferred from Carnarvonshire by order of Denbighshire Quarter Sessions dated 21st May 1890, and the parish of Marford and Hoseley acreage 650, population (264) is transferred from Flintshire by order of Denbighshire Quarter Sessions dated Michaelmas 1871.

Inspected in April, when the force was complete.

The authorised establishment of the force is one chief constable, four superintendents, one of whom is deputy chief constable and another is chief clerk (who, however, at present is included among the inspectors), two inspectors, eight sergeants, and 68 constables. There are also two constables appointed under 3 & 4 Vict. c. 88. s. 19.

All the members of the force, except one, are inspectors under the Contagious Diseases (Animals) Act; and the superintendents are inspectors of explosives.

There has been no change in the number of public-houses, nor in that of refreshment houses with wine licenses, but an increase of one beerhouse, during the year. There was a decrease of 36 persons proceeded against for drunkenness, and of 24 convicted.

Fifty-five members of the force hold certificates from the St. John Ambulance Association.

Four members of the force belonging to the Army Reserve were called up to rejoin the colours, three were still serving with their regiments on 29th September, and one had rejoined the force.

The municipal borough of Wrexham is watched by the county police.

The Inspector visited 12 stations, and found them clean and in good order.

The books and returns were well kept, and the management, numbers, and discipline of the force have been efficiently maintained. A new scale of pay as follows has been adopted :—

RANKS.	On Appoint- ment.	After 1 Year.	After 2 Years.	After 8 Years.	After 4 Years.	After 5 Years.	After 6 Years.	After 8 Years.	After 10 Years.
	Per Annum. £ s. d.	£ s.	£ s. d.	£ s. d.	£ s. d.	£ s. d.	£ s. d.	£ s. d.	£ s. d.
Superintendent A Division -	141 8 9	–	149 0 10	–	156 12 11	–	164 5 0	171 17 1	179 9 2
„ B „	132 6 3	–	138 7 11	–	144 9 7	–	150 11 3	156 12 11	163 14 7
„ C „	104 18 9	–	–	109 10 0	–	114 1 3	–	118 12 6	123 3 9
Inspectors - - -	95 0 0	–	100 0 0	–	105 0 0	–	110 0 0	120 0 0	–
	Per Week. £ s. d.								
Sergeants - - -	1 11 6	–	1 12 8	–	1 13 10	–	1 15 0	–	–
Constables - - -	1 4 0	1 5 0	1 6 0	–	1 7 6	–	1 8 0	1 9 0	1 10 0

COUNTY OF FLINT.

Force - - - 58.*

Area in acres † - - - 163,304	Acres to each constable - - 2,816
Population in 1891 † - - - 76,913	Population to ditto, as per census 1891 1,321

RANKS.	Chief Constable.	Yearly Pay in £ and Shillings.											
		2 Superintendents.						4 Inspectors (including Chief Clerk).				
		Deputy Chief Constable.	Chief Clerk.	1st Class.	2nd Class.	3rd Class.	4th Class.	5th Class.	2nd Class.	3rd Class.	4th Class.	5th Class.
Number of each Rank and Class -	1	1	1	–	–	–	–	1	–	2	–	–	–	1
Rates of Pay of each ditto - -	£ 350	£ 175	£ 120	£ 175	£ 165	£ 155	£ 145	£ 135	£ 120	£ 115	£ 110	£ 105	£ 100	£ 95

RANKS.	Weekly Pay in Shillings and Pence.											
	5 Sergeants.						46 Constables.				
	Merit Class.	1st Class.	2nd Class.	3rd Class.	4th Class.	5th Class.	Acting Sergeants.	1st Class.			2nd Class.	3rd Class.	4th Class.
Number of each Rank and Class -	–	–	2	1	2	–	6	10	5	1	3	10	5	6
Rates of Pay of each ditto - -	s. 35	s. d. 33 10	s. d. 32 8	s. d. 31 6	s. d.		s. d. 30 7	s. d. 30	s. 29	s. 28	s. d. 27 6	s. 26	s. 25	s. 24

* Exclusive of three constables appointed under 3 & 4 Vict. c. 88. s. 19.
† The parish of Marford and Hoseley (acreage 550, population 264) is transferred from Denbighshire by order of Quarter Sessions dated Michaelmas 1871.

Inspected in June, when the force was complete.

The authorised establishment of the force is one chief constable, two superintendents, one of whom is deputy chief constable, four inspectors, one of whom is chief clerk, five sergeants, and 46 constables. There are also three constables appointed under 3 & 4 Vict. c. 88. s. 19.

One Army Reserve man belonging to the force was called up to join his regiment, and was still serving with it on 29th September.

Extra duties performed by the police :—

NATURE OF DUTY.	Chief Constable.	Superintendents.	Inspectors.	Sergeants.	Constables.	TOTAL.
Inspectors under Weights and Measures Act.	1	1	—	—	—	2
Inspectors under Food and Drugs Act -	1	2	3	—	—	6
Inspectors under Explosives Act - -	1	2	1	—	—	4
Inspectors under Contagious Diseases (Animals) Act.	1	2	3	1	1	8
Inspectors of Common Lodging-houses	—	—	1	1	1	3
Assistant Relieving Officers - - -	—	—	- —	1	—	1

There has been an increase of two in the number of public-houses during the year, but a decrease of 17 persons proceeded against for drunkenness, and of 10 in the number convicted.

Thirty-seven members of the force hold certificates from the St. John Ambulance Association.

The Inspector visited 12 stations, and found them clean and in good order. A new station with three cells has been built at Shotton and accommodation for a married constable.

The books and returns were well kept, and the management, numbers, and discipline of the force have been efficiently maintained.

The following new scale of pay has been adopted :—

Constables –

	£	s.	d.	
On appointment - - -	1	4	0	per week.
After 1 year - - -	1	5	0	,,
,, 2 years - - -	1	6	0	..
.. 4 ,, - - -	1	7	6	..
6 ,, - - -	1	8	0	,,
,, 8 ,, - - -	1	9	0	..
,, 10 ,, - - -	1	10	0	..

Acting sergeants, 7d. per week extra.

Sergeants—

On appointment - - -	1	11	6	..
After 2 years - - -	1	12	8	..
,, 4 ,, - - -	1	13	10	..
.. 6 .. - - -	1	15	0	..

Inspectors—

On appointment - - -	95	0	0	per annum.
After 2 years - - -	100	0	0	,,
,, 4 ,, - - -	105	0	0	..
.. 6 .. - - -	110	0	0	..
,, 8 .. - - -	115	0	0	..
,, 10 .. - - -	120	0	0	..

Superintendents—

On appointment - - -	135	0	0	..
After 2 years - - -	145	0	0	..
,, 4 ,, - - -	155	0	0	..
,, 6 ,, - - -	165	0	0	..
,, 8 ,, - - -	175	0	0	..
Deputy chief constable (extra) -	10	0	0	

COUNTY OF MERIONETH.

Force - - - - - 35.

Area in acres - - - 427,810 | Acres to each constable - - - 12,223
Population in 1891 - - 49,212 | Population to ditto, as per census 1891 1,406

RANKS.	Chief Constable.	1 Superintendent.						2 Inspectors.				
		Deputy Chief Constable.	Chief Clerk.	1st Class.	2nd Class.	3rd Class.	4th Class.	1st Class.	2nd Class.	3rd Class.	4th Class.	5th Class.
Number of each Rank and Class	1	1	-	-	-	-	-	2	-	-	-	-
Rates of Pay of each ditto	£ 300	£ 165	-	£ 165	£ 155	£ 145	£ 135	£ 190	£ 115	£ 110	£ 105	£ 100

Weekly Pay in Shillings and Pence.

RANKS.	5 Sergeants.						Acting Sergeants.	26 Constables.					2nd Class.	3rd Class.
	Merit Class.	1st Class.	2nd Class.	3rd Class.	4th Class.	5th Class.		1st Class.						
Number of each Rank and Class	-	2	-	-	2	-	-	12	2	3	3	3	3	-
Rates of Pay of each ditto	-	s. 35	s. d. 33 10	s. d. 32 8	s. d. 31 6	-	-	s. 30	s. 29	s. 28	s. d. 27 6	s. 26	s. 25	s. 24

Inspected in June, when the force was complete.

The authorised establishment of the force is one chief constable, one superintendent and deputy chief constable, two inspectors, five sergeants, and 26 constables.

Extra duties performed by the police:—

NATURE OF DUTY.	Chief Constable.	Super-intendents.	Inspectors.	Sergeants.	Constables.	TOTAL.
Ass'stant Relieving Officers -	—	1	1	1	1	4
Inspectors under the Explosives Act -	1	1	2	3	—	7
Inspectors under Food and Drugs Act -	1	1	2	5	26	35
Inspectors under Contagious Diseases (Animals) Act.	1	1	2	5	26	35

There is an increase of one in the number of public-houses, and of 30 in the number of persons proceeded against for drunkenness, and of 23 convictions, over the numbers for 1900.

One member of the force was called out with the Army Reserve and was still serving with his regiment on 29th September.

Thirty-one members of the force hold certificates from the St. John Ambulance Association.

The Inspector visited 11 stations, and found them clean and in good order.

The books and returns were well kept, and the management, numbers, and discipline of the force have been efficiently maintained.

A new scale of pay as under has been adopted:—

	On Appointment.	After 1 Year's Service.	After 2 Years' Service.	After 4 Years' Service.	After 6 Years' Service.	After 7 Years' Service.	After 8 Years' Service.
Constables per week -	£ s. d. 1 4 0	£ s. d. 1 5 0	£ s. d. 1 6 0	£ s. d. 1 7 6	£ s. d. 1 8 0	£ s. d. 1 9 0	£ s. d. 1 10 0
Sergeants ditto -	1 11 6	—	1 12 8	1 13 10	1 15 0	—	—
Inspectors per annum -	100 0 0	—	105 0 0	110 0 0	113 0 0	—	120 0 0
Superintendents ditto -	135 0 0	—	145 0 0	155 0 0	—	—	165 0 0

COUNTY OF MONTGOMERY.

Force - - - - - - 36.

| Area in acres - | - | - | - 510,111 | Acres to each constable - | - | - 14,154 |
| Population in 1891 | - | - | 58,003 | Population to ditto, as per census 1891 | 1,611 |

RANKS.	Chief Constable.	Yearly Pay in £ and Shillings.										
		1 Superintendent.						Inspectors.				
		Deputy Chief Constable.	Chief Clerk.	1st Class.	2nd Class.	3rd Class.	4th Class.	1st Class.	2nd Class.	3rd Class.	4th Class.	Wanting to complete.
Number of each Rank and Class -	1	1	1	—	—	—	—	—	—	—	—	—
Rates of Pay of each ditto - -	£ 275	£ 130	£ 130	—	—	—	—	—	—	—	—	—

RANKS.	Weekly Pay in Shillings and Pence.							
	5 Sergeants.			28 Constables.				
	1st Class.	2nd Class.	3rd Class.	1st Class.				
Number of each Rank and Class -	1	—	4	8	2	10	3	4
Rates of Pay of each ditto - -	s. 35	s. d. 32 3	s. d. 31 6	s. 30	s. 29	s. 28	s. 25	s. 24

Inspected in June, when the force was complete.

The authorised establishment of the force is one chief constable, one superintendent and deputy chief constable, one inspector, who is chief clerk, five sergeants, and 28 constables.

Extra duties performed by the police.

NATURE OF DUTY.	Chief Constable.	Super-intendent.	Inspectors.	Sergeants.	Constables.	TOTAL.
Inspectors under Contagious Diseases (Animals) Act.	1	1	1	5	28	36
Inspectors under Explosives Act - -	—	—	—	5	—	5
Inspector's under Food and Drugs Act -	—	—	—	2	—	2
Inspectors of Common Lodging-houses -	—	—	—	4	—	4
Assistant Relieving Officers -	—	—	—	1	1	2
Inspectors of Weights and Measures -	1	—	—	—	1	2

There are two more public-houses than in 1900, and 20 persons more were proceeded against for drunkenness, and five more were convicted than in that year.

Eighteen members of the force hold certificates from the St. John Ambulance Association.

The Inspector visited seven stations, and found them clean and in good order.

The books and returns were well kept, and the management, numbers, and discipline of the force have been efficiently maintained.

No. 1.
Eastern Counties,
Midland,
and North Wales
District.

A new scale of pay as under has been adopted :—

Constables—

					£	s.	d.	
On appointment	-	-	-	-		4	0	per week.
After 1 year	-	-	-	-		5	0	,,
,, 2 years	-	-	-	-			0	..
.. 4 years in 1st class	-	-	-	-			6	..
,, 6 ,, ,,	-	-	-	-			0	..
,, 7 ,, ,,	-	-	-	-			0	..
,, 10 ,, ,,	-	-	-	-		1	0	..

Sergeants—

					£	s.	d.	
On appointment	-	-	-	-		1	11	6	..
After 2 years	-	-	-	-		1	12	8	..
,, 5 ,,	-	-	-	-		1	15	0	..

Inspector—

					£	s.	d.	
On appointment	-	-	-	-		97	10	0	per annum.
After 2 years	-	-	-	-		100	0	0	,,
,, 5 ,,	-	-	-	-		110	0	0	,,
,, 10 ,,	-	-	-	-		120	0	0	,,

Superintendent—

					£	s.	d.	
On appointment	-	-	-	-		120	0	0	,,
After 1 year	-	-	-	-		130	0	0	,,
,, 4 years	-	-	-	-		140	0	0	,,
.. 5 ,,	-	-	-	-		150	0	0	,,
,, 8 ..	-	-	-	-		160	0	0	,,
,, 10 ,,	-	-	-	-		170	0	0	..

With allowance of 20*l.* for house rent.

Elvet Garth, Durham,
Sir,   6th April 1902.

   I HAVE the honour to submit herewith the reports of the late Sir Herbert Croft, Inspector of Constabulary for the Northern District.

Owing to his illness and lamented death in February last there is no introductory report, but I have done what I can to edit and put in order the different reports of the County and Borough Police Forces that he inspected last year.

The different Police Forces in the Northern District appear to have been efficiently maintained in respect of management, numbers, and discipline for the year ending 29th of September 1901.

I have, &c.

(Signed)   *J. H. Eden,*
Lt.-Colonel,
H.M. Inspector of Constabulary.

To the Right Honourable,
    CHARLES T. RITCHIE, M.P.,
      His Majesty's Principal Secretary of State
      for the Home Department.

REPORTS of COUNTIES AND BOROUGHS RESPECTIVELY.

COUNTY OF CHESTER.

Force - - - - - 439.

Area in acres - - - 633,101 | Acres to each constable - - 1,442
Population in 1891 - - 31,898 | Population to ditto, as per census 1891   983

RANKS.	Chief Officer.	Deputy Chief Officer.	12 Superintendents.				12 Inspectors.			
			1st Class.		2nd Class.		1st Class.		2nd Class.	
Number of each Rank and Class -	1	1	1	2	1	2	2	2	1	2	2	2
Rates of Pay of each ditto -	£ 656	£ 350	£ 240	£ 210	£ 200	£ 200	£ 186	£ 170	£ 135	£ 125	£ 120	£ 120	£ 110	£ 100

Weekly Pay in Shillings and Pence.

RANKS.	78 Sergeants.						335 Constables.							
	Merit Class.	1st Class.	2nd Class.	3rd Class.	4th Class.	5th Class.	Acting Sergts.	Merit Class.	1st Class.	2nd Class.	3rd Class.	4th Class.	5th Class.	6th Class.
Number of each Rank and Class -	-	38	30	2	12	6	30	63	95	34	33	21	22	39
Rates of Pay of each ditto -	-	s. d. 37 4	s. d. 36 2	s. d. 35 7	s. d. 34 5	s. d. 33 3	s. d. 32 8	s. d. 31 6	s. d. 30 4	s. d. 29 2	s. d. 28 0	s. d. 26 10	s. d. 26 3	s. d. 25 1

I 2

No. 2.
Northern District.

Inspected between Wednesday the 14th and Friday 19th April, both days inclusive, total eight days, when there were vacancies for seven constables.

Authorised Establishment, 439. Variations.—24 constables resigned, one superintendent and one sergeant pensioned, one superintendent and one constable died.

Ambulance.—Four hundred and twelve hold certificates from St. John Ambulance.

Licensing Acts.—An increase of one in public-house, with three less prosecutions and five less convictions.

Drunkenness.—There were 305 fewer prosecutions and 261 fewer convictions.

The books and returns were well kept.

The management, number, and discipline of the forces have been efficiently maintained.

The borough of Crewe is still policed by the county force ; a new station at Budbury was inspected and approved of.

I regret to record the death of the deputy chief constable, Lieut.-Colonel Cope, his loss is felt by all, he was a good, kind-hearted man. Superintendent Leat has been appointed deputy in his place.

BOROUGH OF BIRKENHEAD.

Force - - - - - - 145.

| Area in acres - | - | - | 3,850 | Acres to each constable - - - 26 |
| Population in 1891 - | - | - | 99,857 | Population to ditto, as per census 1891 688 |

RANKS.	Chief Officer.	1 Superintendent.						15 Inspectors.			
		Deputy Chief Officer.	Chief Clerk.	1st Class.	2nd Class.	3rd Class.	4th Class.	1st Class.		2nd Class.	3rd Class.	4th Class.
Number of each Rank and Class -	1	-	-	1	-	-	-	1	1	9	1	1	2
Rates of Pay of each ditto -	£600	-	-	£200	-	-	-	£117	£117	£117	£109	£106	£104

RANKS.	4 Sergeants.						122 Constables.								
	Merit Class.	1st Class.	2nd Class.	3rd Class.	4th Class.	5th Class.	Acting Sergts.	Merit Class.	1st Class.	2nd Class.	3rd Class.	4th Class.	5th Class.	6th Class.	Vacancy.
Number of each Rank and Class -	-	1	1	2	-	-	20	10	17	7	12	22	10	17	1
Rates of Pay of each ditto -	-	40	38	36	-	-	33	32	31	30	29	28	27	25 7	-

Inspected 25th March, when force was complete.

Authorised Establishment, 145. Variations.—Eight constables resigned, five voluntarily, three compulsory ; three were dismissed ; one inspector and one constable pensioned. Total, 13.

Licensing Acts.—Public-houses, six less proceeded against.

There were two less beerhouses, no prosecutions.

CITY AND COUNTY BOROUGH OF CHESTER.

Force - - - - - - - - - 50.

Area in acres - - - 2,960	Acres to each constable - - - 59
Population in 1891 - - - 37,105	Population to ditto, as per census 1891 742

RANKS.	Chief Officer	1 Superintendent						2 Inspectors.				
		Deputy Chief Officer.	Chief Clerk.	1st Class.	2nd Class.	3rd Class.	4th Class.	1st Class.	2nd Class.	3rd Class.	4th Class.	5th Class.
Number of each Rank and Class -	1	-	1	-	-	-	-	1	-	1	-	-
Rates of Pay of each ditto -	£ 350	-	£ s. 114 8	-	-	-	-	£ s. 114 8	-	£ 104	-	-

Yearly Pay in £ and Shillings.

RANKS.	5 Sergeants.						41 Constables.								
	Merit Class.	1st Class.	2nd Class.	3rd Class.	4th Class.	5th Class.	Merit 1st Class.	Merit 2nd Class.	1st Class.	2nd Class.	3rd Class.	4th Class.	5th Class.	6th Class.	Probationary.
Number of each Rank and Class -	-	-	2	2	1 detective	-	3	3	7	6	8	1	6	4	2
Rates of Pay of each ditto -	-	-	35	33	35	-	32	31	30	29	28	27	26	25	24

Weekly Pay in Shillings and Pence.

Inspected Friday 19th April, when the force was complete.

Authorised Establishment.—Fifty. Variations, five.—Three constables resigned, one sergeant and one constable were pensioned.

Licensing Acts.—An increase of one public-house, with three prosecutions and two convictions.

Drunkenness.—A decrease of prosecutions by six, and of convictions by one. Total, 330.

Ambulance.—Thirty-five members hold certificates from St. John Ambulance Association.

The books and returns were were well kept.

The management, numbers, and discipline of the force have been efficiently maintained.

BOROUGH OF CONGLETON.

Force - - - - - - 11.

Area in acres - - - 2,572	Acres to each constable - - - 233
Population in 1891 - - - 10,744	Population to ditto, as per census 1891 977

RANKS.	Chief Officer.'	Yearly Pay in £ and Shillings.										
		Superintendents.						Inspectors.				
		Deputy Chief Officer.	Chief Clerk.	1st Class.	2nd Class.	3rd Class.	4th Class.	1st Class.	2nd Class.	3rd Class.	4th Class.	5th Class.
Number of each Rank and Class -	1	-	-	-	-	-	-	-	-	-	-	-
Rates of Pay of each ditto - -	£ 145	-	-	-	-	-	-	-	-	-	-	-

RANKS.	Weekly Pay in Shillings and Pence.													
	2 Sergeants.						8 Constables.							
	Merit Class.	1st Class.	2nd Class.	3rd Class.	4th Class.	5th Class.	Acting Sergts.	Merit Class.	1st Class.	2nd Class.	3rd Class.	4th Class.	5th Class.	6th Class.
Number of each Rank and Class -	-	1	1	-	-	-	-	1	2	2	2	1	-	-
Rates of Pay of each ditto - -	-	s. d. 31 2	s. 30	-	-	-	-	s. d. 27 2	s. 26	s. 25	s. 24	s. 23	-	-

Inspected the 10th April, when the force was complete.

Authorised Establishment, 11.

Extra Duties.—The chief constable is inspector of common lodging-houses and of weights and measures.

Licensing Acts.—No prosecutions.

Drunkenness.—Fifty-five prosecutions and 36 convictions.

Ambulance.—Six members of the force hold certificates from St. John Ambulance Association.

The cells and offices were clean and in good order.

The books and returns were well kept.

The management, number, and discipline of the force has been well maintained.

BOROUGH OF HYDE.

Force - - - - 33.

Area in acres - . - - 3,07 2 | Acres to each constable - - - 93
Population in 1891 - - - 30,670 | Population to ditto, as per census 1891 929

RANKS.	Chief Officer.	Superintendents.						2 Inspectors.				
		Deputy Chief Officer.	Chief Clerk.	1st Class.	2nd Class.	3rd Class.	4th Class.	1st Class.	2nd Class.	3rd Class.	4th Class.	5th Class.
Number of each Rank and Class -	1	-	-	-	-	-	-	1	1	-	-	-
Rates of Pay of each ditto - -	£ 290	-	-	-	-	-	-	£ 105	£ 100	.	-	-

RANKS.	5 Sergeants.						25 Constables.						
	Merit Class.	1st Class.	2nd Class.	3rd Class.	4th Class.	5th Class.	Acting Sergeants.	Merit Class.	1st Class.	2nd Class.	3rd Class.	4th Class.	5th Class.
Number of each Rank and Class -	-	3	2	-	-	-	-	-	3	8	7	5	-	-
Rates of Pay of each ditto - -	-	s. 34	s. 33	- .	-	-	-	-	s. 28	s. 27	s. 26	s. 25	-	-

Inspected on 12th April.

Authorised Establishment.—Thirty-three.

Extra Duties.—An inspector commands fire brigade, and a sergeant and 10 constables act as firemen and receive extra pay.

Public-houses.—One prosecution, no convictions.

Beerhouses.—Four prosecutions, and one conviction.

Drunkenness.—Ninety-eight were prosecuted and 88 convicted ; a decrease of 38 prosecutions and 29 convictions.

Ambulance.—The whole of the members of the force hold certificates.

The books and returns were well kept.

The management, numbers, and discipline of the force have been efficiently maintained.

BOROUGH OF MACCLESFIELD.

Force - - - - - - - 38.

Area in acres - - - 3,214	Acres to each constable - - - 84
Population in 1891 - - - 36,009	Population to ditto, as per census 1891 947

Yearly Pay in £ and Shillings.

RANKS.	Chief Officer.	Superintendents.						3 Inspectors.				
		Deputy Chief Officer.	Chief Clerk.	1st Class.	2nd Class.	3rd Class.	4th Class.	1st Class.	2nd Class.	3rd Class.	4th Class.	5th Class.
Number of each Rank and Class -	1	-	-	-	-	-	-	1	-	1	1	-
Rates of Pay of each ditto -	£ 300	-	-	-	-	-	-	£ s. 119 12	-	£ s. 109 4	£ 104	-

Weekly Pay in Shillings and Pence.

RANKS.	4 Sergeants.						30 Constables.								
	Merit Class.	1st Class.	2nd Class.	3rd Class.	4th Class.	5th Class.	Merit Class. 1st.	Merit Class. 2nd.	2nd Class.	3rd Class.	4th Class.	5th Class.	6th Class.	7th Class.	
Number of each Rank and Class -	-	1	-	-	1	2	2	1	14	3	1	1	5	2	1
Rates of Pay of each ditto -	-	s. d. 34 6	-	-	s. 33	s. 32	s. 33	s. 31	s. 29	s. 28	s. 27	s. 26	s. 25	s. 24	Vacancy.

Inspected on 11th April, when there was one vacancy for a constable.

Authorised Strength.—Thirty-eight.

Extra Duties.—Chief constable is inspector of hackney carriages, and a sergeant is Coroner's officer.

Public-houses.—Three prosecutions, and two convictions.

Beerhouses.—Two prosecutions, and one conviction.

Drunkenness.—One hundred and sixteen prosecutions, 100 convictions; an increase of 12 prosecutions and three convictions.

Ambulance.—Twenty-eight members of the force hold certificates from St. John Ambulance Association.

The books and returns were well kept.

The management, numbers, and discipline of the force were efficiently maintained.

Force - - - - - - 32.

| Area in acres - - - 3,135 | Acres to each constable - - - 97 |
| Population in 1891 - - - 26,783 | Population to ditto, as per census 1891 836 |

RANKS.	Chief Officer.	Yearly Pay in £ and Shillings.										
		Superintendents.						2 Inspectors.				
		Deputy Chief Officer.	Chief Clerk.	1st Class.	2nd Class.	3rd Class.	4th Class.	1st Class.	2nd Class.	3rd Class.	4th Class.	5th Class.
Number of each Rank and Class -	1	-	-	-	-	-	-	1	1	-	-	-
Rates of Pay of each ditto -	£ 300	-	-	-	-	-	-	£ s. 114 8	£ 104	-	-	-

RANKS.	Weekly Pay in Shillings and Pence.													
	5 Sergeants.						24 Constables.							
	Merit Class.	1st Class.	2nd Class.	3rd Class.	4th Class.	5th Class.	Acting Sergeants.	Detective	1st Class.	2nd Class.	3rd Class.	4th Class.	5th Class.	6th Class.
Number of each Rank and Class -	-	2	2	1	-	-	-	1	6	5	3	2	7	-
Rates of Pay of each ditto -	-	s. 35	s. 33	s. 32	-	-	-	s. 31	s. 31	s. 29	s. 28	s. 27	s. 26	-

Inspected 23rd April, when the force was complete.

Authorised Strength.—Thirty-two ; three constables retired, one was pensioned, and one died.

Public-houses.—Fifty-nine ; with two prosecutions, and two convictions.

Beerhouses.—Fifty-seven ; with two prosecutions, and one conviction.

Drunkenness.—One hundred and six prosecutions, and 100 convictions, being 13 more prosecutions and 19 more convictions.

Ambulance.—Twenty-nine members of the force hold certificates, two less than last year.

The cells and police offices at headquarters and at Millford were clean and in good order.

Books and returns were well kept.

The management and discipline of the force have been efficiently maintained.

BOROUGH OF STOCKPORT.

Force - - - - - - 85.

| Area in acres - | - | - | 2,200 | Acres to each constable | - | - | - | 27 |
| Population in 1891 - | - | - | 70,263 | Population to ditto, as per census 1891 | | | | 836 |

RANKS.	Chief Officer.	Superintendents.						Inspectors.				
		Deputy Chief Officer.	Chief Clerk.	1st Class.	2nd Class.	3rd Class.	4th Class.	1st Class.	2nd Class.	3rd Class.	4th Class.	5th Class.
Number of each Rank and Class -	1	-	1	-	-	-	-	1	1	2	1	-
Rates of Pay of each ditto -	£ 300	-	£ s. 85 16	-	-	-	-	£ s. 122 10	£ 117	£ 110	£ 100	-

RANKS.	9 Sergeant's.						69 Constables.								
	1st Class.	2nd Class.	3rd Class.	4th Class.	5th Class.	6th Class.	Merit Class. 1st. 2nd.		1st Class.	2nd Class.	3rd Class.	4th Class.	5th Class.	6'b Class	7th Class.	Vacancies.
Number of each Rank and Class -	1	1	1	1	2	3	2	21	6	10	4	9	6	3	3	
Rates of Pay of each ditto -	s. 39	s. 37	s. 36	s. 35	s. 34	s. 33	s. 32	s. 31	s. 30	s. 29	s. 28	s. 27	s. 26	s. 25	s. 24	-

Inspected Friday, 12th April, when there were three vacancies which are not yet filled up.

Establishment.—Eighty-five.

Extra Duties.—Chief constable is commander of fire brigade; two inspectors, two sergeants, and 22 constables are firemen. Chief constable and two inspectors inspect explosives and hackney carriages, and the chief and four inspectors inspect under Contagious Diseases (Animals) Act. The chief constable was called on to resign, and was succeeded by Inspector Briddley of Manchester.

Public-houses.—One hundred and thirty; with two prosecutions, two convictions.

Beerhouses.—One hundred and six, with one prosecution.

Drunkenness.—Five hundred and twelve prosecutions, and 506 convictions, being 61 more prosecutions and 68 more convictions.

Ambulance.—Eighty members of the force hold certificates from St. John Ambulance Association.

The books and returns were well kept.

Management and discipline of force efficiently maintained.

COUNTY OF CUMBERLAND.

Force - - - - - - - 197.*

Area in acres - - - 968,136 | Acres to each constable - - - 4,914
Population in 1891 - - 227,373 | Population to ditto, as per census 1891 1,154

RANKS.	Chief Officer.	8 Superintendents.							9 Inspectors.				
		Deputy Chief Officer.	Chief Clerk.	1st Class.	2nd Class.	3rd Class.	4th Class.		1st Class.	2nd Class.	3rd Class.	4th Class.	5th Class.
Number of each Rank and Class -	1	1	1	6	-	-	-		8	-	1	-	-
Rates of Pay of each ditto - -	£ 525	£ s. 202 5	£ s. 127 15	£ s. d. 202 5 5	-	-	-		£ s. d. 120 2 11	-	£ s. d. 112 10 10	-	-

Yearly Pay in £ and Shillings.

RANKS.		26 Sergeants.						155 Constables.						
	Merit Class.	1st Class.	2nd Class.	3rd Class.	4th Class.	5th Class.	Acting Sergeants	Merit Class.	1st Class.	2nd Class.	3rd Class.	4th Class.	5th Class.	6th Class.
Number of each Rank and Class -	-	22	1	3	-	-	-	-	110	10	6	15	12	-
Rates of Pay of each ditto - -	-	s. d. 26 9	s. 25	s. d. 23 3	-	-	-	-	s. d. 30 11	s. d. 29 2	s. 28	s. d. 26 10	s. d. 23 11	-

Weekly Pay in Shillings and Pence.

* There were five additional constables, one sergeant, and four constables appointed under 3 & 4 Vict. c. 88. s. 18.

Inspected between 25th and 27th June, both days inclusive, when the force was complete.

Authorised Establishment.—One hundred and ninety-seven.

Extra Duties :—

NATURE OF DUTY.	Chief Constable.	Super-intendents.	Inspectors.	Sergeants.	Constables.	REMARKS.
Inspectors of Weights and Measures -	1	7	9	20	34	
Inspectors under Explosives Act - -	1	7	8	22	6	Actual expenses paid.
Inspectors under Food and Drugs Act -	1	7	9	20	34	
Inspectors under Contagious Diseases (Animals) Act.	1	7	9	20	34	
Fire Brigade - - - - -	1	8	9	25	154	

Public-houses.—Nine hundred and forty-four ; with 34 prosecutions, and 16 convictions.

Beerhouses.—One hundred and twelve ; with six prosecutions, and five convictions.

Drunkenness.—One thousand three hundred and twenty-three prosecuted, and 1,204 convicted, being nine more prosecutions and 15 more convictions.

Ambulance.—One hundred and sixteen members of the force hold certificates.

The books and returns were well kept.

The management, numbers, and discipline of the force was efficiently maintained.

The chief constable is also chief constable of Westmoreland.

No. 2.
hern District.

CITY OF CARLISLE.

Force - - - - 50.

| Area in acres - - - 2,025 | Acres to each constable - - - 40 |
| Population in 1891 - - - 39,176 | Population to ditto, as per census 1891 783 |

Yearly Pay in £ and Shillings.

RANKS.	Chief Officer.	Superintendents.						2 Inspectors.				
		Deputy Chief Officer.	Chief Clerk.	1st Class.	2nd Class.	3rd Class.	4th Class.	1st Class.	2nd Class.	3rd Class.	4th Class.	5th Class.
Number of each Rank and Class	1	-	-	-	-	-	-	2	-	-	-	-
Rates of Pay of each ditto	£ 350	-	-	-	-	-	-	£ 130	-	-	-	-

Weekly Pay in Shillings and Pence.

RANKS.	5 Sergeants.						43 Constables.														
	Merit Class.	1st Class.	2nd Class.	3rd Class.	4th Class.	5th Class.	Merit.				1st Class.							2nd Class.	3rd Class.	4th Class.	Probation.
Number of each Rank and Class	-	4	1	-	-	-	1	1	3	2	1	4	1	8	3	3	7½	2	4	2	
Rates of Pay of each ditto	-	s. 40	s. 39	-	-	-	s. 37	s. 36	s. 34	s. 32	s. 36	s. 33	s. 32	s. 31	s. 30	s. 29	s. 28	s. 27	s. d. 28 6	s. 24	

[Inspected 5th July, when the force was complete.

Authorised Strength.—Fifty.

Extra Duties.—Chief constable and one constable inspect hackney carriages, explosives, and weights and measures.

Public-houses.—One hundred and twelve, with two prosecutions.

Beerhouses.—Ten.

Drunkenness.—Five hundred and ten prosecutions, and 452 convictions, being 68 more prosecutions and 84 more convictions.

Ambulance.—Forty-one members of the force hold certificates from St. John Ambulance Association.

The books and returns were well kept.

Management, numbers, and discipline of the force efficiently maintained.

COUNTY OF DERBY.

Force - - - 333.*

| Area in acres - - - 644,543 | Acres to each constable - - - |
| Population in 1891 - - - 381,218 | Population to ditto, as per census 1891 |

RANKS.	Chief Officer.	11 Superintendents.						15 Inspectors.				
		Deputy Chief Officer.	Ch'ef Clerk.	1st Class.	2nd Class.	3rd Class.	4th Class.	1st Class.	2nd Class.	3rd Class.	4th Class.	5th Class.
Number of each Rank and Class -	1	1	-	6	2	2	-	5	1	4	5	-
Rates of Pay of each ditto -	£ 550	£ 300	-	£ 210	£ 170	£ 150	-	£ 130	£ 120	£ 106	£ 100	-

Yearly Pay in £ and Shillings.

RANKS.	43 Sergeants.						263 Constables.						
	Merit Class.	1st Class.	2nd Class.	3rd Class.	4th Class.	5th Class.	Merit Class.		1st Class.		2nd Class.	3rd Class.	4th Class.
Number of each Rank and Class -	-	4	8	10	21	-	45	69	13	26	68	19	33	-
Rates of Pay of each ditto -	-	s. d. 37 4	s. d. 35 7	s. d. 33 10	s. d. 32 1	-	s. d. 31 6	s. d. 30 4	s. d. 29 2	s. 28	s. d. 27 5	s. d. 26 3	s. d. 24 6	-

Weekly Pay in Shillings and Pence.

* Exclusive of 14 additional constables appointed under 3 & 4 Vict. c. 84. s. 18.

Inspected 11th, 13th, 14th, 15th and 16th May, when the force was complete.

Authorised Establishment.—Three hundred and thirty-three; two sergeants and six constables have been added to the force.

Public-houses.—One thousand and ninety-seven; with 56 prosecutions, and 41 convictions.

Beerhouses.—Three hundred and ninety-three; with 16 prosecutions, and 10 convictions.

Drunkenness.—Two thousand three hundred and sixty-eight prosecutions, and 2,251 convictions, making 244 more prosecutions, and 117 more convictions.

Ambulance.—Two hundred and ninety members of the force hold certificates from St. John Ambulance Association.

The books and returns were well kept.

The management, numbers, and discipline of the force are efficiently maintained.

The borough of Ilkestone is policed by this county's force.

Extra Duties :—

NATURE OF DUTY.	Chief Constable.	Super-intendents.	Inspectors.	Sergeants.	Constables.
Inspectors under Contagious Diseases (Animals) Act.	The whole force attend to this, and, while so employed, superintendents get 3d. per hour and 2d. per mile, and inspectors, sergeants, and constables get 2d. per hour.				
Inspectors under Chimney Sweepers Act	—	11	—	—	—
Inspectors under Pedlars Act - - -	—	11	—	—	—
Inspectors under Explosives Act -	1	11	—	—	—
Street and Market Inspector at Long Eaton -	—	—	1*	—	—

* He receives 5l. per annum.

BOROUGH OF CHESTERFIELD.

Force - - - - - - - 35.

| Area in acres - - - 1,219 | Acres to each constable - - - |
| Population in 1891 - - - 22,009 | Population to ditto, as per census 1891 |

RANKS.	Chief Officer	1 Superintendent.						2 Inspectors.				
		Deputy Chief Officer.	Chief Clerk.	1st Class.	2nd Class.	3rd Class.	4th Class.	1st Class.	2nd Class.	3rd Class.	4th Class.	5th Class.
Number of each Rank and Class	1	-	1	-	-	-	-	1	1	-	-	-
Rates of Pay of each ditto	£ 300	-	£ s. 92 18	-	-	-	-	£ s. 135 9	£ s. d. 119 16 4	-	-	-

Yearly Pay in £ and Shillings.

RANKS.	4 Sergeants.						27 Constables.							
	Merit Class.	1st Class.	2nd Class.	3rd Class.	4th Class.	5th Class.	Acting Sergeants.	Merit Class.	1st Class.	2nd Class.	3rd Class.	4th Class.	5th Class.	6th Class.
Number of each Rank and Class	-	1	1	1	1	-	-	3	8	3	3	2	3	-
Rates of Pay of each ditto	-	s. d. 43 10	s. d. 40 9	s. d. 39 9	s. d. 38 8	-	-	s. d. 33 3	s. d. 33 3	s. 31	s. 29	s. d. 28 9	Vacancies	-

Weekly Pay in Shillings and Pence.

Inspected 11th May, when there was one vacancy.

Authorised Establishment.—Thirty-five; an increase of one sergeant and two constables.

Public-houses.—Seventy-four, with one prosecution.

Beerhouses.—Fifty-one.

Drunkenness.—Two hundred and fifteen prosecutions, and 213 convictions, making nine less prosecutions than last year.

Ambulance.—Thirty-one members of the force hold certificates from St. John Ambulance Association, eight more than last year.

The cells and police offices were clean and in good order.

Extra Duties.—The chief constable is billet master, inspector of hackney carriages, common lodging-houses, and explosives, and, with a constable, weights and measures.

The books and returns were well kept.

The management, numbers, and discipline of the force are efficiently maintained.

Force - - - - - - - 120.

Area in acres - - - 3,445	Acres to each constable - - - 40
Population in 1891 - - - 94,146	Population to ditto, as per census 1891 733

Yearly Pay in £ and Shillings.

RANKS.	Chief Officer.	1 Superintendent.						6 Inspectors.				
		Deputy Chief Officer.	Chief Clerk.	1st Class.	2nd Class.	3rd Class.	4th Class.	1st Class.	2nd Class.	3rd Class.	4th Class.	5th Class.
Number of each Rank and Class -	1	-	-	1	-	-	-	1	1	2	1	-
Rates of Pay of each ditto -	£ 356	-	-	£ 210	-	-	-	£ s. 124 16	£ s. 119 12	£ s. 114 8	£ s. 109 4	-

Weekly Pay in Shillings and Pence.

RANKS.	16 Sergeants.							96 Constables.									Vacancy.
	Merit Class.	1st Class.	2nd Class.	3rd Class.	4th Class.	5th Class.	1	Acting Sergeants.	Merit Class.	1st Class.	2nd Class.	3rd Class.	4th Class.	5th Class.	6th Class.	
Number of each Rank and Class -	1*	2	4	2	5	1†	1	1‡	17	3	11	9	16	22	6	10	1
Rates of Pay of each ditto -	s. 38	s. 37	s. 35	s. 34	s. 33	s. 32	s. 30	s. 32	s. 32	s. 31	s. 30	s. 29	s. 28	s. 26	s. 25	s. 24	-

* Warrant Officer. † Acting Sergeant. ‡ Detective.

Inspected on 13th May, when there was one vacancy.

Authorised Establishment.—One hundred and twenty.

Extra Duties.—The chief officer is head of fire brigade, and a superintendent, who also inspects hackney carriages, and a constable is drill instructor.

Public-houses.—Two hundred and fifty-four; with seven prosecutions, and six convictions.

Beerhouses.—Ninety-six; with four prosecutions, and three convictions.

Drunkenness.—Seven hundred and seventy-six prosecutions, and 707 convictions, an increase of five prosecutions, and 30 convictions.

Ambulance.—One hundred and seven members, of the force have certificates from St. John Ambulance Association, an increase of twenty.

The cells and police offices at both stations were clean and in good order.

The books and returns well kept.

The management, numbers, and discipline of the force is efficiently maintained.

K 4

BOROUGH OF GLOSSOP.

Force - - - - - 26.

Area in acres - - - 3,050	Acres to each constable - - - 117
Population in 1891 - - - 22,416	Population to ditto, as per census 1891 862

RANKS.	Chief Officer.	Yearly Pay in £ and Shillings.											
		Superintendents.						1 Inspector.					
		Deputy Chief Officer.	Chief Clerk.	1st Class.	2nd Class.	3rd Class.	4th Class.	1st Class.	2nd Class.	3rd Class.	4th Class.	5th Class.	
Number of each } Rank and Class - }	1	-	-	-	-	-	-	1	-	-	-	-	
Rates of Pay of } each ditto - - }	£ 200	-	-	-	-	-	-	£ 115	-	-	-	-	

RANKS.	Weekly Pay in Shillings and Pence.												
	4 Sergeants.						24 Constables.						
	Merit Class.	1st Class.	2nd Class.	3rd Class.	4th Class.	5th Class	Acting Sergeants.	Merit Class.	1st Class.	2nd Class.	3rd Class.	4th Class.	5th Class.	6th Class.
Number of each } Rank and Class - }	-	1	3	-	-	-	-	-	4	4	5	1	3	3
Rates of Pay of } each ditto - - }	-	s. 37	s. 36	-	-	-	-	-	s. 31	s. 30	s. 29	s. 28	s. 27	s. 25

Inspected the 3rd of March, when the force was complete.

Authorised Establishment.—Twenty-six.

Extra Duties.—The chief officer is head of fire brigade, and also inspects hackney carriages, common lodging-houses, explosives, and is also billet master.

Public-houses.—Thirty-four ; with one prosecution, and one conviction.

Beerhouses.—Twenty-seven ; with two prosecutions, and one conviction.

Drunkenness.—Seventy prosecutions and 67 convictions, an increase of 27 prosecutions and 26 convictions.

Ambulance.—Nineteen members of the force hold certificates from St. John Ambulance Association ; two less than last year.

The cells were clean and in good order. Hadfield improved.

The books and returns were well kept.

The management, numbers, and discipline of the force were efficiently maintained.

COUNTY OF DURHAM.

Force - - - - - 618.*

| Area in acres - - - 637,383 | Acres to each constable - - - 1,036 |
| Population in 1891 - - - 684,003 | Population to ditto, as per census 1891 1,101 |

RANKS.	Chief Officer.	13 Superintendents.						19 Inspectors.				
		Deputy Chief Officer.	1st Class.	2nd Class.	3rd Class.	4th Class.	5th Class.	1st Class.	2nd Class.	3rd Class.	4th Class.	5th Class.
Number of each Rank and Class -	1	1	3	2	2	1	2	2	1	2	5	6	5
Rates of Pay of each ditto -	£ 600	£ s. d. 269 3 4	£ s. d. 249 8 4	£ s. d. 240 5 10	£ s. d. 220 10 5	£ s. d. 200 13	£ s. 179 9 2	£ s. d. 189 13 9	£ s. d. 156 17 6	£ s. d. 137 18 6	£ s. d. 118 13 6	£ s. d. 114 1 3	£ s. 109 10

Yearly Pay in £, Shillings, and Pence.

RANKS.	107 Sergeants.							478 Constables.		
	1st Class.	2nd Class.	3rd Class.	4th Class.	5th Class.	6th Class.	Merit Class.	1st Class.	2nd Class.	3rd Class.
Number of each Rank and Class -	13	12	9	8	19	10	22	13	16 26 10 23 38 33 61 80 66	86	18
Pay of ditto -	s. d. 39 8	s. d. 38 6	s. d. 37 11	s. d. 37 4	s. d. 36 9	s. d. 35 9	s. d. 34 5	s. d. 33 8	s. d. 33 10 33 8 33 1 31 6 30 11 30 4 29 4 29 2	s. 28	s. d. 26 3	s. d. 26 1

Weekly Pay in Shillings and Pence.

* Exclusive of three sergeants and 55 constables appointed as additional constables under 3 & 4 Vict. c. 88. s. 19.

Inspected on 17th, 18th, 19th, 20th, 21st, and 22nd of June.

Authorised Strength.—Six hundred and eighteen.

Extra Duties :—

NATURE OF DUTY.	Chief Constable.	Super-intendents.	Inspectors.	Sergeants.	Constables.	REMARKS.
Inspectors of Common Lodging-houses.	—	1	3	2	—	Receive 2l. to 10l. per annum as extra pay.
Assistant Relieving Officers for Tramps.	—	5	2	3	1	Receive 5l. to 15l. per annum as extra pay.
Inspectors under Contagious Diseases (Animals) Act.	1	13	19	97	5	County allowance for not less than five hours, 2s. 6d.; for less than five hours, 1s. 6d.
Inspectors under Explosives Act.	1	13	6	29	—	County Allowance, 3s. 6d. for a day of not less than five hours; with horse, 5s.; without horse, 3s. 6d.

Public-houses.—One thousand five hundred and thirty-six, with 90 prosecutions, and 59 convictions.

Beerhouses.—Three hundred and fifty-six, with seven prosecutions, and four convictions.

Drunkenness.—Eleven thousand six hundred and eighty-two prosecutions, and 11,361 convictions, being 625 more prosecutions, and 404 more convictions.

Ambulance.—Five hundred and twenty-two members of the force hold certificates from St. John Ambulance Association, an increase of five men.

The books and returns were well kept.

The management, numbers, and discipline of the force were efficiently maintained.

L

No. 2.
Northern District.

Since last inspection an increase in the pay of inspectors, sergeants, and constables has been granted by the Standing Joint Committee, and sanctioned by the Home Secretary, as per return below :—

RANK.		Old Rate of Pay.	New Rate of Pay.	Date of Increase.
		Yearly.	*Yearly.*	
		£ s. d.	£ s. d.	
Inspector on appointment	- -	106 9 2	109 10 0	
„ after 2 years	-	111 0 5	114 1 3	
„ „ 5 „	- -	115 11 8	118 12 6	}From 1st July 1901.
„ „ 7 „	- -	120 2 11	127 15 0	
„ „ 10 „	- -	129 5 5	136 17 6	
		Weekly.	*Weekly.*	
		£ s. d.	£ s. d.	
Sergeant on appointment	- -	1 11 6	1 13 3	
„ after 2 years	- -	1 12 8	—	
„ „ 3 „	- -	—	1 14 5	New Grade
„ „ 5 „	- -	1 13 10	1 15 7	
„ „ 8 „	- -	—	1 16 2	New Grade
„ „ 10 „	- -	1 15 0	1 16 9	
„ „ 12 „	- -	—	1 17 4	New Grade
				}From 1st Nov. 1900.
Constable on appointment	- -	1 7 5	1 8 0	
„ after 2 years	- -	1 8 0	1 9 2	
„ „ 5 „	- -	1 8 7	1 9 9	
„ „ 8 „	- -	—	1 10 4	New Grade
„ „ 10 „	- -	1 9 9	—	
„ „ 11 „	- -	—	1 10 11	New Grade
„ „ 15 „	- -	—	1 11 6	New Grade

CITY OF DURHAM.

Force - - - - 16.

Area in acres - - - 880 | Acres to each constable - - - 55
Population in 1891 - - - 14,863 | Population to ditto, as per census 1891 928

RANKS.	Chief Officer.	Superintendents.						Inspectors.				
		Deputy Chief Officer.	Chief Clerk.	1st Class.	2nd Class.	3rd Class.	4th Class.	1st Class.	2nd Class.	3rd Class.	4th Class.	5th Class.
Number of each Rank and Class -	1	-	-	-	-	-	-	-	-	-	-	-
Rates of Pay of each ditto -	£ 204	-	-	-	-	-	-	-	-	-	-	-

Yearly Pay in £ and Shillings.

RANKS.	4 Sergeants.						11 Constables.					
	Merit Class.	1st Class.	2nd Class.	3rd Class.	4th Class.	5th Class.	Service 4 Grade 1st.	1st Class.	2nd Class.	3rd Class.	4th Class.	5th Class.	6th Class.
Number of each Rank and Class -	-	1	1	1	1	-	1	3	3	1	1	-	2	-
Rates of Pay of each ditto -	-	s. 41	s. 36	s. 35	s. 34	-	s. 33	s. 30	s. 29	s. 28	s. 27	-	s. 24	-

Weekly Pay in Shillings and Pence.

Inspected 18th June, when the force was complete.

Authorised Establishment.—Sixteen.

Extra Duties.—The chief is assistant relieving officer for vagrants, billet master, and inspector under weights and measures, with a sergeant as assistant ; he is also inspector of explosives and cattle diseases, and food and drugs.

Public-houses.—Eighty-three, with two prosecutions, and two convictions.

Beerhouses.—Seven.

Drunkenness.—Four hundred and nine prosecutions, and 357 convictions, being 57 more prosecutions, and 45 more convictions.

Ambulance.—Twelve members of the force hold certificates from St. John Ambulance Association ; a decrease of two.

The cells and police offices were clean and in good order.

The books and returns were well kept.

The management, numbers, and discipline of the force are efficiently maintained.

BOROUGH OF GATESHEAD.

Force - - - - - - 115.

Area in acres - - - 3,138 | Acres to each constable - -
Population in 1891 - - - 85,692 | Population to ditto, as per census 1891

RANKS.	Chief Officer.	Deputy Chief Officer.	Chief Clerk.	1st Class.	2nd Class.	3rd Class.	4th Class.	1st Class.	2nd Class.	3rd Class.	4th Class.	5th Class.
		1 Superintendent.						4 Inspectors.				
Number of each Rank and Class	1	-	1	1	-	-	-	1	2	-	-	-
Rates of Pay of each ditto	£ 350		£ s. 98 16	£ s. 135 4	-	-	-	£ s. 127 8	£ s. 119 12	£ 117	-	-

Yearly Pay in £ and Shillings.

RANKS.	1st Class	2nd Class	3rd Class	4th Class	5th Class	6th Class	7th Class	8th Class	Merit Class	1st Class	2nd Class	3rd Class	4th Class	5th Class	6th Class	7th Class	8th Class	9th Class	Vacancy.
	15 Sergeants.								98 Constables.										
Number of each Rank and Class	1	1	1	2	2	2	3	3	1	1	12	9	7	4	17	11	11	9	10	1
Rates of Pay of each ditto	48	41	40	39	38	36	35	34	39	39	38	32	31	30	29	28	27	25 8	24	-

Weekly pay in Shillings and Pence.

Inspected 17th June, when there was one vacancy and one was ill.

Authorised Establishment.—One hundred and fifteen.

Extra Duties.—The chief is assistant relieving officer and inspector under Explosive and Petroleum Acts ; a constable is inspector of hackney carriages.

Public-houses.—One hundred and thirty, with five prosecutions, and one conviction.

Beerhouses.—Forty-two ; no prosecutions.

Drunkenness.—One thousand two hundred and eighty-nine prosecutions and 1,224 convictions, making 291 more prosecutions, and 265 more convictions.

Ambulance.—One hundred and eleven members of the force hold ambulance certificates ; 12 more than last year.

The central station cells and four lock-ups were clean and in good order.

The books and returns were well kept.

The management, numbers, and discipline of the force were efficiently maintained.

BOROUGH OF HARTLEPOOL.

Force - - - - - - 27.

| Area in acres | - | - | - | 739 | Acres to each constable | - | - | - | 28 |
| Population in 1891 | - | - | - | 21,276 | Population to ditto, as per census 1891 | | | | 818 |

RANKS.	Chief Officer.	Yearly Pay in £ and Shillings.										
		Superintendents.						2 Inspectors.				
		Deputy Chief Officer.	Chief Clerk.	1st Class.	2nd Class.	3rd Class.	4th Class.	1st Class.	2nd Class.	3rd Class.	4th Class.	5th Class.
Number of each Rank and Class -	1	-	-	-	-	-	-	-	-	2	-	-
Rates of Pay of each ditto - -	£ 355	-	-	-	-	-	-	-	-	£ s. 109 10	-	-

RANKS.	Weekly Pay in Shillings and Pence.													
	5 Sergeants.						19 Constables.							
	Merit Class.	1st Class.	2nd Class.	3rd Class.	4th Class.	5th Class.	1st Class.					2nd Class.	3rd Class.	4th Class.
Number of each Rank and Class -	-	1	1	2	1	-	2	3	3	1	4	1	1	4
Rates of Pay of each ditto - -	-	s. d. 37 11	s. d. 36 9	s. d. 35 7	s. d. 34 5	-	s. d. 32 3	s. d. 30 11	s. d. 30 4	s. d. 29 2	s. 28	s. d. 26 10	s. d. 25 5	s. d. 24 6

Inspected June 20th, when the force was complete.

Authorised Establishment.—Twenty-seven; an increase of one constable.

Extra Duties.—The chief is billet master, and inspector of explosives and weights, and assistant relieving officer for vagrants. An inspector looks after common lodging-houses.

Public-houses.—Fifty-four, with four prosecutions, and three convictions.

Beerhouses.—Fifteen.

Drunkenness.—Two hundred and forty prosecutions, and 232 convictions, making 51 more prosecutions, and 50 more convictions.

Ambulance.—Twenty-three members of the force hold certificates from ambulance association.

The cells and police offices were clean and well kept.

The books were well kept.

The management, numbers, and discipline of the force were efficiently maintained.

Force - - - - - - - 115.

Area in acres - - - 1,839 | Acres to each constable - - -
Population in 1891 - - 78,391 | Population to ditto, as per census 1891

RANKS.	Chief Officer.	2 Superintendents.						4 Inspectors.				
		Deputy Chief Officer.	Chief Clerk.	1st Class.	2nd Class.	3rd Class.	4th Class.	1st Class.	2nd Class.	3rd Class.	4th Class.	5th Class.
Number of each } Rank and Class - }	1	-	1	1	-	-	-	1	1	1	1	-
Rates of Pay of } each ditto - }	£ 400	-	£ 91	£ s. 188 12	-	-	-	£ s. 127 8	£ s. 194 16	£ 117	£ s. 114 5	-

RANKS.	16 Sergeants.				98 Constables.						
	1st Class.	2nd Class.	3rd Class.	4th Class.	1st Class.	2nd Class.	3rd Class.	4th Class.	5th Class.	6th Class.	Vacancy.
Number of each } Rank and Class - }	3	1	5	3	2	1 Acting.	13	4	2	18	6	9	11	29	1
Rates of Pay of } each ditto - }	£ s. 43	£ s. 39	£ s. 36	£ s. 35	£ s. 34	£ d. 33 7	£ s. 33	£ s. 32	£ s. 31	£ s. 30	£ s. 29	£ s. 28	£ s. 27	£ s. 26	-

Inspected Monday, 17th June, when there was one vacancy and one constable on the sick list.

Authorised Establishment.—One hundred and fifteen ; an addition of five extra men.

Extra Duties.—The chief is assistant relieving officer and assistant inspector of common lodging-houses. Four inspectors and a constable are also assistant inspectors of hackney carriages. An inspector inspects under Cattle Diseases Act.

Public-houses.—One hundred and forty-six, with 12 prosecutions, and seven convictions.

Beerhouses.—Forty-five.

Drunkenness.—One thousand four hundred and one prosecutions, 1,282 convictions, making 122 more prosecutions, and 170 more convictions.

Ambulance.—Ninety-three members of the force hold certificates, and 22 are undergoing instruction.

The cells and offices were in good order.

The books and returns well kept.

The management, numbers, and discipline of the force are efficiently maintained.

BOROUGH OF SUNDERLAND.

Force - - - - - - 166.*

| Area in acres - - - 3,735 | Acres to each constable - - - 22 |
| Population in 1891 - - - 132,334 | Population to ditto, as per census 1891 797 |

RANKS.	Chief Officer.	Yearly Pay in £ and Shillings.										
		5 Superintendents.					3 Inspectors.				
		Deputy Chief Officer.	Chief Officer.	1st Class.	2nd Class.	3rd Class.	4th Class.	1st Class.	2nd Class.	3rd Class.	4th Class.	5th Class.
Number of each Rank and Class -	1	-	1	1	3	-	-	3	1	-	-	-
Rates of Pay of each ditto -	£ 400	-	£ s. 119 12	£ 183	£ s. 166 8	-	-	£ s. 145 13	£ 143	-	-	-

RANKS.	Weekly Pay in Shillings and Pence.												
	21 Sergeants.						136 Constables.						
	1st Class.	2nd Class.	3rd Class.	4th Class.	5th Class.	6th Class.	1st Class.	2nd Class.	3rd Class.	4th Class.	5th Class.	6th Class.	7th Class.	Vacancy.
Number of each Rank and Class -	1	4	5	4	1	2	2	2	3	16	13	11	22	13	14	11	16	30	1
Rates of Pay of each ditto -	s. 43	s. 40	s. 39	s. 38	s. 37	s. 36	s. 35	s. 34	s. 33	s. 33	s. 32	s. 31	s. 30	s. 29	s. 28	s. 27	s. 26	s. 25	-

* Exclusive of River Wear Police, viz., two inspectors, three sergeants, and 21 constables, and 11 constables appointed at private cost.

Inspected on 11th June, when there was one vacancy.

Authorised Establishment.—One hundred and sixty-six.

Extra Duties.—The chief is superintendent of River Wear police.

Public-houses.—Two hundred and thirty-six, with nine prosecutions, and five convictions.

Beerhouses.—One hundred and sixty-seven, with four prosecutions, and three convictions.

Drunkenness.—One thousand two hundred and forty-six prosecutions, and 1,099 convictions, being 142 fewer prosecutions and 140 more convictions.

Ambulance.—One hundred and fifty-eight members of the force hold certificates from ambulance association ; six more than last year.

The cells and police offices were clean and in good order.

The books and returns were well kept.

The management, numbers, and discipline of the force were efficiently maintained.

COUNTY OF LANCASTER.

Force - - - - - 1,641.*

Area in acres	-	- 1,076,762	Acres to each constable - - -
Population in 1891	-	- 1,417,123	Population to ditto, as per census 1891

RANKS.	Chief Officer.	22 Superintendents.						44 Inspectors.					
		Deputy Chief Officer.	Chief Clerk.	1st Class.	2nd Class.	3rd Class.	4th Class.	1st Class.	2nd Class.	3rd Class.	4th Class.	5th Class.	Vacancy.

Yearly pay in £ and Shillings.

RANKS.	Chief Officer.	Deputy Chief Officer.	Chief Clerk.	1st Class.	2nd Class.	3rd Class.	4th Class.	1st Class.	2nd Class.	3rd Class.	4th Class.	5th Class.	Vacancy.
Number of each Rank and Class	1	1	1	10	4	1	2	2	3	12	4	8	9	10	1
Rates of Pay of each ditto -	£ 1,200	£ 600	£ 350	£ 300	£ 280	£ 280	£ 240	£ 220	£ 200	£ 180	£ s. 142 10	£ 135	£ s. 127 10	£ 120

Weekly Pay in Shillings and Pence.

RANKS.	241 Sergeants.						1,309 Constables.						
	1st Class.	2nd Class.	3rd Class.	4th Class.	5th Class.		1st Class.					2nd Class.	3rd Class.	Vacancy.
Number of each Rank and Class	48	37	41	35	33	46	1	311	74	181	135	170	202	334	101	1
Rates of Pay of each ditto -	s. d. 38	s. d. 36 9	s. d. 36 2	s. d. 35 7	's. 35	s. d. 34 8	Vacancy	s. d. 31 6	s. d. 30 11	s. d. 30 4	s. d. 29 9	s. 29 2	s. 28	s. d. 26 3	s. d. 25 1	-

* Exclusive of 14 inspectors and 45 constables appointed under 3 & 4 Vict. c. 88. s. 19.

Inspected between 20th February and 26th March, both days inclusive.

Authorised Strength.—One thousand six hundred and forty-one.

Extra duties :—

NATURE OF DUTY.	Chief Constable.	Superintendent.	Inspectors.	Sergeants.	Constables.	TOTAL.
Inspectors under Contagious Diseases (Animals) Act.	—	21	38	43	—	102
Inspectors under Explosives Act - -	1	19	36	17	—	73
Inspectors under Food and Drugs Act -	—	20	—	—	—	20
Inspectors of Common Lodging-houses -	—	4	6	12	14	36
Inspector of Society for Prevention of Cruelty to Animals.	—	—	1	—	—	1

N.B.—Vacancies are usually kept for 14 men at Morecambe, Lakeside, and Windermere, for summer duty only, from April to Michaelmas.

Public-houses.—Two thousand two hundred and twenty-seven ; with 65 prosecutions, and 38 convictions.

Beerhouses.—One thousand seven hundred and ninety ; with 33 prosecutions, and 19 convictions.

Drunkenness.—Eleven thousand six hundred and sixty-four prosecutions, and 10,599 convictions, making 601 fewer prosecutions, and 178 fewer convictions.

Ambulance.—One thousand three hundred and eleven members of the force hold ambulance certificates.

The books and returns were well kept.

The management, numbers, and discipline of the force have been efficiently maintained.

The following 13 municipal boroughs are policed by the county force, i.e., county borough of Bury, boroughs of Chorley, Eccles, Leigh, Nelson, Colne, Haslingden, Middleton, Rawtenstall, Darwen, Heywood, Mosley, Widnes.

BOROUGH OF ACCRINGTON.

Force - - - - - - - - 43.

| Area in acres - - - 3,426 | Acres to each constable - - - 79 |
| Population in 1891 - - - 38,603 | Population to ditto, as per census 1891 897 |

RANKS.	Chief Officer.	Yearly Pay in £ and Shillings.											
		Superintendents.						3 Inspectors.					
		Deputy Chief Officer.	Chief Clerk.	1st Class.	2nd Class.	3rd Class.	4th Class.	1st Class.	2nd Class.	3rd Class.	4th Class.	5th Class.
Number of each Rank and Class - }	1	-	-	-	-	-	-	.1	2	-	-	-
Rates of Pay of } each ditto . }	£ 350	-	-	-	-	-	-	£ 150	£ 137	-	-	-

RANKS.	Weekly Pay in Shillings and Pence.													
	5 Sergeants.						Constables.							
	Merit Class	1st Class.	2nd Class.	3rd Class.	4th Class.	5th Class	Acting Ser- geants.	Merit Class.	1st Class.	2nd Class.	3rd Class.	4th Class.	5th Class.	6th Class.	Va- cancies.
Number of each Rank and Class - }	-	2	1	1	-	-	-	2	9	6	4	8	4	5	2
Rates of Pay of } each ditto - }	-	s. 40	s. 38	s. 36		-	-	s. d. 32 3	s. d. 31 6	s. d. 30 6	s. d. 30 9	s. d. 29 9	s. 28	s. d. 26 3	-

Inspected, 21st February, when there was one vacancy ; now there are two.

Authorised Establishment.—Forty-three.

Extra Duties.—The chief is inspector under Foods and Drugs and Explosive Acts, and, assisted by a constable, of hackney carriages.

Public-houses.—Forty-seven, with two prosecutions, and one conviction.

Beerhouses.—Forty-six, with three prosecutions, and three convictions.

Drunkenness.—One hundred and sixty-four prosecutions, and 156 convictions, being 144 fewer prosecutions than last year.

Ambulances.—Forty-one members of the force hold certificates ; one more than last year.

The cells and police offices are clean and in good order, books and returns well kept.

Management, numbers, and discipline of the force have been efficiently maintained.

BOROUGH OF ASHTON-UNDER-LYNE.

Force - - - - - - - - - - 45.

Area in acres - - - 1,396	Acres to each constable - - -
Population in 1891 - - - 40,463	Population to ditto, as per census 1891

RANKS.	Chief Officer.	Superintendents.						2 Inspectors.				
		Deputy Chief Officer.	Chief Clerk.	1st Class.	2nd Class.	3rd Class.	4th Class.	1st Class.	2nd Class.	3rd Class.	4th Class.	5th Class.
Yearly Pay in £ and Shillings.												
Number of each Rank and Class -	1	-	-	-	-	-	-	1	1	-	-	-
Rates of Pay of each ditto - -	£230	-	-	-	-	-	-	£ s. 182 12	£ s. 127 8	-	-	-

RANKS.	6 Sergeants.						Constables.								
	Merit Class.	1st Class.	2nd Class.	3rd Class.	4th Class.	5th Class	Merit Class.	1st Class.	2nd Class.	3rd Class.	4th Class.				
Weekly Pay in Shillings and Pence.															
Number of each Rank and Class -	-	1	2	1	2	-	1	3	4	1	3	9	4	4	2	5
Rates of Pay of each ditto - -	-	s. 41	s. 40	s. 39	s. 35	-	s. 36	s. 34	s. 33	s. 32	s. 31	s. 30	s. 29	s. 28	s. 27	s. 26

Inspected 6th March, when the force was complete.

Authorised Establishment.—Forty-five.

Extra Duties.—The chief, assisted by a constable, is inspector of weights. and measures and cattle dealers, and, with the aid of two inspectors, of common lodging-houses and hackney carriages.

Public-houses.—Eighty-seven, with one prosecution.

Beerhouses.—Seventy-seven.

Drunkenness.—Two hundred and twenty-six prosecutions, and 165 convictions, making 57 fewer prosecutions.

Ambulance.—Forty-two members of the force hold certificates ; six more than last year.

The cells and police offices were clean and in good order.

The books and returns were well kept.

The management, numbers, and discipline of the force were efficiently maintained.

M

BOROUGH OF BACUP.

Force - - - - - 26.

Area in acres - - - 6,116 | Acres to each constable - - - 235
Population in 1891 - - - 23,498 | Population to ditto, as per census 1891 903

RANKS.	Chief Officer.	Yearly Pay in £ and Shillings.											
		Superintendents.						1 Inspector.					
		Deputy Chief Officer.	Chief Clerk.	1st Class.	2nd Class.	3rd Class.	4th Class.	1st Class.	2nd Class.	3rd Class.	4th Class.	5th Class.
Number of each Rank and Class	1	-	1	-	-	-	-	1	-	-	-	-
Rates of Pay of each ditto	£ 220	-	£ 78	-	-	-	-	£ s. 107 18	-	-	-	-

RANKS.	Weekly Pay in Shillings and Pence.											
	3 Sergeants.					20 Constables.						
	Merit Class.	1st Class.	2nd Class.	3rd Class.	4th Class.	1st Class.		2nd Class.	3rd Class.	4th Class.	5th Class.	6th Class.
Number of each Rank and Class	-	1	1	1	-	-	3	6	3	5	3	1	-	-
Rates of Pay of each ditto	-	36	30	28	-	-	30	29	28	27	26	Vacancy. -	-

Inspected 19th February, when the force was complete.

Authorised Establishment.—Twenty-six.

Extra Duties.—The chief is inspector of common lodging-houses and hackney carriages, and, with the aid of an inspector, weights and measures, foods and drugs, cattle disease, factory, and explosives.

Public-houses.—Twenty-four, with no prosecutions.

Beerhouses.—Thirty-three, with three prosecutions, and three convictions.

Drunkenness.—One hundred and sixteen prosecutions, and 105 convictions, making 25 more prosecutions.

Ambulance.—Twenty-five members of the force hold certificates; three more than last year.

The cells and police offices were clean and in good order.

The books and returns were well kept.

The management, numbers, and discipline of the force have been efficiently maintained.

BOROUGH OF BARROW-IN-FURNESS.

No. 2.
Northern District.

Force - - - - - - - - - 65.*

| Area in acres - - - 13,987 | Acres to each constable - - - |
| Population in 1891 - - - 51,712 | Population to ditto, as per census 1891 |

RANKS.	Chief Officer.	Yearly Pay in £ and Shillings.										
		2 Superintendents.						3 Inspectors.				
		Deputy Chief Officer.	Chief Clerk.	1st Class.	2nd Class.	3rd Class.	4th Class.	1st Class.	2nd Class.	3rd Class.	4th Class.	5th Class.
Number of each Rank and Class -	1	-	1	1	-	-	-	1	1	1	-	-
Rates of Pay of each ditto -	£ 380	-	£ s. d. 108 8 4	£ s. d. 173 7 6	-	-	-	£ s. d. 136 17 6	£ s. d. 118 12 6	£ s. d. 115 11 8	-	-

RANKS.	Weekly Pay in Shillings and Pence.													
	8 Sergeants.						51 Constables.							
	Merit Class.	1st Class.	2nd Class.	3rd Class.	4th Class.	5th Class.	Merit Class.	1st Class.	2nd Class.	3rd Class.	4th Class.	5th Class.	6th Class.	7th Class.	8th Class.
Number of each Rank and Class -	-	2	1	1	2	2	4	5	6	5	3	5	7	4	6
Rates of Pay of each ditto -	-	s. d. 39 8	s. d. 37 4	s. d. 35 7	s. 35	s. d. 34 5	s. d. 33 10	s. d. 33 8	s. d. 32 1	s. d. 31 8	s. d. 30 4	s. d. 29 2	s. 28	s. d. 27 6	s. d. 26 10

* Exclusive of a sergeant and eight constables appointed at private cost.

Inspected 28th March, when there was one vacancy; since filled up.

Authorised Establishment.—Sixty-five.

Public-houses.—Fifty-five, with three prosecutions, and two convictions.

Beerhouses.—Thirteen, with two prosecutions, 12 convictions.

Drunkenness.—Four hundred and forty-two prosecutions, and 936 convictions, making 145 more prosecutions.

Ambulance.—Fifty members of the force hold certificates.

The books and returns were well kept.

The management, numbers, and discipline of the force have been efficiently maintained.

No. 2.
Northern District.

BOROUGH OF BLACKBURN

Force - - - - - - 140.

| Area in acres - | - | - | 6,974 | Acres to each constable | - | - | - | 49 |
| Population in 1891 | - | - | 120,064 | Population to ditto, as per census 1891 | | | | 857 |

Yearly Pay in £ and Shillings.

RANKS.	Chief Officer.	1 Superintendent.						7 Inspectors.				
		Deputy Chief Officer.	Chief Clerk.	1st Class.	2nd Class.	3rd Class.	4th Class.	1st Class.	2nd Class.	3rd Class.	4th Class.	5th Class.
Number of each Rank and Class -	1	-	-	1	-	-	-	2	2	2	1	-
Rates of Pay of each ditto - -	£ 600	-	-	£ 200	-	-	-	£ 130	£ 124	£ s. 114 8	£ s. 111 16	-

Weekly Pay in Shillings and Pence.

RANKS.	18 Sergeants.						112 Constables.										
	Merit Class.	1st Class.	2nd Class.	3rd Class.	4th Class.	5th Class.	Merit Class.	1st Class.				2nd Class.	3rd Class.	4th Class.	5th Class.	6th Class.	7th Class.
Number of each Rank and Class -	-	8	3	3	3	2	5	9	10	20	12	14	17	4	10	6	4
Rates of Pay of each ditto - -	-	s. 40	s. 38	s. 36	s. 35	s. 34	s. 34	s. 33	s. 32	s. 31	s. 30	s. 29	s. 28	s. 27	s. 26	s. 25	s. 24

Inspected 20th February, when seven constables were on the sick list.

Authorised Establishment.—One hundred and forty.

Extra Duties.—The chief commands fire brigade, with 23 constables. A sergeant inspects hackney carriages.

Public-houses.—Two hundred and forty-eight, with 13 prosecutions, and 10 convictions.

Beerhouses.—One hundred and seventy-two, with nine prosecutions, and seven convictions.

Drunkenness.—Six hundred and fifty-eight prosecutions, and 620 convictions, making 21 fewer prosecutions.

Ambulance.—One hundred and eighteen members of the force hold certificates ; a decrease of two.

The cells and police offices were clean and in good order. Russel Street has been enlarged and improved.

The books and returns were well kept.

The management, numbers, and discipline of the force have been efficiently maintained.

BOROUGH OF BLACKPOOL.

Force - - - - - - 75.

| Area in acres - - - 3,610 | Acres to each constable - - 48 |
| Population in 1891 - - - 23,846 | Population to ditto, as per census 1891 317 |

RANKS.	Chief Officer.	2 Superintendents.						2 Inspectors.				
		Deputy Chief Officer.	Chief Clerk.	1st Class.	2nd Class.	3rd Class.	4th Class.	1st Class.	2nd Class.	3rd Class.	4th Class.	5th Class.

Yearly Pay in £ and Shillings.

RANKS.	Chief Officer.	Deputy Chief Officer.	Chief Clerk.	1st Class.	2nd Class.	3rd Class.	4th Class.	1st Class.	2nd Class.	3rd Class.	4th Class.	5th Class.
Number of each Rank and Class -	1	-	1	1	-	-	-	2	-	-	-	-
Rates of Pay of each ditto -	£ 500	-	£ s. 109 4	£ 170	-	-	-	£ 120	-	-	-	-

Weekly Pay in Shillings and Pence.

RANKS.	10 Sergeants.					Acting Sergeants.	Merit Class.	59 Constables.					
	1st Class.	2nd Class.	3rd Class.	4th Class.	5th Class.			1st Class.				2nd Class.	3rd Class.	4th Class.

RANKS.	1st Class.	2nd Class.	3rd Class.	4th Class.	5th Class.	Acting Sergeants.	Merit Class.	1st Class.				2nd Class.	3rd Class.	4th Class.
Number of each Rank and Class -	1	2	1	3	1	2	-	3	4	17	20	12	3	-
Rates of Pay of each ditto -	s. 42	s. 40	s. 37	s. 36	s. 35	s. 34	-	s. d. 32 8	s. d. 30 11	s. d. 29 9	s. d. 29 2	s. d. 26 10	s. d. 25 8	-

Inspected 25th February, when the force was complete.

Authorised Establishment—Seventy-five.

Public-houses.—Sixty-seven, with six prosecutions, and two convictions.

Beerhouses.—Thirty-seven.

Drunkenness.—Two hundred and eighty-four prosecutions, and 271 convictions, making 20 fewer prosecutions.

Ambulance.—Seventy-two members of the force hold certificates; three less than last year.

The police cells were clean and in good order.

The books and returns were well kept.

The management, numbers, and discipline of the force have been efficiently maintained.

Extra Duties :—

NATURE OF DUTY.	Chief Constable.	Inspectors.	Sergeants.	Constables.	TOTAL.	Remarks.
Inspector of Weights and Measures -	1	—	—	—	1	25l. per annum extra pay.
Assistant Inspector of Weights and Measures.	—	—	1	—	1	3s. 6d. per week extra pay.
Inspector of Hackney Carriages -	1	—	—	—	1	
Inspector of Boats - - -	1	—	—	—	1	
Inspector of Bathing Machines -	1	—	—	—	1	
Inspectors under Explosives Act -	1	1	—	—	2	
Superintendent of Fire Brigade -	—	1	—	—	1	40l. per annum extra pay.
Inspector under Petroleum Act -	1	—	—	—	1	
For Fire Brigade duties, when necessary.	—	—	—	3	3	

COUNTY BOROUGH OF BOLTON.

Force - - - - - - - - 163.

Area in acres - - -	15,270	Acres to each constable - - -	91
Population in 1891 - - -	146,465	Population to ditto, as per census 1891	882

RANKS.	Chief Officer.	2 Superintendents.						6 Inspectors.				
		Deputy Chief Officer	Chief Clerk.	1st Class.	2nd Class.	3rd Class.	4th Class.	1st Class.	2nd Class.	3rd Class.	4th Class.	5th Class.
Number of each Rank and Class -	1	-	1	-	-	1	-	1	1	3	1	-
Rates of Pay at each ditto -	£ 400	-	£ s. 111 8	-	-	£ s. 189 11	-	£ s. 134 16	£ s. 119 12	£ s. 114 8	£ s. 110 10	-

Yearly Pay in £ and Shillings.

RANKS.	20 Sergeants.						128 Constables.							
	Merit Class.	1st Class.	2nd Class.	3rd Class.	4th Class.	5th Class.	Merit Class.	1st Class.	2nd Class.	3rd Class.	4th Class.	5th Class.	6th Class.	7th Class.
Number of each Rank and Class -	-	6	4	6	4	-	3 5 1	51	7	5	10	21	18	17
Rates of Pay of each ditto -	-	s. d. 38 6	s. d. 36 6	s. d. 34 10	s. 33	-	s. d. s. d. s. d. 34 32 6 31 6	s. d. 31 6	s. d. 30 6	s. d. 29 6	s. d. 28 6	s. d. 27 6	s. d. 26 6	s. 26

Weekly Pay in Shillings and Pence.

Inspected 4th March, when the force was complete.

Authorised Establishment.—One hundred and sixty-three.

Extra Duties.— A constable is inspector of hackney carriages and explosives.

Public-houses.—One hundred and forty-two, with five prosecutions, and one conviction.

Beerhouses.—One hundred and fifty-one.

Drunkenness.—Five hundred and fifty-six prosecutions, and 498 convictions, making 15 fewer prosecutions.

Ambulance.—One hundred and twenty-seven members of the force hold certificates, being one less than last year.

The cells and police offices were clean and in good order.

The books and returns were well kept.

The management, numbers, and discipline of the force have been efficiently maintained.

BOROUGH OF BOOTLE.

Force - - - - - 72.

Area in acres - - - 1,590 | Acres to each constable - - - 22
Population in 1891 - - - 49,217 | Population to ditto, as per census 1891 683

Yearly Pay in £ and Shillings.

RANKS.	Chief Officer.	Superintendents.						3 Inspectors.				
		Deputy Chief Officer.	Chief Clerk.	1st Class.	2nd Class.	3rd Class.	4th Class.	1st Class.	2nd Class.	3rd Class.	4th Class.	5th Class.
Number of each Rank and Class -	1	-	1	-	-	-	-	Chief 1	2	-	-	-
Rates of Pay of each ditto -	£ 400	-	-	-	-	-	-	£ s. 167 10	£ 150	-	-	-

Weekly Pay in Shillings and Pence.

RANKS.	7 Sergeants.						61 Constables.									
	Merit Class.	1st Class.	2nd Class.	3rd Class.	4th Class.	5th Class.	Merit Class 1st.	Merit Class 2nd.	3rd Class.	4th Class.	5th Class.	6th Class.	7th Class.	8th Class.	9th Class.	
Number of each Rank and Class -	-	1	5	1	-	-	1	4	3	13	10	9	3	4	7	4	3
Rates of Pay of each ditto -	-	s. 45	s. 43	s. 40	-	-	s. d. 35 2	s. d. 34 2	s. 34	s. 33	s. 32	s. 31	s. 30	s. 29	s. 28	s. 27	s. d. 25 7

Inspected 19th March, when the force was complete.

Authorised Establishment.—Seventy-two.

Extra Duties.—The chief and two inspectors inspect food and drugs and contagious diseases (animals).

Public-houses.—Forty-nine, with two prosecutions, and one conviction.

Beerhouses.—Eight.

Drunkenness.—Six hundred and forty-four prosecutions, and 603 convictions.

Ambulance.—Sixty members of the force hold certificates ; two more than last year.

The cells and police offices were clean and in good order.

The books and returns were well kept.

The management, numbers, and discipline of the force have been efficiently maintained.

COUNTY BOROUGH OF BOLTON.

Force - - - - - - - 163.

Area in acres - - - 15,270	Acres to each constable - - - 91
Population in 1891 - - - 146,465	Population to ditto, as per census 1891 882

RANKS.	Chief Officer.	Yearly Pay in £ and Shillings.										
		2 Superintendents.						6 Inspectors.				
		Deputy Chief Officer	Chief Clerk.	1st Class.	2nd Class.	3rd Class.	4th Class.	1st Class.	2nd Class.	3rd Class.	4th Class.	5th Class.
Number of each Rank and Class -	1	-	1	-	-	1	-	1	1	8	1	-
Rates of Pay at each ditto -	£ 400	-	£ s. 111 8	-	-	£ s. 159 11	-	£ s. 124 16	£ s. 119 12	£ s. 114 8	£ s. 110 10	-

RANKS.	Weekly Pay in Shillings and Pence.													
	20 Sergeants.						133 Constables.							
	Merit Class.	1st Class.	2nd Class.	3rd Class.	4th Class.	5th Class.	Merit Class.	1st Class.	2nd Class.	3rd Class.	4th Class.	5th Class.	6th Class.	7th Class.
Number of each Rank and Class -	-	6	4	6	4	-	3	5	1	51	7	5	10	21	18	17
Rates of Pay of each ditto -	-	s. d. 38 6	s. d. 36 8	s. d. 34 10	s. 33	-	s. 34	s. d. 32 8	s. d. 31 8	s. d. 31 6	s. d. 30 6	s. d. 29 6	s. d. 28 6	s. d. 27 6	s. d. 26 6	s. 25

Inspected 4th March, when the force was complete.

Authorised Establishment.—One hundred and sixty-three.

Extra Duties.— A constable is inspector of hackney carriages and explosives.

Public-houses.—One hundred and forty-two, with five prosecutions, and one conviction.

Beerhouses.—One hundred and fifty-one.

Drunkenness.—Five hundred and fifty-six prosecutions, and 498 convictions, making 15 fewer prosecutions.

Ambulance.—One hundred and twenty-seven members of the force hold certificates, being one less than last year.

The cells and police offices were clean and in good order.

The books and returns were well kept.

The management, numbers, and discipline of the force have been efficiently maintained.

BOROUGH OF BOOTLE.

Force - - - - - 72.

Area in acres - - - 1,590	Acres to each constable - - - 22
Population in 1891 - - - 49,217	Population to ditto, as per census 1891 683

RANKS.	Chief Officer.	Superintendents.						Inspectors.				
		Deputy Chief Officer.	Chief Clerk.	1st Class.	2nd Class.	3rd Class.	4th Class.	1st Class.	2nd Class.	3rd Class.	4th Class.	5th Class.
Number of each Rank and Class -	1	-	1	-	-	-	-	Chief 1	2	-	-	-
Rates of Pay of each ditto - -	£ 400	-	-	-	-	-	-	£ s. 167 10	£ 150	-	-	-

Yearly Pay in £ and Shillings.

RANKS.	7 Sergeants.						61 Constables.								
	Merit Class.	1st Class.	2nd Class.	3rd Class.	4th Class.	5th Class.	Merit Class.		3rd Class.	4th Class.	5th Class.	6th Class.	7th Class.	8th Class.	9th Class.
							1st.	2nd.							
Number of each Rank and Class -	-	1	5	1	-	-	1	4	3	13	10	9	3	4	7	4	3
Rates of Pay of each ditto - -	-	s. 45	s. 43	s. 40	-	-	s. d. 35 2	s. d. 34 3	s. 34	s. 33	s. 32	s. 31	s. 30	s. 29	s. 28	s. 27	s. d. 25 7

Weekly Pay in Shillings and Pence.

Inspected 19th March, when the force was complete.

Authorised Establishment.—Seventy-two.

Extra Duties.—The chief and two inspectors inspect food and drugs and contagious diseases (animals).

Public-houses.—Forty-nine, with two prosecutions, and one conviction.

Beerhouses.—Eight.

Drunkenness.—Six hundred and forty-four prosecutions, and 603 convictions.

Ambulance.—Sixty members of the force hold certificates; two more than last year.

The cells and police offices were clean and in good order.

The books and returns were well kept.

The management, numbers, and discipline of the force have been efficiently maintained.

No. 2.
Northern District.

BOROUGH OF BURNLEY.

Force - - - - - 97.

Area in acres - - - 3,923 | Acres to each constable - - - 40
Population in 1891 - - - 87,016 | Population to ditto, as per census 1891 906

RANKS.	Chief Officer.	1 Superintendent.						6 Inspectors.				
		Deputy Chief Officer.	Chief Clerk.	1st Class.	2nd Class.	3rd Class.	4th Class.	1st Class.	2nd Class.	3rd Class.	4th Class.	5th Class.
Number of each Rank and Class -	Vacant.	-	1	-	-	-	-	1	1	1	2	1
Rates of Pay of each ditto -	-	-	£ s. d. 115 5 4	-	-	-	-	£ s. d. 130 17 4	£ 130	£ s. d. 124 7 4	£ s. 118 6	£ s. 112 15

Yearly Pay in £ and Shillings.

RANKS.	9 Sergeants.						79 Constables.									
	Merit Class.	1st Class.	2nd Class.	3rd Class.	4th Class.	5th Class.	Merit Class.	1st Class.	2nd Class.	3rd Class.	4th Class.	5th Class.	6th Class.	7th Class.	8th Class.	9th Class.
Number of each Rank and Class -	-	4	1	1	1	2	4	31	1	3	7	3	8	4	4	14
Rates of Pay of each ditto -	-	s. d. 37 3	s. 36	s. d. 35 5	s. d. 34 3	s. d. 33 8	s. d. 32 2	s. 31	s. d. 30 5	s. d. 29 8	s. d. 29 1	s. d. 28 6	s. d. 27 11	s. d. 27 4	s. d. 26 3	s. 25

Weekly Pay in Shillings and Pence.

Inspected 22nd February, when the force was complete.

Authorised Establishment.—Ninety-seven.

Extra Duties.—The chief commands fire brigade with 21 men, an inspector inspects weights and measures, and common lodging-houses, foods and drugs, and hackney carriages.

Public-houses.—Eighty-four, with two prosecutions, and one conviction.

Beerhouses.—Ninety-five, with four prosecutions, and two convictions.

Drunkenness.—Four hundred and twenty-two prosecutions, and 375 convictions, making 14 more prosecutions.

Ambulance.—Sixty-one members of the force hold certificates; nine fewer than last year.

The cells and police offices were clean and in good order.

The books and returns were well kept.

The management, numbers, and discipline of the force have been efficiently maintained.

BOROUGH OF CLITHEROE.

Force - - - - - 11.

Area in acres - - - 2,381 | Acres to each constable - - - 216
Population in 1891 - - - 10,815 | Population to ditto, as per census 1891

RANKS.	Chief Officer.	Yearly Pay in £ and Shillings.											
		Superintendents.						Inspectors.				
		Deputy Chief Officer.	Chief Clerk.	1st Class.	2nd Class.	3rd Class.	4th Class.	1st Class.	2nd Class.	3rd Class.	4th Class.	5th Class.
Number of each Rank and Class -	1	-	-	-	-	-	-	-	-	-	-	-
Rates of Pay of each ditto -	£ 180	-	-	-	-	-	-	-	-	-	-	-

RANKS.	Weekly Pay in Shillings and Pence.												
	2 Sergeants.						Constables.						
	Merit Class.	1st Class.	2nd Class.	3rd Class.	4th Class.	5th Class.	Merit Class. 1st.	Merit Class. 2nd.	1st Class.	2nd Class.	3rd Class.	4th Class.	5th Class.	6th Class.
Number of each Rank and Class -	-	1	1	-	-	-	1	2	1	2	1	-	-	-
Rates of Pay of each ditto -	-	s. d. 36 8	s. 22	-	-	-	s. d. 30 10	s. d. 30 10	s. d. 27 4	s. d. 26 3	s. 25	-	-	-

Inspected 18th February, when the force was complete.

Authorised Establishment.—Eleven, but a reservist is still serving in South Africa.

Public-houses.—Twenty-two ; with one prosecution.

Beerhouses.—Twelve.

Drunkenness.—Thirty-seven prosecutions, and 34 convictions, being four fewer prosecutions.

Ambulance.—Nine members of the force hold certificates.

The cells and police offices were clean and in good order.

The books and returns were well kept.

The management, numbers, and discipline of the force have been efficiently maintained.

Extra Duties :—

NATURE OF DUTY.	Chief Constable.	Super-intendents.	Inspectors.	Sergeants.	Constables	TOTAL.
Inspectors of Common Lodging-houses -	1	—	—	2	—	3
Inspectors of Weights and Measures -	1	—	—	—	1	2
Inspector of Markets and Fairs -	1	—	—	—	—	1
Inspector of Food and Drugs -	1	—	—	—	—	1
Inspector of Explosives -	1	—	—	—	—	1
Inspector under Contagious Diseases (Animals) Act.	1	—	—	—	—	1*

* 5l. a year extra pay.

　　　　　N

No. 2.
Northern District.

BOROUGH OF LANCASTER.

Force - - - - - - 40.

| Area in acres - - - 1,577 | Acres to each constable - - - 47 |
| Population in 1891 - - - 31,038 | Population to ditto, as per census 1891 940 |

RANKS.	Chief Officer.	Yearly Pay in £ and Shillings.											
		Superintendents.						1 Inspector.					
		Deputy Chief Officer.	Chief Clerk.	1st Class.	2nd Class.	3rd Class.	4th Class.	1st Class.	2nd Class.	3rd Class.	4th Class.	5th Class.
Number of each Rank and Class -	1	-	-	-	-	-	-	1	-	-	-	-
Rates of Pay of each ditto - -	£ 300	-	-	-	-	-	-	£ s. d. 104 8 8	-	-	-	-

RANKS.	Weekly Pay in Shillings and Pence.												
	6 Sergeants.						32 Constables.						
	Merit Class.	1st Class.	2nd Class.	3rd Class.	4th Class.	5th Class.	Merit Class.	1st Class.	2nd Class.	3rd Class.	4th Class.	5th Class.	Probation Class.
Number of each Rank and Class -	1	1	1	1	1	1	1	4	8	5	1	4	8	1
Rates of Pay of each ditto - -	s. d. 37 2	s. 37	s. d. 36 2	s. 35	s. 33	s. d. 32 7	s. d. 31 2	s. d. 30 7	s. 30	s. 29	s. 28	s. 27	s. 25	s. 24

Inspected 17th March, when the force was complete.

Authorised Establishment.—Forty.

Extra Duties.—The chief is inspector of hackney carriages, Weights and Measures, Food and Drugs, Explosives, and Contageous Diseases (Animals) Acts, and common-lodgings, with five sergeants and a constable as assistants.

Public-houses.—Sixty-three ; with three prosecutions, and three convictions.

Beerhouses.—Sixteen.

Drunkenness.—One hundred and nineteen prosecutions, and 108 convictions, making 17 fewer prosecutions.

Ambulance.—Thirty-nine members of the force hold certificates.

The cells and police offices were clean and in good order.

The books and returns were well kept.

The management, numbers, and discipline of the force have been efficiently maintained.

CITY OF LIVERPOOL.

Force - - - - 1,360.*

Area in acres - - - 15,092 | Acres to each constable - -. -
Population in 1891 - - - 629,443 | Population to ditto, as per census 1891

RANKS.	Chief Officer.	Superintendents.					59 Inspectors.										
		Deputy Chief Officer.	Chief Clerk.	1st Class.	2nd Class.	3rd Class	Chief			1st Class.	2nd Class.	3rd Class.	4th Class.	Sub			
							1st Class.	2nd Class.	3rd Class.					1st Class.	2nd Class.	3rd Class.	4th Class.
Number of each Rank and Class -	1	1	1	1	5	4	3	3	3	4	15	17	1†	2	3	5	3‡
Rates of Pay of each ditto -	£ 1,650	£ 750	£ 500	£ 370	£ 280	£ 240	£ 215	£ 190	£ 165	£ 165	£ 150	£ 135	£ 95	£ 135	£ 125	£ 115	-

Yearly Pay in £ and Shillings.

RANKS.	185 Sergeants.					1,103 Constables.								
	1st Class.	2nd Class.	3rd Class.	4th Class.	5th Class.	Merit Class.			1st Class.	2nd Class.	3rd Class.	4th Class.	5th Class.	6th Class.
						1	2	3						
Number of each Rank and Class -	35§	44	47	48	3†	8‡	186§	176	199	125	109	112	121	56§	9†
Rates of Pay of each ditto -	s. 42	s. 40	s. 38	s. 36	s. 27	-	s. 33	s. 32	s. 31	s. 30	s. 29	s. 28	s. 27	s. d. 25 7	s. 22

Weekly Pay in Shillings and Pence.

† Reserve. ‡ Vacancies. § Long Service. ‖ Probationary.
* Excluding 343 constables in the dock force, two inspectors, and 26 sergeants; total, 371.

Inspected 20th, 21st and 22nd May.

Authorised Strength.—Reduced to 1,360 from 1,460. Eighty of the men are mounted.

Extra Duties.—An inspector and two constables collect money for reformatories and industrial schools ; a sergeant and two constables inspect children trading in streets ; an inspector, a sergeant, and four constables inspect explosives.

Public-houses.—One thousand eight hundred and five ; with 52 prosecutions, and 31 convictions.

Beerhouses.—Two hundred and thirty-seven ; with three prosecutions, and two convictions.

Drunkenness.—Four thousand two hundred and seventy-seven prosecutions, with 4,059 convictions, being 141 more prosecutions.

Ambulance.—One thousand four hundred and sixty-two members of the force hold certificates.

The Bridewell, head-quarters, and divisional stations were found clean and in good .

The books and returns were well kept.

The management, numbers, and discipline of the force have been efficiently maintained.

No. 2.
Northern District.

CITY OF MANCHESTER.

Force - - - - 1,006.

Area in acres - - - 12,911	Acres to each constable - - - 12
Population in 1891 - - - 505,368	Population to ditto, as per census 1891 505

RANKS.	Chief Officer.	6 Superintendents.				46 Inspectors.						
		Deputy Chief Officer.	Chief Clerk.	1st Class.	2nd Class.	Chief.	1st Class.	2nd Class.	3rd Class.	4th Class.	5th Class.	6th Class.
Number of each Rank and Class -	1	-	1	1	4	1	2	10	4	5	5	20
Rates of Pay of each ditto -	£ 1,000	-	£ 140	£ 290	£ 210	£ 180	£ 180	£ 130	£ s. 194 16	£ s. 119 12	£ 117	£ s. 111 16

Yearly Pay in £ and Shillings.

RANKS.	116 Sergeants.					836 Constables.							
	1st Class.	2nd Class.	3rd Class.	4th Class.	5th Class.	Acting Sergeants.	Merit Class.	1st Class.	2nd Class.	3rd Class.	4th Class.	5th Class.	6th Class.
Number of each Rank and Class -	25	6	9	56	2 Vacancies	11 7	110 1	129	2	146 51	1	50 87	104 188	5 Vacancies
Rates of Pay of each ditto -	s. 40	s. 39	s. 37	s. 35	-	s. d. 34 6 33	s. d. 33 6 32 6	s. 33	s. d. 31 6	s. 31 30	s. d. 29 6	s. 29 28	s. 27 26	-

Weekly Pay in Shillings and Pence.

Inspected, 23rd and 24th May, when the force was complete.

Authorised establishment.—One thousand and six.

Extra Duties.—

Public-houses.—Four hundred and eighty-five ; with 29 prosecutions, and 21 convictions.

Beerhouses.—One thousand seven hundred and six ; with 125 prosecutions, and 98 convictions.

Drunkenness.—Seven thousand three hundred and seventy-five prosecutions, and 6,431 convictions, making 1,131 more prosecutions.

Ambulance.—Eight hundred and sixty-eight members of the force hold certificates, being 95 more than last year.

Nine lock-ups and cells were visited and found to be clean and in good order.

Books and returns were well kept.

The management, numbers, and discipline of the force have been efficiently maintained.

Force   -   -   -   158.

Area in acres - - - - 4,730	Acres to each constable - - - 29
Population in 1891 - - 131,463	Population to ditto, as per census 1891 832

RANKS.	Chief Officer.	3 Superintendents.						6 Inspectors.				
		Deputy Chief Officer.	Chief Clerk.	1st Class.	2nd Class.	3rd Class.	4th Class.	1st Class.	2nd Class.	3rd Class.	4th Class.	5th Class.
Number of each Rank and Class -	1	1	1	1	-	-	-	3	2	1	-	-
Rates of Pay of each ditto -	£ 400	£ 156	£ s. d. 90 11 4	£ 143	-	-	-	£ s. 117 13	£ s. 113 2	£ s. 108 11	-	-

Yearly Pay in £ and Shillings.

RANKS.	15 Sergeants.						13 Constables.						
	Merit Class.	1st Class.	2nd Class.	3rd Class.	4th Class.	5th Class.	Merit Class.			1st Class.		2nd Class.	3rd Class.	4th Class.	5th Class.	6th Class.
Number of each Rank and Class -	-	3	6	2	3	1	1	1	2	23	42	31	3	18	5	7
Rates of Pay of each ditto -	-	s. 37	s. d. 34 10	s. d. 33 8	s. d. 32 6	s. 40	s. d. 33 4	s. d. 31 2	s. d. 30 2	s. d. 31 2	s. 30	s. 29	s. d. 28 6	s. d. 27 6	s. d. 25 6	s. 25

Weekly Pay in Shillings and Pence.

Inspected 6th March, when the force was complete, but an inspector and three constables were sick.

Authorised Establishment.—One hundred and fifty-eight.

Extra Duties.—The chief, an inspector, a sergeant, and two constables inspect weights and measures.

Public-houses.—One hundred and eighty-one; with one prosecution, and one conviction.

Beerhouses.—Two hundred and five; with six prosecutions, and five convictions.

Drunkenness.—Six hundred and ninety-five prosecutions, and 659 convictions, being 160 fewer prosecutions.

Ambulance.—One hundred and fifty members of the force hold certificates.

The books and returns were well kept.

The management, numbers, and discipline of the force have been efficiently maintained.

No. 2.
Northern District.

BOROUGH OF PRESTON.

Force - - - - - 116.

Area in acres - - - - 4,089	Acres to each constable - - - 35
Population in 1891 - - 107,573	Population to ditto, as per census 1891 927

Yearly Pay in £ and Shillings.

RANKS.	Chief Officer.	2 Superintendents.						7 Inspectors.				
		Deputy Chief Officer.	Chief Clerk.	1st Class.	2nd Class.	3rd Class.	4th Class.	1st Class.	2nd Class.	3rd Class.	4th Class.	5th Class.
Number of each Rank and Class -	1	-	1	1	-	-	-	2	1*	1†	3	-
Rates of Pay of each ditto - -	£ 450	-	£ 145	£ 165		-	-	£ s. 119 12	£ s. 114 8	£ s. 114 8	£ 104	-

Weekly Pay in Shillings and Pence.

RANKS.	13 Sergeants.						93 Constables.						
	Merit Class.	1st Class.	2nd Class.	3rd Class.	4th Class.	5th Class.	Merit Class.	1st Class.	2nd Class.	3rd Class.	4th Class.	5th Class.	6th Class.
Number of each Rank and Class -	1	1*	1‡	1†	1	2 6	5	16	20 12	4	6	11 13	3 1* 1† 1*
Rates of Pay of each ditto - -	s. 33	s. 35	-	s. 36	s. 36	s. 35 s. 33	s. 32	s. 31	s. 30 29	s. 28	s. 27	s. 26 25	s. 24 36 33 33

* Detective.   † Warrant.   ‡ Merit.

Inspected on 7th March, when the force was complete.

Authorised Establishment.—One hundred and sixteen.

Extra Duties.—A superintendent inspects cattle diseases, two inspectors common lodging-houses. A superintendent and six inspectors inspect hackney carriages and explosives.

Public-houses.—Two hundred and seven; with 10 prosecutions, and six convictions.

Beerhouses.—Two hundred and six; with eight prosecutions, and six convictions.

Drunkenness.—Three hundred and ninety-eight prosecutions, and 297 convictions, being 203 fewer prosecutions.

Ambulance.—Ninety-nine members of the force hold certificates.

The cells and police offices were clean and in good order.

The books and returns were well kept.

The management, numbers, and discipline of the force have been efficiently maintained.

COUNTY BOROUGH OF ROCHDALE.

Force - - - - - - - 88.

No. 2.
Northern District.

Area in acres - - - - 4,184 | Acres to each constable - - - 51
Population in 1891 - - 71,401 | Population to ditto, as per census 1891 881

Yearly Pay in £ and Shillings.

| RANKS. | Chief Constable | 2 Superintendents. | | | | | | 5 Inspectors. | | | | |
		Deputy Chief Constable.	Chief Clerk.	1st Class.	2nd Class.	3rd Class.	4th Class.	1st Class.	2nd Class.	3rd Class.	4th Class.	5th Class.
Number of each Rank and Class	1	1	1	-	-	-	1	1	1	1	1	1
Rates of Pay of each ditto	£ 400	£ 135	s. d. 93 12	-	-	-	-	£ 130	£ s. 120 11	£ s. 109 4	£ 104	Vacancy. -

Weekly Pay in Shillings and Pence.

| RANKS. | 11 Sergeants. | | | | | | Constables. | | | | | |
	Merit Class.	1st Class.	2nd Class.	3rd Class.	4th Class.	5th Class.	1st Class.	2nd Class.	3rd Class.	4th Class.	5th Class.	6th Class.
Number of each Rank and Class	-	3	4	1	3	-	11	13	3	8	9	11	10	4
Rates of Pay of each ditto	-	s. 36	s. 35	s. 34	s. 33	-	s. 33	s. 31	s. 30	s. 29	s. 28	s. 26	s. 25	s. 24

Inspected 11th March, when the force was complete, but now there is a vacancy for an inspector.

Authorised Establishment.—Eighty-eight.

Extra Duties.—

NATURE OF DUTY.	Chief Constable.	Inspectors.	Sergeants.	Constables.	TOTAL.
Inspectors of Weights and Measures	1	1	1	—	3
Inspectors of Hackney Carriages	1	1	—	—	2
Inspectors of Common Lodging-houses	1	1	—	—	2
Inspectors under Diseases of Animals Act	1	1	—	—	2
Inspectors under Explosives Act	1	1	—	—	2
Billet Master	1	—	—	—	1
Fire Brigade	1	1	1	17	20

Public-houses.—One hundred and forty-two; with five prosecutions, and three convictions.

Beerhouses.—One hundred and fifty-seven; with nine prosecutions, and seven convictions.

Drunkenness.—Three hundred and sixty-three prosecutions, and 329 convictions, making 64 more prosecutions.

Ambulance.—Seventy-four members of the force hold certificates.

The cells and police offices were clean and in good order.

The books and returns were well kept.

The management, numbers, and discipline of the force have been efficiently maintained.

N 4

No. 2.
·Northern District.

BOROUGH OF ST. HELEN'S.

Force - - - - 87.*

| Area in acres - - - 7,282 | Acres to each constable - - 83 |
| Population in 1891 - - - 72,446 | Population to ditto, as per census 1891 852 |

RANKS.	Chief Officer.	1 Superintendent.						4 Inspectors.				
		Deputy Chief Officer.	Chief Clerk.	1st Class.	2nd Class.	3rd Class.	4th Class.	1st Class.	2nd Class.	3rd Class.	4th Class.	5th Class.
Yearly Pay in £ and Shillings.												
Number of each Rank and Class -	1	--	1	-	-	-	-	2	1	1	-	-
Rates of Pay of each ditto -	*s.* 350	-	£ 180	-	-	-	-	£ 180	*s. d.* 134 16	*s. d.* 109 4	-	-

RANKS.	9 Sergeants.						72 Constables.							
	Merit Class.	1st Class.	2nd Class.	3rd Class.	4th Class.	5th Class.	Acting Sergeants.	Merit Class.	1st Class.	2nd Class.	3rd Class.	4th Class.	5th Class.	6th Class.
Weekly Pay in Shillings and Pence.														
Number of each Rank and Class -	-	5	2	2	-	-	-	6	4	4	3	11	4	3
Rates of Pay of each ditto -	-	*s. d.* 37 8	*s. d.* 36 6	*s. d.* 34 2	-	-	-	*s.* 32	*s. d.* 30 10	*s. d.* 29 8	*s. d.* 28 6	*s. d.* 27 4	*s. d.* 26 2	*r.* 25

* Exclusive of three constables appointed at private cost.

Inspected 21st March, when the force was complete.

Authorised Establishment.—Eighty-seven.

Fire Brigade.—The chief is nominally head of the brigade. The superintendent, who commands it, is not in the force, and there are other auxiliaries.

Extra Duties.—

NATURE OF DUTY.	Chief Constable.	Super-intendents.	Inspectors.	Sergeants.	Constables.	TOTAL.
Fire Brigade - - -	1	—	—	1	6	8
Inspectors of Weights and Measures -	1	—	—	1	1	3
Inspector of Food and Drugs -	1	—	—	—	—	1
Inspector of Hackney Carriages -	1	—	—	—	—	1
Inspectors under Explosives Act -	1	—	3	—	—	4
Inspectors of Common Lodging-houses and Bakehouses.	1	—	3	—	—	4
Inspectors under Cattle Diseases Act -	1	—	3	—	—	4
Inspectors under Shop Hours Act -	1	—	4	—	—	5
Inspector of Meat, &c. -	—	—	—	—	1	1

Public-houses.—Four hundred and sixty-six; with four prosecutions, and three convictions.

Beerhouses.—One hundred and two; with one prosecution, and one conviction.

Drunkenness.—Seven hundred and eighty-three prosecutions, and 755 convictions, being 126 fewer prosecutions.

Ambulance.—Eighty-one members of the force hold certificates.

The cells and police offices were clean and in good order.

The books and returns were well kept.

The management, numbers, and discipline of the force have been efficiently maintained.

Force - - - - 330.

Area in acres - - - 5,171	Acres to each constable - - 10
Population in 1891 - - 198,139	Population to ditto, as per census 1891 600

RANKS.	Chief Officer.	Yearly Pay in £ and Shillings.										
		2 Superintendents.					14 Inspectors.					
		Deputy Chief Officer.	Chief Clerk.	1st Class.	2nd Class.	3rd Class.	4th Class.	1st Class.	2nd Class.	3rd Class.	4th Class.	5th Class.
Number of each Rank and Class -	1	-	1	1	-	-	-	1	7	5	1 Vacancy.	-
Rates of Pay of each ditto - -	£ 500	. -	£ 150	£ 200	-	-	-	£ 140	£ 130	£ s. 111 10		-

RANKS.	Weekly Pay in Shillings and Pence.													
	34 Sergeants.							Constables.						
	Merit Class.	1st Class.	2nd Class.	3rd Class.	4th Class.	5th Class.	Acting Sergeants.	1st Class.	2nd Class.	3rd Class.	4th Class.	5th Class.	6th Class.	7th Class.
Number of each Rank and Class -	-	6	4	12	12	-	-	126	20	23	30	39	28	28
Rates of Pay of each ditto - -	-	s. 40	s. 39	s. 37	s. 35	-	-	s. 31	s. 30	s. 29	s. 28	s. 27	s. 26	s. 25

Inspected 14th March, when the force was complete, but five sergeants and nine men were on sick list.

Authorised Establishment.—Three hundred and thirty.

Extra Duties.—Ten inspectors inspect explosives, and a superintendent, 10 inspectors, and 29 sergeants inspect weights and measures; and an inspector and sergeant hackney carriages.

Public-houses.—One hundred and ten; with four prosecutions, and one conviction.

Beerhouses.—Four hundred and twelve; with 11 prosecutions, and five convictions.

Drunkenness.—Two thousand six hundred prosecutions, and 2,511 convictions, making 148 more prosecutions.

Ambulance.—Two hundred and seventeen members of the force hold certificates, making 13 more than last year.

The books and returns were well kept.

The management, numbers, and discipline of the force have been efficiently maintained.

BOROUGH OF SOUTHPORT.

Force - - - - - 70.

| Area in acres - - - 6,527 | Acres to each constable - - 52 |
| Population in 1891 - - - 41,406 | Population to ditto, as per census 1891 690 |

RANKS.	Chief Officer.	Yearly Pay in £ and Shillings.										
		2 Superintendents.						2 Inspectors.				
		Deputy Chief Officer.	Chief Clerk.	1st Class	2nd Class.	3rd Class.	4th Class.	1st Class.	2nd Class.	3rd Class.	4th Class.	5th Class.
Number of each Rank and Class -	1	-	1	1	-	-	-	2	-	-	-	-
Rates of Pay of each ditto -	£ 860	-	£ s. 119 12	£ s. 143	-		-	£ s. 124 16	-	-	-	-

RANKS.	Weekly Pay in Shillings and Pence.											
	10 Sergeants.						55 Constables.					
	Merit Class.	1st Class.	2nd Class.	3rd Class.	4th Class.	5th Class.	Merit Class.	1st Class.	2nd Class.	3rd Class.	4th Class.	5th Class.	6th Class.
Number of each Rank and Class -	-	6	1	1	2	-	1	1	3	1	6	15	11	9	3
Rates of Pay of each ditto -	-	s. d. 38 6	s. d. 37 6	s. d. 36 6	s. d. 35 6	-	s. d. 34 6	s. d. 33 6	s. d. 32 6	s. 33	s. 31	s. 30	s. 29	s. 28	Vacancies.

Inspected 19th March, when the force was complete, but two constables were on sick list.

Authorised Establishment.—Seventy.

Extra Duties.—The chief inspects explosives and cattle diseases, and an inspector hackney carriages.

Public-houses.—Twenty-five ; with one prosecution, and one conviction.

Beerhouses.—Twenty-six.

Drunkenness.—One hundred and eighty-nine prosecutions, and 151 convictions, making 54 more prosecutions.

Ambulance.—Sixty-five members of the force hold certificates.

The cells and police offices were clean and in good order.

The books and returns were well kept.

The management, numbers, and discipline of the force have been efficiently maintained.

BOROUGH OF WARRINGTON.

Force - - . - - 69.*

Area in acres - - - - 3,117	Acres to each constable - - - 45
Population in 1891 - - 55,068	Population to ditto, as per census 1891 798

RANKS.	Chief Officer.	2 Superintendents.						2 Inspectors.				
		Deputy Chief Officer.	Chief Clerk.	1st Class.	2nd Class.	3rd Class.	4th Class.	1st Class.	2nd Class.	3rd Class.	4th Class.	5th Class.
Number of each Rank and Class -	1	-	1	1	-	-	-	1	1	-	-	-
Rates of Pay of each ditto - -	£ 390	-	£ 143	£ 156	-	-	-	£ s. 120 18	£ s. 114 6	-	-	-

Yearly Pay in £ and Shillings.

Weekly Pay in Shillings and Pence.

RANKS.	8 Sergeants.						Constables.								
	Merit Class.	1st Class.	2nd Class.	3rd Class.	4th Class.	5th Class.	Merit Class. 1st.	Merit Class. 2nd.	1st Class.				2nd Class.	3rd Class.	4th Class.
Number of each Rank and Class -	-	3	3	1	1	-	5	5	9	4	2	15	9	6	1†
Rates of Pay of each ditto -	-	s. 38	s. 37	s. 35	s. 34	-	s. 33	s. 32	s. 31	s. 30	s. 29	s. 28	s. 27	s. 26	s. 25

* Exclusive of a sergeant and two constables appointed at private cost. † Probationary.

Inspected 18th March, when the force was complete.

Authorised Establishment.—Sixty-nine.

Extra Duties.—The chief, an inspector, and a constable inspect hackney carriages, also explosives.

Public-houses.—Eighty-seven; with one prosecution, and one conviction.

Beerhouses.—Thirty-nine; with one prosecution, and one conviction.

Drunkenness.—Two hundred and sixty-five prosecutions, and 246 convictions, making 37 fewer prosecutions.

Ambulance.—Sixty-eight members of the force hold certificates.

The cells and police offices were clean and in good order.

The books and returns were well kept.

The management, numbers, and discipline of the force have been efficiently maintained.

BOROUGH OF WIGAN.

Force   - - - -   68.

Area in acres - - - -	2,188	Acres to each constable - - -	32
Population in 1891 -	55,013	Population to ditto, as per census 1891	779

Yearly Pay in £ and Shillings.

RANKS.	Chief Officer.	2 Superintendents.						4 Inspectors.				
		Deputy Chief Officer.	Chief Clerk.	1st Class.	2nd Class.	3rd Class.	4th Class.	1st Class.	2nd Class.	3rd Class.	4th Class.	5th Class.
Number of each Rank and Class -	1	-	1	1	-	-	-	2	1	1	-	-
Rates of Pay of each ditto - -	£ 325	-	£ s. d. 121 13 4	£ 165	-	-	-	£ s. d. 122 10 8	£ s. d. 117 16 3	£ s. d. 106 7 10	-	-

Weekly Pay in Shillings and Pence.

RANKS.	8 Sergeants.						Constables.							
	Merit Class.	1st Class.	2nd Class.	3rd Class.	4th Class.	5th Class.	Merit Class.	1st Class.		2nd Class.	3rd Class.	4th Class.	5th Class.	6th Class.
Number of each Rank and Class -	-	2	6	-	-	-	3	13	1	1	4	10	4	14 3
Rates of Pay of each ditto - -	-	s. d. 37 6	s. d. 33 3	-	-	-	s. d. 33 2	s. 32	s. d. 31 2	s. 31	s. 30	s. 29	s. 28	s. d. 26 10 s. d. 26 8

Inspected 22nd March, when the force was complete.

Authorised Establishment.—Sixty-eight.

Extra Duties.—The chief is head of fire brigade, with an inspector, sergeant, and 11 constables.

Public-houses.—One hundred and thirty-nine ; with six prosecutions, and one conviction.

Beerhouses.—Sixty.

Drunkenness.—Two hundred and thirty-eight prosecutions, and 166 convictions, making 62 more prosecutions.

Ambulance.—Fifty-two members of the force hold certificates.

The cells and police offices were clean and in good order.

The books and returns were well kept.

The management, numbers, and discipline of the force have been efficiently maintained.

COUNTY OF NORTHUMBERLAND.

Force - - - - - - 227.*

Area in acres - - - 1,273,561	Acres to each constable - - 5,614
Population in 1891 - - 259,765	Population to ditto, as per census 1891 1,144

RANKS.	Chief Officer	7 Superintendents.						6 Inspectors.				
		Deputy Chief Officer.	Chief Clerk.	1st Class.	2nd Class.	3rd Class.	4th Class.	1st Class.	2nd Class.	3rd Class.	4th Class.	5th Class.
												Yearly Pay in £ and Shillings.
Number of each Rank and Class -	1	1	1	1	2	3	-	3	2	1	-	-
Rates of Pay of each ditto -	£ 500	£ s. 255 5	£ s. 200 15	£ s. 200 15	£ s. d. 191 12 6	£ s. 182 10	-	£ s. 127 15	£ s. d. 121 13 4	£ s. 109 10	-	-

RANKS.	19 Sergeants.						Constables.											
	Merit Class.	1st Class.	2nd Class.	3rd Class.	4th Class.	5th Class.	Actg. Sergt.	Merit Class.	1st Class.	2nd Class.	3rd Class.	4th Class.	5th Class.	6th Class.	7th Class.	8th Class.	9th Class.	10th Class.
Number of each Rank and Class -	-	13	5	4	3	4	1	1†	31	11	30	12	16	2	14	25	23	25	4‡
Rates of Pay of each ditto -	-	s. d. 38 6	s. d. 37 11	s. d. 36 9	s. 35	s. d. 33 3	s. d. 33 3	s. d. 33 3	s. d. 31 6	s. d. 30 4	s. d. 29 9	s. d. 29 2	s. d. 28 7	s. 28	s. d. 27 5	s. d. 26 10	s. d. 25 3	s. d. 23 11	-

* Exclusive of two Inspectors, four sergeants, and 21 constables, total 27, under 3 & 4 Vict. c. 88. s. 19.
† Detective. ‡ Vacancy.

Inspected between 11th and 14th June, both days inclusive, when the force was complete.

Authorised Establishment.—Two hundred and twenty-seven.

Extra Duties :—

NATURE OF DUTY.	Chief Constable.	Super-intendents.	Inspectors.	Sergeants.	Constables.	TOTAL.
Inspectors under Contagious Diseases (Animals) Act.	1	6	5	14	2	28
Inspectors under Food and Drugs Act -	—	5	—	1	—*	6
Inspectors under Explosives Act - -	—	6	5	3	2	16
Inspectors of Fishery - - -	—	—	1	4	1	6
Inspectors under Weights and Measures Act.	1	5	2	4	2	14 .

Public-houses.—Five hundred and seventy ; with 15 prosecutions, and eight convictions.

Beerhouses.—Eighty-seven.

Drunkenness.—Three thousand six hundred and fifty prosecutions, and 3,585 convictions, making 83 fewer prosecutions.

Ambulance. — Two hundred and nine members of the force hold certificates.

The books and returns were well kept.

The management, numbers, and discipline of the force have been efficiently maintained.

No. 2.
Northern District.

BOROUGH OF BERWICK-ON-TWEED.

Force - - - - - - - 17.

Area in acres	-	-	-	6,930	Acres to each constable	-	-	-
Population in 1891		-	-	13,377	Population to ditto, as per census 1891			

RANKS.	Chief Officer.	Yearly Pay in £ and Shillings.											
		Superintendents.						Inspectors.					
		Deputy Chief Officer.	Chief Clerk.	1st Class.	2nd Class.	3rd Class.	4th Class.	1st Class.	2nd Class.	3rd Class.	4th Class.	5th Class.	
Number of each Rank and Class -	1	-	-	-	-	-	-	-	-	-	-	-	
Rates of Pay of each ditto - -	£ 125	-	-	-	-	-	-	-	-	-	-	-	

RANKS.	Weekly Pay in Shillings and Pence.												
	3 Sergeants.						9 Constables.						
	Merit Class.	1st Class.	2nd Class.	3rd Class.	4th Class.	5th Class.	Actg. Sergts.	Merit Class.	1st Class.	2nd Class.	3rd Class.	4th Class.	5th Class.	6th Class.
Number of each Rank and Class -	-	2	1	-	-	-	-	1	4	4	-	-	-	-
Rates of Pay of each ditto - -	-	s. d. 29 6	s. d. 28 6	-	-	-	-	-	s. d. 27 6	s. d. 26 6	s. d. 25 6	-	-	-	-

Inspected 10th June, when the force was complete.

Authorised Establishment.—Seventeen.

Extra Duties.—The chief is inspector of foods and drugs.

Public-houses.— Eighty four ; with four prosecutions, and four convictions.

Beerhouses.—Two.

Drunkenness.—One hundred and ninety prosecutions, and 173 convictions, being two more prosecutions.

Ambulance.—Nine members of the force hold certificates.

The new station is completed and satisfactory, and was opened by the Mayor on 31st May.

The books and returns were well kept.

The management, numbers, and discipline of the force have been efficiently maintained.

CITY OF NEWCASTLE-ON-TYNE.

Force - - - - - - - 300.

| Area in acres | - | - | - | 5,371 | Acres to each constable | - | - | - | 17 |
| Population in 1891 | - | | - | 186,300 | Population to ditto, as to census 1891 | - | 621 |

| RANKS. | Chief Officer. | Yearly Pay in £ and Shillings. | | | | | | | | | | |
| | | 3 Superintendents. | | | | | | 7 Inspectors. | | | | |
		Deputy Chief Officer.	Chief Clerk.	1st Class.	2nd Class.	3rd Class.	4th Class.	1st Class.	2nd Class.	3rd Class.	4th Class.	5th Class.
Number of each Rank and Class -	1	-	-	1	1	2	-	1	6	-	-	-
Rates of Pay of each ditto -	£ 800	-	-	£ 250	£ 180	£ 160	-	£ 120	£ s. 124 16	-	-	-

| RANKS. | Weekly Pay in Shillings and Pence. | | | | | | | | | | | | | |
| | 28 Sergeants. | | | | | | 250 Constables. | | | | | | | |
	Merit Class.	1st Class.	2nd Class.	3rd Class.	4th Class.	5th Class.	Long Service.				1st Class.	2nd Class.	3rd Class.	4th Class.	5th Class.
Number of each Rank and Class -	-	11	7	5	10	5	36	35	35	16	29	30	34	22	12 Probationary.	1 Vacancy.
Rates of Pay of each ditto -	-	s. 42	s. 40	s. 38	s. 36	s. 35	s. 33	s. 32	s. 31	s. 30	s. 29	s. 28	s. 27	s. 26	s. 25	

Inspected on 11th June, when the force was complete.

Authorised Establishment.—Three hundred.

Extra Duties.—The chief is director of fire brigades, with 30 auxiliaries.

Public-houses.—Three hundred and eighty-nine ; with five prosecutions, and two convictions.

Beerhouses.—One hundred and sixty-seven ; with three prosecutions, and three convictions.

Drunkenness.—Four thousand eight hundred and nine prosecutions, and 4,389 convictions, being 255 more prosecutions.

Ambulance.—Two hundred and forty-one members of the force hold certificates ; 41 more than last year.

The cells and police offices were clean and in good order.

The books and returns were well kept.

The management, numbers, and discipline of the force have been efficiently maintained.

No. 2.
Northern District.

BOROUGH OF TYNEMOUTH.

Force - - - - - - 65.

Area in acres - - - 4,317 | Acres to each constable - - -
Population in 1891 - - 46,588 | Population to ditto, as per census 1891

RANKS.	Chief Officer.	Yearly Pay in £ and Shillings.										
		Superintendents.						3 Inspectors.				
		Deputy Chief Officer.	Chief Clerk.	1st Class.	2nd Class.	3rd Class.	4th Class.	1st Class.	2nd Class.	3rd Class.	4th Class.	5th Class.
Number of each Rank and Class,-	1	-	-	-	-	-	-	1	1	1	-	-
Rates of Pay of each ditto -	£ 390	-	-	-	-	-	-	£ s. 137 16	£ s. 132 12	£ 117	-	-

RANKS.	Weekly Pay in Shillings and Pence.														
	10 Sergeants.						51 Constables.								
	1st Class.	2nd Class.	3rd Class.	4th Class.	5th Class.		Merit. Class.	1st Class.	2nd Class.	3rd Class.	4th Class.	5th Class.	6th Class.		
Number of each Rank and Class -	2	2	1	1	1	1	1	1	1	5	3	7	8	5	2	9	8	2
Rates of Pay of each ditto -	s. 42	s. 41	s. 39	s. 36	s. d. 35 6	s. 35	s. 34	s. d. 33 6	s. d. 32 6	s. 33	s. 32	s. 31	s. 30	s. 29	s. 28	s. 27	s. d. 25 6	s. 24

Inspected 15th June, when the force was complete.

Authorised Establishment.—Sixty-five.

Extra Duties—

NATURE OF DUTY.	Chief Officer.	Super-intendents.	Inspectors.	Sergeants.	Constables.	TOTAL.
Assistant Relieving Officer - - -	1*	—	—	—	—	1
Billet Master - - - - - -	1	—	—	—	—	1
Fire Brigade - - - - - -	1	—	—	2	10	13
Inspector of Explosives - - -	1	—	—	—	—	1
Inspector under Petroleum Act - -	1	—	—	—	—	1
Inspector under Contagious Diseases (Animals) Act.	1	—	—	—	—	1
Inspector of Common Lodging-houses -	1	—	—	—	—	1

Public-houses.—Six hundred and thirty-three; with three prosecutions, and two convictions.

Beerhouses.—Thirty-one; with two prosecutions, and convictions.

Drunkenness.—Two thousand and six prosecutions, and 1,875 convictions, making 472 more prosecutions.

Ambulance.—Sixty-two members of the force hold certificates; 11 more than last year.

The cells and police offices were clean and in good order.

The books and returns were well kept.

The management, numbers, and discipline of the force have been efficiently maintained,

Force - - - 202.*

Area in acres - - - 527,221	Acres to each constable - - - 2,669
Population in 1891 - 2,172,291	Population to ditto, as per census 1891 1,081

Yearly Pay in £ and Shillings.

RANKS.	Chief Officer.	7 Superintendents.						8 Inspectors.				
		Deputy Chief Officer.	Chief Clerk.	1st Class.	2nd Class.	3rd Class.	4th Class.	1st Class.	2nd Class.	3rd Class.	4th Class.	5th Class.
Number of each Rank and Class -	1	1	-	2	1 (Vacancy.)	1	2	1	1	2	4	-
Rates of Pay of each ditto - -	£ 600	£ 300	-	£ 200	-	£ 270	£ 150	£ 130	£ 120	£ 112	£ 100	-

Weekly Pay in Shillings and Pence.

RANKS.	27 Sergeants.						169 Constables.								
	Merit Class.	1st Class.	2nd Class.	3rd Class.	4th Class.	5th Class.	Merit Class.	1st Class.					2nd Class.	3rd Class.	
Number of each Rank and Class -	-	6	10	5	6	-	38	22	17	28	8	21	14	14	2 (Vacancies.)
Rates of Pay of each ditto - -	s. d. -	s. d. 36 9	s. d. 35	s. d. 33 3	s. d. 33 1	-	s. d. 30 11	s. d. 29 9	s. d. 29 2	s. d. 28 7	s. d. 28	s. d. 27 5	s. d. 26 3	s. d. 24 6	-

* Exclusive of an inspector and 25 constables, appointed under 3 & 4 Vict. c. 88, s. 19, to look after weights.

Inspected 30th and 31st May inclusive, when the force was complete.

Authorised Establishment.—Two hundred and two.

Extra Duties.—All the men, including the chief, are inspectors under Contagious Diseases (Cattle) Act.

Public-houses.—Six hundred and sixty-two ; and no prosecutions.

Beerhouses.—Three hundred and forty ; and no prosecutions.

Drunkenness.—Nine hundred and ninety- six prosecutions, and 869 convictions, being 95 fewer prosecutions.

Ambulance.—One hundred and ninety-three members of the force hold certificates, being 10 more than last year.

Headquarters and five divisional stations and four locks-ups were inspected, and were clean and in good order.

The books were well kept.

The management, numbers, and discipline of the force have been efficiently maintained.

BOROUGH OF NEWARK.

Force - - - 16.

Area in acres - - - - 1,932 | Acres to each constable - - - 128
Population in 1891 - - 14,457 | Population to ditto, as per census 1891 963

RANKS.	Chief Officer.	Superintendents.						1 Inspector.				
		Deputy Chief Officer.	Chief Clerk.	1st Class.	2nd Class.	3rd Class.	4th Class.	1st Class.	2nd Class.	3rd Class.	4th Class.	5th Class.
Number of each Rank and Class -	1	-	-	-	-	-	-	1	-	-	-	-
Rates of Pay of each ditto -	£ 200	-	-	-	-	-	-	£ s. 100 2	-	-	-	-

Yearly Pay in £ and Shillings.

RANKS.	2 Sergeants.						12 Constables.						
	Merit Class.	1st Class.	2nd Class.	3rd Class.	4th Class.	5th Class.	Acting Sergeants.	Merit Class.	1st Class.		2nd Class.	3rd Class.	4th Class.
Number of each Rank and Class -	-	1	1	-	-	-	-	1	1	2	1	-	4	3
Rates of Pay of each ditto -	-	s. 36	s. 33	-	-	-	-	s. 30	s. 30	s. 29	s. 28	-	s. 26	s. d. 24 6

Weekly Pay in Shillings and Pence.

Inspected 1st June, when the force was complete.

Authorised Establishment.—Sixteen.

Extra Duties.—The chief inspects common lodging-houses and explosives.

Public-houses.—Fifty-five; with no prosecutions.

Beerhouses.—Twenty-two; with no prosecution.

Drunkenness.—Forty-seven prosecutions, and 44 convictions, being 25 fewer prosecutions.

Ambulance.—All the members of the force hold certificates.

CITY OF NOTTINGHAM.

Force - - - - 272.*

Area in acres - - - 10,935 | Acres to each constable - - - 40
Population in 1891 - - 213,877 | Population to ditto, as per census 1891 786

RANKS.	Chief Officer.	6 Superintendents.						12 Inspectors.				
		Deputy Chief Officer.	Chief Clerk.	1st Class.	2nd Class.	3rd Class.	4th Class.	1st Class.	2nd Class.	3rd Class.	4th Class.	5th Class.
Number of each Rank and Class -	1	1	1	1	1	2	-	1	3	1	2	1	4
Rates of Pay of each ditto -	£ 750	£ 200	£ 190	£ 175	£ 175	£ 165	-	£ s. 137 16	£ s. 135 4	£ s. 124 16	£ s. 122 4	£ s. 119 12	£ 117

Yearly Pay in £ and Shillings.

RANKS.	45 Sergeants.						217 Constables.						
	1st Class.	2nd Class.	3rd Class.	4th Class.	5th Class.		1st Class.		2nd Class.	3rd Class.	4th Class.	5th Class.	6th Class.
Number of each Rank and Class -	19	5	8	2	6	3	68	19	17	34	25	7	26	21
Rates of Pay of each ditto -	s. 40	s. 39	s. 33	s. 37	s. 36	s. 35	s. 33	s. 32	s. 31	s. 30	s. 29	s. 28	s. 27	s. 26

Weekly Pay in Shillings and Pence.

* Exclusive of a constable appointed at private cost.

Inspected 29th May, when the force was complete.

Authorised Establishment.—Two hundred and seventy-two..

Extra Duties.—Six constables attend to the castle museum, one to the arboretum, and an inspector inspects hackney carriages.

Public-houses.—Four hundred and fifteen ; with 10 prosecutions, and four convictions.

Beerhouses.—One hundred and eighty ; with four prosecutions, and three convictions.

Drunkenness.—Nine hundred and seventy-five prosecutions, and 901 convictions, being 343 fewer prosecutions.

Ambulance.—One hundred and ninety-seven members of the force hold certificates.

The cells and police offices were clean and in good order.

The books and returns were well kept.

The management, numbers, and discipline of the force have been efficiently maintained.

No. 2.
Northern District.

COUNTY OF WESTMORELAND.

Force - - - - - - 36*.

Area in acres - - 500,511	Acres to each constable - - 13,901
Population in 1891 - 51,785	Population to ditto, as per census 1891 1,438

RANKS.	Chief Constable.	2 Superintendents.						2 Inspectors.				
		Deputy Chief Clerk.	Chief Clerk.	1st Class.	2nd Class.	3rd Class.	4th Class.	1st Class.	2nd Class.	3rd Class.	4th Class.	4th Class.
Number of each Rank and Class - }	1	--	1	1	--	1	-	2	-	-	-	--
Rates of Pay of each ditto - }	£ 175	-	£ s. d. 45 11 8	£ s. d. 202 5 5	-	£ s. d. 174 17 11	-	£ s. d. 190 2 11	-	-	-	-

Weekly Pay in Shillings and Pence.

RANKS.	5 Sergeants.						26 Constables.							
	Merit Class.	1st Class.	2nd Class.	3rd Class.	4th Class.	5th Class.	Acting Sergeants.	Merit Class.	1st Class.	2nd Class.	3rd Class.	4th Class.	5th Class.	6th Class.
Number of each Rank and Class - }	-	3	-	2	-	-	-	-	22	1	1	-	1	-
Rates of Pay of each ditto - }	-	s. d. 36 9	-	s. d. 33 3	-	-	-	-	s. d. 30 11	s. d. 29 2	s. 28	-	s. d. 23 11	-

* Exclusive of two additional constables.

Inspected 2nd, 3rd, and 4th July inclusive, when the force was complete.

Authorised Establishment.—Thirty-six.

Extra Duties :—

NATURE OF DUTY.	Chief Constable.	Super-intendents.	Inspector.	Sergeants.	Constables.	Remarks.
Inspectors of Weights and Measures -	1	2	2	5	14	
Inspectors of Explosives - - -	1	2	2	5	14	
Inspectors of Food and Drugs -	1	2	2	5	14	Actual ex-penses paid.
Inspectors under Contagious Diseases (Animals Act).	1	2	2	5	14	
Inspectors of Fertilisers and Feeding Stuffs.	1	2	2	5	3	
Fire Brigade - - - -	1	2	2	5	26	

No. 2.
Northern District.

Public-houses.—One hundred and ninety-four ; with two prosecutions, and one conviction.

Beerhouses.—Twenty-one ; no prosecutions.

Drunkenness.—Ninety-seven prosecutions, and 85 convictions, being 32 fewer prosecutions.

Ambulance.—Twenty members of the force hold certificates.

Head-quarters and other divisional stations were inspected, and six lock-ups and the site for the lock-up at Patterdale were visited.

The books and returns were well kept.

The management, numbers, and discipline of the force have been efficiently maintained.

The borough of Appleby is policed by the county force.

The chief constable, Sir John Dunn, is also chief constable of Westmoreland.

BOROUGH OF KENDAL.

Force - - - - 16.

Area in acres - - - - 2,622	Acres to each constable - - - 163
Population in 1891 - - 14,430	Population to ditto, as per census, 1891 991

RANKS.	Yearly Pay in £ and Shillings.											
	Chief Constable.	Superintendents.						1 Inspector.				
		Deputy Chief Constable.	Chief Clerk.	1st Class.	2nd Class.	3rd Class.	4th Class.	1st Class.	2nd Class.	3rd Class.	4th Class.	5th Class.
Number of each Rank and Class -	1	-	-	-	-	-	-	1	-	-	-	-
Rates of Pay of each ditto - -	£ 180	-	-	-	-	-	-	£ 91	-	-	-	-

RANKS.	Weekly Pay in Shillings and Pence.												
	2 Sergeants.						12 Constables.						
	Merit Class.	1st Class.	2nd Class.	3rd Class.	4th Class.	5th Class.	Acting Sergeants.	Merit Class.	1st Class.	2nd Class.	3rd Class.	4th Class.	5th Class.	6th Class.
Number of each Rank and Class -	-	2	-	-	-	-	-	1	3	4	1	-	2	1
Rates of Pay of each ditto - -	-	s. 30	-	-	-	-	-	s. 29	s. 28	s. 27	s. 26	-	s. 24	s. 22

Inspected 2nd July, when the force was complete.

Authorised Establishment. —Sixteen.

Extra Duties.—The chief inspects explosives and cattle disease and weights and measures.

Public-houses.—Thirty-seven ; and no prosecutions.

Beerhouses.—Six ; with no prosecutions.

Drunkenness.—Sixty-two prosecutions, and six convictions, one more prosecution.

Ambulance.—Fifteen members of the force hold certificates.

The books and returns were well kept.

The management, numbers, and discipline of the force have been efficiently maintained.

COUNTY OF YORK, EAST RIDING.

Force - - - - - 134.*

| Area in acres | - | - | - | 738,630 | Acres to each constable | - | - | - | 5,512 |
| Population in 1891 | - | | - | 128,370 | Population to ditto, as per census 1891 | | | | 957 |

RANKS.	Chief Constable	Yearly Pay in £ and Shillings.											
		Superintendents.						4 Inspectors.					
		Deputy Chief Constable	Chief Clerk.	1st Class.	2nd Class.	3rd Class.	4th Class.	1st Class.	2nd Class.	3rd Class.	4th Class.	5th Class.
Number of each Rank and Class -	1	1	1	1	2	–	4	–	–	4	–	–
Rates of Pay of each ditto -	£. 450	£ s. d. 199 19 9	£ s. 149 16	£ s. 149 16	£ s. d. 145 4 9½	–	£ s. d. 130 0 7	–	–	£ s. d. 100 7 6	–	–

RANKS.	Weekly Pay in Shillings and Pence.											
	16 Sergeants.						116 Constables.					
	Merit Class.	1st Class.			2nd Class.	3rd Class.	Acting Sergeants.	Merit Class.	1st Class.		2nd Class.	3rd Class.	4th Class.	5th Class.
Number of each Rank and Class -	–	9	2	4	1	–	–	44	21	38	4	7	–	–
Rates of Pay of each ditto -	–	s. d. 22 3	s. d. 21 6	s. d. 30 4	s. d. 29 3	–	–	s. 28	s. d. 26 3	s. d. 25 1	s. d. 23 4	s. d. 22 3	–	° –

* One constable is appointed at private cost.

Inspected 8th, 11th, and 20th July, when the force was complete.

Authorised Strength.—One hundred and thirty-four.

Extra Duties.—

NATURE OF DUTY.	Super-intendents.	Inspectors.	Sergeants.	Constables.	TOTAL.
Inspectors under Contagious Diseases (Animals) Act.	8	4	—	—	12
Inspectors under Food and Drugs Act -	8	—	—	—	8
Inspectors under Explosives Act - -	8	—	—	—	8
Inspectors of Common Lodging-houses -	2	1	—	—	3
Assistant Relieving Officers - -	2	1	—	—	3
Honorary Water Bailiffs for Yorkshire Fishing Board.	—	—	2	19	21

Public-houses.—Four hundred and forty-seven ; with 18 prosecutions, and 13 convictions.

Beerhouses.—Fifty-one ; with one prosecution.

Drunkenness.—Five hundred and ninety-one prosecutions, and 562 convictions, two less prosecutions.

Ambulance.—One hundred and ten members of the force hold certificates, an increase of two.

Head-quarters and six divisional stations were inspected, and Bridlington lock-up.

The books and returns were well kept.

The management, numbers, and discipline of the force have been efficiently maintained.

BOROUGH OF BEVERLEY.

Force - - - - 15.

| Area in acres | - | - | - | 2,404 | Acres to each constable | - | - 160 |
| Population in 1891 | - | - | - | 12,539 | Population to ditto, as per census 1891 | | 836 |

Yearly Pay in £ and Shillings.

RANKS.	Chief Constable.	Superintendents.						1 Inspector.				
		Deputy Chief Constable.	Chief Clerk.	1st Class.	2nd Class.	3rd Class.	4th Class.	1st Class.	2nd Class.	3rd Class.	4th Class.	5th Class.
Number of each Rank and Class -	1	-	-	-	-	-	-	-	1	-	-	-
Rates of Pay of each ditto -	£ 225	-	-	-	-	-	-	-	£ 90	-	-	-

Weekly Pay in Shillings and Pence.

RANKS.	3 Sergeants.						11 Constables.					
	Merit Class.	1st Class.	2nd Class.	3rd Class.	4th Class.	5th Class.	Merit Class.	1st Class.	2nd Class.	3rd Class.	4th Class.	5th Class.
Number of each Rank and Class -	-	3	-	-	-	-	1	3	1	2	3	1	-	-
Rates of Pay of each ditto -	-	s. 32	-	-	-	-	s. d. 29 2	s. 28	s. 26	s. 25	s. 24	s. 23	-	-

Inspected 8th July, when the force was complete.

Authorised Establishment.—Fifteen.

Extra Duties.—The chief is inspector of weights and measures, food and drugs, and common lodging-houses.

Public-houses.—Forty-four; with one prosecution, and one conviction.

Beerhouses.—Twelve.

Drunkenness.—Fifty-seven prosecutions, and 56 convictions, a decrease of 53 prosecutions.

Ambulance.—Fourteen members of the force hold certificates, an increase of two.

The books and returns were well kept.

The management, numbers, and discipline of the force have been efficiently maintained.

CITY OF HULL.

Force - - - 331.*

| Area in acres | - | - | - | 9 202 | Acres to each constable | - | - 27 |
| Population in 1891 | - | - | 200,651 | Population to ditto, as per census 1891 606 |

RANKS.	Chief Constable.	Deputy Chief Constable.	7 Superintendents.						10 Inspectors.				
			Chief Clerk.	1st Class.	2nd Class.	3rd Class.	4th Class.		1st Class.	2nd Class.	3rd Class.	4th Class.	5th Class.
Number of each Rank and Class	1	1	1	1	1	1	1	1	2	3	1	2	1	1
Rates of Pay of each ditto -	£ 600	£ 225	£ s. 161 4	£ s. d. 201 1 4	£ s. 174 4	£ s. 148 4	£ s. 148	£ s. 137 16	£ s. 122 12	£ s. 119 12	£ 117	£ s. 114 8	£ s. 109 4	Vacancy.

Yearly Pay in £ and Shillings.

RANKS.	40 Sergeants.							273 Constables.							
	Merit Class.	1st Class.	2nd Class.	3rd Class.	4th Class.	5th Class.		Merit Class.	1st Class.	2nd Class.	3rd Class.	4th Class.	5th Class.	6th Class.
Number of each Rank and Class								1 2 6 4 6 11 15 67	9	18	14	25	36	23	9 7 6
Rates of Pay of each ditto -	s. 46	s. 44	s. 43	s. 41	s. 40	s. 38 s. 37 s. 36 s. 34		s. 40 s. 39 s. 38 s. 37 s. 36 s. 35 s. 34	s. 33	s. 32	s. 31	s. 30	s. 29	s. 28	s. 27 s. 26 s. 25 s. 24

Weekly Pay in Shillings and Pence.

_ Exclusive of one constable appointed at private cost.

Inspected on 9th July, when there were seven vacancies.

Authorised Strength.—Three hundred and thirty-one.

Extra Duties.—The whole force act as a fire brigade.

Public-houses.—Three hundred and one; with six prosecutions, and six convictions.

Beerhouses.—One hundred and sixty-three; with one prosecution, and one conviction.

Drunkenness.—One thousand eight hundred and fifty-one prosecutions, and 1,809 convictions, a decrease of 131 prosecutions.

Ambulance.—Two hundred and eighty-six members of the force hold certificates.

Head-quarters and four other stations were visited, and cells were clean and in good order.

The books and returns were well kept.

The management, numbers, and discipline of the force have been efficiently maintained.

COUNTY OF YORKS, NORTH RIDING.

Force - - - 248.*

Area in acres - - 1,355,990	Acres to each constable - - 5,467
Population in 1891 - - 250,157	Population to ditto, as per census 1891 1,008

RANKS.	Chief Constable	11 Superintendents.						17 Inspectors.				
		Deputy Chief Constable.	Chief Clerk.	1st Class.	2nd Class.	3rd Class.	4th Class.	1st Class.	2nd Class.	3rd Class.	4th Class.	5th Class.
Number of each Rank and Class	1	1	1	3	2	4	—	2	1	8	6	—
Rates of Pay of each ditto -	£ 450	£ s. d. 240 5 10	£ s. d. 189 13 9	£ s. d. 290 10 8	£ s. d. 179 9 2	£ s. d. 159 13 9	—	£ s. d. 129 5 5	£ s. d. 134 14 2	£ s. d. 120 3 11	£ s. d. 104 18 9	—

RANKS.	27 Sergeants.						194 Constables.										
	Merit Class.	1st Class.	2nd Class.	3rd Class.	4th Class.	5th Class.	Merit Class.	1st Class.								2nd Class.	3rd Class.
Number of each Rank and Class	—	5	2	1	13	6	1	1	42	15	2	15	23	30		33	34
Rates of Pay of each ditto -	—	s. d. 35 7	s. d. 35	s. d. 34 5	s. d. 33	s. d. 33 1	s. d. 31 6	s. d. 30 11	s. d. 30 4	s. d. 29 9	s. d. 29 2	s. d. 28 7	s. d. 28	s. d. 27 5		s. d. 26 3	s. d. 25 1

* There are also three inspectors, two sergeants, and 18 constables as additional constables.

Inspected between 7th and 15th, when the force was complete.

Authorised Strength.—Two hundred and forty-eight.

Extra Duties :—

NATURE OF DUTY.	Chief Constable.	Super-intendents.	Inspectors.	Sergeants.	Constables.	TOTAL.
Inspectors under Cattle Diseases Acts -	1	10	20	19	40	90
Inspectors of Weights and Measures -	—	—	3	—	—	3
Inspectors under Explosives Act -	—	10	15	6	—	31
Inspectors under Food and Drugs Act -	—	—	3	—	—	3
Inspectors of Common Lodging-houses -	—	5	7	3	2	17

Public-houses.—Nine hundred and fifty-four ; with 20 prosecutions, and 15 convictions.

Beerhouses.—Sixty-four.

Drunkenness.—Eight hundred and twenty-four prosecutions, 794 convictions, a decrease of 47 prosecutions.

Ambulance.—Two hundred and twenty-two members of the force hold certificates, a decrease of two men.

The books and returns were well kept.

The management, numbers, and discipline of the force have been efficiently maintained.

Force   -   -   -   - 96.*

Area in acres - - - 2,824	Acres to each constable - - 29
Population in 1891 - - - 75,532	Population to ditto, as per census 1891 786

Yearly Pay in £ and Shillings.

RANKS.	Chief Constable.	Superintendents.						Inspectors.				
		Deputy Chief Constable.	Chief Clerk.	1st Class.	2nd Class.	3rd Class.	4th Class.	1st Class.	2nd Class.	3rd Class.	4th Class.	5th Class.
Number of each Rank and Class	1	-	-	-	-	-	-	1	3	1	-	-
Rates of Pay of each ditto -	£ 150	-	-	-	-	-	-	£ s. 119 12	£ s. 114 8	£ s. 105 6	-	-

Weekly Pay in Shillings and Pence.

RANKS.	11 Sergeants.						79 Constables.							
	Merit Class.	1st Class.	2nd Class.	3rd Class.	4th Class.	5th Class.	Merit Class.	1st Class.			2nd Class.	3rd Class.	4th Class.	5th Class.
Number of each Rank and Class	-	2	8	1	-	-	3	1	19	22	14	6	8	5
Rates of Pay of each ditto -	-	s. 36	s. 35	s. 34	-	-	s. 33	s. 32	s. 31	s. 30	s. 29	s. 28	s. 27	s. d. 25 8

* Exclusive of eight additional constables.

Inspected 17th July, when there were two vacancies.

Authorised Establishment.—Ninety-six.

Extra Duties.—The chief is relieving officer for vagrants and inspector of common lodging-houses ; a sergeant inspects hackney carriages.

Public-houses.—Seventy-nine ; with four prosecutions, and four convictions.

Beerhouses.—Thirty-five.

Drunkenness.—Seven hundred and 'sixty-three prosecutions, and 759 convictions, a decrease of 16 prosecutions.

Ambulance. — Ninety-nine members of the force hold certificates, an increase of three men.

The cells and police offices (three) were clean and in good order.

The books and returns were well kept.

The management, numbers, and discipline of the force have been efficiently maintained.

No. 2.
thern District.

BOROUGH OF SCARBOROUGH.

Force - - - - - - - 50.*

Area in acres - - - - 2,348	Acres to each constable - - - 47
Population in 1891 - - - 33,776	Population to ditto, as per census 1891 689

RANKS.	Chief Officer.	Superintendents.						3 Inspectors.				
		Deputy Chief Officer.	Chief Clerk.	1st Class.	2nd Class.	3rd Class.	4th Class.	1st Class.	2nd Class.	3rd Class.	4th Class.	5th Class.
Number of each Rank and Class -	1	-	1	-	-	-	-	-	1	2	-	-
Rates of Pay of each ditto -	£ 325	-	£ 104	-	-	-	-	-	£ 117	£ s. 111 16	-	-

Weekly Pay in Shillings and Pence.

RANKS.	5 Sergeants.						40 Constables.										
	Merit Class.	1st Class.	2nd Class.	3rd Class.	4th Class.	5th Class.	Merit Class.		1st Class.	2nd Class.	3rd Class.	4th Class.		5th Class.	
Number of each Rank and Class -	-	1	1	2	1	-	3	5	1	2	1	6	5	9	6	2
Rates of Pay of each ditto -	-	s. d. 38	s. d. 37 11	s. d. 36 9	s. d. 35 7	-	s. d. 33 6	s. 32	s. d. 31 6	s. d. 30 11	s. d. 29 9	s. d. 29 2	s. d. 28 7	s. 28	s. d. 27 5	s. d. 24 6

*Exclusive of an additional constable appointed at private cost, and two additional during summer season.

Inspected 15th July, when the force was complete.

Authorised Strength.—Fifty, an increase of one.

Public-houses.— One hundred and sixty-four; with six prosecutions, and five convictions.

Beerhouses.—Twenty-four; with one prosecution, and one conviction.

Drunkenness.—Two hundred and two prosecutions, and 268 convictions, a decrease of 19 prosecutions.

Ambulance.—Forty members of the force hold certificates.

The books and returns were well kept.

The management, numbers, and discipline of the force have been efficiently maintained.

CITY OF YORK.

Force - - - - - - - 80.

Area in acres - - - - - 3,729 | Acres to each constable - - - 47
Population in 1891 - - - 67,926 | Population to ditto, as per census 1891 849

RANKS.	Chief Constable.	Yearly Pay in £ and Shillings.										
		1 Superintendent.						5 Inspectors.				
		Deputy Chief Constable.	Chief Clerk.	1st Class.	2nd Class.	3rd Class.	4th Class.	1st Class.	2nd Class.	3rd Class.	4th Class.	5th Class.
Number of each Rank and Class -	1	–	–	1	–	–	–	1	1	1	1	1
Rates of Pay of each ditto -	£ 350	–	–	£ 180	–	–	–	£ s. 131 18	£ s. 124 16	£ 117	£ s. 114 8	£ s. 109 4

RANKS.	Weekly Pay in Shillings and Pence.												
	9 Sergeants.						62 Constables.						
	Merit Class.	1st Class.	2nd Class.	3rd Class.	4th Class.	5th Class.	Merit Class.	1st Class.	2nd Class.	3rd Class.	4th Class.	5th Class.	6th Class.
Number of each Rank and Class -	–	1	2	2	2	2	3	11	6	9	16	4	9
Rates of Pay of each ditto -	–	s. 39	s. 38	s. 37	s. 35	s. 34	s. 33	s. 32	s. 30	s. 29	s. 28	s. 26	s. 25

Inspected on 6th June, when there were two vacancies.

Authorised Establishment.—Eighty.

Extra Duties.—The chief is inspector of explosives, hackney carriages, and weights and measures.

Public-houses.—One hundred and ninety-eight; with 13 prosecutions, and seven convictions.

Beerhouses.—Thirty-nine; with one prosecution, and one conviction.

Drunkenness.—Four hundred and sixteen prosecutions, and 371 convictions, nine fewer prosecutions.

Ambulance.—Seventy-three members of the force hold certificates, an increase of two.

The cells and police offices were clean and in good order.

The books and returns were well kept.

The management, numbers, and discipline of the force have been efficiently maintained.

COUNTY OF YORK, WEST RIDING.

Force - - - - - - - 1,225.

Area in acres - - - 1,674,902	Acres to each constable - - -
Population in 1891 - - 1,129,830	Population to ditto, as per census 1891

		Yearly Pay in £ and Shillings.												
RANKS.	Chief Con- stable.	23 Superintendents.							41 Inspectors.					
		Deputy Chief Constable.	Chief Clerk.	1st Class.	2nd Class.	3rd Class.	4th Class.		1st Class.	2nd Class.	3rd Class.	4th Class.	5th Class.	
Number of each Rank and Class -	1	-	1	1	2	1	1	2 3 3 1	4	8	6	14	8	1
Rates of Pay of each ditto - -	£ 1,000	-	£ 500	-	£ 250	£ 240	£ 220	£ 200 £ 180 £ 160	£ s. d. 129 5 5	£ s. d. 121 13 4	£ s. d. 115 11 8	£ s. d. 111 0 5	£ s. d. 108 9 2	Vacancy.

		Weekly Pay in Shillings and Pence.											
RANKS.	179 Sergeants.						980 Constables.						
	1st Class.	2nd Class.	3rd Class.	4th Class.	5th Class.		1st Class.	2nd Class.	3rd Class.	4th Class.	5th Class.	6th Class.	
Number of each Rank and Class -	19	14	13	35	39	57 2	205	67 44	122	144	101	100	143 53
Rates of Pay of each ditto - -	s. d. 37 4	s. d. 36 9	s. d. 36 2	s. d. 35 7	s. d. 34 5	s. d. 33 3 Vacancies.	s. d. 31 6	s. d. 30 11 s. d. 30 4	s. d. 29 9	s. d. 29 2	s. d. 28	s. d. 26 2	s. d. 25 1 Vacancies.

Inspected between 24th of April and 9th May.

Authorised Establishment.—One thousand two hundred and twenty-five.

Extra Duties :—

NATURE OF DUTY.	Chief Constable.	Super- intendents.	Inspectors.	Sergeants.	Constables	TOTAL.
Inspectors under Contagious Diseases (Ani- mals) Act.	1	22	1	—	—	24
Inspectors under Food and Drugs Act -	1	22	1	—	—	24
Petroleum Inspectors - - -	—	3	—	—	—	3
Inspectors under Explosives Act - -	—	22	6	1	—	29
Inspectors of Common Lodging-houses -	—	1	2	—	—	3

Public-houses.—Two thousand three hundred and fifty-three ; with 99 prosecutions, and 62 convictions.

Beerhouses.—Nine hundred and eighty-two ; with 38 prosecutions, and 27 convictions.

Drunkenness.—Twelve thousand six hundred and seventy-seven prose-cutions, and 12,284 convictions, an increase of 501 prosecutions.

Ambulance.—Seven hundred members of the force hold certificates, an increase of 33 men.

The books and returns were well kept.

The management, numbers, and discipline of the force have been efficiently maintained.

The following nine municipal boards are policed by the West Riding Constabulary, viz., Batley, Brighouse, Keighley, Harrogate, Morley, Ripon, Pontefract, Orsett, and Todmorden.

BOROUGH OF BARNSLEY.

Force - - - - - - 40.

Area in acres - - - - 2,386	Acres to each constable - - -
Population in 1891 - - - 35,427	Population to ditto, as per census 1891

RANKS.	Chief Constable	Superintendents.						2 Inspectors.				
		Deputy Chief Constable.	Chief Clerk.	1st Class.	2nd Class.	3rd Class.	4th Class.	1st Class.	2nd Class.	3rd Class.	4th Class.	5th Class.
Number of each Bank and Class -	1	-	-	-	-	-	-	2	-	-	-	-
Rates of Pay of each ditto -	£300	-	-	-	-	-	-	£109 4s.	-	-	-	-

Yearly Pay in £ and Shillings.

RANKS.	6 Sergeants.						31 Constables.							
	Merit Class.	1st Class.	2nd Class.	3rd Class.	4th Class.	5th Class.	Merit Class.	1st Class.	2nd Class.	3rd Class.	4th Class.	5th Class.	6th Class.	
Number of each Bank and Class -	-	1	2	2	1	-	1	11	8	3	5	2 Vacancies.	-	-
Rates of Pay of each ditto -	-	36s.	35s.	34s.	33s.	-	39s. 2d.	38s.	37s.	36s.	33s.	-	-	-

Weekly Pay in Shillings and Pence.

Inspected 9th May, when there were two vacancies.

Authorised Establishment.—Forty.

Extra Duties.—The chief is captain of fire brigade, and nine of the force are firemen.

The chief inspects hackney carriages and common lodging-houses, and inspector under Animals Diseases Act.

Public-houses.—Sixty-eight; with two prosecutions, and two convictions.

Beerhouses.—Forty-one; with five prosecutions, and four convictions.

Drunkenness.—Three hundred and ninety-two prosecutions, and 385 convictions, an increase of 131 prosecutions.

Ambulance.—Thirty-three members of the force hold certificates.

The books and returns were well kept.

The management, numbers, and discipline of the force have been efficiently maintained.

CITY OF BRADFORD.

Force - - - - 390.

Area in acres - - - 22,843 | Acres to each constable - - -
Population in 1891 - - - 265,718 | Population to ditto, as per census 1891

Yearly Pay in £ and Shillings.

RANKS.	Chief Constable	6 Superintendents.						14 Inspectors.				
		Deputy Chief Constable.	Chief Clerk.	1st Class.	2nd Class.	3rd Class.	4th Class.	1st Class.	2nd Class.	3rd Class.	4th Class.	5th Class.
Number of each Rank and Class -	1	1	1	1	1	1	1	1	2	2	1	8
Rates of Pay of each ditto -	£ 500	£ 190	£ 130	£ 170	£ 170	£ 170	£ 170	£ 150	£ 130	£ s. 124 16	£ s. 114 8	£ s. 109 4

Weekly Pay in Shillings and Pence.

RANKS.	43 Sergeants.						227 Constables.												
	Merit Class.	1st Class.	2nd Class.	3rd Class.	4th Class.	5th Class.	Merit Class	1st Class.				2nd Class.				3rd Class.			Vacancies.
Number of each Rank and Class -	-	2	7	9	24	-	11	3	28	18	19	22	20	19	18	34	61	70	4
Rates of Pay of each ditto -	-	40	38	36	34	-	35	34	33	33	31	30	29	28	27	26	25	24	

Inspected 26th April, when the force was complete, but one sergeant and 13 constables were on the sick list.

Authorised Establishment.—Three hundred and ninety, an increase by 36 men to meet the extended area here.

Public-houses.—Two hundred and seventy-two; with six prosecutions, and three convictions.

Beerhouses.—Three hundred and forty-five; with seven prosecutions, and five convictions.

Drunkenness.—Four hundred and ninety-eight prosecutions, and 453 convictions, a decrease of 170 prosecutions.

Ambulance.—Three hundred and sixty-six members of the force hold certificates, an increase of 109.

The books and returns were well kept.

The management, numbers, and discipline of the force have been efficiently maintained.

BOROUGH OF DEWSBURY.

Force - - - - - 37.

| Area in acres - | - | - | - | - 1,468 | Acres to each constable | - | - | - | 39 |
| Population in 1891 - | - | - | - 29,847 | Population to ditto, as per census 1891 | | | 806 |

		Yearly Pay in £ and Shillings.										
RANKS.	Chief Constable.	Superintendents.						2 Inspectors.				
		Deputy Chief Constable.	Chief Clerk.	1st Class.	2nd Class.	3rd Class.	4th Class.	1st Class.	2nd Class.	3rd Class.	4th Class.	5th Class.
Number of each Rank and Class	1	-	-	-	-	-	-	1	1	-	-	-
Rates of Pay of each ditto -	£ 300	-	-	-	-	-	-	£ s. 124 16	£ s. 109 4	-	-	-

		Weekly Pay in Shillings and Pence.										
RANKS.	4 Sergeants.						30 Constables.					
	Merit Class.	1st Class.	2nd Class.	3rd Class.	4th Class.	5th Class.	1st Class.			2nd Class.	3rd Class.	4th Class.	5th Class.	6th Class.
Number of each Rank and Class	-	1	1	2	-	-	5	6	2	4	5	5	1	1	1 Vacancy.
Rates of Pay of each ditto -	-	s. d. 38 6	s. d. 36 9	s. d. 32 8	-	-	s. 32	s. 31	s. 30	s. 29	s. 28	s. d. 26 6	s. 25	s. 24	-

Inspected 30th April, when the force was complete.

Authorised Establishment.—Thirty-seven.

Extra Duties.—The chief is inspector of contagious diseases (animals), also of lodging-houses and hackney carriages, Explosives and Shop Hours Act.

Public-houses.—Fifty ; no prosecutions.

Beerhouses.—Forty three ; with three prosecutions, and no convictions.

Drunkenness.—One hundred and thirty-nine prosecutions, 136 convictions, an increase of four prosecutions.

Ambulance.—Thirty-six members of the force hold certificates.

The cells and police offices were clean and in good order.

The books and returns were well kept.

The management, numbers, and discipline of the force have been efficiently maintained.

BOROUGH OF DONCASTER.

Force - - - - - - 36.

| Area in acres | - | - | - | - 1,691 | Acres to each constable | - | - | - 47 |
| Population in 1891 | - | - | - 25,923 | Population to ditto, as per census 1891 720 |

RANKS.	Chief Cons'able.	Superintendents.						3 Inspectors.				
		Deputy Chief Constable.	Chief Clerk.	1st Class.	2nd Class.	3rd Class.	4th Class.	1st Class.	2nd Class.	3rd Class.	4th Class.	5th Class.
Number of each Rank and Class -	1	-	1	-	-	-	-	-	-	2	-	-
Rates of Pay of each ditto - -	£ 250	-	£ s. d. 109 14 7	-	-	-	-	-	-	£ s. d. 114 1 3	-	-

Yearly Pay in £ and Shillings.

RANKS.	5 Sergeants.					27 Constables.								
	Merit Class.	1st Class.	2nd Class.	3rd Class.	4th Class.	Merit Class.	1st Class.						2nd Class.	3rd Class.
Number of each Rank and C'ass -	-	-	-	5	-	2	1	2	2	8	5	5	1	1
Rates of Pay of each ditto - -	-	-	-	s. d. 34 5	-	s. d. 33 3	s. d. 32 1	s. d. 31 6	s. d. 30 11	s. d. 30 4	s. d. 29 2	s. d. 28 10	s. d. 25 3	s. d. 25 1

Weekly Pay in Shillings and Pence.

Inspected 7th May, when the force was complete.

Authorised Establishment.—Thirty-six.

Extra Duties.—The chief is relieving officer for vagrants, and a sergeant inspects hackney carriages.

Public-houses.—Seventy-six[; with two prosecutions and two convictions.

Beerhouses.—Thirty-five.

Drunkenness.—One hundred and forty-seven prosecutions, 103 convictions, an increase of 10 prosecutions.

Ambulance.—Thirty-three members of the force hold certificates, an increase of three.

The cells and police offices were clean and in good order.

The books and returns were well kept.

The management, numbers, and discipline of the force have been efficiently maintained.

Scale of pay for Inspectors, Sergeants, and Constables.—

RANK.	SERVICE.	Per Diem.	Per Week.	Per Annum.	REMARKS.
		s. d.	£ s. d.	£ s. d.	
Inspector - -	On appointment	6 0	2 2 0	109 10 0	
„	After 2 years -	6 3	2 3 9	114 1 3	
„ - -	„ 4 „ -	6 6	2 5 6	118 12 6	
„	„ 6 „ -	6 9	2 7 3	123 3 9	
„ - -	„ 8 „ -	7 0	2 9 0	127 15 0	
Sergeant - -	On appointment	4 9	1 13 3	86 13 9	
„ - -	After 2 years -	4 11	1 14 5	89 14 7	
„	„ 4 „ -	5 1	1 15 7	92 15 5	
„ - -	„ 6 „ -	5 4	1 17 4	97 6 8	
„	„ 8 „ -	5 7	1 19 1	101 17 11	Increased one penny per day by the Watch Committee, 31st October 1900.
Constable - -	On appointment	3 7	1 5 1	65 7 11	
„	After 6 months -	3 8	1 5 8	66 18 4	
„ - -	„ 12 „ -	3 10	1 6 10	69 19 2	
„	„ 2 years -	4 0	1 8 0	73 0 0	
„ - -	„ 4 „ -	4 2	1 9 2	76 0 10	
„	„ 6 „ -	4 4	1 10 4	79 1 8	
„ - -	„ 8 „ -	4 5	1 10 11	80 12 1	
„	„ 10 „ -	4 6	1 11 6	82 2 6	
"MERIT" CLASS for Courageous Conduct in addition to the above rates, for sergeants and constables only - - -		0 2	0 1 2	3 0 10	

Boot Allowance, 9d. per week to all ranks.

Leave of Absence.—Inspectors, 14 days per annum.

    „   Sergeants and constables, 10 days per annum.

    „   All ranks, 1 day per month.

BOROUGH OF HALIFAX.

Force - - - - - 107.

Area in acres - - - - 8,725 | Acres to each constable - - - 86
Population in 1891 - - - 91,778 | Population to ditto, as per census 1891 908

RANKS.	Chief Constable.	1 Superintendent.						5 Inspectors.				
		Deputy Chief Constable.	Chief Clerk.	1st Class.	2nd Class.	3rd Class.	4th Class.	1st Class.	2nd Class.	3rd Class.	4th Class.	5th Class.
Number of each Rank and Class -	1	-	-	-	-	-	-	1	1	1	2	-
	£			£				£	£	£	£	
Rates of Pay of each ditto - -	400	-	-	160	-	-	-	125	120	115	110	-

Weekly Pay in Shillings and Pence.

RANKS.	15 Sergeants.						86 Constables.									
	Merit Class.	1st Class.	2nd Class.	3rd Class.	4th Class.	5th Class.	Merit Class.	1st Class.							2nd Class.	3rd Class.
Number of each Rank and Class -	-	1	3	2	2	7	1	11	5	4	16	1	3	22	6	15
Rates of Pay of each ditto - -	-	41	36	35	34	33	33	32	31	30	29	28 6	28	26 6	26	24

Inspected 24th April, when the force was complete.

Authorised Establishment.—One hundred and seven.

Extra Duties.—A sergeant is inspector of explosives, common lodging-houses, and hackney carriages.

Public-houses.—One hundred and twenty-five; with one prosecution, and one conviction.

R

No. 2.
Northern District.

Beerhouses.—One hundred and sixty-eight; with three prosecutions, and three convictions.

Drunkenness.—Two hundred and thirteen prosecutions, and 155 convictions.

Ambulance.—Ninety-nine members of the force hold certificates, an increase of four.

The books and returns were well kept.

The management, numbers, and discipline of the force are efficiently maintained.

BOROUGH OF HUDDERSFIELD.

Force - - - - - - - 120.*

| Area in acres | - - - 11,852 | Acres to each constable | - - - |
| Population in 1891 - | - - 95,420 | Population to ditto, as per census 1891 |

Yearly Pay in £ and Shillings.

RANKS.	Chief Constable.	2 Superintendents.						6 Inspectors.				
		Deputy Chief Constable.	Chief Clerk.	1st Class.	2nd Class.	3rd Class.	4th Class.	1st Class.	2nd Class.	3rd Class.	4th Class.	5th Class.
Number of each Rank and Class -	1	-	1	1	-	-	-	2	3	2	-	-
Rates of Pay of each ditto -	£ 350	-	£ s. 124 16	£ 175	-	-	-	£ 150	£ 130	£ s. 114 8	-	-

Weekly Pay in Shillings and Pence.

RANKS.	14 Sergeants.						97 Constables.										
	Merit Class.	1st Class.	2nd Class.	3rd Class.	4th Class.	5th Class.	Long Service.					1st Class.	2nd Class.	3rd Class.	4th Class.	5th Class.	6th Class.
Number of each Rank and Class -	-	2	1	7	2	1	1	3	8	11	16	14	11	9	2	5	6	7	4
Rates of Pay of each ditto -	-	s. 38	s. 37	s. 36	s. 35	s. 34	s. 35	s. 34	s. 33	s. 32	s. 31	s. 30	s. 29	s. 28	s. 27	s. 26	s. 25	s. 24	Vacancies.

* Exclusive of one additional constable appointed at private cost.

Inspected on 25th April.

Authorised Establishment.—One hundred and twenty.

Extra Duties :—

NATURE OF DUTY.	Chief Constable.	Super-intendents.	Inspectors.	Sergeants.	Constables.	TOTAL.
Fire Brigade - - - -	1	—	1 (in command)	3	17	22
Inspectors of Common Lodging-houses -	1	1	—	1	—	3
Inspectors of Hackney Carriages -	1	—	—	1	—	2
Inspectors of Explosives - - -	1	—	1	—	—	2
Inspectors of Petroleum - - -	1	—	1	—	—	2
Inspectors under Contagious Diseases (Animals) Act.	1	1	1	4	—	7
Inspectors under Shop Hours Act -	1	1	—	1	—	3

Public-houses. —One hundred and sixty-five; with seven prosecutions, and five convictions.

Beerhouses.—One hundred and nine; with two prosecutions, and no convictions.

Drunkenness.—Two hundred and sixteen prosecutions, and 206 convictions, a decrease of 42 prosecutions.

Ambulance.—One hundred and two members of the force hold certificates, a decrease of 14.

The books and returns were well kept.

The management, numbers, and discipline of the force have been efficiently maintained.

CITY OF LEEDS.

Force - - - - - - 507.

Area in acres - - - 21,572 | Acres to each constable - - -
Population in 1891 - - - 367,505 | Population to ditto, as per census 1891

Yearly Pay in £ and Shillings.

RANKS.	Chief Constable	9 Superintendents							16 Inspectors					
		Deputy Chief Constable	Chief Clerk	1st Class	2nd Class	3rd Class	4th Class		1st Class	2nd Class	3rd Class	4th Class	5th Class	
Number of each Rank and Class	1	1	1	1	2	1	3	1	1	3	1	1	3	8
Rates of Pay of each ditto	£800	£250	£130	£250	£230	£200	£170	£140	£150	£137 16	£130	£124 16	£122 4	£114 8

Weekly Pay in Shillings and Pence.

RANKS.	57 Sergeants						434 Constables													
	Merit Class	1st Class	2nd Class	3rd Class	4th Class	5th Class	1st Class			2nd Class	3rd Class	4th Class	5th Class	6th Class	7th Class	8th Class	9th Class	10th Class	11th Class
Number of each Rank and Class	-	2	17	10	28	-	8	1	13	6	45	4	91	65	3	23	47	58	60
Rates of Pay of each ditto	-	44	40	38	36	-	38	37	36	35	34	33	32	31	30	29	28	27	26

Inspected on 27th and 29th April, when 20 men were on sick list.

Authorised Establishment.—Five hundred and seven.

Public-houses.—Three hundred and forty-one; with 13 prosecutions, and 10 convictions.

Beerhouses.—Four hundred and four; with nine prosecutions, and six convictions.

Drunkenness.—One thousand eight hundred and eighty-nine prosecutions, and 1,677 convictions, an increase of 233 prosecutions.

Ambulance.—Four hundred and seventy-five members of the force hold certificates, an increase of 33.

The books and returns were well kept.

The management, numbers, and discipline of the force have been efficiently maintained.

Extra Duties returned as nil.

SCALE OF PAY.

RANK.	Pay per Annum.	Pay per Week.	
	£ s. d.	s. d.	
Fire Superintendent - -	250 0 0	—	---
Superintendent - - -	250 0 0	—	Chief Superintendent and Deputy Chief Constable (50l. per annum allowed for house, &c.).
.. - - -	220 0 0	—	Detective Superintendent.
.. - - -	220 0 0	—	After 5 years.
" - - -	200 0 0	—	After 3 years' service in rank.
" - - -	170 0 0	—	On appointment.
Chief Inspector (Chief Clerk) -	130 0 0	—	Increasing to 150l.
Inspector—1st Class - -	130 0 0	—	After 5 years' service in rank.
" - 2nd " - -	122 4 0	—	After 3 years' service in rank.
" 3rd " - -	114 8 0	—	On appointment.
Sergeant—1st Class - -	—	38 0	After 4 years' service in rank.
" 2nd " - -	—	36 0	After 2 years' service in rank.
" 3rd " -	—	34 0	On appointment.
Constable—Good Conduct Class	—	32 0	Of 10 years' service.
" " "	—	31 0	Of 7 years' service.
" " "	—	29 0	Of 5 years' service.
" " "	—	28 0	Of 3 years' service.
" 1st Class	—	26 0	After 12 months in 2nd Class.
" 2nd "	—	25 0	After 6 months in 3rd Class.
" 3rd "	—	24 0	On attestation.

No. 2.
Northern District.

If a constable be fined, and reduced from one class to another, he will have to serve the ordinary period before he is re-promoted.

Superintendents and inspectors allowed 32*s.* per annum in lieu of boots.

Sergeants and constables   ,,   26*s.*   ,,

Uniform clothing supplied gratis.

Sergeants and constables in the fire brigade receive extra pay at the rate of 4*s.* per week.

In the detective department sergeants and constables receive 4*s.* per week extra pay as detectives. All officers and constables in the detective department also receive 3*s.* per week in lieu of uniform and clothing.

Divisional superintendents are found quarters, coal, gas, &c., for 3*s.* 10*d.* per week.

Sectional station officers are found quarters, coal, gas, &c., for 2*s.* 0*d.* per week.

Ordinary night and day duty, 8 hours per diem.

LEAVE OF ABSENCE WITH PAY.

Superintendents - - - - - 21 days per annum.
Inspectors - - - - - 17 ,,
Sergeants - - - - - - 13 ..
Constables (of six months' service and upwards, the
last three of which they must be free of fine) - 10 ,,

In addition to this annual leave, inspectors, sergeants, and constables are allowed one day's leave per month.

Any constable who shall resign his appointment within six months of the expiration of his annual leave shall forfeit one week's pay.

Men on joining are appointed as probationers until they are reported fit for duty, when they will be attested and appointed 3rd class constables.

Probationary constables receive pay at the rate of 24*s.* per week.

G. G. TARRY, Major,
Chief Constable.

BOROUGH OF ROTHERHAM.

Force - - - - - - 57.

Area in acres - - - - 6,000 | Acres to each constable - - - 113
Population in 1891 - - - 42,061 | Population to ditto, as per census 1891 793

Yearly Pay in £ and Shillings.

RANKS.	Chief Constable.	Superintendents.						2 Inspectors.				
		Deputy Chief Constable.	Chief Clerk.	1st Class.	2nd Class.	3rd Class.	4th Class.	1st Class.	2nd Class.	3rd Class.	4th Class.	5th Class.
Number of each Rank and Class -	1	..	-	-	-	-	-	1	1	-	-	-
Rates of Pay of each ditto -	£ 435	-	-	-	-	-	-	£ s. 135 4	£ s. 114 8	-	-	-

Weekly Pay in Shillings and Pence.

RANKS.	9 Sergeants.						45 Constables.							
	Merit Class.	1st Class.	2nd Class.	3rd Class.	4th Class.	5th Class.	Merit Class.	1st Class.	2nd Class.	3rd Class.	4th Class.	5th Class.	6th Class.	7th Class.
Number of each Rank and Class -	-	1	2	2	4	-	1	4	2	7	8	7	6	5
Rates of Pay of each ditto -	-	s. d. 43 2	s. 41	s. 40	s. 34	-	s. d. 38 2	s. d. 33 2	s. 32	s. 31	s. 30	s. 29	s. 28	s. 27	s. 26

Inspected 8th May, when the force was complete.

Authorised Establishment.—Fifty-seven.

Extra Duties.—The chief and a sergeant inspect hackney carriages, and a sergeant common lodging-houses.

Public-houses.—Seventy-six ; with five prosecutions, and two convictions.

Beerhouses.—Sixty-six ; with two prosecutions, and one conviction.

Drunkenness.—Six hundred and fourteen prosecutions ; 579 convictions, an increase of 19 prosecutions.

Ambulance.—Fifty-three members of the force hold certificates, an increase of 10 men.

The books and returns were well kept.

The management, numbers, and discipline of the force have been efficiently maintained.

CITY OF SHEFFIELD.

Force - - - - 515. *

| Area in acres | - | - | - 19,651 | Acres to each constable | - | - | '- 42 |
| Population in 1891 | - | | - 324,243 | Population to ditto, as per census 1891 697 | | | |

Yearly Pay in £ and Shillings.

RANKS.	Chief Constable	4 Superintendents.						23 Inspectors.				
		Deputy Chief Constable.	Chief Clerk.	1st Class.	2nd Class.	3rd Class.	4th Class.	1st Class.	2nd Class.	3rd Class.	4th Class.	5th Class.
Number of each Rank and Class	1	-	-	1	2	1	-	1	2	2	1	17
Rates of Pay of each ditto -	£ 800	-	-	£ 250	£ 200	£ 165		£ 135	£ 130	£ 125	£ s. 119 12	£ 115

Weekly Pay in Shillings and Pence.

RANKS.	44 Sergeants.						443 Constables.							
	Merit Class.	1st Class.	2nd Class.	3rd Class.	4th Class.	5th Class.	Merit Class.	1st Class.	2nd Class.	3rd Class.	4th Class.	5th Class.	6th Class.	7th Class.	8th Class.
Number of each Rank and Class	-	4	2	13	26	-	9	67	37	37	39	55	59	37	58	45 Vacancies.
Rates of Pay of each ditto -	-	s. 42	s. 40	s. 38	s. 36	-	s. d. 34 6	s. 33	s. 32	s. 31	s. 30	s. 29	s. 28	s. 27	s d 26 7	

* Exclusive of one superintendent, five sergeants, and five constables appointed at private cost.

Inspected 10th May, when 10 men were on the sick list.

Authorised Establishment.—Five hundred and fifteen.

Extra Duties.—An inspector, sergeant, and three constables look after common lodging-houses and hackney carriages, and a sergeant is cattle inspector.

Public-houses.—Five hundred and eleven ; with 12 prosecutions, and nine convictions.

Beerhouses.—Six hundred and thirty-two ; with 13 prosecutions, and 11 convictions.

Drunkenness.—One thousand two hundred and ninety-two prosecutions, and 1,209 convictions, a decrease of 12 prosecutions.

Ambulance.—Three hundred and ninety-nine members of the force hold certificates, and 70 men are going through a course of instruction.

The books and returns were well kept.

The management, numbers, and discipline of the force were efficiently maintained.

This scale of pay adopted on 28th March 1901 :—

Superintendents—			Pension Stoppage.
200*l.* to 250*l.* per annum	- - -	-	2¼ per cent.

Chief Inspector—

165*l.* per annum	-	On appointment	-	-	..
180*l.*	..	-	- After 3 years	-	-	..

Inspectors—

5th class,	115*l.* per annum	On appointment	-	-	..
4th „	125*l.* „	-	After 3 years in 5th class	-	..
3rd · „	135*l.* „	-	„ 3 „ 4th „	-	..
2nd „	150*l.* „	-	„ 3 „ 3rd „	-	..
1st „	160*l.* „	-	„ 3 „ 2nd „	-	..

Sergeants—

4th class,	36*s.* per week	-	On appointment	-	- 10*d.* per week.
3rd „	38*s.* „	-	After 3 years in 4th class	- 11*d.* „
2nd „	40*s.* „	-	„ 3 „ 3rd „	- 1*s.* „
1st „	42*s.* „	-	„ 3 „ 2nd „	- 1*s.* „

Constables—

Probationers,	25*s.* 7*d.* per week	On appointment	-	- 7*d.* per week.
4th class,	27*s.* „	After 1 year's service	- 8*d.* „
3rd „	28*s.* „	„ 2 years' service	- 8*d.* „
2nd „	29*s.* „	„ 4 „	- 8*d.*
1st „	30*s.* „	„ 6 „	- 9*d.* ..
Long service,	31*s.* „	„ 8 „	- 9*d.*
„	32*s.* „	„ 11 „	- 9*d.*
„	33*s.* „	„ 15 „	- 9*d.*

Uniform clothing is supplied free to all ranks doing duty in uniform.

Rent Assistance is allowed as follows, viz. :—

2*s.* per week to all sergeants paying *necessarily* a rent exceeding 7*s.* 6*d.* per week ; and 2*s.* per week to all constables paying *necessarily* a rent exceeding 6*s.* 6*d.* per week.

1*s.* per week to all sergeants paying *necessarily* a rent exceeding 6*s.* 6*d.* per week ; and 1*s.* per week to all constables paying *necessarily* a rent exceeding 5*s.* 6*d.* per week.

" Allowances " being only granted to *recoup expenses* entailed by varying requirements of service, are not in any sense " pay," and consequently are neither reckoned for purposes of pension, nor are they subject to the deductions which the Police Act, 1890, requires to be made from pay.

CITY OF WAKEFIELD.

Force - - - - 52.

Area in acres - - - - 1,800 | Acres to each constable - - - 39
Population in 1891 - - - 36,815 | Population to ditto, as per census 1891 800

RANKS.	Chief Constable.	Yearly Pay in £ and Shillings.											
		Superintendents.						3 Inspectors.				
		Deputy Chief Constable.	Chief Clerk.	1st Class.	2nd Class.	3rd Class.	4th Class.	1st Class.	2nd Class.	3rd Class.	4th Class.	5th Class.
Number of each Rank and Class	1	-	-	-	-	-	-	1	-	-	-	-
Rates of Pay of each ditto	£ 350	-	-	-	-	-	-	£ s. 111 16	-	-	£ 102	-

RANKS.	Weekly Pay in Shillings and Pence.												
	6 Sergeants.					42 Constables.							
	Merit Class.	1st Class.	2nd Class.	3rd Class.	4th Class.	Merit Class.	1st Class.			2nd Class.	3rd Class.	4th Class.	5th Class.	6th Class.
Number of each Rank and Class	-	1	3	1	1	6	6	5	2	5	6	2	6	4
Rates of Pay of each ditto	-	s. 35	s. 34	s. 33	s. 32	s. 33	s. 31	s. 30	s. 29	s. 28	s. 27	s. 26	s. 25	s. 24

Inspected 3rd May, when the force was complete.

Authorised Establishment.—Fifty-two.

Extra Duties.—The chief and an inspector inspect common lodging-houses, hackney carriages, and explosives.

Public-houses.—One hundred and twenty; with two prosecutions, and one conviction.

Beerhouses.—Thirty-four; no prosecutions.

Drunkenness.—Five hundred and ninety-two prosecutions, and 589 convictions, an increase of 69 prosecutions.

Ambulance.—Forty-two members of the force hold certificates, an increase of one.

The books and returns were well kept.

The management, numbers, and discipline of the force have been efficiently maintained.

No. 3.—SOUTH OF ENGLAND AND SOUTH WALES DISTRICT.

ANNUAL REPORT of Captain *H. D. Terry*, His Majesty's Inspector of Constabulary for the South of England and South Wales District, for the Year ended the 29th of September 1901.

Ripley House, Ripley, Surrey,

Sir, 19th November 1901.

I have the honour to submit my reports on the Constabulary and Police Forces of the South of England and South Wales District for the year ended the 29th of September 1901, and to inform you that they have been efficiently maintained during that period in respect to management, numbers, and discipline.

The aggregate strength of the police forces in the district is 7,357 of all ranks (an increase of 207 over that of 1900), and the population, according to the census of 1901, protected by them is 6,327,077, being an average of a fraction under 860 persons to each constable. There are also 200 of all ranks appointed at private cost, 121 in the counties, and the remainder in the boroughs.

The vacancies in the county forces on the 29th of September 1901 were 85 of all ranks, and 25 in the borough forces.

Fourteen municipal boroughs, not having separate police forces, with a population ranging from 10,216 to 49,439 are policed by the constabulary of the counties in which they lie. Their names, acreage, and population are given below.

Boroughs, with Population exceeding 10,000, which do not maintain separate Police Forces.

Name of Borough.	Area in Acres.	Population.	County Policed by
Maidenhead	2,123	10,607	Berks.
Newbury	1,813	11,002	Berks.
Torquay	3,862	33,751	Devon.
Poole	4,749	19,461	Dorset.
Gloucester	2,311	47,789	Gloucester.
Cheltenham	4,678	49,439	Gloucester.
Bournemouth	2,414	47,003	Hants.
Chatham	4,336	31,594	Kent.
Faversham	684	10,478	Kent.
Taunton	1,203	18,026	Somerset.
Lewes	1,030	11,249	Sussex (East).
Worthing	1,405	20,006	Sussex (West).
Newport	511	10,216	Isle of Wight.
Pembroke	4,618	14,978	Pembroke.

The population of the 21 counties in the district is, according to census of 1891, 4,538,697, and the strength of their constabulary forces 4,525, being an average of a fraction over 1,003 persons to each constable. The population, according to census of 1891, of the 39 boroughs having separate police forces, is 1,788,380, and the strength of the forces 2,832, being an average of a fraction over 631 persons to each constable.

The gross cost of police for the year ended 31st March 1901 was 748,579*l.* 9*s.* 10½*d.* The amount received from the Exchequer Contribution Account towards pay and clothing was 279,642*l.* 13*s.* 3*d.*, and the cost to the local rates 408,045*l.* 6*s.* 6*d.*

The average daily strength of the force (exclusive of "additional" constables) was 7,117, the net cost of police per constable 82*l.* 17*s.* 10*d.*, and per inhabitant 1*s.* 10*d.*

as lugs.

Monmouth.   Maidstone.   Hove.
Somerset.   Margate.   Cardiff.
Sussex (West).   Rochester.   Swansea.

The following alterations have taken place in two police areas in the district during the year, viz. :—

The transfer to the city of Exeter of part of the parish of St. Thomas (acreage 1,235, population 8,175) from the county of Devon, and the transfer of an area (acreage 854, population 1,130) from the county of Hants to the city of Winchester.

Three hundred and one members of the police force in the district belonging to the Army Reserve have been called up since the commencement of the War in South Africa, of whom 148 are still serving with the colours, 131 rejoined their force, 15 died in South Africa, one was accidentally killed, four were disabled by wounds, one whose services were not required, and one "dismissed for misconduct in South Africa."

Four thousand four hundred and twenty-six members hold certificates of efficiency to render " first aid " from the St. John Ambulance Association.

The following changes have taken place during the year :—

Inspector M. Nicholls of the Borough of Reading force, was appointed chief officer of the Borough of New Windsor force on the 16th August 1901, in the place of Mr. R. J. Carter, appointed chief officer of Hanley, Staffordshire.

Mr. W. B. Gentle, deputy chief officer of the Reading force was appointed chief officer of the Brighton force on the 27th September 1901, in the place of Mr. T. Carter, retired on pension.

Mr. R. L. Williams was appointed chief officer of the City of Exeter force on 1st June 1901, in the place of Mr. John Short, retired on pension.

Mr. Evan Lewis, sergeant-clerk of the Birmingham force, was appointed chief officer of the Neath force on 29th November, 1900, in the place of Mr. R. Kilpatrick, appointed chief officer of Chesterfield.

Mr. H. N. Knox Knott, who held the rank of inspector in the Borough of Dover police, was appointed chief officer of that force on 30th June 1901, in the place of Mr. T. Osborn Sanders, retired on pension.

New constabulary stations have been built, or are in course of building, or are to be built at Falmouth in Cornwall ; at Brixham, Crownhill, Teignmouth, and in the Borough of Devonport, in Devon ; at Hartley Row, Odiham, in Hants ; at Aberdillery, Castleton, and Newbridge, in Monmouthshire ; at Uckfield and Bexhill (a second station) in Sussex (East) ; at Crickdale (Swindon division) in Wilts ; at New Quay and Talybont in Cardiganshire ; at Ammanford in Carmarthenshire ; at Pontywaith, Cilfynydd, Caeran, Resolven, Caerphilly, Ton Pentre, Abercynon, and Merthyr, in Glamorgan. shire ; and at Horfield and Eastville stations in the city of Bristol.

Nothing has yet been done to the station at Old Milford in Pembrokeshire, a second station is required here at Hakin across the water. The new station at Neyland in this county has been completed and occupied.

At Swansea the central station and that at Goat Street are completely out of date, and the Watch Committee promised they should be rebuilt, but after a second inspection nothing has been done.

I found nothing had been done at Folkestone.

There has been an increase during the year of 41 in the number of licensed houses having full licenses, and 106 in the number having off licenses.

Three thousand three hundred and thirty-three more persons were proceeded against for drunkenness, and 4,741 more convicted.

The following augmentations and reductions have taken place during the year :—

AUGMENTATIONS and REDUCTIONS in the STRENGTH of the POLICE FORCES
made during the year ended 29th September 1901.

COUNTIES.						BOROUGHS.			
Name of Force Augmented.	Super-intendents.	In-spectors.	Ser-geants.	Con-stables.	Total.	Name of Force Augmented.	Ser-geants.	Con-stables.	Total.
Dorset	—	—	—	1	1	Devonport	—	6	6
Gloucester	—	1	2	13	16	Exeter	1	9	10
Hants	—	2	1	18	21	Weymouth	—	1	1
Kent	1	—	3	36	40	Southampton	—	9	9
Somerset	—	—	1	4	5	Winchester	1	5	6
Surrey	—	—	4	35	39	Gravesend	—	4	4
Sussex (East)	—	—	—	3	3	Margate	—	3	3
Sussex (West)	—	—	1	3	4	Ramsgate	—	2	2
Wilts	—	—	1	9	10	Rochester	—	2	2
Glamorgan	—	—	3	10	13	Tunbridge Wells	—	7	7
						Eastbourne	—	4	4
						Ryde	—	1	1
						Neath	—	3	3
Total					152	Total			58

COUNTY.			BOROUGH.		
Name of Force Reduced.	Constables.	Total.	Name of Force Reduced.	Sergeants.	Total.
Devon	2	2	Bath	1	1
Total		2	Total		1

I cannot conclude this report without bringing to notice that there is still no deputy chief constable appointed in Radnorshire, in accordance with section 7 of the Police Act of 1839.

The usual tables are submitted.

I have, &c.
(Signed)   *H. D. Terry*, Captain,
H.M. Inspector of Constabulary,
South of England and South Wales District.

To the Right Hon. C. T. Ritchie, M.P.,
His Majesty's Principal Secretary of State
for the Home Department.

REPORTS of COUNTIES and BOROUGHS RESPECTIVELY.

No. 3.
South of England
and South Wales
District.

COUNTY OF BERKS.

Force - - - 173.*

| Area in acres † | - | - | - 455,453 | Acres to each constable | - | - | - 2,632 |
| Population in 1891 † | - | - 164,124 | Population to ditto, as per census 189. | 952 |

| RANKS. | Chief Constable. | Yearly Pay in £ and Shillings. | | | | | | | |
| | | 11 Superintendents. | | | | | | 4 Inspectors. | |
		Deputy Chief Constable.	Chief Clerk.	1st Class.	2nd Class.	3rd Class.	4th Class.	1st Class.	2nd Class.
Number of each Rank and Class	1	1	1	2	1	4	2	2	2
Rates of Pay of each ditto	£ 600	£ 220	£ 130	£ 200	£ 150	£ 145	£ 135	£ 103	£ 95

| RANKS. | Weekly Pay in Shillings and Pence. | | | | | | | | | |
| | 23 Sergeants. | | | | 134 Constables. | | | | | |
	1st Class.	2nd Class.	3rd Class.	4th Class.	1st Class.				2nd Class.	3rd Class.	Vacancies.
Number of each Rank and Class	6	1	10	6	73	10	5	13	20	11	2
Rates of Pay of each ditto	s. 33	s. d. 31 10	s. d. 30 8	s. d. 29 6	s. d. 28 7	s. d. 27 5	s. d. 26 3	s. d. 25 1	s. d. 23 11	s. d. 22 9	-

* Exclusive of two additional constables appointed under 3 & 4 Vict. c. 88. s. 19.
† The parish of Combe (population 92, acreage 3,313) is transferred (29th September 1895) from Hants; and Charnham Street (population 451, acreage 1,944) is transferred from Wilts. The parish of Shalbourne (population 901, acreage 1,755) is transferred (29th September 1895) to Wilts.—Local Government Board Confirmation Act.

Inspected in March.

Establishment.—One chief constable, 11 superintendents (one of whom acts as deputy chief constable, and one as chief clerk), four inspectors, 23 sergeants, and 134 constables. There are vacancies for two constables, and one superintendent has been substituted for an inspector. There are also two " additional" constables (an increase of one).

Thirty-seven members hold certificates from the St. John Ambulance Association.

Extra Duties :—

NATURE OF DUTY.	Chief Constable.	Super-intendents.	In-spectors.	Ser-geants.	Con-stables.	REMUNERATION.
Chief Inspector under Contagious Diseases (Animals) Act.	1	—	—	—	—	52l. per annum, travelling expenses.
Inspectors under Contagious Diseases (Animals) Act.	—	9	3	7	—	2s. 6d. per diem each when so employed.
Inspectors of Weights and Measures.	—	3	—	—	—	10l. per annum each.
Inspector of Food and Drugs -	—	1	—	—	—	2s. per diem when so employed.
Inspectors under Explosives Act.	—	9	1	—	—	One superintendent, 5l. per annum.
Assistant Relieving Officers for Vagrants.	—	3	1	1	—	One superintendent, 10l.; two superintendents, 5l. each; one inspector, 5l.; and one sergeant, 7l. 10s. per annum.

No. 3.
South of England
and South Wales
District.

Army Reserve, 29th September 1899–1901.—Five members were called up, of whom four are still serving with colours, and one has returned from South Africa, but is at present a patient in Netley Hospital.

The boroughs of Maidenhead and Newbury are policed by the county constabulary.

There is an increase of two in the number of public-houses, and decrease of one in beerhouses, and five in refreshment rooms. Five more persons were proceeded against for drunkenness, and five fewer convicted.

The clothing and appointments were complete and serviceable, and the books and returns well kept.

The stations visited were clean and in good order.

The management, numbers, and discipline have been efficiently maintained.

A new scale of pay, as under, was sanctioned 27th May 1901 :—

Constables—	£	s.	d.	
3rd class — on joining force	1	2	9	per week.
2nd class—after 1 year's service	1	3	11	,,
1st class—after 3 years' service	1	5	1	..
,, ,, 5 ,, ,,	1	6	3	::
,, ,, 7 ,, ,,	1	7	5	..
,, ,, 8 ,, ,,	1	8	7	..
Sergeants—				
On promotion to that rank	1	9	6	..
After 2 years in that rank	1	10	8	..
,, 5 ,, ,,	1	11	10	..
,, 8 ,, ,,	1	13	0	..
Inspectors—				
On promotion to that rank	95	0	0	per annum.
After 2 years in that rank	100	0	0	,,
,, 4 ,, ,,	105	0	0	::
,, 6 ,, ,,	110	0	0	::
,, 8 ,, ,,	115	0	0	..
Superintendents—				
On promotion to that rank	135	0	0	,,
After 2 years in that rank	145	0	0	..
,, 4 ,, ,,	150	0	0	::
,, 6 ,, ,,	160	0	0	,,
,, 8 ,, ,,	170	0	0	..
,, 10 ,, ,,	180	0	0	..
,, 12 ,, ,,	190	0	0	::
,, 14 ,, ,,	200	0	0	,,

The deputy chief constable to receive 20l. per annum in addition to his pay as a superintendent.

COUNTY BOROUGH OF READING.

Force - - - - - - 75.*

| Area in acres - - - - 5,878 | Acres to each constable - - - 78 |
| Population in 1891 - - - 60,054 | Population to ditto, as per census 1891 800 |

RANKS.	Chief Officer.	5 Inspectors.				
		Chief.	1st Class.	2nd Class.	Detective.	5th Class.
Number of each Rank and Class -	1	1	2	1	1	-
Rates of Pay of each ditto - -	£ 400	£ 130	£ 100	£ 95	£ s. 98 16	-

Yearly Pay in £ and Shillings.

Weekly Pay in Shillings and Pence.

RANKS.	9 Sergeants.						60 Constables.							
	Merit Class.	1st Class.	2nd Class.	3rd Class.	4th Class.	5th Class.	Detective.	Merit Class.	1st Class.	2nd Class.	3rd Class.	4th Class.	5th Class.	6th Class.
Number of each Rank and Class -	-	1	4	3	1	-	1	22	5	9	9	12	2	-
Rates of Pay of each ditto - -	-	s. 35	s. 34	s. d. 32 6	s. 31	-	s. d. 32 6	s. 30	s. 29	s. d. 27 6	s. 26	s. d. 24 6	s. 23	-

* Exclusive of five constables not paid by rates.

Inspected 11th March.

Establishment.—One chief constable, five inspectors, nine sergeants (one of whom acts as chief clerk), 60 constables. There are also five constables not paid by rates. The strength of the force is the same as last year, but no superintendent is on the strength this year. There is one inspector more, one sergeant less, and one constable more.

The scale of pay is unaltered.

Seventy-eight members hold certificates from the St. John Ambulance Association.

Extra Duties.—The chief clerk is inspector under the Food and Drugs Act, receiving 10l. 10s. per annum. The chief constable, four inspectors, and nine sergeants carry out the provisions of the Contagious Diseases (Animals) Act, and the chief constable is inspector of hackney carriages, common lodging-houses, and explosives without remuneration. One sergeant is coroner's officer.

Army Reserve, 29th September 1899–1901.—Five members were called up, of whom one is still serving with the colours ; two have rejoined certified fit for duty. One, who was dangerously wounded and lost the use of his legs, will not be able to rejoin, also one who has lost his right hand.

Licensing Acts.—An increase of one in the number of public-houses.

Twenty-eight more persons were proceeded against for drunkenness, and 17 more convicted.

Inspector M. Nicholls of this force was appointed chief officer of the borough police of New Windsor on 16th August 1901.

The clothing and appointments were complete and serviceable, and the books and returns well kept.

The offices and cells were clean and in good order.

The management, numbers, and discipline of the force have been efficiently maintained.

BOROUGH OF NEW WINDSOR.

Force - - - - - - - 21.

| Area in acres | - | - | - | - 2,702 | Acres to each constable | - | - | - 129 |
| Population in 1891 | - | - | - 12,327 | Population to ditto, as per census 1891 | 587 |

					Yearly Pay in £ and Shillings.								
RANKS.	Chief Officer.	Superintendents.						Inspectors.				
		Deputy Chief Officer.	Chief Clerk.	1st Class.	2nd Class.	3rd Class.	4th Class.	1st Class.	2nd Class.	3rd Class.	4th Class.	5th Class.
Number of each Rank and Class -	1	-	-	-	-	-	-	-	-	-	-	--
Rates of Pay of each ditto -	£ 150	-	-	-	-	-	-	-	-	-	-	-

					Weekly Pay in Shillings and Pence.							
RANKS.	3 Sergeants.						17 Constables.					
	Merit Class.	1st Class.	2nd Class.	3rd Class.	4th Class.	5th Class.	Acting Sergeants.	1st Class.		2nd Class.	3rd Class.	4th Class.	5th Class.
Number of each Rank and Class -	-	1	1	1	-	-	-	1	1	8	1	6	-	--
Rates of Pay of each ditto -	-	£ 37	£ 35	£ 33	-	-	-	£ 35	£ 33	£ 31	£ 29	£ 25	-	-

Inspected 12th March.

The Authorised Establishment is one chief officer, three sergeants, and 17 constables.

The pay of all classes of sergeants and constables was increased by 2s. per week on 7th August 1901.

Mr. Martin Nicholls, who held the rank of inspector (acting also as chief clerk) in the Borough of Reading police force, was appointed chief officer of New Windsor, at a salary of £150 per annum, on the 16th August 1901, in place of Mr. R. J. Carter, who has been appointed chief officer of Hanley, Staffordshire.

Eighteen members hold certificates from the St. John Ambulance Association.

Extra Duties.—The chief officer is inspector of hackney carriages, and under the Contagious Diseases (Animals) Act, without remuneration.

Army Reserve, 29th September 1899–1901.—One member was called up who is still serving with the colours.

There is no change in the number of licensed houses, but 13 more persons were proceeded against for drunkenness than last year, and 17 more convicted.

The clothing and appointments were complete and serviceable.

The offices and cells were clean and in good order, and the books and returns well kept.

The management, numbers, and discipline of the force have been efficiently maintained.

COUNTY OF CORNWALL.

Force - - - - 228.*

Area in acres - - - 862,685	Acres to each constable - - - 3,784
Population in 1891 - - 297,097	Population to ditto, as per census 1891 1,303

RANKS.	Chief Constable.	Yearly Pay in £ and Shillings.										
		7 Superintendents.						10 Inspectors.				
		Deputy Chief Constable and Clerk.	Chief Clerk.	1st Class.	2nd Class.	3rd Class.	4th Class.	1st Class.	2nd Class.	3rd Class.	4th Class.	5th Class.
Number of each Rank and Class -	1	1	-	1	3	2	-	6	4	-	-	-
Rates of Pay of each ditto - -	£ 400	£ 210	-	£ 170	£ 160	£ 144	-	£ s. 107 10	£ s. 97 10	-	-	-

RANKS.	Weekly Pay in Shillings and Pence.												
	25 Sergeants.						185 Constables.						
	Sergeant-Major.	1st Class.	2nd Class.	3rd Class.	4th Class.	5th Class.	Special Class.	Merit Class.	1st Class.	2nd Class.	3rd Class.	4th Class.	5th Class.	6th Class.
Number of each Rank and Class -	1	11	13	-	-	-	6	17	70	56	36	-	-	-
Rates of Pay of each ditto - -	s. 33	s. 32	s. 30	-	-	-	s. 29	s. 27	s. 26	s. 24	s. 21	-	-	-

* Exclusive of two constables appointed under 3 & 4 Vict. c. 88. s. 19.

Inspected in April.

Establishment.—One chief constable, seven superintendents (one of whom acts as deputy chief constable and clerk), 10 inspectors, 25 sergeants, and 185 constables.

There are also two constables appointed under 3 & 4 Vict. c. 88. s. 19.

The strength of the force is unaltered.

One hundred and seventy-four members hold certificates from the St. John Ambulance Association.

Army Reserve, 29th September 1899–1901.—Three members were called up, of whom one has rejoined, certified fit ; one is still serving with the colours, and one is on sick furlough.

Extra Duties.—The chief constable, superintendents, and inspectors act as inspectors under the Contagious Diseases (Animals) Act. Six superintendents are inspectors under the Food and Drugs, Petroleum, and Explosives Acts. Two superintendents, six inspectors, eight sergeants, and two constables are assistant relieving officers. Seven superintendents grant pedlars' certificates, receiving 5l. per annum each.

There is a decrease of one in the number of public-houses during the year, of two in beerhouses, and six in refreshment houses ; and 118 fewer persons were proceeded against for drunkenness, and 115 fewer convicted.

The clothing and appointments were complete and serviceable, and the books and returns well kept.

The outlying stations and cells were clean and in good order.

A new station is to be built at Falmouth.

The management, numbers, and discipline of the force have been efficiently maintained.

A new scale of pay, as under, was adopted and sanctioned 18th July 1901 :—

RANK.	Gross Pay.	
	Per Year.	Per Month.
	£ s. d.	£ s. d.
Deputy chief constable - - -	210 0 0	17 10 0
„ „ „ on appointment -	190 0 0	15 16 8
Superintendent, 1st class - -	170 0 0	14 3 4
„ on appointment - -	160 0 0	13 6 8
„ 2nd class - -	144 0 0	12 0 0
Inspectors, after 5 years - - -	107 10 0	8 19 2
„ on appointment -	97 10 0	8 2 6
Sergeant-Major, after 5 years -	91 0 0	7 11 8
„ on appointment -	85 16 0	7 3 0
Sergeant, after 5 years - -	83 4 0	6 18 8
„ on appointment - -	78 0 0	6 10 0
Constables, after 26 years - -	75 8 0	6 5 8
„ merit class - - -	70 4 0	5 17 0
„ 1st class - - -	67 12 0	5 12 8
„ 2nd „ - - -	62 8 0	5 4 0
„ 3rd „ - - -	54 12 0	4 11 0

BOROUGH OF PENZANCE.

Force - - - - - 13.*

Area in acres - - - - 355   Acres to each constable - - - 27
Population in 1891 - - - 12,432   Population to ditto, as per census 1891 - 956

RANKS.	Chief Officer.	Superintendents.						Inspectors.				
		Deputy Chief Officer.	Chief Clerk.	1st Class.	2nd Class.	3rd Class.	4th Class.	1st Class.	2nd Class.	3rd Class.	4th Class.	5th Class.
Number of each Rank and Class -	-	-	-	-	-	-	-	-	-	-	-	-
Rates of Pay of each ditto -	£ 175	-	-	-	-	-	-	-	-	-	-	-

Yearly Pay in £ and Shillings.

RANKS.	2 Sergeants.						10 Constables.						
	1st Class.	2nd Class.	3rd Class.	4th Class.	5th Class.	6th Class.	Acting Sergeants.	Merit Class.	1st Class.	2nd Class.	3rd Class.	4th Class.	Va-cancy.	6th Class.
Number of each Rank and Class -	2	-	-	-	-	-	-	-	4	3	1	1	1	-
Rates of Pay of each ditto -	£ 31	-	-	-	-	-	-	-	£ 26	£ 25	£ 24	£ 23	..	-

Weekly Pay in Shillings and Pence.

* Exclusive of five constables not paid by rates.

Inspected 12th April.

Establishment.—One chief officer, two sergeants, 10 constables, and five constables additional. There is a vacancy for one constable.

There is no alteration in the strength of the force or scale of pay.

One member holds a certificate from the St. John Ambulance Association.

Extra Duties.—The chief officer is inspector of weights and measures ; allowance, 10l. per annum. He is also inspector under the Food and Drugs, Explosives, and Contagious Diseases (Animals) Acts, and of common lodging-houses. The chief officer, sergeants, and six constables form a fire brigade ; allowances : the chief officer receives 5l. per annum, and the others 3l. each per annum.

There has been no change in the number of licensed houses, but a decrease of 12 in the number of persons proceeded against for drunkenness, and 12 in the number convicted.

The offices and cells were clean and in good order, the books and returns well kept, and the clothing and appointments complete and serviceable.

The management, numbers, and discipline of the force have been efficiently maintained.

CITY OF TRURO.

Force - - - 12.

Area in acres - - - - 1,127 | Acres to each constable - - - 94
Population in 1891 - - 11,131 | Population to ditto, as per census 1891 928

RANKS.	Chief Officer.	Superintendents.						Inspectors.				
		Deputy Chief Officer.	Chief Clerk.	1st Class.	2nd Class.	3rd Class.	4th Class.	1st Class.	2nd Class.	3rd Class.	4th Class.	5th Class.
Number of each Rank and Class -	1	-	-	-	-	-	-	-	-	-	-	-
Rates of Pay of each ditto - -	£ 180	-	-	-	-	-	-	-	-	-	-	-

Yearly Pay in £ and Shillings.

RANKS.	3 Sergeants.						8 Constables.						
	1st Class.	2nd Class.	3rd Class.	4th Class.	5th Class.	6th Class.	Acting Sergeants.	Merit Class.	1st Class.	2nd Class.	3rd Class.	4th Class.	5th Class.	6th Class.
Number of each Rank and Class -	1	2	-	-	-	-	-	-	3	1	-	1	2	-
Rates of Pay of each ditto - -	s. 30	s. 29	-	-	-	-	-	-	s. d. 26 8	s. d. 24 6	s. d. 23 4	s. d. 22 2	s. 21	s. d. 19 10

Weekly Pay in Shillings and Pence.

Inspected 11th April.

The authorised establishment is one chief officer, three sergeants, and eight constables.

The strength of the force and the scale of pay are unaltered.

Eight members of the force hold certificates from the St. John Ambulance Association.

Extra Duties.—The chief officer is inspector of weights and measures, common lodging-houses, and hackney carriages; also inspector under the Contagious Diseases (Animals), Food and Drugs, Explosives, and Petroleum Acts, without remuneration. One sergeant is assistant inspector of weights and measures; allowance, 5l. per annum.

There has been a decrease of seven in the number of beerhouses, and an increase of six in refreshment houses during the year.

Nine fewer persons were proceeded against for drunkenness, and 11 fewer convicted.

The offices and cells were clean and in good order, the clothing and appointments complete and serviceable, and the books and returns well kept.

The management, numbers, and discipline of the force have been efficiently maintained.

COUNTY OF DEVON.

Force   -   -   -   420.*

| Areas in acres † - - - 1,644,268 | Acres to each constable - - - 3,915 |
| Population in 1891 † - 418,804 | Population to ditto, as per census 1891 997 |

Yearly Pay in £ and Shillings.

RANKS.	Chief Constable.	14 Superintendents.						1 Inspector.				
		Deputy Chief Constable.	Chief Clerk.	1st Class.	2nd Class.	3rd Class.	4th Class.	1st Class.	2nd Class.	3rd Class.	4th Class.	5th Class.
Number of each Rank and Class -	1	1	1	5	7	-	-	1	-	-	-	-
Rates of Pay of each ditto - -	£ 400	£ s. 235 1	£ s. 170 6	£ s. 170 6	£ 146			£ s. 89 14	-	-	-	-

Weekly Pay in Shillings and Pence.

RANKS.	48 Sergeants.							356 Constables.					
	Sergeant-Major.	1st Class.	2nd Class.	3rd Class.	4th Class.	5th Class.	Acting Sergeants.	Merit Class.	1st Class.	2nd Class.	3rd Class.	Vacancy.
Number of each Rank and Class -	1	35	12	-	-	-	-	12	113	115	43	40	33	1
Rates of Pay of each ditto - -	s. d. 31 6	s. d. 29 9	s. d. 27 5	-	-	-	-	s. d. 26 3	s. d. 25 1	s. d. 23 1	s. d. 22 2	s. 21	s. d. 20 5	-

* Exclusive of two additional constables appointed under 3 & 4 Vict. c. 88. s. 19.

† The parish of Church Staunton (acreage 5,456, population 472) has been transferred (29th September 1899) to Somerset, and an area (acreage 9,950, population 1,846) is transferred (30th September 1896) from Dorset ; an area (acreage 851, population 4,893) is transferred (9th November 1896) to the borough of Plymouth, and parts of the parishes of Pilton and Tawstock (acreage 857, population 705) are transferred (9th November 1899) to Barnstaple.

Inspected in April.

Establishment.—One chief constable, 14 superintendents (one of whom acts as deputy chief constable, and one as chief clerk), one inspector, 48 sergeants, and 356 constables.   There are also two constables appointed under 3 & 4 Vict. c. 88. s. 19.

· On the extension of the City of Exeter, on the 9th November 1900, one sergeant and six constables were transferred from the county to the city force, but subsequently the county force was increased by one sergeant and four constables, giving a decrease to the force of two.

Three hundred and thirty-two members hold certificates from the St. John Ambulance Association.

Army Reserve, 29th September 1899–1900.—Two members were called up, who both died while serving with the colours.

Extra Duties.—

NATURE OF DUTY.	Chief Constable.	Super-intendents.	In-spectors.	Ser-geants.	Con-stable.	REMUNERATION.
Inspectors under Contagious Diseases (Animals) Act.	1	13	—	—	—	} 9d. per mile one way when engaged on these duties.
Inspectors under Explosives Act.	—	13	—	—	—	
Inspectors under Food and Drugs Act.	—	12	—	5	—	Out-of-pocket expenses.
Assistant Relieving Officers for Vagrants.	—	—	1	15	2	From 20s. to 80s. per annum.
Inspectors of Hackney Carriages.	—	—	—	—	2	From 20s. to 27s. per annum.

The municipal borough of Torquay is policed by the county constabulary.

There has been a reduction during the year of 26 in the number of public-houses, seven in beerhouses, and four in refreshment houses ; but 148 more persons were proceeded against for drunkenness, and 153 more convicted.

The clothing and appointments were complete and serviceable, and the books and returns well kept.

The outlying stations and cells were clean and in good order. New stations are to be built at Brixham, Crownhill, and Teignmouth. The latter is out of date and badly planned, prisoners having to be taken through the sergeant's house to the cells.

The management, numbers, and discipline of the force have been efficiently maintained.

A new scale of pay, as under, has been sanctioned, to take effect 1st September 1901 :—

Rank, &c.	No.	Per Day.		Per Week.			Per Year.		
		s.	*d.*	*£*	*s.*	*d.*	*£*	*s.*	*d.*
Constables—On appointment, 3rd class - -	53	3	0	1	1	0	54	15	0
„ After 2 years 2nd „ - -	25	3	2	1	2	2	57	15	10
„ „ 4 „ 1st „ - -	32	3	4	1	3	4	60	16	8
„ „ 6 „ - - -	84	3	6	1	4	6	63	17	6
„ „ 10 „ at the - - - -	162	3	10	1	6	10	69	19	2
50 Merit Class at the discretion of the Chief Constable (instead of 12). Amount additional to Constable of any grade or class.	—	0	2	0	1	2	—		
Sergeants—On appointment - - -	18	4	1	1	8	7	74	10	5
„ After 3 years - - -	14	4	3	1	9	9	77	11	3
„ „ 6 „ - - -	7	4	5	1	10	11	80	12	1
„ „ 8 „ - - -	5	4	7	1	12	1	83	12	11
„ „ 10 „ - - -	3	4	9	1	13	3	86	13	9
Clothing (Chevrons) extra -	—	—		—			—		
Sergeant-Major—On appointment - -	1	5	0	1	15	0	91	5	0
„ „ After 3 years - -	—	5	2	1	16	2	94	5	10
Inspectors—On appointment - - -	1	5	3	1	16	9	95	16	3
„ After 5 years - - -	—	5	6	1	18	6	100	7	6
Two additional to be appointed—in lieu of two Sergeants—Pay.	—	—		—			—		
Ditto Clothing - - -	—	—		—			—		
Superintendents—On appointment - -	3	8	0	2	16	0	146	0	0
„ After 5 years - -	2	8	6	2	19	6	155	2	6
„ „ 10 „ - -	5	9	0	3	3	0	164	5	0
„ „ 15 „ - -	3	9	10	3	8	10	179	9	2
Deputy Chief Constable—On appointment - -	—	11	6	4	0	6	209	17	6
„ „ After 5 years -	—	12	4	4	6	4	225	1	8
„ „ „ 10 „ -	1	12	10	4	9	10	234	4	2
Chief Constable—On appointment - -	—	—		—			400	0	0
„ After 5 years - - -	1	—		—			450	0	0
„ „ 10 „ - -	—	—		—			500	0	0
„ „ 15 „ - -	—	—		—			550	0	0

No. 3.
South of England
and South Wales
District.

BOROUGH OF BARNSTAPLE.

Force - - - - - - - 14.

| Area in acres | - - 2,374 | Acres to each constable - - - 169 |
| Population in 1891 | - - 13,763 | Population to ditto, as per census 1891- 983 |

RANKS.	Chief Officer.	Superintendent.						1 Inspector.				
		Deputy Chief Officer.	Chief Clerk.	1st Class.	2nd Class.	3rd Class.	4th Class.	1st Class.	2nd Class.	3rd Class.	4th Class.	5th Class.
Number of each Rank and Class -	1	-	-	-	-	-	-	1	-	-	-	-
Rates of Pay of each ditto - -	£175	-	-	-	-	-	-	£91	-	-	-	-

Yearly Pay in £ and Shillings.

RANKS.	1 Sergeant.							11 Constables.						
	Merit Class.	1st Class.	2nd Class.	3rd Class.	4th Class.	5th Class.	Acting Sergeants.	Merit Class.	1st Class.	2nd Class.	3rd Class.	4th Class.	5th Class.	6th Class.
Number of each Rank and Class -	1	-	-	-	-	-	-	4	2	2	3	-	-	-
Rates of Pay of each ditto - -	s. 31	-	-	-	-	-	-	s. 27	s. d. 24 6	s. 22	s. 22	-	-	-

Weekly Pay in Shillings and Pence.

Inspected 18th April.

Establishment.—One chief officer, one inspector, one sergeant, and 11 constables. An inspector has been appointed during the year, and there is one sergeant less than last year.

Thirteen members of the force hold certificates from the St. John Ambulance Association.

Extra Duties.—The chief officer and inspector are assistant relieving officers, receiving 2l. 2s. per annum each. The chief officer is inspector of markets, lighting, and hackney carriages, and under the Contagious Diseases (Animals), Food and Drugs, Petroleum, and Explosives Acts, without remuneration.

Licensing Acts.—There is a decrease of two in refreshment houses, and 14 fewer persons were proceeded against for drunkenness, and 13 fewer convicted.

The clothing and appointments were complete and serviceable, the books and returns well kept, and the offices and cells clean and in good order.

The management, numbers, and discipline of the force have been efficiently maintained.

COUNTY BOROUGH OF DEVONPORT.

Force - - - - - - - - 83.

Area in acres	-	-	1,760
Population in 1891	-	-	54,803

Acres to each constable -	-	-	21
Population to ditto, as per census 1891 -			661

Yearly Pay in £ and Shillings.

RANKS.	Chief Officer	Superintendent.						3 Inspectors.				
		Deputy Chief Officer.	Chief Clerk.	1st Class.	2nd Class.	3rd Class.	4th Class.	1st Class.	2nd Class.	3rd Class.	4th Class.	5th Class.
Number of each Rank and Class	1	-	-	-	-	-	-	1	1	1	-	-
Rates of Pay of each ditto	£280	-	-	-	-	-	-	£127 8	£120 18	£111 16	-	-

Weekly Pay in Shillings and Pence.

RANKS.	10 Sergeants.						69 Constables.									
	Merit Class.	1st Class.	2nd Class.	3rd Class.	4th Class.	5th Class.	Merit Class.	1st Class.	2nd Class.	3rd Class.	4th Class.	5th Class.	6th Class.	7th Class.	8th Class.	9th Class.
Number of each Rank and Class	1	5	2	2	-	-	2	2	13	9	7	2	6	2	3	5 / 11
Rates of Pay of each ditto (s. d.)	39 2	38	37	35	-	-	33 8	31 8	33 6	31 6	30 6	29 6	28 6	27 6	26 6	25 6 / 24 6 / 23 6

Inspected 16th April.

The authorised establishment, which has been augmented during the year by six constables, is one chief officer, three inspectors, 10 sergeants, and 69 constables. The chief officer receives an increase of 10*l.* per annum to his pay.

Eighty-one members hold certificates from the St. John Ambulance Association.

Extra Duties.—The chief officer is inspector under the Petroleum and Explosives Acts; allowance, 10*l.* per annum.

Army Reserve, 29th September, 1899–1901.—One member was called up, who has rejoined the force, certified fit for duty.

There is no change in the number of licensed houses; but 47 more persons were proceeded against for drunkenness, and 44 more convicted.

The clothing and appointments were complete and serviceable, the books and returns well kept, and the offices and cells clean and in good order.

A new police station is to be built in the borough.

The management, numbers, and discipline of the force have been efficiently maintained.

The following revision of the scale of pay was adopted 31st March, 1901:—

The chief constable on appointment to receive 250*l.* per annum, increasing annually by 10*l.* to a maximum of 300*l.* per annum.

Inspectors.—On appointment 109*l.* 4*s.*, increasing by annual increments of 1*s.* per week to a maximum of 135*l.* per annum.

Sergeants.—On appointment 1*l.* 14*s.* per week, with an annual increase of 1*s.* per week for the second, third, fourth, and fifth years respectively, to a maximum sum of 1*l.* 18*s.*

Constables.—On appointment 1*l.* 3*s.* 6*d.* per week, annually increasing by 1*s.* from the second to eighth years to 1*l.* 10*s.* 6*d.*; for the ninth, tenth, and eleventh years to 1*l.* 11*s.* 6*d.*; and for twelfth and subsequent years to a maximum sum of 1*l.* 12*s.* 6*d.*

Members of the merit class to receive 1*s.* 2*d.* per week in addition.

T 3

No. 3.
South of England
and South Wales
District.

CITY AND COUNTY BOROUGH OF EXETER.

Force - - - - - - - 64.

| Area in acres* - - - 3,118 | Acres to each constable - - 48 |
| Population in 1891 * - - 45,579 | Population to ditto, as per census 1891 72 |

RANKS.	Chief Officer.	Superintendent.						5 Inspectors.				
		Deputy Chief Officer.	Chief Clerk.	1st Class	2nd Class.	3rd Class.	4th Class.	1st Class.	2nd Class.	3rd Class.	4th Class.	5th Class.
Number of each Rank and Class -	1	-	-	-	-	-	-	1	1	1	-	-
Rates of Pay of each ditto -	£ 250	-	-	-	-	-	-	£ s. 130 10	£ s. 101 8	£ s. 92 6	-	-

Yearly Pay in £ and Shillings.

RANKS.	7 Sergeants.						53 Constables.							
	Merit Class.	1st Class.	2nd Class.	3rd Class.	4th Class.	5th Class.	1st Class.							2nd Class.
Number of each Rank and Class -	-	1	1	5	-	-	26	1	4	3	2	6	3	8
Rates of Pay of each ditto -	-	s. 34	s. 33	s. 30	-	-	s. d. 28 6	s. d. 27 6	s. d. 26 6	s. d. 25 6	s. d. 24 6	s. d. 23 6	s. d. 22 6	s. d. 21 6

Weekly Pay in Shillings and Pence.

* Part of the parish of St. Thomas (acreage 1,255, and population 8,175) was transferred (9th November 1900) from the county of Devon.

Inspected 20th April.

Establishment.—One chief officer, three inspectors, seven sergeants, and 53 constables. To meet the increase of population on account of the extension of the city boundaries, the force was augmented, in November 1900, by the transfer of one sergeant and six constables from the county of Devon constabulary, and a further increase of three constables on 27th December 1900, being a total increase of one sergeant and nine constables.

The scale of pay is unaltered.

Mr. R. L. Williams was appointed chief officer on the 1st June 1901, at a salary of 250l. per annum, in the place of Mr. John Short, retired on pension.

Thirty-six members hold certificates from the St. John Ambulance Association.

Extra Duties.—The chief officer is inspector of public buildings and general traffic, and one inspector is inspector of hackney carriages, common lodging-houses, and under the Explosives Act.

There has been an increase during the year of 20 in the number of public-houses, and two in the number of beerhouses.

Fifty-two more persons were proceeded against for drunkenness, and 31 more convicted.

The clothing and appointments were complete and serviceable, the books and returns well kept, and the stations and cells clean and in good order.

The management, numbers, and discipline of the force have been efficiently maintained.

COUNTY BOROUGH OF PLYMOUTH.

No. 3.
South of England
and South Wales
District.

Force - - - - - 136.

Area in acres* - - - 2,391	Acres to each constable - - 17	
Population in 1891* - - 88,941	Population to ditto, as per census 1891 654	

Yearly Pay in £ and Shillings.

RANKS.	Chief Officer.	Superintendents.						6 Inspectors.				
		Deputy Chief Officer.	Chief Clerk.	1st Class.	2nd Class.	3rd Class.	4th Class.	1st Class.	2nd Class.	3rd Class.	4th Class.	5th Class.
Number of each Rank and Class	1	-	-	-	-	-	-	2	2	2	-	-
Rates of Pay of each ditto -	£ 410	-	-	-	-	-	-	£ s. 131 19	£ s. 123 8	£ s. 114 12	-	-

Weekly Pay in Shillings and Pence.

RANKS.	12 Sergeants.						117 Constables.									
	1st Class.	2nd Class.	3rd Class.	4th Class.	5th Class.	6th Class.	1st Class.			2nd Class.	3rd Class.	4th Class.	5th Class.	6th Class.	7th Class.	8th Class.	Vacancy.
Number of each Rank and Class	5	3	4	-	-	-	24	10	20	7	7	7	9	6	7	19	1
Rates of Pay of each ditto -	s. d. 40 9	s. d. 38 6	s. d. 36 4	-	-	-	s. d. 33 6	s. d. 32 10	s. d. 32 3	s. d. 31 2	s. d. 30 1	s. 29	s. d. 27 11	s. d. 26 10	s. d. 25 11	s. d. 23 6	-

* An area (acreage 851, population 4,893), was transferred on 9th November 1896 from the county of Devon.

Inspected 16th April.

Establishment.—One chief officer, six inspectors (one of whom acts as chief clerk), 12 sergeants, and 117 constables. The strength of the force is unaltered, but one sergeant has been substituted for a constable. There is a vacancy for one constable.

The pay of the chief officer has been increased by 10*l*. 5*s*. per annum.

Fifty-three members hold certificates from the St. John Ambulance Association.

Extra Duties.—The chief officer, one inspector, three sergeants, and 26 constables form a fire brigade. Allowances: to inspector, 15*l*. per annum; to sergeants, 2*l*. each per annum; and to constables, 1*l*. 10*s*. each per annum.

Army Reserve, 29th September 1899–1901.—One member was called up, who is still serving with the colours.

There is a decrease in the number of public-houses of one, also of one in beerhouses, and one in refreshment houses; also of 10 in the number of persons proceeded against for drunkenness, and 22 in the number convicted.

The clothing and appointments were complete and serviceable, the books and returns well kept, and the offices and cells clean and in good order.

The management, numbers, and discipline of the force have been efficiently maintained.

A revised scale of pay, as under, was adopted 18th April 1901:—

Inspectors—

		£	s.	d.	
1st class, after 4 years	- -	131	19	0	per annum.
2nd „ „ 2 „ -	- -	123	8	8	,,
3rd „ on appointment	- -	114	12	4	,,

Sergeants—

1st class, after 4 years -	- -	105	19	4	,,
2nd „ „ 2 „ -	- -	100	2	0	,,
3rd „ on appointment -	- -	94	9	4	,,

T 4

Constables—

			£	s.	d.	
1st class, after	12 years,	two badges	1	13	6	per week.
,, ,,	10 ,,	one badge	1	12	10	,,
,, ,,	8 ,,	-	1	12	3	..
2nd class ,,	7 ,,	-	1	11	2	..
3rd ,, ,,	6 ,,	-	1	10	1	..
4th ,, ,,	5 ,,	-	1	9	0	..
5th ,, ,,	4 ,,	-	1	7	11	..
6th ,, ,,	3 ,,	-	1	6	10	..
7th ,, ,,	2 ,,	-	1	5	11	..
8th ,, on appointment -		-	1	3	6	..

BOROUGH OF TIVERTON.

Force - - - - - 11.*

Area in acres - - - - 17,680 | Acres to each constable - - - 1,607
Population in 1891 - - 10,892 | Population to ditto, as per census 1891 990

RANKS.	Chief Officer.	Yearly Pay in £ and Shillings.										
		Superintendents.						Inspectors.				
		Deputy Chief Officer.	Chief Clerk.	1st Class.	2nd Class.	3rd Class.	4th Class.	1st Class.	2nd Class.	3rd Class.	4th Class.	5th Class.
Number of each Rank and Class	1	-	-	-	-	-	-	-	-	-	-	-
Rates of Pay of each ditto	£ 150	-	-	-	-	-	-	-	-	-	-	-

RANKS.	Weekly Pay in Shillings and Pence.												
	2 Sergeants.						Acting Sergeants.	8 Constables.					
	Merit Class.	1st Class.	2nd Class.	3rd Class.	4th Class.	5th Class.		Merit Class.	1st Class.	2nd Class.	3rd Class.	4th Class.	5th Class.	6th Class.
Number of each Rank and Class	-	1	1	-	-	-	-	-	7	-	1	-	-	-
Rates of Pay of each ditto	-	31s.	28s.	-	-	-	-	-	26s.	-	23s.	-	-	-

* Exclusive of four constables not paid by rates.

Inspected 23rd April.

The authorised establishment is one chief officer, two sergeants, and eight constables; there are also four constables "additional."

The scale of pay is unaltered, except that the chief officer has an increase of 25l. per annum.

Eight members hold certificates from the St. John Ambulance Association.

Extra Duties.—The chief officer is captain of the fire brigade (allowance, 15l. per annum) and inspector of common lodging-houses, and under the Food and Drugs and Explosives Acts, without remuneration. The two sergeants are sergeants at mace; allowance, 2l. 10s. each per annum.

There is an increase of one in the number of refreshment houses, and two more persons were proceeded against for drunkenness, the number convicted being the same as last year.

The clothing and appointments were complete and serviceable, the books and returns well kept, and the offices, all cells, clean and in good order.

The management, numbers, and discipline of the force have been efficiently maintained.

COUNTY OF DORSET.

Force   -   -   - 176.*

Area in acres †   -   -   - 624,088 | Acres to each constable   -   -   - 3,546
Population in 1891 † -   -   - 172,214 | Population to ditto, as per census 1891   978

RANKS.	Chief Constable.	11 Superintendents.					Inspectors.				
		Deputy Chief Constable.	Chief Clerk.	1st Class.	2nd Class.	3rd Class.	1st Class.	2nd Class.	3rd Class.	4th Class.	5th Class.
Number of each Rank and Class - }	1	1	1	2	4	1	2	–	–	–	–	–
Rates of Pay of each ditto - }	£ 400	£ s. 190 2	£ s. 161 4	£ s. 161 4	£ s. 147 10	£ 111	£ s. 104 18	–	–	–	–	–

RANKS.	23 Sergeants.				141 Constables.						
	Sergt.-Major.	1st Class.		2nd Class.			1st Class.			2nd Class.	3rd Class.
Number of each Rank and Class - }	1	4	2	2	1	4	8	19	11	11	14	25	1	42	18
Rates of Pay of each ditto - }	s. d. 32 8	s. d. 33 10	s. d. 32 8	s. d. 31 6	s. d. 30 4	s. d. 29 2	s. d. 28 7	s. d. 26 3	s. d. 25 8	s. d. 25 1	s. d. 24 6	s. d. 23 11	s. d. 23 4	s. d. 22 2	s. 21

* Exclusive of two additional constables appointed under 3 & 4 Vict. c. 88. s. 19.
† Parts of the parishes of Wyke Regis and Radipole (with an acreage of 559, population 7,462) have been transferred (9th November 1895) to the borough of Weymouth. The parish of Wambrook (acreage 1,587, population 231) is transferred (1st April 1896) to Somerset, and the parishes of Goathill (acreage 298, population 54), Pointington (acreage 1,090, population 134), Sandford Orcas (acreage 1,104, population 222), Seaborough (acreage 685, population 71), and Trent (acreage 1,818, population 419) have been transferred (31st March 1896) from Somerset. An area (acreage 9,930, population 1,646) has been transferred (30th September 1896) to Devon.

Inspected in August.

Establishment.—One chief constable, 11 superintendents (one of whom acts as deputy chief constable, and one as chief clerk), 23 sergeants, 141 constables, and two constables appointed under 3 & 4 Vict. c. 88. s. 19. The strength of the force has been increased by one constable.

The rank of inspector has been abolished. There are now three more superintendents, four more sergeants, and three fewer constables than last year.

One hundred and sixty-seven members hold certificates from the St. John Ambulance Association.

Extra Duties.—

NATURE OF DUTY.	Chief Constable.	Super-intendents.	In-spectors.	Ser-geants.	Con-stables.	REMUNERATION.
Inspector of Weights and Measures.	1	—	—	—	—	Nil.
Inspectors under Contagious Diseases (Animals) Act.	1	7	8	· 15	3	Chief constable, 25l.; super-intendents and inspectors, 10l.; sergeants, 4l. per annum.
Inspectors under Food and Drugs Act.	1	7	3	—	—	Nil.
Inspectors under Petroleum and Explosives Acts.	1	6	3	—	—	Nil.
Assistant Relieving Officers -	—	7	3	—	—	One superintendent, 5l. per annum.
Inspectors of Hackney Car-riages and Pleasure Boats.	—	1	—	2	—	5l. per annum each.
Javelin Men - · · ·	—	—	—	2	22	2s. per diem each when em-ployed.

The borough of Poole is policed by the county constabulary.

A pensioner was employed as a special constable for duty at Swanage during the summer months.

U

Army Reserve, 29th September, 1899–1901.—Six members were called up, of whom two have rejoined (one certified fit, the other has been invalided), three are still serving with the colours, and one did not wish to rejoin.

There is no change in the number of licensed houses, and the number of persons proceeded against for drunkenness and the number convicted is the same as last year.

The clothing and appointments were complete and serviceable, and the books and returns well kept.

The outlying stations and cells were clean and in good order.

The management, numbers, and discipline of the force have been efficiently maintained.

A revised scale of pay, as under, has been sanctioned 12th March 1901 :—

Length of Service with the rank of Superintendent.	Class.	Rank.	Gross Pay.		
			Daily.	Yearly.	Monthly (28 days).
			s. d.	£ s. d.	£ s. d.
On appointment - -	—	Deputy Chief Constable.	9 9	177 18 9	13 13 0
5 years - - -	—	,, ,,	10 1	184 0 5	14 2 4
10 ,, - - -	—	,, ,,	10 5	190 2 1	14 11 8
15 ,, - - -	—	,, ,,	10 9	196 3 9	15 1 0
On appointment -	1st	Superintendent - -	8 6	155 2 6	11 18 0
5 years - - -	,,	,, - -	8 10	161 4 2	12 7 4
10 ,, - - -	,,	,, - -	9 2	167 5 10	12 16 8
15 ,, - - -	,,	,, - -	9 6	173 7 6	13 6 0
On appointment -	2nd	,, - -	7 9	141 8 9	10 17 0
5 years - - -	,,	,, - -	8 1	147 10 5	11 6 4
10 ,, - - -	,,	,, - -	8 5	153 12 1	11 15 8
15 ,, - - -	,,	,, - -	8 9	159 13 9	12 5 0
On appointment -	3rd	,, - -	5 9	104 18 9	8 1 0
5 years - - -	,,	,, - -	6 1	111 0 5	8 10 4
10 ,, - - -	,,	,, - -	6 5	117 2 1	8 19 8
15 ,, - - -	,,	,, - -	6 9	123 3 9	9 9 0

Class.	Rank.	Daily.	Weekly.	Yearly.	Monthly.
		s. d.	£ s. d.	£ s. d.	£ s. d.
—	Sergeant-Major, on appointment - -	4 8	1 12 8	85 3 4	6 10 ·8
—	,, ,, 5 yrs. in rank of Sergeant	4 9	1 13 3	86 13 9	6 13 0
—	,, ,, 10 ,, ,, ,,	4 11	1 14 5	89 14 7	6 17 8
1st	Merit Sergeant, on appointment - -	4 7	1 12 1	83 12 11	6 8 4
,,	,, ,, 5 yrs. in rank of Sergeant	4 8	1 12 8	85 3 4	6 10 8
,,	,, ,, 10 ,, ,, ,,	4 10	1 13 1	88 4 2	6 15 4
,,	Ordinary Sergeant, on appointment -	4 5	1 10 11	80 12 1	6 3 8
,,	,, ,, 5 yrs. in rank of Sergeant	4 6	1 11 6	82 2 6	6 6 0
,,	,, ,, 10 ,, ,, ,,	4 8	1 12 8	85 3 4	6 10 8
2nd	Merit Sergeant, on appointment - -	4 3	1 9 9	77 11 3	5 19 0
,,	,, ,, 5 yrs. in rank of Sergeant	4 4	1 10 4	79 1 8	6 1 4
,,	,, ,, 10 ,, ,, ,,	4 6	1 11 6	82 2 6	6 6 0
,,	Ordinary Sergeant, on appointment · -	4 1	1 8 7	74 10 5	5 14 4
,,	,, ,, 5 yrs. in rank of Sergeant	4 2	1 9 2	76 0 10	5 16 8
,,	,, ,, 10 ,, ,, ,,	4 4	1 10 4	79 1 8	6 1 4
1st	Merit Constable, on appointment to 1st Class.	3 7	1 5 1	65 7 11	5 0 4
,,	,, ,, 5 years in 1st Class -	3 8	1 5 8	66 18 4	5 2 8
,,	,, ,, 10 ,, ,, -	3 9	1 6 3	68 8 9	5 5 0
,,	Ordinary Constable, on appointment to 1st Class.	3 5	1 3 11	62 7 1	4 15 8
,,	,, ,, 5 years in 1st Class -	3 6	1 4 6	63 17 6	4 18 0
,,	,, ,, 10 ,, ,, -	3 7	1 5 1	65 7 11	5 0 4
2nd	Merit Constable - .. - - -	3 4	1 3 4	60 16 8	4 13 4
,,	Ordinary - - - -	3 2	1 2 2	57 15 10	4 8 8
3rd	Ordinary Constables - - - -	3 0	1 1 0	54 15 0	4 4 0

BOROUGH OF WEYMOUTH.

Force - - - - - 29.

| Area in acres * | - | - 1,012 | Acres to each constable - | - | - 35 |
| Population in 1891* | - | - 21,328 | Population to ditto, as per census 1891 | | 735 |

RANKS.	Chief Officer.	Superintendents.						2 Inspectors.				
		Deputy Chief Officer.	Chief Clerk.	1st Class.	2nd Class.	3rd Class.	4th Class.	1st Class.	2nd Class.	3rd Class.	4th Class.	5th Class.
					Yearly Pay in £ and Shillings.							
Number of each Rank and Class -	1	-	-	-	-	-	-	1	1	-	-	-
Rates of Pay of each ditto -	£ 275	-	-	-	-	-	-	£ s. 119 12	£ 104	-	-	-

RANKS.	4 Sergeants.						22 Constables.							Vacancy.
	Merit Class.	1st Class.	2nd Class.	3rd Class.	4th Class.	5th Class.	Acting Sergeants.	Merit Class.	1st Class.	2nd Class.	3rd Class.	4th Class.	5th Class.	
				Weekly Pay in Shillings and Pence.										
Number of each Rank and Class -	-	1	1	1	1	-	-	2	3	1	5	4	6	1
Rates of Pay of each ditto -	-	s. d. 38 6	s. 35	s. 33	s. d. 31 7	-	-	s. d. 30 9	s. d. 28 7	s. 27	s. 26	s. 25	s. 24	-

* Parts of the parishes of Wyke Regis and Radipole (acreage 559, population 7,462) were transferred (9th November 1895) from the county of Dorset.

Inspected 24th August.

Establishment.—One chief officer, two inspectors, four sergeants, and 22 constables. The strength of the force has been augmented by one constable, and there is a vacancy for one constable.

The scale of pay is unaltered, but the chief officer receives an increase in salary of 25*l.* per annum.

Twenty-three members hold certificates from the St. John Ambulance Association.

Extra Duties.—The chief officer is inspector under the Contagious Diseases (Animals), Explosives, and Food and Drugs Acts, and of hackney carriages.

There is an increase of one in the number of public-houses, and of 11 in refreshment houses. Thirteen fewer persons were proceeded against for drunkenness, and 10 fewer convicted.

The clothing and appointments were complete and serviceable, the books and returns well kept, and the offices and cells clean and in good order.

The management, numbers, and discipline of the force have been efficiently maintained.

COUNTY OF GLOUCESTER.

Force - - - - - 369.*

Area in acres † - - - 797,875	Acres to each constable - - - 2,162
Population in 1891 † - - 365,842	Population to ditto, as per census 1891 991

RANKS.	Chief Constable	11 Superintendents.								6 Inspectors.				
		Deputy Chief Constable.	Chief Clerk.	1st Class.	2nd Class.	3rd Class.	4th Class.	5th Class	6th Class	1st Class.	2nd Class.	3rd Class.	4th Class.	5th Class.
Number of each } Rank and Class	1	1	1	2	1	1	3	2	1	3	1	2	-	-
Rates of Pay of } each ditto - . }	£ 570	£ 290	£ 180	£ 180	£ s. 162 18	£ s. 154 6	£ 140	£ s. 128 11	£ s. 122 17	£ 100	£ s. 97 5	£ s. 91 5	-	-

RANKS.	47 Sergeants.								304 Constables.					
	1st Class.	2nd Class.	3rd Class.	4th Class.	5th Class.	6th Class.	Acting Sergeants	Merit Class.	1st Class.	2nd Class.	3rd Class.	4th Class.	5th Class.	6th Class.
Number of each } Rank and Class	29	18	-	-	-	-	-	-	103	116	10	30	45	-
Rates of Pay of } each ditto - . }	s. d. 31 10	s. d. 29 11	-	-	-	-	-	-	s. d. 27 11	s. d. 24 11	s. d. 23 11	s. d. 22 11	s. d. 21 11	-

* Exclusive of five inspectors, one sergeant, and 18 constables appointed under 3 & 4 Vict. c. 88. s. 19.
† The parishes of Cutsdean (acreage 1,560, population 126), Daylesford (acreage 670, population 126), and Evenlode (acreage 1,619, population 248) are transferred from Worcestershire by order of quarter sessions, dated 1st May 1890 ; and the parish of Teddington (acreage 747, population 99) is also transferred from Worcestershire by order of quarter sessions, dated 1st November 1880. The district of Avonmouth (acreage 900, population 714) has been transferred to the borough of Bristol. An area of 4,902 acreage and 58,854 population was transferred to the borough of Bristol on the 1st November 1897. The parishes of Kemble (acreage 3,322, population 482), Poole Keynes (acreage 1,216, population 122), and Somerford Keynes (acreage 1,572, population 341) were transferred from the county of Wilts on 1st April 1897.

Inspected in June.

The authorised establishment is one chief constable, 11 superintendents (one of whom acts as deputy chief constable and one as chief clerk), six inspectors, 47 sergeants, and 304 constables. The force was augmented 7th January 1901 by one constable, and again in May by one inspector, two sergeants, and 12 constables, to meet the estimated increase of population since the census of 1891, about 10,000 of the city of Gloucester, the boundaries of which city have been extended, 9th November 1900.

Two hundred and sixty-nine members hold certificates from the St. John Ambulance Association.

Extra Duties :—

NATURE OF DUTY.	Chief Constable.	Superintendents.	Inspectors.	Sergeants.	Constables.	REMUNERATION.
Inspectors of Weights and Measures.	1	—	3	—	—	Chief constable, 30l. per annum.
Inspectors under Contagious Diseases (Animals) Act.	1	11	9	47	77	One superintendent, 30l. per annum ; others, 1s. 6d. per visit.
Inspector of Petroleum - -	—	1	—	—	—	Included in above, 30l. per annum.
Inspectors of Explosives, and under Food and Drugs Act.	—	11	9	47	104	Nil.
Inspectors of Hawkers' Licences.	—	The whole force.				Nil.
Assistant Relieving Officers -	—	3	1	4	3	One superintendent, 5l. ; one ditto, 3l. ; one inspector, 8l. ; one sergeant, 5l. ; and one ditto, 3l. per annum.
Keepers of Court-houses -	—	1	—	2	—	One superintendent, 1l. ; one sergeant, 5l. ; and one ditto, 1l. per annum.
Javelin Men - - - -	—	1	1	—	20	Nil.
Inspectors of Hackney Carriages and Streets.	—	—	1	—	1	Inspector, 10l. ; constables, 20l. per annum.
Sergeants-at-Mace - - -	—	—	—	—	4	Nil.

The county borough of Gloucester and the borough of Cheltenham are policed by the county constabulary.

Army Reserve, 29th September 1899–1901.—Seventeen members were called up, of whom 13 are still serving with the colours. Three have rejoined certified fit, and one died at Piershill Barracks, Edinburgh, on 30th August 1901.

There has been a decrease during the year of one in the number of public-houses. two in beerhouses, and three in refreshment houses. An increase of 16 in the number of persons proceeded against for drunkenness, and 44 in the number convicted.

The clothing and appointments were complete and serviceable, and the books and returns well kept.

The stations and cells visited were clean and in good order.

The management, numbers, and discipline of the force have been efficiently maintained.

A new scale of pay, as under, was adopted 1st January 1901.

No. 3.
South of England
and South Wales
District.

Ranks and Classes.		Annual Pay.	Monthly.		
			Gross Pay.	Deduction for Pension Fund at 2½ per cent.	Net Pay.
		£ s. d.	£ s. d.	£ s. d.	£ s. d.
Chief Constable (agreed to June 30th, 1891)		570 0 0	47 10 0	1 3 9	46 6 3
Deputy Chief Constable.	after 7 years' service	220 0 0	18 6 8	0 9 2	17 17 6
	" 6 " "	217 2 0	18 1 10	0 9 1	17 12 9
	" 5 " "	214 5 0	17 17 1	0 8 11	17 8 2
	" 4 " "	211 8 0	17 12 4	0 8 10	17 3 6
	" 3 " "	208 11 0	17 7 7	0 8 8	16 18 11
	" 2 " "	205 14 0	17 2 10	0 8 7	16 14 3
	" 1 " "	202 17 0	16 18 1	0 8 5	16 9 8
	on appointment	200 0 0	16 13 4	0 8 4	16 5 0
First Class Superintendents.	after 7 years' service	180 0 0	15 0 0	0 7 6	14 12 6
	" 6 " "	175 16 0	14 13 0	0 7 4	14 5 8
	" 5 " "	171 10 0	14 5 10	0 7 2	13 18 8
	" 4 " "	167 4 0	13 18 8	0 7 0	13 11 8
	" 3 " "	162 18 0	13 11 6	0 6 9	13 4 9
	" 2 " "	158 12 0	13 4 4	0 6 7	12 17 9
	" 1 " "	154 6 0	12 17 2	0 6 5	12 10 9
	on appointment	150 0 0	12 10 0	0 6 3	12 3 9
Second Class Superintendents.	after 7 years' service	140 0 0	11 13 4	0 5 10	11 7 6
	" 6 " "	137 2 0	11 8 6	0 5 9	11 2 10
	" 5 " "	134 5 0	11 3 9	0 5 7	10 18 2
	" 4 " "	131 8 0	10 19 0	0 5 6	10 13 6
	" 3 " "	128 11 0	10 14 3	0 5 4	10 8 11
	" 2 " "	125 14 0	10 9 6	0 5 3	10 4 3
	" 1 " "	122 17 0	10 4 9	0 5 1	9 9 8
	on appointment	120 0 0	10 0 0	0 5 0	9 15 0
Inspectors	after 5 years' service	100 0 0	8 6 8	0 4 2	8 2 6
	" 4 " "	99 5 0	8 5 5	0 4 2	8 1 3
	" 3 " "	97 5 0	8 2 1	0 4 1	7 18 0
	" 2 " "	95 5 0	7 18 9	0 4 0	7 14 9
	" 1 " "	93 5 0	7 15 5	0 3 11	7 11 6
	on appointment	91 5 0	7 12 1	0 3 10	7 8 3
Sergeants	after 5 years' service	83 4 0	6 18 8	0 3 6	6 15 2
	on appointment	78 0 0	6 10 0	0 3 3	6 6 9
Constables	1st class	72 16 0	6 1 4	0 3 0	5 18 4
	2nd class after 3 years' service	65 0 0	5 8 4	0 2 8	5 5 8
	3rd " " 2 "	62 8 0	5 4 0	0 2 7	5 1 5
	4th " " 1 "	59 16 0	4 19 8	0 2 6	4 17 2
	5th " on appointment	57 4 0	4 15 4	0 2 5	4 12 11

No. 3.
South of England and South Wales District.

CITY AND COUNTY BOROUGH OF BRISTOL.

Force - - - - - - - - - - 499.*

Area in acres † - - - - 9,563 | Acres to each constable - - - 19
Population in 1891 † - - 281,156 | Population to ditto, as per census 1891 563

RANKS.	Chief Officer	5 Superintendents						21 Inspectors.				
		Deputy Chief Officer.	Chief Clerk.	1st Class.	2nd Class.	3rd Class.	4th Class.	Chief Inspector.	1st Class.	2nd Class.	3rd Class.	4th Class.
Number of each Rank and Class -	1	1	1	1	1	1	-	1	13	2	2	2
Rates of Pay of each ditto -	£ 800	£ 290	£ 170	£ 245	£ 240	£ 180	-	£ 180	£ 130	£ 119 12	£ 117	£ 114 8

(Yearly Pay in £ and Shillings.)

(Weekly Pay in Shillings and Pence.)

RANKS.	66 Sergeants.						406 Constables.							
	1st Class.	2nd Class.	3rd Class.	4th Class.	5th Class.	6th Class.	Detective Constables.	Merit Class.	1st Class.	2nd Class.	3rd Class.	4th Class.	5th Class.	Va-cancies.
Number of each Rank and Class -	31	4	2	19	1	9	1 2 2 2 2	54	89	76	40	74	23	37	4
Rates of Pay of each ditto -	40	39	38	37	36	35	40 28 37 36 34	33	32	31	29	27	26	24	-

* Exclusive of three sergeants and 13 constables not paid by rates.
† The district of Avonmouth (acreage 900, population 714) and an area (acreage 4,902, population 58,864) was transferred (1st November 1897) from the county of Gloucester.

Inspected 22nd June.

The authorised establishment is one chief officer, five superintendents (one of whom acts as deputy chief officer, and one as chief clerk), 21 inspectors, 66 sergeants, and 406 constables; also three sergeants and 13 constables not paid by rates.

There are vacancies for four constables.

One hundred and seventy-one members hold certificates from the St. John Ambulance Association.

Extra Duties.—Three superintendents are inspectors under the Explosives Act, without remuneration, four inspectors are inspectors under the Petroleum Act (allowance, 6l. 5s. each per annum), and one is inspector of hackney carriages, without remuneration.

The three sergeants (additional) and 13 constables (additional) form a fire brigade.

Army Reserve, 29th September 1899-1901.—Twenty-eight members were called up, nine of whom have rejoined the force, certified fit. One died in South Africa, two are home on furlough and will shortly rejoin the force, and 16 are still serving with the colours.

Licensing Acts.—There has been a decrease of three in the number of public-houses during the year, and a decrease of three in beerhouses.

Eighty-two more persons were proceeded against for drunkenness, and 71 more convicted.

The clothing and appointments were complete and serviceable, and the books and returns well kept. New stations are to be built at Horfield and Eastville and the central station reconstructed.

The offices and cells were clean and in good order.

The management, numbers, and discipline of the force have been efficiently maintained.

A revised scale of pay, as under, was adopted in February 1901.

Rank.	Pay.	Promoted in Class.
Chief Inspector - -	180*l.* per annum -	On appointment.
,, ,, -	190*l.* ,, -	After 1 year in rank.
,, ,, - -	200*l.* ,, -	,, 2 years in rank.
Inspectors—		
4th class -	44*s.* per week -	On appointment.
,, ,, - -	45*s.* ,, -	After 1 year in rank.
3rd ,, - -	46*s.* ,, - -	,, 3 years in rank.
2nd ,, - - -	48*s.* ,, - -	,, 5 ,, ,,
1st ,, -	50*s.* ,, - -	,, 7 ,, ,,
Sergeants—		
4th class - -	35*s.* ,, - -	On appointment.
3rd ,, - - -	36*s.* ,, - -	After 2 years in rank.
,, ,, -	37*s.* ,, - -	,, 3 ,, · ,,
2nd ,, - - -	38*s.* ,, - -	,, 4 ,, ,,
,, ,, -	39*s.* ,, - -	,, 5 ,, ,,
1st ,, - - -	40*s.* ,, - -	,, 6 ,, ,,
Constables—		
5th class -	24*s.* ,, - -	On appointment.
4th ,, - - -	26*s.* ,, - -	After 1 year in rank.
3rd ,, -	27*s.* ,, - -	,, 2 years in rank.
2nd ,, - - -	29*s.* ,, - -	,, 4 ,, ,,
1st ,, -	31*s.* ,, - -	,, 6 ,, ,,
,, ,, - - -	32*s.* ,, - -	,, 10 ,, ,,
Long Service Class -	33*s.* ,, - -	,, 15 ,, ,,

Superintendents on appointment receive 170*l.* per annum, which is increased by annual increments of 10*l.* until the maximum of 250*l.* is reached, with free house, coal, and gas.

COUNTY OF HANTS.

Force   -   -   -   423.*

Area in acres† -   -   -   - 945,528 | Acres to each constable - - - 2,235
Population in 1891† -   - 347,793 | Population to ditto, as per census 1891 822

RANKS.	Chief Constable.	15 Superintendents.						4 Inspectors.				
		Deputy Chief Constable.	Chief Clerk.	1st Class.	2nd Class.	3rd Class.	4th Class.	1st Class.	2nd Class.	3rd Class.	4th Class.	5th Class.
Yearly Pay in £ and Shillings.												
Number of each Rank and Class -	1	1	1	4	3	3	4	4	-	-	-	-
	£	£ *s.*	£ *s.*	£ *s.*	£ *s.*	£ *s.*	£ *s.*	£ *s.*				
Rates of Pay of each ditto -	600	197 14	150 11	179 9	150 11	150 11	130 15	109 10	-			

RANKS.	50 Sergeants.						353 Constables.						
	Merit Class.	1st Class.	2nd Class.	3rd Class.	4th Class.	5th Class.	Acting Sergeants.	Merit Class.	1st Class.	2nd Class.	3rd Class.	4th Class.	5th Class.	6th Class.
Weekly Pay in Shillings and Pence.													
Number of each Rank and Class -	-	1	21	28	-	-	-	-	130	130	93	-	-	-
		s.	£ *s.*	£ *s.*				*s.*	*s. d.*	*s.*			
Rates of Pay of each ditto - -	-	35	33 3	31 6	-	-	-	-	28	24 6	21	-	-	-

* Exclusive of four additional constables appointed under 3 & 4 Vict. c. 88. s. 19.
† The parishes of Bramshaw East (acreage 1,518, population 273), Martin (acreage 3,535, population 413), Melchet Park (acreage 236, population 37), Plaitford (acreage 1,322, population 164), South Damerham (acreage 4,480, population 532), Toyd Farm with Allenford (acreage 640, population 16), West Willow (acreage 1,404, population 631), Whichbury, part in Wilts (acreage 1,768, population 141), are transferred (30th September 1895) from Wilts. The parish of Dochenfield (acreage 578, population 259) is transferred (30th September 1895) to Surrey, and the parish of Combe (acreage 2,112, population 92) is transferred to Berks. An area (acreage 2,980, population 20,709) has been transferred to the borough of Southampton on 9th November 1895. An area (acreage 854, population 1,130) was transferred to the city of Winchester on 9th November 1900.

No. 3.
South of England
and South Wales
District.

Inspected in July.

The authorised establishment, which was augmented during the year by two inspectors, one sergeant, and 18 constables (six of whom are mounted constables), is one chief constable, 15 superintendents (one of whom acts as deputy chief constable, and one as chief clerk), four inspectors, 50 sergeants, 353 constables, and four constables appointed under 3 & 4 Vict. c. 88. s. 19. There are vacancies for nine constables. -

The scale of pay is unaltered.

Two hundred and sixty members hold certificates from the St. John Ambulance Association.

Extra Duties :—

NATURE OF DUTY.	Chief Constable.	Superintendents.	Inspectors.	Sergeants.	Constables.	REMUNERATION.
Assistant Relieving Officers - -	—	10	—	9	3	
Inspectors under Contagious Diseases (Animals) Act.	1	14	4	48	—	
Inspectors of Common Lodging-houses	—	7	—	3	—	Nil.
„ Explosives - -	—	14	—	—	—	
„ Petroleum - - -	—	9	—	—	—	
„ County Bridges - -	—	14	4	48	350	

The borough of Bournemouth is policed by the county constabulary.

Army Reserve, 29th September 1899-1901.—Forty members were called up, of whom 23 have rejoined the force certified fit, thirteen are still serving with the colours, two died in South Africa, one joined the Irish Guards, and one whose services were not required.

There is a decrease of two in the number of public-houses and three in beerhouses, and an increase of nine in refreshment houses. Seventy-two more persons were proceeded against for drunkenness, and 138 more convicted.

The clothing and appointments were complete and serviceable, and the books and returns well kept.

The stations and cells visited were clean and in good order. The additional accommodation at the Kingsclere police station has been completed. A sub-divisional station is being built at Hartley Row, Odiham, with accommodation for one sergeant and two constables (married) and with two cells.

The management, numbers, and discipline of the force have been efficiently maintained.

COUNTY BOROUGH OF PORTSMOUTH.

Force - - - - - - 226.

Area in acres	-	- 4,320	Acres to each constable	-	-	-	20
Population in 1891	-	- 159,251	Population to ditto, as per census 1891				705

Yearly Pay in £ and Shillings.

RANKS.	Chief Officer.	1 Superintendent.						14 Inspectors.				
		Deputy Chief Officer.	Chief Clerk.	1st Class.	2nd Class.	3rd Class.	4th Class.	1st Class.	2nd Class.	3rd Class.	4th Class.	5th Class.
Number of each Rank and Class -	1	-	-	1	-	-	-	1	4	3	6	-
Rates of Pay of each ditto - -	£ 350	-	-	£ 160	-	-	-	£ 130	£ 135	£ 115	£ 110	-

Weekly Pay in Shillings and Pence.

RANKS.	22 Sergeants.						188 Constables.													
	Merit Class.	1st Class.	2nd Class.	3rd Class.	4th Class.	5th Class.	Corporal.	Merit Class.	1st Class.	2nd Class.	3rd Class.	4th Class.	5th Class.	6th Class.	7th Class.	8th Class.	9th Class.	10th Class.	11th Class.	Detectives.
Number of each Rank and Class -	-	6	7	9	-	-	1	1	3	25	22	25	23	13	3	6	6	40	13	3
Rates of Pay of each ditto - -	-	s. 39	s. 37	s. 35	-	-	s. 34	s. 33	s. 33	s. 32	s. 31	s. 30	s. 29	s. 28	s. 27	s. 26	s. 25	s. 24	s. 23	s. 34

Inspected 10th July.

Establishment.—One chief officer, one superintendent, 14 inspectors, 22 sergeants, and 188 constables. There are four sergeants less than last year, but a corresponding increase of one in the number of inspectors, and three in the number of constables.

Two hundred and seventeen members hold certificates from the St. John Ambulance Association.

Extra Duties.—One inspector is inspector of hackney carriages, without remuneration, and two inspectors are assistant relieving officers: allowance, 10*l.* each per annum.

The detective staff consists of one inspector, one sergeant, and eight constables.

Army Reserve, 29th September 1899–1901.—Seven members were called up, of whom four have rejoined the police force certified physically fit, one died in South Africa of enteric fever, and two are still serving with the colours.

There has been an increase of three in the number of public-houses during the year, but a decrease of 12 in the number of beerhouses. A decrease of 44 in the number of persons proceeded against for drunkenness, and 48 in the number convicted.

The clothing and appointments were complete and serviceable, and the books and returns well kept.

The police offices and cells were clean and in good order.

The management, numbers, and discipline of the force have been efficiently maintained.

A new scale of pay, as under, was adopted 9th April 1901.

SCALE OF PAY.

Superintendent, on appointment, 150*l.* per annum, rising by annual increments of 5*l.* to 200*l.*

		£	s.	d.	
Chief Inspector	- - - -	130	0	0	per annum.
Inspectors—					
On appointment -	- - -	110	0	0	,,
After 2 years -	- - -	115	0	0	,,
,, 5 ,,	- -. -	120	0	0	,,
,, 7 .. -	- -	125	0	0	,,
,, 10 .. -	- -	130	0	0	..
Sergeants—					
On appointment	- - -	1	15	0	weekly.
After 3 years -	- - -	1	17	0	,,
,, 6 ,, -	- - -	1	19	0	..
Constables—					
On appointment -	• - -	1	3	0	
After 1 year -	- - -	1	4	0	..
,, 2 years -	- - -	1	5	0	
,, 3 ,,	- - -	1	6	0	
.. 4 ..	- - -	1	7	0	
.. 5 ,, •	- - -	1	8	0	.. (star).
.. 6 ,, •	- •- -	1	9	0	..
,, 8 years -	- - -	1	10	0	
,, 10 ,,	- - -	1	11	0	,, (star).
,, 15 ,, -	- - -	1	12	0	,, (star).

Merit Class for long service and good conduct after 20 years' service, with 1*s.* per week extra. (Chevron.)

Boot Allowance.—Inspectors, 32*s.* per annum ; sergeants and constables, 23*s.* per annum.

X

PLAIN CLOTHES STAFF.

		£	s.	d.	
Detective Inspector—					
On appointment	- - -	110	0	0	per annum.
After 2 years	- - -	115	0	0	„
„ 5 „	- - -	120	0	0	„
„ 7 „	- - -	125	0	0	„
„ 10 „	- - -	130	0	0	„
Allowance for plain clothes	- -	0	2	0	per week.
Incidental expenses	- - -	0	3	0	„
Detective and Clerk Sergeants—					
On appointment	- - -	1	17	0	..
After 3 years -	- - -	1	19	0	..
„ 6 „	- ▪ -	2	1	0	..
Detective Constables—					
On appointment	- - -	1	10	0	..
After 1 year -	▪ - -	1	11	0	..
„ 2 years -	- - -	1	12	0	..
.. 3 „	- - -	1	13	0	..
.. 6 .. -	- - -	1	14	0	..

COUNTY BOROUGH OF SOUTHAMPTON.

Force - - - - - - - - 134.*

Area in acres †	- - -	4,984	Acres to each constable	- -	37
Population in 1891 † -	-	86,034	Population to ditto, as per census 1891		642

RANKS.	Chief Officer.	Superintendents.						8 Inspectors.				
		Deputy Chief Officer.	Chief Clerk.	1st Class.	2nd Class.	3rd Class.	4th Class.	Chief Inspector.	1st Class.	2nd Class.	3rd Class.	4th Class.
Number of each Rank and Class -	1	-	-	-	-	-	-	1	4	2	1	-
Rates of Pay of each ditto -	£ 500	-	-	-	-	-	-	£ 160	£ 125	£ 115	£ 110	-

Yearly Pay in £ and Shillings.

Weekly Pay in Shillings and Pence.

RANKS.	15 Sergeants.						111 Constables.‡							
	Merit Class.	1st Class.	2nd Class.	3rd Class.	4th Class.	5th Class.	Merit Class.	1st Class.	2nd Class.	3rd Class.	4th Class.	5th Class.	6th Class.	7th/Class.
Number of each Rank and Class -	-	6	4	5	-	-	21	24	12	5	2	14	31	2
Rates of Pay of each ditto -	-	*s. d.* 37 6	*s.* 36	*s.* 34	-	-	*s.* 32	*s.* 30	*s.* 29	*s.* 28	*s.* 27	*s.* 26	*s.* 25	*s.* 23

* Exclusive of two constables not paid by rates.
† An area (acreage 2,980, and population 20,709) was transferred (19th November 1895) from the county of Hants.
‡ One constable returned from the seat of war appointed on the strength in addition till a vacancy occurs.

Inspected 9th July.

The authorised establishment, which has been augmented by nine constables, is one chief officer, eight inspectors (one of whom acts as chief clerk), 15 sergeants, and 110 constables. There are also two constables not paid by rates.

There is no alteration in the scale of pay.

The detective staff, consisting of one inspector, one sergeant, and four constables, receive 2s. 6d. each per week in addition to their pay. Three constables perform the duties of acting sergeant, receiving 6d. each per week in addition to their pay.

Forty-four members hold certificates from the St. John Ambulance Association. In future the force will not be examined by this association, but one of the police surgeons will give 10 lectures a year to the whole of the force.

No. 3.
South of England
and South Wales
District.

Extra Duties.—The chief officer is assistant relieving officer (allowance 20l. per annum), one inspector is inspector of hackney carriages (allowance 12l. per annum), and one sergeant is assistant inspector of the same (allowance 8l. per annum).

Army Reserve, 29th September 1899–1901.—Seventeen members were called up, of whom 10 are still serving with the colours, one died in South Africa, and six have rejoined the police force. Two of these have been suffering from phthisis (one is out of danger, the other reported by police surgeon as not likely to recover).

There is an increase of one in the number of public-houses; but 91 fewer persons were proceeded against for drunkenness, and 76 fewer convicted.

The clothing and appointments were complete and serviceable, and the books and returns well kept.

The offices and cells were clean and in good order.

The management, numbers, and discipline of the force have been efficiently maintained.

CITY OF WINCHESTER.

Force - - - - 27.

Area in acres* - - - - 1,903 | Acres to each constable - - - 70
Population in 1891*. - - 20,203 | Population to ditto, as per census 1891 748

RANKS.	Chief Officer.	Deputy Chief Officer.	Chief Clerk.	1st Class.	2nd Class.	3rd Class.	4th Class.	1st Class.	2nd Class.	3rd Class.	4th Class.	5th Class.
			Superintendents.					Inspectors.				
Number of each Rank and Class	1	–	–	–	–	–	–	–	–	–	–	–
Rates of Pay of each ditto	£300	–	–	–	–	–	–	–	–	–	–	–

Yearly Pay in £ and Shillings.

Weekly Pay in Shillings and Pence.

RANKS.	1st Class.	2nd Class.	3rd Class.	4th Class.	5th Class.	6th Class.	Acting Sergeants.	Merit Class.	1st Class.	2nd Class.	3rd Class.	4th Class.	5th Class.	6th Class.
	4 Sergeants.							22 Constables.						
Number of each Rank and Class	2	2	–	–	–	–	–	–	10	1	11	–	–	–
Rates of Pay of each ditto	s. 36	s. d. 33 6	–	–	–	–	–	–	s. 28	s. d. 26 6	s. 23	–	–	–

* An area (acreage 854, population 1,130) was transferred from the county of Hants on 9th November 1900.

Inspected 8th July.

Establishment.—One chief officer, four sergeants, and 22 constables. The strength of the force has been increased by one sergeant and five constables, and the pay of the chief officer increased by 25l. per annum.

Nine members hold certificates from the St. John Ambulance Association.

Army Reserve, 29th September 1899–1901.—One member was called up, who has rejoined the force, certified fit.

Extra Duties.—The chief officer is billet master, and inspector of hackney carriages, and under the Explosives Act, without remuneration.

There is an increase of two in the number of public-houses, and two in beerhouses; but 29 fewer persons were proceeded against for drunkenness, and 22 fewer convicted.

<table>
<tr><td>No. 3.
South of England
and South Wales
District.
——</td><td>The clothing and appointments were complete and serviceable, and the books and returns well kept.

The offices and cells were clean and in good order.

The management, numbers, and discipline of the force have been efficiently maintained.</td></tr>
</table>

COUNTY OF HEREFORD.

Force - - - - - 80.*

Area in acres†	-	- 534,194	Acres to each constable	- - - 6,777
Population in 1891†	-	- 96,097	Population to ditto, as per census 1891	1,201

	Yearly Pay in £ and Shillings.											
RANKS.	Chief Constable.	7 Superintendents.						Inspectors.				
		Depy. C.C. and Chief Clerk.	Chief Clerk.	1st Class.	2nd Class.	3rd Class.	4th Class.	1st Class.	2nd Class.	3rd Class.	4th Class.	5th Class.
Number of each Rank and Class -	1	1	-	1	1	3	1	-	-	-	-	-
Rates of Pay of each ditto - -	£ 400	£ s. 187 8	-	£ 149	£ s. 139 18	£ s. 130 15	£ s. 120 9	-	-	-	-	-

	Weekly Pay in Shillings and Pence.																	
RANKS.	14 Sergeants.						58 Constables.										
	Merit Class.	1st Class.	2nd Class.	3rd Class.	4th Class.	5th Class.	1st Class.							2nd Class.		3rd Class.
Number of each Rank and Class -	-	3	1	1	2	7	26	5	1	5	2	3	4	5	5	3
Rates of Pay of each ditto - -	-	s. d. 33 3	s. d. 32 1	s. d. 31 6	s. d. 30 4	s. 28	s. d. 26 10	s. d. 26 3	s. d. 25 8	s. d. 25 1	s. d. 24 6	s. d. 23 11	s. d. 23 4	s. d. 22 9	s. d. 22 2	s. 21

* Exclusive of two constables appointed under 3 & 4 Vict. c. 88. s. 19.
† The parish of Edvin Loach (acreage 533, population 48) is transferred (29th September 1803) from Worcestershire; and the parish of Fwddog Hamlet (acreage 2,101, population 79) is transferred (29th September 1893) to Monmouthshire.—Local Government Board Provisional Order Confirmation Act.
The parishes of Acton Beauchamp (acreage 1,518, population 216) and Rural Mathon (acreage 3,056, population 379) were transferred from, and the parish of Stoke Bliss (acreage 1,169, population 149) transferred to, Worcestershire (30th September 1897).

Inspected in June.

The authorised establishment, which is the same strength as last year, is one chief constable, seven superintendents (one of whom acts as deputy chief constable and chief clerk), 14 sergeants, and 58 constables. There are also two constables appointed under 3 & 4 Vict. c. 88. s. 19.

Fifty-two members hold certificates from the St. John Ambulance Association.

Extra Duties.—

NATURE OF DUTY.	Chief Constable.	Super-intendents.	In-spectors.	Ser-geants.	Con-stables.	REMUNERATION.
Inspectors, Contagious Diseases (Animals) Act.	→	7	—	5	—	One superintendent 10l. per annum, the remainder 2s. 6d. each case, up to 10s. a week.
Inspectors, Explosives Act ·	—	6	—	1	—	Nil.
Inspectors, Food and Drugs Act.	—	6	—	—	—	Nil.
Assistant Relieving Officers -	—	3	—	1	—	Two 10l., one 8l., and one 4l. per annum.
Inspectors of Lodging-houses	—	—	—	2	—	1l. per annum each.

Army Reserve, 29th September 1899–1901.—One member was called up, who has rejoined the force, certified fit for duty.

There is a decrease of one in the number of public-houses, but an increase of one in beerhouses. A decrease of 28 in the number of persons proceeded against for drunkenness, and 29 in the number convicted.

The clothing and appointments were complete and serviceable, and the books and returns well kept.

The stations and cells visited were clean and in good order.

The management, numbers, and discipline of the force have been efficiently maintained.

A revised scale of pay, as under, was adopted 1st January 1901 :—

No. 3.
South of England
and South Wales
District.

RANK.	Period.	Per Day.	Per Week.	REMARKS.
		s. d.	*£ s. d.*	
Constables—3rd class	On appointment	3 0	1 1 0	3rd class constables to be promoted to second class after six months' service, and after passing examination as efficient.
„ 2nd „	„ „	3 2	1 2 2	
„ „ „	After 1 year's service	3 3	1 2 9	
„ 1st „	On appointment	3 4	1 3 4	
„ „ „	After 1 year's service	3 5	1 3 11	
„ „ „	„ 2 „ „	3 6	1 4 6	
„ „ „	„ 3 „ „	3 7	1 5 1	
„ „ „	„ 4 „ „	3 8	1 5 8	
„ „ „	„ 5 „ „	3 9	1 6 3	
„ „ „	„ 6 „ „	3 10	1 6 10	
Sergeants—2nd class	On appointment	4 0	1 8 0	Sergeants in charge of sub-divisions 3d. a day additional.
„ 1st „	„ „	4 4	1 10 4	
„ „ „	After 3 years' service	4 6	1 11 6	
			Per annum.	
			£ s. d.	
Superintendents—3rd class	On appointment	6 7	120 2 11	
„ 2nd „	„ „	7 2	130 15 10	
„ „ „	After 3 years' service	7 5	135 7 1	
„ 1st „	On appointment	7 8	139 18 4	
„ „ „	After 3 years' service	7 11	144 9 7	
„ „ „	„ 6 „ „	8 2	149 0 10	
„ „ „	„ 9 „ „	8 5	153 12 1	
„ „ „	„ 12 „ „	8 8	158 3 4	
„ „ „	„ 15 „ „	8 11	162 14 7	
„ „ „	„ 18 „ „	9 2	167 5 10	
„ as D.C.C.	—	—	20 0 0	Additional.

CITY OF HEREFORD.

Force - - - 33.

Area in acres -	- - 5,031	Acres to each constable -	- 152
Population in 1891 -	- - 20,267	Population to ditto, as per census 1891	614

		Yearly Pay in £ and Shillings.										
RANKS.	Chief Officer.	Superintendents.						2 Inspectors.				
		Deputy Chief Officer.	Chief Clerk.	1st Class.	2nd Class.	3rd Class.	4th Class.	1st Class.	2nd Class.	3rd Class.	4th Class.	5th Class.
Number of each } Rank and Class - }	1	-	-	-	-	-	-	1	1	-	-	1
Rates of Pay of } each ditto - }	£ 250	-	-	-	-	-	-	£ s. 93 12	£ 78	-	-	-

		Weekly Pay in Shillings and Pence.												
RANKS.	5 Sergeants.						Acting Sergeants.	25 Constables.						
	Merit Class.	1st Class.	2nd Class.	3rd Class.	4th Class.	5th Class.		Merit Class.	1st Class.	2nd Class.	3rd Class.	4th Class.	5th Class.	6th Class.
Number of each } Rank and Class - }	-	1	1	3	-	-	-	-	10	1	5	1	3	5
Rates of Pay of } each ditto - }	-	s. 35	s. 34	s. 31	-	-	-	-	s. 30	s. 29	s. 28	s. d. 26 6	s. 25	s. d. 23 6

Inspected 10th June.

Establishment.—One chief officer, two inspectors, five sergeants, and 25 constables. The strength of the force is the same as last year, but there is one sergeant more, and one constable less.

Twenty-two members hold certificates from the St. John Ambulance Association.

Army Reserve, 29th September 1899–1901.—One member was called up, who is still serving.

Extra Duties.—The chief officer is inspector of hackney carriages, billet master, and inspector under the Contagious Diseases (Animals) and Explosives Acts without remuneration. He is also superintendent of the fire brigade, receiving an allowance for attending fires in the city of 10s. 6d., in the county 21s.

The number of public-houses and refreshment rooms is the same as last year, but there is one beerhouse less than last year. Twelve more persons were proceeded against for drunkenness, and one more convicted.

The clothing and appointments were complete and serviceable, the books and returns well kept, and the offices and cells clean and in good order.

The management, numbers, and discipline of the force have been efficiently maintained.

A new scale of pay, as under, was adopted 26th June 1901.

Constables—

	£	s.	d.	
On appointment	1	3	6	per week.
After 1 year	1	5	0	,,
,, 3 years	1	6	6	..
5 ,,	1	8	0	..
8 ,,	1	9	0	..
10 ..	1	10	0	..

Sergeants—

On appointment	1	11	0	..
After 2 years	1	12	6	..
,, 5 ,,	1	14	0	..
,, 8 ,,	1	15	0	..
Merit class	0	1	0	..

Inspectors—

On appointment	1	16	0	..
After 2 years	1	18	0	..
,, 4 ,,	2	0	0	..
7 ..	2	2	0	..

For special acts of bravery and meritorious conduct, stripes and badges will be awarded at the discretion of the Watch Committee, without increase of pay.

C;OUNTY OF KENT.

Force - - - 516.*

Area in acres † - - - - 912,858	Acres to each constable - - 1,769
Population in 1891 † - - 479,525	Population to ditto, as per census 1891 929

Yearly Pay in £ and Shillings.

RANKS.	Chief Constable.	14 Superintendents.						11 Inspectors.				
		Deputy Chief Constable.	Chief Clerk.	1st Class.	2nd Class.	3rd Class.	4th Class.	1st Class.	2nd Class.	3rd Class.	4th Class.	5th Class.
Number of each Rank and Class -	1	1	1	5	7	–	–	11	–	–	–	–	–
Rates of Pay of each ditto -	£ 500	£ 219	£ s. 182 10	£ s. 182 10	£ s. 164 5	–	–	£ s. 114 1	–	–	–	–

Weekly Pay in Shillings and Pence.

RANKS.	55 Sergeants.						435 Constables.							
	1st Class.	2nd Class.	3rd Class.	4th Class.	5th Class.	6th Class.	Corporals.	1st Class.	2nd Class.	3rd Class.	4th Class.	5th Class.	6th Class.	7th Class.
Number of each Rank and Class -	35	20	–	–	–	–	48	144	160	83	–	–	–	–
Rates of Pay of each ditto -	s. d. 33 8	s. d. 31 6	–	–	–	–	s. 28	s. d. 26 3	s. d. 24 6	s. d. 22 9	–	–	–	–

* Exclusive of two additional constables appointed under 3 & 4 Vict. c. 88. s. 19.
† The parish of Lamberhurst (portion of East Sussex), with area 1,937 acres and population 1,158, is transferred from East Sussex for police purposes, by order of quarter sessions, dated October 1857.

Inspected 19th to 28th March inclusive.

The authorised establishment, which has been augmented during the year by one superintendent, three sergeants, and 36 constables, is one chief constable, 14 superintendents, 11 inspectors, 55 sergeants, and 435 constables. There are vacancies for 16 constables.

There are two constables " additional," an increase of one.

The scale of pay is unaltered.

One hundred and five members hold certificates from the St. John Ambulance Association.

Extra Duties :—

NATURE OF DUTY.	Chief Constable.	Super-intendents.	In-spectors.	Ser-geants.	Con-stables.	REMUNERATION.
Inspectors under the Contagious Diseases (Animals) Act.	1	12	11	55	47	Superintendents and inspectors, 3s.; sergeants and constables, 2s.; and travelling expenses for each fresh outbreak visited.
Inspectors under the Sale of Food and Drugs Act.	—	12	—	—	—	3s. 6d. and travelling expenses per journey to analyst, and 6d. for each sample submitted to him.
Javelin Men at assizes and quarter sessions.	—	—	—	2	18	2s. each per day when so employed.

The boroughs of Chatham and Faversham are policed by the county constabulary.

Army Reserve, 29th September 1899-1901.—Thirty-seven members were called up, of whom 16 are still serving with the colours, one was killed in action, one died of disease, and 19 rejoined, but one of these was discharged medically unfit, and two have been called upon to resign since rejoining.

There are two more public-houses, ten fewer beerhouses, and 20 more refreshment houses than last year.

Twenty-six more persons were proceeded against for drunkenness, and 54 more convicted.

The clothing and appointments were complete and serviceable, and the books and returns well kept.

The outlying stations and cells visited were clean and in good order.

The management, numbers, and discipline of the force have been efficiently maintained.

No. 3.
South of England
and South Wales
District.

CITY AND COUNTY BOROUGH OF CANTERBURY.

Force - - - - - - - 26.

Area in acres - - - 3,971 | Acres to each constable - - 152
Population in 1891 - - 23,062 | Population to ditto, as per census 1891 887

RANKS.	Chief Officer.	Superintendents.						1 Inspector.				
		Deputy Chief Officer.	Chief Clerk.	1st Class.	2nd Class.	3rd Class.	4th Class.	1st Class.	2nd Class.	3rd Class.	4th Class.	5th Class.
Number of each Rank and Class	1	-	-	-	-	-	-	1	-	-	-	-
Rates of Pay of each ditto	£ 230	-	-	-	-	-	-	£ 100	-	-	-	-

Weekly Pay in Shillings and Pence.

RANKS.	4 Sergeants.						20 Constables.							
	1st Class.	2nd Class.	3rd Class.	4th Class.	5th Class.	6th Class.	Merit Class.	1st Class.					2nd Class.	
Number of each Rank and Class	2	1	1	-	-	-	2	3	1	9	1	1	1	2
Rates of Pay of each ditto	s. d. 36 6	s. d. 34 8	s. d. 32 6	-	-	-	s. d. 31 8	s. d. 30 8	s. d. 30 6	s. d. 29 6	s. d. 25 6	s. d. 27 6	s. 25	s. 24

Inspected on 20th March.

Establishment.—One chief officer, one inspector, four sergeants, and 20 constables.

Twenty-three members hold certificates from the St. John Ambulance Association.

Extra Duties.—The chief officer is inspector of weights and measures, alllowance 65l. per annum; of hackney carriages, allowance 5l. 5s. per annum; and under the Petroleum, Explosives, and Contagious Diseases (Animals) Acts, without remuneration.

There has been no change during the year in the number of licensed houses. Eleven fewer persons were proceeded against for drunkenness, and 11 fewer convicted.

The clothing and appointments were complete and serviceable, the offices and cells clean and in good order, and the books and returns well kept.

The management, numbers, and discipline of the force have been efficiently maintained.

A new scale of pay, as under, was adopted 20th June 1901:—

Constables—
    £ s. d.
On appointment - - - - 1 4 0 weekly.
After 1 year - - - - 1 5 0 „
„ 2 „ - - - - 1 6 0 „
„ 4 „ - - - - 1 7 6 „
„ 6 „ - - - - 1 8 6 „
„ 8 „ - - - - 1 9 6 „
„ 12 „ - - - - 1 10 6 „

Sergeants—
On appointment - - - - 1 12 6
After 2 years - - - - 1 13 6 „
„ 4 „ - - - - 1 14 6 „
„ 6 „ - - - - 1 15 6 „
„ 8 „ - - - - 1 16 6 „

Inspector—
On appointment - - - - 2 0 6 „
After 2 years - - - - 2 2 0 „
„ 4 „ - - - - 2 6 0 „
„ 6 „ - - - - 2 8 0 „

In addition to the above there is 2d. per diem granted to constables and sergeants for meritorious conduct.

BOROUGH OF DOVER.

Force - - - 57.*

No. 3.
South of England
and South Wales
District.

Area in acres - - - - - 1,256 | Acres to each constable - - - 22
Population in 1891 - - 33,300 | Population to ditto, as per census 1891 584

RANKS.	Chief Officer.	Superintendents.						2 Inspectors.				
		Deputy Chief Officer.	Chief Clerk.	1st Class.	2nd Class.	3rd Class.	4th Class.	1st Class.	2nd Class.	3rd Class.	4th Class.	5th Class.
Number of each Rank and Class -	1	-	-	-	-	-	-	2	-	-	-	-
Rates of Pay of each ditto -	£ 200	-	-	-	-	-	-	£. s. 109 4	-	-	-	-

Yearly Pay in £ and Shillings.

RANKS.	8 Sergeants.						46 Constables.							
	Merit Class.	1st Class.	2nd Class.	3rd Class.	4th Class.	5th Class.	Acting Sergeants.	Merit Class.	1st Class.	2nd Class.	3rd Class.	4th Class.	5th Class.	6th Class.
Number of each Rank and Class -	8	-	-	-	-	-	-	-	17	17	11	1	-	-
Rates of Pay of each ditto -	s. 36	-	-	-	-	-	-	-	s. 33	s. d. 30 6	s. d. 27 6	s. 25	-	-

Weekly Pay in Shillings and Pence.

* Exclusive of one constable not paid by rates.

Inspected 27th March.

Establishment.—One chief officer, two inspectors, eight sergeants, and 46 constables. One constable is also borne "additional" to the strength. There is one inspector more and one sergeant less than last year; the strength of the force remaining the same.

The scale of pay is unaltered, except that the inspectors receive 109*l.* 4*s.* per annum instead of 130*l.* Mr. H. N. Knox Knott, an inspector in this force, was appointed chief officer on 30th June 1901, with a salary of 200*l.* per annum, in the place of Mr. Thomas Osborn Sanders retired on pension.

Fifty-one members hold certificates from the St. John Ambulance Association.

Extra Duties.—The chief officer is captain of the fire brigade, inspector of explosives, hackney carriages, and billet master. He is also assistant relieving officer; allowance, 5*l.* per annum. One sergeant is inspector of markets, and toll collector; allowance, 5*s.* per week.

Army Reserve, 29th September 1899-1901.—Two members were called up, who have rejoined the force, certified fit.

There is an increase of one in the number of public-houses; but a decrease of two in the number of persons proceeded against for drunkenness, and an increase of five in the number convicted.

The clothing and appointments were complete and serviceable, the books and returns well kept, and the offices and cells clean and in good order.

The management, numbers, and discipline of the force have been efficiently maintained.

Y

BOROUGH OF FOLKESTONE.

Force - - - - - 40.

| Area in acres | - | - | - | 2,482 | Acres to each constable - | - | - | 62 |
| Population in 1891 | - | · | - | 23,905 | Population to ditto, as per census 1891 | | | 567 |

RANKS.	Chief Officer.	Superintendents.						2 Inspectors.				
		Deputy Chief Officer.	Chief Clerk.	1st Class.	2nd Class.	3rd Class.	4th Class.	1st Class.	2nd Class.	3rd Class.	4th Class.	5th Class.
Number of each Rank and Class -	1	-	-	-	-	-	-	2	-	-	-	-
Rates of Pay of each ditto - -	£300	-	-	-	-	-	-	£ s. 122 4	-	-	-	-

Weekly Pay in Shillings and Pence.

RANKS.	5 Sergeants.						32 Constables.							
	Merit Class.	1st Class.	2nd Class.	3rd Class.	4th Class.	5th Class.	Acting Sergeants.	Merit Class.	1st Class.	2nd Class.	3rd Class.	4th Class.	5th Class.	6th Class.
Number of each Rank and Class -	-	2	1	1	1	-	16	3	1	1	7	3	1	-
Rates of Pay of each ditto - -	-	s. 38	s. 37	s. 36	s. 35	-	s. 32	s. 31	s. 30	s. 29	s. 28	s. 26	s. 25	-

Inspected on 27th March.

... The authorised establishment is once chief officer, two inspectors, five sergeants, and 32 constables.

The rate of pay of the inspectors at present serving in this force was increased, 3rd July 1901, from 42s. per week to 47s. per week, and to be further increased by 1s. per week each year to a maximum of 50s. No other alteration has been made in the scale of pay.

All the members of the force hold certificates from the St. John Ambulance Association.

Army Reserve, 29th September 1899–1901.—No members were called up.

The station here is very much out of date, there being no ventilation or artificial lighting to the cells, the windows opening on to the public thorough-fare, within reach of anyone. A new court house is required. There is some talk of building new municipal buildings, in which case an attempt may be made to postpone the building of a new police station until the whole can be considered together.

There has been an increase of one in the number of public-houses ; an increase also of one in the number of persons proceeded against for drunkenness, and two convictions more during the year.

The clothing and appointments were complete and serviceable.

The management, numbers, and discipline of the force have been efficiently maintained.

BOROUGH OF GRAVESEND.

Force - - - - - 40.

| . Area in acres - - - - - 1,256 | Acres to each constable '- - - 31 |
| Population in 1891 - - - 23,876 | Population to ditto, as per census 1891 597 |

RANKS.	Chief Officer.	Superintendents.						1 Inspector.				
		Deputy Chief Officer.	Chief Clerk.	1st Class.	2nd Class.	3rd Class.	4th Class.	1st Class.	2nd Class.	3rd Class.	4th Class.	5th Class.
Number of each Rank and Class -	1	-	-	-	-	-	-	1	-	-	-	..
Rates of Pay of each ditto -	£ 275	-	-	-	-	-	-	£ s. 114 8	-	-	-	:

Yearly Pay in £ and Shillings.

RANKS.	7 Sergeants.						31 Constables.						
	Merit Class.	1st Class.	2nd Class.	3rd Class.	4th Class.	5th Class.	Acting Sergeants.	Merit Class.	1st Class.	2nd Class.	3rd Class.	4th Class.	5th Class.	6th Class.
Number of each Rank and Class -	-	5	1	1	-	-	-	1	13	4	2	-	11	-
Rates of Pay of each ditto -	-	s. 36	s. 35	s. 32	-	-	-	s. d. 30 2	s. 31	s. 29	s. d. 28 3	-	s. d. 24 2	-

Weekly Pay in Shillings and Pence.

Inspected 22nd March.

The authorised establishment, which has been augmented during the year by four constables, is one chief officer, one inspector, seven sergeants, and 31 constables.

The scale of pay is unaltered.

Twenty-nine members hold certificates from the St. John Ambulance Association.

Extra Duties.—The chief officer is superintendent of the fire brigade, inspector of weights and measures, hackney carriages, common lodging-houses, and under the Contagious Diseases (Animals) and Explosives Acts, coroner's officer, and billet master, without remuneration. He is also assistant relieving officer; allowance, 10l. per annum.

Army Reserve, 29th September, 1899–1901.—One member was called up, who has rejoined the force, certified fit.

The number of licensed houses is the same as last year, but there is an increase of 37 in the number of persons proceeded against for drunkenness, and 33 in the number convicted.

The clothing and appointments were complete and serviceable, and the books and returns well kept.

The offices and cells were clean and in good order.

The management, numbers, and discipline of the force have been efficiently maintained.

BOROUGH OF MAIDSTONE.

Force - - - - - 43.

| Area in acres | - | - | - | - | 4,008 | Acres to each constable | - | - | - | 93 |
| Population in 1891 | | - | | - | 32,145 | Population to ditto, as per census 1891 | | | | 745 |

RANKS.	Yearly Pay in £ and Shillings.			Weekly Pay in Shillings and Pence.										
	Chief Officer.	2 Inspectors.		6 Sergeants.			34 Constables.							
		1st Class.	2nd Class.	1st Class.	2nd Class.	3rd Class.	1st Class.	2nd Class.	3rd Class.	4th Class.	5th Class.	6th Class.	7th Class.
Number of each Rank and Class - }	1	1	1	3	2	1	13	1	1	4	10	2	2
Rates of Pay of each ditto - " }	£ 240	£ 130	£ s. 98 16	s. 36	s. 34	s. 32	s. 30	s. 30	s. 29	s. 28	s. 26	s. 25	s. 24

Inspected 19th March.

Establishment.—One chief officer, two inspectors, six sergeants, and 34 constables.

The strength of the force is the same as last year.

The chief officer has an increase of pay, 10l. per annum.

Thirty-nine members hold certificates from the St. John Ambulance Association.

Extra Duties.—The chief officer, inspectors, and sergeants carry out the provisions of the Contagious Diseases (Animals) Act.

Army Reserve, 29th September 1899–1901.—Three members were called up, of whom one is still serving with the colours, one died of enteric fever, and one rejoined the force, but resigned, and joined the Isle of Wight Constabulary.

There has been no change in the number of licensed houses; but there is a decrease of 49 in the number of persons proceeded against for drunkenness, and 48 in the number convicted.

The clothing and appointments were complete and serviceable, and the books and returns well kept.

The offices and cells were clean and in good order.

The management, numbers, and discipline of the force have been efficiently maintained.

A revised scale of pay, as under, was adopted 7th November 1900 :—

RANK.	Per Annum.	Per Week.	REMARKS.
	£ s. d.	£ s. d.	
Chief Officer - - -	280 0 0	—	And allowances.
Chief Inspector - -	180 0 0	—	"
Inspector, 4th class - -	98 16 0	—	On appointment.
" 3rd " - -	104 0 0	—	After 2 years in rank.
" 2nd " -	109 4 0	—	" 4 "
" 1st " - -	117 0 0	—	" 6 "
Sergeants, 3rd ", -	—	1 12 0	On appointment.
" 2nd " - -	—	1 14 0	After 2 years in rank.
" 1st " -	—	1 16 0	" 4 "
Constables, 4th class - -	—	1 4 0	On appointment.
" 3rd " -	—	1 5 0	After 1 year's service.
" 2nd " - -	—	1 6 0	" 2 years' "
" 1st " -	—	1 7 0	" 3 " "
" " " - -	—	1 8 0	" 4 " "
" " " -	—	1 9 0	" 6 " "
" " " - -	—	1 10 0	" 8 " "
" " " -	—	1 11 0	" 10 " "

BOROUGH OF MARGATE.

Force - - - - - 38.

| Area in acres - - - - 759 | Acres to each constable - - - 20 |
| Population in 1891 - - 18,417 | Population to ditto, as per census 1891 482 |

Yearly Pay in £ and Shillings.

RANKS.	Chief Officer.	Superintendents.						2 Inspectors.				
		Deputy Chief Officer.	Chief Clerk.	1st Class.	2nd Class.	3rd Class.	4th Class.	1st Class.	2nd Class.	3rd Class.	4th Class.	5th Class.
Number of each Rank and Class	1	-	-	-	-	-	-	1	1	-	-	-
Rates of Pay of each ditto -	£ 190	-	-	-	-	-	-	£ 130	£ s. 119 12	-	-	-

Weekly Pay in Shillings and Pence.

RANKS.	6 Sergeants.						29 Constables.							
	Merit Class.	1st Class.	2nd Class.	3rd Class.	4th Class.	5th Class.	Acting Sergeants.	Merit Class.	1st Class.				2nd Class.	3rd Class.	4th Class.
Number of each Rank and Class -	-	4	2	-	-	-	1	1	5	3	4	4	3	3	3	2	-
Rates of Pay of each ditto -	-	s. d. 37 6	s. d. 34 10				s. d. 33 4	s. d. 33 2	s. d. 32 2	s. 31	s. d. 29 10	s. 28 8	s. d. 27 6	s. d. 26 4	s. d. 25 2	s. 24	-

Inspected 28th March.

The authorised establishment, which has been augmented during the year by three constables, is one chief officer, two inspectors, six sergeants and 29 constables (one of whom is acting-sergeant).

Thirty-six members hold certificates from the St. John Ambulance Association.

Extra Duties.—The chief officer is inspector of weights and measures, and under the Contagious Diseases (Animals) Act; allowance for these duties, 20l. per annum; assistant relieving officer, allowance 5l. 5s. per annum; Inspector of hackney carriages, common lodging-houses, and under the Shop Hours and Explosive Acts, without remuneration. One sergeant is assistant inspector of weights and measures, allowance 2s. 6d. per week.

There is an increase of one in the number of public-houses, five in beer-houses, and one in refreshment-houses, of three in the number of persons proceeded against for drunkenness, and five in the number convicted.

The clothing and appointments were complete and serviceable, and the books and returns well kept.

The offices and cells were clean and in good order.

The management, numbers, and discipline of the force have been efficiently maintained.

A new scale of pay, as under, was adopted 10th December 1900:—

Constables—

	£	s.	d.	
On appointment (3rd class) - -	1	4	0	weekly.
After 1 year's service (2nd class) on the recommendation of the chief constable -	1	5	2	„
After 2 years' service (1st class) 6th grade, on the recommendation of the chief constable - - - - -	1	6	4	..
After 4 years' service (1st class) 5th grade, on the recommendation of the chief constable - - - - -	1	7	6	..
After 6 years' service (1st class) 4th grade, on the recommendation of the chief constable - - - - -	1	8	8	..

Constables—continued.   £   .   d

    After 8 years' service (1st class) 3rd grade,
    on the recommendation of the chief
    constable -   -   -   -   -   -   1   9 10 weekly.

    After 10 years' service (1st class) 2nd
    grade, on the recommendation of the chief
    constable   -   -   -   -   -   -   1 11   0

    After 12 years' service (1st class) 1st
    grade, on the recommendation of the chief
    constable   -   -   -   -   -   -   1 12   2   ..

Sergeants—

    On promotion (4th class) on the recom-
    mendation of the chief constable   -   -   1 13 10   ..

    After 1 year's service (3rd class) on the
    recommendation of the chief constable -   1 14 10   ..

    After 4 years' service (2nd class) on the
    recommendation of the chief constable -   1 16   0   ..

    After 6 years' service (1st class) on the
    recommendation of the chief constable -   1 17   6   ..

Inspectors—

    On appointment -   -   -   -   -   2   2   0   ..
    After 2 years' service -   -   -   -   2   4   0   ..
    „ 4 „   „   -   -   :-   -   2   6   0   ..
    „ 6 „   „   -   -   -   -   2   8   0   ..
    „ 8 „   „   -   -   -   -   2 10   0   ..

BOROUGH OF RAMSGATE.

Force -   -   -   -   - 48.*

Area in acres - - - - 2,343	Acres to each constable - - - 48
Population in 1891 - - 24,733	Population to ditto, as per census 1891 515

			Yearly Pay in £ and Shillings.									
RANKS.	Chief Officer.	1 Superintendent.						Inspectors.				
		Deputy Chief Officer.	Chief Clerk.	1st Class.	2nd Class.	3rd Class.	4th Class.	1st Class.	2nd Class.	3rd Class.	4th Class.	5th Class.
Number of each Rank and Class -	1	-	1	-	-	-	-	-	-	-	-	-
Rates of Pay of each ditto -	£ 325	-	£ s. 101 4	-	-	-	-	-	-	-	-	-

				Weekly Pay in Shillings and Pence.					
RANKS.	7 Sergeants.						39 Constables.		
	Merit Class.	1st Class.	2nd Class.	3rd Class.	4th Class.	5th Class.	1st Class.	2nd Class.	3rd Class.
Number of each Rank and Class -	-	3	1	2	1	-	7 1 2 2 6 6 14	1	1
Rates of Pay of each ditto -	-	s. d. 37 6	s. 36	s. d. 34 10	s. 38	-	s. s. s. d. s. d. s. d. s. d. 32 31 29 10 28 8 27 6 26 4	s. 25 2	s. 24

Inspected on the 28th March.

    The authorised establishment of the force, which has been augmented by two constables during the year, is one chief officer, one chief clerk, seven sergeants, and 39 constables. There are also one sergeant and three constables not paid by rates.

The scale of pay is unaltered, except that the chief officer receives an increase of 25l. per annum.

All the members of the force hold certificates from the St. John Ambulance Association.

Five members of the force belonging to the Army Reserve were called up 29th September 1899-1901, who have rejoined the force, certified fit for duty.

Extra Duties.—The chief officer is assistant relieving officer ; allowance, 5l. 5s. per annum. He is also billet master, inspector of smoke nuisances, and under the Petroleum Act, and, with the seven sergeants, carries out the provisions of the Contagious Diseases (Animals) Act.

There is no change in the number of licensed houses.

Nine more persons were proceeded against for drunkenness, and 15 more convicted during the year.

The clothing and appointments were complete and serviceable, and the books and returns well kept.

The police offices and cells were clean and in good order.

The management, numbers, and discipline of the force have been efficiently maintained.

CITY OF ROCHESTER.

Force   -   -   -   - 42.

| Area in acres - - - - | 2,909 | Acres to each constable - - - | 69 |
| Population in 1891 - | 26,290 | Population to ditto, as per census 1891 | 626 |

RANKS.	Chief Officer.	Superintendents.						2 Inspectors.				
		Deputy Chief Officer.	Chief Clerk.	1st Class.	2nd Class.	3rd Class.	4th Class.	1st Class.	2nd Class.	3rd Class.	4th Class.	5th Class.
Number of each Rank and Class -	1	-	-	-	-	-	-	2	-	-	-	-
Rates of Pay of each ditto - -	£ 185	-	-	-	-	-	-	£ s. 109 4	-	-	-	-

RANKS.	5 Sergeants.						34 Constables.							
	Merit Class.	1st Class.	2nd Class.	3rd Class.	4th Class.	5th Class.	Acting Sergeants.	Merit Class.	1st Class.	2nd Class.	3rd Class.	4th Class.	5th Class.	6th Class.
Number of each Rank and Class -	-	8	2	1	-	-	-	10	5	3	9	2	4	-
Rates of Pay of each ditto - -	-	s. 34	s. 34	s. 33	-	-	-	s. 31	s. 30	s. 29	s. 28	s. 26	s. 24	-

Inspected 23rd March and also on 12th September.

Establishment.—One chief officer, two inspectors, five sergeants, and 34 constables. The strength of the force has been augmented by two constables during the year, which now shows an increase of one sergeant and one constable.

Twenty-eight members (an increase of six for the year) hold certificates from the St. John Ambulance Association.

Extra Duties.—The chief officer is inspector of common lodging-houses, allowance 5l. per annum ; of food and drugs, allowance 5l. per annum ; of fire hose, allowance 5l. per annum ; and under the Contagious Diseases (Animals), Shop Hours, and Hackney Carriages Acts, without remuneration.

In future 10 per cent. of this force will be reserved for the employment of ex-soldiers who possess the necessary qualifications.

Licensing Acts.—There are two fewer refreshment houses than last year. Five more persons were proceeded against for drunkenness, but 51 fewer convicted.

The clothing and appointments were complete and serviceable, and the books and returns well kept.

The offices and cells were clean and in good order.

The management, numbers, and discipline of the force have been efficiently maintained.

A new scale of pay, as under, was adopted 25th March 1901 :—

	£	s.	d.	
Constables—				
On appointment	1	4	0	weekly.
After 18 months	1	6	0	„
„ 3 years	1	8	0	..
.. 6 „	1	9	0	..
:: 8 ::	1	10	0	..
„ 10 „ (merit class)	1	11	0	..
Sergeants—				
On appointment	1	12	0	..
After 2 years	1	13	0	..
„ 3 „	1	14	0	..
.. 4 ..	1	15	0	..
:: 5 ..	1	16	0	..
Inspectors—				
On appointment	2	0	0	..
After 2 years	2	2	0	..
„ 4 „	2	4	0	..

BOROUGH OF TUNBRIDGE WELLS.

Force - - - - - - - - - 56.

Area in acres - - - - 3,399 | Acres to each constable - - - 60
Population in 1891 - - 27,895 | Population to ditto, as per census 1891 498

RANKS.	Chief Officer.	Superintendents.						2 Inspectors.				
		Deputy Chief Officer.	Chief Clerk.	1st Class.	2nd Class.	3rd Class.	4th Class.	1st Class.	2nd Class.	3rd Class.	4th Class.	5th Class.
Number of each Rank and Class -	1	-	-	-	-	-	-	2	-	-	-	-
Rates of Pay of each ditto -	£ 350	-	-	-	-	-	-	£ 134	-	-	-	-

Yearly Pay in £ and Shillings.

RANKS.	4 Sergeants.						49 Constables.								
	Merit Class.	1st Class.	2nd Class.	3rd Class.	4th Class.	5th Class.	Merit Class.	1st Class.	2nd Class.	3rd Class.	4th Class.	5th Class.	6th Class.	7th Class.	Vacancies.
Number of each Rank and Class -	-	3	1	-	-	-	2	1	6	8	15	1	7	2	6
Rates of Pay of each ditto -	-	s. 36	s. 37	-	-	-	s. d. 33 3	s. d. 33 3	s. 33	s. 31	s. 30	s. 28	s. 26	s. 24	-

Weekly Pay in Shillings and Pence.

constables, is one chief officer, two inspectors, four sergeants, and 49 constables. There are vacancies for six constables.

The scale of pay is unaltered, except that the chief officer has an increase of 50*l.* per annum.

Thirty-eight members hold certificates from the St. John Ambulance Association.

Extra Duties.—The chief officer is inspector of hackney carriages and under the Contagious Diseases (Animals) Act, coroner's officer and billet master without remuneration.

Army Reserve, 29th September 1899–1901.—Seven members were called up, of whom five are still serving with the colours, and two have rejoined certified fit.

There is an increase of two in the number of public-houses, and two in beerhouses. Eleven more persons were proceeded against for drunkenness, and 12 more convicted.

The clothing and appointments were complete and serviceable ; the books and returns well kept, and the offices and cells clean and in good order.

The management, numbers, and discipline of the force have been efficiently maintained.

COUNTY OF MONMOUTH.

Force - - - - - 180.*

Area in acres † - - - 344,649	Acres to each constable - - - 1,914
Population in 1891 † - - - 203,426	Population to ditto, as per census 1891 1,130

	Yearly Pay in £ and Shillings.										
RANKS.	Chief Constable	6 Superintendents.					5 Inspectors.				
		Deputy Chief Constable and Chief Clerk.	1st Class.	2nd Class.	3rd Class.	4th Class.	1st Class.	2nd Class.	3rd Class.	4th Class.	5th Class.
Number of each Rank and Class -	1	1	4	1	-	-	2	1	1	1	-
Rates of Pay of each ditto -	£ 480	£ 260	£ 240	£ 200	-	-	£ s. 127 15	£ s. 118 12	£ s. 115 11	s. 19	-

	Weekly Pay in Shillings and Pence.														
RANKS.	24 Sergeants.						144 Constables.								
	Merit Class.	1st Class.	2nd Class.	3rd Class.	4th Class.	5th Class.	1st Class.	2nd Class.	3rd Class.	4th Class.	5th Class.	6th Class.	7th Class.	8th Class.	Vacancies.
Number of each Rank and Class -	-	4	12	4	1	3	5	1	42	18	18	19	20	15	12
Rates of Pay of each ditto -	-	s. d. 37 4	s. d. 36 3	s. 35	s. d. 33 10	s. d. 33 3	s. d. 31 6	s. d. 30 11	s. d. 30 4	s. d. 29 9	s. d. 29 2	s. 28	s. d. 26 3	s. d. 25 1	-

* Exclusive of three sergeants and 15 constables appointed under 3 & 4 Vict. c. 88. s. 19.
† Fwddog Hamlet (area acreage, 2,101, population, 79) was transferred from the county of Hereford, 29th September 1891.

Inspected in June.

Establishment.—One chief constable, six superintendents (one of whom acts as deputy chief constable and chief clerk), five inspectors, 24 sergeants, and 144 constables. There are also three sergeants and 15 constables appointed under 3 & 4 Vict. c. 88. s. 19. There are vacancies for 12 constables, of which number eight are reservists still serving with the colours in South Africa.

No. 3.
South of England
and South Wales
District.

There is no change in the strength of the force, but one sergeant has been substituted for a constable.

Thirty members hold certificates from the St. John Ambulance Association.

Extra Duties:—

NATURE OF DUTY.	Chief Constable.	Super-intendents.	Inspectors.	Sergeants.	Constables.	REMUNERATION.
Inspectors under the Contagious Diseases (Animals) Act.	1	5	5	10	—	Chief constable, 10l. per annum. Chief clerk, 20l. per annum. Blue returns, 1s. each. Red returns, 2d. each for other officers.
Inspectors under the Explosives Act.	—	5	1	—	—	Three superintendents receive 10l. each, one 6l., and one 5l. per annum; inspector, 6l. per annum.
Assistant Relieving Officers.	—	—	1	1	—	Inspector, 10l.; sergeant, 6l. per annum.
Inspection of Common Lodging-houses.	—	1	—	—	—	6l. per annum.

Army Reserve, 29th September 1899–1901.—Ten members were called up two of whom rejoined the force and eight are still serving with the colours.

There is an increase of one in the number of public-houses, but a decrease of three in beerhouses and two in refreshment-houses. An increase of 53 in the number of persons proceeded against for drunkenness, and 73 in the number convicted.

The clothing and appointments were complete and serviceable, and the books and returns well kept.

The stations and cells visited were clean and in good order.

New constabulary stations are in progress of building at Aberdillery (with Petty Sessional Court House), Castleton, and Newbridge.

The management, numbers, and discipline of the force have been efficiently maintained.

A revised scale of pay, as under, was adopted 17th April 1901:—

RANK.	Period of Service.	Daily.	Weekly.	Annually.
		£ s. d.	£ s. d.	£ s. d.
Deputy Chief Constable	- - -	0 1 1	0 7 7	20 0 0
Superintendents - -	On appointment -	0 8 9	3 1 4	160 0 0
	After 1 year -	0 9 7	3 7 1	175 0 0
	„ 2 years - -	0 11 0	3 16 9	200 0 0
	„ 8 „ - -	0 11 6	4 0 7	210 0 0
	„ 4 „ - -	0 12 1	4 4 5	220 0 0
	„ 5 „ -	0 13 2	4 12 1	240 0 0
Inspectors - - -	On appointment -	0 5 9	2 0 3	104 18 9
	After 2 years - -	0 6 4	2 4 4	115 11 8
	„ 5 „ -	0 6 10	2 7 10	124 14 2
Sergeants - -	On appointment -	0 4 8	1 12 8	85 3 4
	After 2 years - -	0 5 0	1 15 0	91 5 0
	„ 5 „ -	0 5 2	1 16 2	94 5 10
Constables - -	3rd Class on appointment -	0 3 7	1 5 1	65 7 11
	2nd „ after 1 year's service	0 3 9	1 6 3	68 8 9
	1st „ „ 2 years' „	0 4 0	1 8 0	73 0 0
	After 4 years' service - „	0 4 2	1 9 2	76 0 10
	„ 7 „ „ -	0 4 3	1 9 9	77 11 3
	„ 10 „ „ -	0 4 4	1 10 4	79 1 8
Merit pay - -	Inspectors, Sergeants, and Constables.	0 0 2	0 1 2	3 0 10

BOROUGH OF NEWPORT (MON.).

Force - - - - - 91.

Area in acres - - - - 4,463 | Acres to each constable - - 49
Population in 1891 - - 54,707 | Population to ditto, as per census 1891 601

RANKS.	Chief Officer	1 Superintendent.						2 Inspectors.				
		Deputy Chief Officer.	Chief Clerk.	1st Class.	2nd Class.	3rd Class.	4th Class.	1st Class.	2nd Class.	3rd Class.	4th Class.	5th Class.
Number of each Rank and Class	1	-	-	1	-	-	-	1	1	-	-	-
Rates of Pay of each ditto	£ 400	-	-	£ 180	-	-	-	£ s. 135 4	£ s. 114 8	-	-	-

Yearly Pay in £ and Shillings.

RANKS.	12 Sergeants.						73 Constables.							
	Merit Class.	1st Class.	2nd Class.	3rd Class.	4th Class.	5th Class.	Merit Class.	1st Class.	2nd Class.	3rd Class.	4th Class.	5th Class.	6th Class.	7th Class.
Number of each Rank and Class	-	3	1	2	2	3	16	9	15	9	6	7	8	5
Rates of Pay of each ditto	-	s. 40	s. 39	s. 38	s. 37	s. 36	s. d. 33 6	s. 32	s. 31	s. 30	s. 29	s. 28	s. 27	s. 26

Weekly Pay in Shillings and Pence.

Inspected on 25th June.

The establishment is one chief officer, one superintendent, two inspectors, 12 sergeants, and 75 constables. The chief inspector was in April last promoted to superintendent; and two constables to be sergeants.

The pay of the chief officer has been increased from 375l. to 400l. per annum.

- Seventy-nine members of the force hold certificates from the St. John Ambulance Association.

Army Reserve, 29th September 1899-1901.—Three members were called up; one is still serving with the colours, and two have rejoined certified fit.

Extra Duties.—The chief officer and one inspector are inspectors of hackney carriages, the inspector receiving 5l. per annum. The chief officer and inspectors carry out the provisions of the Explosives and Petroleum Acts without remuneration, and one sergeant is assistant relieving officer, allowance, 8l. per annum.

There is an increase of one in the number of public-houses, and a decrease of one in beerhouses during the year; and 42 fewer persons were proceeded against for drunkenness, and 53 fewer convicted.

The clothing and appointments were complete and serviceable; the offices and cells clean and in good order, and the books and returns well kept.

The management, numbers, and discipline of the force have been efficiently maintained.

A new scale of pay, as under, was adopted on 9th April 1901 :—

Inspectors—	£	s.	d.	
On appointment - -	2	4	0	per week.
After 1 year - - -	2	6	0	,,
,, 2 years - - -	2	8	0	,,
,, 3 ,, - -	2	10	0	,,
,, 6 ,, - - -	2	12	0	,,

No. 3.
South of England
and South Wales
District.

Sergeants—

	£	s.	d.	
On appointment	-	1	16	0 per week.
After 1 year	-	1	17	0 ,,
,, 2 years	-	1	18	0 ,,
,, 3 ,,	-	1	19	0 ..
,, 4 ..	-	2	0	0 ..

Constables—

	£	s.	d.	
On appointment	-	1	6	0 ..
After 1 year	-	1	7	0 ..
,, 2 years	-	1	8	0 ..
,, 3 ,,	-	1	9	0 ..
,, 4 ..	-	1	10	0 ..
,, 7 ,,	-	1	11	0 ..
,, 10 ,,	-	1	12	0 ..
Merit class	-	1	13	6 ..

COUNTY OF SOMERSET.

Force - - - - 344.

| Area in acres * | - | - | - | 1,035,404 | Acres to each constable | - | - | 3,009 |
| Population in 1891 * | - | - | 372,612 | Population to ditto, as per census 1891 | 1,083 |

RANKS.	Chief Constable	Yearly Pay in £ and Shillings.										
		16 Superintendents.						Inspectors.				
		Deputy Chief Constable	Chief Clerk.	1st Class.	2nd Class.	3rd Class.	4th Class.	1st Class.	2nd Class.	3rd Class.	4th Class.	5th Class.
Number of each Rank and Class	1	1	1	2	4	4	4	-	-	-	-	-
Rates of Pay of each ditto	£ 500	£ 300	£ 168	£ 180	£ 145	£ 135	£ 135	-	-	-	-	-

RANKS.	Weekly Pay in Shillings and Pence.												
	59 Sergeants.						268 Constables.						Vacancies in all Ranks.
	1st Class.			2nd Class.	3rd Class.	4th Class.	5th Class	Merit Class.	1st Class.			2nd Class.	3rd Class.	
Number of each Rank and Class	16	1	2	14	3	6	15	24	59	56	48	39	29	26	2
Rates of Pay of each ditto	s. d. 32 3	s. d. 32 1	s. d. 30 11	s. d. 32 1	s. d. 30 11	s. d. 29 9	s. d. 28 7	s. d. 28	s. d. 26 10	s. d. 25 8	s. d. 24 6	s. d. 23 4	s. d. 22 2	s. 21	-

* The parishes of Goathill (acreage 298, population 54), Poinтington (acreage 1,020, population 125), Sandford Orcas (acreage 1,104, population 223), Seaborough (acreage 585, population 71), and Trent (acreage 1,818, population 419), have been transferred (31st March 1896) to Dorset. The parishes of Gasper with Stourton (acreage 1,298, population 173), Maiden Bradley with Yarnfield (acreage 1,881, population 51), and Kilmington (acreage 2,876, population 369), are transferred to Wilts. The parish of Wambrook (acreage 1,947, population 221) is transferred (1st April 1896) from Dorset, and the parish of Church Staunton (acreage 5,436, population 672) is transferred (29th September 1896) from Devon. Part of the parish of Wembdon (acreage 121, population 994), and part of the parish of Bridgwater (acreage 57, population 233), was transferred to Bridgwater, 9th November 1896.

Inspected in May.

The authorised establishment, which was augmented during the year by one sergeant and four constables, is one chief constable, 16 superintendents, 60 sergeants, and 267 constables. One superintendent acts as deputy chief constable, and one as chief clerk. There are two vacancies in all ranks.

Two hundred members hold certificates from the St. John Ambulance Association.

Extra Duties :—

NATURE OF DUTY.	Chief Constable.	Super-intendents.	Inspectors.	Sergeants.	Constables.	REMUNERATION.
Inspectors under the Contagious Diseases (Animals) Act.	1	16	—	—	—	Superintendents paid according to work done, but not to exceed 20l. per annum each.
Assistant Relieving Officers.	—	8	—	8	—	1 superintendent, 15l.; 4 ditto, 10l.; 1 ditto, 5l.; 1 ditto, 3l.; and 1 ditto, 1l. per annum. 2 sergeants, 10l.; 1 ditto, 8l.; 1 ditto, 7l. 10s.; 1 ditto, 5l.; 1 ditto, 8l.; 1 ditto, 2l. 2s.; and 1 ditto, 1l. per annum.
Inspectors under the Petroleum and Explosives Acts.	—	16	—	—	—	8l. paid to 1 superintendent.
Inspectors of Common Lodging-houses.	—	2	—	—	—	1 superintendent, 10l.; 1 ditto, 5l.

The borough of Taunton is policed by the county constabulary.

Army Reserve, 29th September 1899–1901.—Fifteen members were called up, of whom 12 are still serving with the colours, and three have rejoined the force certified fit.

There is an increase of one in the number of public-houses, but a decrease of seven in beerhouses, and an increase of two in refreshment-houses. Nineteen fewer persons were proceeded against for drunkenness, and 15 fewer convicted.

The clothing and appointments were complete and serviceable, and the books and returns well kept.

The stations visited and cells were clean and in good order.

The management, numbers, and discipline of the force have been efficiently maintained.

A revised scale of pay, as under, was adopted 26th May 1901 :—

Limit to Ranks and Classes.	Ranks, Classes, and Grades.	Weekly Pay.	Monthly Pay.	Yearly Pay.
		£ s. d.	£ s. d.	£ s. d.
1	Chief Constable - - -	—	41 13 4	500 0 0
1	Deputy Chief Constable - -	—	21 13 4	260 0 0
	First-class Superintendents over 18 years in rank.	—	15 0 0	180 0 0
4	First-class Superintendents over 12 years in rank.	—	13 15 0	165 0 0
	First-class Superintendents under 12 years in rank.	—	12 18 4	155 0 0
	Second-class Superintendents over 12 years in rank.	—	12 1 8	145 0 0
12	Second-class Superintendents over 6 years in rank.	—	11 5 0	135 0 0
	Second-class Superintendents under 6 years in rank.	—	10 8 4	125 0 0
	Sergeants over 8 years in rank - -	1 12 1	6 19 0	83 8 4
40	„ „ 6 „ „ -	1 10.11	6 13 11	80 7 8
	„ „ 3 „ „ -	1 9 9	6 8 11	77 7 0
	„ under 3 „ „ -	1 8 7	6 3 10	74 6 4
20	First-class Sergeants :— A First-class Sergeant will receive 2d. per day in addition to the rate of pay to which he may be entitled by service as Sergeant.			
	First-class Constables over 8 years in Class	1 6 10	5 16 3	69 15 4
	„ „ „ 5 „ „	1 5 8	5 11 2	66 14 8
	„ „ „ 2 „ „	1 4 6	5 6 2	63 14 0
	„ „ under 2 „ „	1 3 4	5 1 1	60 13 4
266	Merit-class Constables (50) :— A Merit-class Constable will receive 2d. per day in addition to the rate of pay to which he may be entitled as Constable.			
	Second class Constables - -	1 2 2	4 16 0	57 12 8
	Third-class Constables - - -	1 1 0	4 11 0	54 12 0
344	Authorised strength.			

CITY AND COUNTY BOROUGH OF BATH.

Force - - - - - - - - 85.

Area in acres	-	-	-	-	3,382	Acres to each constable	-	-	39
Population in 1891	-	-	-	51,844		Population to ditto, as per census 1891			609

Yearly Pay in £ and Shillings.

RANKS.	Chief Officer.	Superintendents.						5 Inspectors.				
		Deputy Chief Officer.	Chief Clerk.	1st Class.	2nd Class.	3rd Class.	4th Class.	1st Class.	2nd Class.	3rd Class.	4th Class.	5th Class.
Number of each Rank and Class -	1	-	-	-	-	-	-	1	1	-	3	-
Rates of Pay of each ditto -	£ 350	-	-	-	-	-	-	£ s. 114 8	£ s. 109 4	-	£ s. 100 2	-

Weekly Pay in Shillings and Pence.

RANKS.	12 Sergeants.						67 Constables.							
	Merit Class.	1st Class.	2nd Class.	3rd Class.	4th Class.	5th Class.	Detectives.	1st Class.	2nd Class.	3rd Class.	4th Class.	5th Class.	6th Class.	On probation.
Number of each Rank and Class -	-	4	8	-	5	-	2	29	10	5	2	3	12	2
Rates of Pay of each ditto -	-	s. d. 34 6	s. 33	-	s. 31	-	s. 31	s. 29	s. 28	s. 27	s. 26	s. 23	s. 24	s. 22

Inspected 10th May.

The authorised establishment, which has been reduced by one sergeant, is one chief officer, five inspectors, 12 sergeants, and 67 constables (of whom two are detectives).

The chief officer receives an increase of 50l. per annum.

Thirty-nine members hold certificates from the St. John Ambulance Association.

Extra Duties.—Four inspectors are assistant relieving officers, receiving 21l. per annum divided between them ; one inspector is inspector under the Reformatory and Industrial Schools Act, receiving 10 per cent. on all money collected by him ; one inspector is coroner's summoning officer, allowance 5s. for each inquest held.

Army Reserve, 29th September 1899–1901.—Three members were called up, who have rejoined the force, certified fit for duty.

Licensing Acts.—There is an increase of one in the number of public-houses.

The same number of persons as last year were proceeded against for drunkenness, and eight more were convicted.

The clothing and appointments were complete and serviceable, and the books and returns well kept.

The offices and cells were clean and in good order.

The management, numbers, and discipline of the force have been efficiently maintained.

A revised scale of pay, as under, was adopted 1st April 1901 :—

No. 3.
South of England
and South Wales
District.

Inspectors—

	£	s.	d.	
On appointment	1	18	6	weekly.
After 2 years	2	0	0	,,
,, 5 ,,	2	2	0	::
,, 8 ..	2	4	0	..

Sergeants—

	£	s.	d.	
On appointment	1	11	0	..
After 2 years	1	12	0	,,
,, 5 ,,	1	13	0	..
,, 8 ,,	1	14	6	::

1s. a week merit, detectives same scale as sergeants.

Constables—

	£	s.	d.	
On appointment	1	3	0	::
After 6 months	1	4	0	..
,, 2 years	1	5	0	..
.. 4 ,,	1	6	0	::
6 ,,	1	7	0	,,
,, 8 ,,	1	8	0	::
,, 10 ,,	1	9	0	..

1s. a week merit, for long service or meritorious conduct.

EXTRAS.

	s.	d.	
One constable as drill instructor	1	0	weekly.
,, ,, ,, assistant clerk	2	6	,,
,, ,, ,, plain clothes	2	6	,,

BOROUGH OF BRIDGWATER.

Force - - - - - 15.

Area in acres - - - 925	Acres to each constable - - - 61
Population in 1891 - - 13,663	Population to ditto, as per census 1891 911

Yearly Pay in £ and Shillings.

RANKS.	Chief Officer.	Superintendents.						Inspectors.				
		Deputy Chief Officer.	Chief Clerk.	1st Class.	2nd Class.	3rd Class.	4th Class.	1st Class.	2nd Class.	3rd Class.	4th Class.	5th Class.
Number of each Rank and Class -	1	-	-	-	-	-	-	-	-	-	-	-
Rates of Pay of each ditto -	£ 175	-	-	-	-	-	-	-	-	-	-	-

Weekly Pay in Shillings and Pence.

RANKS.	2 Sergeants.						12 Constables.							
	1st Class.	2nd Class.	3rd Class.	4th Class.	5th Class.	6th Class.	Acting Sergeants.	Merit Class.	1st Class.	2nd Class.	3rd Class.	4th Class.	5th Class.	6th Class.
Number of each Rank and Class -	1	1	-	-	-	-	-	-	4	-	4	1	2	1
Rates of Pay of each ditto -	s. d. 33 3	s. d. 31 6	-	-	-	-	-	-	s. d. 27 6	s. d. 26 10	s. 25	s. d. 24 6	s. d. 23 4	s. d. 22 2

Inspected on 13th May.

Establishment.—One chief officer, two sergeants, and 12 constables.

Nine members hold certificates from the St. John Ambulance Association.

Army Reserve, 29th September 1899–1901.—One member was called up to join his regiment, but has rejoined the police force, certified fit for duty.

Extra Duties.—The chief officer is assistant relieving officer, receiving 5*l.* per annum. He is also billet master, inspector of markets, hackney carriages, common lodging-houses, and under the Contagious Diseases (Animals) Act, and coroner's officer, without remuneration.

Licensing Acts.—No change in public and beerhouses, increase of one in refreshment.

Drunkenness.—Three more persons proceeded against during the year, and five fewer convicted.

The clothing and appointments were complete and serviceable, and the books and returns well kept.

The offices and cells were clean and in good order.

The management, numbers, and discipline of the force have been efficiently maintained.

A new scale, as under, was adopted 20th June 1901 :—

Constables are engaged on probation for a period not exceeding 12 months, and then, if their conduct and general ability are satisfactory, they may be appointed with the previous service added.

Constables—

	£	s.	d.	
On probation, not exceeding 12 months	1	1	0	per week.
6th class, on appointment	1	2	2	,,
5th ,, after one year in 6th class	1	3	4	,,
4th ,, ,, ,, ,, 5th ,,	1	4	6	,,
3rd ,, ,, ,, ,, 4th ,,	1	5	8	,,
2nd ,, ,, two years in 3rd ,,	1	6	10	,,
1st ,, ,, ,, ,, 2nd ,,	1	7	6	,,

Sergeants—

	£	s.	d.	
4th class, on appointment	1	9	9	,,
3rd ,, after two years in 4th class	1	11	6	,,
2nd ,, ,, ,, ,, 3rd ,,	1	13	3	,,
1st ,, ,, ,, ,, 2nd ,,	1	15	0	,,

Merit class, with badge and 1*s.* per week, open to all sergeants and constables after 15 years' meritorious service.

Uniform and 2*s.* 6*d.* per calendar month for boots.

All advances in class with increase of pay are made on the recommendation of the chief constable, but no constable will be advanced in class by length of service, unless his conduct has been satisfactory since the last advance.

By special recommendation for meritorious service, a sergeant or constable may be advanced in class at any time.

COUNTY OF SURREY.

Force - - - 270.*

Area in acres † - - - - 375,152 | Acres to each constable - - 1,389
Population in 1891 † - - 189,089 | Population to ditto, as per census 1891 700

RANKS.	Chief Constable.	Yearly Pay in £ and Shillings.										
		7 Superintendents.						8 Inspectors.				
		Deputy Chief Constable.	Chief Clerk.	1st Class.	2nd Class.	3rd Class.	4th Class.	Chief Clerk.	1st Class.	2nd Class.	3rd Class.	4th Class.
Number of each Rank and Class - }	1	1	-	1	1	2	2	1	2	4	-	-
Rates of Pay of each ditto - }	£ 600	£ s. 344 14	-	£ 200	£ s. 180 13	£ 175	£ s. 160 12	£ s. 175 8	£ 117	£ s. 110 8	-	-

RANKS.	Weekly Pay in Shillings and Pence.											
	26 Sergeants.						228 Constables.					
	Merit Class.	1st Class.	2nd Class.	3rd Class.	4th Class.	5th Class.	Acting Sergeants.	1st Class.			2nd Class.	3rd Class.	Vacancies.
Number of each Rank and Class - }	-	11	2	6	7	-	-	45	13	41	27	49	31	26
Rates of Pay of each ditto - }	-	s. d. 33 3	s. d. 32 1	s. d. 30 11	s. d. 29 9	-	-	s. d. 29 3	s. 28	s. d. 26 10	s. d. 25 8	s. d. 24 1	s. d. 22 9	-

* Exclusive of seven constables appointed under 3 & 4 Vict. c. 8d. s. 19.
† The parish of Dockinfield (acreage, 878 ; population, 269) was transferred (30th September 1898) from the county of Hants.

Inspected in April.

The authorised establishment, which has been augmented during the year by four sergeants and 35 constables, is one chief constable, seven superintendents (one of whom acts as deputy chief constable), eight inspectors (one of whom acts as chief clerk), 26 sergeants, 228 constables, and seven constables appointed under 3 & 4 Vict. c. 88. s. 19. There are vacancies for 26 constables. The scale of pay is unaltered.

Ninety-nine members hold certificates from the St. John Ambulance Association.

Army Reserve, 29th September 1899–1901.—Two members were called up, who are still serving with the colours.

Extra Duties.—Seven superintendents, eight inspectors, and 22 sergeants carry out the provisions of the Contagious Diseases (Animals) Act, receiving an allowance of 2d. per mile each way for travelling expenses.

During the year there has been an increase of 32 in the number of public-houses, three in beerhouses, and 24 in refreshment houses.

Forty-one more persons were proceeded against for drunkenness, and 62 more convicted.

The clothing and appointments were complete, and the books and returns well kept.

The outlying stations and cells visited were clean and in good order.

The new station at Horley is complete.

New stations are required at Ripley, Cobham, and Chobham.

The management, numbers, and discipline of the force have been efficiently maintained.

A A

BOROUGH OF GUILDFORD.

Force - - - - 19.

| Area in acres | - | - | - | - | 604 | Acres to each constable | - | - | - | 32 |
| Population in 1891 | | - | | - | 14,316 | Population to ditto, as per census 1891 | | | | 754 |

RANKS.	Yearly Pay in £ and Shillings.	Weekly Pay in Shillings and Pence.										
	Chief Officer.	4 Sergeants.			14 Constables.							
		1st Class.	2nd Class.	3rd Class.	Merit Class.	1st Class.	2nd Class.	3rd Class.	4th Class.	5th Class.	6th Class.
Number of each Rank and Class -	1	1	1	2	2	1	2	1	2	5	1
Rates of Pay of each ditto - -	£ 280	s. 40	s. d. 37 6	s. 35	s. 33	s. d. 30 6	s. 30	s. 29	s. 28	s. 25	s. 22

`Inspected 1st April.

Establishment.—One chief officer, four sergeants, and 14 constables.

The strength of the force and the scale of pay are unaltered, except that sergeants after 10 years' service in that rank are to receive pay at the rate of 40s. per week. This revision to take effect from 22nd July 1901.

Twelve members hold certificates from the St. John Ambulance Association.

Extra Duties.—The chief officer is inspector of weights and measures, allowance 30l. per annum ; also of hackney carriages, common lodging-houses, and under the Food and Drugs, Petroleum, and Explosive Acts, without remuneration.

Army Reserve, 29th September 1899–1901.—Two members were called up, of whom one was killed in action at Rensburg (4th January 1900), and one rejoined the force, but he has since resigned and joined the Matabeleland Constabulary.

There is a decrease of one in the number of public-houses ; but an increase of 14 in the number of persons proceeded against for drunkenness, and 10 in the number convicted.

The clothing and appointments were complete and serviceable, the offices and cells clean and in good order, and the books and returns well kept.

The management, numbers, and discipline of the force have been efficiently maintained.

BOROUGH OF REIGATE.

Force - - - 33.

| Area in acres | - | - | - | - | 5,994 | Acres to each constable | - | - | - | 181 |
| Population in 1891 | | - | | - | 22,646 | Population to ditto, as per census 1891 | | | | 686 |

RANKS.	Yearly Pay in £ and Shillings.												
	Chief Officer.	Superintendents.						2 Inspectors.				
		Deputy Chief Officer.	Chief Clerk.	1st Class.	2nd Class.	3rd Class.	4th Class.	1st Class.	2nd Class.	3rd Class.	4th Class.	5th Class.
Number of each Rank and Class -	1	-	-	-	-	-	-	1	1	-	-	-
Rates of Pay of each ditto - -	£ 325	-	-	-	-	-	-	£ s. 119 18	£ s. 114 14	-	-	-

RANKS.	Weekly Pay in Shillings and Pence.												
	4 Sergeants.						25 Constables.						
	1st Class.	2nd Class.	3rd Class.	4th Class.	5th Class.	6th Class.	Acting Sergeants.	Merit Class.	1st Class.	2nd Class.	3rd Class.	4th Class.	5th Class.	6th Class.
Number of each Rank and Class -	1	1	2	-	-	-	-	-	11	1	2	9	2	-
Rates of Pay of each ditto - -	s. 40	s. 38	s. 36	-	-	-	-	-	s. 32	s. 31	s. 30	s. 28	s. 27	-

Inspected 3rd April.

Establishment. — One chief officer, two inspectors, four sergeants, and 26 constables, the strength of the force being the same as last year.

Thirty members hold certificates from the St. John Ambulance Association.

Extra Duties.—The chief officer is assistant relieving officer, allowance 20l. per annum ; also inspector of weights and measures, common lodging-houses, hackney carriages, and under the Contagious Diseases (Animals), Petroleum, Explosives, Shop Hours, and Public Health Acts, without remuneration.

There is no change in the number of public-houses and beerhouses during the year, but an increase of two in the number of refreshment rooms.

The number of persons proceeded against for drunkenness was 33 less than last year, and 25 less convicted.

The clothing and appointments were complete and serviceable, and the books and returns well kept.

The offices and cells were clean and in good order.

The management, numbers, and discipline of the force have been efficiently maintained.

A revised scale of pay, as under, was adopted 26th August 1901 :—

	Weekly.			Annual.		
	£	s.	d.	£	s.	d.
Inspectors—						
On appointment	2	2	0	109	10	0
After 2 years	2	4	0	114	14	4
,, 4 ,,	2	6	0	119	18	7
,, 6 ,,	2	8	0	125	2	11
,, 8 ..	2	10	0	130	7	2
Sergeants —						
On appointment	1	14	0	88	12	11
After 2 years	1	15	0	91	5	0
,, 4 ,,	1	16	0	93	17	2
,, 6 ,,	1	17	0	96	9	4
;, 8 ..	1	18	0	99	1	6
,, 9 ,,	1	19	0	101	13	7
,, 10	2	0	0	104	5	9
Constables—						
On appointment	1	5	0	65	3	7
After 1 year	1	7	0	70	7	11
,, 2 years	1	8	0	73	0	0
,, 4 ,,	1	9	0	75	12	2
,, 7 ..	1	10	0	78	4	4
,, 10	1	11	0	80	16	6
,, 13 ..	1	12	0	83	8	7

In exceptional cases of ability or meritorious service the Watch Committee may, on the recommendation of the chief constable, advance the pay of an inspector by 2s. or 4s., and that of a sergeant or constable by 1s. or 2s. per week, in addition to the above scale, with the decoration of the merit badge in the cases of sergeant and constable. Eightpence per week is allowed each man in lieu of boots and lamp oil provided. Detectives are allowed 3s. per week for plain clothes and uniform provided.

No. 3.
South of England
and South Wales
District.

COUNTY OF SUSSEX (EAST).

Force - - - - - - 192.

Area in acres* - - - - 513,508 | Acres to each constable - - - 2,674
Population in 1891* - - - 164,836 | Population to ditto, as per census 1891 858

RANKS.	Chief Constable.	9 Superintendents.						Inspectors.				
		Deputy Chief Constable.	Chief Clerk.	1st Class.	2nd Class.	3rd Class.	4th Class.	1st Class.	2nd Class.	3rd Class.	4th Class.	5th Class.
Number of each Rank and Class -	1	1	1	1	5	1	-	-	-	-	-	-
Rates of Pay of each ditto -	£ 480	£ 160	£ 150	£ 143	£ 135	£ 120	-	-	-	-	-	-

Weekly Pay in Shillings and Pence.

RANKS.	22 Sergeants.						160 Constables.			
	Merit Class.	1st Class.	2nd Class.	3rd Class.	4th Class.	5th Class.	1st Class.	2nd Class.	3rd Class.	Va-cancies.
Number of each Rank and Class -	-	4	7	8	3	-	34	17	30	21	15	21	21	11
Rates of Pay of each ditto -	-	s. d. 33 3	s. d. 32 1	s. d. 30 11	s. d. 29 9	-	s. 28	s. 27	s. 26	s. 25	s. d. 24 6	s. d. 23 6	s. d. 22 6	-

* The parish of Aldrington (acreage 761, population 2,235) is transferred (26th September 1893) to the town of Hove (Local Government Board Order, No. 30,228). A portion in Sussex, East) of the parish of Lamberhurst (acreage 1,937, population 1,158) is transferred to Kent for police purposes, by order of quarter sessions, dated October 1857. The liberty of the Sluice, in the parish of Bexhill (acreage 881, population 117), and Petit Iham, or liberty of St. Leonards, Winchelsea, in the parish of St. Leonards, Hastings, are non-corporate members of the Cinque Port of Hastings, not forming part of the county borough, but are under the exclusive jurisdiction of the borough police. An area (acreage 2,575, and population 10,849) was transferred (1st November 1897) to borough of Hastings.

Inspected in May.

The authorised establishment, which has been augmented during the year by three constables, is one chief constable, nine superintendents (one of whom acts as deputy chief constable, and one as chief clerk), 22 sergeants, and 160 constables.

There are vacancies for 11 constables.

Ninety-two members hold certificates from the St. John Ambulance Association.

Extra Duties.—The chief constable, eight superintendents, and 11 sergeants are inspectors under the Contagious Diseases (Animals) Act; remuneration: travelling actually incurred, when less than eight hours away from his regular duties, 1s. 6d., and from eight hours and upwards, 3s. 6d. The chief constable and superintendents are inspectors under the Explosives Act; superintendents receiving 5l. each per annum.

The borough of Lewes is policed by the county constabulary.

Army Reserve, 29th September 1899-1901.—Eight members were called up, of whom two are still serving with the colours, and six have rejoined the force, certified fit for duty.

There has been an increase of four in the number of public-houses, 121 in the number of beerhouses, and one in that of refreshment houses during the year; but a decrease of 38 in the number of persons proceeded against for drunkenness, and 38 in the number convicted.

The clothing and appointments were complete and serviceable, and the books and returns well kept.

The outlying stations and cells visited were clean and in good order.

A new station is to be built at Uckfield for superintendent, sergeant, and two constables; plans were at the Home Office at the time of my inspection. A second station is also being built at Bexhill, which seaside resort has much increased of late.

The management, numbers, and discipline of the force have been efficiently maintained.

COUNTY BOROUGH OF BRIGHTON.

No. 3.
South of England
and South Wales
District.

Force - - - - - - - 185.*

Area in acres - - - - 2,529	Acres to each constable - - - 13
Population in 1891 - - 115,873	Population to ditto, as per census 1891 626

RANKS.	Chief Officer.	4 Superintendents.						8 Inspectors.				
		Deputy Chief Officer.	Chief Clerk.	1st Class.	2nd Class.	3rd Class.	4th Class.	1st Class.	2nd Class.	Vacancy.	4th Class.	5th Class.
Yearly Pay in £ and Shillings.												
Number of each Rank and Class -	1	-	1	1	2	-	-	2	5	1	-	-
Rates of Pay of each ditto -	£ 400	-	£ 180	£ 165	£ 145	-	-	£ 130	£ 104	-	-	=

RANKS.	14 Sergeants.						158 Constables.							
	1st Class.	2nd Class.	3rd Class.	4th Class.	5th Class.	6th Class.	1st Class.				2nd Class.	3rd Class.	4th Class.	Vacancy.
Weekly Pay in Shillings and Pence.														
Number of each Rank and Class -	4	4	3	3	-	-	56	11	12	20	17	41	-	1
Rates of Pay of each ditto -	s. 38	s. 36	s. 35	s. 34	-	-	s. 32	s. 31	s. 30	s. 29	s. d. 26 6	s. 24	-	-

* Exclusive of one superintendent and two constables not paid by rates.

Inspected 1st June.

Establishment.—One chief officer, four superintendents (one of whom acts as chief clerk), eight inspectors, 14 sergeants, and 158 constables. There are also one superintendent and two constables not paid by rates.

There are vacancies for one inspector and one constable.

The strength of the force is the same as last year, but an inspector has been substituted for a sergeant.

Mr. W. B. Gentle (deputy chief constable of the borough of Reading) was, on the 27th September, appointed chief officer in the place of Mr. Carter retired on pension.

One hundred and seventy-one members hold certificates from the St. John Ambulance Association.

Extra Duties.—One inspector, one sergeant, and 34 constables form a fire brigade ; allowances: one sergeant, 2l. 2s. per quarter ; the inspector and two constables, 1l. 19s. per quarter ; and 32 constables, 1l. 13s. per quarter.

Army Reserve, 29th September 1899–1901.—Seven members were called up, of whom four are still serving with the colours, one has rejoined, certified fit, one resigned, and one was dismissed for misconduct while serving in South Africa.

There is an increase of one in the number of public-houses, and a decrease of two in beerhouses, and one in refreshment houses.

Four more persons were proceeded against for drunkenness during the year, and 19 more convicted.

The clothing and appointments were complete and serviceable, and the books and returns well kept.

The offices and cells were clean and in good order.

The management, numbers, and discipline of the force have been efficiently maintained.

A A 3

No. 3.
South of England
and South Wales
District.

BOROUGH OF EASTBOURNE.

Force - - - - - - 66.

Area in acres - - - - 5,410 | Acres to each constable - - - 85
Population in 1891 - - - 34,969 | Population to ditto, as per census 1891 555

RANKS.	Chief Officer.	Yearly Pay in £ and Shillings.										
		Superintendents.						3 Inspectors.				
		Deputy Chief Officer.	Chief Clerk.	1st Class.	2nd Class.	3rd Class.	4th Class.	1st Class.	2nd Class.	3rd Class.	4th Class.	5th Class.
Number of each Rank and Class	1	-	-	-	-	-	-	-	-	-	2	1
Rates of Pay of each ditto -	£ 300	-	-	-	-	-	-	-	-	-	£ s. 114 8	£ s. 109 4

RANKS.	12 Sergeants.						50 Constables.					
	Merit Class.	1st Class.	2nd Class.	3rd Class.	4th Class.	5th Class.	Merit Class.	1st Class.	2nd Class.	3rd Class.	4th Class.	Vacancies.
Number of each Rank and Class	-	1	5	6	-	-	2	6	13	8	5	9	4	3
Rates of Pay of each ditto -	-	s. 39	s. 36	s. d. 33 10	-	-	s. d. 31 5	s. d. 30 10	s. d. 29 8	s. d. 28 6	s. d. 27 4	s. d. 26 2	s. 25	-

Weekly Pay in Shillings and Pence.

Inspected 24th May.

The authorised strength of the force, which has been augmented during the year by four constables, is one chief officer, three inspectors, 12 sergeants, and 50 constables. There are vacancies for three constables.

Fifty-eight members hold certificates from the St. John Ambulance Association.

Extra Duties.—The chief officer and two inspectors are inspectors of common lodging-houses, and under the Contagious Diseases (Animals), Food and Drugs, and Explosives Acts, without remuneration. They are also inspectors of hackney carriages ; allowance to inspectors, 5l. each per annum.

Army Reserve, 29th September 1899–1901.—Six members were called up, of whom two are still serving with the colours, one died in South Africa, three rejoined certified fit for duty (one of these has resigned).

Licensing Acts.—An increase of one in the number of public-houses during the year. Seven fewer persons were proceeded against for drunkenness, and eight fewer convicted.

The clothing and appointments were complete and serviceable, and the books and returns well kept.

The police offices and cells were clean and in good order.

The management, numbers, and discipline of the force have been efficiently maintained.

A new scale of pay, as under, was adopted 7th January 1901 :—

	£	s.	d.
Chief Officer - - - - .	300	0	0 per annum.

Inspectors—

		£	s.	d.	
On appointment, 5th class -	-	2	2	0 per week.
After 2 years, 4th „ -	-	2	4	0 „
„ 4 „ 3rd „ -	-	2	6	0 „
„ 6 „ 2nd „ -	-	2	8	0 „
„ 8 „ 1st „ -	-	2	10	0 ..

Clerk Sergeant, Parade Inspector, and Warrant Officer—

		£	s.	d.	
On appointment, 3rd class -	-	1	16	0 ..
After 2 years, 2nd „ -	-	1	18	0 ..
„ 4 „ 1st „ -	-	2	0	0 ..

Section and Detective Sergeants—		£ s. d.		No. 3. South of England and South Wales District.

Section and Detective Sergeants—

    On appointment, 4th class   ·   ·   1 13 10 per week.

      After 2 years, 3rd ' ,,   ·   ·   1 15 ·0   ,,

    ,, 4 ,,   2nd ,,   ·   ·   1 16 ·2   ,,

    ,, 6 ,,   1st · ,,   ·   ·   1 17 4   ,,

    ,, 8 ,,   1st conduct badge   ·   1 18 4   ,,

    ,, 10 ,,   2nd ,,   ,,   ·   1 19 4   ,,

Constables—

    On probation for 12 months   ·   ·   1 5 0   ..

    On appointment, 3rd class   ·   ·   1 6 2   ..

    *After 2 years, 2nd ,,   ·   ·   1 7 4   ..

    ,, 4 ,,   1st ,,   ·   ·   1 8 6   ..

    ,, 6 ,,   1st conduct badge   ·   1 9 8   ..

    ,, 9 ,,   2nd ,,   ,,   ·   1 10 10   ..

    ,, 12 ,,   3rd ,,   ,,   ·   1 11 5   ..

    ,, 15 ,,   4th ,,   ,,   ·   1 12 0   ..

    ,, 20 ,,   5th ,,   ,,   ·   1 13 2.   ..

        Stoppages for sickness, except inspectors, 1*s.* per day.

* Including probationary period, which will be allowed to count towards superannuation if the man is appointed.

"MERIT," OR "DISTINGUISHED" SERVICE CLASS.

There is a "Merit" class open to members of all ranks of the force, who perform specific acts of bravery in the discharge of their duty, or show specially meritorious conduct ; each holder of the rank to wear on his coat sleeve a badge bearing the word "Merit," and he will be granted a gratuity or increase of salary in addition to his ordinary pay, the amount in each case to be fixed by the Watch Committee.

COUNTY BOROUGH OF HASTINGS.

Force -   -   -   -   107.*

Area in acres†   -   -   5,324 | Acres to each constable   -   -   - 49

Population in 1891† - · -   63,189 | Population to ditto, as per census, 1891 590

RANKS.	Chief Officer.	1 Superintendent.					3 Inspectors.				
		Deputy Chief Officer.	Chief Clerk.	1st Class.	2nd Class.	3rd Class.	4th Class.	1st Class.	2nd Class.	3rd Class.	4th Class.	5th Class.
Number of each Rank and Class	1	-	-	1	-	-	-	1	1	1.	-	-
Rates of Pay of each ditto -	£ 400		-	£ s. 163 16	-	-	-	£ s. 134 16	£ s. 114 8	£ s. 109 4	-	-

Yearly Pay in £ and Shillings.

Weekly Pay in Shillings and Pence.

RANKS.	17 Sergeants.						85 Constables.						
	Merit Class.	1st Class.	2nd Class.	3rd Class.	4th Class.	5th Class.	Acting Sergeants.	1st Class.	2nd Class.	3rd Class.	4th Class.	5th Class.	Vacancies.
Number of each Rank and Class	-	2	1	3	3	3	5	3	1	10	11	13	17	13	9	9
Rates of Pay of each ditto -	-	s. d. 38 6	s. d. 37 6	s. d. 36 6	s. d. 34 6	s. d. 32 6	32	31	29 6	28	31	30	28 6	27	26	25

* Exclusive of 25 constables not paid by rates.

† The Hastings police district includes, in addition to the county borough, two non-corporate members of the Cinque Port of Hastings— the liberty of the Sluice (in Bexhill parish), with 381 acres and 117 persons, and Petit Iham, or liberty of St. Leonards, Winchelsea (in the parish of St. Leonards, Hastings), with 46 acres but no population. These areas and population are included in the figures above stated (*see* under Sussex (East), *ante*). An area (acreage 2,575 and population 10,849) was transferred (1st November 1897) from the county of Sussex (East).

Inspected 31st May.

Establishment.—One chief officer, one superintendent, three inspectors, 17 sergeants, 85 constables (12 of whom perform the duties of acting sergeants), and 26 constables " additional to the authorised strength."

There are vacancies for two constables.

Sixty-eight members hold certificates from the St. John Ambulance Association.

Extra Duties.—The chief officer is inspector of hackney carriages and pleasure boats ; allowance, 20l. per annum.

Army Reserve, 29th September 1899-1901.—Four members were called up, of whom three are still serving in South Africa, and one has rejoined the police force certified physically fit.

Licensing Acts.—There has been an increase of one in public-houses during the year, 33 fewer persons were proceeded against for drunkenness, and 19 fewer convicted.

The clothing and appointments were complete and serviceable, and the books and returns well kept.

The offices and cells were clean and in good order.

The management, numbers, and discipline of the force have been efficiently maintained.

A revised scale of pay, as under, was adopted 4th May 1901 :—

	£	s.	d.	
Superintendent	3	3	0	per week.
Inspectors—				
On appointment	2	2	0	,,
After 2 years	2	4	0	,,
,, 4 ,,	2	6	0	,,
,, 6 ,,	2	8	0	,,
8	2	10	0	,,
Station Sergeants—				
On appointment	1	18	6	,,
Section Sergeants—				
On appointment	1	12	6	,,
After 2 years	1	14	6	,,
,, 5 ,,	1	16	6	,,
,, 8 ,,	1	17	6	,,
Constables—				
On appointment	1	5	0	,,
After 1 year	1	6	0	,,
,, 3 years	1	7	0	,,
,, 5 ,,	1	8	6	,,
,, 8 ,,	1	10	0	,,
,, 12 ,,	1	11	0	,,

THE URBAN SANITARY AUTHORITY OF HOVE.

No. 3.
South of England
and South Wales
District.

Force - - - - - - 59.

Area in acres * - - - 1,547 | Acres to each constable - - - 26
Population in 1891* - - - 28,335 | Population to ditto, as per census 1891 - 480

RANKS.	Chief Officer.	Yearly Pay in £ and Shillings.											
		Superintendents.						2 Inspectors.					
		Deputy Chief Officer.	Chief Clerk.	1st Class.	2nd Class.	3rd Class.	4th Class.	1st Class.	2nd Class.	3rd Class.	4th Class.	5th Class.	
Number of each Rank and Class -	1	-	-	-	-	-	-	1	1	-	-	-	
Rates of Pay of each ditto -	£ 400	-	-	-	-	-	-	£ 140	£ 130	-	-	-	

RANKS.	Weekly Pay in Shillings and Pence.												
	8 Sergeants.						48 Constables.						
	1st Class.	2nd Class.	3rd Class.	4th Class.	5th Class.	6th Class.	Acting Sergeants.	Merit Class.	1st Class.	2nd Class.	3rd Class.	4th Class.	5th Class.
Number of each Rank and Class -	2	5	1	-	-	-	-	1	7	15	6	19	-	-
Rates of Pay of each ditto -	s. d. 39 2	s. 39	s. 36	-	-	-	-	s. d. 33 2	s. 33	s. 31	s. d. 28 6	s. 26	-	-

* The parish of Althrington (acreage 761, population 2,238) was transferred (26th September 1893) from the county of Sussex (East).

Inspected June 1st.

The authorised establishment is one chief officer, two inspectors, eight sergeants, and 48 constables. There are vacancies for two constables of the third class.

The pay of the chief officer has been raised from 350l. to 400l. per annum from 11th April 1901.

Forty-one members hold certificates from the St. John Ambulance Association.

Army Reserve, 29th September 1899–1901.—One member was called who rejoined the same day, but is not now a member of the force.

Extra Duties.—The chief is superintendent of the fire brigade, without remuneration, and he and one inspector are inspectors of hackney carriages, boats, and bathing machines.

There is an increase of one in the number of public-houses, of two in beerhouses, and a decrease of four in refreshment houses.

Twelve fewer persons were proceeded against for drunkenness, and eight fewer convicted.

Police Act, 1890.—The town council have adopted a recommendation of the watch committee, fixing under this Act an age limit, below which a member of this force is not allowed to be entitled to retire on pension without a medical certificate, viz. :—

Sergeants and constables - - - - 55 years.
Inspectors - - - - - - - 57 „
Other ranks - - - - - 60 „

The clothing and appointments were complete and serviceable, and the books and returns well kept.

The offices and cells were clean and in good order.

The management, numbers, and discipline of the force have been efficiently maintained.

No. 3.
South of England
and South Wales
District.

A revised scale of pay, as under, was adopted 11th July 1901:—

RANK.	No.	Yearly or Weekly Rate.
		£ s. d.
Chief Officer (no scale) - - - - - -	1	400 0 0
Inspector (no scale) - - - - - -	1	140 0 0
„ (no scale) - - - - - -	1	130 0 0
Sergeants (fourth year and after) - - - - -	4	1 19 0
„ (first three years) - - - - -	1	1 16 0
Clerk Sergeant (no scale) - - - - -	1	1 19 0
Detective Sergeants (no scale) - - - - -	2	1 19 2
Constables—		
Merit class (two grades) with extra pay respectively of 7d. and 1s. 2d. per week	1	1 12 2
Long service class (12 years' approved service) - -	7	1 13 0
1st class (sixth year's service and after) - -	15	1 11 0
2nd „ (fourth and fifth years' service) - -	6	1 8 6
3rd „ (first three years' service) - - -	19	1 6 0
Total - - - - -	59	

(Not limited)

COUNTY OF SUSSEX (WEST).

Force - - - - - - 151.*

Area in acres - - - 402,478 | Acres to each constable - - - 2,665
Population in 1891 - - 140,619 | Population to ditto, as per census 1891 931

RANKS.	Chief Constable.	8 Superintendents.							1 Inspector.				
		Deputy Chief Constable.	Chief Clerk.	1st Class.	2nd Class.	3rd Class.	4th Class.	5th Class.	1st Class.	2nd Class.	3rd Class.	4th Class.	5th Class.
Number of each Rank and Class	1	1	1	1	1	1	1	2	1	-	-	-	-
Rates of Pay of each ditto	£ 415	£ s. 187 1	£ s. 185 7	£ s. 152 1	£ s. 147 10	£ 146	£ s. 133 16	£ s. 118 19	£ s. 112 10	-	-	-	-

Weekly Pay in Shillings and Pence.

RANKS.	15 Sergeants.						126 Constables.									
	Merit Class.	1st Class.	2nd Class.	3rd Class.	4th Class.	5th Class.	1st Class.							2nd Class.		3rd Class.
Number of each Rank and Class	-	4	5	3	3	-	4	18	7	6	16	13	4	2	20	26
Rates of Pay of each ditto	-	s. d. 35 7	s. d. 33 3	s. d. 32 1	s. d. 30 9	-	s. d. 38 7	s. d. 27 5	s. d. 26 10	s. d. 26 3	s. d. 25 8	s. d. 35 1	s. d. 24 6	s. d. 23 11	s. d. 23 4	s. d. 22 3

* Exclusive of one constable appointed under 3 & 4 Vict. c. 88. s. 19.

Inspected in May.

Establishment.—One chief constable, eight superintendents (one of whom acts as deputy chief constable, and one as chief clerk), 15 sergeants, and 126 constables. The strength of the force has been augmented by one sergeant and three constables. There is also one constable appointed under 3 & 4 Vict. c. 88. s. 19.

Eighty members hold certificates from the St. John Ambulance Association.

Army Reserve, 29th September 1899–1901.—Twelve members were called up, of whom five have rejoined, certified fit, and seven are still serving with the colours.

Extra Duties :—

NATURE OF DUTY.	Chief Constable.	Super-intendents.	In-spectors.	Ser-geants.	Con-stables.	REMUNERATION.
Inspectors of Weights and Measures.	—	5	1	2	—	Inspector, 64l. per annum, and 2s. per day when on duty away from office; super-intendents, 3s.; serjeants, 2s. per day when away from their stations.
Inspectors of Petroleum, Explosives, and Common Lodging-houses.	1	7	—	14	—	Nil.
Inspectors under Contagious Diseases (Animals) Act.	1	7	—	14	34	Nil.
Inspectors under Food and Drugs Act.	1	8	1	14	123	Nil.

The borough of Worthing is policed by the county constabulary.

There has been a reduction during the year of three in the number of public-houses, of seven in beerhouses, and three in refreshment houses; and a decrease of 66 in the number of persons proceeded against for drunkenness, and 68 in the number convicted.

The clothing and appointments were complete and serviceable, and the books and returns well kept.

The outlying stations and cells visited were clean and in good order.

The management, numbers, and discipline of the force have been efficiently maintained.

An amended scale of pay, as under, was sanctioned 7th May 1901 :—

WEEKLY SCALE OF PAY.

RANK.	On Appoint-ment.	After Two Years	After Four Years.	After Five Years.	After Six Years.	After Eight Years.	Good Conduct Pay.
	£ s. d.	£ s. d.	£ s. d.	£ s. d.	£ s. d.	£ s. d.	Superintendents and Inspectors may be awarded, by order of the chief constable, for good conduct : 3d. per day after three years' service. After the fourth year 1d. per day in each subsequent year of office. Sergeants may be awarded, by order of the chief constable, for good conduct : 2d. per day after two year's service. 2d. per day more after eight years' service. Constables may be awarded, by order of the chief constable, for good conduct : 1d. per day after four years' service. 1d. per day more after eight years' service. Good Conduct Pay to be forfeited for neglect of duty or misconduct, at the discretion of the chief constable.
Superintendent and Deputy-Chief Constable.	2 16 0	—	—	—	2 19 6	—	
Superintendent—							
1st class - -	2 12 6	—	—	—	—	—	
2nd class - -	2 5 6	—	2 9 0	—	—	—	
Inspector - -	1 12 8	1 15 0	—	—	1 18 6	—	
Sergeants - -	1 9 9	1 10 11	—	1 12 1	—	1 13 8	
Constables—							
1st class - -	1 4 6	1 5 1	—	1 6 3	—	1 7 5	
2nd class - -	1 3 4	—	—	—	—	—	
3rd class - -	1 2 2	—	—	—	—	—	

COUNTY OF ISLE OF WIGHT.

Force - - - - - - 55.

Area in acres	-	-	- 92,550	Acres to each constable	-	-	- 1,682
Population in 1891		-	- 67,720	Population to ditto, as per census 1891			1,231

RANKS.	Chief Constable.	Yearly Pay in £ and Shillings.											
		3 Superintendents.						2 Inspectors.					
		Deputy C.C. and Chief Clerk.	Chief Clerk.	1st Class.	2nd Class.	3rd Class.	4th Class.	1st Class.	2nd Class.	3rd Class.	4th Class.	5th Class.
Number of each Rank and Class -	1	1	-	1	1	-	-	2	-	-	-	-
Rates of Pay of each ditto -	£ 250	£ s. 165 11	-	£ s. 130 11	£ s. 130 15	-	-	£ s. 118 12	-	-	-	-

RANKS.	Weekly Pay in Shillings and Pence.											
	7 Sergeants.						43 Constables.					
	1st Class.	2nd Class.	3rd Class.	4th Class.	5th Class.	6th Class.	1st Class.			2nd Class.	3rd Class.	Vacancies.	4th Class.	5th Class.
Number of each Rank and Class -	6	1	-	-	-	-	20	6	8	1	4	3	-	-
Rates of Pay of each ditto -	s. d. 33 3	s. d. 30 11	-	-	-	-	s. 28	s. d. 26 10	s. d. 25 8	s. d. 24 6	s. 21	-	-

Inspected in August.

Establishment.—One chief constable, three superintendents (one of whom acts as deputy chief constable and chief clerk), two inspectors, seven sergeants, and 42 constables. There are vacancies for three constables of the 3rd class.

There is no alteration in the scale of pay.

Thirty-six members hold certificates from the St. John Ambulance Association.

Extra Duties.—The chief constable, two superintendents, the inspectors, and five sergeants carry out the provisions of the Contagious Diseases (Animals) Act, and two superintendents, the inspectors, and three sergeants are inspectors under the Food and Drugs Act, without remuneration.

The borough of Newport is policed by the county constabulary.

There has been an increase during the year of one in the number of public houses, but a decrease of one in beerhouses ; 14 fewer persons were proceeded against for drunkenness, and 11 fewer convicted.

The clothing and appointments were complete and serviceable, and the books and returns well kept.

The outlying stations and cells visited were clean and in good order.

The management, numbers, and discipline of the force have been efficiently maintained.

BOROUGH OF RYDE.

Force - - - - 15.

| Area in acres | - | - | - | - | 792 | Acres to each constable | - | - | - | 53 |
| Population in 1891 | - | - | - | 10,952 | | Population to ditto, as per census 1891 | 730 |

RANKS.	Chief Officer.	Superintendents.						Inspectors.				
		Deputy Chief Officer.	Chief Clerk.	1st Class.	2nd Class.	3rd Class.	4th Class.	1st Class.	2nd Class.	3rd Class.	4th Class.	5th Class.
Number of each Rank and Class }	1	-	-	-	-	-	-	-	-	-	-	-
Rates of Pay of each ditto - - }	£ 154	-	-	-	-	-	-	-	-	-	-	-

RANKS.	2 Sergeants.						12 Constables.							
	1st Class.	2nd Class.	3rd Class.	4th Class.	5th Class.	6th Class.	Acting Sergeants.	Merit Class.	1st Class.	2nd Class.	3rd Class.	4th Class.	5th Class.	6th Class.
Number of each Rank and Class - }	1	1	-	-	-	-	-	-	6	1	2	1	2	-
Rates of Pay of each ditto - - }	s. d. 33 6	s. d. 34 6	-	-	-	-	-	-	s. 29	s. 28	s. 27	s. 26	s. d. 23 6	-

Inspected August 12th.

Establishment.—One chief officer, two sergeants, and 12 constables.

The strength of the force has been increased by one constable.

Eight members hold certificates from the St. John Ambulance Association.

Extra Duties.—The chief officer is inspector of hackney carriages and weights and measures, also under the Food and Drugs and Explosive Acts, without remuneration.

There has been an increase during the year of two in the number of public-houses, and two in beerhouses, but a decrease of five in refreshment houses.

Eleven fewer persons were proceeded against for drunkenness, and three fewer convicted.

The clothing and appointments were complete and serviceable, and the books and returns well kept.

The offices and cells were clean and in good order.

The management, numbers, and discipline of the force have been efficiently maintained.

COUNTY OF WILTS.

Force - - - 246.*

Area in acres † - - - 863,810	Acres to each constable - - - 3,511
Population in 1891 † - - 246,737	Population to ditto, as per census 1891 1,003

RANKS.	Chief Con-stable.	Yearly Pay in £ and Shillings.														
		10 Superintendents.									14 Inspectors.					
		Deputy Chief Constable.	Chief Clerk.	1st Class.	2nd Class.	3rd Class.				4th Class.	1st Class.	2nd Class.	3rd Class.	4th Class.	5th Class.
Number of each } Rank and Class - }	1	1	1	1	1	2	1	1	1	1	6	8	—	—	—
Rates of Pay of } each ditto - - }	£ 600	£ s. 195 7	£ s. 135 7	£ s. 176 2	£ s. 175 15	£ s. 155 7	£ s. 145 18	£ s. 145 11	£ s. 145 7	£ s. 135 11	£ s. 93 8	£ s. 89 9	—	—	—

RANKS.	Weekly Pay in Shillings and Pence.													
	32 Sergeants.							189 Constables.						
	Merit Class.	1st Class.	2nd Class.	3rd Class.	4th Class.	5th Class.	Acting Ser-geants.	Merit Class.	1st Class.	2nd Class.	3rd Class.	4th Class.	Va-cancies.	6th Class.
Number of each } Rank and Class - }	—	15	17	—	—	—	—	62	50	42	12	13	9	—
Rates of Pay of } each ditto - - }	—	s. d. 32	s. d. 29 6	—	—	—	—	s. d. 27 6	s. 25	s. d. 23 8	s. d. 22 9	s. 21	—	—

* Exclusive of five additional constables appointed under 3 & 4 Vict. c. 88. s. 19.

† The parishes of Bramshaw East (acreage 1,818, population 273), Martin (acreage 3,535, population 418), Melchet Park (acreage 336, population 37), Plaitford (acreage 1,972, population 164), South Damerham (acreage 4,480, population 532), Toyd Farm with Allenford (acreage 846, population 16), West Wellow (acreage 1,404, population 631), and Whichbury (part in Wilts) (acreage 1,768, population 141) are transferred to Hants (30th September 1895). Charmham Street (acreage 1,944, population 481) is transferred (30th September 1895) to Berks. Shalbourne (acreage 1,765, population 201) is transferred from Berks (30th September 1895). Maiden Bradley with Yarnfield (acreage 1,281, population 51), Stourton with Gasper (acreage 1,298, population 173), and Kilmington (acreage 2,876, population 349) are transferred (30th September 1895) from Somerset. The parishes of Kemble (acreage, 2,322, population 483), Poole Keynes (acreage 1,216 population 129), Somerford Keynes (acreage 1,572, population 251), were transferred (1st April 1897) to the county of Gloucester.

Inspected in May.

The authorised establishment, which has been augmented during the year by one sergeant, and nine constables, is one chief constable, 10 superin-tendents (one of whom acts as deputy chief constable, and one as chief clerk), 14 inspectors, 32 sergeants, and 189 constables. There are vacancies for nine constables. There are also five constables appointed under 3 & 4 Vict. c. 88. s. 19.

Ninety members of the force hold certificates from the St. John Ambulance Association.

Army Reserve, 29th September 1899–1901.—Six members were called up of whom three have rejoined, certified fit, and three are still serving with the colours.

Extra Duties :—

NATURE OF DUTY.	Chief Constable.	Super-intendents.	In-spectors.	Ser-geants.	Con-stables.	REMUNERATION.
Inspectors under the Con-tagious Diseases (Animals) Act.	1	10	14	—	—	Chief constable, 1s. per week for each division infected; superintendents, 3s. 6d.; chief clerk, 3d.; and con-stable of district, 9d. per outbreak.
Inspectors under the Explo-sives, Petroleum, and Food and Drugs Acts.	—	—	9	—	—	Nil.
Assistant Relieving Officers -	—	7	7	8	—	Five superintendents, 10l.; two ditto, 8l.; five inspec-tors, 10l.; one at 6l.; one ditto, 5l.; one sergeant, 6l.; two ditto, 5l.
Escort to Judges - - -	—	1	—	—	24	Superintendent, 4s. 6d.: con-stables, 3s. per diem.
Towns Police Clauses Act -	—	5	1	—	—	One superintendent, 30l.; four ditto, 5l.; inspector, 3l. per annum.

The number of licensed houses is the same as last year, and there is a decrease of 104 in the number of persons proceeded against for drunkenness, and 86 in the number convicted.

No. 3.
South of England
and South Wales
District.

The clothing and appointments were complete and serviceable, and the books and returns well kept.

The outlying stations and cells visited were clean and in good order.

Land has been purchased at Crickdale (Swindon Division) for a police station, and the plans approved by the Secretary of State.

The management, numbers, and discipline of the force have been efficiently maintained.

A new scale of pay, as under, was sanctioned 6th August 1901.

GRADES.	Pay per Annum (365¼ days).	Daily.	Weekly.
	£ s. d.	£ s. d.	£ s. d.
Chief Constable - - - -	600 0 0	1 12 10¼	11 9 11¾
Deputy Chief Constable—			
On appointment - - -	195 0 0	0 10 8½	3 14 9
After 5 years - - -	200 0 0	0 10 11½	3 16 8
Superintendents—			
1st class on appointment - - -	175 0 0	0 9 7	3 7 1
After 5 years - - -	180 0 0	0 9 10¼	3 9 0
2nd class on appointment - -	155 0 0	0 8 6	2 19 5
After 5 years - - -	160 0 0	0 8 9	3 1 4
„ 10 „ - - -	165 0 0	0 9 0½	3 3 3
„ 15 „ - - -	170 0 0	0 9 4	3 5 2
„ 20 „ - - -	175 0 0	0 9 7	3 7 1
3rd class on appointment - -	145 0 0	0 7 11	2 15 7
After 5 years - - -	150 0 0	0 8 2½	2 17 6
„ 10 „ - - -	155 0 0	0 8 6	2 19 5
4th class on appointment - -	135 0 0	0 7 5	2 11 9
After 5 years - - -	140 0 0	0 7 8	2 13 8
„ 10 „ - - -	145 0 0	0 7 11	2 15 7
Inspectors—			
On appointment - - -	89 8 4	0 4 11	1 14 3
After 5 years - - -	92 8 4	0 5 1	1 15 5
„ 10 „ - - -	95 8 4	0 5 3	1 16 7
„ 15 „ - - -	98 8 4	0 5 5	1 17 9
Sergeants—			
1st class - - - -	83 9 9	0 4 7	1 12 0
2nd „ - - - -	76 19 3	0 4 2½	1 9 6
Constables—			
Merit class - - -	71 14 11	0 3 11	1 7 6
1st „ - - -	65 4 5	0 3 7	1 5 0
2nd „ - - -	61 14 10	0 3 4½	1 3 8
3rd „ - - -	59 7 0	0 3 3	1 2 9
4th „ - - -	54 15 9	0 3 0	1 1 0

CITY OF SALISBURY.

Force - - - - 18.

| Area in acres - | - | - | 600 | Acres to each constable | - | - | - 33 |
| Population in 1891 - | - | - | 15,533 | Population to ditto, as per census 1891 - | | | 8·63 |

RANKS.	Chief Officer.	Yearly Pay in £ and Shillings.										
		Superintendents.						Inspectors.				
		Deputy Chief Officer.	Chief Clerk.	1st Class.	2nd Class.	3rd Class.	4th Class.	1st Class.	2nd Class.	3rd Class.	4th Class.	5th Class.
Number of each Rank and Class -	1	-	-	-	-	-	-	-	-	-	-	-
Rates of Pay of each ditto -	£ 175	-	-	-	-	-	-	-	-	-	-	-

RANKS.	Weekly Pay in Shillings and Pence.												
	3 Sergeants.						14 Constables.						
	1st Class.	2nd Class.	3rd Class.	4th Class.	5th Class.	6th Class.	Acting Sergeants.	Merit Class.	1st Class.	2nd Class.	3rd Class.	4th Class.	5th Class.	6th Class.
Number of each Rank and Class -	2	1	-	-	-	-	-	-	5	1	5	1	2	-
Rates of Pay of each ditto -	s. 33	s. 30	-	-	-	-	-	-	s. 28	s. 27	s. 26	s. 23	s. 21	-

Inspected May 1st.

Establishment.—One chief officer, three sergeants, and 14 constables.

The strength of the force and the scale of pay are unaltered.

Extra Duties.—The chief officer is inspector of weights and measures, allowance, 20l. per annum; under the Explosives Act, allowance, 6l. per annum; Food and Drugs Act, allowance, 4l. per annum; and assistant relieving officer, allowance, 15l. per annum.

The number of licensed houses is the same as last year; but there is an increase of one in the number of persons proceeded against for drunkenness, and a decrease of five in the number convicted.

The clothing and appointments were complete and serviceable, and the books and returns well kept.

The offices and cells were clean and in good order.

The management, numbers, and discipline of the force have been efficiently maintained.

COUNTY OF BRECON.

Force - - - - 44.*

Area in acres	-	-	- 469,894	Acres to each constable	-	-	- 10,657
Population in 1891	-	-	- 51,393	Population to ditto, as per census 1891			1,168

RANKS.	Chief Constable	2 Superintendents.						1 Inspector.				
		Deputy Chief Constable	Chief Clerk	1st Class.	2nd Class.	3rd Class.	4th Class.	1st Class.	2nd Class.	3rd Class.	4th Class.	5th Class.
Yearly Pay in £ and Shillings.												
Number of each Rank and Class	1	-	-	2	-	-	-	1	-	-	-	-
Rates of Pay of each ditto	£ 300	-	-	£ 150	-	-	-	£ s. 91 17	-	-	-	-

RANKS.	9 Sergeants.						31 Constables.						
	Merit Class.	1st Class.	2nd Class.	3rd Class.	4th Class.	5th Class.	Acting Sergeants.	1st Class.	2nd Class.	3rd Class.	4th Class.	5th Class.	6th Class.
Weekly Pay in Shillings and Pence.													
Number of each Rank and Class	-	4	1	4	-	-	-	12	11	5	3	-	-
Rates of Pay of each ditto	-	s. d. 26 4	s. d. 24 4	s. d. 22 4	-	-	-	s. 28	s. 27	s. 25	s. 22	-	-

* Exclusive of five constables appointed under 3 & 4 Vict. c. 88. s. 19.

Inspected in June.

Establishment.—One chief constable, two superintendents (one of whom acts as deputy chief constable), one inspector, nine sergeants, and 31 constables. There are also five constables appointed under 3 & 4 Vict. c. 88. s. 19.

The strength of the force and the scale of pay are the same as in last year.

Eight members hold certificates from the St. John Ambulance Association.

Army Reserve, 29th September 1899–1901.—One member was called up, who has rejoined the force, certified fit.

Extra Duties.—One superintendent is captain of the fire brigade, allowance, 5l. per annum; one superintendent and three sergeants are assistant relieving officers, allowance, an average salary of 3l. 16s. per annum; and two sergeants are inspectors of common lodging-houses, receiving 5l. per annum each.

There has been a reduction of one in the number of public-houses during the year, but an increase of three in beerhouses, and decrease of two in refreshment houses. Eight fewer persons were proceeded against for drunkenness, and eight fewer convicted.

The clothing and appointments were complete and serviceable, and the books and returns well kept.

The outlying stations and cells visited were clean and in good order.

The management, numbers, and discipline of the force have been efficiently maintained.

C c

No. 3.
South of England
and South Wales
District.

COUNTY OF CARDIGAN.

Force - - - - - 41.

| Area in acres - - - 443,071 | Acres to each constable - - - 10,807 |
| Population in 1891 - - 63,467 | Population to ditto, as per census 1891 1,548 |

RANKS.	Chief Constable.	2 Superintendents.						1 Inspector.				
		Deputy Chief Constable.	Chief Clerk.	1st Class.	2nd Class.	3rd Class.	4th Class.	1st Class.	2nd Class.	3rd Class.	4th Class.	5th Class.
Number of each Rank and Class	1	1	—	1	—	—	—	1	—	—	—	—
Rates of Pay of each ditto	£ 275	£ s. 160 11	—	£ s. 141 8	—	—	—	£ s. 91 5	—	—	—	—

Yearly Pay in £ and Shillings.

RANKS.	5 Sergeants.						32 Constables.				
	Merit Class.	1st Class.	2nd Class.	3rd Class.	4th Class.	5th Class.	1st Class.				2nd Class.		3rd Class.	4th Class.
Number of each Rank and Class	—	2	1	1	—	—	9	6	1	5	5	5	1	5	—
Rates of Pay of each ditto	—	s. d. 33 10	s. d. 33 1	s. d. 29 9	—	—	s. d. 29 3	s. 28	s. d. 27 5	s. d. 26 3	s. d. 25 1	s. d. 23 11	s. d. 22 9	—

Weekly Pay in Shillings and Pence.

Inspected in August.

Establishment.—One chief contable, two superintendents (one of whom acts as deputy chief constable), one inspector, five sergeants, and 32 constables. One inspector has been appointed during the year, and there is one constable less, but the strength of the force is not altered.

Thirty-six members hold certificates from the St. John Ambulance Association.

Extra Duties.—

NATURE OF DUTY.	Chief Constable.	Super-intendents.	In-spectors.	Ser-geants.	Con-stables.	REMUNERATION.
Inspector of Weights and Measures	—	1	—	—	—	25l. per annum (Cardigan division).
" " "	—	1	—	—	—	20l. per annum for Aberystwith division.
Assistant Relieving Officers	—	—	1	2	—	4l. per annum each - -
Inspector of Common Lodging-houses.	—	—	1	—	—	1l. per annum.
Inspectors under Explosives Act.	1	2	1	4	10	Nil.
Inspectors under Food and Drugs Act and Contagious Diseases (Animals) Act.	1	2	—	—	—	Nil.

Licensing Acts.—A decrease of 18 in the number of public-houses, and two in beerhouses.

Twenty-nine more persons were proceeded against for drunkenness, and 19 more convicted.

The clothing and appointments were complete and serviceable, and the books and returns well kept.

The new police station at New Quay has not yet been commenced, owing to the extension of the original scheme, so as to include provision for a petty sessional room and police cells at Tallybont. A station is also required at Llandyssul (divisional head-quarters) as well as a petty sessional court. At present the court is held on property, a part of which is licensed.

The management, numbers, and discipline of the force have been efficiently maintained.

A new scale of pay, as under, was sanctioned and adopted 18th April 1901:—

Constables—

				£	s.	d.	
On appointment, 3rd class	-	-	-	1	2	·9	per week.
After 2 years in the force, 2nd class	-	1	3	11	„
„ 3 „ „ „	-	1	5	1	..
„ 6 „ „ 1st class	-	1	6	3	„
„ 2 „ „ „	-	1	7	5	„
„ 4 „ „ „	-	1	8	0	..
„ 15 „ „ „ (long service)	-	1	9	2	„

Sergeants—

On appointment	-	-	-	-	1	9	9	„
After 2 years as sergeant	-	-	1	10	11	..
„ 3 „ „	-	-	1	12	1	..
„ 6 „ „	-	-	1	13	10	..
„ 15 „ „ (long service)	-	1	14	5	„

Inspectors—

On appointment	-	-	-	-	1	15	0	..
After 5 years as inspector	-	-	1	.18	6	„
„ 10 „ „	-	-	2	2	0	..

Superintendents—

On appointment	-	-	-	-	130	15	10	per annum.
After 5 years' service	-	-	141	8	9	„
„ 10 „ „	-	-	150	11	3	„
Travelling allowance	-	-	30	8.	4	„
D.C.C. (extra)	-	-	10	0	0	..

Chief Constable—

On appointment	-	-	-	250	0	0	..
After 8 years' service	-	-	275	5	5	„
Travelling allowance	-	-	50	3	9	..

COUNTY OF CARMARTHEN.

Force - - - - - 90.*

Area in acres	-	-	-	582,659	Acres to each constable	-	-	-	6,474
Population in 1891	-	120,266	Population to ditto, as per census 1891	1,336

Yearly Pay in £ and Shillings.

RANKS.	Chief Constable.	3 Superintendents.						4 Inspectors.				
		Deputy Chief Constable.	Chief Clerk.	1st Class.	2nd Class.	3rd Class.	4th Class.	1st Class.	2nd Class.	3rd Class.	4th Class.	5th Class.
Number of each Rank and Class	1	1	-	2	-	-	-	1	2	-	-	-
Rates of Pay of each ditto -	£ 400	£ 200	-	£ 190	-	-	-	£ s. 114 16	£ s. 100 2	-	-	-

Weekly Pay in Shillings and Pence.

RANKS.	12 Sergeants.						64 Constables.						
	Chief Clerk.	1st Class.	2nd Class.	3rd Class.	4th Class.	5th Class.	Acting Sergeants.	Merit Class.	1st Class.	2nd Class.	3rd Class.	4th Class.	5th Class.	6th Class.
Number of each Rank and Class	1	5	1	4	1	6	-	-	21	4	12	6	19	2
Rates of Pay of each ditto -	s. d. 31 6	s. d. 36 2	s. 35	s. d. 34 5	s. d. 33 3	s. d. 32 8	-	-	s. d. 29 9	s. d. 29 2	s. 28	s. d. 26 10	s. d. 25 1	s. d. 23 11

* Exclusive of one constable appointed under 3 & 4 Vict. c. 88, s. 19.

No. 3.
South of England
and South Wales
District.
——

Inspected in August.

Establishment.—One chief constable, three superintendents (one of whom acts as deputy chief constable), four inspectors, 18 sergeants (one of whom acts as chief clerk), and 64 constables. A reservist who· has rejoined is borne as a supernumerary until the 2nd November next. There is one constable appointed under 3 & 4 Vict. c. 88. s. 19.

There is no alteration in the authorised strength of the force or scale of pay.

Seventy-seven members hold certificates from the St. John Ambulance Association.

Extra Duties.—Two sergeants are assistant relieving officers, allowance, 13l. per annum, which is paid into the superannuation fund. The chief constable, three superintendents, three inspectors, seven sergeants, and nine constables are inspectors under the Explosives Act ; one superintendent, one inspector, one sergeant, and 15 constables act in lieu of ¡javelin men, receiving out-of-pocket expenses ; one superintendent is captain of the fire brigade, allowance 20l. per annum ; and three superintendents are inspectors under the Contagious Diseases (Animals) Act, receiving 13l. per annum.

Army Reserve, 29th September 1899–1901.—One member was called up, who has rejoined, certified fit.

There has been a reduction of one in the number of public-houses, four in beerhouses, and one in refreshment houses ; but an increase of 49 in the number of persons proceeded against for drunkenness, and 41 in the number convicted.

The clothing and appointments were complete and serviceable, and the books and returns well kept.

The outlying stations and cells visited were clean and in good order.

A new station is to be built at Ammanford.

Plans of the additions to the Llanelly police station have been approved, and are to be commenced forthwith.

The management, numbers, and discipline of the force have been efficiently maintained.

BOROUGH OF CARMARTHEN.

Force - - - - - - 12.

Area in acres - - - - - 5,157	Acres to each constable - - - 429
Population in 1891 - - 10,300	Population to ditto, as per census 1891 858

RANKS.	Chief Officer.	Superintendents.						Inspectors.				
		Deputy Chief Officer.	Chief Clerk.	1st Class.	2nd Class.	3rd Class.	4th Class.	1st Class.	2nd Class.	3rd Class.	4th Class.	5th Class.
				Yearly Pay in £ and Shillings.								
Number of each Rank and Class -	1	-	-	-	-	-	-	-	-	-	-	-
Rates of Pay of each ditto -	£ 150	-	-	-	-	-	-	-	-	-	-	-

RANKS.	2 Sergeants.						9 Constables.					
	1st Class.	2nd Class.	3rd Class.	4th Class.	5th Class.	6th Class.	Acting Ser- geants.	Merit Class.	1st Class.	2nd Class.	3rd Class.	4th Class.	5th Class.	6th Class.
	Weekly Pay in Shillings and Pence.											
Number of each Rank and Class -	2	-	-	-	-	-	-	5	1	2	1	-	-
Rates of Pay of each ditto -	s. 31	-	-	-	-	-	-	27	26	25	24	-	-

Inspected 29th August.

Establishment.—One chief officer, two sergeants, and nine constables ; the strength of the force being unaltered.

The pay of the sergeants and constables has been increased by 1s. per week each.

Ten members hold certificates from the St. John Ambulance Association.

Extra Duties.—The chief officer is market inspector, allowance, 5l. per annum ; assistant relieving officer, allowance, 7l. per annum ; captain of the fire brigade, allowance, 5l. per annum ; inspector of weights and measures, allowance, 5l. per annum ; under the Food and Drugs Act, allowance, 5l. per annum ; and of common lodging-houses, and under the Contagious Diseases (Animals) and Explosives Acts, without remuneration. One sergeant is assistant inspector of weights and measures, receiving the fees prescribed by the Act.

There has been a reduction of four in the number of public-houses, and there are no beerhouses or refreshment houses. Thirteen more persons were proceeded against during the year for drunkenness, and 14 more convicted.

The clothing and appointments were complete and serviceable, the books and returns well kept, and the offices and cells clean and in good order.

The management, numbers, and discipline of the force have been efficiently maintained.

COUNTY OF GLAMORGAN.

Force - - - - 438.*

Area in acres - - - 504,376	Acres to each constable - - 1,151
Population in 1891 - - 456,841	Population to ditto, as per census 1891 1,043

Yearly Pay in £ and Shillings.

RANKS.	Chief Constable.	6 Superintendents.						17 Inspectors.							
		Deputy Chief Constable.	Chief Clerk.	1st Class.	2nd Class.	3rd Class.	4th Class.	1st Class.	2nd Class.	3rd Class.	4th Class.	5th Class.	6th Class.	7th Class.	8th Class.
Number of each Rank and Class -	1	1	1	1	1	2	-	1	1	-	-	-	-	-	-
Rates of Pay of each ditto -	£ 550	£ 260	£ 140	£ 240	£ 175	£ 160	-	£ 140	£ 134	£ 131	£ 128	£ 122	£ 116	£ 113	£ 110

Weekly Pay in Shillings and Pence.

RANKS.	42 Sergeants.						272 Constables.									
	Merit Class.	1st Class.	2nd Class.	3rd Class.	4th Class.	5th Class.	Acting Sergeants.	Merit Class.				1st Class.				2nd Class.	3rd Class.	Vacancy.
Number of each Rank and Class -	-	4	15	10	13	-	25	34	10	5	2	20	56	57	49	42	57	1
Rates of Pay of each ditto -	-	s. d. 37 4	s. d. 36 2	s. 35	s. d. 33 8	-	s. d. 32 1	s. d. 31 6	s. d. 30 11	s. d. 30 4	s. d. 29 2	s. d. 30 4	s. d. 29 9	s. d. 29 2	s. 28	s. d. 26 3	s. d. 25 1	-

* Exclusive of three inspectors, 24 sergeants, and 12 constables appointed under 3 & 4 Vict. c. 88. s. 19.

Inspected in July and August.

The authorised establishment, which has been augmented during the year by three sergeants and 10 constables, is one chief constable, six superinten. dents (one of whom acts as deputy chief constable, and one as chief clerk),

No. 3.
South of England
and South Wales
District.

17 inspectors, 42 sergeants, and 372 constables. There is a vacancy for one constable. There are also three inspectors, 24 sergeants, and 12 constables appointed under 3 & 4 Vict. c. 88. s. 19.

The chief constable has received an increase to his pay of 50l. per annum.

Two hundred and ninety-seven members hold certificates from the St. John Ambulance Association.

Extra Duties :—

NATURE OF DUTY.	Chief Constable.	Super-intendents.	Inspec-tors.	Ser-geants.	Con-stables.	REMUNERATION.
Chief Inspector of Weights and Measures.	1	—	—	—	—	30l. per annum.
Chief Clerk for checking Weights and Measures Returns.	—	—	1	—	—	30l. „ „
Inspectors of Explosives	—	4	4	2	—	44l. 8s., divided annually.
„ „ Common Lodging-houses.	—	2	5	1	—	42l. „ „
Inspectors of Hackney Carriages.	—	3	5	—	—	38l. 10s. „ „
Care of Fire Appliances	—	2	8	15	42	67l. „ „
Inspectors of Street Lamps	—	—	1	2	3	9l. 5s. 6d. „ „
„ „ Food and Drugs	—	5	—	—	—	3s. 4d. per 1,000 of population.
„ under Fertilisers and Feeding Stuffs Act.	—	5	—	—	—	5l. each per annum.
Inspectors of Petroleum	—	1	—	—	—	10l. per annum.
„ „ Seats for Shop Assistants Act.	—	—	17	—	—	5l. each per annum.
Inspectors of Weights and Measures.	—	—	—	3	—	8s. „ „ day.
Adjusters of Weights and Measures.	—	—	—	2	2	2s. 6d. each per day when employed.
Inspectors under Contagious Diseases (Animals) Acts.	—	The whole force.			—	Out-of-pocket expenses refunded.

Army Reserve, 29th September 1899–1901.—Nine members were called up, of whom five are still serving with the colours, one was killed in action, one re-enlisted for 21 years, two were severely wounded.

There is an increase of nine in the number of public-houses, and one in refreshment houses, and a decrease of 16 in beerhouses during the year. Two thousand one hundred and ninety-four more persons were proceeded against for drunkenness, and 2,196 more convicted.

The clothing and appointments were complete and serviceable, and the books and returns well kept.

The outlying stations and cells visited were clean and in good order. A new station, with accommodation for one constable, is nearly completed at Pontygwaith ; at Cilfynydd, Caerau, and Resolven, with accommodation for one constable each, new stations have been just begun to be erected ; one at Caerphilly for two constables about a quarter completed ; at Merthyr the alterations are completed ; at Mountain Ash the new station is nearly completed. New stations are to be built also at Merthyr, Ton Pentre, and Abercynon.

The management, discipline, and numbers of the force have been efficiently maintained.

A new scale of pay, as under, was adopted 29th April 1901 :—

RANK.	Daily.			Weekly.			Annually.		
	£	s.	d.	£	s.	d.	£	s.	d.
Chief Constable	—			—			550	0	0
Travelling allowance	—			—			150	0	0
Superintendents { On appointment	0	8	9	3	1	4	160	0	0
After 1 year	0	9	7	3	7	1	175	0	0
„ 2 years	0	11	0	3	16	2	200	0	0
„ 3 „	0	11	6	4	0	7	210	0	0
„ 4 „	0	12	1	4	4	5	220	0	0
„ 5 „	0	13	2	4	12	2	240	0	0
Deputy Chief Constable (extra)	0	1	1	0	7	7	20	0	0

Scale of pay—*continued*.

RANK.		Daily.	Weekly.	Annually.
		£ s. d.	£ s. d.	£ s. d.
Inspector and Chief Clerk.	On appointment	0 7 8	2 13 8	140 0 0
	After 1 year	0 7 11	2 15 7	145 0 0
	„ 2 years	0 8 3	2 17 6	150 0 0
	„ 3 „	0 8 5	2 19 5	155 0 0
	„ 4 „	0 8 9	3 1 4	160 0 0
Inspectors	On appointment	0 6 0	2 2 2	110 0 0
	After 1 year	0 6 2	2 3 4	113 0 0
	„ 2 years	0 6 4	2 4 6	116 0 0
	„ 3 „	0 6 6	2 5 8	119 0 0
	„ 4 „	0 6 8	2 6 10	122 0 0
	„ 5 „	0 6 10	2 7 11	125 0 0
	„ 6 „	0 7 0	2 9 1	128 0 0
	„ 7 „	0 7 2	2 10 3	131 0 0
	„ 8 „	0 7 4	2 11 5	134 0 0
	„ 9 „	0 7 6	2 12 7	137 0 0
	„ 10 „	0 7 8	2 13 8	140 0 0
Sergeants	On appointment	0 4 8	1 12 8	85 3 4
	After 2 years	0 5 0	1 15 0	91 5 0
	„ 5 „	0 5 2	1 16 2	94 5 10
	Merit class (extra)	0 0 2	0 1 2	—
Acting Sergeants		0 4 7	1 12 1	83 8 7
Constables	3rd class on appointment	0 3 7	1 5 1	65 7 11
	2nd class after 1 year	0 3 9	1 6 3	68 8 9
	1st „ „ 2 years	0 4 0	1 8 0	73 0 0
	„ „ „ 4 „	0 4 2	1 9 2	76 0 10
	„ „ „ 7 „	0 4 3	1 9 9	77 11 3
	„ „ „ 10 „	0 4 4	1 10 4	79 1 8
	Merit class (extra)	0 0 2	0 1 2	—

Sergeants, merit class, 15 per cent ; constables, merit class, 15 per cent.

COUNTY BOROUGH OF CARDIFF.
Force - - - - - - 239.*

Acrea in acres - - - 6,064	Acres to each constable - - - 25
Population in 1891 - - 128,915	Population to ditto, as per census 1891 539

Yearly Pay in £ and Shillings.

RANKS.	Chief Officer.	4 Superintendents.						9 Inspectors.				
		Deputy Chief Officer.	Chief Clerk.	1st Class.	2nd Class.	3rd Class.	4th Class.	1st Class.	2nd Class.	3rd Class.	4th Class.	5th Class.
Number of each Rank and Class -	1	-	1	2	1	-	-	1	1	4	2	1
Rates of Pay of each ditto - -	£ 800	-	£ 156	£ 240	£ 180	-	-	£ s. 163 5	£ 156	£ 130	£ s. 122 4	£ 117

Weekly Pay in Shillings and Pence.

RANKS.	29 Sergeants.									196 Constables.												
	Detective.	1st Class.	2nd Class.	3rd Class.	4th Class.	5th Class.	6th Class.	7th Class.	8th Class.	Detective.	Merit Class.	1st Class.	2nd Class.	3rd Class.	4th Class.	5th Class.	6th Class.	7th Class.	8th Class.	9th Class.	Vacancies.
Number of each Rank and Class -	1	3	2	1	2	14	2	2	2	2	24	6	19	24	2	34	23	12	6	13	24	6
Rates of Pay of each ditto - -	s. d. 45	s. d. 43 6	s. 43	s. 42	s. d. 41 6	s. 40	s. 39	s. 38	s. 37	s. 38	s. 35	s. 34	s. d. 33 6	s. d. 32 6	s. d. 31 6	s. 31	s. 30	s. 29	s. 28	s. 27	s. 26	-

* Exclusive of three constables not paid by rates.

Inspected on 27th July.

Establishment.—One chief officer, four superintendents (one of whom acts as chief clerk), nine inspectors, 29 sergeants, and 196 constables. There are

No. 3.
South of England
and South Wales
District.

vacancies for six constables, who are reservists, still serving with the colours. Three constables are borne " additional " to the establishment.

The chief officer receives an increase to his pay of 100*l.* per annum.

Two hundred and thirty-one members hold certificates from the St. John Ambulance Association.

Army Reserve, 29th September 1899-1901.—Fourteen members were called up, of whom six are still serving with the colours, and six have rejoined the police force, one was accidentally killed at Pembroke Dock by a rifle bullet, and one died from enteric fever in South Africa.

Licensing Acts.—An increase during the year of one in public-houses, and a decrease of two in beerhouses, and two in refreshment houses. Six hundred and seventy-one fewer persons were proceeded against for drunkenness, and 190 fewer convicted.

The clothing and appointments were complete and serviceable, and the books and returns well kept.

The offices and cells were clean and in good order.

The new divisional Roath station has been completed and occupied since March 1901, having six cells and accommodation for seven single and one married inspector, and is satisfactory.

The management, numbers, and discipline of the force have been efficiently maintained.

A new scale of pay, as under, was adopted 18th December 1900 :—

RANK.	Service.	Weekly Pay.	Annual Pay.
		£ s. d.	£ s. d.
Superintendents - -	On appointment - -	3 1 8	160 0 0
	After 1 year - - -	3 5 4	170 0 0
	„ 2 years - - -	3 9 2	180 0 0
	„ 3 „ - - -	3 13 0	190 0 0
	„ 4 „ - - -	3 16 11	200 0 0
	„ 5 „ - - -	4 0 9	210 0 0
	„ 6 „ - - -	4 4 7	220 0 0
	„ 7 „ - - -	4 8 5	230 0 0
	„ 8 „ - - -	4 12 4	240 0 0
	„ 10 „ - - -	4 16 2	250 0 0
Chief Inspectors - -	- - - -	3 0 0	156 0 0
Inspectors - - -	On appointment - -	2 5 0	117 0 0
	After 2 years - -	2 7 0	122 4 0
	„ 4 „ - - -	2 10 0	130 0 0
	„ 6 „ - - -	2 12 0	135 4 0
Detective Sergeants - -	- - - -	2 2 0	109 4 0
Detective Constables - -	On appointment - -	1 16 0	93 12 0
	After 1 year - - -	1 17 0	96 4 0
	„ 2 years - - -	1 18 0	98 16 0
Sergeants - - -	On appointment - -	1 16 0	93 12 0
	After 1 year - - -	1 17 0	96 4 0
	„ 2 years - -	1 18 0	98 16 0
	„ 3 „ - - -	1 19 0	101 8 0
	„ 4 „ - - -	2 0 0	104 0 0
Constables - - - -	On appointment - -	1 6 0	67 12 0
	After 1 year - - -	1 7 0	70 4 0
	„ 2 years - -	1 8 0	72 16 0
	„ 3 „ - - -	1 9 0	75 8 0
	„ 4 „ - - -	1 10 0	78 0 0
	„ 7 „ - - -	1 11 0	80 12 0
	„ 10 „ - -	1 12 0	83 4 0

MERIT CLASSES.

There are two Merit Classes, each carrying 1*s.* 6*d.* per week, for detective sergeants, detective constables, sergeants, and constables. They are awarded for exemplary conduct and vigilance.

BOROUGH OF NEATH.

Force - - - 17.

| Area in acres | - | - | - 1,439 | Acres to each constable | - | - 85 |
| Population in 1891 | | - | - 11,113 | Population to ditto, as per census 1891 | | 654 |

RANKS.	Chief Officer.	Superintendents.						Inspectors.				
		Deputy Chief Officer.	Chief Clerk.	1st Class.	2nd Class.	3rd Class.	4th Class.	1st Class.	2nd Class.	3rd Class.	4th Class.	5th Class.
Number of each Rank and Class -	1	-	1	-	-	-	-	-	-	-	-	-
Rates of Pay of each ditto -	£ 150	-	£ s. 87 2	-	-	-	-	-	-	-	-	-

Weekly Pay in Shillings and Pence.

RANKS.	3 Sergeants.						12 Constables.							
	Merit Class.	1st Class.	2nd Class.	3rd Class.	4th Class.	5th Class.	Acting Sergeants.	Merit Class.	1st Class.	2nd Class.	3rd Class.	4th Class.	5th Class.	6th Class.
Number of each Rank and Class -	-	1	1	1	-	-	-	-	4	4	4	-	-	-
Rates of Pay of each ditto -	-	s. d. 37 3	s. 35	s. d. 32 8	-	-	-	-	s. d. 31 6	s. d. 29 2	s. d. 26 6	-	-	-

Inspected 1st August.

The authorised establishment, which has been augmented by three constables during the year, is one chief officer, one chief clerk, three sergeants, and 12 constables.

The scale of pay is unaltered.

Six members hold certificates from the St. John Ambulance Association.

Extra Duties.—The chief officer is inspector of weights and measures, common lodging-houses, hackney carriages, and under the Contagious Diseases (Animals), Explosives, and Petroleum Acts; also superintendent of the fire brigade, without remuneration. The chief clerk is assistant inspector of weights and measures, without remuneration.

Licensing Acts.—There has been no change.

Fifty-two more persons were proceeded against for drunkenness during the year, and 50 more convicted.

Mr. Evan Lewis, formerly a sergeant clerk in the City of Birmingham Force, was appointed chief officer of this borough on the 29th November 1900, in the place of Mr. Robert Kilpatrick, appointed chief officer of Chesterfield.

The clothing and appointments were complete and serviceable, the books and returns well kept, and the offices and cells clean and in good order.

The management, numbers, and discipline of the force have been efficiently maintained.

D D

No. 3.
South of England
and South Wales
District.

COUNTY BOROUGH OF SWANSEA.

Force - - - - - - - 104.*

Area in acres - - - 5,087	Acres to each constable - - - 49
Population in 1891 - - 90,349	Population to ditto, as per census 1891 868

Yearly Pay in £ and Shillings.

RANKS.	Chief Officer.	2 Superintendents.						5 Inspectors.				
		Deputy Chief Officer.	Chief Clerk.	1st Class.	2nd Class.	3rd Class.	4th Class.	1st Class.	2nd Class.	3rd Class.	4th Class.	5th Class.
Number of each Rank and Class	1	1	1	-	-	-	-	3	1	1	-	-
Rates of Pay of each ditto -	£ 525	£ 210	£ 147					£ s. 136 10	£ s. 131 6	£ s. 136 2	-	-

Weekly Pay in Shillings and Pence.

RANKS.	13 Sergeants.						83 Constables.								
	1st Class.	2nd Class.	3rd Class.	4th Class.	5th Class.	6th Class.	Detectives.	1st Class.	2nd Class.	3rd Class.	4th Class.	5th Class.	6th Class.	7th Class.	8th Class.	9th Class.
Number of each Rank and Class	2	3	2	2	3	1	2	1	23	18	18	6	4	4	5	2
Rates of Pay of each ditto -	s. 43	s. 40	s. 39	s. 38	s. 37	s. 36	s. 36	s. 34	s. 33	s. 32	s. 31	s. 30	s. 29	s. 28	s. 27	s. 26

* Exclusive of one sergeant and nine constables not paid by rates.

Inspected 1st August.

Establishment.—One chief officer, one deputy chief officer, one chief clerk, five inspectors, 13 sergeants, and 83 constables.

One sergeant and nine constables are borne " additional " to the established numbers.

Thirty-eight members hold certificates from the St. John Ambulance Association.

Extra Duties.—The chief officer, inspectors, and one superintendent are inspectors under the Contagious Diseases (Animals), Petroleum, and Explosive Acts, without remuneration. The chief officer and two sergeants are assistant relieving officers ; allowance to the chief officer, 10l. per annum. One inspector is inspector of hackney carriages ; allowance, 10l. per annum. The chief officer, one superintendent, one sergeant, and 18 constables form a fire brigade ; allowance, sergeants 3s., others, 1s. 6d. a week.

Licensing Acts.—A decrease of two in the number of public-houses, and an increase of two in beerhouses, and one in refreshment houses.

Twenty-one more persons were proceeded against for drunkenness, and 12 more convicted during the year.

Army Reserve, 29th September 1899–1901.—Three members were called up, who are still serving with the colours.

The clothing and appointments were complete and serviceable, the books and returns well kept, and the offices and cells clean and in good order.

The management, numbers, and discipline of the force have been efficiently maintained.

The central station and that of Goat Street are completely out of date, and the Watch Committee promised they should be rebuilt, but after a second inspection nothing has been done.

Sergeants—

On appointment	-	-	-	1 15 0 ..
After 1 year	-	-	-	1 16 0 ..
„ 2 years	-	-	-	1 17 0 ..
„ 3 „	-	-	-	1 18 0 ..
.. 4 ..	-	-	-	1 19 0 ..
„ 5	-	-	-	2 0 0 ..

Constables—

On appointment	-	-	-	1 6 0 ..
After 1 year	-	-	-	1 7 0 ..
„ 2 years	-	-	-	1 8 0 ..
.. 3 „	-	-	-	1 9 0 ..
4 ..	-	-	-	1 10 0 ..
„ 5 ..	-	-	-	1 11 0 ..
„ 10 ..	-	-	-	1 12 0 ..
„ 15 „	-	-	-	1 13 0 „

Detective constables and constables in the clerical department receive
1s. per week extra.
The whole of the detectives are also allowed 3s. each per week extra for
outlays.

COUNTY OF PEMBROKE.

Force - - - - - 71.

Area in acres	-	-	- 392,710	Acres to each constable	-	-	- 5,531
Population in 1891	-		- 88,296	Population to ditto, as per census 1891			1,243

		Yearly Pay in £ and Shillings.										
RANKS.	Chief Constable.	3 Superintendents.						1 Inspector.				
		Deputy Chief Constable.	Chief Clerk.	1st Class.	2nd Class.	3rd Class.	4th Class.	1st Class.	2nd Class.	3rd Class.	4th Class.	5th Class.
Number of each Rank and Class -	1	1	-	2	-	-	-	1	-	-	-	-
	£	£		£				£ s.				
Rates of Pay of each ditto -	390	190	-	180	-	-	-	102 10	-	-	-	-

		Weekly Pay in Shillings and Pence.											
RANKS.	11 Sergeants.						55 Constables.						
	Merit Class.	1st Class.	2nd Class.	3rd Class.	4th Class.	5th Class.	Acting Ser- geants.	Merit Class.	1st Class.	2nd Class.	3rd Class.	4th Class.	5th Class.	6th Class.
Number of each Rank and Class -	-	8	2	1	-	-	-	-	25	9	7	8	2	4
		s. d.	s. d.	s. d.					s.	s. d.	s. d.	s. d.	s. d.	s. d.
Rates of Pay of each ditto -	-	32 8	31 6	30 4	-	-	-	-	28	26 10	25 8	24 6	23 4	22 2

Inspected in July.

Establishment.—One chief constable, three superintendents (one of whom acts as deputy chief constable), one inspector, 11 sergeants, and 55 constables.

The strength of the force and the scale of pay are the same as last year.

Fifty-one members hold certificates from the St. John Ambulance Association.

Extra Duties. — The whole force carry out the provisions of the Contagious Diseases (Animals) Act ; the superintendents, inspector, and sergeants are inspectors under the Food and Drugs Act ; the chief constable, superintendents, inspector, sergeants, and one constable are inspectors under the Explosives Act. One superintendent and 11 constables act in lieu of javelin men ; allowance, 5s. per day each when so employed. The inspector and two sergeants are assistant relieving officers : allowance to inspector, 8l. per annum.

The municipal borough of Pembroke is policed by the county constabulary.

There is an increase during the year of four in the number of public-houses, and one in beerhouses. Sixty-five more persons were proceeded against for drunkenness, and 59 more convicted.

The clothing and appointments were complete and serviceable, and the books and returns well kept.

The constabulary station at Neyland has been completed and occupied.

Plans have been prepared for the necessary alterations at Fishguard. Nothing has yet been done to the station at Old Milford, and a second station is required here across the water at Hakin, as recommended a year ago. A new station also is required at Narberth in place of the present one, which is completely out of date.

The remaining outlying stations and cells visited were clean and in good order.

The management, numbers, and discipline of the force have been efficiently maintained.

COUNTY OF RADNOR.

Force - -. - - 18.*

Area in acres - - - 301,164 | Acres to each constable - - 16,731
Population in 1891 - - 21,791 | Population to ditto, as per census 1891 1,210

RANKS.	Yearly Pay in £ and Shillings.		Weekly Pay in Shillings and Pence.							
	Chief Constable.	1 Inspector.	3 Sergeants.			13 Constables.				
		1st Class.	1st Class.	2nd Class.	3rd Class.	Acting Sergeants.	1st Class.	2nd Class.	3rd Class.	
Number of each Rank and Class	1	1	1	1	1	1	1	1	9	1
Rates of Pay of each ditto -	£ 275	£ 95	s. d. 33 10	s. d. 32 8	s. d. 31 6	s. d. 28 7	s. d. 26 10	s. 28	s. d. 26 3	s. d. 23 11

* Exclusive of two sergeants and three constables appointed under 3 & 4 Vict. c. 88. s. 19.

Inspected in June.

The authorised establishment is one chief constable, one inspector, three sergeants, and 13 constables (two doing the duties of acting sergeants) ; one of the acting-sergeants is chief clerk, receiving an allowance of 10*l*. per annum extra to his pay.

There are two sergeants and three constables " additional " to the establishment, being a reduction of two constables during the year.

Nineteen members hold certificates from the St. John Ambulance Association.

Army Reserve, 29th September 1899–1901.—Two members were called up, one of whom has rejoined the force, certified fit, the other is still serving with the colours.

Extra Duties.—The inspector and two sergeants are assistant relieving officers, receiving 5*l*. each per annum ; the chief constable is inspector under the Explosives Act, and the whole force carry out the provisions of the Contagious Diseases (Animals) Act ; remuneration, 6*l*. per annum, to be distributed as the chief constable directs.

There is a decrease of one in the number of public-houses, of one in beerhouses, and an increase of one in refreshment houses during the year. Twenty fewer persons were proceeded against for drunkenness, and 19 fewer convicted.

The stations and cells visited were clean and in good order, and books and returns well kept.

The clothing and appointments were complete and serviceable.

The management, numbers, and discipline of the force have been efficiently maintained.

The following new scale of pay was adopted 5th July 1901 :—

Inspector—

	£	s.	d.	
On appointment - - -	95	0	0	per annum.
After 5 years - - - -	100	0	0	,,

Sergeants—

	£	s.	d.	
On appointment - - -	1	10	4	per week.
After 2 years - - -	1	11	6	,,
„ 5 „ - - -	1	12	8	..
„ 8 „ - - -	1	13	10	,,

Acting Sergeants—7*d*. per week in addition to their pay, of whatever grade, as a constable.

Constables—

	£	s.	d.	
On appointment - - -	1	3	4	per week.
After 2 years - - - -	1	3	11	,,
„ 5 „ - - -	1	5	1	..
„ 10 „ - - -	1	6	10	..
„ 12 „ - - -	1	8	0	..

Clerk, 10*l*. per annum extra to his pay.

TABLE I.--AUTHORISED STRENGTH

RETURN showing the AUTHORISED STRENGTH of the several POLICE FORCE
of Companies and Private Persons)

District No 1.—MIDLAND, EASTERN COUNTIES,

Number.	COUNTIES AND BOROUGHS.	Authorised Strength of Police in 1871.	Population in 1871.	Proportion of Population to each Constable in 1871.	Authorised Strength of Police in 1881.	Population in 1881.	Proportion of Population to each Constable in 1881.	Population in 1891.
	ENGLAND.							
1	BEDFORDSHIRE - -	94	124,786	1,327	91	101,201	1,101	102,906
2	Bedford - - -	16	16,850	1,053	18	19,532	1,085	28,023
3	Luton - - -	-	-	-	24	23,959	998	30,056
4	BUCKINGHAMSHIRE -	124	167,365	1,349	131	162,120	1,237	173,227
5	Wycombe - -	4	4,811	1,203	7	10,618	1,516	13,435
6	CAMBRIDGESHIRE -	70	90,495	1,292	70	86,875	1,239	85,303
7	Cambridge - -	45	30,078	668	51	35,372	693	36,983
8	ELY, ISLE OF - -	52	56,971	1,095	53	54,070	1,020	63,340
9	ESSEX - - - -	285	305,825	1,073	293	303,204	1,034	335,136
10	Colchester - -	27	26,343	975	32	28,395	887	34,559
11	HERTFORDSHIRE -	117	159,658	1,364	139	157,677	1,134	177,478
12	St. Albans - -	8	8,298	1,037	11	10,930	993	12,898
13	HUNTINGDONSHIRE -	52	63,771	1,226	52	59,614	1,328	55,015
14	LEICESTERSHIRE -	109	174,091	1,597	146	199,200	1,364	201,464
15	Leicester - -	92	95,220	1,035	120	122,351	1,011	174,624
16	LINCOLNSHIRE - -	269	352,849	1,311	289	353,983	1,224	338,808
17	Boston - - -	15	14,526	968	15	14,926	995	14,593
18	Grantham - -	5	5,028	1,005	14	16,886	1,206	16,746
19	Great Grimsby -	17	20,244	1,190	31	29,682	957	51,934
20	Lincoln - - -	25	26,776	1,071	34	37,312	1,097	41,491
21	Louth - - -	9	10,500	1,166	9	10,690	1,187	10,040
22	NORFOLK - - -	231	307,329	1,330	236	301,217	1,276	318,202
23	Great Yarmouth -	39	41,819	1,072	46	48,466	1,053	49,344
24	King's Lynn - -	19	16,562	871	22	18,475	839	18,360
25	Norwich - - -	95	80,386	846	97	87,843	905	100,970
26	NORTHAMPTONSHIRE -	116	172,339	1,486	131	186,213	1,421	203,281
27	Northampton - -	44	41,168	935	52	51,880	997	61,012
28	OXFORDSHIRE - -	101	143,013	1,415	101	141,300	1,363	130,985
29	Banbury - - -	5	4,122	824	5	3,600	720	12,768
30	Oxford - - -	36	31,404	872	38	35,929	945	45,742
31	PETERBOROUGH (Liberty)	21	25,173	1,198	9	9,283	1,031	10,078
32	Peterborough (City)	-	-	-	18	21,219	1,178	25,171
33	RUTLANDSHIRE - -	13	22,073	1,697	13	21,434	1,648	20,659

OF POLICE FORCE.

In the Counties and Boroughs (exclusive of the Additional Constables appointed at the Expense in each Year from 1892 to 1901.

AND NORTH WALES.

Proportion of Population to each Constable in 1891.	Authorised Strength of Police in each Year.										Number.
	1892.	1893.	1894.	1895.	1896.	1897.	1898.	1899.	1900.	1901.	
1,068	96	96	97	98	98	98	99	99	100	100	1
1,001	30	32	32	32	34	36	36	42	42	42	2
1,000	30	30	30	30	31	31	31	35	35	35	3
1,185	146	143	143	144	148	148	150	154	154	154	4
1,221	12	12	13	13	13	14	14	14	15	15	5
1,214	70	70	70	70	70	70	70	70	71	71	6
698	53	53	53	55	55	55	55	55	63	63	7
1,030	62	62	62	62	62	62	62	62	65 ·	65	8
1,021	354	354	354	355	355	370	370	384	390	393	9
864	40	40	40	40	40	40	46	46	46	46	10
1,036	173	192	192	192	192	193	204	248	248	248	11
921	14	14	14	15	15	16	16	16	19	19	12
1,060	52	52	52	52	52	52	52	54	54	54	13
· 1,457	157	157·	157	160	160	160	163	166	167	167	14
1,093	158	158	164	· 170	176	188	194	200	206	215	15
1,134	299	299	299	305	305	305	305	305	315	315	16
973	15	15	15	15	15	15	15	15	15	15	17
1,116	15	15	15	15	15	15	15	16	16	16	18
1,018	52	54	55	56	59	59	59	59	63	65	19
1,037	41	42	44	44	45	46	49	49	49	49	20
1,004	10	10	10	10	10	10	10	10	10	10	21
1,248	240	240	240	240	240	240	241	242	242	242	22
981	53	53	53	53	57	57	57	57	57	57	23
798	23	23	23	23	23	23	23	23	23	23	24
886	114	114	114	114	115	115	117	117	117	120	25
1,383	152	152	152	152	162	162	162	162	166	166	26
859	71	77	77	77	77	82	82	86	86	113	27
1,240	109	109	109	109	109	109	111	111	111	111	28
1,064	12	12	12	12	12	12	12	12	12	13	29
832	55	56	56	59	59	60	60	62	62	62	30
1,120	9	9	9	9	9	10	10	10	10	10	31
1,049	24	24	24	24	27	27	27	30	30	30	32
1,476	14	14	14	14	14	14	14	15	15	15	33

TABLE I.—AUTHORISED STRENGTH

District No. 1.—MIDLAND, EASTERN COUNTIES,

Number.	COUNTIES AND BOROUGHS.	Authorised Strength of Police in 1871.	Population in 1871.	Proportion of Population to each Constable in 1871.	Authorised Strength of Police in 1881.	Population in 1881.	Proportion of Population to each Constable in 1881.	Population in 1891.
·	ENGLAND—*continued.*							
34	SHROPSHIRE -	122	213,742	1,751	137	210,590	1,537	209,860
35	Shrewsbury - -	24	23,406	975	25	26,478	1,059	26,967
36	STAFFORDSHIRE	483	682,564	1,413	536	773,524	1,443	858,391
37	Hanley - - -	31	39,976	1,289	41	48,354	1,179	54,946
38	Newcastle - under - Lyme.	12	15,948	1,329	15	17,506	1,166	18,452
39	Walsall - - -	32	46,447	1,451	49	58,808	1,200	71,789
40	Wolverhampton -	69	68,291	989	73	75,738	1,037	82,662
41	SUFFOLK (EAST) -	115	175,483	1,525	126	176,980	1,404	183,478
42	Ipswich - - -	37	42,947	1,160	50	50,762	1,015	57,360
43	SUFFOLK (WEST) -	90	114,706	1,274	93	112,397	1,195	121,708
44	WARWICKSHIRE - -	179	223,673	1,249	246	278,219	1,130	300,462
45	Birmingham - -	400	343,787	859	520	400,757	770	478,113
46	Coventry - -	38	37,670	991	40	42,111	1,052	52.724
47	Leamington - -	23	20,910	909	28	22,976	820	26,930
48	WORCESTERSHIRE -	192	270,666	1,409	213	302,553	1,301	297,631
49	Kidderminster -	16	19,473	1,217	21	24,270	1155	24,303
50	Worcester - -	31	32,236	1,071	33	40,353	1,028	42,908
	NORTH WALES.							
1	ANGLESEY - - -	25	51,040	2,041	28	50,964	1,820	50,098
2	CARNARVONSHIRE -	61	103,112	1,690	70	119,195	1,702	115,886
3	DENBIGHSHIRE - -	63	105,102	1,668	79	108,931	1,378	120,807
4	FLINTSHIRE - -	41	76,312	1,861	51	80,373	1,575	76,913
5	MERIONETHSHIRE -	27	46,598	1,725	34	52,483	1,543	49,312
6	MONTGOMERYSHIRE -	31	67,623	2,181	33	65,798	1,993	58,003
	TOTAL in each Year.	4,297	5,461,575	1,271	4,939	5,905,576	1,196	6,372,721
	Annual Increase	-	-	-	-	-	-	-

AND NORTH WALES—*continued.*

Proportion of Population to each Constable in 1891.	Authorised Strength of Police in each Year.										Number.
	1892.	1893.	1894.	1895.	1896.	1897.	1898.	1899.	1900.	1901.	
1,342	162	162	162	162	162	163	163	165	165	165	34
729	37	37	37	37	37	37	37	37	37	37	35
1,383	621	630	641	650	655	671	685	687	690	690	36
1,075	54	54	54	54	54	56	56	58	58	60	37
1,153	16	16	17	17	18	18	18	18	18	18	38
1,040	71	71	75	75	75	75	78	78	78	78	39
1,008	82	84	84	84	87	87	93	93	93	93	40
1,248	147	149	151	151	151	160	160	165	165	165	41
989	58	58	58	61	62	67	67	67	68	67	42
1,210	100	100	100	100	104	105	105	111	113	113	43
1,097	275	277	281	283	286	290	298	331	304	304	44
797	670	670	670	670	700	700	700	700	700	800	45
995	55	55	55	55	53	67	67	68	88	88	46
792	34	36	36	36	36	36	38	40	40	40	47
1,051	283	283	286	287	293	301	308	345	351	357	48
992	25	25	25	25	25	27	27	27	28	29	49
1,019	43	43	47	47	47	47	47	47	51	51	50
1,789	28	28	28	29	29	30	30	30	30	30	1
1,561	76	77	77	77	77	77	80	80	80	82	2
1,529	79	79	79	79	81	81	81	82	82	83	3
1,481	52	52	52	52	53	53	54	58	58	58	4
1,406	35	35	35	35	35	35	35	35	35	35	5
1,611	36	36	36	36	36	36	36	36	36	36	6
1,126	5,704	5,840	5,880	5,922	6,012	6,113	6,197	6,384	6,442	6,598	
—	153	46	40	42	90	101	84	187	58	156	

E E

TABLE I.—AUTHORISED STRENGTH

District No. 2.—

Number.	COUNTIES AND BOROUGHS.	Population in 1891.	Proportion of Population to each Constable in 1891.	Authorised Strength of Police in each Year.									
				1892.	1893.	1894.	1895.	1896.	1897.	1898.	1899.	1900.	1901.
1	CHESHIRE - - -	463,108	1,178	303	412	412	412	435	435	436	439	439	439
2	Birkenhead - -	99,857	891	112	112	112	112	120	120	120	145	145	145
3	Chester - - -	37,105	824	45	45	45	45	47	50	50	50	50	50
4	Congleton - -	10,744	976	11	11	11	11	11	11	11	11	11	11
5	Hyde - - - -	-	-	-	-	-	-	-	-	-	32	33	33
6	Macclesfield -	36,009	947	38	38	38	38	38	28	38	38	38	38
7	Stalybridge - -	26,783	1,030	26	26	30	30	30	32	32	32	32	32
8	Stockport - -	70,263	949	74	74	74	75	75	76	78	84	85	85
9	CUMBERLAND - -	227,373	1,215	187	187	192	197	197	197	197	197	197	197
10	Carlisle - - -	39,176	955	41	41	41	45	45	48	48	50	50	50
11	DERBYSHIRE - -	382,343	1,351	287	292	297	303	307	309	316	321	323	333
12	Chesterfield - -	22,009	1,295	17	30	30	30	30	30	30	30	30	35
13	Derby - - - -	94,146	941	100	100	100	100	105	105	105	105	120	120
14	Glossop - - -	22,416	1,018	22	22	26	26	26	26	26	26	26	26
15	DURHAM - - -	685,327	1,373	499	530	530	530	574	574	574	574	618	618
16	Durham - - -	14,863	928	16	16	16	16	16	16	16	16	16	16
17	Gateshead - -	85,692	1,008	87	87	93	93	101	101	101	104	110	115
18	Hartlepool - -	21,271	1,063	20	20	23	23	23	25	25	26	26	27
19	South Shields -	78,391	1,136	79	79	79	79	90	90	90	100	105	115
20	Sunderland - -	131,015	955	137	137	143	143	147	154	150	162	166	166
21	LANCASHIRE - -	1,563,073	1,155	1,465	1,495	1,532	1,570	1,478	1,515	1,584	1,578	1,601	1,618
22	Accrington - -	38,603	1,103	37	37	37	40	40	40	42	43	43	43
23	Ashton-under-Lyne	40,463	1,038	39	40	40	40	41	42	44	44	44	45
24	Bacup - - - -	23,498	903	26	26	26	26	26	26	26	26	26	26
25	Barrow-in-Furness -	51,712	958	57	57	57	57	57	57	57	60	60	65
26	Blackburn - -	120,064	952	126	126	127	133	133	133	138	140	140	140
27	Blackpool - -	23,846	795	30	36	42	42	48	59	59	75	75	75
28	Bolton - - -	115,002	966	119	119	122	122	122	125	138	166	166	167
29	Bootle - - -	49,217	849	64	64	64	65	65	66	66	72	72	72
30	Burnley - - -	87,016	1,087	80	80	81	81	91	96	96	96	97	96
31	Clitheroe - -	10,815	1,081	10	10	10	10	11	11	11	11	11	11
32	Lancaster - -	31,038	1,149	27	27	29	29	30	32	30	32	33	40
33	Liverpool - -	517,980	411	1,293	1,294	1,294	1,294	1,460	1,460	1,460	1,460	1,460	1,360
34	Manchester - -	505,368	490	1,031	1,031	1,031	1,031	1,031	1,031	1,031	1,000	1,000	1,005
35	Oldham - - -	131,463	1,011	133	142	156	156	156	156	158	158	158	158
36	Preston - - -	107,573	1,025	110	110	112	112	112	116	116	116	116	116
37	Rochdale - - -	71,401	978	73	73	73	76	76	81	81	81	81	88

)F POLICE FORCE—*continued.*

TORTHERN.

Number.	COUNTIES AND BOROUGHS.	Population in 1891.	Proportion of Population to each Constable in 1891.	Authorised Strength of Police in each Year.									
				1892.	1893.	1894.	1895.	1896.	1897.	1898.	1899.	1)00.	1901.
	LANCASHIRE—*continued.*												
38	St. Helens -	71,288	1,018	71	75	81	82	83	85	85	85	87	87
39	Salford	198,139	600	330	330	330	330	330	330	330	330	330	330
40	Southport -	41,406	881	47	51	55	58	60	60	60	60	70	70
41	Warrington -	52,743	1,014	52	54	54	54	60	67	67	67	69	69
42	Wigan	55,013	887	62	62	62	62	62	65	65	65	68	68
43	NORTHUMBERLAND -	259,765	1,352	192	192	1?3	199	199	206	208	220	227	227
44	Berwick-on-Tweed	13,377	1,029	13	13	13	13	13	13	13	13	13	13
45	Newcastle-on-Tyne	186,300	684	278	278	278	278	290	290	296	296	300	300
46	Tynemouth -	46,588	913	51	53	53	53	57	57	57	57	57	65
47	NOTTINGHAMSHIRE	217,489	1,194	182	190	190	190	193	194	197	199	201	202
48	Newark	14,457	1,032	14	14	14	14	15	15	15	15	15	16
49	Nottingham	213,877	968	224	224	224	239	239	248	256	256	272	283
50	WESTMORELAND -	51,668	1,565	33	34	34	34	33	33	36	36	36	37
51	Kendal	14,430	1,030	14	14	14	14	16	16	16	16	16	16
52	YORK (EAST RIDING)	128,977	1,152	114	114	114	117	120	121	123	123	134	134
53	Beverley	12,539	964	13	13	13	13	14	14	14	14	15	15
54	Hull -	200,044	722	277	277	277	277	302	302	331	331	331	331
55	YORK (NORTH RIDING) -	251,061	1,201	209	215	216	216	219	227	230	240	248	250
56	Middlesbrough	75,532	993	76	76	80	80	86	86	90	90	96	96
57	Scarborough	33,776	888	38	38	40	40	44	46	46	49	49	50
58	York -	67,004	931	72	76	78	78	79	79	79	79	80	80
59	YORK (WEST RIDING) -	1,220,583	1,191	1,050	1,086	1,139	1,178	1,199	1,198	1,210	1,224	1,210	1,225
60	Barnsley	–	–	–	–	–	–	–	40	40	40	40	40
61	Bradford	216,361	845	256	255	256	256	256	276	276	280	354	390
62	Dewsbury	29,847	994	30	30	32	34	35	35	36	36	37	37
63	Doncaster	25,933	960	28	28	34	34	34	34	34	34	36	36
64	Halifax	89,832	1,069	84	90	90	90	91	95	101	101	101	107
65	Huddersfield	95,420	851	112	112	112	112	112	120	120	130	120	120
66	Leeds -	367,505	869	423	450	451	451	451	484	491	500	500	507
67	Rotherham -	42,061	935	46	48	48	48	48	50	52	53	53	57
68	Sheffield	324,243	842	386	386	407	407	437	440	465	465	465	115
69	Wakefield -	33,146	828	40	40	40	40	44	46	46	46	46	52
	TOTAL in each year	10,685,221	Average Population. 929	11,730	11,944	12,147	12,283	12,615	12,815	13027†	13,200	13,531	13,597
	Annual Increase -	–	–	233	214	203	136	332	250	212	169	331	66

† This includes the 40 reserve men in West Riding of Yorkshire.

TABLE I.—AUTHORISED STRENGTH

District No. 3.—SOUTH OF ENGLAND

Number.	COUNTIES AND BOROUGHS.	Authorised Strength of Police in 1871.	Population in 1871.	Proportion of Population to each Constable in 1871.	Authorised Strength of Police in 1881.	Population in 1881.	Proportion of Population to each Constable in 1881.	Population in 1891.
	ENGLAND.							
1	BERKSHIRE - -	116	133,808	1,153	135	155,676	1,112	163,782
2	Reading - -	40	32,324	808	40	48,769	1,051	60,054
3	Windsor - -	16	11,769	735	18	12,273	682	12,327
4	CORNWALL - -	193	313,510	1,624	198	307,658	1,450	297,097
5	Penzance - -	7	10,414	1,487	11	12,409	1,128	12,432
6	Truro - - -	6	11,049	1,841	11	10,619	965	11,131
7	DEVONSHIRE - -	348	411,814	1,183	370	420,512	1,097	431,403
8	Barnstaple - -	10	11,659	1,165	12	12,282	1,023	13,058
9	Devonport - -	46	49,449	1,074	50	48,939	978	54,803
10	Exeter - - -	45	34,650	770	62	37,665	607	37,404
11	Plymouth - -	83	68,758	828	91	73,794	811	84,248
12	Tiverton - -	7	10,024	1,432	7	10,462	1,495	10,892
13	DORSETSHIRE - -	335	163,730	1,212	140	177,254	1,114	180,651
14	Weymouth - -	14	13,259	947	18	13,715	762	13,866
15	GLOUCESTERSHIRE -	288	380,275	1,320	312	403,596	1,296	424,558
16	Bristol - - -	303	182,552	602	374	206,874	553	221,578
17	HAMPSHIRE - -	258	336,218	1,302	279	314,012	1,291	367,776
18	Portsmouth - -	95	113,569	1,195	130	127,989	984	159,251
19	Southampton -	64	53,749	839	66	60,051	910	65,325
20	Winchester - -	17	16,366	962	19	17,780	936	19,073
21	HEREFORDSHIRE -	62	101,160	1,631	70	101,428	1,358	95,682
22	Hereford - -	30	18,347	611	30	19,821	661	20,267
23	KENT - - - -	300	381,653	1,272	300	432,478	1,355	479,525
24	Canterbury - -	21	20,962	998	22	21,848	986	23,062
25	Dover - - -	28	28,506	1,018	34	30,270	890	33,300
26	Folkestone - -	13	12,698	976	20	18,816	949	23,905
27	Gravesend - -	26	21,295	817	29	23,302	803	23,876
28	Maidstone - -	29	26,196	903	30	29,623	987	32,145
29	Margate - -	14	11,995	856	21	16,030	763	18,417
30	Ramsgate - -	16	14,640	915	24	22,683	945	24,733
31	Rochester - -	28	18,352	655	29	21,307	735	26,290
32	Tunbridge Wells -	25	19,410	776	29	24,119	838	27,895
33	MONMOUTHSHIRE -	99	162,550	1,641	109	177,960	1,558	203,347
34	Newport - -	37	27,069	731	49	38,469	720	54,707

Proportion of Population to each Constable in 1891.	Authorised Strength of Police in each Year.										Number.
	1892.	1893.	1894.	1895.	1896.	1897.	1898.	1899.	1900.	1901.	
1,011	162	162	172	172	172	173	173	·173	173	173	1
923	65	66	66	68	70	75	75	75	75	75	2
616	21	21	21	21	21	21	21	21	21	21	3
1,357	219	219	219	219	219	220	220	220	228	228	4
956	13	13	13	13	13	13	13	13	13	13	5
1,012	11	11	12	12	12	12	12	12	12	12	6
1,042	417	424	424	424	424	422	422	422	422	420	7
1,088	12	12	13	13	13	13	13	13	14	14	8
1,015	59	59	63	63	67	70	73	77	77	83	9
667	56	56	52	52	52	52	52	54	54	64	10
818	114	114	118	119	125	135	136	136	136	136	11
990	11	11	11	11	11	11	11	11	11	11	12
1,095	165	166	168	170	171	172	172	173	175	176	13
815	17	17	18	18	23	25	25	28	28	29	14
1,114	381	384	384	384	396	397	343	353	353	369	15
564	393	393	393	393	397	402	499	499	499	499	16
1,234	308	321	333	346	346	347	377	383	402	423	17
983	174	193	195	196	202	206	206	206	226	226	18
827	79	81	85	91	115	119	119	122	125	134	19
1,004	19	19	19	19	19	19	19	21	21	27	20
1,211	79	79	79	79	79	79	79	79	80	80	21
614	33	33	33	33	33	33	33	33	33	33	22
1,255	382	382	412	428	432	441	450	476	476	516	23
887	26	26	26	26	26	26	26	26	26	26	24
876	38	39	39	42	46	47	51	58	57	57	25
854	31	32	32	36	36	36	40	40	40	₋40	26
702	34	34	35	36	36	36	36	36	36	40	27
868	37	37	37	37	37	37	37	43	43	43	28
708	26	27	27	31	31	31	35	35	35	38	29
883	28	29	31	31	35	35	36	39	46	48	30
822	34	35	36	36	36	36	36	36	40	42	31
697	41	41	41	48	48	48	48	49	49	56	32
1,432	142	156	156	156	156	156	164	164	180	181	33
805	75	75	75	76	78	82	85	91	91	91	34

TABLE I.—AUTHORISED STRENGTH

District No. 3.—SOUTH OF ENGLAND

Number.	COUNTIES AND BOROUGHS.	Authorised Strength of Police in 1871.	Population in 1871.	Proportion of Population to each Constable in 1871.	Authorised Strength of Police in 1881.	Population in 1881.	Proportion of Population to each Constable in 1881.	Population in 1891.
	ENGLAND—*continued.*							
35	SOMERSETSHIRE -	286	368,280	1,287	307	367,157	1,19)	374,430
36	Bath - - -	89	52,557	590	86	51,814	602	51,844
37	Bridgwater - -	7	12,059	1,722	12	12,007	1,000	12,436
38	SURREY - - -	123	137,152	1,115	147	164,740	1,087	188,830
39	Guildford - -	12	9,106	758	12	10,858	905	14,316
40	Reigate - - -	16	15,916	994	22	18,662	848	22,646
41	SUSSEX (EASTERN DIVISION).	125	157,304	1,278	165	187,113	1,093	177,923
42	Brighton - -	109	92,471	825	153	107,546	763	115,873
43	Eastbourne - -	-	-	-	-	-	-	34,969
44	Hastings - -	29	29,291	1,010	44	42,258	960	52,340
45	Hove - - -	23	11,277	490	33	20,804	630	26,097
46	SUSSEX (WESTERN DIVISION).	92	111,367	1,210	101	131,436	1,203	140,619
47	WIGHT, ISLE OF -	-	-	-	-	62,712	-	67,720
48	Ryde - - -	12	11,260	938	14	11,461	818	10,952
49	WILTSHIRE - -	201	244,274	1,215	211	244,178	1,157	249,464
50	Salisbury - -	13	12,903	992	14	14,792	1,057	15,533
	SOUTH WALES.							
1	BRECONSHIRE - -	36	54,056	1,501	36	52,489	1,436	51,393
2	CARDIGANSHIRE -	35	73,441	2,098	39	71,212	1,801	63,467
3	CARMARTHENSHIRE -	50	105,222	2,104	57	114,350	2,006	120,266
4	Carmarthen - -	12	10,488	874	12	10,514	876	10,300
5	GLAMORGANSHIRE -	165	276,302	1,801	203	341,833	1,740	456,841
6	Cardiff - - -	55	60,536	718	96	82,761	862	128,915
7	Neath - - -	9	9,319	1,035	10	10,409	1,041	11,113
8	Swansea - -	57	51,702	942	72	76,430	911	90,349
9	PEMBROKESHIRE -	50	81,566	1,631	50	90,882	1,613	88,296
10	RADNORSHIRE - -	16	25,430	1,589	17	23,528	1,384	21,791
	TOTAL in each Year	4,411	5,237,058	Average Population, 1,179	5,052	5,772,431	Average Population, 1,143	6,326,583
	Annual Increase -	59	-	-	77	-	-	-

OF POLICE FORCE—*continued.*

AND SOUTH WALES—*continued.*

Proportion of Population to each Constable in 1891.	Authorised Strength of Police in each Year.										Number.
	1892.	1893.	1894.	1895.	1896.	1897.	1898.	1899.	1900.	1901.	
1,145	328	335	335	335	338	340	338	339	339	344	35
603	86	86	86	86	86	86	86	86	86	85	36
1,036	12	12	12	12	12	15	15	15	15	15	37
1,032	203	203	203	203	203	215	215	231	231	270	38
894	16	17	17	17	18	18	18	18	19	19	39
907	25	30	30	30	30	30	33	33	33	33	40
1,092	173	172	174	174	177	177	181	185	189	192	31
658	174	175	175	175	185	185	185	185	185	185	42
920	38	44	50	50	56	56	56	62	62	66	43
842	66	67	70	78	85	86	107	107	107	107	44
621	43	43	47	47	50	53	57	57	59	59	45
1,090	132	132	132	134	134	138	138	142	147	151	46
1,231	55	55	55	55	55	55	55	55	55	55	47
782	14	14	14	14	14	14	14	14	14	15	48
1,118	223	223	223	223	223	224	224	224	236	246	49
970	18	18	18	18	18	18	18	18	18	18	50
1,223	42	42	43	44	44	44	44	44	44	44	1
1,627	39	39	39	39	39	39	40	40	41	41	2
1,647	73	73	77	77	83	83	83	90	90	90	3
858	12	12	12	12	12	12	12	12	12	12	4
1,380	331	345	370	390	390	393	401	415	425	438	5
811	159	179	199	199	199	219	219	239	239	239	6
1,010	11	11	12	13	13	13	14	14	14	17	7
912	99	99	99	100	100	102	104	104	104	104	8
1,358	65	65	66	66	66	66	66	69	71	71	9
1,282	17	17	17	18	18	18	18	18	18	18	10
Average Population, 1,044	6,156	6,275	6,413	6,508	6,625	6,726	6,878	7,033	7,150	7,357	
—	98	119	138	95	117	101	152	155	117	207	

TABLE II.—RANKS, NUMBER,

RETURN of the Ranks, Number, Rates of Pay, and Travelling Allowances of

District No. 1.—MIDLAND, EASTERN COUNTIES,

Number.	COUNTIES AND BOROUGHS.	Established Strength, 29th September 1900.	1901.	Chief Officers.	Assistant Chief Constable.	Chief Clerks.	Superintendents.	Inspectors.	Sub-Inspectors and Sergeants.	Assistant Clerks.	Constables.	Additional Constables.	Chief Officers. Pay.	Allowances.	Deputy Chief Constable.
													£. s. d.	£. s. d.	£. s. d.
	ENGLAND.														
1	BEDFORDSHIRE - -	100	100	1	–	1	5	5	11	–	77	1	350 – –	100 – –	180 – –
2	Bedford - - -	42	42	1	–	–	–	2	6	–	33	–	300 – –	- - -	- - -
3	Luton - - -	35	35	1	–	–	–	2	5	–	27	–	240 – –	- - -	- - -
4	BUCKINGHAMSHIRE -	154	154	1	–	1	5	6	23	–	118	8	350 – –	150 – –	180 – –
5	Wycombe - -	14	15	1	–	–	–	3	1	–	11	–	208 – –	- - -	- - -
6	CAMBRIDGESHIRE -	71	71	1	–	1	4	2	6	–	57	1	350 – –	100 – –	150 – –
7	Cambridge - -	63	63	1	–	–	–	3	8	–	51	–	400 – –	- - -	- - -
8	ELY, ISLE OF -	65	65	1	–	1	3	2	8	–	50	–	350 – –	75 – – Travelling. 12 – – Office.	150 – –
9	ESSEX - - -	390	393	1	–	1	13	12	51	–	315	4	600 – –	110 – –	250 – –
10	Colchester - -	46	46	1	–	–	–	4	6	–	35	8	355 4 –	- - -	- - -
11	HERTFORDSHIRE -	248	248	1	–	1	6	8	29	–	203	9	600 – –	100 – –	220 – –
12	St. Albans - -	19	19	1	–	–	–	–	3	–	15	–	160 – –	- - -	- - -
13	HUNTINGDONSHIRE -	54	54	1	–	1	4	1	4	–	43	–	250 – –	70 – –	160 – –
14	LEICESTERSHIRE -	167	167	1	–	1	7	7	23	–	128	–	650 – –	140 – –	160 – –
15	Leicester - -	206	215	1	–	1	3	6	32	–	172	–	600 – –	- - -	- - -
16	LINCOLNSHIRE -	315	315	1	–	–	22	11	38	–	243	6	700 – –	200 – –	- - -
17	Boston - - -	15	15	1	–	–	–	–	3	–	11	–	150 – –	- - -	- - -
18	Grantham - -	16	16	1	–	–	–	–	3	–	12	–	170 – –	- - -	- - -
19	Great Grimsby - -	63	65	1	–	1	1	2	11	–	49	–	300 – –	- - -	- - -
20	Lincoln - - -	49	49	1	–	–	–	2	8	–	38	–	360 – –	- - -	- - -
21	Louth - - -	10	10	1	–	–	–	–	2	–	7	–	140 – –	- - -	- - -
22	NORFOLK - - -	242	242	1	–	1	13	9	21	–	197	–	600 – –	100 – –	190 – –
23	Great Yarmouth -	57	57	1	–	–	–	4	7	–	45	–	400 – –	- - -	- - -
24	King's Lynn - -	23	23	1	–	–	–	1	4	–	17	7	150 – –	- - -	- - -
25	Norwich - - -	117	120	1	–	1	–	3	18	–	97	–	350 – –	- - -	110 – –
26	NORTHAMPTONSHIRE -	166	166	1	–	1	6	9	19	–	130	1	450 – –	100 – –	205 – –
27	Northampton - -	89	113	1	–	1	–	6	18	–	87	–	350 – –	- - -	- - -
28	OXFORDSHIRE - -	111	111	1	–	–	7	5	10	–	88	2	408 15 –	100 – –	220 – –
29	Banbury - - -	12	13	1	–	–	–	–	3	–	9	–	160 – –	- - -	- - -
30	Oxford - - -	62	62	1	–	1	–	3	9	–	48	2	300 – –	- - -	- - -
31	PETERBOROUGH (Liberty).	10	10	–	–	–	1	–	1	–	8	–	50 – –	Actual travelling expenses.	- - -
32	Peterborough (City)	30	30	1	–	–	–	1	5	–	23	–	200 – –	- - -	- - -

AND RATES OF PAY.

the several POLICE FORCES in the Counties and Boroughs, 29th September 1901.

AND NORTH WALES.

Chief Clerk.	Superintendents.			Inspectors.		Sub-Inspectors and Sergeants.		Constables.		Number.
	Maximum.	Minimum.	Allowances.	Maximum.	Minimum.	Maximum.	Minimum.	Maximum.	Minimum.	
£. s. d.	£. s. d.	£. s. d.	£. s. d.	£. s. d.	£. s. d.	s. d.	s. d.	s. d.	s. d.	
135 – –	160 – –	135 – –	– –	110 – –	95 – –	32 8	28 7	27 5	21 –	1
• •	• •	• •	• •	None fixed.	100 – –	37 4	32 8	31 6	24 6	2
• •	• •	• •	•	125 – –	98 16 –	37 4	32 8	31 6	24 6	3
160 – –	152 12 –	137 10 –	• •	110 – –	99 – –	31 –	28 6	28 –	20 10	4
• •	• •	• •	• •	• •	•	34 8	28 –	30 –	21 –	5
• •	• •	• •	44 11 3 for forage, &c. Carts provided.	105 – –	90 – –	30 11	27 5	27 5	21 7	6
• •	• •	• •	• •	135 4 –	114 8 –	43 –	32 10	33 10	23 7	7
• •	140 – –	130 – –	60 – –	105 – –	80 – –	30 4	26 10	26 10	21 –	8
135 – –	200 – –	135 – –	50 – – for forage, &c. Carts provided.	115 – –	100 – –	33 10	30 4	29 2	22 2	9
• •	• •	• •	• •	138 – –	95 – –	43 3	32 1	31 6	23 11	10
190 – –	200 – –	135 – –	• •	115 – –	100 – –	34 10	30 4	30 2	21 7	11
• •	• •	• •	• •	• •	• •	36 –	30 4	29 9	23 4	12
• •	150 – –	120 – –	50 2 6 for forage, &c. Carts provided.	105 – –	90 – –	30 11	28 7	27 5	21 7	13
• •	185 – –	140 – –	• •	120 – –	105 – –	34 5	33 3	30 2	23 4	14
175 10 –	182 – –	143 – –	• •	132 12 –	119 12 –	40 –	34 –	34 –	24 –	15
125 – –	180 – –	110 – –	50 – – for forage, &c. Carts provided.	110 – –	90 – –	32 –	30 –	29 –	24 –	16
• •	• •	• •	• •	• •	• •	33 –	29 –	29 6	23 –	17
• •	• •	• •	• •	• •	• •	33 6	30 –	29 –	23 6	18
• •	163 16 –	137 16 –	• •	130 – –	109 4 –	40 –	34 –	33 –	24 –	19
• •	• •	• •	• •	123 10 –	110 10 –	39 –	34 –	33 –	24 6	20
• •	• •	• •	• •	• •	• •	32 6	29 –	26 9	23 –	21
• •	170 – –	135 – –	• •	100 – –	90 – –	31 6	30 4	28 –	22 2	22
• •	• •	• •	• •	119 12 –	93 10 –	36 –	32 –	30 –	23 –	23
• •	• •	• •	• •	105 – –	95 – –	35 –	30 11	30 4	23 4	24
• •	• •	• •	• •	130 – –	110 – –	38 –	34 0	31 –	24 –	25
135 – –	175 – –	135 – –	50 – – for forage, &c. Carts provided.	116 14 –	95 – –	35 –	30 –	31 –	22 –	26
135 – –	• •	• •	• •	145 12 –	104 – –	40 –	30 –	33 –	22 –	27
• •	173 5 –	125 5 –	• •	121 16 –	95 16 –	33 3	28 7	28 3	19 10	28
• •	• •	• •	• •	• •	• •	32 8	25 1	28 –	21 –	29
109 4 –	• •	• •	• •	135 – –	88 – –	38 –	32 –	31 11	22 6	30
10 – –	175 – –	135 – –	• •	• •	• •	35 –	30 –	31 –	22 –	31
• •	• •	• •	• •	• •	• •	38 –	35 6	33 6	25 –	32

TABLE II.—RANKS, NUMBER,

District No. 1.—MIDLAND, EASTERN COUNTIES,

Number.	COUNTIES AND BOROUGHS.	Established Strength, 29th September		RANK AND NUMBER.									YEARLY PAY		
		1900.	1901.	Chief Officers	Assistant Chief Constable.	Chief Clerks.	Superintendents.	Inspectors.	Sub-Inspectors and Sergeants.	Assistant Clerks.	Constables.	Additional Constables.	Chief Officers. Pay.	Chief Officers. Allowances.	Deputy Chief Constable.
													£. s. d.	£. s. d.	£. s. d.
	ENGLAND—*continued.*														
33	RUTLANDSHIRE	15	15	1	–	–	1	1	1	–	11	–	250 – –	35 – –	105 – –
34	SHROPSHIRE	165	165	1	–	1	8	3	20	–	132	8	400 –	{ Travelling and house rent. 200 – – }	177 5 –
35	Shrewsbury	37	37	1	–	1	–	1	4	–	30	–	270 – –	. . .	. . .
36	STAFFORDSHIRE	690	690	1	–	1	17	22	82	–	567	16	800 – –	150 – –	315 – –
37	Hanley	58	60	1	–	1	–	3	5	–	50	3	300 – –	. . .	. . .
38	Newcastle - under - Lyme.	18	18	1	–	1	–	–	3	–	13	–	180 – –	. . .	. . .
39	Walsall	78	78	1	–	–	–	6	11	–	60	–	300 – –	. . .	. . .
40	Wolverhampton	93	93	1	–	1	1	11	4	–	75	–	450 – –	. . .	. . .
41	SUFFOLK (EAST)	165	165	1	–	1	6	10	10	–	137	9	400 – –	100 – –	175 11 3
42	Ipswich	68	67	1	–	–	1	2	7	–	56	–	324 – –	. . .	. . .
43	SUFFOLK (WEST)	113	113	1	–	1	5	9	8	–	89	4	300 – –	75 – –	159 18 –
44	WARWICKSHIRE	304	304	1	–	1	8	10	33	–	251	–	400 – –	150 – –	220 – –
45	Birmingham	700	800	1	–	1	7	25	72	–	694	16	800 – –	. . .	300 – –
46	Coventry	88	88	1	–	–	–	5	8	–	74	–	350 – –	. . .	. . .
47	Leamington	40	40	1	–	–	–	3	6	–	30	–	300 – –	. . .	. . .
48	WORCESTERSHIRE	351	357	1	–	1	10	11	46	–	288	5	600 – –	170 – –	200 15 –
49	Kidderminster	28	29	1	–	–	–	1	5	–	22	2	312 – –	. . .	. . .
50	Worcester	51	51	1	–	–	–	2	7	–	41	–	335 – –	. . .	. . .
	NORTH WALES.														
1	ANGLESEY	30	30	1	–	–	1	1	4	–	23	–	275 – –	50 – –	121 – –
2	CARNARVONSHIRE	80	82	1	–	–	4	3	13	–	61	1	370 – –	{ Actual travelling expenses. }	175 – –
3	DENBIGHSHIRE	82	83	1	–	1	3	2	8	–	68	2	350 – –	100 – –	179 9 –
4	FLINTSHIRE	58	58	1	–	1	2	3	5	–	46	3	350 – –	60 – –	175 – –
5	MERIONETHSHIRE	35	35	1	–	–	1	2	5	–	26	–	300 – –	50 – –	165 – –
6	MONTGOMERYSHIRE	36	36	1	–	1	1	1	5	–	28	–	275 – –	80 – –	130 – –
	TOTALS	6,442	6,598	55	–	29	176	252	770	–	5,316	118			

ND RATES OF PAY—*continued*.

ND NORTH WALES—*continued*.

Chief Clerk.	Superintendents.			Inspectors.		Sub-Inspectors and Sergeants.		Constables.		Number.
	Maximum.	Minimum.	Allowances.	Maximum.	Minimum.	Maximum.	Minimum.	Maximum.	Minimum.	
£. *s. d.*	£. *s. d.*	£. *s. d.*	£. *s. d.*	£. *s. d.*	£. *s. d.*	*s. d.*	*s. d.*	*s. d.*	*s. d.*	
- -	- -	- -	- -	110 - -	100 - -	33 10	31 6	29 2	23 4	.33
- -	150 11 3	130 15 10	52 - - for horse, forage, &c. Carts provided.	100 7 6	95 16 3	35 -	29 9	28 -	22 2	34
- -	- -	- -	- -	130 - -	100 - -	33 11	31 7	29 -	23 5	35
315 - -	285 - -	145 - -	60 - - for horse, forage, &c. Carts provided.	135 - -	105 - -	39 8	34 6	32 8	25 1	36
91 15 -	- -	- -	- -	137 3 -	101 16 -	39 4	35 7	33 11	25 -	37
87 19 -	- -	- -	- -	- -	- -	37 11	32 8	33 10	23 11	38
- -	- -	- -	- -	123 10 -	104 - -	37 6	31 6	31 6	24 -	39
105 - -	245 - -	160 - -	- -	135 - -	105 - -	39 8	34 5	32 8	25 1	40
88 4 2	170 - -	135 - -	50 - -	110 - -	95 - -	33 3	30 4	28 -	22 2	41
140 - -	- -	- -	- -	115 - -	100 - -	35 7	32 1	30 11	23 11	42
71 9 -	170 - -	135 - -	50 - -	100 - -	90 - -	33 3	30 4	28 -	22 2	43
200 - -	200 - -	140 - -	60 - - Carts provided.	115 - -	100 - -	33 3	29 9	29 2	23 4	44
240 - -	250 - -	160 - -	- -	150 - -	109 4 -	42 -	34 -	34 -	24 -	45
- -	- -	- -	- -	140 - -	117 - -	38 -	32 10	31 10	24 7	46
- -	- -	- -	- -	135 4 -	110 1 4	38 6	34 4	32 -	21 -	47
100 7 -	182 10 -	136 17 6	50 3 9 for horse and forage. Carts provided.	118 12 -	100 7 6	35 -	29 9	29 2	22 2	48
- -	- -	- -	- -	117 - -	106 12 -	37 -	29 2	32 -	22 2	49
- -	- -	- -	- -	124 16 -	104 - -	37 -	31 -	33 -	24 -	50
- -	- -	- -	45 - -	90 - -	82 2 -	29 -	27 -	26 -	22 -	1
- -	165 - -	135 - -	- -	120 - -	100 - -	35 -	31 6	30 -	24 -	2
105 - -	179 9 -	104 18 9	54 15 -	120 - -	95 - -	35 -	31 6	30 -	24 -	3
120 - -	175 - -	135 - -	50 - -	120 - -	95 - -	35 -	31 6	30 -	24 -	4
- -	165 - -	135 - -	50 - -	120 - -	100 - -	35 -	31 6	30 -	24 -	5
- -	170 - -	120 - -	20 - - for rent of house.	120 - -	97 10 -	35 -	31 6	30 -	24 -	6

TABLE II.—RANKS, NUMBER,

District No. 2.—

Number	COUNTIES AND BOROUGHS.	Established Strength, 29th September.		RANK AND NUMBER.									YEARLY PAY		
				Chief Officers.	Assistant Chief Constables.	Chief Clerks.	Superintendents.	Inspectors.	Sub-Inspectors and Sergeants.	Assistant Clerks.	Constables.	Additional Constables.	Chief Officers.		Assistant or Deputy Chief Constable.
		1900.	1901.										Pay.	Allowances.	
													£. s. d.	£. s. d.	£. s. d.
1	CHESHIRE	439	439	1	1	–	11	13	78	–	335	12	650 – –	250 – –	350 – –
2	Birkenhead	145	145	1	–	1	1	15	5	–	123	42	600 – –	. . .	. . .
3	Chester	50	50	1	–	1	–	3	5	.	41	–	350 – –	. . .	. . .
4	Congleton	11	11	1	–	–	–	–	2	–	8	–	145 – –	23 – –	. . .
5	Hyde	33	33	1	–	–	–	2	5	–	25	–	230 – –	12 – –	. . .
6	Macclesfield	38	38	1	–	1	–	3	4	–	30	–	300 – –	15 – –	. . .
7	Stalybridge	32	32	1	–	–	–	2	5	–	24	1	200 – –	. . .	. . .
8	Stockport	85	85	1	–	1	–	5	9	–	69	–	300 – –	. . .	. . .
9	CUMBERLAND	197	197	1	1	1	6	9	26	–	153	5	525 – –	112 10 –	202 5 5
10	Carlisle	50	50	1	–	–	–	2	5	–	42	–	350 – –	. . .	. . .
11	DERBYSHIRE	325	333	1	1	1	10	15	43	–	263	14	550 – –	100 – –	300 – –
12	Chesterfield	30	35	1	–	1	–	2	4	–	27	–	300 – –	. . .	. . .
13	Derby	120	120	1	–	1	1	6	16	–	96	–	350 – –	. . .	. . .
14	Glossop	26	26	1	–	–	–	1	4	–	20	–	200 – –	. . .	. . .
15	DURHAM	618	618	1	1	1	12	19	107	–	478	62	600 – –	100 – –	269 3 4
16	Durham	16	16	1	–	–	–	–	4	1	11	–	204 – –	61 3 –	. . .
17	Gateshead	110	115	1	–	1	1	4	15	–	93	6	350 – –	10 – –	. . .
18	Hartlepool	26	27	1	–	–	–	2	5	–	19	1	255 – –	37 12 –	. . .
19	South Shields	105	115	1	–	1	1	4	15	–	93	–	400 – –	12 – –	. . .
20	Sunderland	166	166	1	–	1	4	3	21	–	136	37	400 – –	70 – –	. . .
21	LANCASHIRE	1,639	1,618	1	1	1	21	44	241	–	1,309	62	1,200 – –	. . .	600 – –
22	Accrington	43	43	1	–	–	–	3	5	–	34	–	350 – –	. . .	. . .
23	Ashton-under-Lyne	48	45	1	–	–	–	2	6	–	36	–	330 – –	. . .	. . .
24	Bacup	26	26	1	–	1	–	1	3	–	20	–	220 – –	30 – –	. . .
25	Barrow-in-Furness	60	65	1	–	1	1	3	8	–	51	7	380 – –	. . .	. . .
26	Blackburn	140	140	1	–	1	1	7	18	–	113	–	500 – –	. . .	. . .
27	Blackpool	75	75	1	–	1	1	2	10	–	59	–	500 – –	25 – –	. . .
28	Bolton	166	167	1	–	1	1	6	20	–	138	–	400 – –	. . .	. . .
29	Bootle	72	72	1	–	1	–	3	7	–	61	–	400 – –	15 15 –	. . .
30	Burnley	97	96	1	–	1	–	6	9	–	79	–	350 – –	12 – –	. . .
31	Clitheroe	11	11	1	–	–	–	–	2	–	8	–	180 – –	. . .	. . .
32	Lancaster	33	40	1	–	1	–	1	6	–	32	–	300 – –	. . .	. . .
33	Liverpool	1,460	1,360	1	1	1	10	59	185	–	1,103	463	1,650 – –	. . .	750 – –
34	Manchester	1,000	1,006	1	–	1	6	46	116	–	836	1	1,000 – –	. . .	. . .
35	Oldham	158	158	1	1	1	1	6	15	–	133	–	400 – –	10 – –	156 – –

	Superintendents.			Inspectors.		Sub-Inspectors and Sergeants.		Constables.		
AND ALLOWANCES.						WEEKLY PAY.				
Chief Clerk.	Maximum.	Minimum.	Allowances.	Maximum.	Minimum.	Maximum.	Minimum.	Maximum.	Minimum.	Number.
£. s. d.	£. s. d.	£. s. d.	£. s. d.	£. s. d.	£. s. d.	s. d.	s. d.	s. d.	s. d.	
- -	240 - -	170 - -	55 - -	140 - -	100 - -	36 2	33 3	31 6	25 1	1
- -	200 - -	- -	- -	117 - -	104 - -	40 -	36 -	33 -	25 7	2
114 8 -	- -	- -	- -	114 8 -	104 - -	35 -	33 -	32 -	24 -	3
- -	- -	- -	- -	- -	- -	31 2	30 -	27 2	23 -	4
- -	- -	- -	- -	105 - -	100 - -	34 -	33 -	28 -	25 -	5
119 12 -	- -	- -	- -	114 8 -	104 - -	37 -	32 -	32 -	24 -	6
- -	- -	- -	- -	130 - -	104 - -	35 -	32 -	31 -	26 -	7
85 16 -	- -	- -	- -	- -	110 - -	39 -	33 -	32 -	24 -	8
127 15 -	202 5 5	174 17 11	60 - -	120 2 11	112 10 10	36 9	33 3	30 11	23 11	9
- -	- -	- -	- -	130 - -	114 8 -	40 -	34 -	37 -	24 -	10
- -	210 - -	150 - -	77 - -	130 - -	100 - -	37 4	32 1	32 6	24 6	11
92 1 8	- -	- -	- -	125 9 -	119 16 4	42 10	38 8	33 3	25 9	12
200 - -	- -	- -	- -	124 16 -	109 4 -	38 -	30 -	32 -	24 -	13
- -	- -	- -	- -	115 - -	- -	37 -	36 -	31 -	25 -	14
- -	249 8 4	159 13 9	70 - -	136 17 6	109 10 -	39 8	33 8	33 10	25 1	15
- -	- -	- -	- -	- -	- -	41 -	34 -	33 -	24 -	16
98 16 -	135 4 -	- -	- -	127 8 -	117 - -	42 -	34 -	33 -	24 -	17
- -	- -	- -	- -	121 13 4	103 8 4	39 1	33 3	32 8	24 6	18
91 - -	158 12 -	- -	10 - -	127 8 -	114 8 -	42 -	32 7	33 -	26 -	19
119 12 -	182 - -	166 8 -	- -	145 12 -	143 - -	42 -	33 -	33 -	25 -	20
350 - -	300 - -	200 - -	100 - -	150 - -	120 - -	38 6	34 5	31 6	25 1	21
- -	- -	- -	- -	150 - -	127 - -	40 -	35 -	32 8	26 3	22
- -	- -	- -	- -	132 12 -	127 8 -	41 -	35 -	36 -	26 -	23
78 - -	- -	- -	- -	107 18 -	- -	36 -	33 -	30 -	24 -	24
103 8 4	173 7 6	- -	15 - -	136 17 6	115 11 8	39 8	34 5	33 10	26 10	25
- -	200 - -	150 - -	- -	130 - -	111 16 -	40 -	34 -	34 -	24 -	26
109 4 -	170 - -	- -	40 - -	120 - -	- -	42 -	34 -	32 8	25 8	27
140 8 -	175 - -	135 - -	- -	127 8 -	110 10 -	38 6	33 -	34 -	25 -	28
- -	- -	- -	- -	180 - -	120 - -	45 -	36 -	35 2	25 7	29
115 5 4	- -	- -	- -	130 17 4	113 15 0	37 2	33 8	32 2	25 -	30
- -	- -	- -	- -	- -	- -	36 8	32 -	30 10	25 -	31
- -	- -	- -	- -	104 8 8	- -	37 -	32 7	31 2	24 -	32
500 - -	370 - -	240 - -	- -	215 - -	115 - -	42 -	27 -	33 -	22 -	33
140 - -	290 - -	180 - -	- -	150 - -	111 16 -	40 -	33 -	33 6	26 -	34
90 11 4	143 - -	- -	- -	117 13 -	108 11 -	40 -	32 6	32 4	25 -	35

Table II.—RANKS, NUMBER,

District No. 2 —

Number.	COUNTIES AND BOROUGHS.	Established Strength, 29th September. 1900.	1901.	Chief Officers.	Assistant Chief Constables.	Chief Clerks.	Superintendents.	Inspectors.	Sub-Inspectors and Sergeants.	Assistant Clerks.	Constables.	Additional Constables.	Chief Officers. Pay.	Allowances.	Assistant or Deputy Chief Constables.
													£. s. d.	£. s. d.	£. s. d.
	LANCASHIRE—continued.														
36	Preston	116	116	1	-	1	1	7	13	-	93	-	450 - -	20 - -	. .
37	Rochdale	81	88	1	1	1	-	5	11	-	69	-	400 - -	12 - -	135 - -
38	St. Helens	87	87	1	-	1	-	5	9	-	72	4	350 - -	.	. .
39	Salford	330	330	1	-	1	1	14	34	-	279	-	500 - -	.	. .
40	Southport	70	70	1	-	1	1	2	10	-	55	-	360 - -	20 - -	. .
41	Warrington	69	69	1	-	1	1	2	8	-	56	3	390 - -	.	. .
42	Wigan	68	68	1	-	1	1	4	8	-	53	-	325 - -	.	.
43	NORTHUMBERLAND	227	227	1	1	1	5	6	29	-	184	30	500 - -	50 - -	255 10 -
44	Berwick	13	13	1	-	-	-	-	3	-	9	-	135 - -	70 - -	.
45	Newcastle-on-Tyne	300	300	1	-	-	4	7	38	-	250	19	600 - -	.	.
46	Tynemouth	65	65	1	-	-	-	3	10	-	51	1	290 - -	10 - -	.
47	NOTTINGHAMSHIRE	201	202	1	1	-	6	8	27	-	159	6	600 - -	100 - -	300 - -
48	Newark	15	16	1	-	-	-	1	2	-	12	-	200 - -	10 - -	.
49	Nottingham	272	283	1	1	1	4	12	45	-	217	1	750 - -	.	200 - -
50	WESTMORLAND	36	37	1	-	1	2	2	5	-	26	2	175 - -	37 10 -	.
51	Kendal	16	16	1	-	-	-	1	2	-	12	-	160 - -	3 - -	.
52	YORK (EAST RIDING)	134	134	1	1	1	7	4	16	-	104	-	450 - -	.	.
53	Beverley	15	15	1	-	-	-	1	2	-	11	-	225 - -	.	.
54	Hull	331	331	1	1	1	5	10	40	-	273	1	500 - -	.	225 - -
55	YORK (NORTH RIDING)	248	250	1	1	1	9	17	27	-	194	22	450 - -	211 - -	240 5 10
56	Middlesbrough	96	96	1	-	-	-	5	11	-	79	8	450 - -	40 - -	.
57	Scarborough	49	50	1	-	1	-	3	5	-	40	1	325 - -	20 - -	.
58	York	80	78	1	-	-	1	5	9	-	62	-	350 - -	10 - -	.
59	YORK (WEST RIDING)	1,210	1,225	1	1	1	23	41	179	-	980	11	1,000 - -	.	500 - -
60	Barnsley	40	40	1	1	-	-	2	6	-	31	-	300 - -	27 12 -	.
61	Bradford	354	390	1	1	1	4	14	42	-	327	-	500 - -	.	190 - -
62	Dewsbury	37	37	1	-	1	-	2	4	-	30	-	300 - -	12 - -	.
63	Doncaster	36	36	1	-	1	-	2	5	-	27	-	250 - -	.	.
64	Halifax	101	107	1	-	-	1	5	15	-	85	-	400 - -	.	.
65	Huddersfield	120	120	1	-	1	1	6	14	-	97	1	350 - -	.	.
66	Leeds	500	507	1	1	1	7	16	57	-	424	-	800 - -	.	250 - -
67	Rotherham	53	57	1	-	-	-	2	9	-	45	-	425 - -	12 - -	.
68	Sheffield	465	515	1	-	-	3	24	44	-	443	9	800 - -	.	.
69	Wakefield	46	52	1	-	-	-	3	6	-	42	-	350 - -	30 - -	.
	TOTAL	13,531	13,597	69	18	44	176	540	1,774	-	10,989	832			

Superintendents.			Inspectors.		Sub-Inspectors and Sergeants.		Constables.		Number.
Maximum.	Minimum.	Allowances.	Maximum.	Minimum.	Maximum.	Minimum.	Maximum.	Minimum.	
£. s. d.	£. s. d.	£. s. d.	£. s. d.	£. s. d.	s. d.	s. d.	s. d.	s. d.	
165 – –	– –	– –	119 12 –	104 – –	38 9	33 –	36 –	24 –	36
– –	– –	– –	130 – –	104 – –	36 –	33 –	32 –	24 –	37
– –	– –	– –	130 – –	109 4 –	37 8	34 –	32 –	25 –	38
220 – –	– –	– –	140 – –	111 16 –	40 –	35 –	31 –	25 –	39
143 – –	– –	– –	124 16 –	– –	38 6	35 6	34 6	28 –	40
156 – –	– –	– –	120 18 –	114 8 –	38 –	34 –	33 –	25 –	41
165 – –	– –	– –	122 10 8	106 7 10	37 6	33 3	33 2	25 8	42
219 – –	173 7 6	– –	133 16 8	109 10 –	38 6	33 3	33 3	23 11	43
– –	– –	– –	– –	– –	29 6	28 6	27 6	25 6	44
250 – –	160 – –	– –	130 – –	124 16 –	42 –	35 –	33 –	25 –	45
– –	– –	– –	137 16 –	117 – –	42 –	34 –	33 6	24 –	46
220 – –	150 – –	65 – –	130 – –	100 – –	36 9	32 1	30 11	24 6	47
– –	– –	– –	100 2 –	– –	36 –	33 –	30 –	24 6	48
175 – –	165 – –	– –	137 16 –	117 – –	40 –	35 –	33 –	26 –	49
202 5 5	174 17 11	60 – –	120 2 11	112 10 10	36 9	33 3	30 11	23 11	50
– –	– –	– –	91 – –	– –	30 –	– –	29 –	23 –	51
199 19 9	120 2 11	55 – –	110 5 2½	89 14 7	33 3	29 2	28 –	22 2	52
– –	– –	– –	95 – –	85 – –	32 –	30 –	29 2	23 –	53
201 1 4	137 16 –	– –	132 12 –	109 4 –	46 –	34 –	40 –	24 –	54
220 10 5	159 13 9	– –	129 5 5	104 18 9	35 7	32 1	31 6	25 1	55
– –	– –	– –	119 12 –	105 6 –	36 –	34 –	32 –	25 8	56
– –	– –	– –	122 4 –	104 – –	38 –	33 10	32 6	24 6	57
150 – –	– –	– –	131 16 –	109 4 –	39 –	34 –	33 –	24 –	58
250 – –	160 – –	– –	129 5 5	106 9 2	37 4	33 3	31 6	25 1	59
– –	– –	– –	109 4 –	– –	36 –	32 –	29 2	25 –	60
170 – –	– –	10 – –	150 – –	109 4 –	40 –	34 –	35 –	24 –	61
– –	– –	– –	124 16 –	109 4 –	38 6	32 8	32 –	24 –	62
– –	– –	– –	127 15 –	109 10 –	40 3	33 3	32 8	25 1	63
160 – –	– –	– –	125 – –	110 – –	41 –	33 –	33 –	24 1	64
175 – –	– –	– –	150 – –	114 8 –	38 –	34 –	35 –	24 –	65
250 – –	140 – –	– –	150 – –	114 8 –	44 –	36 –	38 –	26 –	66
– –	– –	– –	135 4 –	114 8 –	43 2	34 –	33 2	26 –	67
250 – –	200 – –	– –	165 – –	115 – –	42 –	36 –	34 6	25 7	68
– –	– –	– –	122 – –	102 – –	38 –	32 –	32 –	24 –	69

TABLE II.—RANKS, NUMBER,

District No. 3.—SOUTH OF ENGLAND,

Number.	COUNTIES AND BOROUGHS.	Established Strength, 29th September.		RANK AND NUMBER.								YEARLY PAY		
		1900.	1901.	Chief Officers.	Assistant Chief Constable.	Chief Clerks.	Superintendents.	Inspectors.	Sergeants.	Constables.	Additional Constables.	Chief Officers.		Assistant or Deputy Chief Constable.
												Pay.	Allowances.	
	ENGLAND.											£. s. d.	£. s. d.	£. s. d.
1	BERKSHIRE - - -	173	173	1	-	1	10	4	23	134	2	600 - -	150 - -	- - -
2	Reading - - -	75	75	1	-	-	-	5	9	60	5	400 - -		
3	Windsor - - -	21	21	1	-	-	-	-	3	17	-	150 - -		
4	CORNWALL - - -	228	228	1	-	1	6	10	25	185	2	400 - -	150 - -	
5	Penzance - - -	13	13	1	-	-	-	-	2	10	5	175 - -		
6	Truro - - -	12	12	1	-	-	-	-	3	8	-	150 - -		
7	DEVONSHIRE - -	422	420	1	-	1	13	1	48	356	2	400 - -	200 - -	
8	Barnstaple - -	14	14	1	-	-	-	1	1	11	-	175 - -		
9	Devonport - -	77	83	1	-	-	-	3	10	69	-	260 - -		
10	Exeter - -	54	64	1	-	-	-	3	7	53	-	250 - -		
11	Plymouth - -	136	136	1	-	-	-	6	12	117	-	410 - -		
12	Tiverton - -	11	11	1	-	-	-	-	2	8	4	150 - -		
13	DORSETSHIRE - -	175	176	1	-	1	10	-	23	141	2	400 - -	150 - -	
14	Weymouth - -	28	29	1	-	-	-	2	4	22	-	275 - -		
15	GLOUCESTERSHIRE -	353	369	1	-	1	10	6	47	304	24	570 - -	180 - -	
16	Bristol - - -	499	499	1	-	1	4	21	66	406	16	800 - -	100 - -	
17	HAMPSHIRE - -	402	423	1	-	1	14	4	50	353	4	600 - -	150 - -	
18	Portsmouth - -	226	226	1	-	-	1	14	22	188	-	350 - -		
19	Southampton - -	125	134	1	-	-	-	8	15	110	2	500 - -	50 - -	
20	Winchester - -	21	27	1	-	-	-	-	4	22	-	200 - -		
21	HEREFORDSHIRE - -	80	80	1	-	1	6	-	14	58	2	400 - -	100 - -	
22	Hereford - -	33	33	1	-	-	-	2	5	25	-	250 - -		
23	KENT - - -	476	516	1	-	1	13	11	55	435	2	500 - -	200 - -	
24	Canterbury - -	26	26	1	-	-	-	1	4	20	-	230 - -		
25	Dover - -	57	57	1	-	-	-	2	8	46	1	200 - -		
26	Folkestone - -	40	40	1	-	-	-	2	5	32	-	300 - -		
27	Gravesend - -	36	40	1	-	-	-	1	7	31	-	275 - -		
28	Maidstone - -	43	43	1	-	-	-	2	6	34	-	240 - -	12 - -	
29	Margate - -	35	38	1	-	-	-	2	6	29	-	190 - -		
30	Ramsgate - -	46	48	1	-	-	1	-	7	39	4	325 - -		
31	Rochester - -	40	42	1	-	-	-	2	5	34	-	185 - -		
32	Tunbridge Wells -	49	56	1	-	-	-	2	4	49	-	350 - -		
33	MONMOUTHSHIRE -	180	180	1	-	1	5	5	24	144	18	450 - -	100 - -	
34	Newport - -	91	91	1	-	-	1	2	12	75	-	400 - -		

Maximum.	Minimum.	Allowances.	Inspectors.		Sergeants.		Constables.		Number.
			Maximum.	Minimum.	Maximum.	Minimum.	Maximum.	Minimum.	
£. s. d.	£. s. d.	£. s. d.	£. s. d.	£. s. d.	s. d.	s. d.	s. d.	s. d.	
200 - -	130 - -	. .	105 - -	95 - -	33 -	29 6	28 7	22 9	1
. .	. .	. .	120 - -	98 16 -	35 -	31 -	32 6	23 -	2
. .	. .	. .	. .	. .	37 -	33 -	35 -	25 -	3
170 - -	144 - -	. .	107 10 -	97 10 -	33 -	30 -	29 -	21 -	4
. .	. .	. .	. .	. .	31 -	. .	26 -	23 -	5
. .	. .	. .	. .	. .	30 -	29 -	25 8	19 10	6
225 1 -	146 - -	75 - -	89 14 -	. .	31 6	27 5	26 3	20 5	7
. .	. .	. .	91 - -	. .	31 -	. .	27 -	22 -	8
. .	. .	. .	127 - 8	111 16 -	39 2	35 -	33 8	23 6	9
. .	. .	. .	130 - 10	92 6 -	34 -	30 -	28 6	21 6	10
. .	. .	. .	131 19 -	114 12 -	40 9	36 4	33 6	23 6	11
. .	. .	. .	. .	. .	31 -	28 -	26 -	23 -	12
190 2 -	104 18 -	. .	. .	. .	32 8	28 7	26 3	21 -	13
. .	. .	. .	119 12 -	104 - -	38 6	31 7	30 9	24 -	14
220 - -	122 17 -	52l. to 62l.	100 - -	91 5 -	31 10	29 11	27 11	21 11	15
290 - -	170 - -	. .	180 - -	114 8 -	40 -	35 -	40 -	24 -	16
197 14 -	180 15 -	. .	109 10 -	. .	35 -	31 6	28 -	21 -	17
160 - -	. .	. .	130 - -	110 - -	39 -	35 -	34 -	23 -	18
. .	. .	. .	160 - -	110 - -	37 6	34 -	32 -	23 -	19
. .	. .	. .	. .	. .	35 -	33 6	28 -	23 -	20
149 - -	120 2 -	50l. to 60l.	. .	. .	33 3	28 -	26 10	21 -	21
. .	. .	. .	93 12 -	78 - -	35 -	31 -	30 -	23 6	22
219 - -	164 5 -	. .	114 1 -	. .	32 8	31 6	28 -	22 9	23
. .	. .	. .	100 - -	. .	36 6	32 6	31 8	24 -	24
. .	. .	. .	109 4 -	. .	38 -	. .	32 -	25 -	25
. .	. .	. .	122 4 -	. .	38 -	35 -	33 -	25 -	26
. .	. .	. .	114 8 -	. .	36 -	32 -	30 2	24 2	27
. .	. .	. .	130 - -	98 16 -	36 -	32 -	30 -	24 -	28
. .	. .	. .	130 - -	119 12 -	37 6	34 10	33 4	24 -	29
101 4 -	. .	. .	. .	. .	37 6	34 10	32 -	24 -	30
. .	. .	. .	109 4 -	. .	36 -	32 -	31 -	24 -	31
. .	. .	. .	124 - -	. .	37 -	34 -	33 2	24 -	32
260 - -	200 - -	60l. to 65l.	127 15 -	107 19 -	37 4	32 8	31 6	25 1	33
180 - -	. .	. .	135 4 -	114 8 -	40 -	36 -	33 6	26 -	34

G g

TABLE II.—RANKS, NUMBER

District No. 3.—SOUTH OF ENGLAND

Number.	COUNTIES AND BOROUGHS.	Established Strength, 29th September 1900.	Established Strength, 29th September 1901.	Chief Officers.	Assistant Chief Constables.	Chief Clerks.	Superintendents.	Inspectors.	Sergeants.	Constables.	Additional Constables.	Chief Officers. Pay. £. s. d.	Chief Officers. Allowances. £. s. d.	Assistant or Deputy Chief Constable. £. s. d.
	ENGLAND—continued.													
35	SOMERSETSHIRE	339	344	1	–	1	15	–	59	268	–	500 – –	100 – –	
36	Bath	86	85	1	–	–	–	5	12	67	–	350 – –		
37	Bridgwater	15	15	1	–	–	–	–	2	12	–	175 – –		
38	SURREY	231	270	1	–	–	7	8	26	228	7	500 – –	100 – –	
39	Guildford	19	19	1	–	–	–	–	4	14	–	250 – –		
40	Reigate	33	33	1	–	–	–	2	4	26	–	325 – –		
41	SUSSEX (EAST)	189	192	1	–	1	8	–	22	160	–	460 – –	100 – –	
42	Brighton	185	185	1	–	1	3	8	14	153	3	400 – –		
43	Eastbourne	62	66	1	–	–	–	3	12	50	–	300 – –		
44	Hastings	107	107	1	–	–	1	3	17	85	26	400 – –		
45	Hove	59	59	1	–	–	–	2	8	48	–	400 – –		
46	SUSSEX (WEST)	147	151	1	–	1	7	1	15	126	1	415 – –	100 – –	
47	WIGHT, ISLE OF	55	55	1	–	–	3	2	7	42	–	250 – –	50 – –	
48	Ryde	14	15	1	–	–	–	–	2	12	–	154 – –		
49	WILTSHIRE	236	246	1	–	1	9	14	32	189	5	600 – –	100 – –	
50	Salisbury	18	18	1	–	–	–	–	3	14	–	175 – –		
	SOUTH WALES.													
1	BRECONSHIRE	44	44	1	–	–	2	1	9	31	5	300 – –	50 – –	
2	CARDIGANSHIRE	41	41	1	–	–	2	1	5	32	–	275 – –	50 – –	
3	CARMARTHENSHIRE	90	90	1	–	–	3	4	18	64	1	400 – –	40 – –	
4	Carmarthen	12	12	1	–	–	–	–	2	9	–	150 – –		
5	GLAMORGANSHIRE	425	438	1	–	1	5	17	42	372	39	550 – –	150 – –	
6	Cardiff	239	239	1	–	1	3	9	29	196	3	800 – –		
7	Neath	14	17	1	–	1	–	–	3	12	–	150 – –		
8	Swansea	104	104	1	–	1	1	5	13	83	10	525 – –		
9	PEMBROKESHIRE	71	71	1	–	–	3	1	11	55	–	390 – –	25 – –	
10	RADNORSHIRE	18	18	1	–	–	–	1	3	13	5	275 – –		
	TOTAL	7,150	7,357	60	–	19	166	209	912	5,991	200			

AND RATES OF PAY—*continued*.

AND SOUTH WALES—*continued*.

	Superintendents.			Inspectors.		Sergeants.		Constables.		
AND ALLOWANCES.						WEEKLY PAY.				
Chief Clerk.	Maximum.	Minimum.	Allowances.	Maximum.	Minimum.	Maximum.	Minimum.	Maximum.	Minimum.	Number.
£. s. d.	£. s. d.	£. s. d.	£. s. d.	£. s. d.	£. s. d.	s. d.	s. d.	s. d.	s. d.	
165 - -	260 - -	125 - -	55l. to 75l.	- -	- -	33 3	28 7	28 -	21 -	35
. .	. .	. .	. .	114 8 -	100 2 -	34 6	31 -	31 -	23 -	36
. .	. .	. .	. .	. .	. .	33 3	31 6	27 6	22 2	37
. .	254 15 -	160 12 -	- -	176 8 -	110 8 -	33 3	29 9	29 2	22 9	38
. .	. .	. .	. .	. .	. .	40 -	35 -	32 -	23 -	39
. .	. .	. .	. .	119 18 -	114 14 -	40 -	35 -	32 -	27 -	40
150 - -	160 - -	120 - -	70 - -	. .	. .	33 3	29 9	28 -	22 6	41
150 - -	165 - -	145 - -	. .	130 - -	104 - -	38 -	34 -	32 -	24 -	42
. .	. .	. .	. .	114 8 -	109 4 -	39 -	33 10	31 5	25 -	43
. .	163 16 -	. .	. .	124 16 -	109 4 -	38 6	32 6	32 -	25 -	44
. .	. .	. .	. .	140 - -	130 - -	39 2	36 -	32 2	26 -	45
135 7 -	187 1 -	118 12 -	. .	112 10 -	. .	35 7	29 9	28 7	22 2	46
. .	165 11 -	130 15 -	. .	118 12 -	. .	33 3	30 11	28 -	21 -	47
. .	. .	. .	. .	. .	. .	35 6	34 6	29 -	23 6	48
135 7 -	195 7 -	135 11 -	. .	92 8 -	89 9 -	32 -	29 6	27 6	21 -	49
. .	. .	. .	. .	. .	. .	33 -	30 -	28 -	21 -	50
. .	150 - -	. .	40 - -	91 17 -	. .	35 4	33 4	28 -	23 -	1
. .	160 11 -	141 8 -	30l. to 50l.	91 5 -	. .	33 10	29 9	29 2	22 9	2
. .	200 - -	190 - -	50 - -	124 16 -	100 2 -	36 2	31 6	29 9	23 11	3
. .	. .	. .	. .	. .	. .	31 -	-	27 -	24 -	4
140 - -	260 - -	140 - -	65 - -	140 - -	110 - -	37 4	32 8	32 1	25 1	5
156 - -	240 - -	156 - -	. .	163 5 -	117 - -	45 -	37 -	38 -	26 -	6
87 2 -	. .	. .	. .	. .	. .	37 2	32 8	31 6	26 6	7
147 - -	210 - -	. .	. .	136 10 -	126 2 -	42 -	36 -	36 -	26 -	8
. .	190 - -	180 - -	25 - -	102 10 -	. .	32 8	30 4	28 -	22 2	9
. .	. .	. .	. .	95 - -	. .	33 10	31 6	28 7	23 11	10

rict No. 1.—MIDLAND, EASTERN COUNTIES, AND NORTH WALES.

	Population. Census		Number of Public Houses.			Number of Beer and Cider Houses.			Refreshment Houses with Wine Licenses.			Number of Persons Drunk, and Drunk and Disorderly.		
	1881.	1891.	Houses.	Proceeded against.	Convicted.	Houses.	Proceeded against.	Convicted.	Houses.	Proceeded against.	Convicted.	Proceeded against.	Convicted.	Discharged.
D.	101,201	102,906	443	3	3	335	1	1	21	-	-	155	151	4
	19,532	28,023	59	-	-	85	-	-	5	-	-	91	91	-
	23,959	30,056	98	2	2	51	-	-	10	-	-	98	92	6
BE	162,120	173,227	809	15	6	465	-	-	73	-	-	328	304	27
	10,618	13,435	65	-	-	25	-	-	3	-	-	24	20	4
C	86,875	83,303	387	6	5	290	2	2	15	-	-	54	54	-
	35,372	36,983	199	1	1	58	-	-	22	-	-	40	40	-
	54,070	63,340	289	4	3	262	4	3	19	-	-	88	74	14
	303,204	335,136	1,097	25	14	684	16	11	149	-	-	771	730	41
	28,395	34,559	112	4	4	67	3	1	-	-	-	71	65	6
	157,677	177,478	775	14	9	612	5	4	100	-	-	450	417	33
	10,930	12,898	59	3	3	34	-	-	-	-	-	75	69	6
BE	59,614	55,015	303	5	4	255	3	2	32	-	-	110	106	4
	199,200	201,464	772	27	19	345	3	1	64	-	-	687	662	25
	122,351	174,624	292	8	8	482	1	1	71	-	-	386	375	11
	353,983	338,808	1,088	33	25	489	6	6	9	-	-	1,588	1,568	20
	14,926	14,593	47	4	3	40	-	-	13	-	-	168	95	73
	16,886	16,746	49	1	-	38	-	-	13	-	-	37	29	8
y	20,682	51,934	51	11	4	109	7	4	1	-	-	624	607	17
	37,312	41,491	114	7	7	81	1	1	23	-	-	149	146	3
	10,890	10,040	27	2	2	22	-	-	7	-	-	34	34	-
	301,217	318,202	1,281	12	9	423	2	2	34	-	-	438	416	22
uth	48,466	49,334	173	2	1	108	1	1	4	-	-	294	285	9
	18,475	18,360	158	5	4	10	-	-	-	-	-	88	80	8
	87,843	100,970	540	13	9	49	-	-	29	-	-	188	167	21
HIRE	186,213	203,281	623	11	8	451	1	-	77	-	-	488	469	19
	51,880	61,012	86	2	2	380	4	4	16	-	-	284	178	6
	141,300	130,985	577	4	2	259	2	2	48	-	-	168	156	12
	3,600	12,758	45	3	1	42	1	1	-	-	-	57	57	-
	35,929	45,712	139	-	-	127	-	-	12	-	-	175	172	3

Table III.—LICENSED HOUSES AND DRUNKENNESS—*continued.*

District No. 1.—MIDLAND, EASTERN COUNTIES, AND NORTH WALES—*continued.*

Number	COUNTIES AND BOROUGHS.	Population. Census 1881	Population. Census 1891	Number of Public Houses. Houses	Proceeded against	Convicted	Number of Beer and Cider Houses. Houses	Proceeded against	Convicted	Refreshment Houses with Wine Licenses. Houses	Proceeded against	Convicted	Number of Persons Drunk, and Drunk and Disorderly. Proceeded against	Convicted	Discharged
	ENGLAND—*continued.*														
31	PETERBOROUGH (Liberty)	9,383	10,078	41	–	–	22	–	–	–	–	–	26	26	–
32	Peterborough (City)	21,219	25,171	67	1	1	87	1	–	–	–	–	51	48	3
33	RUTLANDSHIRE	21,434	20,659	75	1	1	55	1	1	–	–	–	28	23	5
34	SHROPSHIRE	210,590	209,860	702	21	14	313	4	3	74	–	–	1,538	1,466	72
35	Shrewsbury	26,478	26,967	144	4	3	26	–	–	23	–	–	145	138	7
36	STAFFORDSHIRE	773,521	858,391	2,066	60	37	2,466	47	37	277	–	–	6,596	6,273	23
37	Hanley	48,354	54,946	56	4	3	217	4	2	23	–	–	492	443	49
38	Newcastle-under-Lyme	17,506	18,542	66	3	2	65	1	1	16	–	–	278	275	3
39	Walsall	58,808	71,789	174	7	3	144	5	4	37	–	–	283	195	88
40	Wolverhampton	75,738	82,662	207	2	2	264	5	5	5	–	–	364	315	49
41	SUFFOLK (EAST)	176,980	183,478	541	5	4	292	10	1	80	–	–	262	250	12
42	Ipswich	50,762	57,360	153	–	–	149	2	–	3	–	–	189	185	4
43	SUFFOLK (WEST)	112,397	121,706	430	3	3	224	4	3	53	–	–	132	111	21
44	WARWICKSHIRE	278,219	277,566	789	18	12	546	9	6	105	–	–	1,291	1,170	121
45	Birmingham	400,757	478,113	645	16	5	1,386	34	16	191	–	–	3,249	2,836	413
46	Coventry	42,111	58,479	278	5	2	37	1	1	–	–	–	134	111	23
47	Leamington	22,976	26,930	86	3	2	26	–	–	18	–	–	62	62	1
48	WORCESTERSHIRE	302,553	314,772	986	40	33	618	29	24	142	–	–	2,781	2,644	137
49	Kidderminster	21,270	24,803	102	10	10	48	1	1	11	–	–	186	168	18
50	Worcester	40,353	42,908	176	–	–	86	–	–	9	–	–	175	171	4
	NORTH WALES.														
1	ANGLESEY	50,964	50,098	178	3	2	1	–	–	8	–	–	250	221	2
2	CARNARVONSHIRE	119,195	115,886	395	24	11	13	–	–	51	–	–	796	712	84
3	DENBIGHSHIRE	108,931	120,807	409	16	13	181	5	3	12	–	–	937	888	49
4	FLINTSHIRE	80,373	76,913	384	11	9	102	4	2	2	–	–	306	300	6
5	MERIONETHSHIRE	52,483	49,212	124	9	8	5	1	2	9	–	–	242	227	15
6	MONTGOMERYSHIRE	65,798	58,003	213	11	4	32	2	–	6	–	–	298	259	39
	TOTAL	5,905,576	6,372,724	20,219	500	337	14,101	235	161	2,029	–	–	29,300	27,323	1,977

TABLE III.—LICENSED HOUSES AND DRUNKENNESS—*continued.*

District No. 2.—NORTHERN.

COUNTIES AND BOROUGHS.	Population. Census 1881.	Population. Census 1891.	Number of Public Houses. Houses.	Proceeded against.	Convicted.	Number of Beer and Cider Houses. Houses.	Proceeded against.	Convicted.	Refreshment Houses with Wine Licenses. Houses.	Proceeded against.	Convicted.	Number of Persons Drunk and Drunk and Disorderly. Proceeded against.	Convicted.	Discharged.
· · ·	405,503	431,898	878	33	21	669	13	11	184	-	-	1,325	1,683	142
ead · · ·	84,006	92,857	141	5	3	185	3	1	-	-	-	848	680	168
· · ·	36,794	37,107	153	3	2	57	-	-	13	-	-	359	330	29
on · · ·	11,116	10,744	58	1	-	10	-	-	12	-	-	55	36	19
· · ·	-	30,670	49	1	-	90	4	-	15	-	-	98	88	10
field · ·	37,514	36,009	128	3	2	68	2	1	16	-	-	116	100	16
ige · ·	25,977	26,783	59	2	2	65	2	1	5	-	-	106	100	6
t · · ·	50,533	70,268	130	2	2	146	1	-	20	-	-	512	506	6
ND · · ·	214,764	227,373	944	34	16	133	7	5	47	-	-	1,323	1,204	119
· · ·	36,585	39,176	112	2	-	16	-	-	-	-	-	510	452	58
E · · ·	340,843	381,218	1,097	56	41	723	20	13	114	-	-	2,368	2,251	117
eld · ·	12,212	22,009	74	1	-	61	1	1	10	-	-	215	213	2
· · ·	81,175	94,146	254	7	6	275	5	4	20	-	-	776	707	69
· · ·	19,574	22,416	34	1	1	51	2	2	9	-	-	70	67	3
· · ·	596,104	689,003	1,536	90	59	670	9	5	141	-	-	11,682	11,361	321
· · ·	14,932	14,863	83	2	2	12	-	-	8	-	-	409	357	52
d · · ·	65,808	85,692	180	5	1	96	-	-	9	-	-	1,289	1,224	65
ol · · ·	16,998	21,276	54	4	3	30	-	-	2	-	-	240	232	8
ields · ·	56,875	78,391	146	12	7	121	-	-	19	-	-	1,401	1,282	119
nd · · ·	116,536	132,334	236	9	5	285	5	4	-	-	-	1,246	1,099	147
· · ·	1,385,187	1,417,123	2,277	65	38	2,722	38	24	362	-	-	11,664	10,599	1,065
on · · ·	31,434	31,603	47	2	1	68	3	3	11	-	-	164	156	8
nder-Lyne ·	37,040	40,463	87	1	-	99	-	-	22	-	-	226	165	61
· · ·	25,034	23,498	24	-	-	50	3	3	3	-	-	116	105	11
n-Furness ·	47,259	51,712	55	3	2	63	3	2	45	1	-	942	936	6
rn · ·	104,014	120,064	248	13	10	202	9	7	38	-	-	658	620	38
ol · · ·	14,229	23,846	67	6	2	67	-	-	2	-	-	284	271	13
· · ·	105,414	146,465	142	5	1	438	12	5	25	-	-	566	498	68
· · ·	27,374	49,217	49	2	1	11	-	-	3	-	-	644	693	41
· · ·	63,339	87,006	84	2	1	186	4	2	2	-	-	422	375	47
· · ·	10,176	10,815	22	1	-	15	-	-	3	-	-	37	34	3
· · ·	24,239	31,038	63	3	3	30	-	-	11	-	-	119	108	11
· · ·	552,548	629,443	1,805	52	31	280	3	2	101	2	2	4,277	4,059	218

TABLE III.—LICENSED HOUSES AND DRUNKENNESS—*continued.*

District No. 2.—NORTHERN—*continued.*

Number.	COUNTIES AND BOROUGHS.	Population. Census 1881.	1891.	Number of Public Houses. Houses.	Proceeded against.	Convicted.	Number of Beer and Cider Houses. Houses.	Proceeded against.	Convicted.	Refreshment Houses with Wine Licenses. Houses.	Proceeded against.	Convicted.	Number of Persons Drunk, and Drunk and Disorderly. Proceeded against.	Convicted.	Discharged.
	LANCASHIRE—*continued.*														
34	Manchester - - -	373,583	505,368	485	29	21	2,293	146	118	168	1	1	7,395	6,431	944
35	Oldham - - -	111,343	131,463	181	1	1	283	6	5	39	–	–	695	659	36
36	Preston - - -	96,537	107,572	207	10	6	243	8	6	32	–	–	398	297	101
37	Rochdale - - -	68,868	71,401	142	5	3	201	9	7	7	–	–	363	329	34
38	St. Helens - - -	57,403	72,446	146	4	3	127	1	1	11	–	–	783	755	28
39	Salford - - -	176,235	198,139	110	4	1	848	13	5	36	–	–	2,600	2,511	89
40	Southport - - -	32,206	41,406	25	1	1	52	–	–	21	–	–	189	151	38
41	Warrington - -	42,552	55,068	87	1	1	112	1	1	12	–	–	265	246	19
42	Wigan - - -	48,194	55,013	139	6	1	109	–	–	8	–	–	238	166	70
43	NORTHUMBERLAND - -	230,611	259,765	570	15	8	165	1	1	19	–	–	3,650	3,585	65
44	Berwick - - -	13,998	13,377	84	4	4	6	–	–	3	–	–	190	173	17
45	Newcastle-on-Tyne	145,359	186,300	389	5	2	254	4	4	56	–	–	4,809	4,389	420
46	Tynemouth - -	44,118	46,588	163	3	2	69	2	2	16	–	–	2,006	1,875	131
47	NOTTINGHAMSHIRE -	191,222	217,291	661	16	13	341	–	–	34	–	–	1,091	1,072	19
48	Newark - - -	14,018	14,457	55	–	–	41	–	–	9	–	–	47	44	3
49	Nottingham - -	186,575	213,877	415	10	4	597	5	3	51	–	–	975	901	74
50	WESTMORLAND - -	50,488	51,785	194	2	1	29	–	–	9	–	–	97	85	12
51	Kendal - - -	13,690	14,430	37	–	–	14	–	–	–	–	–	62	60	2
52	YORK (EAST RIDING) -	139,945	128,370	447	18	13	90	1	–	29	–	–	591	562	29
53	Beverley - - -	11,425	12,539	44	1	1	15	–	–	3	–	–	57	56	1
54	Hull - - - -	165,690	200,651	301	6	6	512	1	1	2	–	–	1,851	1,809	42
55	YORK (NORTH RIDING) -	253,473	250,139	954	20	15	160	–	–	43	–	–	824	794	30
56	Middlesbrough - -	55,934	75,532	79	4	4	91	–	–	–	–	–	763	759	4
57	Scarborough - -	30,504	33,776	164	6	5	42	–	–	29	–	–	202	168	34
58	York - - - -	61,789	67,926	198	13	7	114	1	1	27	–	–	416	371	45
59	YORK (WEST RIDING) -	1,119,897	1,129,830	2,358	99	62	1,785	44	28	274	–	–	12,677	12,284	393
60	Barnsley - - -	–	35,427	68	2	2	89	5	4	13	–	–	392	385	7
61	Bradford - - -	194,495	266,164	272	6	3	775	7	5	76	–	–	498	453	45
62	Dewsbury - - -	29,637	29,847	50	–	–	80	3	2	6	–	–	139	136	3
63	Doncaster - - -	21,139	25,933	76	2	2	59	–	–	19	–	–	147	103	44
64	Halifax - - -	81,117	91,778	125	1	1	313	3	3	8	–	–	213	155	58
65	Huddersfield - -	86,502	95,420	165	7	4	149	2	–	23	–	–	216	206	10
66	Leeds - - - -	309,126	367,505	341	13	10	841	10	7	–	–	–	1,889	1,677	212
67	Rotherham - -	34,782	42,061	76	5	2	114	2	1	3	–	–	614	579	35
68	Sheffield - - -	284,508	324,243	511	12	9	1,210	13	11	73	–	–	1,292	1,209	83
69	Wakefield - - -	30,805	36,815	120	2	1	77	–	–	19	–	–	592	589	3
	TOTAL - -	9,458,896	10,685,221	21,700	761	482	20,215	437	312	2,452	3	3	94,793	88,525	6,268

Table III.—LICENSED HOUSES AND DRUNKENNESS—*continued*.

District No. 3.—SOUTH OF ENGLAND AND SOUTH WALES.

Number	COUNTIES AND BOROUGHS.	Population. Census		Number of Public Houses.			Number of Beer and Cider Houses.			Refreshment Houses with Wine Licenses.			Number of Persons Drunk, and Drunk and Disorderly.		
		1881.	1891.	Houses.	Proceeded against.	Convicted.	Houses.	Proceeded against.	Convicted.	Houses.	Proceeded against.	Convicted.	Proceeded against.	Convicted.	Discharged.
	ENGLAND.														
1	BERKSHIRE - - -	155,676	164.124	666	8	5	360	3	1	62	–	–	332	305	27
2	Reading - - -	48,760	60,054	115	2	1	152	1	1	14	–	–	204	178	26
3	Windsor - - -	12,273	12.327	46	–	–	38	–	–	–	–	–	65	55	10
4	CORNWALL - - -	307,678	297,097	623	21	18	87	1	1	30	–	–	563	552	11
5	Penzance - - -	12,409	12,432	27	1	1	17	–	–	–	–	–	34	34	–
6	Truro - - -	10,619	11,131	35	5	4	6	1	1	8	–	–	34	32	2
7	DEVONSHIRE - - -	420,512	418,804	1,327	27	14	242	2	2	123	–	–	1,440	1,370	70
8	Barnstaple - -	12,282	13,763	69	3	3	3	–	–	7	–	–	21	19	2
9	Devonport - -	48,939	54,803	126	4	3	101	1	1	21	–	–	336	327	9
10	Exeter - - -	37,665	45,579	156	3	1	33	–	–	3	–	–	221	187	34
11	Plymouth - - -	73,794	88,941	145	5	4	162	5	3	39	–	–	372	298	74
12	Tiverton - - -	10,462	10,892	32	1	1	4	–	–	10	–	–	21	19	2
13	DORSETSHIRE - -	177,254	172,214	529	10	5	244	3·	2	46	–	–	356	317	39
14	Weymouth - -	13,715	21,328	82	1	1	25	–	–	16	–	–	55	50	5
15	GLOUCESTERSHIRE	403,594	365,842	942	20	15	921	12	11	95	–	–	910	805	105
16	Bristol - - -	206,874	281,156	468	5	4	804	11	7	2	–	–	1,168	1,082	86
17	HAMPSHIRE - - -	314,012	347,793	972	40	26	706	16	9	245	–	–	1,945	1,695	250
18	Portsmouth - -	127,989	159,251	321	1	1	518	8	5	9	–	–	671	600	71
19	Southampton - -	60,051	86,084	221	7	5	281	6	3	4	–	–	659	599	60
20	Winchester - -	17,780	20,203	99	4	3	41	–	–	21	–	–	60	42	18
21	HEREFORDSHIRE - -	101,428	96,097	273	5	3	147	2	2	33	–	–	199	172	27
22	Hereford - - -	19,821	20,267	106	7	3	9	–	–	6	–	–	104	42	62
23	KENT - - - -	434,478	479,525	1,378	38	33	874	11	9	229	–	–	2,270	2,165	105
24	Canterbury - -	21,848	23,062	155	4	2	16	–	–	14	–	–	63	55	8
25	Dover - - -	30,270	33,300	180	4	3	15	–	–	3	–	–	145	101	44
26	Folkestone - -	18,816	23,905	89	3	3	41	1	1	11	–	–	116	109	7
27	Gravesend - -	23,302	23,876	89	8	6	41	1	1	22	–	–	402	359	43
28	Maidstone - -	29,623	32,145	76	2	–	108	1	1	–	–	–	102	83	19
29	Margate - - -	16,030	18,417	84	–	–	58	–	–	15	–	–	100	69	31
30	Ramsgate - - -	22,683	24,733	103	2	2	27	3	2	28	–	–	131	126	5
31	Rochester - - -	21,307	26,290	81	–	–	49	1	1	5	–	–	295	237	58
32	Tunbridge Wells -	24,119	27,895	41	1	–	76	1	–	26	–	–	146	146	–
33	MONMOUTHSHIRE - -	177,960	203,426	649	50	28	324	18	12	63	–	–	1,657	1,592	65
34	Newport - - -	38,469	54,707	92	6	2	88	1	–	18	–	–	428	384	44

TABLE III.—LICENSED HOUSES AND DRUNKENNESS—*continued.*

District No. 3.—SOUTH OF ENGLAND AND SOUTH WALES—*continued.*

Number	COUNTIES AND BOROUGHS.	Population. Census. 1881.	1891.	Number of Public Houses. Houses.	Proceeded against.	Convicted.	Number of Beer and Cider Houses. Houses.	Proceeded against.	Convicted.	Refreshment Houses with Wine Licenses. Houses.	Proceeded against.	Convicted.	Number of Persons Drunk, and Drunk and Disorderly. Proceeded against.	Convicted.	Discharged.
	ENGLAND—*cont.*														
35	SOMERSETSHIRE - -	467,157	372,612	965	17	10	656	11	7	92	-	-	852	795	57
36	Bath - - - -	51,814	51,844	169	6	6	77	5	4	34	-	-	96	92	4
37	Bridgwater - -	12,007	13,668	56	1	-	29	1	-	13	-	-	75	64	11
38	SURREY - - - -	164,740	189,089	572	12	4	300	6	5	137	-	-	648	581	67
39	Guildford - - -	10,858	14,316	42	1	1	29	-	-	18	-	-	93	64	29
40	Reigate - - -	18,662	22,646	41	2	2	34	-	-	16	-	-	76	64	12
41	SUSSEX (EAST) - -	187,113	164,836	437	10	8	231	3	3	2	-	-	364	347	17
42	Brighton - - -	107,546	115,873	303	2	2	281	2	2	121	-	-	347	304	43
43	Eastbourne - -	-	34,969	43	4	1	70	4	3	4	-	-	101	95	6
44	Hastings - - -	42,258	63,189	138	1	1	59	5	5	5	-	-	213	191	22
45	Hove - - -	20,804	28,335	30	1	-	16	-	-	37	-	-	63	60	3
46	SUSSEX (WEST) - -	131,436	140,619	463	6	5	259	6	5	5	-	-	573	553	20
47	WIGHT, ISLE OF - -	62,172	67,720	248	5	4	93	-	-	8	-	-	86	83	3
48	Ryde - - - -	11,461	10,952	65	1	1	11	-	-	27	-	-	31	30	1
49	WILTSHIRE - - -	244,178	246,737	669	7	4	348	1	1	68	-	-	367	341	26
50	Salisbury - - -	14,792	15,533	67	-	-	5	-	-	2	-	-	67	43	24
	SOUTH WALES.														
1	BRECONSHIRE - -	52,489	51,393	333	29	18	53	-	-	21	-	-	363	344	19
2	CARDIGANSHIRE - -	71,212	63,467	295	12	9	2	-	-	18	-	-	248	228	20
3	CARMARTHENSHIRE -	114,350	120,266	658	34	23	29	1	-	4	-	-	528	499	29
4	Carmarthen - -	10,514	10,300	91	5	1	-	-	-	-	-	-	50	45	5
5	GLAMORGANSHIRE -	341,833	456,841	1,258	110	75	434	31	25	137	-	-	10,585	10,079	506
6	Cardiff - - -	82,761	128,915	192	15	9	94	3	-	70	-	-	581	183	398
7	Neath - - -	10,409	11,113	55	3	2	32	2	2	3	-	-	283	280	3
8	Swansea - - -	76,430	90,349	298	14	9	77	4	3	4	-	-	682	577	105
9	PEMBROKESHIRE - -	90,882	88,296	474	40	32	5	-	-	18	-	-	614	579	35
10	RADNORSHIRE - -	23,528	21,791	105	6	3	13	-	-	11	-	-	192	179	13
	TOTALS - -	5,873,911	6,327,077	18,464	642	430	9,855	195	141	2,093	-	-	33,803	30,906	2,897

H H

TABLE IV.—RETURN OF PRICES PAID FOR CONSTABLES' CLOTHING, 1901.

District No. 1.—MIDLAND, EASTERN COUNTIES, AND NORTH WALES.

Number	COUNTIES AND BOROUGHS	Dress Coat or Tunic.	Trousers, per Pair.	Great Coat.	Helmet.	Cap.	Cape.	Boots, per Pair, or Boot Allowance.	Serge Suit.	REMARKS.
		£. s. d.	£. s. d.	£. s. d.	£. s. d.	£. s. d.	£. s. d.	£. s. d.	£. s. d.	
	ENGLAND.									
1	BEDFORDSHIRE -	1 1 9	- 13 6	1 9 6	- 5 8a	- 7 -b	- 18 6	1 19 -	- 16 9	a. Summer. b. Winter.
2	Bedford -	1 1 -	- 13 10	1 6 -	- 6 9	- 6 -	- 16 -	{- 19 3 / - 16 6}a	- 14 6	
3	Luton -	1 2 -	- 13 -	1 8 -	- 7 -	—	- 16 6	1 19 -	- 18 6	
4	BUCKINGHAMSHIRE -	1 2 4	{- 11 - / - 13 6}	1 6 -	- 9 6	—	- 16 -	1 6 -	- 13 -	
5	Wycombe -	1 4 -	- 12 -	1 6 -	- 7 6	—	- 17 6	1 6 -	- 10 9	
6	CAMBRIDGESHIRE -	1 4 -	- 13 3	1 10 -	- 7 6	- 4 9	- 19 6	1 10 -	- 15 -	
7	Cambridge -	1 2 -	{- 16 9 / - 13 -}	1 10 -	- 8 -	- 6 6	1 6 9	1 19 -	- 14 -	
8	ELY, ISLE OF -	1 - -	- 12 -	1 2 -	- 5 8	—	- 12 3	1 6 -	- 16 6	
9	ESSEX -	1 - 3	- 12 -	1 2 -	- 6 3	- 8 6	- 17 -	1 6 -	- 11 -	
10	Colchester -	- 18 11	{- 12 3 / - 13 9}	1 9 -	- 5 8	- 4 9	- 18 -	- 16 -*	- 12 -	
11	HERTFORDSHIRE -	1 3 9	{- 14 - / - 11 6}	1 7 6	{- 7 4 / - 4 9}	—	- 16 6	1 6 -	- 13 6	
12	St. Albans -	1 3 -	- 14 -	1 10 -	- 7 -	- 6 -	- 18 -	{- 17 6 / - 19 9}*	- 17 6	
13	HUNTINGDONSHIRE -	1 - 6	- 12 -	1 7 6	{- 6 - / - 0 -}	—	- 16 3	1 10 -	1 - 4†	
14	LEICESTERSHIRE -	1 2 -	- 12 6	1 2 6	- 5 9	—	- 18 -	- 16 6*	- 16 8	
15	Leicester -	1 1 6	{- 13 6 / - 10 6}	1 6 -	{- 7 - / - 6 -}	—	1 1 6	1 6 -	- 13 -	
16	LINCOLNSHIRE -	1 2 2	{- 8 9 / - 13 3}	1 11 6	- 7 -	- 4 9	- 16 6	1 6 -	- 11 3	
17	Boston -	1 8 -	- 17 -	1 12 9	- 4 6	- 5 8	- 19 6	1 10 4	1 - -	
18	Grantham -	1 10 -	- 17 6	1 14 6	- 9 3	- 6 -	1 - -	1 14 8	1 16 -†	
19	Great Grimsby -	1 10 -	{- 15 - / - 14 6}	1 18 -	- 6 6	—	- 19 6	1 10 4	- 15 -	
20	Lincoln -	1 10 6	- 16 11	1 18 -	- 7 9	—	- 19 6	1 10 4	- 14 6	
21	Louth -	1 10 -	{- 15 - / - 13 -}	1 16 -	- 8 6	- 5 -	- 16 6	1 19 -	- 18 6	
22	NORFOLK -	1 2 3	{- 12 4 / - 10 -}	1 7 6	- 5 9	—	- 16 6	1 6 -	- 18 -	
23	Great Yarmouth -	1 1 6	{- 12 - / - 11 9}	1 8 -	- 5 8	—	- 16 6	{- 10 6 / - 18 6}*	- 10 3	
24	King's Lynn -	1 - -	- 12 6	1 8 -	- 8 6	- 5 6	- 16 -	- 18 -*	1 1 -†	
25	Norwich -	- 17 6	- 11 5	1 4 4	- 5 2	- 6 6	- 15 6	1 10 -	- 10 9	
26	NORTHAMPTONSHIRE	- 19 0	{- 10 3 / - 9 3}	1 6 0	- 8 3	{- 3 6 / - 4 -}	- 17 3	1 6 -	1 - 3†	
27	Northampton -	1 - -	{- 12 6 / - 10 6}	1 5 9	- 6 -	- 5 6	- 16 -	1 16 -	- 17 6	
28	OXFORDSHIRE -	- 19 6	{- 12 - / - 11 -}	1 4 3	- 5 6	--	- 14 9	1 19 -	- 11 6	
29	Banbury -	1 4 6	- 13 -	1 8 -	- 7 3	--	- 18 -	1 6 -	- 13 9	
30	Oxford -	- 19 3	{- 12 - / - 11 0}	1 6 0	- 6 3	—	- 16 0	- 15 -*	- 12 6	
31	PETERBOROUGH (Liberty).	- 19 6	{- 9 3 / - 10 3}	1 6 0	- 8 3	{- 3 6 / - 4 -}	- 18 9	1 6 -	1 - 3†	
32	Peterborough (City)	- 18 3	- 11 -	1 3 0	- 6 6	- 4 -	- 17 6	1 6 -	- 19 2†	
33	RUTLANDSHIRE -	1 7 6	- 14 9	1 10 6	- 7 -	—	- 17 -	1 16 -	1 1 4†	

* These prices are paid for boots supplied : all other figures in the column show allowances when boots are not supplied.
These prices are paid for serge suits complete ; all others in the column are for jackets only.

TABLE IV.—RETURN OF PRICES PAID FOR CONSTABLES' CLOTHING, 1901—*continued.*

District No. 1.—MIDLAND, EASTERN COUNTIES, AND NORTH WALES—*continued.*

Number.	COUNTIES AND BOROUGHS.	Dress Coat or Tunic.	Trousers, per Pair.	Great Coat.	Helmet.	Cap.	Cape.	Boots, per Pair, or Boot Allowance.	Serge Suit.	REMARKS.
	ENGLAND—*cont.*	£. s. d.	£. s. d.	£. s. d.	£. s. d.	£. s. d.	£. s. d.	£. s. d.	£. s. d.	
34	SHROPSHIRE	- 19 -	- 12 -	1 5 -	- 7 3	- 6 2½	- 16 -	1 6 -	- 11 -	
35	Shrewsbury	1 8 -	- 16 -	1 12 -	- 7 5	- 4 3	- 17 6	1 10 4	- 11 6	
36	STAFFORDSHIRE	1 - 2	- 11 10	1 10 3	- 5 3	- 3 9	- 13 7	1 16 -	- 9 -	
37	Hanley	1 2 6	- 13 -	1 8 -	- 6 6	—	- 16 -	1 10 4	- 16 -	
38	Newcastle-under-Lyme.	1 1 -	{- 13 9 / - 10 6}	1 5 -	- 6 -	- 6 9	- 17 -	1 10 4	- 14 -	
39	Walsall	1 1 6	- 13 9	1 13 6	- 6 -	—	- 16 -	- 15 9	—	
40	Wolverhampton	1 1 6	- 14 -	1 6 -	- 4 9	- 4 10	- 18 -	1 16 -	- 11 6	
41	SUFFOLK (EAST)	1 - 6	{- 13 - / - 9 3}	1 4 -	{- 6 6 / - 6 3}	—	- 17 -	1 6 -	- 14 -	
42	Ipswich	1 6 6	{- 16 1 / - 15 1}	1 14 6	- 6 6	—	- 18 3	1 10 -	- 19 4	
43	SUFFOLK (WEST)	1 - -	- 11 9	1 10 -	- 5 6	—	- 17 -	1 6 -	- 10 3	
44	WARWICKSHIRE	- 19 6	{- 13 3 / - 11 6}	1 5 -	- 5 -	—	- 14 3	- 16 -*	- 11 6	
45	Birmingham	- 19 5	{- 13 - / - 12 5}	1 10 -	- 7 9	- 3 3	- 19 -	1 10 -	- 12 6	
46	Coventry	1 2 3	- 12 6	1 9 -	- 10 -	—	- 16 -	1 10 -	- 11 9	
47	Leamington	1 5 -	- 16 -	1 15 -	- 8 6	—	- 18 -	1 15 -	- 15 -	
48	WORCESTERSHIRE	{1 2 4 / 1 - 3}	{- 13 9 / - 11 6}	{1 12 - / 1 6 9}	{- 7 - / - 6 6}	{- 5 3 / - 3 11}	{- 15 6 / - 16 9}	{1 10 5 / 1 10 5}	{- 11 6 / - 11 9}	} The lower line shows prices paid by the borough of Dudley, which, though watched by the county police, makes a separate arrangement in regard to clothing.
49	Kidderminster	1 - -	{- 13 9 / - 11 -}	1 6 -	- 8 9	- 5 6	- 16 -	1 10 4	- 12 -	
50	Worcester	1 3 3	{- 13 6 / - 13 -}	1 8 9	- 7 9	- 5 9	- 16 9	{- 14 6 / - 16 6}*	- 15 -	
	NORTH WALES.									
1	ANGLESEY	- 16 6	{- 10 9 / - 10 -}	1 3 -	- 6 -	- 5 -	- 15 -	1 6 -	- 17 6	
2	CARNARVONSHIRE	- 19 -	- 12 6	1 4 -	- 7 9	- 4 1½	- 14 6	1 10 5	1 3 -†	
3	DENBIGHSHIRE	- 19 3	- 13 1	1 3 3	- 6 6	- 5 6	- 16 6	1 10 3	- 11 3	
4	FLINTSHIRE	1 - 6	- 13 -	1 6 6	- 9 3	- 6 -	- 15 -	1 6 -	- 16 -	
5	MERIONETHSHIRE	- 19 6	{- 12 3 / - 10 -}	1 4 9	- 6 -	- 4 -	- 16 6	1 10 5	- 12 9	
6	MONTGOMERYSHIRE	1 3 -	- 13 9	1 9 9	- 6 6	- 5 -	- 17 6	1 6 -	1 1 3†	

* These prices are paid for boots supplied; all other figures in the column show allowances when boots are not supplied.
† These prices are paid for serge suits complete; all others in the column are for jackets only.

TABLE IV.—RETURN OF PRICES PAID FOR CONSTABLES' CLOTHING, 1901—*continued.*

District No. 2.—NORTHERN.

Number.	COUNTIES AND BOROUGHS.	Dress Coat or Tunic.	Trousers, per Pair.	Great Coat.	Helmet.	Cap.	Cape.	Boots, per Pair, or Boot Allowance.	Serge Suit.	REMARKS.
		£. s. d.	£. s. d.	£. s. d.	£. s. d.	£. s. d.	£. s. d.	£. s. d.	£. s. d.	
1	CHESHIRE · · ·	- 19 3	- 11 10 dress. - 10 6 undress.'	1 7 -	- 8 3	- 4 8	- 15 -	1 6 -	{ - 11 9 / 1 - 3 }	Jacket.
2	Birkenhead · ·	- 19 -	- 11 9	1 5 9	- 5 6	- 4 -	- 15 9	1 6 -	- 12 -	
3	Chester · ·	- 16 11	- 11 6	1 8 -	- 5 6	- 13 -	—	1 6 -	—	
4	Congleton · ·	- 19 -	- 11 9	1 5 6	—	—	—	1 10 -	─ ·	·
5	Hyde · ·	- 19 9	- 12 6	1 6 -	—	—	—	1 10 -	—	
6	Macclesfield · ·	- 19 -	- 11 9	1 5 6	- 5 9	—	—	1 8 -	─ ·	·
7	Stalybridge · ·	1 1 -	- 13 -	—	—	- 6 3	- 17 6	1 - 6	—	
8	Stockport · · ·	—	- 12 9	1 4 9	- 7 7	—	—	1 6 -	- 12 6	Jacket.
9	CUMBERLAND · ·	- 18 3	- 10 9	1 2 -	- 5 2	- 4 -	- 18 3	2 5 7	- 19 6	
10	Carlisle · · ·	1 1 6	- 12 6	1 8 -	- 5 6	- 5 6	- 16 6	2 3 4	1 12 6	Suit.
11	DERBYSHIRE · ·	- 18 6	- 11 -	1 3 6	- 4 7	—	- 15 -	1 - -	- 10 9	
12	Chesterfield · ·	1 2 -	- 14 -	1 10 -	- 6 6	- 18 6	- 18 -	- 14 6	- 17 6	
13	Derby · · ·	1 3 -	- 13 6	1 13 -	- 7 3	—	- 16 6	1 10 -	- 12 6	
14	Glossop · ·	1 3 -	- 14 6	1 12 -	- 7 9	—	—	1 6 -	—	
15	DURHAM · ·	- 18 2	- 9 11	1 2 -	- 5 9	- 3 6	- 14 7	1 10 -	1 - -	
16	Durham · · ·	1 1 6	- 13 6	1 13 -	- 8 -	- 6 -	1 2 6	1 6 -	-12 -	Jacket.
17	Gateshead · ·	—	- 11 -	—	- 5 3	—	—	1 6 -	- 12 -	
18	Hartlepool · ·	1 12 -	- 16 9	1 18 6	- 7 6	—	1 - -	1 10 -	- 15 9	Jacket.
19	South Shields · ·	—	{ - 12 6 / - 11 - }	1 6 6	—	—	- 19 -	- 16 6	- 13 -	Jacket.
20	Sunderland · ·	1 3 -	{ - 12 6 / - 13 9 }	1 14 -	- 7 6	- 6 6	- 18 6	- 16 6	- 14 6	
21	LANCASHIRE · ·	1 - 10	- 13 3	1 8 4	- 5 11	—	{ - 18 - / - 17 3 }	1 8 -	—	
22	Accrington · ·	1 1 -	- 12 6	—	- 6 6	—	—	1 10 5	—	
23	Ashton-under-Lyne ·	1 - -	- 12 4	1 5 6	- 5 9	—	—	—	—	
24	Bacup · · ·	1 - -	- 12 -	1 6 6	- 5 -	- 4 -	- 15 6	1 6 -	1 2 3	Suit.
25	Barrow-in-Furness ·	1 1 -	- 12 6	1 9 -	- 5 6	—	- 16 6	1 10 5	- 13 6	Jacket.
26	Blackburn · ·	- 15 6	- 10 2	—	- 5 3	—	—	1 6 -	—	
27	Blackpool · ·	1 1 9	- 13 4	—	- 3 11	—	- 17 3	1 6 -	—	
28	Bolton · · ·	1 7 9	- 13 1	1 16 11	-. 6 -	- 5 6	- 18 6	1 10 -	1 3 11	Jacket.
29	Bootle · · ·	1 1 6	{ - 14 - / - 10 6 }	1 6 -	- 5 9	- 5 -	- 16 6	1 10 4	1 5 9	Suit.
30	Burnley · · ·	1 1 9	{ - 12 - / - 10 6 }	—	—	—	—	{ Per week. / - - 6 }	- 12 -	Jacket.
31	Clitheroe · · ·	{ 2 5 - / 1 3 6 }	{ 1 1 - / - 13 6 }	—	—	{ - 12 6 / - 5 11 }	{ Mackntsh. / 1 19 6 }	1 6 -	—	
32	Lancaster · · ·	1 6 -	- 12 6	1 18 -	- 8 6	- 4 4	- 16 6	1 - 6	1 6 6	Jacket.
33	Liverpool · · ·	- 15 2½	- 13 6	1 4 9	- 7 9	—	- 14 6	1 6 -	- 10 8½	Jacket.
34	Manchester · ·	1 - 3	{ S. - 11 9 / W. - 16 - }	1 4 r	- 6 9	—	- 17 -	1 10 -	- 11 9	Jacket.

TABLE IV.—RETURN OF PRICES PAID FOR CONSTABLES' CLOTHING, 1901—*continued.*

District No. 2.—NORTHERN—*continued.*

Number.	COUNTIES AND BOROUGHS.	Dress Coat or Tunic.	Trousers, per Pair.	Great Coat.	Helmet.	Cap.	Cape.	Boots, per Pair, or Boot Allowance.	Serge Suit.	REMARKS.
		£. s. d.	£. s. d.	£. s. d.	£. s. d.	£. s. d.	£. s. d.	£. s. d.	£. s. d.	
	LANCASHIRE—*continued.*									
35	Oldham	1 - 6	- 13 1	1 3 8	- 6 -	- 5 -	- 15 9	1 19 -	- 14 3	Jacket.
36	Preston	1 5 -	- 14 -	1 7 6	- 4 9	—	- 16 6	1 6 -	- 16 6	Jacket.
37	Rochdale	- 19 6	{ S. - 12 / W. - 10 -	} 1 5 -	- 7 6	- 6 6	- 17 -	1 6 -	1 1 3	
38	St. Helens	- 19 -	- 11 5	1 3 3	- 7 6	—	—	1 10 5	—	
39	Salford	1 1 -	- 12 -	1 7 6	- 6 -	—	—	1 6 -	—	
40	Southport	—	- 11 5	1 5 -	- 8 6	- 17 6	—	1 6 -	- 14 9	Jacket.
41	Warrington	1 3 -	- 13 9	1 3 -	- 8 6	- 5 3	- 15 6	1 3 -	- 15 6	Jacket.
42	Wigan	- 19 9	- 11 9	1 5 -	- 7 9	- 3 -	- 16 6	1 10 -	- 11 10	Jacket.
43	NORTHUMBERLAND	- 17 6	- 11 -	1 3 3	- 6 -	- 4 -	- 16 9	2 5 6	- 10 -	
44	Berwick-on-Tweed	—	- 15 -	—	—	- 5 10	—	1 16 -	- 15 6	Jacket.
45	Newcastle-on-Tyne	- 18 9	- 11 -	1 8 6	- 4 10	- 3 7	- 17 6	1 6 -	- 19 6	Jacket.
46	Tynemouth	—	{ S. - 11 6 / W. - 12 4	} 1 11 - / 1 16 -	} —	- 4 6	- 18 9	{ Per week. / - - 5	} 1 5 9	Jacket.
47	NOTTINGHAMSHIRE	1 1 -	- 12 6	1 5 -	- 8 -	—	- 16 10	1 4 -	- 15 -	Jacket.
48	Newark	1 6 -	- 15 -	1 8 6	- 8 -	—	- 16 -	{ Per week. / - - 9	} - 15 6	Jacket.
49	Nottingham	—	- 13 -	1 13 6	—	- 4 6	—	1 19 -	- 13 -	
50	WESTMORLAND	- 18 3	- 10 9	1 3 -	- 5 2	- 4 -	- 15 3	2 5 7	- 19 6	
51	Kendal	- 19 -	- 12 6	1 3 -	- 7 6	- 4 9	- 16 -	1 6 -	- 12 6	Jacket.
52	YORK (EAST RIDING)	{ (a) 1 4 6 / (b) 1 2 6	} - 12 3	{ 1 5 6 / 1 9 -	} —	- 4 8	- 17 6	1 12 -	—	(a) Sergeant. / (b) P.C.
53	Beverley	1 - 6	- 13 6	—	—	- 5 3	—	1 6 -	- 13 6	
54	Hull	1 3 6	- 13 6	—	- 5 6	- 4 6	- 18 3	1 6 -	—	
55	YORK (NORTH RIDING)	1 - 9	- 11 6	1 12 9	- 5 9	- 4 6	- 14 6	2 - -	- 19 3	Jacket.
56	Middlesbrough	1 8 6	- 16 6	1 12 6	—	- 3 8	—	1 15 -	1 11 9	
57	Scarborough	—	- 11 3	—	—	- 5 9	—	- 18 6	- 5 9	
58	York	1 - -	- 12 6	1 5 6	- 8 6	—	- 15 3	1 - -	- 12 -	
59	YORK (WEST RIDING)	- 15 11	- 10 4	1 5 3	- 6 3	- 3 -	- 16 6	1 10 -	- 10 3	Jacket.
60	Barnsley	- 19 6	- 12 6	1 6 6	- 7 4½	- 6 9	- 14 9	1 10 -	- 11 9	Jacket only.
61	Bradford	1 6 6	- 17 9	1 12 9	- 4 9	- 5 3	- 17 9	1 6 -	- 19 3	Jacket.
62	Dewsbury	- 19 6	- 12 6	1 3 6	—	- 4 -	- 16 6	1 10 -	—	
63	Doncaster	1 9 6	- 15 -	—	- 6 6	- 3 6	—	{ Per week. / - - 5	} —	
64	Halifax	1 6 -	{ - 14 9 / - 14 -	} 1 13 6	- 5 3	{ 1 7 6 / 1 - -	} 1 - -	1 6 -	1 - -	Jacket.
65	Huddersfield	1 4 5	- 11 3	1 15 7	- 5 -	- 9 6	1 3 8	- 14 6	1 3 1	
66	Leeds	- 17 9	- 11 -	1 - 3	- 6 -	- 3 9	- 14 11	1 6 -	- 11 8	Jacket.
67	Rotherham	1 1 -	- 19 10	1 10 6	- 6 3	- 5 -	- 17 11	1 16 -	- 16 3	Jacket.
68	Sheffield	1 7 6	{ - 16 9 / - 13 9	} 1 13 6	- 5 9	- 4 9	- 19 -	1 10 -	- 19 -	Jacket.
69	Wakefield	—	- 12 6	1 8 6	- 7 6	—	—	1 6 -	1 7 3	Suit.

TABLE IV.—RETURN OF PRICES PAID FOR CONSTABLES' CLOTHING, 1901—*continued.*

District No. 3.—SOUTH OF ENGLAND AND SOUTH WALES.

Number.	COUNTIES AND BOROUGHS	Dress Coat or Tunic.	Trousers, per Pair.	Great Coat.	Helmet.	Cap.	Cape.	Boots, per Pair, or Boot Allowance.	Serge Suit.	REMARKS.
	ENGLAND.	£. s. d.	£. s. d.	£. s. d.	£. s. d.	£. s. d.	£. s. d.	£. s. d.	£. s. d.	
1	BERKSHIRE · · ·	1 2 - {	$-\frac{12}{9}\frac{6}{7}$ }	—	- 6 3	—	—	1 6 -	—	
2	Reading · · ·	- 19 9 {	$-\frac{11}{8}\frac{3}{6}$ }	} 1 13 6	- 7 6	—	- 17 -	1 10 4	- 12 9	Jacket.
3	Windsor · · ·	- 19 - {	$-\frac{12}{10}\frac{-}{-}$ }	—	—		- 15 9	- 17 6	—	
4	CORNWALL · · ·	1 - - {	$-\frac{11}{9}\frac{6}{6}$ }	} 1 6 -	- 5 0	—	—	1 6 -	—	
5	Penzance · · ·	1 10 -	- 18 -	1 15 -	- 7 9	- 4 11	- 15 6	1 10 -	1 3 -	
6	Truro · · ·	1 11 - {	$-\frac{17}{14}\frac{-}{-}$ }	} 1 12 -	- 7 6	- 6 -	- 18 -	1 6 -	- 13 6	Jacket.
7	DEVONSHIRE · · ·	- 19 10 {	$-\frac{12}{9}\frac{10}{-}$ }	} 1 6 -	- 7 -	—	{ $-\frac{6}{13}\frac{-4}{10}$ }	} 1 5 -	- 19 8	
8	Barnstaple · ·	1 7 6	- 16 6	2 5 -	- 8 6	—	- 19 6	1 15 -	1 6 6	
9	Devonport · ·	—	- 14 6	1 8 6	- 5 8	—	- 16 -	1 14 8	- 13 · 6	
10	Exeter · · ·	—	—	1 3 6	- 8 11	{ $-\frac{11}{6}\frac{9}{-}$ }	- 16 -	1 19 -	1 1 -	
11	Plymouth · · ·	1 1 5	- 9 7	1 13 6	- 5 10½	- 4 7½	- 13 6	1 6 -	- 12 6	Jacket.
12	Tiverton · · ·	1 8 6	- 16 -	1 15 6	- 7 6	—	1 1 6	1 6 -	- 18 -	Jacket.
13	DORSETSHIRE · ·	- 19 -	- 19 -	1 3 -	- 6 9	- 5 9	- 16 -	1 6 -	- 12 -	Jacket.
14	Weymouth · ·	1 1 -	- 11 9	1 8 6	- 8 -	- 6 9	- 16 6	{ Per pair - 13 6 }	1 3 6	
15	GLOUCESTERSHIRE ·	· —	- 13 6	1 5 -	- 5 -	—	—	- 15 -	- 14 8	Jacket.
16	Bristol · · ·	- 17 3	- 11 6	1 3 6	- 6 3	- 2 9	- 15 6	1 10 4	- 9 6	Jacket.
17	HAMPSHIRE · · ·	1 1 3 {	$-\frac{12}{12}\frac{-}{3}$ }	} 1 13 -	- 5 3	- 4 6	{ $-\frac{14}{14}\frac{-}{6}$ }	} 1 6 -	- 12 -	Jacket.
18	Portsmouth · ·	- 19 3 {	$-\frac{11}{11}\frac{9}{6}$ }	} 1 8 6	{ $-\frac{6}{5}\frac{-}{6}$ }	} —	- 13 9	1 3 -	- 13 6	Jacket.
19	Southampton · ·	1 7 6	- 14 5	1 14 3	- 7 3	—	- 18 11	1 6 -	- 15 11	Jacket.
20	Winchester · ·	1 1 - {	$-\frac{12}{10}\frac{6}{6}$ }	} —	- 8 7	1 5 -	- 16 0	{ $\frac{1}{-}\frac{2}{17}\frac{-}{-}$ }	- 15 9	Jacket.
21	HEREFORDSHIRE ·	- 18 6 {	$-\frac{11}{8}\frac{6}{6}$ }	} 1 3 6	- 5 -	—	- 17 0	1 6 -	- 13 6	
22	Hereford · · ·	1 3 6	- 13 6	1 8 6	- 7 9	- 7 6	- 18 9	1 10 -	- 18 6	
23	KENT · · · ·	- 19 3	- 10 10	1 2 -	{ $-\frac{5}{6}\frac{3}{-}$ }	} —	- 14 3	1 10 5	- 10 3	Jacket.
24	Canterbury · ·	1 2 -	- 12 9	1 3 3	- 5 3	- 4 6	- 15 -	- 16 -	- 12 9	Jacket.
25	Dover · · ·	1 6 - {	$-\frac{14}{12}\frac{6}{6}$ }	} 1 16 -	- 4 9	—	1 1 -	2 12 -	- 18 -	
26	Folkestone · ·	1 15 10 {	$-\frac{17}{16}\frac{11}{6}$ }	} 1 19 6	- 6 11	—	—	{ Per pair - 16 - }	—	
27	Gravesend · · ·	- 19 10	- 11 6	1 7 -	- 5 3	- 6 9	- 16 6	- 14 6	1 8 3	
28	Maidstone · · ·	- 18 11	- 11 6	1 3 6	- 5 10	- 6 6	- 13 9	1 14 8	- 11 6	Jacket.
29	Margate · · ·	—	- 12 6	—	- 5 9	—	—	1 16	1 3 2	
30	Ramsgate · · ·	1 - 9 {	$-\frac{13}{13}\frac{6}{8}$ }	} 1 12 9	- 6 6	- 5 6	- 15 9	1 19 -	- 14 -	Jacket.
31	Rochester · · ·	1 2 6	- 15 6	1 8 6	- 9 3	- 4 6	- 19 -	1 10 4	- 17 6	
32	Tunbridge Wells ·	- 19 3 {	$-\frac{11}{10}\frac{10}{6}$ }	} 1 5 -	- 6 6	—	- 16 6	- 18 -	- 13 -	Jacket.

TABLE IV.—RETURN OF PRICES PAID FOR CONSTABLES' CLOTHING, 1901—*continued.*

District No. 3.—SOUTH OF ENGLAND AND SOUTH WALES—*continued.*

Number.	COUNTIES AND BOROUGHS.	Dress Coat or Tunic.	Trousers, per Pair.	Great Coat.	Helmet.	Cap.	Cape.	Boots, per Pair, or Boot Allowance.	Serge Suit.	REMARKS.
		£. s. d.	£. s. d.	£. s. d.	£. s. d.	£. s. d.	£. s. d.	£. s. d.	£. s. d.	
	ENGLAND—*cont.*									
33	MONMOUTHSHIRE	1 - -	- 13 6	1 6 6	- 5 1	—	.—	1 10 5	—	
34	Newport	1 - 6	- 11 9	1 4 9	- 5 9	—	- 15 8	1 6 -	- 13 6	Tunic.
35	SOMERSETSHIRE	1 2 3	- 11 9	1 13 3	- 6 3	—	1 - -	1 5 -	- 10 5	Jacket.
36	Bath	1 5 6	- 13 3	1 16 9	- 7 6	—	- 19 6	1 14 -	- 13 6	
37	Bridgwater	1 1 6	- 13 6	1 7 6	- 8 -	- 6 9	- 17 6	1 6 -	1 1 3	
38	SURREY	1 2 6	{ -13 2 / -11 - }	1 6 -	{ - 6 3 / - 4 9 }	—	- 15 -	1 6 -	- 17 -	
39	Guildford	- 13 6	- 13 6	1 6 6	- 7 -	—	- 16 6	1 14 8	1 - 9	
40	Reigate	- 19 6	{ -14 - / -13 - }	1 3 -	- 5 9	—	- 16 3	1 14 6	- 18 -	
41	SUSSEX (EAST)	1 - 6	- 18 8	1 10 6	- 6 -	- 5 6	- 15 -	1 16 -	- 13 3	Jacket.
42	Brighton	1 2 6	- 15 -	1 13 6	{ - 5 9 / - 5 3 }	—	- 19 6	1 10 -	1 15 6	
43	Eastbourne	1 1 3	- 13 6	1 11 6	- 6 3	—	—	1 16 -	- 13 3	Jacket.
44	Hastings	1 - -	{ -13 3 / - 9 3 }	1 2 6	- 5 3	- 4 -	- 18 -	1 10 -	- 14 7	
45	Hove	1 1 -	- 13 3	1 13 9	- 6 6	- 7 11	- 16 6	{ Per pair -17 9 }	- 18 6	
46	SUSSEX (WEST)	- 19 3	{ -12 - / -10 - }	1 4 9	- 7 -	—	- 15 10	1 6 -	- 12 6	Jacket.
47	WIGHT, ISLE OF	1 2 6	- 12 -	1 7 -	- 6 -	- 5 3	- 15 6	1 6 -	- 13 -	Jacket.
48	Ryde	1 4 3	- 13 6	1 10 -	- 7 3	—	—	1 12 6	—	
49	WILTSHIRE	- 19 10	{ -11 9 / -10 - }	1 7 3	{ - 5 - / - 5 6 }	—	- 17 7	1 6 -	- 11 -	Jacket.
50	Salisbury	1 2 -	- 13 6	1 6 -	- 5 7½	—	- 18 -	1 12 -	1 4 6	
	SOUTH WALES.									
1	BRECONSHIRE	1 4 -	{ -12 - / -10 - }	1 6 6	- 6 6	- 6 6	- 18 -	1 6 -	1 1 -	
2	CARDIGANSHIRE	- 19 6	- 12· 6	—	—	—	—	1 6 -	—	
3	CARMARTHENSHIRE	1 - -	{ -12 - / -10 9 }	1 4 9	- 6 6	- 4 6	- 15 9	1 10 4	- 17 3	
4	Carmarthen	1 3 6	{ -13 6 / -13 - }	1 8 -	- 7 3	- 4 -	- 16 -	{ Per week - - 6 }	1 6 -	
5	GLAMORGANSHIRE	- 18 11	- 11 9	1 7 6	- 5 9	- 3 4	- 15 6	1 6 -	- 17 3	Jacket.
6	Cardiff	1 - 10	{ -13 9 / -10 2 }	1 5 -	- 6 6	- 5 -½	{ -16 3 / -15 6 }	1 11 8	- 16 6	Jacket.
7	Neath	1 7 9	- 15 10	—	- 6 -	- 6 6	—	1 6 -	- 14 6	Tunic.
8	Swansea	- 17 3	{ -11 2 / - 9 6 }	1 3 -	- 7 2½	- 3 4	- 18 6	1 6 -	- 10 6	Jacket.
9	PEMBROKESHIRE	1 3 -	- 15 -	1 14 -	- 6 6	—	- 17 6	1 6 -	- 18 6	
10	RADNORSHIRE	1 - 6	- 13 6	1 6 -	- 6 1	- 4 6	- 15 -	1 6 -	- 14 6	

TABLE V.—(A.) COST OF THE POLICE, UNDER THE DIFFERENT

District No. 1.—MIDLAND

№	1. NAME OF POLICE FORCE.	2. Salaries and Pay.	3. Travelling Expenses, including Allowances and Cost of Removal of Constables.	4. Clothing and Accoutrements.	5. Harness, Horses, and Forage.	6. Rents, Rates, and Taxes, Purchase of Buildings, &c., less Amount received from Constables as Rent.	7. Printing and Stationery.
		EXPENDITURE					
	ENGLAND.	£. s. d.	£. s. d.	£. s. d.	£. s. d.	£. s. d.	£. s. d.
1	BEDFORDSHIRE - - -	7,901 3 -	100 - -	491 10 10	287 7 7	1,444 14 3	194 2 4
2	Bedford - - - -	3,146 3 7	11 15 7	267 4 -	3 13 1	344 10 5	31 17 3
3	Luton - - - -	3,890 6 9	10 14 8	148 9 6	—	37 1 -	42 8 4
4	BUCKINGHAMSHIRE - - -	11,446 16 11	440 9 1	784 14 8	349 17 10	1,689 9 8	95 13 7
5	Wycombe - - - -	1,902 15 3	—	79 16 10	—	18 5 7	7 5 5
6	CAMBRIDGESHIRE - - -	5,366 8 8	581 3 4	436 4 9	205 7 -	252 16 6	79 9 2
7	Cambridge - - - -	4,986 1 -	3 18 2	415 - 4	3 5 -	43 6 -	71 16 1
8	ELY, ISLE OF - - -	4,781 9 1	300 18 11	356 11 11	38 10 9	404 6 11	31 7 11
9	ESSEX - - - - -	30,181 16 10	1,482 11 11	3,047 7 6	1,317 3 7	3,838 18 1	237 16 1
10	Colchester - - -	4,500 8 11	9 1 -	234 3 -	31 19 1	466 7 7	20 2 -
11	HERTFORDSHIRE - - -	17,968 13 9	471 16 9	1,767 8 1	984 9 9	2,775 13 11	258 5 4
12	St. Albans - - -	1,315 5 6	13 10 -	131 8 11	—	60 11 -	26 18 -
13	HUNTINGDONSHIRE - - -	4,213 11 1	245 4 5	295 16 6	255 17 2	593 16 5	33 6 9
14	LEICESTERSHIRE - - -	13,552 15 10	576 6 2	1,499 10 4	547 5 11	1,922 11 1	140 4 -
15	Leicester - - -	17,171 19 5	467 15 3	1,356 1 9	44 12 6	707 1 5	154 5 10
16	LINCOLNSHIRE - - -	24,594 5 5	1,855 1 2	1,493 4 -	989 14 10	1,504 12 7	141 3 5
17	Boston - - - -	1,168 2 3	—	86 8 9	—	13 19 2	11 1 5
18	Grantham - - -	1,189 13 -	- 19 -	147 12 4	—	—	10 10 2
19	Great Grimsby - -	5,105 - 8	—	399 2 -	31 13 6	—	54 6 -
20	Lincoln - - - -	4,162 7 3	7 3 5	239 4 9	—	142 11 3	34 16 6
21	Louth - - - -	787 1 4	—	50 1 9	—	—	16 14 10
22	NORFOLK - - - -	18,139 16 10	755 8 6	1,440 10 9	873 16 -	1,446 10 7	191 17 8
23	Great Yarmouth - -	4,670 12 1	43 3 6	255 - 3	1 18 -	154 14 8	34 16 10
24	King's Lynn - - -	2,262 13 6	20 - 1	209 14 2	2 6 6	1 7 7	22 18 5
25	Norwich - - - -	8,942 5 6	13 14 6	430 12 3	—	98 10 11	105 16 9
26	NORTHAMPTONSHIRE - -	12,732 1 7	642 19 8	1,046 3 7	407 11 8	2,191 18 4	182 15 11
27	Northampton - - -	7,979 4 4	15 15 6	653 6 11	—	337 3 10	96 12 9

* Column 6 includes the cost of erecting and furnishing buildings, the purchase of land, and the interest and repayment of principal of loans; but expenditure defrayed out of loans is excluded.

HEADS OF SERVICE, FOR THE YEAR ENDED 31st MARCH 1901.

EASTERN COUNTIES, AND NORTH WALES.

	EXPENDITURE.				INCOME.			
8. Postage, Telegrams, and Telephone Charges.	**9.** Extra Police Borrowed on Special Occasions.	**10.** Other Miscellaneous Charges.	**11.** Deficiency of Police Pension Fund.	**12.** Gross Total Cost of Police.	**13.** Sums received for Services of Additional or Lent Constables.	**14.** Other Receipts credited to the Police Fund.	**15.** Amount received from Exchequer Contribution Account; Pay and Clothing.	**16.** Balance of Cost falling on Local Rates (being Amount in Col. 12, less Amount in Columns 13, 14, and 15).
£. s. d.	£. s. d.	£. s. d.	£. s. d.	£. s. d.	£. s. d.	£. s. d.	£. s. d.	£. s. d.
1	17 1 -	—	622 18 9	1,184 12 11	12,143 10 8	134 5 5	4,087 6 6	3,843 10 10	4,118 7 11
2	30 19 6	5 19 6	187 13 5	143 6 11	4,113 2 3	—	8 15 7	1,629 15 10	2,474 10 10
3	17 14 3	11 3 7	391 10 -	—	3,479 10 1	—	265 - 3	1,427 15 2	1,786 14 9
4	83 9 9	—	420 17 -	816 9 6	16,196 18 -	509 - 8	250 15 1	5,840 16 8	9,526 5 7
5	3 19 3	—	33 - 1	—	1,345 3 3	—	—	641 6 -	703 17 3
6	40 13 6	217 16 8	140 13 4	295 13 6	7,506 8 5	1,106 12 10	69 12 6	2,830 17 6	3,470 5 7
7	36 13 6	159 9 3	243 13 6	509 16 4	6,469 17 2	40 19 3	5 11 6	2,556 12 1	3,866 14 4
8	24 1 -	13 7 10	46 9 4	—	5,999 5 8	—	—	2,532 11 -	3,466 14 8
9	394 14 11	—	594 5 3	2,380 11 4	41,855 5 6	731 18 -	3,001 12 5	15,628 6 8	22,303 8 5
10	13 13 9	42 16 -	367 16 8	—	5,776 8 -	574 7 -	6 11 10	2,035 3 1	3,160 6 1
11	543 14 9	55 9 8	515 16 11	481 17 6	25,843 3 5	553 19 3	1,662 1 8	9,368 2 1	14,159 - 5
12	11 15 11	—	10 3 1	43 6 5	1,613 3 10	—	—	701 2 5	912 1 5
13	34 15 11	—	49 10 3	639 12 8	6,161 10 3	46 6 3	47 4 6	2,160 1 3	3,907 15 3
14	180 3 3	—	309 8 6	—	18,722 5 6	—	1,733 12 4	7,117 12 6	9,871 - 8
15	49 16 6	—	264 5 7	577 2 11	20,763 1 2	477 11 6	5 5 11	8,689 7 2	11,590 16 7
16	386 13 6	—	407 2 9	500 - -	31,871 17 8	190 17 5	375 9 2	13,093 14 8	18,211 16 5
17	4 10 5	—	91 15 6	392 18 2	3,768 15 8	—	—	611 6 6	1,157 9 2
18	4 15 1	2 12 6	45 7 6	—	1,401 9 7	—	3 4 6	638 - 7	761 4 6
19	21 15 -	—	176 16 7	—	5,788 14 9	—	39 - -	2,791 1 1	2,958 13 5
20	34 10 11	18 8 10	47 7 -	—	4,676 14 11	—	—	2,208 19 5	2,467 15 6
21	7 3 8	—	54 3 3	—	915 4 3	—	—	419 9 2	495 15 1
22	183 9 3	—	197 3 9	2,973 9 9	26,182 2 1	128 7 4	29 6 2	9,214 8 6	16,810 - 1
23	5 15 -	—	319 4 2	237 8 10	5,832 13 4	—	227 - 1	2,475 5 6	3,130 7 9
24	7 - -	10 10 -	190 13 7	365 13 11	3,112 19 9	480 13 10	—	922 1 6	1,710 4 5
25	35 16 2	—	332 12 10	926 19 6	10,986 10 7	—	—	4,706 6 10	6,180 3 9
26	211 18 1	33 3 8	574 17 8	1,375 4 1	19,387 14 3	266 14 6	142 3 5	6,594 19 9	12,383 16 9
27	29 3 4	—	187 19 -	121 3 3	3,373 7 10	—	9 17 -	3,739 1 6	5,632 9 2

TABLE V.—(A.) COST OF THE POLICE, UNDER THE DIFFERENT HEADS

District, No. 1.—MIDLAND,

Number.	1. NAME OF POLICE FORCE.	EXPENDITURE.					
		2. Salaries and Pay.	3. Travelling Expenses, including Allowances and Cost of Removal of Constables.	4. Clothing and Accoutrements.	5. Harness, Horses, and Forage.	6. Rents, Rates, and Taxes, Purchase of Buildings, &c., less Amount received from Constables as Rent.	7. Printing and Stationery.
		£. s. d.	£. s. d.	£. s. d.	£. s. d.	£. s. d.	£. s. d.
	ENGLAND—*continued.*						
28	OXFORDSHIRE - - - -	8,853 1 10	313 17 5	634 18 10	363 17 6	413 7 8	82 10 1
29	Banbury - - - -	971 14 9	—	87 4 2	—	—	16 11 10
30	Oxford - - - -	6,484 8 3	14 9 4	360 - 8	—	646 12 1	76 12 4
31	PETERBOROUGH (Liberty) -	843 14 -	45 19 2	34 11 -	20 4 -	54 16 8	15 6 -
32	Peterborough (City) - -	2,550 10 6	—	145 11 4	—	386 2 -	14 4 -
33	RUTLANDSHIRE - - -	1,266 6 3	45 1 1	94 7 2	—	90 13 7	7 1 9
34	SHROPSHIRE - - -	12,172 8 11	1,100 17 7	1,092 10 6	416 2 -	295 8 1	149 7 5
35	Shrewsbury - - -	2,865 19 11	—	211 6 8	—	450 8 8	26 2 11
36	STAFFORDSHIRE - -	33,488 10 10	2,089 7 5	3,477 14 3	1,183 1 10	8,052 1 1	707 15 4
37	Hanley - - - -	4,767 6 9	—	368 11 1	51 19 -	217 11 7	58 14 9
38	Newcastle-under-Lyme - -	1,508 17 8	9 17 -	92 7 -	—	55 8 1	27 15 9
39	Walsall - - - -	5,932 2 1	20 - -	393 4 2	22 1 -	342 5 10	111 3 2
40	Wolverhampton - - -	6,867 18 4	43 18 9	735 13 9	54 17 6	559 4 -	114 9 9
41	SUFFOLK (EAST) - - -	11,642 18 11	965 4 8	821 10 8	282 12 10	644 18 7	397 17 7
42	Ipswich - - - -	5,276 6 6	- 8 -	547 7 -	16 9 4	93 19 1	28 16 2
43	SUFFOLK (WEST) - -	8,062 12 10	670 - 4	631 5 10	280 - -	1,267 10 8	217 17 9
44	WARWICKSHIRE - -	22,936 15 9	1,890 12 2	1,722 2 9	177 10 11	5,306 18 1	141 1 3
45	Birmingham - - -	58,631 7 9	1,512 2 8	5,285 17 5	896 17 11	6,334 - 7	703 10 -
46	Coventry - - - -	7,062 8 -	—	670 11 6	—	132 4 11	102 14 11
47	Leamington - - - -	3,406 17 5	5 3 1	360 5 8	—	19 10 8	44 10 5
48	WORCESTERSHIRE - -	25,894 18 9	847 1 8	2,138 17 11	558 13 1	9,850 5 6	151 8 8
49	Kidderminster - - -	2,374 19 2	—	109 8 6	—	220 13 6	26 18 7
50	Worcester - - -	4,237 16 -	8 19 -	323 17 10	2 10 -	173 4 8	39 9 6
	NORTH WALES.						
1	ANGLESEY - - - -	2,196 8 3	183 10 7	92 12 -	—	1,331 13 10	26 18 11
2	CARNARVONSHIRE - -	6,080 4 6	607 5 7	500 13 -	215 14 6	502 19 5	82 18 9
3	DENBIGHSHIRE - - -	6,095 7 4	196 15 7	332 1 11	269 8 4	1,012 15 10	87 18 -
4	FLINTSHIRE - -	4,580 6 8	238 11 6	376 14 10	13 15 1	1,886 13 6	61 15 11
5	MERIONETHSHIRE - -	2,689 12 4	145 11 9	198 19 3	—	211 10 -	43 12 -
6	MONTGOMERYSHIRE - -	2,880 12 -	276 11 8	221 19 10	25 11 8	1,234 6 6	46 6 3
	TOTAL - - - £.	592,995 18 7	22,354 17 5	45,241 6 -	11,931 - 9	71,954 13 8	7,268 12 9

* Column 6 includes the cost of erecting and furnishing buildings, the purchase of land, and the interest and repayment of principal of loans; but expenditure defrayed out of loans is excluded.

OF SERVICE, FOR THE YEAR ENDED 31ST MARCH 1901--*continued.*

EASTERN COUNTIES, AND NORTH WALES—*continued.*

	- - - - - - EXPENDITURE.					INCOME.			
	8. Postage, Telegrams, and Telephone Charges.	9. Extra Police Borrowed on Special Occasions.	10. Other Miscellaneous Charges.	11. Deficiency of Police Pension Fund.	12. Gross Total Cost of Police.	13. Sums received for Services of Additional or Lent Constables.	14. Other Receipts credited to the Police Fund.	15. Amount received from Exchequer Contribution Account; Pay and Clothing.	16. Balance of Cost falling on Local Rates (being Amount in Col. 12, less Amount in Columns 13, 14, and 15).
	£. s. d.	£. s. d.	£. s. d.	£. s. d.	£. s. d.	£. s. d.	£. s. d.	£. s. d.	£. s. d.
28	92 15 6	—	173 7 7	480 13 9	11,027 10 2	141 19 6	1,540 4 3	4,489 – 4	4,866 6 1
29	4 14 8	1 10 –	46 17 6	—	1,128 12 11	—	—	478 3 8	650 9 3
1	38 9 5	17 12 1	691 18 8	190 – –	7,440 8 10	322 7 7	458 13 7	2,687 4 5	3,992 3 3
31	13 12 2	—	14 1 6	126 9 7	1,177 14 –	9 7 7	9 17 8	439 11 2	718 17 7
32	87 9 2	25 2 7	18 19 1	—	3,177 18 8	—	14 19 –	1,287 3 2	1,875 16 6
33	7 12 3	—	31 17 9	—	1,542 – 10	—	14 19 –	679 14 7	862 6 3
34	166 17 9	—	346 12 10	—	15,640 6 1	737 7 4	2,090 5 10	6,261 5 5	6,641 7 6
35	13 19 –	78 8 1	108 10 2	—	3,749 15 5	78 8 1	39 – –	1,527 12 1	2,104 15 3
36	736 14 9	16 13 –	2,907 15 –	—	72,889 12 6	1,066 1 1	6,344 10 10	28,505 11 6	36,741 10 1
37	26 14 5	—	225 17 1	—	5,716 5 8	47 2 11	—	2,319 5 7	3,349 17 2
38	20 4 –	12 14 11	112 – –	—	1,840 4 5	—	5 2 4	786 13 4	1,048 8 9
39	94 10 7	26 10 2	242 18 11	—	7,186 17 –	—	—	3,146 15 4	4,040 1 8
40	111 10 –	—	333 17 3	—	8,781 9 4	—	274 1 7	3,695 11 11	4,811 15 10
41	308 3 1	—	96 7 4	826 10 –	15,857 3 8	628 13 6	1,318 1 5	5,883 2 11	8,126 5 10
42	11 11 2	—	181 1 9	316 9 5	6,472 8 5	—	88 11 –	2,764 7 10	3,619 9 7
43	101 11 7	—	296 18 1	452 – –	12,060 17 1	277 12 10	93 11 9	4,211 13 1	7,467 19 5
44	186 8 1	80 6 8	701 15 5	854 10 8	33,494 1 9	882 4 2	2,278 19 7	12,102 – 8	18,326 17 4
45	269 13 6	—	4,902 8 1	—	77,526 16 11	1,688 10 11	2,064 15 1	29,163 10 –	44,720 – 11
46	14 11 3	—	459 19 6	386 6 4	8,849 16 5	—	—	1,977 – –	6,872 16 5
47	20 19 5	8 4 3	327 7 10	231 8 8	4,452 7 5	18 1 3	8 10 4	1,688 17 11	2,507 17 11
48	406 16 8	—	1,346 9 7	—	41,196 11 7	44 11 11	2,835 19 3	13,973 15 –	24,342 5 5
49	8 7 7	7 1 9	74 15 –	37 – 6	3,849 4 7	—	31 11 7	1,176 10 1	1,641 2 11
50	10 1 –	—	26 19 6	18 11 –	4,341 10 6	—	1 13 –	2,900 2 –	2,639 16 6
1	24 – 7	28 – 1	104 5 10	—	3,987 11 –	26 17 6	24 3 6	1,141 2 8	2,795 7 4
2	71 9 –	88 7 9	297 4 7	—	8,536 17 1	28 4 3	386 19 1	3,237 14 1	4,873 19 8
3	77 1 1	9 7 9	141 17 6	31 8 4	8,273 1 8	54 18 3	396 10 1	3,187 8 11	4,633 6 5
4	60 9 8	6 12 11	136 1 7	—	7,361 2 8	9 14 1	14 1 3	2,403 5 8	4,934 1 8
5	38 17 4	—	528 16 –	49 17 5	3,906 18 1	10 14 5	—	1,442 14 5	2,453 7 3
6	55 2 2	—	367 5 8	312 18 1	6,122 14 10	—	48 17 4	1,497 18 –	3,575 19 6
	6,486 9 4	1,063 15 6	25,312 14 6	18,781 9 9	503,250 18 3	13,000 5 9	39,734 16 10	306,040 2 7	444,575 13 1

TABLE V.—(A.) COST OF THE POLICE, UNDER THE DIFFERENT HEADS

District No. 2.—

Number.	NAME OF POLICE FORCE.	2. Salaries and Pay.	3. Travelling Expenses, including Allowances and Cost of Removal of Constables.	4. Clothing and Accoutrements.	5. Harness, Horses, and Forage.	6. Rents, Rates, and Taxes, Purchase of Buildings, &c., less Amount received from Constables as Rent.*	7. Printing and Stationery.
		£. s. d.	£. s. d.	£. s. d.	£. s. d.	£. s. d.	£. s. d.
1	CHESHIRE - - - - -	38,288 14 10	1,704 1 6	1,786 2 5	676 13 8	8,134 4 6	273 15 -
2	Birkenhead - - - -	12,089 13 4	—	540 4 4	—	70 7 8	147 13 1
3	Chester - - - - -	3,990 19 8	3 - 4	290 12 6	—	5 4 -	46 5 9
4	Congleton - - - -	813 11 8	2 14 1	68 12 6	—	25 1 -	—
5	Hyde - - - - -	2,481 9 1	35 4 10	163 11 11	6 16 6	181 10 -	39 2 2
6	Macclesfield - - - -	3,164 15 -	5 19 11	188 10 3	2 10 -	815 4 11	13 19 4
7	Stalybridge - - - -	2,424 2 9	4 19 6	222 12 2	—	107 2 -	39 10 1
8	Stockport - - - -	6,553 9 4	15 19 9	472 18 4	96 - -	13 14 6	77 6 5
9	CUMBERLAND - - - -	17,794 15 -	316 7 8	1,151 16 8	651 2 9	2,084 8 -	46 7 11
10	Carlisle - - - -	4,408 2 11	—	141 9 -	15 19 -	297 11 2	52 13 6
11	DERBYSHIRE - - - -	27,478 15 3	1,404 3 3	1,834 - 8	902 - 3	3,395 15 10	408 - 2
12	Chesterfield - - - -	2,591 5 9	11 8 10	182 14 9	—	31 4 -	54 13 3
13	Derby - - - - -	9,190 9 3	238 17 2	786 2 4	147 2 3	487 19 10	97 11 2
14	Glossop - - - -	3,118 8 -	1 2 11	141 3 10	6 19 4	119 13 9	30 12 11
15	DURHAM - - - -	53,696 1 4	1,636 1 1	3,920 19 1	10 - -	6,912 16 9	262 1 -
16	Durham - - - -	1,412 13 7	13 11 6	106 1 -	—	136 11 7	19 8 9
17	Gateshead - - - -	9,430 1 2	66 19 10	675 12 7	18 5 9	287 8 1	86 9 4
18	Hartlepool - - - -	2,232 14 5	—	118 17 3	—	—	25 15 7
19	South Shields - - - -	8,667 7 8	—	534 1 3	65 18 2	2,187 7 8	150 2 6
20	Sunderland - - - -	12,301 - -	—	867 - -	—	943 - -	130 - -
21	LANCASHIRE - - - -	135,590 9 3	4,501 11 5	9,206 5 6	1,827 5 -	27,969 4 7	1,026 2 5
22	Accrington - - - -	3,653 6 2	44 19 8	263 14 2	—	178 9 8	39 17 11
23	Ashton-under-Lyne - -	3,319 7 6	58 7 5	219 17 8	—	151 11 1	74 5 8
24	Bacup - - - -	2,082 1 6	7 - -	83 19 6	—	147 17 5	16 5 10
25	Barrow-in-Furness - -	8,978 - 1	187 15 3	438 15 9	—	700 8 8	53 15 9
26	Blackburn - - - -	11,451 - 6	61 18 6	330 13 5	17 12 6	595 1 7	114 10 11
27	Blackpool - - - -	6,169 7 7	141 1 6	320 9 6	37 13 10	1,750 11 5	119 17 1
28	Bolton - - - -	14,341 17 6	20 5 3	1,254 7 10	17 11 5	773 19 6	104 2 6½
29	Bootle - - - -	6,141 8 1	44 11 10	471 16 11	158 16 9	769 8 5	89 13 6
30	Burnley - - - -	7,711 13 2	57 15 11	489 7 -	—	734 2 2	83 13 10
31	Clitheroe - - - -	911 18 5	1 6 5	49 9 3	—	89 19 10	7 3 11
32	Lancaster - - - -	2,969 7 4	—	195 6 10	—	109 5 -	44 7 7
33	Liverpool - - - -	148,967 6 11	779 2 10	11,816 15 8	2,893 1 11	8,156 11 11	1,249 8 4

* Column 6 includes the cost of erecting and furnishing buildings, the purchase of land, and the interest and repayment of principal of loans; but expenditure defrayed out of loans is excluded.

OF SERVICE, FOR THE YEAR ENDED 31st MARCH 1901—*continued.*

NORTHERN.

	EXPENDITURE				INCOME			
	8. Postage, Telegrams, and Telephone Charges.	9. Extra Police Borrowed on Special Occasions.	10. Other Miscellaneous Charges.	11. Deficiency of Police Pension Fund.	12. Gross Total Cost of Police.	13. Sums received for Services of Additional or Lent Constables.	14. Other Receipts credited to the Police Fund.	15. Amount received from Exchequer Contribution Account; Pay and Clothing.	16. Balance of Cost falling on Local Rates (being Amount in Col.12, less Amount in Columns 13, 14, and 15).
	£. s. d.	£. s. d.	£. s. d.	£. s. d.	£. s. d.	£. s. d.	£. s. d.	£. s. d.	£. s. d.
1	638 11 11	47 6 2	608 10 6	896 11 9	52,870 9 8	790 7 6	1,406 18 3	19,467 – 3	31,206 6 8
2	79 15 2	—	1,184 10 9	—	14,082 4 4	—	62 16 –	6,299 18 10	7,729 9 6
3	—	—	115 17 6	103 11 11	4,555 11 8	—	—	1,983 2 6	2,572 9 2
4	2 6 5	—	43 – 10	—	941 6 6	—	—. .	434 14 11	506 11 7
5	20 7 4	—	322 7 6	—	3,300 9 6	96 4 10	38 2 8	1,520 6 11	1,743 15 4
6	—	—	47 18 8	—	4,218 13 1	28 10 1	47 4 1	1,669 14 4	2,473 9 7
7	4 – –	2 1 5	127 17 8	—	2,924 5 7	84 10 4	13 10 –	1,348 11 –	1,577 14 3
8	17 18 10	—	518 8 8	—	7,765 15 10	—	174 7 1½	3,513 13 10	4,077 14 10½
9	77 10 –	—	173 17 8	342 4 –	22,589 9 6	1,140 12 6	1,800 19 2	9,152 10 8	10,445 6 2
10	8 18 –	—	92 11 1	—	5,016 16 8	—	157 19 6	2,391 8 4	2,357 8 10
11	402 9 9	—	1,074 19 8	—	36,800 2 10	1,001 17 3	268 5 9	14,110 7 6	21,419 12 4
12	16 14 7	14 19 10	230 6 7	—	3,184 12 7	—	—	1,386 3 9	1,748 8 10
13	31 16 7	177 10 3	309 18 9	—	11,437 2 7	31 10 2	96 3 –	4,779 6 2	6,530 1 8
14	26 9 7	6 9 3	55 13 4	—	2,495 13 11	—	35 6 –	1,076 8 7	1,383 18 4
15	386 10 2	—	1,574 11 –	617 5 10	68,006 6 3	4,310 2 7	4,764 9 1	25,066 9 –	33,345 5 7
16	16 16 5	32 17 1	29 11 5	—	1,788 11 4	—	—	761 13 11	996 17 5
17	24 15 5	—	619 15 –	—	11,309 7 2	225 4 8	215 19 10	4,835 11 1	5,925 11 7
18	15 9 7	—	152 – 11	—	2,535 – 9	—	—	1,165 6 1	1,369 14 6
19	68 7 7	—	402 1 4	—	12,065 6 4	2 18 9	430 12 11	4,460 11 3	7,162 3 6
20	78 – –	—	177 – –	—	15,986 – –	936 – –	—	6,811 – –	8,239 – –
21	2,965 19 5	—	5,344 – 11	4,666 4 5	193,296 2 11	2,718 16 6	13,021 17 7	69,462 12 6	106,092 16 4
22	6 5 –	—	59 17 9	—	4,466 10 4	—	77 3 10	2,005 16 5	2,383 8 1
23	18 3 8	—	131 19 6	—	4,872 13 6	46 12 7	30 15 –	1,912 18 7	2,582 6 4
24	20 15 –	—	63 10 9	—	2,420 10 9	—	37 8 11	1,097 13 4	1,285 8 11
25	4 14 4	6 15 5	283 13 1	—	7,632 18 4	914 9 10	171 14 9	2,733 17 –	3,812 16 9
26	84 5 3	—	275 18 2	—	12,934 – 10	116 17 3	110 5 6	5,961 13 11	6,735 4 2
27	23 16 2	—	339 1 10	—	9,111 18 11	106 12 11	146 4 –	3,297 9 1	5,361 12 11
28	98 6 3½	—	337 18 3½	—	16,928 8 7½	92 5 10	178 9 6	7,788 2 8	8,869 10 7½
29	31 15 7	—	291 4 11	—	7,999 3 –	—	299 3 8	3,289 6 3	4,410 13 1
30	26 3 –	—	1,165 8 8	32 10 –	10,262 13 9	—	1,425 4 1	4,013 18 5	4,823 11 3
31	14 6 7	—	22 16 10	—	1,098 1 3	8 9 11	8 18 5	490 10 9	590 2 2
32	10 6 1	—	397 13 4	—	3,726 8 3	—	—	1,545 13 3	2,180 14 11
33	2,029 8 9	—	4,572 5 11	4,558 – 7	185,122 2 10	40,855 11 9	1,399 11 4	63,424 15 10	79,442 – 11

TABLE V.—(A.) COST OF THE POLICE, UNDER THE DIFFERENT HEADS

District No. 2.—

Number.	1. NAME OF POLICE FORCE.	EXPENDITURE.					
		2. Salaries and Pay.	3. Travelling Expenses, including Allowances and Cost of Removal of Constables.	4. Clothing and Accoutrements.	5. Harness, Horses, and Forage.	6. Rents, Rates, and Taxes, Purchase of Buildings, &c., less Amount received from Constables as Rent.	7. Printing and Stationery.
		£. s. d.	£. s. d.	£. s. d.	£. s. d.	£. s. d.	£. s. d.
	LANCASHIRE—continued.						
34	Manchester - - - -	84,091 16 11	763 16 5	5,068 10 5	674 18 3	1,855 2 6	1,344 5 2
35	Oldham - - - -	12,701 15 1	77 13 1	774 1 3	—	48 11 8	190 - 11
36	Preston - - - -	9,728 5 2	63 7 3	774 19 9	52 11 -	221 14 8	137 16 9
37	Rochdale - - - -	6,869 3 3	18 19 4	151 15 7	31 14 6	835 - 10	82 10 .
38	St. Helens - - - -	7,359 5 --	11 9 4	353 1 3	—	494 16 8	37 13 3
39	Salford - - - -	26,479 13 4	436 1 3	1,916 17 6	11 8 -	4,385 3 5	360 5 10
40	Southport - - - -	3,830 4 6	—	443 1 9	18 - -	223 17 1	96 3 -
41	Warrington - - - -	3,830 1 1	20 7 6	435 6 1	128 13 10	355 12 1	58 8 6
42	Wigan - - - .	5,680 17 10	—	463 3 9	15 - -	174 1 5	61 5 3
43	NORTHUMBERLAND - -	20,425 7 7	743 19 5	1,406 1 3	576 10 1	3,521 3 6	275 11 8
44	Berwick - - - -	965 11 6	6 7 7	133 7 10	—	322 7 8	11 17 5
45	Newcastle-on-Tyne -	26,082 15 5	142 16 4	1,429 8 1	437 6 11	4,177 - 2	422 6 5
46	Tynemouth - - -	5,140 16 4	44 7 9	532 13 6	—	969 19 4	128 12 5
47	NOTTINGHAMSHIRE -	16,864 11 1	508 1 5	896 18 -	553 7 6	895 6 10	194 10 2
48	Newark - - - -	1,230 5 4	—	59 12 8	—	32 14 2	14 13 10
49	Nottingham - - ! -	22,696 13 3	184 13 -	1,900 6 7	272 19 1	1,463 - 11	233 13 2
50	WESTMORLAND - - -	3,370 - -	91 19 10	216 16 6	276 19 8	275 10 3	15 10 3
51	Kendal - - - -	1,315 15 6	—	62 - 4	—	36 3 10	20 1 3
52	YORK (EAST RIDING) -	10,442 18 3	575 2 10	905 - 4	645 - -	3,256 3 -	161 9 4
53	Beverley - - - -	1,195 19 6	—	111 15 8	—	4 14 5	10 3 4
54	Hull - - - -	27,977 2 5	—	1,083 10 6	21 19 -	969 4 1	84 19 -
55	YORK (NORTH RIDING) -	22,461 11 9	1,961 16 -	1,616 1 1	973 13 5	4,444 - 6	158 13 6
56	Middlesbrough - - -	5,340 3 4	6 14 6	585 16 8	—	215 16 8	44 14 6
57	Scarborough - - -	4,022 2 5	13 15 10	349 19 11	14 - 7	352 7 6	56 9 9
58	York - - - -	6,623 - 6	80 6 4	453 2 4	63 13 1	66 14 7	98 9 3
59	YORK (WEST RIDING) -	96,474 6 3	5,095 8 9	5,391 6 5	475 6 -	13,357 1 4	960 5 2
60	Barnsley - - - -	2,774 18 10	7 3 6	105 10 9	4 9 9	116 - 10	55,16 2
61	Bradford - - - -	23,313 19 -	364 19 6	3,173 4 9	76 15 10	1,346 16 3	591 9 2
62	Dewsbury - - - -	3,087 3 3	30 11 11	215 5 6	—	61 13 4	48 5 4
63	Doncaster - - - -	3,023 1 6	30 11 6	300 5 10	8 5 3	47 16 5	25 3 3
64	Halifax - - - -	5,308 1 -	26 15 11	595 17 4	15 5 6	1,215 - 5	78 19 3
65	Huddersfield - - -	9,589 1 2	78 12 1	904 14 6	57 - -	788 18 -	107 18 10
66	Leeds - - - -	43,840 1 10	2,874 14 9	1,520 7 10	93 5 5	307 3 11	570 9 5
67	Rotherham - - - -	4,583 7 7	79 9 5	306 17 4	21 - 6	47 13 11	83 14 2
68	Sheffield - - - -	38,685 12 6	—	3,311 10 4	74 7 3	1,175 7 8	286 18 3
69	Wakefield - - - -	4,049 18 5	47 17 1	276 15 3	—	456 13 4	37 13 1
	TOTAL - - - £.	1,158,836 - 3	26,147 5 6	75,530 11 5	12,960 10 6	116,348 13 3	12,056 15 3½

* Column 6 includes the cost of erecting and furnishing buildings, the purchase of land, and the interest and repayment of principal of loans ; but expenditure defrayed out of loans is excluded.

OF SERVICE, FOR THE YEAR ENDED 31st MARCH 1901—*continued.*

NORTHERN—*continued.*

	EXPENDITURE.					INCOME.			
	8. Postage, Telegrams, and Telephone Charges.	9. Extra Police Borrowed on Special Occasions.	10. Other Miscellaneous Charges.	11. Deficiency of Police Pension Fund.	12. Gross Total Cost of Police.	13. Sums received for Services of Additional or Lent Constables.	14. Other Receipts credited to the Police Fund.	15. Amount received from Exchequer Contribution Account; Pay and Clothing.	16. Balance of Cost falling on Local Rates (being Amount in Col. 12, less Amount in Columns 13, 14, and 15).
	£. s. d.	£. s. d.	£. s. d.	£. s. d.	£. s. d.	£. s. d.	£. s. d.	£. s. d.	£. s. d.
34	374 3 4	—	6,320 2 2	5,836 4 8	105,839 3 10	3,013 16 9	4,715 10 3	43,636 10 10	54,463 6 -
35	38 4 3	—	731 4 -	—	14,811 10 3	337 6 ˜	715 1 9	6,778 19 7	6,780 2 10
36	54 10 2	—	331 1 11	543 6 1	11,796 12 8	118 17 9	93 3 10	5,096 2 3	6,487 8 5
37	59 18 9	89 14 2	586 3 1	- 15 7	8,715 19 1	96 18 4	405 6 4	3,443 9 6	4,769 4 11
38	21 3 11	5 6 10	186 17 6	—	8,469 18 9	353 - 11	221 18 4	3,699 18 3	4,095 1 3
39	196 18 3	—	1,512 1 -	489 3 1	35,667 5 7	1,153 15 -	335 5 6	14,016 11 4	20,161 13 9
40	27 17 9	34 13 5	575 5 -	—	7,888 2 6	—	58 7 6	2,789 8 4	5,060 6 8
41	60 14 5	—	382 19 8	—	7,172 3 2	—	214 15 11	3,036 1 8	3,921 5 7
42	21 1 4	—	135 16 3	325 9 7	6,866 15 5	—	74 10 7	3,067 - 10	3,725 4 -
43	301 10 -	4 3 10	738 13 10	319 10 -	26,312 10 2	1,973 19 7	1,019 11 3	9,879 17 3	13,640 3 1
44	19 17 1	˙	45 17 9	187 3 6	1,632 15 4	—	9 10 5	551 10 7	1,161 14 4
45	167 13 9	265 19 4	3,271 11 3	—	36,530 17 3	487 9 5	870 9 3	12,994 6 -	22,488 13 1
46	40 11 6	—	270 11 5	—	7,137 11 1	101 6 1	64 1 -	2,867 3 8	4,305 - 4
47	330 7 7	—	278 15 11	—	20,606 18 6	523 13 6	744 13 -	8,468 12 -	10,871 1 -
48	3 - -	6 17 8	60 13 3	22 3 8	1,484 19 6	. —	16 3 5	643 16 7	775 19 6
49	100 4 3	202 1 8	632 6 11	552 5 8	28,328 6 6	65 17 6	207 9 9	12,398 10 5	15,656 7 10
50	33 5 10	—	21 13 6	187 7 7	4,859 3 5	309 - 8	417 1 -	1,776 19 1	2,156 1 8
51	6 15 7	—	130 13 8	37 7 11	1,468 17 1	—	19 15 11	617 9 3	861 11 11
52	100 17 9	1 3 6	247 6 6	835 6 4	17,173 13 10	—	226 11 9	5,496 6 6	11,450 14 7
53	9 12 6	111 1 7	19 3 9	. —	1,463 16 9	111 1 7	—	629 13 6	722 - 8
54	105 1 9	—	613 6 -	679 3 -	31,623 10 9	172 17 5	674 3 11	14,070 9 1	16,606 - 4
55	3 16 7	—	434 3 9	—	32,046 14 9	2,113 17 8	690 5 -	10,787 16 5	18,456 16 8
56	33 14 6	37 9 6	465 8 9	—	9,700 18 5	777 19 4	230 6 5	3,962 18 4	4,710 1 4
57	43 13 3	—	183 9 -	286 9 9	8,301 7 11	10 3 6	—	3,176 4 6	3,114 19 11
58	48 6 11	190 1 3	402 1 6	31 11 10	8,033 6 6	3 7 7	119 3 6	3,489 13 5	4,420 4 -
59	1,816 7 11	—	4,997 14 3	—	126,555 16 1	1,501 16 4	3,093 18 7	56,930 11 1	66,029 10 1
60	26 3 -	8 3 11	313 11 8	—	3,410 17 5	31 10 7	109 1 6	1,427 18 6	1,842 6 10
61	214 - 4	—	1,388 17 10	—	35,488 3 3	213 16 6	595 14 3	15,587 14 9	19,090 16 9
62	7 5 -	—	94 5 9	—	3,534 9 8	19 - -	25 3 11	1,594 4 4	1,896 1 5
63	17 16 10	849 5 4	144 7 8	—	4,516 18 7	843 19 11	76 11 8	1,400 4 3	1,988 3 10
64	80 15 4	—	642 5 5	—	10,962 17 1	—	14 13 3	4,375 - -	6,573 4 10
65	36 2 7	—	862 13 1	—	12,424 - 3	—	406 16 -	4,029 - -	7,988 4 3
66	174 16 8	—	742 5 10	1,170 1 -	50,902 6 6	849 3 3	1,066 8 -	22,414 9 1	26,582 7 3
67	59 17 6	12 8 3	438 3 3	—	5,651 16 9	53 19 3	47 16 3	2,356 19 7	3,193 1 10
68	143 19 8	—	4,036 9 10	643 15 1	48,223 - 7	3,309 13 1	1,453 7 -	19,957 7 1	34,502 14 5
69	10 8 6	—	300 11 10	4 3 11	5,184 - 5	—	53 15 6	2,001 17 3	3,128 7 8
	11,931 1 4½	3,131 9 6	55,444 8 4½	23,886 4 3	1,491,872 3 -¼	71,565 13 7	46,354 16 5½	586,746 6 3	787,205 6 9

II 4

TABLE V.—(A.) COST OF THE POLICE, UNDER THE DIFFERENT HEADS

District No. 3.—SOUTH OF ENGLAND

Number	NAME OF POLICE FORCE	2. Salaries and Pay.	3. Travelling Expenses, including Allowances and Cost of Removal of Constables.	4. Clothing and Accoutrements.	5. Harness, Horses, and Forage.	6. Rents, Rates, and Taxes, Purchase of Buildings, &c., less Amount received from Constables as Rent.	7. Printing and Stationery.
	ENGLAND.	£. s. d.	£. s. d.	£. s. d.	£. s. d.	£. s. d.	£. s. d.
1	BERKSHIRE · - - - ·	15,077 3 1	511 1 3	815 6 5	386 14 6	969 10 9	120 7 2
2	Reading · - -	6,639 1 6	33 3 3	431 5 1	93 11 6	313 9 5	45 4 4
3	Windsor · - -	1,583 10 7	6 12 2	123 10 1	5 16 -	55 12 9	16 15 -
4	CORNWALL · - - -	14,969 19 3	709 11 6	816 14 3	—	2,980 3 4½	99 12 2½
5	Penzance · - -	964 18 -	—	82 19 3	—	20 4 9	9 - 3
6	Truro · - -	873 - 8	—	123 14 6	—	—	15 6 2
7	DEVONSHIRE · - -	28,543 11 -	2,465 11 5½	1,517 17 5	54 4 6½	4,397 3 1½	243 19 2
8	Barnstaple · - -	1,017 - 11	3 12 1	136 - -	—	—	3 16 3
9	Devonport · - -	6,141 13 10	—	580 4 6	—	6 - -	13 13 6
10	Exeter · - -	4,806 14 11	—	564 - 3	—	1,314 18 3	37 16 4
11	Plymouth · - -	10,473 3 3	11 15 8	433 16 3	—	145 18 9	54 15 9
12	Tiverton · - -	306 10 7	—	86 9 6	1 - 6	19 1 4	3 6 4
13	DORSETSHIRE · - -	12,617 16 2	616 8 8	794 16 8	762 6 4	2 824 17 3	92 4 5
14	Weymouth · - -	2,263 7 6	—	335 1 7	—	—	93 3 10
15	GLOUCESTERSHIRE · - -	23,373 19 9	1,104 19 1	1,544 12 7	34 7 4	7,016 14 4½	290 17 4
16	Bristol · - -	40,129 19 4	601 18 7	2,086 12 1	253 14 11	2,535 19 1	214 19 11
17	HAMPSHIRE · - -	27,883 1 2	1,486 10 4	2,593 4 11	1,262 14 6	6,870 3 4	336 4 10
18	Portsmouth · - -	15,966 10 3	229 19 11	1,704 5 5	302 13 6	524 9 6	150 6 2
19	Southampton · - -	10,930 16 10	39 13 9	789 8 11	143 6 3	430 - 2	79 14 7
20	Winchester · - -	1,780 2 6	—	197 7 -	—	—	25 17 8
21	HEREFORDSHIRE · - -	6,173 3 3	175 7 9	470 4 4	466 4 1	409 7 8	34 18 5
22	Hereford · - -	2,322 - 11	—	156 9 6	5 9 6	151 6 1	23 18 7
23	KENT · - - -	36,866 12 2	1,085 6 8	3,351 14 4	953 9 11	4,773 2 9	329 6 3
24	Canterbury · - -	2,124 14 10	5 19 1	129 16 4	—	88 5 -	23 16 8
25	Dover · - -	4,988 9 3	—	559 13 -	—	45 14 3	41 7 7
26	Folkestone · - -	3,441 16 7	14 8 6	567 7 9	—	—	37 14 6
27	Gravesend · - -	3,049 14 2	—	270 - 5	—	58 16 -	64 6 8
28	Maidstone · - -	3,590 15 4	—	286 8 10	13 - -	38 6 8	51 15 3
29	Margate · - -	3,009 - 5	34 16 1	227 10 4	27 9 8	40 8 4	38 13 4
30	Ramsgate · - -	4,060 3 10	4 1 4	337 16 10	84 3 -	39 3 5	54 9 3
31	Rochester · - -	3,076 2 6	11 - 6	76 18 4	—	40 - -	20 - -
32	Tunbridge Wells · - -	4,077 14 2	—	326 13 3	73 5 10	—	13 13 10

* Column 6 includes the cost of erecting and furnishing buildings, the purchase of land, and the interest and repayment of principal of loans; but expenditure defrayed out of loans is excluded.

OF SERVICE, FOR THE YEAR ENDED 31st MARCH 1901—continued.

AND SOUTH WALES.

	EXPENDITURE.					INCOME.			
	8. Postage, Telegrams, and Telephone Charges.	9. Extra Police Borrowed on Special Occasions.	10. Other Miscellaneous Charges.	11. Deficiency of Police Pension Fund.	12. Gross Total Cost of Police.	13. Sums received for Services of Additional or Lent Constables.	14. Other Receipts credited to the Police Fund.	15. Amount received from Exchequer Contribution Account; Pay and Clothing.	16. Balance of Cost falling on Local Rates (being Amount in Col. 12, less Amount in Columns 13, 14, and 15).
	£. s. d.	£. s. d.	£. s. d.	£. s. d.	£. s. d.	£. s. d.	£. s. d.	£. s. d.	£. s. d.
1	152 13 7	—	304 18 6	—	16,325 15 2	—	1,457 2 1	6,968 19 11	7,899 13 2
2	60 6 8	—	170 10 3	251 16 2	8,042 6 1	430 1 1	—	3,331 10 10	4,380 14 2
3	4 2 2	78 17 9	210 13 6	11 3 4	2,106 14 4	84 12 1	—	840 11 4	1,181 10 11
4	73 19 5½	—	812 1 10	1,119 9 7	21,282 10 3½	150 - -	3,504 2 6	8,081 16 7	9,546 11 9½
5	1 14 4	—	15 2 3	—	1,113 19 2	—	—	499 18 -	614 1 3
6	—	—	50 9 -	21 7 3	1,082 19 7	—	—	483 19 8	598 19 11
7	296 17 6	—	389 8 -	3,547 8 10	41,562 1 -½	109 2 6	2,961 1 4	14,915 3 2	23,576 14 -½
8	11 1 2	4 18 2	33 3 -	116 5 2	1,294 16 9	—	—	871 9 1	753 7 8
9	—	—	131 11 6	121 17 -	6,993 18 4	—	—	3,243 18 10	3,743 19 6
10	32 4 2	27 8 -	76 11 5	491 12 -	6,753 7 3	—	—	2,450 1 6	4,303 5 9
11	63 17 9	—	262 16 10	816 6 11	12,962 14 2	54 - -	—	5,872 6 3	6,626 7 11
12	3 10 11	—	39 1 4	77 2 -	1,036 2 6	—	—	443 12 8	592 9 10
13	154 17 7	—	187 2 8	1,345 18 3	19,406 8 -	121 12 -	2,366 8 2	6,287 6 5	10,631 1 5
14	2 9 9	14 - 11	222 13 9	154 17 10	3,081 15 2	—	9 8 7	1,109 14 7	1,962 12 -
15	332 15 9½	1 8 10	456 6 9½	225 18 10½	36,384 1 9	265 16 -	10,430 4 6	11,806 9 -	13,881 12 2
16	316 13 7	—	684 15 -	2,585 1 11	49,709 14 5	135 12 1	459 6 3	21,072 14 8	28,042 1 5
17	517 2 5	—	3,617 12 9	1,832 10 4	46,439 4 5	818 8 -	3,673 2 10	12,631 17 7	24,515 16 -
18	143 5 3	—	1,078 9 1	1,178 1 8	22,092 19 11	—	113 3 11	8,500 - -	13,479 16 -
19	104 17 3	—	431 10 10	1,801 10 -	14,839 17 6	329 18 10	210 5 4	5,375 3 11	8,626 9 5
20	17 18 3	—	165 5 -	55 12 7	2,342 2 11	—	349 18 8	870 4 9	1,021 19 6
21	21 10 1	—	173 19 11	720 7 3	8,645 3 9	151 2 10	480 8 2	3,189 11 6	4,844 - 3
22	38 6 7	19 3 6	56 18 3	387 11 1	3,231 6 2	—	1 7 -	1,290 7 9	1,939 11 5
23	494 6 1	—	1,720 6 0	3,731 15 1	52,163 18 3	239 5 4	3,408 17 2	17,586 11 10	30,918 3 11
24	22 11 10	—	64 14 -	57 17 6	2,527 16 3	—	9 17 11	1,170 18 6	1,346 18 10
25	69 2 9	—	165 3 10	173 9 7	6,043 - 3	—	120 2 -	2,622 17 3	3,300 1 -
26	10 - -	—	123 10 3	249 - 4	4,438 18 1	—	2 - -	1,999 8 2	2,437 9 11
27	13 - -	—	162 3 6	256 18 3	3,896 19 -	—	41 16 1	1,623 17 9	2,231 5 2
28	23 7 11	—	108 12 8	136 - 4	4,339 12 -	—	—	1,849 7 5	2,490 4 7
29	20 10 9½	—	64 19 6	—	3,463 8 5½	—	10 - -	1,563 18 4	1,889 10 1½
30	24 0 3	—	131 9 3	28 9 -	4,733 15 1	354 3 6	1 5 -	1,854 4 4	2,524 2 5
31	7 - -	—	80 2 5	84 15 6	3,395 19 2	—	—	1,588 7 5	1,807 11 10
32	19 9 1	—	368 15 4	92 9 8	4,972 - 2	—	49 11 -	2,195 6 6	2,727 2 6

0.37.

K K

TABLE V.—(A.) COST OF THE POLICE, UNDER THE DIFFERENT HEADS

District No. 3.—SOUTH OF ENGLAND

№	NAME OF POLICE FORCE	2. Salaries and Pay.	3. Travelling Expenses, including Allowances and Cost of Removal of Constables.	4. Clothing and Accoutrements.	5. Harness, Horses, and Forage.	6. Rents, Rates, and Taxes, Purchase of Buildings, &c., less amount received from Constables as Rent.	7. Printing and Stationery.
		£. s. d.	£. s. d.	£. s. d.	£. s. d.	£. s. d.	£. s. d.
	ENGLAND—*continued.*						
33	MONMOUTHSHIRE · · ·	14,305 13 9	614 15 9	1,175 12 7	103 5 3	3,212 13 6	111 10 2
34	Newport · · · ·	7,487 17 6	27 13 —	534 9 4	—	165 11 5	112 5 10
35	SOMERSETSHIRE ·	24,318 4 11	987 6 6	2,092 11 6	871 — 7	2,197 15 —	149 12 8
36	Bath · · · ·	6,700 11 —	—	535 5 11	—	319 19 9	64 14 1
37	Bridgwater · · · ·	1,110 12 6	—	88 2 5	—	15 — —	8 19 1
38	SURREY · · · ·	17,947 17 9	469 18 5	1,650 9 6	228 10 —	5,910 9 —	217 10 6
39	Guildford · · · ·	1,539 — —	—	101 — —	—	48 — —	31 12 —
40	Reigate · · · ·	2,904 3 —	5 3 9	147 7 10	—	24 14 9	22 16 7
41	SUSSEX (EAST) · · ·	13,728 9 5	1,094 11 7	976 6 —½	94 7 3	3,854 17 10½	259 4 5½
42	Brighton · · ·	14,481 9 8	5 7 —	1,582 18 2	12 14 —	845 17 10	94 2 6
43	Eastbourne · · ·	5,081 19 —	43 10 11	323 1 10	—	73 3 11	13 5 10
44	Hastings · · ·	8,842 3 11	37 7 8	727 14 10	79 9 5	643 17 8	66 8 1
45	Hove · · · ·	4,906 2 9	35 15 11	191 3 3	16 12 7	400 — —	75 14 1
46	SUSSEX (WEST) · · ·	10,654 3 9	675 8 3	640 17 10	332 18 3	1,600 12 6	60 3 1
47	WIGHT, ISLE OF · · ·	4,002 6 5	181 1 2	360 9 11	26 19 —	769 14 9	47 1 11
48	Ryde · · · ·	1,129 — 6	—	103 — 6	—	117 16 4	12 16 3
49	WILTSHIRE · ·	17,190 7 4	286 3 7	1,151 5 7	432 11 9	1,334 6 8	127 5 —
50	Salisbury · ·	1,375 15 2	—	89 9 9	—	18 1 3	2 8 1
	SOUTH WALES.						
1	BRECONSHIRE · · · ·	3,953 4 1	215 8 7½	340 12 3	—	308 15 3	56 9 11
2	CARDIGANSHIRE · · ·	3,194 5 5	36 1 5½	327 19 6	34 15 —	334 18 4	35 — 9
3	CARMARTHENSHIRE · · ·	7,446 2 1	175 12 9	632 12 1	210 — —	416 7 9	118 19 11½
4	Carmarthen · · ·	883 5 8	—	66 12 6	—	19 11 4	4 19 5
5	GLAMORGANSHIRE · · ·	37,922 3 7	1,855 14 3	2,882 5 1	123 18 —	5,336 18 6	46 5 10
6	Cardiff · · · ·	20,537 5 4	797 — 2	1,211 12 3	52 10 6	1,034 — 7	220 15 1
7	Neath · · · ·	1,191 7 3	26 6 6	84 7 3	—	745 — 10	57 10 1
8	Swansea · · · ·	9,486 15 4	50 — —	541 16 7	84 — —	335 10 —	76 17 6
9	PEMBROKESHIRE · · ·	5,401 16 9	160 19 7	465 13 10	8 14 4	265 11 3	53 1 10
10	RADNORSHIRE · · · ·	1,464 12 9	79 — 11	86 4 8	18 8 —	73 16 4	6 1 3
	TOTAL · · · £.	551,734 2 1	16,981 7 2½	41,406 2 —½	7,741 5 6½	66,095 1 11	4,905 2 5½

* Column 6 includes the cost of erecting and furnishing buildings, the purchase of land, and the interest and repayment of principal of loans ; but expenditure defrayed out of loans is excluded.

OF SERVICE, FOR THE YEAR ENDED 31st MARCH 1901—*continued.*

AND SOUTH WALES—*continued.*

	EXPENDITURE.					INCOME.			
	8. Postage, Telegrams, and Telephone Charges.	9. Extra Police Borrowed on Special Occasions.	10. Other Miscellaneous Charges.	11. Deficiency of Police Pension Fund.	12. Gross Total Cost of Police.	13. Sums received for Services of Additional or Lent Constables.	14. Other Receipts credited to the Police Fund.	15. Amount received from Exchequer Contribution Account; Pay and Clothing.	16. Balance of Cost falling on Local Rates (being Amount in Col. 12 less Amount in Columns 13, 14, and 15).
	£. s. d.	£. s. d.	£. s. d.	£. s. d.	£. s. d.	£. s. d.	£. s. d.	£. s. d.	£. s. d.
33	86 1 1	—	337 11 8	—	19,994 3 9	1,582 5 2	—	7,190 4 -	11,221 14 7
34	45 14 1	28 16 -	960 3 2	—	9,362 10 4	38 16 -	3 10 3	4,077 13 11	5,242 11 2
35	187 19 6	—	1,669 6 11	2,436 2 7	34,911 1 2	—	5,669 9 3	13,049 3 4	16,192 8 7
36	29 15 10	—	188 10 2	848 8 10	8,627 5 7	—	33 6 6	3,053 - -	5,550 19 1
37	3 1 7	5 1 5	17 14 5	163 6 10	1,411 18 3	—	—	587 4 4	824 13 11
38	150 6 5	—	468 15 1	580 2 11	27,733 19 7	297 8 7	2,591 - 5	8,970 14 7	15,873 16 -
39	6 10 1	—	69 10 -	—	1,795 12 1	—	—	813 - -	982 12 1
40	7 8 7	—	228 18 4	—	3,350 12 10	—	—	1,447 15 3	1,902 17 7
41	274 1 8	32 15 11	543 3 4	1,312 5 1	22,190 1 7½	692 10 -	1,661 11 9½	7,082 3 8	12,803 16 2
42	14 1 6	—	328 3 1	967 3 2	18,912 - 10	48 2 6	52 9 9	7,734 16 9	10,276 11 10
43	46 15 5	—	383 5 5	434 9 1	6,409 11 5	—	145 3 3	2,615 3 5	3,649 4 9
44	89 - 6	—	29 10 10	—	10,315 13 11	—	—	4,628 6 3	5,687 7 8
45	19 9 11	—	165 15 6	225 11 7	6,036 9 7	19 6 1	44 6 7	2,495 1 1	3,477 15 10
46	123 - 4	55 1 -	459 6 1	927 1 10	15,533 12 11	97 14 10	1,396 19 11	5,256 15 6	8,790 2 8
47	69 2 6	22 6 10	33 16 5	147 13 11	5,666 11 10	53 8 4	339 7 2	2,339 6 3	3,044 10 1
48	10 11 6	—	26 - 6	41 16 0	1,440 1 7	—	171 - 8	626 16 8	643 4 3
49	211 5 7	—	220 8 11	1,347 5 2	22,300 19 7	233 18 -	717 18 8	8,494 4 6	12,854 18 5
50	—	9 1 11	162 13 6	57 13 6	1,715 3 2	2 10 7	111 16 7	99 9 1	1,501 6 11
1	22 10 6	—	27 2 3½	—	4,624 3 9	368 4 -	113 2 9	2,001 15 2	2,341 - 10
2	35 10 3	- 13 -	10 12 6½	—	3,919 14 2	—	—	1,726 1 6	2,193 12 8
3	78 19 1	—	352 19 -½	—	9,438 13 9	—	309 11 1	3,584 16 4	5,524 6 4
4	4 14 3	—	15 9 9	—	994 12 11	—	—	476 19 1	519 13 10
5	159 17 9	182 10 6	1,502 5 11	—	50,015 19 5	3,935 16 4	1,480 19 11	18,045 6 6	26,553 16 8
6	127 15 3	—	526 5 6	—	24,507 4 8	145 12 -	448 10 11	10,633 15 3	13,279 6 6
7	11 12 4	—	48 10 9	—	2,167 15 -	—	—	631 10 7	1,536 4 5
8	111 5 11	—	1,055 15 8	—	11,343 1 -	48 16 6	164 16 6	4,743 12 8	6,384 13 4
9	61 15 9	—	63 16 10	538 12 11½	7,090 3 1½	—	—	2,983 16 3	4,086 7 10½
10	26 10 -	—	8 16 7	—	1,762 10 6	42 13 8	—	775 8 8	944 8 2
	5,092 9 7½	502 3 9	22,506 3 6	31,613 11 9	745,579 9 10½	10,836 18 8	50,055 11 5½	279,643 13 2	408,045 6 6

METROPOLITAN

TABLE V. (A.)—COST OF THE POLICE UNDER THE DIFFERENT

1. NAME OF POLICE FORCE.	EXPENDITURE					
	2. Salaries and Pay.	3. Travelling Expenses, including Allowances and Cost of Removal of Constables.	4. Clothing and Accoutrements.	5. Harness, Horses, Forage.	6. Rents, Rates, and Taxes, Purchase of Buildings, &c., less Amount received from Constables as Rent. *	7. Printing and Stationery.
	£. s. d.	£. s. d.	£. s. d.	£. s. d.	£. s. d.	£. s. d.
London, Metropolitan - - -	1,374,076 14 9	20,424 10 3	78,008 5 6	11,908 4 -	129,633 4 3	8,095 9 4

* Column 6 includes the cost of erecting and furnishing buildings, the purchase of land, and the interest and repayment of principal of loans; but expenditure defrayed out of loans is excluded.
Of the amount shown here 113,778l. represents the cost of sites, new buildings, &c., under the head of police stations, and 6,993l. under that of police courts.

METROPOLITAN

TABLE V.—(B.) COMPARATIVE TABLE OF THE NUMBER AND COST

1. NAME OF POLICE FORCE.	2. Population by Census of 1891.	3. Rateable Value.	4. Acreage.	5. Number of Inhabited Houses by Census of 1891.	6. Length of Streets, Squares, &c., in Miles.	7. Average Daily Strength of the Force, exclusive of Additional Constables.
		£.				
London, Metropolitan - - -	5,595,628	43,906,086	447,066	791,860	9,914	13,646

POLICE.

HEADS OF SERVICE, FOR THE YEAR ENDED 31st MARCH 1901.

	EXPENDITURE				INCOME			
8. Postage, Telegrams, and Telephone Charges.	9. Extra Police Borrowed on Special Occasions.	10. Other Miscellaneous Charges.	11. Deficiency of Police Pension Fund.	12. Gross Total Cost of Police.	13. Sums received for Services of Additional Constables.	14. Other Receipts credited to the Police Fund.	15.† Amount received from Exchequer Contribution Account; and Clothing.	16. Balance of Cost falling on Local Rates (being Amount in Col. 12, less Amount in Columns 13, 14, and 15).
£. s. d.	£. s. d.	£. s. d.	£. s. d.	£. s. d.	£. s. d.	£. s. d.	£. s. d.	£. s. d.
6,757 7 10	—	111,301 3 8	190,870 3 6	1,866,965 2 1	218,419 14 2	89,171 19 3	730,164 19 8	823,195 9 -

† Includes 6,200l. received from the vote.

POLICE.

OF POLICE FORCE, FOR THE YEAR ENDED 31st MARCH 1901.

NUMBER OF POLICE, Col. 7, EMPLOYED IN ORDINARY POLICE DUTIES.					13. Net Cost of Police. *	NET COST OF POLICE EMPLOYED IN ORDINARY POLICE DUTIES.			REMARKS.
8. Per 10,000 Inhabitants.	9. Per £.10,000 Rateable Value.	10. Per 100 Acres.	11. Per 100 Inhabited Houses.	12. Per Mile of Street.		14. Per Constable.	15. Per £. Rateable Value.	16. Per Inhabitant.	
					£. s. d.	£. s. d.	d.	s. d.	
24·36	3·10	3·04	1·73	1·37	1,302,810 - 11	96 9 5	7·12	4 7·87	

* Exclusive of (a) rents, rates, and taxes, purchase of buildings, &c.; (b) deficiency of Police Pension Fund; (c) sums received for services of additional constables; and (d) other receipts credited to the Police Fund. The amount stated in the column is therefore the amount in Column 12 of the Table V. (A.), less the amount in Columns 6, 11, 13, and 14 of that table.

CITY OF

TABLE V.—(A.) COST OF THE POLICE, UNDER THE DIFFERENT

| 1. | EXPENDITURE - - - - - - - - - | | | | | |
NAME OF POLICE FORCE.	2. Salaries and Pay.	3. Travelling Expenses, including Allowances and Cost of Removal of Constables.	4. Clothing and Accoutrements.	5. Harness, Horses, Forage.	6. Rents, Rates, and Taxes, Purchase of Buildings, &c., less Amount received from Constables as Rent.	7. Printing and Stationery.
	£. s. d.	£. s. d.	£. s. d.	£. s. d.	£. s. d.	£. s. d.
City of London	110,066 3 6	360 10 5	3,387 1 1	—	13,175 3 7	470 4 -

* Column 6 includes the cost of erecting and furnishing buildings, the purchase of land, and the interest and repayment of principal of loans ; but expenditure defrayed out of loans is excluded.

CITY OF

TABLE V.—(B.) COMPARATIVE TABLE OF THE NUMBER AND COST

1. NAME OF POLICE FORCE.	2. Population by Census of 1891.	3. Rateable Value.	4. Acreage.	5. Number of Inhabited Houses by Census of 1891.	6. Length of Streets, Squares, &c., in Miles.	7. Average Daily Strength of the Force, exclusive of Additional Constables.
City of London	37,705	4,888,214	668	5,819	43	1,001

LONDON POLICE.

HEADS OF SERVICE, FOR THE YEAR ENDED 31st DECEMBER 1901.

EXPENDITURE.					INCOME.			
8.	9.	10.	11.	12.	13.	14.	15.	16.
Postage, Telegrams, and Telephone Charges.	Extra Police Borrowed on Special Occasions.	Other Miscellaneous Charges.	Deficiency of Police Pension Fund.	Gross Total Cost of Police.	Sums received for Services of Additional Constables.	Other Receipts credited to the Police Fund.	Amount received from Corporation of City of London Contribution Account towards Pay and Clothing, Fines and Penalties.	Balance of Cost falling on Local Rates (being Amount in Col. 12, less Amount in Columns 13, 14, and 15).
£. s. d.	£. s. d.	£. s. d.	£. s. d.	£. s. d.	£. s. d.	£. s. d.	£. s. d.	£. s. d.
271 2 6	—	5,245 5 1	26,823 6 10	159,796 16 -	10,638 7 7	1,507 15 4	36,837 10 3	110,818 2 10

LONDON POLICE.

OF POLICE FORCE, FOR THE YEAR ENDED 31st DECEMBER 1901.

NUMBER OF POLICE, Col. 7, EMPLOYED IN ORDINARY POLICE DUTIES.					13. Net Cost of Police. *	NET COST OF POLICE EMPLOYED IN ORDINARY POLICE DUTIES.			REMARKS.
8. Per 10,000 Inhabitants.	9. Per £. 10,000 Rateable Value.	10. Per 100 Acres.	11. Per 100 Inhabited Houses.	12. Per Mile of Street.		14. Per Constable.	15. Per £. Rateable Value.	16. Per Inhabitant.	
					£.	£. s. d.	d.	£ s. d.	
365·48	2·04	149·85	17·20	30·85	107,654	107 10 11	5½	2 17 1	

* Exclusive of (a) rents, rates, and taxes, purchase of buildings, &c.; (b) deficiency of Police Pension Fund; (c) sums received for services of additional constables; and (d) other receipts credited to the Police Fund. The amount stated in the column is therefore the amount in Column 12 of the Table V. (A.), less the amounts in Columns 6, 11, 13, and 14 of that table.

TABLE V.—(B.) COMPARATIVE TABLE OF THE NUMBER AND COST

District No. 1.—MIDLAND, EASTERN COUNTIES,

Number.	1. NAME OF POLICE FORCE.	2. Population by Census of 1891.	3. Rateable Value.	4. Acreage.	5. Number of Inhabited Houses by Census of 1891.
	ENGLAND.		*s.*		
1	BEDFORDSHIRE - - - -	102,906	687,307	297,605	23,186
2	Bedford - - - - -	28,023	148,091	2,223	5,546
3	Luton - - - - - -	30,056	146,349	3,134	6,223
4	BUCKINGHAMSHIRE - - -	173,227	1,075,820	478,691	37,663
5	Wycombe - - - -	13,435	42,763	687	2,456
6	CAMBRIDGESHIRE - - -	83,303	383,169	312,003	18,708
7	Cambridge - - - -	36,983	238,802	3,233	7,893
8	ELY, ISLE OF - - - -	63,340	421,743	238,107	14,336
9	ESSEX - - - - - -	335,136	1,620,816	908,072	70,947
10	Colchester - - - -	34,559	148,332	11,331	6,444
11	HERTFORDSHIRE - - - -	177,478	1,067,804	367,406	36,812
12	St. Albans - - - -	12,898	59,932	997	2,633
13	HUNTINGDONSHIRE - - -	55,015	418,021	234,162	12,619
14	LEICESTERSHIRE - - - -	201,464	1,377,179	524,200	43,579
15	Leicester - - - -	174,624	848,075	8,586	35,705
16	LINCOLNSHIRE - - - -	338,808	2,108,913	1,680,981	103,944
17	Boston - - - - -	14,593	51,123	2,765	3,335
18	Grantham - - - -	16,746	72,238	1,833	3,464
19	Great Grimsby - - -	51,934	236,345	2,832	11,189
20	Lincoln - - - - -	41,491	180,702	3,747	8,916
21	Louth - - - - -	10,040	37,324	2,749	2,424
22	NORFOLK - - - - -	318,202	1,917,742	1,302,882	72,751
23	Great Yarmouth - - -	49,334	201,348	3,567	10.997
24	King's Lynn - - - -	18.360	84,093	3,061	4,161
25	Norwich - - - -	100,970	369,026	7,558	23,268
26	NORTHAMPTONSHIRE - - -	203,281	1,346,680	583,637	44,344
27	Northampton - - -	61,012	355,335	1,311	11,774
28	OXFORDSHIRE - - - -	130,985	735,946	471,340	28,646
29	Banbury - - - -	12,768	61,049	4,634	2,726
30	Oxford - - - - -	45,742	307,000	4,714	9,255

OF POLICE FORCES, FOR THE YEAR ENDED 31st MARCH 1901.

AND NORTH WALES.

	6. Length of Streets, Squares, &c., in Miles.	7. Average Daily Strength of the Force, exclusive of Additional Constables.	8. Net Cost of Police. *	NET COST OF POLICE EMPLOYED IN ORDINARY POLICE DUTIES.		REMARKS
				9. Per Constable.	10. Per Inhabitant.	
			£.	£. s. d.	s. d.	
1	—	100	5,332	53 6 4	1 –	
2	36	41	3,616	83 3 10	2 6	
3	36	35	3,177	90 15 5	2 1	
4	—	153	12,861	84 1 2	1 5	
5	9	15	1,327	88 9 4	1 11	
6	—	71	5,782	81 8 8	1 4	
7	84	64	5,870	91 14 4	3 2	
8	—	65	5,594	86 1 2	1 9	
9	—	390	32,312	83 17 –	1 11	
10	80	46	4,729	102 16 1	2 8	
11	—	230	20,169	87 13 9	2 3	
12	16	18	1,510	83 17 9	2 4	
13	—	54	5,034	93 4 5	1 9	
14	—	166	15,066	90 9 8	1 6	
15	170	206	18,996	92 4 3	2 2	
16	—	315	29,300	93 – 4	1 8	
17	21	15	1,361	90 14 8	1 8	
18	17	16	1,399	87 8 9	1 8	
19	52	63	5,749	88 9 1	2 2	
20	48	49	4,534	92 10 7	2 2	
21	14	10	915	91 10 5	1 11	
22	—	242	21,604	89 5 5	1 4	
23	120	57	5,093	89 7 –	2 –	
24	22	23	2,365	98 9 6	2 5	
25	100	117	9,861	84 5 8	1 11	
26	—	158	15,411	97 10 11	1 6	
27	36	113	8,904	78 15 11	2 11	
28	—	111	8,451	76 2 8	1 3	
29	25	13	1,129	86 16 11	1 9	
30	54	61	5,823	95 9 2	2 6	

* The amount stated in this column is the amount in Column 12 of the Table V. (A.) less the amounts in Columns 6, 11, 13, and 14 of that table.

L L

Table V.—(B.) COMPARATIVE TABLE OF THE NUMBER
31st MARCH

District No. 1.—MIDLAND, EASTERN COUNTIES,

Number.	1. NAME OF POLICE FORCE.	2. Population by Census of 1891.	3. Rateable Value.	4. Acreage.	5. Number of Inhabited Houses by Census of 1891.
	ENGLAND—*continued.*		£.		
31	PETERBOROUGH (Liberty) - -	10,078	100,179	51,587	2,517
32	Peterborough (City) - -	25,171	139,055	1,884	5,296
33	RUTLANDSHIRE - - - -	20,659	187,271	97,273	4,486
34	SHROPSHIRE - - - - -	209,860	1,523,858	858,276	44,200
35	Shrewsbury - - - -	26,967	144,282	3,525	5,594
36	STAFFORDSHIRE - - -	858,391	4,115,001	731,542	167,121
37	Hanley - - - - -	54,946	236,085	1,768	10,316
38	Newcastle-under-Lyme - -	18,452	57,383	672	3,635
39	Walsall - - - - -	71,789	263,242	8,711	13,851
40	Wolverhampton - - -	82,662	364,896	3,525	16,101
41	SUFFOLK (EAST) - - - -	183,478	791,045	549,744	40,287
42	Ipswich - - - - -	57,860	280,288	8,110	12,307
43	SUFFOLK (WEST) - - - -	121,708	582,084	390,855	27,228
44	WARWICKSHIRE - - - -	277,566	1,531,728	570,788	59,618
45	Birmingham - - - -	478,113	2,400,845	12,705	95,470
46	Coventry - - - -	58,479	270,261	4,147	13,209
47	Leamington - - - -	26,930	180,828	2,816	5,536
48	WORCESTERSHIRE - - -	314,772	1,834,167	463,613	60,891
49	Kidderminster - - -	24,803	84,932	1,213	5,184
50	Worcester - - - -	42,908	184,508	3,185	9,307
	NORTH WALES.				
1	ANGLESEY - - - - -	50,098	203,616	175,836	12,112
2	CARNARVONSHIRE - - -	115,886	551,058	360,451	26,118
3	DENBIGHSHIRE - - - -	120,807	488,125	429,493	25,015
4	FLINTSHIRE - - - -	76,913	444,046	163,304	16,770
5	MERIONETHSHIRE - - -	49,212	223,644	427,810	10,933
6	MONTGOMERYSHIRE - - -	58,003	383,335	510,111	12,590
	TOTAL - - -	6,372,634	4,309,431	13,298,070	1,374,388

AND COST OF POLICE FORCES, FOR THE YEAR ENDED
1901—*continued.*

AND NORTH WALES—*continued.*

	6. Length of Streets, Squares, &c., in Miles.	7. Average Daily Strength of the Force, exclusive of Additional Constables.	8. Net Cost of Police. *	NET COST OF POLICE EMPLOYED IN ORDINARY POLICE DUTIES.		REMARKS.
				9. Per Constable.	10. Per Inhabitant.	
			£.	£. s. d.	s. d.	
31	—	10	968	96 16 –	1 11	
32	31	30	2,777	92 11 8	2 6	
33	—	15	1,452	96 16 5	1 4	
34	—	165	12,597	76 6 10	1 2	
35	30	37	3,182	86 – –	2 4	
36	—	664	60,734	91 9 4	1 5	
37	35	60	5,452	90 17 4	1 11	
38	17	18	1,779	98 16 8	1 11	
39	65	78	6,844	87 14 10	1 10	
40	86	93	7,948	85 9 3	1 11	
41	—	165	12,539	75 19 10	1 4	
42	75	67	5,973	89 3 –	2 1	
43	—	118	9,860	87 5 1	1 7	
44	—	298	24,679	82 16 3	1 9	
45	270	692	67,568	97 12 9	2 9	
46	55	88	8,311	94 8 10	2 10	
47	33	40	4,156	103 18 –	3 1	
48	—	349	28,966	82 19 11	1 10	
49	28	28	2,570	88 12 4	2 –	
50	60	51	4,648	91 2 8	2 1	
1	—	30	2,604	86 10 –	1 –	
2	—	80	7,558	93 11 1	1 8	
3	—	82	6,725	82 – 2	1 –	
4	—	58	5,450	93 19 6	1 5	
5	—	35	3,633	103 16 –	1 5	
6	—	36	3,526	97 18 10	1 2	
	†1,675	6,401	556,773	86 19 7	1 9	

* The amount stated in this column is the amount in Column 12 of the Table V. (A.), less the amounts in Columns 6, 11, 13, and 14 of that table.
† Boroughs only.

TABLE V.—(B.) COMPARATIVE TABLE OF THE NUMBER
31st MARCH

District No. 2.—

Number	1. NAME OF POLICE FORCE.	2. Population by Census of 1891.	3. Rateable Value.	4. Acreage.	5. Number of Inhabited Houses by Census of 1891.	6. Length of Streets, Squares, &c., in Miles.
			£.			
1	CHESHIRE · · · · ·	431,898	3,159,754	· 633,101	85,047	—
2	Birkenhead · · · ·	99,857	555,004	3,850	17,495	106·
3	Chester · · · · ·	37,105	200,105	2,960	7,481	24·
4	Congleton · · · ·	10,744	32,776	2,572	2,500	25
5	Hyde · · · · ·	30,670	119,448	3,072	6,559	24
6	Macclesfield · · · ·	36,009	105,768	3,214	8,292	43
7	Stalybridge · · · ·	26,783	104,225	3,185	5,775	28·50
8	Stockport · · · ·	70,263	296,023	2,200	15,616	79½
9	CUMBERLAND · · · ·	227,373	1,496,618	968,136	44,732	—
10	Carlisle · · · ·	39,176	203,598	2,025	7,624	50
11	DERBYSHIRE · · · ·	381,218	1,973,845	644,543	73,750	—
12	Chesterfield · · · ·	22,009	92,551	1,219	4,171	33
13	Derby · · · · ·	94,146	458,313	3,445	19,199	75½
14	Glossop · · · ·	22,416	61,036	3,050	4,829	33
15	DURHAM · · · · ·	684,008	3,478,989	687,383	123,283	—
16	Durham · · · · ·	14,863	55,213	880	2,625	20
17	Gateshead · · · ·	85,692	359,562	3,138	10,879	61
18	Hartlepool · · · ·	21,276	71,877	739	3,283	21
19	South Shields · · · ·	78,391	371,032	1,839	9,999	78·5
20	Sunderland · · · ·	132,334	584,726	3,735	18,590	148
21	LANCASHIRE · · · ·	1,417,123	8,045,551	1,076,752	280,049	—
22	Accrington · · · ·	38,603	170,019	3,426	8,115	40
23	Ashton-under-Lyne · ·	40,463	168,961	1,340	8,542	34
24	Bacup · · · · ·	23,498	80,375	6,116	5,265	51·50
25	Barrow-in-Furness · ·	51,712	257,354	10,987	7,477	49
26	Blackburn · · · ·	120,064	482,072	6,974	24,491	160
27	Blackpool · · · ·	23,846	386,860	3,610	4,921	74½
28	Bolton · · · · ·	146,465	693,732	15,270	30,523	183
29	Bootle · · · · ·	49,217	487,555	1,590	8,314	41
30	Burnley · · · · ·	87,016	364,620	4,015	17,789	84
31	Clitheroe · · · ·	10,815	41,352	2,381	2,290	13·95
32	Lancaster · · · ·	31,038	173,436	3,507	6,025	· 43
33	Liverpool · · · ·	629,443	4,042,525	15,092	111,973	424
34	Manchester · · · ·	505,368	3,196,008	12,911	100,241	689
35	Oldham · · · · ·	131,463	580,290	4,730	20,315	122
36	Preston · · · · ·	107,572	400,754	4,030	22,333	90

NORTHERN.

	7. Average Daily Strength of the Force, exclusive of Additional Constables.	8. Net Cost of Police. *	Net Cost of Police employed in Ordinary Police Duties.			Remarks.
			9. Per Constable.	10. Per £. Rateable Value.	11. Per Inhabitant.	
		£.	£. s. d.	d.	s. d.	
1	439	41,743	95 1 9	3¼	1 11·⁄	
2	145	13,959	96 5 4·55	6·03	2 9·54	
3	48	4,346	90 10 10	5·22	2 4	
4	11	916	83 5 5¼	3¼	1 8¼	
5	31	2,933	94 12 3	6·00	1 10·95	
6	38	3,327	87 11 –	7	1 10	
7	31	2,719	87 14 2	6·26	2 -½	
8	80	7,577	94 14 3	6	2 1¼	
9	197	17,170	76 – 6	1¼	1 6	
10	50	4,561	91 4 5	5·37	2 3·94	
11	329	32,135	97 13 5	3¹¹⁄₁₆	1 8	
12	30	3,103	103 8 8	8³⁄₁₆	2 9	
13	112	10,851	96 17 8	5·68	2 3¼	
14	26	2,375	91 6 11	9¹⁄₁₆	2 1¾	
15	618	51,801	83 16 4½	3¼	1 6	
16	16	1,630	101 17 6	7·08	2 2	
17	110	10,471	95 3 9½	6¼	2 5¼	
18	26	2,535	97 10 –	8·46	2 4·59	
19	100	9,375	93 15 –	6¹⁄₁₆	2 4½	
20	162	13,732	84 15 3	6¼	2 0½	
21	1,591	142.919	89 16 7	4·26	1 9	
22	43	4,210	97 18 1	6	2 2	
23	45	4,328	96 3 6¼	6¼	2 1¼	
24	26	2,235	85 19 2·77	6·67	1 10·82	
25	54	5,837	97 5	5·44	2 3	
26	132·37	12,081	91 10 5½	6	2 0¼	
27	74	7,108	96 1 –	4·4	5 11·53	
28	159·59	15,883	99 10 5·7	5·49	2 2·02	
29	72	6,930	96 5 –	3·41	2 9·79	
30	96	8,080	84 3 4	5·32	1 10½	
31	11	991	90 1 10	5·75	1 9·99	
32	40	2,071	51 15 9	2·88	1 2·7	
33	1,353	130,152	96 3 10	7½	4 1¼	
34	1,000	90,718	90 14 4	6·81	3 7	
35	153	13,511	85 10 3	5·38	2 0·67	
36	116	10,819	93 5 4	6·4	2 0·13	

* Exclusive of sums received for services of additional constables ; of rents, rates, and taxes, other receipts, &c., purchase of buildings, &c., and of deficiency of Police Pension Fund. The amount stated in the column is therefore the amount in Column 15 of the Table VI. (A.), less the amounts in Columns 2, 3, 11, and 14 of that table.

TABLE V.—(B.) COMPARATIVE TABLE OF THE NUMBER
31ST MARCH

District No. 2.—

Number.	1. NAME OF POLICE FORCE.	2. Population by Census of 1891.	8. Rateable Value.	4. Acreage.	5. Number of Inhabited Houses by Census of 1891.	6. Length of Streets, Squares, &c., in Miles.
	LANCASHIRE—continued.		£.			
37	Rochdale	71,401	353,064	6,584	16,420	114
38	St. Helens	72,446	345,066	7,282	12,331	65
39	Salford	198,139	949,497	5,195	39,153	238
40	Southport	41,406	343,022	7,526	7,546	60
41	Warrington	55,068	238,853	3,117	12,361	50
42	Wigan	55,013	305,921	2,188	9,978	33
43	NORTHUMBERLAND	259,765	1,912,205	1,273,561	46,050	—
44	Berwick	13,377	63,838	6,930	2,122	40¼
45	Newcastle-on-Tyne	186,300	1,222,398	5,371	25,432	186
46	Tynemouth	46,588	216,687	4,317	6,328	36
47	NOTTINGHAMSHIRE	217,291	1,341,912	527,221	45,959	—
48	Newark	14,457	69,538	1,932	3,181	15
49	Nottingham	213,877	1,003,000	10,935	45,974	175
50	WESTMORLAND	51,785	471,462	500,451	10,358	—
51	Kendal	14,430	64,321	2,622	2,952	18
52	YORK (EAST RIDING)	128,370	1,191,931	738,630	27,301	—
53	Beverley	12,539	48,467	2,404	2,834	14
54	Hull	200,651	1,004,702	9,202	57,233	116
55	YORK (NORTH RIDING)	250,139	1,827,731	1,355,616	51,353	—
56	Middlesbrough	75,532	327,051	2,824	13,311	67
57	Scarborough	33,776	223,191	2,348	7,237	35
58	York	67,926	394,763	3,729	13,791	51
59	YORK (WEST RIDING)	1,129,830	6,123,829	1,669,345	235,933	—
60	Barnsley	35,427	122,000	2,286	7,066	52
61	Bradford	266,164	1,396,067	22,843	57,233	338½
62	Dewsbury	29,847	126,074	1,468	6,561	32
63	Doncaster	25,933	143,570	1,691	5,393	20
64	Halifax	91,778	477,446	13,636	22,112	148
65	Huddersfield	95,420	454,954	11,852	20,943	130
66	Leeds	367,505	1,741,373	21,572	78,086	353
67	Rotherham	42,061	181,683	6,000	7,996	60
68	Sheffield	324,243	1,470,860	19,651	69,922	326
69	Wakefield	36,815	190,114	2,438	7,793	50
	TOTAL	10,685,221	59,698,517	10,355,333	2,120,071	5870·45

AND COST OF POLICE FORCES, FOR THE YEAR ENDED 1901—*continued.*

NORTHERN—*continued.*

	7. Average Daily Strength of the Force, exclusive of Additional Constables.	8. Net Cost of Police. *	Net Cost of Police employed in Ordinary Police Duties. 9. Per Constable.	10. Per £. Rateable Value.	11. Per Inhabitant.	Remarks.
		£.	£. s. d.	d.	s. d.	
37	88	7,376	83 16 4·36	5·01	1 11·21	
38	84	7,300	88 1 10	5	1 10¾	
39	325	29,436	90 11 5	7·4	2 11½	
40	70	6,966	99 10 3	5	3 4	
41	69	6,601	95 13 5	6·63	2 4¾	
42	68	6,293	92 10 10	7·33	2 3·4	
43	219	21,479	98 1 6½	2·69	1 7¾	
44	13	1,173	90 4 7½	4½	1 9 5/12	
45	298	31,315	105 1 8	6·14	3 4·34	
46	65	5,992	92 3 8	6·63	2 6¾	
47	199	18,444	92 13 8	3·29	1 8¼	
48	15	1,363	90 17 4	4½	1 10½	
49	262	25,950	99 – 10	6	2 5	
50	35	3,500	76 – 6	1	1 4	
51	16	1,415	88 8 9	5¼	1 11¼	
52	134	13,852	103 7 5	2·79	2 1·89	
53	15	1,347	89 16 –	6·7	2 1·8	
54	331	29,038	87 14 6	6·94	2 10½	
55	248	24,801	100 – 1	3¼	2 0	
56	96	8,377	87 5 3	6¼	2 2½	
57	50	4,672	93 8 9½	5·02	2 9·2	
58	80	7,831	97 17 9	4¾	2 3½	
59	1,097	109,602	99 18 2	4·29	1 11·49	
60	40	3,154	78 17 –	6·20	1 9·36	
61	354	33,311	94 1 11	5·72	2 6·08	
62	36·5	3,439	92 18 11	6·5	2 3·2	
63	36	3,549	98 11 8	5¾	2 5¼	
64	101	9,733	96 7 4	4·9	2 –	
65	118	11,228	95 3 0·6	5·92	2 4·24	
66	503	46,610	92 13 3¾	6½	2 6½	
67	55	5,502	100 – 8	7·26	2 7	
68	455	42,642	93 14 9·75	6·95	2 7·56	
69	52	4,669	89 15 9	6	2 3	
	13,197·46	1,233,092	93 8 8·95	4·95	2 3·69	

* Exclusive of sums received for services of additional constables; of rents, rates, and taxes, other receipts, &c., purchase of buildings, &c., and of deficiency of Police Pension Fund. The amount stated in the column is therefore the amount in Column 15 of the Table VI. (A.), less the amounts in Columns 2, 3, 11, and 14 of that table.

TABLE V.—(B.) COMPARATIVE TABLE OF THE NUMBER
31st MARCH

District No. 3.—SOUTH OF ENGLAND

	1. NAME OF POLICE FORCE.	2. Population by Census of 1891.	3. Rateable Value.	4. Acreage.	5. Number of Inhabited Houses by Census of 1891.
	ENGLAND.		**£.**		
1	BERKSHIRE - - - - -	164,124	1,008,405	455,453	34,268
2	Reading - - - - -	60,054	352,118	5,878	11,465
3	Windsor - - - - -	12,327	81,661	—	2,240
4	CORNWALL - - - - -	297,097	1,054,688	862,685	65,483
5	Penzance - - - -	12,432	56,413	355	2,566
6	Truro - - .. - -	11,131	47,690	1,127	2,512
7	DEVONSHIRE - - - -	418,804	2,110,127	1,644,268	84,699
8	Barnstaple - - - -	13,763	50,955	2,374	2,832
9	Devonport - - - -	54,803	263,418	1,760	5,097
10	Exeter - - - - -	45,579	235,201	3,118	8,680
11	Plymouth - - - -	88,941	456,357	2,391	9,633
12	Tiverton - - - - -	10,892	52,249	17,680	2,265
13	DORSETSHIRE - - - -	172,214	809,196	624,088	38,264
14	Weymouth - - - -	21,328	93,578	1,012	2,640
15	GLOUCESTER - - - -	365,842	2,081,780	797,875	89,010
16	Bristol - - - -	281,156	1,561,891	9,563	35,355
17	HAMPSHIRE - - - -	347,793	2,270,903	945,528	69,025
18	Portsmouth - - - -	159,251	806,663	4,320	29,353
19	Southampton - - - -	86,034	487,179	4,984	12,221
20	Winchester - - - -	20,203	109,482	1,903	3,531
21	HEREFORDSHIRE - - - -	96,097	593,270	534,149	21,168
22	Hereford - - - -	20,267	108,934	5,031	4,145
23	KENT - - - - -	479,525	2,696,254	912,858	93,464
24	Canterbury - - -	23,062	103,378	3,971	4,627
25	Dover - - - -	33,300	189,066	1,256	5,809
26	Folkestone - - - -	23,905	217,606	2,482	4,123
27	Gravesend - - - -	23,876	114,845	1,256	4,186
28	Maidstone - - - -	32,145	156,901	4,008	6,007
29	Margate - - - -	18,417	152,608	759	3,272
30	Ramsgate - - -	24,733	142,137	2,343	4,958
31	Rochester - - - -	26,290	119,712	2,909	5,076
32	Tunbridge Wells - - -	27,995	263,614	3,399	5,230

AND COST OF POLICE FORCES, FOR THE YEAR ENDED
1901—*continued.*

AND SOUTH WALES.

	6. Length of Streets, Squares, &c., in Miles.	7. Average Daily Strength of the Force, exclusive of Additional Constables.	8. Net Cost of Police.	NET COST OF POLICE EMPLOYED IN ORDINARY POLICE DUTIES.		REMARKS.
				9. Per Constable.	10. Per Inhabitant.	
			£.	£. s. d.	s. d.	
1	—	173	13,913	80 8 5	1 8	
2	70	76	7,047	92 14 5	2 4	
3	10	21	1,955	93 1 10	3 2	
4	—	228	13,528	59 6 8	– 11	
5	18	13	1,098	84 1 6	1 9	
6	14	12	1,061	88 8 4	1 11	
7	—	419	30,447	72 13 4	1 5	
8	20	14	1,208	86 5 8	1 9	
9	45	83	6,866	82 14 5	1 11	
10	35	64	5,047	78 17 2	2 2	
11	60	136	11,246	82 13 9	2 5	
12	76	11	940	85 9 1	1 8	
13	—	176	12,737	72 7 4	1 4	
14	17	29	2,916	100 11 –	4 2	
15	—	350	18,445	52 14 –	1 –	
16	145	484	43,994	90 17 11	3 –	
17	—	388	28,354	73 1 6	1 7	
18	108	226	20,477	90 12 1	2 6	
19	60	122	11,968	98 1 11	2 9	
20	25	27	1,836	68 – –	1 10	
21	—	80	6,883	86 – 11	1 5	
22	50	32	2,691	84 1 10	2 7	
23	—	481	40,000	83 3 3	1 8 .	
24	25	26	2,371	91 3 10	2 –	
25	42	57	5,704	100 1 4	3 5	
26	26	40	4,188	104 14 –	3 6	
27	19	36	3,538	98 5 6	2 11	
28	40	43	4,165	96 17 2	2 7	
29	17	36	3,413	94 16 1	3 1	
30	54	47	4,321	91 18 8	3 5	
31	24	40	3,271	81 15 6	2 6	
32	70	49	4,830	98 11 5	3 6	

* Exclusive of sums received for services of additional constables ; ot rents, rates, and taxes, purchase of buildings, &c., and of deficiency of Police Pension Fund. The amount stated in the column is therefore the amount in Column 15 of the Table VI. (A.), less the amounts in Columns 2, 3, 11, and 14 of that table.

Table V.—(B.) COMPARATIVE TABLE OF THE NUMBER
31st MARCH

District No. 3.—SOUTH OF ENGLAND

Number	1. NAME OF POLICE FORCE.	2. Population by Census of 1891.	3. Rateable Value.	4. Acreage.	5. Number of Inhabited Houses by Census of 1891.
	ENGLAND—*continued.*		£.		
33	MONMOUTHSHIRE - - -	203,426	974,906	344,649	38,467
34	Newport - - - - -	54,707	352,873	4,463	8,600
35	SOMERSETSHIRE - - -	372,612	1,986,347	1,035,404	80,218
36	Bath - - - -	51,844	307,686	3,382	8,933
37	Bridgwater - - - -	13,663	47,822	925	2,604
38	SURREY - - - - -	189,089	1,507,704	375,152	36,080
39	Guildford - - - -	14,316	91,219	604	2,808
40	Reigate - - - - -	22,646	199,304	5,994	3,952
41	SUSSEX (EAST) - - - -	164,836	1,052,337	513,508	34,318
42	Brighton - - - -	115,873	831,377	2,529	19,543
43	Eastbourne - - - -	34,969	312,620	5,410	5,190
44	Hastings - - - -	63,189	458,870	5,324	8,165
45	Hove - - - -	28,335	358,816	1,547	4,414
46	SUSSEX (WEST) - - -	140,619	888,114	402,478	28,499
47	WIGHT, ISLE OF - - - -	67,720	401,754	92,550	13,382
48	Ryde - - - -	10,952	72,139	792	2,402
49	WILTSHIRE - - - - -	246,737	1,153,005	863,810	54,242
50	Salisbury - - - -	15,533	74,735	609	3,222
	SOUTH WALES.				
1	BRECONSHIRE - - - -	51,393	277,141	469,894	10,953
2	CARDIGANSHIRE - - - -	63,467	283,226	443,071	15,660
3	CARMARTHENSHIRE - - -	120,266	449,690	582,659	24,995
4	Carmarthen - - - -	10,300	40,308	5,157	2,082
5	GLAMORGANSHIRE - - -	456,841	2,664,851	504,376	82,081
6	Cardiff - - - -	128,915	1,066,246	6,064	20,476
7	Neath - - - -	11,113	48,920	1,439	2,183
8	Swansea - - - -	90,349	362,527	5,087	16,305
9	PEMBROKESHIRE - - -	88,296	462,053	392,710	19,092
10	RADNORSHIRE - - -	21,791	172,109	301,164	4,552
	TOTAL - - -	6,327,077	35,750,378	13,234,227	1,226,572

AND COST OF POLICE FORCES, FOR THE YEAR ENDED
1901—*continued.*

AND SOUTH WALES—*continued.*

	6. Length of Streets, Squares, &c., in Miles.	7. Average Daily Strength of the Force, exclusive of Additional Constables.	8. Net Cost of Police.	NET COST OF POLICE EMPLOYED IN ORDINARY POLICE DUTIES.		REMARKS.
				9. Per Constable.	10. Per Inhabitant.	
			£.	£. s. d.	s. d.	
33	—	172	15,199	88 7 4	1 6	
34	65	91	9,165	100 14 3	3 4	
35	—	336	24,607	73 4 4	1 4	
36	50	86	7,435	86 9 –	2 10	
37	16	15	1,283	82 4 2	1 9	
38	—	231	18,353	79 9 1	1 11	
39	13	19	1,747	91 18 11	2 5	
40	50	33	3,326	100 15 9	2 11	
41	—	178	14,669	82 8 2	1 9	
42	88	185	16,298	88 1 11	2 10	
43	51	66	5,756	87 4 2	3 3	
44	50	104	9,672	92 11 5	3 1	
45	39	59	5,347	90 12 6	3 9	
46	—	147	11,511	78 6 1	1 7	
47	—	55	4,366 ·	79 7 7	1 3	
48	17	15	1,109	73 18 8	2 –	
49	—	230	18,668	81 3 3	1 6	
50	8	18	1,525	84 14 5	2 –	
1	—	44	4,034	91 13 7	1 7	
2	—	41	3,594	87 13 2	1 1	
3	—	90	8,704	96 14 2	1 5	
4	· 7	12	975	81 5 –	1 10	
5	—	424	39,262	89 16 10	1 8	
6	97	239	22,879	95 14 6	3 · 6	
7	· 9	14	1,423	101 12 10	2 6	
8	61	106	10,793	101 16 5	2 4	
9	—	70	6,216	88 16 –	1 4	
10	—	18	1,646	91 8 10	1 6	
	1,692	7,117	589,965	82 17 10	1 10	

* Exclusive of sums received for services of additional constables; of rents, rates, and taxes, purchase of buildings, &c., and of deficiency of Police Pension Fund. The amount stated in the column is therefore the amount in Column 15 of the Table VI. (A.), less the amounts in Columns 2, 3, 11, and 14 of that table.

TABLE VI.—STATISTICS OF INCOME AND EXPENDITURE OF POLICE

MIDLAND

Number.	1. NAME OF POLICE FORCE.	INCOME.				EXPENDITURE.			9. Excess of Income over Expenditure	10. Excess of Expenditure over Income.
		2. Stoppages from Pay.	3. Exchequer Contribution.	4. Other Receipts.	5. TOTAL.	6. Pensions, Gratuities, Allowances, &c.	7. Other Payments.	8. TOTAL.		
	ENGLAND.	£. s. d.	£. s. d.	£. s. d.	£. s. d.	£. s. d.	£. s. d.	£. s. d.	£. s. d.	£. s. d.
1	BEDFORDSHIRE - - -	184 5 3	830 15 -	303 17 8	1,318 17 10	2,565 10 10	3 - -	2,567 10 10	—	1,248 13 -
2	Bedford - - - -	84 11 1	231 4 9	140 9 9	456 5 7	599 12 6	—	599 12 6	—	143 6 11
3	Luton - - - - -	83 12 3	138 1 5	322 19 3	545 12 11	340 12 -	—	340 12 -	205 - 11	—
4	BUCKINGHAMSHIRE - -	336 10 6	1,066 8 5	1,038 16 -	2,441 14 11	3,258 4 5	—	3,258 4 5	—	816 9 6
5	Wycombe - - - -	33 9 -	36 15 4	79 8 9	149 13 1	44 16 3	—	44 16 3	104 16 10	—
6	CAMBRIDGESHIRE - -	131 12 4	426 - 1	412 11 10	970 4 3	1,265 17 9	—	1,265 17 9	—	295 13 6
7	Cambridge - - -	136 7 -	450 16 3	291 - 10	878 4 1	1,398 4 1	—	1,398 4 1	—	520 - -
8	ELY, ISLE OF - - - -	117 14 2	405 1 4	216 19 3	739 14 9	1,234 18 2	—	1,234 18 2	—	495 3 5
9	ESSEX - - - - -	732 1 10	3,284 - 10	937 17 5	5,054 - 1	6,334 11 5	—	6,334 11 5	—	1,280 11 4
10	Colchester - - - -	119 15 6	335 - 11	234 5 7	689 2 -	569 13 -	—	569 13 -	19 9 -	—
11	HERTFORDSHIRE - -	477 7 5	1,155 - 11	871 5 5	2,503 13 9	2,985 11 3	—	2,985 11 3	—	481 17 6
12	St. Albans - - -	30 17 3	84 13 5	50 6 11	165 17 7	209 4 -	—	209 4 -	—	43 6 5
13	HUNTINGDONSHIRE - -	97 6 -	335 1 10	123 12 5	556 - 3	996 12 11	—	996 12 11	—	439 13 8
14	LEICESTERSHIRE - - -	340 8 -	930 5 -	1,235 12 2	2,506 5 2	2,345 14 6	91 2 1	2,236 16 6	169 8 8	—
15	Leicester - - - -	516 3 3	978 8 6	411 9 9	1,906 - 6	2,483 2 7	—	2,483 2 7	—	577 2 1
16	LINCOLNSHIRE - - -	740 2 7	1,842 14 4	1,928 12 6	4,511 9 5	5,004 14 4	23 10 5	5,028 4 9	—	516 15 4
17	Boston - - - -	30 - 7	*	33 2 2	63 2 9	456 - 11	—	456 - 11	—	392 18 2
18	Grantham - - -	36 1 8	41 16 -	79 19 9	157 17 5	61 4 4	—	61 4 4	96 13 1	—
19	Great Grimsby - - -	162 8 3	275 4 11	607 1 2	1,044 14 4	655 13 5	—	655 13 5	389 - 11	—
20	Lincoln - - - -	162 2 1	208 18 11	272 13 5	644 14 5	475 14 6	—	475 14 6	168 19 11	—
21	Louth - - - - -	19 3 5	29 2 6	64 9 3	112 15 2	65 - -	—	65 - -	47 15 2	—
22	NORFOLK - - - - -	440 18 6	1,801 3 5	409 3 9	2,651 5 8	6,624 15 5	—	6,624 15 5	—	3,973 9 6
23	Great Yarmouth - -	126 13 5	369 9 1	166 15 1	661 17 7	1,019 6 5	—	1,019 6 5	—	357 8 10
24	King's Lynn - - -	61 5 8	226 7 11	110 11 4	398 4 11	742 2 8	—	742 2 8	—	343 17 9
25	Norwich - - - -	302 9 7	767 10 11	229 6 -	1,299 6 6	2,226 6 2	—	2,226 6 2	—	926 19 8
26	NORTHAMPTONSHIRE - -	318 7 6	1,083 19 8	277 18 10	1,680 6 -	3,043 9 1	—	3,043 9 1	—	1,363 3 1
27	Northampton - - -	222 15 7	599 16 8	785 4 4	1,607 16 7	1,724 5 3	—	1,724 5 3	—	116 8 8

PENSION FUNDS IN THE LOCAL FINANCIAL YEAR 1900–1901.

DISTRICT.

Number	1. NAME OF POLICE FORCE	INCOME 2. Stoppages from Pay.	3. Exchequer Contribution.	4. Other Receipts.	5. TOTAL.	EXPENDITURE 6. Pensions, Gratuities, Allowances, &c.	7. Other Payments.	8. TOTAL.	9. Excess of Income over Expenditure	10. Excess of Expenditure over Income
	ENGLAND—continued.	£. s. d.	£. s. d.	£. s. d.	£. s. d.	£. s. d.	£. s. d.	£. s. d.	£. s. d.	£. s. d.
28	OXFORDSHIRE - - -	239 12 3	720 19 4	606 6 4	1,566 17 11	2,047 11 8	—	2,047 11 8	—	480 13 9
29	Banbury - - -	27 12 1	87 7 4	72 19 6	187 19 11	207 1 7	—	207 1 7	—	49 1 8
30	Oxford - - -	138 16 2	346 9 8	350 12 3	835 18 1	1,008 6 3	—	1,008 6 3	—	172 8 2
31	PETERBOROUGH (Liberty) -	20 16 6	99 11 3	56 15 8	177 3 5	312 13 -	—	312 13 -	—	135 9 7
32	Peterborough (City) -	63 16 10	144 10 4	179 - 5	387 7 7	328 10 8	- 2 6	328 13 2	58 14 5	—
33	RUTLANDSHIRE - - -	31 7 2	70 7 1	139 4 2	240 18 5	149 18 8	- 1 -	149 19 8	90 18 9	—
34	SHROPSHIRE - - -	311 5 4	961 4 11	1,530 7 11	2,802 18 2	2,738 11 4	2 12 -	2,741 3 4	61 14 10	—
35	Shrewsbury - - -	70 15 -	179 10 4	347 10 7	597 15 11	536 12 4	—	536 12 4	61 3 7	—
36	STAFFORDSHIRE - - -	1,372 7 3	3,599 5 1	4,871 5 9	10,043 1 1	9,298 1 10	9 11 1	9,307 12 11	735 8 2	—
37	Hanley - - -	165 1 2	251 10 10	689 17 6	1,106 9 6	514 7 5	—	514 7 5	592 2 1	—
38	Newcastle-under-Lyme -	26 12 11	116 10 9	265 10 9	408 14 5	329 14 8	- 6 9	330 1 5	78 13 -	—
39	Walsall - - -	207 7 6	377 11 10	492 9 8	1,077 9 -	884 8 -	—	884 8 0	193 1 -	—
40	Wolverhampton - -	202 13 11	537 17 4	690 17 7	1,431 8 10	1,375 15 5	7 5 5	1,383 - 10	48 8 -	—
41	SUFFOLK (EAST) - - -	293 4 8	824 16 3	275 - 5	1,393 1 4	2,382 19 8	1 0 10	2,384 - 6	—	990 19 2
42	Ipswich - - -	143 16 2	367 14 6	138 14 5	649 5 2	873 12 1	- 2 6	873 14 7	—	224 9 5
43	SUFFOLK (WEST) - - -	202 14 3	511 5 3	165 5 -	879 4 6	1,391 3 2	—	1,391 3 2	—	511 18 8
44	WARWICKSHIRE - - -	649 18 1	1,656 4 10	1,319 11 4	3,625 14 3	4,496 13 9	—	4,496 13 9	—	870 19 6
45	Birmingham - - -	1,845 16 7	3,730 9 7	4,332 1 9	9,908 7 11	9,681 9 2	68 7 5	9,749 16 7	158 11 4	—
46	Coventry - - -	200 10	489 16 11	69 11 4	729 10 1	1,117 13 8	23 14 1	1,141 7 9	—	411 17 8
47	Leamington - - -	96 10 3	231 18 1	193 1 0	521 9 4	735 10 2	3 3 6	738 13 8	—	217 4 4
48	WORCESTERSHIRE - - -	658 11 7	1,484 19 5	2,586 10 4	4,680 1 4	3,402 4 -	4 0 4	3,406 4 4	1,273 17 -	—
49	Kidderminster - - -	61 3 -	145 9 7	128 14 6	335 7 1	358 - 1	- 19 -	358 19 1	—	23 12 -
50	Worcester - - -	107 19 4	341 2 3	140 6 11	489 8 6	546 9 6	- 19 2	547 8 8	—	58 - 2
	NORTH WALES.									
1	ANGLESEY - - -	87 12 2	† 199 12 -	229 9 10	486 14 0	178 16 4	—	178 16 4	307 17 8	—
2	CARNARVONSHIRE - -	164 6 4	380 5 8	417 11 2	962 3 2	914 12 2	—	914 12 2	37 11 0	—
3	DENBIGHSHIRE - - -	153 5 10	464 6 1	604 1 5	1,221 13 4	1,240 13 4	—	1,240 13 4	—	19 - -
4	FLINTSHIRE - - -	113 11 3	312 4 7	471 14 6	897 10 4	834 8 3	—	834 8 3	63 2 1	—
5	MERIONETHSHIRE - -	67 19 -	206 3 6	237 16 9	511 19 5	561 16 10	—	561 16 10	—	49 17 5
6	MONTGOMERYSHIRE - -	67 1 2	247 3 1	332 6 3	646 10 6	969 7 7	- 1 -	959 8 7	—	312 18 1
	TOTAL - - -	14,006 5 3	35,710 9 2	33,561 5 7	83,277 - -	96,937 - 8	238 19 1	97,175 19 9	4,962 7 5	18,861 7 2

* Exchequer contribution not received in financial year.   † Two years.

Table VI.—STATISTICS OF INCOME AND EXPENDITURE OF POLICE

NORTHERN

	1.	INCOME.				EXPENDITURE.			9.	10.
Number.	NAME OF POLICE FORCE.	2. Stoppages from Pay.	3. Exchequer Contribution.	4. Other Receipts.	5. TOTAL.	6. Pensions, Gratuities, Allowances, &c.	7. Other Payments.	8. TOTAL.	Excess of Income over Expenditure.	Excess of Expenditure over Income.
		£. s. d.	£. s. d.	£. s. d.	£. s. d.	£. s. d.	£. s. d.	£. s. d.	£. s. d.	£. s. d.
1	CHESHIRE - - -	670 11 1	2,386 5 8	1,862 10 3	5,311 7 -	5,889 3 2	17 15 -	5,906 18 2	—	595 11 2
2	Birkenhead - - -	437 2 2	1,039 12 -	1,186 18 6	2,663 12 8	2,741 17 3	—	2,741 17 3	—	78 4 7
3	Chester - - -	131 11 1	324 19 5	290 - 7	746 11 1	1,012 19 7	—	1,012 19 7	—	266 8 6
4	Congleton - - -	30 4 -	22 3 6	60 17 9	112 5 3	6 5 -	—	6 5 -	106 - 3	—
5	Hyde - - -	70 13 5	57 7 5	95 2 -	223 2 10	—	—	—	223 2 10	—
6	Macclesfield - -	94 4 4	141 2 10	394 3 4	629 10 6	318 16 7	—	318 16 7	310 13 11	—
7	Stalybridge - -	69 19 -	169 19 8	203 12 1	442 10 9	493 3 10	1 7 2	494 11 -	—	52 - 3
8	Stockport - -	196 11 3	322 13 7	471 1 2	989 6 -	880 10 7	—	880 10 7	108 15 5	—
9	CUMBERLAND - -	404 17 3	1,180 2 10	1,454 - -	3,039 - 1	3,363 16 8	18 7 5	3,382 4 1	—	343 4 -
10	Carlisle - -	142 7 6	246 9 6	261 7 7	650 4 7	559 9 1	—	559 9 1	90 15 6	—
11	DERBYSHIRE - -	694 13 -	1,759 8 -	2,709 9 4	5,163 10 4	5,019 12 3	—	5,019 12 3	143 18 1	—
12	Chesterfield - -	73 6 4	73 6 9	328 11 5	475 4 6	700 - -	—	700 - -	—	224 15 6
13	Derby - -	295 - 6	610 9 5	559 9 6	1,464 19 5	1,658 3 10	—	1,658 3 10	193 4 5	—
14	Glossop - -	63 8 5	70 - 2	176 1 6	309 10 1	104 13 4	- 4 7	104 17 11	204 12 2	—
15	DURHAM - - -	1,395 3 7	3,440 17 5	4,478 14 7	9,314 15 7	9,916 4 6	15 16 11	9,932 1 5	—	617 5 10
16	Durham - -	34 16 9	82 16 5	196 5 5	313 18 8	236 19 4	—	236 19 4	76 19 4	—
17	Gateshead - -	224 19 4	408 10 4	708 7 2	1,341 16 10	1,103 3 8	- 4 -	1,103 7 8	238 9 2	—
18	Hartlepool - -	58 9 3	190 5 -	200 4 9	448 19 -	842 16 3	3 18 3	846 14 6	—	97 15 6
19	South Shields - -	270 4 5	483 5 8	932 2 8	1,686 12 9	1,234 5 9	—	1,234 5 9	451 7 -	—
20	Sunderland - -	387 15 11	834 19 11	1,104 6 8	2,327 2 6	2,224 4 8	—	2,224 4 8	102 17 10	—
21	LANCASHIRE - -	4,066 17 10	9,897 12 2	7,801 6 3	21,765 16 3	27,492 12 5	15 3 -	27,507 15 5	—	5,751 19 2
22	Accrington - -	107 11 -	110 2 7	473 15 7	691 9 2	91 13 5	—	91 13 5	599 15 9	—
23	Ashton-under-Lyne	104 3	222 11 -	264 9 -	591 3 9	502 11 7	4 16 7	507 8 2	83 15 7	—
24	Bacup - - -	57 17	50 6 4	132 10 1	240 15 10	—	—	—	240 15 10	—
25	Barrow-in-Furness	170 12	*	476 - 9	646 12 10	368 3 1	—	368 3 1	278 9 9	—
26	Blackburn - -	363 3 1	701 19 4	1,194 5 1	2,349 7 6	1,737 4 2	—	1,737 4 2	512 3 4	—
27	Blackpool - -	190 - 7	150 11 8	575 3 4	905 15 7	117 13 4	—	117 13 4	788 2 3	—
28	Bolton - - -	403 12 8	832 4 4	796 - 8	2,033 17 8	2,077 1 4	9 13 8	2,086 15 -	—	52 17
29	Bootle - - -	165 11 7	162 2 7	480 1 5	807 15 7	60 12 -	—	60 12 -	747 3 7	—
30	Burnley - -	231 16 8	168 2 7	884 9 9	1,304 8 -	33 10 -	—	33 10 -	1,271 18 -	—
31	Clitheroe - -	24 19 2	22 10 11	44 - -	91 10 1	7 3 10	—	7 3 10	84 6 3	—
32	Lancaster - -	72 10 4	96 6 7	105 19 10	276 16 9	131 10 8	—	131 10 8	145 6 1	—
33	Liverpool - -	5,976 6 5	9,803 13 1	7,578 9 2	21,358 8 8	26,144 11 10	161 15 -	26,306 6 10	—	4,947 18 2
34	Manchester - -	2,529 10 -	6,066 6 3	1,682 19 10	10,268 16 1	17,486 16 10	7 1 7	17,493 17 5	—	7,225 1 4
35	Oldham - -	303 18 -	*	813 12 9	1,117 10 9	1,534 5 3	—	1,534 5 3	—	416 14 6
36	Preston - -	223 15 5	662 4 5	427 10 3	1,313 10 1	1,905 3 11	—	1,905 3 11	—	591 13 10
37	Rochdale - -	212 16 4	439 18 9	474 5 1	1,127 - 2	1,157 16 9	—	1,157 16 9	—	30 16 7
38	St. Helens - -	224 12 2	187 1 4	549 4 6	960 16 -	19 14 6	—	19 14 6	941 2 6	—

* Exchequer contribution not received in financial year.

DISTRICT.

<table>
<tr><th rowspan="3">Number.</th><th colspan="1">1.</th><th colspan="4">INCOME.</th><th colspan="3">EXPENDITURE.</th><th>9.</th><th>10.</th></tr>
<tr><th rowspan="2">NAME OF POLICE FORCE.</th><th>2.
Stoppages from Pay.</th><th>3.
Exchequer Con-tribution.</th><th>4.
Other Receipts.</th><th>5.
TOTAL.</th><th>6.
Pensions, Gratuities, Allowances, &c.</th><th>7.
Other Payments.</th><th>8.
TOTAL.</th><th>Excess of Income over Expenditure.</th><th>Excess of Expenditure over Income.</th></tr>
<tr></tr>
<tr><td></td><td></td><td>£. s. d.</td><td>£. s. d.</td><td>£. s. d.</td><td>£. s. d.</td><td>£. s. d.</td><td>£. s. d.</td><td>£. s. d.</td><td>£. s. d.</td><td>£. s. d.</td></tr>
<tr><td></td><td>LANCASHIRE—continued.</td><td></td><td></td><td></td><td></td><td></td><td></td><td></td><td></td><td></td></tr>
<tr><td>39</td><td>Salford - - -</td><td>821 9 7</td><td>1,884 6 5</td><td>1,813 14 10</td><td>4,519 10 10</td><td>4,960 11 -</td><td>48 1 11</td><td>5,008 12 11</td><td>—</td><td>489 2 1</td></tr>
<tr><td>40</td><td>Southport - -</td><td>161 10 5</td><td>353 13 9</td><td>489 15 8</td><td>1,004 19 10</td><td>1,096 18 10</td><td>1 9 2</td><td>1,098 8 -</td><td>—</td><td>93 8 2</td></tr>
<tr><td>41</td><td>Warrington -</td><td>162 15 9</td><td>286 15 4</td><td>483 11 9</td><td>933 3 10</td><td>673 4 -</td><td>- 13 3</td><td>673 17 3</td><td>259 5 7</td><td>—</td></tr>
<tr><td>42</td><td>Wigan - - -</td><td>123 11 2</td><td>410 18 7</td><td>338 6 4</td><td>878 16 1</td><td>1,204 5 8</td><td>—</td><td>1,204 5 8</td><td>—</td><td>325 9 7</td></tr>
<tr><td>43</td><td>NORTHUMBERLAND -</td><td>526 4 2</td><td>1,413 16 5</td><td>1,961 4 2</td><td>3,901 4 9</td><td>4,264 7 7</td><td>—</td><td>4,264 7 7</td><td>—</td><td>363 2 10</td></tr>
<tr><td>44</td><td>Berwick - -</td><td>21 12 6</td><td>108 1 3</td><td>107 1 9</td><td>236 15 6</td><td>424 4 -</td><td>—</td><td>424 4 -</td><td>—</td><td>187 8 6</td></tr>
<tr><td>45</td><td>Newcastle-on-Tyne -</td><td>770 17 5</td><td>1,544 10 1</td><td>1,745 9 9</td><td>4,060 17 3</td><td>3,872 9 -</td><td>—</td><td>3,872 9 -</td><td>188 8 3</td><td>—</td></tr>
<tr><td>46</td><td>Tynemouth - -</td><td>138 11 10</td><td>257 13 11</td><td>334 2 1</td><td>730 7 10</td><td>562 16 -</td><td>- 3 9</td><td>562 19 9</td><td>167 8 1</td><td>—</td></tr>
<tr><td>47</td><td>NOTTINGHAMSHIRE -</td><td>449 12 7</td><td>1,020 9 10</td><td>1,151 8 3</td><td>2,621 10 8</td><td>2,371 12 1</td><td>—</td><td>2,371 12 1</td><td>249 18 7</td><td>—</td></tr>
<tr><td>48</td><td>Newark - -</td><td>33 12 5</td><td>80 14 5</td><td>71 10 6</td><td>185 17 4</td><td>208 - -</td><td>—</td><td>208 - -</td><td>—</td><td>22 2 8</td></tr>
<tr><td>49</td><td>Nottingham -</td><td>707 17 11</td><td>1,424 11 10</td><td>898 2 11</td><td>3,030 12 8</td><td>3,727 5 4</td><td>—</td><td>3,727 5 4</td><td>—</td><td>696 12 8</td></tr>
<tr><td>50</td><td>WESTMORLAND - -</td><td>71 18 6</td><td>234 3 4</td><td>245 15 10</td><td>551 17 8</td><td>709 5 3</td><td>—</td><td>709 5 3</td><td>—</td><td>157 7 7</td></tr>
<tr><td>51</td><td>Kendal - - -</td><td>28 10 3</td><td>87 16 4</td><td>126 7 11</td><td>242 14 6</td><td>268 13 4</td><td>1 9 1</td><td>270 2 8</td><td>—</td><td>27 7 11</td></tr>
<tr><td>52</td><td>YORK (EAST RIDING) -</td><td>260 19 -</td><td>773 11 4</td><td>271 8 8</td><td>1,305 19 -</td><td>1,941 9 10</td><td>—</td><td>1,941 9 10</td><td>—</td><td>635 10 10</td></tr>
<tr><td>53</td><td>Beverley - -</td><td>29 17 9</td><td>59 19 9</td><td>82 19 3</td><td>172 16 9</td><td>129 14 -</td><td>—</td><td>129 14 -</td><td>43 2 9</td><td>—</td></tr>
<tr><td>54</td><td>Hull - - - -</td><td>764 16 5</td><td>1,612 1 2</td><td>1,357 - 9</td><td>3,734 - 4</td><td>4,360 4 2</td><td>53 4 2</td><td>4,413 8 4</td><td>—</td><td>679 8 -</td></tr>
<tr><td>55</td><td>YORK (NORTH RIDING) -</td><td>567 12 5</td><td>1,320 15 5</td><td>1,790 14 8</td><td>3,679 2 6</td><td>4,225 6 10</td><td>- 11 6</td><td>4,225 18 4</td><td>—</td><td>546 15 10</td></tr>
<tr><td>56</td><td>Middlesbrough -</td><td>242 7 6</td><td>449 9 10</td><td>999 11 1</td><td>1,692 8 5</td><td>1,344 4 5</td><td>4 4 5</td><td>1,348 8 10</td><td>443 19 7</td><td>—</td></tr>
<tr><td>57</td><td>Scarborough -</td><td>116 18 10</td><td>315 2 5</td><td>225 10 8</td><td>657 11 11</td><td>914 2 2</td><td>9 19 6</td><td>924 1 8</td><td>—</td><td>266 9 9</td></tr>
<tr><td>58</td><td>York - - -</td><td>207 8 3</td><td>484 4 3</td><td>613 18 10</td><td>1,305 11 4</td><td>1,427 10 -</td><td>—</td><td>1,427 10 -</td><td>—</td><td>121 18 8</td></tr>
<tr><td>59</td><td>YORK (WEST RIDING) -</td><td>2,756 8 10</td><td>7,066 18 -</td><td>10,642 14 6</td><td>20,466 1 4</td><td>17,770 18 -</td><td>3 16 6</td><td>17,774 14 6</td><td>2,691 6 10</td><td>—</td></tr>
<tr><td>60</td><td>Barnsley - -</td><td>83 1 10</td><td>66 18 4</td><td>183 17 11</td><td>333 18 1</td><td>—</td><td>—</td><td>—</td><td>333 18 1</td><td>—</td></tr>
<tr><td>61</td><td>Bradford - -</td><td>1,055 18 7</td><td>1,592 2 -</td><td>1,502 15 5</td><td>4,150 16 -</td><td>4,045 19 10</td><td>8 15 4</td><td>4,054 15 2</td><td>96 - 10</td><td>—</td></tr>
<tr><td>62</td><td>Dewsbury - -</td><td>85 2 9</td><td>138 7 1</td><td>632 16 3</td><td>856 6 1</td><td>348 19 8</td><td>2 18 6</td><td>351 18 2</td><td>504 7 11</td><td>—</td></tr>
<tr><td>63</td><td>Doncaster - -</td><td>89 4 5</td><td>160 1 10</td><td>315 13 3</td><td>564 19 6</td><td>343 14 10</td><td>—</td><td>343 14 10</td><td>221 4 8</td><td>—</td></tr>
<tr><td>64</td><td>Halifax - -</td><td>253 10 1</td><td>512 16 3</td><td>1,054 9 1</td><td>1,820 15 10</td><td>1,242 5 4</td><td>—</td><td>1,242 5 4</td><td>578 10 6</td><td>—</td></tr>
<tr><td>65</td><td>Huddersfield -</td><td>280 18 9</td><td>532 1 7</td><td>882 17 -</td><td>1,695 17 4</td><td>1,493 1 9</td><td>—</td><td>1,493 1 9</td><td>202 15 7</td><td>—</td></tr>
<tr><td>66</td><td>Leeds - - -</td><td>1,439 1 6</td><td>2,569 14 0</td><td>625 10 1</td><td>4,634 5 7</td><td>6,602 6 9</td><td>—</td><td>6,602 6 9</td><td>—</td><td>1,968 1 2</td></tr>
<tr><td>67</td><td>Rotherham - -</td><td>129 5 6</td><td>147 19 2</td><td>514 15 4</td><td>792 - -</td><td>41 17 8</td><td>—</td><td>41 17 8</td><td>750 2 4</td><td>—</td></tr>
<tr><td>68</td><td>Sheffield - -</td><td>523 13 9</td><td>2,180 11 2</td><td>4,204 6 1</td><td>6,908 11 -</td><td>7,511 3 2</td><td>40 2 11</td><td>7,551 6 1</td><td>—</td><td>642 15 1</td></tr>
<tr><td>69</td><td>Wakefield - -</td><td>115 2 11</td><td>329 2 10</td><td>389 19 9</td><td>834 5 6</td><td>827 - 4</td><td>11 9 1</td><td>838 9 5</td><td>—</td><td>4 3 11</td></tr>
<tr><td></td><td>TOTAL - - -</td><td>32,490 7 8</td><td>72,961 19 10</td><td>78,565 19 11</td><td>183,888 7 5</td><td>197,687 - 1</td><td>443 2 3</td><td>198,130 2 4</td><td>14,471 1 -</td><td>28,712 15 11</td></tr>
</table>

* Exchequer contribution not received in financial year.

M M 4

Table VI.—STATISTICS OF INCOME AND EXPENDITURE OF POLICE

SOUTHERN

Number.	1. NAME OF POLICE FORCE	INCOME.				EXPENDITURE.			9. Excess of Income over Expenditure.	10. Excess of Expenditure over Income.
		2. Stoppages from Pay.	3. Exchequer Contribution.	4. Other Receipts.	5. TOTAL.	6. Pensions, Gratuities, Allowances, &c.	7. Other Receipts.	8. TOTAL.		
	ENGLAND.	£. s. d.	£. s. d.	£. s. d.	£. s. d.	£. s. d.	£. s. d.	£. s. d.	£. s. d.	£. s. d.
1	BERKSHIRE - - -	383 5 4	975 1 1	1,088 10 6	2,446 16 11	2,961 4 8	11 2 10	2,972 7 6	—	525 10 7
2	Reading - - -	178 1 8	402 13 9	246 11 -	837 6 5	1,079 2 7	—	1,079 2 7	—	251 16
3	Windsor - - -	44 13 4	102 3 1	73 19 10	221 16 2	321 8 2	—	321 8 2	—	99 12 -
4	CORNWALL - - -	416 8 5	1,387 6 10	1,203 8 3	3,007 3 6	4,126 13 1	—	4,126 13 1	—	1,119 9 7
5	Penzance - - -	26 10 10	58 2 -	124 8 1	208 1 11	132 - -	—	132 - -	76 1 11	—
6	Truro - - -	21 11 10	78 15 9	73 18 10	174 6 5	238 1 6	—	238 1 6	—	63 15 1
7	DEVONSHIRE - - -	714 6 11	2,712 18 4	1,153 8 7	4,580 13 10	8,208 6 -	4 12 10	8,212 18 10	—	3,632 5 -
8	Barnstaple - - -	25 3 4	93 17 7	35 5 6	154 6 5	284 5 4	—	284 5 4	—	129 18 11
9	Devonport - - -	177 17 5	406 5 2	288 4 5	872 7 1	1,000 3 8	2 1 3	1,002 4 11	—	129 17 10
10	Exeter - - -	102 - 11	338 3 11	34 14 1	474 18 11	966 10 11	—	966 10 11	—	491 12 -
11	Plymouth - - -	314 19 11	770 8 9	320 13 1	1,406 1 9	2,222 8 8	—	2,222 8 8	—	816 6 11
12	Tiverton - - -	16 16 -	54 11 9	41 - 2	112 7 11	84 1 4	- 8 4	84 9 8	27 18 3	—
13	DORSETSHIRE - - -	332 3 9	1,318 2 3	710 9 10	2,360 15 10	3,762 15 -	- 4 9	3,763 19 9	—	1,403 3 11
14	Weymouth - - -	55 15 2	169 10 3	86 2 3	311 8 1	486 4 -	—	486 4 -	—	174 15 11
15	GLOUCESTERSHIRE - -	644 16 1	1,586 3 3	1,547 7 7	3,778 6 10	4,037 2 4	—	4,037 2 4	—	258 15 6
16	Bristol - - -	1,217 - -	3,331 3 3	2,468 6 11	6,916 15 2	9,499 15 1	2 2 -	9,501 17 1	—	2,585 1 11
17	HAMPSHIRE - - -	839 7 11	2,106 6 10	1,275 3 5	4,220 18 5	6,043 8 9	—	6,043 8 9	—	1,822 10 7
18	Portsmouth - - -	583 5 9	1,458 19 1	1,194 17 9	3,237 2 7	4,415 4 3	—	4,415 4 3	—	1,178 1 8
19	Southampton - - -	297 3 7	866 19 6	279 3 1	1,443 6 2	2,583 6 2	—	2,583 6 2	—	1,140 - -
20	Winchester - - -	55 15 11	135 9 4	28 13 5	219 18 8	398 19 -	—	398 19 0	—	179 - 4
21	HEREFORDSHIRE - - -	155 1 11	636 1 4	172 5 6	863 8 9	1,583 16 -	—	1,583 16 -	—	720 7 3
22	Hereford - - -	65 11 10	214 17 2	69 6 2	349 15 2	737 6 3	—	737 6 3	—	387 11 1
23	KENT - - -	949 16 7	3,044 3 10	1,233 9 4	5,227 9 9	8,959 4 10	—	8,959 4 10	—	3,731 15 1
24	Canterbury - - -	61 19 11	127 12 10	89 7 9	279 - 6	336 18 -	—	336 18 -	—	57 17 6
25	Dover - - -	151 3 8	303 2 5	97 1 5	551 7 6	724 17 1	—	724 17 1	—	173 9 7
26	Folkestone - - -	84 10 1	261 14 1	91 17 3	438 1 5	694 11 9	—	694 11 9	—	256 10 4
27	Gravesend - - -	87 5 1	310 16 1	302 1 6	700 2 8	915 10 6	—	915 10 6	—	215 7 10
28	Maidstone - - -	96 18 -	278 2 2	279 16 2	654 16 4	790 16 8	—	790 16 8	—	136 - 4
29	Margate - - -	86 17 11	142 6 11	151 6 3	380 11 1	292 18 4	- 17 -	293 12 4	86 18 9	—
30	Ramsgate - - -	102 1 5	345 7 2	221 19 11	669 8 6	773 14 7	—	773 14 7	—	203 6 1
31	Rochester - - -	84 19 -	191 19 3	71 6 2	348 4 10	459 19 8	—	459 19 8	—	111 14 10
32	Tunbridge Wells - -	117 2 2	255 16 9	173 17 5	546 16 4	606 12 3	30 13 9	639 6 -	—	92 9 8
33	MONMOUTHSHIRE - - -	381 2 3	870 3 1	1,411 7 -	2,662 12 3	3,313 15 5	—	3,313 15 5	348 16 10	—
34	Newport - - -	218 18 2	359 3 8	376 19 11	955 1 9	758 7 8	—	758 7 8	196 14 1	—

PENSION FUNDS IN THE LOCAL FINANCIAL YEAR 1900-1901—*continued.*

DISTRICT.

№	1. NAME OF POLICE FORCE	INCOME				EXPENDITURE			9. Excess of Income over Expenditure	10. Excess of Expenditure over Income
		2. Stoppages from Pay.	3. Exchequer Contribution.	4. Other Receipts.	5. TOTAL.	6. Pensions, Gratuities, Allowances, &c.	7. Other Receipts.	8. TOTAL.		
	ENGLAND—*continued.*	£. s. d.	£. s. d.	£. s. d.	£. s. d.	£. s. d.	£. s. d.	£. s. d.	£. s. d.	£. s. d.
35	SOMERSETSHIRE - - -	603 4 7	2,353 5 9	1,320 1 -	4,276 11 4	6,857 6 10	—	6,857 6 10	—	2,580 15 6
36	Bath - - - - -	180 4 2	584 19 8	187 3 7	952 7 6	1,800 16 4	—	1,800 16 4	—	848 8 10
37	Bridgwater - - -	31 8 -	116 2 3	29 9 8	176 19 11	340 6 9	—	340 6 9	—	163 6 10
38	SURREY - - - - -	520 3 4	1,294 16 9	1,306 6 11	3,121 5 -	3,623 15 10	77 12 1	3,701 7 11	—	580 2 11
39	Guildford - - - -	43 1 -	79 2 -	78 9 7	190 12 7	172 - -	—	172 - -	27 13 7	—
40	Reigate - - - -	80 5 7	139 15 8	160 5 6	380 6 9	321 16 8	—	321 16 8	58 10 1	—
41	SUSSEX (EAST) - -	372 13 6	1,141 8 10	741 2 5	2,255 3 9	3,575 14 7	4 14 3	3,580 8 10	—	1,325 5 1
42	Brighton - - - -	460 17 11	1,236 5 10	1,343 7 5	3,040 11 2	4,007 19 4	—	4,007 19 4	—	967 8 2
43	Eastbourne - - -	141 1 1	146 13 6	414 13 8	702 8 3	575 17 2	—	575 17 2	126 11 1	—
44	Hastings - - - -	282 14 8	412 10 5	399 10 8	1,094 15 9	888 2 8	6 16 -	894 18 8	199 17 1	—
45	Hove - - - - -	163 19 1	294 19 9	43 3 6	502 1 4	616 1 9	—	616 1 9	—	114 - 5
46	SUSSEX (WEST) - - -	256 3 11	991 12 3	463 5 2	1,612 2 4	3,548 7 6	- 16 3	3,549 4 2	—	937 1 10
47	WIGHT (ISLE OF) - -	125 16 1	297 13 7	274 11 6	698 - 2	774 17 8	—	774 17 8	—	76 17 6
48	Ryde - - - - -	30 5 11	81 - 3	56 7 10	167 14 -	213 4 -	—	213 4 -	—	45 10 -
49	WILTSHIRE - - - -	431 11 9	1,230 13 2	615 5 6	2,277 10 5	3,624 15 7	—	3,624 15 7	—	1,347 5 2
50	Salisbury - - - -	34 3 1	99 9 1	30 5 1	163 16 3	279 18 6	—	279 18 6	—	116 2 3
	SOUTH WALES.									
1	BRECONSHIRE - - -	37 11 11	†496 4 9	364 18 6	947 15 2	638 3 7	—	638 3 7	309 11 7	—
2	CARDIGANSHIRE - -	79 7 7	175 3 1	306 5 9	560 16 5	235 12 8	—	235 12 8	325 3 9	—
3	CARMARTHENSHIRE - -	186 4 9	408 2 5	599 14 8	1,194 1 10	766 1 8	—	766 1 8	428 - 2	—
4	Carmarthen - - -	28 4 10	73 14 7	70 1 11	172 1 4	161 4 -	—	161 4 -	10 17 4	—
5	GLAMORGANSHIRE - -	896 18 2	2,075 18 1	1,848 8 5	4,824 4 8	4,697 3 5	—	4,697 3 5	127 1 3	—
6	Cardiff - - - -	601 5 5	886 6 10	1,270 9 6	2,758 1 9	1,686 8 11	—	1,686 8 11	1,071 12 10	—
7	Neath - - - -	39 13 5	68 11 5	161 - 2	270 5 -	147 9 11	- 5 -	147 14 11	111 10 1	—
8	Swansea - - - -	265 7 4	573 17 9	647 2 8	1,486 7 9	1,436 18 8	—	1,436 18 8	49 9 1	—
9	PEMBROKESHIRE - -	69 - 1	314 4 9	436 11 4	809 16 2	916 12 6	10 14 9	927 7 3	—	117 11 1
10	RADNORSHIRE - -	28 1 9	92 13 1	337 18 -	448 12 10	213 4 -	—	213 4 -	235 8 10	—
	TOTAL - -	15,141 19 -	40,908 19 5	30,443 7 11	86,494 6 4	112,931 7 1	163 1 6	114,964 8 7	3,827 16 7	31,417 18 10

† Two years.

N N

TABLE VII.—EMPLOYMENT OF MATRONS AT POLICE STATIONS WHERE FEMALE PRISONERS ARE DETAINED IN CUSTODY.

MIDLAND DISTRICT.

1. CITY OR BOROUGH.	2. No. of Stations where Females are detained.	3. No. of Stations where there is a Resident Matron (or Matrons).	4. Are the Matron's Services available by Night as well as by Day, if there are Females in the Cells?	5. Where no Resident Matron is employed, are Female Prisoners seen by a Female— (a) When first brought to the Station; (b) At what Intervals afterwards?	6. REMARKS. In this Column should be stated the Arrangements made where no Resident Matron is employed; whether there is a Female Attendant, how she is summoned when wanted, &c.
Bedford	1	—	—	—	The wife of the officer living at or in charge of the station attends to female prisoners as required.
Luton	1	—	—	Yes, but not again unless required.	
Chepping Wycombe	1	—	—	—	A female searcher is summoned by messenger as required.
Cambridge	1	1	Yes	—	
Colchester	1	—	—	Not necessarily, but as required.	
St. Albans	1	—	—	—	A female searcher is summoned by messenger when required.
Leicester	7	—	—	—	A female searcher is summoned by messenger when required.
Boston	1	—	—	—	A female searcher is summoned by messenger when required.
Grantham	1	—	—	Yes, and at meal times.	
Great Grimsby	2	—	—	—	Females prisoners are seen by the wives of officers on reserve duty when required.
Lincoln	8	—	—	—	A female searcher is summoned by messenger when required.
Louth	1	—	—	—	Female prisoners are attended to by wife of head constable.
Great Yarmouth	2	—	—	Yes, and in cases of illness.	
King's Lynn	1	—	—	—	Female prisoners are attended to by wife of head constable.
Norwich	1	—	—	—	Female prisoners are seen every hour from 7 a. m. to 10 p.m., and at night if required, by a woman who lives close to the police station.
Northampton	1	—	—	—	A female searcher is summoned by messenger if required.
Peterborough	1	—	—	—	The wife of the head constable searches female prisoners in cases of felony, and occasionally otherwise.
Banbury	1	—	—	—	The wife of the head constable searches female prisoners in cases of felony, and occasionally otherwise.
Oxford	1	1	Yes	—	A female searcher is summoned by messenger as required.
Shrewsbury	1	—	—	—	
Hanley	1	—	—	—	The wife of the town'hall keeper searches female prisoners charged with larceny, and lives on the premises.
Newcastle-under-Lyme	1	—	—	—	A female searcher is summoned by messenger if required.
Walsall	1	—	—	—	A female searcher is summoned by messenger if required.
Wolverhampton	2	1	Yes	—	
Ipswich	1	—	—	Yes, and remain, as long as required.	
Birmingham	14	1	From 8 a.m. till the court rises at central station.	—	At divisional stations female searchers are summoned by messengers as required.
Coventry	—	—	—	—	Arrangements made with county authorities pending the completion of new police premises for the city.
Leamington	1	1	Yes	—	
Kidderminster	1	—	—	—	A female searcher is summoned by messenger as required.
Worcester	1	1	Yes	—	

TABLE VII.—EMPLOYMENT OF MATRONS AT POLICE STATIONS WHERE FEMALE PRISONERS ARE DETAINED IN CUSTODY – *continued.*

SOUTHERN DISTRICT.

1. CITY OR BOROUGH.	2. No. of Stations where Females are detained.	3. No. of Stations where there is a Resident Matron (or Matrons).	4. Are the Matron's Services available by Night as well as by Day, if there are Females in the Cells?	5. Where no Resident Matron is employed, are Female Prisoners seen by a Female— (a) When first brought to the Station; (b) At what Intervals afterwards?	6. REMARKS. In this Column should be stated the Arrangements made where no Resident Matron is employed; whether there is a Female Attendant, how she is summoned when wanted, &c.
Reading	1	1	Yes	(a) Yes; (b) when required.	Wife of inspector; lives at police station; responsible to watch committee; inspector receives coal; gas free in remuneration.
Windsor	1	1	Yes	„ Yes; „ when required.	Wife of reserve constable; resides on the premises; responsible to head constable; husband receives coal; gas free in remuneration.
Penzance	1	—	Yes	„ Yes; „ when required.	Wife of constable; summoned by messenger; responsible to head constable; remuneration, 1s. for searching, 2s. for day or night attendance.
Truro	1	—	Yes	„ Yes; „ when required.	Female searcher, wife of constable; responsible to head constable; summoned by messenger; remuneration, 1s. by day, 2s. by night attendance.
Barnstaple	1	1	Yes	„ Yes; „ when required.	Wife of constable; summoned by messenger; responsible to watch committee; remuneration, 1s. 6d. each prisoner searched.
Devonport	1	1	Yes	„ Yes; „ when required.	Wife of ex-constable; summoned by messenger; responsible to watch committee; remuneration, 2s. by day, 2s. 6d. by night attendance.
Exeter	1	1	Yes	„ Yes; „ when required.	Widow of constable; summoned by messenger; responsible to city council; remuneration, 1s. for each prisoner searched.
Plymouth	1	1	Yes	„ Yes; „ when required.	Wife of mace-bearer; summoned by messenger; responsible to chief constable; remuneration, 12l. per annum.
Tiverton	1	1	Yes	„ Yes; „ frequently	Wife of head constable; summoned by messenger; responsible to head constable; remuneration, 1s. for each prisoner.
Weymouth	1	—	—	„ Yes; „ when required.	Wife of ex-police-sergeant; summoned by constable on reserve duty; responsible to watch committee; remuneration,1s. for searching; attendance, 2s. by day, 2s. 6d. by night.
Bristol	2	—	Yes	„ Yes; „ when required.	Three matrons are employed; summoned by messenger; responsible to chief constable; on duty 8 hours each; remuneration, 14s. per week.
Portsmouth	1	—	Yes	„ Yes; „ when required.	Female attendant, wife of constable; summoned by messenger; responsible to chief constable; remuneration, 4d. per hour when in attendance.
Southampton	4	4	Yes	„ Yes; „ when required.	Reside at station houses; wife of inspector; remuneration, 1s. for each female prisoner.
Winchester	1	1	Yes	„ Yes; „ when required.	Wife of constable; summoned by constable in charge; responsible to head constable; remuneration, 2s. 6d. per week.
Hereford	—	—	Yes	„ Yes; „ when required.	Female searcher employed when required.
Canterbury	1	1	Yes	„ Yes; „ when required.	Wife of ex-prison warder; responsible to chief constable; remuneration, 1s. by day, and 2s. 6d. by night.
Dover	1	—	Yes	„ Yes; „ when required.	Two female attendants are employed; summoned when required by a constable; responsible to watch committee; remuneration, 10l. per annum each.
Folkestone	1	—	Yes	„ Yes; „ when required.	Female attendant, wife of pensioned constable; summoned by messenger; responsible to watch committee; remuneration, 2s. each prisoner searched.
Gravesend	1	—	Yes	„ Yes; „ when required.	Female attendant, wife of police sergeant; summoned by messenger; responsible to chief constable; remuneration, 8s. per week.

E VII.—EMPLOYMENT OF MATRONS AT POLICE STATIONS WHERE FEMALE PRISONERS ARE DETAINED IN CUSTODY—*continued.*

SOUTHERN DISTRICT—*continued.*

CITY OR BOROUGH.	2. No. of Stations where Females are detained.	3. No. of Stations where there is a Matron Resident (or Matrons.)	4. Are the Matron's Services available by Night as well as by Day, if there are Females in the Cells?	5. Where no Resident Matron is employed, are Female Prisoners seen by a Female— (a) When first brought to the Station; (b) At what Intervals afterwards?	6. REMARKS. In this Column should be stated the Arrangements made where no Resident Matron is employed; whether there is a Female Attendant, how she is summoned when wanted, &c.
one	1	—	Yes	(a) Yes; (b) when required.	Female attendant, daughter of constable; summoned by police; responsible to watch committee; remuneration, 1s. each prisoner.
te	1	—	Yes	„ Yes; „ when required.	Female attendant, wife of retired tradesman; summoned by police; responsible to watch committee; remuneration, 1l. per week.
ate	1	—	Yes	„ Yes; „ when required.	Female attendant, wife of tradesman; summoned by messenger; responsible to chief constable; remuneration, 1s. each searching, 5s. per night when required.
ster	—	—	Yes	„ Yes; „ when required.	Female attendant, wife of hall-keeper; summoned by constable; remuneration, 1s. each prisoner searched, 2s. 6d. for attendance per day or night.
idge Wells	1	—	Yes	„ Yes; „ when required.	Female attendant, wife of constable; summoned by messenger; responsible to chief officer; remuneration, 30s. per annum.
rt (Mon.)	1	1	Yes	„ Yes; „ when required.	Wife of constable; responsible to chief constable; remuneration, 17s. 6d. per week.
	1	—	Yes	„ Yes; „frequently	Female attendant, wife of constable; summoned by messenger; responsible to watch committee; remuneration, 9l. 2s. per annum.
water	1	—	Yes	„ Yes; „ when required.	Female attendant; summoned by constable; responsible to chief officer; remuneration, 1s. 6d. for searching, 4d. per hour when in attendance.
ord	1	1	Yes	„ Yes; „ when required.	Wife of constable; responsible to chief officer; remuneration, 1s. each prisoner searched.
te	2	1	Yes	„ Yes; „ when required.	Resident matron is wife of constable; female attendant is wife of caretaker, and summoned by police; remuneration, 1s. 6d. per prisoner.
ton	4	3	Yes	„ Yes; „ when required.	Resident matrons are wives of constables; female attendant is wife of caretaker, and summoned by police; remuneration, 1s. for attending and searching each prisoner, 2s. 6d. in case of sickness.
ourne		2	Yes	„ Yes; „ when required.	Wives of inspector and sergeant; responsible to watch committee; remuneration, 1s. each prisoner.
ngs		—	—	- -	Female attendant, wife of constable; is employed when necessary.
			Yes	„ Yes; „ when required.	Female attendants, wives of late constable and workmen are employed; summoned by messenger; remuneration, 6 a.m. to 10 p.m., 5d. per hour; 10 p.m. to 6 a.m., 6d. per hour.
		1	Yes	„ Yes; „ when required.	Resides at the station; responsible to chief officer; remuneration, 1s. for each prisoner searched, and 5s. per night attendance.
ury		—	Yes	„ Yes; „ when required.	Female attendant; summoned by messenger; responsible to chief officer; remuneration, 9s. per week and 4d. per prisoner searched by day, 6d. by night.
arthen		1	Yes	„ Yes; „ when required.	Wife of sergeant; responsible to watch committee; remuneration, nil.
ff		8	Yes	„ Yes; „ when required.	Responsible to watch committee; two receive 1l. per week each.
		—	Yes	„ Yes; „ when required.	Female attendant, wife of constable in charge of station.
sea		—	Yes	„ Yes; „ when required.	Female attendant, wife of constable, is called in when required at any time.

Lightning Source UK Ltd.
Milton Keynes UK
UKHW020618120219
337137UK00005B/600/P

9 780428 713249